MW01634024

LEO BAECK INSTITUTE
YEAR BOOK

1984

From a rare photograph taken at a meeting of the Reichsvertretung in 1933 or 1934

From left to right: Jakob Hoffmann, leading Orthodox rabbi; Siegfried Moses, President of the Zionistische Vereinigung für Deutschland; Leo Baeck, President of the Reichsvertretung; Otto Hirsch, Executive Director of the Reichsvertretung; Rudolf Callmann, Member of the Board of the Centralverein deutscher Staatsbürger jüdischen Glaubens; Heinrich Stahl, Chairman of the Berlin Jewish community

From the Archives of the Leo Baeck Institute, New York

LEO BAECK INSTITUTE

YEAR BOOK XXIX

1984

SECKER & WARBURG · LONDON
PUBLISHED FOR THE INSTITUTE
LONDON · JERUSALEM · NEW YORK

FOUNDER EDITOR: ROBERT WELTSCH (1956–1978)
EDITOR: ARNOLD PAUCKER

OFFICES OF THE
LEO BAECK INSTITUTE

JERUSALEM (ISRAEL): 33 Bustanai Street
LONDON: 4 Devonshire Street, W.1
NEW YORK: 129 East 73rd Street

THE LEO BAECK INSTITUTE
was founded in 1955 by the
COUNCIL OF JEWS FROM GERMANY
for the purpose of collecting material on and sponsoring research into the history of the Jewish Community in Germany and in other German-speaking countries from the Emancipation to its decline and new dispersion. The Institute is named in honour of the man who was the last representative figure of German Jewry in Germany during the Nazi period.

The Council of Jews from Germany was established after the war by the principal organisations of Jews from Germany in Israel, U.S.A. and U.K. for the protection of their rights and interests.

THIS PUBLICATION WAS SUPPORTED
BY GRANTS FROM
THE BRITISH ACADEMY
MEMORIAL FOUNDATION FOR JEWISH CULTURE
N M ROTHSCHILD & SONS LIMITED

Published by Martin Secker & Warburg Limited
54 Poland Street, London W1V 3DF
SBN 436 25543 X
Photoset by Wilmaset, Birkenhead, Merseyside
Printed in Great Britain by Richard Clay (The Chaucer Press), Limited, Bungay, Suffolk

Contents

Illustrations

Preface

When last year, the fiftieth anniversary of the 30th January 1933, historians, in a plethora of books and essays, recorded and evaluated the *Machtübernahme* by the Nazis – which also signalled the revocation of Jewish civil rights in Germany – we opted rather in our Year Book for the portrayal of a century of emancipation with its fruits as well as its vicissitudes. This current volume is now devoted to a large degree to the besieged Jewish community under Nazi rule. The Year Book's central theme lends itself to a threefold division; the confrontation of the community with the stark reality of Nazi power; the response from other countries; and, finally, the terrible ordeal of those whom the desperate efforts of their co-religionists and belated succour from abroad were not able to save. An initial essay by Jacob Boas scrutinises internal Jewish policies and does not shy away from bitter divisions and often acrimonious debates; other contributions analyse reactions from overseas (which hovered between selfishness and good intentions, revealing much naivety and frequently a general ignorance of European affairs) or outline the inadequate reception or absorption of those fleeing from the Nazi terror; while in three essays Konrad Kwiet, Sybil Milton and Henry Friedlander depict the nightmare of self-destruction, expulsion, deportation and death.

In juxtaposition is this volume's second theme, which begins with the Early Enlightenment and the gradual entry of Jews into European culture in a time of optimism. The striving for cultural adaptation, the assimilation of language and literature, the disputes between Jews and Gentiles on terms of intellectual equality and by well-matched opponents, are shown in such erudite contributions as those of Steven and Henry Schwarzschild and Ze'ev Levy. We return to the subject of the first section when in some of the vagaries of a Hans Joachim Schoeps we meet the influence of German fascism on some German Jews.

Linked with the central theme is also Ernst Lowenthal's fourth survey of Jewish communal and regional historiography with which this Year Book ends. When German cities and local historians remember their erstwhile Jewish fellow-citizens they come inevitably to deal with – though often cursorily and sketchily – the fate of the remnant, torn from their homes and transported to their deaths in the camps of the East.

There will be two sequels to the matter under discussion here. For the autumn of 1985 the Leo Baeck Institute has convened in Berlin an international conference on 'Self-Assertion in Adversity – The Jews in National Socialist Germany, 1933–1939'; and in Year Book XXX, to be issued at the same time, we shall publish a further session organised by the New York Institute, at the 98th Annual Meeting of the American Historical Association in San Francisco on the 'Resettlement of German Jews'. In this Year Book Michael Blakeney observes in passing how the attitude of the United Kingdom changed in 1938 all the way from a niggardly to a generous response. And it does not seem inappropriate to quote here what *The Times* of London on the 20th August 1983 had to say in a leader after the death of the renowned art historian Sir Nicholas Pevsner, that he was "one of those great spirits who made English culture an indebted beneficiary of the tragic persecution of German Jewry".

The theologian and historian Hermann Greive met his death tragically on 25th January 1984 while teaching at the Martin-Buber-Institut of Cologne University, where he was Professor of Judaistik. He was forty-eight. Greive was an outstanding representative of a new generation of German academics who have so much to give to Jewish studies. In a distinguished career, cut brutally short, he had numerous works of impeccable scholarship to his credit, from *Theologie und Ideologie. Katholizismus und Judentum in Deutschland und Österreich 1918–1935* (1969) to *Die Juden, Grundzüge ihrer Geschichte im mittelalterlichen und neuzeitlichen Europa* (1979) and his *Geschichte des modernen Antisemitismus in Deutschland* (1983). He was co-editor of *Briefe und Tagebücher Theodor Herzls* (1983ff.). Hermann Greive was closely connected with the Leo Baeck Institute as an adviser and he contributed to its symposium volumes and the Year Book. The Institute mourns a colleague; I mourn a friend.

Yet again we can put before the reader a rather substantial volume of the Year Book, and this due to generous donations by a number of benefactors, to defray specific extra costs. The Leo Baeck Institute extends its thanks to them for making it possible by these gifts to enlarge Year Book XXIX, and the two forthcoming volumes, XXX and XXXI, with the express purpose of broadening our scope and in particular giving space to recent research of younger scholars specialising in German-Jewish history.

For many years the Editor has been in the debt of friends and colleagues for their support and for having given unstintingly of their time. In addition to all those mentioned before grateful thanks are due to Hans Feld, London, Peter Freimark, Hamburg, Albert Friedlander, London, John Grenville, Birmingham, Leo Kahn, London, Marion Kaplan, New York, Dovid Katz, Oxford, Ian Kershaw, Manchester, Cécile Lowenthal-Hensel, Berlin, George Mosse, Wisconsin/Jerusalem, Siegbert Prawer, Oxford, Michael Riff, New York, Walter Röll, Trier, Ernst Schulin, Freiburg, Joshua Sherman, New York, Joseph Walk, Jerusalem, Hans Walz, Hanover, and Christa Wichmann, London.

London *Arnold Paucker*

In the Third Reich

German-Jewish Internal Politics under Hitler 1933–1938

BY JACOB BOAS

"They can condemn us to hunger but they cannot condemn us to starvation."

This declaration, capturing all the pathos of the Jewish position in the early days of the Hitler regime, appeared in the 6th April issue of the *C.V.-Zeitung*, German Jewry's most widely disseminated newspaper.* Sandwiched between the anti-Jewish boycott of 1st April 1933 and the publication of the non-Aryan laws less than a week later, it came from Ismar Elbogen, the dean of Jewish historians, and ambiguous as Elbogen's sentiment may seem today, in that uncertain era when Jews could hardly believe that the first steps had been taken which were to lead to stripping them of every mark of civilised existence, the strange mixture of resignation and optimism sounded neither naive nor unfounded. As no one knew what the future might bring, it was impossible to determine what end the anti-Jewish Nazi policy might serve.

For the moment, the most pessimistic interpretations seemed to have been exaggerated. Following the boycott of the 1st April and the non-Aryan legislation the worst appeared to be over. These two initial stimuli intended to eject Germany's Jews from the national body failed to live up to the expectations of the antisemites. The Law for the Restoration of the Professional Civil Service, for example, was enforced only at the higher levels and did not affect the greater number of Jews (who had already been effectively barred from the higher ranks). One estimate put the number of Jews dismissed over a six-year period at 5,433; these included teachers and university professors, who in Germany were considered part of the civil service.[1] In addition, despite persecution and the Law against the Overcrowding of German Schools (25th April 1933), which introduced a *numerus clausus* for Jews in the general German school system, a large number of Jews continued to frequent German schools. As late as May 1938, twenty-five percent of all Jewish school children were still attending non-Jewish schools. A year before the percentage had stood at 38.7.[2] And although the Law Regarding Admittance to the Profession of Law threatened non-Aryan lawyers with the loss of their practices, it was not until 27th September 1938 (Fifth Ordinance to the *Reich* Citizenship Law) that all Jewish lawyers were disbarred and reduced to "consultants".

*I want to thank Dr. Arnold Paucker for his helpful comments on an earlier draft of this article; also Alicia K. Wicks for her generous assistance.

[1]G. Warburg, *Six Years of Hitler. The Jews under the Nazi Regime*, London 1939, p. 59.

[2]S. Adler-Rudel, *Jüdische Selbsthilfe unter dem Naziregime 1933–1939 im Spiegel der Berichte der Reichsvertretung der Juden in Deutschland*, Tübingen 1974 (Schriftenreihe wissenschaftlicher Abhandlungen des Leo Baeck Instituts 29), pp. 28, 30.

The boycott, like the non-Aryan legislation, failed to deliver on its promise. Not the least among that policy's disabling factors was the consideration that the complete elimination of the Jews from the economy would have spelled disaster, as was well noted by the representatives of big business in Hitler's government. The presence of von Hindenburg and the possible repercussions of foreign opinion were still sufficiently important at the time in soft-pedalling the more restrictive aspects of the campaign.* A notable lack of enthusiasm was actually detectable among the masses, and some opposition was even registered in the press and radio.[3] What is more, some Jewish firms seem to have substantially benefited from the Nazi takeover and the restoration of something resembling economic normalcy. Jewish clothing and textile manufacturers were given contracts for supplying the armed services, and at the beginning of 1938 there were nearly 40,000 Jewish-owned firms still doing business in Germany, some with important functions in the rearmament and import trade.[4] A social historian of the Third *Reich* summed up: "Despite boycotts many Jewish shopkeepers managed to stay in business until 1938, a year in which some of them were actually beginning to experience boom conditions".[5]

That same year, however, dubbed by Hitler "The Year of Understanding", witnessed a gruelling series of persecutions. From imposed changes of name to the brutal evacuation of Polish Jews residing in Germany,** the persecution mounted in intensity, reaching its peak in the pogrom of the 10th/11th November, the *Kristallnacht*.

Evidently, until the end of 1938, National Socialism had no fixed plans for the Jews.[6] Lacking authoritative direction, the Jewish Question became from the very beginning a popular subject to engage the attention of ambitious Party members. Those Nazis spoiling to widen their influence could point with contempt to the failure of the radicals in carrying through the boycott. At the

* For foreign reaction (*viz* the USA) see the following essay by Deborah E. Lipstadt, 'The American Press and the Persecution of German Jewry', in this volume of the Year Book – (Ed.).

[3]See Herbert Freeden, *Vom geistigen Widerstand der deutschen Juden. Ein Kapitel jüdischer Selbstbehauptung in den Jahren 1933/38*, Jerusalem 1963, pp. 5–6.

For the economics of the boycott, see Helmut Genschel, *Die Verdrängung der Juden aus der Wirtschaft im Dritten Reich*, Göttingen 1966, pp. 59, 64, 73–80. Genschel points out, for example, that Jewish-owned department stores, the butt of so much propaganda, continued doing business; the giant Hermann Tietz concern in June 1933 even received a subsidy of 14.5 million RM. Genschel also noted that many card-carrying Nazis openly flouted Party directives against shopping in "Jewish" department stores. *Ibid.*, p. 123.

[4]Lucy S. Dawidowicz, *The War against the Jews 1933–1945*, New York 1975, pp. 82, 96. Citing figures furnished by the *Frankfurter Zeitung*, the newspaper of the *Zionistische Vereinigung für Deutschland* reported at the end of 1935 that ladies' apparel was still about 50% in Jewish hands – in Berlin, roughly 80% – while the Jewish share of the capital's market in men's clothing had dropped only about 10% from the pre-Hitler days, from 70% to 60%.

[5]Richard Grunberger, *The 12-Year Reich. A Social History of Nazi Germany*, New York-Chicago-San Francisco 1971, p. 457.

** See the contribution by Sybil Milton, 'The Expulsion of Polish Jews from Germany: October 1938 to July 1939', in this section of the current volume of the Year Book – (Ed.).

[6]For Nazi Jewish policy, see Karl A. Schleunes, *The Twisted Road to Auschwitz. Nazi Policy Towards German Jews 1933–1939*, London 1970; Uwe Dietrich Adam, *Judenpolitik im Dritten Reich*, Düsseldorf 1972.

same time, Hitler's control over Jewish policy would not make itself felt again until after the *Kristallnacht*,[7] and into this void stepped a less extreme faction – advocates of "dissimilation", i.e., the legal confinement of Jews to their own sphere, backed by such government ministers as Hjalmar Schacht and Count Schwerin von Krosigk, Hitler's Finance Minister; the Nuremberg Laws of September 1935 seemed to bear out the moderate position, even to the significant neglecting to mention economic apartheid.

But the period in which a centrally directed Jewish policy was absent came to an end in 1938 when the radicals again seized the initiative. Moderates like Schacht, War Minister von Blomberg and Commander-in-Chief von Fritsch were driven from office, as the regime could confidently boast of a string of victories, not the least of which was an upsurge in the economy. Goebbels's failure to exploit the November pogrom resulted in a dimming of his image in the Nazi hierarchy, and thus it was into the hands of Göring that were gathered the reins of a sharper, that is, more clearly, more pointedly, coordinated Jewish policy.[8]

The ambiguous position of German Jewry in the years 1933–1938 was not solely the result of the improvised nature of Nazi Jewish policy. Far more unbalancing was the illusion fostered by this policy that the nation's Jews might be allowed to fill their own place, with a specific autonomy, within the overall German national context.

It is impossible to say whether National Socialist leaders ever seriously entertained such plans, but the fact remains that in the period 1933–1938 they did little to demolish the hopes many Jews had placed in its eventuality. Bolstering Jewish optimism were a number of factors tending to underline this belief. For instance, Jews experienced little or no interference with their school system. Besides being responsible for teaching the curriculum in force in German schools, they were allowed to complement the standard courses with their own material; private Jewish schools even continued to receive state subsidies until March 1939.[9] Officially there were no efforts made to prevent Jews from synchronising their occupational patterns with those prevailing in the non-Jewish community.[10] Jews were not hindered in the practice of their religion, nor in the functions of their institutions: when in September 1933 they established the *Reichsvertretung der*

[7]Schleunes, *op. cit.*, p. 216.

[8]Raul Hilberg, *The Destruction of the European Jews*, Chicago 1961, p. 23. See also, Ernst Marcus, 'The German Foreign Office and the Palestine Question in the Period 1933–1939', *Yad Washem Studies on the European Jewish Catastrophe and Resistance*, II (1958) p. 194; and Schleunes: "In the final analysis, the Kristallnacht was the product of the lack of coordination which marked Nazi planning on Jewish policy and the result of a last-ditch effort by the radicals to wrest over this policy." *Op. cit.*, p. 236.

[9]E. C. Helmreich, 'Jewish Education in the Third Reich', in *Journal of Central European Affairs*, XV (July 1955), No. 2, pp. 141, 144. For Jewish schools under Hitler, see also Hans Gärtner, 'Problems of Jewish Schools in Germany during the Hitler Regime (With Special Reference to the Theodor Herzl Schule in Berlin)', in *LBI Year Book I* (1956) pp. 123–141.

[10]Though there was no official interference with Jewish efforts at occupational retraining, practical obstacles abounded. German employers, for example, were reluctant to hire Jewish apprentices or labourers, and since Jews could not purchase land, agricultural training was restricted to tiny holdings still in Jewish hands. Hence young Jews often had to go abroad for their agricultural training.

deutschen Juden to represent their interests with the Nazi authorities the procedure involved a simple act of registration with the Ministry of the Interior.[11]

Similarly, Jewish cultural work was not only left unmolested but actually received encouragement from the Nazi bureaucracy. On 16th June 1933, the Prussian Ministry of Science, Art and Popular Enlightenment approved the formation of the *Kulturbund deutscher Juden* – "because the members of the Jewish race", declared the Ministry's Cultural Adviser Hans Hinkel, "being foreigners, deserve every opportunity for creative expression".[12] Two years later, as the arbiter of Jewish cultural affairs in Goebbels's Propaganda Ministry, Hinkel supervised the coordination of Jewish cultural activities in one roof organisation empowered to negotiate Jewish cultural matters, the *Reichsverband der jüdischen Kulturbünde.*[13]

The argument for autonomy was two-way. On the Jewish side, it found a skilled dialectician in Robert Weltsch, the editor of the Zionist newspaper, the *Jüdische Rundschau.* Jews no less than Germans, argued Weltsch before the relevant authorities at the Propaganda Ministry, should have the opportunity to express their fundamental being, an end which could best be served, he suggested, by leaving the Jewish press, the press by and for Jews, relatively undisturbed.[14]

Whatever his Nazi audience may have thought of Weltsch's line of reasoning, it is certain that during the first five years of Nazi rule Jewish journalism by and large continued to function independently.[15] Which is not to say that it was

[11]Kurt Jakob Ball-Kaduri, *Das Leben der Juden in Deutschland im Jahre 1933*, Frankfurt a. Main 1963, p. 41. There seems to be unanimous agreement that a great deal of real autonomy existed. Interview with Max Gruenewald, 14th October 1974, New York; interview with Herbert A. Strauss, 14th October 1974, New York; see also, K. Y. Ball-Kaduri, 'Evidence, its Value and Limitations', in *Yad Washem Studies on the European Jewish Catastrophe and Resistance*, III (1959), p. 87.

[12]Quoted in *Jüdische Rundschau*, XXXVIII (29th September 1933).

[13]See *C.V.-Zeitung*, XIV (9th May 1935); *Jüdische Rundschau*, XXXX (20th August 1935). The *Israelitisches Familienblatt*, citing figures supplied by Hinkel, asserted that the *Kulturbund* had 110,000 members and 600 artists. Herbert Freeden noted that Hinkel was not unknown to intercede with the authorities on behalf of his Jewish charges; in the course of time, however, his control became stricter and stricter. *Jüdisches Theater in Nazideutschland*, Tübingen 1964 (Schriftenreihe wissenschaftlicher Abhandlungen des Leo Baeck Instituts 12), p. 40. What was true of Jewish cultural life was true of "autonomy" in general: it was always under the watchful eye of Gestapo supervision. For example, the Gestapo gradually began to attend the meetings of the decision-making bodies in the community and to demand written reports. Interview with Adolf Leschnitzer, 15th October 1974, New York. The Gestapo, wrote Kurt Tuchler, knew everything that was happening in the community. *Erlebnisse und Beobachtungen in den ersten vier Hitlerjahren*, 1945, in Yad Washem Archives, Jerusalem, p. 3. Thus the leaders of the *Centralverein deutscher Staatsbürger jüdischen Glaubens* decided to discontinue their official meetings because no real work could be done in the presence of the Gestapo; they would meet "unofficially" in a private home instead, usually the Chairman's. Ernst Herzfeld, *Meine letzten Jahre in Deutschland, 1933–1938*, 1945, in: Yad Washem Archives, Jerusalem, p. 2.

[14]Robert Weltsch, *An der Wende des Modernen Judentums. Betrachtungen aus fünf Jahrzehnten*, Tübingen 1972, Veröffentlichung des Leo Baeck Instituts, p. 48.

[15]"In their relationship to Jewish papers the Nazi authorities were incalculable, and the real motives for their comparatively liberal attitude have not yet been discovered." Robert Weltsch, 'A Goebbels Speech and a Goebbels Letter', in *LBI Year Book X* (1965), p. 285. For the Jewish press under Nazism, see Margaret T. Edelheim-Muehsam, 'The Jewish Press in Germany', in *LBI Year Book I* (1956), pp. 163–175 and, by the same author, 'Reactions of the Jewish Press to the Nazi Challenge', in *LBI Year Book V* (1960), pp. 309–329.

altogether free from government interference. On the contrary, there was "constant supervision" and *Nachzensur*– "after-censorship" rather than outright censorship. The editors of the community's publications could never be sure of the ground under their feet. They not only had to select their subject matter with the utmost circumspection, if the message was to clear Nazi check-points it had to be couched in a special language, "the secret language of the persecuted". But as language of this sort, designed to keep the authorities at bay, leaves the field wide open to misinterpretation, the reader, especially today's reader, must approach it greatly forearmed with caution and understanding.

The comparatively free hand left to Jews in the conduct of their own affairs also extended to the sphere of intramural politics. Never dormant in the community, politics in the pre-1933 era had steadily been pushing inward from its position at the perimeter of Jewish life towards its centre, particularly in Berlin where political conflict was more pronounced than elsewhere in the *Reich.*[16] Still, the substance of politics conspired to keep political strife within reasonable bounds. Rarely were Jewish politicians required to break new ground. Politics was an affair of the rich and well-to-do, of those with academic degrees and business pedigrees.

As it no longer was "politics as usual" in post-1933 Germany, so it no longer was "politics as usual" in the Jewish community. The problems and issues facing German Jewry in the pre-Hitler era – concerning Jewish schools, vocational training, religion and welfare – burst their conventional mould during the Nazi ascendancy, and resolute leadership to deal with far more serious problems was urgently required. But this question of who should direct and control Jewish life, and by what authority and principles, plunged the community into recurrent political strife – a bitter contest that did not disappear until the community itself had disappeared.

The struggle for supremacy in the Jewish community was between two forces: on one side were the advocates of the "German-Jewish way", bent on maintaining the status quo, while on the other were the growing ranks of the Zionist faithful, ideologically committed to a national, i.e. "racial", conception of Jewry and to the creation of a Jewish homeland in the Middle East.

In 1933 the *Centralverein deutscher Staatsbürger jüdischen Glaubens*, German Jewry's largest organisation, carried the standard of the "German-Jewish way", and the *Zionistische Vereinigung für Deutschland* (ZVfD), the "general" Zionist organisation, that of the "national" Jews.[17] The former had its uneasy allies in the liberals

[16]See Ernst Herzfeld, *Meine letzten Jahre in Deutschland, op. cit.*, p. 12. See also, Kurt Loewenstein, 'Die innerjüdische Reaktion auf die Krise der deutschen Demokratie', in *Entscheidungsjahr 1932. Zur Judenfrage in der Endphase der Weimarer Republik*, zweite revidierte und erweiterte Auflage. Ein Sammelband herausgegeben von Werner E. Mosse unter Mitwirkung von Arnold Paucker, Tübingen 1966 (Schriftenreihe wissenschaftlicher Abhandlungen des Leo Baeck Instituts 13), pp. 400–401. This article focuses on Berlin.

[17]"General" Zionists as opposed to the small group known as *Staatszionisten* in Germany and as Revisionists elsewhere. Revisionism, created in 1925 by Vladimir Jabotinsky, stood to the right of the general Zionism of the ZVfD, which supported Weizmann's policy of cooperation with England. Revisionism, on the other hand, believed in the use of violence to bring about a Jewish Palestine and was virulently anti-British. The leader of the *Staatszionisten* was Georg Kareski.

(liberals both in the Jewish religious sense and in their German political attitudes) of the community administrations, who were everywhere in power; and the latter had its own similarly queasy supporters in these same ruling bodies, though everywhere in the minority.

Competition between Zionists and "assimilationists",[18] Zionism's epithet for *Centralverein* followers, harked back to pre-Hitler days, when the *Centralverein* had easily maintained a dominant position. But with Hitler's victory conditions changed, and in the subsequent German-Jewish political history Zionism claimed for itself an ever greater share of power, basing its demand on the reputed failure of the pre-1933 liberal leaders to prepare Jews for the coming of Nazism. The day after Hitler's appointment the ZVfD's newspaper, the *Jüdische Rundschau*, wrote that the struggle for Jewish rights could only be waged by those whose commitment to Jewish *Volkstum* had always been beyond reproach, to wit, the Zionists.[19] The members of the ruling clique, Zionists asserted, did not even pretend to be devoted to Judaism: money, and the claim of being "better Germans" had lifted them to political office.[20] Blinded by their liberal shibboleths, misunderstanding Jewish destiny, they had washed their hands of the Jewish Question. Hopelessly set in their ways, hidebound in their beliefs, they had ridiculed the creative force of nationalism, interfered with the construction of Palestine,[21] and dragged their feet on the problems of Jewish schools and occupational retraining. In short, the Zionist indictment concluded, these leaders were the "ewig Gestrigen",[22] perennially behind the times, incorrigible purveyors of the old "apologetic-assimilationist dialectic".[23]

Zionists made up for years of being slighted; for the paltry allocations to their schools and *Hechaluz*,[24] the Zionist instrument which prepared young Jews for a life of labour in Palestine, and for the anti-Zionist resolutions in the *Centralverein*, (the last one as late as 1928). Its ranks swollen with the so-called "March Zionists" (meaning those Jews who had hurriedly crossed over to Zionism in the wake of Hitler's election victory in early March), the ZVfD now aspired to complete mastery of the Jewish community. By mid-1935, encouraged by the

[18]Concerning the Jewish press in Germany from 1918 to 1938, Herbert A. Strauss wrote: "Its editorials and news columns reflected the major issues of each period, understanding them in the light of the two options available to German Jewry in those fateful years, the Zionist and (what we may call for want of a better term) the German-Jewish 'mainstream' to which the derogatory term 'assimilationist' would apply only from the point of view of their opponents, not in their own eyes . . ." 'The Jewish Press in Germany, 1918–1938 (1943)', p. 16. Dr. Strauss kindly provided me with a rough English translation of this article, which appeared in Hebrew as 'Haitonuth hayehudit beGermania bishnim 1918–1939 (1943)', in *Itonut Yehudit shehayta*, Yehuda Gothelf, ed., Tel-Aviv 1973.

[19]*Jüdische Rundschau*, XXXVIII (31st January 1933).

[20]*Jüdische Rundschau*, XXXVIII (16th June 1933): XXXX (12th February 1935).

[21]*Jüdische Rundschau*, XXXVIII (29th March 1933).

[22]*Jüdische Rundschau*, XXXVIII (21st July 1933); XXXX (12th March 1935).

[23]*Jüdische Rundschau*, XXXVIII (25th July 1933).

[24]For example, in 1932 the liberals in the Berlin Assembly voted only 2,000 RM for the *Hechaluz*. *Jüdische Rundschau*, XXXXI (10th October 1936). To save money, in the early thirties these same liberals wanted to dismantle the Jewish elementary schools, which were a "thorn in their side". See Selma Schiratzky, *Die Schule 'Rykestrasse' in Berlin, eine jüdische Volksschule in der Hitlerzeit*, 1956, in: Yad Washem Archives, Jerusalem, p. 2.

pro-Zionist bent of Nazi Jewish policy,[25] the ZVfD considered itself the legitimate spokesman for all German Jewry. At its convention held in Berlin during the first week of May it unanimously adopted a resolution which boldly proclaimed: "The Zionist movement in Germany demands the right to influence decisively the entire Jewish life in Germany".[26] It would not be Zionism's final bid for power.

But the *Centralverein*, as the dominant political power in the community, not only faced attack from "national" Jews; it also had to contend with "national" German Jews, with assailants to its right. On 30th May 1933 Jewish Berliners were privy to a strange sight. On large advertising pillars usually cluttered with Nazi propaganda, the membership of the *Centralverein* was branded for conspiring with the ZVfD to lead German Jewry back to the ghetto.[27] The posters, urging "Join us!", had been put up by the *Verband nationaldeutscher Juden*, a small band of extreme Jewish German nationalists led by Max Naumann.

A Berlin lawyer and a recipient of the Iron Cross First and Second Class, Naumann was wont to indict those Jews whose "Germanness", as he put it, did not "fill their entire being".[28] Characteristically, in 1933 his *Verband* launched the *Aktionsausschuss der jüdischen Deutschen* to defend Germany against "atrocity propaganda" from abroad. The Committee, promoting a resurgent and aggressive national Germany,[29] was joined by three other groups whose perfervid nationalism ranked second to none: the *Reichsbund jüdischer Frontsoldaten* (R.j.F.), the *Deutscher Vortrupp, Gefolgschaft deutscher Juden*, and the youth formation *Schwarzes Fähnlein*,[30]

The life of the *Aktionsausschuss* was unusually short. Two months after its inception in April 1933, a leadership quarrel led to a parting of the ways between the *Verband* and the numerically far superior *Reichsbund*. The other groups quickly followed suit, leaving the Naumann association to fend for itself until the end of 1935 when the Gestapo suppressed both the *Verband* and the *Vortrupp*.

But for Nazi antisemitism, many of the followers of the *Verband nationaldeutscher*

[25]See below, pp. 19–20 and notes 85 and 89.

[26]*Jüdische Rundschau*, XXXX (7th May 1935).

[27]See *C.V.-Zeitung*, XII (1st June 1933).

[28]Max Naumann, *Vom mosaischen und nicht mosaischen Juden*, Berlin 1921, p. 28.

[29]See *Jüdische Rundschau*, XXXVIII (7th April 1933); *Israelitisches Familienblatt*, XXXV (6th April 1933). The full title of the *Aktionsausschuss* was: *Aktionsausschuss der jüdischen Deutschen gegen die anti-deutsche Hetze*.

[30]According to Hans Joachim Schoeps, founder of the *Deutscher Vortrupp*, his organisation had about three hundred members. *"Bereit für Deutschland!" Der Patriotismus deutscher Juden und der Nationalsozialismus. Frühe Schriften 1930 bis 1939. Eine historische Dokumentation*, Berlin 1970, p. 27. "Bereit für Deutschland!" was the *Vortrupp*'s official slogan – "Was auch geschehe: Bereit für Deutschland!" *Der Deutsche Vortrupp. Blätter einer Gefolgschaft Deutscher Juden*, No. 1 (October 1933), p. 2. In 1934 the *Schwarzes Fähnlein* had approximately 1,000 members. George L. Mosse, *Germans and Jews. The Right, the Left, and the Search for a 'Third Force' in Pre-Nazi Germany*, New York 1970, p. 104. For a study on the *Vortrupp*, see Carl J. Rheins, 'Deutscher Vortrupp, Gefolgschaft deutscher Juden 1933–1935', in *LBI Year Book XXVI* (1981), pp. 207–229. On the *Verband nationaldeutscher Juden*, see, by the same author, 'The Verband nationaldeutscher Juden 1921–1933', in *LBI Year Book XXV* (1980), pp. 243–268, and on the *Schwarzes Fähnlein*, also by Rheins, see 'The Schwarzes Fähnlein, Jungenschaft, 1932–1934', in *LBI Year Book XXIII* (1978), pp. 173–197. The history of the *Reichsbund jüdischer Frontsoldaten* has been admirably traced by Ulrich Dunker, *Der Reichsbund jüdischer Frontsoldaten 1919–1938. Geschichte eines jüdischen Abwehrvereins*, Düsseldorf 1977.

Juden and perhaps all of those in the *Deutscher Vortrupp* would have made inspired National Socialists. Certainly much less extreme but likewise committed to rescuing Jews from the Scylla of the *Centralverein* and the Charybdis of the ZVfD was the short-lived *Erneuerungsbewegung der jüdischen Deutschen*. Led by Bruno Woyda, an official of the Berlin Executive and former editor of the *Jüdisch-Liberale Zeitung*, Woyda made use of that paper's 13th November 1933 issue to publicise his movement's programme. Appealing for an end to inaction and indecision, the Renewal Movement urged the re-awakening of German-Jewish consciousness, which it identified as a cross between the soldierly virtues of the Jewish front-fighter – simplicity and comradeship – and the honesty and spontaneity of the Youth Movement. In closing, the Renewal Movement exhorted all Jews sincere in their devotion to Germany to unite behind a "German-feeling leadership".[31]

The *Erneuerungsbewegung* found little support among Jews. The Jewish press blamed it for contributing to that very divisiveness its existence was meant to cure,[32] and though the movement continued to exist until 1935, little more was heard of it after December 1933.

One of the signatures on the Renewal Movement's proclamation belonged to Ludwig Freund, the Executive Director of the R.j.F. By far the largest of all conservative groups, the Jewish veterans association also vied for the contested right of representing Germany's Jews. With 30,000 members in sixteen provincial branches, plus 14,000 young people in affiliated youth and sports groups,[33] the R.j.F. considered itself eminently qualified to fill this role. Citing a proven record of sacrifice – 12,000 war dead, according to its own figures – the R.j.F. prided itself both on initiating young Jews into the time-tested ethos of the German soldier and on its pioneering efforts in the areas of physical fitness and occupational retraining.[34]

The R.j.F. could point to some modest victories in the struggle for Jewish rights. Because of the immunity of Jewish war veterans from the liabilities of the April 1933 non-Aryan legislation, the R.j.F. leader Leo Löwenstein credited his organisation with having kept thousands of Jews in their jobs. Löwenstein also drew attention to the decree promulgated by the *Reich* Minister of Labour in August 1933 which entrusted the *Reichsbund* with the representation of all non-Aryan war casualties *vis-à-vis* the authorities.[35]

It was the Nazi rise to power that allowed the R.j.F. to abandon its former neutrality in Jewish affairs,[36] and the change in the organisation's policy was expressed by Ludwig Freund in his remarks on the future of German Jewry:

[31] I am indebted to Dr. Klaus Herrmann of Sir George Williams University for making the programme of the *Erneuerungsbewegung* available to me.

[32] See *Israelitisches Familienblatt*, XXXV (30th November 1933); *C.V.-Zeitung*, XII (16th November 1933); *Jüdische Rundschau*, XXXVIII (28th November 1933).

[33] Leo Löwenstein, 'Die Linie des Reichbundes jüdischer Frontsoldaten', in *Wille und Weg des deutschen Judentums*, Berlin 1935, pp. 7, 10.

[34] See Dunker, *op. cit.*, pp. 81–104.

[35] Löwenstein, *loc. cit.*, p. 9.

[36] *Ibid.*, p. 10.

> "A leader in this struggle [the struggle for equal rights] now can only be that individual who, analogous to the new political type in Germany, is capable of standing up for his convictions with his entire being and life."[37]

Perceiving itself as the chosen instrument to effect this "new political type", the R.j.F. aspired to taking the Jewish community in hand. To begin with, it introduced the *Führerprinzip* in its own ranks. At the same time it embarked on a vigorous correspondence with the agencies and leaders of the New Order, omitting neither von Hindenburg nor Hitler. Unsolicited, it petitioned, among other things, for Jewish service in the *Wehrmacht*; the enrollment of all Jewish youths into one organisation and their military training under R.j.F. auspices. It further proposed that the community's current political formations be liquidated and replaced by a central organisation of "absolute loyalty" to the regime, structured along authoritarian lines.[38]

Evidently Zionists did not measure up to the "absolute loyalty" standard, for they were told they were no longer welcome in the R.j.F.[39] This rule, which in effect predated 1933 but until then had not been rigidly enforced, cast Zionism as the principal Jewish villain in the German-Jewish drama. Zionism not only was considered "un-German" and therefore an obstacle to the peaceable and honourable understanding between Germans and Jews; worse, Zionism had made light of the R.j.F. figures of Jewish war fatalities, putting their faith instead in those supplied by antisemitic sources.[40]

The R.j.F. vied for the leadership of German Jewry as late as February 1936. Its bid came in response to a similar challenge mounted by the Zionists.[41] But by then it had virtually exhausted its store of available sympathy, and its attempt at leadership collapsed. The R.j.F.'s long record of service to the nation and its endless protestations of "absolute faith" in Germany no longer passed current with the authorities. In respect to its brethren, the R.j.F.'s material basis for its claim to leadership had been removed with the "surrender" at Nuremberg in September 1935 of the thousands of Jews it once boasted of having kept in their jobs.

The political battle for community control swept across the entire plain of Jewish organisational and institutional life. Nowhere, however, was it more

[37] *Israelitisches Familienblatt*, XXXV (24th May 1933).

[38] See Dunker, *op. cit.*, pp. 132–144. Conceding that Nazism often required Jews to act and speak in ways which concealed their actual motivations, the laborious efforts of the R.j.F. to curry favour with the authorities and to create a special niche for itself in the New Germany nevertheless seem to have been excessively suppliant. To what extent the R.j.F. leadership reflected the attitude of the rank and file is, of course, difficult to ascertain. Dunker does not address the question. Dr. Arnold Paucker in a letter to the author of this article, suggests that it did not. See also his review of Dunker's book, 'Jews for the Fatherland', in *The Times Literary Supplement*, 28th July 1978, p. 869.

[39] *Jüdische Rundschau*, XXXIX (22nd June 1934).

[40] *Israelisches Familienblatt*, XXXVI (1st March 1934). In June 1934 the ZVfD in turn decided that it could not cooperate with the R.j.F. Describing the latter as an "anti-zionistische[r] Kampfbund", ZVfD members were no longer allowed to participate in the R.j.F. or in its sports groups. At the same time, ZVfD members were also prohibited from belonging to the *Staatszionisten*. See *Israelitisches Familienblatt*, XXXVI (21st June 1934).

[41] *Israelitisches Familienblatt*, XXXVIII (13th February 1936). A week later the *Israelitisches Familienblatt* called for the depoliticisation of the R.j.F.

bitterly contested than within, and between, the two principal rivals for power, the *Reichsvertretung der deutschen Juden* (after the Nuremberg Laws: the *Reichsvertretung der Juden in Deutschland*) and the *Jüdische Gemeinde zu Berlin.*

The *Reichsvertretung der deutschen Juden* was the self-appointed political representative of Germany's Jews *vis à vis* Nazi authorities,[42] though the latter never officially recognised it as such. It was the creation of roughly two dozen prominent German Jews,[43] and an instrument of the three major organisations of German Jewry, the *Centralverein*, the R.j.F., and the ZVfD. No popular elections preceded its formation and the traditional centres of active Jewish life, the Jewish communities, received only token representation in it. Yet, at its constituent meeting, held in Berlin on 17th September 1933, all major Jewish organisations and institutions, including the communities, were won over to its support. Rabbi Leo Baeck, its newly installed president, terminated the conference with a most fervent appeal to German Jews to close ranks in the face of an assault unmatched for its ferocity in Western Jewry's recent past.[44]

Harmony and solidarity – the qualities apostrophised by Baeck in his closing address – proved in short supply during the entire lifespan of the *Reichsvertretung.* The R.j.F. opposed cooperation with the ZVfD, which it considered to be less than one hundred percent loyal to Germany;[45] Zionists, in turn, feared being swamped by anti-Zionist forces.[46]

To be sure, the Essen triumvirate credited with initiating the *Reichsvertretung* – Rabbi Hugo Hahn, the banker Georg Hirschland, and the lawyer Ernst Herzfeld – were staunch supporters of the *Centralverein*; indeed, Herzfeld served as its last Director. But these three belonged to the Jewish Agency wing of the *Centralverein*; that is to say, they supported the construction of Palestine without, however, sharing the racial conception of Jewry of their Zionist associates in the Agency. In fact, the creation of the Jewish Agency in Germany owed much to the trail-blazing efforts of the two men who filled the top posts in the *Reichsvertretung* Leo Baeck and Otto Hirsch, respectively its President and Executive Director. Leo Baeck even assumed the presidency of the *Keren Hayessod*, the principal funding agency for the construction of Palestine.

It would be wrong, however, to equate the pro-Palestine sympathies thus manifested with pro-Zionism *per se.*[47] Among the *Centralverein* leaders the

[42]"Paramount, of course, was the task of representing the German Jews before the government of Reich, Länder and the Department chiefs." Max Gruenewald, 'The Beginning of the "Reichsvertretung"', in *LBI Year Book I* (1956), p. 61.

[43]See Hugo Hahn, 'Die Gründung der Reichsvertretung', in Hans Tramer (ed.), *In Zwei Welten. Siegfried Moses zum Fünfundsiebzigsten Geburtstag*, Tel-Aviv 1962, pp. 97–105. See also Klaus Drobisch, Rudi Goguel, Werner Müller (unter Mitwirkung von Horst Dohle), *Juden unterm Hakenkreuz, Verfolgung und Ausrottung der deutschen Juden 1933–1945*, Frankfurt a. Main 1973, p. 116.

[44]Hahn, *loc. cit.*, pp. 103–104. Naumann's *Verband* and Separatist Orthodoxy remained aloof however, though the latter joined the *Reichsvertretung* on an informal basis in 1936.

[45]See *Jüdische Rundschau*, XXXIX (16th February 1934); *Israelitisches Familienblatt*, XXXVI (1st March 1934).

[46]Zionists had boycotted the preliminary talks centring on the founding of the *Reichsvertretung.* See Herzfeld, *op. cit.*, p. 15, and Hahn, *loc. cit.*, pp. 102, 103.

[47]The *Jüdische Rundschau*, XXXXI (16th June 1936) observed that the warmer non-Zionists waxed toward Palestine, the cooler they acted towards the Zionist organisation.

proposition that the goals of Zionism had little or no bearing on the problems or needs of German Jewry qualified as dogma. The Jews they meant to benefit with their support for the "upbuilding" of Palestine in pre-Hitler Germany lived to the east of them, the so-called *Ostjuden*. The attitude that Palestine was not quite the place for a German Jew died hard, even after 1933.[48]

The ZVfD nevertheless decided to join the *Reichsvertretung*, evidently in the hope of furthering its own ambitious plans. However, these expectations soon collided with the solidly resisting force of anti-Zionist sentiment within the *Reichsvertretung*. As a result, the ZVfD was compelled to settle for co-equal status with non-Zionists, the principle of power-sharing adopted by the *Reichsvertretung* in August 1936; based on the practice of the "expanded" Jewish Agency, this agreement allocated half of all seats to Zionists and the other half to non-Zionists. By that time, however, the mathematics of shared power was of little consequence, the rout of non-Zionists in the *Reichsvertretung* being virtually complete.[49]

The Zionists, far from seeking the destruction of the *Reichsvertretung*, were determined simply to recast what was essentially an instrument of the *Centralverein* in their own image. In their aim they were rather less drastic than the *Jüdische Gemeinde zu Berlin*, which sought the outright destruction of the *Reichsvertretung*.

Jewish Berlin occupied a position within German Jewry analogous to that of Berlin to the *Reich* as a whole. With one-third of all Jews and another third in the *Preussischer Landesverband jüdischer Gemeinden*, which it dominated, Berlin towered over all the other Jewish communities in Germany. Jews in the German capital contributed the most taxes; they had the biggest budget and the most extensive administrative apparatus. Not surprisingly, Berlin considered itself the most logical candidate for the contested throne of German Jewry.

A strong-willed leader was prepared to press the city's claim. He was Heinrich Stahl, formerly a leading figure in the insurance business. Stahl took charge of the city's Jewish community in June 1933 at the age of sixty-five. Prominent in *Reichsvertretung* affairs, he was invited to Essen, the industrial hub of the Ruhr, to participate in the important final deliberations centring on its actual structure. There Stahl learned to his chagrin that while Berlin was expected to foot a substantial part of the bill for the new creation, it was assigned only a modest participatory role. Realising that such negligence was a deliberate attempt to by-pass the communities, above all that of Berlin, Stahl gave vent to his pique at the afternoon session, held at the banker Georg Hirschland's villa in Werden am Ruhr. Upon learning that Leo Baeck and Otto Hirsch were the leading candidates being considered for the top posts in the *Reichsvertretung*, he took Rabbi Hahn aside and told him: "Baeck, whom we honour and esteem as a man of great learning, does not have our confidence in political matters, and Otto Hirsch", he

[48]Thus the *C.V.-Zeitung*, XIV (13th October 1935) deplored the "politicisation" of Palestine and the inadequate attention being given to other possible emigration sites. See also, *C.V.-Zeitung*, XV (6th February 1936).

[49]The new programme of the *Reichsvertretung*, adopted after the promulgation of the Nuremberg Laws, included entry into the *Keren Hayessod* and a statement to the effect that the hope of Jewry now lay with Palestine. See *C.V.-Zeitung*, XIV (26th September 1935).

added, alluding to the latter's Swabian dialect, "does not enter the picture because to us Berliners he speaks a foreign language".[50]

Though Stahl's objection to Baeck might have had no other than personal grounds,[51] the real reason for his opposition was of course directly related to the failure to provide Berlin with a substantial role in the *Reichsvertretung*, one commensurate with its overall standing in the Jewish community. But, by the same token, the original backers of the *Reichsvertretung* voiced the suspicion that Berlin lacked the foresight and political know-how to steer German Jewry through an uncharted future.[52] Thus they forced Berlin to accept the pre-arranged distribution of power and, without recourse, Stahl grumblingly accepted the promise that he would be given an important post in the *Reichsvertretung* and that Berlin was to become its permanent seat.[53]

While agreeing to these minor concessions, Berlin remained dissatisfied. At a community evening shortly before the founding session of the *Reichsvertretung*, three thousand Jewish Berliners heard Bruno Woyda and Moritz Rosenthal, the "enfant terrible" of the liberals, expound all the familiar reasons why Berlin rather than the *Reichsvertretung* should be first among German Jewry.[54] At the constituent meeting itself, the delegates of the communities, pleased no more than Berlin by the stratagems in Essen, banded together to demand the transfer of all authority to the communities and Berlin. Several influential participants quickly interceded in behalf of the *Reichsvertretung*, narrowly averting its stillbirth.[55] Two months later, pushing for Berlin,[56] the *Erneuerungsbewegung* renewed the campaign; again to no avail.

With that, the ascendancy of the *Reichsvertretung* seemed secure. Yet three and a half years later it faced the boldest challenge ever to its authority. This challenge

[50]Quoted in Hahn, *loc. cit.*, p. 102. Werner Cahnmann, a former *Centralverein* official, attributed considerable importance to these regional differences, pointing out that the leaders of the *Centralverein* came primarily from Berlin. Being Prussians, their German nationalism was usually somewhat more pronounced than that of, say, South Germans. Interview with Werner Cahnmann, 16th October 1974, New York.

[51]According to Hans Klee, whose father, Alfred Klee, was a prominent member of the *Jüdische Volkspartei* on the Berlin Executive, Stahl was not on the best of terms with Baeck. Hans Klee, *Georg Kareski und die Jüdische Volkspartei*, 1958, in: Yad Washem Archives, Jerusalem, p. 7.

[52]*Ibid.*, p. 13. "In taking this line, the initiators of 'Reichsvertretung' were also motivated by their desire to counter the claim of the leaders of the Berlin *Kehillah* [community], who considered themselves as the natural titleholders and demanded for themselves a leading share in the total representation of Jews in Germany". Max Gruenewald, 'The Beginning of the "Reichsvertretung"', *loc. cit.*, p. 58. Hans Klee expressed himself rather more strongly: "It was a downright conspiracy against the communities". *Op. cit.*, p. 5.

[53]Herzfeld, *op. cit.*, p. 13. Herzfeld conceded that Berlin's claim that it had been forced into supporting the *Reichsvertretung* was not without foundation. *Ibid.*, p. 22.

[54]See *Israelitisches Familienblatt*, XXXV (14th September 1933). The *Israelitisches Familienblatt*, a newspaper with no particular ideological affiliation, opposed Berlin's claim to leadership.

[55]See Franz Meyer (in K. Y. Ball-Kaduri), 'The National Representation of Jews in Germany – Obstacles and Accomplishments at its Establishment', in *Yad Washem Studies on the European Jewish Catastrophe and Resistance*, II (1958), p. 169.

[56]Moritz Rosenthal of the liberals admitted as much. See *Jüdische Rundschau*, XXXVIII (1st December 1933). Though Berlin claimed it had nothing to do with the *Erneuerungsbewegung*, it provided it with a forum by placing a community evening at its disposal. See *Israelitisches Familienblatt*, XXXV (23rd November 1933).

originated with Georg Kareski, the founder and leader of the *Staatszionisten* (Revisionists). Kareski had a well-deserved reputation as a provocative and disruptive, not to say subversive, influence both in the Berlin Jewish community and the world of German Zionism. A member of the Berlin Executive, which he served as financial director, he had looked on in undisguised disapproval as Stahl, bowing to pressure, endorsed the formation of the *Reichsvertretung* with Berlin in a subordinate position. A year later, he was scheming to take over the ZVfD-administered *Palästina-Amt*, the agency of World Zionism charged with allocating Palestine immigration certificates in Germany. Rebuffed, he struck again in late 1935, mounting a drive, with Gestapo backing, for the leadership of the *Reichsverband der jüdischen Kulturbünde*, and again failing. Undaunted, he resumed the offensive early in 1937, taking aim at the *Reichsvertretung* itself.[57]

That winter Kareski, supported by Stahl and the *Preussischer Landesverband*, accused the *Reichsvertretung* of fiscal irresponsibility and of lacking the necessary authority to speak for the community at large.[58] After months of back-and-forth squabbling, the situation came to a head on 15th June, at one of those infrequent sessions of the *Reichsvertretung* Council, the belated adjunct created in August 1936 to represent the previously slighted communities and provincial associations. A heated debate raged from 10.30 a.m. until 7.00 p.m., while the Gestapo, apprised of the meeting by Stahl four months in advance, quietly took notes.[59] Kareski charged the *Reichsvertretung* with having been illegitimately founded. Supported by Stahl, he criticised the financial practices of the *Reichsvertretung*, coupling a demand for a thoroughgoing investigation into those practices with administrative and organisational reforms designed to enhance the influence of the communities at the expense of the ideological formations. For itself Berlin desired a leading role in all the *Reichsvertretung* committees, and the Kareski-Stahl combination threatened Berlin's withdrawal from that body if it failed to meet these demands. Startled by this resounding condemnation, the majority of the *Reichsvertretung* Council quickly responded with a vote of confidence for its Presidium, and a committee was set up to deal with the Kareski allegations and the reform proposals.[60]

Meanwhile, the Jewish Department of the Gestapo was quietly manoeuvring Leo Baeck to step down as President of the *Reichsvertretung* so as to make room for its own candidate – Georg Kareski.[61] When Baeck refused to be intimidated by such a move, the Gestapo, with Kareski present, then insisted on the resignation of the entire Presidium, the top decision-making body of the *Reichsvertretung*. Replying that German Jewry could not be led by "borrowed authority",[62] Baeck

[57]Kareski's story has been well told by Herbert S. Levine, 'A Jewish Collaborator in Nazi Germany: The Strange Career of Georg Kareski, 1933–37', in *Central European History*, Vol. XIII, No. 3, September 1975, pp. 251–281.

[58]See *Israelitisches Familienblatt*, XXXIX (21st January 1937): Levine, *loc. cit.*, p. 273.

[59]Herzfeld, *op. cit.*, p. 36.

[60]See *Israelitisches Familienblatt*, XXXIX (17th June 1937); *Jüdische Rundschau*, XXXXII (18th June 1937).

[61]See K. Y. Ball-Kaduri, *Einige Bemerkungen zum Konflikt zwischen der Reichsvertretung und der Jüdischen Gemeinde Berlin*, 1944, in Yad Washem Archives, Jerusalem, p. 1.

[62]Quoted in Gruenewald, 'The Beginning of the "Reichsvertretung"', *loc. cit.*, p. 63.

once more resisted. The result of Baeck's stand was that two weeks later Stahl, swallowing his pride, meekly voiced his support for the *Reichsvertretung*, to the surprise of many Council members.[63] (Incidently, the fiscal critic Georg Kareski himself was caught tampering with the funds of the Jewish People's Bank (*Iwriah*), resulting in its liquidation, Kareski's ousting from the Berlin Executive and his subsequent departure from Germany.[64])

Berlin's 1937 attempt to destroy the *Reichsvertretung* was an apt demonstration of political expediency in action. Only a lapse in moral commitment could explain the anomalous case of the liberal Heinrich Stahl who according to one source had spent 40,000 RM of his own money in the 1930 community elections to ensure the defeat of what he then called "Jewish Nazis", to wit, the Zionist opposition[65], allying himself with the extremist on the right-wing of Zionism, Georg Kareski.[66]

The explanation for Stahl's turnabout shows a less opportunistic cast when considered from the standpoint of the different directions within German Zionism. The overwhelming majority of the German Zionists were in the ZVfD, disciples of the so-called "Blumenfeld Method", also known by the shorthand of "Meinekestrasse", after the location of the organisation's Berlin headquarters. Palestine-centred, geared to educational work, progressive, in the mainstream of

[63]Herzfeld, *op. cit.*, pp. 37–38; see also *Jüdische Rundschau*, XXXXII (9th July 1937). Even so, this was not the end of Berlin's power-seeking. In 1939, Stahl submitted a ten-page broadside to the Nazi overseers of Jewish affairs in which he denounced the *Reichsvertretung* as a hotbed of political intrigue and do-nothing organisation, requesting that its mandate be transferred to Berlin. Soon thereafter, turning a deaf ear to Berlin's entreaties, the authorities supervised the creation of the *Reichsvereinigung der Juden in Deutschland*, the ill-starred successor to the *Reichsvertretung*. K. J. Ball-Kaduri, *Vor der Katastrophe. Juden in Deutschland 1934–1939*, Tel-Aviv 1967, pp. 254–256.

In 1939, as in 1937, Berlin did have a case, though it went to extreme lengths to prove it. Through no fault of its own, the *Reichsvertretung* never performed the very function for which it had been primarily brought into being: the representation of Jews before the authorities. Additionally, the *Reichsvertretung* was hamstrung because it was to a large extent dependent upon the financial contributions from the communities and upon funds from abroad. For example, in 1937 the *Reichsvertretung* spent a total of 3.8 million RM, with a deficit of 250,000 RM. Of this money, 2.5 million RM had come from abroad. See *Jüdische Rundschau*, XXXXIII (14th January 1938). That same year, the Berlin budget was 14 million RM. *C.V.-Zeitung*, XVI (30th December 1937). A sizeable chunk of the *Reichsvertretung* budget came from the provincial associations, with Berlin and Prussia contributing the most. The *Reichsvertretung*, lamented the *Jüdische Rundschau* of 10th August 1934, has remained a "general staff without an army", at the mercy of the large communities and provincial associations.

The *Reichsvertretung's* importance was its connection with the *Zentralausschuss für Hilfe und Aufbau*, the agency which dealt with such diverse programmes as emigration, vocational training, credit assistance, and Jewish schools. In April 1935, the *Zentralausschuss* was formally incorporated into the *Reichsvertretung*. See Meyer, *loc. cit.*, p. 170; see also, G. Lubinsky, *ibid.* (see note 55), p. 173.

[64]According to Jakob Ball-Kaduri's brother, Fritz Ball, Kareski covered up deficits of the Iwriah Bank, of which he was the founder, by forcing a payment of 50,000 RM from the cashier of the Berlin Jewish community. Kareski apparently had a weakness for speculation; twice before he had been involved with banking institutions which had collapsed. K. Y. Ball-Kaduri, *Einige Bemerkungen*, p. 2.

[65]Benno Cohn, *Soziologische Betrachtungen über die Führung des deutschen Judentums vor und nach dem Jahre 1933*, 1944, in Yad Washem Archives, Jerusalem, p. 2.

[66]Herbert S. Levine suggests a possible additional motive for the Stahl/Kareski axis: Stahl may well have availed himself of Kareski's "talent for 'fixing things with the police' ". Apparently Stahl had "some difficulty with the Gestapo because of his support of Social Democratic anti-Nazi efforts in 1932". Levine, *loc. cit.*, pp. 264–265.

West European Zionism, the Blumenfeld orientation played down community politics. The reverse held for the minority position in the ZVfD represented by the *Jüdische Volkspartei*. Confined to Berlin, the *Jüdische Volkspartei* took an active part in community politics, and none more so than its controversial founding-member, Georg Kareski.[67]

The two elements in the ZVfD did not mesh, and the presence of Kareski further complicated relations.[68] Kareski, for example, had an unseemly habit of collectively branding the ZVfD leadership as "the reds in Meinekestrasse", not infrequently within earshot of Herr Kuchmann, a familiar and durable Nazi prop at many Jewish gatherings of an official nature.[69] Kareski's removal from the mainstream organisation seemed only a matter of time; and it came in August 1933, in the aftermath of an "obscure incident" involving a militant attempt, which he apparently led, to occupy the Jewish welfare office in Berlin. Kareski's refusal to bow to the ZVfD demand that he quit the Berlin Executive was followed by his expulsion from the parent body. The role he had played in the affair at the welfare office, coupled with his espousal of Revisionism, not only deepened the rift between the *Jüdische Volkspartei* and the ZVfD leadership, but also fomented a split within the ranks of the *Jüdische Volkspartei* itself:[70] three of its fourteen members in the Berlin Assembly broke away to form an independent unit known as the *Zionistische Fraktion*. When two *Fraktion* members on the Berlin Executive quit that body in the course of 1933 in a show of revulsion against Kareski, his collaborators in the *Jüdische Volkspartei* and Berlin's support of the *Erneuerungsbewegung*, the road was cleared for the Kareski-dominated *Jüdische Volkspartei* in the Executive.[71] In the revision of the Executive that followed the introduction of representational parity in November 1935, reducing it from twelve to seven members,[72] all three Zionist positions went to the *Jüdische Volkspartei*.

[67]See Meyer, *loc. cit.*, p. 170; Kurt Tuchler, *Erlebnisse und Beobachtungen in den ersten vier Hitlerjahren*, 1945, in Yad Washem Archives, Jerusalem, pp. 5–6; Klee, *op. cit.*, p. 1. In November 1934, the *Jüdische Volkspartei* changed its name to *Jüdischer Volksbund*. We, however, shall continue to refer to it by its old name.

[68]Meyer, *loc. cit.*, p. 171. Franz Meyer was a member of the *Reichsvertretung* and of the Executive of the ZVfD in Breslau.

[69]Levine, *loc. cit.*, pp. 259–260. See also, Tuchler, *op. cit.*, p. 6, though Tuchler does not mention Kareski by name.

[70]The sources are somewhat confusing here. Benno Cohn puts the departure of the two *Zionistiche Fraktion* members (Arthur Rau and Siegfried Moses) in the summer of 1933. *Op. cit.*, p. 1. On the other hand, there is no mention of Siegfried Moses, the Chairman of the ZVfD, leaving the Berlin Executive until November 1933, the reason given being Berlin's support of the *Erneuerungsbewegung*. See *Israelitisches Familienblatt*, XXXV (23rd November 1933). Nor was I able to find any references in the Jewish press to Rau's departure. The *Israelitisches Familienblatt*, being closer to the actual events, is more likely to be correct than Cohn. Steering a mid-course, in the text I have combined the reasons.

[71]See *Jüdische Rundschau*, XXXX (12th November 1935).

[72]The original intent was to expand rather than decrease the Executive – this, to reduce Kareski's influence. Kareski objected, and possibly alerted the Nazi authorities to the existence of a law of 1847 prohibiting such an expansion and, in fact, mandating its reduction. See Levine, *loc. cit.*, p. 265.

Tuchler credits Stahl with bringing about a smooth transition, claiming that Stahl was a "real leader personality" whose achievements have been underrated. *Op. cit.*, pp. 2–3. Benno Cohn, at the time the Executive Director of the ZVfD, agreed with this assessment. *Op. cit.*, p. 1. Not Joachim Prinz, however. Rabbi Prinz, a fervent advocate of emigration, repeatedly preached the need for

A similar struggle took place inside the liberal camp, which was divided into two parts: the *Centralverein*, which fought discrimination, and the community liberals, who took aim at Zionism and Orthodoxy. However, with the emergence of a younger generation in the *Centralverein* sympathetic to Palestine, a chasm opened up between the *Centralverein* leadership and the community liberals. Thus in the last (Berlin) community elections before Hitler, a group of pro-Palestine "young liberals" had opposed "old liberals" like Stahl, Moritz Rosenthal and Wilhelm Kleemann, Stahl's predecessor as Chairman of the Executive. Diverging social backgrounds further breached the gap: academicians, serving with pay, generally held sway in the *Centralverein*, while well-to-do businessmen, serving without remuneration, dominated the community liberals.[73]

The respective struggles within the liberal and Zionist camps produced the 1937 combinations Stahl-Kareski-Berlin versus *Centralverein*-ZVfD-*Reichsvertretung*. Precluded from participating in community politics by the *Jüdische Volkspartei*, "Meinekestrasse" Zionists discovered that they had more in common with pro-Palestine *Centralverein* leaders in the *Reichsvertretung* than with their ideological brethren in the Berlin Executive. And, conversely, the circle of "Friends of Palestine" in the *Centralverein* was closer to the general Zionists in the *Reichsvertretung* than to the community liberals in Berlin.[74] (For these reasons, too, the R.j.F. after 1933 replaced the *Centralverein* as the political antipode to the ZVfD.[75])

Berlin left no stone unturned in its pursuit of power. But the ZVfD, too, claimed custody of the disputed body of German Jewry, and the two contestants, Berlin and Zionism, inevitably came to bitter blows. Bristling with invective, the *Jüdische Rundschau* told its readers that an anti-Zionist dictatorship of liberals ran Berlin.[76] Berlin, Zionists claimed, was unresponsive to the needs of Jewish schools, particularly Zionist schools,[77] neglected occupational retraining, youth and cultural matters.[78] Of a total budget of 12,000,000 RM, only three to four percent went to "Zionist" departments – i.e. museums, libraries, archives, the community's least important administrative branches.[79] Zionists complained

---

Jews to leave Germany, which put him in opposition to the established leadership, including Stahl. Stahl happened to be present at one of those sermons, and when a day later Prinz visited him at his house and explained why Jews had to emigrate and proposed that the rich subsidise the poor in this expensive undertaking, Prinz reports that Stahl "grew only angrier . . . He was a rich man, independent and highly respected, and he lived in a splendid villa not far from my house. As I entered the house I saw that his famous collection of Impressionists had been removed from the wall. I enquired about the paintings. He replied that he had sent them to his son in Belgium because they were no longer safe here. I looked at him with great amazement and said: 'Evidently to save the paintings is more important; to save Jews is not'. I never saw him again. It must be said to his honor that he was a victim of his own convictions. He died in Theresienstadt". Joachim Prinz, 'A Rabbi under the Hitler Regime', in *Gegenwart im Rückblick. Festgabe für die Jüdische Gemeinde zu Berlin 25 Jahre nach dem Neubeginn*, eds. H. A. Strauss and K. R. Grossman, Heidelberg 1970, pp. 237–238.

[73]Cohn, *op. cit.*, pp. 1–2.

[74]*Ibid.*, p. 2; Meyer, *loc. cit.*, p. 170.

[75]Ball-Kaduri, 'The National Representation', p. 176.

[76]*Jüdische Rundschau*, XXXIX (2nd February 1934); XXXVIII (17th September 1933).

[77]*Jüdische Rundschau*, XXXX (17th May 1935); XXXX (24th May 1935).

[78]*Jüdische Rundschau*, XXXIX (1st May 1934).

[79]*Jüdische Rundschau*, XXXIX (31st May 1934); XXX (14th May 1935).

that Berlin was opposed to anything that smacked of change; it put up barriers against Judification,[80] monopolised the community evenings and the newspaper,[81] and stubbornly resisted rejuvenation from the top down.[82]

The introduction, however, of equal representation in the Berlin Executive in November 1935 and in the *Reichsvertretung* in August 1936, and the concurrent virtual elimination of Palestine as a haven for Jewish emigrants,[83] blunted the overall Zionist offensive. Even so, what not so long before had represented only a minor ideological current in the community now virtually ruled the mainstream. Once the despised stepchild of German Jewry, Zionists had lived to see their theories vindicated and their programme appropriated piecemeal, even though they never left off bemoaning the dearth of Zionist spirit with which that programme was enacted.[84]

Two trump cards held by Zionism facilitated its rapid rise. One was Palestine; the other was the "most-favoured-nation treatment" accorded it by a Nazi officialdom appreciative of its unsparing efforts in behalf of Jewish emigration.[85] Of the 138,000 Jews who had left Germany by the summer of 1938, 38,000 had opted for Palestine, the majority with the indirect assistance of the *Haavara* (Transfer Agreement), the special arrangement worked out in August 1933 between Nazi Germany and the agencies of World Zionism. (The agreement permitted Jews who wished to leave Germany for Palestine to transfer their money in German goods, thus circumventing the prevailing restrictions on the export of capital; they were to be reimbursed in British pounds upon arrival in Palestine.[86])

[80]*Jüdische Rundschau*, XXXIX (2nd February 1934).

[81]*Jüdische Rundschau*, XXXIX (27th April 1934).

[82]*Jüdische Rundschau*, XXXIX (24th April 1943).

[83]Stung by Arab rioting in the spring of 1936, the British launched the Peel Commission to study the Palestine problem. Its 500-page report, which came out in 1937, recommended the tripartition of Palestine into separate Arab and Jewish states, with the third part to remain in British hands. The Commission also recommended the imposition of severe restrictions on Jewish emigration to the area. Only 8,000 Jews, for example, were to be allowed to settle in Palestine during the period August 1937 to March 1938. See *C.V.-Zeitung*, XVI (8th July 1937).

[84]See *Jüdische Rundschau*, XXXIX (4th May 1934); Tuchler, *op. cit.*, p. 3. Berlin claimed to have carried out the Zionist programme better than the Zionists themselves ever could have. See *Jüdische Rundschau*, XXXIX (10th May 1934); XXXXI (10th October 1936).

[85]"Fest steht, dass sich während der ersten Phasen der nationalsozialistischen Judenpolitik nicht selten eine Situation entwickelte, in welcher es den Nationalsozialisten angebracht erechien, eine pro-zionistische Haltung einzunehmen oder vorzugeben". Hans Lamm, *Über die innere und aüssere Entwicklung des deutschen Judentums im Dritten Reich*, Ph.D. diss., Univ. of Erlangen 1951, p. 140. Similarly, Eliahu Ben Elissar writes: "Les seuls Juifs avec lesquels, en fin de comte, divers organismes du Troisième Reich, et particulièrement le ministère des Affaires étrangères et celui de l'Economie, établiront de véritables relations de travail, seront bel et bien les sionistes et les Juifs palestiniens". *La Diplomatie du IIIe Reich et les Juifs*, Paris 1969, p. 87. See also, Hannah Arendt, *Eichmann in Jerusalem: A Report on the Banality of Evil*, rev. and enl. edn., New York 1970, pp. 59–60.

[86]For the *Haavara*, see the three lengthy essays (by Werner Feichenfeld, Dolf Michaelis, and Ludwig Pinner) in *Haavara-Transfer nach Palästina und Einwanderung deutscher Juden 1933–1939*, Tübingen 1972 (Schriftenreihe wissenschaftlicher Abhandlungen des Leo Baeck Instituts 26). The 38,000 figure is from Feilchenfeld, 'Die Durchführung des Haavara-Transfers', pp. 37–38. Herbert A. Strauss puts the five-year total (1933–1938) at 43,200. "Jewish Emigration from Germany. Nazi Policies and Jewish Responses (II)', in *LBI Year Book XXVI* (1981), p. 346 (Table I). For Part I of this essay, see *LBI Year Book XXV* (1980), pp. 313–361. For the diplomacy of the *Haavara*, see Ellisar, *op. cit.*, pp. 85–95.

The idea of a national home for Jews in the Middle East was bound to appeal to a certain type of Nazi–"idealists", scrupulous constructionists of National Socialist glosses on *Volk* and *Raum*, who were wont to identify with the national aspirations of the Jewish people.[87] Well aware of this particular current in Nazi thought, the ZVfD in the spring of 1933 commissioned Kurt Tuchler, a member of the *Jüdische Volkspartei* on the Berlin Executive, to fire the imagination of such broad-minded Nazis for the Jewish enterprise in Palestine. Tuchler found an interested party in Baron Leopold Itz von Mildenstein, the *Judenreferent* in the S.S.; and later that spring the two men, accompanied by their wives, embarked on their Palestinian jaunt. Upon his return the Baron, who also dabbled in journalism, persuaded the editors of *Der Angriff*, Goebbels's newspaper, to devote a series of illustrated articles to this curious fact-finding journey. Having learned a little Hebrew, von Mildenstein also brought back with him a collection of records from Palestine; to Tuchler's astonishment, strains of familiar Hebrew folk songs greeted him on entering the Baron's office in 1934. To commemmorate the voyage of a Nazi to Palestine, *Der Angriff* even had a medal struck showing the Swastika on one side and the Star of David on the other.[88]

Bizarre as this example might seem, in essence it summarised some of the Alice-in-Wonderland quality of the Nazi-Zionist dialogue. It was a fact that in the opening years of the Hitler regime, the Nazi leaders favoured Zionists over non-Zionists,[89] and Zionists themselves proclaimed that of all Jewish groups, only they could approach the Nazis in good faith, as "honest partners".[90] By making a distinction between race-minded, emigration-conscious Zionists and "assimilationists"–bent, as they said, on destroying National Socialism –powerful Nazis like Reinhard Heydrich, Chief of the *Sicherheitsdienst*, the intelligence arm of the S.S., indirectly backed Zionist attempts to take control of the community. Heydrich echoed the official S.S. position that the activities of Zionists should be encouraged, those of non-Zionists discouraged. Consequently, Zionists were granted privileges denied to other groups. A police decree of March 1935, for example, instructed officers to be more tolerant of the doings of Zionist youth groups than of those non-Zionist ones. As well, access to Nazi functionaries generally proved easier for Zionists than for others; and, forbidden to display the national colours, a special provision in the Nuremberg Laws permitted Jews to

[87]See Arendt, *op. cit.*, pp. 41–42.

[88]See Tuchler, *op. cit.*, pp. 2, 6. For a more detailed treatment of the von Mildenstein-Tuchler voyage to Palestine, see this author's 'A Nazi Travels to Palestine', in *History Today*, vol. 30 (January 1980), pp. 33–38. Von Mildenstein's articles (in which he used the pen name "von Limm") ran in *Der Angriff* from 24th September until 9th October 1934.

[89]See Schleunes, *op. cit.*, pp. 178–181; 193–194. Herzfeld also reports that in the last months of 1936 the Gestapo acted more leniently towards Zionists than towards "assimilationists". *Op. cit.*, p. 32. The *Israelitisches Familienblatt* of 21st March 1935 cited authoritative Nazi sources urging favouritism towards pro-emigration groups like the Zionists. See also, Kurt T. Grossmann, 'Zionists and non-Zionists under Nazi rule in the 1930's, in *Herzl Year Book. Essays in Zionist History and Thought*, IV (1961–1962), pp. 329–344, especially the appendices; and Hans Mommsen, 'Der Nationalsozialistische Polizeistaat und die Judenverfolgung vor 1938', in *Vierteljahrshefte für Zeitgeschichte*, Heft 1 (Januar 1962), pp. 68–87. Of particular interest are the documents, reproduced by Mommsen, from the Bayerische Politische Polizei, pp. 77–87.

[90]*Jüdische Rundschau*, XXXVIII (7th April 1933).

hoist their own banner, that is to say, the Zionist standard, the current flag of Israel.[91]

Needless to say, German Zionism held no brief for National Socialism. If both agitated for a Jewish exodus from Germany, they did so for radically different reasons and purposes. It should hardly need repeating that Zionist principles differed from those of National Socialism as night differs from day. Zionism believed in the existence of different races, but not in the superiority of one race over another. Zionist nationalism, as elaborated by the ZVfD, harked back to an earlier period, the Mazzini-type conception of nationalism as a liberating force leading, ultimately, to the harmonious coexistence of all the world's peoples. And although Zionism, like National Socialism, repudiated individualism, rootlessness and decadence, unlike National Socialism it never lost sight of the individual human being independent of race. Nor did the sanctification of the soil as the mainspring of spiritual and national well-being preclude Germany's Zionists from advocating the peaceful coexistence of Arab and Jew in a Palestinian bi-national state.

Yet much of the idiom through which Zionism expressed its main ideas bore a striking, if superficial, resemblance to the *völkisch* ideas of the day.[92] As much may be gathered from the following excerpt of a statement from a ZVfD position paper submitted to the Nazi authorities on 21st June 1933:

> "Zionism believes that a rebirth of a national life, as has occurred in German life through the adherence to Christian and national values, must also become a reality for the Jewish national entity. For Jews, too, racial origins (*Abstammung*), religion, community of fate and consciousness of their special racial nature (*Artbewusstsein*) must exercise the decisive influence on how they shape their life. This requires that they overcome the egoistic individualism of the Liberal Era through community spirit and a willingness to shoulder responsibility."[93]

Zionists were not unaware of the vexing parallelism between their own brand of *völkisch* thought and that of National Socialism and went to great lengths to dissociate themselves spiritually from the latter. Nevertheless, at bottom it was this elemental consonance with currently popular *völkisch* modes of thought,[94] in addition to the existence of Palestine as a potential haven, which enabled Zionists

[91]Paragraph 4 of the Law for the Protection of German Blood and German Honour stated: "1. Jews are not permitted to display the German flag or the national colours; 2. They are, however, permitted to show the Jewish colours. The exercise of this right is protected by the State". Paragraph 5.3 described the penalty for infringing "1": up to one year's imprisonment plus fine, or one of these.

[92]Benno Cohn summarised the problem faced by Zionism as follows: "Dabei war beim Auftreten vor den jüdischen Massen in jenen Jahren stets die Gefahr einer . . . ideologischen Gleichschaltung mit den Nazis gegeben. Die Zionisten hatten ja die Assimilation immer verurteilt und zur Auswanderung, zur Alija, zur Schaffung eines neuen Volkszentrums aufgerufen. Die zionistischen Sprecher mussten sich daher sehr hüten, in ihren Reden nicht etwa eine Assoziation zu den Parolen der Nazis und ihrer Rassentheorien aufkommen zu lassen". 'Einige Bemerkungen über den deutschen Zionismus nach 1933', in *In Zwei Welten, op. cit.*, p. 46.

[93]Cited in Klaus J. Herrmann, *Das Dritte Reich und die deutsch-jüdischen Organisationen 1933–1934*, München 1969, p. 16.

[94]The *C.V.-Zeitung*, for example, frequently harped on the similarities between Zionism and the Nazi Weltanschauung. In a May 1934 leader, Eva Reichmann-Jungmann observed that in 1933 the attraction of Zionism was great – "tempting and seductive". *C.V.-Zeitung*, XIII (31st May 1934). Taking issue with Jewish nationalism Alfred Hirschberg, that paper's Editor-in-Chief, saw it as assimilation to the times. *C.V.-Zeitung*, XIII (6th December 1934).

to gain the upper hand in the prolonged struggle for supremacy in the Jewish community. Even though the Jewish newspapers frequently reminded their readers that humanitarian values must take precedence over those contingent on race and might, such caveats were bound to ring a trifle hollow against a background pulsating with ideas that appeared to carry all before them. The seemingly endless victory parade of National Socialism suggested the hand of Providence, and the temptation for Jews to appropriate for their own use certain aspects of its style, thought, rhetoric, and behaviour was great and not always averted. Warning Jews against the dangers of "brown assimilation", the Executive Director of the Berlin Jewish community, Walter Breslauer, wrote in a 1934 *C.V.-Zeitung* leader:

> "The National Socialist State excludes Jews from its culture . . . but it leaves them their freedom in the internal Jewish sphere and in no way expects that within this sphere Jews appropriate and duplicate its store of ideas – ideas of totality, leadership principle, the rejection of 'liberal' opinions. A 'brown assimilation' is thus in no way enjoined upon Jews; national Jewish and German-Jewish circles have equal cause to keep their distance from it, which unfortunately does not always happen on either side."[95]

Despite the considerable residual strength of Jewish liberalism – "the majority of German Jews clung to the principles of liberalism with something like desperation"[96] – the enticements of contemporary ideas proved strong indeed. The proliferation of *völkisch* ideas and influences was not entirely absent in the Jewish community, and ran the gamut from political rhetoric to the "one-pot" meals of the Jewish Winter Relief; from teach-ins on leadership to the penchant of Jewish youth formations for flags, emblems and bunting; from the downgrading of intellectual pursuits to the upgrading of physical labour.[97]

Significantly, the attraction of the National Socialist "store of ideas" mentioned by Breslauer was particularly glaring in the *Israelitisches Familienblatt*, the newspaper that up until its final days considered itself the trustee of neutral Jewish opinion. The *Familienblatt* not only had kind words for Italian fascism[98]; it also spoke highly of *Gleichschaltung* and *Führerprinzip*, exhorting Jews to step up to the times by grafting these principles of modern statecraft onto their own unruly body politic.[99] And its leading article of 10th August 1933 rued the fact that so

[95] *C.V.-Zeitung*, XIII (1st November 1934).

[96] Mosse, *op. cit.*, p. 103.

[97] "There is little doubt that the existing youth organisations and clubs had for a time substituted symbols, flags, marching songs, etc., for similar forms of expression of the Hitler youth". Solomon Colodner, 'Jewish Education under National Socialism', *Yad Washem Studies on the European Jewish Catastrophe and Resistance*, III (1959), pp. 166—167. "The Labor Service, the welfare work for the unemployed, the labor camps, the domestic service year, and other such institutions based on collective education were not without influence". Rudolph Stahl, 'Vocational Retraining of Jews in Nazi Germany 1933–1938', *Jewish Social Studies*, 1 (April 1939), No. 2, p. 180. See also, in connection with labour's upgrading, by the author, 'Germany or Diaspora? German Jewry's Shifting Perceptions in the Nazi Era (1933–1938)', in *LBI Year Book XXVII* (1982), pp. 121–122.

[98] See *Israelitisches Familienblatt*, XXXVI (11th January 1934). Despite its vaunted neutrality in Jewish affairs, the *Israelitisches Familienblatt* gradually began displaying a marked bias toward Zionism, demanding that it be given more, though not all, power in the community. See *Israelitisches Familienblatt*, XXXVII (6th June 1935); XXXVII (13th June 1935).

[99] See, for example, Arno Herzberg, 'Anschluss an die Zeit', *Israelitisches Familienblatt*, XXXV (8th June 1933); *Israelitisches Familienblatt*, XXXVI (1st February 1934), praising the fusion of *Volk* and *Staat*, as well as the suppression of niggling parliamentary debate; and the 12th April 1934 headline, 'Wir fordern Gemeindereform an Haupt und Gliedern: Führerprinzip auch bei uns!'

little of the regenerative spirit currently abroad in the "new state" had filtered down to the Jewish community. (In all this, however, it would be well to bear in mind the special conditions, alluded to earlier, under which the Jewish press toiled.)

The chief casualty of the changing mood in the community was the *Centralverein*, the stubborn conscience of Jewish liberalism. Already on the defensive before 1933, Hitler's sweep to power dealt it a crushing blow. The "unflinching cultivation of German identity" and the sharp vigil it kept to safeguard the still tender shoots of emancipation, the very heart of the *Centralverein* programme, shrivelled under the heat of the supercharged illiberal climate of Nazi Germany. At last, concluded a study of the influence of *völkisch* ideas on Germany Jewry, albeit too sweepingly, "the *C.V.-Zeitung* found itself the sole spokesman for a liberalism which had been rejected by most Germans and Jews alike".[100]

The *Centralverein*, in picking over every bit of ideological terrain, yielded but grudgingly. It responded testily to Zionist claims that it had forfeited its right to lead German Jewry by accusing the ZVfD of *Schadenfreude*.[101] What German Jewry needed least of all, the *C.V.-Zeitung* cautioned in December 1933, was a "revolution" of its own.[102] Elsewhere, Jews were reminded that leaders were not made overnight.[103] Lastly, turning vice into virtue, the organisation blandly dismissed charges of ineptitude with the argument that sometimes it took more courage not to act than to act.[104]

To the degree that its ideological position crumbled over the years, the *Centralverein* resorted to stressing pragmatism over ideology, representing itself to the community as the "creative centre of German Jewry".[105] But with each new piece of anti-Jewish legislation, with every Nazi act of terror and intimidation, insult and slight, the *Centralverein* lost ground, until, at last, it was compelled to espouse a goodly portion of the Zionist point of view[106] and practically all of its programme.

The simultaneous waxing and waning of the respective fortunes of the ZVfD and the *Centralverein* betokened a general shift in Jewish socio-political attitudes. The liberal persuasion, with its emphasis on the self-realising individual and the

[100]Mosse, *op. cit.*, p. 102.

[101]The *C.V.-Zeitung*, XIV (26th September 1935) spoke of "Siegesfanfaren" and "ill-concealed joy" on the part of Zionism. The *Centralverein* accused Zionists of a "brutal exploitation of a calamity", said the *Jüdische Rundschau*, XXXX (19th March 1935). Friendly to Zionism, Rabbi Max Gruenewald of the *Reichsvertretung* wrote in the *Jüdische Rundschau*, XXXX (15th November 1935): "Weder eine völlig palästinazentrische Einstellung noch die Erbitterung über ein jahrelanges Unverständnis auf der Seite der verantwortlichen Führung gab das Recht dazu, dass die Judenheit in Deutschland so von führenden Zionisten entblösst wurde, wie das tatsächlich geschehen ist".

[102]*C.V.-Zeitung*, XII (21st December 1933); XII (18th May 1933).

[103]*C.V.-Zeitung*, XII (15th June 1933).

[104]*C.V.-Zeitung*, XII (29th June 1933).

[105]*C.V.-Zeitung*, XIII (25th October 1934); XIV (3rd May 1935).

[106]The process by which non-Zionists came to adopt much of the Zionist "line" has been traced back to the period of the Weimar Republic, especially its last year. See Peter M. Baldwin, 'Zionist and Non-Zionist Jews in the Last Years Before the Nazi Regime', in *LBI Year Book XXVII* (1982), pp. 87–108.

political forms to which it had given rise, was being supplanted by an appreciation of the complex of values – broadly designated as *völkisch* – derived from *Volkstum*. It would be a mistake, however, to interpret this new-fashioned receptivity to *völkisch* ideas and ideals as showing nothing more than mimesis. Rather, it must be understood in the sense of furnishing Jews with a powerful heuristic model for exploring and coming to grips with their own collective identity as Jews.

As the champion and embodiment of *Jewish Volkstum*, the ZVfD emerged as the uncontested beneficiary of this changing outlook. There are numerous indications that Zionism provided an attractive alternative to a liberalism that seemed to have passed the point of no return. For instance, the circulation figures of the *Jüdische Rundschau* quadrupled.[107] Financial contributions to Zionism in the period 1933–1936 tripled over those collected during 1931–1932 – and this from a much impoverished base.[108] Indicative, too, of the new outlook in the community was the change in attitude toward Palestine on the part of a number of influential "German-Jewish" spokesmen and organisations. Thus, in 1903 Heinrich Stahl had returned from a trip to Palestine convinced that the place could not be made fit for human habitation; in 1936 he believed that only Palestine could save the Jews.[109] Eva Reichmann-Jungmann likewise returned full of praise for the Jewish settlements after visiting Palestine around the beginning of 1938.[110] And by the end of 1935 even the R.j.F. claimed to be furthering the work there.[111]

Zionism made converts prodigiously among Jewish youth also. Already at the end of 1934, the ZVfD claimed that eighty percent of all organised young Jewish men and women were enrolled in Zionist youth groups.[112] In June 1935, the formerly neutral *Verband der jüdischen Jugendvereine Deutschlands* came out in favour of the building-up of Palestine. In March 1936, the *Verband* reported that it had decided to integrate itself into the Zionist movement.[113] With the erstwhile groundswell rising to a mighty wave, by the end of 1935 Zionism could justly claim that it had gained the confidence of the broad Jewish masses.[114]

It is of course impossible to ascertain with any degree of certainty how many German Jews in the first five years of Nazism shifted their allegiance to Zionism or repudiated their former liberal convictions. Whatever the precise dimensions of this re-orientation may have been, there can be little doubt that a shift of some sort took place in those years, and that it was by no means negligible. After 1933, more and more Jews began speaking of themselves as a *Volk* and of their

[107]Strauss, 'Jewish Press', *loc. cit.*, p. 34 (from roughly 10,000 before 1933 to approximately 38,000 by the end of 1933). Robert Weltsch, the editor of the *Jüdische Rundschau* during the Nazi years, fixed his paper's pre-1933 circulation at 5,000 to 7,000 per issue. Lamm, *op. cit.*, p. 175, note 1.

[108]Arendt, *op. cit.*, p. 59.

[109]*Jüdische Rundschau*, XXXXI (12 April 1936); XXXXI (8th May 1936).

[110]*C.V.-Zeitung*, XVII (24th February 1938).

[111]See *Jüdische Rundschau*, XXXX (10th October 1935).

[112]*Israelitisches Familienblatt*, XXXVI (6th December 1934).

[113]*Israelitisches Familienblatt*, XXXVII (8th August 1935); XXXVIII (5th March 1936).

[114]See *Jüdische Rundschau*, XXXX (17th December 1935). It should be remembered, though, that the growth of Zionism predated 1933. In 1926, 18,000 Jewish Berliners voted for Zionism; by 1930, their number had risen to 30,000. See *Jüdische Rundschau*, XXXX (17th April 1935).

community as a *Volksgemeinde*, which is another way of saying that they began seeing themselves as a separate and distinct nationality. The confusion, turmoil and disorientation of the pre-1933 period had prepared the soil for this transformation, but it took Hitler's accession to power to bring it to a head. Hence it was not just the existence of Palestine but the entire sweep of recent German – and beyond that of recent European – history that determined the relative ease with which a large number of Jews slipped from a liberal role into Zionism, an ideology decidedly more attuned to the times.

The American Press and the Persecution of German Jewry

The Early Years 1933–1935

BY DEBORAH E. LIPSTADT

I

In recent years, much of the debate regarding what has come to be known as the Holocaust has focused upon the question of when the world became aware of the fact that the Jews of Europe were being systematically murdered. It is generally acknowledged that by the end of 1942 most of the information was available not only to those privy to secret information but also to the general public.[1] Controversy still persists about what was known regarding the Final Solution and precisely when it was known.[2] There is, however, no question about the degree of information which was available regarding the persecution of the Jews during the early years of the Nazi regime. There was an established foreign press corps in Germany throughout the 1930s. American reporters remained in Germany until the very end of 1941. Some were even there through part of 1942 when they were exchanged for Germans who had been interned in the United States.[3] Although there was some key information that was unavailable to them, such as the true conditions in the concentration camps, there was much that they knew, witnessed and shared with their readers in America.

The initial incidents of persecution evoked a strong reaction from American reporters stationed in Germany and from the editorial boards of various American newspapers. Predictably, the American press was interested in the entire orbit of events connected with the rise of the new German regime. Antisemitic persecution was an important, but certainly not central, element of their reports. It is ironic, but understandable, that antisemitism evoked more

[1]Walter Laqueur, *The Terrible Secret. An Investigation into the Suppression of Information about Hitler's 'Final Solution'*, London-Boston 1980; Martin Gilbert, *Auschwitz and the Allies*, London-New York 1981.

[2]Documents recently released in the second volume of the *Official History of British Intelligence in the Second World War*, London 1981, indicate that the Allies were aware of the existence of Auschwitz and six other death camps in the spring of 1942. Martin Gilbert claims that they did not know until much later than that. Walter Laqueur, 'The Untold Story of World War II', in *New Republic* (14th October 1981), No. 184 pp. 18–20.

[3]Gregg Stadler, United Press reporter stationed in Germany, was not exchanged until the spring of 1942. When he returned to the United States he wrote a series of reports in which he described the position of the Jews as that of victims of an "open hunt". *New York Times*, (hereafter cited as *NYT*) 18th May, 1942. Joseph Grigg, who was also a United Press staff correspondent, gave distressingly vivid reports of mass graves and massacres of Jews when he was exchanged in June 1942. *New York Herald Tribune*, 2nd June 1942.

interest during the early periods of Nazi rule than it did in subsequent years. Eventually less attention would be paid to it except on those occasions, e.g. the promulgation of the Nuremberg Laws and the *Kristallnacht*, when a major event occurred. This relegation of antisemitism to what those associated with the press call a "sidebar" may be explained by a number of factors. Initially, this news was shocking. Ultimately American newspaper readers became inured to it. It became an "old" story. Once the war began in 1939 and even more once America entered the conflagration, there were other stories, such as the deaths of American soldiers, which seemed far more pertinent than reports and rumours of massacres, gas chambers and death camps.

This paper will examine the reaction of the American press to Nazi antisemitism during the first three years of Hitler's rule. The initial period of the Nazi regime is of course crucial in terms of Nazi anti-Jewish policy, as by the end of 1935 the foundation of Nazi antisemitic policy had been laid. During this period, as the American public learned about Hitler and Nazism, many of its early perceptions formed the basis of what would eventually become the American attitude towards Nazi Germany in general and its persecution of the Jews in particular.

This study will analyse the manner in which this news was transmitted to the public, the attention accorded it and whether the press understood and explained to its readers that the persecution of the Jews was something intrinsic to Nazi ideology and not simply a passing revolutionary phenomenon. During these years the new rulers were intent on consolidation and establishing Nazi Germany as a respected member of the family of nations. They were then most vulnerable to public criticism and most susceptible to foreign pressure. The new leaders tested the world. Would internal persecution and abrogation of external commitments be countenanced? Would there be a strong outcry, official criticism and the imposition of sanctions? Or would the world maintain a diplomatic distance?[4]

Reporters influenced foreign perceptions of Nazi Germany through both their news stories and the private information they relayed to diplomats stationed in Germany. Ambassadors and consular staff appear to have relied on them regularly as sources regarding the inner workings of the government.[5]

The diplomatic staff of both the German and American governments were aware of the influence of the newspapers on American public opinion.

[4]The American Consul General in Germany, George Messersmith believed that most of the leaders of the Nazi Party had a "complete disregard of what the outside world thinks". Messersmith to Hull, Decimal Files, Department of State, National Archives (hereafter cited as DS.) DS. 862.4016/568 as quoted in Shlomo Shafir, *The Impact of the Jewish Crisis on American German Relations, 1933–1939*, Ph.D. dissertation, Georgetown University, 1971, p. 76. Nonetheless German officials abroad regularly sent reports on attitudes in the countries in which they were stationed. *Reichsbank* President Hjalmar Schacht was an example of a German official who was sensitive to public opinion abroad.

[5]At the end of March 1933 Messersmith wrote to Secretary of State Hull that "American correspondents in Berlin have brought to my attention cases of maltreatment of all sorts of persons of various nationalities which they have personally investigated and found correct but which more recently they have not been able to publish. . . I have confidence in the correspondents who have been giving this information. *Foreign Relations of the United States: Diplomatic Papers*, 1933, II, Washington, 1949, p. 340. (hereafter cited as *FRUS*).

Consequently there were attempts made to sway their reports. The Germans, quite naturally, hoped to persuade them to print sympathetic stories on Germany. The American foreign service staff on certain occasions urged the press to adopt a particular tone when it was felt to be in the interests of American policy.[6] This was especially the case during the first months of Nazi rule when American reporters in Germany were urged by American diplomats to moderate the tenor of their stories.

By examining the news stories that were filed from Germany and the editorial reaction to them we hope to illuminate early American attitudes towards the Nazi regime and the manner in which some of those attitudes were formed.

II

When the Nazis came to power and began to institute their antisemitic policy, the isolation of the Jews from German life was effected through administrative, legal and economic measures.* These were coupled with "individual" acts of terror and brutality. Although the first antisemitic laws were not initiated until 7th April 1933; from the earliest moments of Hitler's rule violence against Jews was an inherent facet of German life. There had been outbreaks against Jews prior to the March elections and now they increased in intensity. American Ambassador Sackett, who was then about to retire from his post, wrote to Secretary of State Hull that "democracy" in Germany had been the recipient of a "blow from which it may never recover".[7] The intensification of attacks against the Jews certainly did not escape the attention of the American press. The *Poughkeepsie News* observed on 11th March 1933 that:

> "Hitlerism is beginning to reveal itself in one of its most brutal aspects in the indignities that its adherents have been heaping upon the Jews since the victory of the Nazis in the Reichstag elections last Sunday. While apparently the full extent of the results of antisemitic agitation has not become known, the instances that have found their way into cable dispatches indicate that Jewish merchants have been harried, boycotts urged against them, and threats or [*sic*] bodily violence made."[8]

Edmund Taylor, of the *Chicago Tribune*, provided a stark description:

> "On the nights of March 9th and 10th bands of Nazis throughout Germany carried out wholesale raids to intimidate the opposition, particularly Jews. As hundreds have sworn in affidavits, men and women were insulted, slapped [and] punched in the face, hit over the head with blackjacks, dragged out of their homes in nightclothes and otherwise molested. Large numbers of socialists and communists were flung into prison including Reichstag Deputies, who were deprived of their parliamentary immunity, to make certain of their non-appearance at the Reichstag session. The arrest of innocent Jews was sanctioned as 'protective jailing' . . .

[6]Messersmith to Hull, 25th March 1933. DS. 862.4016/496 as cited in Shafir, *op. cit.*, p. 77; Messersmith to Hull, 31st March 1933, *FRUS*, 1933, II, pp. 341, 346; Telephone conversation between Phillips and Gordon, 2nd April 1933, *FRUS*, II, p. 346.

*For a survey of the internal Jewish situation, broadly for the period covered by this paper, see the preceding essay by Jacob Boas, 'German-Jewish Internal Politics under Hitler 1933–1938', in this volume of the Year Book – (Ed.).

[7]Sackett to Hull, 9th March 1933, *FRUS*, 1933, II, pp. 206–209.

[8]*Poughkeepsie News*, 11th March 1933.

> 'You are taken off to jail and put to work in a concentration camp where you may stay a year without any charge being brought against you.' Never have I seen law-abiding citizens living in such unholy fear."[9]

Taylor's vivid anti-Nazi reporting eventually resulted in his arrest and expulsion from Germany.

H. R. Knickerbocker observed in the *New York Evening Post*, that:

> "Not even in Czarist Russia, with its 'pale', have the Jews been subject to a more violent campaign of murderous agitation than in Germany since the rise of National Socialism. Hardly an issue of the Nazi newspapers appeared without more or less open incitement to pogroms. An indeterminate number have been killed.
> Hundreds of Jews have been beaten or tortured.
> Thousands of Jews have fled.
> Thousands of Jews have been or will be deprived of their livelihood.
> All Germany's 600,000 Jews are in terror."[10]

The conditions which were depicted by these reporters were difficult for those removed from the scene to fathom. This did not seem to be the Germany of Beethoven, Goethe and Schiller. These reports seemed too unbelievable to be true.

III

During the first weeks of Nazi rule the American public demonstrated a decided ambivalence regarding the accuracy of the reports which were emerging from Germany. The press, together with government officials and the public at large, condemned German actions but also questioned the reliability of the terror stories which they heard. For many Americans, particularly those reading these reports in the safety and security of their homes, the accounts seemed beyond the bounds of credibility. Incredulity marked the American public reaction in 1933 and continued to do so until 1945. As late as 1945 Americans demonstrated a "show me" attitude before they accepted the news of persecution and murder as true.[11] Although in these early years the news which emerged from Germany was not nearly as horrifying as that which would come in the 1940s many Americans harboured an attitude of cynicism and scepticism.[12]

Some papers seem to have tempered their criticism with a desire to avoid being unduly offensive to the new regime because they, along with many other Americans, including those in the State Department, believed Nazi Germany preferable to "a revolution in Germany", which would result in a Communist regime.[13]

Despite initial doubts regarding veracity, the abundance of detail and eyewitness accounts which corroborated one another constituted irrefutable evidence of intense persecution. The *Pittsburgh Sun* typified the American reaction

[9] *The Jews in Nazi Germany. A Factual Record*, New York 1933, p. 21.
[10] H. R. Knickerbocker, *New York Evening Post*, 15th April 1933.
[11] *Washington Post*, 16th April 1945.
[12] *Washington Post*, 21st March 1943.
[13] *Los Angeles Times*, 7th March 1933 (hereafter cited as *LAT*).

to two months of Nazi rule when it observed that "acts of revolting cruelty . . . have been committed".[14] Some papers were concerned that they did not have access to all the details and had to depend on "unverified" reports. Nonetheless within a few weeks they felt that they had heard enough to be convinced that a "tide of Nazi fury" had engulfed German Jewry.[15] The *Toledo Times* typified the press attitude of rather grudging belief. It acknowledged that even though the "stories which have trickled through [from Germany] cannot be checked and officially verified" it was willing to believe that they were accurate.

> "They bear the stamp of authenticity for they are consistent. Detail added to detail, obtained in this fashion, like pieces fitted into a jigsaw puzzle, constructs a recognizable picture of abuse of power, of unrestrained cruelty, of suppression of individual rights, of violent racial and religious prejudices."[16]

Other editorials were more reserved. The *Augusta* (Maine) *Journal* acknowledged, that there "seems to be evidence to support the charges [of brutality against Jews] in the main". But it then reminded readers that "many of the cruelties charged against Germany in war propaganda were later proved not to have existed".[17] The link with atrocity reports of the First World War as a means of casting doubt on the current spate of stories was of course to become a common feature of the American public's reaction to the news of the Final Solution. (By the time the war began "myriads of people decided", according to *Journalism Quarterly*, "that they would not be such simpletons that they would be fooled again" as they had been in the previous war by the tales of atrocities committed by German forces.[18])

The *Columbus* (Ohio) *Journal* also associated reports of "destruction of property, beatings and blacklisting" with the "exaggerated . . . stories the allies told about German atrocities during the war". It was, nonetheless, convinced that the stories must be true in some measure because "when there is so much smoke there must be some fire".[19] The *St. Louis Post Dispatch* demonstrated a similar ambivalence. It acknowledged that while the reports from refugees of "beatings, torture, murder, the looting of homes and stores" might be "somewhat exaggerated" they nonetheless "command attention" because they are so "uniform in tenor".[20] The *New York Times*, which was initially "confused" by the reports, quickly became convinced of their veracity and declared Germany a "nation gone completely mad".[21]

Many of the doubts expressed can be attributed in measure to the tactics adopted by German officials. German leaders denied the atrocities and accused foreign reporters of gross exaggeration. When they could not deny them they disavowed responsibility for them. As quickly became evident during 1933,

[14]*Pittsburgh Sun*, 24th March 1933.
[15]*Poughkeepsie News*, 11th March, 1933.
[16]*Toledo Times*, 23rd March 1933.
[17]*Augusta* (Maine) *Journal*, 25th March 1933.
[18]Vernon Mckenzie, 'Atrocities in World War II – What We Can Believe', *Journalism Quarterly*, IXX (September 1942), pp. 268–276.
[19]*Columbus Journal*, 24th March 1933.
[20]*St. Louis Post Dispatch*, 24th March 1933.
[21]*NYT*, 2nd April 1933.

Germany adhered to a pattern designed to inject calculated confusion into the reports of persecution. They did so in part by shedding doubt on the reporter's accuracy. The *Los Angeles News* counselled its readers not to fall prey to these tactics. On 24th February 1933 an editorial in the paper noted that Berlin had prepared a set of "instructions to German embassies and consulates abroad regarding their relations to the press".

> "After March 5, German representatives are to deny any 'unfavourable' news items emanating from Germany. If certain occurrences cannot be denied or foreign protests are voiced – for instance, in case of anti-semitic activities – a stereotyped statement is to be made to the effect that 'the German government regrets exceedingly the unfortunate occurrences and disapproves of it thoroughly. The perpetrators will be severely punished.' And that will be that."[22]

On 27th March, Hitler's foreign press chief Ernst Hanfstaengl was asked by an interviewer, "are the reports of alleged Jew baiting true or untrue?" His answer was explicit and, as it turns out, entirely untrue. "A few minutes ago, when I met him at the Munich aerodrome after his arrival from Berlin, the Chancellor authorized me to tell you that these reports are every one of them, base lies." Göring also attacked those who had spoken "these horrible lies".[23] He declared that there were "no plundered, no broken-up shops, no warehouses destroyed, robbed or interfered with". The reports of attacks were also stigmatised as untrue by Foreign Minister von Neurath and *Reichsbank* President Hjalmar Schacht. Edwin James, writing in the *New York Times* described Germany's official position.

> "The German government takes the position that a few individual acts of violence have been grossly exaggerated. And at the same time it is stated on behalf of Chancellor Hitler that these acts of violence by Nazis have been condemned and that official orders have been issued to prevent their recurrence."[24]

The *Philadelphia Ledger* was not swayed by German denials. It found the "account of outrages perpetrated by the Hitlerites upon defenseless Jews too convincing to accept the blanket denials" offered by German officials.[25] Other papers concurred. The *Hartford Courant* believed that Göring's statement "cynically evaded the issue".[26] The *Philadelphia Record* dismissed the "absurd statements" by German officials.

> "This posturing will deceive no one. The situation at present seems to be that after many days of brutal attacks on individual Jews, on Jewish stores and on Jewish places of worship, a halt will be called to physical violence and a campaign of legal violence begun."

[22]*LAT*, 24th February 1933.

[23]*The Yellow Spot*, New York 1933, p. 33. Ernst Hanfstaengl, a graduate of Harvard, was appointed to head a press bureau which was designed to influence foreign correspondents in general and those from America in particular. His mother was a member of a prominent Back Bay Boston family, the Sedgwicks. Ernst Hanfstaengl, *Hitler. The Missing Years*, London 1957, pp. 40, 74, 121, 188, 210–211, 222. *The Christian Science Monitor*, 24th March 1933 (hereafter cited as *CSM*); Moshe Gottlieb, 'The First of April Boycott', *American Jewish Historical Society Quarterly*, LVII (June 1968), p. 519.

[24]*NYT*, 26th March 1933.

[25]*Philadelphia Ledger*, 28th March 1933.

[26]*Hartford Courant*, 28th March 1933.

The *Record* went on to predict accurately the tactics the Nazis would adopt.

> "Jewish beatings may stop. But the 'law' will be used to deprive Jews of personal and political rights, to prevent them from practicing any of the learned professions, to divorce them from German economic life, to expel them, where possible, from this country, to seize their bank deposits and property."[27]

But it was not only the German authorities who issued denials. American officials did as well. In late March Secretary of State Cordell Hull suggested at a news conference that the situation in Germany may not have been "accurately" and "authoritatively" reported. In a telegram to Ambassador Sackett he indicated that he did not believe that the "gravity" of the press reports was borne out by the facts.[28] Hull may have genuinely believed that this was the case but he also believed that it was best that foreign forces should not interfere in Germany's affairs. He had received and would continue to receive testimony indicating that the situation was quite grave. Much of this information would come to him directly from American officials stationed in Germany. George Gordon, American *Chargé d'Affaires* in Germany reported to Hull that "numerous sources" had concurred in the opinion that the situation as concerned the persecution of the Jews was "rapidly taking a turn for the worse".[29] Nonetheless, Hull continued to reassure the American public and American Jews in particular that "many reports of of the acts of terror and atrocities which have reached this country have been exaggerated". He explicitly stated why he felt it so necessary to assure the public that the situation was not as bad as reported. "I fear that the continued dissemination of exaggerated reports may prejudice the friendly feelings between the peoples of the two countries and be of doubtful service to anyone." Gordon, who believed in the "deterrent effect" on the Germans of disseminating information on what was taking place, emphasised to Hull the extreme sensitivity displayed by the German press to criticism from abroad. In the end Gordon also adopted the position that despite such German sensitivities "outside intercession under the present circumstances would be very unwise".[30]

A few days earlier Hull had told Jewish leaders that while some "physical mistreatment of Jews" had occurred, this "phase may be considered virtually terminated". He predicted that the situation would soon be ameliorated and "revert to normal". Hull believed it to be his responsibility to "try to calm down the situation created by a lot of extremists in Germany and inflamed by a lot of extremists in this country".[31] Hull's convictions about the impending return to normalcy seem to have been responsible, at least in part, for convincing some of the press that the situation was now under control. The *Los Angeles Times* had told its readers that "amazing tales of oppression" were being brought out of

[27] *Philadelphia Record*, 28th March 1933.

[28] Hull to Sackett, 21st March 1933, *FRUS*, 1933, II, pp. 327. Memorandum of press conference of Secretary of State, 22nd March 1933, *FRUS*, 1933, II, p. 327.

[29] Gordon to Hull, 30th March 1933, *FRUS*, 1933, II, p. 335.

[30] Telephone call between Gordon and Phillips, 31st March 1933, *FRUS*, 1933, II, p. 342; Gordon to Hull, 23rd March 1933, *FRUS*, 1933, II, pp. 328–330; Gordon to Hull, 26th March 1933, DS. 862.4016/116 as cited in Shafir, *op. cit.*, p. 54.

[31] *NYT*, 27th March 1933.

Germany by Americans who were visiting or living there. Subsequent to Hull's reassurances, it counselled readers that these reports were "exaggerated". On 27th March a page one exclusive in the *Los Angeles Times* told that "German violence was subsiding" and announced that the "raids on Jews [had been] declared over".[32] The *Christian Century*, which would emerge as one of the more outspoken and strident sceptics regarding the accuracy of the reports on Jewish persecution, called for a "tighter curb on emotions until the facts are beyond dispute".[33] It is interesting to note that this *Christian Century* editorial which was entitled 'A Need for Light not Heat' appeared after the 1st April boycott of Jewish businesses. Apparently not even the national boycott could convince the *Christian Century* that the persecution of Jews was really happening in Germany.

In contrast, the *New York Evening Post* took issue with the "confused denials" given the press by German leaders and with Hull's reassurances.[34] The *Post* refused to accept the State Department's claims of an amelioration in the situation because the embassy dispatches on which these were based had not been released. Had the *Post* actually been given them it would have had even more reason to doubt German denials and State Department reassurances.

Correspondents made a concerted effort to moderate the tone of their reports so as not to be accused of fomenting hysteria. Their reporting was generally quite accurate and, according to some observers, "more truthful and less sensational" than that of many European newspapers.[35]

Generally it appears that by April 1933 most of the American press acknowledged that things were amiss as far as Jews in Germany were concerned. They were not sure just how amiss. Both readers and editorial boards in the United States were not sure how accurate the American foreign correspondents were. They were also unsure whether this was to be a permanent condition or just the "natural" aftermath of a change in ruling powers. Confusion about what the persecution represented was understandable at this early stage of Nazi rule. The Nazi authorities worked hard to make it appear that they had no role in the outbreaks. It was both easy and convenient to assume that it was but a passing phenomenon and the work of over-zealous adherents. However, some of the press as well as members of the State Department continued to be "confused" about the "permanence" of Nazi antisemitic policy well into the late 1930s. There was a decided inclination on the part of many Americans, including those in policy-making positions, to hope and insist that persecution and the tribulations inflicted on German Jewry would end once Hitler established a firm rule over the country. Some continued to believe this until 1938 when it became clear that violence was a permanent and irrevocable part of the Nazi methodology, particularly as it related to Jews.[36]

[32]*LAT*, 16th March 1933, 26th March 1933, 27th March 1933.

[33]*Christian Century*, 5th April 1933, p. 443.

[34]*New York Post*, 27th March 1933.

[35]Shafir, *op. cit.*, p. 43.

[36]A thorough examination of the press coverage of the *Kristallnacht* shows that as late as 1938 the American press was surprised at the extent to which violence was intrinsic to the Nazi system. See Deborah E. Lipstadt, 'Pious Sympathies and Sincere Regrets. The American News Media and the Holocaust', *Modern Judaism*, II (Winter 1982), pp. 53–72.

IV

Once the American correspondents in Germany and editors assessing the situation from afar were convinced that the reports of brutalities were essentially correct they condemned Germany's actions. They demonstrated no ambivalence in stating that such behaviour was unacceptable and inherently in conflict with American values and behaviour. The *Columbus Dispatch* cautioned that when the new German ambassador, Hans Luther, took up his position and set out to ascertain American public opinion regarding Hitler's policies towards Jews he would not be able to:

> "go astray as to the facts in this matter. American sentiment and judgement is just what it would logically be expected to be, in view of our national origin, our constitution and the traditions which have guided the United States in its development . . ."[37]

There was no doubt among most Americans that Nazi-type behaviour would not be tolerated in the USA. Yet they were confused as to whether this was a matter in which America could properly involve itself. They were worried that if the USA did react in some fashion it would indicate an American commitment to resolving European affairs.

The suggestions for possible American responses varied markedly. Some editorials observed that there was ample precedent for a forceful reaction. Others argued that German treatment of Jews was strictly a German domestic matter and outside the area of American concern. This view was strongly supported by the State Department which wanted to remain as detached as possible. As the situation became more ominous, calls for American intervention diminished in number. During the early months of Nazi rule there were newspapers such as the *Youngstown* (Ohio) *Vindicator* which urged the State Department to issue a "vigorous protest", and wanted America to warn the Germans that American "assistance or cooperation . . . would be impossible" if persecution were "countenanced". This, the paper believed, would indicate to the Germans the depth of American antipathy. It would also "prove a help to Hitler" in restraining those of his followers who took his exhortations "too literally".[38] The belief that the terror was the handiwork of underlings who took Hitler too seriously was symptomatic of an attempt to separate Hitler from his more radical followers and present him as the voice of moderation amid a cacophony of extremism.

The *Boston American* concurred with the need for a vigorous American protest "lest our silence be regarded as a tacit approval of these infamies".[39] The *Manchester* (New Hampshire) *Herald* predicted, incorrectly as would soon become apparent, that there would be a "movement for letting down of the immigration bars in the interest of refugee Israelites driven from Germany".[40] Not only was there to be no such movement but there would be demands for a further

[37] *Columbus Dispatch*, 16th April 1933.
[38] *Youngstown Vindicator*, 22nd March 1933.
[39] *Boston American*, 20th March 1933.
[40] *Manchester Herald*, 24th March 1933.

strengthening of those barriers. It soon became clear that the most prevalent form of aid America would be asked to render was that of admitting refugees. At this stage even those newspapers with few, if any, doubts about the bleak future facing Germany's Jews and the extent to which antisemitism was fundamental to Nazi ideology, began to voice their doubts about American abilities to aid the refugees materially.

The *New York Times* sympathised with expelled Jewish academics but was unequivocal in its belief that nothing could be done for them in the USA.[41] The limits imposed by immigration laws and the dire problems already confronting American universities posed insurmountable obstacles. The firm belief that there was little America could do to increase the number of refugees permitted to enter the country on an annual basis remained the dominant American position throughout the period. With few exceptions the American press echoed this sentiment along with the White House and Congress.[42]

The *Duluth* (Minneapolis) *Tribune* differentiated between those issues against which Americans might freely protest and those that were "none of our business". In the latter category it placed Hitler's "iron fist rule" and his "crushing of opposition parties". However his "cruel . . . oppression" of Jews, his "bigotry and intolerance" were the "business and concern of every nation in the world which lay claim to being civilized".[43] The *Philadelphia Public Ledger* and *St. Louis Post Dispatch* were convinced that there was "ample precedent" for a strong reaction.[44]

The *Columbus* (Ohio) *Dispatch*'s reaction typified that of most of the American press and public. It counselled Hans Luther that American public opinion would condemn "any law or official order abrogating or abridging rights with regard to any class of citizens". While the paper warned Luther that America "cannot sympathize with denial of rights and privileges on such grounds [of religious beliefs and affiliations] in other lands" it made no suggestions for any form of retaliatory action or official condemnation.[45]

As matters in Germany grew ever more ominous there was a marked increase in the ranks of those who counselled inaction. Diverse arguments were used to justify this response. They included, among others, the contention that this was a German domestic matter and America's record was likewise sullied by acts of

[41]*NYT*, 2nd July 1933.

[42]The only time during this entire period of 1933–1945 when the press took a position which was at odds with public opinion on the question of immigration was during the debate over the Wagner Rogers bill. This bill, which was deliberated on in the winter and spring of 1939, would have allowed 20,000 additional German children to enter the United States in addition to those already allowed in under the existing quotas. The bill died in committee and never reached the floor of the Senate or House. 'Admission of German Refugee Children', *Joint Hearings Before a Subcommittee on Immigration, U.S. Senate and Subcommittee on Immigration and Naturalization, House of Representatives*, 20th-21st April 1939; *Congressional Record*, vol. 85, 76th Congress, 1st Sess., pp. 1457–1458, 2338–2341, 2805, 3865–3868, 4817–4819, and Apprendix, pp. 641–642, 656–666, 835–836, 1073–1074, 1681–1682, 1886–1887, 2057–2059, 2792–2794, 3299; *Congressional Record*, vol. 84, Pt. 14, 76th Congress, 1st Sess., p. A–3237.

[43]*Duluth Tribune*, 5th March 1933.

[44]*Philadelphia Public Ledger*, 23rd March 1933; *St. Louis Post Dispatch*, 24th March 1933.

[45]*Columbus Dispatch*, 16th April 1933.

discrimination and Americans therefore could not condemn others. The basic reason, whether it was explicitly stated or not, for counselling inaction, was that Americans genuinely feared being lured into the turmoil of European affairs. Although in 1933 no one thought in terms of war there was still a significant residue of pain and anger over having become involved in the First World War. This was bound to strengthen American isolationism and foster the sentiment that what happened in other regions of the world, Europe in particular, was not an American concern.

V

As reports of the assaults, harassment and terror continued fewer expressions of outright denial or doubt about their veracity were to be found in the American press. Although there were those who still questioned their complete reliability it was increasingly accepted that terror – both physical and legal – had found a permanent niche in Nazi Germany. Although the press generally believed in the fact of persecution, it was unsure whether the humiliations inflicted on Jews could be interpreted as official German policy. Various newspapers equivocated on whether the government was directly responsible for these excesses, whether it had instigated them, condoned them, tolerated them or simply been unable to contain them. There was significant division of opinion as to whether these outrages were to be interpreted as signs of Nazi weakness or strength. Those who believed them to reflect the inherent weakness of the regime argued that it was clear that Hitler was unable to control his underlings. Those who contended that the terror was indicative of the strength of the regime took the position that Nazi Germany believed that it could afford to act with impunity because there was no external force which was strong enough or cared sufficiently to challenge German behaviour.

At first the Nazi leadership was seemingly quite sensitive to the charges of terrorism and brutality. It often informed observers that it was not responsible and promised that lapses in discipline would not be tolerated. Such protestations were repeatedly contradicted not only by the recurring cycle of terror but also by the frequent predictions by Hitler and others in the Nazi hierarchy that the Jewish community in Germany would be eradicated. No one could have then foreseen the actual extent of the tragedy which would befall German Jewry. Nonetheless what was predictable, even after a few months of Nazi rule, was that the status of German Jews would seriously deteriorate and that their future was bleak. Some reporters, especially the better informed, recognised this. Other representatives of the American press, particularly the editorial boards who evaluated the situation from their distant American perspective, seemed far more inclined to accept Nazi protestations of innocence. They believed that the attacks on Jews represented only a temporary aberration.

During the inital period of Nazi rule American officials' denials also helped foster an aura of ambiguity regarding Hitler's role in the persecution. The State Department, and Cordell Hull in particular, believed that America had a vested interest in strengthening Hitler's hand. In their estimation Hitler was the best alternative to chaos and Communism. American officials in Germany reported to the State Department that an internal struggle in the party between the "violent radical wing" and the "more moderate sections" was taking place and that "Hitler . . . represents the element of moderation in the Nazi party". Gordon asked Hull to reinforce Hitler's position. "I believe that if in any way you can strengthen his hands even indirectly, he would welcome it." When Hull assured the Jewish community that the situation in Germany was improving he depicted Hitler as a moderating force.

> "Hitler, in his capacity as leader of the Nazi party, issued an order calling for his followers to maintain law and order, to avoid molesting foreigners, disrupting trade and to avoid the creation of possibly embarrassing international incidents."[46]

Outbreaks against Jews had been "viewed with serious concern by the German government". This attitude was reflected in the press. Some papers tended to separate Hitler from his "radical" followers. The *Los Angeles Times*, for example, believed Hitler "probably not responsible" for the actions against the Jews. The *Columbus Journal* found it "difficult to believe that Hitler is countenancing the anti-racial activities". Rather than attributing them to the *Führer* the newspaper decided " the abuses must be the unauthorized sallies of irresponsible mobs of youthful Nazis". Similarly the *Youngstown* (Ohio) *Vindicator* believed that "always in matters of this kind a demagogue's followers take him too literally and get out of hand".[47]

Exonerating Hitler made it feasible to believe that once he consolidated his political forces he would gain control over those engaged in excesses. The *Chicago Tribune*, which considered antisemitism to be the most unfortunate aspect of Nazism, believed Hitler would bring his storm troopers under control and order would soon reign. The *Tribune*'s sympathy towards Germany was based on what it perceived as the "determination of the German people to overcome [the] communist menace". Despite the *Tribune*'s sympathetic attitude towards what it saw as anti-Communism, the paper still expressed its horror at Hitler's antisemitism. In addition to the reports by Edmund Taylor, Sigrid Schultz sent sharply critical reports to the paper. During the grim days of March 1933 headlines proclaimed 'Jews face drastic Boycott. Hitler's Nazis declare War on World Jewry'. By 1934 the paper had begun to play down the persecution of the Jews and strengthen its appeal for appeasement on the part of the Western Democracies, no matter how terrifying the new Germany appeared. Colonel McCormick was convinced that the Allies' behaviour at Versailles was responsible in great measure for the rise of Nazism. Sigrid Schultz disagreed fiercely. "Our alleged unkindness at Versailles had nothing to do with Germany's dedication to another war."[48]

There were those American newspapers which harboured no doubts about

[46]Gordon to Hull, 25th March 1933, *FRUS*, 1933, II, p. 331; Hull to Gordon, 26th March 1933, *FRUS*, 1933, II, p. 334.

[47]*LAT*, 21st March 1933; *Columbus Journal*, 24th March 1933; *Youngstown Vindicator*, 22nd March 1933.

[48]*Chicago Tribune*, 4th February 1933, 13th March 1933, 24th March 1933; Shafir, *op. cit.*, p. 33; Jerome Edwards, *The Foreign Policy of Colonel McCormick's Tribune*, Nevada 1971, p. 92.

Hitler's role in the terror. The *St. Louis Post Dispatch* sarcastically observed that "Hitler's right hand carefully avoids knowing what his left is doing". The *Louisville Post, San Francisco Chronicle* and *New York Times* had no doubt that Hitler was firmly in control.[49]

There was some editorial speculation that the experience of power would force the German leader to mend his ways. It was widely assumed that he would abandon his hysterical and bombastic condemnations of the Jews. The *Christian Science Monitor*, which adopted a most equivocal attitude towards the entire spectrum of events in Germany, expected Hitler to become a "lamb within a fortnight". The *Los Angeles Times* predicted that as Hitler consolidated his power he would become "less jumpy and theatrical". Rather charitably it interpreted his antisemitic ravings as a sign that he was "unsure of himself". The *Chicago Tribune* also expected him to settle down shortly.[50]

The *Detroit Free Press* was uncertain whom to blame. It had no doubt that "Jew baiting seems to be going on without restraint if not by actual command of high authorities". Ignoring the reams of pronouncements issued by Hitler on the Jews it called on him to clarify his position.

> "If Chancellor Hitler has authorized nothing of this sort, the sooner he intervenes the better for the reputation of his regime and the better for its relations with other nations including the United States. If Hitler is winking at wanton plunderings, persecutions and outrages, then he is planting the first seeds of failure."[51]

As a result of the 1st April boycott the debate in the press over the degree of government complicity intensified. Germany tried to foster the impression that the Nazi party and not the government conducted the boycott. Not all American observers were convinced however; Frederick Birchall, *New York Times* correspondent in Berlin, reported that despite government assertions to the contrary there was nothing spontaneous or unofficial about the boycott. In a front-page leader Birchall contended that irrespective of the fact that it had been "repeatedly asserted that the Nazi show [boycott] was merely 'tolerated' and not participated in by the government", the government had issued precise and public instructions as to the manner in which the boycott was to be conducted.[52] Prior to the boycott the *Los Angeles Times* had exonerated Hitler. A few days after the boycott it declared that "in fairness to Hitler" it must be noted that he did not sanction the boycott or the violence. His antisemitic declarations were, according to the *Los Angeles Times*, "understood to be rhetorical" and the violence was the work of "over-enthusiastic and poorly disciplined followers". If Hitler had agreed to the boycott of German-Jewish business establishments then surely it had only been with "reluctance".[53] The paper neither offered any substantive proof of Hitler's innocence nor did it comment on a statement he made that very day

[49] *St. Louis Post Dispatch*, 24th March 1933; *Louisville Post*, 22nd March 1933; *San Francisco Chronicle*, 20th March 1933; *NYT*, 30th March 1933.
[50] *CSM*, 7th March 1933; *LAT*, 25th March 1933; *Chicago Tribune*, 13th March 1933, 24th March 1933.
[51] *Detroit Free Press*, 23rd March 1933.
[52] *NYT*, 1st April 1933, 5th April 1933.
[53] *LAT*, 30th March 1933, 6th April 1933.

which should have eliminated any doubts about Hitler's and his government's commitment to antisemitism:

> "We must meet the natural demand of Germany for the intellectual leadership according to our own kind of elimination of the preponderance of Jewish intellectuals from our cultural and spiritual life. True intellectual achievements have never been made by racial aliens, but always by strictly Aryan Germanic spiritual forces."[54]

VI

The debate about government complicity in the persecution continued past the boycott and the promulgation of the first antisemitic laws into the spring. Some American opinion-makers vacillated in their evaluation of Hitler. Walter Lippmann, himself a Jew, one of the most widely read and influential columnists of the period, had severely criticised Hitler after he came to power. He was subsequently reassured by Hitler's statements and particularly by a conciliatory speech the German leader made in the middle of May. As a result of that speech Lippmann believed the German leader intent on pursuing peace. Lippmann dismissed those who thought Hitler was insincere and described his words as the voice of a civilised people coming through "foreign din and hysteria and animal passion of a great revolution". Shortly before writing this column praising Hitler's conciliatory attitude Lippmann had devoted another column to Nazi Germany. Written in the aftermath of the infamous book burning in May 1933, it warned of Hitler's preparations for war. Lippmann argued that there were but two things holding the German leader back from starting a conflict: the French army and the persecution of the Jews. Persecution of the Jews, "by satisfying the lust of the Nazis who feel they must conquer somebody and the cupidity of those Nazis who want jobs, is a kind of lightning rod which protects Europe".[55] As Ronald Steel has observed, "while the analysis was not illogical, the idea that a pogrom against the Jews offered protection to Europe was, to say the least, peculiar coming from a Jewish writer".[56]

Even stranger were Lippmann's comments on a speech of Hitler's in mid-May. In addition to describing it as "statesmanlike" and declaring it the voice of "a genuinely civilized people" he argued that the German people should not be judged solely on the basis of the behaviour of Nazi radicals. He urged his readers to recognise what he called the "dual nature of man". Every individual, group or nation could be both good and evil. "To deny", he argued in defence of Germany, "that Germany can speak as a civilized power because uncivilized things are being said and done in Germany, is in itself a deep form of intolerance". To bolster his argument he cited the supposed defects and shortcomings of other peoples.

> "Who that has studied history and who cares for the truth would judge the French people by what went on during their terror? Or the British people by what happened in Ireland? Or the Catholic church by the Catholic church of the Spanish Inquisition? Or Protestantism by the Ku Klux Klan or the Jews by their parvenus?"[57]

[54] *NYT*, 7th April 1933.
[55] Walter Lippmann, 'Today and Tomorrow', *LAT*, 12th May 1933.
[56] Ronald Steel, *Walter Lippmann and the American Century*, New York 1980, p. 330.
[57] Walter Lippmann, 'Today and Tomorrow', *LAT*, 19th May 1933.

Boycott Day, 1st April 1933
SA man posted in front of a Jewish-owned business

By courtesy of Dr. Sybil Milton, New York

Boycott Day, 1st April 1933

By courtesy of Institute of Contemporary History and Wiener Library, London

Lippmann's main objective was to call attention to what he considered legitimate German grievances about the Versailles Treaty. Yet this did not, as Steel has rightly noted, force him to describe Hitler's speech as "statesmanlike" and the "authentic voice of a genuinely civilized people". Worst of all was his invidious comparison linking French terror, Ku Klux Klan lynchings and Nazi brutality with the "flashiness of Jewish 'parvenus'". Coming from one of the most influential opinion-makers in America it certainly was more than unfortunate. Coming from a Jew it seemed almost to indicate a degree of self-hatred. Most importantly however, it tended to suggest that Jewish behaviour was in some way responsible for antisemitism in general and Nazi persecution in particular. Lippmann was not the first to propound such theories; nor was this the first time he himself had argued that Jews could be blamed for the existence of antisemitism.[58] (Ultimately Lippmann's views were to be echoed by many Americans. In April 1938 approximately 60% of those polled believed that the persecution of the Jews in Europe was either entirely or partly their own fault.)[59] Lippmann's article shocked many readers, including Felix Frankfurter, Lippmann's mentor and strong supporter. Frankfurter was so incensed that he did not communicate with Lippmann for more than three and a half years.[60]

Lippmann's ambivalence is revealed more in what he did not say during this period than by what he did say. Although he wrote his column on a continuous basis and commented on the broadest spectrum of foreign and domestic affairs he barely referred to Jews. (In later years he never once mentioned the death camps, ghettos or massacres.) In the aftermath of the *Kristallnacht* he devoted two columns to Europe's problems of over-population. Europe needed to be relieved of a million people a year. The best alternative was to send them to an "unsettled territory where an organized community life in the modern sense does not yet exist". The area which Lippmann believed most appropriate was Africa. His failure to suggest that American immigration laws be altered to allow more Jews to enter the United States reflected the predominant opinion of the American press and public. In contrast many of his colleagues, such as those on the *New Republic* and *Nation*, were vigorously demanding a change in American immigration laws in order to allow oppressed Jews to enter the United States.[61]

Other voices echoed Lippmann's suggestion that the Jews' behaviour was the cause of their suffering. The *Christian Science Monitor*, in an editorial comment on the 1st April boycott, blamed the boycott on the protests of World Jewry and on the fact that "Jews spread lies against Germany". The "stringent measures

[58]Steel notes that the "crudeness" and the "cruelty" of Lippmann's attacks on his fellow Jews are in marked contrast to the sensitivity he displayed towards other minority groups and those suffering discrimination. It is "inconceivable", according to Steel, that Lippmann would have written anything "comparable about the Irish, Italians, or the blacks" despite the fact that none of these groups was without its own *nouveaux riches*. Steel, *op. cit.*, pp. 191–192.

[59]Henry Cantril, *Public Opinion*, Princeton 1951, p. 381.

[60]Steel, *op. cit.*, p. 332.

[61]*Time* magazine let Lippmann, whom it described as "America's most influential Jewish pundit", speak for it when it quoted Lippmann as suggesting that Jews be sent to Africa. If Lippmann, a Jew, did not believe America could solve the problem by letting in refugees who could fault *Time* or anyone else for thinking likewise. *Time*, 5th December 1938, p. 18.

[against them were, therefore] easily justified". This was a case of an "eye for an eye" and reflective of the fact that Jews failed to heed the commandment of Jesus to "love one another" and Spinoza's saying that "it is rational to repay persecution with love".

It also suggested that it was the Jews' "commercial clannishness which . . . gets them into trouble", and recommended that Jews both "within Germany and without might give some attention to this problem". The editorial's references to this particular biblical text, to Jesus and Spinoza as well as its claims that Jewish suffering stemmed from "commercial clannishness" seemed particularly inappropriate and suggested that the *Christian Science Monitor*'s view of the contemporary Jewish agony was refracted through the prism of Christianity's long-standing theological view of Judaism.

The *Christian Century* also suggested that the Jewish problem originated in the behaviour of Jews:

> "May we ask if Hitler's attitude may be somewhat governed by the fact that too many Jews in Germany are radical, too many are communists? May that have any bearing on the situation? There must be some reason other than race or creed – just what is the reason? It is always well to try to understand."[62]

This was not the only time that the *Christian Century*, the most prominent American Protestant journal, had voiced such opinions. Although here it left the rhetorical questions unanswered it had already more than answered them a few weeks earlier in an article written by a German Jew living in America, who had severely attacked his co-religionists, also accusing them of bringing their present suffering on themselves – but by supporting "reactionary [!] parties". They had also instigated hostility by setting themselves up as aliens, by eating particular foods, keeping Saturday as a holiday and doing other things which aroused "suspicion and envy".[63]

The *Christian Science Monitor* had joined Lippmann in its assessment of Hitler's mid-May speech, which it found "realistic and statesmanlike".[64] In contrast the *New York World Telegram* reacted quite differently. It opined that "Hitler by his brutal and cowardly terrorism against Jews, against German culture, against labor unions is planting international dynamite".[65]

[62] *CSM*, 4th April 1933. For a complete analysis of the *CSM*'s attitude towards the persecution of the Jews in 1933 see my article 'A Road Paved with Good Intentions: The *Christian Science Monitor*'s Reaction to the First Phase of Nazi Persecution of Jews', *Jewish Social Studies*, XLV, No. 2 (Spring 1983), pp. 95–112; *Christian Century*, 26th April 1933, p. 574.

"Radical" is, of course, a misnomer unless it is taken to imply simply "left of centre". As Arnold Paucker has shown for the Weimar Republic close to two thirds of the German Jews opted for the left liberal *Deutsche Demokratische Partei* and less than a third voted Socialist. Not until 1932, with the collapse of the liberal centre, did a major "strategical" Jewish shift occur, largely to Democratic Socialism. Nazi accusations were groundless; only a small percentage of Jews tended to be extreme Radicals or Communists. Cf. Arnold Paucker, 'Jewish Defence against Nazism in the Weimar Republic', in *The Wiener Library Bulletin*, XXVI (1972) Nos. 1/2, pp. 26–27.

[63] *Christian Century*, 12th April 1933, pp. 492–495.

[64] *CSM*, 17th May 1933, 18th May 1933; *Documents on German Foreign Policy, 1918–1945, Series C: The Third Reich, First Phase, I, January–October, 1933*, Washington, D.C., 1957, pp. 451–455. For the German text of the speech see *Verhandlungen des Reichstags*, vol. 457, pp. 47–54.

[65] *New York World Telegram*, 19th May 1933; Margaret K. Norden, 'American Editorial Response to the Rise of Adolf Hitler. A Preliminary Consideration', *American Jewish Historical Society Quarterly*, LVII (October 1968), p. 293.

Even those papers which unequivocally condemned Germany's behaviour sometimes failed to recognise that Jews were not harassed because of specific offences they had committed or because they had concentrated in one particular profession or area of the economy. The *Columbus Dispatch*, which had warned Ambassador Luther that Americans would not tolerate Germany's persecution of one segment of its population, because it was antithetical to America's fundamental beliefs about freedom and democracy, believed the "policy of the Hitler government" was directed towards "the large Jewish element in the financial, commercial, professional and official life of present-day Germany".[66] It failed to see that Nazi attacks were aimed at the Jewish entity.

VII

The public debate as to the trustworthiness of the reports emanating from Germany continued. The German government persisted in its attempts to create a favourable image in America. It did so, according to the American consul general in Berlin, by exerting "real pressure" on American businessmen and exchange professors to "send statements which would not give a really correct picture of the situation". It also tried to discredit the reliability of American reporters. An impassioned defence of the American correspondents and the reports they were sending appeared in the *Macon* (Georgia) *Telegraph* at the end of May. It was written by Mark Etheridge who was then in Germany on an Oberlaender Trust fellowship "for the express purpose of having Americans know the truth about Germany". The editor of the *Telegraph* was sensitive to the possibility that Etheridge might be accused of exaggeration and falsification. He therefore prefaced the article with a reminder that Etheridge "assumed the obligation to tell the truth if he told anything in accepting the fellowship". Etheridge's article was a clarion call against doubt:

> "Let me reaffirm what I have said before: it is my conviction that the stories which come to you through . . . [the accredited news] agencies are true, I know the correspondents here in Germany. They are educated, responsible high-type men. Two of them have won the Pulitzer prize for the best of foreign correspondence in the past two years. Another framed the code of ethics for journalists which was sanctioned at Geneva. Another was formerly acting managing editor of the *New York Times*. The press corps here is, upon the whole, a body of outstanding journalists who because what they wrote was being watched and criticized, have not only endeavored to verify the minutest particular of what they wrote, but have leaned backward in reporting the truth. You may bank upon what you have read from them."

Etheridge then went on to defend the integrity of Louis Lochner, the Associated Press reporter whose stories had been attacked by the Germans.

> "The head of the Associated Press bureau is Louis Lochner . . . His wife is German . . . He loves Germany; he likes the German people enormously. He has lived here 12 years. He knows Germany and Germany's reactions better than he knows the United States . . . You know how absurd it is for anybody to pretend that a man who enjoys in the newspaper world such a reputation . . . is in the employ of the communists or Socialists or anybody else except the Associated Press. You know too, since you know A.P. men, how ridiculous it is for the German

[66] *Columbus Dispatch*, 16th April 1933.

government to pretend that what he sends out is distorted. His professional reputation is at stake; his position is at stake; the integrity of the A.P. is at stake. The same thing goes for the United Press. I need only to tell you that the former head of the bureau here, who was a Jew, asked, at the inception of the present trouble, to be relieved so that the government could have no possible ground for saying that the dispatches of the United Press were biased. It strikes me that demonstrates a pretty high sense of honor, and so I say, you may rely upon what you read in the American press about isolated instances."[67]

Etheridge was echoed by Michael Williams, editor of the Catholic periodical, *Commonweal*, in an appeal to the League of Nations on 21st May:

> "The situation of the Jews in Germany is deplorable beyond words. Israel in Germany is perishing under a yoke only comparable to that under which its forefathers groaned in Babylon and Egypt.
> Don't be deceived by false denials concerning the persecution of the Jews under the Hitler regime; guard against its paid and voluntary propaganda. Pay no heed to certain journalists who seem to learn only what the dictatorship desires them to believe."[68]

On 30th May the *New York Times* also responded to what it saw as a persistent need to substantiate the reports of brutalities. It cited the conclusions of a "group of eminent American lawyers" who had visited Germany. In an editorial the *Times* commented that "these leaders of the American bar, including two former Secretaries of State, affirm that the first reports of outrages upon German courts and lawyers have been 'confirmed authentically' ". The lawyers told of "judges violently dragged from the bench and lawyers forced out of practice for no reason except hatred of their race and religion". A few weeks later the *Times* observed:

> "More shocking than the practice of Nazi terror is denial of such terror. Just when Hitler is saying that terror never existed and calm reigns in Germany a Collier reporter found Jewish persecution in full swing and life in Berlin like sitting on an edge of a volcano."[69]

By June even the *Los Angeles Times* had reversed its stand and now branded Hitler's denial of antisemitic persecution as "feeble and unconvincing". In August a series of front page stories in the *Los Angeles Times* described a "campaign of indignities" against Jewish women who kept company with German men. In October it condemned the banning of Mendelssohn's music and the attacks on foreigners by Nazi storm troopers who, unlike "over zealous patriots in other countries . . . have official status". No longer could one differentiate between Hitler and his followers. Hitler's victory at the ballot box did not constitute an endorsement of "peace and honor and equality among nations" as Hitler claimed. What really was endorsed was "Hitler's program, lock stock and barrel, antisemitism and . . . all".[70]

Even those journals which demonstrated an ambivalent and even somewhat benevolent attitude towards Nazi Germany had few doubts about the facts. Colonel Robert R. McCormick, the influential publisher of the *Chicago Tribune*, published an account of his visit to Germany in August 1933. He described a

[67] *Macon Georgia Telegram*, 25th May 1933; *The Jews in Nazi Germany*, *op. cit.*, pp. 20–21; Shafir, *op. cit.*, pp. 76–77.
[68] *The Jews in Nazi Germany*, *op. cit.*, p. 16; see also *CSM*, 19th May 1933.
[69] *NYT*, 30th May 1933, 24th June 1933.
[70] *LAT*, 2nd June 1933, 29th August 1933, 31st August 1933, 3rd September 1933, 6th October 1933, 14th October 1933, 11th November 1933.

prevailing reign of terror which placed "suspected Communists, former opposition members and all Jews . . . in constant danger".[71] That same week the *Christian Century*, which had been and would remain rather sceptical about the accuracy of the reports, set aside its doubts in an article by Paul Hutchinson, one of the editors of the journal, who had just returned from Germany, noting that "the actual brutalities inflicted on Jews, socialists, communists and pacifists have been even more severe than the American press has published".[72]

The Nazi policy of denying these outbreaks or describing them as spontaneous continued. This appears to have had less of an effect as the year wore on but did, at times, inject a note of confusion, particularly evident in a series of news stories which reached America in September 1933, when the *New York Times* carried two reports. One told of two German towns which had promoted specific incidents of discrimination. Here the city authorities were reprimanded by the district governor with the official concurrence of Wilhelm Frick, *Reich* Minister of the Interior. Those inclined to perceive restraint being exercised in Germany could point to such developments as evidence. On 27th September Karl Schmitt, Minister for Economics, "emphatically discountenanced" the boycott of Jewish business establishments. *Times* reporter Guido Endreis claimed that Schmitt's remarks were an indication that more "responsible elements in the Hitler government are taking sane counsels on this issue". Earlier in the month Goebbels admitted in a speech that "uncontrollable elements had occasionally caused incidents but these had been isolated". All this was conducive to the fostering of false notions of moderation in Nazi ranks. However, the day after Schmitt's remarks were publicised an unnamed "high ranking German official" made it clear that the call by the Minister for Economics for a hands-off policy did not represent any deviation from "Nazism's plan to rear a purely 'Aryan' State".

The *New York Times* editorial board was apparently not deceived or placated by Schmitt's comments. It observed that while it was significant that Schmitt disapproved of the boycott of Jewish businesses his criticism should not be understood as indicative of a forthcoming policy change. In fact deterioration of the Jews' situation should be anticipated, not amelioration. By now it was obvious that a recurring cycle of terror existed in Germany. "Hitherto . . . any sign of relaxation in one place has been counterbalanced by an outburst of unreason along another section of the anti-Jewish front." All that could be expected, the *Times* predicted, was a "new display of spiritual ferocity against the Jews".[73]

There were other events, which bewildered the outsider during the first year of Nazi rule. In December the *New York Times* reported on anti-Jewish excesses that

[71] *Chicago Tribune*, 9th August 1933, 11th August 1933, 12th August 1933 (reprinted in *LAT*, 23rd August 1933, 24th August 1933). The *Tribune* continued to criticise the Nazis throughout 1934. After that it softened its view of Hitler somewhat and paid altogether less attention to Nazi Germany. Sigrid Schultz, the *Tribune*'s correspondent in Berlin, continued to send detailed critical reports on Nazism and Jewish suffering. Although McCormick's views differed from hers, her articles generally appeared uncensored. Edwards, *op. cit.*, pp. 93–94.

[72] *Christian Century*, 16th August 1933, pp. 1031–1033.

[73] *NYT*, 20th September 1933, 28th September 1933, 29th September 1933.

had taken place in Fürth and in Nuremberg. The paper revealed that it had received these reports in July but had not then been able to obtain corroboration. Since then independent substantiation had been received. According to the report Jews had been forced to endure insults, beatings and indignities which included making them pull out weeds along a railway track with their teeth. The reporter then noted that two days prior to the incident Hitler had met Streicher in Nuremberg. Mention of this fact seemed to be the journalist's way of indicating that Hitler had apparently approved of these actions. However he also noted that four days after the incident a proclamation signed by Hess, as Hitler's representative, appeared in Nuremberg. It warned SA and SS members not to "let themselves be carried away by such spies who aim at provoking prohibited actions".[74]

These various reports were likely to confirm the optimists in the view that moderation was in the offing. The pessimist would have dismissed them as camouflage, while a great many readers probably did not know at all what to make of them. Although segments of the press continued to demonstrate an ambiguous attitude towards Nazi Germany there were those journalists who well understood the degree to which antisemitism was fundamental to Nazi policy.[75] In the light of the uncertainty about Hitler's intentions and the ignorance as to the extent to which antisemitism was integral in his philosophy, it is instructive to examine how in the last few months of 1933 two journalists of the *New York Times*, managed to cut through the calculated ambiguity created by the Nazis and analyse the likely future of the Jews. While they could not have predicted what would be the ultimate outcome of the cycle of persecution which began in 1933 these reporters sensed the drastic change in German-Jewish life and had no illusion as to the central position antisemitism occupied in Nazi ideology.

In August Otto Tolischus embarked on a systematic survey of Jewish life in the small towns and rural areas of South-Western Germany. He found that antisemitism was "likely to be worst where the influence of the Nazi press is still felt and where the Jews are without the protection of either metropolitan anonymity or rural neighborliness. The most brutal mistreatment is frequently reported in such suburban towns."

Contrary to the common notion, it was not financial ruin or physical abuse which posed the greatest threat to German Jews. "The worst part of the fate of small-town Jews is likely to be a growing spiritual and social isolation." Tolischus graphically described the "social ostracism" which made Jews and their children feel as "if [they] were in an enemy country". He predicted that a Jew in such a position will, if he is an optimist, hope to "be able to hold out until the situation

[74] *NYT*, 24th December 1933.

[75] Among such reporters of discernment were Louis Leo Snyder, the Berlin correspondent for the *New York Herald*'s Paris edition and whose dispatches from Germany condemned Hitler far more fiercely than did the *Herald*'s editorials; Edgar Ansell Mowerer, Berlin correspondent for the *Chicago Daily News*; Hamilton Fish Armstrong, editor of *Foreign Affairs* and a correspondent for a number of different publications; Dorothy Thompson, whose syndicated column appeared in a myriad of different newspapers including the *Philadelphia Public Ledger* and the *New York Evening Post*; Pierre van Passen of the *New York World*; Sigrid Schultz of the *Chicago Tribune*, and *NYT* correspondents Birchall and Tolischus, Norden, *op. cit.*, p. 290.

improves". If, however, he is a "pessimist he will look around for a buyer of his store at any price and prepare to emigrate". The dejection of an increasing number of German Jews was shown by the fact that the "Jewish exodus from Germany is gaining in momentum".

In an editorial comment on the Tolischus survey the *Times* observed that despite diminution of physical abuse, hostility was ever present. Even when there was "no open pressure or calculated discrimination" against the Jews, the atmosphere in places such as the one described by Tolischus "has been poisoned". As far as Jews were concerned a "policy of cruelty and shame" existed.[76]

Two weeks later Birchall used the conclusion of the Nazi rally in Nuremberg as an opportunity to express how

> "difficult [it was] within the limits of news dispatches to make plain to the United States, where two and two still make the normal four, how different is this new brown world that is striving to make the total something else and thinks it is doing it".

This reporter was well aware of the German policy of calculatingly misleading the world. This was true over a broad spectrum of matters, including the Nazi pretence of being "peace loving". Moreover he dismissed the hopes of those who predicted that Nazism would have a short life span. It was destined to last a "very long time", and would not desert its extremist cause.

> "There will be no moderation of Nazi policy in the direction of greater liberality . . . Especially there will be no relenting in the Nazi hostility towards supposed enemies and particularly towards the Jews. Aryanism is now the keystone of Nazi policy as all along it has been the principal tenet of Adolf Hitler's personal faith. It is also in Germany the most popular of the Nazi principles and of all the Nazi tendencies is the most warmly defended by the Germans. Its corollary is persecution even to extermination – the word is the Nazis' own – of the non-Aryans, if that can be accomplished without too great world disturbance."[77]

These forebodings were followed by Tolischus with a description of the despair afflicting the German-Jewish community. Most would emigrate if they could find room in another Western country. They faced

> "the surrender of the achievements of generations and a return to manual labor. The knout of the Egyptians is modernized in the decrees of Hitler. For those who want to leave the change is necessary whether they go to Palestine or elsewhere. They must go as pioneers willing to do any kind of work or perish . . . For those who remain the change is necessary because the Jews are in practice barred from all higher schooling and all the 'academic' professions. According to the best estimates, only the owners of the big and medium businesses who are still supported by both their employees and business connections will be able to survive. The majority of the others are doomed to ruin and demotion to the position of manual laborer . . . The Jews will be compelled by economic necessity to collect in the larger communities and build their own lives on one another in a sort of modern version of the ancient ghetto."[78]

The *New York Times*' final comment for 1933 on Nazi antisemitism was succinctly summarised in the headline of an article 'Year of Hitler nears End with small Hope for Jews' which drew heavily on the observations of Tolischus and Birchall.

[76]*NYT*, 23rd August 1933, 24th August 1933.
[77]*NYT*, 6th September 1933.
[78]*NYT*, 22nd September 1933.

It acknowledged that life was difficult for Socialists, Marxists, pacifists, democrats and anyone else the regime designated as "liberal". It was, however, "non-Aryans", i.e. Jews, who had received the most "crushing and devastating" blow. Although physical persecutions left the most marked scars, the Jews' suffering could not be assessed solely on the basis of that burden. Legal persecution, social isolation, incessant propaganda attacks and the terrible suffering experienced by their children was as painful and devastating as the physical abuse.

> "The actual physical assaults that marked the early days of Nazi rule have ceased, but in most other respects the situation had become worse instead of being ameliorated and there seems to be no reason to expect any betterment."

Jews no longer felt themselves to be part of Germany and were desperately seeking a way to successfully establish themselves in other countries. "Only a few still believe in the possibility of better things to come."[79]

VIII

1934 was a year during which news about Germany's persecution of its Jews was not prominently featured in the American press. This was to some extent because the policy of direct harassment and physical violence was held in partial check ,though Jews in small towns in particular faced constant threats. Antisemitic propaganda continued of course unabated and Streicher devoted an entire issue of *Der Stürmer* to ritual murder. But on the surface and in the eyes of many a student of the German scene things seemed to have reached a relative calm or, at the least, achieved an even keel. (Some Jews who had left Germany during the first wave of Nazi violence even returned to Germany.)

But the more astute outside observer sensed that little had changed. By August 1934 both American Ambassador Dodd and British Ambassador Sir Eric Phipps had recognised the firm resolve of the Nazi Party to remove all Jews from Germany. Birchall again offered Americans trenchant analysis regarding the situation in Germany as it pertained at the end of 1934.

> "The fact is, personal freedom in Germany today comprises freedom to obey orders and to be quick about it. Hesitation in compliance, even if it is a matter of giving the Nazi salute, except in the case of foreigners, may bring anything from a blow in the face to confinement in a concentration camp."

The situation for Jews remained disheartening despite the fact that no

> "additional laws relating to Jews have been decreed in the last year but the Jews had already been thoroughly dealt with in the preceding year. They are barred from all official positions. In law and medicine the small nucleus retained in the first general clearance still remains in practice but no more can be admitted, because German Jews can take university degrees only if they become foreigners".[80]

[79] *NYT*, 24th December 1933.

[80] William E. Dodd, Jr., and Martha Dodd (eds.), *Ambassador Dodd's Diary, 1933–1938*, New York 1941, pp. 157, 248, 288; *NYT*, 12th December 1934.

On some occasions events in Germany did occupy the front page of American newspapers. The murder in June of Röhm and other SA leaders, accompanied as they were by the ruthless elimination of prominent opponents of the regime – some of them victims of private Nazi vendettas – created a great stir in America. The expulsion of the noted columnist, Dorothy Thompson, from Germany did so as well. She had gone to Berlin in August 1934 and was ordered out of the country ten days later. According to Ambassador Dodd the reason for her dismissal lay in an interview with Hitler in 1932 and her reports in 1933 condemning his antisemitic campaign. Thompson explained her expulsion:

> "My first offense was to think that Hitler was just an ordinary man. That is a crime against the reigning cult which says that Mr. Hitler is a Messiah sent of God to save the German people – an old Jewish idea. To question this mystic mission is so heinous that, if you are German you can be sent to jail. I fortunately am an American so I merely was sent to Paris . . ."[81]

But the comparative lack of anti-Jewish outrages made most newspapers ignore German Jewry during 1934 and the first half of 1935. Their readers might well assume that the brutality of the first year of Nazi rule had been quashed by the government. Hope prevailed in America that despite the killings of June 1934 Germany had begun its long trek back to the path of moral behaviour and responsible leadership. The events of 1935 were to prove just the opposite, certainly as far as the Jews were concerned.

IX

1935, the watershed year in the legal and physical war to "eliminate" the German-Jewish community, saw the promulgation of the Nuremberg Laws. It was nevertheless a period when Germany was most susceptible to foreign pressure, anxious as it was to forge economic agreements with other countries. It also looked towards the 1936 Olympics as a means of winning foreign admiration and support. American Ambassador Dodd described it as a time when the Nazis were committed to introducing the "new Germany to the world".[82] The rest of the world had sufficient opportunities during 1935 to voice its revulsion at German behaviour.

1935 was the year in which the American Olympic Committee reached its final decision about the Berlin games, and the press reflected keen American interest. The July riots in Berlin and the Nuremberg Laws were to complicate, to a degree, the discussion about the Olympics. They would also demonstrate to the more astute Americans who did not deceive themselves as to the prospects for Jewish life in Germany the extent to which the Nazis were intent on weaving their intricate web of physical and legal measures around the Jewish population.

[81] *NYT*, 26th August 1934. The North American Newspaper Alliance for whom Thompson wrote her column issued her own report on her expulsion on 26th August 1934. It was front page news in many American newspapers. Marian K. Sanders, *Dorothy Thompson. A Legend in Her Own Times*, Boston 1973, p. 200.

[82] Dodd to Hull, 30th January 1936, DS. 860.4016/1610; see also *FRUS*, 1936, II, p. 197.

When on 15th July anti-Jewish riots erupted on Berlin's fashionable Kurfürstendamm,[83] they were witnessed by foreign journalists and tourists and reports were featured in the American and British press. Surprise and outrage was heightened by the fact that these outbreaks had taken place in the German capital and not in some small town or village where they could be explained away as indiscipline on the part of some local SA acting on their own. Berlin was, after all, the home base of most of the American reporters in the country.[84]

Once again there was discussion in the press whether Hitler could legitimately be held accountable for this new wave of attacks. The *San Francisco Chronicle* said they sprang from the "discontent of Nazi radicals with the moderate policy of the Hitler/Schacht system". The *Los Angeles Times* argued that they indicated that the radical elements had "temporarily gained the upper hand". United Press reporters subscribed to such a moderate versus radical dichotomous explanation and, in fact, considered the antisemitic campaign "just a side show" organised and tolerated for the benefit of extremist elements. Catholics and Jews, they argued, had borne the "brunt of the Nazi party struggle between conservatives and extremists."[85]

Generally the riots were attributed to the influence of party extremists. The *Williamsport Pennsylvania Sun* argued that in light of the radicals' power the most the German government could do was to "content itself with mildly deploring the outbreaks". The *Boston Evening Transcript* wondered if the rioters were able to work unheeded because "the government . . . did not dare to interfere with the lawless among its followers".[86] Some papers exonerated Hitler from any direct responsibility but did believe that the *Führer* and Nazi leadership were at least indirectly "responsible for the disgraceful aftermath of its vicious propaganda". The *Winston Salem North Carolina Journal* argued likewise that the racial campaign was now being carried along by "the force of its own momentum", for although "officialdom have frowned" upon the riots they had persisted nonetheless. The *Trenton Times Advertiser* posited a similar explanation in an editorial entitled 'Hitler's Frankenstein'. The monster created by Hitler had "grow[n] out of control". The riots were the product of "subordinates who apparently disobeyed orders and did exactly what they wanted to do". Seemingly they "brought dismay to Hitler".[87]

Such articles absolving the Nazi governing elite also tended to stress the difference between the party and the government; between the extremists who would engage in such violence and the moderates who only wished to resolve Germany's problems and finally between Hitler who was, according to one

[83]The disturbances were touched off by a performance of the antisemitic Swedish film 'Pettersson and Bendel' in a Kurfürstendamm cinema. (Oddly enough the film is based on a novel by W. Hammenhög which was comic rather than anti-Jewish in intent.)

[84]Moshe Gottlieb, 'The Berlin Riots of 1935 and the Repercussions in America', *American Jewish Historical Quarterly*, LX (March 1970), pp. 302–328.

[85]*San Francisco Chronicle*, 25th July 1935; *LAT*, 12th August 1935.

[86]*Williamsport Sun*, 18th July 1935; *Boston Evening Transcript*, 20th July 1935.

[87]*Evansville Indiana Courier*, 19th July 1935; *Winston Salem Journal*, 23rd July 1935, *Trenton Times Advertiser*, 4th August 1935.

paper, striving "desperately to restore order from chaos" and less respectable personalities such as Streicher who indulged in "mob tyranny and butchery".[88]

Certain antisemitic acts were obviously timed to divert attention from other problems and some decisions affecting Nazi policy towards Jews resulted from divisions of opinion between various party factions. There were those Nazi leaders who were opposed to precipitous measures that might both "inflame opinion abroad" and "create economic and financial disturbances". There were Nazi leaders who were upset by the July riots and the outspoken vulgar tactics of men such as Streicher. At the other end of the spectrum there were those who sought the "complete subordination" of the Jews including citizenship restrictions, loss of property rights and prohibitions on business and social relations with non-Jews. The Nazi leadership balanced its *modus operandi* between these two groups; however, decisions seemed to have been weighted in favour of the radical antisemites. The American press tended during these early years to interpret much of Nazi antisemitic action in terms of party factions.

In the debate on who instigated the riots, American press commentators differed as to whether they were genuinely spontaneous. Some held the government directly responsible, others argued that under a totalitarian Nazi regime there was no such thing as "spontaneous". As the *Mobile Alabama Press Register* put it, "the Nazi rank and file have never been caught yet in a spontaneous act". The *New York Post* was convinced that if the riots were not official they would not have happened.

It was generally agreed by those who argued that Hitler was not directly responsible that someone who had no reason to fear official repercussions instigated these carefully planned outbreaks and the person most frequently credited was Streicher. According to the *Baltimore Sun* the riots certainly were planned and "directed by somebody who, to say the least, feared no untoward consequences from above", and the *Birmingham Alabama Herald* did not doubt that the government had given, at the least, its "tacit approval".[89]

The *New York Herald Tribune* believed the outbreaks reflected the extremists' displeasure with Hitler's attempt to pursue a moderate course. The *Canton Ohio Repository* stated that it was "believed generally that Chancellor Hitler personally is committed to a policy of moderation" and that the riots were proof of the difficulty he was experiencing in "controlling the action of his subordinates". The *Dallas Times Herald* ascribed to Hitler many of the "good qualities that a dictator must have in order to prevent the country from suffering all the ill effects of tyranny", yet he permitted "a defenseless minority to be persecuted". The *Wilmington* (Delaware) *Journal* depicted Hitler as "remaining on the sidelines" and wondered if the riots meant that his "men have gotten out of [his] . . . control". Once again Hitler was absolved as the instigator and cast in a more passive role.[90]

[88] *Winston Salem Journal*, 23rd July 1935.

[89] *Mobile Press Register*, 21st July 1935; *New York Post*, 17th July 1935; *Baltimore Sun*, 27th July 1935; *Birmingham Herald*, 20th July 1935.

[90] *Scranton Repository*, 24th July 1935; *Dallas Times Herald*, 17th July 1935; *Wilmington Journal*, 24th July 1935.

Not all the press subscribed to this view. Some harboured no doubts about the degree of his complicity. The *Rochester Democrat and Chronicle* argued that although "Hitler's hand appears only indirectly in the test campaign to suppress Jews . . . he is its source". The *Christian Century* had no doubts about what was going on. It was a "myth" to believe Hitler unaware or not responsible. "There is no greater Jew hater than Adolf Hitler, that is his primary obsession." The *New York Post* was also totally unambivalent. Anyone who accepted the government explanation that the riots were "spontaneous" and "unofficial" proves "himself as a Nazi sympathizer or a fool".[91]

Once again the American press tried to determine whether the expressions of antisemitism were indicative of Nazi strength or weakness. In the words of the *Cleveland Plain Dealer*, Hitler's "four years of grace in which to create the Teutonic new age are fast slipping away". The *Boston Post* wondered if the riots were not a sign that "Hitler [was] in trouble". The *Troy New York Record* believed they demonstrated that "Nazi rule is crumbling".[92] The view that the riots were a sign of weakness was indicative of the tendency to judge Nazi Germany by "normal" standards. Upheaval and violence in the capital itself, particularly when attributed by the government to enemies of the regime, surely revealed the existence of a genuine threat to stability.

Even the *New York Times* whose front page proclaimed "antisemites firmly in the saddle" and whose reporters believed that it was Hitler and his followers' consciousness of their power and not their weakness which led them to this new radical offensive, fell prey to the "weakness not strength" interpretation and surmised that "all is not well" within Hitler's regime and that the "Reichsführer's power seems to be waning".[93]

The outrage expressed in America and in other countries was doubtless one of the reasons for certain soothing pronouncements at the end of July which hinted at a change in German policy concerning the Jews. The optimists were reassured. The *Washington Star* believed the new policy a "sign that reason" had returned to the Teutonic state. There was general pleasure expressed in a number of papers that the "campaign against Jews and Catholics . . . had been called off" as a result of the "impact of foreign opinion". Other papers echoed the *Star*'s view.[94]

Not everyone was so easily placated. The *New York Times* was convinced that the "off again, on again" antisemitic policies of Germany were premeditated.

> "The art of riding two horses at the same time has been practiced by politicians of all times and all climes. Never has it flourished as it does today in the Nazi . . . capital. Berlin has no difficulty in staging anti-Jewish riots and then denouncing such riots as the work of enemies of the Nazi regime. Berlin appoints a notorious antisemite as chief of police and his first act is to call off antisemitic demonstrations. Berlin spares the Jewish businessman but lets it be known

[91] *Rochester Democrat and Chronicle*, 22nd July 1935; *Christian Century*, 11th September 1935; *New York Post*, 17th July 1935.

[92] *Cleveland Plain Dealer*, 21st July 1935; *Boston Post*, 29th July 1935; *Troy Record*, 24th July 1935.

[93] *NYT*, 23rd July 1935, 24th July 1935.

[94] *Washington Star*, 30th July 1935; *Philadelphia Ledger*, 31st July 1935; *Pittsfield Eagle*, 30th July 1935; *Louisville Courier Journal*, 31st July 1935; *Memphis Commercial Appeal*, 31st July 1935; *Galveston Texas News*, 31st July 1935; *Davenport Iowa Democrat*, 31st July 1935; *Schenectady Gazateer*, 1st August 1935; *Syracuse Herald*, 31st July 1935.

> that the taint of Jews' Jewish blood makes a man unfit to serve in the army. Then Berlin starts a drive against Jewish business but Minister of War von Blomberg lets it be known that non-aryans may serve in the army. The Nazi right hand makes a point not to know what the Nazi left hand is doing."[95]

The *New York Post* also saw no amelioration. In fact it anticipated that a "new terror more vicious and perhaps even more inhuman than the old" would soon beset German Jewry. The *Milwaukee Journal* interpreted German actions as a change in tactics not policies. These were tactics which might officially eschew physical violence but which would relegate Jews to a "living death" and "slow starvation" by cutting them off "entirely from [their] place in the community". The *Baltimore Sun* was also unimpressed by the changes in policy. It cautioned readers against being blinded by manoeuvres which were clearly designed for foreign consumption. It stressed that "fanaticism is the essence of fascism".[96] The *Washington Post* echoed the views of the *New York Times*, *Baltimore Sun*, *New York Post* and *Milwaukee Journal*. Germany was "within striking distance of complete terror".[97]

X

The promulgation of the Nuremberg Laws made plain that the July riots were really the herald of a period of intensification of anti-Jewish persecution. The American press had less difficulty in grasping the implications and the severity of these laws. Although most of the press recognised the decrees as a new step in severity some still believed them to be "nothing but" a means of deflecting the attention of the German people from their domestic problems. Others argued that Hitler was in a precarious position and needed the laws to bolster his stature. According to both the *Memphis Commercial Appeal* and the *Cleveland News* the laws were "symptomatic of internal difficulties".[98]

This time the world was confronted with Nazi government measures and most of those who had adhered to the "moderate versus extremist" approach now abandoned it. One exception was J. E. Williams, editorial columnist for the *Christian Science Monitor* who believed that the laws were a "concession to the extremists" and a "notable triumph" for the "radical wing of the party". On the other hand Tolischus declared the moderate versus extremist discussion "largely academic" because the campaign against the Jews was in such "an advanced state", and all that remained to be done was to "legalize what is already accomplished". The laws were a "milestone in a pilgrimage", that had a choice of two destinations: emigration or a "living death".[99]

The condemnation was now universal. Jews were considered to be a "people without a country" and the laws were seen as absolutely "out of keeping with the modern world and in keeping with the Middle Ages". Yet much of the press failed

[95] *NYT*, 4th August 1935.
[96] *New York Post*, 31st July 1935; *Milwaukee Journal*, 4th August 1935; *Baltimore Sun*, 1st August 1935.
[97] *Washington Post*, 4th August 1935.
[98] *Memphis Commercial Appeal*, 18th September 1935; *Cleveland News*, 17th September 1935.
[99] *CSM*, 17th October 1935; *NYT*, 8th October 1935.

to grasp that these laws were not "merely an extension" of earlier proscriptions but legally placed the Jews in an unprotected and second-class status. Furthermore the fact that antisemitism was now "formally rooted in law" gave the decrees a particular import in German eyes. Ambassador Dodd reminded Secretary of State Hull of the "sanctity with which law is regarded and the discipline with which it is observed in Germany".[100]

This inability to follow the legal, political and ideological implications of the laws was exemplified by the reaction of the *Los Angeles Times* and the *St. Louis Post Dispatch*. The *Times* wondered:

> "What practical change this will make in the status of Jews in Germany [?] . . . Generally speaking nobody has any civil rights in Germany, such rights having been reduced in effect to the status of revocable privileges; and nobody votes in the sense in which voting is understood in democratic countries."

In a similar vein, the *St. Louis Post Dispatch*, after decrying Jews' loss of citizenship, hastened to add:

> "There are no citizens of Nazi Germany, however whose rights are unimpaired . . . The penalties imposed on the Jews, official scapegoats of the Nazi regime, are only part of the burdens borne by all the people under their Fascist dictatorship."[101]

The *Times* and *Post Dispatch* were correct, Jews had already lost many of their rights in common with the German population. But what had previously occurred could be attributed to unauthorised actions or to an individual law designed to make life difficult for Jews. The enactment of the Nuremberg Laws should have left no doubt in the minds of outside observers that there was no future for the Jew in Germany. The argument posed by both papers, that no one had any rights in Germany, foreshadowed a response which would typify the American reaction to the news of the Final Solution – to treat this as simply part of the entire orbit of war-related atrocities. War was the ultimate atrocity. Jews were suffering but so were a multitude of other people.

Most of the American press certainly had no inkling that this legal programme for the "blood and honour" of the German *Reich* was categorically different from the previous antisemitic acts. Its ramifications extended much further than the German policy of economic persecution. While the inability to earn their "daily bread" had immediate implications for Jews, the objective of these laws was ominous in a different and possibly more significant way. The essence of Nazi ideology was contained within them. They constituted the point of departure for the destruction which was to follow.

XI

By the end of the first few years of Nazi rule most reporters had obviously assimilated the nature of the deep changes which had taken place in Germany. Other segments of the press had found it difficult, at any rate until the Nuremberg

[100]Dodd to Hull, 7th September 1935, DS. 862, 4016/1550.
[101]*LAT*, 18th September 1935; *St. Louis Post Dispatch*, 17th November 1935.

Laws to decide if the Nazi government was behind the excesses of antisemitism or was only reluctantly tolerating them. Its supposed efforts to stop them were interpreted by some as genuine and by others as a means of camouflaging its support. Although the news reports which appeared in the American press in 1933 allowed readers to reach a variety of conclusions, ultimately the preponderance of reports and eyewitness accounts should have laid to rest most of the doubts about government complicity. The inclination to believe, which was so strong in 1933 but continued, rather naively, in some measure thereafter, that the government was not behind their actions and that they were not sanctioned by it did not express the reality of the situation but was the wish dream of the American press. Many Americans hoped against hope that Hitler would in the last resort prove himself to be a mature leader who eschewed methods of terror. There was a pronounced desire by the American papers to place Hitler outside the course of events. One can only speculate on the reasons for this attitude. In the eyes of many Americans Hitler represented a bulwark against Communism. He was engaged in rectifying the economic chaos which had prevailed in Germany. Bad as he was, those around him – Streicher, Goebbels, Göring – seemed even worse. Some Americans clearly harboured the deeply felt wish that this brash, bombastic leader would ultimately mend his ways and take his place among the world's responsible statesmen. To acknowledge otherwise – that no moderation would be forthcoming also meant to accept that a German-instigated world-wide conflagration might yet ensue. By September 1935 much of the press had begun to recognise the Nazi reality. For others it took until November 1938 to do so. Some of the press and much of the American public did not fully comprehend the nature of Nazi antisemitism until 1945 when it had already taken its full toll of European Jewry.

Jewish Fate in German Drama 1933–1945

BY ANAT FEINBERG

In late November 1933 a Jewish journalist, Meyer Weisgal, an ardent Zionist and fund-raiser, approached the famous director, Max Reinhardt, with a most unusual proposal – the putting together of a very unconventional theatrical spectacle. "In my halting German", writes Weisgal in his autobiography, "I said: 'Dieses Schauspiel muss Hitler unsere Antwort geben'"[1], planning the production for a world-wide tour. Some three years later, on the 7th January 1937, an audience gathered at the Manhattan Opera House, especially reconstructed for this production, to witness an epic-dramatic parable, based largely on the Bible, about the sufferings and survival of the Jewish people.

Werfel's *Der Weg der Verheissung* is only one of several plays written in the German language from 1933 to 1945 which depict the Jewish experience, past and contemporary. This article provides a survey of some of these unique plays, all of them written, and most of them produced, during the time when German theatres, operating in line with the Nazi *Kulturpolitik*, became yet another stage for the dissemination of fascist propaganda.[2]

The table on the following page lists fourteen of these plays and supplies information on the time and place of origin as well as first production. The plays are listed chronologically, or, to be more precise, according to the date of completion.

I. PRELIMINARY REMARKS

A study of this table reveals a number of interesting facts.

Most playwrights were established figures in pre-1933 German and Austrian theatre. Hasenclever and Werfel, for instance, were amongst the notable exponents of Expressionist drama. Carl Zuckmayer had enjoyed the success of *Der Fröhliche Weinberg* and *Der Hauptmann von Köpenick*. Brecht had already written some of his didactic plays and Ferdinand Bruckner had gained fame as the founder of the *Renaissance-Theater* in Berlin. Even the poetess Else Lasker-Schüler had tried her hand at drama (*Die Wupper*, *Arthur Aronymus und seine Väter*).

[1]Meyer Weisgal, . . . *So Far. An Autobiography*, London–Jerusalem 1971, p. 117.

[2]For drama in Nazi Germany see, for example, Hilde Haider-Pregler, 'Das Dritte Reich und das Theater', in *Maske und Kothurn*, XVII (1971), pp. 203–214; F. N. Mennemeier, *Modernes Deutsches Drama*, Munich 1975, II, pp. 95–139; Hugo F. Garten, *Modern German Drama*, London 1959, pp. 219–238; Joseph Wulf, *Theater und Film im Dritten Reich. Eine Dokumentation*, Gütersloh 1964. Herbert Freeden's *Jüdisches Theater in Nazideutschland*, Tübingen 1964 (Schriftenreihe wissenschaftlicher Abhandlungen des Leo Baeck Instituts 12) is devoted to the limited theatrical activities of the Jews in Nazi Germany.

TABLE OF PLAYS[3]

Author	*Title*	*Composed in*	*First Production*
Ferdinand Bruckner 1891–1958	*Die Rassen.* Schauspiel in drei Akten	Paris: May–November 1933	Zürich: Schauspielhaus, 30th November 1933
Friedrich Wolf 1888–1953	*Professor Mamlock.* Schauspiel	Switzerland and France: Spring, 1933	Warsaw: Kaminsky Theatre, 1934, in Yiddish. Première in German: Zürich: Schauspielhaus, 8th November 1934
Bertolt Brecht 1898–1956	*Die Rundköpfe und die Spitzköpfe.* Ein Greuelmärchen	France and Denmark: 1931–1934	Copenhagen: Riddersalen, 4th November 1936, in Danish. Some scenes performed by A. Granach and amateurs, Moscow 1935
Franz Werfel 1890–1945	*Der Weg der Verheissung.* Ein Bibelspiel in vier Teilen	Austria: 1934–1935	New York: Manhattan Opera House, 7th November 1937, in English
Gerhart Hauptmann 1862–1946	*Die Finsternisse.* Requiem	Germany: February, 1937	Göttingen: Deutsches Theater, 5th July 1952
Bertolt Brecht 1898–1956	'Die jüdische Frau' in *Furcht und Elend des Dritten Reiches*	Denmark and France: 1935–1938	Paris: Salle d'Jena, 21st May 1938 (as *99%*; 8 scenes, one being 'Die jüdische Frau')
Friedrich Wolf 1888–1953	*Das Schiff auf der Donau.* Ein Drama aus der Zeit der Okkupation Österreichs durch die Nazis	France: 1938–1939	Berlin: Hebbel-Theater, 2nd February 1955
Walter Hasenclever 1890–1940	*Konflikt in Assyrien.* Komödie in drei Akten	London: 1938	London: International Theatre Club, 31st March 1939, in English. Göttingen: Deutsches Theater, 15th September 1957
Fritz Hochwälder 1911–	*Esther.* Ein altes Märchen	Switzerland: Summer, 1940	No performance to date.
Else Lasker-Schüler 1869–1945	*Ichundich.* Eine theatralische Tragödie	Jerusalem: 1940–1941	Düsseldorf: Grosses Schauspielhaus, 10th November 1979
Rudolf Leonhard 1889–1953	*Geiseln.* Tragödie	France: Le Vernit camp, Autumn, 1941	Berlin: Hebbel-Theater, December 1946
Franz Werfel 1890–1945	*Jacobowsky und der Oberst.* Komödie einer Tragödie	On the flight from Europe to the USA: 1941–1942	New York: Theatre Guild, 14th March 1944, in English. Première in German: Basle, 17th October 1944
Nelly Sachs 1891–1970	*Eli.* Ein Mysterienspiel vom Leiden Israels	Sweden: Winter 1943	Frankfurt a. Main: "Die Neue Bühne" an der Goethe Universität, 6th February 1962: Dortmund: Städtische Bühnen, 14th March 1962
Carl Zuckmayer 1896–1977	*Des Teufels General*	USA: Vermont, 1944–1945	Zürich: Schauspielhaus, 12th December 1946

Twelve of these plays were written in exile. Of these some were conceived while the dramatists were actually on their flight to freedom, others – like *Geiseln* and *Das Schiff auf der Donau* – while their authors were interned in camps. The only two plays written in the authors' homeland were Werfel's *Der Weg der Verheissung* and Hauptmann's *Die Finsternisse*. Hauptmann wrote this fragmentary play in 1937 as a tribute to a Jewish friend who had died, but destroyed the manuscript in 1945.[4]

All the playwrights, except Hauptmann and Brecht, were of Jewish origin with at least one Jewish parent. A number of them, like Werfel and Wolf, for example, had fought for their country in the First World War. During the 1920s some of them had entertained pacifist, others Communist ideas: Brecht became involved in left-wing politics, Wolf joined the *Kommunistische Partei Deutschlands* (KPD) in 1928.

Not all these plays were produced immediately on completion. Nelly Sachs's *Eli* and Hauptmann's *Die Finsternisse* were first produced long after the war was over. Lasker-Schüler gave a reading of *Ichundich* at the Berger Club in Jerusalem in summer 1941,[5] yet the first full stage production of the play had to wait until 1979. In his preface to the 1948 edition of his play,[6] Leonhard reports that he had read it aloud to his fellow-internees and that the reading had an enormous impact on many of them. However, a full stage production was possible only after the war. Of all the plays only Hochwälder's *Esther* has not yet been performed.

Most successful among the plays which enjoyed immediate production were, no doubt, Wolf's *Professor Mamlock* and Werfel's *Jacobowsky und der Oberst*. Wolf's play was produced in more than ten countries between 1934 and 1942, among them the USSR, Japan, Spain, Israel, Norway and the city of Shanghai.[7] The 1937 New York production of the Jewish Theatre Unit had a relatively long run (76 performances), yet the critics had their reservations. Amazing to us and yet quite typical of the general opinion in America at that time was the view expressed in the *Brooklyn Daily Eagle* on 14th April 1937: "As reasonably as Friedrich Wolf writes, as honestly and intelligently and eloquently as his play is put together, the facts remain the same and *all the world knows them*."[8]

It was in the same city, towards the end of the war, that the English version of Werfel's *Jacobowsky und der Oberst*, directed in a comic vein by the young Elia

---

[3]Among the most helpful sources for the preparation of this table were Hans Christof Wächter, *Theater im Exil. Sozialgeschichte des deutschen Exiltheaters 1933–1945*, Munich 1973, pp. 265–281; Ursula Ahrens, Bio-Bibliographie der Exildramatik 1933–1945', in *Theater im Exil 1933–1945*, Akademie der Künste, Berlin 1973, pp. 145–152. I am grateful to Mr. Norbert Baensch, Chefdramaturg of the Deutsches Theater in Göttingen, who made available to me the stage manuscript of Hasenclever's play and the excellent 'Programmheft' published on the occasion of the 1957 German première of the play.

[4]For the play and the story behind it see, S. D. Stirk, 'Gerhart Hauptmann's Play *Die Finsternisse*', in *Modern Language Quarterly*, IX (1948), pp. 146–151; W. A. Reichart, 'In Memoriam Max Pinkus', in *Gerhart Hauptmann Jahrbuch*, Goslar 1948, pp. 160–173; A. Meetz, 'Gerhart Hauptmann's Requiem *Die Finsternisse*', in *Germanisch-Romanische Monatsschrift*, XL (1959), pp. 29–47.

[5]Nachwort to Else Lasker-Schüler's *Ichundich*, ed. Margarete Kupper, Munich 1980, p. 80.

[6]Rudolf Leonhard, *Geiseln*, Berlin 1948, p. 5.

[7]For the complete list see Wächter, *Theater im Exil*, p. 277.

[8]Emphasis is mine. For the difficulties of Exile-Drama in the USA see Wächter, *Theater im Exil*, pp. 171–190; and Henry Marx, 'Exil-Theater in den USA', in *Theater im Exil 1933–1945*, ed. Lothar Schirmer, Berlin 1979, pp. 215–235.

Kazan, was a great success. Over 400 performances were recorded in New York and in the provinces (on a national tour) and the play won the New York Drama Critics Circle Award for the best foreign play of 1943/1944.

Some 154 performances of Werfel's other play, *The Eternal Road*, were given in New York in 1937. Despite the great interest in the production, Weisgal, the producer, had to halt the run of this huge "musical drama"[9] owing to financial difficulties. Full houses from nine performances a week brought in $24,000, yet Weisgal had to raise another $7,000 per week just to keep the show going "without mentioning such a trifling matter as profit".[10] The over-ambitious theatrical visions of Reinhardt and the designer Norman Bel Geddes, who had previously co-operated on another large-scale spectacle, *The Miracle*, undermined Weisgal's "Zionist undertaking".[11]

Of special interest is the history of the production of Bruckner's *Die Rassen* and Wolf's *Professor Mamlock* in Switzerland, (acquiring an increasingly vital role in the activities of the so-called "Exil Theater")[12], which had to face Swiss fascists and Nazi provocateurs. Protests against Bruckner's play started on the night of the third performance. The Swiss "Frontists" who actually opposed the production of the play, were indirectly helped by the intervention of the German Ambassador to Switzerland. About a year later, the German government tried to stop the run of Wolf's anti-fascist play *Professor Mannheim*.[13] When the German appeal failed to have the desired effect, the Swiss "Frontists" planned a mass-demonstration which, in spite of the presence of the police, ended in violent clashes between socialists and fascists. Twenty-eight people were wounded. The police arrested some 120 rioters, among them the Swiss fascist leader, Henne, yet all were released soon afterwards.[14]

II. HISTORY RECORDED IN DRAMA

The fact that these two plays succeeded in stirring up audiences and politically-orientated people outside the theatre ironically accorded extremely well with the aims of both Bruckner and Wolf. Indeed, the two plays can be

[9] Weisgal, . . . *So Far*, p. 120. Lotte Lenya, whose husband, Kurt Weill, composed the music to Werfel's play, tells about this extravagant production in 'Gespräche mit Lotte Lenya', *Theater im Exil*, ed. Schirmer, pp. 243–244.

[10] Weisgal, . . . *So Far*, p. 137.

[11] *Ibid.*, p. 131.

[12] Louis Naef speaks of two periods in the activities of the "Exil-Theater" in Switzerland: he calls the period 1933–1939 "die provokative Phase" and notes the turning away from politically-orientated drama to the classics with the beginning of the war. See Louis Naef, 'Theater der deutschen Schweiz', in H. Ch. Wächter, *Theater im Exil*, pp. 241–264; the same, 'Theater der deutschen Schweiz – nationales oder Exil-Theater?' in *Theater im Exil* (Akademie der Künste), pp. 13–17.

[13] Wolf's play was performed under three different names: *Der Gelbe Fleck* in Warsaw; *Professor Mannheim* in Zürich ("da es Schwierigkeiten mit einem Herrn Mamlock gab, der zufälligerweise in der Schweiz lebte". Roman Szydlowski, 'Über Bertolt Brecht, Friedrich Wolf und das Projekt in Engels', *Theater im Exil* (Akademie der Künste), p. 60; and as *Professor Mamlock*. A film version of *Professor Mamlock* was produced in the USSR in 1938.

[14] For details about the riots see Roman Szydlowski, 'Über Bertolt Brecht, Friedrich Wolf und das Projekt in Engels', *Theater im Exil* (Akademie der Künste), pp. 59–60.

considered as the first of a group of plays written with a clearly polemical goal in the playwright's mind. Wolf's plays, Bruckner's *Die Rassen*, Brecht's two plays and Leonhard's *Geiseln* were initially designed to open up people's eyes to the infamous crimes perpetrated by the Nazis and to warn of possible greater evil if fascist hysteria was not restrained. For these playwrights, as for the director, Piscator, the theatre was a cultural-political weapon for engaging the masses and provoking them to action.[15] Generically considered, the mode of all but one is dramatic realism. Brecht's play about the Roundheads and the Peakheads is a parable, a forerunner in many respects of Frisch's *Andorra*, with a considerable number of explicit references to Hitler's race theory.

The time span of *Die Rassen* (March/April 1933) allows Bruckner to follow up, step by step, the racist measures taken by the Nazis after the burning of the *Reichstag*.[16] The Jewish student, Siegelmann, apparently modelled on a real character,[17] undergoes all the agonies which were common to many Jews in the Germany of 1933. Siegelmann is expelled from the university, despised and tortured by his former colleagues. In a "Blitzaktion" Nazi students storm his room, stick side locks to his temples, hang a placard round his neck on which is written "Ich bin Jude", cut his trousers and beat him down to the street.

Mental torture, humiliation and physical suffering mark the fate of Professor Mamlock in Wolf's play, which covers the period from May 1932 to April 1933. Wolf's extension of the time span to include the period just before the re-election of Hindenburg, when National Socialism was definitely on the rise, intensifies the tragedy of the Jewish doctor who, like so many other Jews, failed to see what was inevitably in store for him. Ironically, as if to prove Wolf right, a Jewish dentist, by the name of Professor Mamlok (sic) turned up after the première in Zürich claiming that the drama, based, as it were, on his own life-story, led to his being removed from his position in Berlin, and eventually forced him into exile. Wolf succeeded in re-creating an atmosphere of horror. Stormtroopers break into his private lodging and the clinic; Hitler's voice is heard over the wireless screaming that the "Untermenschen" contaminate the Aryan race; Professor Mamlock, like Siegelmann in Bruckner's play, appears with the placard "Jew" round his neck; his half-Jewish daughter, Ruth, returns from her school, in a state of shock, "einen grossen gelben Fleck mitten auf dem Rücken".[18]

Interestingly, a few months after Wolf began writing his play, a macabre comedy entitled *Kultur* by Theodore Wächter was given its première on Broadway, New York. The protagonist, as in Wolf's play, is a German-Jewish surgeon who suffers from the racial restrictions imposed by the fascists. At the end of the play he is asked to help save the mortally sick dictator, and succeeds where others had failed by giving him a (Jewish!) blood transfusion. The doctor is

[15]Günther Rühle considers the political dramatists Bruckner, Wolf, Brecht and the director Erwin Piscator to be the most important positive examples of German theatre in exile, "die nicht nur die Position von 1931/32 perpetuiert haben . . . sondern . . . ihr System im Exil weiter ausgebaut haben". *Theater im Exil*, ed. Schirmer, p. 202.

[16]See a comparison of Bruckner's plot with historical events in Günther Rühle, *Zeit und Theater 1933–1945*, Frankfurt a. Main 1980, VI, pp. 819–835.

[17]*Ibid.*, p. 823.

[18]Friedrich Wolf, *Professor Mamlock, Dramen*, Frankfurt a. Main 1980, p. 270.

offered full rehabilitation, but nonetheless, unlike Mamlock, decides to emigrate.

The reality of horror also pervades 'Die jüdische Frau', one of twenty-eight episodes in Brecht's *Furcht und Elend im Dritten Reich*, which describe various aspects of life in Hitler's Germany. In a Germany overwhelmed by suspicion and fear, husband and wife become alienated from one another as Hitler's racist ideology infects intimate relationships. The only common language the married couple still have before the wife leaves her non-Jewish husband in order to spare him unpleasantness is that of pretence and self-deception.

The awareness of an impending disaster which looms over this short episode turns into physical reality in Wolf's *Das Schiff auf der Donau* and in Leonhard's *Geiseln*. In Wolf's play, written after Hitler's annexation of Austria, the Jewish characters describe how the Nazis forbade customers to buy medicine at Jewish pharmacies lest they be poisoned; how uniformed Nazis stormed Jewish flats, smashed up all they could find and dragged away their Jewish victims; and how people were sent to concentration camps. Finally, Leonhard's play acquaints us with the horrors of a camp. The plot, based on a report which Leonhard, himself interned, had read in the newspapers, depicts the case of ten men, Jews and Communists, who are accused of plotting against the regime and are brutally executed. Though the play was not meant to protest against the extermination of the Jews only, Leonhard describes some instances which were specifically part of the Jewish experience, as for example, the separation of Jewish prisoners from others.

While all these plays, so solidly based on real facts, are marked by a sharp, sober vision of the inevitable doom of the Jews, Brecht in his parable *Die Rundköpfe und die Spitzköpfe* seems to have distorted the racial issue through his Marxist perspective. Brecht's 'Lehrstück' is concerned with the corruption and evil of capitalist society more than with racial discrimination. For the "Tschich"-Jewish-landlord de Guzman, who is led through the streets wearing a placard on which is written "Ich bin ein Tschich", is in the end no better than the rich Roundheads – the master race; "the racial theory is explained as a mere trick to deceive the common people, and the rich peakheads in the end fraternise with the rich roundheads", remarks Martin Esslin in his commentary on the parable, and adds: "In other words, if the Marxist interpretation of Nazi policy had been correct, the rich Jews would have been spared by Hitler and would in the end have emerged as having been on his side all the time!"[19]

Whilst these plays attempt to reflect in a realistic manner the accelerating terror in the German *Reich*, most of the other eight plays are far more stylised and use a more figurative approach to Jewish experience under the Nazis. In each case the allegoric framework or mystical symbolism enables the playwright to examine contemporary events in a more universal context. In this way the Holocaust is portrayed as merely another pogrom in a history of endless persecution. The immediate appeal for political activity, resistance and struggle is missing in these symbolic plays which see the Jew as the object of eternal persecution, an archetypal victim, as it were.

[19]Martin Esslin, *Brecht. A Choice of Evils*, 3rd rev. edn., London 1980, pp. 182.

The two allegories based on the biblical Esther story transfer the plot-context to the contemporary scene: Hasenclever's *Konflikt in Assyrien*, a comedy, implicitly places the biblical figures in Hitler's Germany, while Hochwälder's *Esther*, which he suggested should be played in the style of *commedia dell'arte*, places the old story in "ein zeitlos korruptes Rumänien".[20] Considering the fact that they were written in 1938 and 1940 respectively, both "comedies" are somewhat naive in their handling of the crisis in the relationship between the Jews and the "master race". Both allegories make use of racist jargon, refer to confiscation of Jewish property, to sudden nocturnal actions against the Jews – all of which merely typify the early stages of Nazis persecution.

The discrepancy between the enormity of the crimes against the Jews and the depiction of Jewish harassment in later plays such as Werfel's *Jacobowsky und der Oberst* and, even more so, in Zuckmayer's *Des Teufels General*, is striking. "Der Ewige Jude" in Werfel's *Jacobowsky . . . Komödie einer Tragödie* casually mentions that he survived two years imprisonment in Dachau, and Jacobowsky protests against the indifference of the Western World that did nothing to rescue those oppressed by Hitler, Jews and non-Jews alike. In Zuckmayer's play Jewish fate in Nazi Germany is a minor issue. The only Jew in *Des Teufels General* does not appear on stage. He is said to have been interned in Buchenwald and to have committed suicide in his despair.

In comparison with the warnings of the earlier plays, on the one hand, and early post-Holocaust plays such as Ingeborg Drewitz's concentration camp play *Alle Tore waren bewacht* (1951) or Siegfried Freiberg's *Das kleine Weltwirtshaus* (1948), on the other hand, the portrayal of Jewish experience during the Holocaust in those plays written between 1940–1945 appears inadequate. This is, of course, due to the lack of information about the camps, the killings and the later stages of the "Final Solution". However, would these playwrights actually have been able to depict the monstrosity of the Holocaust had they indeed been aware of its dimensions?

As suggested, this inability or failure to record the atrocities that were committed against the Jews is matched by a symbolic style of dramatic presentation. The biblical basis of three of these plays gives to contemporary events a timeless, universal dimension. Hochwälder qualifies the time of his action as "zeitlos"; Werfel adds to *Der Weg der Verheissung* the following statement: "Dieses Beispiel ereignet sich unter einer zeitlosen Gemeinde Israel/ in einer zeitlosen Nacht der Verfolgung."[21] Werfel's *Der Weg der Verheissung*, Hasenclever's *Konflikt in Assyrien* and Hochwälder's *Esther* convey basically the same message: Jewish destiny has been, is, and will be one of existence on the brink of cataclysm.

Drawing on the rich symbolism of Jewish mysticism Nelly Sachs depicts martyrdom as well as redemption. *Eli*, which she significantly subtitled "Ein Mysterienspiel vom Leiden Israels", was written in 1943, and attests to the

[20]Fritz Hochwälder, 'Als Bühnen-Schriftsteller im Exil', in *Theater im Exil*, ed. Schirmer, p. 53. Hochwälder tells about his first attempts at play-writing in Swiss exile in 'Bericht', in *Theater im Exil* (Akademie der Künste), pp. 17–18.

[21]Title page of the Fischer edition of the play, *Die Dramen*, Frankfurt a. Main 1959, II, p. 91.

intense prophetic vision of the poetess in exile.[22] Both Nelly Sachs and Else Lasker-Schüler tried at the height of the Holocaust to underline its universal nature. Whereas Nelly Sachs focuses on the pattern of Jewish existence constantly on the brink of catastrophe, Lasker-Schüler concentrates on the persecutor. *Ichundich*, written in her unmistakably idiosyncratic style, is a poetic-dramatic collage, intermingling the real (Hitler, director Reinhardt, the poetess, spectators) with the biblical (Saul, David) and the figurative. Jewish experience is subordinated to the wider poetic vision of the play, which is an attempt to approach the Nazi nightmare on a metaphysical level, in the tradition of the archetypal demonic ordeal in Goethe's *Faust*.[23]

Symbolical figures derived from Jewish tradition, Jewish mysticism and Christian mythology can be found in some of these plays. Of particular interest is the figure of "Der Ewige Jude". Ahasver, who appealed to German writers in previous generations (Hauff, Chamisso, Lenau) appears in Hauptmann's *Die Finsternisse* and in Werfel's *Jacobowsky und der Oberst* and conveys in both plays alike, the quintessence of the drama. The legendary Ahasver in Hauptmann's play expresses one of the main ideas underlying this requiem: "Ich trage von Ewigkeit zu Ewigkeit diese Last. Joel [the individual] ist tot. Aber Israel stirbt nicht."[24] Werfel's "Ewiger Jude" is, as he himself seems to suggest, an incarnation of Jewish history: generations of suffering and survival of which Jacobowsky is just one instance. Werfel's Eternal Jew represents only "one possibility", ("Es gibt zwei Möglichkeiten"), one fate, one choice. The other option, or the alternative approach to fate is suggested by the Christian figure of "Der Heilige Franziskus".[25]

On the whole then, one can observe a development from the dramatists' concern with individual fate based on facts and actual experience in a given historical framework, to a metaphorical representation of experiences not bound by time, seen in the perspective of collective destiny.

III. A MIRROR TO PERSECUTED AND PERSECUTOR

a) *The Jewish spectrum*

Two basic groups of Jews emerge from these plays: Jews who have tried, at times with temporary success, to assimilate themselves to their non-Jewish environment, and Orthodox Jews who, in good and bad times, cling firmly to their faith.

In almost all these plays there is at least one representative of assimilated

[22]Discussions of the play are offered by Johannes Edfelt and Walter A. Berendsohn in *Nelly Sachs zu Ehren*, Frankfurt a. Main 1961.

[23]The play has been discussed by Heinz Thiel, '*Ich und Ich* – Ein versperrtes Werk?', in *Lasker-Schüler*, ed. Michael Schmid, Wuppertal 1969, by Otto Köhler in *Frankfurter Hefte*, 9th September 1962, and by M. Kupper in her 'Nachwort' to the edition of the play.

[24]Gerhart Hauptmann, *Die Finsternisse*, in *Sämtliche Werke*, VIII (*Nachgelassene Werke*), ed. Hans-Egon Hass, Frankfurt a. Main 1963, p. 401.

[25]For exegeses of Werfel's play see, for instance, A. D. Klarmann, 'Allegory in Werfel's *Das Opfer* and *Jacobowsky and The Colonel*', in *German Review*, XX (1945), pp. 195–217; F. A. Krügel, *Suffering and the Sacrificial Ethos in the Dramatic Works of Franz Werfel*, Diss., University of Minnesota 1959.

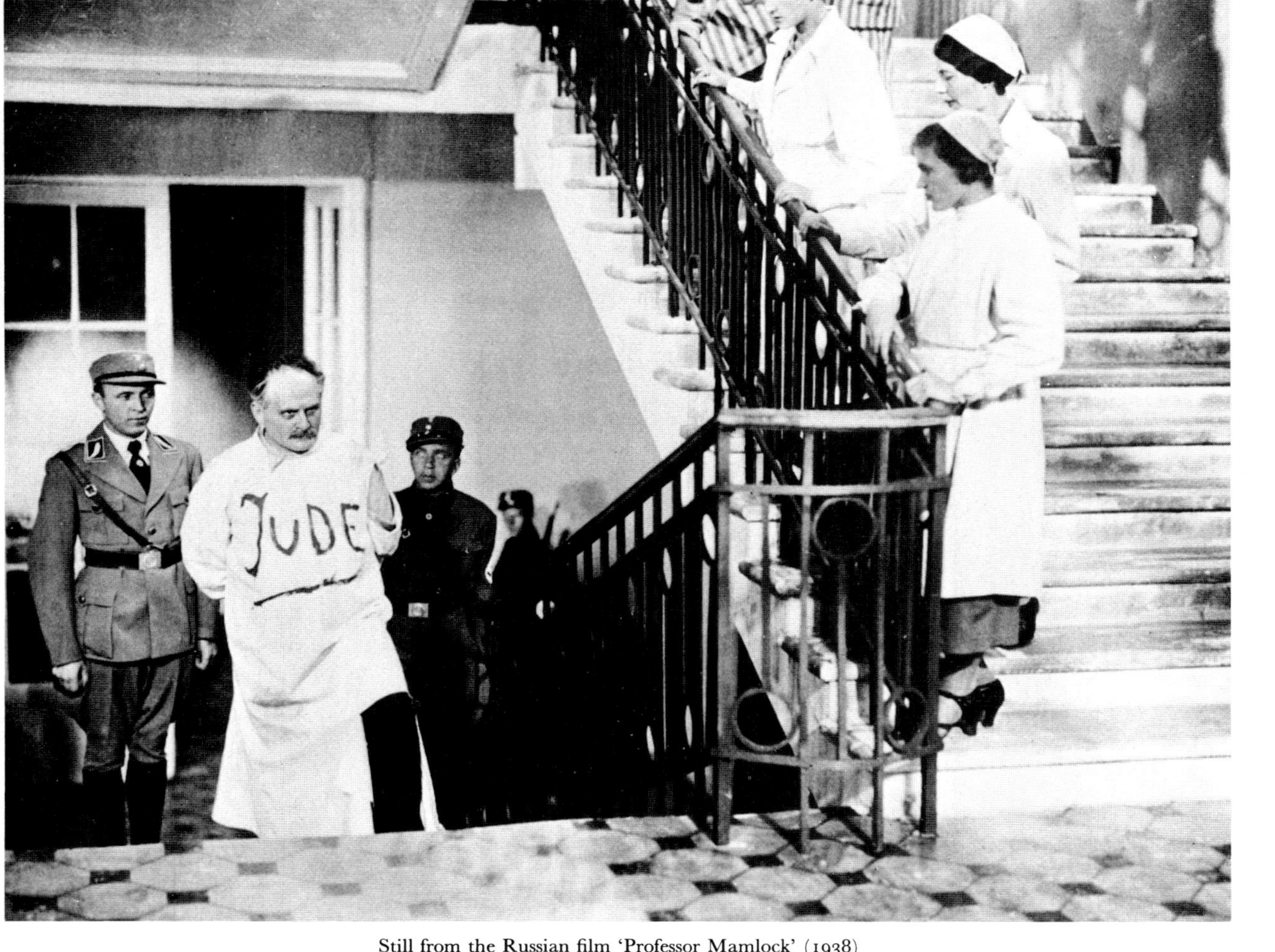

Still from the Russian film 'Professor Mamlock' (1938)

By courtesy of the National Film Archive, London

Jewry, mostly German. That this should be the case is, in fact, not surprising, considering that large sections of German Jewry desperately desired and were only too eager to believe that they belonged to the German people. Wolf's Mamlock may serve as a typical example, as the playwright himself explicitly suggested in 1936.[26] Awarded the Iron Cross, First Class, highly respected by his medical colleagues, married to a German, he loves Germany, his homeland, ("ich liebe auch unser Land, in dem ich geboren bin"),[27] refuses to see the looming dangers and prefers to keep politics out of his clinic. Even when he is advised by well-wishers to save himself and his family by fleeing Germany, he firmly sticks to his life-long belief: "Wir bleiben in Deutschland, wir können nicht mehr aus diesem Land, wir sind ein Teil dieses Landes. Nehmt ihr uns alles, unsere Arbeit, unsere Ehre, unsere Heimat, dann bleibt uns nur ein Weg . . ."[28] When, at the end of the play, he follows this "one way" by committing suicide, he realises on the verge of dying that another way had been open to him: the way of active resistance, which his own Communist son had chosen to follow, despite his father's persistent objections. For the German-loving Mamlock this was only a theoretical option which he was incapable of taking.

The assimilated Jewish *Geheimrat* Max in *Die Rassen* toys with the illusion that he can continue to live in Germany as before, by adopting a racist ideology of his own. He classifies the Jews in two categories and argues the superiority of German Jewry over the rootless Jewish refugees who came from the East (*Ostjuden*), undermined the reputation and endangered the existence of the well-established German Jews. The tailor, Levi, in Hasenclever's comedy, who in order to evade the racial restrictions adopts an Assyric name for himself and his shop, even confesses that he and others like him are willing to abide by the absurd regulation imposed by Authority. Another way out is suggested in Brecht's parable by de Guzman and Isabella: the peakheaded landlord declares himself a Catholic and his sister wishes to enter the San Barabas convent.

Brecht's de Guzman may be seen as a representative of the well-to-do Jews who because of their prosperity and position were the most hated group in a Germany facing dire economic problems. Other examples of wealthy Jews are *Geheimrat* Max in *Die Rassen* and "Der Reiche", the rich Jew in Werfel's bible play who keeps on wondering in amazement "Warum können wir nicht sein wie die anderen?"[29] A moving example of a well-off, assimilated Jew is offered by Hauptmann in the requiem he wrote for his departed Jewish friend, the rich Silesian industrialist, Max Pinkus. The few who assembled for a meal on the eve of the funeral talk of the deceased as having been a noble and generous aristocrat, loyal to his emperor ("Kaisertreu") and to his local community, a patron of the arts, "nach Sprache und Seele war er ein Deutscher".[30] His son, who refuses to acknowledge the fact that only a few courageous friends dare to pay their last

[26]"Denn dieser Mamlock ist nicht irgendeiner, er ist einer von Millionen, er ist der Typus von Millionen 'Demokraten' . . ." in 'Ein *Mamlock*? – 12 Millionen Mamlocks!', Wolf, *Dramen, op. cit.*, p. 458.

[27]Wolf, *Professor Mamlock, Dramen*, p. 267.

[28]*Ibid.*, p. 286.

[29]Franz Werfel, *Der Weg der Verheissung, Die Dramen*, Frankfurt a. Main 1959, II, p. 97.

[30]Gerhart Hauptmann, *Die Finsternisse, op. cit.*, p. 406.

respects to his father, continues to hang on to the illusion of belonging: "Aber wir gerade sind keine Juden in diesem Sinne mehr! Wir haben den Starrsinn aufgegeben! Wir sind ganz aufgegangen in der europäischen, in der deutschen Kultur!"[31]

In Hauptmann's play, as well as in many others, occasional reference is made to the fact that the assimilated Jews were steeped in German culture. Werfel's Jacobowsky is angry with himself for not being able to detach himself from German culture despite the ordeal brought on him by the Germans. "Die deutsche Kultur stösst einem immer wieder auf . . . Leider . . .",[32] he says and recalls time and again Goethe, Mozart and Beethoven; on one occasion he sings a Schubert Lied to himself. Jacobowsky's confessional statement: "In meiner Familie wurde leider das körperliche Training zugunsten einer völlig nutzlosen Intelligenz missachtet"[33] characterises no doubt a large number of European Jews.

Jacobowsky's attitude to his fate as a Jewish refugee, pursued from one country to another, always on the verge of disaster, is exceptional: an optimist by nature and full of "joie de vivre", he is, as he confesses, "hypnotised by his own fate". Constantly aware of his Jewish identity, life is an intriguing challenge for him, a fascinating fight for survival. Unlike him or the assimilated Jews who cannot come to terms with fate, the plays depict several Jewish characters who discover their true identity only because of the sudden turn of events. Helena in Bruckner's play becomes aware of her Jewishness when her German lover, Karlanner, breaks off his relationship with her. This traumatic experience results in a profound need to belong to her Jewish brethren, to share their woes and miseries. Similar to Helena's return to her roots is the case of both Esther figures. Following the source episode, Hasenclever's Esther reveals her Jewish identity to the King after her uncle, Mardochai, had urged her to plead on behalf of her people and make the King revoke his decree. Esther confesses her origin, tells the King that their son is of mixed blood (there is no such episode in the biblical source), yet realises herself the full meaning of her newly discovered identity only when the King keeps silent "one moment too long" ("einen Augenblick zu lange hast Du geschwiegen").[34] The silence which falls like a shadow between the suddenly alienated lovers, cries out also in Brecht's episode 'Die jüdische Frau'.

Esther's confession of her true origin in Hochwälder's play is far less dramatic. Moreover, one has the feeling that no profound transformation accompanies this declaration. Hochwälder divulges Esther's true feelings in the surprise ending. Diverging from the source, in the play Esther leaves the King and chooses to follow her uncle and to join her people. The King offered her the crown, provided she kept her identity secret, and did not guarantee to safeguard the Jews forever.

Only one Jewish figure in all these plays decides that no place in Europe is safe any longer and that the only possible refuge is Palestine. Bruckner, who like all Jewish playwrights mentioned in this article was no Zionist, went into exile to

[31] *Ibid.*, p. 408.
[32] Franz Werfel, *Jacobowsky und der Oberst*, Frankfurt a. Main 1979, p. 97.
[33] *Ibid.*, p. 148.
[34] Walter Hasenclever, *Konflikt in Assyrien*, Bühnenmanuskript, Berlin 1957, p. 86.

America and eventually returned to Germany. Siegelmann in *Die Rassen* sees the deeper roots of the problem of Jewish existence in the Diaspora. He explains the miseries that befell many Jewish generations in that "Man wohnt bei den andern, ohne zu Haus zu sein". Furthermore, he speaks of the eternal longings of the Jews for a homeland: "Es ist die Sehnsucht nach einer Rückkehr, als müsste man jederzeit zurrückkehren können, woher man nie gekommen war."[35] Siegelmann who comes from an assimilated Jewish home (with a father the devoted admirer of Wagner) and is totally disenchanted with Germany, waits for his affidavit to emigrate to Palestine.

None of the Orthodox Jewish figures in these plays entertains Zionist ideology. The old Rebstock in Wolf's *Das Schiff auf der Donau*, Mardochai in Hasenclever's play and the 72-year-old Isidor Bernheim in *Geiseln* all put their ultimate hope in the Almighty. Mardochai argues the case of his Jewish brethren to Haman and says that "Ein Volk kann ohne Vaterland leben – aber nicht ohne Gott".[36] When the Nazi soldiers drag off the Viennese chemist Rebstock he takes with him only his personal first-aid box, a shroud and his prayer book. He faces a moral dilemma when forced to choose between telling a lie in order to save the life of a political refugee and abiding by God's commandment. Like old Bernheim in *Geiseln* he keeps turning to the Bible, both for comfort and for the assurance that similar disasters have occurred before. Bernheim, whose faith does not falter even when the sentence of death is pronounced, keeps up the morale of his fellow prisoners by reciting the psalms and crowning the young French idealist Matheron as "young David". The old Jew has a soothing influence on the internees, and ironically the non-Jewish Grübbel expresses his admiration for him, saying "Der Alte spricht wie ein Pastor".[37]

Representatives of the wide range of Jewish views and mentality can all be found in Werfel's *Der Weg der Verheissung*. The Rabbi who tries to hold his community together and help its members to face misery, draws on the Bible to prove that similar crises had befallen Israel more than once and that hardships were divine punishment on the one hand, and a form of strengthening faith on the other. In addition to the Orthodox Jew Werfel introduces the assimilated Jew, "der *Ent*fremdete" (emphasis is mine) who has alienated himself from his people, the rich Jew, and the antagonist, "Der Widersprecher", whose rationalistic, impious approach to history provokes the entire community.

b) *Antisemitism and German Guilt*

Needless to say, the plays record an immense variety of antisemitic statements. These range from echoes of medieval accusation of a Jewish plot to poison the Christian community or the violent rape of innocent Christian maids by Jews, to anti-Jewish allegations in line with the stereotypes set up by the ideologists of the Nazi race theory. The antisemitic Nazi jargon infiltrates not only realistic plays but also Brecht's parable and the allegories based on biblical material. In lieu of

[35] Ferdinand Bruckner, *Die Rassen*, in *Zeit und Theater 1933–1945*, *op. cit.* p. 575.
[36] Hasenclever, *Konflikt in Assyrien*, *op. cit.*, p. 33.
[37] Leonhard, *Geiseln*, *op. cit.*, p. 35.

quotations, which would make up a compendium of antisemitic slogans, it should suffice here to draw attention to a few aspects which deserve special emphasis.

One of the plays permeated with antisemitic expressions is Hasenclever's *Konflikt in Assyrien.* Hasenclever incorporated Nazi slogans in a sophisticated and effective way into the plot-frame of the Esther story, with Haman as the arch-villain racist possessing many of the Nazi attributes. The Jew Mardochai tries to offer a rationally-grounded explanation for antisemitism. He introduces the image of the Jew as a scapegoat for national and economic crises. "Die Völker könnten ohne die Juden gar nicht existieren. Wenn wir nicht da wären, müsste man uns erfinden."[38]

It is the same Mardochai to whom Hochwälder in his version of the Esther story assigns most of the antisemitic text normally given to Haman. In doing so, Hochwälder not only gives his version of the Esther story a unique personal colouring, but sharpens the disparity between the Jews's understanding of his condition and his subconscious refusal to see the approaching catastrophe. Hochwälder's Mardochai, who speaks broken German, occasionally mixed with Yiddishisms, tries hard to conform. One of the King's men makes the point that the Jewish soul is so peculiar that the Jews themselves believe in the antisemitic characteristics attributed to them.

Hochwälder's addition to the source material is Benjamin, Mardochai's nephew, who chooses to dissociate himself from his people in order to fight for the socialist cause, much to the dismay of his conservative uncle.[39] In the plays of the Jewish Communists Wolf and Leonhard in particular, we hear of the fascists' habit of linking anti-Jewish and anti-Communist propaganda. The Nazi officer Müller in *Geiseln* argues that "Juden und Kommunisten, das ist dasselbe. Alle Kommunisten sind Juden, alle Juden können Kommunisten werden . . . Man muss die Feinde ausrotten . . ."[40]

Not one of these plays elaborates the case for collective political or moral guilt. In Nelly Sachs's *Eli* though the suggestion is made that time is redeemed only when Eli's murderer has been identified and his physical being has disintegrated. Michael's vengeance restores the moral order in the universe and opens the way for a mystical Jewish resurrection.

The tendency to demonise Hitler and his followers is recognisable only in *Ichundich.* (Mephisto says: ". . . Satan hat an dieser Nazirass' höllischen Spass!"[41]) In all other plays, including Zuckmayer's *Des Teufels General*, there is no attempt to portray the Germans as an homogeneous people possessed by monstrous evil. Neither can one say that the playwrights present Jewish suffering under the Nazis as an unprecedented event in history. Most dramatists seem inclined to present at least part of the German nation in a milder or even apologetic light. For example, Karlanner, Bruckner's protagonist, joins the NSDAP more out of a desire to conform than out of political conviction. When, at

[38]Hasenclever, *Konflikt in Assyrien, op. cit.*, p. 124.

[39]In Wolf's *Professor Mamlock* it is Rolf, the doctor's son, who turns to Communism against his father's wish. Both Benjamin and Rolf consider the Jewish problem a side-issue of the greater dangers latent in the totalitarian Nazi regime.

[40]Leonhard, *Geiseln, op. cit.*, p. 15.

[41]Else Lasker-Schüler, *Ichundich*, ed. Margarete Kupper, *op. cit.*, p. 30.

the end of the play, he is accused of treachery, he is already resigned to die. It is not the guilt of which he is accused but the awareness of a grave moral error which makes him realise that the crime he committed is irretrievable. Similar in many respects to Karlanner is the Nazi Grelinger in *Geiseln*. Leonhard seeks to evoke our sympathy for this German officer who wishes to alleviate the physical and mental hardships of the ten prisoners. When at the end of the play the victims are shot in the courtyard, Grelinger sees no other way out of his mental anguish but to commit suicide.

In other plays there are examples of Nazis reformed by their encounter with Jewish victims. Dr. Inge in *Professor Mamlock*, formerly an avid follower of Nazi theories, is the only one who supports the Jewish doctor when all his former friends betray him. Significantly, she is the one to be witness to his political legacy. In Wolf's other play the SS soldier, Sepp, defects to the victims' camp, having fallen in love with a young Jewish woman. An interesting character in this play is the priest, disdainfully nicknamed "Judenpfarrer", who pays with his life for helping the victims on the ship.

Perplexing is the attempt to whitewash a Nazi officer in Zuckmayer's play which, unlike the others, was composed towards the end of the Third *Reich*, when information about the atrocities committed at the concentration camps penetrated more and more deeply into the awareness of the world.

IV. CONCLUSION

"Das Theater der Emigration kann nur ein politisches Drama zu seiner Sache machen ... nicht nur seine Bühne, sondern auch sein Drama ist neu aufzubauen." With this clear-cut credo Walter Benjamin started his review of the 1938 Paris production of Brecht's *Furcht und Elend des Dritten Reiches*.[42] Can the plays written about the Jewish predicament between 1933 and 1945 be considered as political drama? It seems that what began as politically-orientated drama, with the aim of informing, warning and provoking to action, in the course of time lost its polemical character in favour of a more symbolical and timeless dramatic presentation of Jewish experience. This development has objective and subjective reasons.

The majority of the playwrights drew on personal experience or stories they heard while still living in Germany at the beginning of the Nazi regime or on their flight to freedom as racial and/or political exiles. In the later stages of the Third *Reich* the dramatists had to rely on indirect experience, and only scanty details of the enormity of the crimes and the Final Solution leaked out.

The most prominent critic in the USA at this time, B. Atkinson, considered any play such as Bruckner's *Die Rassen* and Wolf's *Professor Mamlock* to be "a poorly written horror play" and suggested, expressing thereby the view of a large section of theatre-goers, that any dramatic presentation of the real horror would fall short of reality. "What the playwright should explain to us is not what, for we know

[42]Walter Benjamin in *Die Neue Weltbühne*, Paris, 30th June 1938, quoted in *Brecht in der Kritik*, ed. Monika Wyss, Munich 1977, p. 190.

that, but why."[43] The world was preoccupied with its own struggle against Nazism. There was a tendency, at least in the pre-war period, not to provoke the fascists, either in Germany or at home, by discouraging the production of stringent anti-Nazi plays in their theatres. One of many examples is the case of Bruckner's play, the performance of which was forbidden in London. The German fascists reported with exultation the decision to ban the performance: "Die englische Zensur hat die Aufführung verboten mit der Begründung, dass man in England kein Stück aufführen dürfe, das einen befreundeten Staat herabzusetzen geeignet ist."[44]

Only a few of these plays were box-office successes.[45] The reason for this does not lie only in the reluctance of spectators to spend money on such entertainment. Though some plays were produced in the original German, a high percentage of these plays had to be translated in order to reach the public, and often enough there were endless, sometimes bizarre problems connected with these translations.[46] To this must be added the fact that actors did not find it easy to relate to or feel at ease with the roles assigned to them. One of the ironies in the history of the production of anti-Nazi plays outside Germany during this time was that Jewish actors who had escaped by the skin of their teeth were not only given roles as Jewish victims but also as SS officers.

It is infinitely more difficult to explain the subjective reasons for this development, namely, why the dramatist shunned politically orientated plays and chose to retreat into a more metaphorical presentation of the Jewish fate. As stated at the beginning of this article, most dramatists were of Jewish origin. The present author does not subscribe to the view that these Jewish exiles did not live up to the task which history had, as it were, assigned to them, because initially they were indifferent Jews, in some cases trying even to ignore their ethnic identity. Weisgal reports that Werfel had told him that the Armenians in *Die vierzig Tage des Musa Dagh* (1933) "waren meine Ersatzjuden".[47] Moreover, he says that though Werfel was remote from Judaism, he realised the importance of the mission he was to carry out by writing *Der Weg der Verheissung*.[48] Hasenclever's allegory is the last play the dramatist wrote before committing suicide in the

[43]B. Atkinson, 'Culture under the Nazis', in *New York Times*, 25th April 1937. The reviewer of the New York production of *Die Rassen*, Robert Garland, reproached the playwright for having "made of it a sermon. A sermon which is effective, but a sermon just the same. Too often the piece loses sight of its story and turns itself into a one-sided debate." *New York World-Telegram*, no date is mentioned, (most probably 20th March 1934).

[44]*Die Deutsche Bühnenzeitung*, 11th April 1934, quoted in Joseph Wulf, *Theater und Film im Dritten Reich*, *op. cit.*, p. 245.

[45]See above pp. 59–60.

[46]For example, the story of the American stage adaptation of Werfel's *Jacobowsky und der Oberst*.

[47]Weisgal, . . . *So Far*, p. 120. Weisgal points to the irony that marked the signing of the contract for the production of *The Eternal Road*. "It was a strange document drawn up in a strange and ominous setting: three of the best-known un-Jewish Jewish artists [Reinhardt, Werfel and Weill] gathered in the former residence of the Archbishop of Salzburg, in actual physical view of Berchtesgaden, Hitler's mountain chalet across the border in Bavaria, pledged themselves to give high dramatic expression to the significance of the people they had forgotten about till Hitler came to power." (*ibid.*, p. 121).

[48]For Werfel's attitude to Judaism see Margarita Pazi, 'Franz Werfel 1890–1945', in *Tribüne* (1981), pp. 119–134.

internment camp of Les Milles in France in June 1940.[49] While writing it in exile he confessed in a letter that "Ich habe wieder einen Lebensinn".[50] Nelly Sachs's *Eli* is one of the most poignant examples of her discovery of, and return to, her Jewish heritage.

Even if we admit that the dramatic quality of these plays is uneven, and that they do not reflect the monstrosity of the Holocaust, they nevertheless serve, long before official historiography took over this task, as early "documents" offering insight into a totalitarian society in which the Jews were victimised.

[49]A moving description of Hasenclever's last days appears in Leon Feuchtwanger's *Der Teufel in Frankreich. Erlebnisse*, 1954, pp. 122–129.

[50]Letter to Edith Schäfer, London, 11th July 1938, printed in *Blätter des Deutschen Theaters in Göttingen*, 115, p. 20.

Jewish Refugees in the Netherlands 1933–1940 The Structure and Pattern of Immigration from Nazi Germany

BY BOB MOORE

I

Over the last twenty-five years, several important studies[1] have added a great deal to our knowledge of the structure and organisation of the Jewish emigration from Nazi Germany in the pre-war period. Their analyses of census data and archive material have provided a clearer picture of the trends in emigration than those quoted in more general works on the persecution of the Jews in Germany. Nevertheless, although a great deal is now known about the emigration from Germany, relatively little demographic information exists on the Jews as refugees in Europe. As yet there has been no published analysis on the detailed demography of Jewish refugees in Western Europe and the only work on refugees in the Netherlands to date is Dan Michman's unpublished Hebrew thesis *The Jewish Refugees from Germany in the Netherlands 1933–1940.*[2] The purpose of this article, itself a part of a more detailed survey of the Dutch government's response to the refugees,[3] is to provide at least some of this missing information on the Netherlands and to assess its role as a country of settlement, and perhaps more importantly, as a country of first refuge for Jews from Germany.

The haphazard way in which contemporary statistics on refugees in Europe were compiled, by governments and refugee organisations alike, and the different criteria used in various countries, make comparisons of refugees admitted to those countries difficult. Nevertheless, a number of conclusions can be drawn which add substantially to our knowledge of the refugee emigration from Germany, specifically on the ages, occupations, origins and eventual destinations of the refugees who found their way to Holland. By using the figures provided by Werner Rosenstock and Herbert Strauss, comparisons have been made between the overall figures for the emigration from Germany and those derived from the statistics relating to Holland. Apart from contrasting trends in emigration from

[1]Werner Rosenstock, 'Exodus 1933–1939. A Survey of Jewish Emigration from Germany', in *LBI Year Book I* (1956), pp. 373–390; S. Adler-Rudel, *Jüdische Selbsthilfe unter dem Naziregime 1933–1939. Im Spiegel der Berichte der Reichsvertretung der Juden in Deutschland.* Mit einem Vorwort von Robert Weltsch, Tübingen 1974 (Schriftenreihe wissenschaftlicher Abhandlungen des Leo Baeck Instituts 29); Herbert A. Strauss, 'Jewish Emigration from Germany. Nazi Policies and Jewish Responses', in *LBI Year Book XXV* (1980), pp. 313–361 and in *LBI Year Book XXVI* (1981), pp. 343–409.

[2]Dan Michman, *The Jewish Refugees from Germany in the Netherlands 1933–1940*, unpublished Ph.D. thesis, Hebrew University of Jerusalem 1978. Text in Hebrew, abstract in English. See also note 60.

[3]Bob Moore, *Refugees from Germany in the Netherlands, 1933–40: The Political Problem and Government Response*, unpublished Ph.D. thesis, University of Manchester 1983.

Germany with immigration into Holland it has also been possible to compare the re-emigration of refugees from the Netherlands with the figures for direct emigration from Germany to countries of settlement overseas. However, the object of this comparative approach is not merely to confirm the conclusions reached about the emigration from Germany as a whole, but to assess the way in which factors such as immigration laws and the policies of refugee relief agencies restricted the movement of Jews out of Germany. The analysis therefore commences with a summary of the Dutch legislation affecting refugees coupled with a broad outline of the objectives and policies pursued by the Dutch-Jewish refugee committee, the *Comité voor Joodsche Vluchtelingen* (CvJV)[4] before dealing with the role of the Netherlands as a country of refuge and settlement. Finally, using the statistical comparisons on the age, occupations, origins and eventual destinations of the refugees it has been possible to show how these Dutch factors were instrumental in determining the extent of Jewish immigration from Germany.

Material for this study has been gleaned from several different sources. Conventional Dutch census figures fail to highlight the extent of refugee immigration, and consequently most of the information presented has come from private sources, most notably from the archives of the CvJV. In 1933, the CvJV was established as the chief refugee relief organisation in Holland, co-ordinating, if not controlling, Jewish refugee relief throughout the country from its offices in Amsterdam. Analysing the information in the files of the CvJV with the aid of a computer,[5] it has been possible to explore in some detail the character of refugee re-emigration from Holland between 1936 and 1938. Other statistics have been obtained from the archives of the international Jewish relief agencies and from the reports submitted to the Refugee Survey compiled by Sir John Hope Simpson in 1938.[6] Details on the history and development of Dutch legislation have come almost exclusively from government archives in the various ministeries concerned with immigration policy in the 1930s.

II

Before examining the statistical evidence of Jewish refugees in the Netherlands, it is important to look at the immigration restrictions existing in 1933, and those imposed by Dutch governments between 1933 and 1940. The object is not to explore the reasons behind this legislation but to illustrate its effects on the ability of people to leave Germany and come to the Netherlands. The term "refugee" as a general description of those fleeing Nazi Germany is difficult to define since it has been interpreted, for legal and political reasons, in many different ways. (There is no uniformity of the term's use between countries, or between governments, relief organisations and those who considered themselves

[4]The surviving archives of the CvJV are held by the *Rijksinstituut voor Oorlogsdocumentatie* (State Institute for War Documentation) in Amsterdam, cited as RIOD-CvJV.

[5]Thanks are due to the Computation Department of the Manchester Medical School for the programming and processing of this information. Information from this survey cited as SRE.

[6]Sir John Hope Simpson, *Refugee Survey*, London 1939.

refugees.) But for the purposes of this article, "refugee" has been used in its widest and most common form to include all those who left Germany unwillingly on account of the Nazi regime. Nevertheless, irrespective of the way a refugee was defined, his treatment in countries of refuge in the 1930s was inevitably tied up with immigration law.

Immigration to the Netherlands was based on the Aliens Law of 13th August 1849[7] which, with a few minor amendments, was still in force in 1933. The law stipulated certain conditions which foreigners had to fulfil in order to be admitted, but its provisions insisted only that the potential immigrant or visitor possessed "sufficient means of support" for the duration of his stay. For those designated as immigrants, this term was usually interpreted as the ability to earn a living in Holland sufficient to support the individual breadwinner and his dependents if any. From its promulgation to the beginning of the First World War, the law was never seriously tested as a means of restricting large-scale immigration, since Holland was largely a land of emigration (to the New World) or transmigration (from Eastern Europe to the Atlantic ports).

Having admitted many hundreds of thousands of Belgian war refugees on a temporary basis during the First World War, it was only in the immediate post-war period, with its high levels of unemployment, that the Dutch government found it necessary to impose a visa requirement on all foreigners to restrict immigration. Although this requirement was soon ameliorated by reciprocal treaties with most Western European states, no such agreement was reached with Germany on account of the unstable political and economic conditions which persisted there. Indeed, it was not until 1st February 1926, when the German economy was showing signs of prosperity, that the visa restriction was lifted with a reciprocal treaty similar to those in force for other Western European countries.[8] By and large, it was only the citizens of Eastern European countries and those rendered stateless by the war or the Versailles treaty who were required to have a visa to enter Holland. While the upswing in the German economy had been the major influence in lifting the visa requirement, the need to protect the interests of Dutch workers in Germany and to cut down on the vast amounts of paperwork generated by the volume of traffic between the two countries was also important. The interests of Dutch workers in Germany were also the paramount consideration in the treaties concluded with Germany which guaranteed the rights of workers to look for work and to compete on equal terms in the labour markets in each other's country. The most recent treaty had been signed on 17th November 1930 but was merely one in a long line of agreements and treaties between the two countries which dealt with labour matters. Similar arrangements for entrepreneurs, which allowed for the establishment of businesses on equal terms, had existed since 1906.[9]

[7]Netherlands Statute Book (Stbld) 1849 No. 39. Amended Stbld. 1875 No. 66; Stbld. 1886 No. 64; and Stbld. 1910 No. 66.

[8]United States National Archives, Diplomatic Archives (USNA–DA) 856.55/10 Consular report Rotterdam. 'Conditions of Temporary Admission and Residence of Aliens for Employment in Holland', 8th November 1934.

[9]The *Vestigingsverdrag* of 1906 which allowed Germans to establish businesses in Holland on the same terms as Dutchmen, and vice versa.

At the beginning of 1933, therefore, there was little hindrance to the free movement of people across the German border into Holland, either for tourists or for immigrants. Indeed, the number of immigrants into the country remained minimal in the first years of the Depression as employment and business prospects were uniformly bad in both countries. The checks made by the Dutch immigration service were designed to keep out those who had insufficient resources, such as pedlars and hawkers, or those who were regarded as politically undesirable. In theory, anyone staying in the country for more than a few days, but excluding those obviously on holiday, was obliged to report to the local police in their place of residence, but there was seldom more than a token attempt to enforce this ruling. Thus it was relatively easy to arrive in Holland as a "visitor" and stay on in the country to settle and find employment, as the local police made little attempt to ensure that "visitors" left the country at the end of their stay. Even before 1933, there were known to be people living in Holland who had come as visitors and who had stayed on, but their numbers were considered too small to constitute a problem.

The relative leniency of the immigration and employment laws in Holland helps to explain the influx of people to the country in the months following January 1933.[10] Only in March of that year did the immigration service begin to compile statistics which gave some indication of the Jewish people from Germany entering and leaving the country. By deducting one total from the other they were able to arrive at a figure which provided an estimate for the Jews who had stayed on. However, this check was only carried out at the major border crossing points and was merely a head-counting exercise of those whose religion was given as Jewish in their passports.[11] The decline in the numbers entering the country in the latter half of 1933 and early 1934 identified by these checks forestalled any specific government attempts to limit or alter the immigration procedure, a course of action which was also designed to prevent the disturbance of normal traffic between Holland and Germany and to retain good relations with the new German regime.

It was not until May 1934 that steps were taken to legislate against foreign workers and to tighten up the immigration procedures.[12] With effect from January 1935, employers in certain specified trades had to apply for permits from the police for foreign workers in their employment. The provisions of this law were gradually extended and by 1st October 1936 they covered all forms of remunerative employment except work on the Rhine barges and the Merchant Marine. A law of 22nd April 1937[13] took this a stage further by insisting that all

[10]See Tables I and III.

[11]Justice Ministry archive (Justitie) A69/450 File 1.756 *Het Vluchtelingenprobleem in Nederland 1933–9*. Letter, Chief of the Border Police and Aliens Service (GVD) to Minister of Justice, 20th May 1933.

[12]The restrictions on foreign workers were given the Royal assent on 16th May 1934 and came into operation on 1st January 1935. Stbld. 1934 No. 257. The tighter control on immigration was implemented through a directive from the Minister of Justice. Foreign Ministry Archive (Buiza) League of Nations Archive A194/287 1934. Appendix to the circular from the Ministry of Justice, 30th May 1934, No. 3160G.

[13]Stbld. 1937 No. 628, 22nd April 1937. 'Law for the regulation of the independant establishment of vocations and businesses by foreigners.'

foreign-owned businesses in certain trades be required to have a permit. However, this particular piece of legislation was never applied to more than a few branches of commerce and its provisions were seldom used to prevent firms being established, or to shut existing ones down. It is important to see these pieces of legislation in their wider context as a product of the Depression and an attempt to protect Dutch workers from foreign competition for the few jobs available, thus preventing anti-foreign feeling and any concomitant unrest rather than purely, or even principally, as a measure directed at immigrants from Germany. Nevertheless, the legislation against foreign workers and businesses did have an important effect on the interpretation of Dutch immigration laws. Once the labour law had been introduced, it was no longer enough for someone to say that he was a skilled tradesman and could therefore earn a living in Holland. The permit legislation would now prevent him from obtaining employment, especially as it was the employer and not the employee who had to apply for the permit. While this law did nothing to prevent the entry of the self-employed or businessman, from 1935 onwards the numbers admitted without assistance as immigrants from Germany were drastically reduced.

The other important influence on Dutch immigration law was the tightening of German currency controls on the export of capital and the increasingly burdensome imposition of the so-called "flight tax", (*Reichsfluchtsteuer*) levied on all the assets of those leaving the country.[14] Eventually, no one could take more than 10 Reichsmark out of Germany in currency, which meant that only those with access to funds outside Germany could hope to prove to the Dutch immigration officials that they had sufficient funds to support themselves for a prolonged stay in Holland. Needless to say, some refugees managed to smuggle capital over the border, but the net effect of these restrictions was to make it impossible for the majority of Jews leaving Germany to comply with the Dutch requirement of having "sufficient means of support". Closer police control over Jewish "visitors" from Germany had also made it difficult to stay in the country. A lucky few, with assets outside Germany or with relatives and friends in Holland willing and able to support them, were still able to enter Holland, but for the rest there were only two alternatives. The Dutch border was long and inadequately policed, making it possible for people to avoid the border controls altogether and to slip into Holland illegally. Otherwise, the only way to enter Holland legally was to try and obtain a guarantee of support from the Dutch-Jewish refugee relief organisations.

From the first months of 1933, the Dutch government had avoided any responsibility for refugees. While the increase in immigration was noted in a question to the First Chamber of the States General on 6th April 1933, the Minister of Justice made it clear that Holland was not prepared to make any special provisions for refugees, or provide any financial aid.[15] The fact that

[14]The *Reichsfluchtsteuer*, a measure which pre-dated the Nazi regime and was intended to be an economic device to protect the *Reichsmark*. Its wider application after 1933 by the Nazis remained part economic protectionism and part antisemitism, especially when combined with the other measures to remove Jews from the German economy. Simpson, *op. cit.*, p. 146.

[15]Proceedings of the First Chamber of the States-General (Handelingen le Kamer) 1933, pp. 533–536. Question by de Heer Oudegeest and reply by Minister of Justice Donner.

leading members of the Dutch government were still questioning the state's role in providing benefits for the Dutch sick and unemployed makes it unremarkable that they should reject any assistance to refugees. However, direct questioning of the Minister revealed that very few people had been turned away by the Dutch border officials. The actual figures quoted were 8 from a total of 1,500 refugees, highlighting the relative simplicity of crossing the border in early 1933.

By offering to set up a refugee relief organisation, the Dutch-Jewish community not only ensured an orderly administration of refugee relief in Holland but also provided the Dutch government with an instrument to control refugee immigration to the Netherlands without government agencies becoming directly involved. The Jewish community in Holland, like the government, was anxious that an influx of Jewish refugees from Germany should not provoke anti-foreign or antisemitic tendencies amongst the Dutch population. For the government's part this was an attempt to keep order in the country as a whole, whilst for the Jewish community it was a deliberate attempt to prevent feeling against foreign Jewish refugees from being turned against them, thus jeopardising their own position in Dutch society. In effect, the CvJV made itself responsible for all aspects of Jewish refugee relief, especially in terms of financial aid and it was this commitment which was to play an increasing role in determining refugee immigration to the Netherlands in the second half of the 1930s.

From 1935 until the Dutch border was closed on 17th December 1938,[16] the vast majority of Jewish refugees admitted to Holland were dependent on the resources available to relief agencies for the provision of financial guarantees. In spite of a government commission on the subject, the immigration law was left unaltered,[17] the controls on mass immigration having been established partly through labour legislation and partly by German controls on the export of currency.

In addition to the immigration laws, Holland also carried the tradition of giving asylum to those who were politically or religiously oppressed in other countries. This *Asylrecht* or right of asylum had its origins in the sixteenth century but had been largely superseded by modern immigration law. Its only modern application was in cases where an individual was being actively sought by other countries, the most prominent twentieth-century example being that of the German *Kaiser* who fled to Holland after his abdication in 1918. Under normal circumstances, admissions policy was such that almost anyone could enter the country without the need to apply for asylum. Thus the unwritten principle of *Asylrecht* remained untested, even for those who had no funds when they arrived in the Netherlands as, for the small numbers involved, there was always a charity or political organisation willing to provide a guarantee. Peace-time immigration on the scale of 1933 was previously unknown and the Dutch government was anxious that the *Asylrecht* should not be invoked because, once tested, it would set a yardstick of need for future cases which could be exploited by other countries, allowing them to "manufacture" people who had experienced the required degree of persecution.[18]

[16]This meant the refusal of admission to all refugees, even as visitors, except for a quota of 7,000.
[17]The Donner Commission, headed by a former Minister of Justice.
[18]The Foreign Ministry believed that the Nazis were quite capable of creating a degree of persecution

III

The absence of any accurate government or police records for the number of Jews from Germany admitted to the Netherlands in the period 1933–1940[19] means that official figures for total refugee immigration were little more than estimates based on statistics provided by the immigration service. Dutch census figures did not differentiate between Jews and other Germans who resided in Holland, and the only major sources for refugee statistics were the relief organisations which dealt with the day-to-day assistance of these people. These national figures were collected by international bodies such as the American Jewish Joint Distribution Committee (AJDC) and the League of Nations High Commission for Refugees (Jewish and other) coming from Germany, such as the one given in Table I below.

TABLE I

Total Number and Distribution of Refugees from Germany[19] in 1933

						Of the Jews			
	Number[1]	*Jews*[2]	%	*Others*	%	*Germans*	%	*Others*	%
France	25,000[3]	21,250	85	3,750	15	15,950	75	5,300	25
Palestine	6,500	6,500	100	—	—	5,525	85	975	15
Poland	6,000[4]	6,000	100	—	—	—	—	6,000[5]	100
Czechoslovakia	5,000	3,750	75	1,250	25	1,875	50	1,875[6]	50
Holland	5,000	4,000	80	1,000	20	3,000	75	1,000	25
England	3,000	2,500	83	500	17	2,250	90	250	10
Switzerland	2,500[7]	2,125	85	375	15	1,700	80	425	20
Belgium	2,500	2,000	80	500	20	1,800	90	200	10
Scandinavia	1,500	1,125	75	375	25	900	80	225	20
Austria	800	640	80	160	20	545	85	95	15
Saar & Luxemburg	500	375	75	125	25	320	85	55	15
Others[8]	1,000	800	80	200	20	680	85	120	15
	59,300	51,065	(86)	8,235	(14)	34,545	(68)	16,520	(32)

1) Includes women and children.
2) Jews by confession.
3) Of whom about 22,000 estimated to be in Paris.
4) Including about 50–60 non-Jews who had been politically active in Germany.
5) Including about 100 Germans originally from former German provinces now in Poland whose relatives had opted for Polish citizenship and these German Jews had gone to them.
6) Mostly repatriated Czechs.
7) Not including German travellers in Switzerland who have prolonged their stay to see how the situation in Germany develops.
8) Includes the United States and Spain.

---

in Germany which would give the refugees a right of asylum, if that right was to be given a legal definition.

[19]Lehman Collection, Columbia University, N.Y. Papers of James G. McDonald (High Commissioner for Refugees 1933–1935) File H.1.

While the table shows the importance of Holland as a country of first refuge in 1933, the total figure for Jewish refugees conflicts with the widely accepted 37,000 quoted by Rosenstock. The explanation lies in the methods used to compile the figures, each major relief organisation having been asked by the High Commission to produce a set of figures but given no guidelines on how these should be prepared. Thus some of the "national" figures given in the table relate only to those refugees actually seen by the organisations in question while others contain estimates for unknown immigration. Furthermore, it is not clear whether the figures relate to the number of refugees seen by the organisations during the course of the year or whether they are totals for those resident in those countries at a given date. It seems likely that the table contains elements of both, being running totals for refugees seen by individual committees and therefore susceptible to the "double counting" of people who moved from one country to another in the course of the year, and estimates of the numbers of refugees resident in those countries at the end of 1933. In the course of 1933, a total of 2,245 refugees were recorded as having left Holland, and of these no less than 1,064 went to destinations in other parts of Europe (see below Table XII), the majority to France or Belgium. Thus it is quite possible for them to have been recorded in the files of refugee relief organisations in more than one European country.

The problem of double counting raises the wider question of the accuracy of total numbers. Every European government was anxious to stress what it had done for the refugees, and the figures most widely quoted by official sources were those for the number of admissions rather than the number actually resident in the country at any given time. Thus in June 1938, the CvJV estimate for the total number of refugees in the Netherlands was 13,800 of whom 11,800 were Jews,[20] whereas the Dutch government estimate presented to the Evian Conference was 17,000. At the same time, estimates for the total number of admissions varied between 25,000 and 33,000.[21] Admissions to Holland were not curtailed until December 1938, five weeks after the November pogrom, when the government provided a further 7,000 quota places for refugees but closed the border to any further immigration. If we accept the CvJV figures as being the most accurate of those available we can add perhaps 8,000 to their total of 11,800 Jews in the Netherlands to give an overall total of 19,800 from which has to be deducted the known re-emigration for the period up to the occupation. The statistics of the HICEM and the CvJV show that this amounted to about 1,500 people,[22] giving an approximate total of refugee Jews in the Netherlands of 18,300 at the time of occupation, a total which can be rounded down to 18,000 to take account of natural wastage.

Attempts to reconcile these disparate estimates have only a limited value as the criteria used to compile them varied so much; the inclusion or omission of women and children presents perhaps the best example of on how large a scale errors could occur. Furthermore, the Dutch figures were to an extent contradicted by a detailed survey ordered by the Germans during the occupation to assess the

[20]Simpson, *op. cit.*, p. 347.
[21]*Ibid.*
[22]Leo Baeck Institute Archive, New York, AR-A 1510 4749 16–32, 1938–1943.

numbers of Jewish "immigrants" in the country. Their survey, shown in condensed form in Table II, gives a total of 15,992 Jews or people with "Jewish blood" who had come to the Netherlands after the 30th January 1933. However even these German figures omit people anxious not to be listed as Jewish and may well be understating the true numbers.

TABLE II

Jewish Immigrants to the Netherlands after 30th January 1933 resident on 1st October 1941[23]

	"Full Jews"		*"Part Jews"*		
Nationality	*Men*	*Women*	*Men*	*Women*	*Total*
Germans	5,715	5,751	338	273	12,077
Austrians	7	10	4	2	23
Polish	307	355	2	4	668
Stateless	1,238	962	49	34	2,283
	7,267	7,078	393	313	15,051
Dutch	35	569	6	37	647
Others	112	141	17	24	294
	7,414	7,788	416	374	15,992

This table, perhaps the most comprehensive survey of refugees in the Netherlands, although dated October 1941, nevertheless suggests that many of the estimates for the numbers of refugees in the Netherlands were too high and that admissions for the whole period 1933–1940 did not exceed 25,000 individuals. Indeed, if the total for 1941 is added to the HICEM figures for the total number of assisted re-emigrations from Holland of 5,871[24] (plus 200 for 1940), it gives a combined total of only 22,063. Nevertheless an amount of unrecorded and illegal immigration and emigration remains unquantified as does the grey area of those people considered by the Germans as "racially Jewish" but who were not members of the Jewish community.[25] While the figures for Holland remain no more than estimates they nevertheless highlight the problems of providing an accurate statistical analysis of refugees from Germany in a single country.

Although these total figures are of interest in relation to the overall emigration from Germany, more important are the details which can be gleaned from them.

[23]Interior Ministry Archive (Binza), Refugees-General (A/V1). Report on Foreigners with Jewish Blood in Holland, 1st October 1941. The table appears to include all "racial" Jews and not just members of the Jewish community.

[24]Leo Baeck Institute Archive, AR-A 1510 4749 16–32, 1938–1943. Table of emigrants assisted by the HICEM 1933–1939.

[25]The division of refugee relief in Holland on religious lines meant that the so-called "non-Aryan" Christians were assisted by Catholic and Protestant organisations.

The influences on emigration from Germany can be considered as two-fold. The changing conditions in Germany had a marked effect on the numbers of Jews attempting to leave the Third *Reich* at different times. There were noticeable reductions in emigration during 1934 and the first half of 1935 and, it is claimed, in the period before and during the Olympic Games in Berlin as a result of a reduction in anti-Jewish actions in Nazi Germany. Conversely, the first few months of Hitler's chancellorship, the summer of 1935 and the months before and after the pogrom in November 1938 were periods of widespread persecution.[26] The intention is to show how these trends were reflected in the figures available for the Netherlands and to what extent these were affected by the influence of external factors such as the Dutch immigration law and the policies adopted by the relief agencies.

The figures for overall Jewish emigration from Germany between 1933 and 1937 reproduced in Table III below show a marked decrease in emigration after 1933 and only a marginal increase after 1935. Given the increasing economic harassment from late 1936 onwards it seems that the determining factor in deciding who left Germany had shifted in this period from the conditions inside Germany to the ability to find a country of refuge.

TABLE III

Overall Jewish Emigration from Germany 1933–1937[27]

Year	*A.*	*B.*
1933	37,000	63,400
1934	23,000	45,000
1935	21,000	35,500
1936	25,000	34,000
1937	23,000	25,000
	129,000	202,900

In the case of the Netherlands, 1935 seems to have marked the end of what might be termed "free" immigration to the country. Tighter passport controls had been in operation since the middle of 1934 but the labour legislation which came into force at the beginning of 1935, combined with the German clampdown on the export of currency, made unassisted immigration virtually impossible. The need to have "sufficient means of support", not only to satisfy the immigration authorities but also in practical terms to provide food and shelter, made it essential to have some form of outside help. As we have seen, only a lucky few were able to live independently in Holland. For the rest, the only alternative once

[26]Strauss, in *LBI Year Book XXV* (1980), pp. 331–337.

[27]Rosenstock, in *LBI Year Book I* (1956), pp. 373–390. (A); Martin Broszat, *The Hitler State*, London 1981, p. 361. (B) cites a report from the *Reichsvertretung. Deutsches Zentralarchiv* Potsdam, Rep. 97. which shows steady decline in numbers until 1938.

they had arrived in Holland, usually as visitors, was to approach the Jewish refugee relief organisations for aid to stay in the country. However, the funds of the CvJV were never sufficient to help all those who applied for aid. Their money came from two sources. Collections nationally and among the Jewish community raised a great deal of money, but the amounts collected tended to vary according to the amount of coverage the plight of the Jews in Germany received in the press. Only after November 1938 was the spirit of charity rekindled in Holland, among Jews and non-Jews alike, which allowed the CvJV to meet the increased burdens placed on its resources. In spite of this, the bulk of the finance for its operations came from the international Jewish charities, most notably the AJDC, with contributions also from the Central British Fund for German Jewry and the refunding of re-emigration expenses by the HICEM. The limitations on CvJV finances meant that it had to select cases for assistance very carefully and after mid-1933, only those people who would be in some form of physical danger if they returned to Germany were given assistance to stay in Holland. Even then, assistance was only provided after extensive checks had been made via the Jewish communities in Germany. Thus, with the exception of early 1933, when the policy was somewhat different, the numbers of refugees given material aid by the CvJV provide a yardstick for the levels of persecution in Germany.

TABLE IV

Refugees newly registered by the CvJV 1933–1938[28]

Year	*Number*
1933	4,078
1934	1,191
1935	574
1936	1,110
1937	1,395
1938	3,842
	12,190

While the usefulness of these figures must be questioned on several counts, they nevertheless highlight a marked decline in 1935, which is not evident in the overall figures given by Rosenstock. Moreover, of the 574 people newly registered for aid in 1935, 364 had been in Holland for more than a year before going to the CvJV for assistance. Thus, as Table V shows, the CvJV only provided assistance to 210 refugees who came to Holland in the course of 1935, while denying aid to a further 290 people.

[28]RIOD-CvJV, File 145. CvJV Annual Reports 1935–1938. David Cohen, *Zwervend en Dolend*, Haarlem 1955, *passim*.

TABLE V

New Arrivals in the Netherlands recorded by the CvJV 1935[29]

	J	*F*	*M*	*A*	*M*	*J*	*J*	*A*	*S*	*O*	*N*	*D*	*Total*
Registered for aid	1	1	2	1	6	8	2	22	39	66	33	29	210
Repatriated or not registrated	44	53	27	20	21	12	18	31	34	52	37	41	390
Total	45	54	29	21	27	20	20	53	73	118	70	70	600

The rapid decline in the "serious" cases in the early part of 1935 had led the CvJV to believe that it could wind up its operations at the end of the year, since so few people were now entering Holland or becoming destitute and requiring financial assistance. The question of those who had been in Holland for some time was complicated by a German directive which threatened imprisonment in an "education camp" for any Jews returning to the *Reich* from abroad.[30] Thus even people who had come to Holland for economic reasons in earlier years now had as much claim to CvJV help as those crossing the border in 1935, being in just as much danger if they returned to Germany.

The monthly figures in Table V show an expected seasonal trend for refugee immigration, with more people arriving in the winter months. However, the major change occurs among those who were offered financial aid. For the first seven months of the year only 21 people were registered by the CvJV. It looks, therefore, as if the upswing in immigration from August onwards reflects the impact of the "antisemitic wave" of summer 1935, and the deeply unsettling effects of the Nuremberg Laws which were promulgated in September. If this pattern is applied to the emigration of Jews from Germany as a whole, it would seem that there was a major increase in numbers within a few months, almost comparable to the watersheds of January 1933 and November 1938.

Those not financially assisted by the CvJV who had only been out of Germany for a few days were usually advised to return home, highlighting another facet of refugee relief policy in Holland. Having screened an applicant for assistance, usually within a matter of a few days, their advice to those who were unsuccessful was to return to Germany before the authorities noticed their absence. Many were also given the rail fare for their return journey, this sort of prompted repatriation being by no means uncommon as late as 1938, although in 1934 and 1935 it was allied with a similar trend among Jews from Germany to return home

[29]RIOD-CvJV, File 45. CvJV Annual Report 1935.

[30]Buiza, A185 (KW) 1935, box 506. Letter, CvJV to Foreign Minister, 25th March 1935. Initially this applied only to Prussia.

of their own accord.[31] However, this voluntary repatriation by people who had spent some time away from Germany was largely curtailed by stricter German measures against returning Jews from 1935 onwards.

It can be seen, therefore, that the trend towards repatriation to Germany, evident from the surveys of Jewish emigration and a trend which the Nazis tried hard to discourage, was in no small way assisted by the policies of the CvJV in Amsterdam. From the very beginning, the Dutch government had made it clear that it would not countenance refugees being encouraged to come to Holland or to settle there, and the CvJV, anxious not to offend the government or to compromise its position as (unofficial) advisory body to the government on refugees, had to take account of the government's desires. Thus there was no question of openly helping refugees to find work in Holland after 1933, especially at a time when over 400,000 Dutch workers were without a job.

From 1936 onwards it seems that the external factors had largely taken over in determining how many people were able to leave Germany. Unlike Holland, the immigration restrictions imposed in many other countries effectively excluded Jews from considering flight there. In Holland, the CvJV effectively set the standard for assistance and thus decided who could stay and who had to return. It was only after the November pogrom that the CvJV was finally overwhelmed and the government, which had for so long relied on the system of checks and balances to keep out large numbers of refugees without disadvantaging the day-to-day traffic of people to and from Germany, was forced to close the border to all but a selected few. One point worthy of note is that Jews who arrived in Holland had seldom been in contact with relief organisations inside Germany before leaving, organisations such as the *Hilfsverein*[32] being only too well aware of the difficulties for refugees in other European countries.

The selection policy of the CvJV created a group of people who were described as "economic refugees". These were the individuals and families who had the foresight to leave Germany before their businesses were affected by the Nazis and they themselves came under threat. Others, also designated as "economic" cases, fled from Germany after losing their jobs or livelihoods. Nevertheless, as the CvJV made clear, to qualify for assistance they had to have fled from something worse than economic misery.[33] Even Jews who came to Holland and found work or re-established their businesses were affected by the Depression. Many of the businesses suffered from under-capitalisation. The effects of the recession and cut-throat competition from existing Dutch firms caused many of them to collapse and the owners to look to the CvJV for help, often years after they had first arrived in Holland. Even the businesses which survived for a time by trading with Germany were caught by the German embargo on foreign goods in 1935.

The presence of these people in the Netherlands can be seen as part of the much larger movement within Germany from the smaller towns and villages to the cities. While this movement away from rural areas had existed since before the

[31]The nature of the Dutch-German border made it relatively easy for people to return to Germany via the "green frontier", without using a recognised border crossing.
[32]The *Hilfsverein der Juden in Deutschland*, the chief Jewish relief agency in Germany.
[33]RIOD-CvJV, File 145. CvJV Annual Reports 1935–1937.

First World War, the increased vulnerability of Jewish communities in small towns to the economic, verbal and physical attacks of Nazi Party activists undoubtedly provided an even greater impetus. Jewish businesses and public servants in small communities became targets for discrimination in a way which would have been impossible in the big cities. A move to the big city was thus a logical step for those who found themselves persecuted, offering the chance of better welfare care and a degree of anonymity.[34]

This movement away from the country areas may have been exacerbated by economic restrictions, especially for Orthodox and observant Jews. Laws against ritual slaughter and Nazi attacks on Jewish butchers and bakers left many communities without a supply of kosher food. The only way to obtain such food was to import it or move somewhere where it was more readily available. On the other hand, it is difficult in many cases to see whether it was the departure of the tradesman or his customers which came first.

It can be argued that the movement of Jews to Holland on "economic" grounds was merely the extension of the much larger internal migration taking place within Germany. Jews from the small towns and country districts of Hanover and Westphalia were able to travel shorter distances in coming to Dutch border towns, to areas with which they arguably had a greater degree of affinity, than to the industrial cities of the Ruhr or Berlin.

IV

So far, the term "Jews from Germany" had been deliberately used to describe the refugees because, as Esra Bennathan[35] and Herbert Strauss have shown, the Jews resident in Germany in 1933 were by no means all German nationals. German census returns show that 19·8% of the Jews by religion living in the *Reich* were non-German, the vast majority of them having come from Eastern Europe.[36] They were mainly recent immigrants with Polish nationality although some had lost their Russian citizenship at the end of the First World War and had never bothered to clarify their status. Many had been given Nansen (stateless) passports with which to travel. It seems that several thousand people with these papers had lived in Germany since the end of the war, merely having their residence permits renewed by the German police. Although they had no intention of leaving the country, a mistrust of authority remained which was sufficient to prevent their applying for German citizenship.[37]

It may have been that, as the nucleus of the Orthodox community in Germany

[34]Strauss, in *LBI Year Book XXV* (1980), p. 324.

[35]Esra Bennathan, 'Die demographische and wirtschaftliche Struktur der Juden', in *Entscheidungsjahr 1932. Zur Judenfrage in der Endphase der Weimarer Republik*. Ein Sammelband herausgegeben von Werner E. Mosse unter Mitwirkung von Arnold Paucker, Tübingen 1965 (Schriftenreihe wissenschaftlicher Abhandlungen des Leo Baeck Instituts 13), pp. 87–131.

[36]Strauss, in *LBI Year Book XXV* (1980), p. 321.

[37]*Ibid.*, p. 322. Strauss suggests that this was due to State governments in Germany being slow to process naturalisation papers for Jews. However, notes in the CvJV archives suggest that many of the foreign Jews who came to Holland had made no attempt to regularise their nationality, being content to have German "Foreigners' Papers" renewed each year by the police.

and marked out by their religious observance, these Jews became early targets for spontaneous attacks by the Nazis; alternatively, their attachment to Germany was less strong than that of the German Jews. At any rate Strauss has shown that the non-German Jewish population declined more rapidly after the Nazi takeover than that of the German Jews.[38] Thus it is not surprising to find this trend reflected in the nationalities of refugees who arrived in Holland. Taking the figures from Table IV, the breakdown of these totals by the CvJV into nationalities shows that the non-German Jews were over-represented among the refugees in the first two years of immigration. While some doubt remains about the consistency of these figures, it seems that people were taken at face value when their nationality was assessed. Even if a refugee had no papers to prove his case, he was listed as being German rather than categorised as stateless. Thus Table VI provides a fairly accurate distinction between the German Jews and those of other nationalities.

TABLE VI

Nationalities of Refugees assisted by the CvJV 1933–1935[39]

	Germans	%	*Poles*	%	*Stateless*	%	*Total*
1933	2,967	72·7	745	18·3	366	9·0	4,078
1934	846	71·0	283	23·8	62	5·2	1,191
1935	449	78·3	61	10·6	64	11·1	574
	4,262		1,089		492		5,843

The over-representation of the Eastern European element shows clearly in the first two years and only in 1935 do the percentages correspond roughly to the proportions of Germans to non-Germans in the Jewish communities of the *Reich*. Independent support for these conclusions comes from a survey carried out by the Dutch immigration service which reported that in mid-1934, 26% of the Jews crossing the border into Holland from Germany were of Eastern European origin.[40] The reduction of their numbers in 1935 stemmed mainly from the instructions issued by the Dutch Ministry of Justice in May 1934[41] which insisted that Jewish people with citizenship rights elsewhere should be encouraged to return to their country of origin rather than be admitted to Holland as immigrant refugees.

The admission of refugees in peace-time was interpreted by successive Dutch governments as an undertaking to accept these people as long-term residents and

[38] *Ibid.*, p. 322.
[39] RIOD-CvJV, File 145. CvJV Reports 1933–1935.
[40] Buiza, A194/287 1934. Letter, Chief of the GVD to the Minister of Justice, May 1934. These checks took place at the major rail crossing points of Oldenzaal and Zevenaar.
[41] Buiza, A194/287 1934. Appendix to the circular from the Ministry of Justice, 30th May 1934, No. 3160G.

potential future citizens, in spite of the fact that the authorities regarded Holland primarily as a transit country for those moving on elsewhere. Thus there was a certain antipathy within government agencies toward the admission of the non-German Jews with their "non-western mentality".[42] Even in 1933 it had been realised that the immigration procedures for Poles and stateless people who needed visas were so lax as to be virtually useless. Dutch consular officials in Germany apparently made no enquiries about the true intentions of people applying for visitors' visas, leading the Foreign Office to issue a directive in mid-1933 in an attempt to restrict the issue of visitors' visas to people who might become refugees.[43] However, the fear remained that there had been a major influx of these non-German Jews which the immigration service knew nothing about. The instructions of May 1934 made it virtually impossible for Poles and especially Polish Jews to enter the country and prompted an enquiry into all applications for visas made by Poles from the beginning of 1932 onwards. It was intended that any Poles found to have overstayed their visas or to have obtained such a visa under "false pretences" (posing as a visitor with the intention of remaining in Holland) be expelled from the country. Enquiries however revealed only 200 people who fell foul of this retrospective action, and not the thousands feared by some elements within the government. Plans to deport these people were dropped when their numbers became apparent, as the suggested solution would have done more harm to Holland's international reputation than it would have benefited the labour market and the suppression of potential antisemitism among the Dutch.[44]

These tighter controls stopped virtually all immigration of non-German Jews after 1935. Only in the months following the *Anschluss* of Austria did other nationalities again become involved although the CvJV had continued to deal with small numbers of Poles, Hungarians and Romanians who came to Holland as transmigrants. The incorporation of Austria into the "Greater German *Reich*" created problems for other countries in deciding whether people living in Austria should henceforward be treated as German citizens, with the same rights of access to other countries as Germans from the *Altreich*. Apart from these technical problems, the statistics for refugees are distorted by different interpretations of their national status. The compilers of Table II have demonstrated that they had no doubt that all Austrians were to be listed as Germâns, the few "Austrians" being people who had come to Holland before March 1938. In spite of the distance from Vienna to Amsterdam, the CvJV recorded some significant immigration of Austrians during 1938. Indeed, the table below shows that for the last three months of 1938, Austrian refugees outnumbered those from Germany in October and showed increases during November and December when there was approximately one Austrian refugee for every two German refugees.

[42]Buiza, A194/287 1934. Letter, Minister of Social Affairs to Minister of Justice, 20th February 1934 No. 653AB. This is only one example of the derogatory terminology used by Dutch governmental organisations when referring to non-German Jews.

[43]Ministry of Social Affairs Archive (Socza), Employment and Social Insurance Department 1916–1940. File 145, Letter, Foreign Minister to Dutch Consular Officials, 22nd June 1933.

[44]Buiza, A194/287 1934/1935.

TABLE VII

Refugees registered for Aid by the CvJV 1938[45]

Month	*Germans*		*Austrians*	*Total*
Jan.–Sept.	—	(1811)	—	1,811
October	97		101	198
November	410		191	601
December	824		408	1,232
	1331	(1811)	700	3,842

This analysis of nationality shows the importance of differentiating between "German refugees" and "refugees from Germany" as well as going some way to explaining the differences in treatment meted out to refugees with similar histories. Many Jews admitted to Holland never realised that they had not been allowed in as a special category of refugee, but under the existing immigration law with the CvJV standing as financial guarantor. The use of normal channels meant that it was often nationality which was of vital importance in deciding whether individuals could be admitted or not, irrespective of the amount and degree of persecution they had suffered.

V

In his survey of Jewish emigration, Rosenstock produced a table which compared the number of known emigrants from each area of Germany in 1937 with the distribution of the Jewish population as a whole. His analysis showed an over-representation of emigrants from the cities of Frankfurt a. Main and Cologne and the province of Hesse. This was partially explained by the internal movement of population from the surrounding areas through these large cities on their way out of the country.[46] Conversely, the under-representation of Berlin as a place for emigrants was accounted for by the milder persecution there compared with other areas. This seems all the more surprising in view of the suspicion that Berlin may have been playing host to a greater percentage of the Jewish community in 1937 than the official figure of 31·9%.[47]

The records of the CvJV have preserved detailed information on one group of refugees in Holland who were subsequently helped to re-emigrate overseas between October 1936 and July 1938.[48] While these statistics are distorted in terms of age and occupations towards people able to re-emigrate by meeting the

[45]RIOD-CvJV, File 145. CvJV Annual Report 1938. Cohen, *op. cit.*, p. 102.

[46]Rosenstock, *loc. cit.*, pp. 383–384.

[47]Adler-Rudel, *op. cit.*, p. 150. Strauss, in *LBI Year Book XXV* (1980) p. 324. Both give an estimated 42% of all Jews in Germany resident in Berlin in October 1938.

[48]The SRE data on re-emigrants from Holland is based on the CvJV archive, RIOD-CvJV, Files 95–127 where individual cases are listed according to their date of emigration.

requirements laid down by countries of settlement, the information on their last place of residence in Germany can be taken as a representative sample. In all, this consists of 1,259 individuals of whom 55·1% had arrived in Holland before 1936.

The figures for Holland show how important geography was in determining the choice of refuge. Areas close to the border such as Westphalia and the Prussian Rhine Province as well as the large cities of Hanover, Hamburg, Cologne, Düsseldorf and Berlin are all over-represented in the figures. One slight anomaly is the under-representation of Frankfurt, especially in view of its prominence in the overall emigration. The only explanation rests on the similar under-representation of Hesse and Hesse-Nassau provinces which surround the city. The assumption must be that the closer proximity of the French and Belgian borders drew more of the Jewish refugees from that area. While the figures show the importance of geography in understanding the movement of refugees, and the high level of correlation between the Dutch and German samples, any conclusions have to be tempered by the acceptance that the Dutch sample is small enough to distort the lower percentages.

With the notable exception of Berlin, it would be true to say that the majority of refugees in Holland came from the area of North-West Germany bordered by a line between Hamburg and Cologne. This includes the heavily populated areas of the Ruhr basin as well as the large agricultural districts of Westphalia and Hanover. The over-representation of Berlin must be explained in terms of its transport links and proximity to Holland compared with other Western European countries. While the geographical element may have been paramount, it was by no means the only reason for refugees choosing to come to the Netherlands. Other factors such as family connections, business ties and Holland's tradition of providing asylum as well as her role as a transit point for journeys overseas undoubtedly also played a part in decision making but they remain unquantifiable elements in any numerical analysis.

VI

Statistics on the occupational distribution of refugees in Holland are in general less reliable than those for place of origin. The German census material used by Bennathan and Strauss provides an accurate picture of the German-Jewish community's occupational structure. But the different categorisations used by refugee organisations prevent a worthwhile comparison being made. Table IX reproduces a CvJV survey of refugees assisted in 1933.

Detailed conclusions from such a generalised table are clearly impossible although the large numbers from the liberal professions, skilled workers and domestic servants are worthy of note, given their relative percentages in the occupational structure of the German-Jewish community as a whole. While the Nazi attacks on Jewish lawyers and civil servants in 1933 account for the high proportion of professional people, the presence of so many "workers" and domestic servants came about for different reasons. This table was compiled from the stated occupations of the refugees, the individuals usually giving their real occupation as they saw it. However, the categories are too broad to have any

TABLE VIII

Comparative Table of Last Places of Residence in Germany for Jewish Emigrants 1937 and Jewish Re-emigration from the Netherlands 1936–1938[49]

Province/City	*Jewish Population as % 1933*	*Jewish Re-emigrants from Holland 1936–8*	*(Rosenstock) Jewish Emigrants from Germany 1937*
Prussia			
East Prussia	1·8	1·6	1·5
Brandenburg	1·5	0·1	0·6
Pomerania	1·3	0·4	0·9
Grenzmark	0·6	—	0·2
Lower Silesia } Upper Silesia }	2·8	1·0	2·9
Saxony (prov.)	1·4	0·1	0·9
Schl.-Holstein }	3·1	0·1	0·2
Hanover }		3·1	1·4
Westphalia	3·7	5·7	3·1
Hesse-Nassau	4·1	3·4	5·2
Rhine Province	5·6	9·6	5·4
Cities			
Berlin	31·9	33·0	24·5
Frankfurt a. Main	5·2	4·1	11.4
Breslau	4·0	4·1	4·0
Cologne	3·0	6·1	5·6
Düsseldorf	1·0	4·6	1·1
Essen	0·9	5·1	1·2
Hanover	—	2·0	0·7
Other Provinces			
Saarland	2·6	0·7	1·8
Hesse	3·6	1·7	5·7
Hamburg	3·4	5·0	3·0
Saxony }	4·1	0·7	1·1
Leipzig }		1·6	1·2
Baden	4·1	2·1	5·1
Bavaria	8·3	3·3	7·9
Württemberg	2·0	0·4	3·4
	100·0	100·0	100·0

[49]Rosenstock, *loc. cit.*, p. 383. SRE data did not include children and they do not, therefore, appear in the comparative analysis. See also Table XI where under-16 age groups have been deleted from comparative figures and the percentages adjusted accordingly.

TABLE IX

Occupational Distribution of Refugees registered by the CvJV 1933 (July)[50]

Occupation	*Number*	%
Self Employed Merchants	339	27·2
Liberal Professions & Intellectuals	285	22·9
Skilled Workers	128	10·3
Unskilled Workers	10	0·9
Shopworkers	287	23·0
Domestic Servants	66	5·3
None	130	10·4
	1,245	100.0

meaning in the case of the most popular occupation, that of *Kaufmann*, a term which encompassed a vast array of activity from international businessmen to street traders and hawkers.

A further distortion occurred when the refugees gave more than one occupation. This was usually done in an attempt to enhance the chances of finding employment in the country of refuge or a country of settlement. The files of the CvJV contain details of many refugees who gave two or even three occupations in which he or she had some "experience". It is not unusual to find combinations of farmer/butcher as well as more unlikely pairings such as lawyer/lemonade manufacturer, the idea being to stress practical experience especially in some form of agriculture rather than the more probable primary occupation of retailer, wholesaler or middleman. This accounts to some extent for the relatively large numbers of people who, in later years, claimed to have had some experience in a branch of agriculture, despite the fact that the German census had shown only 1·7% of the Jewish population employed in this section of the economy.[51]

As proficiency in one of the agricultural skills was a useful if not vital prerequisite for Palestine or South America, it is perhaps not so surprising that such a trend should exist. The situation was further complicated by the programmes of the Zionist organisations and the *Stichting Joodsche Arbeid*[44] designed to retrain Jewish youth in various practical skills, and primarily in agriculture. The numbers of genuine Jewish agricultural workers and retrainees among the re-emigrants from Holland confirm the importance of these skills for emigration opportunities overseas but make comparisons with the occupational distribution of the German-Jewish community of relatively little value. An attempt has been made to differentiate between "real" Jewish agriculturalists and those who had been re-trained by the Zionists or by the *Stichting Joodsche*

[50]Wiener Library, CvJV Papers Box 502i. Correspondence of the CvJV with the Central British Fund for German Jewry, 14th March 1935.
[51]Bennathan, *loc. cit.*, p. 104.

Arbeid in Holland.[52] In many cases, people who listed their occupation as farmer also gave their last address in Germany as one of the large cities, indicating that they were almost certainly retrainees.

Table X sets out in some detail the conclusions from the survey of re-emigrants from Holland. It shows the expected preponderance of people described as entrepreneurs or merchants but the categorisation employed can give no indication of social or economic standing. For example, people listed in the clothing trades include employers, the self-employed artisans and the skilled and unskilled employees.

TABLE X

Occupational Distribution of Refugees who Re-emigrated from the Netherlands 1936–1938[53]

Occupational Group	*Re-emigrants*	%
Merchants/Capitalists	117	9·3
Clothing Trades	93	7·4
Medical Profession	38	3·0
Legal Profession	17	1·4
Cultural Professions	29	2·3
Intellectuals	32	2·5
Skilled Workers	101	8·0
Unskilled Workers	12	0·9
White-Collar Workers	73	5·8
Food and Drink Trades	52	4·1
Agriculture	63	5·0
Agricultural trainees	24	1·9
Students	14	1·1
Domestic Servants	36	3·9
Housewives	221	17·6
None	19	1·5
Unknown	318	25·3
	1,259	100·0

The individual headings show a wide diversity, if not an exact categorisation, of re-emigrant occupations. Although the number of doctors is not surprising in view of Nazi attacks on their involvement in the profession, the proportion of skilled workers does require some further explanation. The retraining programmes of the *Stichting Joodsche Arbeid* encompassed a wide range of skills and, as nearly all the trainees had emigration organised for them by the CvJV, they were

[52]For further details of the history and work of the *Stichting Joodsche Arbeid* see, Gertrude van Tijn, 'Werkdorp Nieuwesluis', in *LBI Year Book XIV* (1969), pp. 182–199.
[53]SRE: Occupational structure of Jewish refugees.

duly recorded in the statistics. Also worthy of note are the people described as domestic servants, few of whom had been engaged in this type of work in Germany. In some cases they were wives and daughters of families in Holland where the husband was unable to earn a living, and the women had taken up domestic work in order to earn some money. Alternatively, they were wives and daughters of families still in Germany who had been sent to safety out of the country by finding employment in domestic service abroad. Holland employed many thousands of German domestic servants and this form of employment remained one of the few avenues for finding work open to refugees. Domestic service remained unattractive to Dutch workers as the pay was usually too low to provide a living wage for someone "living out" and was only viable when the employee could make use of the accommodation provided.

The practice of sending wives and daughters out of Germany first was nevertheless an unusual one. In most cases where one family member was sent on ahead this was the husband or son, a trend reflected in the re-emigrants from Holland where 70·3% were men and only 29·7% women. The table shows a strong tendency among the refugees to make themselves as desirable as possible for countries of settlement abroad. Many had arrived in Holland with no real idea of where to go or what to do and were placed by the CvJV. Others had been retrained by the Zionists in Holland, and for the vast majority this meant a Jewish Agency certificate for Palestine. For refugees unable or unwilling to go to Palestine, the CvJV was usually in a position to find another country of settlement where their skills would be accepted. However, the table shows that in the period 1936–1938, when most re-emigration was to overseas countries, it was not only retrainees who were able to get away. Family connections abroad and individual opportunities continued to play a part in assisting some refugees and families to leave Holland and settle elsewhere.

VII

Age was also a major determinant in the emigration and re-emigration of refugees. From the material produced by Strauss it is to be expected that the majority of Jewish refugees would be under 40 years of age, and this is borne out by the assisted refugees and those who re-emigrated from Holland.

The age range of refugees supported by the CvJV in comparison with the German census figures shows the predominance of the 25–39 age range among emigrants, but this is even more strongly visible among the re-emigrants. Conversely, while the 40–54 age range among supported refugees is roughly equivalent to their proportion in the Jewish population as a whole, the number of people from this age range able to re-emigrate was severely limited, a trend even more marked among those over 60. The table supports the view that the Jewish population in Germany was becoming more and more top heavy as younger people left the country. It also demonstrates that, because of the stringent entry requirements imposed by countries of settlement overseas, the countries of first refuge and their relief organisations were having to support an increasing number of older people who could not re-emigrate elsewhere. The older refugees who

TABLE XI

Age Distribution of Jewish Refugees in the Netherlands[54]

Age	*Refugees supported by the CvJV Nov. 1936*	%	*Re-emigrants survey 1936–38*	%	*Jewish pop. in Germany 1933* %
16–25	66	12·7	204	31·8	14·1
25–29	87		147		
30–34	87	47·2	87	50·8	28·7
35–39	72		91		
40–44	57		49		
45–49	36	33·8	29	16·9	37·7
50–54	42		24		
55–59	41		6		
60–64	16		1		
65–69	8	6·3	1	0·5	19·5
70+	9		1		
	521	100·0	640	100·0	100·0

could not learn new skills or were physically unfit for re-emigration to a more extreme climate became almost permanent charges on the resources of the CvJV, since they were in most cases unable to support themselves in Holland. Some were found places in charitable institutions or old people's homes, but only a few were able to settle overseas.

Even the small number over 50 years of age who did manage to leave the country usually had their residence in an overseas country guaranteed by relatives or children who had emigrated earlier and who were now in a position to provide financial support. As the comparison between the figures for immigrants to Holland and those who re-emigrated shows, the attitude of countries of settlement played a large part in determining the numbers and ages of people who were able to escape from the precarious existence in a country of first refuge to the relative security of a country of settlement.

VIII

From the early months of 1933, both the government and the Jewish relief organisations in the Netherlands made it clear that their primary aim was to effect the re-emigration of refugees elsewhere rather than to encourage their settlement in Holland. From the government's point of view, it was undesirable to countenance immigration on any scale when unemployment at home was

[54]Bennathan, *loc. cit.*, p. 104. RIOD-CvJV, File 145. CvJV Annual Report 1936. SRE: Age structure of Jewish refugees.

reaching unprecedented levels. On the other hand, the CvJV was afraid of the consequences of uncontrolled immigration which might promote antisemitism in Holland and thus threaten the Dutch-Jewish community as well as the refugees. At the same time, their resources were limited and the only way to provide assistance to the maximum number of refugees was to expedite the re-emigration of as many as possible.

Many of the Jews who came to Holland en route for destinations elsewhere were never recorded by the Dutch authorities or by the CvJV, because travel arrangements and passage had been organised privately or by relief organisations in Germany. More important, however, were those who had been forced or had chosen to find refuge in Holland. The parlous financial position of many refugees, worsened by the Depression which prevented them from earning a living, made some permanent solution to their problems essential. In 1933, it was relatively easy for refugees to travel between the countries of Western Europe as Table XII indicates. There were many cases of refugees coming to Holland, staying for a few weeks, deciding that conditions for them might be better in France or Belgium, and moving on. Apart from those whose actual destination was known to the CvJV a further 200 people just disappeared from view during the course of 1933. It was merely recorded that they had left the country. The CvJV itself encouraged the movement of people to other countries in Europe, especially in cases where an individual was in danger of being expelled by the Dutch authorities. Although the Dutch police seldom returned people over the German border against their will, rather than have them deported, the CvJV would provide the train fare to Brussels or Paris in the hope that the refugee would meet with better luck there. It was not until 1935 and 1936 that the relief organisations of Western Europe agreed among themselves not to "export" difficult cases if this meant they would merely be transferred from one relief agency to another. The settlement of refugees in Holland by the CvJV was rapidly discontinued once the government expressed its displeasure at a relief agency encouraging settlement, however compelling the circumstances might have been.

The large number of people listed as being repatriated included Polish and Austrian citizens who were given help in returning to their country of origin, having come to Holland from Germany. Nevertheless, most of the total is made up of German Jews being returned to Germany. Although repatriation may seem a strange response, given the potential dangers in Germany, it became the only alternative for those people who came destitute to Holland but whose plight was not considered bad enough to warrant support by the CvJV – victims of the financial constraints placed on relief work.

These absolute figures show a trend in the re-emigration of refugees from Holland similar to that outlined by Rosenstock for the emigration of Jews from Germany. The comparative Table XIII shows the correlation between the percentages of direct emigration from Germany in 1937 with the re-emigration of refugees from Holland.

The survey of re-emigration shows that more than half of those who emigrated in the period 1936–1938 had been in Holland for more than a year before their departure. Furthermore, many seem to have been given little choice in their

TABLE XII

Re-emigration of Jewish Refugees from the Netherlands 1933–1938[55]

Country	*1933*	*1934*	*1935*	*1936*	*1937*	*until end Nov. 1938*
Europe	1,064	201	68	80	60	68
Repatriation	806	269	85	77	55	42
Palestine	92	71	69	41	61	42
United States	11	19	2	9	80	98
Overseas	72	168	81	279	191	389
Unknown	200	8	6	10	46	85
	2,245	736	311	496	493	724
Resettlement in Holland	480	263	20	16	5	—
TOTAL	2,725	999	331	512	498	724

TABLE XIII

Jewish Emigration from Germany and Re-emigration from the Netherlands. Comparative Percentages 1933–1937[56]

	Europe %		*Palestine %*		*Overseas %*	
Year	*Ger.*	*Holl.*	*Ger.*	*Holl.*	*Ger.*	*Holl.*
1933	72–74	86	19	7	7–9	7
1934	35–40	44	37	15	23–28	41
1935	26–31	31	36	27	33–38	42
1936	20–25	20	34	16	41–46	64
1937	25	15	15	15	60	69
(1938)		(17)		(7)		(76)

country of settlement. While most refugees readily accepted any chance of an emigration, in the few cases where individuals expressed unwillingness to leave Holland the CvJV was always in a position to threaten the withdrawal of any further material aid. The correlation between the percentage emigration and re-emigration supports the point made earlier that by 1935 at the latest, the elements of free choice in the country of settlement had disappeared for both Jews in Germany and those living in countries of first refuge. The switch from

[55]RIOD-CvJV, File 145. CvJV Annual Reports 1934–1938.
[56]Rosenstock, *loc. cit.*, *passim*. SRE: Re-emigration of Jewish refugees.

European to overseas destinations was not, as is often claimed, simply due to the ultimate acceptance by the majority of Jews that there was no prospect of an early return to Germany, but equally to the fact that conditions of entry to most European countries had worsened considerably in the period 1934–1935. More and more it seems that destinations were determined not by choice but by the external factors of quota restrictions, financial guarantees and the ability of the individual to earn a living abroad.

Over the five years 1933–1937, the changes in destination are far more marked among the re-emigrants from Holland. Although Palestine can be seen as a major destination in 1935, especially directly from Germany, this was a year of reduced emigration compared with previous years and represented the first year in which people who had begun Zionist training programmes in 1933 were likely to be fully trained. However, this retraining was to an extent short-circuited by the restrictions placed on immigration to Palestine. People with a definite commitment to Zionism tended to leave directly from Germany in the early years, and the policy of the Jewish Agency was to save as many people as possible who were still inside the *Reich* rather than allocate its certificates to those who had already found some form of refuge abroad. Thus the percentage figures for departures to Palestine are consistently higher from Germany than from the Netherlands. The switch to emigration and re-emigration overseas occurs from 1934 onwards and marks the beginning of refugee dispersal throughout the world. Increasing restriction in Europe and Jewish disillusionment with the situation in Germany left the Americas as the only available option. The French and Dutch governments were unwilling to grant settlement rights to refugees in their colonies, and the British Dominions were seldom persuaded to take in more than a guaranteed few.* The lucky minority with family in the United States could apply for quota places with financial guarantees from relatives, but the numbers of German Jews with close living relatives in the U.S. were small, and even then, many of these American relations did not have the money or were for some reason unwilling to act as guarantors. It seems also that U.S. consular officials in Europe took a good deal of persuasion before they would grant final visa applications.[57]

For the remaining refugees it was usually a case of taking whatever was offered. The expertise built up by the CvJV on the entry requirements of settlement countries was invaluable in creating opportunities for the refugees they assisted. Contacts with Jewish communities in the Dominions and South America provided information on employment and business prospects. From the very beginning the HICEM had undertaken to pay 75% of the refugees' travel costs but this was soon increased to 100% when national relief committees pointed out

* In this connection see in particular the following essay by Michael Blakeney, 'Australia and the Jewish Refugees from Central Europe', in this volume of the Year Book – (Ed.).

[57]The CvJV became involved in a lengthy and, at times, acrimonious debate via the High Commissioner for Refugees with the U.S. State Department about the attitude of the U.S. Consul in Rotterdam towards applications for visas made by German Jews. Arthur D. Morse, *While Six Million Died*, London 1968. pp. 140–145 RIOD-CvJV, File 97. Letter, CvJV to The Society of Friends; London, 18th November 1937.

how much of a drain even the 25% was on their resources. Paying for the passage was by no means the end of the story as many South American countries demanded landing money as well. This meant persuading the HICEM to provide the money or paying it themselves, as they did for the non-Jewish partners in mixed marriages whose passage and landing money would not be paid by the HICEM. Help for such cases was also available from the refugee section of the Society of Friends in London. One example of the lengths to which the CvJV went to place their refugees in countries of settlement is highlighted by the case of Argentina. Entry there depended on the possession of landing money, but it was ascertained that checks were only made on second and third class steamer passengers. Thus it was possible, by sending the refugee first class on the steamer, to avoid providing the landing money. This made a considerable saving on each emigration, in spite of the extra cost of the passage. This cheaper method of effecting an emigration freed more money to help other refugees, but the CvJV was still faced with the prospect of equipping the prospective first class passenger with the necessary clothes in order to look the part.[58]

As it became more and more difficult to find countries willing to accept Jewish refugees, the CvJV was occasionally faced with cases where individuals had to leave Holland by order of the immigration officials but had no chance of obtaining a visa for a country of settlement. In such cases, the CvJV adopted the only course open to them. To prevent refugees from having to return to Germany or entering another European country illegally, they arranged for passages to Shanghai which, in spite of its deplorable conditions, became the only place in the world where an entry visa was not required.[59]

IX

In examining the refugee question in the Netherlands, it would be wrong to overestimate its importance in the minds of the general public or the government. Similarly, it would be wrong to see the series of government measures which affected the immigration of Jews from Germany in the 1930s as a planned, coherent "refugee policy". For successive Dutch governments the major issues were protection of the Dutch labour market and economy from the effects of the Depression, the need to maintain internal security and a desire to maintain good political and economic relations with Germany which would in turn secure the rights of the many Dutch workers there. Jewish refugees were seen as important mainly in terms of further competition in the Dutch labour market and economy, and as potential catalysts for political and economic antisemitism among certain sections of Dutch society. The measures which affected immigration from Germany were primarily designed to protect the economy, and not merely imposed because the majority of the immigrants happened to be Jewish. Although the mechanism which kept down the number of immigrant refugees

[58]For a brief summary of the entry requirements of settlement countries see Strauss, in *LBI Year Book XXVI* (1981), pp. 363–382.

[59]Strauss, in *LBI Year Book XXVI* (1981), pp. 383–384. Only after October 1939 was landing money of $400 required.

and placed the onus of selection on the CvJV and its provincial counterparts cannot be said to have been part of a planned "refugee policy", it nevertheless gave the government the best of both worlds, restricting immigration without affecting the normal traffic between the two countries and leaving all refugee relief work in the hands of private charity.

The statistical evidence on refugees in the Netherlands poses many problems of analysis and evaluation but this does not prevent some general conclusions. The number of refugees who came to Holland in the years 1933 to 1938 mirrors the overall picture of emigration from Germany, with decline after 1933 followed by increases after 1935. However, the figures for Holland bring out much more clearly the importance of 1935 as a watershed, with a sharp increase in emigration following the wave of antisemitic actions during the summer and the promulgation of the Nuremberg Laws. This increase, which was itself limited by the aid policies of the CvJV, runs counter to the view of the Nuremberg Laws as a moderating influence on the levels of emigration after the arbitrary violence of the summer months. Indeed the Laws were instrumental in creating a new type of refugee, the "non-Aryan Christians" whose Jewish ancestry rendered them "racially" unacceptable in the Nazi state.

The financial limitations on the work of the CvJV serve to highlight two important aspects of the emigration from Germany. In 1933, many Jews had abandoned their businesses or employment in order to flee from Germany but brought sufficient amounts of capital to re-establish themselves and thus had little or no contact with the CvJV. However, the economic recession pauperised many who would have had no claim to CvJV assistance on the basis of their experiences in Germany, but who had to be given aid as there was no chance of their returning to Germany unpunished after February 1935. Although newly arrived "economic refugees" were advised to return to Germany before their absence was noted, the CvJV was forced to allocate a substantial proportion of its precious funds to helping people who had been in Holland for some time. Following from this was the role of the CvJV in encouraging would-be refugees to return to Germany because they could expect no assistance in Holland. While the statistics show that this procedure continued until 1938, the refugees were advised to contact one of the relief agencies inside Germany in the hope that their emigration be expedited from there. To a certain extent therefore, the phenomenon of Jews returning to Germany was not entirely voluntary but, in the case of the Netherlands, actively promoted by the hard-pressed relief agencies.

The survey of refugees' residence in Germany has shown the importance of geography and proximity to the Dutch border in determining flight to Holland rather than Belgium or France. While this supports the view that entry requirements for all these countries were largely the same, it also shows how a limitrophe country became involved in the *Binnenwanderung* (internal migration) of Jews from the rural areas and small towns to the larger cities. It seems certain that Holland played host to many Jews from rural Hanover and Westphalia who preferred the shorter journey to the relative safety of a Dutch border town rather than the longer journey and the insecurity of life in one of the large German cities.

Finally, the Dutch statistics on re-emigrating Jews suggest that the increasing restrictions imposed on immigration by countries of settlement left the Dutch relief agencies to look after the older and less adaptable of the refugees while the younger ones had greater opportunity to travel elsewhere. Thus the distortions in the age structure of Jews in Germany was mirrored in the age structure of refugees in the Netherlands. Furthermore, the close correlation in the percentages of Jews leaving Holland and directly from Germany reinforce the view that the choice of destination was largely determined by restrictions in countries of settlement rather than by individual choice.

The overall conclusion must be to stress the role of the CvJV in taking responsibility for the refugees in Holland – a responsibility which the government was only too glad to avoid. Thus the onus was placed on the Dutch-Jewish community to do as much as they could for their persecuted co-religionists within the limitations placed upon them by Dutch legislation and by their own finances.[60] While their statistics allow us to assess certain elements in the Jewish emigration from Germany, they cannot bring out the personal suffering of individuals – as victims of Nazi persecution, and as refugees in a foreign country where language and custom were often unfamiliar. Moreover, many of the refugees, unable to bring capital out of Germany or earn a living in Holland, were forced, for the first time in their lives, to live off the charity of others. In reducing refugees to statistics it must always be remembered that each person was in some way unique and therefore had his or her own particular problems which required individual solutions.

[60] For a more detailed account of Jewish refugee relief in the Netherlands see the recently published article by Dan Michman, 'The Committee for Jewish Refugees in Holland (1933–1940)', in *Yad Vashem Studies*, XIV, Jerusalem 1981, pp. 205–232.

Australia and the Jewish Refugees from Central Europe: Government Policy 1933–1939

BY MICHAEL BLAKENEY

I. DEVELOPMENT AND ADMINISTRATION OF AUSTRALIAN IMMIGRATION POLICY TO 1938

a) *Introduction*

Until 1938, escape to Australia was not a significant consideration for the Jewish victims of Nazism. The Jews of Germany and Austria were living in countries which had been considered among the most cultured and enlightened in the world, and the optimistic expectation that the spirit of Goethe and Schiller would reassert itself often caused them to place the most favourable interpretations on the erratic oscillations of Nazi policy. It was frequently the case that when emigration was decided upon by Jews, temporary refuges were sought in countries adjoining Germany. If a more permanent resettlement was envisaged, the United States, with its extensive Jewish community, was the most desirable option, although a very significant obstacle to emigration to the United States was its restrictive immigration laws.

Thus by 1938 persecuted Jews could (apart from *aliyah* to Palestine) follow one of four courses. First, they could remain where they were and trust to an improvement in the political situation. Secondly, they could emigrate to another European country with the intention of returning home when the Nazi menace had receded.* Thirdly, they could apply for an American visa as well as shifting to a more favourable temporary location, hoping to move to America when their preference number became current. Finally, a refugee could abandon the traditional havens and consider starting a new life on the other side of the world.

b) *Australian Immigration Policy to 1933*

The cultural and economic backwardness of Australia might initially have been a deterrent to prospective emigrants, but after they had observed what the sophistication of Europe had wrought, Australia might have been a welcome change. Like the United States, however, Australia had developed a restrictive immigration policy. One of the earliest statutes of the infant federation was the Immigration Restriction Act 1901 which was designed to implement its "White Australia Policy". Section 3 of the Act defined as prohibited immigrants: "Any

*See the preceding essay by Bob Moore, 'Jewish Refugees in the Netherlands 1933–1940', in this volume of the Year Book – (Ed.).

person who when asked to do so by an officer fails to write out at dictation and sign in the presence of the officer a passage of fifty words in length in a European language directed by the officer" and "any person likely to become a charge upon the public". Although the Act contained no restriction on the ground of nationality or race the dictation test was designed to be administered to exclude non-Europeans, as was the "vagrancy" provision.

Following the coming into effect of the United States Immigration Act of 1924 there had been a substantial increase in the number of immigrants from Southern Europe entering Australia. This development precipitated agitation within Australia for the adoption of a quota system on the American model but this expedient was rejected by the government of the day because of the expense of establishing a European immigration service and because of the offence it might have given to foreign States. In the case of Italy, Australia was bound by an agreement made by the British Government for the abolition of visas. To overcome the immediate problem, the Australian Government reached a "Gentleman's Agreement" with Italy to reduce the number of passports which the latter would issue to intending migrants.[1]

The first prospect of any large-scale Jewish refugee immigration to Australia came in 1921 when some 40,000 Jews fled to Poland from the Ukraine as "fugitives from an indescribable anarchy and carnage".[2] The Polish Government announced that it would refuse the entry of further refugees unless it could be guaranteed that they could emigrate westward. The British Secretary of State for the Colonies asked the Australian Government whether it would be prepared to receive any of the Jewish victims.[3] The Government's response was that its immigration requirements were "being met by the immigration of ex-service men whose passages were being paid by the British Government" and that "the immigration of refugee Jews would involve exclusion of some of these British emigrants".[4]

In 1924, primarily in response to the influx of Southern European migrants the Government introduced the requirement that immigrants possess a visa and that they possessed A£40 or its equivalent or that some resident in Australia would be responsible for them. This administrative means of restricting the influx of *Ostjuden* was approved by Alfred Harris, editor of the *Hebrew Standard* who explained:

> "The danger was imminent that the progress of a century might be suddenly undone and Australian Jews swamped by a sudden eruption [of *Ostjuden*] unable to speak English and, in many ways, failing to understand the Australian outlook or prepared to undertake Australian nationality. Fortunately this danger is guarded against through restricting visas."[5]

[1]Memorandum, Dept. Int., 'Alien Immigration – Question of Quota System etc', 23rd October 1935. Dept. Immigration, Corresp. Files, Class 3 'Alien Immigration 1936 Cabinet Decisions', 1935–1938, Aust. Archive Office, CRS A434, Item 49/3/29456.

[2]Cable, High Commissioner's Office (London) to Prime Minister's Department, 19th May 1921, Dept. Immig., Corresp. Files., Class 3 (Non-British European Migrants), 'Admission of Jews to Australia 1921–1938', Aust. Archives Office, CRS A434, Item 49/3/3196.

[3]*Ibid.*

[4]Cable, Prime Minister's Department to High Commissioner's Office, 1st June 1921, *ibid.*

[5]*Hebrew Standard*, 19th October 1928.

The possibility of increased Polish-Jewish emigration was brought to the attention of the Australian Government by the British Passport Control Officer, Warsaw in mid-1925. The Officer reported that "you are no doubt aware that the Polish Jews cannot be considered a suitable type of emigrant and I presume that the Australian Government would strongly object to a large number of them arriving as settlers".[6] Commenting that it was easy for them to obtain permits, he concluded "my private opinion is that it would be a good thing to limit the number of Jewish emigrants from Poland because as a rule they are men of poor physique and it will be difficult for me to take responsibility for the safety of their political views".[7] The British Passport Officer's views and recommendations were accepted by the Australian Government which requested that "the immigration of these people to Australia should be discouraged as far as it may be in the power of the [Officer] discreetly to do so".[8] The Australian Home and Territories Department expressed the concern that "if a large number came they would probably tend to form into communities as they have done in East London" and it recommended that the British Passport Officer discourage their entry by creating difficulties with the language test.[9] Rabbi Francis Cohen, Chief Minister of the Great Synagogue in Sydney, wrote to the Secretary of the Home and Territories Department drawing attention "to the fact the language test is very often being abused by consulates who make it a pretext for hindering Jewish emigration".[10] He pointed out that Canada had accepted 24,722 East European Jews between 1921 and 1926 at a rate well in excess of 4,000 in the preceding three years whereas Australia had averaged only 150 per year.[11] The Secretary of the Department pointed out that the language problem was substantial as was that of supporting indigent immigrants.[12] An unsigned annotation on this correspondence drew the Minister's attention to the desirability "of avoiding transfer to Australia of large numbers of poor Jews as the tendency was for them to live in the poorer portions of the cities and to become exploited by the more enterprising business Jews".[13]

In response to a request from Rabbi Cohen in September 1928 for a statement of Australian policy on non-British immigration,[14] the Minister for Home and Territories informed him that Australia had adopted a quota system for immigrants from Greece, Yugoslavia, Albania, Poland, Czechoslovakia and Estonia.[15] In December of that year Lucien Wolf, a representative of

[6]F. C. Derbyshire to H. E. Spencer, 20th June 1925, copy sent to Secretary Prime Minister's Department 8th August 1925. Dept. Immig. Corresp. Files, Class 3 (Non-British European Migrants), 'Admission of Jews to Australia 1921–1938', Aust. Archives Office, CRS A434, Item 49/3/3196.

[7]*Ibid.*

[8]Secretary Prime Minister's Dept. to Official Secretary (London), 3rd October 1925, *ibid.*

[9]Memorandum Home and Territories Dept. 'Polish Jews', *ibid.*

[10]Cohen to Secretary Home and Territories Dept., 15th October 1926 referring to letter from Vereinigtes Komitee für jüdische Auswanderung (Emigdirect), 1st September 1926, *ibid.*

[11]*Ibid.*

[12]Quinlan to Cohen, 28th October 1926, *ibid.*

[13]*Ibid.*

[14]Cohen to Minister Home and Territories Dept., 13th September 1928, *ibid.*

[15]Quinlan to Cohen, 18th September 1928. *ibid.*

Hias-Ica-Emigdirect met the Director of Migration at Australia House, London, to request an increase in the Jewish quota for Australia and that the quota be allocated to the association who would give a guarantee that the refugees would never become a charge on the public.[16] Although this offer was considered with interest by the Home and Territories Department[17] it was declined.[18]

A detailed consideration of the Australian response in the 1920s to the question of accepting Jewish refugees from Poland is useful in that it represents a fairly faithful precursor to the Australian response to the Jewish refugees in the next decade. First, the reliance upon British perceptions of Australian solutions became typical; secondly, a general prejudice against poor immigrants was manifest; and thirdly, the lack of enthusiasm of the local Jewish community, or its acquiescence in Government decisions became characteristic, although the local community was eventually given the sort of administrative role envisaged by Wolf.

With the onset of the Depression in Australia administrative action was taken to restrict the arrival of migrants. From December 1931 the Department of the Interior restricted the issue of permanent resident permits to those nominated by close relatives who guaranteed their support for five years.[19] The following year the Immigration Act was amended to provide that an alien was a prohibited immigrant if not in possession of a landing permit or otherwise authorised by the Minister. The landing permit system was to become the administrative basis for regulating the arrival of Jewish refugees after 1933.

c) *Immigration Policy 1933–1937*

With the accession to power of Hitler in 1933 it immediately occurred to the Australian Government that "Australia may be selected as a country having attractions" for German Jews.[20] A memorandum prepared for Cabinet by the Minister of the Interior reported that "it is not considered desirable that any special facilities should be given for Jews from Germany to migrate to Australia".[21] The Australian Archives do not disclose the basis of this decision but it characterised the Government's approach to the question until the end of 1938.

In September 1933 the Australian High Commissioner in London, S. M. Bruce, was approached by Simon Marks, a prominent member of the English Jewish community, to seek the assistance of the Australian Government in accepting German-Jewish refugees on a temporary basis. The Government's

[16]Wolf to Australian High Commissioner, 23rd January 1929, *ibid.*

[17]Memorandum, Home and Territories Dept., 'Jewish Immigration to Australia', 23rd April 1929, *ibid.*

[18]Quinlan to Official Secretary (London), 29th April 1929, *ibid.*

[19]*Commonwealth Year Book*, 1931, p. 678.

[20]Memorandum for Cabinet from J. A. Perkins, Interior Min., 'Question of Admission of Jews from Germany', 2nd June 1933, Dept. of Immig. Corresp. File, Class 3 (Non-British European Migrants), "Admission of German Jews Cabinet Decisions re", 1933–1936, Aust. Archives Office, CRS A434, Item 49/3/7034.

[21]*Ibid.*

decision was that no departure could be made from the conditions it imposed on alien immigration.[22] Australian Jewish leaders decided to appeal to the Government to modify this policy and in January 1934 the Victorian Jewish Immigration Questions Commission approached the Sydney Great Synagogue Board with a view to sending a joint delegation to Canberra.[23] The Great Synagogue Board opposed this on the grounds that it could result in publicity harmful to Australian Jewry and was unlikely, in view of the adverse economic conditions, to be attended with success.[24] The objections of the Board were overcome and a delegation presented a petition to the Minister of the Interior, J. A. Perkins, requesting the Government to view favourably the admission of a limited number of German refugees.[25] The memorandum emphasised that the Jewish community did not support mass immigration or group settlements, that it would only sponsor an excellent type of immigrant who would not be a charge on the State and who would bring new skills and not compete with Australians for employment.[26]

At the beginning of 1934 the Government began to issue landing permits to independent migrants with landing money of A£500.[27] This precaution was not considered adequate enough for the Federal Council of the British Medical Society in Australia which suggested that "the Customs authorities refuse admissions through failure to pass a language test".[28] The doctors were concerned at the competition they would be receiving from German practitioners who had become registered in Britain.[29] The Department of the Interior suggested that the question of eligibility to practise was a State, rather than Federal, matter.[30]

With the improvement of economic conditions in 1935 the Department of the Interior, in October of that year, suggested to Cabinet that restrictions on alien immigration be modified.[31] Cabinet accepted the Department's recommendations that in addition to the grant of landing permits to dependants of relatives in Australia, persons with A£500 landing money and expertise required for special industries, the Minister also be given a discretion to authorise intending migrants of "a desirable type" who were not likely to become a burden on the community or interfere with the labour market.[32] "Desirable type" was defined by reference to "general assimilability . . . due consideration being given to the question of

[22]Dept. Interior, Memorandum, 6th November 1933, *ibid.*

[23]Great Synagogue Minutes, 17th January 1934.

[24]*Ibid.*

[25]Great Synagogue Minutes, 31st January 1934.

[26]*Ibid.*

[27]*Commonwealth Year Book*, 1935, p. 562.

[28]Lawes, Gen. Sec. F.C.B.M.A.A. to Sec. Dept. External Affairs, 8th March 1934, Dept. Immigration, Corresp. File, Class 3 (Non-British European Migrants) 'Admission of German Jews Cabinet Decisions re', 1933–1936, Aust. Archives Office, CRS A434, Item 49/3/7034.

[29]See also E. Kunz, *The Intruders. Refugee Doctors in Australia*, Canberra 1975.

[30]Department of the Interior, Memorandum, 1st May 1934, note 28 above.

[31]Department of the Interior, Memorandum to Cabinet, 'Alien Immigration – Question of Quota System etc', 23rd October 1935, Dept. Immigration, Corresp. File, Class 32, "Alien Immigration 1936, Cabinet Decisions", 1935–1938, Aust. Archives Office, CRS A434, Item 49/3/29456.

[32]*Ibid.*, para. 24.

avoiding as far as possible the establishment of alien communities" and special consideration was to be given to "intending immigrants of Northern European race or extraction".[33]

In 1936, following the Nuremberg Laws, an agreement was reached between the British and American Jewish communities to raise £3,000,000 to assist 100,000 young Germans to emigrate. In response to an appeal from the British Council for German Jewry, the German Jewish Relief Fund was established in Sydney under the chairmanship of Sir Samuel Cohen and it was decided that Australian Jewry should contribute A£50,000. In March 1936, T. Paterson, the Minister of the Interior, recommended, on the urging of Jewish community representatives, that the landing money requirement be reduced from A£500 because of the impossibility of raising that amount.[34] The representatives were reported to have offered to advance landing money on behalf of refugees and to guarantee that they would not be allowed to become charges on the community. Cabinet approved that in the case of non-British migrants who were nominated by persons or associations prepared to guarantee that they would not become a charge on the State, and would not engage in employment to the detriment of Australians, landing money was to be reduced to A£50. Landing money for migrants without guarantors was reduced to A£200.[35]

In September 1936 the Council for German Jewry in London requested that the money raised for the German Relief Fund be retained in Australia to cover the A£50 landing money requirement. The change in Government policy necessitated the coordination of Jewish communal support for the refugees. Following meetings with the Assistant Minister of the Interior and local Jewish leaders it was decided, in 1937, to form the Australian Jewish Welfare Society (A.J.W.S.). Sir Isaac Isaacs the Australian Jewish Governor General became the society's patron on the assurance that refugees it sponsored would become British subjects as soon as possible.

Although the Government appeared to have made some important concessions it still maintained a conservative attitude towards the immigration of Jews. A memorandum from the Department of the Interior of August 1936 explained,

> "Jews as a class are not desirable emigrants for the reason that they do not assimilate; speaking generally they preserve their identity as Jews. It would not be desirable that the Government should give its blessing to any scheme involving block nominations of Jews for admission into the Commonwealth. It is considered that individual nominations should be submitted by the representative Jewish Communities in Australia, which should be required, when submitting each nomination, to state the particular avenue of employment in which it was proposed the nominee should be placed. That this should be done is most important, in order that before the acceptance of a nomination this Department may be in a position to satisfy itself that the introduction of the nominee would not be detrimental to Australian workers."[36]

[33] *Ibid.*

[34] T. Paterson, Memorandum to Cabinet, 9th March 1936, 'Question of Admission of Jews from Germany', note 31 above.

[35] *Ibid.*

[36] Department of the Interior, Memorandum 'Question of Admission of Jews into Australia', 6th August 1936, Department of Immigration, Corresp. File, Class 3 (Non-British European Migrants): 'Admission of German Jews Cabinet Decisions re', 1933–1936, Aust. Archives Office, CRS A434, Item 49/3/7034.

The conservatism of the Department of the Interior was complemented by the conservatism of the A.J.W.S. To minimise the possibility of antisemitic opposition to the immigration programme it had been decided that migrants be sent out in batches not exceeding six persons, that each ship be accompanied by an English-language instructor.[37] When in late 1938 it was reported that a ship was to leave Germany with 800 to 900 refugees bound for Australia, the A.J.W.S. cabled London to prevent the ship's leaving.[38] Refugees were requested by the Society to settle in the country, to adopt Australian customs and manners, to anglicise their names, and were required to sign an undertaking to become naturalised as soon as possible.[39]

d) *The Crisis of 1938*

The German annexation of Austria in March 1938 placed impossible strains on the administration of the Australian immigration system. On 6th April the Prime Minister's Department received an urgent request from London for 10,000 additional immigration forms, reporting that the British Consul-General who represented Australian interests in Vienna had received more than that number of applications for emigration to Australia in three weeks.[40] The High Commissioner in London reported that Australia House was receiving approximately 120 inquiries daily.[41] The plight of the refugees received widespread publicity in Australia and considerable sympathy was generated for them.

At this juncture, on 6th April, the Australian High Commissioner in London, S. M. Bruce, reported to the Prime Minister an enquiry from the United States as to whether Australia would be prepared to cooperate in setting up a committee for the purpose of facilitating the migration from Austria of political refugees.[42] Bruce explained that, although representatives on the committee would be designated by the invited Governments, any funding of emergency migration was to be undertaken by private organisations within the respective countries and that no country was expected to receive a greater number of immigrants than was permitted by its existing legislation.[43] The High Commissioner reported that the United Kingdom had drawn attention to certain difficulties in the proposal such as America's own immigration quotas and the desirability of not encouraging "other countries such as Poland to take further steps to get their Jews to leave".[44] He concluded,

[37]Minutes of the German Jewish Refugees Fund, 3rd December 1936; 25th November 1937.

[38]*Sydney Morning Herald*, 4th November 1938.

[39]See 'Report on Activities of Australian Jewish Welfare Society', 'Refugees (Jewish and Others) General Policy File (1938–1940)', Department of the Interior, Corresp. File Class 2 (Restricted Immigration) 1939–1949 Aust. Archives Office, CRS A433, Item 43/2/46; Australian Jewish Welfare Society, 'Form of Guarantee', *ibid.*, IHM 48/3/149605.

[40]High Commissioner's Office to Prime Minister's Department, 6th April 1938, Department of External Affairs (11), Corresp. Files, Alphabetical Series, C.1927–1942, Refugees, General, No. 4, Part 1: Inter-Governmental Committee (Including Evian Conference), 1938–1940, Aust. Archives Office, CRS A981.

[41]Bruce to Lyons (Cable), 5th April 1938, *ibid.*

[42]*Ibid.*

[43]*Ibid.*

[44]*Ibid.*

. . . "suggest in view of desirability responding to any American initiative for co-operative action and the fact that the United Kingdom Government will probably accept, that we should accept, also. Our reply might however await despatch U.K. reply and follow down same lines."[45]

In evaluating the American invitation, the Secretary of the Department of External Affairs observed that "Australia would be subject to criticism if the invitation was refused, especially as the need for increased population for Australia has been recently and consistently stressed by Government and other spokesmen".[46] He concluded that "in all the circumstances it might be advisable for the Commonwealth Government to reply accepting the invitation in principle without waiting on the reply of the United Kingdom".[47] Although the High Commissioner was instructed immediately, on 8th April, to accept the American invitation[48] a Cabinet Minute of the same date noted: "Approved that Commonwealth be represented at Conference proposed by U.S.A. only if Great Britain decides to be represented."[49] At the Cabinet discussion on 8th April, J. McEwen, the new Minister for the Interior, sought to define the current policy on Jewish immigration. It had been noted with some considerable irritation that the United States had erroneously suggested that Australia maintained an annual quota of only 100 for German refugees.[50] McEwen reported that the A.J.W.S. sought permission to introduce up to 500 persons per year and he recommended that the society be granted this number of permits "provided that not more than 20 persons arrive on any one ship".[51] Cabinet approved this request adding that the German quota would include Austrian Jews but it affirmed the existing policy of a case by case approach to immigration with appropriate guarantees and financial collateral.[52] The Prime Minister informed Bruce of Cabinet's modification of immigration policy but emphasised that Australia's representative at the conference would be instructed "that no special facilities can be granted for the admission of groups of Jewish migrants whether from Germany or Austria but that each case would be considered on its merits on applications in the usual form being submitted to the Department of the Interior", and that "there will in all cases be customary safeguards that admission will not be detrimental to Australian workers".[53]

On 4th May the Government's immigration policy was placed on public record by McEwen in a statement to Parliament,[54] but the panic in Europe was beginning to throw this policy into jeopardy. In a memorandum to Cabinet of

[45]*Ibid.*
[46]W. R. Hodgson, Memorandum to Minister, Department of External Affairs, 6th April 1938, *ibid.*
[47]*Ibid.*
[48]Lyons to Bruce, 8th April 1938 (Cable), Department of the Interior (11), Corresp. Files Class 2, (Restricted Immigration) 1939–1945, Refugees (Jewish and Others) – General Policy File (1938–1944) CRS A433, Item 43/2/46.
[49]Prime Minister's Department, Extract from Cabinet Minutes, 8th April 1938.
[50]Bruce to Lyons, note 41 above.
[51]J. McEwen, Memorandum to Cabinet, 'Immigration of Jews to Australia', 8th April 1938, *ibid.*
[52]Secretary Prime Minister's Department to Secretary Department of External Affairs, Memorandum, 8th April 1938, *ibid.*
[53]Lyons to Bruce, 8th April 1938 (Cable), *ibid.*
[54]McEwen, 'White Alien Immigration', C.P.D., vol. 155, pp. 784–785 (4th May 1938).

25th May, McEwen reported that applications for immigration by German Jews without sponsors, in possession of A£200 landing money were running at 300 per week, "and not taking the racial aspect into consideration would mean the issue of approximately 20,000 permits to Jews for this year".[55] McEwen conceded that "there is no doubt that the majority of Jewish applicants if admitted would be able to establish themselves in business or occupations without much difficulty" and he drew attention to the pre-Depression Australian immigration rate of 50,000 persons per year and the fact that unemployment had now fallen to only 8 per cent. In this memorandum McEwen was suggesting that Cabinet had to address the failure of its immigration policy informally to exclude Jews and whether for the first time Australia would have to establish "a quota for Jews who are a race as distinct from a nationality". Although he conceded that only 50 per cent of the applicants had given their race as Jewish he explained "The balance can be judged fairly clearly by means of the names, particularly their first or 'Christian' names, the photographs and statements in accompanying documents". McEwen recommended:

> "If it were decided to limit the number of Jews to be granted permits to enter Australia it would appear desirable to give preference to Austrian and German Jews because of their greater need, and because they have become more assimilated in European ways, say, than the Jews of Poland where they have practically formed a State within a State."[56]

On 9th June Cabinet agreed to establish a quota of 300 landing permits to be granted to Jews per month, that preference be given to Austrians and Germans instead of Poles, and that preference be related to amount of capital, occupation and age and that "discretion [was] to be used in selection as to types (to be judged by photographs and questions of nationality)".[57] Finally it was decided to approach the A.J.W.S. to assist in the selection of the best type of migrant.[58] The Cabinet's decision was communicated to the High Commissioner in London on 22nd June and the Prime Minister, J. Lyons, requested that he advise the British Consuls at Berlin, Vienna, Warsaw and Budapest to exercise discretion in giving publicity to the fact that in the past few months many thousands of applications had been received from Jews residing in Europe for permission to enter Australia "and that, as the number seeking admission is far in excess of the number which the Commonwealth Government considers could readily be absorbed without detriment to Australian workers it has been decided that only a limited, specially selected number should be granted each month".[59] Lyons concluded:

[55] McEwen, Memorandum to Cabinet, 25th May 1938, Department of the Interior (11), Corresp. Files, Class 2 (Restricted Immigration), 1939–1945 Aust. Archives Office, CRS A433, Item 43/2146.

[56] *Ibid.*

[57] *Ibid.*

[58] *Ibid.*

[59] Lyons to Bruce, 22nd June 1938 (Cable), Department of External affairs (11) Corresp. Files, Alphabetical Series, c.1927–1942, Refugees General No. 4, Part 1: Inter-Governmental Committee (including Evian Conference), 1938–1940, Aust. Archives Office CRS A981.

"As there are sufficient applications directly on hand to cover the number likely to be approved during the next twelve months, intending applicants are warned that there is little prospect of further applications being granted during present year except in very special circumstances."[60]

This cable summarised the final Australian position on the admission of European Jews prior to the Inter-Governmental Committee which had been scheduled to commence at Evian-les-Bains in France on 6th July 1938. Bruce was requested to inform the Committee of the quota and that the applications which were running at a rate of 600 per week would be sufficient to provide enough eligible applicants for the next twelve months.[61]

II. AUSTRALIA AND THE EVIAN CONFERENCE

a) *The Road to Evian*

On 23rd March 1938, only eleven days after the German occupation of Austria, President Roosevelt instructed Secretary of State Cordell Hull to ask the British and Dominion Governments and the Governments of France, Belgium Netherlands, Denmark, Sweden, Norway, Switzerland, Italy and the Governments of the other American republics, "if they would be willing to cooperate with the Government of the United States in setting up a special committee composed of representatives of a number of governments for the purpose of facilitating the emigration from Austria and presumably from Germany of political refugees".[62] The resultant letter of invitation from Hull to the various governments considerably circumscribed this initiative by stating that,

"... our idea is that whereas such representatives would be designated by the governments concerned, any financing of the emergency emigration referred to would be undertaken by private organizations within the respective countries. Furthermore it is to be understood that no country would be expected or asked to receive a greater number of immigrants than is permitted by its existing legislation."[63]

In the press conference which announced the President's initiative it was declared that the German and Austrian quotas would become fully available. Until that announcement the United States had admitted only 27,000 Germans between 1933 and 1938 out of a possible quota of 130,000. A Presidential Proclamation of 26th March 1938 announced the merging of the tiny Austrian quota with that of the German,[64] thereby manifesting American good intent within the existing legislation.

The Australian response to the American invitation was conditioned, along with the rest of its diplomacy, to the British response. The Australian delegate to the Evian Conference was to consist of Colonel T. W. White, Minister for Trade and Customs, Alfred Stirling, an External Affairs Officer based in London, and

[60] *Ibid.*
[61] Lyons to Bruce, 4th July 1938 (Cable), *ibid.*
[62] *Foreign Relations of the United States – 1938*, vol. 1, Washington 1955, pp. 740–741.
[63] *Ibid.*
[64] U.S., Department of State, *Press Releases*, vol. XVIII (26th March, 1938), p. 411.

A. W. Stuart-Smith an Australia House official. The delegation was reported to have taken an "early opportunity . . . to establish contact with the United Kingdom delegation".[65] Stirling reported to Canberra:

> "Before setting out for the Conference, the view of the United Kingdom government, as far as I could gather, was that the 'initiative' of President Roosevelt should be encouraged as much as possible, as a sign, however faint, of increased American interest in international affairs, and particularly in Europe. At the same time the Foreign Office felt that little of a practical character could come of the Conference. Difficulties of finance loomed large; it was not expected that governments would do anything in this direction, and the resources of the voluntary refugee organizations were, of course, limited. Secondly . . . it was doubtful whether the United States, or any other country, would be ready to propose any large scale acceptance of refugees . . . Thirdly, there was the fear that if the Conference should by any chance show any great readiness to accept refugees, Poland and Roumania would feel encouraged to get rid of the several millions of Jews within their borders and might start repressive measures to achieve that end. Finally, their attitude towards the United States proposal to constitute yet another organization for the relief of refugees, was one of disapproval. It was not desirable to overlap with the already existing League organizations for refugees from Germany and Austria."[66]

Consultation with Australia and the other Dominions, prior to the Conference was also in Britain's interest since its Palestine Mandate would potentially be the subject of suggestions for Jewish immigration, together with its African Colonies. Although the United States had suggested on 7th May that the first meeting of the proposed Conference be held on 6th July 1938 at Evian in France,[67] a number of weeks passed without any indication from Washington as to what precisely the State Department had in mind as to the scope of the Conference and the procedures that would be adopted. The Foreign Office predicted that "in default of a lead from the United States . . . the outlook for Evian was gloomy . . . the meeting would be chiefly occupied with passing the buck".[68] Speculation on the President's motives in calling for the Conference was not assisted by reports from the United States. *Time* magazine believed that the proposal was designed to express, in a practical way, American disapproval of the *Anschluss*, *Newsweek* thought it was part of the Administration's plan to divert public opinion from isolationism to more "active opposition" to "international gangsters".[69] Other contradictory possibilities were that the President was under pressure from the American Jewish community to intervene on behalf of its co-religionists or that more conservative elements sought international action to deflect attempts to liberalise the immigration laws.[70]

[65]Australian Delegation, Evian, to Department of External Affairs, Memorandum 13th July 1978, Department of External Affairs (11), Corresp. Files, Alphabetical Series, e.1927–1942, Refugees General No. 4, Part 1: Inter Governmental Committee (including Evian Conference), 1938–1940, Aust. Archives Office, CRS A981.

[66]Stirling to Hodgson, 17th July 1938, *ibid.*

[67]S. Adler-Rudel, 'The Evian Conference on the Refugee Question', in *LBI Year Book XIII* (1968), p. 238.

[68]Quoted in A. J. Sherman, *Island Refuge. Britain and the Refugees from the Third Reich*, Berkeley 1973, p. 104.

[69]Quoted in David S. Wyman, *Paper Walls, America and the Refugee Crisis 1938–1941*, Amhurst, Mass. 1965, p. 44.

[70]See Henry L. Feingold, *The Politics of Rescue. The Roosevelt Administration and the Holocaust 1938–1945*, New Brunswick, N.J. 1970, pp. 22–25; Sheldon Spear, 'The United States and the Persecution of the

As Stirling reported, the British prognosis for the success of the Conference was not optimistic. A meeting between the Foreign Office and the Australian and other Dominion High Commissioners disclosed complete opposition to any proposal which might be raised at Evian for government financial assistance for migration or resettlement schemes.[71]

The question of finance was perceived to be critical to the Evian deliberations. The landing money requirements were an insuperable obstacle to refugees who had experienced the confiscatory legislation of the Nazis. Australia House reported that the British Ambassador to Berlin, Sir Nevile Henderson, had mentioned the Evian Conference to the German Foreign Minister von Ribbentrop.[72] The latter, declaring that this was his first news of the event, expressed concern that the Conference might be used as a forum for anti-German propaganda and conveyed the impression that any adverse criticism might result in a worsening of the Jews' predicament.[73] Henderson advised that the British delegates at Evian bring pressure to bear on the German Government by making the reception of German and Austrian Jews in England dependent on the amounts of property they be permitted to export.[74] He concluded:

> "I would deprecate too dogmatic an attitude by British delegates as regards German policy toward Jews. However uncivilised and deplorable, it is, in the Chancellor's eyes, Germany's own business, even though she will probably be the greatest sufferer for it in the end."[75]

This advice was heeded by all delegates and criticism of Germany was avoided in every speech. As Stirling explained, it was hoped that the Conference and the Committee it established would "lead to something more than the question of refugees, to some general appeasement".[76]

b) *By the Waters of Evian*

Delegates from 32 nations participated in the Conference which was opened at the Hotel Royal, Evian-les-Bains on 6th July 1938. Poland and Romania, anxious to arrange the emigration of Jews from their countries, sent observers, and Germany allowed representatives of German and Austrian Jewry to attend in an official capacity. In opening the proceedings the French delegate Henri Bérenger also welcomed the "refugee associations who have come here of their own free will".[77] He explained that "if they were not convened, the reason is that we are not an international conference . . . nor is it a platform for declarations. Rather we

---

Jews in Germany, 1933–1939', *Jewish Social Studies*, vol. 30 (1968), pp. 228–229; Arthur D. Morse, *While Six Million Died*, London 1968, p. 203.

[71]See Sherman, *op. cit.*, p. 106.

[72]Hood to Secretary, Department External Affairs, 13th July 1938, Inter-Governmental Committee, note 65 above.

[73]*Ibid.*

[74]Henderson to Halifax 4th July 1938, Sherman, *op. cit.*, p. 113.

[75]*Ibid.*

[76]Stirling to Hodgson, note 65 above.

[77]Proceedings of the Intergovernmental Committee, Evian, July 6th to 15th, 1938. *Verbatim Record of the Plenary Meetings of the Committee. Resolutions and Reports*, London, July 1938, p. 11.

are simply a body which the President of the United States desired to create between American and the other continents".[78] The various refugee organisations might have been understandably irritated by this patronising welcome since it was they who had borne the primary expense of rescuing the refugees up to the date of the Conference and it was they who Roosevelt envisaged would bear the costs of rescue in the future.

The Australian delegates were appointed to the Credentials Committee and the leader of the Australian delegation, Colonel White, was appointed to the Chairmanship of the important Sub-Committee on the Reception of Those Concerned with the Relief of Political Refugees from Germany (including Austria). This Sub-Committee received memoranda of suggested action from representatives of about 40 private refugee aid agencies. The 20 Jewish private groups in attendance could not unite on any proposed course presenting a "spectacle of Jewish discord and disruption".[79] The Sub-Committee, in what was described as "a humiliating procedure" gave each representative about ten minutes to make his submission.[80] Bérenger in his closing address communicated the Committee's appreciation to White for "the work he did in so short a space of time".[81] This Antipodean contribution to the refugee problem had taken a mere afternoon.[82]

In the opening speech of the Conference, Myron C. Taylor stated that the United States' contribution lay in making the pre-existing German-Austrian quota of 27,370 fully available and managed to avoid using the word "Jew" in his speech. Having established what has been described as a "precedent for inaction",[83] each delegate listed reasons why their nation was unable to receive more refugees. These included existing saturation levels having been reached, the unsuitability of their territories and the economic problems resulting from the Depression. The French delegate lamented that his country had "already almost exhausted her own resources, which unfortunately are not so boundless as her zeal to save the cause of humanity".[84] But he concluded:

> "To what do the Americas and Australia owe their expansion during the last three centuries if not to the constant influx of European emigrants, refugees and exiles . . . It is, therefore, part of the logic of world history that today . . . the initiative and the resources of the new worlds are offered to these fresh swarms of refugees who are being ejected by new revolutions from their old homes."[85]

This historical challenge was emphatically rejected in the speech of Australia's delegate. Conceding that Australia, as well as the United States, owed its development to migration from the Old World, White explained "in Australia's case such migration has naturally been predominantly British; nor is it desired

[78] *Ibid.*
[79] Wyman, *op. cit.*, p. 49.
[80] Adler-Rudel, *loc. cit.*, p. 255.
[81] Proceedings, note 77 above, p. 45.
[82] Stirling to Hodgson, note 65 above,
[83] Saul S. Friedman, *No Haven for the Oppressed. United States Policy Toward Jewish Refugees 1938–1945*, Detroit 1973, p. 59.
[84] *Proceedings*, note 77 above, p. 16.
[85] *Ibid.*

that this be largely departed from while British settlers are forthcoming".[86] Colonel White maintained that,

> "under the circumstances, Australia cannot do more, for it will be appreciated that in a young country man power from the source from which most of its citizens have sprung is preferred, while undue privileges cannot be given to one particular class of non-British subjects without injustice to others. It will no doubt be appreciated also that, as we have no real racial problem, we are not desirous of importing one by encouraging any scheme of large-scale foreign migration."[87]

Before adjourning, the Evian Conference established a permanent Intergovernmental Committee on Refugees and commissioned it to "approach the governments of the countries of refuge with a view to developing opportunities for permanent settlement" and to attempt to persuade the German Government to cooperate in establishing conditions of "orderly emigration".[88] In closing the Conference the Chairman was "happy to report" that,

> ". . . due to the serious spirit of cooperation which had animated this first intergovernmental meeting, due to the deep-rooted conviction that we were dealing with a harrowing human problem, we have been able to recommend to our respective Governments the establishment of machinery that should . . . bring about a real improvement in the lives and prospects of many millions of our fellow men."[89]

The Evian Conference decided to reconvene its executive committee in London on 3rd August 1938 when a permanent organisation would be formed.[90] The meeting of that date appointed George Rublee, a Washington lawyer and personal friend of the President, as director. Earl Winterton, the anti-Zionist leader of the British delegation at Evian was appointed its chairman. Rublee was enthusiastic in initiating negotiations with the Germans on the refugee question but reported considerable British opposition to such an approach.[91] As Stirling reported, Sir Nevile Henderson doubted "the utility of an approach to the German government (which means in the end Herr Hitler) so long as the Czechoslovak question remains in the present critical phase".[92] With the onset of the Munich crisis the Intergovernmental Committee became increasingly irrelevant and was virtually eradicated by the shot that killed vom Rath, Third Secretary of the German Embassy in Paris.

c) *Assessment*

It had been observed by a number of correspondents that Evian spelt backwards gave the word "naive". This was Alfred Stirling's view of those who expected the Conference to achieve something positive.[93] He commented particularly, that

[86] *Ibid.*, p. 19.
[87] *Ibid.*, p. 20.
[88] *Ibid.*, pp. 54–55.
[89] *Ibid.*, p. 41.
[90] Taylor to Hull, 14th July 1938, *Foreign Relations of the United States – 1938*, pp. 754–756.
[91] See generally, John Mendelsohn (ed.), *The Holocaust*, vol. 6, *Jewish Emigration 1938–1940 Rublee Negotiations and the Intergovernmental Committee*, New York 1982.
[92] Stirling to Hodgson, 26th August 1938, note 65 above.
[93] Stirling to Hodgson, note 65 above.

"on the immediate question, that of finding a home for refugees . . . my own impression is that the Conference made little or no progress".[94]

The Evian Conference presented Australia with an opportunity to demonstrate its statemanship, maturity and humanity. Australia had become "a 'blessed word' to the victims of persecution. Her vast spaces, her small populace, and her need for workers for primary and secondary industries"[95] were perceived as "a case where the self-interest of the Dominions, the Imperial interest and the spirit of humanity coincide".[96] The more populous participating nations also looked to Australia to make a significant contribution to alleviating the pressure upon their strained economies.[97] For these reasons Colonel White's speech was later considered to be "the most depressing" of all delegates'.[98] Prior to arriving at Evian, White had given a number of addresses in England encouraging British emigration to Australia.[99] His Evian speech was perceived as being consistent with the proposition that "only Englishmen were wanted in Australia".[100] Particularly to be condemned was the "racial antipathy" apparent at the Conference which was articulated in White's speech.[101]

Australian press reaction to Australia's performance at the Evian Conference ranged across the entire spectrum from strong disapproval to enthusiastic approbation. The *Sydney Morning Herald* and the *West Australian* disagreed with White's declaration that Australia was doing as much as it could to assist the refugees. The *West Australian* maintained that humanitarian considerations were of prime importance and that Australia should be willing to assist in solving the refugee problem.[102] The *Sydney Morning Herald* was particularly critical of the Australian delegate. In an editorial of 9th July 1938 it declared,

> ". . . there cannot but be disappointment with the negative nature of the speech made by the Australian representative . . . The Minister for Trade and Commerce expressed a pious hope for 'a solution of this tragic world problem' . . .
>
> It is a truism that the Commonwealth has no racial problem and has no desire to import one. On the other hand it prides itself on being a democracy with a strong tradition of tolerance, and any undue suggestion of racial intolerance constitutes a betrayal of our cherished traditions."[103]

The *Herald* urged the streamlining of immigration procedures and the establishment of a migration bureau. In addition to the dictates of humanity, the press supporters of a positive immigration policy adduced the self-interested considerations which should have dictated a more generous Australian attitude at Evian. The *Sydney Morning Herald* pointed out that the European refugee crisis presented Australia with a unique opportunity to "obtain some of the best stock

[94] *Ibid.*
[95] Norman Bentwich, 'The Evian Conference and After', *Fortnightly Review* (September 1938), p. 291.
[96] *Manchester Guardian*, 6th July 1938.
[97] E.g. the comments in *The Times*, 8th July 1938; *New Statesman*, 16th July 1938.
[98] G. Warburg, 'None to Comfort the Persecuted', *The Wiener Library Bulletin*, vol. XV (1961), p. 43.
[99] *The Times*, 18th May 1938; *The Times*, 30th June 1938.
[100] *Manchester Guardian*, 8th July 1938.
[101] *Manchester Guardian*, 16th July 1938.
[102] *West Australian*, 11th July 1938.
[103] *Sydney Morning Herald*, 9th July 1938.

and finest minds of Europe".[104] A parallel was drawn between the refugees and the Flemish and Huguenot immigrants who had established the textile industries of England.[105] The Melbourne *Herald* considered that this was the "opportunity to obtain industrious citizens who will . . . become 100 percent democratic Australians" within a generation or two.[106]

Qualifying the enthusiasm, even of supporters of a positive immigration policy, was the considerable middle-ground of opinion which insisted that Australia's living standards be safeguarded and her racial homogeneity be protected.[107] This was the view of Professor Stephen Roberts[108] whose influential eye-witness account of life in Nazi Germany[109] played such a significant role in framing Australian attitudes towards the *Reich* and in generating sympathy for its victims. Labour newspapers and politicians condemned even assisted immigration from Britain at a time of depressed economic circumstances. The yellow press commended Australia's posture at Evian. The Sydney *Truth* warned of the danger to Australian "race, blood and ideals" from the impending deluge of "unwanted and unabsorbable Hebrews".[110] The *Bulletin* agreed with the strict limitation placed on the number of immigrant Jews,[111] warning that "if unrestricted immigration were permitted it would mean the herding into cities – already overcrowded in proportion to the population of the interior – of brooding aliens, ulcerated with hatred of the countries that had driven them out, and grouped in their own colonies which . . . might become the foci of disorder".[112]

It is difficult to assess which of the extremes of press opinion enjoyed the greatest support in Australia. Benjamin suggests that in general the conservative approach of Colonel White enjoyed the widest public support.[113] It is of course difficult to determine public opinion even from newspaper editorials and correspondence, but until a significant number of refugees arrived in Australia there was no touchstone against which this opinion could be tested.

In the formation of policy on Jewish immigration the Government adopted the secretive approach which characterised all its diplomacy at this time. The report of the Australian delegation at Evian, although completed on 31st August 1938 was only presented to Parliament on 1st December 1938 when the pressures arising out of the *Kristallnacht* pogrom had precipitated another change in policy. Even then the report and a copy of the proceedings of the Intergovernmental Committee were only ordered by the Minister for External Affairs to be "laid on the table of the Library"[114] and thus did not become published Parliamentary

[104] *Sydney Morning Herald*, 8th August 1938.
[105] *Sydney Morning Herald*, 18th August 1938.
[106] *Herald*, 14th October 1938.
[107] *Sydney Morning Herald*, 8th August 1938.
[108] *Sydney Morning Herald*, 7th July 1938.
[109] Stephen H. Roberts, *The House that Hitler Built*, London 1937.
[110] *Truth* 16th October, 1938.
[111] *The Bulletin*, 13th July 1938.
[112] *The Bulletin*, 27th July 1938.
[113] D. J. Benjamin, 'Australia and the Evian Conference', *Australian Jewish Historical Society Journal*, vol. V (1961), p. 219.
[114] Commonwealth Parliamentary Debates (henceforth C.P.D.) vol. 158, 1st December 1938, p. 2536.

Papers, open to public scrutiny. The immigration policy which the Government had adopted for the Evian Conference was little different to the one adopted by it at the time of the Ukrainian pogroms of 1921.

III. KRISTALLNACHT 1938

a) *First Reaction*

The November pogrom generated a wave of revulsion against Nazi Germany throughout the non-Fascist world. The British Prime Minister, Neville Chamberlain, expressed his "deep and widespread sympathy for those who are being made to suffer" and the House of Commons passed a motion condemning the persecution.[115] The *Kristallnacht* and world reaction were also headline news in Australia. The pogrom presented "a nauseating picture of twentieth century civilization",[116] defying not only the theory of human progress but also the basic principles of "elementary justice".[117] The Germans were said to have reverted to the "Dark Ages and the Days of Attila".[118] The *Australian Worker* suggested that they were acting on a "lower ethical plane than the anarchy of the Stone Age".[119] The furthest regression perceived was that by the Honorary Secretary of the Legion of Christian Youth who described the Nazi frenzy like "the animal lust seen in the red glare of an infuriated ape's eye".[120] Both within and from outside Australia pressure was being brought to bear on the Government to humanise its immigration policy.

b) *Domestic Pressures*

Despite the campaign of papers such as the *Sydney Morning Herald* and the *West Australian* for a liberalisation of Australia's conservative immigration policy, J. McEwen, the Minister for the Interior, on 21st September 1938 had re-affirmed the Government's policy of admitting refugees within the "white alien" principles and had declared that it was against official policy to discriminate between aliens from different countries.[121]

From mid-1937 some refugees had attempted to evade immigration requirements by booking passages to Australia as tourists. The Department of the Interior had engaged in heated correspondence with the shipping lines insisting that they should not accept bookings from Jewish aliens unless they held return tickets and had landing money of at least A£50.[122] Customs officials were

[115] 341 H. C. Debs. 58, p. 503, 1428–1483.
[116] *Daily Telegraph*, 5th December 1938.
[117] *Argus*, 17th November 1938.
[118] *Sydney Morning Herald*, 12th November 1938.
[119] *Australian Worker*, 16th November 1938.
[120] Quoted, *ibid.*
[121] C.P.D., vol. 157, p. 11 (21st September 1938).
[122] See Department of Interior Memorandum, 'Alien Tourist Visas – Landing Money Requirements', 12th July 1937, Department of the Interior, Corresp. File Class 3, 'Alien Immigration 1936 – Cabinet Decisions 1935–1938', Aust. Archives Office, CRS A434, Item 49/3/29456.

instructed not to permit aliens to leave their ships unless they held landing permits.[123] Government policy was tested by the arrival at Brisbane on 5th October 1936 of the *Niew Holland*, en route to Sydney, and Melbourne. On board were 27 German, Austrian and Czech "tourists" who did not possess landing permits but who requested permanent residence in Australia. The Government's refusal to allow the refugees to disembark at Brisbane was given wide press coverage as was their personable appearance and the fact that they each possessed at least A£200 landing money.[124] By the time the *Niew Holland* reached Sydney the Government announced that it had decided to grant the refugees permits for three months with the promise of a review of their case at the end of the period.[125]

When the reports of the November pogrom reached Australia the press campaign for a modification of Australia's policy towards the refugees intensified. The *Sydney Morning Herald* maintained that it was incumbent on Australia to bear its share of the international responsibility for the refugee problem[126] and the *West Australian* pointed out that there was little overseas sympathy for Australia's "rather prickly attitude to immigration".[127] Even the *Australian Worker* conceded that "Australia must do something" and that Jewish refugees were at least preferable to alien fascist immigrants.[128] Amongst the respectable press the Melbourne *Argus* was virtually the only proponent of the view that the problems created by the *Kristallnacht* should be solved by countries other than Australia.[129]

c) *International Pressures*

Following the *Kristallnacht*, the refugee problem was beginning to impose strains on Anglo-American relations. The United States Ambassador to London, Joseph Kennedy, expressed the view that the appeasement policy was misconceived and that American public opinion considered that Britain was not doing enough to assist the refugees. At a Cabinet meeting on 16th November, in which those issues were discussed, Prime Minister Chamberlain suggested allowing Jewish refugees to come to Britain as a temporary refuge. In discussing other action, the Dominions Secretary expressed the hope that it might be possible to induce the Dominions to accept more refugees, it being noted that the Australian High Commissioner had felt that his Government might increase admissions to 6,000 or 7,000 refugees a year.[130] Five days later, on 21st November the High Commissioner cabled the Australian Prime Minister advocating that the Australian Government announce its willingness to take 30,000 refugees over the next three years.[131] Bruce explained:

[123] *Sydney Morning Herald*, 6th October 1938.
[124] *Sydney Morning Herald, Courier Mail, Argus, Herald*, 6th October 1938.
[125] *Ibid.*, 8th October 1938.
[126] *Sydney Morning Herald*, 18th November 1938.
[127] *West Australian*, 23rd November 1938.
[128] *Australian Worker*, 23rd November 1938.
[129] *Argus*, 17th November 1938.
[130] Sherman, *op. cit.*, p. 176.
[131] Bruce to Lyons, 21st November 1938, Department of the Interior (11), Correspondence Files,

> "Owing to the wave of indignation consequent upon the treatment of Jews in Germany strong feeling is rapidly developing, particularly in the United Kingdom, United States, Scandinavian Countries, Holland and France that an international effort on an unprecedented scale must be made to find means whereby refugees can be absorbed. Many impracticable schemes are being put forward and impossible suggestions made, especially with regard to the possibility of absorption of great numbers in underdeveloped areas of the Dominions and Australia is particularly mentioned.
>
> This movement has already led to an announcement which the United Kingdom Government is making today with respect to the Colonial Empire and we may find ourselves in an embarrassing position if no public statement is made as to our attitude, notwithstanding the fact that the number we are taking at present bears favourable comparison with what is being done by every other country.
>
> It occurs to me that it would be a wise move for the Commonwealth Government to make an announcement, as by declaring our policy we would, I am convinced, put an end to the present and growing suspicions as to what Australia might do and would gradually increase, particularly in the United States, the goodwill towards the prestige of Australia, as the country that had made the most practical and sympathetic solution of a problem that is causing the greatest concern to Governments and arousing increasingly popular feeling."[132]

The High Commissioner ended by referring to the fact that while public opinion was running high in Australia,

> ". . . an immediate announcement of a definite policy, even a bold one, would probably be accepted, whereas if the opportunity is allowed to pass even the present number of refugees to whom we are granting permits may prove an embarrassment to the Government in the future."[133]

Bruce did not mention his discussions with the Dominions Secretary and it is difficult to ascertain whether his cable was actuated by his perception of Australia's best interests or by the anglophile desire to get Britain off the hook. Such was Bruce's immense prestige with the Australian Government that the subsequent Cabinet deliberations were not about whether a new policy should be announced, but about the scope of the gesture. A secret memorandum from the Secretary of the Department of the Interior recommended that Bruce's suggestion of 30,000 refugees over three years be halved to 15,000 over that period[134] and this was the figure subsequently announced in Parliament by McEwen on 1st December 1938.[135]

d) *The Government's Response*

For the Australian Government, the *Kristallnacht* had two immediate political consequences: it weakened press support for its policy of appeasement and it precipitated the first debate of any consequence in Federal Parliament on the refugee question. On 22nd November 1938, the day following the Bruce cable, E. J. Holloway, the Labour member for Melbourne Ports, asked whether the

---

Class 2 (Restricted Immigration), 1939–1945, Refugees (Jewish and Others) General Policy 1938–1944, Aust. Archives Office, CRS A433, Item 43/2146.

[132] *Ibid.*

[133] *Ibid.*

[134] J. A. Carrodus, Secret Memorandum, Department of the Interior, 24th November 1938, *ibid.*

[135] McEwen, C.P.D., vol. 158, pp. 2534–2536.

Australian Government could respond to the "unique and unfortunate" circumstances and "consider whether or not it is justified in taking some small quota of Jewish refugees of a type suitable for absorption in this country".[136] He suggested that the Government "in the interests of all of us, should consider what Australia's attitude shall be towards this international appeal to the humanitarian instincts of the people of democratic countries".[137] Labour party policy was not necessarily in agreement with Holloway's sentiments, as an interjector pointed out[138] particularly because of its concern with the employment implications of refugee immigration.[139] McEwen responded by assuring Holloway "that, as the policy of the Government stands today . . . regard is definitely paid to the needs of these particular people to whom he had referred this evening. I am glad to be able to assure him that, acting directly within the limits of the Government's immigration policy . . . it is possible for us to admit to this country annually some few thousands of the class of people on behalf of whom he has made his plea."[140] The delicacy of the Minister in declining to name the "class of persons" to whom he was referring was not shared by the antisemitic Labour member for Kalgoorlie, A. E. Green, who interjected that "they will grab your farm if you let them in".[141] McEwen referred to his "very sad duty" of having to interview people "who, with tears in their eyes, plead for the admittance of relations at present perhaps confined in concentration camps where, my interviewers explained to me, they are enduring a living death" but, he explained, the Government "must be careful not to admit aliens in such numbers as to create alien blocs or troublesome minorities [and] . . . persons of undesirable character, or those not in good health".[142] The latter category would presumably cover applicants from concentration camps. Finally, McEwen reiterated the Government's inability to "admit persons able to engage only in such occupations as would tend to depress Australian living standards".[143]

Within two weeks of the Minister's disavowal of Government flexibility on immigration came his 1st December statement that Australia would be taking up to 15,000 refugees over the next three years. He explained that in arriving at this figure the Government was "influenced by the necessity that the existing standards of living should not be disturbed and for reconciling with the interests of refugees, the interests of Australia's present population, and of the people of British race who desire to establish themselves in Australia".[144] McEwen also explained that permits would be granted these refugees within the general white alien immigration policy, thus they had to have the approved amount of landing money or be guaranteed by some approved individual or organisation. Also existing labour conditions were to be taken into consideration together with the

[136]C.P.D., vol. 158, p. 1850.
[137]*Ibid.*
[138]C.P.D., vol. 158, p. 1851.
[139]E.g. see Collings, vol. 159, C.P.D., p. 349, 16th May, 1939.
[140]McEwen, C.P.D., vol. 158, p. 1851.
[141]*Ibid.*, See also his comments in C.P.D., vol. 160, pp. 1965–1967, 15th June 1939.
[142]*Ibid.*
[143]*Ibid.*
[144]C.P.D., vol. 158, p. 2535.

special expertise which refugees might have.[145] McEwen did not consider that the quota would constitute a very great increase of the rate at which permits had been issued over the preceding six months.[146] He stated in conclusion that the Government intended that the aliens would be widely distributed to facilitate their assimilation and that it maintained "a steady policy against facilitating or permitting undue aggregation of aliens in any particular towns or centres".[147]

John Curtin, the leader of the Labour Opposition, expressed general support for the Minister's statement particularly in view of the Government's desire not to allow a deterioration in economic or social standards.[148] He felt confident that the "vigilance exercised by the Government over those people will be sufficient to prevent the formation of racial colonies in Australia" and he approved of the application of the pre-existing immigration conditions on the new quota.[149] The following day Colonel T. W. White, who had been leader of Australia's delegation at the Evian Conference, observed that the policy announced by McEwen was in line with that of the participating nations at that conference who generally disapproved "of any large-scale scheme of migration as being calculated to arouse racial feeling" and that the Government was continuing the approved approach of immigration by infiltration.[150] He welcomed the "unhesitating acceptance", by the Leader of the Opposition, "of the principle of the help that Australia is giving to those refugees in their time of trouble", but White expressed the hope that the Opposition "will also adopt a liberal outlook in respect of the admission to Australia of people of our own race".[151]

e) *Press Reactions*

The Government's announcement of its new immigration policy was well received in Britain where *The Times* declared that Australia had "made a characteristically generous contribution to the refugee problem".[152] It expressed the hope that other governments would follow Australia's example.[153] The London *Observer* rhapsodised that the Government's decision was a "striking illustration of how noble compassion can circle the globe".[154] The Melbourne *Herald's* correspondent reported that there were "scenes of joy" in London after evening newspapers had publicised the decision.[155] The following day thousands of refugees visited Australia House in London, made written or telephone enquiries and had approached Australian businessmen and newspaper offices.[156] The German *Nacht-Ausgabe* ridiculed the 15,000 quota, claiming that Australia

[145] *Ibid.*
[146] C.P.D., vol. 158, p. 2356.
[147] *Ibid.*
[148] *Ibid.*
[149] *Ibid.*
[150] C.P.D., vol. 158, p. 2626, 2nd December 1938.
[151] *Ibid.*, pp. 2626–2627.
[152] *The Times*, 2nd December 1938.
[153] *Ibid.*
[154] *Observer*, 4th December 1938.
[155] *Herald*, 2nd December 1938.
[156] *Sydney Morning Herald*, 5th December 1938.

could absorb at least 30 million settlers, it sneered that the trivial quota was because "the fine gentry of Sydney and the six other large towns only want British settlers".[157]

The Australian press supporters of a liberal immigration policy were qualifiedly favourable. The *Sydney Morning Herald* and the *West Australian* commended the Government's action as a useful initiative, but expressed the hope that the quota might be enlarged in the future.[158] The *Sydney Morning Herald* doubted that the quota met world expectations.[159] The anti-refugee *Bulletin*, which following the *Kristallnacht* declared that "Australia cannot be expected to imperil its existence or to receive vast masses of alien refugees for the gratification of German Jews, [and] New York politicians and editors",[160] expressed its satisfaction with the quota, provided it was rigidly enforced.[161]

IV. IMMIGRATION POLICY TO THE OUTBREAK OF WAR

a) *Administration*

In his speech of 1st December 1938, in which he announced the quota of 15,000 refugees over the next three years, the Minister of the Interior did not indicate how many of the quota would be Jews. A memorandum from J. Carrodus, the Secretary of the Ministry suggested that four-fifths of the annual total of 5,000 should consist of Jews.[162] This proposal was confirmed by Cabinet on 31st January 1939 to come into effect from the beginning of that year.[163]

By the outbreak of war in September 1939 when Jewish refugee immigration ceased only a fraction of the promised 15,000 immigrants had entered Australia. One of the reasons for this was the very significant bureaucratic obstacles which intending migrants had to surmount as well as the insistence that the decisions on landing permit applications be taken in Canberra. As George Berger, a victim of these obstacles explained, the intending migrant

> "... had to prove to the Australian Government in Canberra the possession of a comparatively large amount in foreign currency, possession of which was a criminal offence in Nazi Germany, for which Jews were shot. He had to obtain a certificate as to his blameless character from the Nazi President of Police, in whose eye every Jew had to be considered as a criminal. And he had to wait approximately four months until he received a reply from the Department of the Interior in Canberra whether he would be admitted to Australia or not. Then, in the positive case he had to wait until the Department had issued and forwarded the permit certificate – if, by that time he was still free and alive."[164]

In Berger's case it took almost eight months to obtain a permit during which time he had fled from Vienna, been imprisoned in Yugoslavia, crossed Italy and had

[157]Quoted *ibid.*

[158]*Ibid.*, 3rd December 1938; *West Australian*, 5th December, 1938.

[159]*Ibid.*

[160]*Bulletin*, 23rd November 1938.

[161]*Ibid.*, 7th December 1938.

[162]Carrodus, Memorandum, 12th December 1938, Department of the Interior (11), Correspondence Files, Class 2 (Restricted Immigration) 1939–1945, Refugees (Jewish and Others) General Policy 1938–1944, Aust. Archives Office, CRS A433, Item 43/2146.

[163]McEwen, Memorandum to Cabinet, 31st January 1939, Refugees General Policy File, note 1 above.

[164]G. Berger, 'Australia and the Refugees', *Australian Quarterly*, vol. 13, (December 1941), p. 54.

waited in France for three months.[165] During this waiting period applicants in Austria and Germany were under the constant shadow of internment in concentration camps, in addition to the general abuse and terror inflicted upon them by their countrymen. As a result there was an inevitable discrepancy between landing permits issued and the number actually used and the Department of Interior files carry evidence of successful applicants having been interned or dying in Dachau whilst awaiting confirmation of their applications.[166]

The absence of Department of Immigration officials in Europe threw the burden of administration upon the already harassed British Consular officers. The *Sydney Morning Herald* criticised this as totally inadequate in view of the urgency of the situation and it declared that the Government's approach merely "created work for extra civil servants" and did not allow "an appreciable number of approved migrants entrance to Australia within reasonable time".[167] The centralised administration of immigration policy was criticised by the Australian High Commissioner in London who suggested that the selection of migrants could be done in Europe with the aid of the British Consular officers and European Jewish refugee organisations.[168] He also suggested that an immigration official be sent to Europe.[169] A memorandum of T. H. Garrett, the Acting Secretary of the Department of the Interior dated 25th January 1939 detailed the implementation of Bruce's suggestion.[170] Garrett recommended that Australia House be a place of application and that it should decide whether an applicant was a Jew, Aryan or non-Aryan Christian. In the case of migrants possessing in excess of A£3,000 landing money, he recommended that Australia House be allowed to issue permits. In the case of Aryans and Non-Aryan Christians possessing in excess of A£1,000 he recommended the issue of permits by Australia House where there was "no doubt as to suitability in all respects" and in the case of those categories of persons possessing between A£200 and A£1,000 landing money they could only issue landing permits where satisfied that the immigrant could be absorbed without detriment to Australian workers. All other cases, which in fact represented most of the Jewish four-fifths of the total eligible applicants, had to be submitted to Canberra. The Garrett memorandum did not indicate why a distinction was to be drawn between Jewish and non-Jewish applicants. These recommendations were accepted by Cabinet[171] which also resolved to send Garrett to London to implement the policy[172] and he departed for London by ship on 5th April 1939.[173]

[165]G. Berger, 'Australia and the Refugees', *ibid.*, vol. 13, (September 1941), p. 40, note 5.

[166]See Statistical Returns, Department of the Interior (1), Corresp. Files, Annual Single Number Series, 1901–1931, Australian Jewish Welfare Society, Proposals re Control of Jewish Migration (1938–1939), Aust. Archives Office, CRS A434, Item 38/23138.

[167]*Sydney Morning Herald*, 13th November 1938.

[168]Bruce to Lyons, 2nd November 1938, Refugees General Policy File, note 131 above.

[169]Bruce to Lyons, 8th November 1938, *ibid.*

[170]Garrett, Memorandum 25th January 1939, *ibid.*

[171]Press Release 16th February 1939, *ibid.*

[172]Lyons to Duncan, Acting High Commissioner, 9th March 1939, Cable, *ibid.*

[173]*Sydney Morning Herald*, 6th April, 1939.

With the now rapid deterioration of the position of European Jewry a cable from London-based refugee organisations urged the A.J.W.S. to "redouble already great efforts to save a harassed and tormented people".[174] A deputation from the society had sought an increase in the number of permits granted direct to it and to reduce the quota of refugees with landing money of between A£200 and A£1,000 because most of this category came to the Society for assistance and placed a strain on its resources.[175] The Society was informed that its direct quota was to be increased by 250 persons per year and that this number would be deducted from the A£200 to A£1,000 quota.[176]

b) *International pressure*

Criticism of the Government's financial requirements began to increase as the unreality of its insistence that the victims of Nazi rapacity finance their own salvation was appreciated in Australia. The Australian Council of Trade Unions suspected a class bias in the Government's restriction of refugee immigration to "prosperous and middle-class people with capital and ready money, while persecuted trade unionists and workers generally . . . are prevented from coming".[177] The *Sydney Morning Herald* argued similarly:

> "The financial criterion is obviously not all important. Large numbers of the victims of Nazi tyranny have been completely robbed of all their possessions . . . and they will naturally include many individuals of the very type, with outstanding technological or cultural attainments who would enrich the life of this country . . . The plain truth is that the Federal Government has not yet tackled the whole problem of the refugees with that rigour and enthusiasm which it demands."[178]

With the approaching spectre of war the administration of Australian immigration policy was becoming chaotic. Berger mentions the escalation of the landing money requirement to A£5,000 and that corruption played its part, "the names of the solicitors who would understand how to influence officials [being] . . . highly treasured".[179]

In April 1939 the Government decided to increase the number of permits issued to Jews by 1,000 to relieve pressure on the Department of Immigration. A week later the Government was preparing to extend the quota within reasonable limits "because it recognized a moral responsibility in the circumstances and believed that accepting more migrants was in Australia's interests".[180]

In the summer of 1939 comments were made in the British Parliament suggesting that Australia recognise the exceptional circumstances of the times. The Bishop of Chichester expressed the hope that the Australian Government

[174]A.J.W.S. Minutes, 3rd February 1939.

[175]Department of Interior, Notes on Deputation from Jewish Welfare Society, Sydney, 27th February 1939, Refugees General Policy File, note 162 above.

[176]Carrodus to Lesnie (A.J.W.S.), 16th March, 1939, *ibid.*

[177]*Argus*, 9th March 1939.

[178]*Sydney Morning Herald*, 20th June 1939.

[179]Berger, *loc. cit.*, note 164 above, p. 55.

[180]Memorandum, 27th April 1939, Refugees General Policy File, note 162 above.

would increase the quota following a decision of the New South Wales Trades and Labour Council which he considered favoured refugee immigration.[181] In the same debate Lord Noel-Buxton declared that Australia's "potential activity" in solving the refugee problem was very great.[182] In responding to these comments the newly-elected Australian Prime Minister, Robert G. Menzies, declared that the country's refugee quota was a generous one and that "it was unlikely that any extension would be made to existing arrangements."[183]

The outbreak of war in Europe in September 1939 put an effective end to refugee immigration. On 14th September, the Minister for the Interior, Senator Foll announced that the immigration of refugees from enemy countries would henceforth cease.[184] In a further statement of 22nd September he announced that refugees who had already received landing permits would still be admitted and that the cases of those temporarily resident in non-enemy countries would be considered on their merits.[185]

c) *Australian Public Opinion and the Jewish Refugees*

Until the German annexation of Austria in Spring 1938 created the prospect of a substantial Jewish immigration to Australia, public opinion was largely sympathetic toward the plight of the European Jews. It was noted that the Australian press led the world in its outcry against the Nazi boycott of 1st April 1933 and the contemporaneous anti-Jewish legislation.[186] In May 1933 a protest meeting was held at the Sydney Town Hall by the Lord Mayor and the State Premier.[187] In the same month the Presbyterian General Assembly passed a resolution of sympathy and appointed a special day of prayer for the Jews.[188] Most of these reactions occurred in the absence of any Australian familiarity with Jews or refugees. The Australian Jewish population in 1933 was only 23,553 persons, some 0.36 per cent of the total Australian population.[189] It was derived largely from British stock and was well assimilated.[190] With the arrival of the first Jewish refugees at the end of 1938 traditional xenophobia reasserted itself, often in the guise of a concern for living standards and conditions of employment.

In February 1939 the leader of the Federal Labour Opposition, J. Curtin, who had already expressed a concern that the McEwen policy should not lead to any "deterioration of economic or social standards",[191] complained that immigration was "becoming something of a flood and that is not desirable. Industrial standards must be maintained, the amount of landing money must be

[181] 113 H.L. Deb. 55, p. 1036, 5th July 1939.

[182] *Ibid.*, p. 1046.

[183] *Sydney Morning Herald*, 8th July 1939.

[184] C.P.D., vol. 161, p. 530.

[185] *Ibid.*, p. 1015.

[186] James Parkes, *Antisemitism*, London 1963, p. 96.

[187] *Sydney Morning Herald*, 19th May 1933.

[188] *Ibid.*, 23rd May 1933.

[189] See C. Price, 'Jewish Settlers in Australia 1788–1961', *Aust. Jewish Hist. Soc. Jnl.* vol. V (1964), Statistical Appendix 1.

[190] See P. Y. Medding, *From Assimilation to Group Survival*, Melbourne 1968.

[191] *C.P.D.*, vol. 158, p. 2536, 1st December 1938.

investigated further and all professional men should be subject to exacting tests before being allowed to practise in Australia".[192] In May, Senator J. S. Collings, Labour leader in the Senate declared that "if I had my way, not one foreign refugee, man or woman, would be admitted until every good Australian had been taken off the dole or relief work, and given a job under award conditions".[193] In the State legislatures similar views were expressed.

In New South Wales, the Premier raised the additional complaint that Jewish refugees were in danger of becoming a charge on the State[194] and the Sydney department store, David Jones, was reprimanded in State Parliament for allegedly dismissing six Australian employees to assist foreign refugees.[195] In the Victorian Parliament the opposition to the refugees was directed at their alleged readiness to accept employment in sweated industries and of themselves establishing backyard industries where industrial awards were not observed. The principal incident in this "anti-sweating controversy" was a speech by Sir Frank Clarke, President of the Victorian Legislative Council to the Malvern Branch of the Australian Women's National League on 8th May 1939. Clarke fulminated:

> "Hundreds of weedy East Europeans . . . slinking, rat-faced men under five feet in height and with a chest development of about twenty inches . . . worked in backyard factories in Carlton and other localities in the North of Melbourne for two or three shillings a week pocket money and their keep."[196]

The leading Melbourne dailies gave prominence to the economic practices mentioned by Sir Frank and the Prime Minister promised to have them investigated.[197]

Most commentators agreed that Clarke's economic accusations were far too general, as J. C. Dillon, the Member for Essendon in the Victorian Legislative assembly explained, sweating existed "before there was one refugee in Australia and it had not been greatly aggravated as a result of their arrival".[198] After an inquiry, the Federal Government reported that its investigations had not substantiated Clarke's allegations.[199] The Victorian Premier and the Assistant Minister for Labour issued a joint statement declaring that their investigations had found no evidence of sweating in backyard factories.[200] Clarke's response was that it was not worth his while "engaging in a dog fight on the issue".[201] The dispute despite its groundlessness assisted in creating a generally hostile environment for the refugees.

The Melbourne *Age* sought to explain the sweating controversy on the basis of

[192] *Argus*, 9th February 1939.
[193] *C.P.D.*, vol. 159, p. 349, 16th May 1939.
[194] Stevens to Menzies, 31st July 1939. Department of the Interior (11) 1938–1977, Corresp. Files, Class 2 (Restricted Immigration) 1939–1950, Aust. Archives Office, CRS A433, Item 39/2/2197.
[195] N.S.W. *Parliamentary Debates*, vol. 158, p. 3954, 9th March 1939.
[196] *Age*, 9th May 1939; *Argus*, 9th May 1939; *Daily Telegraph*, 9th May 1939.
[197] For a detailed examination of the sweating controversy in Victoria, see U. Wiemann, *German and Austrian Refugees in Melbourne 1933–1947*, M.A., University of Melbourne, 1965, pp. 188–193.
[198] *Age*, 11th May 1939.
[199] *Argus*, 27th June 1939.
[200] *Ibid.*, 30th June 1939.
[201] *Ibid.*, 27th June 1939.

the confusion in the community between two separate categories of European migrant: the refugees from Hitler and the influx of migrants from Southern Europe.[202] Significant opponents of Jewish immigration were small business proprietors agitated at the prospect of a "flood" of competitors who would undercut them.[203]

The most successful opponents of refugee immigration were practitioners in the so-called liberal profession of medicine who lobbied both State and Federal Governments incessantly to protect their trade interests.[204] The Governments of Victoria, New South Wales, Queensland and Tasmania were induced to amend their Medical Acts to prevent the reception of refugee medical practitioners.[205] The treatment of all foreign doctors became a national issue due to the shortage of medical practitioners in country areas, but the medical lobby remained implacably opposed to them.

As with the Australian opposition to Southern European immigration the opposition to the Jewish refugees assumed a pronounced racist flavour. A letter to the *Medical Journal of Australia* warned that the refugee medical practitioners were "possessed of what may be termed Eastern European standards of ethics".[206] The inability of Jews to observe Anglo-Saxon ethical standards was also a theme of Nazi rhetoric. Similarly, it was assumed, in line with Nazi doctrine, that the arrival of the Jews would mean the monopolisation of the industries into which they moved. Allied to this were the expressed fears that Jews would move into and take over various choice areas of the cities. The final racist argument was, paradoxically, that Jewish immigration would stimulate antisemitism. As the Hon. G. Pratten observed in a speech to the New South Wales Legislative Assembly, "we all have many Jewish friends whose friendship we value" but that without any intention of suggestion from that section of the press which was counselling restraint in immigration "a real antisemitic movement is already existent. If this movement is allowed to develop as has been the case in many parts of the world, a revulsion of feeling will come about . . . directed at . . . Jewry as a whole".[207] On being requested by the Hon. A. W. McNamara to say why he picked on the Jews[208] Pratten explained that "whilst there may be many good types of Jews among the arrivals, a percentage of the wrong type have already come".[209] In adducing further details he declared that "the type of Jew at present pouring into this country has the markings of racial prejudice strongly upon him.

[202]*Age*, 12th May 1939.

[203]E.g. Business Brokers Assoc. of N.S.W. to McEwen, 2nd November 1938, Department of the Interior (11), Corresp. Files, Class 2 (Restricted Immigration) 1939–1950. European Refugees, Views of the Public re Admittance of., Aust. Archives Office, CRS A433, Item 43/2/4588.

[204]See 'Migration to Australia of German-Jewish Medical Practitioners', Department of External Affairs (11), 1921–1970, Corresp. Files, Alphabetical Series 1927–1942, Aust. Archives Office, CRS A981; Department of the Interior (11), Corresp. Files, Class 2 (Restricted Immigration) 1939–1950, Premier of New South Wales – Problem of Employment of Alien Refugees (including doctors), 1939–1940, Aust. Archives Office, CRS A433, Item 39/2/2197.

[205]See J. Barrett, 'Medicine in Australia and Refugees', *Aust. Qtly.*, vol. 12 (January 1940), pp. 14–23.

[206]*Medical Journal of Australia*, 16th December 1939.

[207]*N.S.W. Parliamentary Debates*, vol. 156, p. 2511, 8th November 1938.

[208]*Ibid.*, p. 2512.

[209]*Ibid.*

If that was not so, would the situation have grown to such alarming proportions in European countries"?[210] In an impassioned rebuttal of Pratten, the Hon. A. F. Coates expressed the hope "that we shall never again hear the argument that because a person is a Jew, and for no other reason he should be debarred from entering Australia".[211]

Enough has been said to indicate that there was a vociferous opposition to the reception of Jewish refugees. The difficult question to answer is whether this was representative of that amorphous beast: "public opinion". Certainly there were advocates of more liberal Jewish immigration but these were few in number. Most sympathetic commentators agreed that some constraints should be imposed on Jewish immigration. Typical was the reaction of the Australian Council for Civil Liberties which opposed discrimination in the selection of immigrants, but which was satisfied with the outside limit of 15,000 persons over three years. It is difficult to work out whether public opinion followed the Government initiative or whether the Government's immigration policy was an accurate reflection of popular consensus. If the Government is to be condemned, it is for adopting a too pusillanimous attitude at a time when it could have set an example of humanity and compassion.

V. EVALUATION OF AUSTRALIA'S RECORD

Quite a heated debate has developed on the question of the number of European Jews who found refuge in Australia between 1933 and 1939 and whether that figure represents a creditable achievement on the part of the Australian Government of the day. Accuracy is difficult because, as we have seen, not all the landing permits granted could be taken up by the successful applicants, also not all migrants were willing to disclose their religion. The total number of Jewish migrants registered with the A.J.W.S. in December 1941 was estimated at about 8,000[212] but this figure may have involved duplication where refugees registered in more than one State. Bishop Pilcher, Chairman of the Inter-Church Committee for the Aid to Refugees, estimated the total number of refugees in Australia, including non-Aryan Christians, as 6,500.[213] Berger estimated the total number of Jewish refugees admitted to Australia up to the outbreak of hostilities in the Pacific as 8,500.[214] This estimate is quoted by the authoritative study of Tartakower and Grossmann in 1944.[215] They also comment that only 3,000 of the 15,000 permits made available in the Minister for the Interior's December 1938 speech were taken up.[216] Wischnitzer's 1948 study gives the figure of 6,475 from 1938 to the end of the war.[217] Krieger in 1955 estimated a

[210] *Ibid.*
[211] *Ibid.*, p. 2513.
[212] G. Berger, 'Australia and the Refugees', *Aust. Qtly.*, vol. 13 (December 1941), p. 56.
[213] Quoted, *ibid.*
[214] *Ibid.*, pp. 56–57.
[215] Arie Tartakower and Kurt R. Grossmann, *The Jewish Refugees*, New York 1944, p. 326.
[216] *Ibid.*, p. 327.
[217] Mark Wischnitzer, *To Dwell in Safety. The Story of Jewish Migration Since 1800*, Philadelphia 1948, p. 294.

total of 7,100 refugees from Germany and Austria to September 1939.[218] Krieger commented that only 1,000 Jews had arrived up to July 1938 but that one half of the quota of 15,000 had arrived in Australia by the outbreak of war.[219]

Benjamin took issue with these early studies and estimated that 11,245 Jewish refugees had arrived by 31st October 1940 but, conceding that the 1947 Australian census disclosed only an increase of 9,000 Jews on 1933 figures, concluded: "Perhaps 9,000 for the period 1933 to October 1940 is fair. This would allow for failure to disclose religion at the 1947 census and for natural increase."[220] He agreed with the estimate of only 3,000 arrivals from the 15,000 quota.[221] The most comprehensive statistical analysis of Jewish settlement in Australia is that of Price who estimates a total of 3,754 Non-British Jewish males arriving in Australia between 1933 and 1940.[222] Bergman, relying on Price's estimate of the arrival between those years of 3,337 Jewish males from Germany, Austria, Czechoslovakia and Hungary estimates that with the addition of their families a figure of at least 6,500 "seems to be justified" and that "the figure of 7,500 could certainly have been reached".[223] Australia's first Immigration Minister, Arthur A. Calwell, states that "the total number of refugees admitted to Australia between the end of 1938 and 1945 was 6,475" which he explains was "8,525 short of the figure of 15,000 in three years set by the Evian agreement" (sic.).[224] In the latest reference to Australian immigration figures, Herbert A. Strauss in 1981 maintained that "By the end of 1938, 3,300 Central-European immigrants were reported for Australia and a total of 7,000 Nazi victims (of all kinds) is reported to have arrived between 1935 and 1940".[225]

The Australian response to the plight of the European Jews was described by the Minister of the Interior, in his speech of 1st December 1938, as "humanitarian" and sympathetic,[226] an assessment which has been repeated by Krieger.[227] On the other hand the *Sydney Morning Herald* felt that the quota of 15,000 "did not err on the side of generosity" and suggested that the number could have been doubled or trebled.[228] The Australian response may be compared with that of other countries. Between 1933 and October 1939 the United States received 136,000 refugees from the *Reich* and Spain.[229] However, its policy, despite rhetoric to the contrary, did not deviate from a rigid application of the national origins quota system and only in 1939 was its quota for German and

[218] S. W. Krieger, 'Resettlement in Australia', in W. Rosenstock (ed.), *Dispersion and Resettlement. The Story of the Jews from Central Europe*, London 1955, p. 27.
[219] *Ibid.*
[220] Benjamin, 'Australia and the Evian Conference', *loc. cit.*, pp. 230–231.
[221] *Ibid.*
[222] Price, 'Jewish Settlers in Australia 1788–1961', *loc. cit.*, Statistical Appendix II.
[223] G. F. J. Bergman, 'Some Statistics Concerning Migration Following the Evian Conference'. *Aust. Jewish Hist. Soc. Jnl.*, vol. V (1964), p. 338.
[224] A. A. Calwell, *Be Just and Fear Not*, Melbourne 1978, p. 101.
[225] Herbert A. Strauss, 'Jewish Emigration from Germany. Nazi Policy and Jewish Responses (II)', in *LBI Year Book XXVI* (1981), p. 389.
[226] *C.P.D.*, vol. 158, p. 2535.
[227] Krieger, *loc. cit.*, p. 27.
[228] *Sydney Morning Herald*, 20th June 1939.
[229] See M. J. Proudfoot, *European Refugees: 1939–1952*, London 1957, p. 27.

Austrian immigrants fully subscribed.[230] In the same period 50,000 refugees from the *Reich* and 6,000 from Czechoslovakia entered Great Britain.[231] Although the British Government's initial response to the refugees was "niggardly" and "sluggish", in the months following the *Anschluss* it became considerably more compassionate and even generous.[232] On the other hand much of this "generosity" may be attributed to Britain's embarrassment over its restrictive immigration policy in Palestine. The pressure brought to bear on Britain in this way may also explain the pressure which it, in turn, brought to bear on Australia to accept more refugees.

Also in the pre-war period some 40,000 refugees from the *Reich* were admitted to France; 25,000 to Belgium; 23,000 to the Netherlands and 10,000 to Switzerland.[233] These countries saw themselves as transit stations for the refugees rather than as their final destinations. The other Dominions adopted the same sort of policy as Australia toward the refugees. Until 1936 South Africa admitted some 7,000 refugees, but anti-alien and anti-Jewish agitation caused a termination of immigration.[234] Canada had raised immigration barriers at the time of the Depression and like Australia admitted only wealthy refugees, estimated at 4,000 up to the outbreak of war.[235] The restrictiveness of the Dominions stands in uneven contrast to the comparative generosity of the poorer South American nations. Argentina received 22,000 refugees and Brazil, Colombia and Mexico each 20,000.[236] An important sanctuary for stateless refugees was the International Settlement in Shanghai, where entrants did not require visas; it had received some 20,000 refugees by 1941.[237]

In a comparative assessment of the international response to Jewish emigration from Germany, Strauss maintains that "Australia, secure in its global distance from the cosmopolitan culture that created and sustained it, failed in 1938 to follow the motherland in yielding to liberal impulses . . . the November *Kristallnacht* had no repercussions 'down under' ".[238] As we have seen, the *Kristallnacht* did, in fact, bring about some liberalisation of Australian immigration policy but the allegation of illiberalism requires some closer analysis. Benjamin declared that the Australian response must be assessed not "by the admission rates of other countries where problems differed, not even by the enormous number of people then clamouring for help", but by the Australian standards of the time.[239] His conclusion is that judged by those standards, Australia accepted "a very fair intake". An evaluation of the Australian response

[230]See authorities cited in note 70 above.

[231]See Proudfoot, *op. cit.*, p. 27.

[232]The assessment of Sherman, *op. cit.*, pp. 264–267.

[233]See Sir J. Hope Simpson, *Refugees, Preliminary Report of a Survey*, London 1938, p. 52.

[234]See Tartakower and Grossmann, *op. cit.*, p. 325.

[235]See I. Arabella and H. Trooper, ' "The Line Must be Drawn Somewhere", Canada and the Jewish Refugees', *Canadian Historical Review*, vol. 60 (1979), p. 181.

[236]See Tartakower and Grossmann, *op. cit.*, pp. 263–264, 318–327.

[237]See David Krantzler, 'The Jewish Refugee Community of Shanghai, 1938–1945', *The Wiener Library Bulletin*, vol. XXVI (1972–1973), pp. 28–37.

[238]Strauss, *loc. cit.*, p. 388.

[239]Benjamin, *loc. cit.*, p. 220.

to the plight of the Jews fleeing from Nazi persecution requires some analysis of the quality of the response but even by applying a purely quantitative test it should be noted that immediately preceding the Depression the Australian Government envisaged the reception of 450,000 assisted migrants over ten years. The Jewish refugees could have been a substitute for the British migrants who were now leaving Australia at a greater rate than they were arriving.

In 1943 the Ministry of Post War Reconstruction administered a questionnaire which sought responses to the suggestion "that six million Jews now in Europe might be permitted to come to Australia".[240] Of those who responded, 19 per cent were favourable; 6 per cent indifferent and 75 per cent opposed.[241] All Jews who responded were opposed.[242] It is an interesting speculation to ask what response would have been made by Australians if the alternative plans for that six million had been known.

[240] C. Kelly, *The European Refugee in New South Wales 1938–1943*, Canberra 1943.
[241] *Ibid.*, p. 23.
[242] *Ibid.*

The Ultimate Refuge
Suicide in the Jewish Community under the Nazis

BY KONRAD KWIET

"Of all religions, Judaism counts the fewest suicides, yet in none other is education so general . . . But if the Jew manages to be both well instructed and very disinclined to suicide, it is because of the special origin of his desire for knowledge. It is a general law that religious minorities, in order to protect themselves better against the hate to which they are exposed or merely through a sort of emulation try to surpass in knowledge the population surrounding them . . . Primitive in certain respects, in others [the Jew] is an intellectual and man of culture. He thus combines the advantages of the severe discipline characteristic of small and ancient groups with the benefits of the intense culture enjoyed by our great society. He has all the intelligence of modern man without sharing his despair."

I

It was the French-Jewish sociologist Émile Durkheim who made these optimistic remarks at the turn of the century, in 1897, in his famous work *Le suicide*, which marked the beginning of the scientific study of suicide.[1] Inspired by positivism and a faith in progress, he set out to probe the relationship between society and the individual, and the social phenomenon of suicide appeared to him the ideal subject, demonstrating the need for establishing sociology as an independent academic discipline.[2] It is in this context that Durkheim's remarks about the disinclination of Jews to commit suicide have to be understood. But what may have been valid in 1900 ceased to be so a few decades later. When the National Socialists and their collaborators propagated and implemented the "final solution", Durkheim's "great societies" with their "intense culture" adopted the role of passive onlookers. Victims of persecution and extermination, the Jews no longer enjoyed any "advantages" or "benefits of the intense culture". They were driven to despair, and many took their own lives. Indeed, in the years 1933–1945 the suicide rate of German Jews rose to such heights as to take on the character of a mass phenomenon. The present study attempts to shed light on this hitherto largely neglected subject.[3]

[1]Quoted from the English translation, Emile Durkheim, *Suicide. A Study in Sociology*, London [3]1966, pp. 167 ff.

[2]See Jack D. Douglas, *The Social Meanings of Suicide*, Princeton [2]1973, pp. 16 and 64 f.

[3]This article is the expanded version of a lecture which the author delivered on 2nd April 1982 at Washington University in St. Louis, USA, and on 3rd November 1982 at the University of New South Wales in Sydney during a conference on "Perspectives on Death". The topic was treated first as the subject of an "excursus" in a study written by the present author jointly with Helmut Eschwege, *Selbstbehauptung und Widerstand. Deutsche Juden im Kampf um Existenz und Menschenwürde 1933–1945*, Hamburg 1984 (Hamburger Beiträge zur Zeitgeschichte 19).

The suicide wave of German Jews under Nazi rule is a phenomenon with an historical dimension, that is to say, there are precedents going far back into Jewish history, always connected with particular moments of crisis, persecution and despair. Flavius Josephus records the self-immolation of 960 men, women and children – voluntary death as an alternative to slavery and death at the hands of the Romans. This event left its mark, resulting in a traumatic fear, known as the Masada complex.[4] From there, the line can be followed through the High and Late Middle Ages into the modern era. It can be shown that suicides on a mass scale occurred during the persecutions occasioned by the Crusades, the Black Death, the expulsions from Spain and Portugal and the pogroms of the Chmelnicki uprisings in Eastern Europe. There is no saying if, and to what extent, memories of those acts of despair and religious fervour were still alive in Jewish communities of the twentieth century. We can assume, however, that the modern secularised Jew in Central Europe would scarcely have been impelled to suicidal behaviour by such distant historical precedents.

The same consideration is likely to apply to the force of religious tradition. Whether, and to what extent, suicide is a transgression against Jewish law is a question that must be left to the judgement of religious scholars and rabbis who discussed this age-old problem over the centuries in a prolonged debate that has lost none of its relevance. The issue comes to the fore whenever a decision must be made whether or not to grant a Jewish suicide burial in a Jewish cemetery. It would appear that suicide is not explicitly forbidden either in the Bible or in the Talmud.[5] It was only in post-talmudic times, when Jewish law became codified in the *Halachah* that suicide came to be regarded as a punishable act, as a crime against God in the light of Genesis IX: 5 where it is said that human life is in the hand of God alone. Later, the decision to punish suicide as a heinous sin, even worse than murder, came to be taken at a juncture when the Christian Church, too, adopted its stand against suicide. Verdicts to that effect were pronounced by Fathers of the Church in late antiquity and by the Church Councils of the early Middle Ages. In Jewish tradition, however, we find a narrowly defined list of exceptions in which suicide is not condemned, and it is certainly no accident that these cases were discussed in conjunction with the issue of "idol worship". Thus Jews are allowed to let themselves be killed or commit suicide when it is done to avoid being forced to embrace another religion or to commit murder or incest. In this way post-talmudic authorities drew a clear dividing line between suicide and martyrdom, which in certain circumstances was praised as the highest form of *mitzvah*, and the historical examples of suicide clearly fell into this category. We shall return to the religious tradition at the end of this study.

How far, if at all, the suicides of Jews – or other minorities[6] – at times of crisis and persecution can be understood in terms of the modern science of suicideology

[4]Flavius Josephus, *Der Jüdische Krieg*, Munich 1921, pp. 515 ff. See also Y. Yadin, *Masada, Herod's Fortress and the Zealots' Last Stand*, London 1967, pp. 232 f.

[5]Cf. *Encyclopaedia Judaica*, vol. 15, [4]1978, pp. 489–491.

[6]Little is known about suicides by members of other persecuted groups in the Third *Reich*. Repeated references to suicides, especially by detained Communist resistance fighters, can be found in the sources.

with its theories of suicide and aggression is a question that must be left to sociologists, psychologists, psychoanalysts and medical scholars. What I, as a layman in this field, have been able to gather from the immense and controversial literature on the subject[7] suggests that there is no single causal explanation of suicide, but rather a complex web of many related factors. It appears to be generally agreed that – as Durkheim was the first to emphasise – the social context, including the social life history of the individual, has to be taken into consideration. The concern of this study, however, is not to test the validity of current theories of suicide but to present a brief historical account of the suicidal behaviour of German Jews and throw light on the factors motivating such behaviour. To this end we have to place the waves of suicides prompted by Nazi persecution within the context of the general pattern of behaviour. This raises the question of classification.

It has been argued by some authors, especially in the context of the contemporary history of the Netherlands, that suicides of Jews during the holocaust should be regarded as acts of resistance.[8] This point of view encountered considerable opposition and has not been widely accepted. My own point of departure is the recognition that Jews, both individually and collectively, developed a variety of strategies of defence and survival, strategies that were determined by tradition as well as by the prevailing social and personal circumstances.[9] The strategies varied in form and intensity, ranging from emigration, accommodation and collaboration to protest, escape attempts, politically organised resistance and suicide. These basic responses can be divided into two types: conformist and non-conformist behaviour. All modes of behaviour directed to obeying Nazi orders may be regarded as conformist. Or, to put it differently: the National Socialists decreed norms of behaviour for the Jews in keeping with the aims envisaged at various times in the past by official policies or political programmes concerned with the status of the Jews. According to National Socialist expectations reinforced by terror, the Jews were meekly to accept defamation, exclusion, expulsion and eventually deportation and annihilation. That was the meaning of conforming behaviour. Any deviation from this norm was interpreted as a threat to the Nazi regime. As non-conformist we may therefore classify all modes of behaviour designed to work against the regime's ideology and policies. Oppositional non-conformism of this kind certainly represented a "deviation from the prescribed model" and can be defined as resistance in the broader sense, as distinct from resistance in the narrow sense, which was politically organised, that is to say, it was backed by a political programme and a political organisation striving for clarity and seeking to reach and mobilise sections of the population in order to bring about change and overthrow the regime. If these definitions are adopted, then clearly suicide

[7]Among the recent literature on the subject the following may be mentioned, in addition to Douglas, *op. cit.*: C. L. Halton, Sh. McBride Valente and A. Rink, *Suicide. Assessment and Intervention*, New York 1977, and C. Reimer (ed.), *Suicid. Ergebnisse und Therapie*, Berlin – Heidelberg – New York 1982.

[8]Coen J. E. Stuldreher, 'Samen alleen', in *Bericht van de Tweede Wereldoorlog* 54 (1971), pp. 1489 f.

[9]See Konrad Kwiet, 'Problems of Jewish Resistance Historiography' in *LBI Year Book XXIV* (1979), pp. 37–57.

constitutes a "deviation from the prescribed model". Suicide was the ultimate and most radical attempt to elude Nazi terror. And there can be no doubt: Jewish suicides did interfere with the smooth technical-bureaucratic process of exclusion and extermination. This transgression – which can be described as resistance – was not tolerated. The Nazis sought to prevent Jewish suicides. Wherever Jews tried to kill themselves – in their homes, in hospitals, on the deportation trains, in the concentration camps – the Nazi authorities would invariably intervene in order to save the Jews' lives, wait for them to recover, and then send them to their prescribed deaths.

The description and interpretation of suicide – and this brings us to the last problem area – is severely hampered by the inadequacy of the documentary evidence. The data, fragmentary and hardly verifiable as they are, can be used only with great caution. The official German statistics on suicide, initiated in 1893 as part of the record of causes of death, make no distinction between Jews and non-Jews, so that comparable frequencies cannot be established.[10] For the Second World War the figures are missing altogether. They were collected, but for propaganda reasons not published at the time and must now be regarded as lost. No statistical data on Jewish suicides are available at the West German Federal Office of Statistics.[11] Evidence of suicides among Jews after 1933 can be found in numerous Nazi documents, in contemporary reports, in later testimonies and in some historical works. Yet, these data – in so far as they were accessible to me – do not add up to a comprehensive picture of the suicidal propensity of the German Jews, so that we are unable to make reliable quantitative statements concerning total numbers, motives and social structure. The scattered data available can be compared to the minute pieces of a mosaic, allowing us to reconstruct trends, to make quantitative estimates, to illustrate individual cases and propose a number of hypotheses. An extension of the data base would have required intensive and time-consuming searches which it was not possible to undertake within the scope of the present study, searches concentrating on the records of physicians, hospitals, cemeteries and indemnification offices rather than on the remnants of National Socialist official records. As regards the period prior to 1933, no attempt was made to go beyond the published data, including the official statistics of causes of death of those German constituent states that classified suicides according to religious denomination. The earliest, by no means complete, records of suicides were compiled in the German states in the first half of the nineteenth century, at first using rather unwieldy methods. As the statistical offices came to be established, they received the data collected by the ecclesiastical, police and administrative authorities.

[10]The author wishes to thank the Federal Office of Statistics in Wiesbaden for placing at his disposal a copy of the survey of 'Selbstmorde im Deutschen Reich 1893 bis 1939 bzw. im Bundesgebiet 1946 bis 1980'.

[11]Letter of the Federal Office of Statistics to the author, dated 31st May 1979.

II

If we accept the proposition that the suicide rate within a social group varies in inverse proportion to the degree of its integration,[12] it follows in particular that the suicide rate of German Jews should reflect the trend towards social integration, or conversely towards isolation. Hence it will be useful, before entering upon a survey of conditions during the Nazi era, to outline the development over the preceding hundred years, beginning with the middle of the nineteenth century, at a point when the Jews in Germany had taken the first steps on the path of social integration, but had not yet won equality of legal status. During that period, up to the eve of civic emancipation, the suicide rate among German Jews, with the exception of Bavaria, was lower than among Protestants or Catholics. After that, however, the picture changed very rapidly. Under the Second *Reich* all three religious communities recorded higher suicide rates. But after the granting of civic rights, the increase was disproportionately higher among Jews than among Christians. Before long, the Jewish suicide rate outstripped first the Protestant, then the Catholic rate, thus rising from bottom to top place, well before the outbreak of the First World War. Table I illustrates the changes recorded during the second half of the nineteenth century.

The trend established in Imperial Germany continued under the Weimar Republic. The overall figures dropped temporarily between 1914 and 1918, as is generally the case in war-time,[13] but a closer look at the statistics reveals that this decline was confined to the two main Christian groups, whereas the Jewish suicide rate showed little change. The residual fourth group – in which non-believers and persons of unknown religious affiliation are lumped together – was characterised by erratic fluctuations. These two groups continued to deviate from the norm during the early years of the Weimar Republic, when the suicide rate increased markedly faster among Jews and the residual group than among the two main Christian communities. Jewish suicides in Prussia rose from 161 in 1919 to 204 in 1926, out of a Jewish population of some 400,000. The residual group registered an increase during the same period from 257 to 635 suicides. Table II illustrates the development in Prussia up till 1926, and Table III gives a detailed breakdown for the year 1925, when the Jewish suicide rate in Prussia was 53.2 per 100,000, followed by the non-religious group with 49.9, and far behind by the Christian communities. This picture can be considered representative of the period, except for the relative position of the Jewish and unattached groups, which was liable to fluctuate from year to year.

Among the major German cities the highest suicide rates were recorded in Berlin. The detailed figures given in Table IV show that in Greater Berlin the Jewish suicide rate increased dramatically from 1922 to 1925, rising from a point below the average figure for the whole population of the city to a level substantially above it. The same trend can be illustrated by a different set of data: in 1925 the 172,679 Jews counted in Greater Berlin represented 4·3 per cent of the

[12]Douglas, *op. cit.*, p. 34.

[13]Cf. Ulrich Linse, 'Das wahre Zeugnis. Eine psychohistorische Deutung des Ersten Weltkriegs', in Klaus Vondung (ed.) *Kriegserlebnis*, Göttingen 1980, p. 103.

TABLE I

Suicides (per 100,000) in selected German States according to Religion

	Protestants	*Catholics*	*Jews*
Prussia			
1849–1855	15·9	4·9	4·6
1869–1872	18·7	6·9	9·6
1890	24·0	10·0	18·0
1911	26·1	10·8	31·5
1921–1924	24·6	10·7	39·6
1925	27·9	13·5	53·2
1926	29·4	14·8	50·5
Bavaria			
1844–1856	13·5	4·9	10·5
1884–1891	22·4	9·4	19·3
1901–1910	22·6	10·5	27·1
Baden			
1852–1862	13·9	11·7	8·7
1870–1874	17·1	13·6	12·4
1874–1888	24·2	17·0	21·0
1906–1912	27·8	16·0	33·1
Württemberg			
1846–1860	11·3	7·7	6·5
1873–1876	19·0	12·0	6·0
1881–1890	17·0	11·9	14·2
1908–1912	21·0	11·7	25·0
Saxony			
1908–1910	30·9	38·1	42·1

Sources: Durkheim, *op. cit.*, p. 154; *Handwörterbuch der Staatswissenschaft*, vol. 7, [4]1926, p. 444; *Zeitschrift des preußischen Statistischen Landesamts*, 67 (1928), and 68 (1929); Arthur Ruppin, *Soziologie der Juden*, vol. 1, Berlin 1930, pp. 246 f.; Max Sichel, 'Der Selbstmord bei den Juden – einst und jetzt', *Zeitschrift für Demographie und Statistik der Juden*, 1 (1924), No. 5/6, pp. 91–107, here pp. 93 f.

total population of the *Reich* capital. By comparison, the number of Jewish suicides as a proportion of all suicides in Greater Berlin rose from some 3 per cent in 1922 to 6·6 per cent in 1925.[14]

The Jewish suicide rate in Berlin in the mid 1920s was remarkably high by comparison with major cities outside Germany also. As can be seen in Table V,

[14]The departure from the norm is also documented for Frankfurt a. Main. Out of 1,054 suicides which came to the notice of the authorities in the years 1914–1923, 86 were committed by Jews, a proportion of 8·2 per cent, whereas, according to the census of 1910 Jews accounted for only 6·3 per cent of the population. The situation in Frankfurt was investigated by Sichel, *loc. cit.* (Table I).

TABLE II

Suicides in Prussia

			Protestants	*Catholics*	*Jews*	*Others**	*Deutsches Reich*	
1896	6497	(20·5)	5140	1059	81	217	10888	(20·6)
1913	9178	(22·2)	7073	1740	133	232	15664	(23·2)
1914	8770	(20·8)	6774	1573	171	252	14773	(21·8)
1915	6776	(16·1)	5180	1273	140	182	11260	(16.6)
1916	6904	(16·4)	5241	1239	147	277	11748	(17·3)
1917	6426	(15·1)	5028	1105	131	162	10734	(16·4)
1918	6120	(14·4)	4782	1009	135	194	10159	(15·7)
1919	6784	(17·2)	5293	1073	161	257	11555	(18·4)
1920	7964	(20·7)	6067	1280	167	328	13729	(21·7)
1921	7559	(19·9)	5737	1215	150	457	12729	(20·6)
1922	8022	(21·4)	6060	1275	133	557	13317	(21·8)
1923	7863	(20·9)	6063	1191	152	457	13148	(21·3)
1924	8590	(22·6)	6540	1426	205	419	14338	(23·1)
1925	9164	(24·1)	6792	1613	215	484	15273	(24·5)
1926	9746	(25·3)	7155	1767	204	635	16480	(26·2)

* Non-believers and those of unknown religious affiliation.

Source: *Statistisches Jahrbuch für den Freistaat Preußen*, 22 (1926), pp. 50 f.; various years of *Statistiken des Deutschen Reiches*, and *Vierteljahrshefte zur Statistik des Deutschen Reiches*.

TABLE III

Suicides in Prussia 1925 according to Religion

	total	*male*	*female*	*per 100,000 Prussia*	*Berlin*
Protestants	6,792	4,780	2,012	27·9	42·3
Catholics	1,613	1,247	366	13·5	31·7
Other Christians	60	43	17	13·3	18·1
Jews	215	136	79	53·2	67·8
Unknown/non-believers	484	392	92	49·9	53·8
Total population of Prussia	38,120,000				
Jews	404,000	(1·06%)			

Source: *Zeitschrift des preußischen Statistischen Landesamts*, 67 (1928), p. 481.

TABLE IV

Suicides in Berlin
(as from 1921 Greater Berlin)

	total	*per 100 000*	*of which Jews*	*per 100 000*
1895	480	28.8		
1905	708	34.9		
1913	811	38.5	Not possible to check	
1914	780	36.6		
1915	607	28.6		
1916	622	29.5		
1921	1353	35.2		
1922	1685	43.9	61	31.7
1923	1666	43.5	72	41.7
1924	1730	45.4	96	55.5
1925	1730	45.4	117	67.8
1926	1890	46.9		
1927	1798	44.7		
1928	1659	41.3		
1929	1823			
1930	2024			
1931	2083		Not possible to check	
1932	1908			
1933	2262			

Source: *Statistik des Deutschen Reiches*, Bd. 275, p. 171; Bd. 276, p. 393; Bd. 307, p. 57; *Vierteljahrshefte zur Statistik des Deutschen Reiches*, 8 (1899); 16 (1907); *Statistisches Jahrbuch für das Deutsche Reich*, 45 (1926); *Statistisches Jahrbuch für den Freistaat Preussen*, 29 (1933); *Zeitschrift des preussischen Statistischen Landesamt*, 67 (1928); 68 (1929); 69 (1930); *Statistische Taschenbücher der Stadt Berlin.*

Jewish suicide rates in four Central and East European cities as well as in New York were well below the Berlin figure, and – with the exception of Vienna – also considerably lower than the corresponding figures for Christians, with the exception of Protestants in Budapest who equalled the Berlin Jewish suicide rate. However, the highest rate by far was scored by the Christian population of the USA.

The rising trend of Jewish suicides in Germany, and above all in Berlin, caused alarm among Jewish representatives and organisations. Towards the end of 1925 a debate on this problem was initiated, in the course of which reference was made for the first time to a "suicide epidemic among German Jews". The section for economic statistics of a *Jüdisches Wissenschaftliches Institut* in Berlin was prompted to embark on an investigation of the Jewish propensity to suicide.[15] Newspapers

[15] *Jüdische Rundschau*, 21st October 1927, p. 594. It was not possible to trace this investigation the results of which, however, have been evaluated by Ruppin, *op. cit.*, pp. 246 f. Ruppin's figures for a number of foreign cities are given in Table V below.

TABLE V

Suicides in major Cities (per 100,000)

		Protestants		*Catholics*	*Jews*
Berlin	1925	45		32	68
Lodz	1923/25 per annum		14		7
	1927		24		13
Warsaw	1925		35		18
	1927		44		17
Vienna	1926		46		51
	1927		48		41
Budapest	1925	68		53	48
New York	1925		(79*)		23

* This figure applies to the whole of the USA in 1923.
Source: Ruppin, *op. cit.*, pp. 247 f.

and periodicals carried reports and commentaries. Fritz Salomon devoted his leading article in *Der Schild* of 11th December 1925 to this problem under the heading 'Appalling Suicide Figures. The Fairy Tale of the Rich Jews'. Meetings were organised. Early in 1926 the seven Berlin Lodges of the *B'nai B'rith* called an anti-suicide rally. According to the report in *Jüdische Rundschau*,[16] "the Temple was filled with a capacity crowd". In his address, Fritz Kahn, President of the Jehuda Halevi Lodge, interpreted the suicides as an indication of a process of disintegration that was besetting German Jewry. " 'We must indict ourselves', he said, 'because we connived at the development in our German fatherland of a Jewishness without Judaism, which can offer no moral support to the losers, to those in the grip of despair.' In conclusion Dr. Kahn called for an all-out effort in order to raise the level of Jewish awareness and assist the victims of penury and persecution." The next speaker was Leo Baeck. He, too, warned against any tendency to condemn those who had committed suicide, and went on to present moral-religious guidelines for a defensive strategy. "After profound and closely argued remarks about the ethical personality which alone can give a meaningful shape to life, Dr. Baeck arrived at the following conclusion: drawing on your own resources to impart value and purpose to life – that is the essence of being Jewish." Hans Goslar, on behalf of religious-Orthodox Zionism, castigated the "social conceit of many Jews". He called for more love of one's neighbour and solidarity, and demanded that greater efforts should be made in organising Jewish welfare and credit assistance. Ludwig Holländer, the Director of the *Centralverein*, put forward some further suggestions on how to bring down the incidence of suicide, which were referred to the appropriate bodies "for discussion and implementation".

[16] *Jüdische Rundschau*, 9th February 1926, p. 85.

Two months before, the C.V. had already gone into action by launching an appeal for a "relief campaign on the largest possible scale", in order to counter the worsening "plight of the Jewish middle income groups" and "forestall new misery . . . and new suicides". The effect in practical terms – if any – which all the appeals and relief measures may have had on the Jewish suicide rate is hard to assess in the absence of relevant statistical data. It appears that from 1927 on German suicide statistics were no longer broken down according to religious affiliation. The general suicide figures, in any case, continued to rise after 1926/1927.[17] The effects of the world economic crisis, which in 1929 brought the Weimar Republic's phase of economic stabilisation to an abrupt end, were reflected in a rising suicide rate which, it may be assumed, affected the Jews no less than the rest of the population.

The statistical data on suicide in Imperial Germany and the Weimar Republic reveal rising suicide rates among all groups, the religious communities as well as those without religious affiliation, however with the Jewish graph deviating significantly from the non-Jewish trend. The denominational suicide statistics make these deviations and distinctions manifest, but cannot explain them.

With their entry and rapid rise into the German middle class, the Jews embraced the corresponding middle-class values and life-style: the marriage age rose, fewer marriages were contracted, the birth rate fell, life expectancy increased. It is known that marital and social status, number of children and age structure all have a bearing on the incidence of suicide. Moreover, the initial stage of embourgeoisement involved a large-scale Jewish migration from rural environments into the towns, a transplantation which also promoted suicidal tendencies. The occupational structure – with Jews dominant in trade and commerce and the liberal professions – tended in the same direction. It was in particular the economic involvement of Jews at all levels of the economy that rendered them vulnerable, and more so than ever at times of crisis. In October and November 1925 – that is, at a time of relative economic stability – 16 Jewish suicides were recorded in Berlin, nine of which were attributed to economic distress. Eight of these nine were men, and the police reports gave their occupations as follows: 3 merchants, 1 factory owner, 1 banker, 1 coffee house proprietor, 1 itinerant trader, 1 manual worker.[18]

Finally, the old cultural and religious ties, which for centuries had been a vital means of protection were largely abandoned. The privilege of entry into German society was granted at a price, and that price was the abandonment of the Jewish identity. During the period of emancipation this demand was made from the outset, and the vast majority of German Jews complied. Religion was declared *Privatsache*, a private concern, Jews became "German citizens of the Jewish faith", who went out of their way to proclaim their loyalty and proud allegiance to the German "fatherland". The disintegration of the former homogeneous and solid group structure, together with the process of growing into the non-Jewish society, itself in the throes of modernisation and social change, gave rise to psychological

[17] *C.V.-Zeitung*, 27th November 1925, p. 755; and cf. Table II above.
[18] Salomon, *loc. cit.* See above p. 143.

disturbances. In the 1920s several observers, among them the physician Max Sichel,[19] held that of all attempts to explain the high Jewish suicide rate, "most likely to carry conviction is the one that takes account of the peculiar Jewish character". According to Sichel, "Jews are especially susceptible to the psychological disorders that are known to be accompanied by suicidal tendencies, notably constitutionally conditioned melancholia, middle-age depressions, many psychopathic disorders with a depressive element as well as personality patterns characterised by a precarious psychological equilibrium".

Arthur Ruppin included in his work on the sociology of the Jews a section on suicide,[20] in which he accepted the psychological interpretation, while leaving open the question as to whether Jewish susceptibility was hereditary – due in Sichel's words to a "congenital morbid disposition" – or rather the result of social pressures.

However that may be, in the eyes of the vast majority of German Jews the Wilhelminian Empire marked a period of social betterment and economic success. The faith in the German-Jewish "symbiosis" lived on in the Weimar Republic. Yet, underneath the surface of these conscious beliefs a mood of crisis began to spread. The socio-cultural effects of assimilation could not be overlooked. A declining birth rate and aging population, defections from Jewish congregations, conversions and mixed marriages gave cause for laments and pessimistic forecasts. Even before the outbreak of the First World War there was talk of the "disintegration" and "doom" of German Jewry. The growth of antisemitism intensified the mood of insecurity, and with the decay of liberalism during the last phase of the Weimar Republic the majority of German Jews lost what was their political home, while inflation and economic crisis threatened and destroyed the livelihood of many. All these symptoms of crisis reinforced an atmosphere of apprehension. As Monika Richarz put it: "The Jewish bourgeoisie felt economically threatened and at the same time politically and socially isolated."[21]

One would expect this distinctive situation of the German Jews to be reflected in their suicide rate. Indeed, the deviations of the Jewish from the national suicide curve seem to indicate that the Jews' adjustment to German society and their integration were never complete. In entering society, the Jews had moved predominantly into the ranks of the bourgeoisie, into the towns, and into occupations in the fields of commerce and the professions. But in doing so, they had developed a social structure and vocational pattern that set them apart from the rest of the population. As a result, they were over and over again singled out for attack. As an urbanised middle-class section of the population, their suicide rate was naturally higher than the national average. Whether the gap would have progressively narrowed with the passage of time – as has frequently been asserted – must remain an open question. So much is certain that assimilated Jews had to face particularly heavy odds in the struggle for a secure existence and

[19] Sichel, *loc. cit.*, p. 107.
[20] Ruppin, *op. cit.*, p. 245.
[21] Monika Richarz, *Jüdisches Leben in Deutschland*, III, *Selbstzeugnisse zur Sozialgeschichte 1918–1945*, Stuttgart 1982, Veröffentlichung des Leo Baeck Instituts, p. 14.

social recognition. Proceeding from this insight, we may conclude with Donald Niewyk that "the deeply wounded self-esteem of declassed German Jews was a more significant cause of suicide than anti-Semitism per se".[22]

III

A new "era" began when both the bourgeoisie and the organised labour movement forsook the political scene, and the Jews thus lost the two social forces that at one time had promoted and supported their emancipation. When the Nazis took control in 1933, they declared antisemitism a state doctrine and lost no time in taking action on the old slogans for a Germany rid of Jews. During the first years of the Third *Reich*, the anti-Jewish programme was implemented in public and by traditional means, that is to say, by moral defamation, social segregation and expulsion. During the Second World War the work was continued in secret by organised mass murder. Both in Germany and abroad the predominant reaction of society to these events was one of apathy and silence. Germany's Jews became aware of their growing isolation. The various stages of this process of intensifying persecution accompanied by the collapse of the German-Jewish symbiosis and the failure of international solidarity were reflected in the Jewish suicide figures.

It is worth noting in this context that the national suicide rate was not affected by the change of regime but continued after 1933 at the high levels recorded during the closing years of the Weimar Republic, a social continuity vividly demonstrating that the slogans of "national revolution" and *Volksgemeinschaft* were not enough to build a social order in which fewer people were driven to take their own lives. In the so-called "peacetime years" of the Third *Reich* 117,818 persons killed themselves (as shown in Table VI). The suicide rate per 100,000 inhabitants varied in those years between 28·0 and 28·9, more than twice the British suicide rate (12·4 in 1936).[23]

The picture presented by the incidence of suicide among the Jews stands in stark contrast to the national trend. It would be possible to reconstruct a Jewish suicide curve which documents the close correlation between persecution and suicide. The peaks of such a graph would be shown to coincide successively with the anti-Jewish boycott proclaimed after the National Socialist accession to power, the annexation of Austria, the *Kristallnacht* pogroms of November 1938, and finally the deportations of 1942 and 1943.* Precise numerical data are not available, but estimates based on the extant evidence suggest that roughly 10,000 German Jews and persons of Jewish descent committed suicide or made suicide attempts under Nazi rule. The first antisemitic terror wave reached its peak with the notorious "Jew boycott" of 1st April 1933. The first measures of organised persecution had a profound effect on Jewish morale. Defamation and isolation,

[22]Donald L. Niewyk, *The Jews in Weimar Germany*, Baton Rouge-London 1980, p. 20.

[23]Richard Grunberger, *Das zwölfjährige Reich. Der Deutschen Alltag unter Hitler*, Wien – München – Zürich 1972, p. 236 (English original edition: *A Social History of the Third Reich*, London 1971).

* On the deportations see also the essay by Henry Friedlander, 'The Deportation of the German Jews. Post-War Trials of Nazi Criminals', in this section of the current volume of the Year Book – (Ed.).

TABLE VI

Suicides in the Third Reich (1933–1939)

	numbers			per 100,000 inhabitants		
year	*total*	*male*	*female*	*total*	*male*	*female*
1933	18,723	13,104	5,619	28·7	41·4	16·8
1934	18,801	13,335	5,466	28·7	41·7	16·8
1935	18,422	12,878	5,544	28·6	40·7	15·7
1936	19,288	13,443	5,845	28·6	40·9	17·9
1937	19,614	13,687	5,927	28·9	41·3	16·8
1938	19,415	13,364	6,051	28·0	39·4	17·1
1939	22,278	15,245	7,053	28·1	39·3	17·3
1939/1945			*No data available*			

Source: Statistisches Bundesamt Abt. VII D–*Selbstmorde im Deutschen Reich 1893 bis 1939 bzw. im Bundesgebiet 1946 bis 1980.*

physical violence, arrests and dismissals from the civil service drove many Jews to suicide. At Weißensee, one of three Jewish cemeteries in Berlin, 77 suicides were buried in 1933.[24] Newspapers and books published by Jewish exiles spread the news of a suicide wave. The highest figures were recorded in April and May 1933. It is likely that between 300 and 400 Jews took their own lives in response to the anti-Jewish boycott. The swelling numbers of suicides elicited a joint appeal for courage and endurance from the *Rabbinerkonferenz* and representatives of the Jewish community.[25]

One such Jewish suicide was taken up by Nazi propaganda in a disgustingly triumphant manner. In the summer of 1933 Fritz Rosenfelder committed suicide at Bad Cannstadt, leaving behind a farewell letter. A local Nazi propaganda sheet published the letter in full and appended its own comment.[26] The letter ran as follows:

> "My dear friends, Herewith my last farewell. A German Jew had been unable to go on living with the knowledge that the movement to which national Germany is looking for salvation considers him a traitor to the fatherland. I leave without hate or anger. One fervent wish is uppermost in my mind: may reason assert itself before long. But until that happens I am debarred from any activity in keeping with my sentiments, and so I have chosen a voluntary death in order to shock my Christian friends into awareness. This step of mine may reveal to you what we German Jews are feeling and thinking today. How much I would have preferred to lay down my life for my fatherland. Do not mourn me, but endeavour to enlighten the people and to make sure that truth shall prevail in the end. In this way you will render me the greatest honour. Yours, Fritz."

[24]Martin Riesenburger, *Das Licht verlöschte nicht*, Berlin 1960, p. 39.

[25]E.g. L. Feuchtwanger (ed.), *Der gelbe Fleck. Die Ausrottung von 500 000 deutschen Juden*, Paris 1936, pp. 261–266. Some of the suicides mentioned in this book appear in two lists of suicides compiled in exile in October 1935 and October 1936. See Wiener Library PC III, Reel 33/34. For a quotation of the appeal see Herbert Freeden 'Anfang vom Ende der deutschen Judenheit', in *Allgemeine*, 4th March 1983, p. 18.

[26]*NSDAP Nachrichtendienst*, Ortsgruppe Duisburg Neudorf-Nord, August 1933, Wiener Library, Germany Suicides and Executions, IV A 30.

And this is the comment of the *NSDAP Nachrichtendienst*:

> "If the Jew Fritz Rosenfelder believed that his words would induce the Germans to change their attitude to the Jewish race, then he has died in vain. But now that he is dead, we in turn think of him 'without hate or anger'. On the contrary, we are pleased with him and have no objection if his racial brethren adopt the same method of taking leave. For when that happens, then indeed 'reason will have asserted itself in Germany', and the Jewish Question will have been solved in a straightforward and peaceful manner. We shall then be ready to march behind the coffins of the departed and to fire three thundering gun salutes into the air in honour of Yaveh . . ."

After the shock of the "Jew boycott" the pressure of persecution eased to some extent and the suicide curve went down again. The fact that this tendency continued even after the promulgation of the Nuremberg Laws in September 1935 supports the theory that this historic turning point was perceived at the time less as a "threat" but rather as a "clarification" of the social and judicial position, as is shown by the official statements of some representatives of German Jewry.[27] Yet, at the level of every-day life the persecution continued, operating chiefly through the methods of defamation and exclusion, which drove more Jews to suicide. In Mannheim 85 Jews were buried between 1st June 1934 and 1st November 1936. According to Rabbi Geis, eleven of them had taken their own lives for "political reasons".[28] In the autumn of 1937 the Berlin Jewish community published a study on deaths in the community which included a survey of suicides. It showed that the Jewish suicide rate had risen further since the 1920s and had reached in 1932–1934 a figure of 70·2 per 100,000, as compared with the non-Jewish suicide rate of 48·8. The Gestapo intervened, however, and the suicide statistics had to be removed from the study.[29]

The suicide graph rose very rapidly again in March 1938. The Nazis followed the occupation of Austria with a vehement campaign of defamation, arrests and exclusion, which shook the large Jewish community in Vienna to its foundations. The persecutions and suicides provided headlines for the foreign press. The *Jewish Chronicle* of 25th March 1938 spoke of 1,700 Jewish suicides. Four days later, in a speech to members of the NSDAP Joseph Goebbels had this to say about foreign press reports:

> "When one hears of foreign press reports these days, one gets the impression that a few thousand Jews are hanging or shooting or poisoning themselves in Vienna every day. Actually there are no more suicides in Vienna than before, with the difference, however, that in the past only Germans shot themselves, now there are Jews doing it, too."[30]

Neither Goebbels nor the *Jewish Chronicle* painted an accurate picture. According

[27]See Abraham Margaliot, 'The Reaction of the Jewish Public in Germany to the Nuremberg Laws', in *Yad Vashem Studies*, XII (1977), pp. 75–107, and 'The Dispute over the Leadership of German Jewry (1933–1938), *ibid.*, X (1974), pp. 129–148.

[28]Hans-Joachim Fliedner, *Die Judenverfolgung in Mannheim 1933–1945*, 2 vols., Stuttgart 1971, here vol. 1, p. 77, note 55.

[29]The author has been unsuccessful in tracing this investigation. References to it can be found in a Dutch report of *Joodse Perscommissie voor byzondere Berichtgeving*, 3rd November 1937, Wiener Library, PC 3, 156.

[30]Quoted by Herbert Rosenkranz, *Verfolgung und Selbstbehauptung. Die Juden in Österreich 1933–1945*, Vienna 1978, p. 40.

to official Austrian suicide statistics, the figures for Jews and non-Jews were as shown in Table VII:[31]

TABLE VII

1938	*January*	*February*	*March*	*April*
Non-Jews	88	62	213	138
Jews	5	4	79	62

Herbert Rosenkranz points out that nearly all the suicides were carried out quietly and inconspicuously.[32] An aged professor of paedriatrics wrote in a farewell letter: "I have saved the lives of 60,000 children, now I have to take my own." Rosenkranz classifies as a "violent protest" the suicide of one Jew, who rushed into a Vienna coffee-house screaming "Heil Hitler", then cutting his throat before the eyes of the customers. That was the only incident of its kind on record. During the following weeks the suicide figures did not drop; in the words of Sir John Hope Simpson: "The way out for many in Vienna was not emigration but suicide."[33]

A few months later the synagogues in Germany and Austria were set alight; shops and flats were destroyed and looted; Jews were insulted, maltreated and killed. About 30,000 Jews were taken to the concentration camps. Steps were taken to make the exclusion of Jews from all economic activities complete, and the pressure intended to drive them out of the country altogether was stepped up. Against the background of the November pogroms suicide figures rose again. The sum total was probably between 300 and 500. Reports came from all regions. To mention a few examples, five Jewish suicides were recorded in Düsseldorf,[34] ten in Nuremberg,[35] while the Mayor of Ingolstadt reported on 1st December 1938: "The operations mounted against the Jews were carried out speedily and without major frictions. In the course of these measures one Jewish married couple drowned themselves in the Danube".[36] From Bad Reichenhall it was reported:

> ". . . On 13th December 1938, the Jewess Klara Dapper, 67, widow of an actor, formerly of Bayerisch Gmain, poisoned herself with Veronal, because during the night of 12th to 13th December 1938 a notice had been affixed to her front door by persons so far unknown, saying: 'Out with all the Jews, at long last'. Dapper lived in a house in Bayerisch Gmain, which she owned. Bayerisch Gmain is now free of Jews . . ."[37]

[31] *Ibid.*
[32] *Ibid.*, p. 41.
[33] John Hope Simpson, *The Refugee Problem*, London 1939, p. 126. Cf. also *Black Book. The Nazi Crimes against the Jewish People*, New York 1946, pp. 128 f.
[34] Kurt Düwell, *Die Rheingebiete in der Judenverfolgung des Nationalsozialismus vor 1942*, Bonn 1968, p. 183.
[35] Arnd Müller, *Geschichte der Juden in Nürnberg 1146–1945*, Nuremberg 1968, p. 243.
[36] Martin Broszat *et al.* (eds.), *Bayern in der NS-Zeit*, vol. 1, *Soziale Lage und politisches Verhalten der Bevölkerung im Spiegel vertraulicher Berichte*, München-Wien 1977, p. 471.
[37] *Ibid.*, p. 476.

What this report concealed, or rather falsified, was the fact that the notice had actually been pinned to Klara Dapper's door three days earlier than stated, during the night from 9th to 10th December, that she had taken the overdose on the following day, that she was left lying unconscious for three days, and that during that time several doctors in nearby Bad Reichenhall refused to attend her. The circumstances prompted the police to initiate an investigation. The resulting report stated:

> "It has been ascertained that she (Klara Dapper) seceded from the Jewish community in 1907. She was deeply disturbed by the measures recently taken against the Jews, and lived in a state of some apprehension that some day she might come to harm, and she stated repeatedly that she would not leave her villa alive if she were to be forced to go . . ."

After the events of the *Reichskristallnacht* and its aftermath the Jewish suicide curve dipped again, though only briefly. With the unleashing of the Second World War the persecution of the Jews was further intensified, and preparations were made for the transition to organised mass murder. Mass deportations saw to it that the areas under German rule and settled by Germans should be made "free of Jews".* To the Jews, already deprived of social status, the notification of impending deportation signified the loss of the last remnant of life in a familiar environment. The official communication requiring them to vacate their homes and get ready for "evacuation" determined many recipients to take their own lives. Thus the suicide curve attained its peak with the deportations.

The Jews in Baden and the Rhine Palatinate were deported in October 1940; they were among the first German Jews to suffer this fate.[38] They were given between quarter of an hour and two hours to prepare themselves for "evacuation to the South of France". On 30th October 1940 the Gestapo in Karlsruhe reported: "A number of women and men used that time to evade transportation by killing themselves".[39] A week later, on 6th November, the Public Prosecutor's Office in Mannheim presented a list of suicides, which included the names of the eight Jews who had killed themselves on the morning of 22nd October in the course of the "Bürckel operation".[40] The Mannheim paediatrician Dr. Eugen Neter remembered the events of those days:

> "The arrest and announcement of impending transportation came as a frightful and stunning shock to those affected. It was inevitable that many a soul failed to stand up to that trial. In the course of the first few hours of the operation, there were several cases of suicide and attempted suicide. There were about ten cases in Mannheim – out of 2,500 deportees – and as many in Baden-Baden where the Jewish community numbered barely 100 members . . ."[41]

* For further details see also the already cited essay by Henry Friedlander, and the survey by E. G. Lowenthal, 'In the Shadow of Doom. Post-War Publications on Jewish Communal History in Germany (IV)', in this volume of the Year Book – (Ed.).

[38]Well before the war, at the end of October 1938, the deportation of Jews of Polish origin living in Germany gave rise to some suicidal acts. In a letter, dated 19th December 1938, Otto Buchholz describes the fate of the deportees and refers to a case of suicide: "Old Frankel . . . in his grief lay down on the rails (dead), and there were many deaths" (Fliedner, *op. cit.*, vol. 2, pp. 72 f.). At the end of 1939, the first Jews were deported to the Lublin "*Reservat*". *Daily Telegraph* of 13th November 1939 reported that 83 Jews, among them 36 women, had killed themselves in Vienna.

[39]Paul Sauer, *Dokumente über die Verfolgung der jüdischen Bürger in Baden-Württemberg durch das Nationalsozialistische Regime 1933–1945*, 2 vols., Stuttgart 1966, here vol. 2, p. 243.

[40]Fliedner, *op. cit.*, p. 76. See also p. 158 of this study.

[41]*Ibid.*, p. 79.

In September 1941 the Yellow Star was introduced, heralding the beginning of the systematic deportations to locations outside Germany. The number of suicides rose dramatically. Hildegard Henschel – the wife of Moritz Henschel, the last chairman of the Berlin Jewish community – reported about the situation in Berlin when the news broke:

> "There had of course been rumours during the preceding days about an impending evacuation on the pattern of Stettin, Schneidemühl and Baden, but nobody thought that they would so soon become reality. The people were thus all the more surprised, but did not resist, although in many cases they put an end to their doubts by taking Veronal."[42]

All Jewish communities were affected by the suicide wave. Only a few examples can be given here. On 15th October 1941 the first transport left Vienna for Lodz. Nineteen Jews who should have gone with this transport took their own lives: either by jumping from windows or by gassing themselves, by hanging, with sleeping tablets, by drowning; or by means unknown. Within the space of three weeks the Gestapo reported 84 suicides and 87 suicide attempts in Vienna.[43] On 20th March 1942 a transport of 1,000 Hesse Jews left for Lublin. A week later the Jewish liaison officer in Mainz, Michael Oppenheim, was summoned to the Gestapo. In his diary he recorded the following interview:

> "Herr Schertel: 'Why so many suicides? How was it that the evacuation scheme (*Abwanderung*) became known in advance in Mainz?' – I: 'The date of the evacuation had already been talked about by Aryans. The Nathan family even had fairly accurate knowledge of the date and destination of the transport.' "

Three days later Oppenheim gave the Gestapo the names of six who had killed themselves, "having known about their imminent migration". In May 1942, Ida Levy refused to vacate her home and killed herself. Oppenheim surmised "suicide by starvation". At the beginning of September 1942 he was asked to draw up a new transportation list and to "keep stretchers ready for the sick, the aged, etc.". The departure of this transport was planned for 19th to 23rd September. Between 6th and 16th September 13 Jews committed suicide in Mainz. Others postponed that decision until their turn came. Oppenheim noted in his diary:

> "1.4.1943: I ask Lißmann to come in a day or two later because of his illness, soon afterwards he kills himself . . .
> 7.4.1943: I summon Ernst Hannemann for the 8th (he takes poison and dies a few days later)."[44]

On 11th December 1941 a transport carrying 1,007 Jews from the Rhineland left Düsseldorf for the Riga Ghetto. According to a confidential report by Police Captain Splitter, the officer in charge – a report betraying a vehement hatred of the Jews and an awareness of the "final solution" – one Jew joined the transport "only slightly injured" after having thrown himself in front of a tram, and an

[42]Hildegard Henschel, 'Aus der Arbeit der Jüdischen Gemeinde Berlin während der Jahre 1941–1943', *Zeitschrift für die Geschichte der Juden*, 9 (1972), pp. 33–52.
[43]Rosenkranz, *op. cit.*, p. 301.
[44]Stadtarchiv Mainz, Tagebuch von Michael Oppenheim. See also Anton Keim (ed.), *Tagebuch einer jüdischen Gemeinde 1941/1943*, Mainz 1969.

elderly woman had managed to get away from the loading ramp and take shelter in a nearby house, but was "noticed" by a charwoman.[45] Another major transport, leaving Düsseldorf on 22nd April 1942 for Izbica-Lublin, did not get off to a smooth start. In Krefeld three Jews – Julius Meier with his wife Auguste Meier and Elsa Frankenberg – committed suicide, another five had absconded and were searched for. The Gestapo found papers indicating that some of them were intending to kill themselves, but was unable to trace the missing persons. In addition a number of Jews had to be left behind, as they had been detailed for forced labour and their deportation would have threatened the power supply of factories "essential for the war effort". And so Adolf Eichmann, the coordinator of the deportations at the *Reichssicherheitshauptampt* (Central Security Office) was informed on 29th April:

> "For these reasons it was necessary . . . to cancel the evacuation of fifty Jews engaged in the labour effort, so that after deduction of the suicides and missing Jews the transport from Düsseldorf numbered 941 Jews at the time of departure."[46]

"Shortfalls" were noted also in subsequent transports. Out of 154 Jews selected for deportation in a transport leaving Koblenz for Lublin on 15th June 1942, one went underground, three – Anny Leven and a married couple, Josef and Helene Cahn – took their own lives, and seven were reported ill and "unfit for travel".[47] At the end of July 1942 two transports with a total of 1,659 Jews were organised. On that occasion five escapes, five deaths and thirteen suicides were recorded.[48] In Bavaria, there were no major "hitches" in the running of the scheme. On 7th December 1941 the Regional Governor of Upper and Central Franconia reported:

> "In the course of the operation mounted for the evacuation of Jews a special train carrying 1,001 Jews and nine children left Nuremberg for Riga. Three Jewesses committed suicide, presumably out of fear of the imminent evacuation."

In his "Monthly Report" of April 1942 he wrote:

> "In the course of the evacuation scheme a special train left Nuremberg on 24th March with 990 Jews, destination Lublin-Izbica. There were no incidents. The Jew Dr. Martin Israel Offenbacher evaded evacuation by suicide (gas)."

A month later his report ran:

> "On 24th March 781 Jews, and on 25th April another 105, were evacuated to the East. The operation was trouble-free, apart from a few suicides and suicide attempts."[49]

At Würzburg the Gestapo was obliged to add several replacements to the deportation list of 28th August 1942, since five elderly Jewesses who had made

[45]'Vertraulicher Bericht über die Evakuierung von Juden nach Riga v. 11.12.–17.12.1941', in *Judendeportation aus dem Reichsgebiet II*, zusammengestellt von der Zentralen Stelle der Landesjustizverwaltungen, n.d.; printed also in H. G. Adler, *Der verwaltete Mensch*, Tübingen 1974, p. 462.

[46]Schreiben der Stapoleitstelle Düsseldorf an das RSHA–Amt IV B 4–, 19th April 1942, in *Judendeportation II*, *op. cit.*

[47]Schreiben der Stapoleitstelle Düsseldorf and das RSHA, 18th August 1942, *ibid.*

[48]*Ibid.*

[49]Quoted by Broszat *et al.*, *op. cit.*, p. 485.

suicide attempts had to be "scratched".[50] In Upper Bavaria 14 Jewish suicides were counted in June and July 1942.[51]

At the Lübbenau cemetery in the Cottbus Administrative Area two Jews were buried who had killed themselves on the eve of their deportation. The headstones bear the names Dr. Max Plessner and Beatrixe Ledermann. At Calau, not far from Lübbenau, stands the house where the well-known actor Joachim Gottschalk was born. A memorial tablet recalls the family's joint suicide. Gottschalk, himself an "Aryan", was married to a Jewess. Threatened with separation, they ended their lives, together with their son, on 6th November 1941.[52]

Less than three weeks before, on 18th October 1941, the first Jews had been "removed" from Berlin. It was a transport of 1,013 men, women and children, bound for Lodz, the first of 180 transports from Berlin.[53] The Berlin correspondent of the Swedish *Social Democraten* learned that on that occasion 200 Jews had evaded deportation by suicide.[54] The Gestapo referred to "waves" of deportations. Two types, "East transports" and "old-age transports" were organised. In this way 35,738 Jews were taken to the death camps in the East, and 14,797 to the "old-age Ghetto" of Theresienstadt (Térezin). The deportation waves were reflected in the suicide figures. On 3rd April 1942 523 Jews were evacuated to the East; 57 killed themselves, On 3rd October 1942 717 Jews were called up for "resettlement" in Estonia; 208 killed themselves.[55] Hildegard Henschel reports:

> "In November 1942 the suicide figure rose alarmingly. A special section of the Jewish hospital had been set aside for a long time, but there were not enough beds for those already close to death when admitted. People lay on wooden stretchers, on benches and similar emergency facilities."[56]

On the situation during the big police raid on 27th February 1943, she writes:

> "It was as if we were paralysed. At first we did nothing until the first suicides were brought in. There were those who had jumped out of windows, others who had thrown themselves in front of cars, others who had taken Veronal or even potassium cyanide . . . It was horrible."[57]

[50] Adler, *op. cit.*, pp. 387 f.

[51] Institut für Zeitgeschichte München, 'Verfolgung und Widerstand in Bayern', *Inventarverzeichnis*: NSDAP und Gestapoleitstelle, München 1975, II, 21 in 38.

[52] Anna Dora Miethe, *Gedenkstätten, Arbeiterbewegung, antifaschistischer Widerstand, Aufbau des Sozialismus*, Leipzig–Jena–Berlin 1974, p. 207.

[53] Wiener Library, PC 4 Section iA, Reel 44.

[54] H. G. Sellenthin (ed.), *Jüdische Gemeinde Berlin*, Berlin 1959, p. 83; Robert Kempner, 'Die Ermordung von 35,000 Berliner Juden', in Herbert A. Strauss and Kurt R. Großmann, *Gegenwart im Rückblick. Festgabe für die jüdische Gemeinde zu Berlin 25 Jahre nach dem Neubeginn*, Heidelberg 1970, pp. 180 ff.; Kurt Jacob Ball Kaduri, 'Berlin wird judenfrei', in *Jahrbuch für die Geschichte Mittel- und Ostdeutschlands*, 22 (1973), p. 202.

[55] Gerald Reitlinger, *Die Endlösung. Hitlers Versuch der Ausrottung der Juden Europas 1939–1945*, Berlin 1956, p. 99. The relevant information was passed to Reitlinger by Dr. Toch. There are no references to suicides in the fragmentary remnants of the deportations lists sent by the Berlin Gestapo to the financial authorities, of which photocopies are available at the General Prosecutor's Office. However, a systematic evaluation of the extensive files of the Ministries of Justice and Finance as well as the RSHA and Stapoleitstelle Berlin may yet yield some quantitative data.

[56] Henschel, *loc. cit.*, pp. 44, 47.

[57] *Ibid.*

Another witness reported:

> "On a single day 87 Jews were buried in Berlin. In one case seven members of a household had decided to commit suicide by taking 25 Veronal tablets each after having learned that they would have to vacate the flat. One of the seven was saved. He hanged himself after being discharged from hospital."[58]

Officials of the *Reichsvereinigung*, too, lost the will to live as the deportations went on. Siegfried Falk was ordered by the Gestapo to cooperate in organising the deportations. He refused and committed suicide together with his wife in December 1941. The same decision was taken by Margarete Hartstein and Meier Spanier. In October 1942 Dr. Julius Schönfeld, the Administrative Director of the Jewish hospital, also committed suicide with his wife after the Gestapo had asked him to put members of his staff on the deportation lists.[59] There was no end to the funerals, as Martin Riesenburger, at the time an auxiliary rabbi, who survived the war by going underground, remembers:

> "On a cold day – it was Tuesday, 23rd March 1943 – a small congregation of mourners assembled in the hall of the cemetery around a coffin that contained the earthly remains of a woman who with staunch loyalty had stood by her world-famous husband who had died eight years before: it was Martha Liebermann, the widow of the great painter and graphic artist Max Liebermann."

Martha Liebermann had poisoned herself with sleeping tablets. She was eighty-five years old.[60]

It is not possible to make reliable quantitative statements about the precise scale of the suicide epidemic. Even a reasonably realistic estimate is difficult to arrive at, since the available evidence is scanty, to some extent conflicting and scarcely testable. Hildegard Henschel was heard as a witness at the Eichmann trial in Jerusalem:

"Prosecutor:	'Was there any possibility of evading deportation?'
Witness:	'Only suicide . . . The suicides started immediately before the first transport to Litzmannstadt, and the number increased very rapidly. People took Veronal, some of them took potassium cyanide . . .'
Prosecutor:	'Frau Henschel, I believe you remember a round figure of suicides between October 1941 and the beginning of 1942?'
Witness:	'There were about 1,200.'
Prosecutor:	'And that only among Berlin Jews?'
Witness:	'Only, indeed . . .' "[61]

The statistician and lawyer Bruno Blau, who had a non-Jewish wife and as a Gestapo detainee was brought, seriously ill, to the Berlin Jewish Hospital where he remained and witnessed the liberation,[62] has stated that in Berlin in 1941/1942 one in four Jewish deaths was due to suicide.[63] Herbert A. Strauss recalls having

[58]Wiener Library, P IIIa No. 1095.

[59]These examples are quoted from E. G. Lowenthal (ed.), *Bewährung im Untergang. Ein Gedenkbuch*, Stuttgart 1956, pp. 47, 69 f., 165, 192.

[60]Riesenburger, *op. cit.*, p. 41.

[61]Bernd Nellessen, *Der Prozeß von Jerusalem. Ein Dokument*, Düsseldorf-Vienna 1964, p. 111.

[62]For Blau's recollections, see Richarz, *op. cit.*, pp. 459–475.

[63]Bruno Blau, 'Die Juden in Deutschland von 1939–1945', *Judaica*, 7 (1951), pp. 271–284.

been informed by the Berlin community shortly before he went underground and a few months before he succeeded in escaping to Switzerland that ten per cent of the Berlin Jews notified of their impending deportation had taken their own lives in 1941/1942, a figure of about 2,000 suicides.[64] The burial of 1,279 suicides was recorded by the Weißensee Jewish cemetery in the years 1941/1943.[65] It is reasonable to assume that suicides were also buried at the other two Jewish cemeteries in Berlin. The total number of Jewish suicides in Berlin during the period of the deportations, then, is likely to lie somewhere between 2,000 and 3,000.[66] In Württemberg a little over 10 per cent of the Jews due to be deported – 260 out of 2,500 – ended their own lives.[67] Taking into consideration the data relating to the other regions, we arrive at a figure of 3,000 to 4,000 suicides in the whole of Germany during the period of the deportations. Moreover, if we add suicides and suicide attempts preceding the period of deportations as well as those that occurred in the concentration camps, in the occupied territories and in exile, we get a likely sum total of just under 10,000. Even the most conservative estimate of 5,000 Jewish suicides during the twelve years of the Third *Reich* would indicate that nearly 1 per cent of the 525,000 Jews living in Germany in 1933 took their own lives. Similarly, the most conservative estimate of 3,000 Jewish suicides during the period of the deportations would indicate that 2.2 per cent of the 134,000 Jews intended for deportation evaded that fate by suicide. In Berlin the proportion would be about 4 per cent. The actual figures can be assumed to be somewhat higher.[68]

In the light of these figures an attempt can now be made to determine the place of suicide in the typology of behaviour sketched in the introductory section of this study. It must be borne in mind, however, that nearly all the data used are based on very rough estimates which have to be handled with great caution. In addition, some of the data may overlap. It is in the nature of things that different modes of action may be practised simultaneously or consecutively.

[64]Herbert A. Strauss, 'Jewish Emigration from Germany. Nazi Policies and Jewish Responses (I)', in *LBI Year Book XXV* (1980), pp. 315–361, in particular p. 320, note 13 and p. 327, note 26.

[65]Riesenburger, *op. cit.*, pp. 39 f.

[66]It appears that Jewish suicides were left out of the official statistics. The data, published only after the end of the war, do show a marked increase in 1942, but there is no evidence in the official figures of a Jewish suicide epidemic. The published overall suicide figures for Berlin for the years 1939 to 1944 are consecutively: 2,109, 1,707, 1,546, 2,001, 1,743, 1,233.

[67]Archivdirektion Stuttgart, *Die jüdischen Gemeinden in Württemberg und Hohenzollern*, Stuttgart 1966, p. 23.

[68]Hans Lamm, *Über die innere und äußere Entwicklung der deutschen Juden im Dritten Reich*, Phil. Diss., Erlangen 1951, p. 343, presents a survey of suicides, based on investigations carried out by him immediately after the end of the war in 38 municipalities, not including either Berlin or Vienna. He arrives at a total number of 1,169 Jewish suicides, including 300 in Frankfurt a. Main, 100 in Cologne, 182 in Munich, 56 in Nuremberg. Figures given in various other publications have to be treated with caution. Paul Sauer, *Die Schicksale der jüdischen Bürger Baden-Württembergs während der nationalsozialistischen Verfolgungszeit 1933–1945*, Stuttgart 1968, p. 265, puts the number of Jewish suicides in Baden-Württemberg at 165, distributed over the lifetime of the Nazi regime as follows: 1933/35 – 32; 1936/37 – 13; 1938/39 – 61; 1940/45 – 59. In Hamburg 308 Jews are known to have killed themselves out of 5,366 deported during the years 1941–1945. Cf. Senat Hamburg, *Die jüdischen Opfer des Nationalsozialismus in Hamburg*, Hamburg 1964, p. 104. Figures totalling 663 for the years 1938–1943 are given for Frankfurt a. Main alone by Adolf Diamant, 'Jiskor für Selbstmörder', in *Allgemeine*, 4th March 1983, p. 18.

The two dominant modes of behaviour were staying put in Germany on the one hand, and emigration on the other. Though diametrically opposed, both responses fitted in with the aims of National Socialist racial policy during the initial years of the Third *Reich*. In other words, until well after the outbreak of the Second World War persecution of the Jews proceeded in keeping with the notions of "traditional" antisemitism. The Nazi regime was prepared to grant the Jewish section of the population – with some exceptions – the possibility of some form of continued existence. The Jews were compelled to accept the *déclassé* status of an "enemy of the people" or be driven out. The majority left Germany. Just under 300,000 Jews succeeded in overcoming the manifold barriers erected against them both in Germany and abroad and obtaining the documents required for emigration. Of these, about 30,000 were caught by the Nazis and their collaborators during the Second World War in the occupied territories and removed, in keeping with the "final solution of the Jewish Question", by then in full swing. As for the Jews who had remained in Germany, the right to any form of existence was denied them from 1940/1941 on. The mass deportations extinguished the remnants of Jewish communities. Some 134,000 Jews were shipped to the death camps.

It was part of the practice adopted by the Nazi regime in the persecution of the Jews that it allowed occasional departures, granted "exceptions" from the very norms it had laid down. Numbers of Jews were able to make use of the opportunity. It was always the question of "exemptions", of the granting of a privilege protecting the favoured individuals from persecution. Several thousands of Jews are likely to have benefited in this way; more accurate estimates are scarcely possible.

Behaviour that can be classified as betrayal or collaboration was exceedingly rare in quantitative terms. No more than a handful of German Jews worked as informers or otherwise for the regime, in particular for the Gestapo.

The opportunities of resistance – "deviation from the prescribed model" – were very limited. Nevertheless, resistance was in evidence at various levels and in various forms. Manifestations of open protest occurred from the outset and continued well into the period of deportations. In speech and writing German Jews and German-Jewish organisations fought back against moral defamation and social discrimination. Several hundreds of instances are documented in the scant extant records, so that it is reasonable to assume that over one thousand transgressions occurred and were punished by the regime.

Flight across the national frontier ranks next to protest. In contrast to the time-consuming procedure of "legal" emigration ordered by the Government, flight was a spontaneous and secret act. There is no telling how many illegal frontier crossings succeeded. At a guess there were several thousands of cases. With the outbreak and extension of the Second World War nearly all the European escape routes were cut, and the escape route that remained led into the underground within Germany. The decision to try that route was often prompted by the deportation call-up. About 10,000 Jews in Germany and 2,000 to 3,000 German refugees in the occupied territories tried to find hiding places. By far the largest single centre of this underground was Berlin, where in the middle of 1943 an estimated 5,000 Jews lived in hiding. When the city was liberated, 1,500 surfaced again. In no other German city are more than fifty Jews known to have survived underground. The fragmentary data available indicate that out of every ten Jews who went underground in Germany three were saved. In Western Europe the chances of survival were somewhat better, in Eastern Europe they were yet worse. Accordingly, this German index figure – which can serve as a yardstick for the attitude of the German population, which alone could offer sanctuary and solidarity – lay between the two extremes.

German Jews, or rather Germans of Jewish descent, also played a part in the politically organised resistance struggle. Their motivation, however, was not specifically Jewish; they were prompted by political convictions which determined their anti-fascism. As dedicated Communists, Social Democrats, Trotskyite or undogmatic Socialists they found their place after 1933 in the various resistance groups. There were probably no more than 2,000 of them. In the middle 1930s the Gestapo had succeeded in virtually wiping out working-class resistance. Anti-fascists of Jewish extraction found some, though limited, opportunity of continuing their resistance struggle in exile, in the Spanish Civil War, in the occupied countries and in the concentration camps. A very few only had an opportunity of joining a resistance group in Germany. In Berlin the Communist-Jewish Herbert Baum Group, with an inner core of 32 members, operated in almost complete isolation.[69]

It is in the light of the character and relative weight of these alternative modes of behaviour that Jewish suicidal tendencies under the Nazi regime must be assessed. As shown above, nearly 10,000 Jews and Germans of Jewish origin are likely to have killed themselves or attempted to kill themselves, the majority during the period of the deportations. Actually, more Jews chose flight into the underground rather than flight into suicide, the only two options open to them in order to evade deportation when the summons had come to vacate their homes and report for "evacuation" to the death camps.

The suicides imposed additional work on the Nazi bureaucracy. Even before the outbreak of the Second World War clear instructions had been given for an "exhaustive" collection of data concerning all cases of suicide in the German *Reich*.[70] In a circular dated 28th February 1939 Himmler reminded the police authorities once again most emphatically that it was their task to investigate all suicides and attempted suicides "according to criminological principles" and to find out "how far they were prompted by indictable offences".[71] The police interrogated relatives and neighbours, and checked the death certificate issued after the post-mortem, as well as the death record card (*Sterbefallkarte*) kept by the register offices. The official documents recorded name, sex and age, place of residence, date and place of death, cause of death, and these data provided the basis for the statistical records of causes of death, of which the suicide statistics

[69]Cf. Helmut Eschwege, 'Resistance of German Jews against the Nazi Regime', in *LBI Year Book XV* (1970), pp. 134–180.

[70]Erich Schmahl, 'Statistik der Selbstmorde und Selbstmordversuche', in Friedrich Burgdörfer, *Die Statistik in Deutschland nach ihrem heutigen Stand*, vol. 1, Berlin 1940, pp. 333–339.

[71]*Ibid.*, p. 334;

formed part. Himmler's decree added the one element that was missing in the *Reich* statistics, and that was the motive for suicide. The decree listed criteria such as economic distress, incurable disease, melancholia and nervous disorders, unhappy love, fear of punishment, family quarrels and other motives, but made no mention of feelings of contrition or shame, weariness of life, loneliness, bereavement or grief. The statistician Erich Schmahl, writing in 1940, named these additional motives. He pointed out that "the leadership of the National Socialist state sets great store by the statistical observation of suicidal acts and their motives" and foreshadowed that "the local and regional records of the last named groupings of suicide statistics will shortly be extended to the entire state territory".[72] Not long after the formulation of these plans the wave of Jewish suicides broke, and one can hardly go wrong in assuming that the official quarters had neither the time nor the incentive to make, let alone publish, an "exhaustive" investigation of the motives.

In the autumn of 1941 the organised deportations started – in the jargon used internally by the SS – "within the framework of the Europe-wide Jew purge" (*gesamteuropäische Entjudung*). The responsible department at the *Reich* Central Security Office – Eichmann's Office IV B 4 – stated explicitly at the end of January 1942:

> "The evacuation of Jews to the East, recently carried out in several regions, marks the beginning of the final solution of the Jewish question in the *Reich* within its old borders, in the Ostmark and in the Protectorate."[73]

The data of the Jews selected for deportation were received by telegram from all regions. The regional Gestapo offices as well as Police directorates, district officers and municipal and parish authorities involved in the evacuations were instructed to "report any shortfalls (through suicide, etc.) without delay".[74] A report was also sent to the Ministry of Finance, which was responsible for the sequestration of the assets and chattels of the deportees. Temporarily, the suicides caused some concern to the finance officials. It was laid down in the 11th Executory Order in pursuance of the *Reich* Citizen Act, issued on 25th November 1941, that the property of any person crossing the state frontier was forfeited to the *Reich*. Zealous finance officials in Baden discovered that, as the law stood, the property of those Jews who had committed suicide in the course of the "Bürckel operation" in October 1940 – "and these cases are very numerous" – could not be seized.[75] The Central Security Office and the Finance Ministry deliberated and hit upon a solution of the problem. The Gestapo in Frankfurt a. Main announced on 21st August 1942:

> "Should a Jew commit suicide because of the evacuation, then the procedure to be followed is the same as if he had been transported. I request however that any successful suicides be specified on the relevant form."[76]

The property, then, was confiscated.

[72]*Ibid.*, p. 334.
[73]'Schreiben des RSHA-IV B 4 v. 31.1.1942 an die Stapoleitstellen', in *Judendeportation, op. cit.*
[74]Gestapo Order, dated 18th November 1941, quoted by Sauer, *Dokumente, op. cit.*, vol. 2, p. 272.
[75]Letter of the Reich Ministry of Finance to the RSHA, *ibid.*, p. 264; see also Adler, *op. cit.*, p. 166.
[76]Express letter of the Gestapo, Frankfurt a. Main, dated 21st August 1942, in: Kommission zur Erforschung der Geschichte der Frankfurter Juden, *Dokumente zur Geschichte der Frankfurter Juden 1933–1945*, Frankfurt a. Main 1963, p. 523.

In some cases the cumbersome bureaucratic procedure even required the announcement of the sequestration of assets in the legal gazette, the *Deutscher Reichs- und Preußischer Staatsanzeiger*. The terse notice published on such occasions said nothing about suicide; it stated that the decision was final and not subject to appeal. Measures were also taken to stop private inquiries about deportees and suicides. The Domicile Registration Offices (*Einwohnermeldeämter*) were instructed to put after the names of "de-registered Jews" the words "moved away, address unknown" or "emigrated".[77] In the files of the Amsterdam SS Centre for "Jewish Emigration", the report of a suicide carries the endorsement "take inventory and other usual measures".[78]

Gestapo officials appeared in the consulting rooms of the few remaining Jewish physicians who were allowed to treat Jewish patients. Dr. Edith Kramer reports that many patients requested prescriptions for sleeping tablets and asked what was the lethal dose. She was often called afterwards to certify her patients' death by suicide or arrange for their admission to the Jewish Hospital if they had survived.[79] Gestapo officials then turned up at the Jewish Hospital to collect the patients whose lives had been saved for the next transport.[80] The situation in Hamburg has been described by Martin Tobar:

> "Attempted suicides accounted for a large proportion of the patients. This fact led to visits by Gestapo officials who wanted to find out where the individuals concerned had procured the means for their attempted suicide. In spite of this increased interest, suicide attempts were often simulated by giving the patients massive doses of Dolantin or similar drugs, especially when we expected a visit from the Gestapo in the near future. However, such measures effected nothing more than a postponement, for those patients had to reckon with all the greater certainly to be included in the next transport. The sick deportees had to be removed as inconspicuously as possible . . . A furniture van arrived outside the building, and the sick deportees had to be packed into it."[81]

Jewish doctors in Cologne dealt with the same problem. Rabbi Zvi Asaria reports:

> "The desperate situation robbed many of their last hope. Each further deportation resulted in further suicides. Talking under their breath, the doctors wondered whether there was any point in saving the lives of their patients, and whether they should not mercifully allow them an easy death."[82]

This attitude seems to have been widespread. Dr Edith Kramer, who in June 1942 was deported to a labour camp at Poznań and later transferred to Theresienstadt, recalls that a gathering of Jewish doctors was convened in Berlin, at which the suicide wave was discussed. No voice was raised against the proposal that the last will of those who had attempted to take their own lives should be

[77]Letter of the Düsseldorf Gestapo, dated 5th May 1942, in *Judendeportation, op. cit.*

[78]Jacob Presser, *Ondergang. De vervolging en verdelging van het Nederlandse jodendom*, deel 2, S'-Gravenhage 1965, p. 509.

[79]Edith Kramer, 'Hell and Rebirth. My Experience during the Time of Persecution', unpublished manuscript.

[80]Wiener Library, P IIIa No. 4.

[81]Forschungsstelle für die Geschichte des Nationalsozialismus in Hamburg, Fst 6262.

[82]Zvi Asaria, *Die Juden in Köln. Von den ältesten Zeiten bis zur Gegenwart*, Cologne 1959, p. 389.

respected by allowing them to die.[83] Yet, not all physicians at the Berlin Jewish Hospital subscribed to that opinion. Dr. Hermann Pineas, the Head of the Neuro-psychiatric Department writes in his recollections:

> "The cases of attempted suicide, which increased on a vast scale during the period when people were summoned to be transported to the camps, were taken to special rooms attached to the medical ward on the ground floor. The preferred method was the use of Veronal or Phandodorm, that is to say in any case one of the barbituric acids, of which those unfortunates had large supplies. Colleagues in the medical ward held different views on the question as to whether it was better to save the lives of such patients or let them quietly go to sleep. At any rate, mortality was enormous."[84]

Some physicians refused to help patients wishing to die. In the autumn of 1942, Camilla Neumann, conscripted for forced labour, was on the verge of suicide, "worn out and weary of life, weary of fear and of all the horror". She goes on to write:

> "I resolved to end my life. I went to our good Dr. Lissner and asked him to prescribe Veronal. He refused. Yet, eight days later he himself took poison. Sixteen tablets I had already, but that quantity was no use, especially as I was determined not ot leave Ludwig behind on his own. At that time Veronal was very much in demand, the Jews paid 1,000 Marks for 30 tablets. But there were other ways of ending one's life, and I talked to Ludwig about it. Ludwig did not want it and raised many objections. At first he said: 'Surely it would be paradoxical to be driven into suicide by fear of death.' Then he said over and over again that he wanted to see Ursel (our daughter) again, and did not wish to lose this chance by committing suicide. Ludwig simply did not *want* to face up to reality, and went on waiting for the 'miracle'. At the same time he suffered terribly. He found it inconceivable that the German people should have allowed things to come to such a pass. He could not understand how a people that had produced men like Bach, Beethoven and Goethe could now pay homage to a Hitler, a Himmler and a Goebbels."[85]

Suicides and waves of suicides were not confined to the *Reich* territory. Some famous emigrés – Ernst Toller, Arnold Zweig and Kurt Tucholsky among them – committed suicide in exile. The link between persecution and suicide is manifest also in the occupied territories. During the invasion of the Netherlands in May 1940, 150 Jews killed themselves. A considerable proportion of them were born in Germany. Several more hundreds of cases were recorded during the mass deportations in 1942/1943.[86] Numbers of refugees killed themselves after the occupation of France.[87] When the first transport bound "for the East" left Paris in July 1942, the number of suicides showed a rapid increase. In Eastern Europe it was chiefly members of Jewish Councils and resistance fighters who resorted to suicide in hopeless situations.

Little is known about suicide in the concentration camps and death camps.

[83]Personal communication from Dr. Edith Kramer. This is the place to thank Mr. and Mrs. Kramer, who in Sydney in 1982 greatly helped the progress of this work by supplying information and source material on a number of points.

[84]Richarz, *op. cit.*, p. 433.

[85]*Ibid.*, p. 418.

[86]Presser, *op. cit.*, vol. 1, pp. 14, 19, 173, 259, 284. See also Louis de Jong, *Het Koninkrijk der Nederlanden in de Tweede Wereldoorlog*, vol. 3, S'-Gravenhage 1971, pp. 450 f., vol. 6/1, pp. 45, 255, 328.

[87]Kurt R. Großmann, *Emigration. Geschichte der Hitler-Flüchtlinge 1933–1945*, Frankfurt a. Main 1969, p. 201 (for names).

Any attempt to establish valid figures of suicidal acts is frustrated by the nature of the SS records of causes of death, which are incomplete and partly falsified.[88] Nor is it possible to ascertain the relative proportion of Jewish and non-Jewish, German and foreign prisoners. Scattered evidence in the meagre extant source material and in the literature provide the basis only for some very general statements. This fragmentary evidence suggests that suicides occurred chiefly during the first phase of detention in the camps. As the stay in the camps lengthened, suicidal tendencies gradually gave way either to a reviving will to live or else to what has been called the "Mussulman syndrome", a state of utter apathy and inaction. It appears that, following the first shock and the adaptation to the inhuman camp conditions, death lost its terror for the majority of inmates and became a familiar feature of everyday life. Living on in the camp meant vegetating on the borderline of life and death, and under such conditions the prospect of voluntary death lost much of its attraction.

The aim of the SS was from the outset to destroy the self-esteem and the will to live of the inmates. The methods for achieving this end were first developed and tested at the Dachau "model camp", with its graduated system of insults, roll calls, interrogations, prison sentences and physical maltreatment.[89] Thousands succumbed to the terror, and not a few were driven to suicide. A striking example of conditions during the initial phase at Dachau is provided by the case of a Würzburg Jew which occupied the police and engaged the interest of the public for several months.

On 22nd July 1933 the livestock dealer Fleischmann was arrested. In a quarrel with an innkeeper over the sale of a horse, he had knocked his opponent on the head with his stick. A doctor had diagnosed concussion. News of the incident spread quickly and gave rise to expressions of anti-Jewish sentiment. Fleischmann was taken into "protective custody", ostensibly "for his own safety" and was brought to Dachau. He was not set free until 6th December, and then was fined 200 Marks by a local court. Fleischmann had the audacity to appeal against the sentence, which "again caused growing agitation among the population". On 13th February 1934 he was again taken into "protective custody" and transferred to Dachau as a "particularly brutal and anti-social element". The fact of his being returned to the camp and the specific description of his character indicated that his death was considered desirable. A few days later the camp command reported his suicide.[90]

Little documentary evidence is available about Buchenwald. When thousands of Jews were taken there after the November pogroms of 1938, there were some suicides. One survivor reported:

> "The following morning I saw the corpses of two suicides. One of them had thrown himself against the electrified barbed wire; the other had died from a guard's bullet. The idea of

[88] Falk Pingel, *Häftlinge unter SS-Herrschaft. Widerstand, Selbstbehauptung und Vernichtung in Konzentrationslagern*, Hamburg 1978, p. 303.

[89] Günther Kimmel, 'Das Konzentrationslager Dachau', in Broszat *et al.* (eds.), *op. cit.*, vol. 2, *Herrschaft und Gesellschaft im Konflikt*, p. 360.

[90] Hauptstaatsarchiv München. Reichsstatthalter Epp 281. Meldung der Bayerischen Politischen Polizei, 9th March 1934.

committing suicide never entered my head while I was in detention, even though I was surrounded by large numbers of men who had lost their senses. Later, mental cases were locked in a washroom behind our barracks, and one of my friends – a neurologist – was told to look after them."[91]

At the Flossenbürg camp, too, the SS guards were out to diminish the number of Jewish prisoners. In that task they were helped by the prisoners themselves. It happened repeatedly that "elderly or debilitated Jews crawled to the wire fence and begged the guards at the watch tower to shoot them".[92] In the death register at Flossenbürg it is noted that up till the summer of 1942, 72 Jewish detainees had died, sixteen of them from gunshot wounds. At Mauthausen numerous suicides were recorded, 177 in 1942 alone; 33 of them had hanged themselves, but the vast majority had run into the electrified fence and were shot by the guards.[93] The same method – in the camp jargon "running into the wire" – was also predominant in Auschwitz.[94] At the Auschwitz trial in Frankfurt one witness testified:

"When there still were prisoners held in camp area B I b at Birkenau it was my job as a carrier of dead bodies to walk along the fence every day and pick up the bodies of those who had been shot. As a rule, they were suicides, people who had run into the fence during the night. Numbers varied a great deal. When transports came from the Netherlands, the number was very high. I remember that on one occasion there were as many as thirty. When the transports came from Slovakia the number was low, perhaps five to ten. The average would have been around eight to twelve daily. Mostly it was new arrivals who ran into the fence, but there were also some who had been at the camp for some time."[95]

This testimony corrects the assertion – which has repeatedly been made – that suicide at the camps was only a marginal phenomenon.[96]

The collapse of life expectancy and future prospects caused a young German Jews to commit suicide at Auschwitz. For half a year Fredy Hirsch had acted as a camp leader (*Lagerkapo*) at the so-called "Czech family camp" at Birkenau. On the strength of his experience and his authority he was able to care in particular for the education of the young.[97] There, about 5,000 Jews from Theresienstadt lived under privileged conditions in a section of the camp screened from the other compounds. They had been led to believe that they would remain exempted from the "selections" and allowed to continue their "ghetto existence". When at the beginning of March 1944, the SS dropped the pretence and announced their imminent transport to the gas chambers, Hirsch killed himself. His suicide is said to have frustrated a planned rising. Czechoslovak Jews in other parts of the camp had made preparations to respond to the liquidation of the "family camp" by setting fire to their hutments, thus signalling to other prisoners, above all to the

[91] Rita Thalmann and Emmanuel Feinermann, *Crystal Night, 9–10 November 1938*, London 1974, p. 129.
[92] Toni Siegert, 'Das Konzentrationslager Flossenbürg', in Broszat *et al.*, *op cit.*, vol. 2, pp. 461 f.
[93] Hans Maršálek, *Die Geschichte des Konzentrationslagers Mauthausen*, Vienna 1974, pp. 166 f.
[94] See *Auschwitz. Geschichte und Wirklichkeit des Vernichtungslagers*, Hamburg 1980, p. 84; *Hefte von Auschwitz*, 1 (1959), pp. 34 ff.; 9 (1966), pp. 37 and 67; 10 (1967), p. 86; 14 (1973), p. 116; Wieslaw Kielar, *Anus Mundi. Five Years in Auschwitz*, Harmondsworth 1982, pp. 70 f.
[95] Hermann Langbein, *Der Auschwitz-Prozeß. Eine Dokumentation 1*, Vienna 1965, pp. 115 f.
[96] Cf. for instance Victor E. Frankl, *Man's Search for Meaning*, New York 1977, pp. 27 f.
[97] Pingel, *op. cit.*, pp. 215–218.

members of the Jewish special squads (*Sonderkommandos*) in the crematoria, who were in the know, that the rising was due to begin. It was assumed that Hirsch would take over the leadership.[98] The circumstances of his suicide have been described by two Czechoslovak Jews who succeeded in escaping from Auschwitz in April 1944:

> "On 6th March 1944 we learned that the Crematorium was being prepared for the Czechoslovak Jews. I went at once to Fredy Hirsch to pass the news to him, and I appealed to him to take action without delay. He answered: 'I know my duty.' Before sunset I crept once again to the Czechoslovak camp and was told that Fredy Hirsch was dying. He had poisoned himself with Luminol. The next day, 7th March 1944, when he was in a coma, he and 3,791 of his comrades with whom he had arrived at Birkenau on 7th September 1943 were taken in lorries to the Crematorium, where the lot of them were gassed. The younger ones sang as they went to their deaths. The resistance had not come off. Certain men of the special squads had waited in vain."[99]

We cannot in this context go into further detail about the harrowing events at Auschwitz, Treblinka, Sobibor and the other death camps (where, incidentally the German-Jewish aspect is most difficult to disentangle), but special mention must certainly be made of Theresienstadt, which in many respects occupied a special place among the camps. About 140,000 Jews passed through the camp. Some 33,500 died there, another 88,000 were transferred to different camps. Suicide was strictly prohibited. Offenders who survived were taken to the ill-famed "small fortress", and the same punishment was meted out to others. Relatives were punished in keeping with the principle of "kinship liability"; fellow prisoners who kept silent about a suicidal act, contrary to the camp regulations, which made reporting such incidents mandatory, were called to account. This affected the camp doctors in particular, who frequently hushed up suicides by stating "heart failure" as the cause of death.[100] The precise number of suicides and suicide attempts cannot be ascertained, but is likely to be higher than the data established by H. G. Adler, who refers to 273 suicides and 211 suicide attempts at Theresienstadt, with two cases in 1941, 254 in 1942, 164 in 1943, 54 in 1944 and none in 1945.[101]

With the above figures in mind, one may venture to draw conclusions. Even allowing for the "hidden figure" of hushed-up suicides, the number of suicides and attempted suicides in the camps appears to be relatively low, compared with the total number of prisoners. This can be taken as a sign of the prisoners' will to live. The falling suicide rate confirms the observation made at the outset that suicidal tendencies decline as the length of the period of detention increases.

[98] Hermann Langbein, ... *nicht wie die Schafe zur Schlachtbank. Widerstand in den Konzentrationslagern*, Frankfurt a. Main 1980, pp. 198 f.

[99] This report, dated 20th April 1945, is published in Heiner Lichtenstein, *Warum Auschwitz nicht bombardiert wurde*, Cologne 1980, p. 155. One surviving member of the Jewish Special Squad in his recollections has expressed disappointment over the frustration of the resistance plan and criticised Hirsch's conduct. See Filip Müller, *Auschwitz Inferno. The Testimony of a Sonderkommando*, London 1979, pp. 104 and 106 ff.

[100] Personal communication from Dr. Edith Kramer.

[101] H. G. Adler, *Theresienstadt 1941–1945*, Tübingen 1960, pp. 316, 532. Adler's figure of "about 50 cases" for 1944 is here amended to 54, so as to ensure that the annual figures add up to the total of 484.

Adler points out that up to the end of 1943 there were only 58 suicides motivated by the fear of transfer to another camp. The Jewish suicide rate appears to have been higher at Theresienstadt that at other camps. This peculiarity can be explained as a result of the characteristic social and age structure of the inmates. Apart from its function as a transit camp, Theresienstadt was regarded as a privileged "old age ghetto". The prisoners came predominantly from Germany, Austria and the German-speaking areas of Bohemia and Moravia. In spite of national differences and internal animosities which were manifest within the "captive society" of Theresienstadt, one common element remained dominant throughout, and that was assimilation. The close links with the German language and culture were unmistakably demonstrated by the social mix of the Jews sent to Theresienstadt: they were people over sixty-five; Jews disabled or decorated in the First World War, with their families; persons with two Jewish grandparents and who belonged to the Jewish religious community (*Geltungsjuden*); Jews from mixed marriages; baptised Jews; finally the group of prominent Jews, representing the Jewish establishment. Nearly half the prisoners were over sixty.[102] The average age of those who killed themselves sixty-two.[103] In the other extermination camps the elderly were as a rule put to death immediately on arrival. Only the younger ones, those "fit for work" stood a chance of survival, however limited.

IV

Here a parallel can be observed to the situation of the Jews who committed suicide before the onset of the deportations. Here again old age and a high degree of assimilation were crucial factors. Or, in other words, the predominance of the elderly and their progressive isolation and loss of social status are reflected in the high suicide rate. The age structure of German Jewry was already abnormal under the Empire and in the Weimar Republic. By 1933, 16·3 per cent of German Jews were over sixty years of age. By 1941, as a result of Nazi persecution and emigration, which affected chiefly the younger age groups, the proportion of those over sixty had risen to 36·4 per cent.[104] Nearly all reports and accounts of contemporary witnesses have noted the relatively advanced age of those who sought death. Their average age was probably between sixty and seventy. A rough indication of the age structure is given in Table VIII, which is based on the evaluation of four lists of suicides:

Equally characteristic is the occupational structure which demonstrates social affinity with the middle and upper bourgeoisie. In 1933 it was in the first place civil servants dismissed on racial grounds who committed suicide. Members of the professions, lawyers and physicians, artists and merchants also figure largely. In the following years the suicides included a growing proportion of businessmen who saw their livelihood destroyed. Some references to occupation can be found in the two lists enumerating nearly 100 Jewish suicides compiled in exile and

[102] *Ibid.*, p. 44.
[103] *Ibid.*, p. 316.
[104] Strauss, *loc. cit.*, p. 318.

TABLE VIII

Age	*Mannheim Oct. 1940*[105]	*Baden & Württemberg 1935–1942*[106]	*Rhineland Summer 1942*[107]	*Vienna Oct. 1942*[108]
Under 31	—	—	—	—
31–40	—	1	1	—
41–50	1	4	1	1
51–60	1	5	1	4
61–70	4	8	4	6
71–80	2	4	1	2
over 80	—	—	—	5

covering the period up till 1936.[109] Out of 52 cases in which the occupation is stated we find 13 businessmen, 10 laywers, 9 medical men, 9 artists/journalists, 7 civil servants, 2 livestock dealers, 1 bank manager, 1 commercial employee. Sauer's list for Baden and Württemberg mentions one single manual worker, a tobacco worker, apart from a food wholesaler, a jewelry manufacturer, a university professor, a bank manager, an appeal court judge, regional court judges, medical specialists and businessmen.[110] In other regions, too, businessmen, retired public servants, some of them forcibly pensioned off before reaching retirement age, as well as déclassé members of the professions are to the fore in the suicide statistics.

Another circumstance pointing to the high degree of assimilation of the Jewish suicide victims was the fact that so many of them were not members of the Jewish religious community. Some were baptised, others regarded themselves as non-believers. Thus of nine "Jewish" suicides admitted to hospital in Vienna on 15th October 1941, only three belonged to the Jewish religious community. Four were Roman Catholic, one Old-Catholic, and one *konfessionslos*, attached to no religious community. Similar records for 15th May 1942 show that five out of eleven Jewish suicides were non-believers.[111] Dr. Eugen Neter confirmed the same phenomenon for Baden. In his report on suicides during the "Bürckel operation" he noted:

> "These cases of suicide – some of them occurred during the journey [to the Gurs camp] – involved without exception Jews alienated from Judaism, who had left the community or were baptised. There was an element of tragedy in the fate of these people: the road into exile

[105] The report of the Mannheim Prosecutor's Office on eight suicides which occurred on 22nd October 1940 in the course of the "Bürckel Operation", is cited by Fliedner, *op. cit.*, vol. 2, p. 76.
[106] Sauer, *Schicksale*, *op. cit.*, pp. 266 f.
[107] See notes 47 and 48 above.
[108] These figures refer to the first Vienna deportation list of 15th October 1941, reported by Rosenkranz, *op. cit.*, p. 301.
[109] See note 25 above.
[110] Sauer, *Schicksale*, *op. cit.*, pp. 266 f.
[111] Rosenkranz, *op. cit.*, p. 30.

threw them back (to Judaism and Jewishness), that is to a fate from which, dying, they distanced themselves: they did not want to be Jews any longer and had Jewishness forced upon them."[112]

Only very few Orthodox Jews appear to have committed suicide in Germany. Long before the Third *Reich* came into being the vast majority of Central and West European Jews had severed their ties with traditional Judaism in the course of emancipation. In Eastern Europe on the other hand, above all in Poland and Lithuania, the Jewish population was still firmly attached to their religious and national traditions. At the centres of East European Jewry, therefore, suicide remained a marginal phenomenon, with the exception of some members of Jewish councils and resistance fighters. In the few cases where Orthodox Jews did kill themselves it was not in order to avoid forcible conversion. The Nazis had barred that traditional way of escape. Orthodox Jews took their own lives when they were compelled to watch their families being butchered, or when they feared that they would not be buried in accordance with the law in a Jewish cemetery. Thus the norms and traditions of Judaism were operative in the Orthodox, but not in the secularised centres of the Jewish communities.

Some Orthodox Jews, in interpreting the Torah, went to the length of extolling death in the gas chambers as an act of "faith and sacrifice" for the greater glory of God.[113] In contrast, the attitude of the secularised German Jews who took their own lives was one of despair. Their faith in the reality of a German-Jewish symbiosis had been uprooted by the Nazi terror. Through their suicide they offered a sacrifice to that faith to which many of them clung to the last moment. That moment of truth, of final and decisive rejection, came for those people – people mostly of the older age groups, who had decided to stay on in Germany – when the deportation orders were delivered.

Sociologists have pointed out that the propensity to suicide increases with advancing age: loneliness, emptiness, uselessness and grief take their toll. "Social anxiety" manifests itself in depression and suicide. According to psychoanalysts, the struggle for love induces anger against those who withhold love and recognition, and aggression against the unloved self. The Jews in Germany strove for a long time to win acceptance and recognition, but it was in vain. The psychoanalyst could argue that the narcissistic, self-directed anger of the Jews erupted in suicide. Yet, contemporary sources reporting the suicides speak a language different from that of the theorists. They speak of careful preparations, of conversations and memories of a happy German childhood, of people remembering their children who have left Germany, and of those who in the final hours turn for solace to the German classics, inspired in their farewell to life by the words of Goethe and Schiller, by the music of Bach and Beethoven.

Such states of mind are documented by the fragmentary extant sources. Four testimonies have been selected here. Ilse Rewald, a young Berlin Jewess, who survived underground, remembers:

[112]Fliedner, *op. cit.*, vol. 2, p. 79.

[113]Cf. Nathan Blumenthal, 'Magical Thinking among the Jews during the Nazi Occupation' in *Yad Vashem Studies*, V (1963), pp. 221–236, and Joseph Walk, 'The Religious Leadership during the Holocaust', in *Patterns of Jewish Leadership in Nazi Europe 1933–1945*, Jerusalem 1979, p. 387.

"One did not really pity those who killed themselves with Veronal. If anything, they were admired for the courage with which they had taken the decision not to go on with a life that had ceased to be a real life. One woman in the arms factory where I was engaged in forced labour sold her Persian carpet and used the money to buy sleeping tablets. Later, when the list was sent to her, she showed no agitation at all . . . When on the next day she did not turn up in the factory, it was clear to all of us that she had found her solution."[114]

On 19th August 1942, Helene Waldeck, aged eighty, killed herself with sleeping tablets at the Mannheim Jewish hospital. In her farewell letter she wrote:

"I am ending my life, which I find no longer bearable, of my own free will. It is too much to bear for an eighty-year-old person who through all these years has led a decent life. I hope I shall be successful in what I am trying to do, I have had the tablets for many years. I had them already when my daughter took her own life, and when I should have gone with her, then I would have been spared a lot. I wish to thank the house where I was looked after at the end, I have to thank the nurses, the gentlemen, the doctor, they were caring and kind to me, but against the incitement campaign they were powerless. That I cannot see my children again makes this step harder for me, but they will understand."[115]

Heinrich Mugdan – classified as part Jewish (*Mischling ersten Grades*) by the Nazis – aided the suicide of his eighty-three year old Jewish grandmother. At the end of August 1942 he recorded in his diary:

". . . she told me of the early days, of her happy childhood, of her wonderful lovable mother; then she talked about her own dear little ones . . . On one occasion she asked for Thekla's monologue,[116] and we looked for the place in *Wallenstein*, or rather, she looked for it . . . 'I learned a hundred of Schiller's poems by heart, and I still know them all more or less' . . . And then she washed herself very thoroughly . . . , put on her final garments, plaited her hair, removed her false teeth and lay down . . . She prayed for a long time, and so that I could hear. I stood at the window, feeling so guilty . . . Then she took a large quantity of sleeping tablets. Even so, she could not fall asleep . . . 'I am praying for all of you. I am sure, it will work. Things will be better for you some day.' . . . In the end she fell asleep . . ."[117]

Finally, a report by Edith Wolff, a German-Jewish resistance fighter, describing the preparations for suicide of an elderly couple in Berlin, whose children had emigrated:

"One day, at the end of February 1943, Frau and Herr Kleinberger called at our place for a short visit at night, as they were going on a journey. They told us that they still wanted a really good meal with music and wine. They had received the deportation order and had already procured an antidote. We realised immediately that that medicine was poison and that their journey was one into death. There was nothing we could do about it, nor did we wish to interfere . . ."[118]

[114]Ilse Rewald's report is included in Jochen Köhler, *Klettern in der Großstadt. Volkstümliche Geschichten vom Überleben in Berlin 1933–1945*, Berlin [2]1981, p. 187.
[115]See Fliedner, *op. cit.*, vol. 2, p. 114.
[116]Schiller, *Wallenstein's Tod*, Act 4, Scene 12, in which the Duke's daughter announces her intention to follow her lover who had solved a conflict of conscience by seeking a hero's death in battle.
[117]Richarz, *op. cit.*, pp. 398 f.
[118]Yad Vashem, 01/247, p. 6.

The Expulsion of Polish Jews from Germany October 1938 to July 1939

A Documentation

BY SYBIL MILTON

The expulsion of Polish Jews from Germany on 28th and 29th October 1938, was overshadowed at the time and in subsequent historical analyses by the ferocity of the pogrom that followed on 9th and 10th November 1938.[1] Although the *Kristallnacht* has often been perceived as a pivotal moment in the evolution of Nazi policy from emigration to extermination,[2] it was the forced repatriation of Polish Jews that was a paradigm for later Nazi anti-Jewish measures. Furthermore, the plight of the expelled Jews trapped in no-man's land foreshadowed war-time international indifference to the murder of European Jews.

The expulsion affected approximately 18,000 Polish-Jewish residents in Germany.[3] On 31st March 1938, the Polish government had announced that the passports of Polish citizens residing abroad for more than five years would require revalidation. The German government believed that this measure was aimed particularly at Polish Jews in Germany and annexed Austria, who would remain trapped there stateless and impoverished. On 6th October 1938, the Polish government announced that the decree would take effect on 30th October, the deadline for passport revalidation.

The almost simultaneous failure of the Evian Conference during the summer of 1938 and the territorial changes in the Sudetenland, Hungary, and Slovakia following the Munich Conference in September 1938, had already resulted in the eviction of several thousand native and refugee Jews from these regions. Their bank accounts were frozen, their assets and property confiscated, and they were abandoned in border zones in improvised camps. These first chaotic deportations in mid-October involved about 3,000 Czech Jews in territories under German, Slovak, or Hungarian control. A joint memorandum of November 1938 described

[1]Most monographic literature gives only peripheral attention to the October 1938 expulsion. The rare exceptions include H. G. Adler, *Der verwaltete Mensch. Studien zur Deportation der Juden in Deutschland*, Tübingen 1974, pp. 91–105, and the extensive documentation section in Adolf Diamant, *Chronik der Juden in Dresden*, Darmstadt 1973, pp. 355–401, and in John Mendelsohn (ed.), *The Holocaust, vol. 3, The Crystal Night Pogrom*, New York–London 1982.

[2]Joseph Tenenbaum, 'The Crucial Year 1938', *Yad Washem Studies on the European Jewish Catastrophe and Resistance*, II, Jerusalem 1958, pp. 49–77; and Shaul Esh, 'Between Discrimination and Extermination', *ibid*, pp. 79–93.

[3]Exact figures on the Polish-Jewish population in greater Germany are not available for 1938, nor is it known how many Polish Jews left or were expelled between 1933 and 1938. The figure of 18,000 Jews represents about 25 per cent of the number of Polish Jews residing in 1933 Germany.

their plight: "Batches of them are driven from time to time to the Czech frontier, where they are usually refused admission, with the result that a number of them have been compelled to remain, under conditions of indescribable hardship, in temporary camps."[4]

Just before the new Polish passport regulations took effect, the Gestapo and German Foreign Office decided to deport Polish Jews from Germany on 28th October 1938.[5] The Jews were rounded up, and shipped to the Polish frontier in sealed and guarded trains; they usually left their property and assets behind. The Poles admitted them during the first day of the expulsion, but refused them entry thereafter, thus becoming accomplices in their plight. The expellees camped in no-man's land or were held in refugee detention centres on Polish territory near the border without permission to enter the interior of Poland. Emigration was foreclosed for most because of their status as stateless persons. Most of the Polish Jews had lived in Germany for many years, although they had been unable to acquire German citizenship. Even members of the younger generation, born and educated in Germany, and speaking only German, were still Polish citizens. Families were separated when wives and under-age children were left behind or sent back from the border. Young adults were often sent to different places than were their parents, especially if they were residing in different German towns on 28th October 1938. There were no visiting privileges between police detention centres or between refugee camps.

Although those Polish Jews arrested at the end of October were located through the centralised files created by German census records and residence registry cards, the pattern of the expulsions varied locally. (This was also true after 1941, especially for the deportation of Jews living in protected mixed marriages.) Thus, the *Regierungspräsident* of Frankfurt a. Main ordered that Polish Jews holding valid passports together with their wives and under-age children be arrested and sent to Poland in collective transports. In Baden, however, only men above the age of eighteen were affected by the expulsion order.[6] In Nuremberg, women and children were separated from the men and sent in a separate train two days later; but this train was turned back from the border and the travellers were released after paying the return fare.[7]

After initial detention in jails and other collecting points, the expellees were allowed to pack at the very most food for two days, small quantities of cash (usually 10 RM), and a minimum of their belongings. The traumatic effect of having to choose from a lifetime of possessions in a very few minutes caused enormous anguish. Fur-lined coats and blankets provided immediate relief

[4]American Jewish Joint Distribution Committee Archives, New York (hereafter Joint or JDC, NY), November 1938 memorandum about the "position of Jews in and from Sudeten German Areas", 3 pages.

[5]*Documents on German Foreign Policy, Series D, 1937–1945*, V, pp. 111–112 (Doc. 84), and V, pp. 117–120 (Docs. 91–92).

[6]Kommission zur Erforschung der Geschichte der Frankfurter Juden (eds.), *Dokumente zur Geschichte der Frankfurter Juden, 1933–1945*, Frankfurt a. Main 1963, p. 423; and Paul Sauer, *Die Schicksale der jüdischen Bürger Baden-Württembergs während der nationalsozialistischen Verfolgungszeit, 1933–1945*, Stuttgart 1969, p. 286.

[7]Leo Baeck Institute, New York (hereafter LBI, NY): Bernhard Kolb, Die Juden in Nürnberg, Nürnberg 1946, partly published ms., last page (addenda to page 63).

against the harsh winter climate, but baggage restrictions and the speed of departure did not always permit logical choices in packing. The uncertainty was compounded since many expellees did not know where they would be going. During the journey the deportees were crowded into trains with locked windows guarded by armed police and SS men. Occasionally local Jewish communities provided food, drink and money to the benumbed and hungry travellers.[8] Deportations were coordinated from all over Germany to several specific Polish border stations in Upper Silesia and Poznań province; this journey required bureaucratic synchronisation between the police and railway authorities. The round-ups of 1938 taught the SS how to organise the technical details for the later war-time deportations.

Although there were few fatalities on the journey, there was both panic and chaos at the Polish-German border. Over 8,000 Polish Jews were dumped at the border between Neu-Bentschen and Zbaszyn. The town of Zbaszyn in Poznań province had only 5,432 inhabitants, including 54 Jews, during the 1921 census and was ill-equipped to deal with the flood of arrivals who outnumbered them 2:1.[9] About 4,000 families crossed the border through fields and swamps between Beuthen and Kattowitz in Upper Silesia; similarly 1,500 people from Berlin and Königsberg were left stranded at Chojnice (Konitz). Similar incidents occurred at the Dworsky-Mlyn frontier post, and 4,000 Polish Jews were loaded onto German steamers and smaller vessels at Danzig, but only 1,500 were permitted to land in the port of Gdynia, compelling the others to remain on the ships.[10] The family of Sendel Grynszpan was in the convoy for Hanover to Zbaszyn and reached Lodz on 1st November 1938. The latter city had been the site of anti-Jewish riots and pogroms in September 1935, when several Jews were killed and hundreds injured. The Grynszpan's son, Herschel, a refugee in Paris, revenged his family's expulsion by assassinating the German diplomat Ernst vom Rath, ostensibly the provocation for the pogrom of 9th and 10th November 1938.

In the winter of 1938, the overcrowded refugee camp at Zbaszyn housed the largest group of detainees, ranging from 5,000 to 8,000 people from infants to the elderly. They slept in condemned military stables "still with the strong stench of the animals at one time kept there", and in unheated barracks. Most of the refugees (over 60 per cent) had neither money nor change of clothing. The absence of minimal comforts extended from the wretched housing to the overcrowded mess halls with inadequate utensils and tableware. In addition, unemployment, lack of privacy, and detention in the border zone created widespread demoralisation and the break-up of families.[11]

[8]The feeding of the deportees before their departure from Bochum is described in Ottilie Schönewald's memoirs, quoted in Martin Gilbert, *Final Journey. The Fate of the Jews in Nazi Europe*, New York 1979, pp. 18–21, and Rita Thalmann and Emmanuel Feinermann, *Crystal Night. 9–10 November 1938*, New York 1974, pp. 26–32. See also Document I about provisions for the Jews expelled from Chemnitz.

[9]In 1938, Zbaszyn had 4,000 inhabitants and six Jewish families. See JDC, NY: German-Polish refugee files: Troper report from Zbaszyn, 13th–14th November 1938, 7 pp.

[10]'Niemandsvolk im Niemandsland', *Jüdische Presszentrale*, Zürich, 11th November 1938 (vol. 21, No. 1013), pp. 8–9.

[11]JDC, NY: Troper report.

Between 30th October and 10th November 1938, several similar refugee camps in border zones holding from 50 to 2,000 Jewish expellees were created on the borders of Slovakia, the Sudetenland, and Hungary. Reporting on conditions at the Mischdorf camp near Bratislava, HICEM stated in late November 1938: "More than 300 refugees found themselves in an open field for one week, in a temperature which went as low as 20 degrees below zero during the daytime and 50 degrees below zero at night".[12] Similarly a two-lane highway connecting Kosice and Lundenburg held a "tent colony pitched 100 yards from the Czech border".[13] Despite supplies brought in by Joint and local Jewish relief organisations, conditions did not substantially improve. These encampments, originally considered temporary, became semi-permanent by July 1939; eventually, the Nazis occupied these regions and deported those Jews still confined in the camps.

Property belonging to foreign Jews was registered and inventoried during the early summer of 1938. During November and December 1938 the intermittent and stalemated negotiations between the Polish and German governments about the repatriation and fate of the abandoned property of the expelled Jews was resolved in the agreement announced on 24th January 1939.

This bilateral agreement allowed the 5,000–6,000 wives and under-age children left behind during the October expulsion to rejoin their husbands and parents in Poland. It also permitted up to 1,000 expellees with sufficient assets to return to Germany at one time to settle their personal and financial affairs before 31st July 1939. They could liquidate their personal and business assets and property and would be allowed to take household goods, professional, and personal possessions with them back to Poland without any fines or taxes. The money from the sale of their property would be deposited in blocked accounts in the Dresdner Bank and later diplomatic agreement would be reached about the transfer of these liquidated assets to Poland.[14] Although mutual government concessions were involved in successfully concluding the diplomatic negotiations, it is unclear whether the deportees benefited from this agreement. Many of those expelled owed rent and other business debts to German creditors; this money could have been collected against their abandoned and sequestered property or could have been subtracted from the sale of their assets. Obviously, even if small amounts of money were obtained and some personal and business property retained in early 1939,[15] this was again lost in the confiscatory measures that accompanied Nazi rule in occupied Poland after 1st September 1939. Furthermore those Polish Jews, approximately 8,000, who still resided in

[12]JDC, NY: Czechoslovak refugee files: Marie Schmolka (head of HICEM, Prague), Report on the situation of 2,000 Czech refugees, 13th December 1938, 7 pages.

[13]*Jewish Chronicle*, London, 4th November 1938, pp. 18–19; and JDC, NY: German-Polish and Czechoslovak refugee files, 1938–1940. Also 'Unwanted Jews pass Holiday in No-man's Land', *New York Herald Tribune*, 26th December 1938.

[14]National Archives, Washington, D.C. (hereafter NARS, DC): CDF 862.4016/2069 and CDF 862.4016/2078; both documents reproduced in Mendelsohn *op. cit.*, 3, pp. 303–327. See also NARS, DC RG238/NG 2654: Memorandum from Himmler to the *Reich* Chancellery, 8th February 1939 reporting on the agreement.

[15]See Document X.

Germany were affected by the Aryanisation of Jewish property after the November 1938 pogroms.

During the summer of 1939 the *Reichsvertretung* interceded on behalf of Polish and stateless Jews still threatened with expulsion and on 20th June 1939 formally requested an extension of the July deadline.[16] After the war began in September 1939, these remaining Polish Jews were arrested and deported to Sachsenhausen, Buchenwald, and other concentration camps.

The expulsion of Polish Jews in annexed Austria took place only in the summer of 1939. Immediately after *Anschluss*, the Polish Ambassador in Berlin, Jozef Lipski, negotiated a confidential agreement whereby Poland agreed to ignore the expropriation of Jewish property in Austria and the harassment of the Jews in exchange for the return of Polish oil industry shares held by Austrian Jews.[17] This made Poland an accessory in the increasingly brutal antisemitic measures directed against Polish Jews in former Austria. In October 1938, although threatened with expulsion, the Polish and stateless Jews received a four-week reprieve, a direct result of the negotiations between Dr. Löwenherz and Dr. Rothenberg of the Jewish community of Vienna and SS *Obersturmführer* Eichmann.[18] Holders of invalidated Polish passports were released from Gestapo jails but had to report daily to the police. Jews taken to the Polish border by sealed train on 28th–29th October 1938, were refused entry by Polish authorities and their return fares were charged to the Jewish community of Beuthen. On 8th May 1939, Himmler ordered all Polish Jews without exit visas and without valid passports to leave the *Reich* before 31st July 1939. Failure to leave would result in internment in a concentration camp. Consequently more than 3,000 Polish Jews were arrested for eventual transport, but overcrowding in the jails led to the cancellation of the order. On 8th July 1939, Himmler and Best exempted certain categories of Jews from deportation and expulsion. These exempted stateless Jews included: 1) old and sick Jews; 2) Jews married to German women; and 3) Jews preparing to emigrate within six months. These Jews were ordered to be released from jail and were free, but supervised by the police to whom they had to report daily.[19] Only after the invasion and occupation of Poland were Polish Jews from Austria taken into custody, deported to concentration camps, and their property confiscated.

The expulsion of Polish Jews from Germany is important for an understanding

[16]H. G. Adler, *Der verwaltete Mensch*, pp. 835–837.

[17]Emanuel Melzer, 'Relations between Poland and Germany and their Impact on the Jewish Problem in Poland, 1935–1938', *Yad Vashem Studies*, XII, Jerusalem 1977, pp. 217–224.

[18]NARS, DC: RG 238/PS 3934, affidavit of Dr. W. Bienenfeld, Deputy Chairman of the Vienna Jewish community, p. 6 (about the conversations of 27th-29th October 1938). Also Microfilm T 84/R13 – 39863: Daily report of the Gestapo Headquarters, Vienna, 27th–28th October 1938; and Central Archives for the History of the Jewish People, Jerusalem: Papers of the Vienna Jewish community, No. 2507: Memorandum by Dr. Löwenherz about a conversation with Eichmann on 29th October 1938. See also Herbert Rosenkranz, *Verfolgung und Selbstbehauptung. Die Juden in Österreich, 1938–1945*, Vienna 1978; and Jonny Moser, *Die Judenverfolgung in Österreich, 1938–1945*, Vienna-Frankfurt a. Main-Zürich 1966.

[19]NARS, DC: RG 238/PS 1941. Report from Dr. Fischer, *Reich* Plenipotentiary in Vienna, to Heinrich Himmler, 9th May 1940, recapitulating the difficulties since 1938 in expelling Polish Jews from Austria.

of later Nazi policies. It was the first sizable deportation of Jews requiring the coordination of railways, police, diplomats, and treasury officials. Polish inability and unwillingness to dissolve the refugee camp at Zbaszyn symbolised Germany's ability to make other nations partly liable for anti-Jewish measures. Although international welfare and tangible aid by agencies like the Joint did help the internees, many were stranded in camps along international borders. Furthermore, the expulsion led to the assassination of vom Rath and provided the Nazis with an excuse for the subsequent violence of the *Kristallnacht*. The October expulsion was a turning point in the persecution of the Jews.

THE DOCUMENTS

I

Letter from Julius Rosenzweig (born 1909 – died in the Warsaw Ghetto) to his younger sister Celia; Warsaw, 19th August 1939. The twelve page hand-written letter is in almost grammatical German, but occasional errors are the result of the writer's recent intensive use of Yiddish and Polish. The opening and closing paragraphs have been deleted.[20] Report on the expulsion of Polish Jews from Chemnitz.
Source: LBI, NY: Celia Rosenzweig Collection, AR 7128/1.

Warsaw, 19th August 1939

Dear Cilli,

Our expulsion happened as follows: The day in question, the 27th October, was bad from the beginning. Early in the morning I went to the Labour Exchange to get my [unemployment] benefit payment and was told that I would receive only RM 5.50 per week from now on instead of RM 12.50. When I came home, the second blow was waiting for me: a letter from the landlord, informing us we were not allowed to have any lodgers. In the afternoon I went to Herschberg to give him an English lesson. After we had finished I waited while Herschberg shaved. We then wanted to go into town together. I sat in his room while he was in the bathroom. Suddenly the doorbell rang, and I heard Herschberg talking with two men, whom he then brought into the room where they quietly sat down. I continued to read my paper. Suddenly I noticed that one of them wore a swastika and I had a dark suspicion that they might be from the Gestapo. He remarked that "he takes a long time to shave; he's probably tearing his hairs out one by one". He went into the bathroom and asked Herschberg who the man in the room was (meaning me). Herschberg gave him my name and, in answer to the next question, mentioned that I was a Polish citizen. The man came back, asked me for my passport (which terrified me), and identified himself as a Gestapo-man. He asked me where I lived; when I told him Moritzstrasse 2, he said that they had been looking for me for quite a long time. He kept my passport. In the meantime Herschberg was ready. The officials told us to put on our coats and come with

[20] All translations from German by Sybil Milton. Italics, apart from foreign words, denote words underlined in the original. Letter reproduced by permission of Celia Rosenzweig, New York. The Rosenzweigs arrived in Germany in 1904 after a journey via Port Arthur during the Russo-Japanese War and a civil marriage in London. They initially lived in Offenbach a. Main, later moving to Leipzig and Chemnitz. Her father was an import-export merchant who had fallen into financial difficulties in the early 1930s and had already been expelled to Poland in 1935. There were four children, including Julius and Celia. Celia held a Palestine certificate in 1938, which she never used and went to England in 1939 and eventually to the United States. Her brother, Julius, was born in Germany in 1909 and in 1938 worked as the sales representative for an oriental carpet factory. After the expulsion of her family, their apartment and possessions were sealed and Celia went to court in January 1939 and was allowed to auction off the household furniture for 600 RM before she left for England. Her mother's fate is not known; she probably perished in the Warsaw Ghetto.

them. In answer to our question where we were going, they said: to Palestine, and added that we had had five years time [to go there].[21]

We thought it was a joke, especially when we were told to take along food for twenty-four hours. In answer to my objection that I had to go home first to get the food and let my mother know, I was told that I was going to see my mother anyway. Then we left, one official went ahead with me, the other followed with Herschberg. While we were walking he asked me all sorts of questions, tried again to make me believe that we were being sent to Palestine, and added that I could thank my co-religionists for it. We came to Jakobsstrasse and suddenly found ourselves in front of Zweisinger's dance hall. In front of it stood a police car from which quite a number of Jews emerged. We were led into the hall, where many more Jews were already assembled. We talked among ourselves and speculated on what was going to happen to us. In the meantime more and more Jews were arriving, old and young men, women and children, accompanied by *Schupos* in uniform or plainclothes Gestapo-men.[22] The entrance was guarded by *Schupos* with guns, and many *Schupos* and higher police officers were wandering around the hall. One very young police officer, who seemed to be in charge, threw his weight about and abused us (though only verbally). By then Mother had arrived, and she told me that *Schupos* had come to our apartment and told her to dress warmly and also to take along food for twenty-four hours. The many thousands of Jews who were rounded up in Germany on the 27th and 28th October have never been told the real reason. Miss Kind came along with Mother. The *Schupos* never asked about the Aptekers.[23] It came out only gradually what was going on. I was handed a printed form, which stated that according to statute such-and-such, by order of the *Reichsführer* SS, we were expelled from Germany and had to leave the German *Reich* by 29th October.[24] The evacuation to Poland would be regulated by the Chief of Police. That, of course, was quite a blow. To be expelled so unexpectedly, and without knowing why: without being able to take anything with us, [we were to leave] just as we were. I personally had nothing with me, not

[21]Nazi propaganda before 1939 intermittently used slogans reflecting government policy of encouraging Jewish emigration. The phrase "Juden raus nach Palästina" appeared on mock railway tickets and children's antisemitic board games. See LBI, NY: National Socialism 1933–1945 Collection, AR 120/29. In this instance, the reassurances about emigration to Palestine were expedient for pacifying prisoners and ensuring the Gestapo and police an easier job of guarding the frightened arrestees.

[22]*Schupo* is the abbreviation for *Schutzpolizei*, the uniformed metropolitan Protective Police. For further information on police in the Third *Reich* see Henry Friedlander, 'The SS and Police', in Alex Grobman, Daniel Landes, and Sybil Milton (eds.), *Genocide: Critical Issues of the Holocaust*, Chappaqua, NY – Los Angeles 1983, pp. 150–154.

[23]Between 15,000 and 20,000 Polish Jews were expelled from Germany on 28th and 29th October 1938. It is estimated that approximately 4,000 wives and under-age children were stranded in Germany. There are no precise statistics about how many Polish Jews escaped the October raid. The Aptekers were illegal subtenants of the Rosenzweigs.

[24]The printed form is found in Manfred Unger, 'Die Endlösung in Leipzig. Dokumente zur Geschichte der Judenverfolgung, 1933–1945', *Zeitschrift für Geschichtswissenschaft*, XI, No. 5 (1963), p. 952 (Document 1); and H. G. Adler, *Der verwaltete Mensch*, p. 95. The Order [S.V. 7 2255/38-509-27] issued by the *Reichsführer* SS and Chief of the German Police, 26th October 1938, prohibiting the residence of Jews of Polish nationality is found in Joseph Walk (ed.), *Das Sonderrecht für die Juden im NS-Staat. Eine Sammlung der gesetzlichen Massnahmen und Richtlinien*, Heidelberg – Karlsruhe 1981, p. 247 (entry 569). It is reproduced in Helmut Eschwege (ed.), *Kennzeichen J. Bilder, Dokumente, Berichte zur Verfolgung und Vernichtung der deutschen Juden, 1933–1945*, Frankfurt a. Main 1979, p. 97 (Document 2); in *Dokumente zur Geschichte der Frankfurter Juden, 1933–1945*, pp. 422–423; and in *Documents on German Foreign Policy, Series D: 1937–1945* (Washington, D.C., 1949–1962), V, pp. 111–112 (Document 84) and V, pp. 117–120 (Documents 91 and 92).

even a winter coat. I was wearing my summer coat. What was going to happen to all the assets, the factories, businesses, shops, houses, flats? The hall became more and more crowded; some people who had not been found at home the first time, were being searched for again and again. It became later and later, we sat around the table of the dance hall from which Jews had been banned and which had now become our prison.

The noise in the hall got louder and louder, and the police officer had more and more opportunities to yell at the Jews not to run around so much but to sit down quietly and not to make so much noise. Enormous quantities were consumed that night; I don't think the place ever did such big business as that night, they must have made a mint. In the meantime it seems to have become known in the town what was going on. Many people came to say good-bye to friends and acquaintances. Others brought suitcases and things for the people assembled in the hall. Many had telephoned home and so were able to have things brought to them. Others had received permission to go home and fetch things, among them Mother, who claimed she had to go home to get medicines and clean underwear. She was away for several hours but did not bring much because she was terribly nervous being watched constantly by four policemen. That was around 2 a.m.: the Aptekers were no longer in the apartment. It appears that they hid somewhere in town. Mother did bring her fur-lined coat, which was important, and also a suitcase with underwear for herself and me, and some medicine. As it turned out later, it was probably fortunate that we could not take along more. Incidentally, only women received permission to go home; and not all of them, for the later it became, the more difficult it got to obtain that permission.[25] And when the 28th October began to dawn, nobody was permitted to leave. Despite tiredness, nobody was able to sleep, and we kept ourselves going by drinking a lot of coffee. You could not even go to the lavatory without the permission of the police. At the entrance a *Schupo* stood guard. Towards morning, it became noisier and noisier in the hall because obviously the evacuation was to start very soon. Before we dressed we were told we were going to be taken to the railway station. *We were not allowed to open windows; if we tried, they would shoot.*

When we went out into the street it was raining heavily. In the hallway and in the street people were standing around watching, others were peering out of their windows. We were loaded into police cars and raced to the station. Here again people were watching, but there were also Jews who had come to say good-bye. We were taken to platform 13. A special train stood ready. It took a long time before we could board it. A loudspeaker announced that all railway workers who had nothing to do with platform 13 were to leave immediately. (So that they should not find out what was going on!)[26] Finally we started towards Beuthen. It was 10 a.m., 28th October. We travelled the whole long day. It was a disagreeable, exhausting trip. Despite the previous warning, we did open the windows once in a while. Our provisions were soon consumed, and it was even harder to obtain something to drink. Some policemen were very friendly and brought us water at various stations; others refused, even the first-aid orderlies did not give us any water. We got on quite well with the *Schupos* and *Kripos* on the

[25]The relative courtesy extended to women reflects Nazi attitudes that women were less likely to cause trouble – and women, being responsible for the household, were more logical choices for packing suitcases. See Sybil Milton, 'Women and the Holocaust', in Renate Bridenthal, Atina Grossmann, and Marion A. Kaplan (eds.), *Women in Weimar and Nazi Germany*, New York 1984, (in press).

[26]The railway fares for the expulsion of Polish Jews from Saxony are discussed in Adolf Diamant, *Chronik der Juden in Dresden*, pp. 373–374; issues involving the railways after 1939 in Raul Hilberg, 'German Railroads, Jewish Souls', *Society* (November–December 1976), pp. 60–74; and *idem*, *Sonderzüge nach Auschwitz*, Mainz 1981.

train; they even joked with us.[27] Especially the *Schupos* were very decent, while the *SS-men, as we came to know later, were nothing but criminals*. Around 10 or 11 o'clock in the evening we reached Beuthen where, on another track, trains full of Jews from Leipzig and Dresden were already waiting.[28] Incidentally, one *Schupo* told us that there were *altogether 493 people from Chemnitz*. On the train were approximately 800 people, including Jews from Plauen, Glauschau, Zwickau, and all the other smaller villages around Chemnitz.[29] In Beuthen the Jewish community had organised the distribution of hot drinks and sandwiches. The *Schupo* nearest us also partook of this meal. We stopped for a very long time in Beuthen. We left around midnight; ten minutes later we came to a small station, our final destination. There we were gruffly told to get out of the train. Not all those who had luggage had taken it to their compartments; many had entrusted it to the freight car. Now they all wanted to get their things. There was a terrible crush and a typically Jewish lack of discipline in front of the baggage car.[30] Some people got their things, then the police had enough and *refused to hand out any more* (*this was the Upper Silesian police*). Miss Kind's case, with which I wanted to help her, was among them. (All the suitcases were later sent to Kattowitz, where they arrived months later, and were handed over to their owners by the Committee.)[31] Then we walked through the small station building out into the dark street. *Flanked by SS, we walked four abreast, and the SS kept urging us to walk faster, – without regard for the women and old people who were carrying suitcases*. The SS constantly insulted us, calling us Jewish swine, Jewish riff-raff. The walk seemed to be endless. The SS rushed us more and more; there were now no houses, we were in open country and did not know where we were being herded to. The suitcases grew heavier and heavier. Since I had nothing to carry, I offered to help a woman to carry her case for part of the way. It was sheer agony. The SS did not permit us to put the luggage down even for a moment in order to change hands. That might have made it too easy for us! They yelled, if you can't carry it, leave the junk behind. And many people did throw their cases away because they could no longer carry them. Not only our group was treated like that; those from the Leipzig and Dresden convoys had to suffer similar hardships. On and on it went, in the darkest night. Like ghosts in the night, it was terrible to see this veritable Exodus. As we were marching along we heard crying and wailing in front of us, which kept coming closer. I could not imagine what it might be. What was happening? Were people being shot? At last we came to the spot from where it came. There was an *enormous crush, crying,*

[27] *Kripo* is the abbreviation for *Kriminalpolizei*, the Criminal Police, the traditional detective force headed by the Prussian police officer Arthur Nebe. The behaviour of the perpetrators is discussed by Henry Friedlander, 'The Perpetrators', in *Genocide*, pp. 155–157.

[28] NARS, DC: CDF 862.4016/1828, report from David H. Buffum, American Consul in Leipzig to the Secretary of State, 30th October 1938, 7 pages. See Document II of this article.

[29] The statistics of the number of Jews expelled from Chemnitz is given as 322 and an additional 160 Polish Jews from the villages around Chemnitz in Adolf Diamant, *Chronik der Juden in Chemnitz*, Frankfurt a. Main 1970, p. 129. Diamant qualifies his statistics with the comment that the expulsion included only 78% of the Polish Jews in Chemnitz. It is possible that additional coaches were attached to Julius Rosenzweig's train, accounting for the discrepancy with Diamant's figures. Definitive statistics are not possible based on the available literature. See also Adolf Diamant, *Zur Chronik der Juden in Zwickau*, Frankfurt a. Main 1971 (im Selbstverlag), pp. 59–65.

[30] The negative assessment of Jewish personality reveals the absorption of Nazi prejudices by the author of the letter. Born and brought up in Germany in a family residing there for almost twenty-five years, his prejudices against *Ostjuden*, Poles, and Jews show the extent of his assimilation and identification with his German milieu. See Steven E. Aschheim, *Brothers and Strangers. The East European Jew in German and German Jewish Consciousness, 1800–1923*, Madison 1982.

[31] Committee is either the General Aid Committee for Jewish Refugees from Germany in Poland or the American Joint Distribution Committee.

wailing, and on the part of the SS threats, shoving, and beating. We had come to a stream, and the SS pushed everybody into it; people were falling all over each other, and the SS helped along with *rubber truncheons, horse whips, and the butts of their guns, and threatened to shoot anyone who dared to turn back.* Those who wanted to use their flashlights in this pitch darkness were also threatened with being shot because the SS swine did not want the Poles to know what was going on. The river was the border between Germany and Poland. When we climbed out of the water, with wet and muddy trousers and shoes, we were on Polish soil, in an open field with clay soil. In this rainy weather that was anything but pleasant. Now no one knew what to do, for no one knew which way to go. At long last we decided on a certain direction and after a while came to a Polish border guard who did not want to let us pass, although those who spoke Polish explained everything and pointed out that some of us were Polish citizens and all of us carried valid passports. That did not help at all because we had already crossed the "green border", and that meant we had crossed illegally. He would not let us pass and started to set his dog on us to drive us back. Again much crying, wailing, and jostling. Of course we were afraid to go back to Germany because we were sure we would be shot. Finally the guard turned his back on us and we continued further into Poland. Again negotiations started and *again he loosed his dog at us. Back in the direction of Germany.* When he turned his back on us, we turned around again. Later he called more soldiers, all armed, *all shouting contradictory orders.* We did not know what to do. Once we marched on for a bit, then we had to stop again. We stood on one side, the soldiers stood facing us on the other side. *The soldiers trained their guns on us*, and in our panic we thought they would shoot us. But perhaps they only wanted to torment us. Again we started to walk on and suddenly we realised that the soldiers were gone and we were alone; we also realised that they had led us in a circle and we were again walking towards Germany. Again much sobbing and crying, for to go back to Germany would have meant our destruction; we would have been killed outright or sent to concentration camps.[32] After these long hours of exertion many more suitcases were thrown away or left behind; (but everything that was abandoned on the Polish side was later picked up and soon returned to the refugees, while everything left behind on the German side was welcome loot for the Germans). Alone, we again tried to find our way into Poland; and again we were joined by a soldier who led us on a lengthy march to a piece of no-man's land where we could at last rest. It must have been around 4 in the morning. We sat down on trunks and stones and stayed there for about two hours. In front of us were three Polish border guards and, facing them, three SS-men. They carried on a lively conversation about us. The SS declared that we belonged to Poland; the Poles objected that we would take food out of their mouths. When daylight came we had to walk again and were led to a large meadow. By then it was 6 a.m., Saturday, 29th October. Our only good luck was that it did not rain too hard. Otherwise not all would have lived through this terrible night. We stood around on this meadow for quite a while and many felt sick from standing about in the fine drizzle. *Behind us was a line of Polish soldiers*; in front of us, SS and *Schupos.* What now? We did not know. It seems that *during the night Poles and Germans discussed what to do with us.* In short, we were again in the hands of the Germans, and the games of the previous night started all over again. Again we had to march in columns flanked by SS and police who forced us to move on and cursed us; again the

[32] Julius Rosenzweig could not know, of course, that all of them were to be trapped in Poland after the German invasion. He perished in the Warsaw Ghetto uprising of 1943. Information from Celia Rosenzweig, interview September 1982. Polish-Jewish men still in Germany in 1939 were sent to Sachsenhausen.

trouble with the luggage because they did not give us time to change from one hand to the other. Slowly we reached inhabited country; people gaped at us on the street and through windows. The SS hurried us more and more, and at last we were on a broad country road that led to the border. This was now the legal border post; we were rid of the Nazis and the Poles took over. At the end the Nazis lined up in three rows: one row SS, one police, and one customs officers, all with drawn guns, to make sure that nobody re-entered Germany. The Poles took charge very quickly; no passports had to be shown and the luggage was checked only cursorily. Then a Polish police officer took over. We passed a restaurant from which the group from Leipzig waved at us and called out to us. We were taken to an old school building in Tarnowitz, where we could buy coffee and sandwiches. The Jewish community of Kattowitz immediately sent a lorry full of food, without cost, enough for the whole day. The school was very crowded and not very pleasant (a typical Polish pigsty), but at least we could rest and, after two sleepless nights, get some sleep at last. That, however, was too much to hope. Just as we settled down, partly on straw, and partly on hard benches, we had to get ready to continue the journey. We were transported by truck to the train depot in Rivca. There we were given railway tickets to whichever place we wanted. We chose Warsaw, although most of the Chemnitz group went to Galicia. At Kattowitz we had to change trains. Here the Jewish community was already in action and distributed hot drinks. The community worked very efficiently all day long, even though it was the Sabbath. Our train left for Warsaw on Saturday, 29th October 1938, at 6:30 in the evening; we arrived there Sunday morning at 6:30 a.m. We had to wait two more hours in the station until somebody from the Rescue Committee came to fetch us.[33] We were then taken to the Committee [offices]. There we met the Fostel and Langmann families. The people from Frankfurt did not have such a horrible border crossing as the people evicted from Saxony; the Jews expelled from other parts of Germany also had easier experiences. On the advice of the Committee we spent the first night in rather unpleasant lodgings. But we slept quite well; after all we'd had three sleepless nights, since we also could not sleep on the train from Kattowitz to Warsaw. The next day Mother disappeared, while I was in town with Father. The Committee had sent her to Otvock, about 35 km. from Warsaw, where she was supposed to stay. We learned about this in the afternoon and immediately went there. By then it was late at night and Father and I stayed three days in Otvock and tried to find out where she was. We finally found out on Wednesday. She was taken to a reception centre with a number of other refugees, where she spent her days but had private lodgings for the night. I too spent a day there and slept in private quarters. Many families offered to take in refugees. Thursday Mother and I were taken to Falencia, where I stayed until 1st December; Mother is still there.

Well, I think I have written enough for now; you now know everything that happened. The expulsion of the Jews is really the fault of the Polish government, since it announced that anybody who had not come to Poland by 29th October, i.e., did not have a "blue stamp", would lose his Polish citizenship. Hitler did not

[33] Aleksander Hafftka, *The Activity of the General Aid Committee for Jewish Refugees from Germany in Poland: 1 November 1938–1 July 1939*, General Aid Committee for Jewish Refugees from Germany in Poland, Warsaw 1939, 63 pages mimeographed; and LBI, NY: Wilhelm Graetz Collection, ORT Report, 'Problem of Relief to the Polish Jewish Deportees from Germany', (Paris, 8th December 1938, 9 pages typed), AR 4121/IV 15; and TOZ report about 'Work on behalf of the Polish Deportees from Germany', (undated, 2 pages typed), AR 4121/VIII. Also Raphael Mahler, 'Mikhtavei E. Ringelblum mi-Zbaszyn ve'al Zbaszyn', (Letters of E. Ringelblum from and about Zbaszyn), *Yalkut Moreshet*, II, No. 2 (April 1964), pp. 17–31; and E. Ringelblum, 'Zbaszyn', *Folkshilf*, No. 1–3 (No. 97–99), pp. 88–93 (in Yiddish).

want to be saddled with so many stateless Jews and responded with a unique counter-measure. Within 24 hours he had rounded up ca. 25,000 Jews and chased them across the border, all in one day.[34] That you were returned to Germany shortly before you reached the border is probably due to the fact that it was too late. Poland would not have admitted anyone who had not crossed the border by midnight of 29th October.

II

Report No. 608 from David H. Buffum, American Consul in Leipzig, to Cordell Hull, Secretary of State. Leipzig, 30th October, 1938. The typed seven-page report about the "forced exodus of Polish Jews from Leipzig to Poland" is marked "strictly confidential". *Source*: National Archives, Washington, D.C.: State CDF 862.4016/1828.

I have the honor to refer to the mass movement of Polish Jews from Leipzig to the Polish border reported to the Department primarily in this office's code message of October 28, 1938 which reads in paraphrased form, as follows:

> "There is taking place today a summary expulsion from Leipzig to Poland of Polish Jews. Radical measures towards this end were started at five o'clock this morning, and it is said that three trainloads of Polish Jews have already been despatched towards the Polish border. The authorities have combed schools, homes, shops and even an old ladies home for Polish Jews and their occupants have been marched in the direction of the railway station. It is estimated that there are six thousand Polish Jews in Leipzig most of whom are connected with the fur business here. American interests are not as yet directly affected, but one American merchant reports that all his employees being Jews of Polish citizenship have been placed under arrest. It is anticipated that the fur trade here will be direly affected by this forced exodus."

This decidedly hectic exodus probably constitutes a shift of a people without counterpart insofar as speed of execution is concerned, for it was carried out at a virtually delirious tempo. By 8 p.m. of the same day the drive was initiated, the high bulk of Polish Jews resident by thousands in the long famous fur trade city of Leipzig were definitely on their outward way, probably none of whom knew even approximately whither.[35] Apparently the radical features of the plan surprised

[34]Julius Rosenzweig's figure of 25,000 is exaggerated for October 1938, when the figures of Joint and other agencies range from 15,000–18,000 expellees. His figure might well be accurate for the summer of 1939 when this letter was written. In early 1939, women and children not expelled were pushed across the border and Jews who had escaped by hiding were also subsequently caught and evicted. This meant that an additional 3–4,000 Polish Jews from Germany were deported during the first six months of 1939. Furthermore the Austrian Polish Jews whose expulsion was rescinded in October 1938 were evicted in May 1939; this added about 3,000 people more to the number of Polish Jews who were sent across the Polish border. For information on the May 1939 Austrian expulsion, see NARS, D.C.: T 84/R13-39863, daily report of the Gestapo Headquarters, Vienna, 27th–28th October 1938; *Widerstand und Verfolgung in Wien, 1934–1945* Vienna 1975, III, pp. 263–264 (Docs. 123–124); and LBI, NY: C. I. Kapralik, 'Wien, 1938–1939', London 1972, unpublished 40 page typescript memoirs based on contemporary diaries and documents.

[35]See Wilhelm Harmelin, 'Jews in the Leipzig Fur Industry', in *LBI Year Book IX* (1964), pp. 239–266. Buffum's report indicates that Leipzig, like Württemberg, expelled whole families, whereas in Baden only males above the age of eighteen were evicted leaving women and children behind. See Hans-Joachim Fliedner, *Die Judenverfolgung in Mannheim, 1933–1945. Dokumente*, Stuttgart-Berlin-Köln-Mainz 1971, II, pp. 71–74; and Sauer, *Die Schicksale der jüdischen Bürger Baden-Württembergs*, pp. 251–252.

local police authorities fully as much as the victims, for it has been ascertained that the former were routed from their beds at 2 a.m. on the morning of October 28, 1938 by a general alarm call from Berlin headquarters; that a few hours were devoted to list checking, and that a systematic and apparently relentless round-up was put into motion at 5 a.m. the same day – a round-up which is reported to have been not devoid of casualties.[36]

The fundamental reason behind this precipitate exodus is claimed to have been a decree promulgated by the Polish government two weeks ago stipulating that all Poles residing in foreign countries for five years or more must return to Poland by October 31, 1938 for passport regularities or forfeit their claims for Polish citizenship.[37] Exact stipulations of the alleged decree could not be ascertained in Leipzig. According to police authorities here it was of very recent enactment and of above enumerated gist. On the other hand, several Polish citizens interviewed maintained that they had never heard of any such decree and that in their opinion it had never been officially promulgated. At all events it seems logical to assume that the Polish government would not enact a decree of such potential possibilities three days before the punitive phase would be applicable, and just why the German government should wait until the 11th hour to apply countermeasures, probably could be explained only with difficulty and not by this office. It is the German claim that the alleged decree can be considered in the light of an attempt on the part of the Polish government to deposit a somewhat unwieldy parcel of undesirable nationals on Germany's doorstep. Insofar as countermeasures are concerned, it can be considered as an established fact that the only warning thereof received by persons involved here was the ringing of their door bells at an early hour followed by brusque demands to get into clothes, take a little money, some food and pass the keys of their homes to neighbors, as the persons summoned were told that they were about to leave the country.

The matter goes much further behind any Polish decree as intimated or the vigorously retaliatory action on the part of Germany. It actually can be considered as a reappearance on the scene of the ubiquitous minority ghost who came into being at Versailles on June 28, 1919. Practically all of the persons so peremptorily dismissed can be considered as Poles from a technical standpoint only as they were mostly residents of former Austria and parts of prewar Germany, such as Galicia and Upper Silesia that were designated to Poland by the Versailles Treaty and to former Austria by the Treaty of St. Germain. As it is understood that a high majority of them had no knowledge whatsoever of the Polish language, national customs in Poland or a means of livelihood other than where they were, probably very few among them had ever entertained even the remotest idea of proceeding to Poland for permanent residence. The compulsion from Germany is a "fait accompli", although there are unconfirmed rumors that the refugees involved have not been accepted as yet by Poland, and if the short notice decree supposition on the part of Poland is correct, it is considered quite possible that it would be difficult to find particularly ethical reasons on either side to justify such radical action. It is interesting to note that although the Versailles Treaty has been vehemently and repeatedly expounded from many a national socialistic rostrum as the root of all evil insofar as Germany and Europe are

[36]No statistics of the fatalities or injuries during the round-ups could be ascertained.

[37]Polish Legislation of 31st March and 6th October 1938 is reproduced in Jan Szembek, *Diariusz i Teki Jana Szembeka*, London 1972, IV, pp. 432 and 447; also in Waclaw Jedrzejewicz (ed.), *Diplomat in Berlin, 1933–1939. Papers and Memoirs of Jozef Lipski* New York–London 1968, pp. 461–462. An overall view of the problem is found in Melzer, 'Relations between Poland and Germany . . .', *loc. cit.*, pp. 193–229.

concerned, it was Germany yesterday that forcibly insisted upon one of the stipulations of the Versailles Treaty.

The speed with which the drive was executed was probably without parallel in the civilized world. Most of the victims were given half an hour to get dressed and wind up their personal affairs. It is estimated that 3,500 Polish Jews have already left Leipzig on four special trains. Police estimate that total evacuation from Saxony to date comes close to 12,000 persons. The exodus was replete with harrowing scenes such as separation of children from their parents, husbands from wives and cases of swooning from hunger, thirst, and the wild excitement of being herded, in most cases penniless, to an unknown destination. The death of one woman from heart failure has been confirmed. There are rumors of others.

There was certainly no lack of police, but in the general confusion of departure large numbers of intended victims eluded the vigilance of their custodians at the main station and fled for protection to the Polish Consulate in Leipzig and many in desperation appealed to this office for help. Letters were issued by this Consulate to those who were on the waiting list in Berlin for immigration visas and it is known that in seven instances they were allowed to remain.

Although without enjoying the rights of asylum, the Polish Consulate proved to be the only "Mecca" in the city and hundreds of bewildered persons streamed there for protection. I am informed by the Polish Consul that 1,300 Polish Jews spent last night on the Polish consular premises, which consists of a combined office and residence in a villa in the center of the city. Women and children were placed in the attic, others in the office section, in the dwelling quarters, on stairs, and in corridors. The cellar was filled to overflowing. The garden was a bedlam of humanity and most of the excited occupants shivered under makeshift tents, bushes, or whatever shelter that could be found during the course of a long night marked by a fall drizzle of rain.

It is expected in fur circles here that the exodus will have a chaotic effect upon the fur business for which Leipzig has been widely known for centuries. Over fifty percent of persons engaged in the fur trade here constituted Polish Jews and with its barred windows and empty streets the famous "Leipzig Bruehl" now has the appearance of a deserted village. There will be unfulfilled contracts, empty buildings, unpaid rents, disrupted bank accounts, and ruined stocks, in the opinion of several fur merchants interviewed. Forcibly abandoned stocks owned by Polish Jews at Leipzig go into several millions of marks, according to the trade, and losses from lack of vigilance could be appreciable ones.

While this despatch was being typed, a sensational development has occurred, or at least has just been brought to my attention, to the effect that the Polish Jewish refugees are being returned. One thousand are said to have arrived in Leipzig with empty stomachs and badly shaken nerves after a far from enjoyable weekend. There are rumours to the effect that during the course of negotiations in Warsaw the Polish Government threatened reciprocal treatment of Germans in Poland; there are others to the effect that the Polish Government made certain guarantees as to the citizenship status of the persons involved. Whatever the reasons, the exodus is in reversed direction.

III

Report No. 784 from A. J. Drexel Biddle, Jr., U.S. Ambassador in Warsaw to Cordell Hull, Secretary of State. Warsaw, 5th November, 1938. Typed seven-page report about the "mass expulsion of Polish Jews from Germany"...[38]
Source: National Archives, Washington, D.C.: CDF 862.4016/1824.

[38]Deletions of references to earlier American despatches and telegrams.

As reported in my despatch No. 757 of October 22, 1938, an Order of the Polish Minister of the Interior was promulgated on October 15, 1938, providing for the inspection of all Polish travel documents issued abroad by Polish Consulates. According to information obtained from a prominent official of the Polish Foreign Office, this Order . . . was designed primarily to prevent the wholesale expulsion of Polish Jews from Germany. This Order provided that all Polish passports theretofore issued to Polish citizens abroad were to be examined and stamped, if considered valid, by Polish Consulates, and it was further provided that the validating stamp was to be refused if any occasion for doubt arose regarding the authenticity or validity of the passport in question or if circumstances were found to exist which might act to deprive the holder of his citizenship. The decree was to enter into effect fourteen days after its promulgation, i.e., on October 29 at midnight, and it has been learned that it was the Polish Government's intention to refuse admission into the country after that date of all holders of nonvalidated passports.

When the Polish Government learned that it was the German Government's intention forcibly to repatriate a large number of Polish Jews prior to the enforcement of the Polish Order, and as a direct result thereof, the Polish Government immediately approached the German Government and offered to discuss the matter. It was proposed that an extension of the date of enforcement of the Order be made to November 15 with a view to coming to some mutually satisfactory arrangement. The proposal, however, was refused by the German Government and on October 28 the expulsion began. This movement continued throughout the night of the 28th and the following day and resulted in the entry of almost 15,000 refugees into Poland according to information received from the Jewish Relief Committee.

As the Department was informed in my telegram No. 244 of October 30,[39] the Polish Government began to take certain retaliatory measures in view of the fact that the German Government had refused all attempts at diplomatic negotiations and during the day of October 29 it appears that about 1,000 Germans residing in Poland, principally in Lodz, were placed under arrest and orders issued for their deportation to Germany. (This information is from journalistic sources.) It was only after this drastic measure had been taken by the Polish Government that the German Government offered to discontinue the expulsion and to allow the matter to become the subject of negotiations between the two Governments. On the morning of October 30 an official communique was published by the Polish Telegraphic Agency (PAT) reading as follows:

> "As a result of the exchange of views between the Polish and the German Governments negotiations will be opened next week to discuss the problem of Polish citizens of Jewish nationality inhabiting Germany. The negotiations will also cover the question of the return to Germany of Polish citizens recently expelled from Germany.
>
> In this connection all further expulsions of Polish citizens of Jewish nationality from Germany has been suspended, and transports which have already reached the frontier have been withdrawn.
>
> The Polish Government on its part has suspended the inaugurated expulsion of German citizens from Poland."

On November 2 these negotiations were commenced in Berlin between special delegations appointed by the two Governments. It will be noted from the

[39]NARS, DC.: State CDF 862.4016/1803; facsimile reproduced in John Mendelsohn (ed.), *The Holocaust. Crystal Night*, 3, pp. 9–10.

Vienna 1938. Jews seeking passports at Polish Consulate

By courtesy of Joint Distribution Committee, New York

Jews at the German–Polish frontier post at Zbaszyn, October–November 1938

By courtesy of National Archives, Washington, D.C.

Refugee camp in no man's land between Hungary and Czechoslovakia, winter 1938–1939

By courtesy of Joint Distribution Committee, New York

Refugees at Zbaszyn, October–November 1938

By courtesy of YIVO Institute, New York

Jewish refugees receiving food in a deserted flour factory (in the background the church of Zbaszyn)

By courtesy of Institute of Contemporary History and Wiener Library, London

communique that the Polish Government intends to discuss the return of these refugees to Germany although to date there is no indication that Germany will receive them.

From reports which have reached the Embassy through various reliable sources, it appears that the German action was most unexpected and took the Polish Government by surprise. Early on the morning of October 28 it is said that thousands of Polish Jews in Germany were routed out of their beds by the police who put them aboard trains bound for the Polish frontier. The refugees, mostly male Jews, were allowed to take with them only ten marks per person and a certain amount of food. At the frontier it is said that the Polish authorities were unwilling at first to allow the refugees to pass since they had come in such large groups and in such disorder. Subsequently, however, they were allowed to enter and were assigned to such quarters as were available. In Silesia it was reported that most of the immigrants were forced to walk for miles to the frontier and that they were treated rather brutally by their German guards. Most of them arrived in miserable condition and doctors and Red Cross nurses were rushed by the Polish Government to that section to take care of them. For want of better accommodations the refugees, it is understood, were put temporarily in the mines of the district. At Zbaszyn, on the main railway line from Berlin to Warsaw, it has been learned that the refugees were handled very roughly and that as a result they arrived in Poland in great disorder. Many had lost what few belongings they had managed to bring with them including their travel documents. Many were hysterical, and it is said that a few died of fright and several cases of temporary insanity were reported.

The arrival of these thousands of destitute individuals created an enormous problem for the Polish Government. Fortunately, various Jewish societies were able to lend some aid and they assisted the Government in making it possible, through small grants of money, to send a great many of the refugees to the interior of the country where they were received by Jewish communities. The Polish government, as previously reported, was very lenient in allowing the refugees to proceed and this report has been confirmed by the local Jewish press. Although the Government has not allowed any comment on this subject to appear in the press other than official communiques, the Jewish *Nasz Przeglad* of November 3 carried an item expressing the appreciation of the Jewish people for the benevolent attitude taken by the Polish Government.

The groups of refugees at Katowice in Silesia and at Chojnice in Pomorze were liquidated very quickly (they numbered approximately 7,000), but of the 7,000 or more said to have arrived at Zbaszyn, approximately 5,000 are still detained there.

A prominent official of the Polish Foreign Office in discussing this German expulsion Order with an officer of the Embassy staff, stated that while the Polish Government recognized the right of every sovereign state to deport aliens considered undesirable by that state, on the other hand, the Government considered that the manner in which this expulsion has been accomplished by Germany was nothing short of brutal. The same official has informed me subsequently that Poland is making every effort to conduct the present negotiations with Germany with a view to obtaining the restoration of, or adequate compensation for, the property of the refugees which has been confiscated by the German Government. In the course of the discussion on this subject, this officer indicated that the Polish Government hopes to link these negotiations eventually with those involving the credit of 120 million zlotys recently granted by Germany to Poland for the purchase of industrial machinery. The Department will recall that in my strictly confidential despatch No. 728 of

October 13, 1938, on the subject of the negotiations regarding this German credit to Poland, I mentioned the fact that other negotiations had been initiated simultaneously between Poland and Germany looking to the compensation for Polish Jews in Vienna who faced the loss of their respective properties and that, although these two sets of negotiations had been conducted separately, it was probable that the two might converge and be treated together. By such an arrangement it would be possible to earmark a part of the extensive German credit for the Polish Jewish refugees. It has been suggested that interest bearing notes could be issued by the Government against a part of the credit as payment to the refugees.

My aforementioned informant estimates that prior to the commencement of the expulsion there were between 60 and 70 thousand Jews of Polish nationality residing in Germany.

IV

Letter from SS *Obergruppenführer* Werner Best of the *Reichsführer* SS and Chief of the German Police in the Ministry of the Interior to Hans Heinrich Lammers, Chief of the *Reich* Chancellery; Berlin, 29th October 1938. Four-page typed letter with marginalia by Lammers. *Source*: National Archives, Washington, D.C.: RG 238/NG 2654; also 1522/373329-52[40]

Berlin, 29th October 1938

S-V 7 No. 2295/38-509-27 (file number of the Interior Ministry) Rk 21309 B. (written in ink, file number of the *Reich* Chancellery). Re: Order prohibiting residence of Jews of Polish nationality.

On 6th October 1938, the Polish Government issued and on 15th October 1938, published a decree whereby all passports must bear a control stamp in order to remain valid. Passports which do not have this stamp no longer can be used for entry into Polish territory. With this decree the Polish Government obviously intended to make it impossible for numerous Polish Jews living abroad – particularly in Germany – to return to Poland. This would mean that some 70,000 Polish Jews in *Reich* territory would have to be tolerated permanently in Germany.[41]

On 26th October 1938, the Foreign Office instructed the German Embassy in Warsaw to make representations at once to the Polish Government and demand a binding statement to the effect that the Polish Government would admit holders of Polish passports from Germany into Poland even if the passports did not bear this validation stamp. The German Government would find itself compelled, as a precautionary measure, to expel all Polish Jews from *Reich* territory on very short notice.

The police responsible for the registration of aliens were instructed by the Foreign Office to issue immediate orders on a large scale to Jews of Polish nationality prohibiting further residence in *Reich* territory. The 29th October 1938 was set as the final date for leaving *Reich* territory, because after that date the Polish passport decree was in force. On 28th and 29th October 1938, some 15,000 Polish Jews throughout the *Reich* – particularly male adults – were taken into custody for deportation and brought in special transports to the Polish border.

Although these Polish Jews were in possession of valid Polish passports and the

[40]The above translation is a revised version of the text published in *Documents on German Foreign Policy, Series D*, V, pp. 117–119 (Doc. 91). Best was the head of the Legal Section of the Gestapo in 1938 and later served as plenipotentiary in Denmark.

[41]Note in margin: "Please see that I am kept currently informed. L[ammers], Nov. 1."

Polish passport decree is not to take effect until 30th October 1938, the Polish border police authorities – evidently on instructions from Warsaw – refused to receive the Polish Jews when they crossed the border into Poland. Through the massing of thousands of Polish Jews in a few border towns on the German–Polish frontier, some very disagreeable conditions resulted. In the night of 28th to 29th October 1938, we succeeded in pushing some 12,000 Polish Jews into Poland, partly by way of the frontier stations, partly surreptitiously (über die grüne Grenze).

The Polish Government issued instructions this afternoon to expel *Reichsdeutsche* immediately from Poznań and Pommerellen in reprisal. A report on the scope of these measures cannot yet be given, because so far no transports have arrived at the German border. According to German border police, however, these counter-measures of the Polish Government are supposedly confined to the expulsion of German Jews.

Meanwhile, diplomatic negotiations conducted by the Foreign Office with the Polish Government resulted in agreement by the two Governments not to expel each other's citizens. On the question of the treatment of Polish Jews, German-Polish negotiations are to take place in Warsaw at the beginning of next week. As a result of this agreement, the German border police have been instructed to desist from further removals of Polish Jews to Poland and to free all Polish Jews still in deportation custody by suspending the prohibition of residence issued against them, and permit them to return to their homes.

(signed) W. K. Best

V

Memorandum by State Secretary of the German Foreign Office Ernst von Weizsäcker; Berlin, 8th November 1938.
Source: National Archives, Washington, D.C.: RG 238/NG 2799; also 147/78712-13.[42]

The Polish Ambassador came to see me today, to get the German-Polish talks about the treatment of Polish Jews in Germany going again, which, in his opinion, have reached an impasse. I told Lipski that as far as I knew the talks had not been broken off and were not in such a state that the two of us had to cut the knot.[43] The salient question, namely, how to treat the people that had been expelled by us to Poland seemed about to be solved. A problem for which I too did not yet see any solution was what to do with those Polish Jews still in Germany, but the members of the German delegation were still examining this problem. What we most certainly could not accept was that as a consequence of their expatriation a hunk of 40,000 to 50,000 stateless formerly Polish Jews should be dropped into our lap. Lipski stated that my figures were exaggerated and described the great sacrifice Poland is supposedly making if she admits those who had now been expelled. Lipski claimed that this created an extremely heavy domestic political burden for Poland and also a burden for him personally, since he had done so much to act in our interests.

I told Lipski that to accept Polish property – and that is what the Polish Jews are – does not seem to me such a great sacrifice. Besides, Lipski ought to consider

[42]The above translation amends the translation published in *Documents on German Foreign Policy, Series D*, V, p. 122 (Doc. 95).

[43]Freiherr Ernst von Weizsäcker was State Secretary of the German Foreign Office, April 1938 – April 1943. Josef Lipski was the Polish Ambassador in Germany, 15th November 1934–1st September 1939.

the case of vom Rath. It would not surprise me if this incident were to lead to a considerable intensification of German measures against Polish Jews.[44]

VI

Letter of complaint about an excessively high bill for railway fares for the expelled Polish Jews, from the *Polizeipräsident*, Leipzig (signed Stollberg) to the Fares' Office of the *Reichsbahn* Directorate in Halle/Saale; no date, carbon copy.

Source: Facsimile from the Stadtarchiv Frankfurt a. Main reproduced in Diamant, *Chronik der Juden in Dresden*, p. 373.

On orders from the *Reichsführer* SS and Chief of the German Police in the Ministry of Interior of 27th October 1938 (SV 7 No. 2555/38-509-27) the immediate removal of approximately 1,650 persons by train from Leipzig to Beuthen (Upper Silesia) occurred. This was accomplished on Friday, 28th October 1938, with four special trains departing from the Central Railway Station in Leipzig.

Because of the especially difficult conditions occasioned by the short notice and rapidly implemented operation, there was no guarantee that the individual transports of the hurriedly arranged special trains could be fully occupied, and thus the required minimum of 500 persons was not reached on any of the transports.

The composition of the individual trains was as follows:

Time	*Adults*	*Children*		*Escorts*
		4–10 years	Under 4	
Train 1, 9 a.m.	371	17	22	17
Train 2, 10:55 a.m.	423	25	23	17
Train 3, 12:32 p.m.	356	19	27	17
Train 4, 20:02 p.m.	344	38	25	16
Total	1,464	99	97	67

For each transport from Leipzig to Beuthen (Upper Silesia), the Police Presidium paid 4,325 RM transport costs to the Cashier's Office at the main train station in Leipzig, since it was determined that the minimum fee to be paid for 500 people was set at 8.65 RM per person, or 40% of the full price of a trip of 540 km.

Because the total costs of 17,300 RM are especially high relative to the transported persons, I am therefore requesting that the figures be re-checked and that a corresponding adjustment of the fares be made and also instructions for the reimbursement of any overpayment be issued.[45]

[44]Herschel Grynszpan assassinated Ernst vom Rath in Paris on 5th November 1938, after learning about his family's expulsion from Hanover to Lodz. See Martin Gilbert, *Final Journey*, pp. 18–25; Rita Thalmann and Emmanuel Feinermann, *Crystal Night*; and Heinz Lauber (ed.), *Judenpogrom. "Reichskristallnacht" November 1938 in Grossdeutschland*, Gerlingen 1981.

[45]After re-calculating the fare base, the *Reichsbahn* Directorate in Halle reimbursed the Police President's Office for 1,440.60 RM on 22nd November 1938. Diamant, *Chronik der Juden in Dresden*, p. 374.

VII

Letter from [Herbert] von Dirksen to [Ernst] Wörmann,[46] on official embassy letterhead. Dated: London, 30th November 1938.
Source: LBI, NY: Max Kreutzberger Collection, AR 7183/Box 17, file 7: photocopies of E 523624–26 of German Foreign Office Records.

I have not yet thanked you for your letter of 21st November regarding our participation in a settlement of the Jewish emigration question, since a special reply was superfluous after Mr. [Karl-Heinz] Abshagen's trip to Berlin and Vienna.[47] Mr. Abshagen has now returned today and reported to me about the results of his trip as well as his discussions with Mr. Pell.[48] I have telegraphed the Foreign Office about this, so that I have very little new to add. I would like to state now how much I welcome our decision to remove as many Jews as possible from Germany in an orderly manner; I believe that we thus serve not only our own interests with our willingness to expedite Jewish emigration, but I am convinced that our decision also has very positive consequences abroad, here in England too.

I am appending a carbon of a note about Abshagen's conversations with Mr. Pell about the Polish attitude in the Jewish question; it is very interesting in several respects.

With best wishes,
Yours,
Dirksen (signed).

Aide-Memoire

Mr. Abshagen informed me as follows about his conversations with Mr. Pell of the local refugee committee:

The Polish Government is now extraordinarily busy in the matter of the Polish Jews and is exacting blackmail, so to speak. In both Washington and the Hague as well as here, they have made representations to the effect that the question involving the threatened expulsion of Polish Jews from Germany must be settled before the general Jewish refugee question from Germany can be tackled. If an immediate solution of the Polish Jewish question is not forthcoming, the consequences would be to so excite the Polish population that extensive anti-Jewish pogroms could be expected. Mr. Pell, characterising such actions as obvious extortion, added that Secretary of State Hull probably often made very unpleasant remarks to Ambassador Dieckhoff about the German government policy on the Jewish question, but that everything he said to Mr. Dieckhoff would be child's play compared to what the Polish Ambassador had to hear from Mr. Hull, when he made his previously mentioned démarche.

[46]Herbert von Dirksen was Ribbentrop's successor as German Ambassador in London. Ernst Wörmann was the second man in the German Embassy in London holding the rank of Minister, 1936–1938; he became Director of the Political Department of the Foreign Office with the title of Under State Secretary, April 1938–April 1943.

[47]Karl-Heinz Abshagen was a journalist and friend of Robert Pell. He was used as a confidential intermediary by Wörmann to arrange contact between Dirksen, Schacht, and Rublee.

[48]Robert Pell served as the head of the Division of European Affairs of the US State Department and was also a member of the American delegation to the Evian Conference and the Intergovernmental Committee (hereafter IGC). See Henry L. Feingold, *The Politics of Rescue. The Roosevelt Administration and the Holocaust, 1938–1945*, New Brunswick, New Jersey 1970; and John Mendelsohn, 'The Holocaust. Rescue and Relief Documentation in the National Archives', *The Annals of the American Academy of Political and Social Science*, 450 (July 1980), pp. 237–249.

Mr. Pell subsequently said to Mr. Abshagen, that the British and American governments most strongly disapprove in general of the politics of the Polish Government during the last several weeks; by this he was not only referring to the operation involving the Polish Jews residing in Germany, but also to Poland's attempt to separate Carpatho-Ukrainian territory from Czechoslovakia as well as the recent Polish surprise move signing a treaty with Soviet Russia.[49]

Mr. Pell believed that the Polish government would some day bitterly regret that it pursued these policies; if there ever was a German-Polish quarrel, no one would lift a finger to help Poland.

London, 30th November 1938. (signed) von Dirksen.

VIII

Letter from Emanuel Ringelblum to Raphael Mahler about conditions in the Zbaszyn refugee camp; Srodborow, 6th December 1938.
Source: *Yalkut Moreshet*, vol. II, No. 2 (April 1964), pp. 24–25.[50]

I am on vacation in Srodborow. I worked in Zbaszyn for five weeks. Apart from Ginzberg,[51] I am among the select few who managed to hold out for so long. I have neither the strength nor patience to describe everything we went through in Zbaszyn. I do not think any Jewish community has ever experienced so cruel and merciless an expulsion as this one. I saw a woman, still half-crazed, who was evicted from her home in Germany still in her pyjamas. Another woman, approximately fifty years old, was paralysed and carried out of her house to the border on an armchair held by young Jewish men. A man suffering from sleeping sickness was carried across the border on a stretcher, cruelty unmatched in history.

During these five weeks, we (Giterman, Ginzberg, and I;[52] and after ten days, Ginzberg and I) built a whole town with a supplies department; infirmaries; carpentry workshops; tailoring, barber, and shoemaking shops; a legal and emigration department; a post office with fifty-three employees; a welfare office; a petty claims court; a police department; and a cleaning and sanitation service. In addition to the 10–15 people from Poland, we have employed almost 500 refugees from Germany in these departments. The most important thing is that there is no feeling of condescension in this welfare; it is not a situation where some give and others receive. The refugees see us as brothers who hurried to help in a moment of need. Almost all important posts are held by refugees, who administer the departments. Our relationship with them is friendly, since we do not patronise them with philanthropy. For this reason no hard feelings exist. Every complaint of bad treatment is investigated, and more than one "philanthropist" has been sent away by us.

[49]Reference is to the Polish-Soviet Communiqué of 26th November 1938; see Gerhard L. Weinberg, *The Foreign Policy of Hitler's Germany. Starting World War II, 1937–1939*, Chicago-London 1980; Gordon A. Craig, 'The German Foreign Office from Neurath to Ribbentrop', in Gordon A. Craig and Felix Gilbert (eds.), *The Diplomats, 1919–1939, The Thirties*, New York 1963, 2, pp. 406–436; and Henry L. Roberts, 'The Diplomacy of Colonel Beck', *ibid.*, pp. 579–614.

[50]Translation by Dalia Levi and Rabbi J. Schachter, New York. The letters from Emanuel Ringelblum to Raphael Mahler, written in Yiddish, were published in a Hebrew translation with an introduction by Mahler in his article, 'Letters of E. Ringelblum from and about Zbaszyn', *Yalkut Moreshet*, II, 2 (April 1964), pp. 17–28. I would like to thank Mr. Samuel Frankel, Director of the Moreshet Archives, for making copies of the original Yiddish letters available to me.

[51]Ginzberg was the manager of the Zbaszyn refugee centre.

[52]Isaac Giterman was the representative of the Joint Distribution Committee in Poland.

Vast cultural activities have developed. The first thing we introduced was the use of Yiddish. It has become the vogue of the camp. We have also organised courses in Polish, and they are attended by about 200 people. We have set up several reading rooms and a library; the religious groups have set up a Talmud Torah school. There are also concerts and an active choir.

Even so, numerous problems still exist! Although service of the mid-day meal has improved, many people still have to wait for a long time before being served, and the weather has now become very cold. People still feel that they are in a camp. For the past five weeks, people have slept on straw mats in large dormitories. Although the halls are heated, there is no possibility to change clothes. The "public bath" has raised its price to 50 zloty [*ca.* $15] per bath and not everyone can bathe.

Many men who left their wives and children behind in Germany are now receiving terrible news from home.[53] People are going temporarily insane and agonise about their futures in Poland once they leave this camp.

The upkeep costs us 10,000 zlotys a day.[54] How long can we afford this? The government is not giving us a cent. We paid in full for straw we received during the first days from the district government. The future is envisaged in desperate terms. People in the camp have received notices that they have lost their Polish citizenship. We are all worried about their future and how long the status quo can continue. It seems that we are not going to accept Germany's terms and actions. This camp will become a propaganda vehicle; and no Jew will be allowed into Poland. We are the true antisemites. We will evacuate Zbaszyn only when the internees have the possibility of immigration. Zbaszyn has become a symbol for the defencelessness of Polish Jews. Jews have been humiliated to the level of lepers, to fourth-class citizens, and as a result we are all affected by this terrible tragedy. Zbaszyn was a heavy moral blow to the Jewish population of Poland . . .[55]

When I return to my normal routine in a few days, I will write further about everything.

IX

Covering letter from M. C. Troper, European Executive Council of Joint in Paris to J. C. Hyman, Executive Director of Joint in New York; Paris, 1st December 1938.
Two-page letter about Joint expenditures and conditions of the homeless refugees in Poland, also contains a seven-page single-space report from Isaac Giterman of the Warsaw office of Joint about Zbaszyn.
Source: Archives of the Joint Distribution Committee, New York.[56]

Paris, 1st December 1938

Dear Mr. Hyman:

. . . In the meantime you have undoubtedly received my brief report on my visit to Zbaszyn. Subsequently, at my request, Mr. Giterman of our Warsaw

[53] The pogrom of 9th–10th November 1938.
[54] *Ca.* $2,000–2,500 per day.
[55] The deletions refer to Ringelblum's historical studies and the activities of the History Committee of the YIVO Institute in New York City.
[56] Especial thanks to Rose Klepfisz, Archivist at Joint for making this material available. Both the cover letter and report have been condensed. The rough English translation of Giterman's report was prepared by the Warsaw office of Joint; I have edited and corrected occasional grammatical lapses in the original.

office, prepared a more detailed statement, dealing not only with the situation in Zbaszyn, but with the entire problem of the 18,000 or more expelled Polish Jews from Germany. This report was translated by someone in the Warsaw office, and not wanting to lose time in getting it to you, I am sending you herein two copies which I have not attempted to edit. Although to date the JDC has appropriated only 130,000 zlotys (we authorized an expenditure of up to $30,000), it can readily be seen that this is no indication of what may yet occur, or the additional amounts which the JDC will be called upon to contribute, in view of the fact that funds from local sources may suddenly drop off. From the beginning of the emergency to the present time we have impressed upon the local population the importance of their furnishing the major part of the requirements, and thus far our efforts have been successful. However, you can understand that as time passes and the situation becomes more chronic, it will be more difficult to stimulate the same response from the people themselves. This will undoubtedly place a heavier burden on JDC, and what this will mean in dollars, we cannot foretell at the moment.

In Zbaszyn alone, the cost per day for the 5,500 refugees amounts to about 12,000 zlotys or over $2,000. Naturally, if the responsibility of caring for these people not only in Zbaszyn but in the cities of the interior to which a good number of refugees have gone, falls on JDC, substantially larger amounts will have to be made available.

In passing through Zbaszyn last Saturday, a delegation of the Refugee Committee came to the train. They advised me that some attempts were being made to provide heat, but that the situation in general was pretty desperate. They also mentioned that the Government had agreed to permit 50 children from Zbaszyn to go to relatives in the interior, and that old men and women over 65 years of age, of whom there are 350, were also being permitted to enter the interior. Under present circumstances this is regarded as quite a concession on the part of the Government, but there continues to be great dissatisfaction among the refugees who must remain in Zbaszyn . . .

Under separate cover I am sending you a few pictures taken in Zbaszyn.* You can understand, of course, that the military police prohibited the taking of photographs generally, and it was most difficult to get even those we are forwarding to you. Most of them were taken in the stables where the refugees live – stables that had previously been condemned for the use of horses.

Sincerely yours,
M. C. Troper
Chairman, European Executive Council

Enclosure: Seven-page report entitled 'Jews Exiled from Germany to Poland', by Isaac Giterman.

. . .

The number of the arrived homeless

It is difficult to give an accurate estimate of the number of expelled people as no registration took place, when the people were pushed over the frontier . . .

The number of the exiled is estimated at 17–18 thousand. According to our information during the night from October 28th to 29th: through the frontier crossing in Katowice 6,000 persons were expelled; in Chojnice – above 1,500, and in Zbaszyn and Drowski Mlyn – 8,500 persons, that is to say, about 16,000 in all. It is, however, not improbable, that the real number is even greater. At present we know about the following towns where large numbers of homeless are

* No photos were found in the Joint Archives.

sheltered: Cracow – 2,800; Warsaw – 1,200; Posen – 1,200; Lemberg – 1,000; Lodz – 600; Zbaszyn – 6,000. Others departed to various places in the country. In Stanislawow, Tarnopol, Tomaszow, Chorzow, etc., there are above 100 refugees respectively.

The reception of the homeless

During the whole day of October 28th, the news of the approaching arrival of refugees were not clear . . . Only late at night the first tidings arrived from Katowice that they had been informed from Bytom that during the night many thousands of persons would be pushed across the frontier. Taking with me the sum of 4,000 zlotys which was available at the moment, I immediately left for Katowice.

. . . The worst happened at Rodziankowo, 16 km. from Katowice where at 12 points between 2 and 4 a.m., 2,500 persons have been driven across the frontier. They have been beaten with terrible cruelty and shot at on a way of 5–6 km. in order to compel them to run. [sic] Arriving in Rodziankowo I found several persons lying ill on the ground. Some of them had broken hands and legs, since they ran into pits and holes. Many of the ill were still in the fields. First aid was given by 1 Polish and 8 Jewish doctors from Katowice. The German police did not allow them to take luggage out of the railway cars. Many persons have strewn all their things on the way. The things left on the Polish side were subsequently gathered by cars sent by the Jewish community in Katowice. It should be admitted here that the attitude of the Polish population was very humane. The local Christians have actively helped in organising aid for the expelled.

All refugees have been brought with cars and vans, placed at the disposal of the committee by the Jewish proprietors, to Katowice, and subsequently everybody left to places chosen by themselves.

Besides those driven over the frontier at Rodziankowo, 3,500 persons have crossed the frontier in trains at Bytom. As already stated, at Katowice 5,000 persons entered Poland. They have all been evacuated in the course of a day and a half. The Silesian voivoda [district official] declared that he did not wish refugees to stay in Silesia where antisemitism is particularly strong, and he helped much to transport them to other places. No registration was performed by the authorities, nor was anybody asked for his papers, and tickets were granted to any place in the country . . . It must be admitted the attitude of the police towards the homeless was not only correct, but humane in every respect . . . In antisemitic Katowice, where thousands of refugees were walking in the streets and on the stations, I did not notice . . . the slightest sign of antisemitism. It is noteworthy that some Christians even brought gifts for the refugees.

. . .

The situation which I found in Zbaszyn

. . . About 2,500 persons, many of them infirm and suffering were standing, or at best lying on the bare ground in the halls of the station building. Thousands were sheltered in the so-called barracks, horse stables, 10 men in every box. Most of those billeted in the barracks we found at 3 a.m. out of doors; they received nothing but bread and butter because nothing else was available on the spot. The barracks were filled with the sick, although above 100 persons in a serious condition have been sent to hospitals in adjacent towns.

To complete the picture it will suffice to say that most of the exiled have been taken without warning from their houses and promised to be released after half an hour. Therefore most refugees had nothing with them. Even among those who were more provident many have lost their things while being driven 9 km. over the frontier. We found some people in underwear or pyjamas only, for they had not even been allowed to dress. Families were broken up . . . In such a situation, most had only 10 marks in their pockets; above 8,000 people have been driven over the frontier, 2,000 who had money for railway fares left in the first two days. Just before our arrival, one of them committed suicide by throwing himself in front of a train.

Conditions under which we organized our relief for the homeless

Our first impression was that nothing could be done here. It would be impossible to organise any relief under the prevailing conditions. The number of refugees was twice the number of inhabitants of the town. There were only 6–7 Jewish families on the spot. Leaving aside the horrible shelter conditions, there was not even the possibility to warm some milk for a child nor for cooking food for the homeless. There were no plates, vessels, knives, or forks. For one and half days, our office was located literally in the street. It was a sight that could drive anyone to despair . . .

Concurrently with caring for food and nursing of those ill who have been left to the TOZ[57] doctors, we had to prepare the first party of 1,000 persons to be sent to various towns of the country. We chose first the old, infirm, and children. It was endeavoured to obtain free passages, but to cut the delays we covered the whole cost of 25,000 zlotys. Here however the unforeseen happened: they were forbidden to leave Zbaszyn. All 1,000 persons who were already seated in the coaches had to return in the dark to the barracks.

The despair of 6,000 sufferers when they have been apprised after all their misfortunes that they have got into a concentration camp is beyond description. I mounted a roof of a barrack and tried to appease the homeless. I had to struggle against the despair which threatened to submerge me too.

On the following day we suffered another blow. More than 2,000 persons lodged at the railway station had to leave in the rainy evening and we had to install them in the dark in lodgings which we got with the greatest difficulty. These lodgings were scarcely better than barracks. In the first days there was an imminent danger that these 2,000 would be compelled to leave the private houses where they have been accommodated. To lodge them in the barracks was physically impossible . . . The local police commander saved the situation . . . At the same time however the homeless have been forbidden to leave the barracks and sentries were posted before the barracks and the other houses. The gravest ordeal was when the authorities demanded that the homeless be vaccinated against typhus, because of the severe side-effects of the vaccine . . .

What has been done to alleviate the situation of the homeless

Despite all our efforts, we could not create tolerable conditions for the homeless. To this very day, thousands of people rest on the floor of the cold and filthy barracks and similar buildings . . . Even to this day conditions are entirely unbearable . . . Each person now at least has a straw bag to sleep on and his own spoon, tumbler, and basin. The children and infirm receive milk every day, there is enough linen for everybody, and some receive clothing . . .

The atmosphere among the homeless

. . . After initial despair at the prohibition against leaving Zbaszyn, it is now an almost normal Jewish town. There are organised discussions of Zionist youth and classes in Polish language. On Saturday, songs have been heard in the barracks. A confirmation has been celebrated and the Torah was read. Most touching was

[57]TOZ is the acronym for *Towarzystwo Ochrony Zdrowia* (Society for the Safeguarding of Health) created in 1921. It was subsidised by the American Joint Distribution Committee and OSE (*Oeuvre de Secours aux Enfants*). It provided total health care for Jews throughout Poland and included summer camps for children, hospitals, and public health clinics.

the request of all children below the age of 16 to be allowed to gather in a certain place and arrange some games . . .

It should be pointed out that the homeless were saved from an utter spiritual and moral collapse thanks to the warmth and care with which they have been surrounded by the delegates of the committees who came from all parts of Poland to Zbaszyn . . .

The work of the various committees for Zbaszyn

The report praises the response of Polish Jews to the tragedy at Zbaszyn, and mentions in particular the contributions of Joint, the Posen Committee, and the Central Relief Committee in Warsaw. Giterman calls this "a colossal rally of compassion and helpfulness". He also describes a "stream of volunteers willing to work; from every town 60–70 persons came . . . In the first days they had no time for eating and sleeping." He praises a Dr. Steier, the practising physician of Kalisz who left his work at the local hospital and was for the whole time active as store-manager at Zbaszyn. He sleeps in the store on the bare ground . . . His praise extends to help from the local Christian populace who showed sincere humane feelings and deep sympathy with the poor exiled Jews.

Expenditure on the work in Zbaszyn

Expenses amount to more than 8,000 zlotys a day. Besides the feeding and medical aid the committee has to pay rent for premises as well as for people living in private lodgings. Up till now, the JDC has spent 35 thousand zlotys on relief work in Zbaszyn until November 18th, out of the 150,000 zlotys given for this purpose. Besides this, more than 100,000 zlotys were spent by various committees on clothing. The percentage of JDC expenditure for this is relatively small and covers only the first few days until the committees were established. During the last weeks all expenses connected with relief work in Zbaszyn have been covered by the Central Committee in Warsaw . . . Substantial aid by JDC will be indispensable when the question of finding work for the refugees in Poland is faced . . .

X

Letter from the Saxonian Minister of the Interior to the *Reichsführer* SS and Chief of the Police in the *Reich* Ministry of the Interior, Berlin; Dresden, 31st December 1938.
Source: Diamant, *Chronik der Juden in Dresden*, p. 385.

Dresden, 31st December 1938

After my previous reports of 1st, 2nd, and 24th November, and 6th and 9th December, 1938, have remained unanswered, in which I urgently requested guidelines for handling economic questions arising from the expulsion operation, I must point out the following:

I ordered the sealing of residences and of some business premises of the expelled Jews in order to spare the *Reich* avoidable damage claims from the evicted Jews and the Polish government. Such claims were expected because the Polish Consul General in Leipzig had already given notice in principle. The securing of these premises has neither been approved nor disapproved of by you until now. With each passing week it results in increased damages for the Aryan creditors of the evicted Jews, damages which I can no longer justify. The Police and I are faced by growing mountains of very urgent complaints. The simple cases, where debts of expelled Jews were unknown or barely known, grow more complicated daily, often because the expellees naturally do not pay regular rents, but on the other hand, rent taxes must still be paid by the landlords. In many cases, there are already claims for damages advanced by attorneys, who represent the interests of their injured fellow nationals. Before long we can count on compensation and damage suits filed against the government. Until now, I have not considered myself empowered to empty the apartments in so far as the apartments' owners have not filed certified powers of attorney.

However, as I have stated, I can no longer justify current conditions and intend to release police officials as of 10th January 1939, to settle questions raised by the expulsion. I am assuming that none of the evicted Jews will return to Germany and am ordering that only the interests of the affected German nationals be given consideration, and that no further regard be paid to potential damage claims by the expellees and the Polish Government. I will permit court bailiffs to decontrol and sell off the property of the evicted Jews, in so far as the owners wish this and that no liabilities be levied against the police.

I request the return of individual cases.

(Signature)

XI

Letter from Dr. H. M. Hürzeler, Swiss Consulate in Leipzig, to the *Reich* Plenipotentiary in Saxony: Leipzig, 26th January 1939.
Source: Diamant, *Chronik der Juden in Dresden*, p. 387.

Leipzig, 26th January 1939

Gentlemen:

I have the honour to approach you about the following matter. Mr. N. Pindos, Dresden A 24, Nürnberger Platz 6, informs me that as the legally appointed agent for the Aryan Swiss citizen Julie Mayer of Vitznau, Switzerland, he has difficulty in emptying the property located at Dresden, Plauener Platz 2, owned by Mrs. Mayer and occupied by the Polish citizen of Jewish descent, Samuel Liptscher.

Liptscher was thrust across the border at the end of October along with other Polish Jews and his apartment sealed. The dwelling remains sealed up to now, so that it cannot be viewed by prospective tenants, nor can it be rented. Rent has also not been paid. The sealing occurred on orders from the Saxon Minister of Interior in Dresden in his letter of 22nd November 1938. His letter has remained unanswered until now.

I therefore urge that you reply to this request and take the necessary steps to release the apartment without delay, so that my fellow Swiss citizen suffers no additional damage from the previously enacted measures.

(Signed) Dr. H. M. Hürzeler
Vice-Consul

XII

Letter from Dr. W. K. Best, *Reichsführer* SS and Chief of the German Police to Dr. Hans Lammers, Chief of the *Reich* Chancellery; Berlin, 3rd February 1939.
Source: *Documents on German Foreign Policy, Series D*, V, p. 169 (Document 127).

Berlin, 3rd February 1939

Re: Order prohibiting the residence of Jews of Polish nationality; my previous letter of 2nd December 1938.[58]

[58] *Ibid.*, pp. 137–138 (Doc. 107), 2nd December 1938 letter from Heydrich to Lammers about the initial negotiations between the German and Polish governments, 2nd–10th November 1938, for an agreement regulating property questions and repatriation of the expellees.

The negotiations between the German and Polish governments have led to the agreement of which a copy is enclosed, and the agreement was put into force on 24th January 1939, by an exchange of notes between the Foreign Office and the Polish Embassy.[59] The concession made by Germany in permitting Polish Jews expelled at the end of October to return temporarily to *Reich* territory in order to wind up their personal and business affairs is offset by the fact that the Polish government has pledged itself to receive into Poland the expelled Polish Jews' wives and children under 18 years of age who are still in *Reich* territory. They are estimated to be some 5,000 to 6,000 in number. Care has been taken to see that all the Polish Jews who are now being permitted to return temporarily leave *Reich* territory definitely with their wives and children at the expiration of the time limit. No agreement could be reached with the Polish government regarding the treatment of the remaining Polish Jews some 7,000 to 8,000 still in Germany (the number of Polish Jews in the *Reich* in 1933 was about 70,000) since the Polish Government refuses to make any commitments with respect to the non-enforcement of Polish Law about the revocation of citizenship. It must therefore be expected that the rest of the Polish Jews still in *Reich* territory will shortly become stateless through revocation of their citizenship. The attempt will be made by means of the Foreigners Department of the Police to get as many of these Polish Jews as possible to leave *Reich* territory.

Signature: Dr. Best

XIII

Letter from SS *Obergruppenführer* Dr. Werner Best of the *Reichsführer* SS and Chief of the German Police, Berlin, to the Minister of Interior for Saxony in Dresden, Berlin, 8th July, 1939. *Source*: Diamant, *Chronik der Juden in Dresden*, p. 398, facsimile from Stadtarchiv Frankfurt am Main.

Berlin, 8th July, 1939

Re: Residence prohibition for Jews of Polish nationality.

The German border post at Neu-Bentschen commented on the 5th May 1939 report of the Dresden-Bautzen Sub-office of the Security Service as follows:

Polish Jews arriving as temporary returnees to German territory, rarely possess adequate funds to buy tickets from Poland to their destinations inside Germany. The Jewish Relief Committee in Zbaszyn (Bentschen) only provided them with tickets to reach Neu-Bentschen. To continue the journey from there, they must request money by telegram or telephone from relatives or acquaintances. In contrast to the Security Service (SD)[60] report of 5th May 1939, we have not

[59]The agreement stipulated that Polish Jews temporarily readmitted to Germany would be allowed to take away personal property and to liquidate other property without hindrance, the proceeds to be transferred through a special foreign exchange account to be set up between the two governments. Temporary returnees to Germany were not to exceed 1,000 persons at any one time and the opportunity for such temporary return would expire on 31st July 1939. See Doc. XIII, 8th July 1939 letter from Best to Saxonian Interior Minister; and also NARS, DC: Report from A. J. Drexel Biddle, Jr., US Ambassador in Warsaw to Secretary of State, Cordell Hull, Warsaw, 5th January 1939, NARS, DC: State CDF 862.4016/2069, published in Mendelsohn, *The Holocaust. Crystal Night*, 3, pp. 303–308; and Biddle Report No. 922 of 27th January 1939, NARS, DC: State CDF 862.4016/2078 *ibid.*, pp. 311–327.

[60]SD is the abbreviation for *Sicherheitsdienst* or Security Service headed by Reinhard Heydrich. It was a party formation created by the SS in 1931 to gather intelligence about the enemies of the Nazi movement. For further information on the Security Service see Friedlander, 'The SS and Police', *loc. cit.*, pp. 150–151.

observed that anyone remained without money. Judging by the money sent, it can scarcely be assumed that Jews will not have adequate financial means during their further stay on *Reich* territory.

It would mean a severe burden for the small Border Police station at Neu-Bentschen, if in addition to the present passport control, they would also have to inspect tickets and check cash reserves. Finally, it would seriously hamper these officials from performing their other more important tasks for the Security Service (SD).

In order to curtail unnecessary stays by Jews in Germany, I have limited travel permits to only two weeks after 31st May 1939. I assume that the Jews will have adequate means at their disposal for this period, so that they will not be a financial burden to anyone. If sporadic instances occur, where they are without cash, they must be helped by the appropriate local Jewish community.

I therefore request that for the brief interval until 31st July we refrain from the proposed type of inspection.

The suggestion [for inspection] would not be implemented either, since German border posts have for some time past still permitted the return of Polish Jews for only two weeks and after 31st July we no longer expect permission for further returnees to be granted. If the return trip of Polish Jews causes difficulties in individual cases because of lack of cash and if the Jewish community does not assume transport costs for these persons, they will be expelled to Poland in collective prison transports.

(Signature) Dr. Best

XIV

Letter from Emil Israel Engel, Executive Secretary of the Board of the Jewish community of Vienna, to Department II, Office for Foreigners of the Police Presidium in Vienna; Vienna, 30th May 1939; re: arrest of Polish Jews.
Source: *Widerstand und Verfolgung in Wien: 1938–1945*, III, pp. 263–264 (Document 123); original in Dokumentationsarchiv des österreichischen Widerstandes, Vienna, DOW 8496.

During the past week, a number of now stateless Jews – former holders of Polish citizenship which they lost as a result of the Polish legislation of October 1938 – were requested to leave German *Reich* territory as soon as possible; the time allotted to these persons for departure was often measured only by days. Many persons were also taken into custody with the stipulation that they be delivered to the Polish border.

The Jewish community of Vienna entrusted by the appropriate authorities with the direction and organisation of Jewish emigration from the *Ostmark*[61] and also with the regulation of preparations for issuing travel documents, confirms from their own observations that all Jews residing in Vienna, including naturally also those who are not citizens of the *Reich*, are most anxiously seeking to obtain emigration possibilities. Official instructions stipulated that the forms required for the release of travel documents be given only to those persons who can

[61] *Ostmark* was the territory of Austria annexed in March 1938. In October 1938, orders expelling Polish Jews from Vienna were rescinded. See Rosenkranz, *op. cit.*, p. 158. Also NARS, D.C.: RG 238/PS 3934, affidavit of Wilhelm Bienenfeld, Deputy Chairman of the Jewish community of Vienna, 4th May, 1946, p. 6: "On 30th October 1938, orders were given that stateless Jews and Polish citizens depart from Vienna within 24 hours. Dr. Löwenherz and Dr. Rothenberg in discussions with SS *Obersturmführer* Eichmann stated that this was impossible since departure approval could not be received during this short time period. This led to a four-week extension of the deadline."

produce proof of possible emigration to a specific country. During the last months, there were a large number of persons, among them Jewish emigrés, who after the loss of their Polish citizenship could emigrate only with the help of foreign passports.

However, those who would still have to wait after receipt of their visas, were not in a position to acquire foreign passports and could not receive passports from the Polish consulate in Vienna. There is no possibility that these persons would be allowed to enter by the Polish border authorities, but that they would be held accountable by *Reich* officials for want of valid emigration documents.

Therefore, it is requested that when extending residence permits for stateless Jews, who were originally holders of Polish citizenship, they should also be given the possibility for acquiring travel documents. However, for those persons who are presently detained (in custody) and are still holders of Polish citizenship and can thus cross the Polish border because of legal provisions, the Jewish community declares it is ready to cover travel costs when these individuals do not have their own funds and requests that the authorities refrain from further arrest and expulsion in these cases.

The Deportation of the German Jews Post-War German Trials of Nazi Criminals

BY HENRY FRIEDLANDER

In 1943 the Allied leaders – Roosevelt, Churchill, and Stalin – issued the Moscow Declaration, warning the "Hitlerite Huns" that there would be retribution for Nazi crimes.* They vowed to punish those who had committed "atrocities, massacres, and executions" in the territories occupied by Germany. After the German capitulation, the four occupying powers – France, Great Britain, the United States, and the Soviet Union – signed the London Agreement to establish the International Military Tribunal for the trial of the major war criminals at Nuremberg. The United States also created Military Tribunals at Nuremberg for the trial of cabinet and sub-cabinet Nazi leaders. At the same time, the four military governors established military commissions in their zones of occupation for the trial of lesser Nazis. Further, the Allies extradited Nazi criminals for trial in countries formerly occupied by Germany. Thus many of the men responsible for the murder of the European Jews faced their judges immediately after the end of the war. For example, Göring, Ribbentrop, and Kaltenbrunner were convicted by the International Military Tribunal and sentenced to death in Nuremberg. The chiefs of the *Einsatzgruppen* and of the concentration camp system were tried and convicted by the U.S. Military Tribunals at Nuremberg. Concentration camp administrators and guards were tried and convicted by American and British military commissions in Dachau and Lüneburg. The commandant of Auschwitz was extradited to Poland and executed in the camp he had once headed.[1]

Allied law applied only to crimes committed against Allied nationals. Allied courts assumed no jurisdiction for those committed against German nationals, including the German Jews. Of course, German Jews had been murdered together with Jews from other European countries. No distinction had been made between German and other Jews at the places of execution in Eastern Europe. German Jews had been shot together with Russian Jews in Minsk, with Latvian

*This article is a revised version of a paper delivered at the Leo Baeck Institute, New York, 1982. I would like to thank the following for information and documentation: Dr. Adalbert Rückerl, Leitender Oberstaatsanwalt der Zentralen Stelle der Landesjustizverwaltungen, Ludwigsburg; Hans-Jörgen Klingberg, Leitender Oberstaatsanwalt bei dem Kammergericht, Berlin; Matthias Priestoph, Oberstaatsanwalt bei dem Landgericht, Berlin; Daniel P. Simon, Director of the Berlin Document Center; and Sybil Milton, Chief Archivist of the Leo Baeck Institute, New York.
I dedicate this essay to the memory of my grandmother, Julie Friedländer née Lewiesohn, who was born in Posen in 1858 and deported from Berlin to Theresienstadt in 1942.

[1]Henry Friedlander, 'Nuernberg and other Trials', in *Genocide: Critical Issues of the Holocaust*, eds. Alex Grobman, Daniel Landes, and Sybil Milton, New York–Los Angeles 1983, pp. 381–383.

Jews in Riga, and with Lithuanian Jews in Kovno. German Jews had been gassed together with Polish Jews in Belzec, Chelmno, Sobibor, and Treblinka; in Auschwitz they had been murdered together with Jews from every country in Europe. The men responsible for these killings were tried and sentenced in Allied courts. In this way the killers of the German Jews did face their Allied judges. But the Allies did not assume jurisdiction over the crime of deporting the German Jews to their death in the East. This specific crime – the deportations that made the killings possible – had taken place on German soil and had been directed against German nationals.* Crimes committed against German Jews in Russia and Poland could be tried in Allied courts; those committed against them in Germany had to be tried in German courts.[2]

Late in 1945 the Allies slowly re-established the German judicial system. First, they purged it of its Nazi elements: Nazi laws were invalidated and Nazi judges were disqualified. Second, they re-opened the ordinary courts: Magistrate Courts (*Amtsgerichte*, or AG), District Courts (*Landgerichte*, or LG), and Circuit Courts (*Oberlandgerichte*, or OLG), together with the offices of State Attorney (*Staatsanwaltschaft*, or StA); all special and party tribunals, including the People's Court, were dissolved, and the former Supreme Court, the *Reichsgericht*, remained closed permanently.[3] This re-established judicial system operated under the rules of the German Code of Criminal Procedures (*Strafprozessordnung*, or StPO) in force since 1877.[4] The courts applied the customary German law, purged of its Nazi additions. Continental law, unlike Anglo-Saxon common law, is based exclusively on statutory penal codes. In Germany this remained the Penal Code (*Strafgesetzbuch*, or StGB) of 1871.[5]

The German courts were re-established to deal with ordinary crimes. Nazi crimes were reserved for Allied courts. In December 1945 the Allies issued Control Council Law No. 10 to provide "a uniform legal basis in Germany for the

*On the deportations see also the essay by Konrad Kwiet, 'The Ultimate Refuge. Suicide in the Jewish Community under the Nazis', and the survey by E. G. Lowenthal, 'In the Shadow of Doom. Post-War Publications on Jewish Communal History in Germany (IV)', in this volume of the Year Book – (Ed.).

[2]Adalbert Rückerl, *NS-Verbrechen vor Gericht*, Heidelberg 1982; Henry Friedlander, 'The Judiciary and Nazi Crimes in Postwar Germany', *Simon Wiesenthal Center Annual*, 1 (1984), pp. 27–44.

[3]For the various laws and regulations, see *The Statutory Criminal Law of Germany with Comments*, ed. Eldon R. James, Washington 1947, pp. 209–215; *Justiz- und NS-Verbrechen. Sammlung deutscher Strafurteile wegen nationalsozialistischer Tötungsverbrechen*, eds. Adelheid L. Rüter-Ehlermann and C. F. Rüter, 22 vols., Amsterdam 1968 ff., Registerheft, pp. 71 ff. (Hereafter cited as *JuNSV*.) For the re-established German judicial system, see Joachim Reinhold Wenzlau, *Der Wiederaufbau der Justiz in Nordwestdeutschland 1945 bis 1949*, Königstein/Ts. 1979; Friedrich Scholz, *Berlin und seine Justiz*, Berlin–New York, 1982; Karl Loewenstein, 'Reconstruction of the Administration of Justice in American-Occupied Germany', *Harvard Law Review*, 61 (1948), pp. 419–467; *idem*, 'Law and Legislative Process in Occupied Germany', *Yale Law Journal*, 57 (1948), pp. 724–760; Eli E. Nobleman, 'The Administration of Justice in the United States Zone of Germany', *Federal Bar Journal*, 8 (1946), pp. 70–97; Hans Julius Wolff, 'Criminal Justice in Germany', *Michigan Law Review*, 42 (1944), pp. 1067–1081 and 43 (1944), pp. 155–178.

[4]For the StPO, I have used the Beck'sche Kurz-Kommentare (1959 and 1966 edns.) and for current procedures the Beck-Texte im dtv (1981).

[5]For the StGB, I have used the Beck'sche Kurz-Kommentare (1958 edn.) and for a current edn. showing recent changes the *StGB-Vergleich* of the Beck-Texte im dtv (1975). For greater analysis, I have used the *Leipziger Kommentar* (various edns.).

prosecution of war criminals and other similar offenders".[6] This law was designed for proceedings in Allied courts, but it also included a possible exception:

> Such tribunal may, in the case of crimes committed by persons of German citizenship or nationality against other persons of German citizenship or nationality, or stateless persons, be a German court, if authorized by the occupying authorities.[7]

Thus German courts were at times permitted to apply Control Council Law No. 10 as well as the customary German law. Only one crime defined by Law No. 10 applied directly to proceedings in ordinary German courts:

> *Crimes against Humanity.* Atrocities and offenses, including but not limited to murder, extermination, enslavement, deportation, imprisonment, torture, rape, or other inhumane acts committed against any civilian population, or persecution on political, racial or religious grounds whether or not in violation of the domestic laws of the country where perpetrated.[8]

The use of Control Council Law No. 10 offered great advantages, making the conviction of Nazi criminals easier. It made no distinction between the perpetrator and his accomplice, rejected the defence of superior orders, and provided for penalties higher than the penal code. Further, it made conviction possible for deeds not previously prohibited by German law. In 1952, after the establishment of the Federal Republic, the use of Law No. 10 was discontinued.[9] Thereafter, only the German penal code could be applied.

During the immediate post-war years, most trials involving Nazi crimes dealt with relatively simple questions of fact and law. They involved local and random acts of violence against Jews. They did not require a great deal of investigation; they came to trial because the victim, or a relative, had denounced the perpetrator.[10] One case can serve as an example for all:

> *The Case of the Berlin Jewish tailor F.*[11] On 21st July 1944, one day after the attempted assassination of Hitler, a district Nazi party meeting in Berlin-Wedding discussed the appearance of a painted Soviet star with hammer and sickle on the bridge over the river Panke. The group of assembled junior party leaders decided to force the Jewish tailor F., who lived in the district, to remove

[6]Control Council Law No. 10 (20th December 1945), in *Trials of War Criminals before the Nuremberg Military Tribunals*, 14 vols., Washington 1950–1952, 1, pp. xvi–xix. German edn. in *JuNSV*, Registerheft, pp. 73–76. For the problems of translation (no Allied laws were ever issued officially in German), see Loewenstein in *Yale Law Journal*, 57, p. 743.

[7]Control Council Law No. 10, Article III, Section 1d, in *Trials of War Criminals*, 1, p. xvii.

[8]Control Council Law No. 10, Article II, Section 1c, *ibid.*

[9]Rückerl, *NS-Verbrechen vor Gericht*, p. 124.

[10]See the cases listed in Bundesjustizministerium, *Die Verfolgung nationalsozialistischer Straftaten im Gebiet der BRD seit 1945*, Bonn 1964, pp. 78 ff. For a statistical summation, see Der Bundesminister der Justiz, 'Bericht über die Verfolgung nationalsozialistischer Straftaten', Deutscher Bundestag, 4. Wahlperiode, Drucksache IV/3124, pp. 20 ff.

[11]German court records usually provide only initials for the names of defendants, victims, and witnesses; only in major cases are the names of the defendants provided.

the graffiti. Two cell leaders, the future defendants B1 and B2, volunteered to do so. They arrived at F's apartment at 8 p.m. The Jewish tailor, his non-Jewish wife who had recently given birth, and his Aryan mother-in-law were asleep. The men forced entrance, knocked down the protesting women, and dragged F. from the apartment, also beating him severely. At the bridge, the Jewish tailor, dressed only in a night gown, was forced to clean the graffiti with his bare hands. Unable to do so, he was beaten, kicked, and burned with cigars. The scene attracted a mob which encouraged and participated in the abuse. A police officer, who attempted to intervene, was told that "this man belongs to us, and we will finish him". When F. collapsed, he was thrown into the river. B1 and B2 attempted to drown him, but left him at the river bank when air raid sirens signalled an alarm. F. eventually was taken to the Iranische Street Jewish Hospital where he died on 1st August 1944.

B1 and B2 were men in their thirties. Both had been exempted from front line service as essential factory workers. B1 had been a member of the Nazi party since 1932; B2 was a member of the SS who had joined the party in 1940. After the war, B2 was captured by the Americans, turned over to the Soviets, and kept in a POW camp for SS members in Russia until 1950. B1 was arrested by the German police in 1945, turned over to the Soviet police, and kept in a Siberian labour camp until 1948. Both were arrested in this case upon their return to West Berlin.[12]

In 1951, the Berlin District Court convicted both under Control Council Law No. 10. B1 was sentenced to 15 years, and B2 to 12 years. In 1953, the *Bundesgerichtshof* reversed the decision and returned the case, because Law No. 10 no longer applied. Later in 1953, the Berlin District Court again convicted, but this time under the applicable German law. The Court did not convict for murder (*Mord*) or manslaughter (*Totschlag*), which are defined as intentional killings, because it could not prove that the defendants intended to kill F. Instead, the Court convicted for bodily injury resulting in death (*Körperverletzung mit Todesfolge*), and imposed a sentence of 10 years on each defendant.[13]

Most Nazi crimes against German Jews committed on German soil and brought to trial immediately after the war did not involve acts of random violence. More often they concerned bureaucratic measures designed to harass the Jewish victims. Often they resulted in deportation and death. Local officials guilty of such crimes against individual Jews had never thought that they could be indicted long after their victim had disappeared. As defendants they usually claimed that they had only followed legal procedures; their trials did not often lead to conviction. The following case can serve as an example:[14]

The City of Alzey vs. Bertha Franken. During the 1930s the city of Alzey near Mainz embarked on a project of urban renewal. For this purpose it bought real estate in the inner city. This project involved Kloster Street, designated for new

[12]LG Berlin, 10th May 1951, 1 PKLs 3/51, in *JuNSV*, 8, pp. 365–371; *Bundesgerichtshof* (BGH), 12th March 1953, 5 StR 83/52, in *JuNSV*, 11, pp. 235–236; LG Berlin, 14th July 1953, 1 PKs 3/51, in *JuNSV*, 11, pp. 229–234.

[13]For murder, see Art. 211 StGB; for manslaughter, see Art. 212 StGB; for bodily injury resulting in death (*Körperverletzung mit Todesfolge*), see Art. 226 StGB.

[14]OLG Koblenz, 3rd November 1949, Ss 122/49, in *JuNSV*, 10, pp. 539–540 (incl. summary of LG Mainz, 27th July 1949); BGH, 27th June 1952, 2 StR 161/51, in *JuNSV*, 10, pp. 541–542 (incl. summary of LG Mainz, 11th October 1950); LG Mainz, 4th March 1953, 3 Ks 3/52, in *JuNSV*, 10, pp. 527–538.

sewers and wider pavements. Kloster Street No. 8 was the property of a Jewish woman, the late Johanna Koch née Strauss. In the 1930s the property belonged to her three heirs: Albert Koch, who had emigrated to Toledo, Ohio; Luise Koch, an invalid who had died in 1937 owing the city of Alzey 10,000 RM for institutional care; and Bertha Franken née Koch, a resident of Berlin. In March 1941 the city of Alzey – fearful that a private company might preempt the city by purchasing No. 8 and nearby properties – expropriated this real estate. The Alzey Magistrate Court issued the order, and the urban renewal commission set compensation at 4,500 RM. Bertha Franken received her one third share of 1,500 RM. She contested the financial award, demanding an additional 4,800 RM for a total compensation of 9,300 RM. The Magistrate Court granted her appeal, and ordered the city to pay the additional money to the three heirs. The city appealed to the District Court in Mainz.

On 4th November 1941 Dr. H., the mayor of Alzey, wrote an official letter to the Gestapo in Mainz, complaining about the "colossal impudence" of the Jewess Bertha Sara Franken née Koch, and adding: "I therefore request that you persuade the competent authorities in Berlin to effectuate the departure of the Jewess with the next transport to the East." In March 1942 Dr. H. wrote a second official letter. Appealing this time to the regional office of the Nazi party, he requested that they influence Berlin to speed the deportation of Bertha Franken. The regional office appealed to the provincial (*Gau*) office of the party, which involved the party chancellery in Munich. On 2nd June 1942 Bertha Franken was deported to Lublin with Berlin transport No. 14; there were no survivors.

The first trial of Dr. H., the former mayor of Alzey, took place in 1949 before the District Court in Mainz. The Court failed to convict, accepting the defendant's argument that he had signed the letters without reading them. The Koblenz Circuit Court[15] reversed, contending that this defence was "improbable and unbelievable". In his second trial in 1950 the Mainz District Court convicted under Control Council Law No. 10, but only imposed a sentence of 10 months. In 1952 the *Bundesgerichtshof* reversed, because Law No. 10 no longer applied. However, the Court directed the lower court to consider a possible conviction under Article 239 of the penal code: deprivation of liberty (*Freiheitsberaubung*). The Court pointed out "that regardless of the fate that awaited them in the camps of the East, the deportations of the Jews constituted a deprivation of liberty and as such offended against law and justice". The Court thus argued that Article 239 should apply "even if the defendant did not know that the deportations, camouflaged as 'resettlement', were designed to exterminate the Jews".[16] In his third trial in 1953 the Mainz District Court rejected conviction under Article 239. The Court was not convinced that there had existed a causal relationship between the mayor's letters and Bertha Franken's deportation; she would have been deported anyway. Instead, the Court applied Article 49a: solicitation to commit a felony (*Anstiftung*). But because this crime carried a penalty of less than six months, the amnesty of 1949 prevented conviction.

These early cases established a pattern that would be repeated in most post-war trials of Nazi criminals. Perpetrators who were personally involved in physical killings (*tatnahe Täter*) – especially those who acted without orders or

[15] After the abolition of the *Reichsgericht* (RG) by the Allies, the competent OLG functioned as appeals court; after the creation of the Federal Republic the BGH, the highest federal court, replaced them as appeals court in felony cases.

[16] BGH 1952, in *JuNSV*, 10, p. 542.

exceeded their orders (*Exzesstäter*) – would be punished with greater severity than the *Schreibtischtäter* who used bureaucratic means – far removed from the scene of the killings – to accomplish murder.[17]

Unlike the crimes previously discussed, the deportation of German Jews to the East was a crime that did not usually involve acts of malice against individual Jews. It was an administrative crime against groups of Jews; the perpetrators were bureaucrats following orders. The first trial involving a deportation commenced in 1947 and concluded in 1948. It concerned a relatively small number of Jews from Württemberg; they were deported from the county of Hechingen, including the towns of Hechingen and Haigerloch. The perpetrator was the local county administrator (*Landrat*), who simply followed the orders he received. However, this minor case involved many of the issues of fact and law the courts would later face in all deportation trials.

The Hechingen Case.[18] In November 1941 the central office of the Gestapo (*Stapoleitstelle*) in Stuttgart notified the appropriate regional officials about the projected deportation of the Jews from Württemberg. While all arrangements in Stuttgart were carried out by the Gestapo, those in towns, villages, and rural areas came under the responsibility of local officials. The Hechingen *Landrat* thus received a list of Jews to be deported, as well as guidelines for the procedures to be followed. These included directives for the seizure of properties,[19] the items the Jews were permitted to take, the forms to be completed, and the means of delivering the victims to the Stuttgart collecting point. The *Landrat* carried out his orders. He issued orders to all officials under his command (including the police), and supervised their execution. The Jews were taken to Stuttgart, from where – together with other Jews from Württemberg – they were deported to the East. The first transport left Stuttgart for Riga on 1st December 1941. The same procedure applied to two deportations in March and June 1942; the second and third transports went to the Lublin region. A fourth and final transport, following the established procedures, left for Theresienstadt in August 1942. A total of 320 Jews were deported from Hechingen. The Court ascertained that only eight Jews survived: seven in Riga, one in Theresienstadt, and none in Lublin.

After the war the State Attorney indicted the *Landrat* under Control Council Law No. 10. At his trial before the District Court in Hechingen, the *Landrat* advanced a number of arguments in defence of his actions: he had acted on orders, he had acted under duress, and he had only been an unimportant cog in the deportation process. The Court rejected every defence offered by the *Landrat*; it convicted under Law No. 10 and handed down a sentence of 2 years and 6 months. It rejected superior orders as an acceptable defence, because Law No. 10 had specifically invalidated this justification. It also rejected the

[17]For a discussion of various types of Nazi criminality, see Herbert Jäger, *Verbrechen unter totalitärer Herrschaft. Studien zur nationalsozialistischen Gewaltkriminalität*, Olten–Freiburg 1967.

[18]LG Hechingen, 28th June 1947, KLs 23/47, in *JuNSV*, 1, pp. 471–493; OLG Tübingen, 20th January 1948, Ss 54/47, in *JuNSV*, 1, pp. 494–502; LG Tübingen, 12th August 1948, KLs 74/48, in *JuNSV*, 3, pp. 147–157.

[19]Trials involving the confiscation of Jewish properties during the deportations have been rare in the Federal Republic. For one crass example, see LG Munich I, 14th December 1954, 3 KLs 2/54, in *JuNSV*, 13, pp. 13–17. In this case the StA indicted the former head of the Bavarian Aryanisation office under Art. 255 StGB: extortion with the use of violence (*räuberische Erpressung*). The Court did not convict.

defence of duress (*Notstand*), contending that duress does not apply to a public servant whose official duty demands that he resist force to maintain the legal order, adding the prophetic comment: "If one would permit every senior civil servant (*höheren Beamten*) who took part in the deportation of the Jews to plead duress, probably nobody would be convicted for his participation."[20] In the same way it rejected the argument that he had only been a cog in a larger machine of destruction:

"The defendant has also argued that it cannot have been the intention of Control Council Law No. 10 simply to punish every type of participation in the persecution of the Jews. For example, the secretary who typed and mailed the Gestapo's deportation orders, or the engine-driver of the train that conveyed the Jews, cannot be culpable . . . But this does not mean that the *Landrat* is equally innocent. . . The responsibilities of the *Landrat* are very different from those of the secretary or the engine-driver. The duty of the secretary is limited to typing her dictation accurately and promptly; the duty of the engine-driver is limited to bringing the train safe and on time to its destination. Neither secretary nor engine-driver violate their duty if they do their jobs within the framework of the persecution of the Jews. The situation of the *Landrat* is very different. As the senior administrative and police officer of the county he is charged to protect the population of the county from unlawful attacks on their liberty and property; he violates his duty when he participates in an attack on the rights he has been appointed to protect."[21]

In 1948 the Circuit Court in Tübingen reversed this decision on appeal, returning the case for retrial to the District Court in Tübingen, and not to the one in Hechingen that had convicted the *Landrat*. The technical reason advanced by the Circuit Court concerned a 1941 circular of the Württemberg Jewish community (*jüdische Kultusvereinigung*), transmitting the orders of the Gestapo to the Jews of Hechingen and warning them to obey the deportation directives. The Circuit Court reversed because the District Court had failed to evaluate the impact this document might have had on the decisions of the *Landrat*. In addition, the appeals court also rejected the arguments against duress advanced by the lower court. Unlike policemen and firemen sworn to risk their lives to save others, a *Landrat* did not have a similar obligation. The District Court in Tübingen, conducting the second trial in 1948, refused to convict. It did so for three reasons. First, it found that the defendant had acted under duress,[22] accepting without proof the argument that if he had not carried out his orders, the *Landrat* would have been sent to a concentration camp. Second, it found that the *Landrat* had faced a conflict of obligations: a refusal to cooperate would have resulted in his removal from office, thus preventing him from protecting other residents of the county. The Court found that this conflict constituted an extra-legal justification preventing conviction.[23] Third, it did not believe that Control Council Law No. 10 applied in this case. The *Landrat* did not persecute the Jews of Hechingen "on racial or religious grounds" as required by Law No. 10, because he was actually a friend of the

[20]LG Hechingen 1947, in *JuNSV*, 1, p. 488.

[21]LG Hechingen 1947, in *JuNSV*, 1, p. 484.

[22]Art. 52, 54 StGB. For a detailed discussion of the *Befehlsnotstand*, see Jäger, *Verbrechen*, pp. 83 ff. Jäger did not find a single case where a German was penalised for refusing to commit this type of crime.

[23]The complex issues raised by the *übergesetzlicher Rechtfertigungsgrund* do not play a role in deportation cases; the Hechingen trial is virtually the only one in which they have been considered. However, they figured prominently in the post-war Euthanasia trials. See Henry Friedlander, 'Strafrecht und NS-Verbrechen. Die Euthanasie Nachkriegsprozesse', *Vierteljahrshefte für Zeitgeschichte* (in preparation).

Jews and an opponent of antisemitism. As evidence the Court cited letters that Jews who had emigrated before the war had written during the trial in support of the *Landrat*:
"He had always been friendly toward the Jewish population and had, whenever possible, helped them (Letter from Julie Levy)."
"He was an ardent anti-fascist and friend of the Jews . . . He should receive complete vindication, which would reflect the feelings of the surviving Jews from Hechingen and Haigerloch (Letter from Walter B. Frank)."
"Without his help, several members of our family would not have been able to leave Germany and thus save their lives. Considering his character (*Wesensart*), I consider it impossible that he would at any time have shown signs of antisemitism." (Letter from Ruth Grödel Löwengart).[24]

The trials discussed so far have only dealt with events on the fringes of the German-Jewish tragedy. They did not reveal the total crime. The deportation and murder of the German Jews had been systematically prepared, centrally directed, and executed with precision. Before later trials could deal with this premeditated crime, the state attorneys had to investigate the process and procedures employed by the perpetrators.[25] They had to chart the anatomy of the deportations.

Forced deportations replaced forced emigration as the official Nazi policy after the war had closed most borders to voluntary migration.[26] Although no exact figures are available for September 1939, we can assume that approximately 345,000 Jews remained in Greater Germany: *ca.* 185,000 in Germany proper (the so-called *Altreich*), *ca.* 60,000 in Austria (the so-called *Ostmark*), and *ca.* 100,000 in Bohemia and Moravia (the so-called Protectorate).[27] Before the systematic deportations of the German Jews commenced in the autumn of 1941, sporadic

[24]LG Tübingen 1948, in *JuNSV*, 3, pp. 150–151.

[25]See Rückerl, *NS-Verbrechen vor Gericht*, pp. 139 ff.

[26]For the evolution of Nazi policy, see Uwe Dietrich Adam, *Judenpolitik im Dritten Reich*, Düsseldorf 1972; Raul Hilberg, *The Destruction of the European Jews*, Chicago 1961; H. G. Adler, *Der verwaltete Mensch*, Tübingen 1974; Christopher Browning, *The Final Solution and the German Foreign Office*, New York–London 1978.

[27]Historians and the sources do not agree. For example, compare Hilberg, *Destruction*, p. 767; Gerald Reitlinger, *The Final Solution*, New York 1961, pp. 491–493; Lucy S. Dawidowicz, *The War against the Jews*, New York 1975, pp. 374–377. Most tabulations have used the Korherr report commissioned by Himmler: Der Inspekteur für Statistik beim Reichsführer SS, 'Die Endlösung der europäischen Judenfrage', Nuremberg Doc. NO-5194. But his figures, compiled in 1943, are inflated, and do not provide information about 1939. (Compare the figure of 100,000 Jews deported from the *Altreich* up to 1st January 1943, in Korherr report, p. 4, with the figure of 92,306 Jews, in Bruno Blau, 'Die Entwicklung der jüdischen Bevölkerung in Deutschland von 1800 bis 1945', Leo Baeck Institute, New York, manuscript collection, table 73 on p. 345). Almost all statistics concerning Jews during 1939–1945 are based on the Nazi racial definition, regardless of religion.
For Germany proper (*Altreich*), the census of May 1939, four months before the war, recorded 213,000 Jews. See Bruno Blau, 'The Jewish Population of Germany 1939–1945', *Jewish Social Studies*, 12 (1950), pp. 161–172. By September 1939 the numbers of Jews in Germany had dropped to 185,000. See Herbert A. Strauss. 'Jewish Emigration from Germany. Nazi Policies and Jewish Responses (I)', in *LBI Year Book XXV* (1980); Table I on p. 317. For Austria, the deputy chairman of the Vienna Jewish community reported 58,000 Jews in the city in December 1939. See W. Bienenfeld affidavit, 12th April 1946, p. 25, Nuremberg Doc. PS-3934; compare also Jonny Moser, *Die Judenverfolgung in Österreich 1938–1945*, Vienna–Frankfurt–Zürich 1966, pp. 51–52. For the Protectorate, the figures for December 1939 record 97,961 Jews. See H. G. Adler, *Theresienstadt 1941–1945*, Tübingen 1960, p. 7.

expulsions served as an experiment to test various possibilities of forcing the Jews from German territory. Although military conquest had brought millions of additional Jews under German suzerainty, the task of making Germany itself *judenfrei* retained the highest priority.

In October 1939, the first transports of deported Jews left Germany for the *Generalgouvernement* in Poland; their destination was a camp in Nisko on the San river east of Lublin. About 3,000 Jews from Vienna, Mährisch Ostrau, and Kattowitz were involved in these deportations before the Nisko plan was dropped.[28] In February 1940, the first deportations from Germany proper took place. 1,200 Jews were suddenly rounded up in Stettin; they were sent to Piaski near Lublin. In March 1940, 160 German Jews were taken from Schneidemühl to the Lublin region.[29] Thereafter deportations to Poland stopped, because governor Hans Frank persuaded Hitler to prohibit the further dumping of Jews in the *Generalgouvernement.*[30] Blocked in the East, the Nazi authorities moved in the West. In October 1940, about 6,500 Jews from Baden and the Palatinate were shipped across the border into France. The French authorities, surprised by the sudden arrival of these transports in the unoccupied zone, incarcerated the deported Jews in the Gurs internment camp.[31] Early in 1941, Baldur von Schirach persuaded Hitler to permit the deportation of Jews from Vienna to Poland; in February and March about 5,000 Jews were sent from Vienna to the Lublin region.[32]

In October 1941 the systematic deportation of the German Jews commenced. At that time Hitler had already ordered the physical annihilation of the European Jews, and the SS had already started to obey his command.[33] Since late June the SS *Einsatzgruppen* had killed Jews in mass executions in the territories occupied during the invasion of the Soviet Union.[34] But the murder of the Polish Jews had not yet commenced; the installations designed for this purpose had not yet been constructed.[35] The plans to deport the Jews from the territories conquered by Germany in the West and South had not yet been implemented; the

[28]Adler, *Der verwaltete Mensch*, pp. 125–140; Moser, *Judenverfolgung*, pp. 15 ff.

[29]Adler, *Der verwaltete Mensch*, pp. 140–147; Bruno Blau Ms., pp. 342–343; Helmut Eschwege, *Kennzeichen J. Bilder, Dokumente, Berichte zur Verfolgung und Vernichtung der deutschen Juden, 1933–1945*, Frankfurt a. Main 1979, pp. 162–164. See also *Lebenszeichen aus Piaski*, eds. Else Behrend-Rosenfeld and Gertrud Luckner, Munich 1970.

[30]Reitlinger, *Final Solution*, p. 46; Adam, *Judenpolitik*, p. 254; Helmut Krausnick, 'Judenverfolgung', in *Anatomie des SS-Staates*, 2 vols., Munich 1967, 2, p. 292. See also Nuremberg Doc. PS-1941.

[31]Adler, *Der verwaltete Mensch*, pp. 155 ff.; Bruno Blau Ms., p. 343. For Baden, see Paul Sauer, *Die Schicksale der jüdischen Bürger Baden-Württembergs während der nationalsozialistischen Verfolgungszeit 1933–1945*, Stuttgart 1969, pp. 268–282: 4,464 Jews from Baden arrived in Gurs. Of these 1,168 (26.2 per cent) died in Gurs; 491 (11 per cent) emigrated; 777 (17.4 per cent) survived in France; and 2,015 (45.1 per cent) were deported after August 1942 to Auschwitz and Maidanek (13 or 0.3 per cent survived the camps in the East).

[32]Adler, *Der verwaltete Mensch*, pp. 147–152; Moser, *Judenverfolgung*, p. 22.

[33]See Hilberg, *Destruction*, pp. 257 ff. and the rev. edn. *Die Vernichtung der europäischen Juden*, Berlin 1982, pp. 278 ff.; Krausnick, 'Judenverfolgung', pp. 297 ff. But compare also Adam, *Judenpolitik*, chapter 7.

[34]Hilberg, *Destruction*, chapter 7; Helmut Krausnick and Hans-Heinrich Wilhelm, *Die Truppe des Weltanschauungskrieges. Die Einsatzgruppen der Sicherheitspolizei und des SD 1938–1942*, Stuttgart 1981.

[35]See Adalbert Rückerl, *NS-Vernichtungslager im Spiegel deutscher Strafprozesse*, Munich 1977; Ino Arndt and Wolfgang Scheffler, 'Organisierter Massenmord an Juden in nationalsozialistischen Vernichtungslagern', *Vierteljahrshefte für Zeitgeschichte*, 24 (1976), pp. 105–135.

inter-ministerial conference to discuss such plans would not meet in Berlin-Wannsee until 20th January 1942.[36] But the high priority Hitler attached to the removal of all Jews from the Greater German *Reich* forced the bureaucrats charged with carrying out the Final Solution to tackle the problem posed by the German Jews out of sequence. In September 1941 Hitler ordered that the German Jews were to be deported immediately, and the bureaucracy moved to accomplish this task.[37]

The murder of the European Jews was a collective enterprise, and all levels of the German civil service participated (as well as local officials in all countries within the German sphere). But central direction was reserved for *Reich* Leader SS Heinrich Himmler, and especially the *Reichssicherheitshauptamt*, or RSHA, headed by Reinhard Heydrich (later by Ernst Kaltenbrunner). There direction (*federführend*) over Jewish affairs rested with Department IV (*Amt* IV), the Gestapo, headed by Heinrich Müller. In the Gestapo the so-called *Judenreferat*, designated RSHA IV B 4 and headed by Adolf Eichmann, exercised day-to-day control.[38] This office organised, coordinated, and often executed all administrative measures against the Jews; it exercised primary responsibility for all deportations. In the occupied countries it collaborated with the local offices of the security police (except in Russia, Poland, and Serbia, where deportations were not necessary because the killings took place nearby and thus did not require the services of IV B 4); in the allied countries it worked through the police attachés assigned to the German embassies. It delivered the deported Jews to the places of execution in the East, coordinating their arrival with the local police and camp commanders. The task of killing the Jews was the responsibility of Himmler's men in the East; the RSHA – and the *Führer* Chancellery – provided only directives and logistic support.[39]

In Germany the Eichmann office exercised direct control. Directives went to the local offices of the Gestapo, who carried out the anti-Jewish measures in their region. For the deportations, RSHA IV B 4 circulated guidelines with detailed instructions on the procedures to be followed. It also provided railway time-tables, assigned a quota to each locality, and issued orders for the number of transports.[40] In Germany proper, the regional Gestapo offices (*Stapoleitstellen*), and under their direction the district Gestapo offices (*Stapostellen*), organised the

[36]Nuremberg Doc. NG-2586. See also Hilberg, *Destruction*, pp. 263 ff.; Krausnick, 'Judenverfolgung', pp. 321 ff.; and Browning, *Final Solution and German Foreign Office*, pp. 76 ff.

[37]Adam, *Judenpolitik*, pp. 310–311; Adler, *Der verwaltete Mensch*, p. 173.

[38]Der Generalstaatsanwalt bei dem Kammergericht, 1 Js 1/65 (RSHA), Vermerk über das Ergebnis der staatsanwaltschaftlichen Ermittlungen nach dem Stande vom 30. April 1969 in dem Ermittlungsverfahren gegen Friedrich Bosshammer, Richard Hartmann, Otto Hunsche, Fritz Wörn wegen des Verdachtes der Teilnahme am Mord im Rahmen der "Endlösung der Judenfrage" (3 vols., Parts A-C), Part A, pp. 85 ff. [Hereafter cited as GStA bei dem KG, 1 Js 1/65 (RSHA), Vermerk]. The office was first designated IV D 4 Emigration and Removal (*Auswanderung und Räumung*) and later redesignated IV B 4 Jewish Affairs and Removal Matters (*Judenangelegenheiten und Räumungsangelegenheiten*). See Krausnick, 'Judenverfolgung', p. 284.

[39]GStA bei dem KG, 1 Js 1/65 (RSHA), Vermerk, Part B, pp. 255 ff. See also sources cited above in notes 34 and 35.

[40]For copies of these guidelines, see GStA bei dem KG, 1 Js 1/65 (RSHA), Vermerk, Part B, pp. 258–297.

deportations.[41] In Austria, the *Zentralstelle für jüdische Auswanderung Wien* directed the deportations in concert with the Vienna Gestapo; in the Protectorate, its Prague counterpart did so in concert with the Gestapo in Prague and Brünn.[42]

The procedures differed slightly from place to place and over time, but generally followed the guidelines prepared by RSHA. For each transport the Gestapo office compiled a list of persons to be deported. Those designated were ordered to report at a certain time and place; in some areas, especially after the number of evasions increased, they were picked up without notification. For several days they were kept in assembly centres, until the transport was fully collected and the paper work had been completed. They had to leave their apartments in good order, pay their household bills, surrender their keys, and take with them a limited quantity of personal possessions. They had to declare and surrender their money (except 50 RM), their valuables (except wedding rings), and their property. In the assembly centres they were searched for contraband by members of the Gestapo, who also arbitrarily confiscated many permitted items. On the day of deportation, they were taken to the station on foot or by truck, and loaded into sealed 3rd class passenger (later often freight) wagons. During the journey the trains were guarded by units of the *Schutzpolizei*, and sometimes they were also accompanied by members of the Gestapo.[43]

The Eichmann office and the local Gestapo offices used the Jewish organisations to transmit their orders and help to apply them. In Germany proper the Eichmann office required the services of the *Reichsvereinigung der Juden in Deutschland*; in the same way, the regional Gestapo offices used the local Jewish *Kultusgemeinde*, acting as a branch of the *Reichsvereinigung*. In Austria and the Protectorate, where the *Reichsvereinigung* had no jurisdiction, the Gestapo conscripted the services of the Jewish communities of Vienna and Prague. The Jewish organisations were forced to compile the lists for the deportations, or supply the pool of names from which the Gestapo could pick those needed for the next transport. They also notified those selected, and distributed the forms for the property declaration. They also staffed the assembly centres; they supplied food and other necessities for the journey. At first the Gestapo, with the aid of other police and party formations, conducted the round-ups; eventually Jewish monitors (*Ordner*) helped collect those designated for deportation.[44]

No one knows the exact number of Jews deported from Germany. No one knows the exact destination of every transport that left Germany; even the total

[41]For an example of the relationship between regional and district Gestapo offices, see directives concerning deportations from the *Stapoleitstelle* Nürnberg-Fürth to the *Stapostelle* Würzburg, in LG Würzburg, 30th April 1949, KLs 63/48, in *JuNSV*, 4, pp. 469 ff.

[42]The *Zentralstelle* had been established in Vienna in 1938 and in Prague one year later. See Adam, *Judenpolitik*, p. 201.

[43]For procedures in Nuremberg, see LG Nürnberg-Fürth, 10th May 1949, KLs 230/48, in *JuNSV*, 4, pp. 525 ff.; for Düsseldorf, see LG Düsseldorf, 27th May 1949, 8 Ks 21/49, in *JuNSV*, 4, pp. 633 ff.; for Cologne, see LG Köln, 9th July 1954, 24 Ks 3/53, in *JuNSV*, 12, pp. 575 ff. See also Raul Hilberg, *Sonderzüge nach Auschwitz*, Mainz 1981.

[44]See W. Bienenfeld affidavit, pp. 51 ff., Nuremberg Doc. PS-3934; Martha Mosse, 'Erinnerungen', Anlage 2, 23rd–24th July 1958, in Leo Baeck Institute, New York, Max Kreutzberger Research Papers, AR 7183, Box 7, Folder 6; StA Berlin, 1 Js 9/65 (Stapoleit. Bln.), Anklageschrift gegen Otto Bovensiepen u. a., pp. 115–119. See also Hilberg, *Vernichtung*, pp. 320 ff.

number of transports is in doubt.[45] Still, the approximate figures are known. Many documents have survived; a few victims have returned. Thus it is possible to reconstruct the pattern of the deportations.

The imposition of the Jewish star (*Kennzeichnung der Juden*) on 1st September 1941, to take effect on the 15th, was the signal for the start of the deportations.[46] On 14th October 1941, and again on the 24th, Kurt Daluege, the chief of the uniformed police, signed the orders for the first deportations.[47] Between 15th October and 4th November, the first twenty transports, containing a total of 19,953 Jews, left Germany for the ghetto in Lodz (Litzmannstadt). These transports, each containing approximately 1,000 persons, originated in various German cities: four came from Berlin; five each from Vienna and Prague; two from Cologne; one each from Düsseldorf, Frankfurt a. Main, Hamburg; and in addition one with about 500 Jews from Luxemburg.[48]

Lodz was not a logical choice as a destination. It was located in the territory–known as the Wartheland–that had been incorporated into the German *Reich*. Governor Arthur Greiser, determined to Germanise his fiefdom, wanted to expel all Jews. Only when this was not feasible, did he agree to the establishment of the *Gaughetto* in Lodz as an interim solution.[49] The Polish Jews incarcerated there could not claim the protection of the German laws. But the German Jews remained German citizens (*Staatsangehörige*), though with limited rights under the Nuremberg racial laws. Still, they had retained some rights, including property rights, pension rights, and access to the courts.[50] Deportation to Lodz, located within the borders of the German *Reich*, would not automatically invalidate the rights retained by German Jews as citizens. To deprive them of their citizenship and to confiscate their property, the Gestapo had to apply two laws dating from 1933: the "Law Concerning the Confiscation of Communist Property" and the "Law Concerning the Confiscation of Subversive Property".[51] But this was a time-consuming process; each person deported to Lodz had to be declared an enemy of the state.[52]

[45]See GStA bei dem KG, 1 Js 1/65 (RSHA), Vermerk, Part B, p. 365.

[46]Joseph Walk (ed.), *Das Sonderrecht für die Juden im NS-Staat*, Karlsruhe 1981, p. 347. See also Adam, *Judenpolitik*, pp. 333 ff.

[47]Reitlinger, *Final Solution*, p. 87; Adam, *Judenpolitik*, p. 311. See also Nuremberg Doc. PS-3921.

[48]GStA bei dem KG, 1 Js 1/65 (RSHA), Vermerk, Part B, pp. 356–357. See also Adler, *Der verwaltete Mensch*, pp. 168–175. For Berlin, see StA Berlin, 1 Js 9/65 (Stapoleit. Bln.), Anklageschrift Bovensiepen, p. 224; for Düsseldorf, see LG Düsseldorf, 3rd June 1949, 8 Ks 19/49, in *JuNSV*, 5, p. 5; for Cologne, see LG Köln, 9th July 1954, 24 Ks 3/53, in *JuNSV*, 12, p. 581; for Frankfurt, see *Dokumente zur Geschichte der Frankfurter Juden 1933–1945*, Frankfurt 1963, pp. 532–533; for Vienna, see Moser, *Judenverfolgung*, p. 28 and Herbert Rosenkranz, *Verfolgung und Selbstbehauptung. Die Juden in Österreich 1938–1945*, Vienna 1978, p. 285; for the Protectorate, see Adler, *Theresienstadt*, p. 701.

[49]Adam, *Judenpolitik*, p. 289. Himmler had to exert pressure on Greiser to accept the Jews deported from Germany. See Adler, *Der verwaltete Mensch*, p. 173.

[50]Adam, *Judenpolitik*, pp. 296 ff.

[51]'Gesetz über die Einziehung kommunistischen Vermögens', 26th May 1933 (RGBl. I, p. 293) and 'Gesetz über die Einziehung volks- und staatsfeindlichen Vermögens', 14th July 1933 (RGBl. I, p. 479). See LG Münster/Westf., 8th March 1961, 6 Ks 1/55, in *JuNSV*, 17, p. 92. See also Adam, *Judenpolitik*, note 319 on p. 301; Reitlinger, *Final Solution*, pp. 86–87.

[52]See StA Berlin, 1 Js 9/65 (Stapoleit. Bln.), Anklageschrift Bovensiepen, pp. 166–171. Every deported Jew had to sign a declaration invoking these laws to confiscate his property (see sample declaration, *ibid.*, p. 168). The StA Berlin was "surprised" that most witnesses, whose signatures

Considering these disadvantages, it is not clear why Lodz was chosen as the destination for the first deportations. It has been assumed that Hitler's sudden order prevented careful planning. The Baltic states (and Bielorussia), the destination for the next group of transports in November and December, would have been a better choice. There the *Einsatzgruppen* were prepared to kill the arriving Jews; in the Wartheland facilities for killing them had not yet been constructed. Two explanations have been advanced to account for the failure to send the first 20,000 German Jews to the Baltic. First, facilities were not available to receive them; thus the Latvian Jews had to be killed to make room in the Riga ghetto. Second, the railways could not provide the needed transport for this long journey; the chaos following the invasion of Russia prevented the utilisation of trains for the deportations.[53] These arguments, which have some merit, are not fully convincing. As we shall see, the SS *Einsatzgruppen* were prepared to kill the arriving Jews, thus making the question of available space redundant. The railways recovered sufficiently to carry the Jews to the Baltic only three weeks later.

For whatever reasons Himmler picked this destination, he only considered Lodz as an interim solution. In October 1941, while the transports of German Jews were arriving in Lodz, a killing installation was already under construction at Kulmhof (Chelmno) nearby; operations commenced there early in December.[54] Thus when Himmler assured Greiser in September that he planned "to deport [the German Jews] further East next spring" (*sie im nächsten Frühjahr noch weiter nach dem Osten abzuschieben*), he knew that Kulmhof would be available for this purpose.[55]

On 8th November 1941, four days after the last transport left for Lodz, the second phase of the deportations commenced. Henceforth the transports went to the *Reichskommissariat Ostland*, the German administrative region in the occupied Soviet territories that included Lithuania, Latvia, Estonia, and Bielorussia. Unlike the transports that left for Lodz, we do not have an absolutely accurate accounting of those sent to the *Ostland*.[56]

Between 8th November and 15th December, the period during which this phase was supposed to have been completed, twenty-two transports with an

---

appear on surviving copies, could not remember signing them (*ibid.*, pp. 170–171). But this author, who was deported from Berlin on 24th October 1941 with the second transport to Lodz, clearly remembers signing this type of declaration.

53 See Adler, *Der verwaltete Mensch*, pp. 168–175; Reitlinger, *Final Solution*, p. 90.

54 Rückerl, *NS-Vernichtungslager*, pp. 262, 268, 288.

55 Himmler to Greiser, 18th September 1941, cited in Adler, *Der verwaltete Mensch*, p. 173.

56 For compilation of the number and destination of transports to the *Ostland*, I have used GStA bei dem KG, 1 Js 1/65 (RSHA), Vermerk, Teil B, pp. 356–359 and 391 ff. For correction, completion, and confirmation of these figures, I have also used the list of transports arriving in Riga (27th November to 6th February), in Gertrude Schneider, *Journey into Terror*, New York 1979, p. 155; the list of Vienna transports, in Moser, *Judenverfolgung*, p. 34; and the list of Berlin transports, in StA Berlin, 1 Js 9/65 (Stapoleit, Bln.), Anklageschrift Bovensiepen, pp. 224–233 (this Berlin list, excluding the Theresienstadt transports, has been published in Robert M. W. Kempner, 'Die Ermordung von 35 000 Berliner Juden', *Gegenwart im Rückblick. Festgabe für die Jüdische Gemeinde zu Berlin 25 Jahre nach dem Neubeginn*, eds. Herbert A. Strauss and Kurt R. Grossmann, Heidelberg 1970, pp. 185–187). See also Adler, *Der verwaltete Mensch*, pp. 176 ff., and *idem, Theresienstadt*, pp. 45 ff.

approximate total of 22,000 Jews departed for the East. Of these ten went to *Riga* from Berlin, Cologne, Düsseldorf, Hamburg, Hanover, Kassel, Münster, Nuremberg, Stuttgart, and Vienna (*ca.* 10,000 Jews). Another seven went to *Minsk* from Berlin, Brünn, Düsseldorf, Frankfurt a. Main, Hamburg, and Vienna (*ca.* 7,000 Jews). Finally, five transports, originally destined for Riga, went to *Kovno* from Berlin, Breslau, Frankfurt a. Main, Munich, and Vienna (*ca.* 5,000 Jews).

Unlike the Jews sent to Lodz, not all those deported to the *Ostland* arrived in the Riga or Minsk ghettos. In this region, where the *Einsatzgruppen* had been operating since summer, the SS could easily dispose of Jews. This happened to the five transports re-routed to Kovno. They never entered the ghetto; instead they were taken to Fort No. 9 outside the city. There *Einsatzkommando* 3 shot them all in mass executions on 25th and 29th November; they were the first group of German Jews murdered as part of the Final Solution. In the report on its activities in Lithuania during July to November (the so-called Jäger report),[57] *Einsatzkommando* 3 listed dates, places, and numbers executed; the entries for the days in question read as follows:

25.11.41 Kauen-F. IX – 1159 Juden, 1600 Jüdinn., 175 J.-Kind. 2 934
(Umsiedler aus Berlin, München u. Frankfurt a. M.)

29.11.41 Kauen-F. IX – 693 Juden, 1155 Jüdinn., 152 J.-Kind. 2 000
(Umsiedler aus Wien u. Breslau)

In the same way, the first transport of German Jews to arrive in Riga never reached the ghetto. It had left Berlin on 27th November 1941, and arrived in Riga on the 30th, the day *Einsatzkommando* 2 killed most of the remaining Latvian Jews in the city. The German Jews were taken directly to Rumbuli Forest, where they were executed early in the morning before the operation against the Latvian Jews had commenced.[58]

All other transports arriving in Riga and Minsk during November and December 1941 escaped summary execution. However, there were still many casualties. The long journey and the winter cold killed many older persons; in a number of transports the SS killed upon arrival those judged unable to do heavy labour. The survivors entered the ghettos in Riga and Minsk, and also forced labour camps established in Jungfernhof and Salaspils outside Riga.[59]

The Eichmann office had been unable to meet its quota before 15th December, and therefore the deportations to Riga resumed after the Christmas holiday. During January and early February German Jews arrived and entered the ghetto. During this period ten transports with about 10,000 Jews reached Riga: three

[57] Facsimile of Jäger report, in Adalbert Rückerl (ed.), *NS-Prozesse*, Karlsruhe 1972.

[58] See Reitlinger, *Final Solution*, pp. 92–94; Krausnick and Wilhelm, *Truppe des Weltanschauungskrieges*, pp. 583–596.

[59] See witness testimonies in GStA bei dem KG, 1 Js 1/65 (RSHA), Vermerk, Teil B, pp. 391 ff. Also 'Bericht über die Evakuierung von Juden nach Riga' (Düsseldorf transport of 11th December 1941), in Adler, *Der verwaltete Mensch*, pp. 461–465 and Hilberg, *Sonderzüge nach Auschwitz*, pp. 130–138.

each from Berlin and Vienna, two from Theresienstadt, and one each from Dortmund and Leipzig.[60]

A third group of transports left for the *Ostland* between May and December 1942. At that time the *Ostland* was no longer the only destination for deportations from Germany, and only occasional transports arrived there. During this period almost all Jews were killed upon arrival. Twenty transports went to Minsk: one from Cologne, ten from Theresienstadt, and nine from Vienna. The Jews were killed – by mass executions or in gas vans – at Maly Trostinez and other locations outside Minsk. Six transports went to Riga: one from Breslau and five from Berlin. From these only very few persons were selected for the labour camps outside Riga; all others were killed. Two transports went to Estonia: one from Theresienstadt and one from Berlin (including 811 Berlin Jews and 236 from Frankfurt a. Main). Again, only those able to work were selected upon arrival for the labour camps near Reval.[61]

While the frequency of the transports to the *Ostland* decreased, the third phase of the deportations commenced. The new destination was the *Generalgouvernement*. As Belzec, Sobibor, and Treblinka, the camps of Operation Reinhard designed to kill the Polish Jews, began to operate, Governor Frank abandoned his opposition to the arrival of the German Jews. Thus between March and June 1942 numerous transports from Germany reached the Lublin region. The number of transports, their origin, and their destination are not fully known. Lists for some are not available; others only indicate "*nach dem Osten*" as the destination. We know about three transports from Berlin and six from Vienna; and one or more seem to have come from Breslau, Cologne, Darmstadt, Düsseldorf, Frankfurt a. Main, Munich, Nuremberg, and Stuttgart. The largest number – probably thirteen – came from Theresienstadt. The Jews were dumped into the small ghettos and camps of Eastern Poland; Izbica, Piaski, and Trawniki appear most often as the destination. But at least some of these transports seem to have gone directly to Sobibor. The deportations to Lublin ended in late June. Still, in October 1942 an additional five transports from Theresienstadt were sent directly to Treblinka.[62]

The deportations to the *Ostland* and the *Generalgouvernement* did not pose for the civil service the problems concerning citizenship, property, and pensions presented by those that had left for Lodz. On 25th November 1941, as the trains crossed the German border for the East, the bureaucracy issued the "11th Decree to the *Reich* Citizenship Law" (*Elfte Verordnung zum Reichsbürgergesetz*), which

[60]The GStA bei dem KG, 1 Js 1/65 (RSHA), Vermerk, Teil B, p. 358, does not mention Leipzig and Dortmund. Schneider, *Journey into Terror*, p. 155, lists both transports. Reitlinger, *Final Solution*, pp. 92–93, who uses the memoir of a survivor from Dortmund [Jeannette Wolff, *Sadismus oder Wahnsinn*, Dresden 1946] mentions only Dortmund.

[61]See Krausnick and Wilhelm, *Truppe des Weltanschauungskrieges*, pp. 583–596; Adler, *Der verwaltete Mensch*, pp. 195–197.

[62]GStA bei dem KG, 1 Js 1/65 (RSHA), Vermerk, Teil B, pp. 360 and 455 ff.; StA Berlin, 1 Js 9/65 (Stapoleit. Bln.), Anklageschrift Bovensiepen, pp. 224 ff.; LG Köln, 9th July 1954, 24 Ks 3/53, in *JuNSV*, 12, p. 581; LG Düsseldorf, 3rd June 1949, 8 Ks 19/49, in *JuNSV*, 5, p. 5; LG Nürnberg-Fürth, 10th May 1949, KLs 230/48, in *JuNSV*, 4, p. 529; LG Stuttgart, 19th September 1952, Ks 35/50, in *JuNSV*, 22, pp. 761–762; Adler, *Theresienstadt*, p. 50. See also Rückerl, *NS-Vernichtungslager*, pp. 155–157 and *passim*.

provided for automatic loss of citizenship and confiscation of property if a German Jew took up residence in a foreign country (*im Ausland*). Deportation to the East counted as a change of residence. To underline this fact, on 3rd December 1941 the "Directive for the Execution of the 11th Decree" (*Anordnung zur Durchführung der Elften Verordnung*) specifically included the *Ostland* and the *Generalgouvernement* in those foreign areas falling under the provisions of the 11th decree.[63]

In October 1941, a meeting of Gestapo representatives in the Eichmann office discussed procedures for the early deportations. Although Eichmann seems to have ordered the exemption of Jews of mixed parentage (*Mischlinge*), in mixed marriages (*Mischehen*), and over sixty years, the local Gestapo offices disregarded these directives during the winter of 1941–1942. The transports to Lodz and the *Ostland* included large numbers of old people.[64] But during the spring of 1942, possibly because the age of those deported discredited the public explanation that the Jews went East to do heavy labour, this policy changed. Later directives excluded persons over sixty-five, and their spouses if over fifty-five, from deportations to the East; instead, they were to be sent to the *Altersghetto* Theresienstadt in the Protectorate.[65]

Theresienstadt opened in December 1941. At first it served as a transit camp for Czech Jews, who had been sent directly to the East during the winter of 1941–1942; henceforth, they would be deported East only via Theresienstadt. Starting in June 1942, transports of Jews from Germany and Austria arrived in Theresienstadt. They included old people, but also other exempted categories: those with high military decorations, important international connections, non-Jewish spouses or parents.[66] These transports continued until the end of the war. For example, the first *Alterstransport* left Berlin for Theresienstadt on 6th June 1942; the 117th departed on 27th March 1945.[67] Although the death rate of the old was very high in Theresienstadt, many were not permitted to die a semi-natural death there; large numbers were deported from Theresienstadt to the places of execution in the East.[68]

The Gestapo called the deportations to Theresienstadt "change of address" (*Wohnsitzverlegung*). Because Theresienstadt was located in the Protectorate, and thus within the borders of the Greater German *Reich*, the provisions of the 11th decree did not apply; the RSHA found an ingenious way to confiscate property. Imitating the method used to buy a place in a nursing home, they forced the old people to sign a contract with the *Reichsvereinigung*, giving up all property for "perpetual care" in Theresienstadt (*Heimeinkaufvertrag*).[69] This hoax brought the RSHA, who took the money from the *Reichsvereinigung*, vast sums; the deported

[63]Walk, *Sonderrecht für die Juden*, pp. 357 and 358. See also Adam, *Judenpolitik*, pp. 292 ff.

[64]For the meeting in the Eichmann office, see GStA bei dem KG, 1 Js 1/65 (RSHA), Vermerk, Teil B, pp. 257–259; for the age composition of early transports, see witness accounts, *ibid.*, Teil B, pp. 391 ff.

[65]*Ibid.*, Teil B, pp. 263 ff., 276 ff.

[66]Adler, *Theresienstadt*, pp. 39–45 and *passim*.

[67]StA Berlin, 1 Js 9/65 (Stapoleit. Bln.), Anklageschrift Bovensiepen, pp. 224–233.

[68]Adler, *Theresienstadt*, pp. 45 ff.

[69]See sample *Heimeinkaufvertrag*, in Krausnick, 'Judenverfolgung', pp. 329–330.

Deportation of the Jews from Würzburg

By courtesy of Bildarchiv, Preussischer Kulturbesitz, Berlin

Deportation of Jews from Hanau (in front of the main railway station), 30th May 1942

By courtesy of Bildstelle, Hanau, and Bildarchiv, Preussischer Kulturbesitz, Berlin

Deportation of the Jews from Gailingen, either October 1940 (to Gurs) or 1941

By courtesy of Yad Vashem, Jerusalem

Deportation of the Jews from Brandenburg an der Havel, 1942

By courtesy of Bildarchiv, Preussischer Kulturbesitz, Berlin

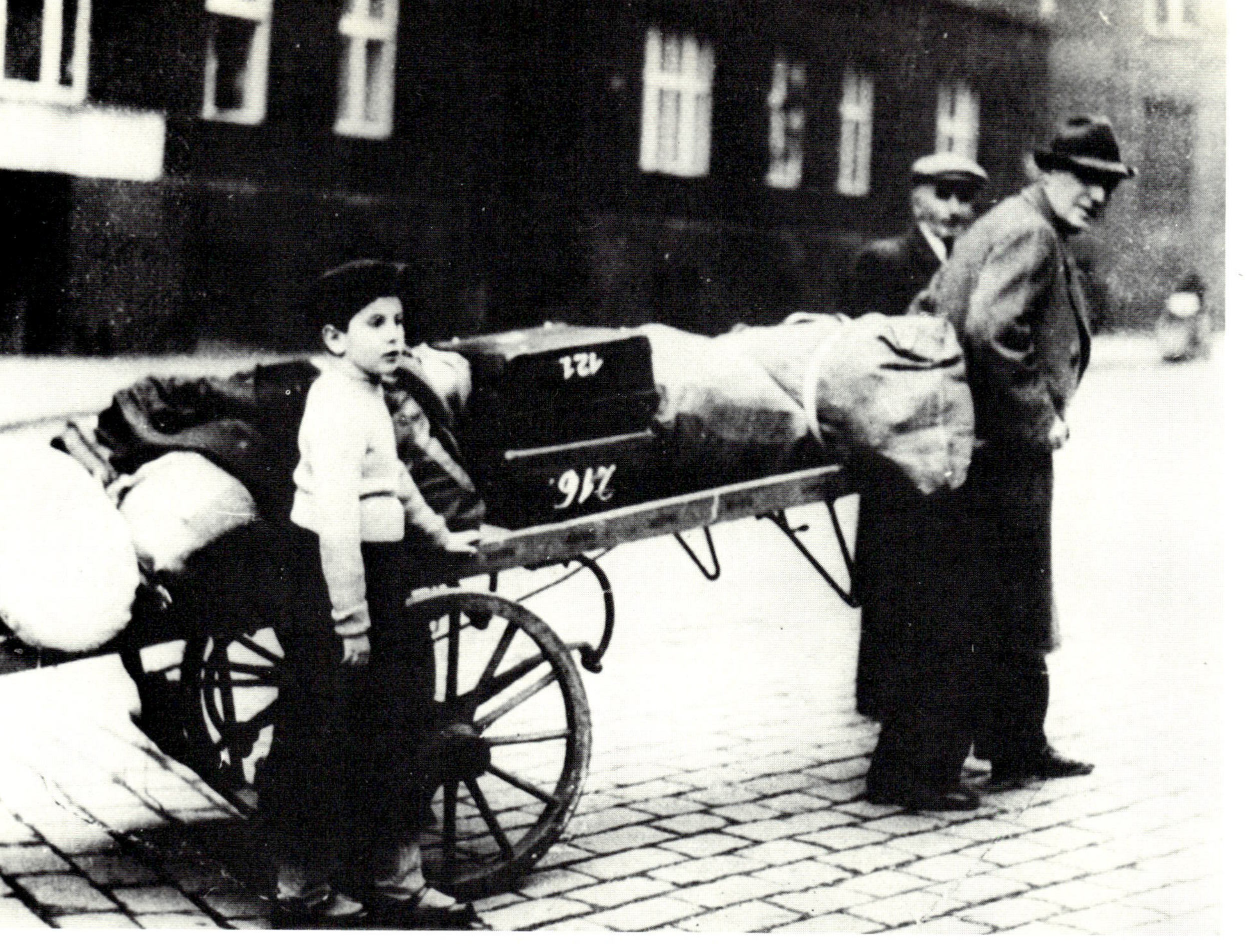

Theresienstadt (Terezin) at dawn
Family reporting for retransport East

By courtesy of Bildarchiv, Preussischer Kulturbesitz, Berlin

old Jews received, in turn, miserable conditions in Theresienstadt and, in addition, a journey to the East.

In the summer of 1942, occasional transports from Germany began to arrive in Auschwitz; starting in January 1943, Auschwitz replaced all other destinations for the deportation of the German Jews. Henceforth, only Auschwitz served as the final goal for transports from Germany.[70] During the first half of 1943, the Gestapo increased its efforts to deport the remaining Jews from Germany; on 30th June 1943, Germany was declared *judenfrei*, and thereafter only smaller transports – including Jews caught in hiding and those from mixed marriages – left for Auschwitz, Theresienstadt, or, after November 1944, concentration camps in Germany proper.[71]

Almost all deported German Jews were murdered. Only an insignificant number returned from the East. Their specific fate differed from place to place, but the final result was always the same.[72]

1) *Lodz (Litzmannstadt)*. Those deported to Lodz shared the fate of the Polish Jews in the ghetto. Many died in the ghetto of starvation, exposure, or disease. But most were deported to Kulmhof (Chelmno) during the round-ups of the spring and autumn of 1942. Kulmhof was an extermination installation using gas vans; there were no survivors. Those remaining were sent to Auschwitz when the ghetto was dissolved in August 1944.[73]

2) *Kovno, Minsk, Reval, and Riga*. Those deported to the *Ostland* were mostly shot by the *Einsatzgruppen*. As we have seen, many were killed upon arrival. This was the fate of everyone on all transports sent to Kovno, and on many sent to Minsk and Riga. Other transports – all those sent to Reval and many of those sent to Minsk and Riga – had a few survivors; some young people able to do heavy labour were placed in forced labour camps like Salaspils near Riga or Jägala in Estonia. From only a minority of transports, mostly those arriving in 1941, did everyone

[70]GStA bei dem KG, 1 Js 1/65 (RSHA), Vermerk, Teil B, pp. 362–363, 514 ff. There could have been exceptions; thus Moser, *Judenverfolgung*, p. 48, believes that a Vienna transport of 31st March 1943 went to Treblinka.

[71]GStA bei dem KG, 1 Js 1/65 (RSHA), Vermerk, Teil B, pp. 362–363. For transports arriving in Auschwitz during the first half of 1943, see 'Kalendarium der Ereignisse im Konzentrationslager Auschwitz-Birkenau (III)', *Hefte von Auschwitz*, 4 (1961): pp. 63–111. The drive to remove all Jews from German soil even led to the transfer of almost all Jews from concentration camps located in Germany proper to Auschwitz. Benedikt Kautsky, *Teufel und Verdammte*, Zürich 1946, was one of those transferred. See also Henry Friedlander, 'The Nazi Concentration Camps', in *Human Responses to the Holocaust*, ed. Michael D. Ryan, New York–Toronto 1981, pp. 33–69.

[72]See, for example, StA Berlin, 1 Ks 2/69 (Stapoleit. Bln.), Überlebende der Berliner Judentransporte, 12 pp. This is a list of names, arranged by transport, of survivors from the Berlin deportations to the East. For a more complete count without names, probably adding those who had died between 1945 and the middle 1960s, see LG Berlin, Strafsache gegen Bovensiepen u. a., 7th April 1971, (500) 1 Ks 2/69 (10/69). From about 35,000 Jews deported from Berlin to the East (not including those sent there via Theresienstadt), the district court found the following to be the number of survivors (arranged by destination): Lodz 20, Kovno none, Riga 31, Reval 11, Minsk 7, Lublin 1, Auschwitz 178. Dr. Wolfgang Scheffler, Free University of Berlin, served as the expert witness for the court. See also summaries of accounts by survivors, in GStA bei dem KG, 1 Js 1/65 (RSHA), Vermerk, Teil B, pp. 391–542. Also Henry Friedlander and Sybil Milton, 'Surviving', in *Genocide*, pp. 233–235.

[73]See Josef Wulf, *Lodz. Das letzte Ghetto auf polnischem Boden*, Bundeszentrale für Heimatdienst, Bonn 1962. See also the Kulmhof trial: LG Bonn, 30th March 1963, 8 Ks 3/62, in *JuNSV*, 21, No. 594.

enter the ghettos in Minsk and Riga (and Jungfernhof near Riga). In 1942 the ghetto in Minsk was dissolved and everyone was shot. In 1943 the ghetto in Riga was dissolved; its inmates were sent to the newly constructed concentration camp Riga-Kaiserwald. In 1943 and 1944 the camps in the *Ostland* closed; the inmates were sent to Maidanek and Stutthof.[74]

3) *The Lublin region.* Those deported to the Lublin region were killed in the extermination camps of Operation Reinhard: Belzec, Sobibor, Treblinka. As we have seen, a few transports went directly to Sobibor or Treblinka. The rest went to the small ghettos near Lublin. These were dissolved in 1942 and early 1943. Some inmates were shot on the spot, but most died in the gas chambers of Belzec or Sobibor. There were no survivors. A few German Jews able to do heavy labour were sent to forced labour camps like Trawniki. In November 1943, the camps in the Lublin region were dissolved; almost all inmates were shot in Maidanek during the so-called *Erntefest.* Only a handful escaped.[75]

4) *Theresienstadt.* For the Czech Jews Theresienstadt was only a transfer camp on the way to the East. But those arriving on old age transports suffered a similar fate. Over 30,000 died in Theresienstadt. The rest were sent to the East on old age transports; they had no chance to survive this second deportation. Only a few German Jews, mostly those with privileged status, survived until liberation.[76]

5) *Auschwitz.* Those sent to Auschwitz had to pass the so-called selection as soon as they arrived. Only the young and able were kept for labour; all others were immediately killed in the gas chambers of Birkenau. Those admitted to the camp were kept in Auschwitz I (*Stammlager*), Auschwitz II (Birkenau), or Auschwitz III (Buna-Monowitz) and its subsidiary camps. Periodically those unable to continue heavy labour were gassed. Auschwitz was evacuated in January 1945; the surviving inmates were sent to concentration camps inside Germany.[77]

The men responsible for the deportation, and thus the murder, of the German Jews survived the war to face their German judges. Although the chief perpetrators were dead or missing,[78] the men of the Gestapo were available for trial. The first large trial, before the District Court of Nürnberg-Fürth early in 1949, involved seven members of the Nuremberg Gestapo.[79] The most important

[74]For Riga, see Schneider, *Journey into Terror, passim.* For Minsk, see Karl Loewenstein, *Minsk. Im Lager der deutschen Juden*, Bundeszentrale für Heimatdienst, Bonn 1961. See also the Minsk *Einsatzgruppen* trials: LG Koblenz, 12th June 1961, 9 Ks 1/61, in *JuNSV*, 17, No. 512 and LG Koblenz, 21st May 1963, 9 Ks 2/62, in *JuNSV*, 19, No. 552. About Minsk also see 'Aus den Akten des Gauleiters Kube', *Vierteljahrshefte für Zeitgeschichte*, 4 (1956), pp. 67–92.

[75]For the account of a survivor from Trawniki and other camps in the Lublin region, see Arnold Hindls, *Einer kehrte zurück*, Stuttgart 1965, Veröffentlichung des Leo Baeck Instituts. For the camps of Operation Reinhard, see Rückerl, *NS-Vernichtungslager, passim.* See also the Treblinka trial: LG Düsseldorf, 3rd September 1965, 8 I Ks 2/64, in *JuNSV*, 22, No. 596.

[76]See Adler, *Theresienstadt*, pp. 39–60 and *passim.*

[77]See Hermann Langbein, *Menschen in Auschwitz*, Vienna 1972. See also the Auschwitz trial: LG Frankfurt, 19th–20th August 1965, 4 Ks 2/63, in *JuNSV*, 21, No. 595. Also Henry Friedlander, 'The Nazi Camps', in *Genocide*, pp. 222–232.

[78]Apart from Hitler, Göring, and Himmler having committed suicide (Heydrich had been assassinated), Kaltenbrunner was hanged in Nuremberg and Eichmann was hanged in Jerusalem; Müller disappeared.

[79]LG Nürnberg-Fürth, 10th May 1949, KLs 230/48, in *JuNSV*, 4, pp. 525–587. In the court decision

defendant was Nuremberg's former Police President and Gestapo chief, Dr. Benno Martin.[80]

Martin was born into a civil service family in 1893. A junior officer and decorated in the First World War, he fought with the Epp Free Corps in the Bavarian civil war of 1919. He studied law, passed his state examinations, and received a doctorate in jurisprudence from Erlangen. In 1923 he joined the Bavarian police, and was posted to Nuremberg; there he served for ten years as *Regierungsrat* in the political police. After the Nazi seizure of power, Martin advanced with spectacular rapidity. Serving as deputy to the stormtrooper who headed the Nuremberg police in 1933, he was appointed Police President – and also chief of the Gestapo – of the *Stadt der Reichsparteitage* in 1934.[81]

Martin joined the Nazi party in May 1933 and the SS in April 1934.[82] But his association with the Nazis pre-dated his membership; during the Weimar Republic he used his position in the police to aid the movement. In 1934, Streicher recognised his past service by admitting him to membership in the "Old Guard".[83] His advancement in the SS was as spectacular as his rise in the police. Starting in 1934 as *Untersturmführer*, he had advanced by 1938 to *Oberführer*, moved in 1941 to *Brigadeführer*, and in 1942 to *Gruppenführer*. Finally, in 1944 he was promoted to *Obergruppenführer* and *General der Polizei*. In December 1942 he left his Nuremberg police job to assume in the same city the office of Higher SS and Police Leader for *Wehrkreis* XIII.[84]

After the war, Martin revised his *vita*. In an autobiographical sketch, he did not mention his past association with Streicher and his acceptance into the "Old Guard". Instead, he implied that he had remained at his post in Nuremberg only to contain Streicher and help the Jews. He claimed that Göring's investigation of Streicher's irregular method of Aryanisation, which led to Streicher's loss of power in Franconia, had been due solely to his efforts.[85] No doubt, Martin represented the interests of the state (and the SS) *vis-à-vis* Streicher and his party cronies. But this was an intra-party rivalry, a fight for personal advancement. Of course, after the war Martin stressed his past differences with Streicher, the Nazi boss of Franconia and publisher of the *Stürmer*; in the same way he distanced himself from his former superior, Reinhard Heydrich, pointing to past differences beween them.[86] Indeed, in an evaluation of 1942, Heydrich praised Martin's competence but attacked his ambition. This also seemed to reflect intra-office

---

published in *JuNSV* only initials are provided for the names of the defendants; for full names, see Herbert Schultheis, *Juden in Mainfranken 1933–1945*, Bad Neustadt 1980, pp. 793–794.

[80]LG Nürnberg-Fürth 1949, in *JuNSV*, 4, pp. 531–533: *vita* of Dr. Martin.

[81]Berlin Document Center [Hereafter cited as BDC], Folder of Dr. Benno Martin: 'Lebenslauf' 1935; 'Fragebogen' 1937.

[82]BDC, Folder Martin: Karteikarte.

[83]BDC, Folder Martin: Martin to Ministerialrat Schachinger, 28th February 1934; Martin to Heydrich, 26th March 1934.

[84]BDC, Folder Martin: Dienstlaufbahn.

[85]Benno Martin, 'Mein Kampf gegen Streicher', reproduced in Bernhard Kolb, 'Die Juden in Nürnberg', pp. 33/1-33/12, Leo Baeck Institute, New York, manuscript collection.

[86]*Ibid.*

rivalries. In a similar evaluation of 1942, however, Martin's other former superior, Kurt Daluege, supported him without qualification.[87]

The state attorney indicted Martin for aiding and abetting (*Beihilfe*) in a felony under Articles 341, 239/III of the penal code: deprivation of liberty resulting in death committed by an official of the state (*Freiheitsberaubung im Amt mit Todesfolge*).[88]

Martin offered a multiple defence: First, he did not consider the deportations illegal. The Jews were considered enemies of the state (*Staatsfeinde*); at that time, he shared this self-evident (*selbstverständlich*) viewpoint. Their deportation was a justified war measure; he pointed to similar measures against the Japanese-Americans in the United States. It was his duty to carry out the deportation orders. Second, he did not know, and could not have imagined, that the Jews would be killed in the East. Third, he acted under duress; failure to obey would have led to his incarceration in a concentration camp.[89]

In a long and careful decision, the District Court in Nürnberg-Fürth rejected every one of Martin's defence arguments.[90] First, the Court ruled that the deportations violated German penal law (*Strafrecht*). Laws and decrees lack legal status if they treat human beings as subhumans and deny them basic human rights.[91] The perpetrators – Hitler and associates – intentionally deprived the Jews of their liberty in order to kill them; they knew that their actions were "illegal and unjust" (*Unrecht*). They did not act in defence of the state; the Court rejected the contention that the Jews had been enemies. There were no military necessities; the perpetrators were simply motivated by hatred against the Jews. Second, Martin was an accomplice.[92] His claim that he did not recognise the illegality of the deportations cannot be accepted; as a senior police functionary acquainted with the leading men of the Third *Reich*, he knew all about the constantly more severe measures imposed on the Jews and had to recognise that they would lead to their destruction. He intended to aid and abet, and he contributed to the success of the crime. As Police President he did not have to be involved actively in the deportations, but could have left this to subordinates in the Gestapo. However, he did direct the deportations; thus duress does not apply. Finally, the Court rejected his contention that his struggle against Streicher and his differences with Heydrich proved that he had

[87]BDC, Folder Martin: Reinhard Heydrich to RFSS Himmler, 21st March 1942; Kurt Daluege to RFSS Himmler, 15th May 1942.

[88]Art. 239 StGB in Par. I provides for imprisonment for anyone who "intentionally and unlawfully" deprives another of his liberty. Par. II provides for imprisonment not to exceed ten years if the confinement lasted for at least one week. Par. III provides for imprisonment for no less than three years "if death is caused by the confinement". Art. 341 StGB increased penalties for an official (*Beamter*) who deprives another of his liberty "illegally". Art. 49 StGB defines the crime of the accomplice: if he "knowingly" aids and abets the perpetrator, he will be judged under the same law, but his sentence *may* be reduced.

[89]LG Nürnberg-Fürth 1949, in *JuNSV*, 4, pp. 553–556.

[90]LG Nürnberg-Fürth 1949, in *JuNSV*, 4, pp. 525–587, especially pp. 558 ff.

[91]See Gustav Radbruch, 'Gesetzliches Unrecht und übergesetzliches Recht', *Süddeutsche Juristen-zeitung*, 1 (1946), pp. 105–108.

[92]From Franconia (Nuremberg, Würzburg, and smaller towns) a total of 4,754 Jews were deported. Of these 1,000 went to Riga, 1,955 to the Lublin region, 73 to Auschwitz, and 1,726 to Theresienstadt. LG Nürnberg-Fürth 1949, in *JuNSV*, 4, p. 529. Because Martin was either absent from Nuremberg in 1942 or preoccupied with his forthcoming appointment as HSSPF, he was convicted as an accomplice only in the matter of the 1,000 Jews deported to Riga on 29th November 1941.

only involved himself to improve the lot of the deported Jews. This defence argument, "suddenly introduced", did not impress the Court; it judged his actions involving Streicher and Heydrich as motivated by "ambition and a desire for status" (*Ehrgeiz und Geltungsbedürfnis*). Martin was thus found guilty under Article 239/III. He was a *Beamter*, and thus Article 341 also applied. Using the milder standards under which an *accomplice* may be judged, the Court imposed a sentence of three years. Martin appealed.

In a strange and unfortunate decision, the highest Bavarian appeals court reversed the conviction.[93] It did hold that it had been against the law to deport the Jews in order to kill them. But the deportations alone, which have been judged illegal since the war, were not considered illegal at the time. During the Third *Reich* the *Schutzhaft* decree of 1933 permitted the detention of persons without judicial review, the Four Year Plan authorised the labour draft, and this legislation – as well as others like the 11th decree – was enforced by the courts. Martin might therefore have assumed that the deportations were legal; if he did so, he cannot be convicted. The District Court did not analyse his awareness sufficiently, and the case must therefore be returned to the lower court. In the second trial, the District Court followed the lead of the appeals court; Martin was not convicted because he lacked the awareness that the deportations were illegal.[94] The state attorney appealed.[95]

The *Bundesgerichtshof* reversed this decision of the District Court, delivering at the same time an implied reprimand to the Bavarian appeals court. The *Bundesgerichtshof* pointed out that even if Martin did not realise that the deported Jews would be killed, he did know "that an entire people were torn from their familiar surroundings only because of their race". Thus he was obviously aware that the deportations possessed the ingredients (*Merkmale*) of an illegal deprivation of liberty.[96]

In the third trial, the District Court avoided all complex legal questions. It followed the lead of the *Bundesgerichtshof*, and rejected the idea that Martin, who had received a classical and Christian education, could have failed to realise the illegality of the deportations. But it did find that he had been an opponent of the hard line represented by Streicher. It credited him with having taken a humane position *vis-à-vis* the Jews, citing the testimony of a prominent former Jewish functionary in favour of Martin. The Court then found that Martin had participated only under duress. It took the absurd position that the SS general had feared commitment to a concentration camp if he did not obey the order to deport the Jews. Using Article 52 of the penal code, the Court failed to convict.[97]

Martin's fellow Nuremberg defendants – as well as nineteen members of the Würzburg Gestapo – were also freed through the application of Article 52 of the penal code.[98] The same excuse of duress prevented the conviction of the Gestapo

[93]Bayerisches Oberstes Landesgericht, 15th November 1950, III 12/50, in *JuNSV*, 4, pp. 588–616.

[94]LG Nürnberg-Fürth, 2nd June 1951, 213 Ks 1/51, in *JuNSV*, 8, pp. 465–505.

[95]In the United States, and in other countries operating under the common law, double jeopardy prevents the state from appealing against felony decisions. In Germany, where the civil law applies, state attorneys commonly appeal against decisions in felony cases.

[96]BGH, 19th December 1952, 1 StR 2/52, in *JuNSV*, 8, 506–514.

[97]LG Nürnberg-Fürth, 1st July 1953, Ks 1/51, in *JuNSV*, 11, pp. 185–203. For duress, see above note 22.

[98]LG Würzburg, 30th April 1949, KLs 63/48, in *JuNSV*, 4, pp. 469–499; LG Nürnberg-Fürth 1951, in *JuNSV*, 8, pp. 465–505.

officer in charge of the Stuttgart Jewish office.[99] In the immediate post-war years only the chief of the Cologne Gestapo, Dr. Emanuel Schäfer, his successor, Franz Sprinz, and the head of the Cologne Jewish office, Kurt Matschke, were convicted; they were found guilty as accomplices in the deportation of 11,500 Jews from Cologne.[100] The Court rejected all excuses, including duress, and convicted under Article 239 of the penal code. Sprinz, who received a sentence of three years, and Matschke, who received two years, were convicted under Article 239/III; Schäfer was convicted under Article 239/II and was sentenced to only one year.[101]

In 1969–1971, the time that the trial of the Berlin Gestapo officers took place, the statute of limitations (*Verjährung*) had expired on all crimes of the Nazi period except murder.[102] As we have seen, the courts had previously ruled that the crime committed by the chief perpetrators – Hitler and his associates – had been murder; but they had also found that the Gestapo men who had acted as accomplices had not aided and abetted in the intentional killings, and could therefore only be convicted for assisting in the deprivation of liberty resulting in death. By 1969, however, the state attorneys had to prove murder.

> The state attorney indicted the former chief of the Berlin Gestapo, Otto Bovensiepen, and his former deputy, Dr. Kurt Venter, as accomplices to the crime of murder committed by the chief perpetrators.[103] They knowingly and with base motives assisted in the deportation and killing of 35,000 Berlin Jews.[104] Bovensiepen was born in 1905, studied law at Bonn, passed his state examinations in 1929 and 1933, and was appointed to the political police in Düsseldorf. He joined the Nazi party in 1925, the SA in 1933, and switched to the SS in 1936; he rose by 1943 to the rank of *Standartenführer*. He headed the Gestapo in Magdeburg, Dortmund, Bielefeld, Köslin, and Halle, before being posted to Berlin in March 1941. He headed the Berlin Gestapo until his removal after a scandal in November 1942.[105] Venter was born in 1911, studied law at Bonn and Marburg, received his doctorate in jurisprudence at Marburg, passed his state examinations, and joined the Gestapo. Serving in Düsseldorf, Koblenz, and Tilsit, he joined the Berlin Gestapo as deputy to the chief in

[99] LG Stuttgart, 19th September 1952, Ks 35/50, in *JuNSV*, 22, pp. 759–769.

[100] LG Köln, 9th July 1954, 24 Ks 3/53, in *JuNSV*, 12, pp. 575–600. In other trials Schäfer and Matschke were also convicted for crimes committed in the occupied territories.

[101] Until 1953 it was not necessary for the application of Art. 239/III StGB to prove a causal relationship between the actions of the defendant and the death resulting from the illegal confinement. It was sufficient to show that the confinement caused the death. But the introduction in 1953 of Art. 56 StGB changed this. Henceforth, 239/III required proof that the defendant caused the death at least through negligence.

[102] Art. 66 StGB. The statute of limitations in Nazi crimes did not start to run until after the Second World War. Still, even for murder it would have expired by the late 1960s if the *Bundestag* had not prolonged it.

[103] There were also six other defendants; all subordinates of Bovensiepen and Venter.

[104] For the legal arguments in the indictment, see StA Berlin, 1 Js 9/65 (Stapoleit. Bln.), Anklageschrift Bovensiepen, pp. 461–481. Art. 211 StGB defines murder in the following way: "A murderer is someone who kills a human being out of bloodthirst (*Mordlust*), for the satisfaction of sexual desires, for greed (*Habgier*) or any other base motives (*niedrigen Beweggründen*), or in a cunning (*heimtückisch*) or cruel (*grausam*) manner or by means causing a common danger, or to make possible or conceal another felony." Premeditation is not required, but intent is.

[105] BDC, Folder Otto Bovensiepen. His highest civil service rank was *Oberregierungsrat*.

December 1941 and remained there until November 1943. He joined the Nazi party and the SA in 1933, and the SS in 1941.[106] In 1969 their trial opened before the District Court in Berlin.

Bovensiepen suffered a heart attack during the trial, and a physician testified that this defendant, sixty-five years old in 1970, would never be able to last through a trial. For him the trial had ended. The trial against Venter continued. But the District Court did not convict. Although suspicion (*Tatverdacht*) that he had committed the crime remained, the Court could not prove that he had assisted in the deportations. The Court accepted his defence argument that he had not supervised, participated, or involved himself in the affairs of the Jewish office; his duties in the Berlin Gestapo had not covered Jewish affairs.[107]

As we have seen, after the majority of German Jews had been deported by the middle of 1943, the Gestapo moved to deport *Mischlinge* and Jews in mixed marriages. Although these people remained officially immune from deportation until early in 1945, when as many as could be found were sent to Theresienstadt, in many places the Gestapo deported them one by one as individuals for one reason or another. A number of trials dealt with the men responsible for these deportations.[108] Unlike the earlier mass deportations, which involved large groups and could be handled in an impersonal way, these individual arrests involved the perpetrator in a direct confrontation with his victim. Thus the certainty of conviction and the length of the sentence increased, because the perpetrator had crossed the line dividing the *Schreibtischtäter* from the killers on the scene. The following case can serve as an example.[109]

The Case of Heinrich Baab. The Frankfurt Gestapo, which had jurisdiction over the *Regierungsbezirk* Wiesbaden, deported about 10,300 Jews between October 1941 and the middle of 1943.[110] Thereafter, only *Mischlinge* or Jews in mixed marriages remained in the city and the district; the Court estimated their number as 800 to 2,000. Many of these were arrested after October 1943; the pretext was usually the violation of one of the many anti-Jewish decrees and sometimes a completely fictitious accusation. Those arrested were almost always deported. These Jews belonged to a protected category, and would not have been deported without the arbitrary arrest. The Frankfurt Gestapo pursued this policy of arrest and deportation with great determination; even members of the RSHA were astonished by their vigour. Baab served in the Gestapo's Jewish office, and he had arrested and deported large numbers of Jews.

[106]BDC, Folder Dr. Kurt Venter. His highest civil service rank was *Regierungsrat*.

[107]LG Berlin, 7th April 1971, (500) 1 Ks 2/69 (10/69).

[108]Two members of the Düsseldorf Gestapo were convicted under Control Council Law No. 10; one received three years and the other received eight years. LG Düsseldorf, 27th May 1949, 8 Ks 21/49, in *JuNSV*, 4, pp. 633–659 and LG Düsseldorf, 3rd June 1949, 8 Ks 19/49, in *JuNSV*, 5, pp. 3–25. Two members of the Darmstadt Gestapo were convicted under Art. 239 StGB; one received two years and seven months and the other received six years. LG Darmstadt, 14th July 1950, 2a Ks 1/49, in *JuNSV*, 22, pp. 659–679 and LG Darmstadt, 23rd May 1951, 2a Ks 1/49, in *JuNSV*, 22, pp. 725–740. In the case of a Gestapo officer from Offenbach a. Main, the Court refused to convict. LG Frankfurt, 30th July 1953, 4 Ks 2/53, in *JuNSV*, 11, pp. 257–273.

[109]LG Frankfurt, 5th April 1950, 51 Ks 1/50, in *JuNSV*, 6, pp. 371–437.

[110]See the list of deportation transports from Frankfurt, in LG Frankfurt 1950, in *JuNSV*, 6, pp. 377–378.

Heinrich Baab was born in 1908, learned the trade of locksmith, passed his examination for journeyman, and was employed in a factory. In 1928 he joined the police and was posted to Stettin. Soon transferred to Frankfurt, his home town, he served in the uniformed police there until 1937. In that year he applied and was admitted to the Gestapo; except for service with an SS *Einsatzkommando* in Poland in the autumn of 1939, he remained with the Frankfurt Gestapo until the end of the war. He served in various departments, including those dealing with the churches, communism, and sabotage; between August 1942 and early summer 1944, he was a member of the Jewish office. Baab entered the Nazi party in 1932, belonged to the SA from 1932 until 1935, and joined the SS in 1937. He held non-commissioned ranks – comparable to his lower civil-service titles – and was only promoted to *Untersturmführer* in January 1945. He fled from Frankfurt at the end of the war, and was captured by the French army. Released from POW camp, he joined his family in Thuringia. In 1947 he left the Soviet zone, returned to Frankfurt, and appeared for his denazification; he was arrested on a warrant from the state attorney. His trial took place in 1950 before the District Court in Frankfurt.[111]

Baab was accused of having been responsible for the arrest and deportation of 105 persons. In some of these cases he admitted his involvement, in others he claimed loss of memory, and in still others he denied all participation.[112] In almost all cases the Court did not accept Baab's denials; it considered his involvement proven. In almost all cases the non-Jewish spouses, relatives, and friends of the deported Jews survived in Frankfurt; they could appear as witnesses and testify about Baab's participation. The following are a tiny sample of these cases:[113]

Case 17: The half-Jewish sixty-five-year-old publisher E. D. Oswalt, who had been married to a Jewish woman who had died in 1937 and was therefore counted as a Jew (*als Jude galt*), frequently forgot to wear his star. He was ordered to appear before the Gestapo and never returned. He was sent to Oranienburg and did not survive. The surprising circumstance that unlike others he was sent to Oranienburg and not to Auschwitz has never been explained. Perhaps Oswalt received preferential treatment because he was owner of the well-known publishing house Rütten and Loening.[114]

Case 36c: The wife of the witness was accused of having ordered a gas mask. [She was sent for by the Gestapo and arrested.] Through petition to Himmler the witness managed to get permission for his wife, who was Swiss, to emigrate to Switzerland. The witness succeeded in getting his [Jewish] wife – who was already on her way to Auschwitz – off the train in Kassel. She was brought back to Frankfurt, and assigned by the defendant to the assembly centre on Hermesweg. There she committed suicide on 28th May 1943.[115]

Case 62: At the beginning of March 1943, the Jewish wife of the Aryan witness, who lived in a privileged mixed marriage, was ordered to appear before the

[111] BDC, Folder Heinrich Baab: 'Lebenslauf', n.d.; 'R.u.S.-Fragebogen', 1938; Karteikarte. See also LG Frankfurt 1950, in *JuNSV*, 6, p. 379.

[112] LG Frankfurt 1950, in *JuNSV*, 6, p. 382. See also Heinrich Baab, 'Erinnerungen', Stadtarchiv Frankfurt, copy in Leo Baeck Institute, New York, Max Kreutzberger Research Papers, AR 7183, Box 7, Folder 2.

[113] See LG Frankfurt 1950, in *JuNSV*, 6, pp. 397 ff.

[114] LG Frankfurt 1950, in *JuNSV*, 6, pp. 407–408.

[115] LG Frankfurt 1950, in *JuNSV*, 6, p. 415.

Gestapo and did not return. The witness, who had been drafted into the Organisation Todt, was notified by his children and immediately came home on leave. He found his apartment sealed and his children taken to a home by the social welfare agency. The witness went to the Gestapo to find out why his wife had been arrested; the defendant replied "because she was born". When the witness later asked what he should do with his under-age children, he was advised by the defendant to send them to the Hadamar home. As is now known, large numbers of *Mischling* children were killed in Hadamar as part of the so-called Euthanasia Programme. The wife was sent to Auschwitz and died there on 9th August 1943.[116]

Case 63c: The Jewish wife was ordered to appear before the defendant for a discussion (*zur Erörterung*). He arrested her, because she had gone to an Aryan hairdresser. She was sent to Auschwitz, where she died.[117]

In all cases the Gestapo used a pretext to arrest and deport the Jews. The following are some typical examples used by Baab:[118]

"Your wife, who is Jewish, has not shown the necessary reticence in her relations with Aryans, and despite repeated warnings has not changed her behaviour." Case 8

"His wife was accused of having provoked the Nazi party by staying for a time at the hotel Frankfurter Hof." Case 9

"[The Jewish wife] was accused of having visited an Aryan physician." Case 14–15

"[The Jewish wife] was arrested because she did not possess the Jewish food ration cards marked with a J." Case 35

"The defendant accused [the Jewish wife] that on one occasion she did not carry her identity card with her to work." Case 40c

"The defendant accused [the Jewish wife] of having used the railway." Case 45

"The defendant accused [the Jewish husband] of having smoked a cigarette in the street, thus insulting the German nation." Case 48

"[The Jewish husband] was accused of having smoked a cigarette in the park." Case 61

"She was accused of visiting Aryan shops and of failing to use the obligatory first name of Sara." Case 73

The Court found Baab guilty in 98 cases. Of these, the majority concerned Jews who did not survive their deportation. If Baab knew that the Jews he deported would be killed, he could be convicted as a murderer. As we have seen, in all deportation trials the defendants escaped conviction for murder by convincing the courts that they had been ignorant of the fate waiting for the deported Jews in the East. Baab attempted the same manoeuvre, but failed to convince the Court. Instead, the Court found that he had known the Jews would be killed. Moreover, it had been his intention to cause their death. The Court based this finding on information supplied by the witnesses, who repeated under oath comments made by Baab. Thus his own words convicted him. The following are a sample of Baab's untranslatable insults to his victims:[119]

[116]LG Frankfurt 1950, in *JuNSV*, 6, p. 430.

[117]LG Frankfurt 1950, in *JuNSV*, 6, p. 431.

[118]See LG Frankfurt 1950, in *JuNSV*, 6, pp. 397 ff. For the various decrees limiting Jews and serving as pretext, see Walk, *Sonderrecht für Juden*, *passim* (for example, the decree of 12th May 1942 concerning the prohibition to visit Aryan hairdressers appears on p. 372).

[119]LG Frankfurt 1950, in *JuNSV*, 6, pp. 383–384 and *passim*.

Er gab einer 70-jährigen Frau auf deren Frage, wann sie zurückkäme, zur Antwort: "Als Urne".

Er drohte an, sie ins KZ zu bringen, damit sie dort "verrecke".

"Wo du hinkommst, gibt es kein zurück mehr."

Als die Zeugin ihn um Erlaubnis bat, ihrem Ehemann eine Hose bringen zu dürfen, erwiderte er: "Der Dreckjud braucht keine Hose, der verreckt ja doch in Auschwitz".

Er drohte an, ihn "dahin zu bringen, wo es kein Wiedersehen mehr gibt".

Die Frau, die in der Haft einen Gallenanfall erlitt, schrieb ihrem Ehemann, dass er ihr gegenüber geäussert hat, sie habe "bald ausgegallt".

Er sagte der Zeugin, sie sehe ihren Ehemann nicht wieder, das sei ein Abschied fürs Leben.

"Der Jud wandert aus nach Buchenwald, das gibt im Schornstein blauen Dunst."

The Court concluded that all Jews and *Mischlinge* committed by Baab to Auschwitz (and other concentration camps) were sent there to be killed. It further found that Baab knew this and that he acted with intent. Thus when the victims were sent to Auschwitz and died there, he was guilty of murder. The Court found this to be true in 55 cases. It therefore sentenced Baab to the obligatory life in prison under Article 211 of the penal code.

The Court also concluded that Baab had intended the same result even in instances where the victims survived. The survival was due to fortunate circumstances; it did not alter Baab's intent. In such instances he had attempted murder, but had not succeeded. The same applied in those instances where the victim had survived Auschwitz, but had perished during or after its evacuation. Baab could not have foreseen this development. The attempt to kill the victim in Auschwitz had failed. The Court found attempted murder in 21 cases, and applied Article 211 in combination with Articles 43 and 44 of the penal code.[120] It sentenced Baab to eight years in prison in each of 21 instances.

The Court also found that Baab had not intended to kill non-Jewish victims – relatives of Jews – he sent to concentration camps. In these instances – a total of 22 cases – it convicted for deprivation of liberty under Article 239 of the penal code, and sentenced for an average of two years in prison in each of 22 instances. Combining these term sentences under Article 74 of the penal code,[121] the Court imposed on Baab a term of fifteen years, to run concurrently with his life sentence.

During the Second World War the Nazis murdered at least 250,000 German, Austrian, and Czech Jews.[122] The deportations from the Greater German *Reich* to the East made these murders possible, but the trials of those responsible did not result in justice. Unlike those who did the actual killings, the *Schreibtischtäter* of the Gestapo were usually able to evade their just rewards.

[120] Art. 43 StGB defines attempt (*Versuch*). Art. 44 StGB provides a lesser sentence for the attempt than for the completed crime. In the case of murder, the sentence for an attempt is to be no less than three years.

[121] Art. 74 StGB provides for a combination of a series of term sentences. The combination, not to exceed fifteen years, must be higher than the highest of the series but lower than their total. Art. 14 StGB defines sentences: life or term; term not to exceed fifteen years.

[122] Hilberg, *Destruction*, p. 767. This total does not include German Jews who had emigrated and were then deported from their places of refuge after they were conquered by the Germans.

Culture and Ideas

Two Lives in the Jewish Frühaufklärung Raphael Levi Hannover and Moses Abraham Wolff

BY STEVEN AND HENRY SCHWARZSCHILD

I. RAPHAEL LEVI

Raphael Levi (1685–1779), who is usually known as Raphael Levi Hannover, from his life-long residence in that city, is a figure of at most secondary importance in Jewish history.* It is then understandable that he has never yet been accorded a full-fledged historical or intellectual biography. On the other hand, as his dates show, he experienced the whole of "the age of the Enlightenment". In fact, he was personally connected with its beginnings in the *Frühaufklärung* through Leibniz and with its end directly through Mendelssohn and indirectly through Kant. Furthermore, living in Hanover and marginally involved in several of its chief history-making episodes at the time, Levi can be shown to have contributed to, certainly to have significantly reacted to, and in his own person to have embodied, the modern European-Jewish symbiosis in its infancy. Further yet, Levi, when studied in detail, turns out to be a thread in a large web of historical and cultural developments in and beyond the eighteenth century, in the Jewish and in the Gentile worlds – from Germany to Eastern Europe, France, England, and even to North America, from the impact of the Thirty Years' War to Ezra Stiles, from Rabbi David Oppenheim (the collector of the bulk of the Bodleian Library's Jewish section)[1] to the British Newtonians and to nineteenth-century utopians. Such a man can be of the highest interest to history, just because, lacking extraordinary stature, he reflects the general forces at work in his time more straightforwardly.

Raphael Levi was born into an Hanoverian, well-established but poor family in Weikersheim a. der Tauber in Franconia. He was sent, in traditional Jewish style,

* An excerpt from this study in French was pre-published in *Le 18e siècle*, 13 (1980), pp. 27–36.

[1] Rabbi David Oppenheim (Worms 1663 to 1736 in Prague) was married to Gründel, daughter of Leffmann Behrens, the patron of Levi. (Cf. below) Leffmann Behrens's son Hertz married the daughter of Samson Wertheimer. (Cf. below, note 5.) Rabbi Oppenheim and the Hanoverian Court Jew Simon Wolf Oppenheimer, who also had a daughter of Leffmann Behrens for wife, were thus brothers-in-law once-removed (*mechuttanim*). (Cf. S. Gronemann, *Genealogische Studien über die alten jüdischen Familien Hannovers* . . . , Berlin 1913, pp. 39f.) Rabbi Oppenheim, Chief Rabbi of Bohemia and a world-wide rabbinic authority, transferred his private library from Prague to Hanover because of government censorship in the former city. Simon Wolf Oppenheimer added to the collection with books that he bought from, among others, his client Prince Eugène of Savoy. The whole collection (cf. its printed catalogue, *Kohelet David*, Hebrew and Latin, ed. Isaac Metz, Hamburg 1826) became the foundation of the Bodleian Judaica collection in Oxford. (Cf. Gronemann, *op. cit.*, pp. 78 ff.) His Hebrew writings in the Bodleian Library are only now being published: *Responsa Nish'al David*, ed. J. Feld, Jerusalem: Hatam Sofer, vol. I (1972), vol. II (1976), vol. III (1982).

to study at a *yeshivah* in Frankfurt a. Main.[2] When his father, Jacob Joseph Levi, son of Mathias, son of Raphael Levi of Hanau,[3] died in 1691, his mother Eva, of a rabbinical family, returned to her native town, Hanover, and Raphael had to break off his studies and rejoin her. (The mother died on 13th November 1706.) To earn a living he became an accountant and bookkeeper for the Hanoverian Court Jew Simon Wolff Oppenheimer.[4] In this way the young man found himself on the outskirts of the international network of immensely wealthy and powerful Jewish financiers, for Oppenheimer headed the local branch of his father Samuel's Vienna-based cartel, and this in turn was personally and commercially intertwined with the even greater cartel of Samson Wertheimer,[5] with the local Hanoverian Court-Jewish family of Leffmann Behrens Cohen,[6] and with virtually every other Jewish banker to the absolute, or aspiringly absolute, rulers of the seventeenth and eighteenth centuries in Europe and beyond.[7] While working in his job, Levi continued to educate himself, as Mendelssohn was to do paradigmatically a generation later, studying mathematics, French, Latin, etc.

The story is often told in the sparse and anecdotal literature on Raphael Levi[8] of how, on his way to the office, he noticed a mistake being made by the workmen in the building of new royal stables[9] – how engineer-major Mölling in charge, impressed by Levi's intelligence, introduced him to the Court scholar and intellectual of Hanover, Gottfried Wilhelm Leibniz – how the philosopher, also

[2]For the history and importance of the Frankfurt *yeshivah* cf. Mordechai Eliav, *Jewish Education in Germany in the Period of Enlightenment and Emancipation* (in Hebrew), Jerusalem 1960, pp. 149f., and Salomon Adler, 'Die Entwicklung des Schulwesens der Juden zu Frankfurt am Main bis zur Emanzipation', *Jahrbuch der Jüdisch-Literarischen Gesellschaft*, XVII (1927), pp. 143–173.

[3]Gronemann, *op. cit.*, p. 130.

[4]For his tombstone cf. *ibid.*, p. 60.

[5]Cf. 'The Appointment of Samson Wertheimer as Imperial Court Factor', in P. R. Mendes-Flohr and J. Reinharz (eds.), *The Jew in the Modern World – A Documentary History*, New York-Oxford 1980, pp. 17 ff., where he is also treated as "Chief Rabbi" of the empire (cf. note 194 below); David Kaufmann, *Samson Wertheimer, der Oberhoffaktor und Landesrabbiner (1658–1728) und seine Kinder*, Vienna 1888, and *Urkundliches aus dem Leben Samson Wertheimers*, Vienna 1892; H. Schnee, *Die Hoffinanz und der moderne Staat. Geschichte und System der Hoffaktoren an deutschen Fürstenhöfen im Zeitalter des Absolutismus . . .*, 3 vols., Berlin 1953–1955, vol. 3, pp. 239 ff.

[6]For Leffmann Behrens (1634–1714), his family connections and rabbinical authority in Hanover and elsewhere, cf. Gronemann, *op. cit.*, pp. 35–52; H. Schnee, 'Der Hof- und Kammeragent Leffmann Behrens als Hoffinanzier der Welfen. Ein Beitrag zur Geschichte der Beziehungen zwischen jüdischer Hochfinanz und modernem Staat', *Niedersächsisches Jahrbuch für Landesgeschichte*, 23 (1951), pp. 116–157; Selma Stern, *The Court-Jew . . .*, Philadelphia 1950, pp. 63–72, 212. For a photograph of his extant tombstone cf. *Monumenta Judaica. Katalog*, Cologne 1963–1964, B. 432.

[7]Cf. Selma Stern, *The Court Jew, op. cit.*, chapt. 1; Schnee, *Die Hoffinanz, op. cit.*, vol. 3, pp. 221 f.; Hermann Kellenbenz, *Sephardim an der unteren Elbe. Ihre wirtschaftliche und politische Bedeutung vom Ende des 16. bis zum Beginn des 18. Jahrhunderts* (*Vierteljahrsschrift für Sozial- und Wirtschaftsgeschichte*, Beiheft 40), Wiesbaden 1958, p. 463. For the economic interaction of the Sephardic "grandees" with the German-Jewish upper class cf. *ibid.*, pp. 466, 469, and for even a request of Venetian Sephardim to establish themselves in business in Hanover in 1706, cf. *ibid.*, p. 471. For the impact of Sephardim on internal Ashkenazic conditions cf. Morris M. Faierstein, 'The Liebes Brief. A Critique of Jewish Society in Germany (1749)', in *LBI Year Book XXVII* (1982), pp. 230 f., 235, 237 f., 240.

[8]*Allgemeine Deutsche Biographie*, Leipzig 1883, vol. 18, p. 505; Ludwig Lazarus, 'Raphael Levi', in *Leben und Schicksal. Zur Einweihung der Synagoge in Hannover*, Hannover 1963, pp. 53–64, and 'G. W. Leibniz und Raphael Levi', *Niedersachsen*, vol. 66 (1966), pp. 244–249.

[9]Of Ludwig Wittgenstein, too, it is reported that he was sensitive to architectural proportions down to one centimetre.

taken with the precocious Jewish youngster, solicited the support of the latter's employer, the Court Jew – and how, as a result, Levi moved into Leibniz's house *c.* 1700 as his amanuensis, pupil, and friend.[10]

Raphael Levi's first significant promotion occurred thus as a result of a partnership between the Court intellectual and the Court Jew. This may be taken as a typical phenomenon, for it was almost invariably on this social level, the thin upper-crust of Court Jews and Court scholars, that any effective Christian-Jewish inter-relationships emerged in early modern times.

One might go so far as to ask oneself whom the King of Hanover would choose if he had to make a choice between the philosopher and the financier. In fact, despite Leibniz's life-long high-flying political and social ambitions, he never – to his continuous chagrin – really "made it" beyond being librarian and historian to the ruling Guelph dynasty, and even in these capacities he rarely found full favour in his patrons' eyes. The Behrens-Wertheimer-Oppenheimer combine, on the other hand, was indispensable to the rulers not only financially but also politically. Early in their respective careers, for example, when Leibniz was sent to Paris on official business (whatever the philosophical and scientific pursuits that he followed privately), it was Behrens who made the financial arrangements for this through his son Hertz there.[11] Throughout his life, many, if not most, of Leibniz's theoretical endeavours – not to speak of his more concrete, mechanical, technological, and historiographical ones – were intended to serve the economic, proto-industrial plans that the mercantilistic regime of Hanover, like most German sovereigns after the Thirty Years' War, made, and the *sine qua non* for them, the money, had typically to be provided by the Court Jews.[12] Leibniz, as a young man, wrote a curious broadsheet, in which he claimed to prove *more geometrico* that the Polish crown must be allotted to the Palatine duke.[13] (Not surprisingly, this philosophical proof somehow did not convince the world.) Leffmann Behrens, on the other hand, financed the political machinations that aimed at obtaining the Polish crown for the King of Hanover, and when, he, too, failed in the attempt, success was achieved by at least acquiring the imperial elector's hat for his patron.[14] In that period of European history, not nationalism in our sense but absolute monarchy was the pervasive political principle, and

[10]Ludwig Grote, *Leibniz und seine Zeit. Populäre Vorlesungen*, Hannover 1869, p. 2 has a picture of Leibniz's house in Hanover, Schmiedestrasse 10; also P. Ritter, 'Bericht eines Augenzeugen über Leibnizens Tod und Begräbnis', *Zeitschrift des Vereins für Niedersachsen* 81 (1916), p. 246.

[11]G. Schnath, *Geschichte Hannovers im Zeitalter der 9. Kur u. englischen Sukzession, 1674–1714* (Veröffentlichungen der historischen Kommission für Hannover, Oldenberg . . . , XVIII), Hildesheim-Leipzig 1938, 2 vols., vol. 1, pp. 105 f, 329. One of Leibniz's political doctrines was that if Hanover was to become a major power it had to place ambassadors at numerous foreign courts.

[12]Cf. Stern, *The Court Jew, op. cit.*, p. 67; for references to Leibniz cf. *ibid.*, pp. 41, 66, 70.

[13]Cf. Carl Haase, 'Leibniz als Politiker und Diplomat', in W. Totok and C. Haase (eds.), *Leibniz – Sein Leben – Sein Wirken – Seine Welt*, Hannover 1966, pp. 204 f.

[14]Stern, *The Court Jew, op. cit.*, pp. 69–72; Gronemann, *op. cit.*, p. 35. Indeed, though Behrens failed in the pursuit of the Polish crown for the King of Hanover, he succeeded on behalf of the King's neighbour. Kurt Grunwald, 'Three Chapters on German-Jewish Banking History', in *LBI Year Book XXII* (1977), p. 194, says that "the purchase of Poland's crown for Saxony's king by Leffmann Behrens is probably the most outstanding example of the 'extra-curricular activities' in which the Court Jews were engaged". Cf. Ragnild Hatton (cf. note 16), chapt. III: 'The Electoral Cap', and Kaufmann, *Samson Wertheimer . . . , op. cit.*, pp. 8 f.

dynastic ambitions easily overrode nationalist solidarity. Thus the French court paid, and the Hanoverian court eagerly accepted, large, though secret, subsidies, for their respective political reasons. The Jews, and Jewish bankers, for reasons of their own, were indifferent to local patriotism, and they, therefore, could and did serve the rulers efficiently. Thus it was the Hanoverian Jewish Court Jews who, from Hertz Behrens in Paris, often through Sephardic intermediaries in Amsterdam and Hamburg, would bring the French subsidies to their recipients. (And when Schnath,[15] in his typically thorough and German way, then condemns such "unpatriotic" behaviour he not only characteristically serves his own current masters of 1938 but also engages in anachronistic historiography.) Ragnhild Hatton, in her biography *George I. Elector and King*,[16] therefore, called Behrens-Cohen's role in the entire career of the King "especially important."[17] In return, he and Wertheimer managed to have Eisenmenger's notorious antisemitic classic suppressed by the government, for example.[18]

How often, if ever, Leibniz and Oppenheimer met at court, how they related respectively to their common master, and how they related to one another are questions on which our records appear silent. It is, in any case, clear that they were colleagues and maintained some sort of equality between them. When Raphael Levi became the protégé of both simultaneously he began to draw direct and considerable benefits from the two great forces in his society – the intellectual-cultural and the financial-political, from the Court philosopher and the Court Jew.

Good historical fiction might speculatively fill the lacuna in our knowledge of the nature of the inter-relationship between two such different persons, embodying two different historical cultures, as the Christian intellectual and courtier Leibniz and the talmudic Jew and Court factor Oppenheimer within the setting of a seventeenth-century court of the ruler of an ambitious principality. Certainly much fiction has been written around the affair of Sophie Dorothea, the wife of Georg Ludwig, with Count Königsmarck. Her lover was murdered, and Georg Ludwig divorced the Duchess in 1694.[19] Like other philosophers of the age, Leibniz managed to have better relations with the ladies at court than with the men: one supposes that "culture" tended to be left to them, while politics and business were pursued by the men even at that early stage of modern economic society.[20] Thus Leibniz edited the *Memoirs of the Duchess Sophie*.[21] (Descartes had similarly close relations with Sophie's sister Elizabeth.) Her daughter-in-law, Sophie Dorothea, also became Leibniz's special patroness, and when she fell from

[15]Schnath, *op. cit.*, pp. 49, 328 f., 535.

[16]Cambridge, Mass. 1978.

[17]*Ibid.*, p. 94.

[18]Kaufmann, *S. Wertheimer . . .*, *op. cit.*, p. 15.

[19]Schnath, *op. cit.*, vol. 2, '1693–1698', Hildesheim 1976, chapt. 3, p. 195, and Hatton, *op. cit.*, pp. 48 ff., 54–69.

[20]Cf. G. E. Guhrauer, *G. W. Leibniz, eine Biographie*, Breslau 1846/Olms 1962, vol. 2, p. 303, and Lougee, *Le Paradis des Femmes – Women, Salons, and Social Stratification in 17th Century France*, Princeton University Press 1976.

[21]Ed. A. Kocher, Publicationen aus den Königlichen Preussischen Staatsarchiven, IV, Leipzig 1879, pp. 1–10; cf. G. Scheel, 'Hannovers Politisches, Gesellschaftliches und Geistiges Leben zur Leibnizzeit', in Totok and Haase (eds.), *op. cit.*, p. 84.

favour – so did Leibniz's political prospects.[22] Leffmann Behrens held debts from all parties involved in the affair – Count Königsmarck and his murderers, not to speak of the monarch.[23] Leibniz was an interested observer of the libertinistic and Machiavellian goings-on at the court.[24] They were described at the time as "choses si extravagantes et exécrables" and as "sexual orgies".[25] (One must still wonder how the Jew reported to his family and associates, when he got home, on the life-style of his clients.)

The Jews were brought into the petty states that emerged out of the Thirty Years' War in order to put these on what was regarded as a sound economic base. In terms of prevailing mercantilist ideas, this meant that agriculture and proto-industrialism were to be nurtured, and policies were pursued that aimed at importing as much money, and exporting as little, as possible. The entrenched guilds resisted such policies. Jews – outsiders, excluded from the Christian guilds, dependent on the rulers for their very lives and residence, with their experiences in financial matters and their international connections – fitted very well into the mechanisms of official policy. In Hanover, then, which comprised *c.* 11,000 people around 1689, and from which Jews had been banned since *c.* 1350, the Court-Jewish family was brought in and settled outside the old city, in Neustadt, "the new town", where, for the rest, government employees and lower nobility settled. Huguenots, too, were cordially welcomed on the same basis.[26] The Jewish family was licensed to bring in relatives, servants, a growing staff of employees, and its religious and educational entourage.[27] And this was the seed out of which the modern Jewish community grew (analagously to many others): they all never lost the stamp of socio-economic bossism that was implanted in them at birth.[28]

One may also wonder – indeed, one can make a good educated guess – how the

[22]Sophie Charlotte became the first queen of Prussia. Through her friendship Leibniz became the founder of the Prussian Academy of Sciences. In this he was helped by the Court preacher and Orientalist Daniel Ernst Jablonski. In addition to several other enterprises of direct Jewish importance Jablonski also gave his "imprimatur" to the curious MS-tract, in Hebrew and in German, that the privileged Jew Simon Wolff Brandes wrote, proving, as was revealed to him directly by God, that *Psalm* 21, with the appropriate *gematriot*, predestined Frederick I to be crowned on precisely 18th January 1701 in – precisely – Königsberg and that he ought to be good to Jews. (Cf. Cécile Hensel, 'Eine jüdische Huldigung an den ersten König in Preussen', *Jahrbuch der Stiftung Preussischer Kulturbesitz*, IV (1966), pp. 192–199.) (Cf. notes 45, 63 below) Jablonski deserves a full Jewish treatment. Here it will merely be mentioned that he published an important edition of the Hebrew Bible (1699) and even sponsored an edition of the Talmud (Berlin-Frankfurt a.d. Oder, 1730 ff.). For a discussion of the city of Lissa, where Jews, Mennonites, and the Bohemian Brethren, Jablonski's original church, co-existed with the major churches cf. W. Grossmann, 'Religious Toleration in Germany, 1648–1750', in *Studies on Voltaire and the 18th Century*, 1982, p. 121.

[23]Cf. Schnath, *op. cit.*, pp. 166, 173, 180.

[24]*Ibid.*, p. 187.

[25]Hatton, *op. cit.*, pp. 67 f.

[26]*Ibid.*, p. 47.

[27]Scheel, *loc. cit.*, pp. 89–96; M. Wiener, 'Zur Geschichte der Juden in der Residenzstadt Hannover . . .', *Jahrbuch für die Geschichte der Juden und des Judentums*, I, ed. L. Philippson etc., Leipzig 1860, pp. 197 f.

[28]On the symbiosis of Jews and early-modern European absolutism, cf. Hannah Arendt, *The Origins of Totalitarianism*, New York 1966, pp. 11–28; Grunwald, *loc. cit.*, pp. 197–199; B. D. Weinryb, 'Economic and Social Factors in the German-Jewish Enlightenment' (in Hebrew), *Knesset*, 1938, pp. 416–436; Adolf Leschnitzer, *Saul und David. Die Problematik der deutsch-jüdischen Lebensgemeinschaft*, Heidelberg 1954, p. 32 *et al.*

old Christian philosopher-scientist and the young traditionalist Jew spent their years together under the same roof.

Leibniz's religious universalism is well-known. Throughout his life he was, theoretically as well as practically, a Christian ecumenist. In the historical period after the Thirty Years' War the split that rent Christendom by dint of the Reformation remained the prime problem of Europe in general and of Germany in particular, for here the religious wars and even their settlement in the Peace of Westphalia left the most immediate and troublesome consequences. Hanover was a particularly sensitive focus for these tensions, as is manifest in the religious oscillations of its ruling dynasty (and, of course, in its eventual accession to the throne of Great Britain). On the active political level Leibniz was, therefore, engaged in one effort or another virtually throughout his life to bring about at least a *modus vivendi*, if not an actual reconciliation, of Roman Catholicism and Protestantism.[29] On the theoretical, theologico-philosophical, level the *ultima linea* of all his thinking and writing can be said to be a close approximation of deism, or at least of natural religion – i.e. the thesis that human reason, when properly employed, can be shown to attain to all of the essence of religious truth – that historic revelations and ecclesiastical rituals connected with that truth may, in one way or another, be quite compatible with but are ultimately unimportant for true religion,[30] – and that, therefore, rational men of all Christian denominations and even of entirely different religious cultures and historical institutions may very well – to use the Christian theological phrase – be saved. (This is the technical definition of "universalism" in Protestant theology.) This is Leibniz's early-Enlightenment translation of the doctrine of "mystical indifferentism", which he learned from Erhard Weigel and others in post-Renaissance and earliest-modern German pietism,[31] according to which, as Albrecht Ritschl put it, "conscience or natural moral law is equated with the eternal word that is the unknown Christ in pagans and Turks too".[32] Leibniz thus declares: "We can today find a better (religion) among the Jews, although theirs, too, is not yet perfect."[33] All Leibniz's metaphysical and other writings can be shown to converge toward this conclusion, not least his *Théodicée* and *Monadologie*. Ernst Cassirer[34] thus calls the *Monadologie* Leibniz's "true mystical theology" and rightly concludes his study with the summary statement that for Leibniz all

[29]Cf. J. Kvačala, note 71 below (Kvačala is also the biographer of Comenius), and Chr. v. Rommel, *Leibniz u. Graf Ernst von Hessen-Rheinfels. Ein ungedruckter Briefwechsel über religiöse und politische Gegenstände* . . . , 1847, 2 vols., etc.

[30]Cf. Guhrauer, *op. cit.*, vol. 2, p. 168; D. E. Mungello, *Leibniz and Confucianism. The Search for Accord*, University Press of Hawaii 1977, p. 71 [and its review by R. Moritz in *Orientalistische Literaturzeitung*, 76/3 (May-June 1981), pp. 230–234].

[31]Cf. note 190 below.

[32]A. Ritschl, *Geschichte des Pietismus*, vol. 2: 'History of Pietism in the Lutheran Church of the 17th and 18th Centuries', Bonn 1884, pp. 294 f.

[33]Jean Baruzi, *Leibniz et l'organisation religieuse de la terre*, Paris 1903, p. 491 (cf. also *ibid.*, pp. 254, 276 ff., 433, 465).

[34]*Leibniz' System in seinen wissenschaftlichen Grundlagen*, Marburg 1912, pp. 84, 446. (Cassirer's as well as his teacher Hermann Cohen's philosophical and religious purposes at the time play no little part in their Leibniz-exegesis.)

religions and cultures participate in "harmonia universalis, id est Deus".[35] Leibniz's pre-established harmony manifested itself on both the metaphysical as well as the social levels: metaphysically, as Cassirer put it,[36] "in Leibniz's system every individual substance is not only a fragment of the universe, it is the universe itself seen from a particular point of view . . . This means that only the highest development of all individual energies – not their levelling, equalisation, and extinction – leads to the truth of being, to the highest harmony, and to the most intensive fullness of reality;" socio-religiously, it manifests itself in tolerance of all religions as parts of totality.[37]

This rationalistic universalism of Leibniz's manifests itself in virtually all his philosophical enterprises – for example, in his mathematical work and in his linguistics (the latter not unconnected with the former). What George Steiner calls his messianic, anti-Babel theory of an universal *Ur*-language[38] is one of the most important precursors of modern theory of computer language[39] and fits into the tradition of what Noam Chomsky has called *Cartesian Linguistics*[40] – i.e. the claim that there is an universal, uniquely differentiating characteristic of the human species that resides in its primary (and primaeval) capacity for and in form of language. He was always on the look-out for research in what was called *characteris universalis* and *lingua universale*.[41] In this age-old tradition of linguistic theory the view has commonly been held that, for obvious biblical reasons, Hebrew is that primordial, "pure" language; Leibniz is, as a matter of fact, rather skittish about this view, although he does not rule it out.[42]

We are not suggesting that these motifs in Leibniz's thinking and work were due to Raphael Levi's influence on him. They long precede Leibniz's acquaintance with Levi. On the contrary, the basic attitude which they display can be said to have made it possible for the Jew Levi to find full-fledged *entrée* to Leibniz; they constitute, as it were, the basis on which further and mutually beneficial results could be and were produced in the inter-action between the two men. For it can be shown that three specific, further extrapolations of Leibniz's universalism were made during the years of Levi's residence in Leibniz's house.

For one thing, the first decade of the eighteenth century is the period during which the political and intellectual groundwork was laid for the eventual accession of the House of Hanover to the throne of Great Britain.[43] This was

[35]The *Monadologie* is dedicated to Prince Eugène of Savoy – also, as we have noted, one of Simon Wolff Oppenheimer's noble clients.

[36]*The Philosophy of the Enlightenment*, Princeton University Press 1951, pp. 32 f.

[37]Cf. F. Vanessen, 'Reim u. Zahl bei Leibniz', in *Autaios* VIII/2 (July 1966), p. 106.

[38]*On Difficulty and Other Essays*, Oxford 1978, pp. 138 f.

[39]Cf. A. Robinet, 'Leibniz, l'automate et la pensée', in *Studia Leibnitiana*, IV (1972), and his *Le défi cybernétique: l'automate et la pensée*, Paris 1973. For the Leibniz-Descartes disagreement on "Adamite" language cf. Ivon Belaval, *Leibniz, Critique de Descartes*, Paris 1960, pp. 181–189.

[40]Noam Chomsky, *Cartesian Linguistics . . .*, New York 1966.

[41]Cf. Harnack, *op. cit.*, pp. 57–59, 98 about Rödike. Cf. also H. Aarsleff, *From Locke to Saussure. Essays on the Study of Language and Intellectual History*, University of Minnesota Press 1982, 'Leibniz on Locke on Language', 'The Study and Use of Etymology in Leibniz'.

[42]A. Foucher de Careil, *Leibniz. La philosophie juive et la cabale*, Paris 1861 (Compte-rendu de l'Académie des Sciences morales et politiques), pp. 31 f.

[43]Cf. Hatton, *op. cit.*, 'The prospect of England', pp. 70 ff.

primarily a matter of assuring the Protestant succession. English Protestantism was, therefore, an important outpost of Hanover-policy. At that time certainly the most advanced theologico-political sector of English Protestantism was represented by John Toland – so much so, indeed, that Toland's mystical deism really broke through the outer boundaries of Protestantism. Toland made several trips to Germany at that time, partly in order to establish contact with individuals and groups of similar outlook and partly in order to tie his interests into the concrete political developments. Leibniz and Toland met and exchanged views in 1701[44] in connection with the arrival of a whole English delegation that brought the Act of Settlement.[45] (Toland exchanged a long series of *Letters to Senera*, 1704, with Sophie Charlotte, Queen of Prussia, whom he called "la reine républicaine".)[46]

Toland represented Christian Unitarianism in a form that radicalised even the Unitarianism of Newton and of his heterodox circle down to William Whiston. (John Maynard Keynes spoke of Newton as "a Judaic monotheist of the school of Maimonides",[47] and Frances Yates calls it "Hebraic piety".[48]) Leibniz certainly had tendencies in the same direction, but, whereas Newton was perfectly clear in his own mind about his Unitarianism and merely wanted to keep it from public knowledge (to the point of breaking with his eccentric and more outspoken disciple Whiston over this), Leibniz kept his unitarian tendencies even from his own full consciousness.[49] Thus Leibniz wrote a whole, early, tract defending trinitarianism against Socinianism,[50] while, on the other hand, there is considerable evidence that he was, unconsciously, propelled toward Unitarianism by the logic of his thinking. Jean Baruzi, that Christian enthusiast for Leibniz, finds himself compelled, for example, to raise the question whether Leibniz believed in the divinity of Jesus in the sense of the theologoumenon of the incarnation,[51] and G. Stammler[52] points to the frequent occurrence of the word "deus" and the extremely infrequent occurrence of "Christus" in Leibniz's writings.

Self-conscious *versus* unself-conscious Unitarianism would have been one significant difference between Leibniz and Toland. Further, Toland also represented most of the genuine Hermetic tradition in early-modern thought,[53]

[44]Cf. Guhrauer, *op. cit.*, p. 170; Hatton, *op. cit.*, p. 76.

[45]Margaret C. Jacob, *The Newtonians and the English Revolution 1689–1720*, Ithaca 1976, p. 230. The secretary of the Prussian Society of Sciences, J. Th. Jablonski, brother of the Court preacher and himself also a friend of Leibniz's, had to report to Leibniz on 28th April 1708 (A. Harnack, 'Bericht des Secretärs der Brandenburgischen Societät der Wissenschaften J. Th. Jablonski an den Präsidenten G. W. Leibniz (1700–1715) nebst einigen Antworten von Leibniz'. *Philosophische und historische Abhandlungen der Königlichen Akademie der Wissenschaften zu Berlin*, Berlin 1897, p. 52) that "Toland was here, but only for a few days, what he accomplished I have not learned".

[46]Franco Venturi, *Utopia and Reform in the Enlightenment*, Cambridge 1971, p. 51.

[47]*Encyclopaedia Britannica*, 1970, vol. 16, 'Newton', p. 421; *Essays in Biography*, London 1961, p. 316. Cf. also H. McLachlan, *Sir I. Newton-Theological Manuscripts*, Liverpool 1950, pp. 16 f., 21, 127, 135.

[48]Frances A. Yates, *The Rosicrucian Enlightenment*, London-Boston 1972, p. 207.

[49]Cf. Ernst Cassirer, 'Newton and Leibniz', *Philosophical Review*, 52 (July 1943), p. 379.

[50]*Defensio trinitatis per nova reperta logica* . . . , 1669.

[51]Baruzi, *op. cit.*, pp. 205 ff., 474 ff.

[52]Georg Stammler, *Leibniz*, Munich 1930, p. 181, note 226.

[53]Cf. Yates, *op. cit.*, and Jacob, *op. cit.*, p. 227.

while Leibniz, who had this also in his cultural background and was, therefore, significantly affected by it,[54] largely suppressed this, too, in his consciousness. Unlike Toland, he held that religious truth could be super-rational but not irrational.[55] Above all, as Margaret Jacob makes clear,[56] Toland's mystical hylozoism was the ideology of English political radicalism, while Leibniz's rationalistic optimism about the nature of God's creation led, like Newton's mechanism, to a mildly meliorist political conservatism and quietism.[57] Indeed, his conservatism even got him into political trouble when, apparently in league with Sophie, he insinuated an anti-Whig pamphlet into England during the succession-debates there.[58]

Despite these differences, Toland and Leibniz got along with one another quite well both personally and intellectually. They had enough in common: the same tendency toward natural religion, if not strict deism – the same background in mystical pietism – and the same goal of political rationalisation. As Heinemann put it: "Toland's relations with Leibniz mark the happiest and greatest time of his life."[59] Certainly Toland's famous and historic clarion-call for Jewish emancipation,[60] his use not only of biblical but also of some selected quasi-rabbinical Jewish sources,[61] and his congenial attitude toward Judaism,[62] must have commended him to Raphael Levi and through him perhaps to Levi's master and patron.

After his king actually became George I of Great Britain and when his other royal patron, Friedrich Wilhelm I of Prussia, also sought to overcome religious dissension in his realm, Leibniz's and D. E. Jablonski's Christian ecumenical efforts were given new impetus.[63]

How Leibniz's philosophical ecumenism spread beyond the confines of Christendom even in his old age is illustrated by his famous intervention in the

[54]Yates, *op. cit.*, pp. 91, 154 f.

[55]Cf. especially Leibniz's *Annotationunculae . . . ad Tolandi*; cf. F. H. Heinemann, 'Toland and Leibniz', *Philosophical Review*, LIV/5 (September 1945), p. 443, and Guhrauer, *op. cit.*, pp. 224–227.

[56]Jacob, *op. cit.*

[57]Cf. Venturi, *op. cit.*, p. 61.

[58]Cf. Hatton, *op. cit.*, pp. 78, 107.

[59]Heinemann, *loc. cit.*, pp. 439–443; cf. Cassirer, *loc. cit.*, p. 90. For Leibniz's influence on Toland cf. R. L. Colie, 'Spinoza and the Early English Deists', *Journal of the History of Ideas*, XX/1 (January 1959), p. 44.

[60]Cf. P. H. Meyer, 'The Attitude of the Enlightenment toward the Jew', *Studies on Voltaire and the 18th Century*, vol. XXVI, Geneva 1963, pp. 1165 f.

[61]Cf. Isaac E. Barzilay, 'John Toland's Borrowings from Simone Luzzatto. Luzzatto's *Discourse on the Jews of Venice* (1638), the Major Source of Toland's Writings on *The Naturalization of the Jews in Great Britain and Ireland* (1714),' *Jewish Social Studies*, XXXI/2 (April 1969), pp. 75–81. Cf. B. Ravid, 'How Profitable the Nation of the Jewes Are . . .', in *Mystics, Philosophers and Politicians . . . in Honor of Alexander Altmann*, eds. J. Reinharz *et al.*, Durham, N.C. 1982 on the use by Menasseh ben Israel of Court Jews as a recommendation to Oliver Cromwell in his famous 'Humble Address' (p. 164, note 15) and his use of Simone Luzzatto's economic arguments throughout.

[62]Cf. the 'Appendix . . . Concerning the Jewish Nation and Religion' in his *Nazarenus* . . ., 1718; and Max Wiener, 'J. Toland and Judaism', *Hebrew Union College Annual*, XVI (1941).

[63]Cf. 'D. E. Jablonski', in *Realencyklopädie für protestantische Theologie und Kirche*, 3, Leipzig 1900, vol. 8, p. 512; and H. R. Trevor-Roper, *Religion, the Reformation and Social Change*, London 1967, pp. 201, 293, for Jablonski, etc.; and Grossmann, *loc. cit.*, pp. 124–127 on the Prussian policy toward dissenters.

Jesuit-Chinese controversy.[64] He held that, as far as natural, universal reason is concerned, Chinese mathematics was the binary system which he himself was advocating[65] and that this rational system constituted the substance of the Hermetic tradition of truth that had been handed down from the biblical patriarchs,[66] beginning with Noah (thus integrating the Chinese into the biblical-Noachitic framework of history)[67] through Pythagoras, Plato, Hermes Trismegistus (the Chinese Fu Hsi),[68] the *Kabbalah*, Bruno, etc.[69] Endowed with such a rational culture, the ethics and politics of the Chinese are lauded by Leibniz, as they would have to be, for being superior to those of Christian Europe.[70] The lively suspicion was even being entertained by Leibniz and some of his friends that the recently discovered Chinese Jews and their ancient Bible would throw light on the descent of the Chinese from ancient Jewish tradition.[71] From the point of view of Raphael Levi's self-interest, it had again to be very welcome that his influential teacher's doctrine proclaimed all rational religion – Roman Catholic, Protestant, Confucian, universally human and, therefore, also Jewish – to be the sufficient and sole basis for a viable society.

This did not remain mere theory on the part of our protagonists. In historical fact, too, the encounter of religions in Hanover resulted in an old-fashioned, mediaeval confrontation between Christianity and Judaism (if a private record, published two centuries later, can be trusted). *Religionsgespräch gehalten am Kurfürstlichen Hofe zu Hannover 1704* . . . ,[72] is a Hebrew report of a formal "disputation" between an apostate, proselytising Jew and a rabbi, within the ducal palace, in the presence of the King (the later George I), his father (?) and

[64]Cf. Guhrauer, *op. cit.*, pp. 95–98; Mungello, *op. cit.*; and *Discourse on the Natural Theology of the Chinese*, tr., ed. H. Rosemont and D. J. Cook, Society for Asian and Comparative Philosophy, monograph No. 4, University Press of Hawaii 1977; p. 2, from Leibniz's *Consilium Aegyptiacum*, in *Sämtliche Schriften und Briefe*, vol. 4; and *Autaios*, VIII/2 (July 1966), 'Sonderheft zum 250. Todestag G. W. Leibniz', pp. 134–203.

[65]Cf. above, p. 235 and *Discourse* . . . , *op. cit.*, p. 15.

[66]Cf. Guhrauer, *op. cit.*, pp. 95 ff. and *Discourse* . . . , *op. cit.*, p. 16.

[67]Cf. Mungello, *op. cit.*, pp. 35 f.

[68]*Discourse* . . . , *op. cit.*, p. 15.

[69]Mungello, *op. cit.*, pp. 48, 122; *Discourse* . . . , *op. cit.*, p. 15. For how these considerations also play a part in Leibniz's well-known "main-stream" works, cf. his *Théodicée*, Nos. 181, 208.

[70]*Discourse* . . . , *op. cit.*, p. 2. (One has to realise, of course, that seventeenth- and eighteenth-century European intellectuals and scholars knew very little, if anything, about Far Eastern cultures. Leibniz's sympathy with China, Montesquieu's *Lettres persanes*, for that matter d'Argens's *Lettres juives* [cf. Meyer, *loc. cit.*, pp. 1181 f.] etc., are "ideal models", in the form of pretended descriptions of distant civilisations, whose purpose it is to criticise the conditions of their own societies.) Cf. Bricaire de la Dixmérie, *Le sauvage de Taïti aux français* . . . , Paris 1770; Moshe Pelli, 'The Beginning of the Epistolary Genre in Hebrew Enlightenment Literature in Germany. The Alleged Affinity between Lettres Persanes and 'Igrot Meshulam', in *LBI Year Book XXIV* (1979), p. 88, note 5. Cf. also John Webb, *An Historical Essay Endeavoring A Probability that the Language of the Empire of China is the Primitive Language*, London 1669. Cf. also T. W. Adorno's interpretation of Gustav Mahler's "chinoiserie" as being code-words for Jewishness and Palestine: *Gesammelte Schriften*, vol. 13, *Mahler – eine musikalische Physiognomik*, Frankfurt a. Main 1971, pp. 291 f.

[71]J. Kvačala, *Neue Beiträge zum Briefwechsel zwischen D. E. Jablonsky und G. W. Leibniz*, Jurjew 1899 (cf. note 29 above), p. 50. Cf. W. C. White, *Chinese Jews* . . . , 2nd edn., New York (Paragon Book Reprint) 1966, pp. 26 f., 39 ff., 154.

[72]Edited by A. Berliner, Berlin 1914.

mother.[73] The disputation is supposed to have been organised by Levi's employer, the Court Jew Lippmann Cohen (i.e. Leffmann Behrens), as a defence-measure against the activities of the apostate and against old-fashioned forcible conversionist sermons in local synagogues.[74] It is noteworthy that the rabbi is described as versed in the New Testament, French, etc.,[75] and that the Queen is described as open-minded toward the Jews.[76] At the end of the disputation she declares the result to be a draw.[77] This accords with what we know to have been the sympathetic relationship between the Queen and Leibniz. Glückel of Hameln, by far the most famous source for Jewish life in that part of the world at the time, also reported the Duchess's sympathy for and association with Jews.[78] The King's own enlightenment, too, is established. Hatton speaks of his "sympathy for non-conformists" and of "the measure of relief he brought to them".[79] In England as well as in Hanover he advanced religious toleration and freedom of thought, for Jews as well.[80] "George was in tune with Early Enlightenment ideas both in domestic and foreign affairs."[81] He welcomed Voltaire himself to his realm.[82] Latitudinarianism and ecumenism were so essential in the Hanoverian dynasty that the refusal of death-bed ecclesiastical ministration became something of a delightful custom[83] – not limited to Leibniz's final remark: "There is nothing I need to confess."[84] A Hanoverian, Hennig Böhmer, published in 1708 *De causa Judaeorum tolerantia*. And, as we know, Raphael Levi was at that very time in and out of the Court librarian's home.

Up to now our arguments for Raphael Levi's inter-actions with and effects on Leibniz have been indirect. That is to say, it seems logical, but we have no concrete evidence, that Leibniz's relationship to Toland, with the latter's deism, Unitarianism, his advocacy of Jewish emancipation and his "accommodationism" to Confucian, natural religion[85] imply the logical extension that Jews also, their basic beliefs and their religious culture, fall easily within the ecumenical framework of Leibniz's rational religion and state. One can, to be sure, easily visualise Leibniz and Levi, sitting together in their common home, reinforcing one another in conversation and with literary references in their shared outlook on the world. But, of course, logical implications are not the same thing as historical facts.

"Literary references" is the cue that leads us to the empirical evidence. Even

[73]*Ibid.*, unpaginated pp. 2 f. of the introduction.
[74]*Ibid.*, pp. 3f.
[75]*Ibid.*, Hebrew pagination p. 12.
[76]*Ibid.*, p. 11.
[77]*Ibid.*, p. 16.
[78]Azriel Shochat, 'The Acculturation of the Jews of Germany in their Environment with the Spread of the Enlightenment' (in Hebrew), *Zion*, XXI (1956), p. 220.
[79]Hatton, *op. cit.*, p. 262.
[80]*Ibid.*, pp. 47, 289 ff.
[81]*Ibid.*, p. 290.
[82]*Ibid.*, p. 291.
[83]*Ibid.*, pp. 47, 91, 332, note 62.
[84]Guhrauer, *op. cit.*, vol. 2, pp. 329 f. He was often nicknamed "Glöw nix" ("Glaube nichts"): Stammler, *op. cit.*, p. 43.
[85]Cf. *Discourse . . .*, *op. cit.*, pp. 11, 15.

relatively early in Leibniz's career, for example in 1689, he had occasion, in his capacity as librarian, to acquaint himself with some classics in Jewish literature – even rabbinical codes and Talmud-translations.[86] Furthermore, throughout his life Leibniz, like the other revolutionary scientists of modernity, from Bruno through Newton and beyond, delved into what Christian Europe thought of as *Kabbalah* in the pursuit of "the Hermetic tradition" of ultimate truth. Thus, in 1687 he paid an extended visit to Baron Knorr de Rosenroth, the classic compiler of Christian *Kabbalah*. Then and thereafter Leibniz read much of the available Jewish literature to which de Rosenroth had drawn his attention, and he took from it what he found useful to his philosophical and religious purposes.[87] The very word "cabalisiren" in German came to mean "to engage in linguistic esotericism".[88]

It was, however, precisely during the period that Raphael Levi was living with him, in the first decade of the eighteenth century, that Leibniz studied systematically the *magnum opus* of all Jewish philosophy, Maimonides' *Guide for the Perplexed*.[89] Foucher de Careil has published *Leibnitii observationes ad Rabbi Mosis Maimonidis librum qui inscribitur 'Doctor Perplexorum'*, dated it, and analysed its usefulness to Leibniz's own philosophical ends.[90] Clearly, Leibniz must have used his amanuensis Levi as his "resource-person" in the study of Maimonides. Not that Levi was at all likely to have studied the *Guide for the Perplexed* at the Frankfurt *yeshivah*. To this day, and certainly in the seventeenth century in Germany, Maimonides, the philosopher, has always been carefully avoided in traditionalist Jewish circles in favour of "Rambam", the legalist.[91] But, even if first stimulated to read the philosophical work by his Gentile philosophical teacher, Levi could, of course, read him in Hebrew with the classical commentaries, and he could explicate him in all detail. Indeed, Maimonides remained the central Jewish intellectual and scientific figure for Levi throughout the rest of his life, as the very titles of his Hebrew books will illustrate.[92]

[86]De Careil, *op. cit.*, pp. 30, 32.

[87]*Ibid.*, pp. 56 ff. Leibniz's own *Animadversiones ad Georg Wachteri librum de Recondita Hebraeorum Philosophia*; de Careil, *ibid.*, pp. 2, 8; K. Müller, 'G. W. Leibniz', in Totok and Haase (eds.), *op. cit.*, p. 41.

[88]Cf. Harnack, *op. cit.*, p. 54.

[89]Cf. S. Levy, 'English Students of Maimonides', *Jewish Annual 5701* (1940–1941), and J. I. Dienstag, 'Christian Translators of Maimonides' *Mishneh Torah* into Latin', *ibid.*, pp. 287 ff. (*Salo W. Baron Jubilee Volume*, vol. 1, American Academy for Jewish Research, 1947.) (It is noteworthy, in view of Levi's later specialised interest in the calendar, that there were many early Latin translations of Maimonides's *Book of the Laws of the Sanctification of the New Moon*.) Cf. also Guhrauer, *op. cit.*, p. 86.

[90]De Careil, *op. cit.*; cf. Jacob Guttmann, 'Der Einfluss der maimonidischen Philosophie auf das christliche Abendland', in W. Bacher etc. (eds.), *Moses ben Maimon. Sein Leben, seine Werke, und sein Einfluss*, vol. I, Leipzig 1908, pp. 224–230; L. E. Goodman, 'Maimonides and Leibniz', *Journal of Jewish Studies*, XXXI/2 (Autumn 1980), pp. 214–236, including a translation of Leibniz's *Observationes*.

[91]Cf. Bialik's famous poem 'Ha-Matmid', in which a *yeshivah* student is expelled because he has been found studying the *Guide*.

[92]This is a truism of the entire history of modern Jewish intellectuality: the *Guide* . . . is always the work that triggers off Jewish philosophy, in all regions and throughout subsequent history. Salomon Maimon, for one, re-named himself after his hero. Mendelssohn was first pushed towards philosophy by the *Guide*, after it had been re-printed in 1742, for the first time since 1553, near his home-town of Dessau in Jessnitz (cf. Alexander Altmann, *Moses Mendelssohn. A Biographical Study*,

Leibniz died 14th November 1716, and Levi lived with him until the end. As the story of how Levi came to the attention of Leibniz in the first place is one episode in his life told relatively often, so the other story of that sort is that Levi was the only person in attendance at Leibniz's clandestine interment in the St. John Church in Neustadt-Hanover.[93] (The story has, as a matter of fact, all the earmarks of a moral fable, told by earlier German liberals and by Jews.) In any case, for the rest of his long life, Levi kept Leibniz's personal and intellectual memory with pious loyalty. In his old age he and the mature Moses Mendelssohn, from 1767 onward, found that they shared common Leibniz-Wolffian views on immortality and other philosophical issues. Mendelssohn visited Levi in Hanover in 1771 and 1777 – the latter also the year in which he attended lectures of Kant's in Königsberg.[94]

Two extant portraits symbolise the Leibniz-Levi symbiosis: one of Leibniz, which he bequeathed to Levi,[95] the other of Levi himself,[96] that depicts him as a typical eighteenth-century gentleman-scholar in wig and ruffles, his books and astronomical paraphernalia at hand.[97]

Levi now settled down in Hanover as a modest teacher of commercial arithmetic and of Jewish studies. (Leibniz, too, had concerned himself with insurance and interest-rates.[98]) The government, therefore, exempted him from

---

University of Alabama 1973, p. 10). Cf. F. Lachover, 'Maimonides and the Beginning of the Hebrew Enlightenment' (in Hebrew), *Moznayim*, III (1938/1939), Tishri-Second Adar, pp. 539–546.

[93]Cf. Johann Heinrich Voss, *Sämtliche Gedichte*, Königsberg 1825, vol. 5, pp. 118 f. (originally published in 1781); *Encyclopaedia Britannica*, 13th edn., 'Leibniz', p. 687, col. 1; Lazarus, 'Leibniz und Levi', *loc. cit.*, p. 244. (For Voss cf. Alfred Dieck, *Die Wandermusikanten von Salzgitter . . .*, Göttingen 1962, vol. 1, p. 39, note 18.) Grote, *Leibniz und seine Zeit, op. cit.*, p. 556, doubts this wide-spread story. Ritter, *loc. cit.*, also militates against it; so does K. Müller, in W. Totok and C. Haase (eds.), *op. cit.*, pp. 59 f. and G. Scheel, *ibid.*, 'Hannover – Politisches, Gesellschaftliches und Geistiges Leben zur Leibnizzeit', p. 85.

[94]On the Mendelssohn-Raphael Levi relationship cf. Altmann, *op. cit.*, pp. 161 ff., 179 ff., 786, note 14 (note that the Yiddish letter from Mendelssohn to an "unknown person", who turns out to be Levi, was in the possession of Rabbi Marcus Adler of Hanover – later Chief Rabbi of Great Britain); James H. Lehmann, 'Maimonides, Mendelssohn, and the Me'asfim', in *LBI Year Book XX* (1975), pp. 87 ff. For the Mendelssohn-Kant relationship, cf. L. W. Beck, *Early German Philosophy*, Harvard University Press 1969, p. 324, and for Mendelssohn as Leibnizian, cf. *ibid.*, pp. 324–339. Cf. Schwarzschild, 'The Jewish Enlightenment Symbiosis', *Jewish Spectator* (Fall 1974), pp. 26 ff.

[95]This portrait is now at the University of Göttingen. Cf. Guhrauer, *op. cit.*, vol. 2, pp: 369–371 and appendix B; L. Schreiner, 'Leibniz im Bilde seiner Zeit', in W. Totok and C. Haase (eds.), *op. cit.*, pp. 74–76 and illustration 8; Lazarus, 'Leibniz und Levi', *loc. cit.*, p. 247.

[96]This portrait by an "unknown painter, *c.* 1670" is now in the Historisches Museum am Hohen Ufer, Hannover: cf. *Führer des Niedersächsischen Heimatmuseums der Hauptstadt Hannover*, 6, p. 98, No. 158.

[97]For pre-Emancipation Jewish acculturation in Germany, cf. Shochat, 'The Acculturation of the Jews in Germany . . .', *loc. cit.*, also especially in matters of clothing, pp. 212, 216 ff., and *With the Changes of Eras* (Hebrew: *'im Chiluffay HaT'kufot*), Jerusalem 1960; Schnee, *Die Hoffinanz . . . , op. cit.*, vol. 3, p. 211. For another Hanoverian Court Jew of approximately this era, who, however, excoriated Jewish acculturation both in matters of clothing and of philosophy, see Isaac Jacob Gans (1723–1798), the grandfather of the Hegel-disciple Eduard Gans: cf. Hanns G. Reissner, *Eduard Gans. Ein Leben im Vormärz*, Tübingen 1965 (Schriftenreihe wissenschaftlicher Abhandlungen des Leo Baeck Instituts 14), pp. 12, 168 f., and Grunwald, 'Three Chapters on German-Jewish Banking History', *loc. cit.*, pp. 10–12. Cf. notes 155 f. below.

[98]Cf. C. Haase, 'Leibniz als Politiker und Diplomat', in Totok und Haase, *op. cit.*, p. 456, note 234.

the special taxes imposed on Jews in business.[99] He married Vogel, daughter of Baruch, and they had seven children, of whom, however, only one daughter, Eva, survived to marry Jacob Heyn from Hameln (probably of the Heine family) and to have her own family.[100]

Even now, though, he continued to maintain close relations with the Jewish bankers in the town. By the 1720s the grandsons of Leffmann Behrens had taken over the international business, including its extension to England in connection with the assumption of the British crown by the Hanoverian dynasty.[101] But now serious trouble overtook them. Unrepaid loans of tremendous magnitude and their own financial machinations drove them into bankruptcy. They were imprisoned and tortured: the synagogues that they personally owned in Hanover, in the Palatinate, and elsewhere were auctioned off; and the court-trials over the issues involved in the bankruptcy lasted for over a century. Raphael Levi himself was hired to translate Hebrew documents that were used in these trials. In the process he made compromise proposals, but these, too, failed.[102] When Michael David, the maecenas of a new local Jewish bankers' family, married the widowed mother of Leffmann Behrens's grandsons,[103] Levi grew close to these oligarchs, too.[104] In 1758 Levi and Simon Wolf Oppenheimer signed Michael David's will as witnesses.[105]

In his scholarly capacity Levi published several books over the decades. They are essentially pedestrian in content and reflect his two areas of expertise – in German on commercial arithmetic, and in Hebrew on Jewish astronomical calendration. By thus putting into literary practice his commercial[106] and philosophico-mathematical training as well as his Jewish learning, Levi served in a double-barreled way the Jewish mercantile class and the religious leadership (typically combined in personal union):

Vorbericht vom Gebrauch der neuerfundenen Logarithmischen Wechseltafeln (Frankfurt-Hannover 1748/1749). *Supplement zu dem im verwichenen 1747ten Jahre herausgegebenen Vorbericht . . . Wechsel-Tabellen vermittels welcher ein Cours aus 2.3. oder mehrer gegeben Datis bloss durch die Addition und Subtraction ausfündig zu machen, zu mehrer Erläuterung derselben . . .* (Frankfurt-Leipzig 1749). *Luchot ha'Ibbur* (Tables of Intercalation),

[99]Once on 9th April 1717 and again on 6th August 1742 (cf. Lazarus, *loc. cit.*, p. 9).

[100]The details of all of the members of Levi's family are listed in Gronemann, *op. cit.*, p. 97, and Wahl, *loc. cit.*, p. 60 (cf. note 148 below).

[101]For their agents in England, cf. Schnee, *Die Hoffinanz . . .*, *op. cit.*, vol. 2, pp. 24, 28 f., 31, 44, 46.

[102]*Ibid.*, pp. 46–55. Schnee supplies no specific documentation for Levi's role in this episode. Generally one must say about Schnee's very thorough work that it carries strong and prejudicial overtones of Teutonic chauvinism, if not antisemitism (cf. F. L. Carsten, 'The Court Jews. A Prelude to Emancipation', in *LBI Year Book III* (1958), pp. 140–156).

[103]*Ibid.*, p. 56. Leffmann-Behrens's grandsons married into the Samson family, themselves Court agents and rabbis of Brunswick, which established the famous Samson Foundation in 1733 and enlarged it up to 1805, by which the Jewish School of Wolfenbüttel was founded in 1786 – and it was to remain important well into the second half of the nineteenth century (Gronemann, *op. cit.*, pp. 47 f., 83).

[104]Gronemann, *op. cit.*, pp. 93, 132.

[105]*Ibid.*, p. 132.

[106]For other, contemporary Jewish educational enterprises for commerce cf. *Monumenta Judaica, op. cit.*, B 367; Kalman Cohen, *Lehrbuch des Kaufmännischen Rechnens*, Düsseldorf 1758; and *Monumenta Judaica*, B 368, 'Lehrgangsplan'; 20th November 1752.

which appeared in two parts: Part I, Leiden 1756 and Part II Hannover, 1757. (As the title indicates, this work consists largely of tables of intercalation, on the basis of detailed astronomical calculations, and of explanations to Maimonides's relevant codification. On p. 38 and on an inserted, personally signed paste-in on the fly-leaf of Part II Levi announces that he is preparing additional parts, in which additional talmudic and Maimonidean problems of the calendar will be explicated, and he protests the reports that Moses Yekutiel of Tiktin has published – as, indeed, was the case – his *Techunat HaShama'yim* on the basis of notes that students had made of Levi's lectures.) *Techunat HaShama'yim* . . . (Celestial Astronomy) (Amsterdam 1756), whose editorial subtitle announces that it comprises an extended explanation of the book "Laws of the Sanctification of the New Moon" in Maimonides's law-code.[107] *Neue compendiöse Allgemeine Cours- und Wechsel-Tafeln, bestehend aus 26 kleinen Tafeln vermittels welchen der Unterschied zwischen allerley Münzarten sowohl der ein als ausländischen durch ganz Europa blos durch eine kleine Addition oder Subtraction, ohne alle übrigen Rechnungen in Procenten und auch stückweise kann bestimmt werden* (Hannover 1760). One more book appeared posthumously – *Rechnungsmethode*, edited by Meyer Aaron,[108] (Hannover 1783), with the explanation[109] that "his death and several other considerations kept him from making it known to the world". (It is notable in this stage of modern European society that Levi's posthumous text is supplemented with an appendix by the Hanoverian government-minister, chamber-secretary, and member of one of the historic, leading families of the country, Otto von Grote, 'About the Four Kinds of Calculating with Fractions'.)[110] Finally, one of Levi's students, Simon ben Nathan Nata Walsch, published *Neveh Kodesh* (The Splendour of Holiness), (Hannover-Berlin 1786), which again deals with calendration, whose introduction claims that here the content of Part III of *Luchot Ha'Ibbur*, which Levi had promised, is presented, as derived from Levi's lectures by the author and another student.[111]

[107]The publishing history of this book is very complicated and controversial.

[108]On Meyer Aaron, cf. Gronemann, *op. cit.*, p. 132. Lazarus, *loc. cit.*, p. 62 called this book "completely lost". The University of California – Berkeley has a copy: QA101/L38. It has Meyer Aaron's name inscribed on the title page and someone's (Aaron's?) thorough marginalia throughout.

[109]*Ibid.*, p. 1.

[110]The Grotes and the Jews of Hanover meet repeatedly in modern history. For Raphael Levi's associate Otto von Grote, cf. Schnath, *op. cit.*, vol. 1, Hildesheim-Leipzig 1938, p. 640 and for his portrait *ibid.*, p. 544; Schnee, *Die Hoffinanz* . . . , *op. cit.*, vol. 2, p. 34, etc. for the profitable relations between the Court Jew and the minister, and *ibid.*, p. XIX, for how the two travelled and worked together in 1692. On the Grote family cf. also Hatton, *op. cit.*, indexed. M(endel) Zuckermann, *Übersicht über den jüdisch-geschichtlichen Inhalt des Königlichen Staatsarchivs zu Hannover (Mitteilungen des Gesamtarchivs der deutschen Juden*, II/2), Leipzig 1910, p. 38, supplies information about O. A. Grote, the ambassador of Hanover to Hamburg, who around 1817, favoured Jewish emancipation. This Count Grote was also von Hardenberg's pro-Jewish liaison-man at the Congress of Vienna, at a time when the city-states of Germany, like Hanover and Frankfurt, were bastions of reaction: cf. I. Kracauer, *Geschichte der Juden in Frankfurt a/M.*, Frankfurt a. Main 1927, vol. 2, pp. 450, 470. Ludwig Grote, the author of *Leibniz und seine Zeit* . . . , *op. cit.*, a retired, very orthodox Lutheran pastor, was presumably also a member of this family.

[111]There are manuscripts and alleged holographs of Levi's writings in various libraries, the Bodleian, Columbia University, the Jewish Theological Seminary, etc. They all seem to be copies of his Hebrew astronomical texts. Cf. Moritz Steinschneider (*Ozrot Chajim*) *Katalog der Michael'schen*

From the point of view of Jewish intellectual history, greatest comparative importance must be assigned to Levi's work *Techunat HaShama'yim.*[112] Sections 1–92 of the book rehearse and explain historic Jewish astronomical calculations. Only the last five sections then go on to say really interesting things. Section 93: traditional astronomy, as used by Maimonides, was, of course, Ptolemaic, not Galilean, but this suffices for the practical purposes of Jewish calendration, although (section 94) one major Aristotelian correction of Ptolemy has long been entrenched. Section 95 summarises Ptolemaic cosmology. Section 96 then presents in brief outline and with an heliocentric diagram "the new astronomy of Copernicus" and its cosmology, which is said to have "endless advantages".[113] And the last section, 97, then asserts that Maimonidean astronomy could be reformulated in Copernican terms – to which Levi carefully adds: "Where I differ from the ancients . . . God knows that . . . our intention is only to establish the

---

Bibliothek . . . , preface by L. Zunz, Hamburg 1848, p. 24, No. 301 (Techunat HaShama'yim); p. 29, No. 345 (*k'llalay yessod ha'ibbur*), p. 74, No. 847 (*Techunat HaShama'yim*), described as a holograph and containing "much more than the printed version"; No. 726, *Luchot ha'ibbur*, 1756; *Chochmat hat'chunah*, Bodleian Neubauer Nos. 2062, 2063 with a plan for a philosophic encyclopaedia, 1726; etc. Cyrus Adler, *Catalogue of the Leeser Library*, Philadelphia 1883, p. 50: *Techunat HaShama'yim* and tables, 1734, *The Calendar of the Christians* 1737, and *Sod ha'ibbur*. (Adler lists the printed works *Luchot Ha'ibbur*, Leiden-Hannover 1756, *Techunat HaShama'yim*, Amsterdam 1756, and the Bodleian numbers above. He describes the Levi-manuscript as bound in a cover, one side of which bears the initials "G. L." [?], the other the date 1737, "The first part apparently in the author's handwriting", in Judaeo-German, tables by a scribe, 73 pp. (The Leeser library was absorbed by the Hebrew Education Association of Philadelphia and ended up in the library of Dropsie University. In the latter's much-neglected holdings I was not able, however, to locate any trace of it.) Columbia University: *Techunat HaShama'yim*, X893/H193 (which they have held since 1935 but know nothing about, except that it is probably not a holograph); Jewish Theological Seminary of America, No. 2607 (cf. *Registry of Jewish Theological Seminary of America*, 1942/1943, pp. 72 f.): *Techunat HaShama'yim*, again asserted to be a holograph, some parts of which are not in the Amsterdam 1756 edition – which sounds like Steinschneider's description of the Bodleian No. 847. Excerpts from and references to *Techunat HaShama'yim* appear to this day in rabbinic works on the Jewish calendar. Meyer Fürth published *Yir'at Shama'yim* ('The Fear of Heaven'), Dessau 1820, again on Maimonides's *Laws of the Sanctification of the New Moon.* He refers (p. 27 *et al.*) to Levi's *Techunat HaShama'yim* and stipulates some corrections. For the rest, he reprints Levi's tables and uses his examples (pp. 42–45). In 1821 Fürth added a second volume, comprising Levi's *Luchot Ha'Ibbur*, Part II. In this second volume Fürth repents his modernism, however, and prays that the modernistic, Mendelssohnian sins "may soon bring our Messiah". *Mishneh Torah*, Warsaw 1881/1882, Vilna 1900, and Jerusalem: Congregation Bnee Yoseph, New York 1975, carry paragraphs 90–92 of *Techunat HaShama'yim* as a super-commentary to chapt. 17 of Maimonides's *Laws of the Sanctification* . . . – For the Walsch family cf. D. J. Cohen, 'An Autographic Letter by Moshe Wallich . . .', *Studies in Bibliography and Booklore*, vol. 14 (1982), pp. 12 f.

[112] Altmann, *op. cit.*, p. 786, note 16, where "1755" should be corrected to 1756. (Professor J. I. Dienstag has drawn our attention to the fact that some copies of this work comprise a 'Final Appendix' which the one at our disposal lacks, pp. 39–40.)

[113] For other early Jewish Galilean astronomy cf. André Neher, 'L'exégèse biblique juive face à Copernic au 16e et au 17e siècles', *Studies Presented to Prof. M. A. Beck*, Amsterdam 1974, pp. 190–196; George Alter, 'Two Renaissance Astronomers. David Gans, Joseph Delmedigo', *Rozpravy Československe Akademie Věd*, 68/11 (1958); and André Neher, *David Gans* . . . (cf. the following note) pp. 27, 362, and esp. p. 364 on Rabbi Jonathan ben Joseph of Rozhany in his book, *S. Yeshu'a ben Yisra'el*, Frankfurt a. Main 1720 and others in Frankfurt. Cf. also *The Heritage of Israel*, F. C. Burkitt at the end of his article on the role of *Kabbalah* in the transmission of Copernicus to Kepler, Bruno and Böhme.

truth . . . Perhaps I will thus find favour in the eyes of God and man."[114] The book ends on what may at first appear to be nothing but a conventional coda: "May it be the will of the great God and Lord that He may protect His great name by returning the exile of His people and fulfil in us the verse, 'The people that walk in darkness will see a great light, the dwellers in the land of the shadow of death will have a shining light upon them.' (*Is.* IX:1) Finished in 'Forgive Thy people Israel, that Thou has redeemed.'" (*Deut.* XXI:8)–*padeeta*=1734.[115]

Apart from writing his books, Levi taught many students during the long years of his modest existence as a private teacher in Hanover. He had Jewish as well as Gentile students. Another of his Jewish students was Berman Berend (Baresh–Behrend Joshua–Isachar Berish), who was to become *Landesrabbiner* (1789–1802).[116] In an article about Levi in *Hannoversche Morgenzeitung* (1846), reprinted in Fürst's *Der Orient*,[117] the story is told of a young Gentile whom Levi taught and helped and who went to work for the King of Hanover and Britain in London. Another student of his was Salomon Haase, from Worms, who later became professor of mathematics at the University of Marburg.[118]

Raphael Levi became involved in non-Jewish history one more time, in 1748. In 1714 Sir Isaac Newton had induced the Royal Society to offer a prize of £20,000 for a solution to a problem that beset Britain's international commerce and politics–the determination of navigational longitudes at sea.[119] The prize was eventually awarded to the London clock-maker John Harrison, but in the interval a whole slew of solutions was offered, some crazy and some just ineffective. When George II visited his dynastic home in Hanover on an extended visit in 1748[120] Raphael Levi also submitted a solution. (It should be remembered that about this time several works of his had appeared in print.) Levi's proposal impressed the monarch and his retinue sufficiently to have an expense-account granted to the Jewish scholar, on which to travel to London and to submit his plan to the

[114]Cf. André Neher, *David Gans (1541–1613), Disciple du Maharal de Prague, assistant de Tycho Brahe et de Jean Kepler*, Paris 1974, pp. 369–372 and plate 2, note 2. The whole of this book is valuable on the inter-action of modern European science and Judaism. Raphael Levi, though dealt with, is unfortunately not indexed.

[115]The Hebrew "padeeta"="that Thou hast redeemed"=1734 by the numerical value of the Hebrew letters.

[116]Cf. Lazarus, 'Raphael Levi', *loc. cit.*; Gronemann, *op. cit.*, p. 64, Hebrew pp. 47 f. He and his father, rabbi in Hanover 1761–1789 (*ibid.*, pp. 61 ff.), are apostrophised in Walsch's *Neveh Kodesh* (cf. note 111) as his teachers and singular scholars. Cf. also Asaria-Helfgott, 'Zur Geschichte des Landesrabbinats in Hannover', *Udim* (Zeitschrift der Rabbinerkonferenz in der Bundesrepublik Deutschland), IV, Frankfurt a. Main 1973, p. 28.

[117]Leipzig, 13th August 1846, pp. 256–258.

[118]F. W. Strieder, *Grundlagen zu einer hessischen Gelehrten- und Schriftstellergeschichte*, Kassel 1785, vol. 5, pp. 203 f. and vol. 15, p. 341; Monika Richarz, *Der Eintritt der Juden in die akademischen Berufe. Jüdische Studenten und Akademiker in Deutschland 1678–1848*, Tübingen 1974 (Schriftenreihe wissenschaftlicher Abhandlungen des Leo Baeck Institute 28), p. 27. Cf. also Selma Stern, *Der Preussische Staat und die Juden*, II/1, Tübingen 1962 (Schriftenreihe wissenschaftlicher Abhandlungen des Leo Baeck Instituts 8/1), p. 167.

[119]Cf. Frank E. Manuel, *A Portrait of Newton*, Cambridge, Mass. 1968, pp. 267 f., and *Greenwich Observatory* . . . , ed. E. G. Forbes, London 1974, vol. I: 'Origins and Early History (1675–1835)', pp. 77–80 *et al.*

[120]Cf. W. R. Rohrbein and A. von Rohr, *Hannover im Glanz und Schatten des britischen Weltreiches* . . . , Hannover 1977, pp. 50 f.

scientists in charge of the project.[121] Levi did, indeed, go to England, though what happened to his submission[122] and how he spent his time there, brief as it was, we do not know.[123] *The Journal Book of the Royal Society*, vol. XIX (1745–1748), p. 498, without mentioning Levi's name, seems to report on his proposal.[124] William Whiston, the Newton-disciple, scholar, and Unitarian activist, who himself worked on the prize-competition repeatedly,[125] especially, together with H. Ditton, *New Method of Discovering Longitude* (London 1714), may be reporting on contact he had with Levi in London in *Memoirs of the Life and Works of Mr. Wm. Whiston* (London 1753), pp. 15f.[126] Whiston, though kept out of the Royal Society by his more duplicitous patron Newton, had close connections with some of its members, and there was one Jew among them, Dr. Jacob de Castro Sarmento (who later apostacised), and he and others in London's Sephardic circles, especially their Chief Rabbi David Nieto, had long concerned themselves intensively not only with modern philosophy and science in general[127] but also with astronomy and calendration in particular.[128] Whiston and Levi may well have been brought together through such intermediaries, for we know independently that the Ashkenazic Court Jews and the network of Sephardic grandees entertained solid connections.[129]

It might seem that we have now finished sketching all that is important about

[121]Zuckermann, *op. cit.*, contains no references to Levi, although pp. 37 f. list some materials of the Hanover chancellery in London concerned with Jewish affairs. A personal inquiry to the archives also drew blank. One might assume that the offices of the Leffmann Behrens banking firm in London looked after Levi's welfare while he was there. Forbes, *loc. cit.*, pp. 115 ff. and 178, illustrates how close the scientific connections were between Hanover and the Greenwich Observatory over long periods and how the religious concerns of people like Johann David Michaelis and Leonard Euler converged with astronomical and navigational concerns. Cf. also Johann Friedrich Euler, *Translatio Epistolae R. Maimonides ad Proselytum* . . . , dissertation, University of Basle, 14th September 1759.

[122]J. Dudley, the librarian and archivist of the Royal Greenwich Observatory, in a letter of 21st August 1979, speculates that the death in 1748 of the Foreign Secretary of the Royal Society, Zollman, may have caused Levi's paper to be lost, since he took charge of such matters, as the "Journal Book" shows.

[123]Daniel E. Baring, *Leben des . . . M. Antonii Corvini* . . . , Hannover 1749, pp. 16 f.; Altmann, *op. cit.*, pp. 116 f.; Lazarus, 'Raphael Levi', *loc. cit.*, p. 63. Levi left for London on 13th April. (The Corvinus-book was written immediately upon the events. The author mentions Levi in connection with a discussion of the navigational problem. He reports having personally spoken with R. Levi and refers to his other books.) Georgio Tonelli reports that Corvinus's teacher Darjes influenced Kant: 'Kant's Critique of Pure Reason Within the Tradition of Modern Logic', in *Akten des 4. Internationalen Kant-Kongresses*, Mainz 1974, Berlin, Part III, pp. 189 f., 'Conditions in Königsberg and the Making of Kant's Philosophy', A. Buchler *et al.* (eds.), in *bewusstsein-G. Funke zueigen*, Bonn 1975; and 'Die Voraussetzungen zur Kantischen Urteilstafel in der Logik des 18. Jahrhunderts', in *Kritik u. Metaphysik. Studien H. Heimsoeth zum 80. Geburtstag*, Berlin 1966, pp. 138, 152.

[124]We are indebted to J. C. Graddon (my late brother-in-law – Steven Schwarzschild) for his help at the Royal Society: cf. 'The Retirement of Mr. J. C. Graddon, assistant editor to the Society', *Notes and Records of the Royal Society of London*, 27/2 (February 1973), pp. 325 f.

[125]Cf. James E. Force, *Whiston Controversies: the Development of Newtonianism in the Thought of Wm. Whiston*, dissertation, Washington University, December 1977, pp. 18–21, 442 ff.

[126]J. Whiston and B. White, 2nd edn.

[127]Jakob Petuchowski, *The Theology of Haham David Nieto* . . . , New York 1954, pp. 24, 29, 50, 59, 138, note 26a, etc.

[128]*Ibid.*, pp. 22 f.

[129]Cf. Kellenbenz, *op. cit.*, p. 469.

Raphael Levi's life and works. The knowledgeable and perceptive reader will have, while reading, grown suspicious however. Is it likely that a Jewish scholar, of whatever stature, who spent the largest part of his life studying philosophy, both general and Jewish, and astronomical mathematics, was basically interested in nothing but tables of currency-exchanges and tables of calendar-determinations? Anyway, the last sentence in *Techunat HaShama'yim*, which we quoted, strikes messianic, adventist overtones, however conventional. Furthermore, the combination of philosophic speculation and the dating of historical periods is the classic basis for eschatological concerns – even in "the age of reason", among Jews no less than among non-Jews. Leibniz, with all his cool prudence and quasi-deism, can be shown to have sipped from the fountains of German mysticism – especially through Erhard Weigel –,[130] and he displayed a remarkable tolerance toward adventist movements throughout his life. During the period of his life when he looked into the *Kabbalah* under the guidance of Baron Knorr de Rosenroth (*Kabbala Denutada*) Leibniz hit on a millenarian date himself: "Putat adventum Mesiae aut regnum interris pertinere circiter ad annum 1832."[131] In 1691, in an exchange with his benefactress, the Duchess, Sophie (mother of George I), he defended a contemporary German Christian millenarian, Fräulein von Asseburg. Using, incidentally, a proto-typically Maimonidean explanation of the social psychology of prophets, he reasoned that such innocent adventists do no harm, whereas forcing them to abjure their beliefs will be harmful to society.[132] Furthermore, as we have also noted earlier, there was always an unarticulated utopian-eschatological agenda that underlay Leibniz's rationalistic philosophising itself, so that he could exclaim: "I seem to be an esotericist. In fact, he who knows me only from my writings does not know me."[133]

Among eighteenth-century philosophers, scientists, writers and religionists generally, adventism was no less rife than at all other times and with other types of mentalities. Sir Isaac Newton's wild millenarianism was continued by his successors, and for example, "in 1707, Tenison wrote to inform the Electress Sophie of Hanover (Leibniz's great friend) that God was at work in the war on the Rhine".[134]

At the end of the period with which we are concerned, Kant entitled an essay 'The End of All Things' and the last, neglected sentence in the *Critique of Pure Reason* implies a feverish adventism: "The critical path alone is still open. If the reader has had the courtesy and the patience to traverse that path in my

[130]Cf. K. Moll, *Der junge Leibniz. I: . . . Der Anschluss an E. Weigels Scientia Generalis*, Stuttgart 1978, and Guhrauer, *op. cit.*, p. 13; G. M. Ross, 'Leibniz and the Nuremberg Alchemical Society', in *Studia Leibnitiana*, VI (1974), and *ibid.*, vol. III (1971), a Weigel-miscellany; Ritter, *Die Umbildung der Theosophie in Metaphysik bei dem jüngeren von Helmont und bei Leibniz*.

[131]De Careil, *op. cit.*, pp. 59 f. Cf. also Yates, *op. cit.*, on Leibniz pp. 91, 154 f.

[132]Guhrauer, *op. cit.*, vol. 2, pp. 40–45, and Baruzi, *op. cit.*, pp. 501 ff.

[133]Guhrauer, *op. cit.*, p. 212. Cf. also Walter Tinner, 'Leibniz: System and Exoterik', in H. Holzhey and W. C. Zimmerli (eds.), *Esoterik and Exoterik der Philosophie. Beiträge zu Geschichte und Sinn philosophischer Selbstbestimmung*, Basel-Stuttgart 1977, and *ibid.*, H. Mettler, 'Lessing und Leibniz. Bemerkungen zur Exoterik anhand dreier Abschnitte aus Leibniz "Von den ewigen Strafen"'.

[134]Jacob, *op. cit.*, p. 255. Cf. also Manuel, *op. cit.*, especially on Leibniz's comments about the Huguenot millenarians in London, p. 210.

company, then he may now judge whether – if he agrees to make his own contribution toward turning that foot-path into an highroad – that which many centuries were unable to achieve may be attained before the end of the present century: namely to bring human reason to complete satisfaction (pacification – *Befriedigung*) with respect to that which has always pre-occupied its desire for knowledge, though up to now unsuccessfully." (Since this is also the final sentence in the B-edition, Kant clearly thought that, given sufficient human effort, the philosophical millennium could be brought about in the thirteen remaining years of the century!) Ramond Ruyer rightly called the eighteenth century "le siècle classique de l'utopie" in Western culture.[135]

One is, then, bound to ask oneself whether Raphael Levi, too, entertained such high-flying ambitions behind his cool, modest pretensions. One would keep one's eyes open for hints of this, even in the absence of documentary evidence.

In fact, Israel Zinberg, in his *A History of Jewish Literature*, in the course of briefly dealing with Raphael Levi, added a little footnote: "In the municipal library of Berlin there is a manuscript of Hanover's 'Calculation of the End and of the Resurrection of the Dead', that has not yet been published." Until now no such piece of writing had been found.[136] A recently discovered Hebrew manuscript of Saadia Gaon's *Book of Doctrines and Beliefs*,[137] written by an anonymous scribe in Amsterdam in 1770, contains on the last four pages, which the scribe would otherwise have had to leave unused, precisely a text under the title cited by Zinberg and in Raphael Levi Hannover's name. We can here only summarise its content:

Maimonides codified the Jewish doctrine of the coming of the Messiah. The well-known rabbinic injunctions against calculating the time of the end do not apply to people who will not, even if their expectations are disappointed, foreswear belief in it. Jews must do whatever they can to hasten the Messiah's coming. "Perhaps God will soon have mercy on us." Taking a number of biblical, post-biblical, talmudic dates and rabbinic statements, and following the classical pattern of messianic speculation as found in Rashi to *Hab.* 2:3, and then fitting these into the established interpretations of the *loci classici* in the Book of *Daniel*, Levi concludes that, among other historical events, also the Protestant Reformation and the European-Turkish wars as "Armageddon" converge to show that the Messiah is scheduled to come in the Jewish year 5543=1783.

This 1770 copy of Levi's millenarian speculation bears no date of composition. We can, however, by means of an historical reconstruction, come quite close to assigning a date to it. We shall see later that Gershom Seixas in New York and through him Ezra Stiles in New Haven knew of its precise content no later than

[135] *L'Utopie et les utopies*, Paris 1950, p. 187. Trevor-Roper, *op. cit.*, is then quite wrong when he holds that after 1660, "in the new Europe there was no place, no need, for utopianism . . . They would not waste their time on the Millennium, the Messiah or the number of the Beast."

[136] Tr. Bernard Martin, Hebrew Union College Press, vol. 6, 1977, pp. 243 f. Hebrew translation, Tel-Aviv 1958, vol. 3, p. 366, note 9–Yiddish original, vol. 5, p. 287, note 19. We have tried to check which library this might be, and whether there are any traces of the manuscript in Germany, but have been unsuccessful.

[137] It was found by Professor Abraham J. Karp of the University of Rochester, N.Y., who kindly allowed us to study it.

Raphael Levi Hannover
Portrait by an unknown painter

By courtesy of Historisches Museum am Hohen Ufer, Hanover

1768 through an English translation. In that English version Levi's name is not mentioned; it has been either suppressed or forgotten. It seems likely that Seixas must have come into possession of the text during one of his sojourns in England.[138] By that time it apparently existed in English and without the author's name. The Hebrew text obviously antedates this. We also know that Levi visited London in 1748, which is for other reasons as well a probable *terminus ad quem* for the composition of 'Calculation of the End . . .'. For one thing, we have seen that Levi had written and saw published most of his writings in the 1740s (thus establishing his name in the learned world, both Jewish and Gentile). Furthermore, *Techunat HaShama'yim*, though published (against the author's wishes) in Amsterdam in 1756, ends with the sentence that we have quoted, which not only articulates as unmistakable a messianic allusion as the circumstances permit but also explicitly dates the author's text as finished in 1734. The Seixas-version of 'Calculation of the End . . .', introduced as "faithfully translated," coincides with the Hebrew version in all respects but one. In English not the East-West split of the Christian Church or Charlemagne but the rise of the Mohammedan Empire and Luther are adduced as historical evidence. (We might infer that there was an original text by Levi, larger than either available to us, which used both sets of historical evidence and, perhaps, others yet.) The English version has asterisks preceding the references to the Moslem and Protestant realms, implying strongly pejorative adjectives. Its last line reads: "Fiat Voluntas Domini Dei Nostri. Amen." These characteristics of the English version may be interpreted as expressions of both the special animus and the vocabulary of the ex-Christian Sephardim. (The Ashkenazic, Hebrew version, on the other hand, picks as significant out of the *Vorlage* more distant historical events in Central Europe.) Now, the Turkish-Christian wars, regarded not only by Raphael Levi but also by Christian Europe in general at the time and by his teacher Leibniz in particular as "Armageddon"-like events,[139] came to a halt, at least for some time and to the advantage of Christendom, with the Treaty of Belgrade of 1739. One may then well hold that Levi originally composed his Hebrew essay in the early-to-middle 1730s. By the time Levi reached London in 1748, and if he met Wm. Whiston, as we have speculated, his and Whiston's adventist speculations must have given rise to interesting discussions between the two men, since Whiston[140] had fixed on the year 1768 and also connected the Jews with it.[141] That the manuscript also reached Amsterdam and was there preserved

[138]Perhaps the possibility ought to be considered that Seixas obtained Levi's 'Calculations of the End . . .' not via England but directly from one of his several German and particularly Hanoverian congregants – for example, the well-known Hyman Levy, born in Hanover in 1721, who became the father-in-law of Seixas's brother Benjamin. (Cf. David de Sola Pool, *Portraits Etched in Stone – Early Jewish Settlers 1682–1831*, New York 1952, pp. 171 f.) But, of course, this would not explain the English translation.

[139]Cf. his *Antiturcia*: cf. Stammler, *op. cit.*, p. 35, and Hatton, *op. cit.*, pp. 29, 43. Friedmann (ed.), *Seder Eliyahu Rabbah* (in Hebrew), Vienna 1901, pp. 113 ff.: "When you see empires in combat with one another, watch for the footsteps of the Messiah." For the Thirty Years' War as Armageddon in the view of the Protestant radicals of the earlier generation cf. Trevor-Roper, *op. cit.*, pp. 247 f.

[140]Cf. Jacob, *op. cit.*, pp. 133, note 87, 167; cf. also on Whiston generally, *ibid.*, pp. 130–134; other Newtonians had fixed on 1736 (*ibid.*, p. 255).

[141]Jews and the Newtonian circle had long since established relations, and calendaric problems as

in Raphael Levi's name, whereas in England and America it was remembered only in the name of "a contemporary German rabbi", may well be due to the fact that, as also the publication of *Techunat HaShama'yim* in Amsterdam illustrates, the Ashkenazic Jews in Holland had got hold of Levi's writings directly and consciously, whereas the Sephardic Jews, after one short visit by him in London, were only dimly aware of and not personally interested in him. The connections between the Jews and the rulers of Hanover, on the one hand, and Amsterdam Jewry, on the other, are, in any case, well documented.[142]

This messianic prophecy of Levi's displays the typical characteristics of its *genre*.[143] For one thing, it is dated close enough to the projected end-time to make the adventist hope realistically relevant to the people then living, while it just happens to be dated slightly the other side of the reasonable expectation of the calculator's death – thus preventing its empirical falsification in his life-time. In the second place, it is kept as esoteric knowledge: it is published neither in its own time nor even until now. In this light we can now also understand Raphael Levi's striking reluctance to publish anything at all really substantial and his vehement insistence that anything published under his name be kept under his own very tight personal rein (like autographing every copy of his books):[144] knowing what we now do, we can discover faint adumbrations of his millenarianism in all sorts of otherwise unsuspicious texts. Tiktin's acrostic introductory poem to *Techunat HaShama'yim* has a line, for example: "May God will to send us soon/liberator and redeemer . . . and may He give us joy in the building of Ariel."

In the century after Sabbatai Zvi millenarianism was heavily repressed among Jews, as Gershom Scholem has shown. In Levi's own time the notorious Emden-Eybeschütz controversy in German Jewry brought the dangers of Sabbatianism to renewed heights of passion. Jacob Emden, like his equally Orthodox but modernising colleague Moses Mendelssohn, opposed messianism for at least three reasons: it conjured Sabbatian dangers; it always tended to be subversive of the religious establishment; and it opened the door to what in later

---

well as messianic speculations were important ingredients of their common concern: cf. Petuchowski, *op. cit.*, pp. 22, 78, 81, 83 ff., 138, note 26a, etc. For Anglo-Jewish conditions on a lower level, cf. T. E. Endelman, *The Jews of Georgian England 1714–1830* . . . , Philadelphia 1979, chapt. 4: 'The Acculturation of the Anglo-Jewish Middle Class', and chapts. 5–6: 'Peddlers and Hawkers', 'Pickpockets and Pugilists'. For the first Jew to be knighted, in 1700 – naturally a foreign money-man – cf. Oskar K. Rabinowicz, *Sir Solomon de Medina*, London 1974.

[142]Cf. Yosef Kaplan, *From Christianity to Judaism. The Life and Work of Isaac Orobio de Castro* (in Hebrew), Jerusalem 1982, p. 177, note 109, on the medical treatment of the Duke of Hanover by the Jewish physician and philosopher Isaac Orobio in Amsterdam, in 1679. The Duke stayed in a Jewish home.

[143]Cf. A. H. Silver, *A History of Messianic Speculation in Israel*, New York 1927.

[144]For a reproduction of Levi's autograph-copyright on his printed books cf. Lazarus, *loc. cit.*, p. 62. Professor A. Karp has shown us his copy of Judah Levi Horovitz (Vilna), *'amuday beth yehudah* (in Hebrew), Amsterdam 1766, which, too, is signed on p. 2 by both author and publisher, as a form of copyright. (Cf. for M. Mendelssohn's introductory approval of the author as "the head of the pious philosophers" and "pious Jew", Altmann, *op. cit.*, p. 367. Mendelssohn had also submitted the book to Rabbi Hirsch of Berlin.) We owe to Mr. David Sparks, librarian at Notre Dame University, the information that the institution of copyrights for limited periods was developed under the 'Statutes of Queen Anne' in 1705 from earlier royal control and then, 1688–1705, so-called "term-catalogues". Parallel Jewish developments seem to have been taking place at the time.

times was to be known as the accusation of Jewish "double loyalty", precisely at a time when Jews sought social acclimatisation. Thus Rabbi Emden at one point rejected a messianic calculation for 1724[145] on grounds of local political loyalty – "for the earthly king is of the same kind as the heavenly". Jonathan Eybeschütz, on the other hand, had close personal relations with the Wertheimer family and through them with Raphael Levi's immediate patrons, the Leffmann Behrens family.[146]

To be sure, Levi was also worried about the rabbinic acceptability of some of his scientific views. But it was science – mathematical astronomy – in the service of chiliasm that really concerned him. We shall see a number of widely dispersed later interpretations of his messianic date of 1783; even at the time it may be taken to symbolise the messianic fever that seethed underneath the quiet surface of the pre-revolutionary period: growing Jewish expectations of socio-political emancipation for 1783 – the American Revolution just passed, the French Revolution in the immediate offing.

Levi died in Hanover on 18th May 1779, in his daughter's house, where he had been working until the end.[147] His tombstone can still be seen in the Jewish cemetery in the Oberstrasse.[148]

We have had to cast our eyes forward in history while trying to date Levi's 'Calculation of the End . . .'. We have thus had some preliminary hints that his speculation was to leave tracks in the sand-dunes of later times. The abbreviated English text of his little tract, without either author's or copyist's name, turns up among the papers of Gershom Seixas, the first American rabbi, in revolutionary New York and its surroundings.[149] Seixas, a fervent American patriot and a thoroughly traditionalist Jew, discerned "signs of the end" on many occasions during his lifetime – the American Revolution as such, 1783 itself perhaps as the date of the U.S.-British treaty and therewith international recognition of the American republic, Napoleon's Sanhedrin later, and so forth.[150]

[145] *'Etz 'Avot*, 27, 41, quoted in Shochat, *loc. cit.*, p. 229. On the Emden-Mendelssohn relationship, cf. Schwarzschild, 'Do Noachites have to Believe in Revelation? . . .', *Jewish Quarterly Review*, LII/4 (April 1962), pp. 307 f. and LIII/1 (July 1962), pp. 30–33, and Blu Greenberg, 'Rabbi Jacob Emden: The Views of an Enlightened Traditionalist on Christianity', *Judaism*, XXVII/3 (Summer 1978), pp. 351 ff., etc.

[146] Cf. D. Kaufmann, *Samson Wertheimer . . .*, *op. cit.*, pp. 83, 88.

[147] Lazarus, 'Leibniz und Levi', *loc. cit.*, p. 249.

[148] Cf. Margret Wahl, 'Der alte jüdische Friedhof in Hannover', in *Hannoverische Geschichtsblätter*, n.s., XV/1–2 (1961), p. 42, No. 307, and photograph=Gronemann, *op. cit.*, p. 307, 173 bb. The inscription on Levi's tombstone is almost identical with his eulogy in the *Memor-book* of the Hanover Jewish community, preserved in the Leo Baeck Institute, New York, Jacobson Collection, III, 29. R. Levi has entries in *Historisch-literarisches Handbuch berühmter und denkwürdiger Personen . . .*, ed. F. C. G. Hirsching, Leipzig 1799, vol. 4, p. 245 ("he left behind the reputation of an honourable man, which is somewhat rare among Jews") – *Lexikon der vom Jahr 1750 bis 1800 verstorbenen teutschen Schriftsteller*, ed. J. G. Meusel, Leipzig 1808, vol. 8, p. 214, – *Fortsetzung . . . zu . . . Gelehrten-Lexikon . . .*, ed. H. W. Rotermund, Delmenhorst 1810, vol. 3, col. 1715.

[149] The manuscript, in the American Jewish Historical Society, is considerably longer than the printed excerpts in *Publications of the American Jewish Historical Society*, vol. 27 ('The Lyons Collection', vol. II), 1920, p. 128.

[150] Cf. Raphael Mahler, 'American Judaism and the Doctrine of the Return to Zion in the Period of the American Revolution' (in Hebrew), section 4; also Th. Kessner, 'G. M. Seixas: His Religious "Calling", Outlook and Competence', *American Jewish Historical Quarterly (A.J.H.Q.)*, 58 (1969), pp. 466 ff.

From among the many interesting details that one can infer from Seixas's paper we here mention only a few. As noted earlier, Levi may have left a Hebrew version of his calculation among the Sephardim in London when he visited there in 1748. Somewhere, at some time, an English version was produced, which fell into the hands of the American Sephardi Seixas. From him or his immediate circle the news reached even Ezra Stiles, the founder of the very Protestant Yale College. Stiles reports in his diary on 10th August 1769 that the Jews in New York have imminent expectations, raised "by a present-day German rabbi", of the second advent.[151] On 7th July 1773 Stiles writes that "I asked (Rabbi Carrigal) if he approved the Compt[a] of the german Rabbi which fixt the Messiah's coming in A. D. 1783 or ten years hence. He s[d] he did not rely on it."[152] Many years afterwards Seixas was still concerned with this calculation, for on the document he asks Dr. Jacob de la Motta (born in 1789, Jewish surgeon in the 3rd Brigade of the 51st Regiment of the N.Y. State Infantry in the War of 1812) to make another copy of it.[153]

The after-waves of Levi's messianism, carried to the shores of North America by Gershom Seixas, continued to roll even long after Seixas's death. A nephew of Seixas's, Abraham B. Seixas, signed as "Secretary, Pro tem." Mordecai Noah's Ararat Proclamation in 1825,[154] which projected the fulfilment of Jewish messianic hopes, at least in an interim way, on the green fields of the American continent. (The German representative of Noah was for a while Eduard Gans, the baptised Jew, disciple of Hegel and professor of law at the University of Berlin[155] – and thus the crooked paths of history brought together again the destinies of the grandson of the Hanoverian Court Jew Isaac Jacob Gans[156] with the indirect student of the scholarly employee of the other Hanoverian Court Jew Behrens, Raphael Levi.) Also, one of Seixas's sons, Joshua, taught Hebrew to Joseph Smith, the founder of the Mormon church, around 1836 in Ohio, for adventist purposes.[157]

[151]Cf. also Mahler, 'American Judaism and the Doctrine . . .', *loc. cit.*, pp. 116 f.

[152]Yale University, Beinecke Rare Books and Manuscripts Library, Stiles diaries, vol. I, p. 42. Rabbi Arthur Chiel has kindly provided us with the full relevant texts; the published diary is heavily excerpted. For Stiles's adventism and Jewish connections, cf. Arthur A. Chiel, 'Ezra Stiles and the Polish Rabbi', *Studies in Jewish Bibliography, History and Literature in Honor of I. Edward Kiev*, ed. Charles Berlin, New York 1971, pp. 83–89; 'E. Stiles – the Education of an Hebraician', *A.J.H.Q.*, LX/3 (March 1971); 'The Rabbis and E. Stiles', *A.J.H.Q.*, LXI/4 (June 1972); 'E. Stiles and the Jews: a Study in Ambivalence', *A Bicentennial Festschrift for Jacob R. Marcus*, ed. B. W. Korn, New York 1976, pp. 63–76. Cf. also Mahler, 'American Judaism and the Doctrine . . . ', *loc. cit.*, pp. 116 f., and about Seixas's Messianism: *ibid.*, pp. 130–132.

[153]On de la Motta cf. C. Reznikoff and U. Engelman, *The Jews of Charleston*, Philadelphia 1950, and Thomas Tobias, 'The Many-Sided Dr. De La Motta', in *The Jewish Experience in America*, vol. II, pp. 64–81, and D. de Sola Pool, *Portraits Etched in Stone . . . op. cit.* pp. 373 ff.

[154]*The Jews of the U.S., 1790–1840*, eds. J. Blau and S. Baron, New York 1963, p. 900; cf. J. D. Sarna, 'The Roots of Ararat . . .', *American Jewish Archives*, XXXII/1 (April 1980), pp. 52 ff.

[155]Cf. Reissner, *op. cit.*, chapt. IX, 'Ganstown, USA'.

[156]Cf. above, note 97. Isaac Gans's portrait is reproduced in *LBI Year Book XXIV* (1979), following p. 232.

[157]Moshe Davis, 'The Holy Land in American Spiritual History', in *With Eyes toward Zion. Scholars Colloquium on American-Holy Land Studies*, ed. M. Davis, New York 1977, pp. 10 f. As Professor R. Popkin has pointed out to us, the Rev. Joseph Wolff, Jewish apostate and adventurer, was invited by John Quincy Adams to address the U.S. Congress in 1837 and predicted the millennium for 1843 (as did the Millerites). Adams is said to have replied: "I think it is a bit too soon".

In England, too, the messianic prophecy for 1783, which Levi left there in 1748, continued to prey on the minds of some Jews well into the nineteenth century. The London Jew Jacob Hart published a book *Beenah le'Ittim* (Understanding for the Times) in 1795 in which he argued – again without mentioning, probably without knowing, Levi's name but rehearsing precisely Levi's cogitations (a son-in-law of Glückel of Hameln, Marcus Moses, had led the Hambro' Synagogue secession in London in 1704)[158] – that when "the end" is near the rabbinic prohibition of messianic calculations lapses. Using Levi's conventional interpretations of *Daniel*, Hart, too, arrives at the messianic date 1783, which he explicitly connects to the American and French Revolutions.[159] And if one wonders, as wonder one must, why a man would proclaim a messianic date of 1783 in a book published in 1795 (!), it turns out that, in another well-entrenched messianological move, Hart stipulated an interim period between the end of normal history and the beginning of the messianic age proper (the model of Marx's transitional period of "socialism") – in his terminology, "the end of the years" and "the end of the generations", to the latter of which he assigned the year 1840.[160]

Nor is France to be excepted from the area to which the waves of Hanoverian enlightenment-messianism spread. Alsace-Lorraine was, of course, always an integral part of the culture and demographic unity of Rhenish-Ashkenazic Jewry. Liefman Calmer Hannover, for example, bore this name because of his place of origin.[161] He was a relative of the family of Glückel of Hameln, herself sister-in-law of Leffmann Behrens. (Jews, like Huguenots, were invited to Hameln out of mercantilist considerations.)[162] And Liefman Calmer became an important personage in Paris.

Like England and Germany, France, too, had had its millenarian enthusiasts in the earlier part of the eighteenth century – the "convulsionaires" and others, who, again using *Daniel* as a favourite text, associated the return of the Jews with the imminent end of history.[163] The genealogy of French millenarian utopianism, identified with the special role of the Jews, from Péreyre to the Abbé Grégoire, i.e. from the middle of the seventeenth to the middle of the nineteenth centuries, is, as Richard Popkin has shown, a persistent presence in France and in the very bosom of its Roman-Catholic culture.[164] On the cooler level of high culture, just as

[158]Cecil Roth, 'Educational Abuses and Reforms in Hannoverian England', *M. M. Kaplan Jubilee Volume . . .*, Eng. section, New York 1953, p. 470.

[159]Professor A. Karp originally drew our attention to both the Seixas and the Hart connections of Raphael Levi's calculation. Cf. Arthur Barnett 'Eliakim b. Abraham (Jacob Hart) – an Anglo-Jewish scholar of the 18th century', *Jewish Historical Society of England. Transactions*, XIV (1940), p. 211; S. Brodetsky, 'Supplementary Note', *ibid.*, pp. 222 f.

[160]Brodetsky, *loc. cit.*, p. 222. Since Hart also had strong connections in Germany and spent time there, it is possible that he may have come across Levi's calculations there, rather than in England: cf. *ibid.*, pp. 211 f., 216. He was the publisher of the Anglo-Jewish anti-Priestley polemicist David Levy.

[161]Cf. A. Hertzberg, *The French Enlightenment and the Jews*, New York 1968, p. 136 and under this name in the index.

[162]Cf. Schnath, *op. cit.*, vol. 2, pp. 246 ff.

[163]Cf. Hertzberg, *op. cit.*, pp. 260–262.

[164]Cf. 'La Péreyre, The Abbé Grégoire and the Jewish Question in the 18th Century', *Studies in 18th Century Culture*, American Society for 18th-Century Studies, vol. 4, 1975, pp. 209–222.

Leibniz in Germany used China as an heuristic tool to proclaim the non-denominational nature of universal truth, so in France "chinoiserie" became the pseudo-anthropological tool for Montesquieu in his *Lettres persanes* (1721) and for the Marquis D'Argens in his *Lettres juives* (1736) and *Lettres chinoises*.[165] (Can one ever forget the latter's commendation of Mendelssohn to Frederick the Great: "Un philosophe mauvais catholique supplie un philosophe mauvais protestant de donner le privilège à un philosophe mauvais juif. Il y a dans tout ceci trop de philosophie pourque la raison ne soit pas du côté de la demande?")[166]

On the Jewish side of this equation Moses Ensheim (*c.* 1760–*c.* 1830) was, in the tradition of *Maskilim*, a mathematician, who had taught Moses Mendelssohn's children in Berlin. Once he had moved to Paris, he was applauded by no less than Joseph Louis Lagrange and Pierre Simon Laplace.[167] He, too, started out philosophically with Maimonides's *Guide* and went on to non-Jewish classical culture. On the surface he, too, gave voice to the sober rationalism of Mendelssohn and became the link between Mendelssohn and Grégoire in the famous Dohm episode on behalf of Jewish emancipation. (Mirabeau had published *Sur M. Mendelssohn* in 1787.) But when the French Revolution erupted and spread abroad, his suppressed chiliasm came to the fore. In *Hame'asef*, the journal of the Berlin Jewish enlighteners, he published in 1790 a messianic ode to the *Assemblée Nationale*: "Oh, House of Jacob . . . Your salvation is approaching and your day of deliverance." When the French armies triumphed over the Germans he composed a 'Cantique à l'occasion de la fête civile, célébrée à Metz le 21 Oct. l'an premier de la république dans le temple des citoyens Israélites', which, in a Hebrew imitation of the *Psalms* and the song of Deborah, begins with the words: "Of the singer, a song of Moses Ensheim, sung on the day on which the hand of the dwellers of our native land triumphed over their enemies."[168]

From Germany we have now tracked Levi chiefly through Britain, France, and the North-American continent. This may then be regarded as the Jewish side of what T. J. Schlereth, in his *The Cosmopolitan Ideal in Enlightenment Thought-Its Form and Function in the Ideas of Franklin, Hume, and Voltaire*[169] calls "the transatlantic scientific community".[170] We have independently confirmed his major points from Jewish sources: "G. Leibniz . . . was the 17th century outstanding cosmopolite."[171] Ezra Stiles belonged to this international network.[172] Like

[165]The use of exotic pseudo-anthropological, actually ideal, models continued also in Germany beyond Leibniz – *viz.* Christian Wolff's 'Rede von der Sittenlehre der Sineser' (1721) (in Fr. Brueggemann, ed., *Das Weltbild der deutschen Aufklärung*, Leipzig 1930, pp. 174 ff. – Cf. D. F. Lach, 'The Sinophilism of Chr. Wolf', *Journal of the History of Ideas*, XIV (1953), pp. 561–574).

[166]Cf. Meyer, 'The Attitude of the Enlightenment towards the Jews', *loc. cit.*, pp. 1181 f., 1186 f.

[167]Cf. Hertzberg, *op. cit.*, p. 175; Graetz, *Geschichte der Juden*, vol. XI, Leipzig 1900, pp. 127, 186.

[168]Hertzberg, *op. cit.*; Graetz, *op. cit.*, the late-nineteenth-century German, approved of these sentiments. Even German Jews in Germany celebrated Napoleon's conquests – for example, the battle of Moscow in 1812 was celebrated by Rabbi Adler in Hanover. (Asaria-Helfgott, *loc. cit.* p. 11.)

[169]University of Notre Dame Press 1977. Cf. also J. F. McDermott, 'The Enlightenment on the Mississippi Frontier, 1763–1804', in *Studies on Voltaire and the 18th Century*, XXVI, Geneva 1963, pp. 1129–1142, which brings the Enlightenment to the present writers' home-town.

[170]*Ibid.*, p. 155.

[171]*Ibid.*, p. XXIV.

[172]*Ibid.*, p. 7.

Leibniz, so also Benjamin Franklin and Ezra Stiles concerned themselves with the idea of a universal language.[173] "Letters" were a literary *genre* of the enlighteners, and they used exotic historical geography for reforming purposes.[174] Socio-economically the enlighteners were far from revolutionaries: they were upwardly mobile; they kept an uneasy alliance with the aristocracy; and "in the opinion of many philosophers, the merchant class apeared as the most obvious promoters of a cosmopolitan economic outlook".[175] The Noachitism that we met in Leibniz, and which is a fundamental, though much neglected, doctrine in Judaism,[176] was in fact pitted by the likes of Voltaire against Jewish tribalism.[177] Schlereth is, on the other hand, not interested in the Jewish side. It does not occur to him that Jews in the eighteenth century could not patronise either the saloons or the coffee-houses in which the enlighteners would congregate. Nor has Schlereth perceived the chiliastic strain that is woven into the rationalistic mind of the Enlightenment. These two *lacunae* in Schlereth's study we have been able to fill.

By now we have gone well beyond Raphael Levi's life-span. Although the story, of course, goes on, we have now to analyse it, however summarily. It was, as we have seen, by no means the life of a man of importance of the first order, either in historical or in intellectual terms. Except for its often interesting personal features many similar stories could be told. It does instantiate a number of broad rules that appertain to the birth and nature of the European-Jewish symbiosis the more for its comparative ordinariness.

In the first place, Salo W. Baron's historiography of modern Europe is fully borne out by our investigation. Baron says:[178]

> "The mid-17th century may indeed be considered a major turning point in both world and Jewish history. For our purposes it certainly may serve as the most convenient dividing line between the pre-Emancipation and the Emancipation eras. The Treaty of Westphalia of 1648, which terminated the Thirty Years' War, proclaimed, on an international scale, the general principle of the liberty of conscience, however hazy and ill-defined . . . Although not directly referring to Jews, this new approach toward mutual toleration of religious diversity opened up new vistas for equal treatment of Jewish subjects, too. Simultaneously, a new era was beginning for the Jewish people by its resettlement in Western Europe and the latter's colonial posessions . . . By the mid-17th century, on the other hand, the burgeoning new forces of Enlightenment and intellectual rapprochement with the Christian world produced not only a Spinoza and a Uriel da Costa but also the more intrinsically Jewish manifestations of the Italian, Dutch, and Berlin Haskalah. The period around 1650, which undoubtedly represented the nadir of Jewish population strength and to superficial observers seemed to presage an inevitable eclipse of Jewry, yet carried in itself the seeds of a new evolution which led to a vigorous rebirth of the ancient people."[179]

[173] *Ibid.*, p. 43.

[174] *Ibid.*, pp. 8, 66, 70 f., 83 f.

[175] *Ibid.*, pp. 12, 100, and all of chapt. 5 on anti-mercantilistic free-trade.

[176] Cf. Schwarzschild, 'Law-Noahide', *Encyclopaedia Judaica*, and Meyer, 'The Attitude of the Enlightenment towards the Jews', *Studies on Voltaire . . .*, *op. cit.*, pp. 1176–1182, and generally.

[177] Schlereth, *op. cit.*, pp. 77 f.

[178] *Social and Religious History of the Jews*, 2nd edn., vol. IX, New York 1965, pp. v–vii.

[179] Cf. also Baron's statements in S. W. Baron, *et. al.* (eds.), *Violence and Defense in the Jewish Experience*, Philadelphia 1977, p. 18 and notes. For Jacob Katz's not very helpful comments on this question of periodisation cf. his *Jews and Freemasons in Europe 1723–1939*, Harvard 1970, p. 234, note 30.

More specifically we have to say that the eighteenth-century Enlightenment, from its beginnings in, for example, Leibniz to its end in Kant created a philosophical ambience, among the élites of the Gentiles and of the Jews, especially in Germany, which comprised rationalised religion and growing, especially mathematical, science, and in which denominational, cultural, and historical separations were increasingly sublated. The Jewish élite consisted of a wide but exclusive network of immensely wealthy and powerful bankers. This network served the centralisation of political power in the hands of the absolute, or aspiringly absolute, rulers of the age. It drew to itself a middle class of rabbis, scholars, and clerks, – so that Shochat[180] can quote contemporary sources as saying of the Jews that they "leben als Printzen, ein Bauer habe mehr Golus (miserable life of exile) als sie", and so that Schnee[181] could truthfully assert that, with respect to their life-style and cultural values, "die Verbindung des Gelehrten-Adels mit der Geldaristokratie wurde zum Adelsideal des späteren Judentums".

The Jewish communities in Central Europe after the Thirty Years' War consisted by and large of a broad underclass, clustering around the special privileges of the Court Jews and subsisting under their self-interestedly benevolent protection. The Gentile class of *clercs* is in turn well personified in Leibniz and Kant – from the court servant, with all the ambitions, dissatisfactions, and achievements of this type,[182] to the university professor, who ardently welcomed the French Revolution. That rising Gentile and Jewish middle class wished to strengthen and to spread its political, commercial, and cultural egalitarianism as the century grew older. In the Gentile world the thrust toward universalising its values took the form of "the age of the revolutions".[183] In the Jewish world it took the form of emancipation and acculturation.

The Gentile intellectuals are, therefore, not surprisingly, surrounded by Jewish disciples. Leibniz had only Raphael Levi; by the end of the Enlightenment Kant was the centre of a whole coterie of Jews – Marcus Herz, Solomon Maimon, Lazarus Bendavid,[184] etc. (a Jewish tradition of Kantianism, which continues to this day). Another way of illustrating this development is to compare the relationship between Leibniz and Levi with that of Lessing and Mendelssohn. All of them were Leibnizians. Lessing wrote his path-breaking play *Die Juden* in 1749. The two Christians were librarians at Wolfenbüttel. But Levi was clearly very much the epigonic pupil of Leibniz, whereas Lessing and Mendelssohn became colleagues, pretty much on an equal level.

What was true of the limited society of the Court Jews in the eighteenth century became the standard for the Jewish communities at large in the nineteeth – in life-style, culture, political aspirations, and in business. Kaufmann unself-consciously apostrophised the *sh'tadlanim*, the Jewish "intercessors", as "an early

[180]Shochat, *With the Changes of Eras*, *op. cit.*, p. 235.

[181]*Die Hoffinanz . . .* , *op. cit.*, vol. 3, p. 209; cf. also *ibid.*, p. 191, and vol. 2, p. 37.

[182]Cf. W. Ohnsorge, 'Leibniz als Staatsbediensteter', Totok and Haase, *op. cit.*, pp. 175 ff.

[183]Cf. Robert Palmer, *The Age of the Democratic Revolution*, Princeton University Press 1969.

[184]From Lazarus Bendavid's *Zur Berechnung und Geschichte des jüdischen Kalenders . . .* , Berlin 1817, one gets the uneasy feeling that he knew about and wanted to refer to Raphael Levi, but he never does – although he refers to Harrison's solution of Newton's navigational problem: p. 37, note 1.

glimmering of the sun" of the Emancipation[185] and as an anticipation of the history of several generations of Jews after them.[186]

These bourgeois emancipationist forces, Jewish and Gentile, transcended national boundaries, crossing even the Channel and the Atlantic. Somehow, as one immerses oneself in the Jewish and Gentile atmosphere of the eighteenth century, one not only disabuses oneself of the banal notion that Moses Mendelssohn was the first modern European Jew but one actually wonders, realising that Mendelssohn had a whole class of predecessors, extending over at least a century, what kept that modernising development from acquiring the full-fledged historical and political force that, in fact, began to be manifested only about 1800.[187]

The philosophical super-structure of this social development had a surface-dimension and a hidden depth. Underneath Leibniz's and Newton's invention of the infinitesimal calculus, underneath Raphael Levi's tables of monetary exchanges and astronomical calculations (as underneath Moses Mendelssohn's use of probability-theory to prove the existence of divine providence and to defend Leibniz's determinism: 'On Probability' (1756) and other mathematical pursuits[188] – while he remained in the employment of Berlin Jewish bankers and silk-manufacturers, brought to Berlin, as he was, by the oligarchs' rabbinical associate, his teacher David Hirsch Fränkel),[189] there seethed what Kant then called "philosophical chiliasm" – Newton's and Levi's mystical speculations about the kingdom of God that was immediately to be established on earth, i.e. a condition in the world in which affluent and serene comfort would extend to all.[190] This is truly a form of "rationalistic mysticism".[191] Of course, not only the ideology but also the material infra-structure on which it was based depended on the political and financial centres of power – Newton's royal mint, Levi's bankers, the monarchs ruling each of these, etc. As Schnee rightly says of the Court Jews, but as is equally true of the Christian intellectual and commercial middle class of early modern times, they were the "Handlanger des Absolutismus".[192] As this was true of the Jewish financiers so it was of the rabbis. Indeed, these two were often united in the same person. For example, in Hanover, after the Court Jew Behrens and his in-law Rabbi Oppenheim, the local rabbi, 1687–1703, was a relative of Behrens, Rabbi Joseph ben Meshullam Süssel Cohen.[193] Wertheimer

[185]Kaufmann, *Samson Wertheimer . . .*, *op. cit.*, p. 13.
[186]Kaufmann, *Urkundliches . . .*, *op. cit.*, p. 83: the Wertheimer "family anticipates the history of several generations" of Jews.
[187]Cf. J. Eschelbacher, 'Die Anfänge allgemeiner Bildung unter den deutschen Juden vor Mendelssohn', in *Beiträge zur Geschichte der deutschen Juden. Festschrift zum 70. Geburtstage M. Philippsons*, Leipzig 1916, p. 177: Mendelssohn "was not the creator of a new age, as he is often celebrated to have been, nor a path-breaker who opened previously untrod paths and brought light into prior darkness. A new age had already begun when he entered it." He refers to Raphael Levi on p. 171.
[188]Cf. Altmann. *Mendelssohn . . .*, *op. cit.*, pp. 120, 267, 666–669, etc.
[189]*Ibid.*, pp. 322 ff. for Mendelssohn's involvement with the Court Jews and commerce.
[190]For English, "scientific" millenarianism, cf. Jacob, *op. cit.*, chapt. 'The Millennium' (pp. 100 ff.).
[191]Cf. Philip Merleau, *Monopsychism, Mysticism, Metaconsciousness*, Hague 1963, pp. 20 ff.
[192]Schnee, *op. cit.*, p. 255; cf. also p. 189.
[193]Z. Asaria-Helfgott, *op. cit.*, p. 27.

was not only appointed Court Jew by the Viennese Emperor but also "Prince of the Land of Israel", "Chief Rabbi", and *Juden-Kaiser*.[194] When, in the later nineteenth and in the twentieth centuries, the underclasses in rapidly developing capitalism in turn increasingly universalised the demands of the bourgeoisie for affluence and equality, the identification of Jewry with the ruling class turned into a persisting danger to it. As Cecil Roth said: "The Court Jews, of whatever country, whether in the 17th or in the 20th century, did their coreligionists more harm than good."[195] The fact is that in the eighteenth and nineteenth centuries the Gentile and the Jewish bourgeoisies laid both the social and the theoretical groundwork for the spread of at least the demand for even broader social emancipation. Their role in the twentieth century is, indeed, another matter.

[194]Kaufmann, *S. Wertheimer . . .*, *op. cit.*, pp. 9 f., 43, 46.
[195]Quoted by Schnee, *op. cit.*, vol. 3, p. 224.

II. MOSES ABRAHAM WOLFF

Moses Abraham Wolff was born in Neuwied in, or within a year of, 1715.[1]

His place of birth is itself an important factor in Wolff's life. Up the Rhine from Frankfurt and Koblenz, there had been a small town by the name of Wied before the Thirty Years' War. It lay in the path of some of the worst military storms of those religious wars, and it was utterly destroyed by them. The ruling house of Wied wanted to rebuild its property after the war was over, and, therefore, it built a new town there in 1653, called Neuwied; its usual Latin name proclaims its history even more precisely: Neo-Veda Vedanus. In building the new town the local government followed principles which many similarly situated German princes at the time followed: with the experience of the religious wars weighing heavily on them, they declared all religious differences irrelevant to the right to settle in the new town,[2] which became, therefore, a haven for religious dissenters of all sorts – particularly Mennonites,[3] *Herrenhuter*, and also Jews. (All of these maintained organised communities in Neuwied well into the twentieth century.)[4] The only criterion for the right of settlement was economic – defined by the usual monetary and especially by mercantilist considerations: did the settlers bring money and pay taxes, and did they practise vocations which were regarded as productive – *viz.* agriculture and export? One German historian called this a

[1]His birth date is commonly cited as "*c.* 1715", for example by Adolf Kober, 'Rheinische Judendoktoren, vornehmlich des 17. und 18. Jahrhunderts, in *Festschrift zum 75 jährigen Bestehen des Jüdisch-Theologischen Seminars Fraenkelscher Stiftung*, Breslau 1929, p. 212. In fact, when he died he was described in the *Memor-book* of the Jewish Community of Bonn as eighty-seven years old: *ibid.*, p. 234. Klaus H. S. Schulte, *Bonner Juden und ihre Nachkommen bis um 1930* . . . Bonn 1976, p. 530, manages to get both Wolff's birthdate and date of death wrong.

[2]As Ragnild Hatton, *George I. Elector and King*, Cambridge, Mass. 1978, p. 93, says: "Memories of invasion and occupation during the Thirty Years War were still alive." Cf. the town of Glückstadt, near Hamburg, which was run on the same principle by Christian IV of Denmark: Hermann Kellenbenz, *Sephardim an der unteren Elbe. Ihre wirtschaftliche und politische Bedeutung vom Ende des 16. bis zum Beginn des 18. Jahrhunderts* (Vierteljahrsschrift für Sozial- und Wirtschaftsgeschichte, Beiheft 40), Wiesbaden 1958, p. 189, Hatton, *op. cit.*, p. 82, and W. Grossmann, 'Religious Toleration in Germany, 1648–1750', in *Studies on Voltaire and the Eighteenth Century*, 1982, pp. 122 f. Cf. also the policies for the settlement of Hameln, 'Raphael Levi', above p. 253.

[3]Cf. C. J. Dyck, *An Introduction to Mennonite History*, Scottsdale, PA. 1967, pp. 93, 119 f., and Grossmann, *loc. cit.*, pp. 121–124.

[4]For example, Friedrich Wolf, the author of the well-known book and film *Professor Mamlock*, was born in Neuwied in 1888: cf. Werner Jehser, *Friedrich Wolf*, 2nd edn. Berlin 1968. Printing has been and remains to this day an important industry in Neuwied, including Jewish and Hebrew printing: 1735–1736 – Isaac b. Samuel Halevy, *Responsa* (in Hebrew), publisher Israel b. Moses; 1737-Loeb b. Samuel Tzvi Hirsch, *Responsa* (on names in divorces) (in Hebrew), printer Johann Balthazar Haupt, publisher "Israel b. Moses Israelita"; etc. (Cf. B. Friedberg, *History of Hebrew Typography in Central Europe* [in Hebrew], Antwerp 1935, p. 108.) For Haupt's Jewish printer Benjamin b. Salman Croneburg in Neuwied cf. *Monumenta Judaica. Handbuch*, Cologne 1963, p. 701. One branch of our own family, Waldeck, also settled in Neuwied: cf. Siegfried Schwarzschild, 'Die Familie Schwarzschild in Frankfurt a. M.', *Jüdische Familien-Forschung*, V/2 (June 1929), p. 136 and Louis Neustadt, *Stammtafeln der von Liebmann Schwarzschild in Frankfurt a. M. (1555–1594) abstammenden Familien*, Frankfurt a. Main 1886, Table X/12.

"Mercantilistische Bevormundungspolitik",[5] and another referred to such settlements as "Exilantenstädte".[6]

Such a policy would, of course, attract and retain the usual upwardly mobile "pariahs" of old-fashion societies – in Europe especially Protestant radicals and Jews. It could be conveniently carried out not in the old, established towns, where the mediaeval guilds and the entrenched Christian bourgeoisie (even in the etymological sense of the word) resisted the centralising forces of absolute rulers, nor in the old, independent cities (imperial or Hanseatic, for example), but in small, often new, towns and villages in the countryside.[7] (Modern Central-European Jewry was, therefore, constituted by two different streams of urban Jews – those who had been essentially urban since the Middle Ages, as in Frankfurt, and those who gravitated from the country-side to the burgeoning cities during the period of industrialisation in the nineteenth and twentieth centuries.)

In the new town of Neuwied one Abraham Wolff settled. He was "privileged", i.e. legally domiciled there together with his family and entourage, no later than 1691. Until at least 1748 he was the official Court Jew – i.e. the supplier of money and material to the Prince of Wied, Count Friedrich Alexander, for in this period of history even petty rulers of this kind organised their sovereignty with the indispensable help of a Jewish financier. Such a financier had in turn to be personally and commercially connected with the large Jewish banking cartels in other parts of Europe, for only through them could the large sums of money be raised that the governments required. As also was the rule with Court Jews, Abraham Wolff was at the same time the head of the local Jewish community. The rabbi of the Jewish community was, until he died in 1750, Eliezer ben Solomon Zalman Lipschütz, from Poland.[8] Wolff and his family possessed "highest social and financial standing" among their co-religionists in the principality of Wied throughout most of the eighteenth century. Abraham's son Samuel was "privileged" in 1732 and head of the Jewish community from 1743–1772. Another son of Abraham's was Moses – usually referred to as Moses Abraham Wolff, though his name was properly, of course, Moses son of Abraham, in full Moses son of Abraham Halevi.[9]

Children of well-to-do Jewish families such as this were given a traditional

[5]Georg Hoffmann, *Die Juden im Erzstift Köln im 18. Jahrhundert mit besonderer Berücksichtigung ihrer Stellung in der Hoffinanz*, Aachen 1928, pp. 26, 30.

[6]Heinrich Stoob, *Forschungen zum Städtewesen in Europa*, Cologne 1970, p. 37, quoted by Grossmann, *loc. cit.*, p. 121.

[7]Cf. the "*Neu*stadt" of Hanover, where the Jews were settled (cf. 'Raphael Levi' above, p. 233), and "*Neu*wied".

[8]*Monumenta Judaica. Handbuch, op. cit.*, p. 712 and note 51.

[9]Wilhelm Levison, *Die Siegburger Familie Levison und verwandte Familien*, Bonn 1952, pp. 118 f.; Schulte, *op. cit.*, p. 533, note 3; Louis Lewin, 'Nachträge und Bemerkungen zu Steinschneiders Verzeichnis der jüdischen Ärzte – Fortsetzung', *Zeitschrift für Hebräische Bibliographie*, ed. A. Freimann, XXIV/1–12 (January–December 1921), p. 6, No. 25, and Moritz Steinschneider, 'Jüdische Ärzte', *ibid.*, XVIII/1–3 (January–June 1915), p. 56, No. 2132. One has to be somewhat careful with family relationships in these situations, and even then one cannot always be entirely sure that all the details are correct, for names are uncertain guides here: there are many different Wolffs – the names are often spelled in inconsistent ways – and the Jews operate under German, Hebrew, Yiddish, and other names, which are also not necessarily kept consistent.

Jewish education of some sort, as Moses's later life will frequently illustrate. In his case it is noteworthy, however, that, starting very early in his life and thus early in the eighteenth century, the larger part of his education was obtained in specifically Christian schools. He was first sent to the Jesuit-school in near-by Koblenz, then to the *Gymnasium* in even nearer Duisburg, and finally he enrolled in the relatively new University of Duisburg to study medicine on 20th September 1733.[10] A Professor Tümmermann is mentioned as one of his teachers there in the *vita* of his eventual dissertation.

No Jews had lived in the city of Duisburg since they had been accused of causing the great plague there in 1350 and killed for it. But when, after the Thirty Years' War, the governments sought to rehabilitate their countries not only economically but also educationally, and when new population groups were, therefore, brought in, some access, however limited, to new schools also tended to be opened to a few members of the new settlements. This is what happened at the University of Duisburg. By government decrees in 1726 and in 1784 "Jewish medical students are to be treated exactly like anyone else".[11] In fact, Jews matriculated and were promoted as physicians long before these dates. Kober[12] lists an Emanuel Israel, interestingly also from Neuwied and a graduate of the *Gymnasium* of Duisburg, as a student here in 1729. Indeed, one Ascher Lazarus was enrolled in 1708, and the first full medical degree was bestowed on a Jew in 1727. *Monumenta Judaica – Handbuch* can thus truthfully assert that "the University of Duisburg was of special significance for Rhenish Jewish doctors".[13]

For some reason Moses Abraham Wolff did not, however, complete his studies at Duisburg. Instead, he earned his degree on 5th October 1737 at the University of Halle with a dissertation *De morborum inconsulta ratione suppressorum revocatione* . . .[14] (*On the Treatment of Diseases Suppressed by an Unknown Cause*).[15] Though it is not clear how long he studied at the universities of Duisburg and Halle respectively, we do know that his was no "external degree",[16] for he had at

[10]University Duisburg File No. 172: matriculations 1652–1818, kindly copied for us by Dr. Schmitz of the Nordrhein-Westfälisches Hauptstaatsarchiv as of 14th August 1978. (The University of Duisburg was dissolved in 1818, its files transferred to the University of Bonn, from whence they finally reached their present disposition in 1937 – a history of modern Germany in itself). Cf. also Wilhelm Rotscheidt, *Die Matrikel der Universität Duisburg 1652–1818*, Duisburg 1938; Adolf Kober, 'Jüdische Studenten und Doktoranden der Universität Duisburg im 18. Jahrhundert. Ein Beitrag zur Geschichte der Aufklärung', *Monatsschrift für Geschichte und Wissenschaft des Judentums (MGWJ)*, 1931, pp. 122 f.; Heinrich Schnee, *Die Hoffinanz und der moderne Staat. Geschichte und System der Hoffaktoren an deutschen Fürstenhöfen im Zeitalter des Absolutismus* . . . , Berlin 1953, vol. 3, pp. 53 f.

[11]Günter von Roden, *Die Universität Duisburg*, Duisburger Forschungen, vol. 12, 1968, p. 170, and W. Ring, *Duisburger Universitätsgeschichte*, 1920, p. 123.

[12]Kober, 'Jüdische Studenten . . .', *loc. cit.*

[13]Köln 1963/1964, pp. 267 f.

[14]British Library No. 7306, f. 10 (13), 30 text-pages.

[15]Kevin Herbert, Professor of classics at Washington University, St. Louis, has greatly helped us with this Latin text. He informs us that it is a sort of German school-Latin, no doubt acquired in the Jesuit school, which Wolff had attended.

[16]Halle was, in any case, the chief German university to go to for an external degree at least until the end of the nineteenth century. Hermann Cohen and Georg Cantor, for example, acquired their degrees in this way: cf. Walter Kinkel, *Hermann Cohen. Eine Einführung in sein Werk*, Stuttgart 1924, p. 40, and Georg Cantor, *Gesammelte Abhandlungen*, ed. E. Zermelo, 1932 (A. Fraenkel, 'Das Leben'), p. 474.

least two teachers in Halle – Professor Friedrich Hoffmann, in medicine, who is mentioned more than once in the dissertation with great servility, and Professor Anton Wilhelm Amo, in philosophy, who composed a German-language congratulatory poem, which is, following a wide-spread practice at the time, printed at the end of the dissertation.[17]

We need not dwell long on the content of Wolff's dissertation. It is a conventional piece of medical work. Diseases are said usually to take their own natural courses. Sometimes, however, radical measures are called for. The author's purpose is to explain how a disease that went into temporary remission, because a second disease had come to the fore, is to be treated when it re-asserts itself. Scientifically it might be of passing interest to note that Wolff emphasises his interest in practice, rather than in theory, and that he forswears belief in the traditional theory of humours in favour of physiological explanations.[18] Historically it is worth noting that he uses the example of an eighteen-year-old Jewish youth, "wholly given to the study of our language and law", whom he cured by his method.[19]

It is again useful to consider the situation of Jews in Halle and at its university at that relatively early time, for this throws much light on the history of European modernisation.

Like Duisburg, the Jewish community of Halle has a long and extremely chequered history. After the expulsion at the end of the Middle Ages, it, too, was "free of Jews" beyond the Thirty Years' War. This was still the case in 1687.[20] But under the rule of Friedrich Wilhelm I of Prussia the new socio-economic policies of which we have spoken made their effects felt here also.[21] Within a very few years, no later than by 1692, Jews were "privileged" in the city and actually quite comfortably settled there.[22] In 1693 they had an official cemetery.[23] In 1721 thirty-seven Jewish families, in 1733 forty-six or forty-nine such families were officially listed as domiciled in Halle.[24]

The religious dissensions which the Reformation and the Thirty Years' War had introduced into Europe, and not only their chief antagonists, Roman Catholics and established Protestants, but also Christian non-conformists and Jews, constituted important threads in the fabric of European society in the seventeenth and eighteenth centuries. The "confessions" went hand-in-hand with various socio-economic roles, and as the latter changed and inter-acted so

[17]For other examples of such poetic *laudationes* cf. Kober, 'Jüdische Studenten . . .', *loc. cit.*, pp. 123 f. Wolff's doctorate is listed in many places: Johann Heinrich Zedler, *Grosses vollständiges Universal-Lexikon* . . . , Leipzig-Halle 1748, vol. 58, p. 779; Johann Carl Heffter, *Museum Disputatorium Physico-Medicum* . . . , Zittau 1763, vol. 1, part 1, p. 474, and in many modern histories of Jews in medicine.

[18]Wolff, *op. cit.*, p. 11.

[19]*Ibid.*, pp. 9 f.

[20]Selma Stern, *Der Preussische Staat und die Juden, op. cit.*, I/1, pp. 6 f. and I/2, pp. 123 ff.; *Jüdisches Lexikon*, 'Halle'.

[21]For the religious policy of the Prussian rulers during the *Frühaufklärung* cf. Grossmann, *loc. cit.*, pp. 124–127.

[22]Stern, *op. cit.*, I/2, pp. 358 f., 364, 366 ff., 376 ff., and II/1, pp. 128, 133 ff., 154, note 2, 156, 165.

[23]*Ibid.*, II/2, part 2, pp. 642 f.; cf. also *ibid.*, pp. 648 f., 653 ff., etc.

[24]*Ibid.*, pp. 158, 536.

also did the former. The different Christian Churches tried to convert their Christian opponents, and all of them always tried to convert Jews. In Halle Johann Heinrich Callenberg, professor of philosophy at the local university and member of one of the important local families, founded the first Protestant institutional mission to the Jews, the Institutum Judaicum in 1724 or 1728, attached to the university.[25] One Jewish convert, under the typical name of Paulus Christianus, was active at the university in 1727, in the particularly offensive ways which many such apostates practised down through the centuries.[26] On the other hand, when the Protestant pietists August Francke[27] and Johann Heinrich Michaelis wanted, for their own religious reasons, to publish a Hebrew Bible, they not only had to bring Jewish printers to town under the legal protection of the university but even a particularly noteworthy Christian convert to Judaism, who went under the new name of Moses son of Abraham.[28]

We have then located Jews in the city and university of Halle, brought there for socio-economic and academico-religious reasons, by the end of the seventeenth century. The relations between Christians and Jews were accordingly variegated. We have noted crossings-over from each side. Economically the Jews – not only their leadership echelon but, under their protection, also the bulk of the community – were not badly off, certainly compared to the bulk of the Christian population. Selma Stern observes repeatedly that they lived in the best houses of the town.[29] The network of Court Jews and their appendages certainly lived generally very well. Even their social relations with non-Jews were increasingly amiable. On their respective religious holidays Jews and Christians would exchange formal greetings in Halle.[30] On the other hand, the tensions that were characteristic of that period of new developments also, of course, affected the Jews detrimentally. The old guilds and the old bourgeoisie opposed the new social, economic, and political trends.[31] There were also internal tensions in the leading political and intellectual circles, of which we will show several manifestations, and, depending on how these tensions were variously resolved, the Jews were left better or worse off. On top of all this, the old forms of religious zeal had not, of course, vanished. Thus in 1724, for example, students at the University of Halle

[25] Cf. J. F. A. de le Roi, *Das Institutum Judaicum in seiner Blüthezeit 1728–1765*, Karlsruhe-Leipzig 1884 (reprinted from *Die evangelische Christenheit und die Juden*). The Institute existed until the 1790s. Its most important successor to this day is the Institutum Delitzschianum. The Callenberg Institute published, among other things, a Yiddish dictionary, dated 14th April 1736 and a detailed annual report by Beyer in 1777 and 1778. (The preface to the second of these cites a founding date of 1728, but the *Jewish Encyclopaedia* and the *Jüdisches Lexikon* give 1724 as the date.)

[26] Stern, *op. cit.*, II/2, pp. 235–238.

[27] For Francke's connections with Leibniz cf. *Autaios*, VIII/2 (July 1966) ('Sonderheft zum 250. Todestag G. W. Leibniz'), p. 136; for the rest, cf. Grossmann, *loc. cit.*, pp. 129–131. A powerful picture of the spirit that pervaded the University of Halle – Wittenberg at that time – mixed of rational science and German mysticism – is drawn in Thomas Mann's *Doctor Faustus* . . . , Stockholm 1947, pp. 137 ff.

[28] Stern, *op. cit.*, II/1, pp. 162, 381–384; II/2, p. 643. For another convert to Judaism in this society at the time, 'Moses Germanus, of Swabia', cf. Leibniz, *Theodicée*, Paris 1969, pp. 56 ff.

[29] Stern, *op. cit.*, II/1, p. 165, I/2, pp. 356 f.

[30] Azriel Shochat, 'The Acculturation of the Jews of Germany in their Environment with the Spread of the Enlightenment' (in Hebrew), in *Zion*, XXI (1956), p. 209.

[31] Cf. Stern, *op. cit.*, II/1, p. 133.

erupted in a pogrom which destroyed the local synagogue, the rabbi's house, and other Jewish homes.[32]

When Moses Abraham Wolff came to Halle, some time between 1734 and 1736, his main concern would have been conditions at the university. It was at the time the best medical school in Germany, in, as Monika Richarz puts it, a town with a substantial community, in a relatively enlightened Protestant country that welcomed Jews.[33] There had been Jewish medical students here since 1714.[34]

Jews could become associated with the University of Halle, both in its medical faculty and as printers, because it was a very special place. Founded at the very time that also Jews came to the city, in 1693, here "a new direction was apparent", as Albert Levi puts it. "Here for the first time a professor lectured in his native German. Here appeared the unique beginning of that *libertas docendi* which was to usher in the Enlightenment, restore the universities, (and) make possible Immanuel Kant in Königsberg . . ."[35] This was due to the impact that the philosophy of Leibniz, from Hanover, of his rationalist successor Christian Wolff, and of the more pietistic thinker Thomasius exercised in this Protestant environment.[36] Christian Wolff and Thomasius set the pace for the university from the start.[37] Because of it "Halle became the centre of free research and tolerance".[38] To be sure, there were internal conflicts within the "liberal camp". Wolff and Thomasius favoured tolerance toward dissenters, while the faculty as a

[32]Cf. *Jewish Encyclopaedia*, vol. 6, p. 175, 'Halle'.

[33]Richarz, *op. cit.*, p. 76, where Moses A. Wolff is mentioned.

[34]Kober, 'Jüdische Studenten . . .', *loc. cit.*, p. 119. Cf. also Guido Kisch, *Rechts- und Sozialgeschichte der Juden in Halle 1686–1730*, Berlin 1970, p. 80, for a list of Jewish physicians from Halle University, and Stern, *op. cit.*, II/1, p. 167, both of which, however, are not aware of Moses A. Wolff there, and *ibid.*, II/2, pp. 639 ff. The British Library volume that contains Wolff's dissertation, 7306, f. 10 (15), also contains the medical dissertation of a Salomon Joachim Bondy Eger, Jew of Prague, dated 25th August 1738. Hans-Jürgen Krüger, *Die Judenschaft von Königsberg in Preussen 1700–1812*, Marburg 1966, lists a Jewish physician from the University of Halle at Königsberg before 1731 (pp. 56 f.), by the name of Abraham Moses Levin, and another, Jakob Hirschberg in 1751.

[35]Albert W. Levi, *Philosophy as Social Expression*, Chicago 1974, p. 174.

[36]Cf. Grossmann, *loc. cit.*, pp. 133–137.

[37]Stern, *op. cit.*, II/1, pp. 5 f., and H. W. Arndt's introduction to Christian Wolff's *Vernünftige Gedanken* . . . (the "German Logic"), *Gesammelte Schriften*, I/1, Hildesheim 1965, p. 22. For Thomasius, heir to German mystical pietism and early enlightener cf. Ernst Troeltsch, *The Social Teaching of the Christian Church*, New York–Evanston 1960, vol. 2, p. 788 and Grossmann, *loc. cit.*, pp. 127 ff. As Eric Werner (*A Voice Still Heard* . . . , Pennsylvania State University Press 1976, p. 125) says: "It remains the unforgotten merit of the pietists to have set both example and pace toward a kind of 'friendship' with a weary and anxiety-ridden Jewry."

[38]Stern *op. cit.*, II/1, p. 7. Wolff's 'Speech about the Ethics of the Chinese' of 1721 (cf. Bruggemann [ed.] *Das Weltbild der deutschen Aufklärung*, Leipzig 1930, pp. 174–195) illustrates the same cosmopolitan, rationalistic posture as Leibniz's Chinese interests. (Cf. D. F. Lach, 'The Sinophilism of Chr. Wolf', *Journal of the History of Ideas*, XIV [1953], pp. 561–574.) Generally, Wolff emphasised, as he entitled chapt. 6 of his *Preliminary Discourse on Philosophy in General*, tr. and intro. R. J. Blackwell, Library of Liberal Arts, 1963, pp. 96 ff., 'The Freedom to Philosophize'. For the ensuing debate about Wolff's rationalistic sinophilism cf. Max Wundt's *Die deutsche Schulphilosophie im Zeitalter der Aufklärung*, Tübingen 1945, p. 235 (and his treatment of Thomasius, pp. 28–61, of Chr. Wolf pp. 133–177). (For Wundt as Nazi cf. Hubert Kiesewetter, *Von Hegel zu Hitler – eine Analyse der Hegelschen Machtstaatsideologie und der politischen Wirkungsgeschichte* . . . , Hamburg 1974, p. 20). Cf. also Werner Schneiders, *Naturrecht und Liebesethik. Zur Geschichte der praktischen Philosophie im Hinblick auf Chr. Thomasius*, Hildesheim 1971.

whole forbade, for example, Jewish books at the university.[39] Friedrich Wilhelm I, himself orthodox and, like the rulers of Hanover and like Leibniz, interested in increasing his political power by, among other things, re-uniting the Christian Churches, at times opposed the liberals. Thus Christian Wolff, who had come to the University of Halle under Leibniz's aegis in 1706, was expelled from both the university and the country in 1723. At times like these the King would also give vent to his hatred of Jews.[40] But also under Thomasius's sway, whose basic differences with Wolff are not so obvious from a later perspective as they loomed at the time, the main thrust toward loosened denominational lines and progressive, even cosmopolitan, social developments continued. A title of his such as *Introduction to the Doctrine of Reason . . . for all Reasonable Human Beings, of whatever Estate or Sex* (1691) proclaims its essential universalism (however eclectic it may have been).

This explains the presence and role not only of Jews but also of Anton Wilhelm Amo – a black professor of philosophy, from African Guinea (Ghana), ex-slave, disciple of Christian Wolff, at the university.[41] It must surely be a unique event that in the earlier part of the eighteenth century, in the heart of Germany, an ex-slave teaches philosophy to and becomes a personal friend of a Jewish medical student, to the point of appending his German congratulatory sonnet to the latter's Latin medical dissertation:[42]

> "Dein aufgeweckter Geist im klugen *meditieren*, Und unermüdter Fleiss im gründlichen Studiren.
> *Hoch Edler*, macht dass Da in der Gelehrten Orden ein *Stern*, ein *Heller Stern*, der ersten Grösse worden,
> Der immer heller wird in neuer Ehren-Schein. So einen grossen Lohn giebt Weisheit ihren Söhnen.
> Genug. Vom Himmel muss die Lust die ungemeyn *Dich* und die *Deinigen* in Lauter Segen Kröhnen.
> Dises sezet seinem Hochgeehrtesten Freunde
> Glückwünschend hinzu.
> Anton Wilhelm Amo
> Von Guinea in *Africa*, der *Philosophie* und Freyen künste *Magister legens*."

The black philosopher, invoking heaven's blessings on Moses son of Abraham Halevi Wolff and on his house,[43] may be only a conventional phrase-monger,

[39]Stern, *op. cit.*, II/1, pp. 150 ff.
[40]*Ibid.*, pp. 8–10.
[41]Cf. Burchard Brentjes, *Anton Wilhelm Amo. Der Schwarze Philosoph in Halle*, Leipzig 1976; *Antonius Guilielmus Amo Afer . . . transl. of his Works*, Halle 1968; *Dictionary of African Biographies*, New York 1977, ed. L. H. Ofusen-Appiah, vol. I, pp. 196 f. Blumenbach discusses Amo in 'Von den Negern', in *Magazin f.d. Neuste aus der Physik u. Naturgeschichte*, ed. J. H. Voigt, IV/3 (Gotha 1787), pp. 10 f. and the Abbé Grégoire, in *De la littérature des Nègres . . .*, Paris 1808, pp. 198–202.
[42]Cf. *A.G.A. Afer . . .*, *op. cit.*, vol. 'Dokumente, Belege', p. 54.
[43]The historians are, as usual, hide-bound in their respective parochialisms. Not a single Jewish or German biographer of Wolff has hitherto even referred to their subject's relations with Amo; black and white German biographers of Amo, on the other hand, though they take cognisance of his poem for Wolff, do not follow up on anything regarding who this Wolff was. This applies also to the politically motivated historians in the German Democratic Republic, Brentjes, *op. cit.*, p. 50, who merely mentions the poem. Cf. its uses in W. Suchier, 'A. W. Amo . . .', in *Akademische Rundschau . . .*, IV/9–10 (June–July 1916), p. 446.

referring to Wolff's immediate kin. It is, however, hard not to discern in that italicised phrase a broader concern also – that Wolff's fellow-Jews, like Amo's own fellow-blacks, together finally achieve the human and social dignity of which they have so long been robbed.

One also wants to know what academic interests these two men must have shared.

In the eighteenth century medicine (and "natural philosophy") were by no means yet so divorced from philosophy as they were to become. In Amo's writings as in those of his teacher Christian Wolff, one finds a lot of material that would not normally find its way into later philosophical literature – "scientific" and medical material included –, and, at the same time, medical science still nourished itself in considerable measure on Aristotle and the scholastic tradition, – what is sometimes referred to as *Barockscholastik*. Thus Amo, like Moses Wolff,[44] accepted Harvey's new theory of blood-circulation, and, as an orientalist and Hebraist,[45] even found it stipulated in the Bible.[46] Moses Wolff, on the other hand, had, as far as one can determine, little theoretical interest, and what he had of it was, as we shall see later, of a very middle-brow, amateurish sort. Presumably he had to listen to lectures in philosophy, including Amo's, while he was a student. One is forced to conclude that it was Amo's wider range of interests, rather than Wolff, that provided common intellectual ground for them.

We can be more specific. As a disciple of Christian Wolff, and among others but preeminently of Leibniz and Descartes, Amo was stuck with a central philosophical problem that afflicted his teachers and Cartesianism to this day: the fundamental problem of dualism. There is declared to be, on the one hand, the world of ideas, mind, thought, etc., and there is, on the other hand, the totally discrete world of matter. Logic and philosophy come to grips with the former, while natural, especially mathematical, science deals with the latter. (The scientific, and even materialistic, side of this dualism was, therefore, much furthered in the immediate wake of both Leibniz and Descartes.) Such disciplinary dualism (transmogrified in our time into "methodological dualism") runs into one crucial problem no later than when trying to deal with human beings. These, presumably, have both a material as well as an intellectual dimension, which, furthermore, certainly seem to operate with some kind of co-ordination. How – so dualism has always had to be asked – can it be explained that two such totally disparate, unconnected substances, mind and matter, tie up with one another? Indeed, what can tie them together, so that they do, in fact, work harmoniously, at least in human beings?

Descartes, in attempting to climb over this philosophical hurdle, resorted to his famous – and absurd – pineal gland. Leibniz proffered a somewhat more complex solution, mixed of his doctrine of "pre-established harmony" and of his doctrine of decreasingly clear understanding, really "imagination", which perceives the metaphysical, immaterial monads as material phenomena. It is to this problem that Amo addresses himself, too, in his inaugural dissertation of 1734, *Apatheia of*

[44]Cf. *Apatheia, op. cit.* (see below), p. 76.
[45]Brentjes, *op. cit.*, pp. 37, 68.
[46]*Apatheia, op. cit.*, p. 76, and Brentjes, *op. cit.*, pp. 103 f.

the Human Soul or the lack of Sensation and of the Capacity of Sensation in the Human Soul and the Presence of both in our Organically Live Bodies . . .[47] – the doctrine that the soul (mind) is, indeed, in a universe which is totally different from and, therefore, "apathetic" to the material universe.[48] This doctrine, like main-line dualism in general, opens up the material universe to the unrestricted investigation of the physical, in biology of medical, research – precisely the subject which was of interest to Moses Wolff and, avocationally, also to Amo. The two "worlds" were then brought together again by Amo in a Cartesian, rather than Leibnizian, fashion, whereas Christian Wolff, while admitting his inability to resolve the conundrum, speculated that Leibniz's pre-established harmony was its most likely explanation.[49]

Once he had finished his studies, Moses Wolff settled in Bonn in 1740. He obtained the formal "privilege" on 10th October 1741,[50] no doubt with the help of his bankers' family. In Bonn he married Sara Meyer, daughter of Assur Meyer, in 1746.[51] Here he practised medicine with great professional and remunerative success for the rest of his long life. Only in the last few years of his old age does he seem to have withdrawn from medical practice.[52] He was known as Moyses Doktor,[53] "Jud Meyer modo Doctor Wolff", and as "Arzt Moses Abraham Neuwied".[54] His success can be measured in monetary terms, through his standing in the Jewish community, and by his high-ranking non-Jewish patients.

[47] *Apatheia, op. cit.*

[48] Martin Knutzen of Königsberg published in 1735 *Commentatio de commercio mentis et corporis per influxum physicum*, in which he sided, as the title implies, more with Descartes than with Leibniz. From this a line can be drawn to Kant. (Cf. Wundt, *op. cit.*, pp. 207–209). The well-known continuity of philosophical history between the Leibniz-Wolffian school and Kant always deserves further penetration. (Cf. H. Heimsoeth, *Studien zur Philosophie Kants . . .*, Cologne 1956, pp. 1–91.) For one thing, much of the German-language philosophical vocabulary that Kant used he inherited from there – together with many problems. Also many of Kant's conceptualisations have their origin in this school-philosophy in which he was raised. He, of course, revolutionised his intellectual inheritance. All of this can be well illustrated with Anton Amo (though we have no reason for thinking that Kant knew of Amo). In *Metaphysische Anfangsgründe der Sitten*, II: *Metaphysische Anfangsgründe der Tugendlehre*, paragraphs XVf., he argues that, since virtue demands that reason determine our actions, we must bring our drives under control and thus become apathetic "toward our feelings and inclinations". He then speaks of "the duty of apathy" and of "moral apathy". Here is the crux of the Kantian revolution: what for his predecessors was "reality" turns into norms, regulatives, for him, or, to put it differently, the Cartesian discreteness of mind and matter becomes Kant's discreteness of noumena and phenomena, reason and sensibility. The problem remains the same for both, however: how can the two, once rent asunder, be re-united in human experience? On the revival of the Stoic notion of apathy in the Enlightenment cf. T. J. Schlereth, *The Cosmopolitan Ideal in Enlightenment Thought. Its Form and Function in the Ideas of Franklin, Hume, and Voltaire*, University of Notre Dame Press 1977. Cf. Walter Benjamin on "apathia" in connection with baroque tragedy, *The Origin of the German Tragic Drama*, NBL, 1977, p. 140.

[49] Cf. Charles A. Corr (of the University of Illinois, Edwardsville, to whom we owe thanks also for other help in his area), 'Christian Wolff and Leibniz', *Journal of the History of Ideas*, XXXVI/2 (April–May 1975), p. 258, and L. W. Beck, 'Lovejoy as a Critic of Kant', *J.H.I.*, XXXIII (1972), p. 258, and G. Fabian, *Beitrag zur Geschichte des Leib-Seele Problems. Lehre von der prästabilierten Harmonie u. von dem psychophysischen Parallelismus in der Leibniz-Wolffschen Schule*, Langensalza 1925, pp. 32–47.

[50] Schnee, *Die Hoffinanz . . .*, *op. cit.*, pp. 53 f., 526, 530.

[51] Schulte, *op. cit.*, pp. 530, 531 f., note 1, 577, note 2.

[52] Kober, 'Rheinische Judendoktoren . . .', *loc. cit.*, p. 212.

[53] Schulte, *op. cit.*, p. 57.

[54] *Ibid.*, pp. 531 f., No. 1. Other listings of him are to be found in Nathen Koren, *Jewish Physicians. A*

He was appointed personal physician to the local ruler, the Elector-Duke and Archbishop Clemens[55] and in 1765 to Clemens's successor Maximilian Friedrich of Cologne.[56] The latter, who had his residence in Bonn, is reputed as "one of the most enlightened men in Germany". When he established an academy in the city he consulted his physician about the professorship in Hebrew[57] – according to one source (though a generally unreliable one) he was actually appointed to that position himself.[58] Moses Wolff was so close to Maximilian Friedrich and to his successor, Maximilian Franz,[59] that he was permitted to live outside, though in a street adjacent to, the ghetto (now called Doetschstrasse),[60] in a house one of whose doors faced the ducal palace, so that he could quickly go from one to the other.[61] He also treated the personnel of the court.[62] We know of one occasion on which he was also given special permission to treat a noble lady in Cologne, on 28th October 1763.[63]

Wolff's medical career and his social standing were so memorable that, in the third quarter of the nineteenth century, he even became the subject of a lower-middle-brow short-story, *Der Leibarzt des Kurfürsten – Eine Historische Novelle* by Karl Heigel.[64] The well-written and interesting tale does not claim to be, and is not, reliable scholarship; rather does it bespeak German liberalism at the time of its composition. Nothing in it is incompatible with known facts, on the other hand. There is talk about "our people" (the Jews) and of *Lichtfreunde*, i.e. enlighteners, *illuminés*.[65] Wolff is described as having abandoned both *Kabbalah* and Newtonian, mathematical science[66] in favour of Bacon's *Novum Organon* and Harvey's medicine.[67] An incident is related of how the Jew Wolff acted, in fact, like "the good Samaritan" in the New Testament.[68] Blacks are mentioned, without prejudice. Duke Clemens accepts him as a good physician and human being after he had first asked: "Wolff, the Jew?", to which the answer comes: "The physician".[69] And the short-story ends with the sentence: "It was a Jewish word: 'Let there be light.' "

Biographical Index, Jerusalem 1973, p. 139. *Jüdisches Lexikon*, Felix Theilhaber's article on Jewish physicians, vol. 4, p. 37, and *Monumenta Judaica, op. cit.*, pp. 267 f. (also all of pp. 264–269).

[55]Schnee, *Die Hoffinanz . . . , op. cit., ibid.*

[56]Lewin, *loc. cit.*

[57]Elijahu Carmoly, *Histoire des médecins juifs anciens et modernes*, Brussels: Encyclographic Society of Medical Sciences, 1844, vol. 1, p. 212.

[58]Richard Landau, *Geschichte der jüdischen Ärzte . . .*, Berlin 1895, p. 122.

[59]Kober, 'Rheinische Judendoktoren . . .', *loc. cit.*, p. 212.

[60]Alfred Levy, *Aus Bonner Archiven. Zur Geschichte der jüdischen Gemeinde. Zum 50jährigen Jubiläum der Synagoge*, Bonn 1929, p. 11.

[61]Kober, 'Rheinische Judendoktoren . . .', *loc. cit.*; Hoffmann, *op. cit.*, p. 29.

[62]Schnee, *loc. cit.*

[63]Kober, 'Jüdische Studenten . . .', *loc. cit.*, p. 123.

[64]In *Sorgenlose Stunden im Kreise beliebter Erzähler*, ed. F. W. Hackländer, 2nd series (with illustrations and one story by Sacher-Masoch), Stuttgart 1875 (and in *Bonner Zeitung*, 1879).

[65]*Ibid.*, p. 2.

[66]*Ibid.*, pp. 3, 20.

[67]*Ibid.*, p. 4. For early Jewish scientific adhesion to Harvey's medicine cf. André Neher, *David Gans (1541–1631) . . .*, Paris 1974, p. 366.

[68]*Sorgenlose Stunden . . . , op. cit.*, p. 12.

[69]*Ibid.*, pp. 20, 24.

The most prominent patient that Dr. Wolff is supposed to have had was Pope Clement XIII in 1768. Clement was afflicted with an eye-disease, which his own doctors could not cure. Archbishop Maximilian Friedrich recommended his own private physician.[70] The antisemitic pope at first rejected the suggestion, but circumstances then forced him to accept it. (Wolff is described as an oculist.)[71] Even then, though, Clement is reported to have refused the Jew entrance to the room in which he was seated; instead, the physician had to diagnose him through a glass partition. The cure was successful.[72] Pope Benedict XIV wrote about Wolff that he was the only "personne de tête" in Bonn.[73]

This story sounds like a moralistic fable. Kober, in fact, denies its historicity, on the ground that it resulted from a misinterpretation of a sentence in Wolff's eulogy in the *Memor-book* of the Jewish community of Bonn.[74] The sentence at issue, translated literally, reads as follows:[75] "(Wolff's) chair (throne) was set up among the great ones of Rome, princes, satraps, and lords, and they believed in Moses." Kober is right, of course, that "the great ones of Rome" could refer to any Roman Catholic dignitaries. In any case, there are obviously two biblical word-games involved in the sentence: as "they believed in Moses" is a paraphrase of *Exodus* XIV: 31d, here punningly applied to Moses Wolff, so "princes and satraps" is an allusion to *Esther* I: 3. By the same token, "the great ones of Rome" could also refer to Wolff's activities in Rome, if any, and to the Pope. The matter cannot be settled in this manner. Auerbach[76] certified the truthfulness of the story on the basis of an eyewitness account from Moses Wolff's own household, transmitted by identified persons to himself. His testimony has the ring of validity about it. And Ludwig von Pastor's *History of the Popes*[77] documents that Pope Clement did, indeed, contract eye-troubles in 1763 and that he was cured in 1768.

Wolff's medical practice made him a very wealthy man. Schnee[78] has compiled some available figures: he was actually put on a salary by the Duke at 400 *Reichsthaler* (*Rtlr*), which was a very large sum itself, and to this were added considerable perquisites for his treatment of courtiers, and occasionally prisoners, etc.[79] In 1750 the government paid him *Rtlr* 1,492+883+219+164, in 1751: 3,806, in 1751/2: 4,000, in 1753/4: 1,742+1,040 as a special grant with which to build a garden. How close the terms were on which the ruler and the Jewish Court physician related to one another is illustrated not only by their living arrangements, which we have mentioned, but also by the fact that Wolff

[70]Carmoly, *op. cit.*, p. 212.

[71]Solomon R. Kagan, *Jewish Medicine*, Boston 1952, p. 71.

[72]B. H. Auerbach, *Geschichte der israelitischen Gemeinde Halberstadt* . . . , Halberstadt 1866, p. 16, note 1, and Carl Brisch, *Geschichte der Juden in Köln und Umgebung* . . . , part 2, Köln 1882, p. 134. The story is also referred to in *The Medical and Health Thesaurus* (in Hebrew), eds. A. Goldstein and M. Schechter, Tel-Aviv 1956, column 1592, under the heading 'physicians to popes'.

[73]Schnee, *loc. cit.*

[74]Kober, 'Rheinische Judendoktoren . . .', *loc. cit.*, pp. 211 f.

[75]*Ibid.*, p. 234.

[76]Auerbach, *op. cit.*, p. 16, note 1.

[77]Ludwig Freiherr von Pastor, *History of the Popes*, London-St. Louis 1961, vol. 36, p. 168.

[78]Schnee, *ibid.*

[79]Schulte, *ibid.*, for prisoners' treatment in 1746.

was bequeathed the sum of 800 Gulden in the Duke's last will (of which 553.20 were actually paid out on 2nd May 1768).

One suspects that there was more here than meets the eye. The relations between the Elector-Duke/Archbishops of Cologne and the Wolff family were not based exclusively on the physician-patient relationship. In the gigantic banking enterprise, which the Court-Jewish house of Leffmann Behrens conducted on behalf of its Hanoverian patrons and their "English policy", it was the Court Jew who arranged, for the most part, the appointment of a bishop for (among others) Cologne favourable to King George.[80] The same goes for the Bishop of Münster (in the course of which debts were contracted whose repayment was disputed for generations).[81] (The chief Court Jew of Cologne was Simon Baruch, the grandfather of Ludwig Börne.)[82] Brothers of Dr. Moses Abraham Wolff were suppliers over a long period for the court in Bonn and Cologne. Schnee raises the possibility[83] that both G. Wolff and J. Wolff, often mentioned in that capacity, were brothers of the physician. (We must keep in mind the variableness of names in that situation, of which we have spoken.) It is a documented fact that Moses's older brother Gumberz, born in Neuwied *c.* 1710, sometimes known as Gumprecht Linz, had lived in Bonn since 1752 and acted as a supplier to the court. (He died in Bonn in 1794.)[84] In Moses Abraham's extremely large estate I.O.U.s of great magnitude were contained, some direct, some apparently bought from other Jewish creditors, and some from high-ranking personages throughout Northern Europe.[85]

All of this evidence tends to show that the physician Wolff was not only established in medical practice with the help of his banking family but that throughout his life he also continued to be connected with their commercial activities as relatively small Court Jews and through them with the large, international Court-Jewish network, at which we have looked from the perspective of Raphael Levi. The symbiosis of the ruling class and the uppermost socio-economic echelon of the Jewish communities in the eighteenth century comprised not only their common economic and political but also, to some extent, their personal and professional lives.

Presumably Wolff also had "private patients", Jews and others. All in all, he clearly was very wealthy throughout his life. He had one very fancy house in Bonn from the outset, and he built an even fancier one in 1781. The tax on it in 1795 was 6,500 *Rtlr.*[86] The details of his estate are impressive:[87] there were 300,000 francs in cash – the contents of his large house, valuable utensils, furniture, art-objects

[80]Schnee, *Die Hoffinanz . . .*, *op. cit.*, vol. 2, p. 11.

[81]*Ibid.*, p. 441.

[82]Zwi Asaria, *Die Juden in Köln . . .*, Cologne 1959, p. 60. For the role of Ludwig Börne's father, Jacob Baruch, in the emancipatory Jewish community of Frankfurt cf. R. Liberles, 'The Jews of Frankfurt: 1750–1870, in *A Tale of Two Cities. Jewish Life in Frankfurt and Istanbul 1750–1870*, ed. V. B. Mann, New York 1982, p. 30.

[83]Schnee, *op. cit.*, vol. 3, *loc. cit.*

[84]Schulte, *op. cit.*, pp. 526–529.

[85]*Ibid.*, pp. 531 f., note 1.

[86]*Ibid.*, p. 603.

[87]*Ibid.*

(which make the place sound, if not Victorian, baroque), etc., were auctioned off to eager Gentile and Jewish buyers – he left large and numerous bequests – and his house itself was taken over by a grandson of his, Abraham Hirsch Wolff, a banker, who was to live in it from 1815 to 1839.[88]

Parallel with Wolff's official, professional and with his private life there went, of course – typically for his class – his life in the local Jewish community. In 1715 the Jewish community of Bonn was permitted by the government to comprise a synagogue, the rabbi's house, and sixteen family-houses, all in the *Judengasse*, behind gates guarded by soldiers. The number of private houses was raised to nineteen in 1773.[89] In 1765 the number of actual domiciled individuals was 200.[90] Wolff paid an annual tax to the Jewish community of 14.33 *Rtlr* between 1773 and 1794,[91] but in addition he is reported to have been generous with charitable contributions in services, goods, and money. In 1766 he gave a Torah-scroll to the congregation (which was still preserved there in 1928).[92] Nonetheless, his eleemosynary expenditures do not sound impressive. He is described in his official eulogy (which may, of course, be somewhat pious) as a fully practising Jew.[93] His palatial home had a permanent *Laubhütte* (presumably a *sukkah*), to which one could walk beneath a covered way[94] through the garden (no doubt the one subsidised by his ducal patron). The ritual arrangements of his burial and mourning, for which he provided, were traditional, except that he followed the innovation for which the Mendelssohnian circle of Berlin *Maskilim* fought, not to inter the dead before the sun has set.[95]

As the eighteenth century grew older, and especially as progressive ideas spread among Christians and Jews, the rule of the Court Jews and their immediate appendages over the internal life of the Jewish communities was increasingly disputed. In Halle Selma Stern reports examples of such social strains.[96] They would typically take the form of religious quarrels (as we have seen to be the case generally in Europe throughout the early-modern centuries). Thus there was a great and a long argument within the Bonn congregation in 1762 about the typical ritual issue of who was to be honoured by being "called up" to the liturgical scripture-readings in the synagogue. The "young people" wanted to break into this charmed circle. Moses A. Wolff was long since *Barnes* (the characteristically Rhenish-Southern German softening of Hebrew *parnass*, Yiddish *parness*, for "head of the congregation"), but even without that title it

[88] *Ibid.*, p. 603.
[89] Cf. Asaria, *op. cit.*, p. 60.
[90] Hoffmann, *op. cit.*, p. 28.
[91] Kober, 'Rheinische Judendoktoren . . .', *loc. cit.*, p. 212.
[92] Schulte, *op. cit.*, *ibid.*
[93] Cf. Kober, 'Rheinische Judendoktoren . . .', *loc. cit.*, pp. 234 f., for Wolff's eulogy in the Bonn *Memor-book*.
[94] Schulte, *op. cit.*, *ibid.*
[95] *Ibid.*, Marcus Herz (Kant's great friend), *An die Herausgeber des hebräischen Sammlers über die frühe Beerdigung der Juden*, Berlin 1787; Isaac Euchel, 'Ist nach jüdischem Gesetz das Übernachten der Todten wirklich verboten?', *Hame'asef*, VI (1790), pp. 38–50, 80–85, 171–176, 245–249 (Breslau 1797), and B. D. Weinryb, 'Enlightenment and German-Jewish *Haskalah*', *Studies on Voltaire and the Eighteenth Century*, vol. XXVII, p. 1839.
[96] Stern, *op. cit.*, II/1, p. 173.

would not take much imagination to figure out on what side of the dispute he arraigned himself. He was, as a matter of fact, usually represented by his brother Gumberz, the Court supplier. The dispute was so severe that it was eventually brought before the government.[97]

It takes equally little imagination to conjecture which side the government favoured. In all pre-revolutionary and Restoration situations in Europe at the end of the eighteenth and the beginning of the nineteenth centuries the governments assumed that the *status quo* was to be preserved not only in general politics but also in religion, even in the despised Jewish "church".[98] As Schulte puts it, "the approximately thirty Jewish businessmen-families in Bonn before the incursion of the revolution belong economically to Bonn's upper class", and they were "favourites of the *ancien régime*".[99]

"Favourites" of the government the Jews were, but they were, of course, favoured mostly, if not exclusively, because of their financial and political usefulness. The absolutist and centralist government used them as potent help against the entrenched interests of the guilds and of the rising middle class. These interests reacted by opposing the very position, certainly any improvement of the position, of the Jews. For various tactical or historical reasons the government might temporarily yield to the anti-Jewish forces, but on the whole it tended to resist them.[100] This in turn did not endear the Jews to the pre-revolutionary elements in society.[101] On 28th February 1784 the Rhine flooded to an exceptional height. Among other places also the Bonn ghetto had to be evacuated. The Jews were given temporary refuge in Christian homes – presumably by business-associates and clients of theirs and by "enlightened" compatriots.[102] At the same time, however, other sectors of the populace used the opportunity to try to plunder the property of the Jews, left exposed to the elements, and the government had to send in troops to suppress the riot.[103]

Moses Wolff was also typical of his time and society in that he had a large family, locally and elsewhere, with whom he appears to have acted in concert all his life. His wife seems to have been a midwife and thus to have helped him also professionally.[104] They had several children (though because of the variety of names under which people went at the time, Hebrew, Yiddish, German, French, Latin, etc., as we noted, it is sometimes difficult to keep the lines straight): Heinrich (Henri) and Salomon (sometimes known as Simon), who followed in their father's professional footsteps[105] in Bonn and in Düren, near Aix-la-

[97]Schulte, *op. cit.*, pp. 58 f.

[98]Cf. e.g. Michael A. Meyer, 'The Religious Reform Controversy in the Berlin Jewish Community, 1814–1823', in *LBI Year Book XXIV* (1979).

[99]Schulte, *op. cit.*, pp. 60, 61, note 87.

[100]Hoffmann, *op. cit.*, p. 30.

[101]*Ibid.*, pp. 31 f.

[102]Cf. the discussion between Heckscher and Kellenbenz, *op. cit.*, pp. 466 f., as to whether Jews in the eighteenth century were in contact only with other Jews and Christian nobles or also with Christian business-associates and scholars.

[103]Brisch, *op. cit.*, p. 142.

[104]Kober, 'Rheinische Judendoktoren . . .', *loc. cit.*, p. 213.

[105]Carmoly, *op. cit.*, *ibid.*

Chapelle, respectively,[106] – Samuel, known as "Jud Wolff" and a very rich man in turn[107] – a daughter who, when married in Frankfurt, was given a dowry by her father of 2,500 Gulden,[108] – and another son, Jacques, born in 1759, who may be taken to symbolise the next generation in the history of Jewish emancipation by virtue of the fact that when, in the course of institutionalising and spreading the French Revolution, Napoleon organised a Jewish consistory in Bonn, he was appointed as a non-rabbinical member of it, on 15th February 1811.[109] We have had occasion earlier to speak of Moses's brother Gumberz in Bonn and one of his grandsons, Moses Hirsch, a banker. Another brother of Dr. Wolff, Joseph, had continued their common father's establishment in their native town of Neuwied, and a third brother, Samuel Abraham Wolff, was head of the Jewish community there 1743–1772.[110] Many other close as well as distant relatives were remembered in his last will.[111] A nephew of his, Simon Meier Cassel, born in Bonn, studied for two years first at the University of Mayence around 1770, then for four years at his uncle's *alma mater* in Halle, then joined his uncle's medical practice in Bonn for five years, and finally he dedicated his dissertation at the University of Giessen to Moses Abraham Wolff in 1781 – only to have himself baptised in the same year.[112] We have also had earlier occasion to take note of the fact that members of the family cooperated in various commercial enterprises, sometimes over considerable distances and periods.

In this biographical sketch of Moses Wolff we have not had occasion to mention intellectual matters since we spoke of his student-days. Little wonder: he had been a very busy physician, a small-time politician, as well as an entrepreneur. We come across a few traces of what the Germans call the culture of the *Bildungsbürgertum*, middle-brow cultural pretensions. These, like other features of Moses's life, sound more as though taken from the life of the rising middle class among Jews and others of the Victorian/Wilhelminian age a century later. Bonn had a *Lese-und Erholungsgesellschaft*: one can almost hear the book review and the discussions in the small-town parlours, with collations following; both Christians and Jews, no doubt with the proper social credentials, belonged to it – Moses among them in 1790, a son of his in 1806, and a grandson of his in 1812.[113] In Moses's estate a number of (unfortunately unspecified) Jewish, philosophical, theological, and other books are listed.[114] Clearly, he must have regarded himself as belonging to the "enlightened" echelon of German Jewry, in

[106]*Zeitschrift für Hebräische Bibliographie*, XVIII/1–3, *loc. cit.*

[107]Kober, 'Rheinische Judendoktoren . . .', *loc. cit.*, p. 213.

[108]Hoffmann, *op. cit.*, p. 29.

[109]Kober, 'Jüdische Studenten . . .', *loc. cit.*, p. 123.

[110]Schulte, *op. cit.*, p. 526. In a letter dated 10th January 1979 the archival director of the *Fürstlich Wiedische Rentkammer* gives the dates of the local Jewish leadership of Abraham Wolff as 1699–1739 and of his son Samuel Abraham Wolff as 1739–1754.

[111]Schulte, *op. cit.*, pp. 531 f., note 1.

[112]Kober, 'Jüdische Studenten . . .', *loc. cit.*, p. 119.

[113]Of such *Lesegesellschaften* R. Liberles says (*loc. cit.*, pp. 26 f.): "Medical doctors, however, were among the few who had obtained formal secular education, and they formed the nuclei of several reading circles established at the turn of the century." At least in Frankfurt, however, they were not a mixture of Christians and Jews (cf. *ibid.*, p. 31).

[114]Schulte, *op. cit.*, *ibid.*

the style of the Mendelssohn circle: his background, life-style, socio-economic interests, and the provisions he made for his own burial, which we have mentioned, lead to this conclusion. It may, again, be taken as symbolic and anticipatory of the socio-intellectual development of the following century that Gumberz Wolff was on close terms with the famous Chevalier von Geldern, himself an extremely interesting product of the European-Jewish pre-symbiosis of the eighteenth century, a Hanoverian, and the ancestor of Heinrich/Henri Heine.[115]

Moses Abraham Wolff died on 19th Ellul 5562=1802[116] in Bonn, eighty-seven years old, and he was buried the next day in the Jewish cemetery across the Rhine, in Schwarzrheindorf. His tombstone is still standing there.[117] His eulogy in the *Memor-book* of the Jewish community, from which we have quoted before, describes him (and his family) as good Jews, him as a physician and "natural scientist" famous among Jews and non-Jews far and wide, a generous philanthropist and communal leader.[118]

Moses Wolff is in every way a paradigmatic figure in what may be called "the Jewish *Frühemanzipation*", on the model of the concept of *Frühaufklärung*.[119] He is not an important but a symptomatic figure in history. He came from the very heart of the class of Court Jews (though on its lower level). He was the product of a university. (In both these respects he differed from Raphael Levi, about whom one mid-nineteenth-century rabbi boasted[120] that he proved the supererogatoriness of a university education for products of rabbinic schools.) He was a part-time, marginal Court Jew and a full-time physician – this the traditional profession, which, unlike the rabbinate, tended to bridge the gap between the ghetto and Christian society: already of the Middle Ages it could be said that "there was not a noble or a prelate who did not keep a Jewish physician".[121] He exercised an influential leadership-role within the Jewish community, with respect to its external relations also. As Kober says,[122] "(t)he well-established connection of Jewish scholarship and medical practice continued for the time being. But these physicians are not only people of limitedly Jewish education . . . The Jewish physicians who studied at German universities became the path-breakers of a new age in history. They were enabled to study at German universities because the age of enlightenment had brought about this change as early as the first quarter of the eighteenth century."

This socio-cultural development had, of course, its socio-economic infra-

[115] *Ibid.*, p. 529.

[116] Brisch, *op. cit.*, *ibid.*, has a false date.

[117] Schulte, *op. cit.*, p. 533, note 3.

[118] Kober, 'Rheinische Judendoktoren . . . ', *loc. cit.*, pp. 234 f.

[119] Cf. Morris M. Faierstein, 'The Liebes Brief. A Critique of Jewish Society in Germany (1749)', in *LBI Year Book XXVII* (1982), for relations with the Christian nobility – of Court Jews and the Jewish bourgeoisie (pp. 229 f.) – and for proto-modernism (p. 241).

[120] S. E. Blogg, *Sefer HaChayim-Israelitisches Andachtsbuch . . .*, Hannover 1848, p. 313, note 1. (Our copy of the 3rd edn., 1862, bears the names of six generations of our family.) Blogg served as chief-editor of the Telgener Press in Hanover, founded under the auspices of the government, from which many Jewish books came forth.

[121] Julius Klein, *The Mesta. A Study in Spanish Economic History*, Cambridge, Mass. 1920, pp. 37 f.

[122] Kober, 'Rheinische Judendoktoren . . . ', *loc. cit.*, p. 217.

structure. The division of labour between the two brothers Moses and Gumberz in Bonn, the physician and the "bespoke" merchant to the ruler, reminds one somewhat of the typical family-arrangement in East-German Junker-families and in families of the English upper-class, where the eldest son would take over the family estate, the next son would go into the army or government, and the third would go into the church. Jews generally fulfilled in modern times what Montesquieu had predicted in Letter 85 of his *Lettres Persanes*:[123] "One notes that those who live in tolerated religions usually make themselves more useful to their fatherland than those who live in dominant religions, because, isolated from honours, unable to distinguish themselves except by their opulence and riches, they devote themselves to acquisitions through work and to the most burdensome jobs of society." Jewish historians, characteristically and unfortunately, limit themselves to the political and socio-cultural side of the story; it seems to take non-Jewish German historians, like Sombart himself and in his wake Schnee and, in our specific instance, Schulte, to analyse the socio-economic side. As Kellenbenz puts it,[124] "therewith we come to the especially touchy subject of (Jewish) cooperation with ducal government". We see in the cases of Raphael Levi and his patrons and of Moses Wolff that there can be no question but that the official leadership of the Jewish communities in (and beyond) the eighteenth century was hand in glove with the absolute, enlightened or unenlightened, rulers. Their social as well as their economic interests necessitated this. The Jewish *Frühaufklärung* is thus the precise counter-part of Protestant pietism and early rationalism, which, too, "developed", as Grossmann quotes Hinrichs,[125] "a new conformity . . . in the service of the absolute state". Since the organised Jewish communities were in turn total dependencies of the Court Jews, it must be said that Jewry as a whole was integrated into the absolutist state-apparatus. Their practical motto was Amo's literary motto (taken from Epictetus): "Necessitatis qui se accommodat sapit, estque rerum Divinorum conscius."[126] (What the socio-political impulses were on "the dark side" of this moon – the footloose Jewish beggars and beggar-bands and the *Lumpenproletariat* in the country-side and in some cities[127] – is a question that, in the nature of the case, is not easily accessible to historical documentation. Scholem has pointed out, in any case, that European-Jewish proto-emancipation occurred on the level of the Court Jews and on the level of the Jewish "underworld.")[128] Official Jewry would

[123] Paris 1960, p. 179. Cf. also a quotation of Grossmann's *loc. cit.*, p. 120: "Good health, abstinence, honesty and an adequate system of education helped nonconformists to advance in industry and trade and may in turn have caused them to increase their numbers relative to other groups."

[124] Kellenbenz, *op. cit.*, p. 460.

[125] *Loc. cit.*, p. 130: C. Hinrichs, *Preussentum und Pietismus*, Göttingen 1971, p. 254. Two sentences of Grossmann's then synthesise this syndrome neatly: "With the *Frühaufklärung* the debate on religious toleration reaches a new plateau" (*loc. cit.*, p. 116); "religious toleration as a human ideal served and was fostered by absolutist territorial rulers" (*ibid.*, p. 135).

[126] Cf. Brentjes, *op. cit.*, p. 67.

[127] Cf. Rudolf Glanz, *Geschichte des niederen jüdischen Volkes in Deutschland. Eine Studie über historisches Gaunertum, Bettelwesen und Vagantentum*, New York 1968, esp. pp. 105, 309, note 63 for Neuwied; O. H. Von Rhyn, *Kulturgeschichte des jüdischen Volkes. Die Juden und das Gaunertum*, Jena 1892; and T. Endleman, *The Jews of Georgian England 1714–1830* . . . , Philadelphia 1979, chapts. 4–6.

[128] 'Jews and Germans', in J. Goldin, *The Jewish Expression*, New York 1970, p. 468.

naturally and invariably be on what we today would call the "liberal" side of the establishment: they were still suffering under many disabilities, and they, therefore, had to put their hopes in rationalistic, enlightened, progressive absolutism. Also, as we have observed, as the structure of Court Jewry grew, co-opting more and more clerks, representatives, servants, and ideologues, and as Gentile and Jewish intellectuals formulated the principles of the society that they knew and liked in increasingly broader, because theoretical, terms, internal stresses in both the Jewish and the Gentile communities also increased between the old governors and those who wanted to get at least their share of power. Gentile society, therefore, erupted in the revolutions of the late eighteenth and the first half of the nineteenth centuries.[129] The Jews welcomed the bourgeois thrusts of the revolutions and made their peace with its Thermidorean successors. (There were very few individual Jews who ever associated themselves with their Left wings.) Their interests motivated them to be eager for political and social rights, not for economic or ideological inversions. It was only in the generation of the *Vormärz*, the children of the first Jewish generation to enjoy limited legal, social, economic, and political emancipation as a result of 1789 or 1812, that an avant-garde of radical Jewish intellectuals came to the fore (and this was to become a paradigmatic phenomenon, to end only in our time). When the houses numbered 764, 796, and 807 in the Bonn ghetto are now remembered as the residences of Heine, Marx, and Moses Hess[130] – then we have run the full course of a movement that began at the end of the Thirty Years' War. But, of course, by that time and later a high Jewish price was also paid for this result. Raphael Levi was still a talmudic scholar. Jakob Hart wrote about the *Zohar*. Marx, on the other hand, got the extremely little that he knew of Jewish matters not even from his own immediate, solidly rabbinical family anymore but from Christian, Reformation students of Hebrew culture. Many leading lights in the Jewish battalions for total emancipation in the later nineteenth century either joined the Christian Church or asserted their total secularity. Even Selma Stern, the foremost Jewish historian of early German-Jewish modernisation, despite her late historian-husband Eugen Täubler's Zionist prominence, operated with the conventional notion of the illumination of assimilation as against the obscurantism of the ghetto and its Judaism.[131] We have seen this to be a false and facile image of pre-emancipation Jewish culture. We need not go back as far as Maimonides or the Maharal of Prague, of whom we had occasion to speak in connection with Raphael Levi: Levi himself moved comfortably in a world in which Galileo, Newton, Leibniz, and Mendelssohn rubbed shoulders with the talmudic rabbis. Moses Abraham Wolff had social links with Anton Wilhelm Amo and, when the time came, dwelled in his *sukkah*. This kind of specifically Jewish universalism was projected again when Moses Hess of Bonn wrote *Rom und Jerusalem*.

[129]Cf. G. Mühlpford, 'K. F. Bahrd und die Radikale Aufklärung', *Jahrbuch für Deutsche Geschichte*, V, Tel-Aviv 1976, pp. 50 ff.

[130]Schulte, *op. cit.*, p. 567.

[131]Stern, *op. cit.*, II/1, pp. 166–174.

A Word List for Teaching Eighteenth-Century Jews Some Fine Points of High German

BY WERNER WEINBERG

In his article 'The Yiddish Written Word in Nineteenth-Century Germany'[1] Steven M. Lowenstein argues conclusively and documents thoroughly the fact that the development from Judaeo-German (Western Yiddish) to standard German as the language of the Jews in Germany was a slow process marked by discernible steps. It was not – as popular opinion has it to this day – a more or less sudden passage from the ghetto to enlightened Europe as a direct consequence of Mendelssohn's German Pentateuch translation.

In the section dealing with the use of the Hebrew alphabet in writing standard German, Lowenstein brings a striking example for the transitional character of this socio-linguistic process:

> "A copy of Mendelssohn's translation of the Psalms printed in Offenbach in 1804–1805 gives clear confirmation of the assumption that most Jews had difficulty with the language [i.e., High German]. The edition contains a lengthy glossary of difficult words. Among the words which had to be explained were such ordinary words as 'Unfall,' 'Busse', 'Gruft', 'Heiden', 'Wut', 'Tyrann' and 'Thron' ".[2]

I believe that the glossary here referred to merits a separate study, which is provided in the present paper. Some pertinent facts concerning the choice of alphabet in Mendelssohn's Pentateuch translation (as distinguished from that for his Psalms translations), as well as an account of the general language situation of the contemporary German Jewry, must precede the presentation and analysis of that glossary.

In 1778 there appeared a forty-page prospectus containing sample chapters of the Pentateuch translation, called *Alim Literufah* (Leaves of Healing; Ezekiel XLVII: 12).[3] In 1780 there followed the Book of Genesis and in 1783 the complete set of the Pentateuch.[4] In all stages the biblical text, translated into standard German, was printed in Hebrew letters (the regular square type, not the special Ashkenazic cursive often called *Weiberdeutsch* [*vajbertajtsh*]). Lowenstein emphasises[5] that Mendelssohn's Pentateuch translation only constitutes "the most famous instance of this type of writing"[6] but was by no means the first

[1] In *LBI Year Book XXIV* (1979), pp. 179–192.
[2] *Ibid.*, pp. 188–189.
[3] Amsterdam, A. S. Proops.
[4] See Herrmann M. Z. Meyer, *Moses Mendelssohn–Bibliographie* (hereafter: Meyer, *Bibliographie*), Berlin 1965, Nos. 248, 250.
[5] *Loc. cit.*, p. 180.
[6] The expression "Moses (or Mosche) Dessau(s) Deutsch" was current for a long time. An early such

instance. In this context Lowenstein leads us to Herbert Paper's transcription of a 1765 standard German text in Hebrew letters[7] in *The Field of Yiddish*,[8] consisting of samples from a translation of Bachya ibn Pakuda's *Chovot Halevavot*. There[9] Paper quotes Steinschneider as calling the ibn Pakuda translation "das erste Buch eines jüdischen Verfassers in dieser [i.e., High German] Sprache" and, for corroborating his opinion, citing Zunz to the same effect, the latter, however, adding: "der erste Versuch aber, in die nationale [i.e., Jewish] Literatur die hochdeutsche Sprache einzuführen, ging im Jahr 1760 von Berlin aus". Zunz's remark is contained in his *Die gottesdienstlichen Vorträge der Juden*,[10] and refers to the *Sefer Millim Leloah* (Book of Words for [or: by] God), a biblical dictionary by Yehuda Leib ben Yoel Minden.[11] In this book, words are first explained in Hebrew and then translated into German, using Rashi script. That Zunz calls it an *attempt* to introduce standard German printed in Hebrew letters may be due to the fact that – unlike the ibn Pakuda translation five years later – Minden's book contains only single words rather than a coherent text. However, Zunz may also be hinting at the fact that Minden's German is sometimes archaising and not free of Yiddish features. Nevertheless, Minden's words are definitely German, and Zunz writes:[12] "In dem Wörterbuch . . . findet man bereits den Gebrauch des Hochdeutschen . . .", adding, "welches Mendelssohn zu verdanken ist". This last remark is somewhat puzzling, seeing that Mendelssohn was neither the first nor the only Jew of his time to employ German, and while the use of German in Mendelssohn's philosophical and literary works up to the time of Minden's book must have constituted a challenge to many Jews to improve their German or take up its study, Mendelssohn had not by then published any High German text in Hebrew letters.

Whether or not Minden was actually the first to publish a work employing that method (earlier examples may still be found), those among the Jews who knew High German are sure to have written it in the Hebrew alphabet in their notes, their private and (internal) business correspondence and for sundry other purposes well before Minden. After all, Jews had used the Hebrew alphabet in all the countries of their diaspora. They learned it in early childhood and it remained for them an adequate and convenient means to render the language of their host countries, whether Greek, Arabic, Italian, Spanish, French or German.

But who were the Jews who spoke German before Mendelssohn? Well, there is the single documented case of the Troubador Süsskind von Trimberg in the thirteenth century. Next, we have the long line of Court Jews who had to deal with

---

naming referring to "the last decade of the eighteenth century" is found, for instance, in *Moritz Lazarus und Heymann Steinthal. Die Begründer der Völkerpsychologie in ihren Briefen*. Mit einer Einleitung herausgegeben von Ingrid Belke, Tübingen 1971 (Schriftenreihe wissenschaftlicher Abhandlungen des Leo Baeck Instituts 21), in the appendix 'Die jüdische Volksschule in Anhalt von 1830–1840', p. 377.

[7]Lowenstein, *loc. cit.*, p. 180, note 3.

[8]I, New York 1954, pp. 143–146.

[9]*Ibid.*, p. 143.

[10]Berlin 1832, p. 466.

[11]Berlin 1760.

[12]Note c to the above quoted place (*op. cit.*, note 10).

the ruler and a variety of German citizens. Parallel to them the *shtadlanim*, who represented the Jewish community before German officialdom, must be mentioned. Further, one must not forget the class of Jewish wandering beggars, vagabonds and worse who, while on the one hand teaching not a little Yiddish to their Christian confrères on the road, acquired much of their German. This is profusely documented for the eighteenth century in Rudolph Glanz's book *Geschichte des niederen jüdischen Volkes in Deutschland.*[13] It quotes entries in police records where the absence of Judaeo-German speech characteristics is noticed with surprise: "redet übrigens die Francken Sprache, doch mit jüdischem Accent", "spricht Hochdeutsch mit e. geringen jüdischen Accent", "der jüdische Accent tritt wenig bei ihm hervor".[14]

Finally, and closest to Mendelssohn's time, we find an elite of well-to-do Jews, mostly in large towns, who enjoyed special privileges and – whether assimilated or not – followed the affluent German classes in dress, housing, mores, education, culture and language. Mendelssohn himself had learned his High German from such Jews in Berlin (augmented of course by intensive study on his own).[15] The use of High German among ordinary Jews probably only began in the last decades of the eighteenth century. Mendelssohn wrote in his letter of 29th August 1782 to *Assistenzrath* Klein about "... dem unter meinen Brüdern seit einiger Zeit aufkommenden Gebrauch der reinen deutschen Mundart".[16]

One must realise that the period of Mendelssohn's activity only marks the initial stage of transition from Judaeo-German to High German in the speech habits of the German Jews. The completion of this process lasted well over a century.[17]

[13]New York 1968.

[14]*Ibid.*, pp. 198–200.

[15]Cf. Moritz Kayserling, *Moses Mendelssohn. Sein Leben und Seine Werke*, Leipzig 1862, pp. 11–13; Alexander Altmann, *Moses Mendelssohn. A Bibliographical Study*, University of Alabama, 1973, pp. 22–24. The German addenda to the periodical *Hame'asef* from 1784 on show an excellent command of the German language by literary members of the Jewish elite.

[16]Cf. *Moses Mendelssohn Gesammelte Schriften, Jubiläumsausgabe* hereafter: *JubA*), 13, p. 80.

[17]This is true of both Judaeo-German speech (even though steadily decreasing and eventually only preserved in vestiges) and of writing High German in Hebrew letters. For the former, see Werner Weinberg, *Die Reste des Jüdisch-deutschen*, Stuttgart 1969, 1973. See further, 'Aus den Jugenderinnerungen Steinthals', in *Lazarus/Steinthal*, *op. cit.*, p. 375: "Wir Kinder kannten ein vierfaches Deutsch: unsere Eltern sprachen das eigentliche Jüdisch-Deutsch mit eingestreuten hebräischen Wörtern ... Die christlichen Knaben sprachen den ... Volksdialekt. Wir jüdische Knaben sprachen weder wie unsere Väter und Mütter, noch auch wie die christlichen Kinder ... Es war ein gemässigtes Judendeutsch ... In der Schule sollten wir Knaben reines Deutsch sprechen, was uns schwer ward, weil es uns geziert schien ..." (This description refers approximately to the years 1830–1835). Compare also the very beginning of Anton Ree's book, *Die Sprachverhältnisse der heutigen Juden* ... Hamburg 1844: "Thatsächlich sprechen noch bis auf den heutigen Tag viele Juden ihre Muttersprache [meant is High German] auf eine Weise, durch welche sie sich entschieden als Juden kenntlich machen." See also Monika Richarz (ed.), *Jüdisches Leben in Deutschland. Selbstzeugnisse zur Sozialgeschichte 1780–1871*, Stuttgart 1976, Veröffentlichung des Leo Baeck Instituts, pp. 53–54: "Diese Beispiele [of emancipation and German education among Jews around 1850] dürfen aber nicht darüber hinwegtäuschen ... daß vor allem die traditionelle Sprache der Juden das Judendeutsch nur sehr langsam schwand. Von den jüdischen Aufklärern ... verfolgt, lebte das Judendeutsch in der Mehrheit der jüdischen Bevölkerung, und vor allem auf dem Lande, noch bis weit über die Jahrhundertmitte fort." – There follow examples of natural Judaeo-German speech from around 1860 and 1870.

Referring to the reasons Yehuda Leib Minden lists for the way he designed his dictionary, Alexander Altmann summarises the status of German among one section of Jews around 1760 as follows:[18] "Here it is clearly stated that German Jews–that is, the educated upper class–spoke German and wanted their children to study the text of Scripture with the help of an adequate German translation."[19]

To further illustrate the acquisition of High German by German Jewry in the second half of the eighteenth century as an incipient and still shaky and unsettled process let me quote yet another passage from Altmann's book, which refers to the time when the Psalm Translation had appeared in 1783: "It has . . . to be borne in mind that the major part of Jewry in central Europe was incapable of understanding, let alone appreciating, the German translation".[20] This statement is aptly supported by a passage from a review of the 1778 specimen of the Pentateuch translation (see above) by the theologian Johann Christoph Doederlein:[21] "We doubt that the author will find many people among his co-religionists in Germany who understand his German. We showed the sample [of the translation] to several Jews of considerable learning. They had difficulty reading the German and making sense of it. As yet only a few are sufficiently advanced in the humanities [*an Geist, Genie und Sprache*] to derive pleasure and benefit from reading good and polished translations."[22] This state of affairs is further confirmed by the rejection of Mendelssohn's Pentateuch translation by the celebrated Rabbi Ezechiel Landau of Prague, a rejection not based on any fault Landau found with Mendelssohn, nor on any principal opposition to a German translation, but on the very excellence of Mendelssohn's literary German: "Because that translator [Mendelssohn] plumbed the depths of language to speak a very profound German to which only the greatest experts in German grammar are accustomed, and because it is hard on the [Jewish school]

For the continued use of the Hebrew alphabet in writing High German among Jews, see again Lowenstein's data (above), e.g., about the printing of Seligmann Baer Bamberger's Book *Amiro Lebeys Yaakauv* up to 1870, a Rödelheim "*techinno*" of 1879 and school exercises in the 1880s (*loc. cit.*, pp. 189–190). It may be added that Rödelheim prayerbooks, containing German directions in Hebrew letters were used right up to the final phase of German Jewry, even in the 1930s, and that this writer still learned "*Jüdischdeutsch*" – then understood to mean Hebrew cursive script applied to standard German – in his Jewish school in the 1920s.

[18]Altmann, *op. cit.*, p. 370.

[19]Again, a good illustration is found in Steinthal's recollections; *Lazarus/Steinthal*, *op. cit.*, p. 377, where he tells how his grandfather, around 1790, gave his sons a copy of Mendelssohn's Pentateuch with the words: "Nun werdet ihr das Chumosch richtig übersetzen lernen."

[20]Altmann, *op. cit.*, p. 377.

[21]From D. Johann Christoph Doederlein's *Theologische Bibliothek* . . . , Band I, Leipzig 1782, p. 156. Two years later, when the Pentateuch had appeared in its entirety, Doederlein, in a review in his *Theologische Bibliothek*, . . . III, 1 (1784), pp. 4–5; expressed his reservation once again: "Allein eben so sehr zweifeln wir, ob unter dem grössten Theil unsrer innländischen Juden so viel Kultur, Kentniß und Geschmack in Absicht auf deutsche Sprache angetroffen wird, als nöthig ist, diese Übersetzung nur verständlich, ich will nicht sagen, schön zu finden. Uns haben es wenigstens einige nicht ungelehrte Glieder einer angesehenen deutschen Synagoge, als wir sie ihnen vorlegten, offenherzig gestanden, daß sie für ihre Kentniß und Bildung zu gelehrt sey, und wir sahen es, daß es ihnen äuserst schwer fiel, nur die mit hebräischen Buchstaben geschriebenen Worte zu entziffern."

[22]Altmann, *op. cit.*, pp. 377–378.

אב · איבר / וועג /

אבדאך · דיא אברע רעקקע / דער באלקן / דאס דאך ·

אהנדן · מיט שטראפע בדענקן · „דער אבר ניכט אהנע אהנדונג הינגעהן לעסט" (שמות ל"ד ז') ·

איספאהן · אוספאהן / אוספאסן ·

אינבריבסטיג · מיט ווארמן הערצן ·

איננע ווערדן · גוואהר ווערדן · | אנמליין · אנגזלט ·

בארבארן · גרוואמע = בעזע מענשן

בוהלן · זיך אים איינם אנדרן ליבע בווערבן · ווירד אבר מייהטנס נור איב שלעכטן פרשטאנדע [פאן פרבאטנר ליבע] גברויכט ·

בוסע · שטראפע · דאפאר ביסן / שטראפע ליידן · איינע לוסט ביסן : איין פרגניגן זא גניסן / דאס עס אם ענדע שמערצן ברינגט ·

בענעדיין · זעגנען / לאבן | בערגן · שיצן · דאפאן פרבערגן ·

ברוט · [פאן ברימן] איינע אנצאל לעבנדר טהירע / זא צו איינר צייט אויס דען אייערן אויסגבריטט ווארדן · זא נון אלס פאם מענשן פראבשייעטע גווירב אויף דיזע ארט זיין לעבן ערהעלט : זא האט מאן אויך אונטר מענשנגשלעכטרן דיא יעניגע / דיא זיך דורך שלעכטע האנדלונגן דען אבשייא גוטר מענשן צוגצאגן / מיט דיזם נאמן בלעגט ·

[illegible]

דיאדעם · קעניגליכע הויפטבינדע · אין דען עלטרן צייטן טרוגן דיא קעניגע שטאט דער קראהנן שטירנבינדן / דיא זא היסן · דאהער מאן יעצט אויך נאך דיא קעניגליכן קראהנן צווויילן זא בנענט · | דיקיגט · דיקקס גביש ·

האדר · שטרייט / צאנק · | הארט · [פאן הארט] פעלזנשוטט ·

הארם · גראם / קוממר / גמיטהסשמערצן ·

הארדן · ווארטן / גדולד האבן / האפן ·

הולד · ליבע / גיטע · דאפאן האלדזיין / יעמאנדן גוט זיין ; האלדהאבן / ליב האבן ·

הולדיגן · צום אברהערן אנערקענגן ·

היידן · אבגעטער / מענשן דיא אבגעטטריא טרייבן ·

הייל · וואהלזיין / גליק · דאפאן אונהייל / אונגליק ; הייקן / גוונד מאכן · | היישן · פארדרן ·

העגן · פלעגן / ווארטן / צו ערהאלטן זוכן · דאהער בילדליך פאן איינם גדאנקן / דעם מאן גערנע נאכהענגט / מיט זיך הערום טרעגט · | העהנן · שפאטטן ·

וואהט · העפטיגר צארן · | וויטן · עטוואס מיט וואוט טהון

וואלן · אומהער געהן · | וואנדללאז · אונפרענדרליך ·

ווירדע · עהרע / אנזעהן · | וויעהנן גלויבן / דער מיינונג זיין ·

זאמט · פיר אינסגזאמט / מיט איינאנדר ·

זייך · קראנק · | זעכקן · זינקן מאכן ·

זעעליגקייט · עוויגס הייל · | טאבן · לערמן ·

טאנד · איין ניכטאיגר דינג / דאס קיינן בשטאנד / קיינן ווערט האט

פארשע · איינע ארט קריגס גווערר ·

טיקקע · בעזר ווילע / בעזע גדאנקן

טיראן · איין גרוזאממר אברהערר ·

Glossary of High German words, 1785–1790

By courtesy of Hebrew Union College – Jewish Institute of Religion, Cincinnati, Ohio

טעהנן · איינן טאָהן פֿאָן זיך געבן ·

טראָהן · דער שטול / אויף וועלכם איין פירשט אלס אבר הערר זיינם פֿאלקס זיצט · דאהער טראהנן / אלס אברהערר זיצן / דיא אבערהערשאפט פֿיהרן / רעגירן ·

טריומף · זיגספֿרייערע · טריומפֿיהרן / זיך דעס זיגס פֿרייען ·

טרימטר · דזא ציכרבלייבזל פֿאן עטוואס דאס פֿרדארבן איזט בזאנדרס פֿאן שטעדטן אונד גראסן גביידן ·

יובלגזאנג · פֿריידנגזאנג | יעהלינגס: פלעצליך / שנעל / גשווינד

לאָדרן · אויפֿפֿלאממן | מאַיעסטעט · קעניגליכֿס אנזעהן

מויל · פֿיר מוילטיר / מוילעזל ·

מיטעררייא · דאס אויפֿלעהנן דער אונטרטהאנן געגן איהרן אברהערן ·

מיינאייד · פֿאן אייד [איין שוואור] אונד מיינן [דער מיינונג זיין / גלויבן] איינע בטהיירונג / פֿאן וועלכר מאן פֿעלשליך גלויבט / דאס זיא איינע ווארהייט בקרעפֿטיגט · איין פֿאלשר שוואור ·

מילדע · גיטע / פֿרייגעביגקייט / וואהלטהעטיגקייט ·

מיריאַדע · איינע צאהל פֿאן צעהן טויזנד ·

ערהן · אויס ערץ · = מיט עהרנר קיילע · = (פזאלם 9. 2.) מיט אייזרנר קיילע ·

עמפערן · זיך עמפאר העבן / הערפֿאר העבן / אויפֿלעהנן / זיך געגן יעמאנד זעצן / בזאנדרס דיהנר געגן העררן ·

עמפפֿאנגן · מאן זאגט פֿאן איינר מוטטר / זיא עמפפֿעננגט דאס קינד / איזט שוואנגר / אונד גבעהרט ענדליך · זיהע (פזאלם 15.7) · | ערדראָסלן · ערווירגן ·

ערקאָהרן · ערוועהלט / דאפֿאן וויללקיהר / דיא וואַהל דעס וויללנס ·

פֿאַרר · איין שטיהר · | פזאַלם · הייליגר גזאנג ·

פֿיהרן · פֿאהרן מעכֿטן · זיהע (פזאלם 9. 18) ·

פֿייערעססע · פֿייערשמידע / פֿייערהערד ווארויף מעטאלל נארביטעט ווירד ·

פילגרים · איין וואנדרר / רייזנדר | פֿעהרליכקייט · פֿיר גפֿאהר

פעטטן · פֿעטשטיקקע / פֿעטטע זייטן ·

פעסטע · (1) פֿיר פֿעסטונג (2) בנעננונג דעס הימלסקרייזעס ·

פפֿאַד · דער פֿוסשטייג ·

פראַמן · גוט זיין · עס פראַממט מיר : עס איזט מיר גוט / ניצליך / אנגנעמען / אנשטענדיג · דאהער איין פראַמר : איין גטר / זיך אונד דער וועלט ניצליכר מאן · | פרהערן · פֿרוויסטן ·

פֿרזעהרן · פֿאן פֿרצעהרן / פֿרדערבן ·

פֿרליימדן · יעמאנדן בעזס נאכֿרעדן ·

פרקינדן · בקאנט מאכֿן / אויסרופֿן ·

פֿררוכטר · פֿאן פֿרריכֿן · עטוואס דאס זיינן גרוך פֿרלאהרן קיינן ווערט מעהר האט · דאפֿאן בילדליך איין מענש פֿאן שלעכֿטם קאראקטר · איין טויגעניכטס ·

צופֿרזיכֿט · פֿרטרויען · | ציהן · פֿיר צייגן / צייגע זאגן ·

רובלאָז · זיהע פֿררוכטר ·

ריגן · פֿאן ריגן [בוועגן] / אין בוועגונג זעצן · דאפֿאן בילדליך אינס גדעכֿטניס רופֿן · ווירד יעדאך נור פֿאם שטראפֿן גזאגט ; אונד מאן ריגט ענטוועדר דאס רעכֿט [דאס איברטרעטן ווארן] אדר דיא זינדע [דיא איברטרעטונג דעס רעכֿטס] אום צו שטראפֿן ·

רייזיג · צום קריגע גריסטעט ·

שאַלק · [אים אלט דייטשן / איין קנעכֿט] איין נידריגער = שלעכֿטר מענש · | שירם · שוץ ·

שמאַך · שאנדע / פֿראכֿטונג ·

שמעהן · שימפֿן / שמאך אנטהון · דאפֿאן פֿרשמעהן / פֿראכֿטן

שעמען · שאַטטנבילדר · | שענע · פֿיר שענהייט ·

Glossary of High German words, 1785–1790

boy to understand it, the teacher . . . is forced to spend the majority of the day . . . explaining German grammar to him. In this way, the day ends and the boy remains ignorant of the principles of the Torah. . . . The young are forced to spend their time with the books of the Gentiles in order to become accustomed to a refined German style so that, thereafter, they can study that [i.e., Mendelssohn's] translation, and our Torah becomes a handmaiden serving the German language . . ."[23]

If the status of High German among Jews was as yet fluid and wavering, their choice of alphabet, when writing it, was even more so. From the standpoint of an author and publisher it was obvious and made good sense that he would employ the German alphabet (Gothic or Latin letters) when a book was intended for a Christian readership, and the Hebrew alphabet, when the book was to be read by Jews. Thus the fact that the Pentateuch translation was printed in Hebrew letters but the Psalm translation in Gothic ones, forms a clear indication of the two different audiences Mendelssohn had in mind for either.[24] When Christian Gottlob Meyer wanted to make the Pentateuch specimen of 1778 accessible to his newly acquired Christian brethren he transliterated the translation into the Gothic alphabet.[25] And hardly had Mendelssohn's complete book of Genesis come off the press, when Professor Josias Friedrich Christian Löffler published it, too, in Gothic letters.[26]

For the reverse reason the young *Maskil* Joel Brill-Loewe[27] of Mendelssohn's circle transcribed Mendelssohn's translation of the Psalms into the Hebrew alphabet (square letters) and published it together with his own (Loewe's) "*Biur*" and Sforno's commentary, to make it both palpable and accessible to his co-religionists. (Do we detect a note of reproach on Loewe's side because Mendelssohn had aimed his translation so clearly at Christians and a handful of upper-class Jews?). Loewe acted with Mendelssohn's less than enthusiastic approval. In a letter of 6th March 1784, Mendelssohn wrote to Moses Fischer (translated from the Judaeo-German): "Here the Book of Psalms with my German translation is being printed by a young man who also adds the commentary of Rabbi Ovadiah Sforno."[28] He went into somewhat greater detail in a letter to Avigdor Levi of 22nd April 1784:[29] "Someone here has anticipated me in printing a *Biur* on Psalms, in which he wants to indicate, in Hebrew, the reasons underlying my translation. Moreover, the German translation is to be

[23]*Hame'asef*, 1786, p. 143; see also Altmann, *op. cit.*, pp. 821, note 106; further Joseph Klausner, *Historiah shel hasifrut ha-ivrit hahadashah*, vol. I, Jerusalem 1930, p. 55, note 4.

[24]Cf. Kayserling, *op. cit.*, p. 318.

[25]*Probe einer jüdisch-deutschen Uebersetzung der Fünf Bücher Moses von Herrn Moses Mendelssohn . . .*, Göttingen 1780. Cf. Meyer, *Bibliographie*, No. 249.

[26]*Die fünf Bücher Mose, zum Gebrauch der jüdischdeutschen Nation nach der Ueberzetzung des Herrn Moses Mendelssohn.* Erstes Buch. Berlin–Stettin, 1780. Cf. Meyer, *Bibliographie*, No. 251: "Im Buche selbst ist der Herausgeber nicht identifiziert; doch siehe Altmann, *Mendelssohn*, S. 389."

[27]Henceforth Loewe. He signs himself Joel Brill, also Joel Löwe (the name Brill being the acronym of *bereb Yehudah Leib* and the last word, in turn, the Yiddish of *Löwe*). In the literature, he is referred to as Brill (also Brüll) or Löwe (Loewe) or both. In an edition of the Pentateuch "nebst einer wörtlichen Übersetzung für Anfänger", Breslau 1799, he is listed as "Joel Brill genannt Löwe".

[28]*JubA*, 19, p. 291; see also Altmann, *op. cit.*, p. 364.

[29]*JubA*, 19, p. 292; here rendered in Altmann's translation, *op. cit.*, pp. 817–818, note 130.

printed in Hebrew characters. I permitted him to do this. I believe that he will do a good job . . . Should he miss my true meaning at times, no harm will be done. One day I intend to do the work myself, please God . . ."[30] Loewe, in turn, wrote in *Hame'asef*:[31] ". . . in meinem Kommentar zu . . . [Mendelssohn's] Psalmen-übersetzung, welchen ich mit Vorwissen, und Genehmigung meines unvergesslichen Lehrers herausgegeben habe . . .".

The year 1804–1805, cited by Lowenstein for the Hebraisation of the script for the Psalm-Translation, already refers to a later edition. Loewe's version, called *Sefer Zemirot Yisrael*, appeared originally in four parts, the first as early as 1785 (i.e., two years after the German-letter edition). The set was completed in 1790.[32] Counting here only the editions that are listed in Meyers *Bibliographie*,[33] we find seven more between 1800 and 1809 alone[34] and three additional ones in 1817, 1832 and 1846, respectively (Loewe himself had died in 1802). But there were more (see below).

The 'Glossary of difficult [German] words'[35] which was added in *Sefer Zemirot Yisrael* for the benefit of the average Jew is distributed over three of the four parts and each is found on four unnumbered pages following the individual title pages in the 1785–1790 edition as follows:

Part I	1st Book of Psalms	1785	105 words[36]
Part II	2nd Book of Psalms	1786	72 words
Part III	3rd Book of Psalms	1788	58 words
Part IV	4th & 5th Book of Psalms	1790	no glossary

The total count of different words is thus 235.[37]

Why did the mass of Jewish readers need this glossary of German words? Their acquisition of the German language was then just beginning, and only a small

[30]See also Kayserling, *op. cit.*, 2nd edn., 1888, p. 323.
[31]Deutsche Zugabe zum 5. Jahrgang, September 1789, p. 3.
[32]Berlin, im Verlag der jüdischen Freyschule.
[33]Nos. 302–314.
[34]No. 304 must be 1800 instead of 1880.
[35]Lowenstein, *loc. cit.*, p. 189.
[36]The number of words given here includes boldface entry words, derived forms and etymons, but not declined or basic forms of the entry word or reference words to other entries.
[37]The three lists were continued throughout the later editions with only slight editorial differences. In comparing the original 1785–1790 edition with one of 1820 (Breslau, "gedruckt und zu haben bei Löbel Sulzbach"), we observe the following changes: Short entries, which in the original edition are often printed in the empty space left in the last line of the previous entry (see below), are now given equal status with longer entries: almost every entry begins with a new line. There are the following orthographic changes: more generous pointing, compound words or words with prefixes more often written together, more consistent doubling of consonants (including double *kuf* for *ck*), which is found only sporadically in the first edition and *tet-tsade* for *tz*, which is missing entirely from the first edition. Further an *ayin* has been inserted to express *e* in the infinitive ending and in many other situations; vowel lengthening by *h* is often omitted (*erklähren*>*erklären*); there are occasional stylistic changes, e.g., in List I under *Obdach*: Oberdecke>obere Decke, in List II under *Buben*: "in noch härterem Verstand">"im noch härteren Verstande", under *Trift*: "Vieh das zusammen ausgetriben wird">"Vieh das zusammengetriben wird". Entries of the second list which were marked with an asterisk in the first edition to signify that they had been forgotten in List I, have now been put into that list in their alphabetical space – however, in List III the asterisked words remain (except for *walten*). No entries of 1785–1790 were omitted in the 1820 lists. In the transcriptions below, the later changes have not been considered.

Jewish elite knew German well. (But even the champion of that elite, namely Moses Mendelssohn, still used Hebrew letters for part of his correspondence in High German[38] and wrote High German notes for himself using Hebrew letters).[39] The interesting fact about Loewe's glossary is that it records a phase of the transition in language habits. Two observations in particular seem to illustrate the transitory character of the period concerning the development toward German. First: Part IV of the series appeared without a glossary; one is tempted to conclude that in Loewe's judgment the German of his readership had sufficiently improved since the publication of Part I to render glossaries to Books IV and V of Psalms unnecessary. But such an inference is probably too rash, and Loewe himself gives us no clues, about his discontinuing the glossary. The fact that at a later date he published a Pentateuch 'nebst einer wörtlichen Übersetzung für Anfänger', i.e., in easy German,[40] shows that in his judgment his fellow Jews were still in the process of perfecting their German. The conclusion that at a given time a glossary was no longer considered necessary rests more substantially on a second observation: in the 1832 editions[41] all glossaries are omitted. The publishers must have had good reason to think that the initial phase of the adoption of High German by the Jews had come to an end (even though a 1825–1828 Dyhernfurth edition still featured the word lists).

This deduction becomes quite plausible when one considers that a generation had passed since the first publication of *Sefer Zemirot Yisrael* and that during this time two powerful forces had been at work, advancing the cause of High German among German Jews. One was governmental decisions by *Länder*, principalities and municipalities that granted differing measures of civil rights to the Jews, part and parcel of which was, as a rule, an edict about replacing Judaeo-German with High German for all official purposes.[42] The second force was the founding of

[38]See *JubA*, 19, Letters 276 and 282. See also Borodianski's remarks in the Introduction, pp. XXV–XXVI.

[39]For instance on a manuscript of his translation of the Psalms, which is described in the forthcoming vol. X of *JubA*.

[40]Breslau, 1797, 1802.

[41]Karlsruhe, Vienna.

[42]In the framework of this essay only a few examples must be listed. Individual and limited official proposals and initiatives date back to the *early* part of the eighteenth century. See, for instance, Selma Stern, *Der preußische Staat und die Juden*, Tübingen 1962–1971 (Schriftenreihe wissenschaftlicher Abhandlungen des Leo Baeck Instituts 7, 8 & 24), I, 1 pp. 107, 118; I,2, 453; II,1. 148; II,2, pp. 54, 146–150, and more. Further, Ismar Freund, *Die Emanzipation der Juden in Preußen*, Berlin 1912, pp. 46–47 (in Friedrich II's 'Generalreglement'.). The *Tolerance Patent* of Emperor Joseph II of 1782 is usually considered the first major document among the edicts combining emancipation with the furthering of High German. There we read in §13: "Bei so vielen der Judenschaft eröffneten Erwerbungs-Wegen und dem dadurch entspringenden mannigfaltigeren Zusammenhange mit Christen fordert die Sorgfalt für die Aufrechterhaltung des gemeinschaftlichen Zutrauens, daß die hebräische, und hebräisch mit deutsch vermengte sogenannte jüdische Sprache, und Schrift abgeschaffet werde. Wir heben daher den Gebrauch derselben in allen öffentlichen inn- und außer gerichtlichen Handlungen ausdrücklich auf, und verordnen, daß sie statt derselben sich künftig der landesüblichen Sprache bedienen" (from the HUC-JIR, Cincinnati, copy of the *Toleranz-Patent* for the *Land* Mähren). In the *Juden-Privileg* of 1792, §28 reads in part: ". . . sollen die Kinder in der deutschen allgemein verständlichen Sprache und Schrift ohne Beimischung hebräischer oder rabbinischer Ausdrücke angeführt werden, und die Juden . . . gerichtlich and außergerichtlich keiner andern als dieser Sprache und Schrift . . . sich bedienen" (from: Ludwig Geiger, *Geschichte der*

modern Jewish schools with German figuring prominently in the curriculum. These schools were in part the direct outcome of those government decrees and in part the fulfilment of the dreams and the fruit of hard work by leading *Maskilim*.[43]

When Lowenstein notes that Loewe's glossary contains "such ordinary words as 'Unfall', 'Busse', 'Gruft', 'Heiden', 'Wut', 'Tyrann', and 'Thron'"[44] his point is of course, that these words are ordinary for later generations, but were obviously not so considered by the majority of German Jews during the half-century from 1780 to 1830.

As we study the glossary, reproduced partly and transcribed fully in the Appendix at the end of this article, we notice that we are dealing not so much with "difficult" words but with a vocabulary that, as a class, was not part of the German of the contemporary, ordinary Jew. It was the literary vocabulary of the educated, even, one could say, those highly educated in German literature. Below, an attempt is made to group some of these words into categories within the vocabulary of high literacy. Meanwhile, let us see what Loewe himself discloses about his intentions in adding the glossary to Mendelssohn's translation. First, there is the neutral title he gave his glossary: 'Explanation of some High German words'. We take note of the fact that he did not speak of "difficult" or "rare" words, but, for reasons of his own, preferred not to characterise the type of words he found it necessary to explain. Notes to the 2nd and 3rd lists tell us that words carrying an asterisk had been forgotten or were not quite correctly explained in the earlier lists. This means that in 1788 Loewe's opinion – that his readership needed a glossary – had certainly not changed from three years before. The note for his first list contains a slight hint at his underlying intention concerning his choice of glossary words: he is convinced that he renders his readers a service by

---

Juden in Berlin, II, Berlin 1871, p. 356). In the first letter from the *Konsistorium* of the short-lived Kingdom of Westphalia (1807–1814) to the Jewish congregations it says: "Alle Aufsätze [Schreiben] an das Konsistorium müssen in der deutschen Sprache . . . mit deutschen Buchstaben deutlich geschrieben sein" (from: Bernhard Brilling, 'Briefe des Königlichen Westfälischen Konsistoriums der Israeliten in Kassel . . .', *Udim*, IV (1973), p. 41. Brilling mentions also a much earlier law for the city of Breslau: ". . . sind alle Handlungsbücher, kaufmännische Rechnungen, die Gemein- und Almosenbücher in deutscher Schrift zu fertigen . . . ; *ibid.*, note 11). §2 of the *Emanzipationsedikt* of 1812 reads in part: ". . . daß sie nicht nur bei Führung ihrer Handelsbücher sondern auch bei Abfassung ihrer Verträge . . . der deutschen . . . Sprache, und bei ihren Namens-Unterschriften keiner andern, als deutscher oder lateinischer Schriftzüge sich bedienen sollen" (from: *Edikt betreffend die bürgerlichen Verhältnisse der Juden in dem Preussischen Staate*, Berlin 1812). And so the stream of edicts of tolerance, emancipation, and civic rights continued (interrupted only during the period of reaction after Napoleon's defeat), almost without exception accompanied by the demand to expedite the acquisition of High German and often making this requirement the condition for granting those rights and privileges.

[43]Prominently among them David Friedländer and Naphtali Herz Wessely. The first of this chain of schools was the Berlin *Freischule*, founded in 1778, whose *Lesebuch* (Berlin 1779), incidentally, still figured a 'Gebräuchliches jüdisches Alphabet im Schreiben', i.e. Judaeo-German cursive script (inserted between pages 8 and 9). There followed the *Königliche Wilhelmschule* of Breslau in 1791 (whose founding director was none other than Joel Brill-Loewe), the *Herzogliche Franzschule* of Dessau in 1799, the *Jacobson-Schule* of Seesen in 1801, and the *Samsonsche Freischule* of Wolfenbüttel in 1807. Cf. Mordechai Eliav, *Hahinukh hayehudi be-Germaniah bimey ha-Haskalah* . . . , Jerusalem 1961, pp. 71 ff, 83 ff., 87 ff., 96 ff., 104 ff.

[44]*Loc. cit.*, p. 189.

explaining those High German words which the translator employed "for the sake of beautiful and vigorous expression" but which in regular life ("im gemeinen Leben") are rarely or never heard and which, therefore, "might be unknown to many" (a polite understatement).

Whether or not there is, woven through the lines of the last remark, another, ever so humble criticism – this time directed at Mendelssohn's all too sophisticated German – the fact is that Mendelssohn, in his endeavour to demonstrate to the Christian world the poetical beauty of the Psalms, uses such an exquisite language that one sometimes wonders whether he was not carried away by his undertaking.

The degree of unfamiliarity of the average German Jew with some of the glossary words (in Loewe's judgment) can be seen especially, when he adds the definite article to a noun for the benefit of the reader to learn its gender. Thus, e.g., in List III: *Ungeheuer* (das), *Gespann* (das), *Hefen* (die), *Seuche* (die), *Söller* (der), *Märe* (die) *Zähre* (die), *Reich* (das).

Some examples of Loewe's literary High German words, arranged by categories are (examples are listed in the order of the three glossaries):

Archaic and Poetical Words (these two categories are often overlapping): *ahnden, umfahn, buhlen, (Lust) büßen, Gruft, Hader, harren, Hort, Huld, holdhaben, huldigen, heischen, hegen, wallen, wandeln, siech, ehern, empfangen (ein Kind), Farr, Feste, frommen ("es frommt mir") versehren, zeihen, ruchlos, Schalk, Schirm (Schutz), Ahnen (Voreltern), Bubenstück, bieder, Gezücht, holdselig, wogen, walten, waschen (schwatzen), Wesen, Leu, Zwinger, betören, weben (sich bewegen), Söller, Märe, erkiesen, verwesen (verwalten), Zähre.*

Infrequent Words, "Choice" Words from Several Synonyma: inbrünstig, inne werden, wähnen, Tand, jählings, lodern, Drangsal, Widersacher, Zwiespalt, ungestüm, Eiland, Denkspruch, Wipfel, öde, Fittig, versiegen, Kerker.

Freely coined compounds:[45] *Landzweig, Ätherwüste, Feierkleidung, Erdengötter, Schattenglück, Schreckgesicht.*

Terms belonging to areas with which Jews were as a rule unfamiliar: Theology: *Buße, Heil, Seligkeit, Zuversicht, Hölle.* Romantic nature: *Wasserfall, Äther ("Himmelsluft"), Hain, rieseln.* Agriculture: *Trift, Flur, Gespann, düngen, Hürden, Senkreben.* Military: *Tartsche, reisig, Geschoß, Kriegsgespann, schleifen (eine Festung)*, Political: *Staat, Reich.*

Rare or Archaic Grammatical Forms: führen (subjunctive of *fahren*), *ergeußt (ergießen), zeuchst* (ziehen).

[45]It seems that the coining of compounds in German was fashionable in Mendelssohn's time. Perusing the first Book of Psalms in his translation, we noticed the following unusual compounds, many of which were probably Mendelssohn's own coinage: *Beutebegieriger* (V, 7), *unglücksschwanger* (VII, 15), *Blutschuldrächer* (IX, 13), *Mordgebeine* (X, 10), *Wundergüte* (XII, 7), *Rachschwerdt* (*ibid.*, 13), *Schutzfels* (XVIII, 3), *Glutflamm* (*ibid.*, 9), *Zornhauch* (*ibid.*, 16), *Speisegaben* (XX, 4), *Todesschattenthal* (XXIII, 5), *Schmachred* (XXXI, 14); *Redlichgesinnte* (XXXIII, 1), *Zehnsaitenpsalter* (*ibid.*, 2), *Todesfährlichkeit* (*ibid.*, 19) *Betrüglichreden* (XXXIV), *Trauersack* (XXXV, 13), *mundverzerrend* (*ibid.*, 16), *Löwengrimm* (*ibid.*, 17), *Lebensurquell* (XXXVI, 10), *Unrechtthäter* (XXXVII, 1), *Redlichwandelnder* (*ibid.*, 14). Perez Sandler, *Habe'ur latorah shel Moshe Mendelssohn vesi'ato*, Jerusalem 1941, p. 71, notes Mendelssohn's partiality to self-coined compounds also in the Pentateuch translation. Thus he lists: *Vorderhauptbinde* (*totafot*, Exodus XIII:16) and *Religionsfeuerglut* (*esh dat lamo*, Deuteronomy XXXIII:2).

"Foreign" words:[46] *Barbaren, benedeien, Diadem, Tyrann, Triumph, Majestät, Myriade, Monarch, Firmament, Residenz, Psalter, Regent.*

A few remarks may precede the rendition of the glossaries:

(1) Loewe did more than define words. He went into etymologies and added derivations. In this he was, however, not always fortunate and we may disagree with either his definitions or derivations and, especially, with some of his etymologies. Among the latter we call attention to the words *Meineid, Frommer, versehren, Verruchter, zeihen, rügen, Hort, Horde, Hölle, zerschellt,* inviting a comparison with the etymologies given in Grimm's *Wörterbuch.*

(2) The German words in Hebrew letters are arranged according to the Hebrew alphabet. This makes for a non-alphabetical order to the German transcription. Hebrew initial *alef* can stand for *a, i, o,* or *u* (while *e* or *ä* are found in the alphabetical place of Hebrew *ayin*); *d (dallet)* follows *g (gimmel); w (vav)* follows *h (he); j (yod)* follows *t (tet)*; etc. Hebrew *pe* can stand for *f, pf, ph,* and *v.*

(3) For the transcription, a German orthography is employed that is indicated by the Hebrew original (one does well to realise that the spelling of neither German nor Judaeo-German was definitely standardised in the eighteenth century);[47] e.g., *bider* (*ie* is indicated by *yod-alef* only in *die* and *sie*), *erklähren, bedihnen, umfahen, Krohne, Trohn, Uebersezer, from (fromm).* Changes in conventional German orthography are made where the Hebrew alphabet falls short of rendering exactly German graphic features, such as *Umlaute ä, ö, ü,* diphthongs *ei, ai, au, eu, äu*; further *y, ch, ck* (for double *kuf*), *qu, sch.* For *samech* ß or *ss* are used in conformance with conventional German orthography. The infinitive, plural and case ending *-n* is changed to *-en* and, altogether, an *e* is inserted where the text – if more elaborately pointed – would probably have a *segol*, or where it might have rendered unstressed *e* by *ayin* (as done in the 1820 edition).[48] Capitalisation is introduced and follows conventional German orthography. The periods or commas after the entry words are omitted.

(4) Probably for reasons of paper economy, no new line is started for short entries that fit into the free space of the last line of the previous entry. The new entry is then separated by a vertical line.

[46]To the native speaker of German, words of Greek or Latin origin, even if fully absorbed and technically belonging to the category of loan words may appear as "not quite German".

[47]Cf. Borodianski in *JubA*, 19, p. xxix.

[48]See note 37; cf. also Borodianski, *loc. cit.*, p. xxx, on Mendelssohn's handling of unstressed *e* in his Judaeo-German orthography.

I,1

APPENDIX

*Erklährung einiger hochdeutscher Wörter**

ob über, wegen.
Obdach die Oberdecke, der Balken, das Dach.
ahnden mit Strafe bedenken. "Der aber nicht ohne *Ahndung* hingehen läßt" (Ex. XXXIV:7).
umfahn umfangen, umfassen.
inbrünstig mit warmen Herzen.
inne werden gewahr werden. / *Antlitz* Angesicht.
Barbaren grausamme=böse Menschen.
buhlen sich um eines anderen Liebe bewerben. Wird aber meistens nur im schlechten Verstande [von verbotener Liebe] gebraucht.
Buße Strafe. Davon *büßen*, Strafe leiden. Eine Lust *büßen*: ein Vergnügen so genießen, daß es am Ende Schmerzen bringt.
benedeien segnen, loben. / *bergen* schützen. Davon *verbergen*.
Brut [von *brüten*] eine Anzal lebender Thiere, so zu einer Zeit aus den Eiern ausgebrütet worden. Da nun alles vom Menschen verabscheuete Gewürm auf diese Art sein Leben erhällt: so hat man auch unter Menschengeschlechtern die jenigen, die sich durch schlechte Handlungen den Abscheu guter Menschen zugezogen, mit diesem Namen belegt.

* Ich glaube verschiedenen unter meinen Lesern einen Gefallen damit zu erzeigen, wen ich ihnen die in den Psalmen vorkommenden hochdeutschen Wörter erklähre, deren sich der Übersezer des schönen und kraftvollen Ausdruks willen bedihnt, die aber im gemeinen Leben, theils selten, theils gar nicht vorkommen, und dahero vielen unbekant sein möchten.

Der Herausgeber.

I,2

Gruft Grube.
Diadem königliche Hauptbinde. In den ältern Zeiten trugen die Könige stat der Krohnen Stirnbinden, die so hißen. Daher man jezt auch noch die königlichen Krohnen zuweilen so benent. / *Dikigt* dickes Gebüsch.
Hader Streit, Zank. / *Hort* [von hart] Felsenschutz.
Harm Gram, Kummer, Gemüthsschmerzen.
harren warten, Geduld haben, hoffen.
Huld Libe, Güte, Davon *holdsein*, jemanden gut sein; *holdhaben*, lib haben.
huldigen zum Oberherrn anerkennen.
Heiden Abgöterer, Menschen die Abgötterei treiben.
Heil Wohlsein, Glük. Davon *Unheil* Unglük; *heilen*, gesund machen. / *heischen*, fordern.
hegen flegen, warten, zu erhalten suchen. Daher bildlich von einem Gedanken, dem man gerne nachhängt, mit sich herum trägt. / *höhnen* spotten.
Wut heftiger Zorn. *wüten* etwas mit *Wut* thun.

wallen umher gehen. / *wandellos*, unveränderlich.
Würde Ehre, Ansehn. / *wähnen* glauben, der Meinung sein.
samt für *insgesamt*, mit einander.
siech krank. / *senken*, sinken machen.
Seeligkeit ewiges Heil. / *toben*, lärmen.
Tand ein nichtig Ding, das keinen Bestand, keinen Wert hat.
Tartsche eine Art Krigs Gewehr.
Tücke böser Wille, böse Gedanken.
Tyran ein grausammer Oberherr.

I,3
töhnen einen Tohn von sich geben.
Trohn der Stul, auf welchem ein Fürst als Oberherr seines Volkes sizt. Daher *trohnen*, als Oberherr sizen, die Oberherrschaft führen, regiren.
Triumf Sigesfreude. *triumfihren*, sich des Siges freuen.
Trümmer die Überbleibsel von etwas das verdorben ist besonders von Städten und großen Gebäuden.
Jubelgesang Freudengesang. / *jählings* plözlich, schnel, geschwind.
lodern aufflammen. / *Majestät* königliches Ansehn.
Maul für *Maultir*, Maulesel.
Meuterei das Auflehnen der Unterthanen gegen ihren Oberherrn.
Meineid von *Eid* [ein Schwur] und *meinen* [der Meinung sein, glauben] eine Betheuerung, von welcher man fälschlich glaubt, das sie eine Warheit bekräftigt. Ein falscher Schwur.
Milde Güte, Freigebigkeit, Wohlthätigkeit.
Myriade eine Zahl von zehn tausend.
ehern aus Erz. "Mit eherner Keule." (Psalm II:9.) mit eiserner Keule.
empören sich empor heben, hervor heben, auflehnen, sich gegen jemand sezen, besonders Dihner gegen Herrn.
empfangen man sagt von einer Mutter, sie *empfängt* das Kind, ist schwanger, und gebährt endlich. Sihe (Psalm VII:15.). / *erdrosseln* erwürgen.
erkohren erwählt, davon *Willkühr*, die Wahl des Willens.
Farr ein Stihr. / *Psalm* heiliger Gesang.
führen fahren möchten. Sihe (Psalm IX:18.).
Feueresse Feuerschmide, Feuerherd worauf Metall bearbeitet wird.

I,4
Pilgrim ein Wanderer, Reisender. / *Fährlichkeit* für Gefahr.
Fetten Fettstücke, fette Seiten.
Feste (1) für Festung (2) Benennung des Himmelskreises.
Pfad der Fußsteig.
frommen gut sein. es *frommt* mir: es *ist* mir *gut*, nüzlich, angemessen, anständig. Daher ein *Frommer*: ein guter, sich und der Welt nüzlicher Man. / *verheeren* verwüsten.
versehren von *verzehren*, verderben.
verleumden jemanden Böses nachreden.
verkünden bekant machen, ausrufen.

Verruchter von *verrichen*. Etwas das seinen Geruch verlohren, keinen Wert mehr hat. Davon bildlich ein Mensch von schlechtem Charakter, ein Taugenichts.

Zuversicht Vertrauen. / *zeihen* für *zeugen*, Zeuge sagen.

ruchlos sihe *Verruchter*.

rügen von *regen* [bewegen], in Bewegung sezen. Davon bildlich ins Gedächtnis rufen. Wird jedoch nur vom Strafen gesagt; und man *rügt* entweder das *Recht* [das übertreten worden] oder die *Sünde* [die Übertretung des Rechts] um zu strafen.

reisig zum Krige gerüstet.

Schalk [im Alt Deutschen, ein Knecht] ein nidriger=schlechter Mensch. / *Schirm* schuz.

Schmach Schande, Verachtung.

schmähen schimpfen, Schmach anthun. Davon *verschmähen*, verachten.

Schemen Schattenbilder. / *Schöne* für Schönheit.

II,1 *Erklährung einiger hochdeutschen Wörter**

Ahnen Voreltern [wird besonders bei vornehmen Familien gesagt].

Untife eine seichte sumpfige Stelle im Wasser.

**Unfall* Unglük. / **albern* närrisch.

Buben (im einzelen ein) *Bube*. Ein Knabe. Wird jedoch im Hochdeutschen nur im gehäßigen Verstande gebraucht, von einem ungezogenen Knaben. In noch härterem Verstande aber auch von lasterhaften erwaksenen Personen. (Davon) ein

Bubenstük die böse That eines solchen Menschen.

bider (eigentlich) fest, dauerhaft. (Daher auch) tauglich (und endlich) from, rechtschafen. (Davon) *Biderman, Biderherz, Bidersin*.

Beute (1) Jeder Gewin. (2) Besonders was man im Krig dem Feinde an beweglichen Gütern abnimt. (Davon) *erbeuten*, auf solche Weise bekommen.

bestehen (heißt unter anderen Bedeutungen auch) überwinden.

Gedicht (sihe *dichten*) eine künstliche Rede [die zur Absicht hat auf die Empfindung zu wirken].

Gefolg (1) ein Haufe mehrer Menschen die einem anderen folgen.
(2) die Manschaft die einen großen Herrn begleitet.

Gezücht (von *Zucht*). Die Jungen oder Nachkommen eines lebendigen Geschöpfs, wird aber nur noch im verächtlichen Verstande gebraucht, wie *Brut* (sihe ersten Theil).

gezükt wie *gezogen*. [wird besonders von Schwerdtern gesagt, die aus der Scheide gezogen sind.]

**Geschoß* Werkzeug zum Schißen.

* Alle die mit einem* bezeichneten Worte, sind solche, deren Erklärung im ersten Theile vergessen wurden.

II,2

dichten (1) (von deuchten, denken) nachdenken, im Nachdenken begrifen sein. (Davon) *erdichten*. Sich etwas erdenken, das nicht wirklich ist. (2) (von dicht machen), zusammen sezen. (Davon) Lügen dichten. (3) Gedanken zusammen sezen, ein Gedicht machen. (Sihe *Gedicht*). (4) verfertigen, hervorbringen [besonders mit der Sprache].

**Drangsal* Bedrückung, Bedrängung. Imgleichen die dadurch verursachte schmerzhafte Empfindung.

Hohn mit Spot verbundene Verachtung. (Davon) *höhnen*, verspotten. / *holdselig* sihe *selig*.

Horde (von *Heerde*) eine Gesellschaft herumwandernder Menschen; [als die Familien einiger morgenländischen Völker, die von der Vihzucht leben]. Im Deutschen verbindet man mit disem Worte gemeiniglich einen verächtlichen Neben-Begrif, daher man einen Haufen ungesiteter räuberischer Leute eine Horde nent.

Hölle (von hohl). Ein hohler, verstekter, verborgener Ort. (Alsdan) die tifsten Räume der Erde. (Ferner) das Grab, (auch) der Zustand nach dem Tode, das Reich der Todten. (Und endlich) der Aufenthalt der Bösen nach disem Leben und der Ort ihrer Bestrafung.

Wogen Meeres-wellen. / *walten* nach Willkühr handeln.

Wasserfall wo das Wasser, entweder durch Röhren geleitet, oder durch die Natur, von einem hohen in einen nidren Ort herabfällt. / *waschen* schwazen.

Widersacher Feinde [die in allen Sachen wider uns sind].

Wesen (im alten Deutschen sein daher jezt) der Name jedes Dinges das wirklich ist.

**Sehne* eine Schnur die Schnellkraft hat. [die man aus-spannen kan, und die beim Loslassen zurükprallt.]

II,3

selig (1) bedeutet eine Menge, ein Reichthum gewisser Dinge, als *redselig*, gesprächig, wortreich. (Ferner) *glükselig, mühselig, armselig, holdselig* und andere mehr [vil Glük, Mühe, Armut, Huld haben]. (2) als ein Adjektivum bedeutet es gut, in einem hohen Grade glüklich, (und ferner) des himmlischen Glüks nach disem Leben theilhaftig, (davon) die *Seligen*, die Guten, die [in jenem Leben] Glüklichen. (Und) die *Seligkeit*. Die künftige Wohlfahrt der Frommen. Das ewige Leben.

Trift (von *treiben*) (1) Das Vih das zusammen ausgetriben wird, eine *Heerde* Schafe, Kühe u.s.w. (2) Der Ort worauf getriben wird, die Weide.

**lallen* wird von Kindern gesagt, die zu reden anfangen.

Landzunge (für) Land-Strich, Stük Landes [indem die verschidenen Provinzen und Städte eben so die Theile des ganzen Staates ausmachen, wie die Zweige die Theiles eines Baumes sind. / **Leu* ein Löwe.

Monarch Allein-Herrscher. Regent. [König oder Kaiser].

Äther eine feine flüßige Materie, die subtiler als die Luft ist, und mit welcher der Raum des Himmels angefüllt sein soll. Die Himmels-Luft. (Davon) die

Ätherwüste, der weite unermeßliche Raum des Himmels, der disen Äther enthält.

Estrich (1) Ein von Steinen oder anderer Materie verfertigtes Pflaster. (2) Der gepflasterte Fußboden eines Zimmers. / *Ergeußt*, von ergißen.

II,4

Posaune eine Art großer Trompeten.

Farr ein junger zweijähriger Oks. Ein Stihr.

Feierkleidung die Kleidung an Fest- und Feiertagen.

Firmament der sichtbare Himmel, an welchem die Sterne glänzen. [Weil man ehedem glaubte der Himmel bestehe aus einer festen Materie, daher stat dises Worts auch zuweilen das Wort *Feste* üblich ist wie Psalm XIX.2.].

Flur (unter anderen Bedeutungen auch) mehrere nebeneinander ligende Äcker.

vermummen durch Verhüllung (Einwiklung] unkentlich machen.

verschlagen (heißt unter anderen Bedeutungen auch) listig.

Zohne (im weitläufigsten Sinne) jede Gegend der Erdkugel, in Betracht ihrer Entfernung von dem Äquator [die Linie unter der Sonne].

Zwiespalt (von zwei und spalten) Trennung, Streit.

Zwinger eine Vormauer in einem Festungs Werke.

zeuchst (von) zihen. (so *verzeuch* von) verzihen, warten.

**zermalmen* zu Staub zerstoßen.

zerschellt in kleinen Schollen [Stücken] zerbrochen.

raffen fortreißen. Schnell und mit Gewalt wegnehmen.

Residenz der Wohnort eines regirenden Herrn.

Staat eine zahlreiche Gesellschaft von Menschen, welche zur Beförderung ihrer Glükseligkeit unter der gemeinschaftlichen Bande einer Regirungsform stehen. (Davon) die *Staaten* die Reiche.

III,1 *Erklährung einiger hochdeutschen Wörter**

Ungeheuer (das), ein Ding welches wegen seiner Größe oder Wildheit Furcht und Entsezen verursacht; in welchem Verstande man sehr große und ungewöhnliche Thire so zu benennen pflegt.

ungestüm heftige Bewegung, starkes Geräusch.

Eiland eine Insel, ein Stük Land das um und um vom Meer umgeben ist.

Anstoß (unter anderen Bedeutungen) ein begangener Fehler.

Beginnen (im figürlichen Verstande) das Unternehmen, Vorhaben.

bethört (1) zum Thoren gemacht. (2) verblendet, verführt.

bescheiden zutheilen, als einen bestimmten Theil anweisen. (Davon) die Sache ist ihm beschiden.

Gefider die vilen Federn an einem Tihre oder sonstigem Dinge.

Gespan (das), so vil Thire einer Art als gewöhnlich zusammen gespant werden; besonders von Pferden. (Davon) *Krigs-Gespan*, was vor Krigswagen gespant wird.

düngen den Erdboden fett und fruchtbar machen. (Davon) der *Dünger*, der Mist, und überhaupt alles, wodurch ein Acker fruchtbar wird.

Diejenigen Wörter die mit *bezeichnet sind, sind solche, deren Erklährung in den früheren Theilen entweder vergessen oder nicht ganz richtig angegeben worden.

III,2

Denk-Spruch ein Ausspruch der an eine wichtige Sache oder Wahrheit erinern soll.

Hain ein kleines Gehölz, Lustwäldchen.

Hürden von Weiden oder sonstigen Zweigen geflochtene Wände, welche den Schafen des nachts zur Sicherheit dihnen, und an einander gesezt werden können.

Hefen (die), dasjenige bei einer Flüßigkeit, das durch die Gährung in die Höhe getriben wird, und sich hernach zu Boden sezt. Es heißt auch die Mutter oder die Berme. (Figürlich) die Hefen austrinken müßen, die Strafe in aller ihrer Schwere leiden.

**walten* (1) thätig sein, wirken. (2) Das Veränderliche an einer Sache nach eigenem Gutdünken bestimmen. (3) regiren, herrschen.

**wallen* gehen, besonders wenn es mit einiger freudigen und tanzenden Bewegung untermischt ist.

**wandeln* (1) eine Veränderung leiden, sich verändern. (2) den Ort verändern, gehen. (3) sich aufführen, seine sittliche Handlungen auf eine gewiße Art einrichten. (Davon) der *Wandel*, die Aufführung.

Wipfel der obere leicht bewegliche Theil der Bäume und Gewäkse.

weben (im Altdeutschen) sich bewegen, besonders, sich langsam bewegen.

Seuche (die) eine jede langwirige Krankheit, (im engeren Verstande) eine anstekende Krankheit.

Söller (der) dasjenige was man gemeiniglich den Boden an einem Hause zu nennen pflegt; das oberste Fachwerk unterm Dache.

III,3

Senk-Reben (oder auch) der *Senker*, im Wein- und Gartenbau, ein Zweig, Reis oder Rebe, welches zur Fortpflanzung in die Erde gebeugt worden, damit es daselbst Wurzel schlage.

täuschen hintergehen, in der Erwartung betrügen.

lüstern ein unmäßiges sinliches Verlangen nach etwas haben.

meistern wegen beßere (wirkliche oder eingebildete) Einsichten die Handlungen eines andern tadeln; den Meister spilen.

Mähre (die) ein Mährchen, eine erdichtete Erzählung, unwahre Geschichte.

Öde leer, unbewohnt und unbebauet, Wüste.

Erden-Götter die Großen und Vornehmen dieser Welt.

erkisen aussuchen, auslesen, erwählen.

Psalter ein sehr altes musikalisches Instrument, das zehn Saiten hatte, und eine Art von Harfe war, womit man den Gesang zu begleiten pflegte.

Fittig der Flügel an einem Vogel. / *feist* fett.

verwesen (von *ver sein*) einem Dinge vorstehen, die Aufsicht über etwas haben, verwalten. (Davon) ein *Verweser*, Verwalter.

versigen (heißt bei Flüßigkeiten) nach und nach in die Erde einzihen und verschwinden, (davon) austroknen.

Zähre (die) ist gleichbedeutend mit Thräne.

Kost die Speise. / *Kerker* (der) ein Gefängnis.

Rotte (eigentlich) mehrere bei einander befindliche lebendige Dinge einer Art. Gewöhnlich braucht man dises Wort aber nur im schlechten Verstande von Personen welche sich zu einer lasterhaften schädlichen Absicht versammelt. (Davon) sich *rotten*, sich in solcher Absicht versammeln, verbinden.

III,4

riseln das sanfte Flißen der Quellen und Bäche.

**Reich* (das) ein Gebiht, eine Provinz, ein Land, so jemandes Herrschaft unterworfen ist.

Regent derjenige welcher andere regiert, die höchste Gewalt in einer Geselschaft ausübt. Ein Fürst.

Ränke (die) Krümmungen, (davon) Kunstgriffe zur Erreichung einer bösen Absicht, oder zum Schaden anderer.

Schatten-Glük dasjenige so nur das Ansehen des Glüks hat, ohne doch wirklich ein Glük zu sein, so wie der Schatten eines Körpers nur das Ansehen desselben aber nicht deßen Wirklichkeit und Festigkeit hat.

schon (zuweilen für) obschon, obgleich.

stolziren seinen Stolz, seinen Hochmuht an den Tag legen, zu erkennen geben.

stiften eine Anstalt auf vile künftige Zeiten errichten, (davon) die *Stiftung*, eine solche Anstalt (und) *Stiftungs Haus* ein dazu errichtetes Gebäude.

schleifen einreißen, zerstören, (wird gewöhnlich nur von festen Schlößern und Städten gebraucht).

schlichten grade machen, eben und glat machen. (2) In Ordnung bringen oder legen (davon) einen Streit und Zank schlichten, beilegen, (und endlich) die öfentliche Ruhe wider herstellen.

Schrekgesicht eine Erscheinung die Furcht und Schrecken verursacht, aber bald verschwindet. Ein Gespenst.

Johann Georg Hamann's Concept of Judaism and Controversy with Mendelssohn's "Jerusalem"

BY ZE'EV LEVY

I. INTRODUCTION

Johann Georg Hamann (1730–1788), the teacher of Johann Gottfried Herder, contemporary and fellow-citizen of Kant in Königsberg, was undoubtedly one of the oddest characters in the spiritual life of Germany during the second half of the eighteenth century. Together with the Swiss Protestant priest Kaspar Lavater (1741–1801) and the German philosopher Friedrich Heinrich Jacobi (1743–1819), he was one of the sworn enemies of the philosophy of Enlightenment in Germany. Hamann's manner of writing was so esoteric, mystical, fragmentary and so full of aphorisms and hints that even his contemporaries found it extremely difficult to understand him.[1] Nowadays it is quite impossible to tackle his writings without resorting to competent interpretative research-work. Although Hamann was never a professional philosopher or theologian, he exercised a remarkable influence on both domains; he became known to his contemporaries as "Der Magus des Norden", alluding to his dwelling-place in Northern Europe (he himself invented the title, hinting at the "Magi of the East" mentioned in the New Testament.[2])

Hamann's influence can be encountered in Herder's philosophical theories on language. His views on poetry as "the mother-tongue of mankind" afterwards inspired Herder's reflections on biblical literature. Several notions of Hamann's also left their traces on the writings of Jewish scholars such as Isaak Bernays in Hamburg at the beginning of the nineteenth century, or Rosenzweig and Buber in the twentieth. Since the latter decades of the nineteenth century Hamann has again aroused considerable attention among German scholars, mainly in the wake of religious and philosophical perspectives that were influenced by Kierkegaard or Dialectical Theology. Despite this renewed interest in his work, it nevertheless seems that Hamann's importance derives mainly from his polemics with Moses Mendelssohn in *Golgatha und Scheblimini*. Hegel noted that *Golgatha und Scheblimini* was Hamann's most important piece of writing.[3] This remark expresses perhaps more respect for Mendelssohn than for Hamann since only his attempt to refute Mendelssohn's concept of Judaism was deemed by Hegel to be

[1]Mendelssohn characterised one of Hamann's first treatises—*Sokratische Denkwürdigkeiten*—as "koernicht aber etwas dunkel"; *Mendelssohn's Gesammelte Schriften*, 1843, IV, 2. Abteilung, p. 99.
[2]Matthew II:1.
[3]G. W. F. Hegel, *Sämtliche Werke*, Jubiläumsausgabe 1930, Band XX, p. 243.

worthy of philosophical interest. In a specific sense the same also holds, perhaps even more so, for Lavater. Were it not for his famous correspondence with Mendelssohn, would he still be remembered today? Similarly Jacobi caught the attention of his contemporaries and of later generations by his *Über die Lehre Spinozas, in Briefen zu Herrn Moses Mendelssohn*; the interest in the *Pantheismusstreit* has not yet died out.

It is therefore noteworthy, in connection with these three adversaries of the philosophy of the Enlightenment that the most salient event in the spiritual and literary life of each of them is associated with Mendelssohn. Their attack on the philosophical foundations of the Enlightenment was accompanied by a penetrating discussion of the essence of Judaism. A distinction is made between the term "attack" in regard to the Enlightenment and "discussion" in regard to Judaism because these foes of the Enlightenment were not professional Jew-baiters; their dispute with Mendelssohn was not fostered by overt antisemitic motives. Sometimes there certainly were such undertones too; they were not free of prejudices, but that was not the distinctive feature of their debates. Those are to be found mainly below the surface , as in their letters, etc. Their ambivalent relations with Mendelssohn are depicted by Altmann in his monumental book on Mendelssohn.[4] The ideological struggle for or against emancipation had not yet begun; it only started after the French Revolution and the Napoleonic wars. These thinkers, unlike people such as Lessing and Dohm, were simply indifferent to the problem of the civil rights of Jews. Hamann formulated this attitude clearly, shortly before his death: "Why should the civil repression (Verstossung) of Jews or Negroes concern us? Their time has not yet come."[5] This was his opinion on the subject. *Golgatha und Scheblimini* represented a critical comment on *Jerusalem* in which Mendelssohn had proclaimed equality of human rights for the Jews against the demands of sovereignty voiced by Christian and Deist authors.

II. MENDELSSOHN AND HIS ANTAGONISTS

In order to understand fully the particular tinge of Hamann's polemical attack on Mendelssohn it will be useful to elucidate the common denominator and the distinctive features of the three religious-philosophical controversies in which Mendelssohn was involved.

1. Mendelssohn's dispute with Lavater was conducted by public correspondence which compelled him, though reluctantly, to respond to an external challenge. He considered it his moral duty to take up the gauntlet thrown down to him.[6]

2. The same holds for the second affair, thirteen years later. This time he was addressed by an anonymous pamphlet – *Das Forschen nach Licht und Recht* – which represented a challenge of a different kind; it did not emanate from an adversary

[4]Alexander Altmann, Moses Mendelssohn. A Biographical Study, London 1973.

[5]*Johann Georg Hamanns Briefwechsel mit Friedrich Heinrich Jacobi*, herausgegeben von Dr. C. H. Gildemeister, Gotha 1868; 10th May 1788, p. 645.

[6]See Mendelssohn's letters to his Jewish and Gentile friends; compare Altmann *op. cit.*, p. 209 f. The details of the affair are of no concern to this study.

of Enlightenment but on the contrary from somebody who considered himself to be, *qua* Deist, an ally of Mendelssohn. It was not the superiority of Christian revelation and miracles which was at stake but the superiority of Deism which the anonymous interlocutor of Mendelssohn,[7] as well as Mendelssohn himself, adhered to philosophically. This time he was asked to abandon Judaism and to convert to Christianity not to reinforce the latter creed but to strengthen the followers of Deism. From this standpoint Mendelssohn's philosophical task was much more difficult and complicated than the refutation of Bonnet's arguments on the truth of Christianity sent to him by Lavater. He had to explain why his essential Deist conception which served as connecting link between him and his Gentile fellow-Deists (Lessing, Abt, Nicolai, Reimarus etc.) did not contradict his attachment to the Jewish religion and the observance of its commands. The explanation had to include the question of the relationship between religion and State, in order to furnish a philosophical argument that Jews may be full-fledged citizens in the modern State and participate in its general cultural life without forsaking Judaism. This could not be accomplished by a letter but necessitated a thorough reply; thus the second challenge gave birth to *Jerusalem*. Although the topic was the elucidation of the particular essence of Judaism in connection with general philosophical truths available to every rational being, the book also treated, on several occasions, the relation between Christianity and Judaism.[8] These two issues occupy Hamann in *Golgatha und Scheblimini*; they will preoccupy the following inquiry too.

3. The third controversy in which Mendelssohn was involved concerned the alleged Spinozism of Lessing; it is not directly relevant to the topics discussed here. I shall, however, mention, some of Hamann's responses because there came into being at the time a kind of alliance between Mendelssohn's three polemists – Lavater, Jacobi, Hamann – which, surprisingly, was also joined by Herder. Hamann wrote to Lavater that his good luck provided him with three "Jonathans" (i.e. good and reliable friends) – Lavater, Herder and Jacobi.[9]

Two important points stand out from this schematic description:

1. Mendelssohn was the focus of *four* controversies three of which were launched by foes of the Enlightenment and one by one of its representatives (namely Krantz, the author of the anonymous pamphlet). Mendelssohn himself participated only in three because he left Hamann's intervention unanswered. His resolution was firm not to be pulled into any dispute on his *Jerusalem*.

2. *Golgatha und Scheblimini* represents an anti-rationalist comment on *Jerusalem*

[7]As to his identity, see Altmann, *op. cit.*, pp. 502–513.

[8]Mendelssohn employed, for the latter purpose, in part the material of his *Gegenbetrachtungen* on Bonnet's views that he had not put to use during his dispute with Lavater.

[9]Johann Georg Hamann, *Briefwechsel*, herausgegeben von Walther Ziesemer und Arthur Henkel, Wiesbaden 1955–1975, 6. Band (Frankfurt a. Main), p. 260. Hamann's extensive correspondence forms an inseparable part of his thought. Apart from six volumes of the scientific edition of his correspondence, published by Ziesemer and Henkel from 1956 to 1975, there have also appeared, mostly in the nineteenth century, various volumes of Hamann's correspondence with Herder, Lavater and Jacobi. Hamann's letters to Jacobi (see note 5) are significant to this study because they are particularly relevant to the subject of Judaism, forming sometimes almost short essays, especially during the "Pantheismusstreit". Quotations hereinafter as in the Ziesemer-Henkel edition, except the letters to Jacobi which will be quoted according to Gildemeister's edition.

which had been a rationalist response to a rationalist challenge. The basic assumptions of the challenge and of Mendelssohn's reply to it were of the same kind while Hamann's philosophical presuppositions were from the very beginning of an utterly different kind, transferring the dispute which had been conducted until then on rational ground, to irrational ground. While Krantz and Mendelssohn employed more or less the same philosophical language, and were *in potentia* capable of understanding each other, notwithstanding their essential disaccord, Hamann spoke in a completely different language.

Mendelssohn and Hamann thus represent two diametrically opposite personalities. It was not only their contrary philosophical beliefs which were, of course, the principal root of their dispute, but also their manner of writing separated one from the other. In contrast to Hamann's fragmentary and esoteric style, Mendelssohn's style (which had been lauded on various occasions by Kant and others for its elegance) weighs every word in order to fix it into a whole speculative system. Perhaps Hamann's disordered writing, abundant with similes and metaphors, also reflects somehow his philosophical idea that poetry, not rational discourse, is the mother-tongue of mankind.

III. THE BACKGROUND AND MOTIVES OF GOLGATHA UND SCHEBLIMINI

Hamann wrote his *Golgatha* as a response to Mendelssohn's *Jerusalem* but it was really the final outcome of several developments. In 1779 a second edition of David Hume's *Dialogues concerning natural religion* was published. Hamann translated them into German, not to gain support for Hume, but in order to use the translation to refute his ideas. The most important follower of Hume in Germany at the time was Johann August Starck who wrote in 1780, also anonymously, *Freimüthige Betrachtungen über das Christentum*. This aroused Hamann's fierce dismay. However, his project of translating Hume did not work out, despite Kant's support, because in the meantime there occurred another philosophical event of enormous impact: In 1781 Kant's *Critique of Pure Reason* appeared. Hamann was a citizen of Königsberg, and for many years had maintained very friendly relations with Kant. He happened to read the *Critique* straight from the press, even before binding, and decided at once to write a critical comment on the book, three weeks before its publication. The disputation with Kant overshadowed the controversy with Hume. He now considered it more urgent to refute Kant's critical philosophy than Hume's scepticism and concepts of natural religion. In this connection one encounters for the first time, in August 1781, the word *Sheblimini* in the title of the planned book: *Scheblimini oder epistolarische Nachlese eines Misologen*. The Hebrew expression *shev lyimini*[10] had captured his mind by way of Martin Luther whose complete works he had also read in 1780. Inspired by Luther's theological concepts, he decided to refute Hume and Kant simultaneously. *Scheblimini* thus represented for Hamann a symbol, or perhaps a code, of Christian religious philosophy in the spirit of

[10]"Sit thou at my right hand", Psalm CX:1.

Luther and the Reformation. Although it was not yet the last adaptation the word *Sheblimini* appeared from then on in all the versions of the projected booklet. The term *Misolog* was a neologism of *Philolog*, to wit not "lover of logos" but "hater of logos". He borrowed the expression from Kant himself who employed it at the end of the *Critique* to denounce the naturalist position that prefers common sense to science: "Es ist blosse Misologie, auf Grundsätze gebracht".[11] Thus Hamann did not hesitate to designate himself a *Misologe*, namely an enemy of reason. All these hidden allusions to Luther and Kant demonstrate very clearly Hamann's esoteric manner of writing. One year later there occurred another change of plan: Mendelssohn had meanwhile published a critical essay on Hume, and in its wake Hamann altered the name of his planned book to *Scheblimini oder epistolische Nachlese eines Metakritikers*. On the 25th August, 1782 he speaks of his plans as follows:

> "The first letter[12] deals with the printed translation of Hume's dialogues, the second with the written translation and Mendelssohn's judgment. The third compares Jews and philosophers. The fourth is a re-hashed translation of the last chapter of the first part of Hume's *On Human Nature*. The fourth will certainly touch on Kant."[13]

Hamann had had the intention not just to limit himself to Mendelssohn's judgment of Hume, that is to say to a general philosophical topic, but to include an explicit comparison of "Jews and philosophers". What he had in mind is quite easy to guess since in the final version of the book he continuously draws inferences from philosophers to Jews and *vice versa*. But this plan too was altered again, this time by the publication of Mendelssohn's *Jerusalem*. First Kant's *Critique* disrupted Hamann's original plan and transferred his main philosophical interest from Hume to Kant; now Mendelssohn brought about a further change. *Jerusalem* left a very strong impression on him; according to his own testimony, in a letter of 4th August 1783, he read it "almost three times". So he abandoned his original plans and in their stead finally prepared two separate publications:

1. The criticism of Hume was replaced by a criticism of Kant.
2. The criticism of Starck was replaced by a criticism of Mendelssohn.

In a letter of 8th December 1783 he fixed the title of the book on Kant: *Metakritik über den Purismus der Vernunft*. He did not wage war so much against Kant's criticism however but directed his main attack against Kant as the representative of the Enlightenment. This is a memorable point: the *Metakritik* against Kant and *Golgatha* against Mendelssohn thus became in some ways "connected vessels" in defeating the same philosophical outlook, namely the philosophy of the Enlightenment. The main thesis of the *Metakritik* that there is no Pure Reason because there is no linguistic purity reminds one paradoxically of certain ideas of Mendelssohn. His conclusions are, of course, different. Mendelssohn sternly

[11] Immanuel Kant, *Kritik der Reinen Vernunft*, B 883. Kant employed the term again in *Grundlagen zur Metaphysik der Sitten* (1785): "*Misologie*, d. i. Hass der Vernunft", *I. Kants sämtliche Werke*, 5. Band, Leipzig 1922, p. 19.

[12] The title – "epistolische Nachlese" – indicates that he intended to publish the book in the form of letters.

[13] See the introduction to *Golgatha und Scheblimini*, erklärt von Lothar Schreiner, *J. G. Hamann's Hauptschriften erklärt*, Gütersloh 1956.

believed that clear and pure language is a pre-condition of clear reasoning. This principle guided his Bible translation. Lucid Hebrew and lucid German are an obligatory basis of adequate philosophical thought.[14] Yet while Mendelssohn was optimistic in this regard, and believed in the possibility of pure language and clear thought, Hamann's position was pessimistic: "Language is the unique organon and criterion, the first and the last, of Reason; it has no other support (Creditif) than tradition (Überlieferung) and usage (usum)".[15] Both books, namely the *Metakritik* (which was published for the first time only in the nineteenth century) and *Golgatha*, deal with problems of theology, language, history and revelation.

The second book was written in January and February 1784 and finally named *Golgatha und Scheblimini. Von einem Prediger in der Wüsten.* The subtitle implied that Hamann considered his assignment to be similar to the mission of John the Baptist who was, so to say, the intermediary between Judaism (the "Old Testament") and Christianity (the "New Testament"). Hamann presents himself as leaning on the common foundation of true Judaism and true Christianity. This is no mere conjecture but an assumption based on explicit remarks in his letters. By the subtitle he also intended to hint that his message is like "a voice in the wilderness"; yet, surprisingly enough, when the book appeared in Berlin anonymously in August 1784 (though Hamann's authorship was well-known), it aroused unusual interest. The reason was undoubtedly that the little book, notwithstanding its esoteric style and continual confusion between quotations and the author's own words,[16] represented the first serious attempt to discuss Mendelssohn's book.

Thus *Golgatha und Scheblimini* not only aims at Mendelssohn and his *Jerusalem* but at the philosophy and theology of the Enlightenment of which Mendelssohn was one of the foremost representatives. It may be that Mendelssohn had acquired his prominent position also on account of his Jewishness. If his philosophical books had been written by a Christian author they probably would not have aroused so much attention. The piquant fact that they were composed by a Jew, and a practising Jew at that contributed much to the admiration of his enlightened contemporaries. Hamann already perceived this sensitive point during his first meeting with Mendelssohn some twenty years before. Although he was then a fervent admirer of Mendelssohn,[17] he had from the very beginning some reservations about *Phaidon*, the very book which established Mendelssohn's

[14]In a similar way, contemporary linguistic philosophy, inspired by Wittgenstein and Austin, proclaimed the "therapeutical" task of philosophy: to cleanse ordinary language of ambiguities, fallacies, errors etc. This will ensure *extempore* better thinking.

[15]Johann Georg Hamann, *Sämtliche Werke*, Historisch-Kritische Ausgabe von Josef Nadler, 6 Bände, Wien 1949–1957, vol. III, p. 284.

[16]Two years later, responding to the "attacks" on his book, Hamann admitted that "Diese kleine musivische Schrift ist aus lauter Stellen des Mendelssohnschen Jerusalems zusammengesetzt . . . womit er seine Unwissenheit des Judentums und seine Feindschaft gegen das Christentum, welche er *religiöse Macht* nennt, zu bemänteln gesucht"; *Golgatha*, Nadler, vol. III, *op. cit.*, p. 319, emphasis in the original.

[17]He addressed him as follows: "A Monsieur Moyse Fils de Mendelson, Sçavant très célèbre à Berlin", see letters of 6th November 1764, 13th September 1770; *Briefwechsel*, ed. Ziesemer-Henkel, 2. Band, 1956, p. 272, 3. Band 1957, p. 5.

main reputation among the enlightened public. He wrote to Herder, on 10th June 1767, just after Mendelssohn's book had appeared: "I have just read Moses Mendelssohn's preface to the Phaedon and I think that it is more beautifully written than thought"; after the publication of the second edition a year later, he commented: "I do not know whether Mendelssohn's Phaedon is improved: yet I almost doubt that it can be".[18] Mendelssohn had expressed his thoughts through the mouth of Socrates while Hamann waged war against the Enlightenment in the name of Socrates. Mendelssohn's "Socrates" symbolises Man's capacity to attain eternal truths by reason, but Hamann attacks anthropocentrism and Man's autonomy. His ideal is complete devotion to God. Man's aspiration to moral behaviour by his own rational faculties is no more than conceit doomed to inescapable failure. Religion educates Man to become aware of his insignificance. This controversial issue achieves its most caustic comment in *Golgatha*. In addition to his polemics with Mendelssohn as philosopher of the Enlightenment there is the Jewish polemical angle against Mendelssohn the defender of Mosaic Law. Mendelssohn supposedly commits a double error: as a philosopher he leans on Reason, as a Jew on the "Law".

Hamann thus polemises against Mendelssohn and the Enlightenment at the same time. Natural religion is an "Unding",[19] i.e. a *contradictio in adjecto*. Through his critique of *Jerusalem* Hamann wishes to reinforce the ideas of Luther against natural religion: "This quadrangle (Judaism–Christianity–Papacy–Lutheranism) is my oldest and my newest subject, and, so help me God, the egg of my Sheblimini".[20] Despite his sincere regret, ten days after Mendelssohn's death, that he had not written to him personally on these matters, he did not consider it so very important since his book concerned the philosophy and theology of the Enlightenment in general rather than Mendelssohn's theories in particular.[21] It is therefore rather surprising that not only Lavater and Jacobi, the foes of Enlightenment, but also Herder and Goethe who led the Enlightenment towards Romanticism acclaimed Hamann's book with delight. It may be – though this is again no more than a conjecture – that this derived from their ambivalent attitude to Mendelssohn. Respect and esteem went together with reservation and ill-will. Perhaps they were vexed by the fact that it was a Jew who led the movement of German Enlightenment. All the polemical involvements in Mendelssohn's life, from Lavater to Jacobi, were implicitly overshadowed by the hidden warning that it does not befit a Jew to guide intellectual life in Germany since its elements are firmly rooted in Christian culture. All this is the more surprising since, as mentioned above, none of Mendelssohn's opponents was directed, at least not openly, by anti-Jewish motives. The young Hamann, on his way to England in 1754, visited the Jewish "Weltweise", and in 1777, during Mendelssohn's two-weeks' stay with Kant in Königsberg, did not miss a day in having long conversations with him.

[18]28th August 1768, *ibid.*, 2. Band, p. 395; p. 420. See also Altmann, *op. cit.*, pp. 168–169.
[19]Letter to Herder of 25th June 1780, *Briefwechsel*, IV, *op. cit.*, p. 195.
[20]*Ibid.*
[21]Letter to Jacobi of 15th January 1786, Gildemeister, *op. cit.*, p. 192.

"On the 24th of July my dear Phaidon Moses Mephiboshet appeared, and on the last day of the vacation he left together with his in-law . . . I expect Moses to come back in another week, and to enjoy his company even more.[22]

Why he nicknamed him "Mephiboshet" is not clear.[23] His correspondence with Mendelssohn during the sixties and the seventies is imbued with a friendly and intimate atmosphere; he tells him about his personal affairs, and inquires about Mendelssohn's doings and family. Both of them spice their letters with a sense of humour. Hamann, e.g., alludes to his name: "Since you know that, unfortunately, my name is not Mordechai, the old address can remain"[24] to which Mendelssohn replies: "The golden age of my faith of which it is said *vegar ze'ev im keves venamer im g'di* has not yet come".[25] Hamann comments: "The golden age of my faith that Mordechai and the Agagi will drink to each other has not yet come".[26]

IV. A CHARACTERISATION OF GOLGATHA UND SCHEBLIMINI

It has been noted in the previous paragraph that the expression *Sheblimini* was meant to hint, code-like, at the pronounced Lutheran elements of Hamann's Christian outlook. The combination of the two expressions – "Golgatha" and "Sheblimini" – symbolises the two poles of Jesus's life: "Golgatha" – his agony, afflictions and crucifixion; "Sheblimini" – his resurrection and seating at the right of God. As a motto to his book, Hamann chose two verses of the Bible; the first one, from Deuteronomy, he quotes is in Mendelssohn's German translation, but the second one, from Jeremiah, is in Luther's:

"Who said unto his father and to his mother, I have not seen him; neither did he acknowledge his brethren, nor knew his children: for they have observed thy word, and kept thy covenant (Deuteronomy XXXIII:9).
Behold, I will feed them with wormwood, and make them drink the water of gall; for from the prophets of Jerusalem is profanity (Heuchelei) gone forth into all the land (Jeremiah XXIII:15)."

Quoting the verse of the Pentateuch – the Torah – in Mendelssohn's translation while quoting the verse of the Prophets in Luther's is deliberate irony: Mendelssohn who bases Judaism on the Torah, on the "Gesetz", abandoned the legacy of the prophets. He is, as it were, indifferent to Prophecy in which Christian hermeneutics strived to discover allusions to Jesus's future revelation and *Kerygma*. Mendelssohn, being concerned with the concept of Judaism, was indeed less interested in prophecy which is of more universal nature, but his motives were of course not such as Hamann tried to insinuate.

[22]4th August 1777, *Briefwechsel*, III, *op. cit.*, p. 365.
[23]He also started another letter to Mendelssohn by "liebster bester Moses Mephiboshet", *ibid.*, p. 375.
[24]11th February 1762, *ibid.*, II, p. 130.
[25]*Ibid.*, p. 134. The quotation of Isaiah is written in Hebrew letters.
[26]*Ibid.*, p. 142. "Agagi" – the biblical surname of Haman.

Moreover, those who deny their fathers (in the first verse), or the profane prophets (in the second verse), represent the philosophers of Enlightenment who lean, like Mendelssohn, their principal spokesman, on Reason alone. Those profane prophets from *Jerusalem*–a transparent allusion to Mendelssohn's book–spread falseness throughout the country. While Hamann usually employed the pejorative term "Babel" to designate the Berlin Enlightenment, he made use, in this case, of a verse by means of which he could stress, at the very opening of his book, his misgivings concerning Mendelssohn's conceptions. Unlike the Jewish philosophers and the followers of Enlightenment, the keepers of God's word and covenant remain faithful to the Scriptures and to tradition. The two verses of the motto thus express a militant theological tendency.

If so many concealed meanings and implications can be derived from the title and the motto alone, it is easy to conjecture how strange, vague and esoteric the text will turn out to be. No wonder that a modern reader needs a competent commentator to guide him through this obscure labyrinth. But there are still more difficulties ahead: Hamann intersperses his text with quotations, part sentences and expressions from *Jerusalem* and other philosophical, theological and literary sources, without bothering to note their origin nor even the fact that they are quotations. One needs therefore to be acquainted with various books that Hamann's contemporaries then more or less knew but which have fallen into oblivion since.

Golgatha represents primarily a response to Mendelssohn's *Jerusalem.* As against the latter's rationalist apologetics of Judaism one encounters in Hamann's book fideistic apologetics of Judaism, in order to prove that Judaism is essentially a preparatory stage towards Christianity. While Mendelssohn said that Jews *can* join general intellectual life without renouncing their peculiar attachment to Judaism, Hamann claims that Judaism *must* join Christian spiritual life because Christianity represents the most consistent realisation of Judaism. He believes Mendelssohn's concept of Judaism to be based on confused concepts that cannot be adjusted to genuine religious belief while true Judaism of the kind Mendelssohn did not comprehend or simply denied, anticipated Christian *Kerygma*.

To be brief, Hamann does not attack Judaism but on the contrary claims to defend it against its falsification by Mendelssohn. The latter was led astray by his rationalist outlook. The paradoxicality of the argument lies in that Hamann the Christian considered it his duty to defend Judaism against Mendelssohn the Jew. The philosophical stages that led him to his criticism of Mendelssohn are firmly linked to his conception of language; let us sum them up for the moment in the following schematic manner:

a. As against Herder's rationalist philosophy of language, Hamann professes an irrational philosophy of language.

b. His concept of language gives birth to his theological conception.

c. This theology is turned, in *Golgatha*, against Mendelssohn's rationalist conception of religion in general, and of Judaism in particular.

This programme may be found in its most succinct formulation in the following sentence:

"Without language there is no reason; without reason there is no religion, and without these three essential components of our nature there is no social spirit and no social bond."[27]

Thus language, reason and religion form the spiritual whole of social life. The decisive point, particularly relevant to this inquiry, consists in that all Hamann's meditations on language, scattered throughout various small essays and reviews are given their final form – philosophically, religiously and historiosophically – in *Golgatha*. Mendelssohn's *Jerusalem* presented a challenge to Hamann which obliged him to order his thoughts; the principal point of departure for his criticism was the assumption that by reducing Judaism to general rational elements – the "Law" – Mendelssohn emptied it of its most important religious element, namely language. Judaism thus becomes paganism which is precisely what Hamann wishes to prevent: Judaism being the cradle of Christianity, it is inconceivable that it be rooted in pagan elements.

V. HAMANN ON LANGUAGE AND MEANING IN MENDELSSOHN'S JERUSALEM

Hamann opens *Golgatha* with quasi-hypocritical compliments to *Jerusalem* but they contain more mockery than sincerity. He comments on Mendelssohn's concept of "Social Contract" (chapter 1 of *Jerusalem*) although he feigns not to understand it. Nevertheless he pretends to find there a common point of departure for both of them in the belief in God's covenant with Abraham. This covenant possesses universal religious significance.[28] But since Mendelssohn does not emphasise the covenant but stresses instead the "Law of Moses" as representing the very essence of Judaism, and, moreover, since Mendelssohn identifies, philosophically, Judaism with the general outlook of rational religion (which is identical with natural religion), Hamann wishes to lean on biblical universalism as a counterbalance to Mendelssohn's legal-rational version of Judaism. He denies that the Torah has been the Law of the ancient Jewish people, to wit some kind of social contract based on natural law but divinely revealed. He also rejects Mendelssohn's attempt "to be able to explain rationally a few statements by the Rabbis",[29] namely Mendelssohn's argument that what had been, until the destruction of the temple, political offences, afterwards became religious transgressions.

Hamann therefore discusses to begin with Mendelssohn's general philosophical conceptions but he does not disregard some of the problems arising in the second chapter of *Jerusalem*. As already said, his statements evoke sometimes quite astonishing associations with certain claims of contemporary analytical and linguistic philosophy. He maintains, e.g., that Mendelssohn's central notions – State, religion, freedom of conscience – are abstract to such a far-reaching degree as to become practically meaningless. They are "drey Wörter, die dem

[27] 'Philologische Einfälle und Zweifel', in: J. G. Hamann, *Sybillinische Blätter des Magus*, Jena–Leipzig 1905, p. 127. See also: J. G. Hamann, *Schriften zur Sprache*, ed. by Josef Simon, Frankfurt a. Main 1967, p. 201.

[28] *Golgatha*, ed. Nadler, III, *op. cit.*, p. 293.

[29] *Ibid.*, "einige Behauptungen der Rabbinen vernünftig erklären zu können".

ersten Anblick nach alles oder vielmehr nichts sagen".[30] It follows that if Mendelssohn's principal concepts are no more than arbitrary linguistic explanations – "Wortschrauben", "Leibnitzische Worterklärung" etc.[31] – they create unavoidable contradictions: among others, the contradiction between the argument (*Jerusalem*, ch. 1) that there exists a universal inalienable right to happiness, based on the rules of Reason and Good, and the argument (*Jerusalem*, ch. 2) of a revealed law, given to the People of Israel only, in order "to bring happiness to the entire nation as well as to its individual members".[32] Mendelssohn, the philosopher of Enlightenment, thus speaks about Man's right to happiness while Mendelssohn, the religious Jew, speaks about Divine Law, destined for the Jewish People only. This is indeed a serious argument which was raised later by various critics of Mendelssohn. If every human being is able to grasp eternal truths through his own faculty of reason why does Mendelssohn ascribe to the commandments, that were accorded to Israel only, the important task to "guide the seeking mind to divine truths – partly eternal partly historical – on which the religion of this people was based"?[33] If such guidance is desirable for a Jew, is it not at the same time desirable for everybody else? Should the "Laws" not urge every human being to meditate on those truths?

Hamann asserts that Mendelssohn does not really understand the terms he deals with. Not only does he misunderstand the word "justice" but he derives his main concept – "Gesetz der Gerechtigkeit"[34] – i.e. the cornerstone of his general philosophical conception as well as of his concept of Judaism, from nature and reason instead of from revelation and language. He thus commits, in his principal terms, what would be called nowadays "linguistic fallacies". All these arguments are a direct outcome of Hamann's "Philosophy of Language":

> "My main question is not: what is Reason? but: what is Language? I suppose that this is the cause of all the paralogisms and antinomies [a reference to Kant's *Critique of Pure Reason* – Z. L.] that are attributed to the former. The result is that one conceives of words as of concepts, and of concepts as of the things themselves. Words and concepts cannot have existence because existence applies to things (Dinge und Sachen) only."[35]

The same criticism also holds for Spinoza's philosophy.

> "Spinozism is an unnatural conjecture which assumes no more than one existing substance that is cause and effect both at the same time, and that can be thought and felt infinitely . . . does it mean that concept and substance are one and the same?"[36]

Although Hamann blurs in this case Spinoza's neat distinction between substance and modes, the decisive criteria of his negative attitude to the philosophies of Spinoza and Kant were guided by linguistic aspects. As against "Spinoza's prejudice in mathematical form" which he characterises as

[30] *Ibid.*, p. 294.
[31] *Ibid.*, p. 296.
[32] Moses Mendelssohn, *Jerusalem and other Jewish writings*, translated and edited by Alfred Jospe, New York 1969, p. 98.
[33] *Ibid.*, p. 99.
[34] *Golgatha, op. cit.*, p. 296.
[35] Letter to Jacobi 14th November 1784, Gildemeister, *op. cit.*, p. 15.
[36] *Ibid*, 16th January 1785, p. 49.

"non-philosophical humbug" etc.[37] he deals neither with physics nor theology but with "language, the mother of Reason and Revelation".[38] He complains that we lack "a grammar of reason",[39] a concept which will reappear in Rosenzweig's *Der Stern der Erlösung* as "Grammatical Thinking" (Das Sprachdenken). Rosenzweig also believed language represented a greater reality than all abstract concepts of thought taken together. Language is no product of human intellect but "God's dowry to mankind"[40] through which Man becomes Man.

Without commenting yet on the philosophical implications of Hamann's argument, or on Mendelssohn's conception in this regard, it ought nevertheless to be noted that the assertion that Mendelssohn does not comprehend the concept of "justice" is not accurate. Mendelssohn links justice with the idea of revelation too although for him revelation involves the Law only. Nor is it true that Mendelssohn ignores language-aspects. A lengthy part of *Jerusalem*, ch. 2, deals with linguistics though his ideas in this domain are certainly outdated by now. Hamann even nicknamed him, on account of his views on language, "der Buchstabenmensch".[41]

Hamann's linguistic claims, however, are not limited to theoretical deliberations but lead to very significant practical conclusions. The following example will suffice: Mendelssohn states (in *Jerusalem*, ch. 1) that rights and actions are subordinated to the authorities of the State; they are entitled to exert coercion in this field. On the other hand, duties between man and his fellow-men, or between man and God, and in the first place opinions and ideas, cannot be enforced by the authorities. Hamann characterises this conception as "Schlangenbetrug der Sprache"[42] that is to say: religious coercion is permissible even if he does not say so explicitly. He does not limit these linguistic matters, which hold such an important place in his philosophical outlook, to "the therapeutical" aspects (to use an expression of Wittgenstein) of laying bare the linguistic fallacies and conceptual errors that supposedly led Mendelssohn astray in *Jerusalem*. He assigns to language also a primordial role in assuring proper conduct of human life which anticipates, to a certain extent, the status of language in modern religious-existentialist philosophies. According to Mendelssohn, social contract is based everywhere on natural law while to the Jewish people this law was divinely revealed. According to Hamann, on the other hand, social contract depends on reason and language – on word and answer, namely on "dem sittlichen Vermögen Ja! oder Nein! zu sagen, und auf der sittlichen Nothwendigkeit, das gesagte Wort wahr zu machen".[43] Man's capacity to respond to questions of ethical decision-making by "yes" or "no", and to keep his word, is deeply rooted "in the natural use of human reason and language",[44] and lies at

[37] *Ibid.*, 28th October 1785, p. 121.
[38] *Ibid.*, p. 122.
[39] *Ibid.*, 5th December 1784, p. 22.
[40] "Die Morgengabe des Schöpfers an die Menschheit", Franz Rosenzweig, *Der Stern der Erlösung*, Heidelberg 1954, II, p. 29.
[41] *Golgatha, op. cit.*, pp. 293, 296, 302.
[42] *Ibid.*, p. 298.
[43] *Ibid.*, p. 300.
[44] *Ibid.*

the base of human relations. One encounters the same idea afterwards in the religious-existentialist philosophy of Kierkegaard when he speaks about "Either-Or". Justice is not a matter of philosophical reasoning but of speaking and doing. Direct and indirect traces of Hamann's philosophy of language are also encountered in the thought of contemporary Jewish philosophers like Buber and Rosenzweig.

Hamann also accuses Mendelssohn of linguistic confusion in his approach to Hobbes; there exists a "Verwandtschaft desjenigen was der eine *Recht* und der andere *Macht* nennt".[45] Hamann tries to exploit the fact that Mendelssohn, notwithstanding his reservations concerning Hobbes's philosophy as such, admitted that under his influence "the concepts of right and duty, of authority and obligation" have been defined and developed systematically for the first time.[46] Hamann deduces that *Jerusalem* is not the true Jerusalem, the city of God, Jerusalem of Judaism and Christianity alike but Jerusalem removed "to the meridian of Babel".[47] In his secret language, Hamann again attacks several adversaries at once: 1. 'Babel' hints at the "Tower of Babel", namely the linguistic confusion – "Hocuspocus" – by which Mendelssohn, "der speculative Buchstäbler", deceives his readers.[48] He thus accuses Mendelssohn of nothing less than deliberate deceit. 2. 'Babel' is the residence of the Berlin Enlightenment to which Mendelssohn addressed his book. 3. Finally, "Babel", i.e. Berlin, is the capital of Friedrich II whose freethinking Hamann detested at all times.[49]

So the whole first part of *Golgatha* supports the claim that Mendelssohn's thought is no more than "conceptual confusion". Thus, if the crucial argument of Mendelssohn, namely that it is obligatory to separate religion and State, turns out to be conceptual confusion, then the whole conceptual system of *Jerusalem* which is based on this argument, of course tumbles down too:

> "Man verwirrt nemlich die Begriffe, und es ist im genausten Verstande eben so wenig der Wahrheit gemäss, als dem Besten der Leser zuträglich, wenn man Staat und Kirche entgegensätzt, die innere Glückseligkeit von der äusseren Ruhe und Sicherheit so scharf abschneidet, wie das Zeitliche vom Ewigen."[50]

As a matter of fact, this sentence is again a paraphrase of Mendelssohn's own words which Hamann turns, without admitting this, against their proper author. What is still more astonishing: the argument of "conceptual confusion" by which Mendelssohn's views are turned into "linguistic fallacies" is also borrowed from *Jerusalem*:

> "Actually it is neither correct nor in man's best interest to distinguish so sharply between the temporal and the eternal. Eternity, in principle, can never be man's portion; his "eternity" is merely an infinitely prolonged temporality. His temporality never ceases; it is an integral and

[45] *Ibid.*, p. 302, emphasised in the original.
[46] *Jerusalem, op. cit.*, p. 14.
[47] *Golgatha, op. cit.*, p. 302.
[48] *Ibid.*
[49] He voiced his disgust on the same occasion in the most pungent manner: "alle Oeuvres diverses einer cynisch-sodomitischen Mundart (an allusion to Friedrich's French writing) die nach b.. und f.. wie nach Pech und Schwefel stinkt, nichts als schwarze Künste eines f.. Diable der Finsternis sind"; *ibid.*, p. 301.
[50] *Ibid.*, p. 302.

essential part of his continuity. To counterpoise man's temporal welfare and his eternal bliss leads to a confusion of concepts which has important practical consequences."[51]

But while Mendelssohn believed that such identity between State and religion ("Church") existed only in the ancient Jewish state, more precisely only until the days of Samuel, hereby continuing the well-known argument of Spinoza, Hamann again interprets Mendelssohn's assertion that there is no complete division between the temporal and the eternal as alluding to the State (which guarantees temporal happiness) and the Church (which guarantees eternal happiness). Despite Mendelssohn's clear assertion that both – Church (in the large sense of the term, i.e. religion) and State – must ensure human happiness, his principal and decisive injunction consists in that they are separate authorities; the most each one of them can accomplish in regard to the other is mutual support. Hamann, however, infers arbitrarily that as a result of such separation none – neither religion nor State – can subsist, like the child in Solomon's judgement.[52] In his esoteric way he thus introduces another hint, namely that Mendelssohn the Jewish "Weltweise" represents the very antithesis of Solomon the Jewish king who was the wisest of all men.

Hamann accuses Mendelssohn – the "Theorist" – of denying that the State should be concerned with the beliefs of its citizens; likewise God should not be concerned with their actions. According to Hamann, this contradicts on the one hand Mendelssohn's own "schemas" on Judaism and Divine Law, and on the other hand pushes him, as it were, to accept the position of Hobbes.[53] The first part of the accusation, namely that the State must not intervene in the beliefs and opinions of its citizens, is certainly correct. The second part touches again one of the most difficult issues of Mendelssohn's Jewish religious philosophy, i.e. how to reconcile his basically deist position, denying God's revelation and providence, with the assertion that God revealed the Law to the People of Israel. Hamann certainly seized on the most vulnerable aspect of Mendelssohn's concept which became afterwards the focal point of all relevant controversies. To dismiss it, however, as conceptual confusion or "Wortspiele physiognomischer und hypokritischer Unbestimmtheit"[54] is to dodge the core of the problem. He terminates the section – once again in an ironical manner that can be apprehended only by competent scholars acquainted with the relevant material – by using Mendelssohn's own words: "Eine Sprachverwirrung der Begriffe bleibt nicht ohne praktische Folgen".[55]

Upto this point Hamann had not yet undertaken any substantial theological discussion on Judaism and Christianity but only tried very hard to undermine in advance Mendelssohn's philosophical authority. Only in the second part of *Golgatha* does he focus on the capital subject-matter, i.e. *Judaism*. He wishes to appear as the advocate of Judaism as opposed to Mendelssohn who "distorts" it.

[51] *Jerusalem*, *op. cit.*, p. 17.
[52] *Golgatha*, *op. cit.*, p. 303.
[53] *Ibid.*
[54] *Ibid.*
[55] *Ibid.*, cf. Mendelssohn's remark on "a confusion of concepts" (above, note 51).

By his plea for true Judaism he endeavours to guarantee a proper spiritual basis for Christianity.

VI. THE ESSENCE OF JUDAISM ACCORDING TO HAMANN

In the opening sentence of the second part of his booklet Hamann proclaims his intention to explain "properly" the essence of Judaism as birthplace of Christianity:

> "Ohne mich und dich, andächtiger Leser! mit der noch speculativeren Anwendung[56] zu ermüden, wünschte ich, unserer beiderseitigen Sicherheit wegen *im obersten Stockwerke*, keinen solchen lockern Grund und sandigen Boden für die neue und harte Theorie des Judentums."[57]

Hamann ostensibly accepts Mendelssohn's assertion that Judaism is the ground floor and Christianity the attic floor. Mendelssohn had claimed that there is no sense in exchanging Judaism for Christianity since if the ground floor collapses nothing will sustain the upper floor.[58] Hamann apparently accepts this which at the time also aroused Kant's critical response[59] but, as is his usual way, turns it upside down. It is Mendelssohn's conception that really undermines Judaism because it is unable to guarantee the requisite firm and secure foundation. Hamann pretends to repair the ground floor which has been damaged by Mendelssohn, thus ensuring the foundation of Christianity.

Moreover, he also appears to agree with Mendelssohn that Judaism does not acknowledge revealed religion. Mendelssohn denied revelation of truths which can be attained anyway by every human being *qua* rational being, and do not need supra-human intervention; in his religious-philosophical outlook he kept only the belief in one single act of revelation, namely of Law (the Torah). Hamann asserts too that there has been only one sole revelation but this is the realisation of God's word in Christ; it expresses the union of the Old and the New Testament.[60] Academic inquiries[61] do not suffice to explain genuine religious phenomena such as the giving of the Law on Mt. Sinai. Judaism has never fully understood the true signification of its law and religion. Therefore the decisive distinction between Judaism and Christianity is not to be found where Mendelssohn looked for it. It consists in the barrier that divides the false conception of Judaism, namely Mendelssohn's, from the true one, namely his, Hamann's. To demonstrate the difference between them let us confront Hamann's words which contain many part sentences of *Jerusalem* with Mendelssohn's parallel statements:

[56]Namely, the application of Mendelssohn's social contract, based on natural law.
[57]*Golgatha, op. cit.*, p. 303, my emphasis.
[58]*Jerusalem, op. cit.*, p. 58.
[59]I. Kant, *Die Religion innerhalb der Grenzen der blossen Vernunft, I. Kants Werke*, Leipzig 1923, VI, p. 591.
[60]*Golgatha, op. cit.*, p. 304.
[61]Another cut at the Berlin academy of sciences, the stronghold of Enlightenment which also gave birth to *Jerusalem*.

Golgatha und Scheblimini	*Jerusalem*
Der charakteristische Unterschied zwischen Judentum und Christentum betrifft also weder un- noch mittelbare Offenbarung, in dem Verstande, worin dieses von Juden	... einen charakteristischen Unterschied zwischen ihr (der jüdischen Religion) und der christlichen Religion[63]
und Naturalisten genommen wird – noch ewige Wahrheiten und Lehrmeinungen – noch Cerimoniel- und Sittengesetze: sondern	Religionslehren und Sätzen, oder ewigen Wahrheiten von Gott und seiner Regierung und Vorsehung[64] Gesetze, Vorschriften, Gebote, Lebensregeln[65]
lediglich zeitliche Geschichtswahrheiten, die sich zu einer Zeit zugetragen haben, und niemals wiederkommen –	Zeitliche, Geschichtswahrheiten; Dinge die sich zu einer Zeit zugetragen haben und vielleicht niemals wiederkommen[66]
Thatsachen die durch einen Zusammenhang von Ursachen und Wirkungen in einem Zeitpunct und Erdraum wahrgeworden,	Sätze, die durch einen Zusammenfluss von Ursachen und Wirkungen in einem Punkte der Zeit und des Raums wahr geworden[67]
und also nur von diesem Punct der Zeit und des Raums als wahr gedacht werden können, und durch Autorität	... also von diesem Punkte der Zeit und des Raums nur als wahr gedacht werden können[68]
bestätigt werden müssen. Autorität kann zwar demütigen, aber nicht belehren; sie kann die Vernunft niederschlagen, aber nicht fesseln.	
Dennoch verschwindet ohne Autorität die Wahrheit der Geschichte mit dem Geschehenen selbst.[62]	Ohne Autorität verschwindet die Wahrheit der Geschichte mit dem Geschehenen selbst[69]

Hamann thus reduces the essential distinction between Judaism and Christianity, or more accurately between two divergent conceptions of Judaism only one of which constitutes an adequate base for Christianity, not to the third stratum in Mendelssohn's concept of Judaism, i.e. the Law, but to the second stratum namely historical truths that depend on authority, and therefore necessitate faith. Faith, as proclaimed by Lavater before, by Jacobi one or two years later, and asserted finally by Kierkegaard in the most striking form – faith alone can truly serve as a base for genuine religiosity. What appears therefore in Mendelssohn's famous conception of the three strata – to wit: eternal truths, historical truths and ceremonial laws – as the first stratum – eternal truths, i.e. the rational elements – is dropped by Hamann as being entirely irrelevant. It is not reason, the highest longing of the Enlighteners, but faith which represents the cornerstone of religion. The irrational overcomes, or ought to overcome, the

[62] *Golgatha, op. cit.*, p. 304.
[63] Moses Mendelssohn, *Schriften zur Philosophie, Aesthetik und Apologetik*, II, Hildesheim 1968, p. 419.
[64] *Ibid.*, p. 458.
[65] *Ibid.*, p. 459.
[66] *Ibid.*, p. 420.
[67] *Ibid.*
[68] *Ibid.*
[69] *Ibid.*, p. 422. (For the English translations see *Jerusalem, op. cit.*, pp. 61, 97, 98, 62 and 64.)

rational. Divine truth cannot be apprehended by the human intellect; it can only be believed in.

Historical truths – Hamann leans again on Mendelssohn's thought for entirely different purposes – should not be limited to events that have happened in the past, but are relevant as well to future happenings. They are grounded in prophecy which again requires belief. The essential distinction between Judaism and Christianity concerns the relationship to those historical truths of the past and the future.[70] It is easy to see where Hamann wishes to lead his readers. Those verses or fragments of verses of the Bible, especially in the books of the prophets, which Christian hermeneutics used to interpret as prophetic hints to Jesus's future revelation, express historical truths. Therefore the "Old Testament" of Judaism heralds the truth of Christianity but its tidings necessitate faith. Hamann who considered himself to be the competent spokesman of Lutheran Protestantism thus continues a traditional line of argument that had been characteristic of Christian hermeneutics since patristic philosophy.

The veracity of historical truths derives – according to both Mendelssohn and Hamann – from three principal sources:

1. Jewish authority, i.e. the authority of the biblical authors: "Jüdische Autorität allein giebt ihnen die erforderliche Authentie."[71]

2. Miracles: "diese Denkwürdigkeiten der Vor- und Nachwelt wurden durch Wunder bestätigt".[72] Mendelssohn too, despite his rationalism, did not reject the possibility of miracles, or perhaps paid some kind of lip service to them. While distinguishing between necessary and contingent eternal truths, he asserted that the former emanate from divine reason; they are not subject to change since otherwise God would contradict himself. The latter emanate from divine will, and are liable to change when performances of extraordinary happenings, i.e. miracles, "are in accord with His holy will and intentions".[73] Mendelssohn was indifferent to the complicated problem of divine reason and divine will that had preoccupied Jewish and non-Jewish philosophy since the Middle Ages.[74] Elsewhere he ascribed to miracles the task of confirming the authenticity of historical truths,[75] but his argument is not wholly clear there. How can a miracle confirm historical truth if the historical event to be confirmed is a miraculous happening? Mendelssohn's qualms as to the status of miracles testify to the theoretical difficulties that he encountered whenever he attempted to bridge the gap between his general deistic philosophical outlook and his Jewish "faith" ("faith" as *double entendre*).

3. The reliability of the witnesses and the chroniclers: "Glaubhaftigkeit der Zeugen und Überlieferer".[76]

[70] *Golgatha, op. cit.*, pp. 304–305.
[71] *Ibid.*, p. 305.
[72] *Ibid.*
[73] *Jerusalem, op. cit.*, p. 62.
[74] Compare with the controversy between the conceptions of the "Ash'aria and the Mu'atazila" as reflected in Maimonides's *Guide of the Perplexed*, translated by Sh. Pines, Chicago 1963, I, ch. 71, p. 177, III, ch. 17, pp. 466–468.
[75] *Jerusalem, op. cit.*, p. 70.
[76] *Golgatha, op. cit.*, p. 305; the "faithfulness" of historical truths; *Jerusalem, op. cit.*, "accepted on faith", p. 98.

Mendelssohn considered historical truths to be valid for both Judaism and Christianity, indeed for all human beings, since they relate to facts – but facts of which only "authority can provide evidence of their historicity".[77] The human intellect judges them by logical inference: a public happening observed by tens of thousands of eye-witnesses, such as the giving of the Torah, possesses more certainty than miracle-stories about Jesus, relying on a few eye-witnesses only. In the first case there is a very high degree of probability, even certainty; in the second case there is not. He continues, perhaps unawares, an idea already to be found in Jewish mediaeval philosophy – *Hahagadda Hane'emenet* of Saadia Gaon or Yehuda Halevi's basic argument of truth in the *Kuzari*. Mendelssohn tried to link this assertion with the general philosophical conception as formulated, to give for one example, in his famous prize essay of 1763: 'Abhandlung über die Evidenz in metaphysischen Wissenschaften'.[78] Yet while Mendelssohn stressed the aspect of historical truth – the particular event of the giving of the Torah – Hamann emphasises instead the aspect of revelation at this particular historical happening. Thus while Mendelssohn conceives of truths, including historical truths, as universal, Hamann conceives of them as particular events. One encounters again the fundamental distinction between reason and action. According to Hamann this is the main difference between the two religions, namely the historical fact of a revealed Law as against the act of revelation, embodying a profound religious experience. Mendelssohn did not attribute to this unique historical fact of divine revelation any particular religious significance but political-legal significance only. This arouses Hamann's anger: Mendelssohn, as it were, neglects the essential principle – the religious signification of God's revelatory act.

VII. ABRAHAM AS THE SYMBOL OF FAITH VERSUS MOSES AS THE MOUTHPIECE OF BELIEF AND UNBELIEF

Hamann presents Abraham as the symbol of faith although he does so by relying mainly on the "New Testament". He anticipates Kierkegaard again who, as is well-known, characterised Abraham as the "Knight of Faith"; the story of the Aqedah symbolises the most authentic expression of Man's existential situation, confined to the single relationship between Man and God.

The symbol of unbelief is Aaron who shared responsibility in the making of the Golden Calf. Moses, finally, is depicted as the symbol of faith and non-faith, the expression of belief and unbelief taken together. He is, *prima facie*, the antithesis of Abraham. He cast all his authority, not to strengthen faith, but to enforce Law. This does not only relate to the theoretical aspect of preferring Law to Faith but Moses indeed committed several times actual acts of unbelief, as recounted in the Bible. Therefore God punished him by preventing him from entering the promised land.[79]

[77] *Ibid.*
[78] Moses Mendelssohn, *Schriften zur Philosophie, Aesthetik und Apologetik*, I, Leipzig 1880, pp. 45–104.
[79] *Golgatha, op. cit.*, p. 305.

But what Hamann really wishes to insinuate is something else. Moses the law-giver is but part of the true and whole image of Moses. He is only Moses as the Jews, and in particular Mendelssohn, see him. But "der ganze Moses samt allen Propheten ist der Fels des christlichen Glaubens, und der auserwählte köstliche Eckstein, der von den Bauleuten verworfen ist".[80] The Jews estranged themselves from the true message of Moses. Aaron and the "Rabbis" ("Häupter der Synagoge") destroyed, by the making of the Golden Calf, the very essence and significance of the law of Moses. Mendelssohn and the Jews praised Moses as the law-giver, but his law – his testament – has not been kept by those to whom it was addressed. Because the Jews did not heed Moses the prophet he remained some kind of pope for them.[81] This claim is in flagrant contradiction to the religious and philosophical Jewish tradition which always considered Moses to be the greatest of the prophets, but Hamann needed it to corroborate his arbitrary argument that only the Christians truly accepted Moses's prophetic message. The Jews turned "the corpse of his rotten law into a relic of superstition, prayer-houses were turned into murder-dens, Beth-El (the "house of God") into Bethaven (the "house of sin"),[82] the city of the bridegroom-of-blood[83] has turned, despite pagan and anti-christian Rome, into a Babylonian whore", and so on.[84]

In short, Abraham is "the father of the faithful"[85] to whom a promise (Verheissung) was given but no legislation[86] while Moses was awarded a legislation which, however, has not been observed by his subjects. Unlike Judaism, Christian belief conceived of Moses as a law-giver, a prophet and a teacher all at once, stressing his prophetic faculties which were deemed to be of special relevance to Christianity. This whole exegetical legerdemain is based on a grave misunderstanding of the prophet's position and role as described in the Bible. The prophet is first of all "the man of spirit"; until the separation of spiritual and political functions with the advent of Saul's kingdom, his main spiritual activity focused on legislative and political leadership. The grandeur of Moses as a prophet, according to the biblical conception, was identical with his function of law-giver. This is an important point. According to Plato, e.g., the philosopher, namely the man of spirit par excellence, ought to govern the State and enact its laws because he is endowed with more intellectual faculties than the rest of the citizens; he distinguishes himself among them by encompassing in his vision the universal and the eternal. The prophet, according to Jewish belief, and this applies above of all to Moses, is an excellent philosopher too, but he is also

[80]*Ibid.*

[81]*Ibid.*, p. 306.

[82]Amos V:5: "Beth-El shall come to Aven"; compare also Joshua VII:2: "Beth-Aven, on the east side of Beth-el". The Hebrew word *miqedem* may also be translated as "formerly" instead of "on the east side". According to *Kings* II, X:29, Jeroboam and Jehu turned Beth-El into a place of sin. Hosea X:5, also mentions "Bethaven".

[83]By this denomination of the circumcised child (Exodus IV:25), Hamann means Jesus whose city is Jerusalem; this is another allusion to Berlin, the stronghold of the Enlightenment, and to Mendelssohn's *Jerusalem*.

[84]*Golgatha*, *op. cit.*, p. 306. As mentioned before, Hamann very often employed the word "Babel" to designate Berlin.

[85]Hamann, *Werke* (ed. Nadler), II, *op. cit.*, p. 214.

[86]*Golgatha*, *op. cit.*, p. 307.

endowed with an additional faculty which is withheld from the Platonian philosopher, to wit: his acting in the name of God. He is inspired by God's spirit.[87] The establishment and government of Plato's ideal State should be handed over to the "Guardians", the wisest and cleverest of the citizens; the State thus becomes the spiritual product of human thought. It is certainly no accident that Plato despaired of its possible constitution, and in the "Laws" he contented himself with outlining the "second-best State". The prophet, on the other hand, as leader of his people – this holds again for Moses and the prophets up to Samuel – expresses the idea that the constitution of a perfect human society is beyond the achievement of a human being, were he even the wisest of men. Therefore the prophet acts under divine guidance. He transmits the "word of God". He is not only an accomplished philosopher but God's messenger. This conception has been formulated in the most systematic and consequential manner in Maimonides's *Guide of the Perplexed.* Hamann has completely missed this important point that Moses as prophet and Moses as law-giver are indivisible. By his artificial and arbitrary separation of the two functions he wished to insinuate that Judaism sticks to Moses's outdated law while Moses's prophecy belongs to Christianity, as a harbinger of those spiritual elements that were embodied afterwards in Jesus's revelation.

In this context an interesting comparison is worthy of being mentioned. Spinoza, in his *Theologico-Political Treatise*, confronted Moses, the law-giver of a single people, with Jesus, the moral teacher of all mankind.

> "Moses does not teach the Jews as a prophet not to kill or to steal, but gives them these commandments solely as a lawgiver and judge"

while

> "Christ . . . his sole care was to teach moral doctrines, and distinguish them from the laws of the State".[88]

Mosaic Law, on the other hand, "aimed not so much at instructing the Jews as at keeping them under constraint".[89] It follows that Hamann endeavours to apply Spinoza's distinction between Moses and Jesus to Moses himself: one Moses as seen by Judaism, namely Mendelssohn's view, and another Moses as seen by Christianity, namely Hamann's view. Whether he has been influenced in this regard by Spinoza, is difficult to ascertain. He knew his writings very well.

> "I do not possess either Spinoza or Hobbes both of whom I have read twenty years ago with true fascination ("wahrer Andacht"); I owe them more thanks than to Shaftesbury and Leibniz".[90]

[87]Plato talked about divine inspiration in connection with poets, but in their case it involves intellectual mediocrity. They only convey divine messages but do not create anything on their own behalf; see *Yon* 531a f., cf. also *Apologia* 22b.

[88]*Theologico-Political Treatise. The Chief Works of Benedict de Spinoza*, vol. I, New York 1951, pp. 70–71.

[89]*Ibid.*

[90]Letter to Jacobi, 14th November 1784, Gildemeister, *op. cit.*, p. 15.

Two weeks later he informs Jacobi that all the principal writings of Spinoza lie on his desk.[91] In his letters he mentions his repeated study of the *Ethics*, *Theologico-Political Treatise*, *On the Correction of the Understanding* and the *Principles of Descartes' Philosophy*. His interest in Spinoza grew in the wake of the strife between Jacobi and Mendelssohn on the alleged Spinozism of Lessing. Hamann, of course, took sides with Jacobi. He recoiled from Spinoza's philosophy because it represented a "Cartesianismus outré";[92] in particular he detested the *Ethics* which aroused his "disgust on account of its tasteless and ridiculous method".[93]

Nevertheless, the above-mentioned similarity between Spinoza's remarks on Moses and Jesus and Hamann's remarks on Moses strengthens the possible conjecture that Hamann may have been influenced by the *Theologico-Political Treatise*. His general error, however, is not confined to his view of Moses but involves likewise his general view of prophecy. When he spoke of "the whole Moses and all the prophets", he completely disregarded all the distinctive features of Hebrew prophecy after Samuel. The later prophets are not rulers or lawgivers in the name of God as was Moses. The period of theocracy that Josephus Flavius believed to be the particular form of government of ancient Israel, had already come to its end by then. Practical political rule belonged to the kings and priests while the prophet took upon himself from then on the assignment of teacher, preacher and moralist. In the new social and political reality he represents, to employ a modern term, the opposition protesting against the deeds of the rulers and proclaiming ethical, social and religious ideals. His fellow-citizens do not heed his warnings and look on him as "the crazy man-of-spirit". No wonder that Spinoza who characterised education towards obedience and God-fearing as the main task of religion, criticised the prophets who disobeyed the authorities and violated regular social relations. Spinoza, the author of the *Ethics*, underrated the ethical message of the Hebrew prophets, notwithstanding its pronounced universal signification.

Jews and Christians thus differ, according to Hamann, not only in their relationship to Jesus but also in their relation to Moses. Disobedience to the Torah of Moses – Hamann emphasises Torah instead of Law – brings about death and exile. This is indeed what happened to the Jews. Obedience to the Torah is followed by life and the promised land. This is in store for the Christians. According to Hamann's christological version, Moses is our contemporary; he helps us to distinguish between unbelieving Jews and believing Christians. Christianity does not believe in philosophical theories, and must not be corroborated philosophically. Otherwise it would be congruent with natural religion. Mendelssohn's view of reason as the common denominator of natural religion and Judaism exasperates Hamann:

> "No, Christianity does not know any other shackles of faith except the stern prophetic word in the oldest documents of mankind and in the Holy Scriptures of genuine Judaism, free of Samaritan segregation and apocryphal Mishna."[94]

[91] 1st December 1784, *ibid.*, p. 20.
[92] 14th November 1784, *ibid.*, p. 15.
[93] 11th January 1785, *ibid.*, p. 42.
[94] *Golgatha, op. cit.*, p. 306.

The expression "shackles of faith" harks back to Mendelssohn's statement that the Articles of Faith (of Maimonides, Chasdai, Albo and Abarbanel), "thank God, they have not been forged into shackles for our beliefs".[95] "The oldest documents of mankind" hints at Herder's book on the Bible[96] about which Hamann had written previously a very critical review.

Hamann grounds his Christian faith in the Bible, and does not hesitate to speak of the Jews as "the chosen people of all the peoples of the world, appointed for the salvation of mankind".[97] He claims to restore, for universal eschatological purposes, the religious foundation of "true Judaism" which has been dropped, as it were, by Mendelssohn, who based Judaism on revealed law alone. If, however, the Jews are God's chosen people, despite violating Moses's Torah and disobeying Samuel, this proves that they were not elected for special virtues and rights but only by God's grace. It is very important for him to show that the election of Israel does not imply any spiritual superiority. In order to restore "true" Judaism, Hamann does not spare any effort to diminish Moses's status as a legislator. The fact that he was obliged to formulate such a detailed legislation serves as further proof that on the one hand Moses was unable to rule his people by his personality but needed multiple paragraphs of authoritarian law to cope with them; on the other hand this proves that the Jews were still imbued with slave-mentality. A law is "a common need of slaves and despots who resemble them."[98] This reminds one again of Spinoza's argument that when the people of Israel left Egypt they had not yet got rid of their slave-mentality; they were not yet able to conduct their affairs as free men but needed a competent ruler. But Spinoza's picture of Moses is utterly different from Hamann's. The law was not a substitute for the inadequacy of Moses as a ruler but, on the contrary, the religious-political law was meant to educate the people to obedience not out of fear but by way of free will and understanding.

> "He then, by the Divine virtue he possessed, made laws and ordained them for the people, taking the greatest care that they should be obeyed willingly and not through fear . . . [Moses] introduced a religion, so that the people might do their duty from devotion rather than fear."[99]

In this inquiry we are not concerned with Spinoza's concept of religion as such but it seemed noteworthy to confront his remarks about Moses's political wisdom in giving the Law to his people with Hamann's slanderous comment that the law was an expression of Moses's "great incompetence" ("so grosse Unfähigkeit") as a ruler.[100] Spinoza, despite his ambivalent and sometimes inimical attitude to Judaism, emphasised the positive aims of Mosaic Law while Hamann,

[95]*Jerusalem, op. cit.*, p. 72; the inclusion of Abarbanel in this connection seems to be an error of Mendelssohn.

[96]J. G. Herder, *Älteste Urkunde des Menschengeschlechts*, Riga 1774.

[97]*Golgatha, op. cit.*, p. 306.

[98]*Ibid.*, p. 307; "ein gemeinschaftliches Bedürfnis für Sclaven und ihnen ähnlichen Despoten".

[99]Spinoza, *op. cit.*, p. 75.

[100]By the way, Goethe afterwards followed Hamann's line of argument; in his biblical studies he also stressed Moses's supposed incompetence; see J. W. Goethe, *Israel in der Wüste; Goethes sämtliche Werke*, Jubiläumsausgabe Cotta, Stuttgart–Berlin 1912, V; see also *Dichtung und Wahrheit*, Goethe's autobiography.

pretending to defend ("true") Judaism, dwelt on its negative nature. His main design was, of course, to refute Mendelssohn who established Judaism on (revealed) law. He therefore added that Moses's wisdom was in part no more than "Egyptian booty", "Midianite cleverness" and "Chinese ceremonials".[101] The hidden implication is quite clear: if Mendelssohn asserted that Mosaic Law is the distinctive feature of Judaism, Hamann now insinuates that, as a matter of fact, this law has almost no original Jewish ingredients by which to support the election of Israel but is some kind of conglomerate of Egyptian, Midianite and . . . Chinese elements. No wonder, he comments, that this "catechism of universal human religion"[102] deteriorated into "the empty babble of Aaron" ("lose Geschwätz Arons").[103]

VIII. JESUS'S REVELATION VERSUS SINAI REVELATION

The Rabbis, as it were, continued the task, inaugurated by Aaron and the priests, and thus lost the "key of knowledge", that is to say they did not comprehend that the covenant with Abraham was the '*Old Covenant*" ("Old Testament") announcing the "*New Covenant*". Christianity was able to conceive of the "old" testament as "old" while Judaism ignored this. Having lost the key, the Rabbis could no longer open "the lock of faith" showing the way to the kingdom of heaven, and they barred the way to Jesus. Reason not only kept them away from the main road, namely faith, but moreover prevented them from drawing the necessary lesson obtainable by the right use of reason. He thus continues a traditional argument of Christian theology, namely that the destruction of the temple and the conquest of the ancient Jewish state rendered "Mosaic Law that was necessarily linked to the property and institutions of the country"[104] superfluous and senseless. That historical fact represented a divine declaration of much more public impact than the volcanic happenings at Mt. Sinai; they constituted a conclusive proof of the advent of the Messiah.[105] Hamann tries to refute Mendelssohn's argument that Mosaic Law, given to the people of Israel through public divine revelation, commits them and their descendants until its official cancellation by a similar public divine revelation in the future. From Mendelssohn's argument it follows that if such public revelation has not yet occurred, Jesus's coming does not represent an act of revelation either, or at least not an equivalent act to God's revelation at Sinai. He, therefore, attempts to assert the contrary: the destruction of the temple, being a historical event, expresses God's will much more blatantly than the spectacle of merely natural phenomena at Sinai – a mountain enveloped in smoke and so on. Interestingly enough, Hamann repeats again a well-known argument of Spinoza, namely that the commandments of the Torah formed the political laws of the ancient Jewish state, and after its disappearance they ceased to be valid. But while Spinoza's

[101] *Golgatha, op. cit.*, p. 307.
[102] *Ibid.* Again an allusion to Mendelssohn's remark that "human knowledge can be reduced to a few fundamental concepts which may be considered axiomatic"; *Jerusalem, op. cit.*, p. 73.
[103] *Golgatha, op. cit.*, p. 307.
[104] *Ibid.*, p. 308.
[105] *Ibid.*

inquiry dealt with secular-political aspects,[106] Hamann dealt with religious-metaphysical aspects; Judaism should have made way for Christianity since the true meaning of the destruction of the temple was a public demonstration of Jesus's Messianism. Spinoza's subject-matter was the *Jewish People* and its ancient commonwealth; Hamann's subject-matter was *Judaism*. The chronological proximity of Jesus and the destruction of the temple always prompted Christian theologians to see a providential link between the two. Unlike Spinoza who was guided in his inquiry by a secular outlook, Hamann followed, in this respect, the footsteps of traditional Christian theology.

Thus both Mendelssohn and Hamann lean on Spinoza's arguments; the political nature of Mosaic Law was a common point-of-departure for all three of them; the status of Mosaic Law in the Diaspora constitutes the dividing line between them. Spinoza considered the Law to have become superfluous, Mendelssohn considered it to have acquired religious-moral signification while according to Hamann it had turned into a stumbling block barring the way to true belief. Mendelssohn rejected Spinoza's view in order to safeguard the distinctive essence of Mosaic Law in the Diaspora while Hamann, rather paradoxically again, accepted it in order to defend the traditional Christian thesis which Spinoza never as much as mentioned, namely that Judaism must cede its place to Christianity. While Spinoza and Mendelssohn both appreciated the constructive role of Mosaic Law in the ancient Jewish commonwealth (despite their divergences as to its later status), Hamann, from the very beginning, dissociated himself from it; it obstructed the straight passage from God's covenant with Abraham, the "Old Testament", to the "New Testament", both grounded in faith. Because Mendelssohn assumedly did not catch the true message Hamann speaks of him as "an uncircumcised Sophist",[107] i.e. his thought has remained pagan.

As against the revelation of Christ – "Golgatha" – which was of universal bearing and eternal nature, God's revelation to Israel, through Moses, in the desert was of particular significance and temporary nature only. If Mendelssohn claims that what distinguishes Judaism is not a religious element but the Law revealed to Moses, how can such a legislation, adapted to a specific historical situation in the desert long ago, still befit the Jewish situation in modern times? This would be an inconceivable miracle. It is therefore unbelievable that the Law should have been the most important feature of Biblical Judaism. The significance of the Bible is to be searched for elsewhere, in its preliminary tidings of Jesus. Hamann again repeats an age-old hermeneutic principle of Christian theology. The "horoscope" of the "heavenly hero, by whose advent everything is and will be completed",[108] is not to be revealed by the stars worshipped by the pagans but in the Scriptures, the Pentateuch and the Prophets. The biblical text must be interpreted correctly and properly.

Moses established a temporary and historically limited theocracy but through it transmitted a universal message. Therefore Moses the lawgiver symbolises

[106] Spinoza, *op. cit.*, pp. 55–56.
[107] *Golgatha, op. cit.*, p. 308.
[108] *Ibid.*

false Judaism while Moses the prophet whose prophecy the Jews neglected, symbolises true Judaism, the cradle of Christianity. In this version Judaism is "der eigentliche ursprüngliche Edelmann des ganzen menschlichen Geschlechts"[109] because it derives its original nobility from Abraham, the forefather of all true believers.

IX. HAMANN ON MENDELSSOHN'S ALLEGED "ATHEISM"

A considerable part of *Golgatha* deals with Mendelssohn's "systematic atheism" which Hamann believes to derive from his deplorable "atticism", i.e. the legacy of Greek philosophy.[110] Although the context of those passages makes it clear that the main targets of his attack were Friedrich II and Lessing, Hamann informs Jacobi that Mendelssohn was deeply hurt by the accusation of "systematic atheism" and "atticism".[111] He admits to being troubled by pangs of conscience,[112] and feels relieved when Johann Heinrich Schultz, a Christian clergyman professing some eccentric religious atheism, also wrote a little treatise against *Jerusalem*. Schultz thus "took his place" and relieved him of the necessity for continuing his critical work. He abhors "polemical bloodshed".[113] He tells Jacobi that Mendelssohn, humorously, compared his polemics with Schultz and Hamann to Abraham's dilemma when Sarah accused him of impotency and Hagar of her pregnancy, and he was obliged to admit both.[114] Hamann expected, however, that the attack on "his old friend Mendelssohn" will encourage him to clarify his views on Spinozism. When Mendelssohn's *Morgenstunden* appeared a year later he believed that his comments were perhaps one of the reasons, maybe even the main one, that urged Mendelssohn to formulate his conception of the Godhead in order to revoke the accusation of atheism.[115] His good intent to avoid "polemical bloodshed" did not last for long, however. When the Jacobi-Mendelssohn controversy reached its boiling-point, two days before Mendelssohn's death, Hamann incited Jacobi to deal with him "not with a warm hand but an ice-cold one".[116] After his excitement over the news of Mendelssohn's death calmed down, he again asserted that his concept of Judaism was better but at least from now on his criticism would not cause sorrow to his late friend.[117]

The fact, nevertheless, remains that if the charge of atheism was directed

[109]*Ibid.*, p. 309.

[110]*Ibid.* Similar distinctions between "Judaism" and "Atticism", and between "Abrahamism" and "Mosheism", are met in the nineteenth century, in the writings of S. D. Luzzatto, the Italian Jewish scholar; *Atticisme e Judaisme*, 1840 and other writings. It is, of course, difficult to ascertain if the latter has been influenced by Hamann though it looks quite possible.

[111]See Hamann's letters to Jacobi, Gildemeister, *op. cit.*, 14th November 1784, p. 13; 1st December 1784, p. 20; 5th December 1784, p. 25; 30th September 1785, p. 144.

[112]*Ibid.*, 1st December 1784, p. 20.

[113]*Ibid.*, 16th January 1785, p. 47. This does not fit in with the fact that most of Hamann's writings display pronounced polemical tendencies; see also Altmann, *op. cit.*, pp. 639–640.

[114]Gildemeister, *op. cit.*, 31st March 1785, p. 70.

[115]*Ibid.*, 30th November 1785, p. 144.

[116]*Ibid.*, 4th January 1786, p. 184.

[117]*Ibid.*, also p. 194; he adds some reminiscences of his meetings with Mendelssohn in Berlin and Königsberg, p. 190.

against the leaders of the Berlin Enlightenment, and not just against Mendelssohn[118] then he had had enough time to make this point clear instead of regretting that he did not do so in time. Moreover, in the same letter he expressed his doubts whether Mendelssohn did understand his *Golgatha*, and was even a little bit alarmed whether he, Hamann, perhaps misunderstood Mendelssohn. But these anxieties were quickly overcome.[119] A month later, having read Mendelssohn's posthumous *An die Freunde Lessings*, he again characterises Mendelssohn by such slanderous epithets as "sophist, liar, mendacious".[120] He searches in vain for the exalted qualities that the Berlin Enlighteners attributed to him; *Morgenstunden* makes him feel "as in an empty arid wilderness with darkness upon the face of the deep, and the spirit of God does not move upon the face of the waters of his writing".[121]

X. PHILOSOPHY OF LANGUAGE – HAMANN VERSUS MENDELSSOHN

Having condemned Mendelssohn's alleged atheism, Hamann turns his attention back to Mendelssohn's philosophical conception of language. Mendelssohn, as it were, adopted the fundamental assumptions of the Enlightenment that proclaimed priority of writing (Schrift) over language (i.e. speech). Written words signify the things themselves. But, claims Hamann, Mendelssohn thus gives orders to language instead of receiving orders from it. Mendelssohn discarded Herder's famous presupposition which Hamann accepted to a certain extent, that the origin of language consists in absorbing sounds.

> "Some people make the assumption that our written alphabet merely represents a series of sounds and that sounds alone can denote objects and ideas. This assumption is completely without foundation. True, for those of us whose sense of auditory perception is highly developed, writing evokes primarily the spoken word. In other words, for us language is the path that leads from writing to object. But this need not always to be the case."[122]

Mendelssohn's proof depends on the awareness that "for a person who was born deaf, writing denotes objects immediately".[123] Mendelssohn's few remarks on the origin and essence of language in *Jerusalem*[124] are but part of much more detailed notes. Linguistic problems always fascinated him as he considered them also to be of relevance to his conception of the "ceremonial law". In *Jerusalem*, however, he restricted these issues to a few pages, in order not to transgress the principal subject-matter i.e. the elucidation of the essential uniqueness of Judaism. His fragmentary and speculative comments on language cannot stand the test of modern linguistics but it ought to be noted that unlike his naive views on

[118] *Ibid.*, 15th January 1786, p. 192, i.e. ten days after Mendelssohn's death.
[119] He arbitrarily exchanges certain words of Mendelssohn: "moral prejudices" instead of "moral truth" etc. (*Jerusalem, op. cit.*, p. 14); he thus distorts Mendelssohn's intentions, *ibid.*, pp. 194–195.
[120] Gildemeister, *op. cit.*, 15th February 1786, p. 220.
[121] *Ibid.*, 3rd April 1786, p. 278.
[122] *Jerusalem, op. cit.*, pp. 79–80.
[123] *Ibid.*, p. 80.
[124] *Ibid.*, pp. 78–83.

"Adamitic language" in *Or Netiva* (the Hebrew comment to his German Bible translation), his remarks on language in *Jerusalem* are of a more rationalist nature. While as an exegete Mendelssohn adopted, perhaps only outwardly, the more or less traditional view that the "lingua Adamica" in which God spoke to Adam was Hebrew,[125] as a philosopher he ascribed, as did the rest of the Enlighteners, to a natural explanation of the origin of language (its correctness is not our concern here). This, of course, aroused Hamann's anger; he was at the time the only important scholar who still defended the thesis of the divine origin of language. He rejected the assumption that written words were direct designations of things. Instead of leading the way towards understanding of reality, language becomes, according to Mendelssohn, an expression of reality. But then, says Hamann, religious language also expresses objective content. Language does not express content at all; it does not relate to objective data but *creates* its content. Were we to employ modern linguistic terminology, notwithstanding the unavoidable anachronism, Mendelssohn considered mainly what F. de Saussure (the "father" of structural linguistics) would have designated as "langue" while Hamann stressed what he would have called "parole" (speech). Saussure, like Chomsky afterwards, emphasised the creative aspect of "language", namely the capability of producing meaningful expressions. Hamann rebuffed Mendelssohn's assertion in a most vehement manner: It is nonsensical to assume that writ signifies things; only "deaf-born philosophers" dare suggest such a conjecture.[126]

There are two sides to Hamann's critique of Mendelssohn's linguistic concepts. On the one hand he once again distorts Mendelssohn's view. The latter asserted that things themselves are original "sight-signs"; later an increasing sophistication of the signifiers takes place. Mendelssohn admitted that "these variations of the modes of writing and notation must have had a significant effect on the development and advancement of our concepts and knowledge".[127] He rightly proclaims that there are many people who lack the "skill of writing" but are nevertheless endowed with very variegated speech much of which cannot even be reproduced accurately in our written language.[128] Such statements refute many of Hamann's criticisms.

On the other hand, several aspects of Hamann's concept of language, and especially religious language, are undubitably closer to certain modern linguistic trends than Mendelssohn's. One ought not to forget that linguistic problems had also been for many years one of Hamann's favourite preoccupations, much more than Mendelssohn's. This applies in particular to the relationship between language and thought. Therefore, as against Mendelssohn's above-mentioned assertion that "language is the path that leads from writing to object",[129] Hamann states that in understanding a religious text one proceeds from spoken language through written language to things. It is not the written word which

[125] *Or Netivah*; *Mendelssohn's Gesammelte Schriften*, Jubiläumsausgabe, *op. cit.*, Bd. XIV, pp. 214 f.

[126] *Golgatha, op. cit.*, p. 310. Hamann hints at Mendelssohn's proposition that "for a person who was born deaf, writing denotes objects immediately".

[127] *Jerusalem, op. cit.*, p. 81.

[128] *Ibid.*

[129] *Ibid.*, p. 80, see also above (note 123). Yet Mendelssohn added that this is not sufficient to prove that this necessarily must be so (*ibid.*).

leads to things, but the utterance that assures a living connection to things. It endows religious texts with meaning. But this involves again the arbitrary assumption that this state of affairs is not limited to religious language alone but that there is not any objective state of affairs at all. According to Mendelssohn there does exist an objective realm of things and concepts that has clear, preordained meanings of which the words are but the signs. This point reveals a surprising similarity between Mendelssohn's conception of language and certain semiological theories of contemporary linguistics (again, with due respect to the obvious shortcomings of such analogies). But according to Hamann, as said before, language creates its meanings, an issue which is discussed in *Golgatha* in the context of religious language.

While Mendelssohn, true to his rationalist outlook, accords priority to reason, Hamann gives preference to imagination. Not discursive prose but poetry is the mother-tongue of mankind. In this regard he is followed by his pupil, Herder, although the latter denied the divine origin of language.[130] The controversy on language, between Hamann and Mendelssohn, may be schematically summed up as follows: By emphasising vocal elements as the original essence of language, Hamann and Herder anticipated certain modern theories, especially in the field of phonology. They differed, however, as to its origin. Both exerted considerable influence on several Jewish thinkers – Hamann on Isaak Bernays (the presumed author of *Der Biblische Orient*) at the beginning of the nineteenth century, and on Rosenzweig and Buber in the twentieth, Herder on Samson Raphael Hirsch, the founder of neo-orthodoxy.

The point of departure for these discussions on the origin of language, with its salient repercussions on theological problems and Biblical Judaism, was the following question, formulated in 1769 by the Berlin Academy of Science: "If one assumes that men depend on their natural faculties alone could they have been capable of inventing language? If this is the case how could it have been achieved?" There evolved three main ways for tackling this question:

A. The naturalistic hypothesis: The origin of language is to be found in natural instincts and expressions that were developed and perfected in Man to such a degree as to form an essential distinction between him and the rest of the animals. Language is one of man's natural spiritual faculties, like reason, and moreover, serves as an instrument to express reason and reflexion. This was, summarily, Herder's answer.

B. The anthropological hypothesis: Language is invented by Man. It is a sign-system, fixed arbitrarily and validated by convention. Although this view was expressly formulated by Wilhelm von Humboldt only at the beginning of the nineteenth century, and has become famous, through Saussure's linguistic theory in the first decade of this century, it displays some striking similarities to Mendelssohn's speculative reflections on language, mentioned above. He asserted that language denotes, by its letters and words, extra-linguistic objective and eternal things and

[130] At the end of the eighteenth century, Salomon Maimon proclaimed, in opposition to this view, that man never should abandon reason to imagination since imagination is liable to deceive him as a thinking being and betray his theoretical wisdom; see *Streifereien im Gebiete der Philosophie* (1793). He thus more or less shared Mendelssohn's point of view.

concepts. Mendelssohn, the spokesman of Enlightenment, ascribed to language, as a central medium of expressing thought, an important place in philosophy. Clear and distinct language is a precondition of clear and distinct thought.[131] In his short essay *Über die Frage: Was heisst Aufklären?*[132] Mendelssohn revealed language as being the yard-stick *par excellence* of culture and education. By its theoretical use, denoting things and concepts, language serves science and reflects the educational standard of a people while by its practical use it signifies objective phenomena of social customs and reflects the cultural standard of the people. Despite the speculative formulation, language thus functions as a distinctive criterion between education and culture, and between theory and praxis.

C. The theological (super-natural) hypothesis: Language is of divine origin. This proposition, ventured by T. P. Süssmilch in 1766, instigated the Academy to announce its prize-question. It was refuted by Herder who won the prize. Süssmilch had claimed that language is indeed the instrument of reason, moreover its prime condition. However, this wonderful instrument could only have been produced by super-human reason. It is impossible to assume that language preceded its invention or that Man, for whom language is the precondition of reason, should have been endowed beforehand with the necessary amount of reason to invent it. Thus there remains only one possible alternative: God alone could have invented language and awarded it, by his divine grace, as a gift to Man. Language, to use Rosenzweig's well-known expression, is "God's dowry to mankind".[133] Hamann adopted this argument but added another layer to its supposedly logical structure which stressed again its irrational and mystical nature: Language is God's invention of which Man – in the course of his historical experience – must discover the hidden meaning. By language will be revealed to him the true contents of reality, especially religious reality.[134] Language results from "Göttlicher Unterricht". By listening to God's voice Man acquired language-capacity. Hamann tried to corroborate this assertion by numerous quotations from *Genesis*.

In this connection another point ought to be mentioned: Reason, by its very nature, is not subordinated to temporal-historical contexts; to paraphrase Mendelssohn, its status is the same as "eternal truths". "Instruction" ("Unterricht"), on the other hand, is an activity performed in time, at certain times. The "Torah"[135] has been given to the People of Israel in a definite historical context – the revelation at Sinai. Hamann's hypothesis of the divine origin of language, i.e. his conjecture that God has "taught" language to Man, can be reconciled more easily with historical tradition than Herder's naturalistic

[131]These were, among others, some of Mendelssohn's motives in *Koheleth-Mussar* and in his Bible translation.

[132]*Mendelssohn's Gesammelte Schriften*, *op. cit.*, 1843, III, pp. 399–403. The essay was published in the same year and by the same journal with Kant's famous response to the question.

[133]*Stern der Erlösung*, *op. cit.*, II, p. 29.

[134]As said before Hamann's writings on language are scattered throughout various small essays; they have been published by J. Simon in a critical edition (*Schriften zur Sprache*, see note 27).

[135]The Hebrew word "Tora" belongs to the same linguistic root as "Hora'a", which means "instruction".

hypothesis or Mendelssohn's rational conception. What is attainable by reason, is attainable forever; that is to say, it is meta-historical. Furthermore, if God instructed Man with language that indicates that God willed it so. Human language thus expresses God's will to establish by its means a "covenant" with Man. So Hamann managed to associate his philosophy-of-language with his focal idea about the "first covenant" with Abraham which we have already encountered in his theological meditations.

Since the origin of language emanates from God, Hamann decrees that all enquiries concerning its beginnings are simply futile. 'God "speaks" to Man, or to all living creatures, through nature and history. To try and understand God's ways is *prima facie* true "philology". Every natural phenomenon or historical event is God's "word". All these words together form a coherent "language". "Nature has been given to us in order to open our eyes, history has been given to us in order to open our ears . . ."[136] This is the crux of language. Hamann distinguishes between "Offenbarung" (revelation) which derives from "Offenheit" (openness), and "Überlieferung" (tradition); the latter leans on fixed modes of apperception that once existed but are now closed to us. Language functions instead: through it "Überlieferungen" are transmitted ("mitgetheilt").[137] Divine revelation is not solely confined to nature and history but there is a still more important revelation – the Holy Scriptures. There revelation endows faith with its principal tenets. We may encounter similar thoughts nowadays in Buber's philosophy, namely that everything that happens in nature and history is "divine speech".[138] Buber puts a sharper edge to Hamann's saying that "history has been given to us to open our eyes"; if Man shuts his ears, God's words do not reach him. It then only appears to him that God does not reveal himself anymore but hides himself from Man. Both – Hamann implicitly, Buber explicitly – point at the difference of divine speech in nature and history, in order to explain its discontinuity in the latter sphere. Both believe that this disruption is only apparent; the "short circuit" in God's dialogue with Man is caused by Man and can be overcome.

The proposition that God speaks to Man through nature and history is of utmost importance to Hamann since language is thus transformed into the basis of social and religious life. It is Man's duty to keep the word of God.

"Without language no reason, without reason no religion, and without these three essential components of our nature there is no social spirit and no social bond"[139] There exist firm connections and interaction between ways of life and language. The strict performance of the commands of the Torah by the Jews, although Hamann criticises Mendelssohn's legalistic view, can be observed in their language too.[140] Without being aware of it, Hamann repeats Mendelssohn's idea of the relationship between language and ways of life, manifesting a people's culture.

[136] *Schriften zur Sprache*, *op. cit.*, p. 71.
[137] *Ibid.*, p. 97.
[138] Martin Buber, *An der Wende. Reden über das Judentum*, Köln–Olten 1952, pp. 98 f.
[139] *Schriften zur Sprache*, *op. cit.*, p. 127.
[140] *Ibid.*, p. 90.

Mendelssohn was attracted by the second hypothesis on language that already hovered in the intellectual climate of the time. His position, albeit sticking to its rational foundation, had not yet got rid of its speculative nature. But he also adopted, inadvertently perhaps, some features of the first hypothesis. The astonishing outcome of the whole affair lies, however, in the fact that Hamann relies, in his criticism of Mendelssohn's concept of language, mainly on Mendelssohn's proper ideas, as, e.g., his assertion that "human knowledge can be reduced to a few fundamental concepts which may be considered axiomatic".[141] The same applies to Mendelssohn's statement that

> "people must have had frequent occasions to transform writing into speech and speech into writing, and thus to compare audible and visible symbols. As a consequence, they must soon have noticed that certain sounds recur in the spoken language quite frequently, just as certain figurative components recur in different hieroglyphic images, and that different combinations produce a multiplicity of meanings.[142]

Hamann applies these opinions of Mendelssohn to the history of the Jewish people.[143] As one can express by means of a few letters all ideas,[144] so, precisely in the same manner, Jewish biblical history constitutes an "Elementarbuch" of the essential contents of all human history.[145] The analogy in itself is, of course, artificial but it is very characteristic of Hamann's favourite line of thought. The facts of Jewish history form the alphabet of divine language, translated into human language. The history of Israel, as narrated by the Bible, constitutes the fundament of human and world history, guided by divine providence. It represents a "Fingerzeig", an expression used by Lessing before him.[146] Hamann probably borrowed it from the Hebrew expression "the finger of God". Biblical language contains mysterious revelatory language that cannot be translated into ordinary and rational language. The "word" is first of all "the word of God".[147]

XI. JEWISH HISTORY ACCORDING TO LESSING, MENDELSSOHN AND HAMANN

Both Mendelssohn and Hamann dissociated themselves from Lessing's small book *Erziehung des Menschengeschlechts*. According to Lessing, Jewish revelation – the childhood of mankind – as well as Christian revelation – the adolescence of mankind – should make way, with the maturation of mankind, to reason which befits maturity. Hamann believed only in one single revelation, namely that of Jesus. Lessing's book implied the degradation of the religion which represented the highest expression of divine revelation, of God's word and of salvation;

[141]*Jerusalem, op. cit.*, p. 73.
[142]*Ibid.*, p. 80.
[143]*Golgatha, op. cit.*, pp. 310–311.
[144]This reminds us incidentally of Humboldt's famous saying that human language makes infinite use of finite means; see also N. Chomsky, *Cartesian Linguistics*, New York–London 1966, p. 24.
[145]*Golgatha, op. cit.*, p. 311.
[146]*Lessings Werke*, Leipzig–Wien 1901, V, p. 622.
[147]Despite the repeated paraphrases of Mendelssohn's *Jerusalem*, Hamann's remarks in this context aim not so much at *Jerusalem* of the Jewish philosopher than at *Erziehung des Menschengeschlechts* of Lessing.

Lessing, as it were, turned religion into an outmoded means of natural ends, of human reason, i.e., into a mere instrument for the intellectual and moral education of mankind. According to Lessing Man not God, becomes the centre of the universe and of history while according to Hamann this centre is embodied in Christ's advent. Ancient Jewish history has already foretold – mainly in the books of the Prophets – Jesus's future revelation.

> "Nicht nur die ganze Geschichte des Judentums war Weissagung; sondern der Geist derselben beschäftigte sich vor allen übrigen Nationen, denen man das Analogon einer ähnlichen dunkeln Ahndung und Vorempfindung vielleicht nicht absprechen kann, mit dem Ideal eines Retters und Ritters, eines Kraft – und Wundermanns, eines Goel's, dessen Abkunft nach dem Fleisch aus dem Stamme Juda, sein Ausgang aus der Höhe aber des Vaters Schoss seyn sollte."[148]

This long and strange sentence demonstrates again Hamann's christological hermeneutics which associates different verses of the New Testament with sayings of Moses, the Prophets, the Psalms etc. that were believed to announce the future coming of Jesus. Jesus will accomplish the construction of the new, free and true Jerusalem that will replace the worldly Jerusalem of the Jewish temple. Mendelssohn had given his book the symbolical name of *Jerusalem* in order to stress Jewish Jerusalem against Christian Jerusalem; Hamann now does the exact contrary. He thus continues his principal argument about "true" and "false" Judaism; Jewish history flows in two channels; but only the true one leads to the Kingdom of Christ. He paraphrases Mendelssohn again: this channel contains "temporal and eternal historical truths".[149] The other channel, the false one, leads to "das Ende und Grab des mosaischen Kirchenstaats" which has become more oppressive than "ägyptische Knecht- und babylonische Gefangenschaft".[150] The conclusion is the same as before: After Jewish theocracy had come to its end, Mosaic Law – which Mendelssohn considered to be the very essence of Judaism – turned into an unbearable yoke because it imprisoned the Jews in a spiritual ghetto. Only the prophetic grain of Moses's Torah shows the way to true freedom, as expressed by Christian *Kerygma*.

XII. THE EPILOGUE OF GOLGATHA UND SCHEBLIMINI

At the end of the book, Hamann imagines himself "resting on the ruins of the philosophical-political Jerusalem",[151] namely Mendelssohn's *Jerusalem*, finally conquered by his assault. Mendelssohn disclaimed Jesus, i.e. the son, and whoever disclaims the son does not reach the father either.[152] This forms the dividing line between Christian belief and Mendelssohnian Jewish unbelief.[153] Mendelssohn, though born and circumcised a Jew, has remained essentially

[148] *Golgatha, op. cit.*, p. 311.
[149] *Ibid.*
[150] *Ibid.*, pp. 311–312.
[151] *Ibid.*, p. 315.
[152] These are, of course, paraphrases of the New Testament. See The first letter of John II:23; The Gospel according to John VIII:23.
[153] *Golgatha, op. cit.*, p. 315.

pagan. His philosophy expresses "pagan, naturalistic and atheistic fanaticism" – once more the same accusation as before – because he is unable to understand that God the Father and God the Son form "one single being". Thus his Jewish monotheism is no more than philosophical deism (quite a correct definition as such) while the true spirit of the Bible has been salvaged by him, Hamann, for the sake of Christianity.

Hamann does not content himself with religious-philosophical criticism of Mendelssohn but also takes up the age-old Christian allegation that the Jews killed God.

Mendelssohn remains at the end without a Messiah because there is no Messiah but Christ whose blood has been shed by his ancestors, with the support of Pontius Pilate and Herod.[154] Through their own fault the Jews missed salvation. They do not understand the true essence of their Judaism which he, Hamann, has saved from distortion by Mendelssohn. The Jew is like an adulterer who betrays his wife, namely genuine Judaism, for the sake of philosophy. "Diese ehebrecherische Philosophie, welche die Hälfte asdodisch redet, und nicht rein jüdisch . . ."[155] The recurrent analogy between Judaism and philosophy was, as shown above, one of Hamann's favourite pleas.

He terminates his booklet with an attempt to refute Mendelssohn's assertion that truth and falsehood belong to the realm of the intellect while good and evil belong to the realm of the will. Although Mendelssohn never expressed this assertion in as unequivocal a manner as did Spinoza before him, the idea can be inferred from his remarks on the impossibility of separating "action and conviction".[156] He asserts that knowledge of truth does not influence, or almost does not, man's actions which are guided by hope of reward and fear of punishment. Yet despite this link between "action and conviction" Mendelssohn thinks it necessary to separate intellect from will, and beliefs from actions:

> "All these excellent notions address themselves not to our ability to believe but to our capacity to understand and reflect. Among the precepts and ordinances of the Mosaic Law, there is none saying 'You shall believe' or 'You shall not believe'. All say 'You shall do' or 'You shall not do'. You are not commanded to believe, for faith accepts no commands; it accepts only what comes to it by reasoned conviction. All commandments of divine law are addressed to man's will, to his capacity to act".[157]

Hamann, on the contrary, believed the concepts of good and evil to depend on knowledge of truth. He therefore finishes *Golgatha* with the question "What is truth?"[158] answering in the traditional Christian way of belief: Truth is peace, accorded to the believer who trusts in God, the peace of mind that surpasses by far any intellectual achievement. This true peace manifests itself in the expectation of Jesus's return. It is interesting that Hamann did not conceive of truth, as was

[154] *Ibid.*

[155] *Ibid.*, p. 316. See Nehemiah XIII:23–24: "In those days also saw I Jews that had married wives of Ashdod, of Ammon and of Moab. And their children spake half in the speech of Ashdod, and could not speak in the Jews' language".

[156] *Jerusalem, op. cit.*, p. 18.

[157] *Ibid.*, p. 71.

[158] *Golgatha., op. cit.*, p. 318.

customary in traditional philosophy, as the point of departure for the possibility of the cognitive *processus* but as the result of belief. One encounters a similar idea, 150 years later, in Rosenzweig's philosophy. He also declared, contrary to nineteeth-century idealist philosophy, and in particular Hegel's, that "Die Wahrheit aber erscheint immer erst am Ende. Das Ende ist ihr Ort. Sie gilt uns nicht für gegeben, sie gilt uns für Ergebnis."[159] As said before, Hamann's ideas influenced Rosenzweig's philosophy in several respects. His "grammatical thinking" has already been mentioned. The most evident similarity consists perhaps in that both of them present themselves as philosophical realists, in the modern sense of the term, namely empiricists.

XIII. CONCLUSION

Attempting to recapitulate the dispute between Hamann's and Mendelssohn's concepts of Judaism, the first obvious conclusion would be that neither the one nor the other arrived at an adequate definition of the essence of Judaism. Mendelssohn adopted the line of rationalist hermeneutics, and reduced the uniqueness of Judaism to revealed law. It should be made clear, *en passant*, that most post-Mendelssohnian Jewish scholars misinterpreted Mendelssohn when they summarised his concept by the simplistic definition: "Judentum ist geoffenbartes Gesetz". One must distinguish, in Mendelssohn's conception, between the essence of Judaism and its uniqueness. Its uniqueness, that which distinguishes it from other monotheistic religions, is indeed Mosaic Law as embodied in the Torah; it was given in a public revelatory act at Mt. Sinai, and binds only the people who were present there and their descendants. The essence of Judaism comprises much more than that although the additional components are common to Judaism and other monotheistic religions. Mendelssohn defined Judaism by three strata, not by one. The first two strata are in principle common to all human beings, only the third one singles out Judaism but without the two others Judaism would not be what it is. Mendelssohn makes us understand though, very discreetly, that the religious concepts of Judaism fit the two first strata – eternal and historical truths attained by reason – far better than Christianity which is based on irrational elements, belief in unconvincing miracles etc. The misleading definition of Mendelssohn's disciples that "Judaism is revealed law" ought therefore to be replaced by some formulation that would make it wholly clear that according to Mendelssohn Judaism conforms to general deistic principles while its particular distinctive feature derives from Mosaic Law. Such a tentative definition implies two hidden propositions: 1. Jewish religion is ultimately more rational than Christianity; 2. Only in Judaism has an act of divine revelation (though revelation of a law, not of truths) indeed taken place. Only the People of Israel have been deemed worthy of such a divine act of grace the like of which did not happen elsewhere. This alleged superiority of Judaism can be easily deduced from between the lines of *Jerusalem* although Mendelssohn, of course, did not say so in an explicit manner. This point did not

[159] *Stern der Erlösung, op. cit.*, III, p. 178.

escape his contemporaries. It kindled most of the annoyance at Mendelssohn's book. This was undoubtedly also the main reason for Hamann's counter-attack.

Contrary to Mendelssohn's rationalistic line of argument which is, of course, not free of theoretical speculations and fallacies, Hamann employs, from the very beginning, a line of irrational and mystical hermeneutics, in the spirit of Lutheran Christianity. He had adopted this line in the wake of a religious crisis in his youth, during his stay in London. It then became clear to him that world, nature and history are the speech of God, revealing himself to Man. God's words are like hieroglyphs, allegories and symbols; the significance of Jewish history, as taught by the Bible, does not consist in what it tells us about ancient Israel but in symbolising a universal, trans-historical truth, namely the covenant between God and Man which reaches its culminating apotheosis in the New Testament.[160]

The hermeneutical foundation, i.e. the exegetical use of biblical verses, in Hamann's works exceeds by far what had been current in philosophical books of his time, including Mendelssohn's *Jerusalem*. His main argument, as has been shown, identified Judaism with the "old covenant", the "Abrahamsbund", the purpose of which was to prepare the way for the "new covenant" where Judaism would accomplish its mission by being integrated into Christianity. Mendelssohn's concept of Judaism fails in that it denies the idea that God, who by his very essence is beyond time, decided, at a definite historical moment, that is to say in time, to incarnate himself as a human being. Judaism has thus renounced true divine speech as manifested by Christ's incarnation and tidings. To sum up, according to Hamann Judaism refuses to be swallowed up by Christianity which is the latter's true preordained task. Therefore Judaism, as conceived by Mendelssohn, is estranged from its true nature, and has turned into false and distorted Judaism.

[160]'Gedanken über meinen Lebenslauf', in *Sybillinische Blätter des Magus*, *op. cit.*, p. 44.

The Symbiotic Relationship between French and German Jewry in the Age of Emancipation

BY JONATHAN I. HELFAND

The majority of French and German Jews in the eighteenth century cherished the same tradition, observed the same laws, and shared a common vision of the future.* As political and intellectual currents began to alter the face of Western Europe and foster new attitudes towards the Jew, French and German Jewry shared this experience too and reacted similarly to common stimuli. True, there were unique circumstances peculiar to each community and even differences between them. On the whole, however, the Jews of France and Germany had more in common than not.[1] Moreover, as Jacob Katz has observed, there was a "reciprocal influence" among Western European Jewries in the age of emancipation. Thus, he notes, "the example and teaching of German reformers like Mendelssohn had their effect on French Jews; and the political advances gained by French Jews through the French Revolution had their impact on German Jewry".[2]

This interrelationship, or "reciprocal influence", between West European Jewries is a basic premise of all modern Jewish historians. Surprisingly, however, little has been done to describe or measure the parameters of this "symbiosis". This paper will attempt just such a study, seeking to analyse the nature of the symbiotic relationship between two Jewries – French and German – during the last decades of the eighteenth century and the first half of the nineteenth century. The foci of this study will be the two principle movements during this period: the *Haskalah* and religious Reform.

I. HASKALAH

The locus of the *Haskalah* movement was Germany; its capital, Berlin. It was here in the latter decades of the eighteenth century that the movement for Jewish Enlightenment, inspired by the example of Mendelssohn, grew and flourished. Admirers of reason and science, devoted to the humanitarian ideals of the European *Aufklärung*, the *Maskilim* – men of the *Haskalah* – sought to transform themselves culturally and, in turn, re-shape the Jew and the Jewish community.[3]

* This paper is based on a lecture delivered at the Leo Baeck Institute, New York, on 29th April 1982.

[1]Jacob Katz, *Tradition and Crisis*, New York 1961, pp. 3–10. The nature of Jewish unity in the diaspora is discussed in Arthur Ruppin, *Soziologie der Juden*, vol. I, Berlin 1930, pp. 49–63 and Ben Zion Dinur, 'Israel in Diaspora', in his *Israel and the Diaspora*, Philadelphia 1969, pp. 1–76.

[2]Jacob Katz, *Out of the Ghetto*, New York 1978, pp. 3–4.

[3]On the attitudes and ideology of the German *Haskalah* see Isaac Eisenstein Barzilay, 'The Ideology of the Berlin Haskalah', *Proceedings of the American Academy for Jewish Research*, XXV (1956), pp. 1–37;

In order to realise their goals, the *Maskilim* proposed changes in education and pedagogy, elimination of what they regarded as Yiddish "jargon", and "productivisation" through vocational re-orientation. They proposed new schools with new curricula and textbooks, encouraged the revival of the Hebrew language as well as the mastery of European languages and culture, and wrote various publications to promote their programme.[4]

The Hebrew journal *Hame'asef* was the principle organ of the *Haskalah*. Published intermittently from 1784 to 1811, it represents the programme of the *Maskilim* and also reflects the process of their radicalisation. Whereas the earlier volumes of the 1780s are more conservative in tone and muted in their criticism of the Jewish establishment, the later volumes are more hostile and even bitter. They reflect the outspoken views of men like David Friedländer, who wrote that Jewish rituals were "time-consuming, expensive, and stigmatised the Jew as a stranger in society. They contributed in no small way to the feeling of hate towards him." Or of Lazarus Bendavid, who spoke of Orthodoxy as a hydra, "all of whose heads must be cut off at once".[5]

The *Haskalah* movement that took root in Germany was not without echoes or parallels in France. French Jewry of the late eighteenth century was actually a conglomerate of three cultural groupings: the Sephardim of the Bordeaux region, the Avignonese Jews in the Papal States, and the Ashkenazim of Alsace-Lorraine. Of the three, the most enlightened was the Sephardic community. When the Sephardic or "Portuguese" Jews began settling in Bordeaux in the sixteenth century, they did so as marranos. Their external culture was Christian; in their language, dress, education and social mores, they were virtually indistinguishable from their Christian neighbours. As these "Portuguese" began to emerge from the shadow of marranism and re-establish Jewish religious and institutional life, their culture and self-image continued to be influenced by their former status.[6] The impact of this cultural affinity on the religious outlook of Sephardic Jews is described by a contemporary author:

> "Les juifs de Bordeaux et de Bayonne, loin de vouloir faire de la Misna et du Talmud, comme les autres juifs, la base fondamentale de leur discipline, rejettent de leur croyance ce qui s'y trouve contraire ou non conforme au bon sens et au sens littéral de la bible, sur lesquels ils fondent les dogmes qui peuvent les intéresser."[7]

---

and 'The Treatment of the Jewish Religion in the Literature of the Berlin Haskalah', *Proceedings of the American Academy for Jewish Research*, XXIV (1955), pp. 39–68. Cf. Israel Zinberg, *History of Jewish Literature*, translated by Bernard Martin, vol. VIII, Cincinnati–New York 1976, pp. 59–87.

[4]In addition to the sources mentioned above, see also Mordechai Eliav, *Ha-hinukh ha-yehudi be-Germania be-yeme ha-haskalah ve-ha-emanzipaziah* (Jewish Education in Germany in the Period of the Enlightenment and Emancipation), Jerusalem 1960, pp. 119–127, 172–173.

[5]David Friedländer, *Sendschreiben an Seine Hochwürden Herrn Oberconsistorialrath und Probst Teller zu Berlin von einigen Hausvätern jüdischer Religion*, Berlin 1799, p. 17; Lazarus Bendavid, *Etwas zur Characteristik der Juden*, Leipzig 1793, p. 55. Quoted in Barzilay, 'The Treatment of the Jewish Religion in the Berlin Haskalah', *loc. cit.*, pp. 58, 60. As Jacob Katz has observed, in the course of time the *Maskilim* "grew to identify themselves with the criticism of their religion". See 'The Influence of Religion and Society on Each Other at the Time of Emancipation', in *Emancipation and Assimilation*, n.p. 1972, p. 80.

[6]Salo W. Baron, *A Social and Religious History of the Jews*, vol. XV, 2nd edn. Philadelphia 1973, pp. 75–122; and Arthur Hertzberg, *The French Enlightenment and the Jews*, New York 1970, pp. 140–163.

[7]Cited in Zosa Szajkowski, 'Hitnagshuyot ha-ortodoxim ve-ha-reformim be-zarfat' (Clashes of the Orthodox and Reformers in France), *Horeb*, XIV–XV (1960), p. 257, note 16.

Considering their background and attitude, it is not surprising that the most prominent representatives of cultural enlightenment came from the Sephardic community. For example, the linguist Jacob Rodrigues Péreire (1715–1780), political agent of the Bordeaux Jews in Paris (and innovator in the instruction of deaf-mutes), was "the first practicing Jew to become a figure of prominence in the intellectual circles of Paris".[8] Other noted intellectuals of Sephardic origin include David Gradis (1724–1811), author of several philosophic tracts; the philosopher Isaac de Pinto (1715–1788); the historian Louis Francia de Beaufleury (1752–1817); and Abraham Furtado (1756–1817), who was to serve as presiding officer at the Assembly of Notables in 1806.[9]

While undoubtedly ranking among the most cultured Jews of the age, these men have little to do with the *Haskalah* movement as such. The eighteenth-century *Haskalah* was a result of the clash and interplay between traditional Jewish culture and Western intellectual trends. Those, like the Sephardim, whose roots were not in the ghetto, could neither experience nor represent the ferment that produced the *Haskalah* movement.[10] At best, the German *Maskilim* and the Sephardim were aware of each other's intellectual achievements and activities. Beyond that, no meaningful exchange seems to have taken place.[11]

Leaving aside the Sephardic aristocrats, there were other enlightened Jews in pre- and post-revolutionary France who can properly be considered part of the *Haskalah* movement. The most famous of these was Zalkind Hourwitz. Born in Lublin in 1840, Hourwitz, like Salomon Maimon, went on a pilgrimage to Berlin.

[8]Hertzberg, *op. cit.*, pp. 141–142. For a biographical study of Péreire with emphasis on the parallels between him and Mendelssohn see Rina (Renée) Neher-Bernheim, 'Jacob Rodrigue Péreire', in *Proceedings of the Seventh World Congress of Jewish Studies: IV, History of the Jews in Europe*, Jerusalem 1981, pp. 57–66. See also Renée Neher-Bernheim, 'Un pionnier dans l'art de faire parler les sourds-muets, Jacob Rodrigue Péreire', in *Dix-huitième Siècle, Juifs et Judaisme*, 13 (1980), pp. 47–61.

[9]Gradis published *Courte dissertation sur l'origine du monde ou Réfutation du système de la Création*, Paris–Bordeaux 1798; *Discussions philosophiques sur la préexistance de la matière . . .*, Paris an VIII [1799]; *Essai de philosophie rationelle sur l'origine des choses*, Bordeaux an X [1801]. See Eliakim Carmoly, *Biographie des Israélites de France*, Frankfurt a. Main 1868, pp. 145–157.

Pinto lived most of his life outside France but wrote in French and is generally regarded as French. However, cf. Hertzberg, *op. cit.*, pp. 154–155.

Beaufleury's *Histoire de l'établissement des Juifs à Bordeaux et à Bayonne depuis 1550*, Paris an VIII [1799], is the first history of Sephardic Jewry in France. See Zosa Szajkowski, 'Louis Francia de Beaufleury a yiddisher fartreter deputet b'es der franzozisher revoluzia' (Louis Francia de Beaufleury A Jewish Substitute Deputy during the French Revolution), *Davke*, XX (1954), pp. 241–248.

Abraham Furtado served as President of the Assembly of Notables in 1806. For his biography see *Archives israélites*, II (1841), pp. 361–368.

There were also enlightened scholars among the Jews from the Papal States. Israel-Bernard de Valabrègue (c. 1714–1779) was interpreter for Hebrew and Oriental languages at the Royal Library. He, like Pinto, wrote a defence of the Jews. Hertzberg, *op. cit.*, pp. 62–64, 176–177; and Zosa Szajkowski, 'La Vita intellettuale profana fra gli Ebrei nella Francia del XVIII secolo', *La Rassegna Mensile di Israel*, XXVII (1961), p. 190. Reprinted in his *Jews and the French Revolutions of 1789, 1830, and 1848*, New York 1970, p. 783.

[10]Malino, *op. cit.*, p. 26, comments on the lack of "a serious confrontation with Judaism" in the writings of the enlightened Sephardic Jews of the period. (See note 64.)

[11]Mendelssohn and Pinto were aware of each other's achievements. Pinto, for example, made use of Mendelssohn's argument for the immortality of the soul in his *Traités* and Mendelssohn admired Pinto's defence of the Jews against the attack of Voltaire. Hertzberg, *op. cit.*, p. 150; Alexander Altmann, *Moses Mendelssohn. A Biographical Study*, London 1973, pp. 425–426.

From there he went to Metz and finally settled in Paris. In 1787 he submitted his now-famous essay, *Apologie des juifs*, for the contest sponsored by the Academy of Metz, ultimately sharing the prize with the Abbé Grégoire and the lawyer Adolphe Thiéry.[12] Hourwitz, however, remained a foreigner among French Jews; indeed, he signed himself "un juif Polonais". His opposition to Jewish communal autonomy and his harsh attacks on Jewish tradition, as much as his foreign origin, won him few friends among French Jews. In 1806 several rabbis threatened to leave the Assembly of Notables if Hourwitz were seated in their midst, and as late as 1937 native French historians opposed any special celebration of the 150th anniversary of his arrival in France.[13]

For authentic native *Maskilim*, one must look to Alsace-Lorraine, home of some 28,000 Jews, reared and trained not unlike their German brethren, speaking the same or a similar Yiddish or Judaeo-German, but joined by politics and fate to France. As political factors began to play a more important role in Jewish life in the latter part of the century, Alsatian and German Jews were set on different paths that emphasised their distinct and separate cultural identities.[14] Thus, the *Maskilim* who emerged in Alsace, though devoted to the cultural enterprise represented by Mendelssohn and his German disciples, maintained a distinct French character. In addition to Hebrew, they chose French, not German, as their vehicle of expression. Politically, they identified with France and, later, with the French Revolution. And, finally, they were the beneficiaries of enlightened French thought and politics, a factor that exerted a strong influence on their attitudes and development. Four names figure prominently in this group: Moses Ensheim, Berr Isaac Berr of Nancy, Isaiah Berr-Bing of Metz, and Cerfberr of Strasbourg.

Moses Ensheim, also known as Moses Metz, was closely associated with the *Haskalah* circles of Berlin; even his biography follows the classic pattern of his Berlin colleagues.[15] Born in 1750 to a poor Metz family, Ensheim received a traditional Jewish education in his youth. Only after his teenage years did he master French and German, as well as the classical languages and even Arabic.

[12]For his biography see Léon Kahn, *Les Juifs de Paris pendant la Révolution*, Paris 1898, pp. 130–150 and, most recently, Frances Malino, 'Zalkind Hourwitz juif polonais', in *Dix-huitième Siècle, Juifs ět Judaisme*, 13 (1980), pp. 79–89.

On the contest see Abraham Cahen, 'L'Emancipation des Juifs devant la Société Royale des Sciences et Arts de Metz en 1787 et M. Roederer', *Revue des Etudes Juives*, I (1880), pp. 83–104.

[13]Robert Anchel, 'Un Juif Polonais en France. Zalkind Hourwitz', *Univers israélite*, XCII, No. 38 (1936/1937), pp. 505–506. According to Anchel the Imperial Commissioner Molé wrote the following note on a letter dated 22nd September 1806: "Plusieurs rabbins disent qu'ils se retireraient de l'assemblée si ces deux individus [i.e. Hourwitz and Moses Ensheim] étaient choisis." According to Kahn (*op. cit.*, p. 131) Hourwitz was excluded because of his "dédain de la tenue et de l'élégance" which was offensive.

As to the celebration Anchel writes: "L'importance de cet événement ne justifierait peut-être pas de cérémonies trop nombreuses ou trop bruyantes . . . [Hourwitz] nous paraît avoir trop souvent manqué de tact, pour ne pas dire plus." As a final evaluation he adds, "il ne suffit pas de venir de l'Est pour apporter la lumière".

[14]On Alsatian culture see Freddy Raphael and Robert Weyl, *Juifs en Alsace, Culture, Société, Histoire*, Toulouse 1977; and *idem.*, *Regards nouveaux sur les Juifs d'Alsace*, Strasbourg 1980.

[15]Henry Léon, *Histoire de Juifs de Bayonne*, Paris 1893, pp. 377–378; *Archives israélites*, VI (1845), pp. 71–72.

An accomplished autodidact, he was hired as tutor in the home of Moses Mendelssohn, a position he held from 1782 to 1785. During that period he greatly impressed his young charge, Joseph, who in later years referred to him as a "profound thinker".[16] Upon his return to France, Ensheim was befriended by Abraham Furtado. Furtado ultimately found Ensheim a position as tutor in his brother Joseph's home in Bayonne. Ensheim remained with the Furtado family until his death in 1839.[17]

As a scholar, Ensheim's particular interest was mathematics. In 1799 he published a book on calculus entitled *Recherches sur les calculs différentials et intégrals*. His Hebrew writings, though scant, clearly align him with the *Haskalah* movement. In 1787 he published *Sheloshah hidot al ta'anugot po'ale batel* (Three Riddles on the Pleasures of Wastrels), a satire on game-playing, which was reprinted in *Hame'asef* two years later.[18] Ensheim's other literary contributions to *Hame'asef* include a poem in honour of the National Assembly,[19] as well as various reports on events in France, among them a translation of Berr Isaac Berr's address to the National Assembly and news of the emancipation of the Sephardic Jews.[20] In 1792 Ensheim composed a Hebrew poem, *La-Menaze'ah Shir*, to mark the anniversary of the Republic and the victory of the French Army in the field. The poem was translated into French by Isaiah Berr-Bing and chanted in the synagogue of Metz on 21st October 1792. The Hebrew text, together with the French translation, was published that year in Metz.[21]

Ensheim never expressed himself in print on the goals of the *Haskalah*, nor was he ever the author of any programmatic essays to instruct his fellow Jews or guide their future. He did, however, aid the Abbé Grégoire with the preparation of his prize-winning essay.[22] Ensheim's identification with the ideas expressed in that essay, in addition to his close association with the Mendelssohn household, made him, like Zalkind Hourwitz, *persona non grata* with some rabbinic members of the Assembly of Notables. Thus, he too was excluded from that body.[23] At the time of his death, Ensheim was eulogised in the French press by a leading proponent of religious Reform, his student Olry Terquem, as the "Nestor" of the Reform

[16]Altmann, *op. cit.*, p. 726.

[17]Léon, *op. cit.*, p. 378.

[18]Metz 1787; *Hame'sef*, 5550 (1790), pp. 69–72.

[19]*Ibid.*, pp. 33–37.

[20]*Ibid.*, pp. 30–32 (speech of Berr Isaac Berr), 187–188 (on the emancipation of Sephardic Jews); 5549 (1789), pp. 365–367 (on the convening of the National Assembly), 367–371 (letter sent by the Jews to the National Assembly), 371–372 (on Abbé Grégoire's speech to the National Assembly).

[21](Moses) Moyse Ensheim, *Cantique composé par le citoyen Moyse Ensheim, à l'occasion de la fête civique célébrée à Metz, le 21 octobre, l'an 1er de la République, dans le Temple des citoyens Israëlites.* See Zosa Szajkowski, 'The Emancipation of Jews During the French Revolution. A Bibliography of Books, Pamphlets, and Printed Documents, 1789–1800', *Studies in Bibliography and Booklore*, V (1959), No. 394. The French translation was done by Isaiah Berr-Bing.

On Ensheim's literary career see Joseph Klausner, *Historiah shel ha-sifrut ha-'ivrit ha-hadashah* (History of Modern Hebrew Literature), vol. I, Jerusalem 1952, pp. 320–321.

[22]Grégoire, acknowledging Ensheim's assistance, calls him "a learned German [sic] Jew and a disciple of Mendelssohn". Henri Grégoire, *Essay on the Physical, Moral, and Political Reformation of the Jews*, translated from the French, London n.d., p. 259, note 14.

[23]Anchel, *op. cit.*, p. 506. Cf. Simon Schwarzfuchs, *Napoleon, the Jews and the Sanhedrin*, London 1979, p. 90.

Movement, an accolade that was repeated by Ludwig Philippson in the pages of the *Allgemeine Zeitung des Judenthums*.[24]

Berr Isaac Berr (1744–1828), son of the syndic of Nancy, distinguished himself as a communal leader throughout his career.[25] In 1789 he represented the Jews of Alsace-Lorraine before the National Assembly and subsequently served as a member of the Assembly of Notables in 1806 and the Grand Sanhedrin in 1807. His literary pursuits in Hebrew and French, as well as his political activities, place him squarely in the tradition of the German *Haskalah*. Indeed, his affinity for that group is evidenced by the fact that he was a subscriber to *Hame'asef*.[26]

Berr's literary career began with a French translation of Rabbi Jacob Perle's prayer for the recovery of Louis XV and his elegy on the king's death.[27] Of greater significance, however, was Berr's translation of Naphtali Herz Wessely's monograph on educational reform, *Divrei Shalom Ve-emet*.[28] This work marked the beginning of his literary efforts to improve Jewish education and to gain civil rights for the Jews.

As syndic of the Jews of Lorraine, Berr played an important role in the discussions and debates on the question of Jewish emancipation. In August 1789 he was one of a delegation of six Jewish representatives from the eastern provinces who appeared before the National Assembly.[29] In October of that year he addressed the National Assembly on behalf of his constituents and presented them with the petition of the Jews of Alsace-Lorraine for equal rights and protection under the new constitution.[30]

Berr, unlike Hourwitz and his German counterparts, supported the idea of

[24]*Allgemeine Zeitung des Judenthums*, III (1839), p. 306. Philippson quotes Terquem's obituary from the *Courrier de la Moselle*. See also Elijahu Tcherikower, 'Ha-maavak le-shivui zekhuyot ha-yehudim be-zeman ha-mahapekhah ha-zarfatit 1789–1791' (The Struggle for Jewish Rights During the French Revolution), in *Yehudim be-'itot mahapekhah* (Jews in Times of Revolution), Tel-Aviv 1958, pp. 67–70.

[25]Carmoly, *op. cit.*, pp. 54–62; Tcherikower, *op. cit.*, pp. 78–79. On Berr's later years see Zosa Szajkowski, 'Zu der geschichte fun die franzozisher yidn' (On the History of French Jews), *Davke*, XXIV (1955), pp. 238–243.

[26]The subscription list for 5545 (1785) lists Ber Arshil of Nancy, another name for Berr Isaac Berr. According to Tcherikower, *op. cit.*, p. 78, note 43, the name derives from the French word for bear – *ours*.

[27]*Prières ordonnées par les Syndics de la Communauté des Juifs de Lorraine, et récitées soir et matin dans leurs Synagogues . . . pour demander à Dieu le rétablissement de la santé du Roi Louis XV, le Bien-âimé. Composées par le Rabin de Lorraine. Et traduites par le Sr. Berr-Isaac Berr, le jeune.* Nancy n.d.; *Plaintes et lamentations sur la mort du Roi Louis XV, de Glorieuse Mémoire, ordonnées par les Syndics de la Communauté des Juifs de Lorraine, et récitées dans leurs Synagogues, après avoir fait distribuer des aumônes. Composées par le Rabin de Lorraine Et traduites par le Sr. Berr-Isaac Berr, le jeune*, Nancy [1774]. See Zosa Szajkowski, *Franco Judaica. An Analytical Bibliography of Books, Pamphlets, Decrees, Briefs and Other Printed Documents Pertaining to the Jews in France 1500–1788*, New York 1962, Nos. 1659, 1660.

[28]*Instruction salutaire adressée aux communautés juives qui habitent paisiblement les villes de la dominion du Grand Empereur Joseph II . . . Traduite de l'Hébreu du célèbre Rabbin Naphtali Hertz Weisel de Berlin*, Berlin 1782. Szajkowski, *Franco Judaica*, No. 1634. A second edition was published in 1790.

[29]*Adresse présentée à l'Assemblée Nationale, le 31 août 1789, par les Députés réunis des Juifs, établis à Metz, dans les Trois Evêchés, en Alsace & en Lorraine*, n.p. [1789]. Berr is one of the signatories on pp. 17–18. Szajkowski, 'The Emancipation of the Jews . . .'. No. 12. See Hertzberg, *op. cit.*, pp. 186–187.

[30]The text of his address is given in Achille-Edmond Halphen, *Recueil des lois, décrets, ordonnances, avis du Conseil d'Etat, arrêtés et règlements concernant les Israélites depuis la Révolution de 1789*, Paris 1851, pp. 183–184. See also Szajkowski, 'The Emancipation of the Jews . . .', No. 16.

continued Jewish communal autonomy along with the extension of civil rights to the Jews. According to the historian Maurice Liber, it was Berr who influenced Thiéry to support Jewish autonomy in the essay he submitted to the contest sponsored by the Metz Academy.[31] Berr himself expressed his position in a letter in response to an anti-Jewish pamphlet by Bishop La Fare of Nancy. Berr suggested that the National Assembly grant Jews all civil rights, except the right to hold office, while allowing them to maintain internal communal autonomy.[32] His position was vigorously attacked by his nephew, the physician Jacob Berr, who labelled his uncle's proposal as "dangerous" and instead demanded emancipation without compromise and the abolition of Jewish communal autonomy.[33]

On the morrow of emancipation, however, Berr Isaac Berr changed his tactics. In a letter addressed to his fellow Jews after 28th September 1791, Berr urged them to adopt cultural, educational, and vocational reforms in response to the new privileges and obligations placed on them by the emancipatory legislation. His essay not only echoes but even cites the programme put forward by the German *Maskilim*. Calling the title "*citoyen actif*" most precious, he reminds his readers that they must also be fit to fulfil their new functions.[34]

> "If we cannot ourselves enjoy all the goodness that the new constitution offers us, inasmuch as it is very difficult to change manners and habits acquired over thirty or forty years, we will at least see our children gather the first fruits of this delicious plant . . . Our education has been faulty in many ways; the famous Rabbi Hartwig Wessely has already rendered us a great service by publishing diverse works in Hebrew on this matter; one of these works, entitled *Instructions salutaires adressées aux Communautés juives de l'Empire*, was published in French in 1782 . . . I urge you, my dear brothers, to pay attention to this author's ideas and you will easily see that our destiny and that of our progeny depends solely on the changes we shall make in our educational system."[35]

Berr goes on to encourage his co-religionists to teach their children Hebrew and, following the pedagogical model of Mendelssohn's *Biur*, to put an end to the use of *jargon* (i.e., Yiddish) by teachers. Ultimately, he envisions a French version of the *Biur*, reducing the number of languages required of students to two – French and Hebrew. Berr also recommends vocational education for the children of the poor to make them productive and useful to society.[36]

[31] Zosa Szajkowski, *Autonomy and Communal Jewish Debts During the French Revolution of 1789*, New York 1959, p. 8. Reprinted in Szajkowski, *Jews and the French Revolutions . . .*, p. 606.

[32] Berr Isaac Berr, *Lettre du sieur Berr-Isaac-Berr, négociant à Nancy, Juif, naturalisé en vertu des Lettres-patentes du Roi . . ., député des Juifs de la Lorraine; à Monseigneur l'évêque de Nancy, Député a l'Assemblée Nationale*, Paris 1790, pp. 17–19. Cf. Hertzberg, *op. cit.*, p. 348. In his *Réflexions sur la régénération complète des Juifs en France*, [Paris 1806], pp. 6–7, Berr blames the lack of a formal communal organisation for the "retardation of [Jewish] civil and moral regeneration".

[33] Jacob Berr, *Lettre du Sr. Jacob Berr, juif, maître en chirurgie à Nancy, à Monseigneur l'Evêque de Nancy, député à l'Assemblée Nationale, pour servir de réfutation de quelques erreurs qui se trouvent dans celle adressée à ce prélat, par le Sr. Berr-Isaac Berr*, [Nancy] 1790. Tcherikower, *op. cit.*, p. 80.

[34] *Lettre d'un Citoyen, membre de la ci-devant Communauté des Juifs de Lorraine à ses confrères à l'occasion du droit de Citoyen actif rendu aux Juifs par le décret de 28 septèmbre 1791.* Published with *Lettre du Sieur Berr-Isaac-Berr, manufacturier, Membre du Conseil municipal de Nancy A M. Grégoire, Sénateur, à Paris*, Nancy 1806, pp. 29–30.

[35] *Ibid.*, p. 34.

[36] *Ibid.*, pp. 35–37.

While thus endorsing the *Haskalah* programme of educational reform and productivisation, Berr strongly condemns as "monsters" those who "for whatever advantages they foresee in the new constitution, permit themselves to change the dogmas of their religion".[37] Berr's opposition to religious reform or change is evident again, fifteen years later, in a letter addressed to the Abbé (by then Bishop) Grégoire. Berr blames the failure of attempts to accelerate the vocational shift of Jews to more "productive" pursuits on the "continual indecision of my brethren" on the one hand, and the "criminal abandonment" of religion by some Jews on the other.[38] In 1806 his reputation as a conservative in religious matters led the liberal members of the Assembly of Notables to defeat his candidacy for chairman in favour of the more "enlightened" Abraham Furtado.[39]

Isaiah Berr-Bing of Metz (1759–1805) was described by Naphtali Herz Wessely as "a man of understanding, young in years and valiant, a writer and clear spokesman . . . one of the élite of our brethren, the holy congregation of Metz". This accolade is offered in Wessely's introduction to Bing's translation of Mendelssohn's *Phaedon* – a translation that Alexander Altmann has described as "a little masterpiece".[40] Wessely's esteem for Bing is echoed by the Abbé Grégoire, who refers to him as "a learned Jew of Metz and my intimate friend".[41] Grégoire was particularly indebted to Bing for his translations of *Behinat olam* of Jedaiah Bedersi and Yehuda Halevi's elegy *Zion ha-lo tishali*, both of which he used in his prize-winning essay.[42]

The publication of an anti-Jewish pamphlet in 1787 gave Bing the opportunity to express his views on Judaism and emancipation. Responding to the attacks on Judaism, he reminds his readers that at a time when the ancient Gauls were still pagans, Judaism had produced a Philo and a Josephus. If that ancient glory had declined, the fault lay with their persecutors, not the Jews. This cultural decline, according to Bing, is exemplified by Yiddish, a "muddled language" that is one of the elements preventing the enlightenment of the Jews.[43]

Bing strongly favours the cultural regeneration of the Jews and also calls for their emancipation. On both subjects, however, he is unwilling to achieve his goal without regard to cost. For example, Bing agrees with his opponent on the necessity of eliminating superstition from religion. But, if by "superstition" the

[37] *Ibid.*, pp. 30–31.

[38] *Ibid.*, 'Lettre . . . A M. Grégoire . . . ,' p. 14. Cf. S. Posener, 'The Immediate Economic and Social Effects of the Emancipation of the Jews in France', *Jewish Social Studies*, I (1939), p. 294.

[39] Schwarzfuchs, *op. cit.*, pp. 60, 65.

[40] *Phaedon hu sefer hasharat ha-nefesh le-he-hakham ha-shalem rabbenu moshe mi-Dessau ha-nikra Mendelssohn*, Berlin 5647 [1787]. A second edition appeared in Brünn 1798. Bing also produced French translations of the *Phaedon* and *Nathan der Weise* of Lessing. Cf. Altmann, *op. cit.*, p. 192.

[41] Grégoire, *op. cit.*, pp. 259–260.

[42] *Ibid.*, pp. 277–279, 280–283. The translation of *Behinat olam* was published in Metz 1794. Szajkowski, 'The Emancipation of the Jews . . . ,' No. 419. Cf. David Feuerwerker, *L'Emancipation des Juifs en France*, Paris 1975, pp. 109–110.

[43] *Lettre du Sr. I. B. B., Juif de Metz, à l'auteur anonyme d'un écrit intitulé: 'Le cri d'un citoyen contre les Juifs de Metz'*, Metz 1787. Republished by his son-in-law, Michel Berr in 1805. Zosa Szajkowski, 'Judaica-Napoleonica. A Bibliography of Books, Pamphlets, and Printed Documents, 1801–1815', *Studies in Bibliography and Booklore*, II (1956), No. 9.

On the opposition to Yiddish see Zosa Szajkowski, 'Der kamf kegen Yiddish in Frankreich' (The Struggle Against Yiddish in France), *Yivo Bletter*, XIV (1939), pp. 46–77.

author of the *Cri du citoyen* implies the abandonment of Jewish tradition as a whole, then, writes Bing, "my deepest wish is that we forever cleave to this superstition, the philosophy of Voltaire notwithstanding".[44] As for conditional emancipation, he declares:

> ". . . if we must no longer remain a Community, if we must sacrifice our civil laws, be ruled by the national law, if this revolution so fortuitous to the French does nought but augment our misfortunes, we prefer death a thousand times rather than subscribe to it."[45]

Thus Bing, like Berr, while imbued with the spirit of the *Haskalah*, clearly eschewed the position of Mendelssohn and his disciples, who argued for the abrogation of Jewish communal autonomy. Interestingly, these two families were united in the marriage of Michel Berr (son of Berr Isaac Berr) to Bing's daughter Minette.[46]

Cerfberr of Medelsheim (1730–1793), army contractor, financier, and champion of Jewish rights, was more a peer than a disciple of Mendelssohn. André Neher has observed wryly that on the eve of the French Revolution, the great German Jew was Mendelssohn the philosopher, the great Portuguese Jew was Furtado the economist, and the great Alsatian Jew was the horse-dealer Cerfberr.[47]

In seeking to qualify Jews for civil rights, Cerfberr established factories to employ Jewish workers, thereby diminishing – he hoped – the number of pedlars and petty traders among Alsatian Jews. In 1780 he requested that Mendelssohn write a *mémoire* to be submitted to the *Conseil d'état* defending the Jews and promoting their struggle for civil rights. Ultimately his efforts led to the publication of Christian Wilhelm Dohm's famous essay *Über die bürgerliche Verbesserung der Juden* in 1783. In all probability Cerfberr supplied the notes for this work. Consequently, Dohm's essay reflects the position of Cerfberr and other Alsatian leaders who wished to maintain communal autonomy after the granting of civil rights and not the opposing view of Mendelssohn.[48]

Cerfberr was less a *Maskil* than a maecenas of *Haskalah* and something of a hero to the *Maskilim*.[49] Thus, his success in having the obnoxious *péage corporel*, or

[44]Heinrich Graetz, *Geschichte der Juden*, vol. XI, Leipzig n.d., pp. 184–185.

[45]Cited in Tcherikower, *op. cit.*, p. 74, note 32. Cf. Hertzberg, *op. cit.*, pp. 329–332.

[46]Zosa Szajkowski, 'Michel Berr, The Failure of an Intellectual among the First Generation of Emancipated Jews in France', *Journal of Jewish Studies*, XIV (1963), p. 53. Reprinted in his *Jews and the French Revolutions . . .*, p. 1077.

[47]André Neher, *L'Existence juive*, Paris 1962, p. 248.

On Cerfberr see M. Ginsburger, *Cerf Berr et son époque*, Guebwiller 1908; Renée Neher-Bernheim, 'Cerf-Berr de Medelsheim: le Destin d'une famille durant la Révolution', *Revue des Etudes Juives*, 137 (1978), pp. 61–75.

[48]Altmann, *op. cit.*, pp. 449–451. Writing several decades later, Olry Terquem charged that Cerfberr was prepared to maintain communal autonomy even at the expense of emancipation. *Archives israélites*, IV (1843), pp. 725–726.

[49]For example, he continued to use Yiddish in his business affairs. See Moise Schwab, 'Les livres de comptes de Cerf Berr et de ses fils', *Revue des Etudes Juives*, 61 (1911), pp. 292–294. He also endowed a *yeshivah* in Bischeim, which certainly did not follow the educational philosophy of the *Maskilim*. Cf. M. Ginsburger, 'Une fondation de Cerf Berr', *Revue des Etudes Juives*, 76 (1923), pp. 45–57, and Simon Schwarzfuchs, 'Shalosh te'udot me-haye ha-kehilot ha-yehudiyim be-Alsace-Lorraine' (Three Documents from the Life of the Jewish Communities of Alsace-Lorraine), *Michael*, 4 (1976), pp. 16–17.

Leibzoll, abolished in Metz was celebrated in *Hame'asef* with a poem by Wessely.[50] Cerfberr helped underwrite the publication of Mendelssohn's *Biur* with eighteen subscriptions and was a strong supporter of *Hame'asef*, personally accounting for twelve subscriptions in 1785 and serving as the address for the journal's agent in Alsace, Moses Halphen (the latter possibly related to him by marriage[51]). Cerfberr's financial support undoubtedly accounts, at least in part, for the deference shown him by the editors when he complained of a theological error which appeared in *Hame'asef*. Not only was a retraction made, but a special editorial note was included at the beginning of the next volume.[52]

Cerfberr's complaint serves to underline the strong religious conservatism that typified his behaviour. Indeed, though a supporter of *Hame'asef* and a proponent of civil rights for the Jews, Cerfberr was described by the *Journal de Paris* as a "rigide observateur des moindres rites institués par Moise" and compared, rather unfavourably, with the more enlightened and liberal Abraham Gradis of Bordeaux.[53]

Two lesser-known *Maskilim* of this period are Mayer-Louis Schwabe (1771–1837) and Israël Hyemson Créhange (1769–1844). In a eulogy for Schwabe, Lazare Wogue describes Schwabe's close relationship with Isaiah Berr Bing and Moses Ensheim. For the most part self-educated, he pooled his knowledge with his seniors, Bing and Ensheim, to further their education as well as his own. The scion of a wealthy family, Schwabe ultimately became the president of the Consistory of Metz.[54]

Israël Créhange of Sedan was a friend and contemporary of Schwabe. A student of the famous *Sha'agat Aryeh*, Rabbi of Metz, Créhange was befriended by Bing and was, according to his obituary, one of the *Me'asfim*. A well-to-do merchant, he prepared a catechism for teaching Jewish school children in Sedan and also established a small synagogue in his home.[55]

A recently discovered manuscript at the Leo Baeck Institute Archives in New York is the work of yet another little-known *Maskil*, Joseph (Jessel) Lehman. According to the title-page, Lehman was a "maître d'école" at the school of Isaiah Mayer, *hazzan* in Nancy.[56] The book, entitled *Sefer hovre shamayim* (based on

[50] *Hame'asef*, 5546 (1786), pp. 49–50. On his struggle to eliminate the tax see Zosa Szajkowski, 'The Jewish Problem in Alsace, Metz, and Lorraine on the Eve of the Revolution of 1789', *Jewish Quarterly Review*, XLIV (1954), pp. 219–222. Reprinted in *Jews and the French Revolutions* . . ., pp. 311–314.

[51] *Ibid.*, 5545 (1785), subscription list (unpaginated) includes Cerfberr and his son Lipman (Hippolyte). A list of agents appended to the journal lists Moses Halphen at the address of "Cerf Ber grand fermieur à Strasbourg". Cerfberr's niece was married to a Halphen.

[52] *Ibid.*, 5548 (1788), introduction. Cf. Hertzberg, *op. cit.*, pp. 178–179.

[53] *Journal de Paris*, 22 frimaire an VII, cited in Kahn, *op. cit.*, pp. 9–10.

[54] I. H. Créhange is probably to be identified with Hayamssohn Créhange, resident of Paris, who applied for the Chair of Hebrew Language and Literature at the *Collège de France* in 1799. The application also includes a Hebrew poem in honour of the *Institut National*. [*Archives Nationales* F 19/13556, dossier 36 (Collège de France).] For Schwabe see L. Wogue, *Eloge funèbre de feu Mr. M.-L. Schwabe*, Metz 1837.

[55] *Archives israélites*, V (1844), pp. 753–757. The eulogy was given by the Reformer, Gerson-Lévy.

[56] *LBI Archives, West European Collection*, AR-C 1638, I,b. According to Szajkowski, Lehman was from Ribeauvillé and had also prepared a calendar that included travel directions for Alsace. Zosa Szajkowski, *The Economic Status of the Jews in Alsace, Metz, and Lorraine (1648–1789)*, New York 1954, p. 65, note 152.

a phrase in Isaiah XLVII:13), discusses astronomy, including information on weather, distances of the moon and planets, as well as some popular beliefs and superstitions about the heavens. The work was completed (according to the title-page) on 13th May 1789.

There were, of course, other French Jews who were affected by the *Haskalah*. The subscription lists to *Hame'asef* include over a dozen subscribers in Alsace, in addition to those already mentioned. While not all of these names can be identified, many belong to distinguished Alsatian families. For example, the subscription list for 1785, besides listing Cerfberr (Herz Medelsheim) and his son Lipman, names Mayer Mutzig (Mutzich), probably the son or close relative of Aaron Mutzig, *parnas* of Strasbourg.[57] The subscribers Goudchaux and Gershon Silna of Metz, listed in 1788, can probably be identified with the wealthy Goudchaux family of Metz.[58]

It is, of course, difficult to gauge the size and influence of the *Haskalah* movement in France. Nonetheless, one incident does shed some light on this question. When the distinguished Rabbi of Metz died in 1785, no immediate successor was chosen. According to Abraham Cahen, it was because of "the influence of the biblical studies of Mendelssohn and his school . . . [that] the community could not decide whether to preserve the tradition or abrogate it [and] the post remained unoccupied".[59]

Indeed, it is clear that the ideology and activities of the German *Maskilim* had made a strong impact on their French counterparts. The *Maskilim* of France read the works of their German mentors and translated them for others to read. They subscribed to their journal and echoed their sentiments in matters of education, language, and vocational reform. "In Revolutionary France", wrote Michel Berr in 1806, "the example of Wessely and Friedländer was followed; Jews, becoming French, wanted to sing in the ancient and holy tongue of their ancestors of the events to which they could no longer be indifferent."[60]

For their part, German *Maskilim* took inspiration from the political advances being made by Jews in France. In 1789 Lazarus Bendavid published a translation of nine French pamphlets on the struggle for civil rights by French Jews, including the address of the representatives of Alsace-Lorraine to the National

[57]The name of Aaron ben Mayer Mutzig, *parnas* of the community of Strasbourg, appears on a document dated 1776. Isidore Loeb, 'Les juifs à Strasbourg depuis 1349 jusqu'à la Révolution', *Annuaire de la Société des Etudes Juives*, II (1883), p. 179.

[58]The Hebrew name Loeb ben Jacob Silni, translator of the *Ode hébraïque par M. le Rabbin Cracovie* . . . , Paris 1807, is given in French as Lion Jacob Goudchaux de Metz. Szajkowski, *Judaica Napoleonica*, note 106. Cf. Hertzberg, *op. cit.*, p. 179, for other French subscribers to German publications.

The *Maskil* Elie Halphen Halévy (*c.* 1760–1826) was also active in France. Cantor, scribe, and secretary to the Jewish community in Paris, he was a gifted Hebrew poet and edited the *Israélite Française* (1817–1819). However, his German origin and rather late arrival in France (1801) place him beyond the scope of this study. On Halévy see Zinberg, *op. cit.*, pp. 196–198; and Klausner, *op. cit.*, pp. 322–335.

[59]Abraham Cahen, 'Le Rabbinat de Metz pendant la période française (1567–1871)', *Revue des Etudes Juives*, 13 (1886), p. 106.

[60]J. Mayer and Abraham de Cologna, *Odes hébraïques pour la célébration de l'anniversaire de naissance de S. M. L'Empereur des Français . . . traduite en français par Michel Berr*, Paris 1806, Introduction.

Assembly in August 1789.[61] The following year David Friedländer published a translation of the *Réponse des Juifs de la province de Lorraine* . . . in the *Berlinische Monatschrift*.[62] And, as previously noted, *Hame'asef* reported on the events surrounding the Revolution and the struggle for Jewish emancipation.

Viewed as a whole, however, this symbiotic relationship was heavily one-sided. French Jewry clearly took more than it gave. Moreover, there were striking differences between the German *Haskalah* and the movement it inspired in France. Among the German *Maskilim* who desired change and modernisation there were both moderates and extremists. The extremists, as previously noted, bitterly attacked the religious establishment and often urged drastic changes. Ultimately they determined the character of the *Haskalah* movement in Germany.[63] This radicalisation, which was to become the hallmark of German *Haskalah* and a major factor in the struggle for religious Reform, was virtually absent in France.

There were several notable exceptions to this trend, namely, Zalkind Hourwitz, Moses Ensheim, Michel Berr, and his cousin Jacob Berr. Zalkind Hourwitz's scathing attacks on the religious establishment, as already noted, made him *persona non grata* with the communal leadership and estranged him from the Jewish community.[64] Ensheim, though not a foreigner like Hourwitz, suffered a similar fate. He ended his days at the home of Joseph Furtado, isolated from Jewish communal affairs and intellectual activities. Jacob Berr, who had so stridently attacked his uncle, continued to be active in the Consistory. Some years later, however, a bitter communal dispute broke out when attempts were made to disqualify him from serving in that body after he had married a Christian.[65]

Michel Berr continued an often bitter campaign to change and reform Jewish life in France. In his *Lettres sur les Israélites et le Judaïsme*, published in 1825, the young Berr takes pleasure in the religious Reforms being enacted in Germany, criticising French Jews for their backwardness.[66] Elsewhere Berr proposed that all non-essential elements should be thrown out of the Talmud and only the prophetic and moral ideas maintained.[67] Small wonder that the circle of Berlin *Maskilim* made him an honorary member.[68]

Such radicalism, however, was the exception rather than the rule in France. The prevailing ideological conservatism of the more influential French *Maskilim*

[61]B. L. [Lazarus Bendavid], *Sammlung der Schriften an die Nationalversammlung, die Juden und ihre bürgerliche Verbesserung betreffend*, Berlin 1789. Szajkowski, 'The Emancipation of the Jews . . .', No. 20.

[62]Szajkowski, 'The Emancipation of the Jews . . .', No. 113. Many of the other documents concerning Alsatian Jewry were translated into German locally because of the large German-speaking population there.

[63]Eisenstein-Barzilay, 'The Treatment of the Jewish Religion . . .', *loc. cit.*, pp. 39–57. Cf. the discussion of David Friedländer, Mendelssohn's heir apparent, in Michael A. Meyer, *The Origins of the Modern Jew*, Detroit 1967, pp. 57–84.

[64]Malino, *The Sephardic Jews of Bordeaux. Assimilation and Emancipation in Revolutionary and Napoleonic France*, Tuscaloosa 1978, p. 130, note 17, has noted that Hourwitz was "a pariah within the Ashkenazic community".

[65]*Archives israélites*, VI (1845), p. 703.

[66]P. 1. On Berr see the series of articles by *Tsarphati* [Olry Terquem] in *Archives israélites*, IV (1843), pp. 721–727; V (1844), 109–116, 168–179.

[67]According to Terquem in *Archives israélites*, V (1844), p. 175.

[68]*Lettres sur les Israélites et le Judaïsme*, 'Supplement', p. 2.

is evident in their desire to preserve communal autonomy. It is also a factor in the almost total absence of any attempts to implement institutional changes based on *Haskalah* ideology. While Berr Isaac Berr and others paid lip-service to the need for educational reforms, Jewish education in France lagged far behind the advances being made in Germany. Thus, at the time modern schools were being established in Berlin (*Freischule*–1781), Breslau (1791), Dessau (1799) and Seesen (1801), no new schools were created in France and secular studies were at best kept at a minimum in existing Jewish schools.[69] By 1832, according to Leopold Zunz, over 50 catechisms and manuals of religious instruction had been published, almost all in Germany.[70] In the same period only five such works appeared in France, all of them printed after 1818.[71]

In 1807 the French government noted the slow progress being made in the modernisation of Jewish education and a suggestion was made to establish special schools for Jews.[72] As late as 1817 the consistorial leader Simon Mayer Dalmbert failed in an effort to establish a secular Jewish school in Paris.[73] That same year the Jewish lawyer Joseph Oulif of Metz organised a progressive primary school in that city. Five years later Olry Terquem observed that this independent effort still remained the only project of its kind in France.[74]

The moderation of the French *Maskilim* is attributable primarily to two factors. First, while they shared the same basic intellectual characteristics with the German *Maskilim*, there was, after 1789, an important difference between them. The Germans were strongly motivated by their desire for emancipation and integration into civil society–elusive goals that contributed to their frustration and bitterness.[75] In France, though formal emancipation did not put an end to the disadvantages or lead to immediate integration into French society, it certainly precluded the kinds of tension and disappointment that shaped the second generation of German *Haskalah*.[76]

The second factor is the status of the leaders of the French *Haskalah*. Berr, Bing, Cerfberr, Schwabe, and many of the subscribers to *Hame'asef*, were members of the communal establishment. Their advocacy of cultural change and civic

[69]Eliav, *op. cit.*, pp. 71–118.

[70]Leopold Zunz, *Die gottesdienstlichen Vorträge der Juden, historisch entwickelt*, Frankfurt a. Main 1892, p. 472. For a partial listing of catechisms see E. Schreiber, 'Catechisms,' *Jewish Encyclopedia*, vol. III, pp. 622–623. On the significance of this literature see Jakob J. Petuchowski, "Manuals and Catechisms of the Jewish Religion in the Early Period of Emancipation', in Alexander Altmann (ed.), *Studies in Nineteenth-Century Jewish Intellectual History*, Cambridge, Mass. 1964, pp. 47–64.

[71]Szajkowski, 'Michel Berr . . .', pp. 57–58, notes 25, 26. To these five should be added the above-mentioned catechism of Israël Créhange.

[72]Posener, 'The Immediate Economic and Social Effects . . .', p. 312.

[73]Zosa Szajkowski, *Jewish Education in France, 1789–1939*, ed. by Tobey B. Gitelle, New York 1980, p. 4.

[74]Tsarphati [Olry Terquem], *Troisième lettre d'un Israélite français à ses coreligionnaires*, Paris [1822], p. 21.

[75]Selma Stern-Täubler, 'The Jew in Transition from Ghetto to Emancipation', *Historia Judaica*, II (1940), pp. 102–119, esp., pp. 113–116. Cf. Eisenstein-Barzilay, 'The Treatment of the Jewish Religion . . .', *loc. cit.*, pp. 55–57.

[76]On the nature of emancipation in France as opposed to the situation in Germany see Jonathan I. Helfand, *French Jewry During the Second Republic and Second Empire (1848–1870)*, Ann Arbor, Michigan 1979, pp. 198–202, 328–331. See also Robert A. Kann, 'Assimilation and Antisemitism in the German-French Orbit', in *LBI Year Book XIV* (1969), pp. 96–99 and the discussion by Robert Weltsch in his 'Introduction' to that *Year Book*, xiv–xvii.

improvement was strongly coloured by their own involvement in and commitment to the communal establishment. Thus, while the turbulence of the German *Haskalah* bred other movements of dissent, the French *Maskilim* faded away, leaving behind but a scant record of pamphlets and poetry to mark their place in history.

II. RELIGIOUS REFORM

It is in the sphere of religious Reform that French and German Jewry draw closest together and, paradoxically, move furthest apart. While religious Reform had been on the Jewish agenda since the turn of the century, new leadership and ideological formulations revitalised the movement in the 1830s.[77] The aesthetic Reforms of Jacobson and his heirs in Hamburg and Berlin were now placed in an ideological framework as a generation of university-trained leaders took over. Germany was clearly the home of this new movement. Its leaders – Geiger, Holdheim, Hirsch – were German; its rabbinic conferences took place on German soil; its institutions and publications were found east of the Rhine. French Jews in the 1830s and 1840s who desired Reform looked to their German brethren for models and instruction.

Olry Terquem, the most radical of the French Reformers, published a series of essays in the 1820s and 1830s entitled *Lettres Tsarphatiques*. His proposals to eliminate Hebrew from the liturgy, abolish the second day of the festivals, transfer the Sabbath to Sunday, establish a theological faculty, and change the circumcision ritual, closely parallel the programme introduced by the German Reformers.[78] On several occasions he even compares the advances made in Germany with the lack of progress in France.[79] While Terquem's radicalism failed to convince French Jews, other Frenchmen took up the cudgels for Reform, frequently citing German models and precedents.

Thus, in 1825, when the Central Consistory considered introducing clerical garb in the synagogue, a member recommended that they further follow the example set by the Germans and pray in the national language.[80] Impressed by the intellectual achievements of *Wissenschaft des Judentums*, some Reformers urged

[77]David Philipson, *The Reform Movement in Judaism*, New York 1931, pp. 39–50 and Caesar Seligmann, *Geschichte der jüdischen Reformbewegung von Mendelssohn bis zur Gegenwart*, Frankfurt a. Main 1922, pp. 88–107.

[78]For a discussion of these literary polemics and a brief bibliography see Isidore Loeb, *Biographie d'Albert Cohn*, Paris 1878, pp. 154–157 and Szajkowski, 'Hitnagshuyot . . .', pp. 266, 276–277. Cf. the obituary for Terquem in *Archives israélites*, XXIII (1862), p. 313.

[79]*Troisième lettre d'un Israélite français à ses coreligionnaires*, Paris [1822], p. 22 (on reforming circumcision); *Sixième lettre d'un Israélite français à ses coreligionnaires . . .*, Paris n.d., p. 20 (on homiletics).

[80]*Archives du Consistoire Central*, 1. B.2., minutes of 19th September 1825. The discussion was shelved and raised again on 10th October. Benoît Fould, who had raised the issue, argued: "Nous ne sommes plus des Juifs, mais des citoyens Israélites français." A decade later three distinguished members of the Parisian community – Albert Cohn, Samuel Cahen, and Salomon Munk (all educated west of the Rhine) – requested permission from the Paris Consistory to hold private services on *Rosh Hashanah*. Their purpose was to introduce "several modifications" similar to those "already realised in many cities of Germany". *Archives du Consistoire de Paris*, B 20 (1), 'Temples et réunions de prières', letter of 25th August, 1836.

that the curriculum of the Rabbinical School of Metz be revised to include the study of Zunz, Jost, and Geiger.[81] August Fabius, admiring the dignity and beauty of the German Reform Temples, advised his French co-religionists to follow the "wise Germans." "Honour to them!" he proclaims, for giving their Temples "the simplicity and grandeur that recall so magnificently the days of Jerusalem. They can teach you best, they who have been practising for a quarter of a century."[82]

Perhaps the most fascinating demonstration of German-French symbiosis during this period is the appearance of the bilingual journal *La Régénération – Die Wiedergeburt*. Published in Strasbourg by Simon Bloch, it was dedicated to "the amelioration of the religious and moral condition of the Jews". "The intellectual perfection of man", writes Bloch in the *Prospectus*, "must march together with the progress of civilisation", a goal already promoted by periodicals "für Kultur und moralische Bildung" in "the land of Mendelssohn, Friedländer, Frankel, and Riesser."[83] The goals set forth by Bloch are a combination of the classic programme of the *Haskalah* together with the religious ideals of moderate Reform. He wished to educate the young; to teach Jewish history, literature, morals, and religion; to make youth (particularly Alsatian youth) more useful to society and homeland; and to present Jews and non-Jews with "einem richtigen Begriff" of the Mosaic religion.[84]

La Régénération, which appeared for a year-and-a-half (1836–1837), contained contributions from Karl Rehfuss, Isaak Markus Jost, Michael Creizenach and his son Theodor, Abraham Geiger, and Salomon Formstecher. It included news reports about political and religious progress in Germany, discussions on the need for religious Reform, book reviews, and even poetry. For example, Karl Rehfuss contributed a two-part article on "La Source du Salut", discussing recent developments and changes in German synagogues.[85] The talmudic principle of *aseh shabatkha hol* ("profane the Sabbath rather than require the aid of man") was analysed by Creizenach *père*.[86] And Geiger's article on the status of women in contemporary Judaism was reprinted from his journal.[87] *La Régénération* also published an unfavourable review of the *Neunzehn Briefe über Judentum* (under the pseudonym of Ben Usiel), by the neo-orthodox rabbi, Samson Raphael Hirsch.[88]

[81]Samuel Cahen, *Coup d'oeil sur les dernières Lettres Tsarphatiques*, Paris 1839, p. 6. On the place of the writings of Mendelssohn in the curriculum see Jules Bauer, *L'Ecole Rabbinique de France (1830–1930)*, Paris 1931, pp. 24–26. Mendelssohn remained a hero and exemplar in France. In 1832 the Central Consistory adopted a biography of Mendelssohn for use as a reader in Jewish schools. L. M. Cottard, *Souvenirs de Moïse Mendelssohn*, Paris 1832.

[82]Auguste Fabius, *Offrande au Dieu de l'Univers*, Lyon 1842, pp. 27, 38–39.

[83]*La Régénération – Prospectus*, p. 3.

[84]*Ibid.*, p. 4.

[85]*La Régénération*, I (1836), pp. 97–114, 233–246.

[86]*Ibid.*, pp. 269–271. See also his sermon on pp. 55–61 and his article on principles of faith, pp. 306–312.

[87]*Ibid.*, II (1837), pp. 33–41.

[88]*Ibid.*, I (1836), pp. 223–224. The reviewer observed that the book contained "much that is new and good". Unfortunately, he concluded, "what is good is not new and what is new is not good".

Jost's contribution, 'Extraits d'ouvrages Hébraïques peu connus,' appeared in vol. I, pp.

After the demise of *La Régénération* the cause of religious Reform in France was picked up by the *Archives israélites*, which began publication in 1840. It, too, faithfully chronicled the changes being introduced in Germany and frequently urged French Jews to follow suit. In 1842 the *Archives* reported extensively on the state of religious Reform in Germany and England. The article discusses ritual changes and rationalisations for them as well as such theological issues as the universalisation of the concept of "the end of days".[89]

The Rabbinic Conferences held in Germany in 1844, 1845, and 1846 were followed with great interest in the Franco-Jewish presss. In 1845 L. Schlesinger, a German correspondent of the *Archives israélites*, published several articles on the religious stirrings in Germany. Contrasting the situation in the two countries, he exhorted his French readers not to remain indifferent to this struggle for religious Reform.[90] The Jews of each country, he observes in another report, reflect their cultural environment. They are "enlightened in Germany, the land of philosophy, indifferent and conservative in France, the land of Catholicism by indifference." And, again, "German Jewry is as superior to French as Protestantism is to Catholicism".[91]

While admiring the progress made by German Reform, the *Archives* remained somewhat less than enthusiastic about the extremism shown in some quarters. In 1845 the editor, Samuel Cahen, refrained from endorsing the programme of the Braunschweig Conference and later supported the moderate position of Zacharias Frankel, particularly with regard to the preservation of Hebrew as the language of prayer.[92] One of Schlesinger's reports contrasts Frankel and the radical Holdheim in the following terms: "Frankel aime le Judaisme comme un enfant dorloté aime sa mère; Holdheim traite le Judaisme comme on traite une maîtresse avec laquelle on est brouillé".[93]

In 1842, when Chief Rabbi Emmanuel Deutz died, a prolonged struggle ensued in France over his successor. French Reformers tried to elect a new rabbi in the spirit and image of their German counterparts.[94] The unfavourable comparisons they made between the French and German rabbinates evoked an angry response from Simon Bloch, now editor of the conservative *Univers israélite*. What distinguishes German rabbis from French rabbis, he writes, is not their erudition, but rather the notoriety the Germans achieve by attacking tradition. The enlightened French rabbis eschew such behaviour, preferring anonymity to infamy.[95]

After three years of debate, the Central Consistory resolved to formulate a

---

115–118, 265–269; Formstecher's article on stability and change in Judaism appeared in vol. II, pp. 111–116.

[89] *Archives israélites*, III (1842), pp. 427–436.

[90] *Ibid.*, VI. (1845), pp. 449–451.

[91] *Ibid.*, pp. 710, 714.

[92] *Ibid.*, pp. 354–355, 643, 859–863, 873; V (1844), 513–515.

[93] *Ibid.*, VI (1845), pp. 877–878. He also refers to Holdheim as "un amiable Méphistophelès".

[94] On the debate surrounding the election see Jonathan I. Helfand 'The Election of the Grand Rabbi of France (1842–1846)', in *Proceedings of the Eighth World Congress of Jewish Studies, Division B*, Jerusalem 1982, pp. 139–144.

[95] *Univers israélite*, II (1845), pp. 3–5.

series of proposals for religious Reform as a touchstone for candidates for the vacant position. The list included suggestions to unify the Sephardic and Ashkenazic rites, adopt Sephardic pronunciation; introduce changes to enhance religious ceremonies (e.g., marriage, confirmation); eliminate prayers in conflict with civic and political allegiance; introduce an organ into the synagogue; revise the circumcision ritual in accordance with "progress and science"; abstain from "intolerant" questions on Jewish ancestry at the time of marriages and funerals; institute curricular changes in the Rabbinical Seminary of Metz; and modernise the rabbinate.[96]

This agenda for Reform drawn up by the Consistory reflects the influence of German Reform. Indeed, before the proposals were published in France, a committee of the Consistory submitted copies of a shorter version to several German Reform rabbis in order "to be guided by [their] example and to invoke [their] authority against those . . . who oppose even the most reasonable and legitimate innovations".[97]

In the matter of religious Reform, the symbiotic relationship was not as one-sided as it might appear. As early as 1807 the journal *Sulamith* reported enthusiastically on the decisions of the Grand Sanhedrin.[98] In the 1830s and later, the German-Jewish press frequently commented on religious conditions in France. Geiger, for example, reviewed some of the *Lettres Tsarphatiques* in his journal.[99] He also published selections from the pastoral letter of the newly-elected Liberal rabbi of Strasbourg, Arnaud Aron.[100] Similarly, the *Allgemeine Zeitung des Judenthums* carried reports on the *Tsarphati* polemics as well as the general religious conditions in France.[101]

When the German Reformers convened their first conference in 1844, they considered themselves the heirs of the French Grand Sanhedrin. In fact, the Braunschweig Conference began with a discussion and reaffirmation of the doctrinal decisions of the Sanhedrin. Later, even the proposal to sanction intermarriage was based on an interpretation of the decisions of the Grand Sanhedrin.[102]

German Reformers rendered more than just lip-service to their French

[96]The questions have been published by Renée Neher-Bernheim, *Documents inédits sur l'entrée des Juifs dans la société française (1750–1850)*, Tel-Aviv 1977, vol. II, pp. 298–300; and in Phyllis Cohen Albert, *The Modernization of French Jewry. Consistory and Community in the Nineteenth Century*, Hanover N.H. 1977, pp. 385–386. The answers of Marchand Ennery, who was ultimately elected, are in the Archives of the Leo Baeck Institute, New York, Alsace-Lorraine Collection, pp. 1340–1341 and were published in Jonathan I. Helfand, 'Entre tradition et réforme: Une lettre de Marchand Ennery,' *Archives Juives*, XVI (1980), pp. 31–35.

[97]*Sinai*, I (1846), pp. 74–76. Cf. the report on this consultation in *Univers Israélite*, III (1846), p. 80.

[98]'Reform des Judenthums in Frankreich und Italien', *Sulamith*, II (1807), pp. 3–10.

[99]*Wissenschaftliche Zeitschrift für Jüdische Theologie*, IV (1838), pp. 258–260.

[100]*Ibid.*, I (1835), p. 271.

[101]*Allgemeine Zeitung des Judenthums*, III (1839), pp. 151–152 (on the *Lettres Tsarphatiques*); X (1846), p. 346 (on the use of the organ in French synagogues), pp. 290–291 (on the anti-Reform manifesto of Rabbis Lambert and Goudchaux). Despite his own commitment to Reform, Philippson found Terquem's hostile tone unacceptable.

[102]*Protocolle der ersten Rabbiner-Versammlung abgehalten zu Braunschweig von 12ten bis zum 19ten Juni 1844*, Braunschweig 1844, pp. 19–20, 98. Cf., the report in the *Allgemeine Zeitung des Judenthums*, VIII (1844), p. 372 and Seligmann, *op. cit.*, pp. 110–111.

counterparts. On two occasions, Reform congregations in Germany turned to the French Consistory for guidance in a matter of religious controversy.

In 1831 the lawyer Jacob Dernburg, president of the community council of Mainz,[103] together with three other communal leaders, asked the help of the Consistory in implementing several reforms in their community. They wrote that several fanatics had opposed the introduction of a choir in the synagogue as well as other proposed changes in the rendition of the service. In order to support their case, they requested that the Consistory attest to the fact that such changes had been introduced in Paris and did not violate Jewish tradition.[104] It is important to note that French aid was sought at the very time that the Reformers in Mainz, led by Dernburg, were about to break with the community.[105]

The second such instance took place in December 1847. Moses Haarbleicher, who had succeeded Meyer Israel Bresselau in 1839 as secretary of the Hamburg Temple, asked the Consistory to clarify its stand on intermarriage.[106] The German papers had reported that a marriage between a Catholic and a Jewess who had not converted had taken place in a Paris church with special Papal permission. Haarbleicher, in addition to requesting details in this specific case, asked how the Consistory would deal with the children of such a union and how it would act in the case of a Jewish father and a Gentile mother (i.e., how it would apply the legal principle of matrilineal descent in Jewish law). Haarbleicher's request for an immediate response indicates that he needed the answer not just for theoretical speculation, but for practical application.

While the issue of religious Reformation created a bridge between French and German Jews, it also drove a wedge between the two communities. Because organised French Jewry and its spokesmen seemed to lag behind their German brethren, the Germans tended to ridicule and belittle the French. In return, French Jews, particularly (but not exclusively) traditionalists, criticised the Germans for overstepping the bounds of propriety in their Reform and in their attacks on French Jewry.

On several occasions Philippson used the pages of his journal to express disdain for the French rabbinate and French scholarship. In 1846 the *Allgemeine*

[103]Jacob Dernburg, who became president in 1830, also introduced the confirmation ceremony to the community. See Paul Arnsberg, *Die jüdischen Gemeinden in Hessen*, vol II, Frankfurt a. Main 1971, p. 21. He was the brother of the orientalist Joseph Derenbourg.

There were other important connections between Mainz and French Jewry. Chief Rabbi Marchand Ennery had studied in the *yeshivah* of Rabbi Hirtz Scheur in Mainz, as had Samuel Cahen, editor of the *Archives israélites*. These connections, going back to the French occupation of Mainz, may have influenced the community to turn to France for guidance.

[104]*Archives du Consistoire de Paris*, I. CC. 59. I wish to thank the Consistoire Central Israélite de France and its archivist, Mlle Elisabeth Couteau, for making this, and the following document, available to me.

[105]Arnsberg, *op. cit.*

[106]*Archives du Consistoire de Paris*, I. CC. 60. On Haarbleicher see the obituary in the *Allgemeine Zeitung des Judenthums*, XXXIII (1869), pp. 893–896.

The letter may be referring to the case of Mlle. de Haber, granddaughter of the President of the Central Consistory, Worms de Romilly, who married M. de Grouchy, a maréchal de France, in a church ceremony. The marriage was widely discussed in the Catholic and Jewish press. See the *Archives israélites*, IV (1843), pp. 455, 465–466. According to the *Archives*, however, she had converted.

Zeitung des Judenthums attacked the newly-elected Chief Rabbi, Marchand Ennery, as "an old man who likes repose and inaction". The *Archives israélites* took this occasion to note the tendency of the *Allgemeine Zeitung* and other German journals to deride French Jews for their religious backwardness. Noting that French Jews had been emancipated for fifty years, Samuel Cahen advised his German colleagues to wait and see what would happen to their religious life once they were finally emancipated.[107] Less polite was the response of the conservative *Univers israélite*, which condemned the attack on Ennery as "perfidious and grotesque".[108]

Two years earlier, comments in the *Allgemeine Zeitung* on the inferior quality of Jewish scholarship in France elicited the following stinging response from the *Archives israélites*:

> "No one has rendered justice to the sage doctors [of Germany] more than we: it is we who have for fifteen years popularised the honourable names of Creizenach, Jost, Geiger, and Zunz in France; who more than we has sought to stimulate our young rabbis with the words of these savants . . . If in recent issues we have used several harsh expressions relating to Mons. Geiger . . . it is because we have viewed with pain (and not just in *his* work) a desire to deprecate the works of French Jews in the field of Hebrew philology. This is neither just nor politic on the part of men who have no country . . . Because those who are rebuffed on account of their religion are pariahs. Certainly a country that forces Munk to become an expatriate, that in order to employ Jewish scholars forces them to betray their conscience, that country cannot be the *patrie* of the Jews."[109]

Among the traditionalists, of course, there was little sympathy or respect for the cause of Reform and certainly not for the German brand of radicalism. When the *Aufruf an unsere deutschen Glaubensbrüder* was published in Berlin in 1845, the *Univers israélite* condemned it as "a Jewish New Testament signed by 28 would-be evangelists".[110] Similarly, when French Reformers tried to influence the appointment of a Chief Rabbi, Chief Rabbis Lambert of Metz and Goudchaux of Nancy issued a pastoral letter strongly condemning attempts to reform Judaism. When asked by the Central Consistory to explain this action, Lambert responded that it was his obligation to keep the "disastrous" German Reform Movement out of France.[111]

III. CONCLUSION

French and German Jews entered the Age of Emancipation with a common heritage and a shared dream of progress and equality. In the early years of the *Haskalah* mutual interests and cross-cultural influences created new bonds between them. However, these bonds were not sufficient to overcome divisive historic forces.

Two major factors contributed to the growing distance between French and German Jewry. The first was the conflict created by their competing national

[107] *Archives israélites*, VII (1846), pp. 566–567.
[108] *Univers israélite*, III (1846), p. 101.
[109] *Archives israélites*, V (1844), pp. 862–863.
[110] *Jewish Theological Seminary Archives*, Box 18, envelope "Metz, 1846".
[111] Cited in Philipson, *op. cit.*, p. 271, note 43.

identities. In the past Jewish ties had easily transcended international borders, but the growing affinity of the Jew for his state began to place strains on such contacts. The military and political clashes between France and Germany heightened such tensions between Jews to the east and west of the Rhine. This is particularly true at a time when both French and German Jews were eager to prove their patriotism and fidelity to their respective states. Thus, in the early 1800s the Berrs and Cerfberrs of French Jewry no longer subscribe to *Hame'asef.*[112] And while in the 1830s and 1840s French and German Jews again subscribe to each other's periodicals, national loyalties clearly affect their relationship.[113] Essays and debates on religious Reform in French and German journals are replete with pejorative references to one another's national identity or political status. In one instance, the enlightened editor of the *Archives israélites* goes so far as to blame the anti-Jewish riots of 1848 in Alsace on the *Germanic* character of the local population.[114]

Second, ideological and institutional differences contributed to the growing gap between these erstwhile symbiants. In the early nineteenth century German Jews were still locked in a struggle for emancipation. This struggle stimulated the growth of the movements for religious Reform and *Wissenschaft des Judentums.*[115] French Jews, emancipated by fiat, had little utilitarian need for programmes of regeneration and Reform, or even for *Wissenschaft.* Thus, while German intellectuals agonised over the nature of Jewish identity and the role of Judaism in the modern world, French Jews, believing that their egalitarian dream had been fulfilled, comfortably assimilated, without the *Sturm und Drang* of their German co-religionists. They still, of course, shared common causes and even supported each other's projects. But the intimate relationship generated by the early *Maskilim* waned as French and German Jews, by fate as much as by choice, continued on their separate paths.

[112]In 1809 *Hame'asef* did list several subscribers from Strasbourg, but they include none of the illustrious names of the previous lists. Two of these new subscribers, Engel and Dreyfuss, also appear on the subscription list to Herz Homberg's catechism, *Imre Shefer*, Vienna 1808.

[113]In 1840 the *Archives israélites* listed nine German subscribers out of 100, including Jost, Philippson, and Fürst, all of them newspaper editors. (*Archives israélites*, I (1840), p. 696.) In 1842 there were no additional German subscribers. In 1843 out of a list of 130, only four were from Germany.

[114]*Archives israélites*, IX (1848), pp. 467–469.

[115]As Michael Meyer has observed: "Had political equality in Germay been nearly complete, as in France . . . the reform movement would not have been able to establish itself so easily. *W.d.J.* [*Wissenschaft des Judentums*] would probably also have been severely hampered in its development . . .", 'Jewish Religious Reform and Wissenschaft des Judentums. The Positions of Zunz, Geiger and Frankel', in *LBI Year Book, XVI* (1971), p. 20.

Ludwig Börne and the Formation of a Radical Critique of Judaism

BY ORLANDO FIGES

I

In 1844 Marx published two essays in the *Deutsch-Französische Jahrbücher** under the general heading 'Zur Judenfrage'.[1] The first of these was a critical review of Bruno Bauer's essay 'Die Judenfrage'.[2] Bauer had argued that the Jews could not attain real civil equality until the State had ceased to be Christian, for until that time the Jews could only effectively demand religious privilege. Rather, they should abandon Judaism and attach their cause to the broader struggle for the emancipation of man from religion and the establishment of a free and humanist State. Marx agreed with Bauer's atheism but thought that he had not gone deep enough to distinguish between political and human emancipation. Because the Jews could be emancipated politically without renouncing Judaism, there had to be a difference between political and human emancipation, which demanded, not merely the secularisation of the State, but the absence of religion altogether. Furthermore, religion was to be seen not as the foundation but only as the manifestation of secular deficiencies, so that Bauer's demand that Jews and Christians renounce their religious prejudices could only be fulfilled after the social emancipation of mankind.

Having shown that the problem of Jewish emancipation was social, not theological, in character, Marx's second essay went on to analyse the social problem of the Jews. The secular basis of Judaism was practical need and egoism; its "worldly cult", bargaining; its "worldly god", money. "Very well then!", declares Marx, "Emancipation from huckstering and money, and consequently from practical, real Judaism, would be the self-emancipation of our time".[3] Judaism is an anti-social element which has emancipated the Jews by making money into a world power: "The Jews have emancipated themselves insofar as the Christians have become Jews."[4] Thus the social emancipation of the Jew becomes the "emancipation of society from Judaism".[5]

*The author would like to thank Sir Isaiah Berlin and Dr. Julius Carlebach for invaluable guidance; also Daniel Johnson, Norman Stone, Neil McKendrick and Richard Beardsworth for generous help in the preparation of the manuscript.

[1]Karl Marx, Friedrich Engels, *Collected Works*, London 1975 onwards [hereafter *MEW* (London)] 3, pp. 146–174.

[2]Bruno Bauer, *Die Judenfrage*, Brunswick 1843.

[3]*MEW* (London), 3, p. 170.

[4]*Ibid.*

[5]*Ibid.*, p. 174.

For a number of reasons, these essays have attracted a great deal of attention. For one thing they are important documents for an understanding of the general phenomenon of the radical Jew. The Jews played a role in the development of modern Socialism out of all proportion to their numbers. Hess, Börne, Heine, Marx, Lassalle, Bernstein, Luxemburg, Eisner, Blum and Trotsky were all of Jewish origin. For many, the road to Socialism was a logical escape from the failure to assimilate into European society. Yet their place within the Socialist movement was never an easy one; a factor largely due to the influence of Marx's essays. This is a problem which has attracted much literature[6] and it forms the general context of this paper.

A second point of interest is that Marx's essays have rightly been seen by Istvan Meszaros and others as an important stage in the development of Marx's own Socialist ideology, and, in particular, as a catalyst to the crystallisation of a theory of alienation in the *Economic and Philosophical Manuscripts* of 1844.[7] Thirdly, within this context, there has been a significant linguistic debate between Marxist and Jewish defenders concerning the exact nature of Marx's critique . . . anti-Judaism or anti-commercialism?[8] The debate is not easily resolved; but surely this is the point. Marx's essays are not only essential to his Socialism, but, in themselves, they form a paradigm for the shaping of a "radical critique of Judaism",[9] which symbolises that very ambiguity in the position of the Socialist Jew already referred to. Marx was not unique in reconciling Socialism with anti-Judaism, for the Jewish path to Socialism was taken as much as a result of alienation from the Jewish-commercial world of their backgrounds as it was from the failure to assimilate.

If the "radical critique of Judaism" did not disappear when Marx discovered Capitalism and its vocabulary, this was largely because it took on an ambiguous double-meaning. On the one hand "radical" meant specifically left-wing. Marx, the young Engels, Lassalle and Bakunin are well-known for their use of the word "Jew" as a term of abuse, while Socialists from Fourier to Bakunin (with the exception of the Saint-Simonists) have, alongside their critique of Capitalism, consistently associated Judaism with the heretical and anti-social spirit of

[6]See for eg: Robert Wistrich, *Revolutionary Jews from Marx to Trotsky*, London 1976; George Lichtheim, 'Socialism and the Jews', in *Dissent*, 1968, 314–342; Jacob Toury, *Die politischen Orientierungen der Juden in Deutschland. Von Jena bis Weimar*, Tübingen 1966 (Schriftenreihe wissenschaftlicher Abhandlungen des Leo Baeck Institute 15) Edmund Silberner, *Sozialisten zur Judenfrage*, Berlin 1962; Eduard Bernstein, 'Jews and Social Democracy', in Paul Massing (ed.), *Rehearsal for Destruction*, New York 1967.

[7]Istvan Meszaros, *Marx's Theory of Alienation*, London 1976, pp. 70–76; Nathan Rotenstreich, 'The Bruno Bauer Controversy', in *LBI Year Book IV* (1959), pp. 3–39, p. 23; Hans Liebeschütz, in 'Judentum und deutsche Umwelt im Zeitalter der Restauration', in *Das Judentum in der deutschen Umwelt 1800–1850.* Studien zur Frühgeschichte der Emanzipation herausgegeben von Hans Liebeschütz und Arnold Paucker, Tübingen 1977 (Schriftenreihe wissenschaftlicher Abhandlungen des Leo Baeck Instituts 35), p. 31.

[8]See for eg. on the Marxist side, Dietmar Scholz, 'Politische und menschliche Emanzipation: Karl Marx Schrift "Zur Judenfrage" aus dem Jahre 1844', in *Geschichte in Wissenschaft und Unterricht*, 18, 1967, pp. 1–16; Edward Andrew, 'Marx and the Jews', in *European Judaism*, 3, 1968, pp. 9–14. For the opposite view see Edmund Silberner, 'Was Marx an Anti-Semite?', in *Historia Judaica*, 11, 1949, pp. 3–52.

[9]Julius Carlebach, *Karl Marx and the Radical Critique of Judaism*, London 1978.

commercialism. On the other hand, "radical" meant no more than a radical solution to the Jewish Question, and here the left-wing critique merged with the right-wing racialist attack. This union is a key to Hitler's own radical position concerning the Jews, for he allies the racial fear of "Verjudung" with the economic and social one, which originates in Marx's image of a Judaised Christian society and finds full sociological expression in Werner Sombart.

Ludwig Börne's life (1786–1837) is highly significant on all three points. Born Löb Baruch in the Frankfurt ghetto, Börne's education was typical of a second-generation enlightened Jew brought up on a diet of eighteenth-century rationalism. Under Napoleon this enabled Börne temporarily to gain an administrative post in the Frankfurt police, before losing it with the Restoration. Like many of his Jewish contemporaries, Börne turned to political journalism. Acclaimed as the father of *feuilleton* and hailed as the greatest theatre-critic since Lessing, Börne's influence on the *Jungdeutschland* movement was immense, while his consistent advocacy of a politically committed literature was a great influence on the young Engels.[10]

Börne's output was enormous, and much of it standard reading for the radicals of his day. But he was no genius. Despite several attempts, he never produced a novel or major work. His thinking was dogmatic, practical and often crude. A philosophically considered viewpoint was foreign to his political style. His great rival, Heine, attacked him as a philistine, a "nazarene", who had failed as an artist and sought culture in the proletariat, only to remain bitterly jealous of the great Heine himself. Heine's cruel and arrogant polemic[11] came close to the truth. Börne was a bitter man and this often manifested itself in jealous attacks on Heine. His failure as a writer, his emotional coldness, his miserable failure with women and unimpressive impact on the Paris salons were all accentuated by Heine's dashing success in these fields.

But this was not, as Heine argued, the source of his political radicalism. Börne was the first radical Jew but his emotional development was typical of the Jews who took the Socialist path between his day and that of Marx. His dogmatic and destructive radicalism was the result of a growing sense of alienation from both the Jewish-commercial background he had rejected and the Germany that had rejected him. Here was the true source of Börne's bitterness; being neither German nor Jew, in no-man's-land. Like Marx, Börne found in Socialism a new identity, one that was vague and distant from his Jewishness. And like Marx, Börne's evolving Socialism, although of a far more primitive kind than Marx's, depended for its crystallisation on the formation of a radical and moral critique of Judaism, linked to an equally radical critique of bourgeois society.

Börne was the first to connect the two and in this sense he is the father of the "radical critique of Judaism". This radical critique has been well traced from Marx's generation onwards.[12] Its origins, however, are less clear. The orthodox

[10]Peter Demetz, *Marx, Engels and the Poets*, Chicago 1959, pp. 16–23. Engels wrote an appalling eulogy of Börne ('Ein Abend'), which appeared in the *Telegraph für Deutschland* in 1840. *MEW* (London), 2, pp. 108–109.

[11]Heinrich Heine, *Ludwig Börne: eine Denkschrift*, Hamburg 1840.

[12]Carlebach, *op. cit.*; Silberner, *Sozialisten*, *op. cit.*

explanation is that Marx, in a totally original way, adapted his critique from a purely theological and moral tradition. If this were the case there would be no precedent for the fact that Marx added social and (admittedly crude) economic analyses to the Hegelian framework. It will be argued here that this is untrue, for Börne played a pioneering role in shaping and adding an economic and social "underside" to the moral tradition. This has not yet been recognised, although it shows quite clearly that by the early 1830s Börne had developed a critique of Judaism, which already consisted of the crude ingredients used by Marx.

Hans Liebeschütz, for example, has argued that Marx's concept of Judaism derived totally from the patristic interpretation of the Old Testament and that "the closest parallel, and perhaps the key to the understanding of Marx, is Spinoza's *Tractatus Theologico-Politicus*".[13] This is unlikely. Spinoza's appeal for the creation of a political science free of theological prejudice, and for a logical and scientific study of human society and human religion may have provided a methodological precedent for Marx's sociological approach to Judaism.[14] This would have been supported by Spinoza's assertion that the only concern of the State towards a particular religion could be the social and political behaviour of its followers. However, Spinoza offers only a theological critique of Judaism and provides no precedent for Marx's socio-economic analysis of the Jews. Such evidence would be unlikely to come from Spinoza, who sees his contemporary political ideal in the mercantile community of Amsterdam. Moreover, Spinoza's patristic view of the Old Testament does not connect with his rationalistic approach to political science in the way that Liebeschütz postulates, since Spinoza argues that the crisis between prophecy and reason is unnecessary and falsely stated, given the rule of religious toleration.

Spinoza's real significance lies in the shaping of eighteenth-century theological and moral critique. The influence of the Deists and the French anti-clerical movement has been well traced amongst figures like Peter Annet and Voltaire.[15] Their notion of Judaism as the rotten core of Christianity was orthodox at this time and although it has no direct significance for Marx, it is important for the completion of the moral tradition under Kant and Hegel.

For Kant Judaism was at best a church, but certainly not a religion. It was a collection of people united by a political and legal code based on a system of earthly punishments and rewards, which, combined with the Jews' negation of immortality, encouraged their servility, greed and materialism. Since Judaism had survived only because of the constitutional character of its religious code, neither Jewish history nor religion had any real significance, in which case the solution to the Jewish Question was simply for the Jews to relinquish Jewish law and ally with evangelism.

Hegel also denied Judaism to be a religion in the true Christian-humanist sense

[13]Hans Liebeschütz, 'German Radicalism and the Formation of Jewish Political Attitudes During the Earlier Part of the Nineteenth Century', in Alexander Altmann (ed.), *Studies in Nineteenth-Century Jewish Intellectual History*, Cambridge, Mass. 1964, pp. 141–170, p. 158.

[14]Certainly we know that Marx had been reading the *Tractatus* before writing his essays. See David McLellan, *Marx Before Marxism*, London 1970, pp. 52, 78.

[15]Leon Poliakov, *The History of Anti-Semitism* (tr. M. Kochan), vol. 3, London 1975; Ira Wade, *The Clandestine Organization and Diffusion of Philosophic Ideas in France, 1700–1750*, Princeton 1938.

of David Strauss's *Das Leben Jesu*. As mere slaves to law and God,[16] the Jews had failed to understand the human significance of Christ's teaching and were therefore to blame for the social divisiveness of Christian transcendentalism which Hegel had attacked in the Tübingen fragments. If Christianity was to rediscover the harmony of Greek folk religion, it had to recognise the temporary truth of the Judaic revelation as superseded in the light of its "Unfreiheit des Geistes". Jewish existence was one without self-consciousness and potential for "Bildung", because its religion was vested totally in the Object. Only God had consciousness while the Jews were left alienated from the Spirit and clinging to the dead laws and materialism of this-worldly nature. The biblical Jew, therefore, was a symbol for spiritual alienation, both from the universe and from himself. Unable to master his own existence, he had to be superseded in the realisation of the Spirit.

The Hegelian threat to Judaism was not new, for it only continued the critique from Christianity and Kantian Enlightenment. But it was far more difficult to answer because, rather than criticising Judaism "ab extra", it showed it to be superseded "in the light of standards implicit in Judaism itself".[18] The Christian threat could be met by counter-testimony and the "rationalistic" one by diverting it against Christianity. But a "rationalistic" religion could not be abstracted from Judaism, and neither could a Hegelian one, though Samuel Hirsch and the *Verein für Cultur und Wissenschaft der Juden* tried. Orthodox Judaism and a firm commitment to Hegel were not compatible. In the generation of Hirsch and Eduard Gans this caused much soul-searching. By the generation of Ferdinand Lassalle this was bordering on self-hatred: "I do not like Jews at all, I even detest them in general. I see in them nothing but . . . the characteristics of slaves."[19]

The transition was connected to changes within the Hegelian school. The Young-Hegelian conversion to atheism and political radicalism in the mid–1830s deprived Hegelian Jews of an escape from their dilemma by conversion to Christianity and relegated Judaism one stage further in the dialectical process. The belief in radical change doomed Judaism to destruction because of its a-historical nature. The Jew, subjected to the will of God, was unable to master his own existence and therefore provided no basis for liberty. The belief in atheism as the highest expression of human emancipation had similar implications. For Bauer the Jew was an "exaggerated" representative of the whole of Christian humanity, alienated by religion as a division in consciousness where religious beliefs are opposed to consciousness as a separate power. For Ludwig Feuerbach Judaism was a primitive form of Christianity, dominated by positivism, creation and utilism. The one common theme was the Jew's practical

[16]Carlebach (*op. cit.*, p. 153) has pointed out that the slave image is a recurring theme in the Hegelian tradition. The Jews are slaves to law (Kant), God (Hegel), egoism (Feuerbach) and money (Marx).

[17]For Hegel on Judaism see: Hans Liebeschütz, *Das Judentum im deutschen Geschichtsbild von Hegel bis Max Weber*, Tübingen 1967 (Schriftenreihe wissenschaftlicher Abhandlungen des Leo Baeck Instituts 17); Nathan Rotenstreich, 'Hegel's Image of Judaism', in *Jewish Social Studies* (*JSS*), XV, 1953, pp. 37–52.

[18]Ernst Fackenheim, 'Samuel Hirsch and Hegel', in Altmann, *op. cit.*, pp. 191–201, p. 196.

[19]Quoted in Edmund Silberner, 'Ferdinand Lassalle; From Maccabeism to Jewish Anti-Semitism', in the *Hebrew Union College Annual*, XXIV, 1953, pp. 151–186, p. 175.

approach to the world, making nature "the abject vassal of his selfish interest, of his practical egoism".[20] The Jews approached nature through the stomach, their God was egoism, and the result was the concept of creation. Feuerbach had taken this concept from Mendelssohn's view of Judaism as a religion of works and practices rather than beliefs, but had broadened it to convey the idea of a general attitude to the world based on practicality, or the utilitarian seeking of benefits.[21] Whereas Mendelssohn's use of the word "action" conveyed a behavioural pattern, Feuerbach's was descriptive of a general human nature. "Judaism is worldly Christianity; Christianity spiritual Judaism."[22] The worldliness of Judaism consisted in its inability to adopt a universalistic world view derived from Greco-Roman heathenism because of its particularist national interests, which Feuerbach tried to account for within an analytic-anthropological framework.

Feuerbach's assertion that the Christian dogmas were mere figments of human imagination, and therefore that theology was to be seen as a branch of anthropology, may have influenced Marx's thinking toward the Jews. Moreover, Feuerbach's association of Judaism with utility and egoism might well have helped Marx, within a strictly moral framework, to look for the social manifestation of that egoism in the Jewish attachment to money. Certainly, Marx's essays were written during a period when he was greatly influenced by Feuerbach.[23] However, two points must be made here. Firstly, whereas Feuerbach's interest in Judaism is to provide a general anthropological critique of religion, Marx's interest is to shape a social critique of bourgeois society. Secondly, as Julius Carlebach has pointed out,[24] Marx's theory of antisocial atomistic egoism was one specifically applied to the Jews and only affected Christians insofar as Christian society had been Judaised. Feuerbach's theory, in contrast, was one which, because it threatened to assert the conceptual superiority of the Christian universal spirit (and therefore lead him straight back to Hegel), he was forced to apply to the practical expression of Christianity as well, which by its emphasis on the individual's relationship to God rather than to his fellow men, also became a religion of egoism. Here Feuerbach was forced to make the finer distinction between Jewish ethnocentrism and Christian egoism. Thus while Marx's egoism was specifically "Jewish", Feuerbach's was more universal and idealised, in which case it provides no precedent for Marx's social and economic critique of Judaism.

This brings us back to the crux of our problem. The Hegelian tradition provided no social or economic critique of Judaism. Hegel made the point that Palestine was traversed by all the world's major trading routes, but only to show the difficulties Jews would find in reaching their aim of a separation from alien influences.[25] Bauer put forward the argument, which Marx himself quoted, that:

[20]Ludwig Feuerbach, *Essence of Christianity*, (tr. G. Eliot), New York 1957.
[21]Rotenstreich, 'Bauer Controversy', *loc. cit.*, pp. 25 ff.
[22]Feuerbach, *op. cit.*, p. 120.
[23]Silberner, 'Was Marx an 'Anti-Semite', *loc. cit.*, p. 29.
[24]Carlebach, *op. cit.*, pp. 108–109.
[25]*Ibid.*, p. 94.

"The Jew who, in Vienna for example, is only tolerated, determines the fate of the whole empire by his financial power."[26]

And yet Bauer's solution to the Jewish Question remained theological rather than social. He was interested in the overthrow of the Christian State, not the bourgeois-"Jewish" one; and therefore, Bauer attacked only the Jew as financier, not Judaism as the essence of money.

There was nothing very unusual about this. The association of Jews with money was an ancient one, and had gained common currency during the eighteenth century amongst Christians fearing the power of money over their society. Goethe denied the Jews the ideal society of Greek aestheticism which he put forward in *Wilhelm Meister* because the Jews' economic power threatened to break up the old system of "diversified subordination which, from the highest to the lowest . . . seemed to unite rather than divide individuals and favoured general well-being".[27] Here was the old irrational fear that the entry of Germany into a modern world would Judaise Christian society. As Herder put it, "A ministry where the Jew counts for everything, a house in which the Jew holds the key to the cash desk . . . are undrainable Pontine marshes".[28]

Not surprisingly, the Jews themselves played a part in this tradition during the period of assimilation, when they found that they could defend their position within German culture by condemning the "unacceptable face" of commercial Jewry. This was the price Heine paid for his "ticket to European culture". Amidst a general literary attack on the power of money within society at large (as might be seen in Shelley's *Queen Mab* – which formed a preface to Hess's 'Geldwesen' – and Balzac's *Gobseck*[29]), Heine declared that "das Geld ist der Gott unserer Zeit, und Rothschild sein Prophet".[30]

Nigel Reeves sees Heine's hostility to the Jews as a major influence on Marx's essays.[31] He argues that in 1843/1844 Marx was essentially taking up the anti-philistine motifs of his early, humorous novel *Einige Kapitel aus Scorpion und Felix*, which, Reeves argues, was largely derivative of Heine's *Die Bäder von Lucca*, where Jewish money dealers are lampooned in the figures of Gumpel and Hirsch. This is to misconceive the nature of Heine's critique. Whereas Marx's association of Jewry and money is totally abstract, Heine's is subjective and personal. He is attacking Jews, not Judaism. The true object of Heine's attack is his uncle Salomon: "dieser Mann der . . . Institute stiftet, um heruntergekommene

[26]*MEW* (London), 3, pp. 170–171.

[27]Quoted in Poliakov, *op. cit.*, p. 287.

[28]*Ibid.*, p. 286.

[29]Moses Hess, 'Über das Geldwesen', in *Rheinische Jahrbücher zur gesellschaftlichen Reform*, H. Pultman (ed.) Darmstadt 1845. Reprinted Leipzig 1970; Honoré de Balzac, *Le Roman Gobseck*: "Das Gold ist das Inbild aller menschlichen Kräfte . . . Das Gold ist das geistige Prinzip einer Gesellschaft."

[30]Heine, *Sämtliche Werke*, (E. Elster ed.), 1887–1890, VI, p. 258.

[31]Nigel Reeves, 'Heine and the Young Marx', in *Oxford German Studies*, 7, 1972/1973, pp. 44–97, pp. 57–62. Also on Heine see Siegbert Prawer, 'Heine's Portraits of German and French Jews on the Eve of the 1848 Revolution', in *Revolution and Evolution. 1848 in German-Jewish History*, edited by Werner E. Mosse, Arnold Paucker, Reinhard Rürup, Tübingen 1981 (Schriftenreihe wissenschaftlicher Abhandlungen des Leo Baeck Instituts 39). See also now Prawer's *Heine's Jewish Comedy*, Oxford 1983.

Schacherer wieder auf die Beine zu bringen".[32] If Heine's attack on Rothschild was soon repented it was because he never intended to set up Judaism as the essence of capitalism, and even less to support the revolution which made it its antithesis.

The difference between Marx, on the one hand, and Goethe, Bauer and Heine, on the other, is the vital distinction in the formation of a radical, economic critique of Judaism; it is the distinction between "a conceptual system which was trying to become a science, and elemental feelings as old as man himself".[33] It has often been asserted that the origins of this science, and the major influence on Marx's essays, was Hess's 'Über das Geldwesen'.[34] It is not difficult to understand why. Hess's argument against Judaism, like Marx's, depends on the assumption that social exchange is a "Gattungsact", and, therefore, that man's social evolution from robbery and slavery to commercialism is not yet complete. Money is the mark of man's self-enslavement and cannibalism. The freedom received from the Enlightenment was no more than the individualist-isolationist right of the predatory animal. It was the Jews' world-historic mission to turn man into cannibals:

> "Die Juden, die in der Naturgeschichte der socialen Thierwelt den welthistorischen Beruf hatten, das Raubthier aus der Menschheit zu entwickeln, haben jetzt endlich diese ihre Berufsarbeit vollbracht."[35]

Carlebach, however, has recently shown[36] that Hess's essay was written too late for Marx to have seen it before writing 'Zur Judenfrage', although, Carlebach argues, there are striking similarities between 'Geldwesen' and Marx's *Manuscripts* of 1844. He concludes, therefore, that "while Hess's influence was important in leading Marx towards revolutionary communism, it was insignificant in providing a model for Marx's analysis of Judaism".[37]

As it stands, therefore, there is no precedent for Marx's extension of the moral critique of Judaism onto a social and economic level. But Marx's innovation was not altogether original. A tradition of criticism levelled at Judaism as the essence of heretical capitalism had already been championed by Börne. It was a tradition of which both Hess and Marx were part.

Börne was in this respect a pioneer. As the first radical Jew it was really Börne who initiated the argument that Jewish and human emancipation were inseparable. The Jews had to subordinate their cause to the proletarian revolution, which was Socialist insofar as it required human liberation from the spirit of bourgeois commercialism embodied in what was a "Jewish" July

[32]Letter from Heine to Campe (10th May 1837), quoted in Hanns G. Reissner, 'Begegnung zwischen Deutschen und Juden im Zeichen der Romantik', in *Das Judentum in der Deutschen Umwelt, op. cit.*, pp. 325–357, p. 350.

[33]Poliakov, *op. cit.*, p. 125.

[34]Edmund Silberner, *Moses Hess: Geschichte seines Lebens*, Leiden 1966, pp. 191–192; David McLellan, *The Young Hegelians and Karl Marx*, London 1969, pp. 154–158; Richard Tucker, *Philosophy and Myth in Karl Marx*, Cambridge 1969, p. 112.

[35]Moses Hess, 'Über das Geldwesen', in '*Philosophische und sozialistische Schriften 1837–50*, A. Cornu and W. Mönke (eds.), Berlin 1961, pp. 329–348, p. 345.

[36]Carlebach, *op. cit.*, pp. 110–124.

[37]*Ibid.*, p. 110.

Monarchy. The essence of Judaism was money, and this was a form of alienation which threatened to affect the whole of European society. Thus Börne had integrated his economic critique of Judaism into a broader dialectical framework of capitalism versus a crude form of Socialism, which in many ways presaged the type of critique put forward by Marx.

Great though his influence was in his day, it is unlikely that Marx picked up his critique of Judaism directly from Börne. Marx's friendship with Heine did not lend itself to a wide and sympathetic reading of Börne, whose writings on Judaism were scattered over the entire range of his output. Börne's relationship towards his Jewishness was a complex one and he was probably too confused to work out clearly what his views on the subject were at any one time. Like Marx, Börne's radical critique of Judaism was intractably connected with his own development as a Jew. It is in this context that it must be set.

II

Löb Baruch was born doubly misfortunate; not only was he a Jew, but a Jew from Frankfurt a. Main, where antisemitism had been a fully institutionalised way of life since the "Stättigkeit" of 1616. Limited to 500 households, all crammed within one narrow *Judengasse*, the Jewish community was plagued by countless petty restrictions forced through the Magistry by the Judaeophobic Christian traders. The Jews were forbidden to contract more than twelve marriages each year; they were barred from the professions and guilds; they had to wear specified clothing and were locked into the ghetto after sunset; on walks outside the ghetto, Jews had to stay out of parks and off the pavements and doff their hat to the Christian who ordered "Mach Mores Jud!".[38] Subjected to this pervasive system of apartheid by the burghers of Frankfurt, the Jews were forced to use their economic powers as a lever against the authorities, who depended upon preserving Jewish trade as a form of taxable property. As the young Baruch acutely observed, there was a constant tension between the desires of the burghers and those of the Senate:

> "Man hat trotz dem Hasse, den man immer gegen Juden hatte, sich doch nie entschliessen können, sie gänzlich aus dem Lande zu vertreiben. Denn die Habsucht, die von ihrem Reichtum Nutzen ziehen wollte, war stärker noch als der Hass."[39]

In this context trade was the Jewish ticket for survival, and the Frankfurt Jewish community was predominantly commercial. Out of 505 households resident in 1709, 225 were engaged in trade and 50 in money-changing.[40] Despite their meagre political power, families like Speyer, Sichel, Amschel, Rothschild and Oppenheimer possessed by the end of the eighteenth century, according to Sombart, six million florins distributed between 753 families living in the ghetto.[41]

[38] On the Frankfurt ghetto see Isidor Kracauer, 'Geschichte der Judengasse in Frankfurt am Main', in *Festschrift des Philanthropin*, Frankfurt 1904.

[39] Ludwig Börne, *Sämtliche Schriften*, (5 vols.), I. and P. Rippman (eds.), Düsseldorf-Darmstadt 1964–1968 (hereafter *R*), I, p. 37.

[40] Simon Dubnow, *History of the Jews*, vol. 17, London 1971, p. 215–219.

[41] Werner Sombart, *The Jews and Modern Capitalism* (tr. M. Epstein), London 1913, p. 187.

A striking similarity amongst Jewish radicals of the early nineteenth century is the commercial context from which they emerged. Heine's uncle was a wealthy banker who tried to set Heine up in trade (Harry Heine u. Co. – a title Wolfgang Menzel exploited in his attack on "Jung Palästina"). Hess's father owned a sugar refinery and also tried to force his son into business in Cologne. Lassalle's father was a prosperous silk-dealer. Börne was no exception. His grandfather, Simon Baruch, had been Financial Agent to the Archduke Maximilian and adviser to Maria Theresa on occasion. His father, Jacob, was a trader and money-changer, holding a much respected position within the Jewish community, and several times representing the Jews at diplomatic level.

Like Heine and Hess, this commercial background only alienated Börne from his Jewish roots. Jacob Baruch was a cold, patriarchal and "verschlossener" man,[42] whose overbearing sense of respectability brought him into increasing conflict with his son. In his father's eyes Börne was a failure. Having had a great deal spent on his education in Frankfurt, Berlin, Halle and Heidelberg, Börne, instead of proving himself as a doctor, had nothing to show for himself but a penchant for the theatre and a sharp sense of wit. What Börne wrote, and particularly about the Jews, was an acute embarassment to his father. On several occasions the latter tried to arrange sinecures in Vienna or scholarships to universities, just to bring Börne under control. But, eager to find his "entry ticket" to European culture, what angered Börne about the Jewish community was exactly the sort of materialism and narrowness for which his father stood. In 1807 he wrote to his father from Heidelberg:

> "Ich weiss es, dass Du vollkommen zufrieden sein wirst, wenn ich einst so geschickt werde wie ein Dr. U. oder K., mein ehrliches Auskommen habe, bis endlich nach 20 jährigem Streben mein Ruhm durch den vielgeschäftigen Mund der Tanten und Cousinen bis an die äusserste Stadtmauer dringt, wo mich ein Banquier N. N. beglückt, mir, wenn er den Schnuppen kriegt, ein Rezept abzufordern."[43]

The ironic sense of wit formed to protect Börne from the antisemitism he met outside the ghetto and from the hostility he met from within his own family as the least popular child, was clearly becoming more aggressive and was directed, for the first time, against the Jews themselves, as Börne sought to shape his own identity free from that which was imposed upon him by ghetto existence.

The young Börne (and even the mature Börne for that matter, as the basic psychological make-up of this sad figure never really changed) was a lonely, depressive adolescent, whose diaries were filled with soul-searching fragments of autobiographia (such as the 1802 story *Ludwig Bartel*), and self-indulgent hypochondria, occasionally breaking down into fits of melancholy and references to suicide. Alienated from his father, "wo sich gleichfalls das Geld an die Stelle der Liebe gesetzt findet",[44] having no relationship with his mother, Börne's early years were dominated by the desire to be "was ich nicht bin"[45] and to attach

[42]Karl Gutzkow, 'Börne's Leben', in *Gesammelte Schriften*, vol. 6, Frankfurt a. Main 1845, pp. 1–302, p. 44.

[43]*R* V, p. 606.

[44]Martin Schneider, *Die kranke schöne Seele der Revolution. Heine, Börne, das "Junge Deutschland", Marx u. Engels*, Frankfurt a. Main 1980, p. 99.

[45]*R* IV, p. 49.

himself to mother figures in Henriette Herz and Jeanette Wohl, who remained a platonic friend throughout his life. There were no other women.[46]

To Börne, this loveless, alienated existence meant nothing more than simply being Jewish. The desire to be "was ich nicht bin" was largely the determination to cease being Jewish; just as for Löb Baruch, the novel *Ludwig Bartel* was a semiotic self-projection looking forward sixteen years to when he changed his name to Ludwig Börne. Börne was fortunate in coming (like Hess, Marx and Heine) from the Rhineland where he was in a good position to saturate himself in European culture. And in this context 1802 proved to be something of an *annus mirabilis* for Börne when, his appetite whetted by an early reading of Voltaire, Spinoza and Mendelssohn, he was sent to study with the Orientalist J. W. F. Hezel at Giessen and then on to Berlin to study medicine under Dr. Marcus Herz, husband of the famous Henriette.

The leading light of Henriette Herz's salon was Friedrich Schleiermacher. Börne immediately became infatuated with him and visited him daily. If Henriette was his first experience of love, Schleiermacher was his first true contact with German culture and the Classics.[47] A proponent of the absolute superiority of the Christian religion, who argued that "Judaism is long since dead. Those who yet wear its livery are only sitting lamenting beside the imperishable mummy, bewailing its departure and its sad legacy",[48] Schleiermacher had an obvious appeal for this young Hegelian Jew. Under Schleiermacher's influence, Börne's attitude towards his own Jewishness, and Judaism in general, became immediately more ambiguous. Schleiermacher was, after all, a much more extreme figure for a Jew like Börne to latch on to than Mendelssohn and David Friedländer, under whose influence one could cut off the Jewish beard and deny Judaism as a living religion and yet still retain an inner attachment to the Jewish way of life. This is exactly what Börne did not do. When he revisited the *Judengasse* for the first time in seven years in 1805 Börne felt something deeper than estrangement:

> "Was mich betrifft, war ich in Frankfurth so lebensfroh, wie noch nie, obzwar das Element, in dem ich athmete, mir so fremd war. Die Leute amüsirten mich erstaunlich . . . welch ein Leben das ist, welch ein Handeln. Die alten Juden von Abraham bis zum weisen Salomo sind mir immer vorgekommen, als hätten sie die allgemeine Weltgeschichte travestiren wollen . . . Aber die jetzigen, mein Gott . . . höchstens parodiren sie jene Travestie. Drei Dinge sind, die sie zu schätzen wissen, erstens: Geld, zweitens: Geld, und drittens: Geld. Es ist die Blüthe ihres Witzes, dass sie den Hamlet'schen Monolog übersetzen: Geld oder nicht Geld? das ist die Frage u.s.w."[49]

III

Börne's search for an identity within a German context and his consequent ambivalence towards the Jews – torn, as he was, between a sympathetic identification with its distant past, on the one hand, and a violent reaction against

[46]Karl Franzos, 'Börne und die Frauen', in *Deutsche Dichtung*, 9, 1890–1891.
[47]Schleiermacher's famous translation of Plato's *Symposium* might well have appealed to Börne, eager to love and be loved.
[48]Quoted in Poliakov, *op. cit.*, p. 186.
[49]*R* IV, pp. 120–121.

its contemporary materialism on the other, are reflected in his first major work: *Freimütige Bemerkungen über die neue Stättigkeit für die Judenschaft in Frankfurt am Main* . . . (1808).[50]

On the face of it this was a simple political tract defending the right of Frankfurt's Jews to political emancipation. Dalberg's assumption of power in Frankfurt in 1806 as head of the Napoleonic "Rhine Alliance" had been accompanied by promises of Jewish emancipation. But opposition from the Frankfurt burghers managed to limit the "Stättigkeit" of 1807 to a disappointing compromise, with all the major checks on Jews remaining intact and a new uniform annual tax of 22,000 Gulden imposed. This sparked off a lively literary debate between Israel Jacobson, leader of the Westphalian Jews, and no less a figure than Goethe himself, who was wholly opposed to Jewish emancipation, as is clear from his correspondence with Bettina Brentano at the time.[51]

Börne's attitude was somewhat divided. On the political level his tract was a defence of Jacobson and took a firm stance within the "regenerationist" or "assimilationist" tradition shaped by liberals such as Christian Wilhelm von Dohm, Wilhelm von Humboldt, and Karl von Hardenberg. The Decree, Börne argued, was a fraud as it was based on Christian greed for taxes rather than Christian tolerance. True political emancipation would only come when Christians were prepared to make a real change in their attitudes to Jews and talk of "equal rights, equal responsibilities". This, Dohm had argued in his *Über die bürgerliche Verbesserung der Juden* (1781) – something of a paradigm for the "regenerationist" tradition –, implied that the emancipation of the Jews depended not merely on their own betterment, but also that of society at large. To attack the Jews as usurers and rogues was to forget that they were only so because they had been oppressed and barred from all legitimate professions. Thus the occupational diversification of Jews depended upon the lifting of restrictions on civil rights, land ownership and employment in the professions and crafts; while true assimilation (where between Jews and Christians "es sollen . . . gar keine Verhältnisse mehr stattfinden"[52]) necessitated, according to Börne, religious toleration as a fulfilment of civic equality, and the break up of "feudal" antisemitism and isolationist Jewish Orthodoxy by mixed "Gemeinschaftschule".

Yet as an apologist for the Jewish cause it was clear that Börne was arguing from well outside the ghetto. If his defence of Jewish political emancipation had been based on rational argument, the emotional drive of his polemic was in fact directed against the Jewish community itself, egoistically tied, as he saw it, to the making of money. And here, on the social and economic level, Börne's thinking was highly ambiguous and at times came dangerously close to departing from Dohm's apologist line of thinking altogether. This is perhaps why Börne's father withdrew the essay from publication and had it circulated by manuscript. The

[50] . . . *mit besonderer Hinsicht auf die Kritik der Jacobsonschen Schrift, denselben Gegenstand betreffend*, *R* I, pp. 14–72.

[51] Bettina von Arnim, *Goethe's Briefwechsel mit einem Kinde*, in *Sämtliche Schriften*, vols. 4–6, Berlin 1853, vol. 4, pp. 222–227.

[52] *R* I, p. 18.

Freimütige Bemerkungen have received only scant attention from commentators, while their anti-Jewish stance has gone by wholly unnoticed. The tract may shed interesting light on the formation of a radical critique of Judaism.

Unlike Dohm, Börne sees the Jews' fondness for money not simply as a result of suppression in other fields of activity outside trade, although political emancipation in this area would have helped. The Jewish addiction to money is the result of a more general sense of alienation, not only from the German nation, but also from a higher, transcendental form of spiritualism, which forces the Jew towards theoretical as well as practical egoism:

> "Der Egoismus, der zwar in der Praxis stets seine Rechte behauptet, wird doch zuweilen theoretisch verleugnet. Bei den Juden aber verliert er auch in der Theorie nie seine Herrschaft. Untersucht man die Kosmopolitischen Ansichten des Mittelstandes unter Christen, so wird man finden, dass ein Jeder irgend etwas als Mittelpunkt setzt, entweder seinen Landesherrn oder den Staat überhaupt oder sonst ein anderes, wobei er denn sich selbst höchstens nur als ein Trabant dieser Zentralsonne betrachtet. Unter den Juden aber steht keiner so niedrig, dass er sich nicht als Mittelpunkt der ganzen Welt ansehen sollte."[53]

Alienated from the "Geist" of national identity, the Jew becomes intractably egoistic. He does not say "unsere Armee . . . unser König", but "die Preussen . . . der König", "und das vertrauliche 'unser' wird nur dann ausgesprochen, wenn vom Handel oder vom Gelde die Rede ist".[54] Money becomes not only the mark of Jewish alienation, but also the secret ("vertraulich") centre of his spiritual identity.

This leaves Börne in an ambivalent position. Given that money has become (through alienation and suppression, admittedly) the God of the Jews, Börne finds it difficult to decide whether to pardon them or condemn them. In the end he does both.

On the one hand Jewish materialism is forgiven as "der Rausch des Vergessens"; it is compensation for the life of the ghetto. After his visit to the Frankfurt ghetto in 1805, Börne wrote to Henriette Herz:

> "Trauern sie, liebe Mutter, und alle Grazien und Musen mögen mit trauern, aus allem dem ist nichts geworden. Denn in Frankfurth hat man weder Vergangenheit noch Zukunft, es war mir, als hätte ich mich aus dem Lethe berauscht, Gegenwart, Gegenwart, nichts als Gegenwart."[55]

The Jews' Lethe is money; money soothes the pain of Jewish existence. For Schewa, the tragic hero of Cumberland's play *The Jew* (1819), money is a form of temporal escape; yet the earthly spiritualism which the Jew has built out of money has become a universal one. Börne reviewed the play and commented:

> "Ist Geld etwas anderes als die Hoffnung des Genusses, wie es die wohltuende Erinnerung ist der mühsamen Erwerbung; ist es nicht Vergangenheit und Zukunft, und will man dem armen Juden, der keine Gegenwart hat, auch diese rauben? Ist nicht Geld das Grab, das allen gemein ist und Könige wie Bettler, Glückliche und Unglückliche . . . aufnimmt? Ist es nicht die gemeinschaftliche Verwesung, die Christen und Juden untereinandermengt und ihre Unterscheidungszeichen aufhebt!"[56]

[53]*Ibid.*, p. 28.
[54]*Ibid.*, p. 28.
[55]*R* IV, p. 121.
[56]*R* I, p. 288.

On the other hand, it is when Börne comes to see Jewish materialism within this universal context that he is most critical of it. Having forgiven the suffering Jew his lust for money, Börne then, on a social level, condemns money as a universal form of alienation affecting both Christian and Jew. Money is a putrefying force ("Verwesung") which brings all men to their death ("Grab"). On this social level, as on the psychological level, the Jew must be pardoned as he is no more guilty than the Christian. However, on an ethical level the Jew must be condemned for his materialism, because what distinguishes him from the Christian ("ihre Unterscheidungszeichen aufhebt") is that whereas the Jew is both practically and ethically egoistic, the Christian, by way of spiritual love for community, has an ethical escape from the alienation of money, "dass es ihm (Schewa) an Einsicht nicht gebrach": "Das süsse Glück, seinen Freunden wohlzutun, hat Schewa nie gefühlt."[57] Schewa becomes, for Börne, a tragic figure because he is unable to reach the spiritualism of the Christian, and as a tragic figure he must be sacrificed.

Until, in his later works, Börne makes Schewa, in the form of Rothschild, the social sacrifice of his proletarian-ethical revolution, it is ambiguous whether it is Judaism or the Jew which makes money its ethical essence. In Rothschild it is Judaism which is guilty by social criteria. But is Schewa ethically unable to transcend his materialism to reach the higher spiritual level merely because he is alienated from the community, or is Börne, in Feuerbachian terms (yet as a converted Christian, and therefore in Hegelian terms) trying also to say that there is something inherent in Judaism which holds Schewa back?

Certainly, on many occasions in the *Freimütige Bemerkungen*, Jewish materialism is less a result of external alienation than a form of internal "Krankheit", a word which Börne uses constantly here in relation to the Jews. The only way to purge the Jews of the greed which they fulfil in commerce is to give them the opportunity to be greedy in some other form of activity:

> "Aber alle Arzneien, die man den Juden gegen ihre Krankheit geben will, müssen ihnen angenehm gemacht werden, sie müssen den Geschmack des Gewinstes habe. Ihre Leidenschaft zum Handel muss selbst ein Mittel werden, sie vom Handel abzuziehen."[58]

Greed and egoism are so firmly embedded in the Jew, that it requires some form of Hegelian exorcism to purge him! The Christian business-man is attracted by the object of trade, the Jewish trader is attracted to its principle:

> "Der jüdische Kaufmann aber betrachtet das Prinzip des Handels als Objekt des Handels, d.h., er macht das Geld (ein idealisches) zur Ware und entzieht sich hierdurch den Gefahren, denen der christliche Kaufmann ausgesetzt ist."[59]

Unlike the Christian, the Jew makes no distinction between money and the commodity. Once this inextricable connection is built into a principle, the Jew is unable to redefine his position towards money. Jewish materialism becomes Jewish egomania.

[57] *Ibid.*, p. 288.
[58] *Ibid.*, p. 56.
[59] *Ibid.*, p. 37.

In this position it becomes tempting to abandon the Jew to his own egoism, for the Jews delight not simply in possession, but, rather, in the act of acquisition.[60] Here Börne comes dangerously close to letting go:

> "Aber es ist den Juden mehr um das Gewinnen als um den Gewinst, mehr um das Betriegen als um den Vorteil des Betrugs zu tun. Denn ein Volk wie das jüdische . . . muss von seinem rastlosen Geiste immerfort zur Tätigkeit getrieben werden."[61]

And yet here, at the climax of the *Freimütige Bemerkungen*, the ambiguity still remains unresolved. Börne believes that the Jews are eternally ("immerfort") traders, yet although he sees this as an outcome of their "rastlosen Geiste", he by no means makes it clear whether this is the result of external alienation, or merely the consequence of being "ein Volk wie das jüdische". And in his conclusion Börne is able to keep this ambiguity from conflict by an all-in solution to the Jewish Question: political emancipation of the Jews leading to the emancipation of the Jews from Judaism.

On one level this is primarily a spiritual demand. Börne's utopian image is "die Sehnsucht seines Geistes zu befriedigen, mit Freude und Liebe ergreifen".[62] This is symbolised in the figure of Shylock, whose "Christianisation" Börne sees as a parable for the ethical transcendence of Jewish materialism. Shylock's demand for a pound of flesh is that of the Jewish "Geldteufel"; it is "nicht anderes als die Spiegelung jener Kränkungen seines Volkes, deren sinnträchtigen Ausdruck das 'mürbe geschlagene Herz' enthält".[63] But for Börne, commenting on the play in 1828, the moral of the *Merchant of Venice* is Shylock's "Bildung" towards a de-Judaised spirit. Through avenging his people Shylock learns that only love, not money, can be the spiritual centre of the world:

> "Der Christ hasst den Juden, der Jude vergilt es dem Christen, und indem er es tut, rächt Shylock die verspottete Tugend auch an sich selbst. Er gibt Geld hin, sein Volk zu rächen, und erfährt, dass Gold nicht Herr der Welt ist, wie der Jude glaubt, sondern dass Liebe mächtiger ist als Gold, selbst im Juden."[64]

Shylock has triumphed over "Judaism" though he remains a Jew. Thus "Judaism" is an inner ethical core of egoism that prevents the Jew from seeing the true light of love. Here Börne's imagery is powerful and it is clear that he sees Shylock's liberation as not external, but as an ethical transcendence of something inherent in himself:

> "Shylock ist ein gestiegener Jude, ein Racheengel; er hat sich zu einer Höhe hinauf empfunden, wo er fähig wird, etwas zu tun, das nicht seinem Beutel wuchert, etwas zu tun für alle."[65]

But the spiritual demand for the liberation of the Jew from egoism is also the

[60] It is interesting to note that Max Stirner takes exactly the opposite view to Börne: "der Jude versteht diese (christlichen) Interessen . . . nicht einmal, weil er sich nicht erlaubt, den Dingen keinen Wert beizulegen". (*Der Einzige und sein Eigentum*, H. Helms (ed.), Reclam, 1970, p. 21.)
[61] *R* I, p. 62.
[62] *Ibid.*, p. 62.
[63] Schneider, *op. cit.*, p. 99.
[64] *R.* I, p. 503.
[65] *Ibid.*, pp. 500–501.

social demand for his liberation from trade; and here the ambiguity at the end of the *Freimütige Bemerkungen* is resolved. Shylock's discovery of love necessitates his abandonment of money. Similarly, in the *Freimütige Bemerkungen* Börne sees the purpose of liberating the Jew in agriculture and handicrafts in providing a cure for that social "Krankheit" called commerce which makes him a two-dimensional person:

> "Die Krankheit der Juden aber besteht in einer Hypersthenie der Handels- und Gewinnsucht. Dadurch, dass hier alle ihre Lebensthätigkeit aufgehäuft ist, müssen natürlich die übrigen Teile ihres Organismus geschwächt werden."[66]

The hope of political liberation, leading to occupational diversification, is that it will make the Jews into "full" human beings by diverting them from trade, which Börne sees merely as the social manifestation of the spiritual malaise which is Judaism.

Although this is still a social critique of "Judaism" rather than a Socialist one, the latter would not have been possible without the role of the former in linking spiritual and social emancipation from Judaism. The connection is vital. The ambiguity of the ethical condemnation in Schewa becomes resolved once Börne sees that neither a spiritualisation of the Jew nor his political emancipation in fields outside commerce are, by themselves, enough to purge him of his sickness. The two forms of emancipation are inextricably connected. Ceasing to be "Jewish" must also mean ceasing to be a trader. Thus by social criteria Börne finds, like Marx, that it is Judaism, not the Jew which is guilty.

Here was the root of a solution to the Jewish Question which went beyond assimilation and threatened to make Jewish emancipation a class question. Jewish occupational diversification had not merely to fulfil some Dohmist ideal of political emancipation and civil betterment, both of Jew and state; emancipation had to defeat the alienated spirit of Jewish materialism, embodied in the wealthy Jewish traders. Simple political emancipation was the "wealthy way". For Börne the aim of occupational diversification should be the universal way: a way that depended upon the negation of Judaism in the social field.

IV

The ambiguity of the ethical critique of Judaism had been resolved in the *Freimütige Bemerkungen* on a social level. But it was not yet on a Socialist one. The aim of de-Judaisation was not the salvation of society, threatened by "Verjudung" (at least not yet); it was the salvation of the Jews, and, therefore, was an argument for assimilation. It is the failure of assimilation which marks the divide between Börne's social and Socialist critiques, for it was only when Börne himself failed to find an identity in Germany that the salvation of Jews from "Judaism" became inseparable from the salvation of society from "Judaism" within a Socialist framework.[67]

[66] *Ibid.*, pp. 55–56.

[67] In this sense I have thought it not inconsistent to discuss the *Freimütige Bemerkungen* in connection with other works (the reviews of *Der Jude* and *Merchant of Venice*) written before Börne's political radicalisation.

The search for assimilation was an old Jewish story. But Börne's generation was special. Liberated from the ghetto, many of Börne's contemporaries found themselves in something of a no-mans-land, alienated from their Jewish roots yet unable to become German since, as Jews, they had nothing to give up in exchange. The Jews were stranded in the dilemma of their own identity. Some resolved it by returning to the Jewish fold (the Hess family for example).[68] Others resolved the conflict by burying their Judaism in a kind of "psychological ghetto" and asserting their Germanness. If this failed then Socialism and internationalism often became an alternative path for the Jews. It was a path which Börne pioneered.

Börne's attitude towards his Jewishness is summed up neatly in one of his 'Aphorismen' (1808):

> "Wenn ich nicht selbst ein Jude wäre, so wollte ich manches zum Lobe der Juden sagen; aber die deutsche Eitelkeit zwingt mich, Bescheidenheit zu affektieren."[69]

There is no ambiguity here. What dominates ("zwingt") Börne is the self-imposed determination to be German, which obliges him to bury his Judaism. From an objective, non-Jewish, viewpoint he might regret this, but as a Jew he can see nothing but a handicap in his Jewishness, in which case the desire to become German was a welcome opportunity to eradicate his Jewish identity.[70]

This sort of twisted thinking was not unusual for a generation dominated by "Jewish trouble". Nearly all the Jews of this period found that Judaism had a private, inexplicable, even mystical hold over them. Heine and Gans are well-known in this respect and even Börne joined them on occasion. But the external pressures from German society, where the Jew was a cripple, could not but penetrate the individual psyche. The extremities of Jewish self-hatred were later to become well-known. These were avoided to a large extent in Börne's day where there was always the hope of assimilation, or at least the Jew could convince himself that there was.

Börne belonged to that class of Jew which sought to be more "German" than the Germans. Moritz Saphir remembered a meeting with Börne and Heine in November 1827 in which Börne had argued fiercely that the Christian who had had to earn his Christianity was more Christian than he who was born with it.[71] Börne, himself, put forward the argument in one of his *Briefe aus Paris* that the Jew was more patriotic than the German because he was born without a Fatherland:

> "Ja, weil ich in keinem Vaterland geboren, darum wünsche ich ein Vaterland heisser als ihr, und weil mein Geburtsort nicht grösser war als die Judengasse . . . genügt mir auch die Stadt nicht mehr zum Vaterlande, nicht mehr ein Landgebiet, nicht mehr ein Provinz; nur das ganze grosse Vaterland genügt mir, soweit seine Sprache reicht."[72]

Linguistic nationalism was a common Jewish cry. The only undeniably

[68]Poliakov has argued (*op. cit.*, pp. 256 ff.) that it was generally the poorer Jews who were the first to retreat from assimilation.

[69]*R* I, p. 142.

[70]*Ibid.*

[71]In Hans Houben, *Gespräche mit Heine*, Frankfurt a. Main 1926, p. 119.

[72]*R* III, p. 511.

"German" characteristic to which a Jew could appeal was language, and this is why antisemites emphasised Jewish "Sprachfehler" and talked of "deutschredende Israeliten". But in Börne's case the appeal was not without justification. When Napoleon entered Halle in 1806 Börne fled to Berlin, sacrificed his Bonapartist sympathies and returned to his university to deliver a 'Rede an die Juden', in which he challenged the Jews to fight for their Fatherland. Eight years later Börne was asserting his national arrogance with an article presumptuously entitled 'Was wir wollen':

> "Wir wollen freie Deutsche sein, frei in unserem Hasse, frei in unserer Liebe. Mit dem Leibe nicht, nicht mit dem Herzen einem fremden Volke ergeben . . . Wir sind uns selbst genug."[73]

However, since there was no agreement yet as to what, exactly, "German" meant (other than anti-French and anti-Junker), one could not help but notice, from the "Germans'" point of view, that Börne's desire to be German, like his linguistic claim to nationalism, was purely abstract and therefore meant really little more than the determination to cease being Jewish. Faced with a wave of antisemitic reaction after 1815, culminating in the *Hep! Hep!* riots of 1819, Börne's instinctive reaction was to convert to Christianity rather than lose out as a "German". There was no ambivalence in Börne's decision. For him:

> "Die jüdische Nation gleicht einer ägyptischen Mummie, die ohne Leben den Schein des Lebens trägt und als Leiche doch der Verwesung widersteht."[74]

Personal attacks on him as a Jew could cause violent reactions. One such attack from Eduard Meyer[75] incited Börne to recall with venom an incident in 1807 when, travelling to Heidelberg via Mainz, a customs official had stamped in his passport "Juif de Francfort":

> "Mein Blut stand stille; doch durfte ich nichts sagen noch tun; denn mein Vater war gegenwärtig. Damals schwur ich es in meinem Herzen: 'Wartet nur! ich schreibe euch auch einmal einen Pass, euch und allen!'"[76]

And yet on this occasion Börne was angered as much by Riesser's defence of him,[77] as a Jew, as he was by Meyer's attack itself. What angered him, above all, was the fact that both his critics and defenders could not escape the "magischer Judenkreis" surrounding his name.[78]

Börne's baptism was therefore a great relief. The drive to conversion within the German-Jewish communities of Börne's day was often powered by a complex amalgam of motives: escape from antisemitism; political, social, cultural and professional opportunism; sometimes even a spiritual need to cling to the "talisman of the cross" (Heine) in the wake of despair. But there can be few

[73] *R* I, pp. 164–165.
[74] *Ibid.*, p. 163.
[75] *Gegen Ludwig Börne den wahrheit-, recht- und ehrvergessenen Briefsteller aus Paris, von Dr. Meyer*, Altona 1831.
[76] *R* III, pp. 364–365.
[77] *Börne und die Juden. Ein Wort der Erwiderung auf die Flugschrift des Hrn. Dr. Ed. Meyer gegen Börne*, Altenburg 1832.
[78] *R* III, p. 510.

figures in this period whose desire for baptism was so clearly motivated by the determination to assassinate the Jew within and become submerged in German society. Börne insisted that his baptism was a political act, enabling him to establish a journal free from antisemitic prejudice, but since he kept the whole thing secret his baptism could never have had this effect and his claim is therefore clearly invalidated.

If Börne did not disclose his baptism it was because he felt guilt at having deserted his roots. The Jewish "betrayal complex" was a common one. As Rahel Levin confessed:

> "Ich habe solche Phantasie, als wenn ein ausserirdisch Wesen, wie ich in diese Welt getrieben wurde, mir beim Eingang diese Worte mit einem Dolch ins Herz gestossen hätte: 'Ja, habe Empfindung, sieh die Welt . . . sei gross und edel, ein ewiges Denken kann ich dir auch nicht nehmen'. Eins hat man aber vergessen: 'Sei eine Jüdin!' und nun ist mein ganzes Leben eine Verblutung."[79]

Börne expressed similar feelings of regret and waste after his baptism, manifested in a rapid succession of works concerning the Jews full of frantic attacks on antisemitism and "overdone" declarations of Jewish pride.[80] There was even an abortive novel (*Der Roman*, 1822/1823) in which Börne attempted to purge his guilt through a sympathetic portrayal of the tragic hero, a Jewish Colonel, whose love for a beautiful Christian girl is unreciprocated because of his Judaism. Yet rather like Heine's *Der Rabbi von Bacharach* – a work with a similar psychological role to play for Heine after his conversion – Börne's novel remained a fragment.

This inability to feel Jewish only exacerbated the problem of self-hatred. When Heine and Börne held their famous conversation about baptised Jews, in which they agreed that it was impossible to turn lice into fleas by pouring water over them and attacked "aged daughters of Israel" wearing crosses longer than their noses,[81] they were attacking their own positions as apostates.

Perhaps this is also the context in which one should see the Heine versus Börne polemic. This is a subject which has attracted much literature, but mostly from the viewpoint of Heine scholarship.[82] Seen from Börne's angle, it may be suggested that the polemic had more to do with being Jewish than has hitherto been conceded, and it is interesting to note that the writer coming closest to this suggestion so far is one of the foremost Börne scholars.[83] Inge Rippmann has pointed out that Heine's *Ludwig Börne. Eine Denkschrift* is something of a "Doppelporträt". Not only are there striking similarities in the respective positions of Heine and Börne, as patriots living in exile, and as baptised Jews with "Jewish trouble", but on one occasion in his *Denkschrift* Heine even transposes

[79]Quoted in Simon Dubnow, *Weltgeschichte des jüdischen Volkes*, vol. VIII, Berlin p. 262.

[80]See for eg. the two essays 'Für die Juden' of 1816 and 1819 (*R* I, pp. 170–179 and 871–879 respectively) and the critical review of the antisemitic play *Der kleine Haman*, (1819), *ibid.*, pp. 1030–1039.

[81]Quoted in Carlebach, *op. cit.*, p. 33.

[82]See for eg: Joseph Dresch, *Heine à Paris*, Paris 1956; Friedrich Hirth, *Heinrich Heine. Bausteine zu einer Biographie*, Mainz 1950; Otto Barthelemy, *La Querelle de Heine et de Börne*, Lyons 1935; David Sternberger, *Heinrich Heine und die Abschaffung der Sünde*, Hamburg 1972.

[83]Inge Rippmann, 'Heine's Denkschrift über Börne: Ein Doppelporträt', in *Heine Jahrbuch*, 1973, pp. 41–70.

himself into Börne; the story of bourgeois "satisfaits" fearing for their tea-sets during political unrest, which Heine attributed to Börne, had already been told by Heine in chapter 8, part 3 of the *Reisebilder*.[84] Heine's picture of Börne is highly subjective and the basis of his attack often inconsistent, as he is less interested in Börne the man than Börne the symbol for mediocrity and "Nazarenism". According to Friedrich Hiller, Heine saw in Börne a "bête noire" which he tried to exorcise through his polemic.[85] If that is so then Heine's negation of Börne's "Nazarenism" could have partly been the negation of the Jewish element in himself. Heine's relationship towards his Jewishness was highly ambiguous, and it may be that what he considered "narrow-mindedness" at this time was exactly that which he termed "Jewish", in which case Heine's attack on Platen as a homosexual and Platen's counter-attack on Heine as a Jew form a fitting parallel to this whole affair, for both Heine and Börne saw in each other their own caricature as a Jew. What Heine objected to in Börne was that, as a Jew, he was constantly being associated with him; "Ich will nicht mit ihm etwas gemein haben", Heine told Oscar Wolff.[86] And it is significant, therefore, that Heine's return to a positive identification with Judaism in his last years coincided with a more sympathetic view of Börne.[87]

Börne never experienced this return to Jewishness and he continued, until his death, to attack Heine both personally and politically. He saw in him another Goethe, another flippant, amoral, politically indifferent aesthete:

> "N'offensez pas M. Heine en le croyant capable d'une tendance sérieuse, d'une croyance, d'une conviction; M. Heine sait aussi bien que qui que ce soit, que ne rien craindre, ne rien espérer, ne rien aimer, ne rien vénérer et n'avoir aucun principe, sont les traits constitutifs d'un grand caractère."[88]

The political differences between the two men were a manifestation of their respective emotional developments as Germans and Jews. Heine's return to Jewishness was preceded by a conscious rejection of Hegel in favour of political liberalism and Saint-Simonism. Börne never accepted the latter, which he associated with monarchism and Jews,[89] while his failure as German and as Jew led him to a dogmatic radicalism bent on the destruction of both forms of identity. It was from bourgeois society that Börne, like many Socialists, was alienated. Socially and psychologically he had rejected the bourgeois world of Jewish commerce, yet in terms of profession and status he had not been integrated into that German *Bildungsbürgertum* designated by the holding of an "Amt". As an intellectual proletarian, rather like the Young Hegelians in the 1840s, it was not

[84] *Ibid.*, p. 54.
[85] In Houben, *op. cit.*, p. 209.
[86] *Ibid.*, pp. 242–243.
[87] Alfred Meissner, Adolf Stahr and Fanny Lewald all confirm that Heine, in his last years, deeply regretted his attack on Börne. See *ibid.*, pp. 634–635 and 733–735.
[88] *R* II, p. 892.
[89] The prominent part played in the Saint-Simonist movement by Jews (Rodrigues, Halevy, d'Eichenthal, the Pereire brothers), and capitalist ones at that, led to bitter attacks on the movement from many radical quarters, most famously the Fourierists.

difficult for this radical Jew to integrate his social critique of Judaism into a Socialist critique of bourgeois society.

Börne's hopes for assimilation ran out with the wave of antisemitism that swept the Restoration period. Not only did he lose his job in the Frankfurt police, but he also became the object of constant attacks from nationalist intellectuals in the universities and salons; Meyer, Wolfgang Menzel, Johann Klein, Karl von Simrock (translator of the *Nibelungen*), Georg Gervinus, Friedrich Raumer, Willibald Alexis, Friedrich Förster, – all attacked Börne as a Jew or radical or some combination of the two. This was rubbing salt into a wound that was already deep and bitter. Having failed to find an identity in Germany, Börne sought a new one in a form of radical politics that would transcend nationality altogether. Here Börne's Jewishness could be turned to advantage, for the Jews were the apostles of cosmopolitanism and therefore of freedom:

> "Die Juden sind die Lehrer des Kosmopolitismus, und die ganze Welt ist ihre Schule. Und weil sie die Lehrer des Kosmopolitismus sind, sind sie auch die Apostel der Freiheit. Keine Freiheit ist möglich, solang es Nationen gibt."[90]

Clearly Börne's ideal of freedom needed a party that would not question his nationality; but, more than that, he needed one that would not question his identity at all, for Börne's failure as a "German" was unable to arouse the Jew in him. The mystical appeal which Börne found in the Jew as cosmopolite was totally abstract. He was not interested in being Jewish but in abstracting something out of the historical plight of Jewry which he could use against the Germans. The only significance in being Jewish was that it made him a *Weltbürger*, an abstract identity whose primary role was to relieve Börne from the shame of his inadequate "Germanness":

> "Eins ist, was mir Freude macht: nämlich dass ich ein Jude bin. Dadurch werde ich zum Weltbürger und brauche ich mich meiner Deutschheit nicht zu schämen."[91]

For many Jews Hegelianism provided an escape from the dilemma of their German-Jewish existence. For Gans, a "scientific" comprehension of the historical reality of Jewish culture (such as the *Culturverein* offered) within the context of a Hegelian dialectic of Spirit in world history, could provide a new basis for assimilation by forcing the Jew to recognise, beyond his identity as a Jew, the need for "humanisation in the higher sense". Thus Hegelianism provided an escape from Jewish particularism to a human universality which Gans felt could be found in European culture. It is not surprising, therefore, that the majority of Berlin Jews, seeking cultural and social integration, should find an attractive uniform in Hegel: Gans, Moses Moser, Saphir, Immanuel Wohlwill, Rahel Levin, the Veits and the Mendelssohns.[92]

But the Hegelian balance was a delicate one for Jews. When the ideal vision of universal integration was shattered by the reality of post-war Germany, Gans and his followers were put in a awkward position. No inner reform could seriously

[90] *R* III, p. 758.
[91] *R* I, p. 145.
[92] See Jacob Toews, *Hegelianism: The Path Towards Dialectical Humanism*, Cambridge 1980, pp. 126 ff.

expect to counteract antisemitism. For a while Gans thought in terms of a radical-utopian solution: an emigration of educated Jews to America to found a homeland on an island in the Niagara River, or alternatively, on the Mississippi.[93] When the plans collapsed the *Culturverein* disintegrated from the frustration of its dilemma and its members went their separate ways. Some (Gans, Heine) converted to Christianity. The majority (Isaak Jost, Leopold Zunz, Friedrich List, Moser, Wohlwill) continued to maintain a precarious identity as reformist members of the Jewish community.

Börne never joined the *Culturverein*. His level of alienation was one stage deeper than the Jewish Hegelians. The *Culturverein* disintegrated with the realisation that the delicate balance of Hegelian universalism could not be easily preserved (although its members continued to try and do just this); Börne's starting-point in his search for universalism was the absolute acceptance of this failure. Whereas the *Culturverein* sought in Hegelianism a means of preserving both a German and a Jewish identity, by way of their integration on a higher universal level, Börne sought in a more radical universalism the means by which he could destroy both forms of identity and put in their place an altogether new identity which was their absolute negation. Only after the revolution could the Jew cease to be Jewish; thus Börne's political radicalisation and his universalisation of the Jewish Question within a utopian framework went hand in hand.

V

After 1815 Börne became convinced that antisemitism and the failure of freedom in Germany had one and the same cause: the suppression of the German people by "Könige und Aristokraten":

> "Ich rede aus gleichem Grunde für Juden und gegen Adel, denn dieser verhält sich zum Bürgerstande, wie die christliche Welt zur jüdischen. Beide gründen Vorrechte auf den Zufall der Geburt."[94]

Börne argued that antisemitism was merely a manifestation of the aristocratic suppression of burgher-rights, a form of "Aristokratismus" used by the nobility as a diversion from the class-war. The greatest mistake the Jews could make therefore, was to seek protection against the mob from the nobles, for just as the Indians bait the boa-constrictor with an ox, so the Jews would be the meat driven into the hungry jaws of the revolution.[95] For its part, the people should come to realise that the Jews were in fact its political allies in the class-war:

> "Es wird begreifen lernen, dass man es zum Missbrauche der Freiheit verleitete, um sagen zu können, dass sie keiner Freiheit würdig seien, und dass man sie zum Gefängniswärter der Juden bestellt, weil die Gefängniswärter wie die Gefangenen den Kerker nicht verlassen dürfen. Dass eine Türe mehr den Ausgang versperre, eine weniger, das ist der Unterschied; unfrei sind sie beide."[96]

[93]Hanns G. Reissner, *Eduard Gans. Ein Leben im Vormärz*, Tübingen 1965 (Schriftenreihe wissenschaftlicher Abhandlungen des Leo Baeck Instituts 14), pp. 83–102.
[94]*R* II, p. 505.
[95]*R* III, p. 282.
[96]*R* I, p. 874.

Thus Börne saw antisemitism as the sign of a politically young nation; if the German did not have prejudices he would break down a hundred times a day. As mere prejudice, hatred of the Jews suppressed the German heart and polluted the ideal of German freedom:

> "Der Judenhass ist einer der pontnischen Sümpfe welche das schöne Frühlingsland unsrer Freiheit verpesten."[97]

But if antisemitism was a false consciousness imposed from above, the Jews should realise that the masses were not inherently antisemitic and recognise them as their true political allies. If both united in the cause of freedom against "Aristokratismus" then the obstacle of antisemitism could be overcome.

In this way the Jews became a symbol for the universal fight for freedom. If, as Jacob Katz points out, Börne was the first to use the term "emancipation" in connection with the Jews,[98] he meant it in this utopian and universal context. For Börne, Jewish rights were no more than human rights. The barbarism of the antisemites was in their distinction between civil and human rights:

> "Was ihr Menschenrechte nennt, das sind nur Tierrechte . . . Die Bürgerrechte, diese allein sind Menschenrechte; denn der Mensch wird erst in der bürgerlichen Gesellschaft zum Menschen. Er wird darin geboren, er wird also als Bürger geboren."[99]

If the Germans could not tolerate the Jews it was only because they themselves were slaves and therefore the emancipation of the Jews depended upon the civil and human emancipation of their oppressors:

> "Ist nicht Deutschland das Ghetto Europas? Tragen nicht alle Deutschen einen gelben Lappen am Hute . . . ?"[100]

In this context it was politically wrong to follow the example of Gabriel Riesser and others in isolating the Jewish campaign from the human one. The Jewish way had to be the universal way and it had to be subordinate. When Riesser proposed to start a Jewish political journal Börne was strongly opposed:

> "Wer für die Juden wirken will, der darf sie nicht isolieren; das tun ja eben deren Feinde, zu ihrem Verderben . . . Um ihnen zu helfen, muss man ihre Sache mit dem Rechte und den Ausprüchen der allgemeinen Freiheit in Verbindung bringen. Man muss nur immer gelegentlich, unerwartet von ihnen sprechen, damit der ungeneigte Leser gezwungen werde, sich damit zu beschäftigen, weil es auf seinem Wege liegt."[101]

Börne came to oppose Riesser as strongly as he did the antisemites. Instead of seeing the broader vision of universal rights, the sectarian Jews fought for their rights as though they were defending no more than a cabbage-patch and wrote bulky tomes to prove the wrong that was being done to them when the question of Jewish emancipation was a first principle that needed no further elucidation.[102]

[97] *R* II, p. 498.
[98] Jacob Katz, 'The Term "Jewish Emancipation": Its Origin and Historical Impact', in Altmann, *op. cit.*, pp. 1–25, p. 16.
[99] *R* II, p. 522.
[100] *R* III, pp. 888–889.
[101] *Ibid.*, p. 757.
[102] *R* I, pp. 177–179.

Börne's impatience showed only too clearly that he was no longer interested in the Jews as such. Having placed the Jewish Question within a universal context, Börne found that he could only identify with the Jew as a distant, abstract symbol for freedom:

> "Ich liebe nicht den Juden, nicht den Christen, weil Jude oder Christ: ich liebe sie nur, weil sie Menschen sind und zur Freiheit geboren."[103]

Börne had eradicated the Jewishness from his identity. As an abstraction, the Jew became as distant to Börne as the proletariat itself.

This put the Jews into a very precarious position. The emotional root of that abstraction had been Börne's own hostility to the Jewish preoccupation with trade, which, in the *Freimütige Bemerkungen*, had manifested itself not only in a new level of alienation from his Jewish background, but also in the formation of a social critique of Judaism. The political emancipation of the Jews should entail, by his definition, their social emancipation from "Judaism", which necessitated subordinating the Jewish cause to the universal one, as mere assimilation into the existing political structure would only play into the hands of the Jewish traders. The fate of the Jew and the masses had thus become one abstract entity. But the danger that faced the Jews in this situation, or rather the danger that faced "Judaism", was that if the power of Jewish money interfered with this universal emancipation then it would no longer be a question of the emancipation of the Jews from "Judaism", but, as Marx put it, the "emancipation of society from Judaism".

Clearly "Judaism" could easily turn the Jews into counter-revolutionaries. If the Jewish cause was subordinated to the universal revolution, it followed that "wenn es das Interesse der Revolution gebot, dann wandte sich Börne auch gegen die Juden".[104] As long as the Jews, as victims of "Aristokratismus", recognised the masses as their allies they could remain a revolutionary force. But the Jews were too often concerned with their own sectarian interests and used their economic power to seek an alliance with the oppressors, in which case they were no longer victims of a feudal class structure but had, themselves, become perpetrators of an equally pernicious financial aristocracy which undermined the revolutionary struggle for freedom. Here Börne was evidently moving towards a tertiary class analysis which increasingly saw the Jewish trader as the last prop of feudalism:

> "Denn die Juden und der Adel, das heisst Geld und Vorherrschaft, das heisst dingliche und persönliche Aristokratie, bilden die zwei letzten Stützen des Feudalsystems. Sie halten fest zusammen. Denn die Juden, von dem Volke bedroht, suchen Schutz bei den vornehmen Herren, und diese, von der Gleichheit geschreckt, suchen Waffen und Mauern im Gelde."[105]

The irrational hostility which Börne had shown towards Jewish commerce in 1808 was given a rational basis by the abstraction of the counter-revolutionary Jewish trader from the oppressed Jew, linked to an interrelated distinction

[103] *R* II, p. 537.
[104] Hans Bock, *Ludwig Börne: vom Gettojuden zum Nationalschriftsteller*, Berlin 1962, p. 109.
[105] *R* I, p. 876.

between bourgeois and feudal society in general. By focusing his attack specifically on the Jewish trader as the reactionary force, Börne was shaping his radical economic critique of Judaism, which, in the transition from a binary to a tertiary class analysis, became guilty by social and revolutionary criteria.

But one should go further than this. The radical critique of Judaism was not merely the product of a tertiary class analysis: in many ways it was its cause. Börne did not stumble across such an analysis which he then applied to the Jews in order to find them guilty. Like Marx, Börne shaped his critique of bourgeois society by focusing an economic critique on Judaism which he then made synonymous with bourgeois society.

Börne had already found Judaism guilty when he went to Paris and became famous for his attacks on the bourgeois, and "Jewish", July Monarchy. In *Der ewige Jude* (1821) Börne asked what it was that made the Jewishness of the Jew an eternal obsession of the German, and had answered that it was a spirit of praxis inherent in Judaism which made the Jew the eternal trader. Antisemitism was therefore rooted in economic tension between the masses and a powerful Jewish bourgeoisie:

> "Da die produzierende Kraft überall mit der verzehrenden im Streit liegt, so musste auch eine Verfolgung die Juden treffen."[106]

It was not unusual for radicals to become more critical of the Jews as they focused their attack on bourgeois society. Georg Büchner, by making a Jew sell Woyzeck the dagger to kill Marie, was designating the Jews as petty-bourgeois middle-men, who made the form of alienation (embodied in Woyzeck's act of murder) which he saw the aristocracy imposing on the proletariat economically possible. But Börne went deeper than this; it was not the Jews but Judaism itself, which was inherently commercial. Although the Jews had been responsible for the development of the money system (a point argued in the 70th of his *Briefe aus Paris*), it was now impossible to tell "ob es mehr Wucherer unter den Juden oder unter den Christen gibt".[107] All traders and userers, whether Christian or Jewish, were equally "Blutsauger".[108] What was guilty in Jewry, therefore, was not the Jew, but Judaism, which had Judaised Christian society with the spirit of commercialism and materialism:

> "Ich habe die Handelswelt nicht zu verteidigen, deren Judentümlichkeit – diese Sichtbarwerdung des Gelddämons, diese heraufgestiegene Furie der Habsucht, dieser leibliche Goldteufel – mir in der tiefsten Seele verhasst ist, sie mag in der Gestalt eines Hebräers, eines Muselmannes oder eines Christen mir entgegentreten. Aber ist diese Judentümlichkeit nur allein der Juden Schimpf und Schuld? Ist sie nicht die Stickluft, welche die ganze Handelswelt umdünstet, erhaltend zwar das Leben, weil sie das Leben zurückhält, aber tödlich, wo sie abgesondert erscheint."[109]

[106] *R* II, p. 504.
[107] *Ibid.*, p. 512.
[108] *Ibid.*, p. 512. Hess uses a remarkably similar image in 'Über das Geldwesen': "Das Geld, das wir verzehren und um dessen Erwerb wir arbeiten, ist unser eigenes Fleisch und Blut . . . Wir alle sind . . . Kannibalen, Raubthiere, Blutsauger". (Hess, *op. cit.*, p. 335).
[109] *R* II, pp. 512–513.

Jacob Toury has compared this and other passages in *Der ewige Jude* with Marx's own essays of 1843/1844,[110] and there is no doubt that the extremity of Börne's hatred for the "Judaism" of commerce provides an interesting parallel with Marx's own language on the subject. But it must be emphasised that Marx makes little distinction between Jews and Judaism and has few qualms about crediting the Jews with all the negative attributes of heretical capitalism, whereas Börne consistently argues that it is only Judaism which is guilty, while the Jews themselves are as innocent as the Christians. He opposes the antisemites who accuse the Jews of being "die Priester Merkurs . . . die steckten die Opferpfennige ein".[111] Although the worship of money is specifically "Judaic", the worshippers of money are Christian as well as Jewish, and it is to both that Börne speaks when he asks for the abandonment of the Judaic gods:

> "Werft euern Abgott um, zerstört seine Tempel – und die Fleischgabel entfällt den euch verhassten Leviten."[112]

What the revolution must destroy is not the Jews, but the Judaic enslavement of man to money:

> "Bei den Griechen und Römern war der Handel den Sklaven eigen, ihr aber seid Sklaven des Handels, und nichts verdient ihr als Geld und Verachtung."[113]

Though Börne does not say, like Marx, that all Jews are traders, he does agree with Marx that all traders are "Jews". While writing *Der ewige Jude*, Börne wrote to Jeanette Wohl from Munich:

> "Gestern sagte mir ein hiesiger Jude: 'Ach, Frankfurt ist doch ein ganz anderer Ort wie München, hier ist ja gar kein Leben.' Anfänglich verstand ich ihn nicht, aber bald fiel mir ein, dass er ein Jude ist, der unter Leben Handeln versteht. Ein Handelsmann ist ein Jude, ein Jud ist ein Gaul, und ein Gaul ist ein Schinnes!"[114]

But despite this reservation the similarities between Börne and Marx cannot be overlooked. Like Marx, Börne sets up "Judaism" as the antithesis of his revolutionary dialectic and it is clear that his critique of Judaism was, like Marx's, essential to the shaping of his tertiary and even Socialist class analysis in the 1830s.

When the July Revolution broke out in 1830 Börne came to Paris full of revolutionary enthusiasm for Louis Philippe. Within two years he realised that this was misplaced. The ideal of an emancipation of the proletarian fight for freedom from the clasp of Jewish commerce in alliance with the nobility had been betrayed by the consolidation of a political power elite, dominated by the financial bourgeosie, in increasing opposition to the masses. Börne rapidly deserted the monarchist cause and, under the influence of Lafayette, came to the forefront of the proletarian, revolutionary republican party during the Hambach

[110] Toury, *op. cit.*, Anhang D, p. 355.
[111] *R* II, p. 513.
[112] *Ibid.*
[113] *Ibid.*
[114] *R* IV, p. 546.

Festival and the Silkweavers' strikes in Lyons. The *Briefe aus Paris* are something of a day-by-day account of this process.

According to the orthodox view of Börne, outlined by Hans Bock,[115] Ludwig Marcuse[116] and Gerhard Ras,[117] this transition was dominated by a growing political opposition to the July Monarchy. Börne here is a "verspätete[r] Jakobiner"[118] who sees, merely, that the political ideals of 1789 are not yet fulfilled and therefore "Der Kampf wird zum dritten Male beginnen".[119] There is a certain amount of truth in this view. The central, consistent ideal of Börne's thinking was a "negative" freedom ("der Abwesenheit der Unfreiheit"[120]) which fell largely within the Jacobin tradition. Freedom was the leitmotif of history, whose dialectic consisted of the political tension between "Herrschaft" and "Freiheit". Reaching the latter depended upon the destruction of those political pillars of authority to which social and economic tension could only allude. Social class-war was not the motor of history and could only be a means to the true end of political democracy. What counted was not the unequal distribution of wealth but that of the privilege which wealth carried: "Nicht gegen den Besitz, nur gegen die Vorrechte der Reichen streitet das Volk."[121] And in this sense Börne ultimately rejected much of the social idealism of his time in favour of a "kleinbürgerliche Demokratie" which trusted its political ideals to the petty-bourgeoisie rather than the proletariat. These he saw symbolised in the Hambach Festival and the political struggles of the early 1830s in the German provinces, struggles in which Börne himself was active in Frankfurt and Hesse.

However, although this binary, political class analysis was relevant to feudal Germany, the significance of Börne's *Briefe aus Paris* (1832–1834) is in his formation of a tertiary class analysis, a distinction of which the orthodox view fails to see the full implications. Börne's years in Paris taught him that:

> "Da, aber, wo der Mittelstand sich die Gleichheit erworben, sieht das untere Volk die Ungleichheit neben sich, es lernt seinen elenden Zustand kennen, und da muss früher oder später der Krieg der Armen gegen die Reichen ausbrechen."[122]

And here the economic power of the bourgeoisie was such that, although the destruction of privilege remained the end, the means to that end – the social and economic war – became vastly more significant:

[115]Bock, *op. cit.*

[116]Ludwig Marcuse, *Revolutionär und Patriot. Das Leben Ludwig Börnes*, Leipzig 1929.

[117]Gerhard Ras, *Börne und Heine als politische Schriftsteller*, Den Haag 1926.

[118]Bock, *op. cit.*, p. 221.

[119]Quoted in *ibid.*, p. 200.

[120]*R* III, p. 1088.

[121]*Ibid.*, p. 371.

[122]*Ibid.*, p. 372. Engels put this same point in very similar language fifteen years later: "Die Arbeiterklasse ist notwendig ein Instrument in der Hand des Bürgertums, solange das Bürgertum selber revolutionär . . . ist . . . Aber von dem gleichen Tage, an dem das Bürgertum die volle politische Macht erlangt . . . übernimmt die Bewegung der Arbeiterklasse die Führung und wird zur nationalen Bewegung." (*Marx, Engels, Lenin, Stalin, zur deutschen Geschichte*, Berlin 1953, Bd. II/I p. 51). Engels admired the *Briefe aus Paris* greatly and it is quite possible that he was copying from it on this occasion.

> "Wenn aber diese Vorrechte sich hinter dem Besitz verschanzen, wie will das Volk die Gleichheit, die ihm gebührt, anders erobern, als indem es den Besitz erstürmt?"[123]

What interested Börne in the Silkweavers' strikes, therefore, was not simply that the economic power of the bourgeoisie had deprived the workers of their interests in parliament, but that that economic power had come to dominate the class-war itself; and it was during the Lyons strikes that Börne came closest to the neo-Babouvist tradition: "Es ist wahr, die Krieg der Armen gegen die Reichen hat begonnen!"[124]

Evidently, Börne was at least partly grappling with some form of primitive Socialist critique of bourgeois society. Although he had no vision of a proletarian overthrow of capitalism and sometimes appeared merely to be asking for the bourgeoisie to separate political rights from economic dominance, he (like Balzac, Lamennais and many other figures of the 1830s) made a direct attack on the economic and social structure of power under the July Monarchy and even talked of "Güterverteilung" in the Babouvist vein. In this sense he can be seen as an important bridge between the democratic radicalism of the 1830s and the crystallisation of a proletarian Socialism during the following decade.

As for Marx, Börne's critique of Judaism played a vital role in this transition. Börne had rejected Saint-Simonism less because of its social idealism than because of its support of monarchism and the Jews. The alliance of these two forces was the antithesis of his revolutionary dialectic. It was his critique of the power of Jewish money over the July Monarchy that provided Börne with the means by which he could turn his political opposition to the bourgeoisie into a social, and potentially Socialist one.

Börne saw the "Finanzaristokratie" which dominated the July Monarchy as essentially Jewish; not only because it was a bourgeois embodiment of the Judaic commercial spirit, but also because he was determined to see the dominant capitalists of the day as Jews. Thus the critique had come full circle. In 1808 a social and ethical critique of Jews had been turned into a social critique of Judaism; in 1821 this critique had been integrated into a universal framework for emancipation and Judaism had subsequently been found guilty of heretical capitalism; now, in the *Briefe aus Paris*, the framework had been made at least partly Socialist, but the enemy of the revolution was no longer simply "Judaism", but the financial Jews themselves.

This integration of guilty Jew and guilty Judaism was symbolised by Rothschild, the personal embodiment of the reactionary power of Judaism. For Heine, Rothschild was one of the great revolutionary levellers in the gradual destruction of the old aristocracy – Richelieu, Robespierre and Rothschild![125] But Börne could see in him only the spiritual antithesis of his own revolutionary existence, and on one occasion Börne even recounted how he had dreamt that he had seen the Frankfurt Rothschild hanged.[126] It is often unclear exactly which Rothschild Börne is attacking: James in Paris, Amschel Mayer in Frankfurt or

[123] *R* III, pp. 371–372.
[124] *Ibid.*, p. 371.
[125] Heine, *Werke*, Berlin and Weimar 1968, vol. 5, pp. 185–186.
[126] Heine, *Börne*, pp. 108–109.

even Carl in Naples. The truth of the matter is that he is attacking the whole Rothschild dynasty, not as individuals but as symbols of a Judaised, counter-revolutionary modern-day capitalism:

> "Gegen den Menschen Rothschild habe ich gar nichts, aber weil er Rothschild ist, setze ich ihn den Königen gleich, und das kann ihn doch gewiss nicht verdriessen, wenn er auch nicht zu ihnen gehören möchte, da er am besten weiss, wie tief jetzt ein König unter Pari steht. Aber er ist der grosse Makler aller Staatsanleihen, welcher den Fürsten die Macht gibt, der Freiheit zu trotzen und den Völkern den Mut nimmt, sich der Gewalt zu widersetzen. Rothschild ist der Hohepriester der Furcht, die Göttin, auf deren Altar Freiheit, Vaterlandsliebe, Ehre und jede ... Tugend geopfert werden. Rothschild soll in einer Börsenstunde alle seine Papiere losschlagen, dass sie in den tiefsten Abgrund stürzen; dann eile er in meine Arme, und er soll es spüren, wie fest ich ihn an mein Herz drücke."[127]

Rothschild had penetrated the highest positions of power; having kissed the hand of the Pope, he had become the spiritual essence of the monarchy, the "Judaised" July Monarchy, symbolised in the coronation of Louis Philippe in the "Börsensynagoge":

> "Rothschild hat dem Papste die Hand geküsst... Jetzt kömmt doch endlich einmal alles in die Ordnung, die Gott beim Erschaffen der Welt eigentlich hat haben wollen. Ein armer Christ küsste dem Papste die Füsse, und ein reicher Jude küsst ihm die Hand. Hätte Rothschild sein römisches Anleihen, statt zu 65 p.c. zu 60 erhalten ... hätte er dem Heiligen Vater um den Hals fallen dürfen ... Ich finde das alles sehr schön. Louis-Philippe, wenn er in einem Jahre noch König ist, wird sich krönen lassen; aber nicht zu Reims in St. Remi, sondern zu Paris in 'Notre-Dame de la bourse', und Rothschild wird dabei als Erzbischof fungieren."[128]

The task of the revolution must be to overthrow this Judaised July Monarchy and liberate man from the alienating power of the Rothschilds, "die gefährlichsten Feinde der Völker".

VI

Börne's polemic against Rothschild was the culmination of a long tradition of hostile remarks towards the Jews as traders. Börne's works are pregnant with violent personal and generalised attacks in this field. The Jews are "Söhne des Merkurs", intellectually "kaufmännisch"; they talk "in einem fort von Geld" and "nicht anders".[129] This was not unusual. What was unusual was that Börne transformed this age-old hostility into a scientific attack on Judaism itself, an attack which incorporated both the Hegelian view of Judaism as practical egoism, and the utopian negation of Judaism as representing the alienating spirit of heretical capitalism. The science that Börne's critique was searching for was Socialism and in this sense his writings form the essential framework for Marx on the question of the Jews.

It is indeed unlikely that Marx derived his critique directly from Börne. The linguistic similarities mentioned by Toury, between Marx's essays and *Der ewige Jude*, are probably coincidental. However it is possible that Marx had read

[127] *R* III, p. 351.
[128] *Ibid.*, pp. 482–483.
[129] *R* I, p. 8; *R* I, p. 10; *R* II, p. 714.

Börne's essay and quite likely that he had come across Börne's attacks on the "Jewish" July Monarchy contained in the *Briefe aus Paris*, which was, after all, a standard work for all radicals during the 1830s and championed by the Young Hegelians and Engels in particular. But whether or not Börne had a direct influence on Marx, both men had a remarkably similar critique of Judaism.

Marx and Börne are dealing with a simple revolutionary dialectic. Judaism represents a spirit of greed, egoism and capitalism, which threatens to "Judaise" society and enslave man to a god preventing him from fulfilling his true life. The utopian emancipation of man is the emancipation from Judaism. Unlike Marx, Börne is not an atheist, but he does see in the destruction of Judaism a reconciliation of man with his communal "Menschenseele" and a return to a human, classless society, symbolised in Antiquity, where life is reconciled with Spirit and thought, rather than alienated through power and class:

> "Bei den Alten war das Leben von der Wissenschaft nicht getrennt, sie dachten ihr Leben und lebten ihre Gedanken, und diesen . . . konnte es an Kraft und Dauerhaftigkeit nicht fehlen."[130]

Like Marx, Börne saw this "Erziehung zur Freiheit" as one that had to transcend the arbitrary, political values of bourgeois society itself. Bourgeois society had already been Judaised and its values were subjective and Jewish, not absolute and human. The latter qualities were to be sought in the proletariat, for only they were unpolluted by the Judaic-bourgeois spirit and therefore held the potential for social rather than political "Bildung":

> "Ich finde wahre menschliche Bildung nur im Pöbel, und den wahren Pöbel nur in den Gebildeten."[131]

The working classes were

> "die einzige, welchen das verfluchte Geld nicht die ganze Seele, allen Glauben abgehandelt."[132]

Börne's spiritual identification with the masses was a logical outcome of the repulsion he felt from his commercial, Jewish background and a fulfilment of his adolescent search for love and community. For the same reasons Börne focused on reform Catholicism, in Lamennais's *Paroles d'un Croyant* (1834), as a revolutionary ally of the masses. As the example of Poland had shown, Catholicism could give the proletariat spiritual strength in the struggle for freedom.[133] Under Lamennais's formula, it could be used to interpret Christianity as a form of primal Socialism, ordained by God, and made possible by the spirit of communal love:

> "Gott gab ihm diese Vorschrift: Helft euch einander, denn es gibt Starke und Schwache unter euch, Kranke und die sich wohlbefinden, und doch sollen alle leben."[134]

[130]*R* I, p. 708.
[131]*R* III, p. 181.
[132]*Ibid.*, p. 114.
[133]*R* II, p. 894.
[134]*Ibid.*, p. 1172.

Only the Reformation had corrupted this ideal by delivering religion into the hands of the powerful and justifying economic individualism:

> "Die Reformation war die Schwindsucht, an der die deutsche Freiheit starb, und Luther war ihr Totengräber . . . Religion war eine Waffe in räuberischer oder meuchelmörderischer Hand. Wie haben sie den Gott der Liebe herabgewürdigt, und seine Lehre zum Gesetz ihrer Herrschsucht, zum Regulative ihres habgierigen Krämerrechtes missbraucht!"[135]

Because of his support of Catholicism Börne parted company with the Young Hegelians after 1835, condemning Strauss's questioning of faith as a typically bourgeois occupation. Börne's opposition to Judaism was not based on atheism but, much more specifically, on the secular recognition of the social problem of Judaism. And here Börne represents the central argument and methodological basis of Marx's essays much more squarely than the Hegelians. He had already dealt with the problem making the transition from an atheistic critique of Judaism to a social and economic one, which Marx had to contend with in adapting the Hegelian critique to his own social synthesis in 1843/1844. Börne's critique was still broadly Hegelian, but he radicalised it within a utopian framework (where Judaism became synonymous with heretical capitalism) by means that were more direct than Marx's, yet he came to the same radical conclusions as far as the social destiny of Judaism was concerned. Through the critical analysis of the economic power of Judaism's social organisation Börne shaped another tradition in the radical critique of Judaism.

There is, of course, a very real sense in which the radical critique of "Judaism" was no longer a critique of Judaism as such. Unlike Hegel, Börne and Marx were not specifically interested in the Judaic religion, not merely because they were Jews rebelling against their roots, but because, apart from the hostility which they showed to Jews, their primary aim was to form a more general critique of bourgeois society at large. Feuerbach also was not specifically interested in Judaism; he looked beyond it, using his assessment of Judaism as a tool to shape an *anthropological* critique of religion. But this necessitated the acceptance of Judaism as a religion. This is exactly what Börne and Marx did not do. For both, "Judaism" had very little to do with religion as their critique of it had already given the word a new meaning which was primarily social and if not yet synonymous with capitalism, was at least moving that way.

Marx's critique of Judaism served as an important model for the shaping of a Socialist theory of alienation. "Judaism" already meant something close to "Capitalism" and was certainly presented by Marx as the antithesis in a universal dialectic of human emancipation. The Jew stands for a form of alienation from which the whole of society needs emancipation. The starting-point of Marx's first essay is the principle of *bellum omnium contra omnes*, which splits man into the duality of public citizen and private individual and alienates him from himself, his "Gemeinwesen" and from other men. The spiritual incompleteness of Jewish commercial life represents this alienated existence of the individual within bourgeois civil society, for which Marx already has a rich vocabulary: "Trennung", "sich selbst veräussern", "sich isolieren und sich

[135]*R* III, pp. 924–925.

zurückziehen", "alle Gattungsbände des Menschen zerreissen".[136] Even though Marx's essays pre-date his interest in political economy, they still contain fundamental concepts in the Marxian system; the critique of bourgeois society, the distinction between political and human emancipation, the materialistic approach to history and the call for revolution.[137]

The way in which Marx came to his Socialism was by no means unique. The path from Jewish self-burial to Socialism was a well-trodden one during a period in which Jews found it difficult to resolve the dilemma of their identity through assimilation. During the latter half of the century many Jews followed Hess's example by recognising the falsity of the Jewish dilemma and reconciling a positive commitment to Judaism with Socialism. Yet the position of the Jew within the Socialist movement remained a difficult one and this was due as much to the self-hatred of its Jewish members as it was to the anti-Jewish tradition of the Socialist movement. The case of Ludwig Börne shows that it was also not uncommon for Jews to arrive at their Socialism, both emotionally and intellectually, through a radical critique of "Judaism" which then turned into a more general attack on bourgeois society. In this respect Marx's essays were not unusual, and in a sense second-hand, since Börne had already shaped a tradition of economic attacks on Judaism which Marx made explicit in 1843/1844. In this light, we should look closer at the mechanism by which Jews became Socialists. Börne is a significant figure in the formation of early Socialism, not because of his political radicalism, but because in his treatment of "Judaism" he was essentially searching for a Socialist vocabulary.

[136]Meszaros, *op. cit.*, p. 73.
[137]Carlebach, *op. cit.*, p. 165.

Salomon Ludwig Steinheim's Influence: Hans Joachim Schoeps, A Case Study

BY GARY LEASE

In a century marked both by singular thought and by eccentric figures, Salomon Ludwig Steinheim stands out as one of the oddest figures of all. Born in Westphalia in 1789, the year of the French Revolution, of an old German-Jewish family, Steinheim's life covered the beginning of German Jewry's public struggle in Germany.[1] Thus his life spanned both the political struggle for Jewish emancipation in Germany and the corollary struggle within Judaism to formulate a theological understanding of Jewish belief in relationship to the Christian world around it. His thought, largely forgotten and dismissed even by his contemporaries as the product of a crank,[2] represents a position distinct from most analyses of German-Jewish thought during the nineteenth century. It may well be of value to survey briefly Steinheim's unique contribution to an understanding of Judaism and religion in general, and to trace his influence into our contemporary period, seeking out the consequences his thought may have had in our time.

Brought up in a small village in Westphalia, Steinheim left there at the age of fifteen to attend the famous *Gymnasium*, the *Christianeum*, in Altona near Hamburg in 1804.[3] After three years of study there he enrolled at the University of Kiel in 1807 to study medicine. Three years later, 1810, he and some colleagues from Kiel, including August Detlev Christian Twesten (later successor to Schleiermacher in Berlin in 1835), left Kiel to enroll for the first semester of the University of Berlin. Here he participated in an enthusiastic student discussion group which included largely students of the Protestant faculty of theology. After one year of study at Berlin, he returned to Kiel and completed his medical studies with a doctor's degree in 1811.[4] He returned to Altona and in 1813 put up his board as a doctor of medicine. At the same time he took up an active role in the Jewish community there and became the community doctor for the local synagogue in Altona. His training was soon put to hard use during the typhoid epidemic of 1814 in which he won a solid reputation among the citizens of Altona and

[1]For a brief but penetrating biographical sketch, see Hans Joachim Schoeps, 'Salomon Ludwig Steinheim. Lebenslauf-Werk-Einordnung', in *Salomon Ludwig Steinheim. Zum Gedenken*, Leiden 1966, pp. 3–39. Further materials are collected in the Steinheim *Nachlass*, his personal papers (what survived of them) now housed in the Jewish National and University Library, Jerusalem.

[2]Abraham Geiger, 'Umschau: Salomon Ludwig Steinheim', in *Jüdische Zeitschrift für Wissenschaft und Leben*, 10 (1874), p. 292. Professor Michael Schmaus taught this author long ago how much can be learned from the study of thinkers and movements rejected in their own times. This present study is a small token of appreciation.

[3]Schoeps, 'Salomon Ludwig Steinheim', *loc. cit.*, p. 5.

[4]*Ibid.*, p. 6.

Hamburg by his unceasing care of the sick and his exposure of himself to infection. This was later repeated during the deadly cholera epidemic that swept Germany in 1831 (taking with it such disparate figures as the philosopher, Hegel, and the military theorist, von Clausewitz). During that struggle he almost established the origin and source of the disease, but lacking a microscope he was unable to make a final identification of the bacillus.[5] This period of his life was marked by dedication to his medical work and his efforts for the community.

It was not until 1833 that he turned actively from a deep involvement in medical science and his many researches and publications in that field to the world of Jewish theology and the philosophy of religion. Indeed he felt himself called to be a representative of the Jewish concept of revelation, in contrast to those streams of thought represented on the one hand by Moses Mendelssohn and on the other by a figure such as Samuel Hirsch, a follower of Hegel.[6] At the same time, he also involved himself in the political and cultural struggle for Jewish emancipation, particularly in the northern German provinces. But when in 1840 these efforts for emancipation failed, and his own plans to found a periodical which would pursue the fight for emancipation from the standpoint of the essence of Judaism and not simply from a general humanitarian point of view collapsed, he retreated from public exposure in the German-Jewish world.[7] The first volume of his major publication, *Die Offenbarung nach dem Lehrbegriffe der Synagoge*, appeared in 1835 in response to a debate then currently raging among Christian theologians; this and other publications drew the criticism of his Jewish colleagues.[8] All this time, Steinheim's house was a centre for a highly cultivated society in Northern Germany which included the leading literary figures, humanists and thinkers of the day, and which still lived in the romantic atmosphere of the fast-disappearing age of Goethe.[9]

Finally, in 1845, Steinheim abandoned Altona and his medical practice and moved to Rome. Initially he thought of this only as a brief recuperative visit. But by 1849 his decision was firm to remain in Rome in self-imposed exile and not to return to Germany to live. It did not take long for him and his wife to establish an energetic salon life in Rome, where they became known among the cultured circles as "Philemon and Baucis".[10] From here he maintained a steady and forceful contact with events in Germany and strove to bring his initial work on revelation to a conclusion. He had originally planned it to appear in five volumes, corresponding to the five books of the Torah. But in fact only three more

[5]Salomon Ludwig Steinheim, *Bau- und Bruchstücke einer künftigen Lehre von den Epidemieen und ihrer Verbreitung mit besonderer Rücksicht auf die asiatische Brechruhr*, Altona 1831. See Schoeps's account, 'Salomon Ludwig Steinheim,' *loc. cit.*, p. 7.

[6]Salomon Ludwig Steinheim, *Die Offenbarung nach dem Lehrbegriffe der Synagoge*, vol. II: *Glaubenslehre der Synagoge als exakte Wissenschaft*, Leipzig 1856, pp. vii–viii. And Schoeps, 'Salomon Ludwig Steinheim', *loc. cit.*, pp. 6–8.

[7]*Ibid.*, p. 15.

[8]See Steinheim's account of the key reviews of his early work, all from Christian theologians in Christian publications, in *Offenbarung*, vol. II, *op. cit.*, p. vi; and his description of how representatives of the Jewish Enlightenment reacted to it, p. viii. Schoeps also notes this criticism from within the Jewish community, 'Salomon Ludwig Steinheim', *loc. cit.*, p. 11.

[9]*Ibid.*, pp. 17–20.

[10]*Ibid.*, pp. 21–22.

appeared, the second volume in 1856, the third, presenting a Jewish view of Christianity's history, in 1863 and the fourth in 1865 in which he argued against Luther's, Baur's and other interpretations of the Old Testament. A revered and at the same time odd figure in European Judaism, Steinheim died in the spring of 1866 in Zürich and was buried in the Protestant cemetery on the decision of the baptised son, Max, of an old Jewish friend, the historian Moses Budlinger; later that year his remains were transferred to the Jewish cemetery in Altona.[11]

In general, Steinheim rejected both Jewish Orthodoxy as well as the Reform movement, and this fact certainly influenced the reception of his own thought among Jewish thinkers of the time. His third, or middle position, can be characterised as "an existential faith in a living God, who through his revelation breaks through the contradictions of human reason".[12] In the last analysis this position bears upon the individual and not upon questions which stem from an institutional structure; "thus it was only in the twentieth century, where the religious doubt of the isolated and atomised individual became a common situation", that Steinheim's position gained any chance for understanding and influence.[13]

Steinheim saw himself as a genuine representative of true human science. For over 2,000 years human reason had struggled to come to know itself and its relationship to reality, and based on that knowledge, to predict the action proper to human nature. All religions, all philosophy had been concerned with this problem. And now in the nineteenth century Steinheim found that the major representatives of the perennial struggle to achieve proper and genuine human action were once again caught in a battle of monumental proportions, or as he called it, the battle between the Old and the New. It was into this battle that Steinheim threw himself with the enthusiasm of one who was sure that he had the proper solution, and of one who felt that the question to which he offered his answer was of absolutely vital importance to human existence.[14]

For Steinheim that which is properly and inherently the product of human nature is the "old", that which dissipates and passes away. On the other hand, the "new" is that which is eternal and not subject to change and decay. This

[11]The first burial, in a Christian cemetery, led to rumours that Steinheim had perhaps become a Christian shortly before his death; or at least that such a burial fittingly represented his dangerously close connections to Christian thought and thinkers. Benjamin Rippner, however, set the story straight, establishing that the initial burial in Zürich did not take place at Steinheim's request, and that the final interment was in agreement with Steinheim's actual position at the end of his life: 'Salomon Ludwig Steinheim', in *Monatsschrift für Geschichte und Wissenschaft des Judentums*, 22 (1878), pp. 461–462.

[12]Schoeps, 'Salomon Ludwig Steinheim', *loc. cit.*, p. 29. Steinheim himself saw his position as that of a "mediator" who "dared to demonstrate to each party that neither one understood the true doctrine of religion, and, having tossed away the core, had been nibbling only at the rind": Steinheim, *Offenbarung*, vol. II, p. ix.

[13]Schoeps, 'Salomon Ludwig Steinheim', *loc. cit.*, p. 30. In general, apart from a positive reception on the part of Heinrich Graetz (see below), Steinheim remained without influence throughout the nineteenth century, and until Schoeps attempted a revival in the 1930s, and again in the 1960s (see below) seemed likely to continue unnoticed in the twentieth as well.

[14]Salomon Ludwig Steinheim, 'Vom Bleibenden und Vergänglichen im Judentum', in *Vom Bleibenden und Vergänglichen im Judentum*, Berlin 1935. (*Deutschjüdischer Weg: Eine Schriftenreihe des Deutschen Vortrupps*. Nr. 3. Ed. Hans Joachim Schoeps), p. 12. Steinheim originally wrote this essay in 1842.

fundamental difference between the Old and the New is what led Steinheim on his search for genuine knowledge.[15] The natural inherent ideas stemming from human nature itself, "the so-called instincts of reason", are those which Steinheim calls "the old". They were present at the very beginning of human nature and we find ourselves forced to accept them as "eternal" truths. The difficulty is that these truths are without object and vacuous; it is only when human nature brings these inborn ideas into confrontation with objective reality that they gain content and meaning.[16] And it is precisely this added material, namely the determination of humanity's inborn ideas, these additions to human knowledge, which must be characterised as "something new". For this reason human nature is able to experience a growing consciousness and a learning which leads to human acts. But this new knowledge is subject to change, otherwise it would not be new; and it remains forever differentiated from the aboriginal knowledge, the inborn ideas, of human nature. Thus that knowledge which remains always true is indeed a completed knowledge but also an empty one; that knowledge which changes is a full and lively knowledge but an incomplete one.[17] And therefore "the eternal New, knowledge through experience, must always walk upon that great field of mistake and error. The certainty of knowledge, of knowledge itself, is only available for forms in their highest and most abstract sense, namely numbers and measures; the certainty of insight controls only the most general of truths concerning the existence of the external world; particular existence, and therefore knowledge is always a doubtful, unsteady thing".[18]

Following Kant,[19] Steinheim saw that the only answer to this dilemma lay in a critique of reason, that is, in an investigation of the nature and extent of the human being's ability to think. It must, according to Steinheim, set its own limits and determine the extent to which it is able to establish the truth of reality.[20] If this is possible, then presumably we will be able to judge whether human religious constructions are proper or not. According to Steinheim they are not; human history is filled with the rubble of our attempts to construct an idea of God

[15]*Ibid.*, pp. 13–14.
[16]*Ibid.*, p. 14.
[17]*Ibid.*, p. 16.
[18]*Ibid.*
[19]Salomon Ludwig Steinheim, *Moses Mendelssohn und seine Schule in ihrer Beziehung zur Aufgabe des neuen Jahrhunderts der alten Zeitrechnung*, Hamburg 1840, p. 105: where he expressly accepts Kant's direction making ethics dependent upon physics: "reality cannot be proven"; for Steinheim, Kant is the "destroyer of reason's idolatrous pictures", for he had based God's existence upon a "*Pflichtgebot*", i.e., he had substituted a necessity of action (*Sollen*) for one of essence (*Müssen*). But, agrees Steinheim, such an absolute command in human conscience is not conceivable without God "as the highest good". In general, says Steinheim, "the strict spirit of revelation is entirely the result of a further development of Kant's critique of reason and indeed is its end result"; this is seen in Kant's own words that of all such ideas, Moses's doctrine of creation is the one with which reason must agree: *Moses Mendelssohn, op. cit.*, p. 37. For a more detailed account of Steinheim's use of Kant, and the role his philosophical point of departure played in Steinheim's theological constructions, see Heinz Moshe Graupe's several studies, and particularly his articles, 'Steinheim und Kant; eine Untersuchung zum Verhältnis von Theologie und Religionsphilosophie', in *LBI Year Book V* (1960), pp. 140–176; and 'Die philosophischen Motive der Theologie S. L. Steinheims', in *Salomon Ludwig Steinheim. Zum Gedenken, op. cit.*, pp. 40–76.
[20]Steinheim, *Die Offenbarung nach dem Lehrbegriff der Synagoge*: vol. I: *Ein Schiboleth*, Frankfurt a. Main 1835, p. 70; Steinheim, 'Vom Bleibenden', *loc. cit.*, p. 18.

only according to our own human, and therefore necessary, ways of thought. Such an unaided reason, a "free-born being" is held captive by its own constructions.[21] These constructions themselves fall prey to ever more complicated critical attacks until, in fact, all "dogmas" fall into dust and human reason lies the prisoner of its own limitations.[22] The reason for this is clear: humanity has been unable to perceive the most fundamental and the most precious characteristic of its nature, namely its freedom. This is so, claims Steinheim, because all religions have dismissed the thought of creation; not just a creation of cosmic reality out of the stuff of a world soul (a source which falls back into the trap of human creation, into the trap of the imprisonment of reason), but indeed a creation from nothing.[23]

But how can one establish an act of creation from nothing which, in turn, provides such a fundamental freedom? Beginning again with Kant, Steinheim accepts his description of antinomies posited for human reason. But having done so, Steinheim then expands their application; reason, he contends, is not trapped *a priori* in its antinomies, and thus it must not abandon its efforts to comprehend the essence of reality (*das Ding an sich*). Indeed reason must realise that, precisely in that object which it believes it has comprehended, it finds itself "in clear contradiction to reality", and thus it has not simply gained "nothing", but rather in the opposite of its comprehension it has gained reality: Reason's "certain knowledge is that which is opposed to and contradictory to genuine reality".[24]

It is from this fundamental point of departure that Steinheim sees the solution to the vital battle raging in nineteenth-century religious circles. Because "if there is no freedom in the highest instance, that is in the creation of the world, then clearly there is no other freedom in any action".[25] "This battle is that of freedom with necessity, of morality with carnality; a true doctrine of God with that of idolatry, of revelation with paganism, of the new with the old."[26] This freedom of reason finally allows humanity to break away from the chains of cause and effect and to vanquish reason with a higher understanding by means of a free decision to subordinate that reason to the truth of *revelation*.

But is there a religion of revelation? That is precisely Steinheim's query. His criterion, or *Schiboleth* (the subtitle of his first volume on Revelation), is simple: "the essential and primary characteristic of a revelation must be that nothing similar or correspondent to it may be found in our original religious consciousness, but rather that it be dissimilar and contradictory to that consciousness";[27] or, to be even more clear, "the nature and *Schiboleth* of a divine revelation is that it does not agree with our religious consciousness, but instead it contains teachings and commandments which are foreign to, and at times even contradict that consciousness".[28]

[21]Steinheim, *Offenbarung*, vol. I, p. 66.
[22]*Ibid.*, pp. 68–69.
[23]Steinheim, 'Vom Bleibenden', *loc. cit.*, p. 22.
[24]Steinheim, *Offenbarung*, vol. II, p. 46.
[25]Steinheim, 'Vom Bleibenden', *loc. cit.*, p. 22.
[26]*Ibid.*, p. 23.
[27]Steinheim, *Offenbarung*, vol. I, p. 10.
[28]*Ibid.*, p. 11.

In other words, a revelation can be recognised, and must be accepted as such, when it stands in contradiction to the facts of our consciousness.[29] As for the content of this revelation, that is equally simple: it can only be "a communication or uncovering of unknown and indeterminate facts, a revelation of mysteries";[30] "the spiritual communication of hidden relationships which without this communication could not have been known by any means".[31] In his search for religious certainty, Steinheim had stumbled onto a solution which denies uncertainty because it forbids human participation; reason, by its very nature, cannot establish knowledge of the divine nature which is the origin of all reality, but it can recognise that knowledge when it finds a message which stands in stark contradiction to itself. That which seems to be the most unreasonable claim about God, the world, and human beings must be a revelation for that very reason!

The modern critical situation within Judaism began for Steinheim with the Enlightenment reforms of Moses Mendelssohn. Steinheim's medical and natural scientific background is reflected in his stern analysis of Mendelssohn's achievements: If a cure is continued after the sickness is healed, then you have a new sickness; and this is what happened in Mendelssohnian reform. European Jewry had been saved by Mendelssohn from the *plica polonica*, but then exchanged it for the "powdered and pomaded", beautiful world of Berlin, the philosophical world as it called itself.[32] Everyone, on all sides, had been crying for a "new" revelation, just as that cry can be heard today; this is nothing more than a cry for salvation.[33] The task was and is to "obtain full clarity about believing Israel's calling and Israel's duties in all their truth".[34] Moses Mendelssohn had begun this enormous task, but most certainly did not complete it; the "spiritual revolution" began with him but must still be brought to fruition.[35] Unfortunately, in liberating Judaism from the grip of decaying Orthodoxy, Mendelssohn identified rational monotheism with the holy scriptures; thus commandments which can be understood by reason alone do not need to be revealed.[36]

This is not to disparage Mendelssohn's accomplishments. Before his breath of fresh air swept through eighteenth-century Europe, Judaism was ruled by an authoritarian, dry, wasted service to letters on a page. An unknowledgeable priesthood had enslaved the Jewish people from within as externally they were limited and discriminated against.[37] The schools – Steinheim speaks here from personal experience – were torture chambers; "the true service to Jehovah had been turned into the work of galley slaves, and the servant of God had been turned

[29]Steinheim, *Offenbarung*, vol. I, pp. 165–166. See also *Offenbarung*, vol. II, p. 167: If any other would say that he had not only produced the work, but also the material for that work from nothing, we would think him an obvious liar; but in the God of revelation such a claim is "a truth and a certainty", because without such a power, he would not be God!

[30]Steinheim, *Offenbarung*, vol. I, p. 144.

[31]*Ibid.*, p. 166.

[32]Steinheim, *Moses Mendelssohn*, p. 43; "one had simply changed the actors, and exchanged the old Jewish-Polish propaganda for a new rationalistic line": *ibid.*, p. 44.

[33]*Ibid.*, pp. ix–x.

[34]*Ibid.*, p. 2.

[35]*Ibid.*, pp. 8–9.

[36]*Ibid.*, p. 10.

[37]*Ibid.*, p. 12.

into a servant of men".[38] Mendelssohn led the successful rebellion against this enslavement of the Jews by their own religion; but this victory of rationalism over clericalism, as important as it was, is only a phase in Steinheim's eyes. Clericalism, now moving towards mysticism, will not fool the Jews again; those forces in Judaism which had been strong enough to overcome that clericalism will now also be strong and healthy enough to advance beyond rationalism: beyond both it will construct a new, alternative system.[39]

Some rationalists said that Mendelssohn allowed the law to be revealed in order to smooth the way for his brand of rationalism. Whether he did or not, in Steinheim's view this "levelling" of Judaism meant that there was no longer a higher spirit in history, a genuine teacher, in word and deed, of humanity, nor a teaching for humanity to lead it to perfection.[40] The new, rationalist generation had no depth, no sense; in one case the director of a school teaching the new brand of Reform Judaism, responsible to the Covenant, had his own sons educated elsewhere, while he stayed on as director till his retirement! "If one had first sought the better form for the real content, one had now to search for the real content to fit the better form: first for the old religion one found new symbols; now for the new symbols one must find a religion richer in content . . . The newly formed religion of *common sense* was not able to find the right form . . ."[41] Steinheim's point of departure is his conviction, contrary to Mendelssohn's, that the Old Testament "was not given to reveal the law, but the living God, and that the law is of secondary, subordinate importance". And for this revelation there is no other source but that of the Old Testament; all philosophy, and pagan religions, are in contradiction to this genuine reality.[42]

This is the treasure granted to Judaism over 2,000 years ago and which is promised a final victory in the world's development. In contrast to Mendelssohn's so-called "natural religion", Steinheim calls for "the genuine teaching authority of the Old Testament to be returned to God; we did not actually take it away from Him, but have reduced it to the ridiculous absurdity of a law without a lawgiver. For more than a generation my own life has been dedicated to this restoration."[43] The battle going on in his own day between philosophy and revelation is the battle over whether reason will be the final judge of religion and whether philosophy and theology will become identical (as in Hegel); or whether the whole of humanity will be victorious, setting itself free from the slavery of philosophy and gaining the liberation of revelation.

Philosophy is in fact so dangerous because in it reason makes the claim not only to present the inner human experience in its essence, but also to capture the essence of all reality in its own concepts. But for Steinheim the god of concepts is, with all its attributes, the greatest possible contradiction to the god of experience, or revelation; "the old god, constructed out of inherent human thoughts, was the

[38] *Ibid.*, pp. 15, 18.
[39] *Ibid.*, pp. 29–30.
[40] *Ibid.*, p. 45.
[41] *Ibid.*, pp. 46–48.
[42] *Offenbarung*, vol. II, p. 38.
[43] Salomon Ludwig Steinheim, *Die Offenbarung nach dem Lehrbegriffe der Synagoge*: vol. IV: *Fünf Monomachieen*, Altona 1865, p. 517.

non-god in contrast to the new god whose existence and essence we must first learn".[44] And thus Steinheim also had to stand in opposition to the major movements of nineteenth-century Judaism. Orthodoxy is concerned only with ritual; it is represented by people who seek only stability in tradition and follow only the "colourful cloak of Benjamin" even at the cost of the most fundamental thought in Judaism; therefore the Orthodox direction in Judaism must be combatted. But on the other side those progressives of the Reform movement in nineteenth-century Judaism must be equally opposed, for they wish to make religion into a philosophy. And insofar as they discard the unique character of Judaism they also discard the essential ideas of that Judaism. Therefore the task of the present time is to offer battle to both of these directions in Judaism and hope that its most precious jewel – revelation – which they wish to steal, will not be allowed to sink into the depths of the sea but can be saved both for Judaism and for the world.[45]

The practical consequences are clear to Steinheim. Because of this revelation, Judaism has not only received the gift of freedom and morality, but at the same time has been given a mission. Wherever it finds reason enslaved it must fight to overcome dogmatism and to bring revelation to victory. This is to be achieved through a critical assessment of the self-determination of reason; the insight into reasons's own products and at the same time the recognition of revelation's totally other nature; and finally the persuasion that reason must subordinate itself in faith to the teachings of revelation even though these may in fact be contradictory to our reason.[46] Steinheim is persuaded that the essence of this revelation consists of the unique unity or singularity of God, this God's creation of the universe out of nothing, and the fact that, though this revelation is totally other than what our reason teaches us, it is nevertheless to be accepted precisely *because* of that contradiction.[47]

In practice, this position must lead to a political theocracy.[48] This is so, according to Steinheim, because civil freedom is the foundation of all human action; rare is the one who must fight for his earthly existence, and who is also able to consider seriously the questions of religion and morals.[49] And such civil freedom is precisely the result of our inherently free nature, which is in turn based on God's freedom as made manifest in his act of creation.[50] However, such civil freedom is only possible within a theocracy: "The founding of a Kingdom of God is our task"; without this all history becomes meaningless, "a mockery of the creator and his creation".[51] Such a theocracy is the only way of transcending the

[44]Steinheim, 'Vom Bleibenden', *loc. cit.*, p. 25.
[45]*Ibid.*, p. 28.
[46]Steinheim, *Offenbarung*, vol. I, pp. 70–71, 74.
[47]As stated clearly in the first volume of his major work: "The one God has created the world out of nothing, according to his free decision, and has communicated the full freedom of his nature to our souls, and this is the single possible basis for all truth in knowledge, and all morality in action": *Offenbarung*, vol. I, p. 358.
[48]Besides Steinheim's work on *Moses Mendelssohn*, and *Offenbarung* vol. II, see especially Steinheim, *Die Politik nach dem Begriffe der Offenbarung als Theokratie*, Leipzig 1845.
[49]Steinheim, *Moses Mendelssohn*, p. 41.
[50]Steinheim, *Offenbarung*, vol. II, pp. 325–341, 358.
[51]Steinheim, *Moses Mendelssohn*, p. 57.

contradiction between the gods of this world and the salvation of a higher order; it may take a long time in human history to attain this goal of a Kingdom of God, but it remains the "meta" toward which all human history tends.[52] This is nothing but the idea of a theocracy as found in the Old Testament; for what reason could only guess, the revealed word has shown us in all clarity, both in a two-thousand year past and in a "continuous present"; reason asks, but in this matter revelation answers and demonstrates.[53] The walls separating the kingdoms of this world and the other world must fall; when justice (civil liberties) finally enters the political order, then the theocracy will manifest itself.[54] Such a political order is to be found in the Old Testament, which offers us the best constitution available, a true republic, given by God. This constitution has only one goal, that humanity live free under the law of highest freedom.[55]

Such an order of freedom is in fact the final goal of humanity because human nature is not an original unity, and therefore strives to establish a harmony within itself. Human nature transcends the organisational world of creation (nature) and strives to present a "higher order of things in the invisible world i.e. the order of moral (ethical) harmony, of freedom".[56] The State, composed of human beings, has the same goal; as "an act of the absolute moral law" it is an institution, or occurrence, of a human society in which the postulate of highest reason is to become fact.[57] That is, the content of the higher order, or the invisible world, is to become the content of actual human world; this content has the character of freedom; only in freedom is the new life of humanity to be found, and in freedom humanity becomes the beginning of a new creation.[58] If, however, the human spirit is seen as an emanation or modification of the world soul, then no freedom is possible, and thus no ethics.[59] This would, however, be in stark contradiction to the revelation of creation in the Old Testament, which provides the foundation for freedom, which in turn generates true ethics. For "freedom is undetermined spontaneity, it is the power or ability to act, without any motive or any other direction, i.e., without external motives". The moral principle stands or falls on this principle of freedom; without the absolute freedom of will and the choice, against the laws of nature and reason, to do wrong, then there is no duty which can bind humanity to do right.[60]

Since freedom "is itself a principle and points to a higher spirit, in its absolute free act, as creator of the world, according to choice and consciousness", it is, in its very nature, an inherent and essential constituent of human consciousness and nature.[61] And it is in this freedom that humanity creates the State on earth; the goal of such a State as transcendental is to transfer the beyond into a genuine

[52]*Ibid.*, pp. 51–52.
[53]*Ibid.*, p. 53.
[54]*Ibid.*, p. 61.
[55]*Ibid.*, p. 58.
[56]Steinheim, *Politik*, p. 2.
[57]*Ibid.*, p. 3.
[58]*Ibid.*, p. 28.
[59]*Ibid.*, p. 30. Here Steinheim is most likely polemicising against the doctrines of the *Kabbalah*, as he understood them.
[60]*Ibid.*, p. 31.
[61]*Ibid.*, p. 34.

presence here, to achieve a society of humans which represents the freedom of all.[62] This true State has nothing to do with simply banding together; on the contrary, "the State becomes in its truth, if it should ever realise itself in its full reality, a true religious institution, a general religion, a living empire of free spirits, a State of God, in the biblical language".[63] This religion of revelation should "in no way become a State religion, but must and should become the religion of the State; it should not be *in* the State, but rather an expression of its life in truth, the idea of the State in its fullest development. The State, as an institution of the higher human nature, and thus of the doctrine of revelation, completes and fulfils itself in religion."[64] Only the non-revealed religion can and must be a ruling religion, i.e., maintained by the State's power; that is because it belongs to the State in which it rules. Revealed religion, on the other hand, is the fulfilled idea, in praxis, of the true State; and thus it neither rules nor is ruled.[65] For this to happen, though, the entire human mode of thought must undergo what the New Testament called "rebirth", or a "liberation from the law".[66]

In fact, however, this has yet to occur, though the Old Testament revelation has shown us the way. During the revolutions of the past five hundred years, the ruling religion, Christianity, has claimed that its kingdom is not of *this* world, while the State has constantly harped that its kingdom is not of *that* world, and so we remain to the present day.[67] Our task, then, according to Steinheim, is the hardest task of all: genuine rebirth! The State must become a State in freedom, while in it thrives the religion of the State. This is, for Steinheim, the grand nobility of humanity, that through its creator it has the power to fulfil itself through a *new* creation.[68] As a state religion, Christianity changed revelation's idea of a State in freedom; this idea has survived in only two places: hidden in Judaism and as a ferment in paganism. Thus has begun the history of the third exile and the future work of the *Weltgeist*: making the idea of freedom the principle of the State, thereby forging the theocracy of revelation.[69]

Steinheim is convinced that revelation will triumph as the religion of the world. The pagan, or natural mind, is one of necessity just as its god is a necessary one, and therefore there is no alternative: either you are a pagan philosopher or you are a believer in revelation. It is revelation which saves us from necessity. It genuinely frees us and shows us that *it* (not reason) is our judge and creator.[70] In Steinheim's mind the Jews are a "seminary for the whole world" where one people after another is sent to school to learn this divine lesson of one God and his creation of the world.[71] That this revelation will emerge victorious in the end is

[62] *Ibid.*, pp. 42, 50.
[63] *Ibid.*, p. 59.
[64] *Ibid.*
[65] *Ibid.*, pp. 59–60.
[66] *Ibid.*, p. 85.
[67] *Ibid.*, p. 93.
[68] *Ibid.*, pp. 93–95.
[69] *Ibid.*, p. 97. As the main witness, Steinheim cites Hegel's *Religionsphilosophie*, Berlin 1840, Pt. I, p. 240, in which he describes how religion will become an ethic, i.e., the State, or, in other words, how the basis for State and religion are identical!
[70] Steinheim, *Offenbarung*, vol. I, pp. 359–362.
[71] *Ibid.*, pp. 363–364.

clear to him; then there will be no need for either Judaism or Christianity or any other religion. While proclaiming this prophecy, however, Steinheim could also say that it is his message which is most important and not himself; in his mind it was clearly meaningless how he was to be judged. He was, as he said in one of his last works, "out of shooting range".[72]

Heinrich Graetz, in his monumental history of the Jews, dedicated more room to a discussion of Steinheim and his thought than to any other of his nineteenth-century contemporaries.[73] This is not surprising when one considers that Graetz himself was often in opposition to both Orthodox and Reform Judaism of his time. Though he termed Steinheim's *Offenbarung* an "impressive book" and Steinheim himself a "talented" man who stressed the "metaphysical side" of Judaism,[74] Graetz went even further than Steinheim and rejected the keystone of monotheism as the "primary principle of Judaism". In contrast to Steinheim, Graetz felt that this idea does not exhaust the entire content of Judaism, which, in Graetz's mind, is infinitely richer and deeper.[75] While for Graetz Steinheim's work reveals Jewish thought in all its "salvational power",[76] able to uncover and polish old, unnoticed truths of Judaism; and while, in the judgment of Graetz, no one in his time, or in the time before him, had understood the fundamental nature of Judaism as deeply as Steinheim; yet he scarcely made an impression on his contemporaries. In asking why, Graetz had a ready answer: "Because his life and his actions did not correspond to his thought and his feelings."[77] Hiding himself in Rome, hardly participating in Jewish public and religious life, remaining indifferent to the practical preservation of Judaism – these were all aspects of his total presentation which forced his fellow Jewish critics to neglect his work. And yet, maintained Graetz, the truth recognised by Steinheim, that the Jewish people, because of their apostolic mission, must be both priests and sacrifice, remains true, even though this idea was not allowed to play an actual role in Steinheim's life. In addition, for one who seemed so at home in the world of Jewish thought, Steinheim was always strangely ill at ease with Jewish writings; unacquainted, in depth, with Jewish thought and tradition

[72]Steinheim, 'Vom Bleibenden,' *loc. cit.*, p. 242.

[73]Heinrich Graetz, *Geschichte der Juden*, vol. 11, Leipzig[1]1870, pp. 475–482; in the second edition, Leipzig[2]1900, pp. 431–437. Intriguingly, though, Graetz left no mention of Steinheim in his recently published diaries and correspondence; see *Heinrich Graetz. Tagebuch und Briefe*, herausgegeben und mit Anmerkungen versehen von Reuven Michael, Tübingen 1977. (Schriftenreihe wissenschaftlicher Abhandlungen des Leo Baeck Instituts 34). Though Graetz was in Altona in 1839 (the diaries cover the years 1833–1856) and Steinheim was still living there; and though the correspondence, beginning in 1843, continues until 1891, there is no trace of Steinheim in this sphere of private utterances.

[74]Heinrich Graetz, 'The Structure of Jewish History', in *The Structure of Jewish History and other Essays*, trans. & ed. Ismar Schorsch, New York 1975, p. 67. This is a translation of Graetz's famous piece, 'Die Construction der jüdischen Geschichte', in *Zeitschrift für die religiösen Interessen des Judentums*, 3 (1846).

[75]*Ibid.*, p. 69. And yet Zacharias Frankel, editor of the *Zeitschrift für die religiösen Interessen des Judentums*, criticised Graetz for taking over Steinheim's version of monotheism, which, in Frankel's eyes, "under the guise of the most enthusiastic allegiance to revelation, actually undermines it fully and exposes it to caprice", *ibid.*, p. 304, note 6. In general, Schorsch agrees that Graetz's ideas are derived, in this regard, from Steinheim, *ibid.*, p. 40, note 91.

[76]Heinrich Graetz, *Geschichte der Juden*, vol. 11, Leipzig 1870, p. 475.

[77]*Ibid.*, p. 480.

before the eighteenth century, Steinheim often had trouble assembling proofs for his theses, a lack which occurred to other critics as well.[78] But few other Jewish thinkers gave Steinheim so much time. Graetz's student, Benjamin Rippner, did characterise him as a "genuine martyr of civilisation",[79] but beyond demonstrating that Steinheim had not become a "Judaising Christian"[80] he was unable to establish his influence for following generations.

On the contrary, from the very beginning Jewish critics shredded Steinheim's system and thought. One of his first reviewers, Elias Grünebaum, a zealous Reform Jew acquainted with Geiger, subjected Steinheim's first volume on revelation to a blistering critique. He quickly struck to the heart of Steinheim's theory, establishing that the revelation which Steinheim preaches cannot give evidence of itself, i.e., is unable to point out whether any information about divine matters is a revelation or not. Indeed Grünebaum finds the claim that "healthy human reason" stands in contradiction to revelation to be completely unproven, and if it were proven, it would be the loss of Judaism for, according to Grünebaum, if one were to attempt to attain the highest point of reason then "one would have to worship a God become flesh" and indeed even go that one better and worship at the feet of "the Indian God with its nine incarnations which would certainly be better than a God who had only been incarnated once".[81] In Grünebaum's eyes, Steinheim's work is filled with such ambiguities and lacks any clarity in his use of language. Several of these points may prove interesting.

To begin with, Grünebaum sees a major difference between a revelation and a physically existing thing. He finds Steinheim's argument that we accept as true certain physical situations even though they contradict our reasonable expectations, to be totally inapplicable to the question of revelation. Indeed what is missing for Grünebaum and for any later critic, is the "historical factor" which must be present if one is to establish that a revelation has actually taken place.[82]

[78]*Ibid.* See Steinheim, *Gesänge aus der Verbannung, welche sang Obadiah ben Amos im Laude Ham*, Frankfurt a. Main[2]1837, p. 57: "Ich fürchte nicht die Zeiten des allgemeinen Drangsals; dann halten, wie unterm Joche die Rinder, die gemeinschaftlich Leidenden zusammen." Not so strangely, Graetz himself enjoyed feelings of German national identification which led the editor of the second edition of some volumes from his *Geschichte der Juden* to term him both "ein begeisteter nationaler Jude" as well as a "vortrefflicher preussischer Patriot": Markus Brann, 'Vorwort', in Heinrich Graetz, *Geschichte der Juden*, vol. 11, Leipzig[2]1900. Brann is here referring to the "harsh judgments concerning Germany and Germans which were to be found frequently in the first edition"; these he left out due to personal communication from the late author and on the basis of Graetz's letter to von Treitschke: "Was Ihre Verdächtigung gegen meine Darstellung der Geschichte der Juden in deutschen Ländern betrifft, so will ich nur bemerken, dass sie im Jahre 1869 geschrieben war. Die glorreichen Siege, die durch geniale Führung entstandene Einheit und der Aufschwung erfolgten erst später. Vor diesen Ereignissen galt das Volk allgemein als deutscher Michel, und mein Urtheil richtete sich nach den allgemeinen von deutschen Historikern und Schriftstellern ausgesprochenen Urtheilen. Uebrigens habe ich von selbst in der englischen Uebersetzung meiner Geschichte, welche sich jetzt unter Presse befindet, die vor 1870 wahren, jetzt aber unwahr gewordenen Urtheile geändert," in *Breslauer Zeitung*, Nr. 605 (28th December 1879).

[79]Benjamin Rippner, 'Salomon Ludwig Steinheim', in *Monatsschrift für Geschichte und Wissenschaft des Judentums*, 21 (1877), p. 407.

[80]Benjamin Rippner, 'Salomon Ludwig Steinheim', *ibid.*, 22 (1878), 12.

[81]Elias Grünebaum, 'Review of Steinheim's *Offenbarung*, Vol. I', in *Wissenschaftliche Zeitschrift für jüdische Theologie*, 4 (1840), p. 92.

[82]*Ibid.*, p. 94.

Yehuda Halevi, that mystic of the Middle Ages, was especially careful to use history as a foundation for his presentation of God's revelation to the Jews. The truths of Jewish revelation, from Grünebaum's point of view, cannot be shaken by a contradiction with human knowledge; much less can one prove these truths precisely by means of this contradiction: even that did not occur to Halevi![83]

Another problem for Grünebaum is his insight that Steinheim confuses the fact of revelation with its content. The wonder of the revelation taking place is much different from what has been revealed. To say that a revelation by its occurrence is a contradiction to human reason is one thing; but it is quite another to show that what has been revealed stands in contradiction to human reason. Grünebaum maintains that the whole of Jewish tradition, especially the talmudic tradition, is concerned with showing the agreement between God's revelation and the powers of human reason. It is simply not so that revelation must be a mystery which would not be known to humanity if it had not been revealed by God.[84] On the contrary, Grünebaum claims that you must recognise the possibility of historical change and development in human thought; what may not have been possible for human reason at one point in its history may well be possible for it at a later date. Besides that, he maintains that this is not the point of a revelation at all: the doctrines of the unity of God, the creation of the world, and human freedom probably cannot be philosophically proven, but they are by no means the entirety of revelation. What, asks Grünebaum, do we do with the commandments?[85] The whole of talmudic tradition points out that the commandments in fact are more important for the forming of human life than the doctrines of God's unity and creation.[86] At the same time the Talmud works fundamentally according to the principle that revelation is to be brought into harmony with human reason as much as possible; and according to Maimonides with philosophy.[87] This brings Grünebaum to the conclusion that the "doctrine of the synagogue" upon which Steinheim wishes to base his system is in fact not the doctrine of the synagogue at all, for Jewish tradition rejects the thought that human reason cannot be brought into conjunction with God's revelation.

Grünebaum concludes his critique of Steinheim by pointing out that his distinction between a revelation and a non-revelation leads to the final absurdity that a non-revealed religion is characterised as one which does not have an exactly determined point of origin; but since such a point of origin is the condition for development, therefore any non-revealed religion does not have a development or a history; and yet of course all non-revealed religions have a history. On the other hand, a revealed religion, precisely because it has a clearly determined starting point, must have a history, that is, a continuing development in history; but of course it does not have any such history precisely because this would destroy the character of revelation. For Grünebaum this is pure drivel and, at the very least, a sophistry which confuses and misuses the concept "point of

[83] *Ibid.*, p. 95.
[84] *Ibid.*, p. 99.
[85] *Ibid.*, p. 103.
[86] *Ibid.*, p. 105
[87] *Ibid.*, p. 106.

origin".[88] All of this shows him that if revelation, as Steinheim will have it, is to function as the education of humanity then it is hard to imagine that this eternal wisdom would have been so stupid as to treat the young and the mature person in the same way. And this is just what Steinheim says, for, in fact, revelation cannot change; but Grünebaum finds that revelation, particularly the revelation made available through Jewish scriptures, must be distinguished according to the age in which it confronts humanity.

Thus human reason as it matures will have greater insight into the meaning and content of a revelation; the more mature person certainly will not only understand it differently than a young one, but will also use it differently. Grünebaum finds this wonderful process of distinction at work in the mid-nineteenth century, peeling the hard shell off the rich kernel of God's revelation to the Jews so that the full spirit of that revelation may be known and spread without the bitter and hard covering in which it was initially given. Thus, from Grünebaum's point of view, Steinheim stands in stark contradiction to both the traditions of Jewish Orthodoxy as well as to the efforts of progressive Reform Judaism of the nineteenth century, and though the spirit and intention are to be praised, his actual work is seen as destructive.

Some years after Steinheim's death Abraham Geiger, one of the major leaders in the nineteenth-century Reform movement in Germany, commented on Rippner's attempted restoration of Steinheim and his thought. Though he appraised him as a "noble figure"[89] in nineteenth-century Jewish history, he is equally convinced that not only did his work not achieve acknowledgement and influence during his lifetime, but it is even less likely to gain such acclaim in later years. For Geiger, Graetz was wrong: Steinheim is not the "Philo of our time".[90] We still read Philo with pleasure; no one knows Steinheim's work any longer, and his writings remain without influence.[91] When he asks the question, Why?, as Graetz did, Geiger responds very differently: that Steinheim has been so quickly forgotten is not due to his "lukewarm" religous practices, as Graetz would have it, but to the fact that in not knowing Hebrew, Steinheim never knew the history and writings of the Jews![92] Alienated from Judaism, Steinheim still felt duty bound to be a member of the community of his birth.

Geiger's problem with Steinheim's thought began at the very root of his theory: revelation. In his eyes, Steinheim did not see revelation as a revealing act on the

[88]*Ibid.*, pp. 108–109. See also, for example, Leopold Zunz's criticism: "I cannot agree to the hostile division between revelation and paganism; rather do I see everywhere only emanations of one and the same world spirit (*Weltgeist*); only in the phenomenal world are there antagonisms, even contradictions, but philosophy resolves them . . ." This reference to Steinheim's *Offenbarung*, vol. I is contained in an as yet unedited letter (1st May 1836), in: Nahum N. Glatzer, 'The Beginnings of Modern Jewish Studies', in *Studies in Nineteenth-Century Jewish Intellectual History*, ed. Alexander Altmann, Cambridge, Mass. 1964, p. 35. Graetz, on the other hand, had accepted Steinheim's distinction between the revelation of Judaism and paganism, i.e., other religions: Judaism "negates paganism", in *Structures of Jewish History*, p. 66.

[89]Abraham Geiger, 'Umschau: Salomon Ludwig Steinheim', in *Jüdische Zeitschrift für Wissenschaft und Leben*, 10 (1874), p. 286.

[90]Heinrich Graetz, *Geschichte der Juden*, vol. 11, pp. 477–478: One might call Steinheim the "German Philo among the Jews".

[91]Geiger, *loc. cit.*, p. 287.

[92]*Ibid.*, p. 289.

part of God in which God reveals both himself and his saving relationship to humanity, but rather the act of communication which brings that message to humanity. In this sense Steinheim "had something which was his very own, a philosophy, a revelation, a Judaism, which were his own creation and which he nevertheless attributed to the Synagogue as its doctrine; it was a way to salvation which he had hacked out by himself, but which he felt the whole of humanity had to walk in order to save itself from its evil errors".[93] For Geiger this meant that sooner or later, Steinheim would have ended up (though he did not see this himself) in the Christian camp. This is because he did not really know Jewish history but only the development of Judaism since Mendelssohn, and Geiger quotes a letter from Steinheim in which he said: "Mendelssohn was simply a circumcised pagan".[94] Thus in Geiger's eyes Steinheim would have great difficulty in defending himself against the charge that he was a Judaising Christian; in fact he stood far beyond the walls of nineteenth-century Jewish thought and Jewish life. While acknowledging the man's personal goodness, Geiger nevertheless had to characterise his thought as "unhealthy" and found that his later works did not deepen his initial insights, but rather spread themselves out endlessly; for this reason he was ignored in his lifetime and totally forgotten thereafter. "Is this unjust", asked Geiger, "or is it the action of a neutral judgement on the part of history?"[95]

But Hans Joachim Schoeps did not agree. Born in 1909 in Berlin, Schoeps was certainly one of the most controversial and provocative Jewish thinkers of our century. The similarities between him and Steinheim are astounding. Both were excellent writers and, in fact, Schoeps represents one of the finest German stylists of our time; Steinheim was a poet and Schoeps began his scholarly career as a twenty-year-old in Prague editing the posthumous short stories of Franz Kafka under the direction of the writer Max Brod;[96] both were polymaths, Steinheim working for many years as a leading figure in nineteenth-century medical theory, while Schoeps emerged as an authoritative historian of Prussian history and law while at the same time an acknowledged expert in the area of Christian origins and patristics;[97] both considered themselves lay theologians;[98] both were ignored in their lifetimes, hoping for acknowledgement at a later date;[99] both were deeply involved in debate with Christians and Christian thinkers;[100] both attempted to

[93]*Ibid.*, pp. 290–291.

[94]*Ibid.*, p. 291.

[95]Geiger, *ibid.*, p. 292.

[96]Hans Joachim Schoeps, *Ja-Nein-Trotzdem*, Mainz 1974, pp. 117–119.

[97]See, for example, Schoeps's standard work on the history and theology of Jewish-Christianity, first published in 1949; his study of Pauline theology is, in the author's opinion, but not in his alone, the most profound and provocative work on Paul in this century.

[98]And yet neither knew Hebrew – Geiger complained of this lack in Steinheim, and Scholem made no bones of it in his confrontation with Schoeps (see below).

[99]Schoeps, *Ja-Nein-Trotzdem*, p. 13.

[100]One need only recall that Steinheim's fellow-students in Berlin were almost entirely Christians, and that his first articles, and the first reviews of his work, were in Christian journals; while Schoeps engaged in a long-running feud with Hans Blüher over the differences between Judaism and Christianity, in *Streit um Israel. Ein jüdisch-christliches Gespräch*, Hamburg 1933.

provide a systematisation of Judaism for their contemporary worlds; and both felt themselves violently misunderstood, Steinheim as a Judaising "Christian" and Schoeps as a Jewish "fascist".[101] One cannot begin to understand both Schoeps's position and his fascination with Steinheim without also making clear the world in which he found himself.

Stemming from Sabbatianist forebears,[102] Schoeps felt himself to be the product of a movement in Jewish history which had betrayed believing Jews. In his mind it made no difference whether the principle *sola fide* is announced in the name of Sabbatai Zvi, Martin Luther, or for that matter, Karl Marx. As far as he was concerned, having been betrayed once was enough.[103] His initial philosophical studies, particularly of Max Scheler and Nicolai Hartmann, persuaded him that the highest existential and value categories of life are always the weakest ones; in other words, the true and the good are always and necessarily vanquished.[104] Perhaps, so mused Schoeps, this is why he was always interested in minority movements and minority groups in history.

In any event, it was in the crisis years of 1930 to 1933 that Schoeps, a young Prussian Jew, began to come to grips with what he felt was a unique religious situation. Through his friends at the University of Berlin and later at Leipzig he had come to realise that his whole "existential structure" had always been a Protestant and Lutheran one. At the same time, however, he was and remained a Jew, unable ever to believe in the divinity of the Christian Jesus. And in that situation, and in the existential need of Germany under the threat of the National Socialists, he had to ask himself "how may I experience a god of grace?"[105] This clear existential dialectic, which had drawn him to Karl Barth's theology, also drew him to Steinheim.[106]

In his early work, *Jüdischer Glaube in dieser Zeit*,[107] Schoeps took as a point of departure the persuasion that the very basic truths of religion had already been eliminated from the existential understanding of Western culture.[108] He immediately saw that, for him, the only possible solution was to return to the most fundamental points of this traditional religious thought, namely the revelation of Sinai, and this was precisely what he found in Steinheim. With a certain amount

[101]See the recent study of Schoeps's youth organisation, *Deutscher Vortrupp*, by Carl J. Rheins, 'Deutscher Vortrupp, Gefolgschaft deutscher Juden 1933–1945', in *LBI Year Book XXVI* (1981), pp. 207–229.

[102]Schoeps, *Ja-Nein-Trotzdem*, p. 135.

[103]*Ibid.*, p. 140.

[104]*Ibid.*, p. 141.

[105]*Ibid.*, pp. 138–139.

[106]Alexander Altmann, 'Zur Auseinandersetzung mit der "dialektischen Theologie"', in *Monatsschrift für Geschichte und Wissenschaft des Judentums*, 79 (1935), p. 359, maintains that Schoeps assumed the whole conceptual baggage of dialectical theology for use in his Jewish theology – and in complete naivety! Some twenty years later Altmann saw no reason to revise his initial judgment; Schoeps had introduced a "fully-fledged Barthianism, only slightly modified to suit the Jewish requirements" into his theology. His comment, two decades after the fact, was that, in general, German Jewry felt uncomfortable with "Karl Barth and his Jewish disciple". In 'Theology in Twentieth-Century German Jewry', in *LBI Year Book I* (1956), pp. 209–210.

[107]Hans Joachim Schoeps, *Jüdischer Glaube in dieser Zeit. Prolegomena zur Grundlegung einer systematischen Theologie des Judentums*, Berlin 1932.

[108]Schoeps, *Jüdischer Glaube*, *op. cit.*, p. 1.

of joy he took up Steinheim's call for a theological dialectic between reason and faith, or reason and revelation as the way out of what was increasingly appearing to be a hopeless situation. In his later work on the *Geschichte der jüdischen Religionsphilosophie in der Neuzeit*,[109] he rejected the "natural religion" of Mendelssohn and his followers because it was not the basis for a stand of faith, but simply a pronouncement of reason.[110]

It is fascinating to note that the foreword Schoeps wrote in 1935 for a small edition of Steinheim's works is almost identical in every word to the sketch he presented in a volume of 1966, also dedicated to Steinheim.[111] In both cases he remained persuaded that a future theology of Jewish thought must base itself upon the attempt to solve the dialectical, antinomian view of revelation and reason through a commitment of faith to the act of creation.[112] In fact, the concept of creation became for Schoeps the key dogma in a new Jewish theology. Modern Jews must "believe and confess that God, according to his free will and out of nothing, has created the world through his word".[113] For a Jewish theology such a dogma has fundamental importance. First, it openly rejects any acceptance of an "eternally existing person" in union with God (here against Christianity); and secondly, it denies eternity or self-motion to matter (against "paganism"). It is vital, from Schoeps's point of view, that the Jewish belief in God as the origin of all being be protected; only through a proclamation of the doctrine of creation from nothing is this guaranteed. Since, however, this truth cannot be gained by human knowledge, it is only available through God's work, i.e., revelation. Therefore it is revelation which constitutes "the single possible, genuine, true relationship" between God and humanity.[114] It is here that he found the answer to his initial question of how he might experience a god of grace.

Schoeps's single *caveat* is that one should strive to move beyond Steinheim's epistemological point of departure, placing his dialectical resolution in the phenomenon of human "sin" or the human "fall". From this existential point of view, Schoeps maintains that humanity has fallen from God and its origin, and therefore its reason is not to be trusted; because of these inner contradictions, humanity needs help from outside and this can occur only in revelation. From revelation we learn that human beings may be creatures of God in freedom, but

[109]Berlin 1935.

[110]Advertised on the back-flap of *Geschichte der jüdischen Religionsphilosophie in der Neuzeit*, which had been subtitled "Vol. I", was a further study to be dedicated entirely to the "Religionssystem Salomon Ludwig Steinheims" which would constitute "Vol. II" of Schoeps's history. The three parts of the work were to be entitled: "Die problemgeschichtlichen Voraussetzungen der Steinheimschen Offenbarungslehre"; "Das Offenbarungssystem auf dem Boden des erkenntnis-theoretischen Realismus"; and "Die Lehre in der Zeit." This promised presentation of Steinheim's system never appeared, presumably because Schoeps's publishing house, a part of his *Deutscher Vortrupp* organisation, was closed, along with the *Vortrupp*, at the end of 1935; see Rheins, 'Deutscher Vortrupp', *loc. cit.*, p. 226.

[111]For the first, see 'Nach Hundert Jahren', in *Vom Bleibenden, op. cit.*, pp. 7–10; for the latter, see 'Salomon Ludwig Steinheim', pp. 36–39.

[112]Schoeps, 'Nach Hundert Jahren', *loc. cit.*, p. 10; 'Salomon Ludwig Steinheim', *loc. cit.*, p. 39.

[113]Hans Joachim Schoeps, 'Secessio Judaica – Israel in Ewigkeit', in "*Bereit für Deutschland.*" *Der Patriotismus deutscher Juden und der Nationalsozialismus*, Berlin 1970, p. 285. This essay appeared originally in Schoeps's house organ *Deutscher Vortrupp* in August of 1934.

[114]Schoeps, 'Secessio Judaica', *loc. cit.*, p. 285.

this can only be so if the origin of human nature, and indeed the whole world, stems from God's ultimate act of freedom, namely creation from nothing.[115] In his *Prolegomena* of 1932 he attempted to point a way toward a Jewish theology which would present "revelation as this freedom of human beings to experience God and finally to achieve a return, within time, to the existential situation of the creation in the beginning".[116] To the end Schoeps remained convinced that any Jewish systematic theology must orientate itself on Steinheim and his concept of revelation, for in Schoeps's eyes Steinheim remains "the one consequent suprarational Jewish thinker of the nineteenth century".[117]

Schoeps claimed then, and reasserted that claim later, that the controversies which broke out over his attempt to provide a systematic theology of Judaism were concerned with "the continued existence of Judaism as a religion in our time: Judaism as a third force next to paganism and Christianity".[118] It was in this sense that he founded the *Deutscher Vortrupp* to support his and his Jewish comrades' commitment to Germany and against Hitler.[119] As one might imagine, criticism was not long in coming.

The most pointed of his reviewers was the even-then famous Jewish philosopher and historian Gershom Scholem, who published an open letter to Schoeps in the *Bayerische Israelitische Gemeindezeitung*.[120] Scholem's major point of contention is that Schoeps simply does not know the genuine history of Jewish theology and that to reduce it to the battles between philosophy and theology of the nineteenth century is to do it a disservice. More particularly, he finds that Schoeps's attempt to establish certain "dogmas" which might serve as the foundation of a Jewish theology really is contrary to the spirit and also the substance of Judaism. This is especially so for the teaching of a creation from nothing. Scholem is particularly struck by the fact that an idea, which can receive two such contradictory interpretations as that of Maimonides and that of the *Kabbalah*, must appear very doubtful as a fundamental point of departure for a systematic understanding of Judaism.[121]

Even more alarming for Scholem was Schoeps's orientation to Karl Barth and the concomitant rejection of tradition as an essential category for religious life in Judaism. This was particularly clear in Scholem's eyes when Schoeps made his "historical" confession to Germany and the place of Jews in Germany; from his point of view the problems with which Schoeps tries to wrestle are not the problems of Judaism, but the unfruitful remains of a German Judaism, or a

[115]Schoeps, 'Salomon Ludwig Steinheim', *loc. cit.*, p. 39.
[116]*Ibid.*
[117]Schoeps, *Jüdischer Glaube*, *op. cit.*, p. 45; 'Nach Hundert Jahren', *loc. cit.*, p. 10; 'Salomon Ludwig Steinheim', *loc. cit.*, p. 39.
[118]Schoeps, *Ja-Nein-Trotzdem*, *op. cit.*, p. 34.
[119]On the history, ideology and subsequent fate of the *Deutscher Vortrupp*, see 'Deutscher Vortrupp', *loc. cit.*
[120]*Bayerische Israelitische Gemeindezeitung*, VIII, No. 16 (15th August 1932). Now reprinted in Schoeps, *Ja-Nein-Trotzdem*, *op. cit.*, pp. 36–45.
[121]*Ibid.*, p. 39. One is forcefully reminded of Geiger's criticism of Steinheim: see above, notes 94, 98. Scholem also picks up Altmann's charge that "dogmas" do not fit Judaism well: see Altmann, 'Zur Auseinandersetzung', *loc. cit.*, p. 360, where he points out that Judaism simply does not have the materials from which a "dogmatic" theology could develop.

German-Jewish pietism.[122] The attempt, says Scholem, to reject the question concerning the religious meaning of oral tradition and the fundamental concepts which support that meaning, is simply not possible for a Jewish consciousness. In sum, Scholem judges Schoeps's attempt to connect an historical present with an eternal present on the basis of biblical teaching to be a fantasy.[123]

Of course Schoeps, who showed himself to be a polemicist of the first order in his later works, had to answer Scholem's charges, and he did so in a private letter to his reviewer.[124] Repeating the major thrust of his published work he expressed his concern that Scholem had simply ignored Schoeps's contention, namely that as a result of Western secularisation Jewish existence in our contemporary time has been split into two parts, and that a synthesis of these two schizophrenic sides to Jewish existence is only possible through a dialectic process.[125] To make the question even more poignant and clear, Schoeps emphasises the fact that a contemporary German Jew whose thought structure is critical-Protestant in nature, cannot be rid of the question "whether it is truly the same reverential piety with which our fathers of one hundred and fifty and possibly even as late as fifty years ago lit the Sabbath lights, with which we, in our being and our consciousness so secularised Jews of Western Europe, do the same thing, if we do it at all?"[126] This is a question which cannot be answered through scholarship alone, but can only be answered through the force of personal existence. There simply is no longer a category of Jewishness which transcends the particular time and place of one's existence.[127] And in that moment when the gates of the ghettos were opened, everything became different and the ability of Jewish tradition to maintain an eternal unchanging religious identification ceased to function. That is why current Jewish theology in Schoeps's mind is essentially only a phenomenon of remembrance, and not a creative theology.[128] He remained convinced that the essential way to understand human existence is through the acceptance of God's creation of the world and human nature out of nothing; only this point of departure will allow one to develop a genuine Jewish theology in our current world.

Just as Steinheim called for right-thinking Jews to remain "at their posts",[129] so also Schoeps announced the same task for German Jews living in a world of contradiction and destruction.[130] He clearly recognised that historically German Judaism was being destroyed, but every true Jew who was also a German was called upon to remain true to that divided heritage and stand fast in the face of

[122]Schoeps, *Ja-Nein-Trotzdem*, *op. cit.*, p. 41.
[123]*Ibid.*, p. 45.
[124]Now printed for the first time *ibid.*, pp. 45–54.
[125]*Ibid.*, p. 47.
[126]*Ibid.*, pp. 48–49.
[127]That is, there was no such thing as a Jewish *Volk*, constituted by blood; rather, the unique historical mission given to the Jews is what determines one's Jewish identity: See Schoeps, 'Secessio Judaica', *loc. cit.*, pp. 287–288: To be an Israelite means to be under "ein objektives Schicksal" and to participate in an "objektiven Auftrag". See also, Rheins, 'Deutscher Vortrupp', *loc. cit.*, p. 212.
[128]Schoeps, *Ja-Nein-Trotzdem*, *op. cit.*, p. 53.
[129]Steinheim, 'Vom Bleibenden', *loc. cit.*, p. 29.
[130]Hans Joachim Schoeps, *Wir Deutschen Juden*, Berlin^{2}1934, p. 5.

that destruction. "Whatever may happen: we are committed to Germany!"[131] And this post is to be held even if it is already a post which has been overrun.[132] For Schoeps this constituted a "*Konfession*" which belonged to the Jews of his time; it was a task from which they could not extricate themselves. "We cannot deny the decision which has already been made and we cannot remove the decision made by history; but we can deny its truth and therefore its legitimacy."[133] Echoing Steinheim almost word for word, Schoeps asked whether Jews have not always had something akin to a Jewish missionary call, which tells them that a martyrdom of suffering for truth is their greatest possibility of revealing themselves as genuine Jews?[134] In that moment of crisis Schoeps knew no answer other than that one can be destroyed for truth, and if German Jewry is destroyed, then with it will be destroyed a portion of truth. For whoever enters public life in this world also accepts an historical fate and whoever does that also accepts the possibility of human destruction.

The consequences are clear. Following in Steinheim's footsteps, Schoeps attempted to construct a new and functional systematic theology for Jews in the twentieth century which would allow them to live both as Jews and as members of another culture and another consciousness. "We German Jews", he said, "do not want our own happiness; rather, the happiness of our fatherland is our happiness."[135] A strange and tortuous way from an odd and isolated thinker in the Jewish world of the nineteenth century led in practice to nihilism – a charge hurled by Schoeps himself at Scholem[136] – which attempts to deny itself by raising the moment of its own destruction upon an altar of faith. Using a creation from nothing as a point of departure, Schoeps has brought Steinheim's thought full circle to destruction into nothing: The theological persuasion must have its consequence.

[131] *Ibid.*, p. 7.

[132] At the end of 1935 Schoeps's Jewish youth organisation, *Deutscher Vortrupp*, was dissolved by order of the Nazi government; at the end of 1938 he managed to escape to Sweden, one step ahead of arrest; during the war his parents died in concentration camps; yet none of this changed Schoeps's "fundamental commitment to Germany": Rheins, 'Deutscher Vortrupp', *loc. cit.*, pp. 226, 228.

[133] Schoeps, *Wir Deutschen Juden*, p. 9; 'Secessio Judaica', *loc. cit.*, pp. 287–288. Israel will survive despite all attacks against it; whatever happens to the individual, Israel itself will survive because that is its fate; in closing, Schoeps quotes a line from Martin Luserke: "Persönlichkeiten sterben wie die Fliegen/Das Objektive ist nicht tot zu kriegen."

[134] Steinheim, 'Vom Bleibenden', *loc. cit.*, p. 23; Schoeps, *Wir Deutschen Juden*, *op. cit.*, p. 10. Cf. also Steinheim's poem from 1837: above, note 78. Schoeps was not alone in this stance. See for instance a moving episode reported from Auschwitz in Otto Friedrich, 'The Kingdom of Auschwitz', in *The Atlantic Monthly* (September 1981), p. 56.

[135] Schoeps, *Wir Deutschen Juden*, p. 52.

[136] Schoeps, *Ja-Nein-Trotzdem*, p. 54.

Communal History

Frankfurt Jewry: A Model of Transition to Modernity

BY JAKOB J. PETUCHOWSKI

I

It is as though History had been looking for a laboratory in which to work out the major trends of modern Judaism, and found: Frankfurt a. Main during the last four decades of its existence as a Free City. Name the particular trend in which you are interested, and you are liable to discover that it either first crystallised in Frankfurt or, at the very least, that it was somehow connected with Frankfurt in one of its earliest manifestations.

Radical Reform Judaism? It was theoretically formulated in Frankfurt some years before it was implemented in Berlin.[1] Moderate Reform Judaism or, as it was then called, *fortschreitender Rabbinismus*, Progressive Rabbinism? It was preached by the Frankfurt rabbi, Leopold Stein, from 1844 on.[2] Conservative Judaism? It was Zacharias Frankel's demonstrative departure from the 1845 Frankfurt Rabbinical Conference, protesting that Conference's relegation of Hebrew in the synagogue to the position of a merely "subjective necessity", which gave the impetus to the rise of a school of thought standing midway between unyielding adherence to the past and radical departures from tradition.[3] As for Modern Orthodoxy (or Neo-Orthodoxy), everybody knows that Samson Raphael Hirsch founded it in Frankfurt.[4] Even the rise of *Gemeinde-Orthodoxie*, a form of Orthodoxy which can be practised within the framework of a Jewish community dominated by its Liberal wing, originated in Frankfurt. But that happened at a time when Frankfurt had ceased to be a Free City, and is, therefore, beyond the scope of our present inquiry.[5]

II

Why Frankfurt? It would be easy to take a romantic view, and to insist that, on account of its long history, going back to 1074, and on account of the very distinguished and scholarly rabbis who have presided over the religious life of the

[1]Cf. David Philipson, *The Reform Movement in Judaism*, 3rd edn., New York 1967, pp. 107–139; and Michael A. Meyer, 'Alienated Intellectuals in the Camp of Religious Reform: The Frankfurt Reformfreunde, 1842–1845', in *Association for Jewish Studies Review*, vol. VI (1981), pp. 61–86.

[2]Cf. Robert Liberles, 'Leopold Stein and the Paradox of Reform Clericalism, 1844–1862', in *LBI Year Book* XXVII (1982), pp. 261–279.

[3]Cf. Philipson, *op. cit.*, pp. 189–192.

[4]Cf. Hermann Schwab, *The History of Orthodox Jewry in Germany*, London 1950, *passim*.

[5]Cf. Paul Arnsberg, *Neunhundert Jahre "Muttergemeinde in Israel". Frankfurt am Main 1074–1974*, Frankfurt a. Main 1974, pp. 118 ff.

Frankfurt Jewish community through the centuries, Frankfurt was eminently suited to be the testing-ground where the various trends of modern Judaism were to be worked out before being tried elsewhere. Frankfurt Jewry had always been proud of its unique traditions which distinguished it from all other Jewish communities in the world. In the seventeenth century, Joseph Yuspa Hahn (1570–1637) had dealt with the liturgical procedures adopted by Frankfurt Jewry in his book, *Yosiph Ometz*.[6] He was outdone by Salomon Salman Geiger (1792–1878), the very learned and very Orthodox brother of the famous Reform Jewish theologian, Abraham Geiger. In 1862, Salomon Salman Geiger published his book, *Dibheré Qehilloth*, in which 478 closely printed pages are devoted to the *minhagim*, the liturgical customs unique to Frankfurt Jewry.

And in nearby Rödelheim, lived Wolf Benjamin Heidenheim (1757–1832), the man whom Leopold Zunz had called "the Mendelssohn of the festival prayer-book",[7] and whose printing press turned out edition after edition of the famous *Rödelheim Siddur*, the standard Jewish prayer-book for Orthodox Jewry in Germany and beyond. Indeed, Heidenheim was interested in finding a wide market for his prayer-book and therefore he printed the standard Ashkenazi Rite. But the pages of his prayer-book are peppered with instructions such as "In Frankfurt a. M. wird es nicht gesagt", or "In Frankfurt a. M. sagt man". The latter phrase more often than not introduces nothing more than a very minor verbal change in the prayer as recited by the rest of Jewry. Even the 1929 *Einheitsgebetbuch* of German Liberal Judaism still had to appear in a separate edition for Frankfurt!

No wonder, therefore, that Caesar Seligmann, himself a Frankfurt rabbi from 1902 until 1932, could say: "In Frankfurt, the *esprit de corps* and the magical word about the 'Frankfurt *Qehillah*' managed to maintain their spell even over those who, both in thought and in deed, had removed themselves far from positive Judaism."[8]

But it was more than romanticism and magic which made Frankfurt the stage upon which various forms of modern Judaism took their first steps. One might even claim, without denying the old Frankfurt tradition its share in shaping the mentality of the *Qehillah*'s sons and daughters, that what happened to, and in, the Frankfurt Jewish community in the first five or six decades of the nineteenth century had very little to do with the old-established *Minhag Frankfurt*. The impulses came from elsewhere. The Enlightenment teachings of the Mendelssohn circle found their disciples in Frankfurt as well – in spite of the attack launched, in 1782, on Mendelssohn's Bible translation and commentary by the Frankfurt rabbi, Pinchas Halevi Horowitz (1730–1805). The French occupation of Frankfurt (1806–1815), which brought Frankfurt greater political freedom, also brought some modern ideas which remained even when, with the regaining by Frankfurt of Free City status, Jewish rights were again curtailed. After all, Frankfurt's last traditionalist Chief Rabbi, Salomon Abraham Trier (1758–

[6]First printed in Frankfurt, in 1723; second Frankfurt edition, 1928; reprinted in Jerusalem, in 1965.
[7]Quoted in Paul Arnsberg, *Bilder aus dem jüdischen Leben im alten Frankfurt*, Frankfurt a. Main 1970, p. 134.
[8]Caesar Seligmann, *Geschichte der jüdischen Reformbewegung*, Frankfurt a. Main 1922, p. 105.

1846), who in his latter years felt impelled to defend the commandment of circumcision against the radical Reformers, was himself one of the Frankfurt delegates to Napoleon's *Grand Sanhédrin*.[9]

It also seems that the Prince Primate of Frankfurt, Karl von Dalberg, took an interest in Jewish affairs, and favoured that element within the Jewish community which had espoused the cause of Enlightenment. At any rate, in 1808, von Dalberg had the old Board of the Jewish community replaced by a new Board which was composed of people sympathetic to progress.[10] And then things began to happen in rapid succession, giving rise to different versions of what actually took place. We shall here state the highlights first, then give quotations from two contemporary documents, and finally offer our own interpretations.

III

Already before the period of the French occupation, some Frankfurt Jews had felt the need for a communal school in which secular as well as Jewish subjects would be taught. An attempt to establish such a school was made in 1794, but came to grief because of the opposition of the rabbinate and the Board of those days. However, with the support of Baron Mayer Amschel Rothschild's bookkeeper, Siegmund Geisenheimer, such a school was ultimately established in 1805. It was called the "Jewish Philanthropin". (In later years the adjective was dropped.) Over the years, the time allocated to Jewish studies in this school increasingly diminished – thus, as it were, justifying the worst fears of its opponents. But since the Philanthropin was now *the* Jewish communal school of Frankfurt, the Board of the Jewish community looked askance at the possibility of having any rival Jewish schools. And, since 1808, that Board was composed of quite different people from those who, in 1794, had opposed the very idea of a Jewish school in which secular studies would be taught.[11]

Moreover, in 1807 the Philanthropin had introduced quite non-traditionalist worship services (*Andachtsstunden*), where regular sermons were preached, and prayers were recited in German. Some of the Philanthropin's teachers like Josef Johlson (1777–1851) and Michael Creizenach (1789–1842) doubled as preachers. The latter in particular is said to have been very impressive.[12] The *Andachtsstunden* attracted the parents as well as the pupils; and the image of an alternative Jewish service of worship, quite different from the one conducted in the community's synagogues, was thus presented to an ever widening circle of Frankfurt Jews. The role which the Philanthropin played in the rise of Reform Judaism in Frankfurt cannot be overestimated.

In fact, it was from among the teachers and the sympathisers of the Philanthropin that the membership of the Frankfurt "Friends of Reform",

[9]Cf. Eugen Mayer, *Die Frankfurter Juden*, Frankfurt a. Main 1966, p. 42.

[10]Cf. Arnsberg, *Neunhundert Jahre . . .*, *op. cit.*, pp. 71 f.

[11]Cf. Mordechai Eliav, *Jewish Education in Germany in the Period of Enlightenment and Emancipation* (in Hebrew), Jerusalem 1960, pp. 109 ff. About the Philanthropin see Arthur Galliner, 'The Philanthropin in Frankfurt. Its Educational and Cultural Significance for German Jewry', in *LBI Year Book III* (1958), pp. 169–186.

[12]Cf. Eugen Mayer, *op. cit.*, p. 59.

founded in 1842, was largely recruited. Seeing that Michael A. Meyer has only recently dealt in depth with that particular group,[13] we shall confine ourselves here to the statement formulated by the "Friends of Reform", a statement which declared that the "Friends"

> "1. considered the Mosaic religion capable of continuing development;
> 2. considered the ritual and dietary laws and other physical religious practices, which originated in the ancient polity, to be no longer binding as a religious act or symbol;
> 3. singled out circumcision as such an act;
> 4. did not recognise the Talmud as an authority; and
> 5. did not await or wish for a Messiah who would lead the Jews back to Palestine, but rather regarded the land to which they belonged by birth or civil status as their only fatherland."

However, the version which was adopted as the official declaration, meant to enlist sympathisers elsewhere, diplomatically confined itself to three points, and omitted items 2 and 3 of the original statement, i.e., those rejecting ritual practices in general, and circumcision in particular. It should be noted, however, that, in this reformulation, the first principle was reworded as follows:

> "We recognise in Mosaism the possibility of an unlimited further development."

That notion of an "unlimited further development" became a key factor in the protracted literary warfare to which the publication of that declaration gave rise. Even rabbis and scholars sympathetic to the cause of Reform, including Leopold Stein (1810–1882), who, in 1844, would become the rabbi of Frankfurt, saw in the possibility of an "unlimited further development" the negation of any positive content of Judaism whatsoever; and Leopold Zunz dismissed the Frankfurt "Friends of Reform" with the verdict: "Suicide is no Reform."[14]

While the Frankfurt "Friends of Reform" may have dropped the reference to circumcision from the version of their principles which was meant for public consumption, it was no secret that they were opposed to circumcision. When, therefore, in 1843, a Jewish father in Frankfurt refused to have his son circumcised, it was the Frankfurt "Friends of Reform" who were universally blamed for bringing about this state of affairs. Rabbis all over Germany and beyond, Orthodox and Reform alike, became involved, mainly at the request of the aged Chief Rabbi Salomon Abraham Trier, in this controversy about circumcision, and in the attacks upon the Frankfurt "Friends of Reform". In the Introduction to his edition of the collected rabbinic responsa on the issue of circumcision, the aged Rabbi Trier, by that time eighty-six years old, gives expression to his satisfaction with the fact that "a younger generation, sons of a new age", have come to his aid in this battle. Trier continues:

> "And it is to such a battle that Divine Providence wanted me to call my younger colleagues in the last years of my life. My gaze, already directed to the Hereafter, still had to fall upon a cloudy future, in which a destructive, critical philosophy, dissolving everything into sceptical hypotheses, is aiming at the total destruction of positive Judaism – both with regard to the latter's fundamental element, the life-giving principle of faith, and with regard to its practical components and expressions. In a community, which had ever been distinguished by its true

[13]Cf. Michael A. Meyer's article referred to in note 1 above.
[14]Quoted in Seligmann, *op. cit.*, p. 107.

> religiosity, intelligence and humanity, and which had always reckoned peace and concord among the benefits with which the omniregnant hand of God had made it happy, I was still destined to see how the hydra of religious strife arose. This must necessarily bring about a schism, which will be as corrupting inside as it will be outwardly damaging. I should indeed have been able to expect of the piety of my congregants, and of the humanity of those who seek to bring about this split that they would have spared their very aged rabbi this grievous pain – their rabbi who, for almost half a century, has carried out his sacred duties."[15]

Poor Salomon Trier! He was perhaps more successful in marshalling the opposition to the Frankfurt "Friends of Reform" than he had dared to hope. But 1844, the year in which he published his collection of rabbinic responsa on circumcision, was also the year in which he felt compelled to resign his office – because, in spite of his opposition, the Board of the community had decided to invite Leopold Stein to come to Frankfurt as the Assistant Rabbi of the community. And Stein was a Reform rabbi, albeit of a rather moderate nature.[16]

Stein had previously been the rabbi of Burgkundstadt and Altenkundstadt, and he was also a prolific author, editor, poet and dramatist, as well as a friend of the German poet Friedrich Rückert. In 1840, he had published *Ḥizzuq Habayith*, a book of German prayers and hymns to supplement and, in part, to replace the traditional Jewish liturgy. This book included Stein's *O Tag des Herrn*, which was meant to replace the traditional *Kol Nidré*, and to be sung to the traditional *Kol Nidré* tune. It became widely accepted in Germany, and, in its English translation, across the Atlantic.[17]

The liturgical reforms which Stein introduced upon assuming the Frankfurt position were of a relatively minor character, but sufficient to arouse the opposition of the Orthodox.[18] And when, under Stein's direction, the Main Synagogue was rebuilt and dedicated in 1860, it was a synagogue with an organ; and Stein published a new prayer-book to go with the new synagogue.[19] By modern American standards, Stein's synagogue and prayer-book could easily pass for "Conservative". But nineteenth-century German standards were somewhat different.

During Stein's Frankfurt tenure, the Second Rabbinical Conference was held in Frankfurt, in 1845; and Stein was elected as its President.[20] The main issue at that Conference seems to have been the question, whether it was an "objective necessity" or only a "subjective necessity" to retain the use of Hebrew in the synagogue. By a vote of 15 to 13, with Stein voting with the minority, the Conference decided that Hebrew was only a "subjective necessity". It was a purely theoretical discussion, for, with the sole exception of Holdheim's Berlin Reform Congregation, no German Liberal synagogue ever displaced Hebrew from the position of being the main language of public prayer. (In the United States and, later on, in England the situation was to be different.)

But the fact that a body of rabbis would even theoretically consider the

[15]Salomon Abraham Trier (ed.), *Rabbinische Gutachten über die Beschneidung*, Frankfurt a. Main 1844, pp. v f.

[16]Cf. the article by Liberles referred to in note 2 above.

[17]Cf. Jakob J. Petuchowski, *Prayerbook Reform in Europe*, New York 1968, pp. 338–340.

[18]Cf. Petuchowski, *op. cit.*, pp. 155 f.

[19]See the Preface to that prayerbook, in English translation, in Petuchowski, *op. cit.*, pp. 156–159.

[20]Cf. Philipson, *op. cit.*, pp. 163–193.

abolition of Hebrew so upset the Chief Rabbi of Dresden, Zacharias Frankel (1801–1875), who had come to Frankfurt as a participant, that he left the Conference in protest–going on to develop a theory of "positive-historical" Judaism, in contrast to the Reformers' "critical-historical" Judaism. Frankel's theory was ultimately to become the foundation of Conservative Judaism, both in Europe and in the United States.

Stein's tenure as Frankfurt's rabbi was to be relatively short. While the Frankfurt Senate exercised control over the Board of the Frankfurt Jewish community, that Board, in its turn, wanted to control the rabbi–particularly in public utterances. Stein was chafing under that control; and, notwithstanding the Board's regulations, Stein not only attacked the Board's policy during his sermon at the dedication of the new synagogue in 1860, but he also proceeded, over the Board's objections, to have that sermon printed. When the Board called Stein to task, he resigned from his rabbinical position.[21]

Before we deal with Stein's successor, Abraham Geiger (1810–1874), who served as rabbi in his native Frankfurt from 1863 till 1869, we must go back a few years in time, in order to record an event which happened while Stein was still the rabbi of the Frankfurt community. In 1849, eleven Orthodox members of the Frankfurt community, feeling that their religious needs had been neglected, petitioned the Senate of the Free City for permission to form a private religious association for the holding of services and the maintaining of essential religious institutions. The Senate granted the petition, on condition that the members of the new association would meet their financial obligations towards the over-all Frankfurt Jewish community. Thus was the *Israelitische Religionsgesellschaft* of Frankfurt born, which in 1851, (by which time its membership had reached the one hundred mark) extended a call to the Chief Rabbi of Moravia, Samson Raphael Hirsch (1808–1888). And Hirsch accepted the invitation, exchanging the Moravian chief rabbinate for the position of rabbi of a small, private congregation.[22] Even before the building of his Frankfurt synagogue was completed, in 1853, Hirsch had opened his school.[23] Hirsch's school, gradually built up to include all classes of primary and secondary school, was to rival the Philanthropin in academic performance, and to excel it in the pursuit of Jewish studies. For Samson Raphael Hirsch was not an Orthodox rabbi of the old type. In Nikolsburg, as Chief Rabbi of Moravia, he had acquired the reputation of a "reformer", because he not only believed in the synthesis of Torah and secular culture; he had also practised it.[24] And Frankfurt offered even more scope for that synthesis than Nikolsburg had done.

[21]Cf. Arnsberg, *Neunhundert Jahre*, p. 89.
[22]Cf. Hermann Schwab, *op. cit.*, p. 40.
[23]Cf. Arnsberg, *Neunhundert Jahre*, pp. 103 f.
[24]Cf. Noah H. Rosenbloom, *Tradition in an Age of Reform. The Religious Philosophy of Samson Raphael Hirsch*, Philadelphia 1967, p. 92. About S. R. Hirsch see also Pinchas E. Rosenblüth, 'Samson Raphael Hirsch. Sein Denken und Wirken', in *Das Judentum in der Deutschen Umwelt 1800–1850. Studien zur Frühgeschichte der Emanzipation* herausgegeben von Hans Liebeschütz und Arnold Paucker, Tübingen 1977 (Schriftenreihe wissenschaftlicher Abhandlungen des Leo Baeck Instituts 35), pp. 293–324.

The services in the synagogue of the *Religionsgesellschaft* could vie with the decorum of any Reform synagogue.[25] Like the latter, Hirsch's synagogue, too, had a choir (although, of course, not an organ). It also had regular sermons in *Hochdeutsch*. And in his school, Hirsch could wax as enthusiastic about Friedrich Schiller, on the occasion of the hundredth anniversary of the poet's birth, as any educator in the town.

But the importance of Hirsch's synthesis lay precisely in the fact that, for Hirsch, Torah Law was immutable, as immutable as the Laws of Nature; and "Torah", as Hirsch understood it, covered the entirety of religious legislation, down to the least minutia of custom. It is obvious that Hirsch did not believe in religious evolution. It is equally obvious that Reform Judaism, as it had been developed by his erstwhile friend, Abraham Geiger, and Conservative Judaism, which called for the application of scientific methods to the study of documents which, for Hirsch, were God-given documents, had to be anathema to him. Orthodox Judaism was not to be construed as one of the "wings" or "branches" of Judaism. It, and it alone, is Judaism. Reform and Conservatism are not. Nevertheless, it should be pointed out here that it was not until he had been in Frankfurt for twenty-five years that he called upon his followers to secede from the Frankfurt Jewish community.[26]

Abraham Geiger and Samson Raphael Hirsch had been friends and fellow-students at the University of Bonn. Later they were to become the antipodes of the Jewish religious world. By the time Geiger succeeded Stein as rabbi of the Frankfurt Jewish community, Geiger had become one of the most prominent representatives of the *Wissenschaft des Judentums*, the scientific study of Judaism, for which Hirsch had no use at all. Geiger had even engaged in the critical study of the Bible, which was rare for Jews at that time, and he had developed a view of Judaism which saw the history of Judaism as the history of continuous religious progress and development.

Hirsch and Geiger were no longer on speaking terms. But neither were Stein and Geiger – in spite of their earlier cooperation in the work of the Rabbinical Conferences. For Stein was unable to forgive Geiger the fact that Geiger had accepted the Frankfurt position which Stein had been compelled to give up. Geiger's son, Ludwig, summed up the situation as follows:

> "It was a curious coincidence that Geiger lived and laboured in the same city in which two former friends, Hirsch and Stein, were also active. Yet no contact was established between those who once were so close and had now been separated."[27]

[25]Cf. Petuchowski, *op. cit.*, pp. 123 f.

[26]Cf. Hermann Schwab, 'S. R. Hirsch und die Trennungsorthodoxie', in *Bulletin des Leo Baeck Instituts*, II (1958), No. 5, pp. 24 f; and Eugen Mayer, *op. cit.*, p. 63.

[27]Ludwig Geiger, *Abraham Geiger. Leben und Lebenswerk*. Berlin 1910, p. 203. For re-evaluations of Abraham Geiger's work, undertaken on the occasion of the hundredth anniversary of his death, see Jakob J. Petuchowski (ed.), *New Perspectives on Abraham Geiger*, Cincinnati 1975; and see Jakob J. Petuchowski, 'Abraham Geiger and Samuel Holdheim. Their Differences in Germany and Repercussions in America', in *LBI Year Book XXII* (1977), pp. 139–159. Stein's rabbinate at the Frankfurt Westend-Union congregation is mentioned in Seligmann, *op. cit.*, p. 149; Sally Gans, 'Stein, Leopold', in *Jüdisches Lexikon*, vol. V, col. 706; and Arnsberg, *Bilder*, *op. cit.*, p. 257. All three

Altogether, the seven years which Geiger spent as the rabbi of his native city were not among Geiger's happiest. Frankfurt did not live up to his expectations; and he was glad when the opportunity presented itself for him to become the rabbi of Berlin in 1870.

In the meantime, Hirsch's *Israelitische Religionsgesellschaft* continued to make progress. Ultimately, after the law permitting secession from the local community without renouncing one's Judaism was passed by the Prussian *Landtag*, in 1876, the existence of Hirsch's *Religionsgesellschaft*, coupled with the threat of a large-scale Orthodox exodus from the Frankfurt Jewish community, proved to be a real challenge to the Board of that community, which always contained a Reform majority; and steps were taken to accommodate those Orthodox elements of the community who turned a deaf ear to Hirsch's plea for their secession. But that lies beyond the period which concerns us here.

IV

And now two documents, purporting to describe the Frankfurt Jewish situation in the three or four decades before Hirsch's arrival in Frankfurt. The first one is from an article written by Hirsch himself:

> "And so we have had to look on while Rabbis and executives armed with Government orders and backed up by the police . . . have treated synagogues and public worship and all that Jewish communities hold sacred as if they were so many puppets put in their hands, as if they themselves were some divinity armed with thunder and lightning from which the trembling community had to receive some new law. We had to look on while in the face of this tempest the old prayers with their hopes were silenced, new forms of service adopted, synagogues closed, scrolls of the Torah removed, and those members of the community who remained true to the Torah were banished with their form of service into cellars, into woods, into foreign parts."[28]

Our second document is a leaflet, published in 1877 by Emanuel Schwarzschild (1825–1896), at that time chairman of the Board of the *Israelitische Religionsgesellschaft*. Schwarzschild is reminiscing about his youth, i.e., a number of decades before Hirsch came to Frankfurt:

> "As far as I remember, the administration of the community lay in the hands of the Reformers. 'Let it pasture until it becomes blemished!' (b. *Temurah* 22a) was the principle of the community Board. Once the process of deterioration had progressed, once the Board believed that the ground had been sufficiently prepared, the Board proceeded to invite a Reform rabbi. It was undeterred by the opposition of the old and venerable Rabbi Salomon Trier as well as by the opposition of Baron von Rothschild. The latter had guaranteed a contribution of a quarter of a million *gulden* for the building of a new synagogue – on condition that at least an Orthodox Assistant Rabbi be employed. The Board of the community decided to forgo this munificent donation, rather than extend a call to a man of whom it could have been expected that he

---

references confine themselves to a mere mention of the existence of that congregation and of Stein's ministry there. It would certainly be a *desideratum* of modern Jewish historical scholarship to discover more about that particular congregation, about the German, Jewish and American backgrounds of its members, and about the influence possibly exerted by American Reform Judaism on at least some German Jews at that time.

[28]Samson Raphael Hirsch, *Judaism Eternal*, translated and edited by I. Grunfeld, vol. I., London 1959, pp. 136 f.

would promote Orthodoxy within the community. But the call extended to the Reform rabbi was only the first step. The next step was the introduction of an organ and of the triennial cycle of Pentateuchal readings, as well as several liturgical changes. The consequence was that the Orthodox withdrew from the Main Synagogue and went to the small auxiliary synagogues, of which several were indeed in existence. Here, it was demonstrated all the more just how widespread apostasy had become, how much the ranks of the Orthodox had decreased. The fact that the auxiliary synagogues sufficed, that they were not even sufficiently filled on weekdays, making it necessary for the sextons to stand at the doors in order to recruit the necessary quorum – that, indeed, was the sad aspect of the situation."[29]

Schwarzschild, however, does more than criticise the Board. He does not spare the Orthodox, either, but accuses them of having greatly neglected the Jewish education of the young. Then he continues:

> "When I look around today among my contemporaries, who were born in Frankfurt, I do not find a single one who is Jew enough to don phylacteries. The nearest one, born before me, is four to five years older. The nearest one, born after me, is younger by that many years. And as far as the following decade is concerned, things are hardly any better . . . It follows that, from a certain point in time on, within a period of several years, a *Yehudi* (a real Jew) was produced only intermittently. If this situation had continued, the number of Orthodox in Frankfurt would have been so diminished that today hardly a prayer quorum would have been found.
>
> Just as nothing essential was done for education, so was there a general laxity leading to the decline of the religious institutions. The ritual slaughterers were left to their own devices; the Jewish butchers, with one or two exceptions, were unreliable; and the ritual bath was in a state in which it could hardly be used, sometimes it was even totally useless. But there was no need for it, anyhow. The older people no longer required it, and the younger people no longer wanted to know about it. Those few who still wanted it, travelled elsewhere, to Offenbach and to other places."[30]

Hirsch and Schwarzschild purport to describe the same situation. Both of them, moreover, share the same religious orientation. In fact, the Schwarzschild quotations are taken from a leaflet which Schwarzschild wrote in defence of Hirsch against the Würzburg rabbi, Seligmann Baer Bamberger. The only difference is that Hirsch came to Frankfurt in 1851, whereas Schwarzschild wrote about his own youth, which was spent in Frankfurt. Hirsch's rhetoric, which conjures up, and is meant to conjure up, images of medieval persecutions and the Inquisition, is based on reports, hearsay and imagination. Schwarzschild's report is based on personal experience. It should carry more weight in the evaluation of the situation.

Hirsch and Schwarzschild agree, of course, that things were done which violated traditional Jewish Law. But, while Hirsch wants us to believe that the lay leaders and the non-Orthodox rabbi actively persecuted the Orthodox, Schwarzschild, though stressing the inequity inflicted upon the Orthodox by the appointment of Stein, leads us to infer that the Board had been guilty of a policy of "benign neglect", rather than of active suppression *vis à vis* the institutions necessary for an Orthodox Jewish life, and that the Orthodox themselves were guilty of gross neglect as far as the education of their young and the maintenance of traditional observances were concerned. At that, taking his illustration of the

[29]Emanuel Schwarzschild, *Ein offenes Wort an Seine Ehrwürden Herrn Distrikt-Rabbiner Seeligmann Bär Bamberger zu Würzburg*, Frankfurt a. Main 1877, p. 4.
[30]Schwarzschild, *op. cit.*, pp. 6 f.

people who did, and those who did not, don phylacteries as a chronological yardstick, we would get a period of about ten years during which the state of traditional observance was at its worst. It is well in this connection to recall that, until 1844, Frankfurt Jewry still had an Orthodox Chief Rabbi, one, moreover, who, though old and weak, was powerful enough to rally the entire Jewish world against the Frankfurt "Friends of Reform", and that Samson Raphael Hirsch arrived on the scene only seven years later.

If we look at the level of observance of dietary and other ritual laws in other German cities during that same fourth decade of the nineteenth century, we would find that there was a notable decline also in those communities which were not ruled by a Board composed of Reform sympathisers. It was, in fact, the general decline in traditional observance at that time which was one of the contributing factors in the rise of Reform Judaism – seeing that Reform Judaism was meant to save for Judaism those Jews who had already thrown off the regimen of traditional practice. There is no reason to assume that Frankfurt Orthodox Jews would have been immune from this process even if the Board of the community had been completely Orthodox.

The next point which has to be borne in mind is that it will simply not do to lump all of the Reformers together. When one reads Orthodox descriptions of the Frankfurt situation, one is left with the impression that the members of the community Board, the "Friends of Reform," and Rabbi Leopold Stein were all of the same persuasion. But that is not so – it was, after all, the Board which called Stein to the Frankfurt pulpit; and, while Stein may have been quite unacceptable to the Orthodox, Stein was by no means a friend of Radical Reform Judaism. As we have seen, he sided with Frankel on the question of Hebrew in the synagogue. He also went his own way liturgically, shunning the extremism of other editors of Reform prayerbooks. Thus while in the prayer-book which he edited for the Frankfurt community in 1860, he relegated prayers for a return to Palestine and the restoration of the sacrificial cult to the silent devotion of those who wanted to utter such prayers, he consciously retained for public worship the petitions "for a renewed glory of Zion and Jerusalem".[31] Even after Stein had left the rabbinate of the Frankfurt community, and served as rabbi of the Westend-Union, a congregation of German-American Jews of pronounced Reform tendencies,[32] he continued to stand out from among other Reformers by his belief in a personal Messiah and in the messianic role of Jerusalem. In the Preface to the 1882 edition of his prayer-book, he wrote:

> "As far as Israel's exalted hopes are concerned, we have devoutly retained for the Messiah, who bears our ideal future, his holy place . . . That Temple will find its eternal site in Jerusalem. Where else? Not in Berlin, capital of German Protestantism. Not in Rome, centre of the pagan world of the past, and of the Catholic world of today. But in Jerusalem, the Holy City, in which all nations and religions have an equal share."[33]

But of even greater importance is the fact that Stein had been very prominent,

[31]Cf. Petuchowski, *Prayerbook Reform in Europe*, p. 158.
[32]Cf. the reference to Stein in note 27 above.
[33]Cf. Petuchowski, *Prayerbook Reform in Europe*, p. 179.

in 1843, in attacking the Frankfurt "Friends of Reform".[34] A year later, he occupied the Frankfurt pulpit! If the Board of the community had been identical with the "Friends of Reform", or even only dominated by them, it would have been most unlikely for that Board to appoint Stein, of all people, to the Frankfurt rabbinate within a year of Stein's polemics. There must have been members of the Frankfurt Board, and a sufficient number of them to lead to Stein's appointment, who sided with Stein's "Progressive Rabbinism", rather than with the radicalism of the "Friends of Reform". In other words, the Board was far from representing a uniform "Reform" position, as we are led to believe by Orthodox historians writing about that period.

Still, if the Board consisted of some members who shared Stein's views, it also must have had some members who were more in sympathy with the "Friends of Reform". Robert Liberles is, therefore, quite right in pointing out the division which existed among the ranks of the Frankfurt Reformers, and in attributing the repeated difficulties which Stein had with the Board, as well as his final defeat, to the anti-Stein faction among the Reformers of Frankfurt.[35]

Liberles is also right in raising questions about the historiography of the followers of Samson Raphael Hirsch, imitating the example set by Hirsch himself, who painted the background in darker colours than are warranted by the facts, in order to glorify the achievements of their hero, Samson Raphael Hirsch – who, says Liberles, remains one of the most effective community leaders of German Jewry in the nineteenth century, even "when the myths surrounding Hirsch are peeled away".[36]

V

What all this means in terms of seeing in the religious life of the Jewry of the Free City of Frankfurt a model of the transition to modernity, is that we shall have to get away from the notion that a radical wing of Reform Judaism, represented by the Frankfurt "Friends of Reform", gained control of the Frankfurt Jewish community, and then proceeded to suppress Orthodox Judaism; that Orthodox Jews were thereupon forced to lead some kind of Marrano existence until eleven courageous champions of Orthodoxy founded the *Israelitische Religionsgesellschaft* and invited Hirsch, who, in his turn, single-handedly revived the true faith in the Frankfurt Jewish community.

Instead, we shall probably be closer to the truth when we envisage the following scenario: The ideas of the Enlightenment affected certain segments of Frankfurt Jewry at the end of the eighteenth century and the beginning of the nineteenth century – no less than they affected corresponding segments of the Jewish population in other German cities at that time. Frankfurt happened to have a Prince Primate, Karl von Dalberg, who found it easier to work with that particular segment of Frankfurt Jewry than with those Frankfurt Jews who, in

[34]Cf. Philipson, *op. cit.*, pp. 123 ff.
[35]Cf. Liberles 'Leopold Stein . . .', *loc. cit.*, p. 266.
[36]Cf. Robert Liberles, 'Champion of Orthodoxy: The Emergence of Samson Raphael Hirsch as Religious Leader', in *Association of Jewish Studies Review*, vol. VI (1981), pp. 43–60.

principle, were opposed to secular culture. This gave the "enlightened" Jews a leading position in the administration of the Jewish community – to the intense annoyance of the Orthodox.

The "enlightened" Jews themselves, however, were far from being united ideologically. Some failed to see any meaning at all in the inherited Jewish faith, and either were wholly indifferent to it or converted to Christianity. Others wanted to reform Judaism, and reform it radically. They founded the "Friends of Reform". Still others favoured a less than radical reform of Judaism – a "Progressive Rabbinism", rather than a revolutionary break with the past. They were represented on the Board of the community in sufficient numbers to effect the appointment of Leopold Stein, with whose rejection of Radical Reform Judaism they were in sympathy.

As far as the Orthodox are concerned, they undoubtedly suffered a setback when the adherents of the Enlightenment gained control of the Board of the community, and they were certainly adversely affected when, unlike the situation in pre-Napoleonic times, the Board no longer paid much attention to the institutions essential for *kosher* food and the observance of the laws of levitical purity. But, as Schwarzschild's testimony indicates, there were, in addition to Frankfurt's main Synagogue, several smaller synagogues, which the Orthodox were unable to fill, so that sextons had to stand at the doors to recruit the requisite ten adults for public prayer. It was not the Board which prevented the Orthodox Jews from going to those synagogues, in which no organ was played, and no liturgical texts were changed. They just did not go – even as, again according to Schwarzschild's testimony, there was a time when scions of Orthodox families no longer bothered with the donning of phylacteries; and we cannot imagine the community Board preventing them from doing so.

We are more likely dealing with a situation where, as in other cities, a process of erosion in traditional observance had set in, which was far more due to the *Zeitgeist* than to the composition of the Board of the community. After all, even the most radical members of the Board could not, at the beginning, have been the offspring of Reform families themselves, but must have been people who had given up the Orthodoxy of their parents. And, as we have already noted, with the resignation of Chief Rabbi Salomon Trier in 1844, and the arrival of Samson Raphael Hirsch in 1851, the period during which Orthodox Frankfurt Jews had no prominent local rabbinical authority to which they could turn was one of seven years only. At that, as Liberles has pointed out, the thinning out of the Orthodox ranks was not nearly as thorough as the historians in the Hirsch tradition would have us believe.[37]

Still, it is true that, with the arrival of Hirsch, Orthodox Judaism in Frankfurt was revitalised. For, if one of the major threats confronting Orthodoxy had been, not the putative suppression of Orthodoxy by a community Board committed to Reform, but the supposed inability to be an observant Orthodox Jew and a cultured nineteenth-century European at one and the same time, then Hirsch, both in theory and in practice, demonstrated that the two can indeed be combined.

[37]Cf. Liberles 'Champion of Orthodoxy . . .', *loc. cit.*

Some of the considerations we have adduced may not be unique to Frankfurt, although the case of Samson Raphael Hirsch rather tends to be. They would also apply to the Jewries of other German cities of that time. The fact, however, that they all apply to the Frankfurt situation – and that within the span of a mere four decades or so – would seem to justify our seeing in Frankfurt Jewry, towards the end of Frankfurt's history as a Free City, the model of a transition to modernity, which, in one way or another, was destined to become paradigmatic for Jewish religious developments on both sides of the Atlantic in the nineteenth and twentieth centuries.

In the Shadow of Doom

Post-War Publications on Jewish Communal History in Germany (IV)

BY E. G. LOWENTHAL

In the summer of 1977, when I came to the end of the third instalment, I anticipated that this might mark the provisional completion of the whole series.[1] That expectation has turned out to be premature. Indeed, the interest in the subject, so far from abating, has, if anything, increased still further, as the spate of new publications, approaching the theme from many different angles, has shown. The trend was reinforced by the profound impression created by the television series on the holocaust shown in the Federal Republic in 1979 and by the ensuing discussion which, for all its emotional intensity, was enlightening. Another factor that may have played a part is the emergence of radical tendencies on the West German political scene. It is clearly impossible to apportion precise degrees of influence to the various factors involved. The fact remains that serious efforts are being made to rescue the most recent episodes in the history of the Jews in Germany in general, and of the German-Jewish communities in particular, from oblivion, and throw light on the pattern of events.

As before, interest has been focused above all on what happened in the German cities and regions in 1938 and the following years, that is to say on the period that encompassed the inception, the ruthless execution and the aftermath of the macabrely named "final solution", the programme for the extermination (and driving out) of the Jews. Apart from the broad sweep of history, research on specific themes was often stimulated by local events: there have been public debates and exhibitions; some towns organised visits by former Jewish citizens who had emigrated; and even now belated gestures are being made with the solemn inauguration of memorial sites or tablets marking places where once a synagogue stood or a prominent Jewish citizen lived. In many instances – more often in small localities than in the big cities – such occasions provided an impetus for delving into the background of those happenings and preserving the memory, for the benefit of younger generations in particular, through officially or privately sponsored publications.

Considerable attention has also been devoted to the years 1933–1938. Altogether, the period of persecution under the Nazi regime lends itself with comparative ease to historical investigation owing to the availability of official

[1] See *LBI Year Book XXIII* (1978), pp. 283–308.

sources, ranging from legislation and executive orders to deportation lists.* No comparable source material exists for the preceding seventy to one hundred years which regrettably are all-too often ignored in the recent literature, even though they represent a period – variously described as a time of post-emancipatory integration or, more extravagantly, as the halcyon days of Jewish life in Germany alongside and in intimate relationship with the non-Jewish population – that forms a vital part of German-Jewish history. It has almost become a fashion to terminate the historiography of the Jews in Germany – and of the Jewish communities in particular – with the end of the ghetto period and resume the story only with the onset of Nazi persecution. In this way the opportunities open to an emancipated and integrated Jewry are excluded from consideration. It is not difficult to find political-psychological motives for this omission: a natural reluctance to admit that there ever was a time when a friendlier, more peaceable *modus vivendi* had actually been established. In addition, there is the technical obstacle presented by the paucity of source material. It is not, of course, an insuperable obstacle: a great deal can be achieved by patient search and by imaginative vision combined with methodological rigour, as recent examples have demonstrated.

The publications presented here can be divided into two groups of roughly equal size. There are on the one hand publications by non-Jewish authors – books, pamphlets, essays – commissioned by local government bodies and dealing exclusively with Jews and Jewish institutions, many of them adding appendixes on Jewish customs and festive rites both in the home and in the synagogue. This category further includes "Jewish" chapters in general publications on local history and minor essays in journals of local or regional history.

On the other hand, there are official or semi-official *Festschriften*, often commemorating historic anniversaries of the granting of municipal charters, going back by anything from 500 to 1,200 years and providing accounts of local and regional history, with local government affairs to the fore. Some, by no means all, of such publications incidentally throw light on interesting details of German-Jewish history. A special category is presented by the organisations of persons who fled or were expelled from the former Eastern territories of Germany. In these books with their nostalgic historical surveys the history of the Jewish communities during the period covered from, say, 1850 to the end of the Second World War is nearly always ignored, an omission explained in some instances on the ground that it had proved impossible to get in touch with former Jewish fellow citizens who had emigrated.

The publications in both main groups cannot be considered works of scholarship, nor does it appear that they aspire to such standards. Rather may they be classified as popular literature, which of course does not diminish their significance for the appropriate section of the reading public.

A third, numerically much smaller, group consists of papers originating in the

* On the deportations see the essay by Henry Friedlander, 'The Deportation of the German Jews. Post-War German Trials of Nazi Criminals', and also the essay by Konrad Kwiet, 'The Ultimate Refuge. Suicide in the Jewish Community under the Nazis', in this volume of the Year Book – (Ed.).

universities, most of them set for examination purposes. Within this group a disproportionately high number of Jewish historical studies happens to have been published in Westphalia, often with the accent on personal or social history. In general, however, the papers in this group go scarcely beyond statistics relating to demographic and economic structure. Yet, studies in recent economic history surely ought to take note of the compulsory "Aryanisation" of a vast number of Jewish enterprises in all parts of Germany between 1933 and 1939. This aspect has been completely ignored in the recent literature on German communal historiography, including the publications dealing with Jewish affairs.[2] The topic of "Aryanisation" appears to have remained a "hot potato", and yet, a systematic scholarly examination of the available data referring to the history of the enterprises concerned could throw new light on the part played by the Jews in the development of the German economy, at least since the *Gründerzeit*.

Not many relevant publications were published by Jewish authors during the period under review, and most of these suffer from a lack of balance in that they tend to focus attention on numerically unimportant groups within the body of German Jewry, while neglecting more important groups that have played a substantial part in economic life and communal politics.

A most welcome development has been noted in a number of the smaller localities which in the past had had substantial Jewish populations. In such places some of the older schoolchildren, under the guidance of young teachers or clergymen, engaged in searches to find out what had happened to those former fellow citizens. Such efforts, so far confined to a few places, might well serve as an example to others. Similar endeavours were made in a private capacity by some enlightened non-Jews, who wanted first of all to place on record exactly what had happened in their localities in the years 1938–1942, and beyond this to find out what Jewish life and life with the Jews had been like in earlier, normal times. It must be appreciated that such undertakings reflect the stirrings of the conscience of a later generation which was not involved in those events. Equally gratifying, if exceptional, is the stand taken by a young professor of regional history who, in reviewing an officially sponsored book on local history, castigated the absence of any reference to the part played by the Jewish section of the population.[3]

The following pages, then, will present a multifarious collection of post-war publications on Jewish communal history in Germany. It will be seen that the majority of these investigations relate to medium-sized as well as major towns rather than to the big cities which were the foremost centres of Jewish population, notably Berlin, Hamburg, Frankfurt a. Main, Cologne and Munich, where the collection, sifting and processing of the source material is rendered doubly difficult by its very abundance. As a result there is a lack of scholarly studies of the historical development of the Jewish population of the major cities from the nineteenth century to the advent of the Third *Reich*. This is a pity, since during the

[2]Cf. Helmut Genschel, *Die Verdrängung der Juden aus der Wirtschaft im Dritten Reich* (Göttinger Bausteine zur Geschichtswissenschaft, 38), Göttingen 1966 for a useful introduction to the topic.

[3]See *Vierteljahrsschrift für Sozial- und Wirtschaftsgeschichte*, 1977, p. 325 for a review of *Neustadt a.d. Weinstraße*, published by that town in 1975.

period beginning about 1870 the majority of German Jews were city dwellers.

In arranging the material there would have been some advantage in following the foregoing classification according to the categories of authorship. It was decided nevertheless to follow the method of the previous three instalments, that is to say, to group the contributions geographically according to the Federal States (*Länder*), with the localities within each Federal State arranged in alphabetical order, thus preserving continuity and providing a regionally coherent picture.

I. NORTH RHINE-WESTPHALIA

IA. NORTH RHINE PROVINCE

AACHEN: For the past fifteen years or more the project of a history of the Jews of Aachen has been discussed mostly by non-Jewish circles, with Sebastian Elverfeldt, the Sexton of St. Paul's, in the lead. Apart from a few minor essays in the Jewish press in Germany and America,[4] the only known publication about Aachen Jews is a report by Eric (Erich) Lucas, born 1915 in Aachen, now living in Israel, on his extended family, embracing the Elkan, Keller and Lucas families.[5] He presents a family chronicle interspersed with personal recollections, offering the social historian revealing glimpses of Jewish rural life in Hoengen, Langweiler, Warden and other Rhenish villages, all of them situated between Aachen and Eschweiler/Stolberg. The Jewish groups in these villages – too small to qualify as communities – were looked after by the Orthodox rabbi of Cologne, Dr. Benedikt (Pinchas) Wolf (died 1968 at Petach Tikwah, Israel), who was at the same time chairman of the *Verein für die jüdischen Interessen Rheinlands*, an organisation formed to take care of the religious needs of the many Jewish communities – at least fifty – which did not have a rabbi of their own.

The Lucas family chronicle is supplemented by an appendix listing the deported Jews "born in the municipalities and communes of the former Aachen rural district and the former commune of Setterich". The list contains some 260 names, stating in each case the date of birth and last place of residence, whereas date and place of death are added only in relatively few cases. The documents published as part of the chronicle judiciously amplify points made in the text.

ESSEN: In addition to a number of essays on specific aspects of the history of the Jews of Essen published during the last fifteen years, above all in the quarterly *Das Münster am Hellweg*,[6] a comprehensive work on the history and fate of the Jews

[4]Cf. 'Im Spiegel der Geschichte. Jüdische Gemeinden in Deutschland', see *LBI Year Book XI* (1966), p. 310, note 17; Max Strauß, 'The Jewish Community of Aachen Half a Century Ago', *YIVO Annual of Jewish Social Science*, 1949, pp. 115–123.

[5]Eric Lucas, '"Die Herrschaft". Geschichte einer jüdischen Großfamilie im Kreis Aachen von der Mitte des 19. Jahrhunderts bis zum 2. Weltkrieg', *Heimatblätter des Kreises Aachen*, 36, 1980, Nos. 1–4, published as a pamphlet Aachen 1982, translated from the English by Ernst and Hilde Cassel, with a foreword by Oberkreisdirektor Dr. Friedrich-Wilhelm Janssen.

[6]See *LBI Year Book XXIII*, pp. 286 f., notes 20 and 22 for reports on the Essen and Essen-Steele communities in *Das Münster am Hellweg*, 1970 and 1975, and *ibid.*, 31, 1978, for biographical sketches of Rabbis Salomon Samuel (1894–1922), Paul Lazarus (1914–1919), Hugo Hahn (1922–1939) and Emil Bernhard Cohn (1912–1914).

of Essen appeared in 1980.[7] This work, compiled by Hermann Schröter, former Director of the Municipal Archives, was started as long ago as 1968.

The book features *inter alia* a 'List of Names of Essen Jews, compiled on the basis of the files of the Essen Restitution Office'. In a brief preface to this list – never published before – the author notes that sober matter-of-fact expressions, such as "perished", "declared dead", or "missing" point to a multitude of ineffable tragedies.

The compilation of this book was a particularly laborious enterprise because of the extreme paucity of sources. The list of some 2,500 Essen Jews, with their personal and occupational data, together with deportation lists (Litzmannstadt and Minsk 1941, Izbica and Theresienstadt 1942, Auschwitz 1943) and a comprehensive index of names takes up 320 pages, far more than half the total length. Dispassionate as are the words denoting either banishment or annihilation in case after case, most readers will be drawn in the first place to this section, dealing – as the second noun of the book's title indicates – with the fate rather than the history of Essen Jews.

Yet, this fact will scarcely diminish the interest aroused by the first, historical section of the work, which consists of some thirty articles of moderate length, some of them published previously in *Das Münster am Hellweg* and other journals. Most of these essays deal with prominent personalities among the Essen Jews: merchants, physicians, jurists, rabbis, teachers, artists, scientists. Well-known names appear in these tributes: Blum and Samson, Herzfeld and Krombach, Hirschland and Strauß, Samuel and Hahn, Lekisch and Levy, Marcus and Bezem among many others. In this context Schröter contributes a comprehensive and most useful illustrated survey of schools, synagogues and cemeteries. On the other hand, to be more balanced and precise his brief introductory chapter on 'The Jews in Essen' would have required more specialised advice, especially with regard to intrinsically Jewish matters.

The historical section of the book includes a number of documents from the century preceding 1933: family names in 1847; members of the synagogue congregation in 1910; Jews from the town of Essen and the Essen rural district who fell in the First World War (compiled in 1932); names and addresses of all "non-Aryan" shopkeepers and tradesmen – some 800 of them – in 1935. Essen's large Jewish community was 4,500 strong at the end of 1932 and ranked fourteenth among Germany's major Jewish communities in both 1927 and 1938. It played an important part in the life of the town.

KERPEN, a small town on the left bank of the Lower Rhine, used to have – till the end of 1932, at any rate – two religious minorities besides the Roman Catholic majority, with Protestants outnumbered by Jews. Both in 1871 and 1885 the population included 125 Jews. In 1932, 29 Jewish families were recorded. Yet the *Festbuch* published in 1971 to commemorate the 1,100th anniversary of the first documented reference to the town[8] completely ignores the existence of its Jewish

[7]Hermann Schröter (ed.), *Geschichte und Schicksal der Essener Juden. Gedenkbuch für die jüdischen Mitbürger der Stadt Essen*, published by the City of Essen, Essen 1980, 811 pp.

[8]*Kerpen in Geschichte und Gegenwart. Festbuch aus Anlaß der ersten urkundlichen Erwähnung vor elfhundert Jahren*, published by the Kerpen Municipality, Kerpen 1971, 207 pp.

citizens. Moreover, the period 1933/1945 is barely touched upon, apart from an account of the immediate effects of warfare. What happened to the inhabitants, including the Jewish inhabitants, is not revealed.[9] This sort of historiography can do no good to the reputation of the town.

KREFELD: Since the early 1970s the Municipal Archives under the direction of Guido Rotthoff were known to be working on an account of local Jewish history. The fruit of their labours, a handsome volume entitled *Krefelder Juden* was published in 1980.[10] The omission of the definite article in the title is significant. Indeed, the book does not present a coherent history of the Jewish community; it consists rather of a small number of weighty contributions towards such a history, without, however, covering the hitherto neglected seventy years before 1933, an age of social advancement and cultural achievement. The principal essay by Dieter Hangebruch, taking up more than half the total length of the book, under the heading 'Emigriert – Deportiert' deals with the fate of the Krefeld Jews during the twelve years of the Third *Reich*. A list of Jews residing in Krefeld between 1st April 1933 and 1st January 1945, extending to 148 pages, is likely to be of primary interest to the readers of the book. Here the personal data of some thousand Jews and "non-Aryans" residing in Krefeld are supplied, in every case with a reference to the relevant source, whereas details concerning occupation, career and honorary offices are not presented consistently. At least 700 are likely to have perished following deportation (to Litzmannstadt, Riga, Izbica, Theresienstadt).

Exactly 100 pages are devoted to the anti-Jewish measures adopted by the Nazis in Krefeld, some of them perhaps described in excessive detail.

Foremost among the remaining essays, much shorter than Hangebruch's, is the study by Eleonore Stockhausen on the history of the Krefeld Jewish community in the nineteenth century, in particular during its latter half. The topics covered include Jewish educational institutions up to 1865; the four Chief Rabbis who held office during the century; synagogues, cemeteries and associations; as well as a demographic statistical table for the period ending in 1858. An essay on Krefeld's Jews during the Napoleonic era and the subsequent years of Prussian rule until 1821 is contributed by Klaus H. S. Schulte, who has already made a name for himself with an instructive work on the history of the Jews on the left bank of the Lower Rhine.[11] Finally, Josef Lichtenberg writes about the Jews living at present in the Hüls district of the town.

LECHENICH: The history of the Jews in this country town in the Euskirchen district on the left bank of the Rhine was first touched upon in Schulte's work covering the entire region.[12] A *Festschrift* published in 1979 on the 700th

[9]The author's inquiry to the municipal administrators concerning this omission elicited a reply from the Town Clerk who wrote "that those responsible for the publication of the *Festbuch* have died in the meantime, or are no longer in the employ of the town of Kerpen, owing to their age. I am therefore not in a position to inform you of the motivation of the editors in omitting a mention of the Jewish community and the war years 1933–1945 in the Festbuch *1100 Jahre Kerpen*".

[10]Guido Rotthoff (ed.), *Krefelder Juden*, Krefelder Studien, 2, published by the Town Clerk and the Municipal Archives, Bonn 1980, 424 pp.

[11]Klaus H. S. Schulte, *Dokumentation zur Geschichte der Juden am linken Niederrhein seit dem 17. Jahrhundert*, Düsseldorf 1972, 377 pp. (Cf. *LBI Year Book XXIII*, pp. 283 f.)

[12]Schulte, *op. cit.*

anniversary of the town[13] draws largely on this work for its brief survey of Jewish affairs. It recalls the traditional links of the Jewish inhabitants with the town as they were established over the centuries, and records the existence of the single-form Jewish school and of the synagogue (1886–1938). According to demographic statistics, the number of Jewish citizens was 110 in 1885 and 74 in 1932, roughly 2 per cent of the almost exclusively Roman Catholic population. As regards "events during the years of persecution", the author regrets that it was not possible to arrive at a clear picture (p. 74). According to Schulte, at least eight Jews had been deported from Lechenich.

The *Festschrift* refrains from naming any Jews with the exception of Gerson von Bleichröder, Berlin ("the baron, much liked in Lechenich"), who is credited with having made a substantial contribution to the building of the synagogue. This doubtful conjecture, first put forward by Schulte, needs to be checked. At any rate, Bleichröder (1822–1893), the banker of the Prussian Court, may well have been a close friend of his contemporary, the Lechenich merchant Hermann Simon. Of more enduring interest – though not mentioned – is the fact that Gerson Simon (1858–1931), son of an Orthodox Lechenich family, established a wholesale business in Berlin and in 1928 became chairman of the Berlin Jewish community.

NIEDERAUSSEM, a commune on the left bank of the Rhine, now incorporated in the municipality of Bergheim/Erft, numbered some 600 Jews in 1880 beside 40,000 Catholics and 430 Protestants. As in Kerpen, a chronicle of the commune, published in 1974,[14] completely ignores the existence of the Jews, apart from a purely topographical reference to the "Jüddekirchhoff", the Jewish cemetery. In an attempt to forestall criticism, the author in his foreword states that owing to the short time available for the completion of the chronicle, "many topics worth recording had regretfully to be omitted". Nevertheless, one is left wondering – as in the case of Kerpen – why the fate of the Niederaussem Jews was deemed to be of no account.

WESSELING: The history of the Jewish community of this town, halfway between Cologne and Bonn, today a river port and industrial centre, was already touched upon by Schulte[15] and is now the subject of a booklet,[16] addressed to the "uninstructed", by Christoph Ehmann, a sociologist who for some time was chairman of the Wesseling Society for the Study of the Local Environment. The Jewish community, centred on the synagogue, existed from 1855 to 1940. In 1932 it still numbered some 60 members. The narrative is supplemented by four lists of names of considerable historical interest, relating to the years 1860, 1864, 1904 and 1938, as well as some memorable photographs of the *Hachscharah Kibbutz*, a Jewish agricultural training centre which operated in the years up to 1939 on a

[13] *Lechenich. 700 Jahre Stadtrechte 1279–1979. Festschrift zur 700-Jahrfeier der Stadt*, published by the Bürgergesellschaft, Lechenich 1979, 103 pp.

[14] Kurt Schmitz (ed.), *Niederaussem. Chronik einer Gemeinde*, published on behalf of the Municipality, Niederaussem 1974, 342 pp.

[15] Schulte, *op. cit.*

[16] Christoph Ehmann, *Die Geschichte der jüdischen Gemeinde Wesseling*, Blätter zur Wesselinger Heimatkunde, 1, Wesseling 1980, 80 pp.

site close to the town, and which in the summer of 1938 still accommodated some 45 trainees. The building now houses the Swedish Embassy.

WUPPERTAL: The officially sponsored book on resistance in Wuppertal 1933–1945, published in 1974,[17] has been followed up by a further publication devoted specifically to the fate of the Jews.[18] In this well illustrated pocket book the author, a member of the editorial staff of the Municipal Information Office, has managed to convey in a popular style a useful outline of the subject. A more comprehensive account is being elaborated by a small team of Wuppertal historians. One section of Schnöring's book contains accounts of the experiences of named and unnamed Jews who were taken to Auschwitz, Minsk, Litzmannstadt, Riga, Izbica and Theresienstadt. The total number of these victims is estimated at about 900. Other sections deal with the situation of the Wuppertal Jews before 1933 and with the events and measures preceding the implementation of the "final solution" in Wuppertal and elsewhere. The book also pays tribute to a number of Christians – both clergy and laymen – who extended a helping hand to persecuted Jews.

Several references are found in the book to Else Lasker-Schüler, the distinguished poet and graphic artist born in 1869 at Elberfeld, who for many years had preserved close ties with Wuppertal. After fleeing to Switzerland in 1933, she was deprived of her German citizenship in 1938. She died in 1945 in Jerusalem. The aptly chosen illustrations in Schnöring's book include photographs of the gravestones of her parents, Aaron and Jeannette Schüler, at the Wuppertal Jewish cemetery.

A concise chronicle of the main events in Wuppertal during the years 1933–1945 is added as a useful appendix.

IB. WESTPHALIA

In an officially sponsored collection of essays on the Churches and religious communities in Westphalia[19] the Jews are accorded equality of status. The chapter on Jewry is contributed by Bernhard Brilling, Münster, who has added the Jewish history of the region to the fields in which he has acquired specialised knowledge. His intimate aquaintance with the subject is highlighted by the 120 footnotes which add substantially to the information conveyed by the terse narrative, which runs to just under 40 pages.

The text is divided into two sections, dealing respectively with the development of the Jewish communities from 1815 until their liquidation in 1942, and with the Westphalian Jews' struggle for equality of legal status. This information is supplemented by facts and figures concerning the basic statistics and vocational structure of the Jews. Brilling excels in his account of the Jewish organisational

[17]Cf. *LBI Year Book XXIII*, p. 288.

[18]Kurt Schnöring, *Auschwitz begann in Wuppertal. Jüdisches Schicksal unter dem Hakenkreuz*, Wuppertal 1981, 142 pp.

[19]Bernhard Brilling, 'Das Judentum in der Provinz Westfalen', in *Kirchen und Religionsgemeinschaften in der Provinz Westfalen*, Beiträge zur Geschichte der preußischen Provinz Westfalen, vol. 2 (Veröffentlichungen der Historischen Kommission für Westfalen XXXVIII) Münster 1978, 143 pp.

structure (community institutions and their exponents; officials and leading representatives of the laity; Jewish associations). The differences between Orthodox and Reform Jews in nineteenth-century Westphalia are treated at some length. Compared with the detailed accounts of the early history and the anti-Jewish measures of 1933 to 1945, the treatment of other important topics is somewhat cursory. This applies notably to the Weimar era with its libertarian values, which in Westphalia as elsewhere was an era of Jewish economic and social advancement. Similarly, one misses an account of Jewish reactions to anti-Jewish measures and propaganda both before and after 1933. The fact that 11,500 Westphalian Jews emigrated between 1933 and 1939 is briefly stated, but no mention is made of Jewish self-help during those years, which could be regarded as a feat of spiritual resistance.

Moreover, it would have been useful to have given more information about the spatial residential pattern of the 21,600 Jews recorded in the Province in 1925 – i.e. their distribution among rural and urban environments, among large, medium and small municipalities and communes – as well as about Jewish migration within the Province. The official figure for the Westphalian Jewish population in 1962 is correctly given as 1,161. One should add that by the spring of 1981 that figure had dwindled to 800, including 300 in Dortmund, the rest distributed over eight municipalities: Bielefeld, Gelsenkirchen, Hagen, Herford-Detmold, Minden, Münster, Paderborn and Recklinghausen.

BECKUM: About fifty years ago, this town numbered 1,170 Protestants, 110 Jews and as many "others" out of a population of 10,600. The synagogue congregation was led from 1924 to 1938 by Jakob Jack Raphael, their versatile preacher, teacher and cantor. Raphael was born in Poznań and died in 1971 at Ramat Chen, Israel, in his 74th year. He is not mentioned in the copiously illustrated volume published on the occasion of the 750th anniversary of the town.[20] The book, however, notes that the Jewish community was documented as early as 1699, and that in 1835 it mustered 70 and employed a "Jewish primary teacher". From 1911 to 1919 the Jewish school was part of the State's education system, afterwards it reverted to private status. The book mentions the "purchase" of privately and community-owned Jewish property in November 1938, using the minutes of the relevant meeting of the Municipal Assembly as the only source – without a word of comment! The reader will look in vain for detailed information about the end of the community, that is to say about the fate of its members. On the other hand over six pages are devoted to the lucky circumstances in which the town was saved from destruction in the spring of 1945 and the subsequent period of occupation. In this context it has to be placed on record that in 1975 the Town Council erected a memorial stone in honour of the Beckum Jews who perished in the holocaust. Significantly, the suggestion for this act of remembrance had come from a former Jewish citizen of Beckum who had emigrated to Britain.

BIELEFELD: The Jews of this industrial town in Eastern Westphalia and their community figure in the first volume of the history of the town, written by

[20]Siegfried Schmieder, Egon Ahlmer, Wilheim Winkelmann, *Stadt Beckum. Ereignisse und Entwicklung in 750 Jahren*, Beckum 1974, 352 pp.

Reinhard Vogelsang, the Head of the Municipal Cultural Institute.[21] He presents statistics for the period 1745–1848, during which the community increased from 35 to 174. (For the sake of comparison it is worth noting that by 1932 the figure had risen to over 800, while today there are barely 30 Jews in the town.) The book gives data about the social and occupational structure of the Bielefeld Jews in the first half of the nineteenth century, covering the beginnings of the period of emancipation. The old synagogue in Klosterplatz – shown in a photograph – was demolished in 1907, to be replaced by the new synagogue in Turnerstraße, which was burnt down in November 1938.

The second volume of this history of Bielefeld – whenever it appears – should contain much more, and indeed much more interesting material about the development of the Jewish community and the fate of its members during the span of a century that witnessed progress and achievement as well as crisis and dissolution. The story of those hundred years should establish a link with another official publication, a list of Jews domiciled in Bielefeld before 1933, compiled by Ursula Niemann on behalf of the Municipal Archives, first published as long ago as 1962,[22] and superseded ten years later by an amended and expanded list,[23]

BORGENTREICH is a small town near Paderborn. The history of its Jewish community is the subject of a scholarly paper by the young historian Rudolf Muhs of Freiburg University, which forms part of a comprehensive *Festschrift* on the 700th anniversary of the town.[24] Until the end of last century, the Jewish community, first documented in 1646, consistently outnumbered the Protestants in this predominantly Catholic town. The essay is accompanied by a few photographs of Jewish graves and some facsimile reproductions of documents, one of them relating to the re-launching of the community in 1929.

The text is divided into three sections, covering respectively the period of episcopal rule up till 1802, the Prussian era 1808–1933 and finally the years of doom. The number of Jews in the town declined consistently from 104 in 1840 to 74 in 1861, 53 in 1885, 23 in 1905 and 19 in 1933, which still amounted to 1.1 per cent of the population. On the whole, the paper contrives to highlight significant details – including biographical and occupational data of many individual Jews – without losing sight of the broad sweep of the pattern of events.

DORTMUND: As early as 1808 Jews were granted the unrestricted right to settle in this town. Their numbers were substantial, reaching a peak around 1930 with a figure of some 4,500. It is all the more surprising that so far no comprehensive history of the Dortmund Jewry has been written, as a glance at the bibliography in Ulrich Knipping's history of Dortmund Jews in the Third *Reich*[25]

[21] Reinhard Vogelsang, *Geschichte der Stadt Bielefeld. Von den Anfängen bis zur Mitte des 19. Jahrhunderts*, Bielefeld 1980, 384 pp.

[22] Cf. *LBI Year Book XI*, pp. 318 f.

[23] Ursula Niemann, *Liste der um 1933 in Bielefeld ansässig gewesenen Juden und ihre Schicksale sowie ein Überblick über die Geschichte der jüdischen Gemeinde in Bielefeld*, Bielefeld 1972.

[24] Rudolf Muhs, 'Die jüdische Gemeinde in Borgentreich 1646–1941', in Franz Mürner (ed.), *Stadt Borgentreich 1280–1980*, published on behalf of the Municipality, Borentreich 1980, pp. 221–252.

[25] Ulrich Knipping, *Geschichte der Juden in Dortmund während der Zeit des Dritten Reiches* (Monographien zur Geschichte Dortmunds und der Grafschaft Mark, 8), Dortmund 1977, 255 pp. (Diploma Thesis).

will confirm. The text in Knipping's monograph is supplemented by an Appendix of roughly equal length, which reproduces over thirty relevant documents, notably a list of the members of the Dortmund Jewish community, dated 1st June 1941 (about 1,200 names) and a Theresienstadt list (1942–1944) (331 names).

The text includes several statistical surveys as well as personal reminiscences of some survivors, among them Jeanette Wolff.[26] Brief biographical sketches of some fifty Jews, nearly twenty of whom survived the Nazi regime, are revealing and of considerable historical interest. Knipping's account of all aspects of the persecution of Jews in Dortmund is well supported by authoritative sources. Nor is the internal development of the community in the years 1933–1941 neglected. Facts, names and dates presented here recall a large number of individual incidents which illustrate the bearing, the response, the resolute self-help of the Jews of Dortmund in those grievous times. This account deserves special attention because of its rare combination of brevity with comprehensiveness.

A permanent exhibition on 'Resistance and Persecution in Dortmund 1933–1945' was opened at the beginning of 1981 under the auspices of the City Council. The exhibition was prepared by the Municipal Archives under the guidance of a *Kuratorium* whose thirty members represent various political and religious groups, in particular political organisations of victims of persecution. Two of the members belong to the present-day Jewish community of the town. In the comprehensive catalogue,[27] Chapter Five, dealing with the persecution of the Jews in Dortmund 1933–1945, describes over 100 exhibits illustrating five phases: the situation before 1933, the period of persecution 1933–1938, the *Kristallnacht*, and the systematic extermination of the Jewish population 1939–1945, ending with 'Letters and personal reminiscences of former Dortmund Jews after 1945'. Among the better known representatives of the former synagogue congregation only two are mentioned by name: the teacher Emanuel Goldschmidt (born 1867, died at Theresienstadt 1943), and the barrister Dr. Louis Koppel (born at Hörde 1881, died in New York 1973), for many years chairman of the community. If some exhibits and catalogue entries refer to events beyond the local boundaries, this is clearly in keeping with the educational task of this exhibition, which does not lose sight of the wider context.

GÜTERSLOH: A book on the history of the Jewish community in this town was published officially by the municipality[28] with the support of the energetic *Kreisheimatpfleger* Werner Lenz. What distinguishes this publication is the fact that its author is a Jew who was brought up in this town, Jehuda Barlev, Cologne (formerly Kurt Herzberg, Gütersloh). The book is dedicated to the memory of his parents, Salomon and Klara Herzberg, and an element of reverence is pervasive throughout the text, as well as in the illustrations and the documents reproduced. The Jewish community – until 1938 styled *Israelitische Gemeinde* – numbered some

[26] Bocholt 1888-Berlin 1976. After the Second World War she was a parliamentarian in the Federal Republic and a leading representative of Jewish organisations.

[27] Published by the Municipal Archives, Dortmund 1981, XVI, 336 pp.

[28] Jehuda Barlev, *Juden und jüdische Gemeinde in Gütersloh 1671–1943*, published by the Municipality, Gütersloh 1977, 106 pp.

80 persons in 1924, and still 62 in 1933. Of the latter, over half managed to emigrate in time, but 26 fell victim to the deportations.

The book is remarkable on account of the thorough search for relevant material made by the author in the local archives where aspects of Jewish life in Gütersloh and the surrounding area might be documented, above all the Archives of the Prince zu Bentheim-Tecklenburg at Rheda. The study is supplemented by an instructive pictorial and documentary appendix covering the period from 1700 to the present. However, there are some gaps in the concluding section of the text, due largely to the difficulty of gathering authentic information. Even so, it would have been interesting to be told more about the lives of teachers such as Markus Gottlieb, Arnold Stein and Karl Rosenthal.

Barlev has also contributed brief notes on local Jewish topics in a periodical edited by Werner Lenz.[29]

LIPPE: 'Sorrowful Remembrance' is the title of an essay by Heinrich Bödeker on the Jews of the Lippe region now forming part of North-Rhine Westphalia.[30] Actually, the article gives in the main a potted history of the Jews in Germany as a whole, with the developments specific to Lippe noted only marginally. The information vouchsafed – the number of Jewish inhabitants before 1933 (some 600), the wording of anti-Jewish municipal regulations, the restoration of Jewish cemeteries – is useful as far as it goes, but the reader is entitled to expect more interesting details.

On a gravestone shown in one of the photographs we can read the name and dates of the birth and death of Adolf Sternheim (1871–1950), one of the survivors of Theresienstadt, who at one time played a noteworthy part in both Jewish and general civic life at Lemgo, a former Hanseatic town. Sternheim was clearly more representative of Jewish life in Lippe than was the pacifist Felix Fechenbach murdered by the Nazis in 1933, who came from South Germany to Detmold, where his memory is faithfully preserved, to take over the editorship of the Social Democrat *Lippische Volksblatt*. Today, the joint Jewish community of Detmold and Herford is the only one left in Lippe. At the beginning of 1981 it had 40 members.

MINDEN: Arno Herzig has followed up his earlier monographs on the Jews of Iserlohn and on Jewish emancipation in Westphalia[31] with a paper on the changing social structure of the Jews of Minden in the eighteenth and nineteenth centuries.[32] He describes the situation in Minden as typical of a trend of gradual Jewish integration that was noticeable in various German regions, but tends to be underrated if not altogether ignored in today's historical literature. Indeed,

[29] *Gütersloher Beiträge zur Heimat- und Landeskunde*, edited by Werner Lenz, has occasional essays on Jewish regional affairs, notably three contributions by J. Barlev: 'Levi Bamberger und die Schule in Gütersloh' (December 1974, pp. 743–746), 'Neuenkirchen, die Judengemeinde der Grafschaft Rietberg' (June 1976, pp. 853–865), and 'Die Frühgeschichte der jüdischen Gemeinde Rheda' (December 1979, pp. 1118–1121).

[30] Heinrich Bödeker, 'Schmerzliches Gedenken', *Heimatland Lippe* (bi-monthly of the Lippischer Heimatbund), No. 6, 1978, pp. 269–280. Cf. *LBI Year Book XXIII*, pp. 289 f. for the history of Lippe Jews 1648–1858.

[31] Cf. *ibid.*, p. 288.

[32] Arno Herzig, 'Sozialprofil der jüdischen Bürger von Minden im Übergang vom 18. bis 19. Jahrhundert', *Mitteilungen des Mindener Geschichtsvereins*, 1978, pp. 45–70.

notwithstanding widespread antisemitic stirrings, there were places like Minden, where since the middle of the last century Jews became socially, culturally and – at local government level – also politically integrated within the German civic society. Herzig supports his thesis with photographs and newspaper cuttings and relevant documents from the Municipal Archives.

MÜNSTER: The fifth volume on the history of this town is devoted to the Jews.[33] It is published in conjunction with a documentary folder.[34] In his foreword, Herbert Janssen, the Head of the Municipal Education and Culture Department, notes that "in addition to being used intensively in the history lessons at our schools, the booklets published in this series have encountered considerable interest among the general public" – a claim that is credible. Here the history of the Jews in Münster from the crusades to the present day is told and made clear as a coherent story. A time chart covers eight successive epochs from 1324 to 1961: the first Jewish community; the interlude under Bishop Franz von Waldeck (1535–1554); from the expulsion to the Thirty Years' War; from that war to the beginning of the era of emancipation; the winning of emancipation; Jewish fate in the balance (1870–1933); the road to destruction; finally the new beginning after 1945.

RECKLINGHAUSEN: Until 1978, literature on the Jews of this town was confined to very few publications. A *Festschrift* on the occasion of the centenary of the community was published in 1929[35] by the preacher Isidor Horwitz (born 1890 in Württemberg, emigrated to the USA after twelve years in Recklinghausen); Selig Auerbach, who was rabbi of Recklinghausen from 1934 to 1939 (now living at Lake Placid, USA) wrote an interesting, largely autobiographical essay;[36] lastly, Wilhelm Mummenhoff wrote two brief essays concerned with limited periods.[37]

A more comprehensive study by Heinz Reuter (Castrop-Rauxel) was published in 1979.[38] Taken together, these publications add up to a rounded and reliable picture of the development of the Recklinghausen Jewish community. At the end of 1932 it numbered some 300 (without the affiliated congregations). While taking in both mediaeval occurrences and – more in the nature of an appendix – the rebuilding of a community after 1945 (with a membership of 50 in 1950), Reuter's study, drawing extensively on archival sources, focuses attention on the years 1800 to 1942, which cover progress, decline and destruction of organised Jewish life in Recklinghausen and the neighbouring localities. One poignant and revealing document from the Municipal Archives is designated a

[33]Hans Galen, Joachim Korupka, Helmut Lahrkamp (eds.), *Geschichte original – am Beispiel der Stadt Münster 5: Die Juden*, published by the Municipal Archives and Municipal Museum, Münster 1981.

[34]Diethard Aschoff, *Die Juden in Münster von den Anfängen bis zur Gegenwart. Dokumente, Fragen, Erläuterungen, Darstellung*, with the collaboration of the publishers, Münster 1981.

[35]Isidor Horwitz, *Die Synagogengemeinde Recklinghausen 1829–1929*, Recklinghausen 1929.

[36]Selig Auerbach, 'Das Bezirksrabbinat Recklinghausen', in *Aus Geschichte und Leben der Juden in Westfalen*, Frankfurt a. Main 1962, pp. 125–133.

[37]Wilhelm Mummenhoff, 'Zur Geschichte der Juden in Recklinghausen während der kurkölnischen Zeit', *Vestische Zeitschrift*, 37, 1930, pp. 269–280.

[38]Heinz Reuter, 'Die Juden im Vest Recklinghausen – ihre gesellschaftlichen und politischen Verhältnisse unter besonderer Berücksichtigung der Synagogengemeinde Recklinghausen', *ibid.*, 77/78, 1979, pp. 19–156. ("Vest" is the regional term for an administrative area.)

'List of the Jewish inhabitants of Recklinghausen during the Third *Reich*'. It gives the names, dates of birth and death, and indications of the final fate of 476 Jews. Many instructive statistical surveys relating to the social, occupational and age structure of the Jewish population as well as to community budgets, school attendance and emigration supplement the text of this predominantly socio-economic inquiry.

SOEST had at the beginning of the 1930s still close on 200 Jewish inhabitants, who formed the local synagogue congregation, which for a time ran a Jewish public primary school and employed successively Sally Katzenstein and Harry O. Bernstein as officials. A major work on the Jews of Soest was published in 1971.[39] A documentation on the persecution of Jewish citizens of Soest in the Third *Reich*, published eight years later on the occasion of the unveiling of a memorial tablet at the location of the former synagogue and school in Osthofenstraße,[40] draws extensively on Buß as well as on *Brunsvicensia Judaica*[41] and Knipping's study of the Dortmund Jews.[42]

It is not surprising, then, that material specifically relating to Soest takes up considerably less room than the account of developments in the wider region and in Germany as a whole. The local material comprises reports in the local press, announcements and regulations issued by official quarters and Party authorities, as well as documents on the local repercussions of the "final solution". The opening section sets out to present a history of the Jews of Soest from the thirteenth century to 1933. The last community is likely to have been established during the closing years of the eighteenth century. Its synagogue was dedicated in 1822 (and destroyed in 1938). A new cemetery was established in 1832. Finally, Köhn mentions the Foundations generously endowed by the Soest merchant Philipp Stern in favour of the poor and the local orphanage, which operated from 1869 till 1921.

STEINHEIM, a town situated between Detmold and Holzminden, currently with a population of barely 7,000, may be remembered by some people with a special interest in economic history as the birth place of Simon Hirschland (1807–1885), the founder of the once prominent Essen private bank, which for several generations remained in his family.[43]

A recent monograph on the Steinheim Jews by Johannes Waldhoff[44] is divided into fifty brief chapters covering the period from the Thirty Years' War to the liquidation of the community. One chapter is devoted to the Hirschland family, supplemented by a genealogical table (1681 to 1826).

The number of Jewish inhabitants declined from 130 in 1855 to under 70 in 1932 (which at the time amounted to 2 per cent of the population). A first

[39]Wilfried Buß, *Sosatia Judaica*, Soest 1971, 484 pp. (Diploma Thesis).

[40]Gerhard Köhn, *Die Verfolgung der jüdischen Mitbürger in Soest während des Dritten Reiches* (Veröffentlichungen des Stadtarchivs Soest, 8) Soest 1979, 151 pp.

[41]*Brunsvicensia Judaica*, Brunswick 1966; cf. *LBI Year Book XV* (1970), p. 236.

[42]Knipping, *op. cit.*

[43]*Jüdisches Leben in Deutschland. Selbstzeugnisse zur Sozialgeschichte 1780–1871*, hrsg. und eingeleitet von Monika Richarz, Stuttgart 1976, Veröffentlichung des Leo Baeck Instituts, pp. 236–240.

[44]Johannes Waldhoff, *Geschichte der Juden in Steinheim* (Heimatgeschichtliche und volkskundliche Schriften der Stadt Steinheim, 2), Steinheim 1980, 305 pp.

synagogue built in 1750 was in the 1880s found to be too small and was replaced in 1884 by the second synagogue, a structure with an octagonal cupola, displaying the Magen David. This stately building proclaimed the economic strength of the Steinheim Jews. The dedication of this synagogue in August 1884 is described in all its details. Less room is accorded to an account of the demolition carried out 54 years later in deference to orders from on high: a laborious job involving the use of explosives to bring down the cupola and the gradual dismantling of the strong walls. One distinctive feature of the book is the extensive treatment of the occupational structure and economic situation as well as the harmonious relations between Jews and Christians, continuing well into the 1930s. These subjects are given far more prominence than is customary in this branch of literature. This approach was facilitated by the fact that all the relevant official files have been preserved. At the same time, it was clearly the author's intention to demonstrate that "the history of the Steinheim Jews is an integral part of the history of the town".

WARBURG: A doctoral thesis on the history of the Warburg Jews during the rule of the Prince Bishops, written in the 1920s, was published only in 1978.[45] A recent collection of 20 documents on the pogrom of November 1938 in the Warburg area[46] includes an undated report of SS Regiment 72 to the competent SS authority, which lists the destroyed Jewish shops (73), households (56) and burnt down synagogues (28). Other documents include teleprinter and radio messages, circulars and letters dealing with events in nearly fifty localities in Eastern Westphalia between 9th and 26th November 1938. The originals are kept at the Detmold State Archives and in Yad Vashem, Jerusalem. In the words of the compiler, the publication is intended "to make a contribution to facing up to the past and coming to terms with it".

II. RHINELAND-PALATINATE AND SAAR TERRITORY

The monumental nine-volume documentation relating to the history of the Jewish population in Rhineland-Palatinate and the Saarland from 1800 to 1945, published by the Rhineland-Palatinate State Archives Adminstration under the supervision of its Director, Franz-Josef Heyen,[47] was all but completed by the publication of vol. 2 in 1979, and vols. 1 and 9 in 1982, with vol. 8 forthcoming.[48]

[45]Martha Evers, *Geschichte der Juden in der Stadt Warburg zur fürstbischöflichen Zeit*, unpublished doctoral thesis, Münster 1920, now published in the series 'Warburger Schriften', Warburg 1978, with updated bibliography.

[46]*Das Novemberpogrom 1938 im Raum Warburg*, duplicated, not distributed by the book trade, n.d., 50 sheets.

[47]*Dokumentation zur Geschichte der jüdischen Bevölkerung in Rheinland-Pfalz und im Saarland von 1800 bis 1945*, hrsg. von der Landesarchivverwaltung Rheinland-Pfalz in Verbindung mit dem Landesarchiv Saarbrücken, vols. 1–9 (Veröffentlichungen der Landesarchivverwaltung Rheinland-Pfalz, 12–20), Koblenz 1974–1982. For a review of vols. 3–7 see *LBI Year Book XXIII*, pp. 290 ff.

[48]*Der Weg zur Gleichberechtigung der Juden* (Dokumentation 2, Veröffentlichungen 13), Koblenz 1979, 472 pp.; vol. 1 of the series contains in addition to Heyen's foreword two historical contributions: 'Zur rechtlichen Situation der Juden im 18. Jahrhundert', edited by Georg Friedrich Böhm, and 'Die Juden in der Französischen Zeit 1798/1801 bis 1814', edited by Editha Bucher (Dok. 1, Veröff. 12) Koblenz 1982, 282 pp; *Inventar der Quellen zur Geschichte der jüdischen Bevölkerung in Rheinland-Pfalz und im Saarland 1800/1815–1945*, Gemeinschaftsarbeit unter der Redaktion von Theresia Zimmer (four sub-volumes, Dok. 9, Veröff. 20/1–4), Koblenz 1982, XX, 1708 pp.

Oddly enough, vol. 1 of the series was the penultimate to be published. That is the way it happened, says Heyen unapologetically in his "foreword" to the whole series, which in actual fact has turned out to be a thoughtful afterword, discussing points of principle and topical implications. Heyen recalls the decisions taken in 1969 to launch the series as a ten-year project. In describing the method adopted, he refers to the inherent limitations imposed by circumstances, in particular by the loss of most of the documents of the Jewish communities as well as of letters and diaries in private archives, even though supplementary documentation might yet prove useful. The project – Heyen emphasises – was meant to cover not only the period of persecution, but also

> "the epoch, beginning in the early years of the nineteenth century, when Jewish life in Germany developed into an increasingly integrated part of the life of the population as a whole . . . It is right to consider the nineteenth century in its entirety, in order to assess the way in which, quite apart from developments at national level, everyday life, the humdrum daily round, is affected on the one hand by the multifarious roots, motivations and currents of antisemitism of every hue – religious, racist, nationalist-*völkisch*, economic, social and cultural – and on the other hand by possibilities of overcoming antisemitism through a will for tolerance, through an awareness of the relativity and plurality of religious values."

At the end of his foreword Heyen asks whether a documentation prepared by Jews would have been different. He leaves the question unanswered, but affirms, that

> "it is good and right that Germans and Christians should occupy themselves intensively with this aspect of German history. Indeed, our work is intended as a contribution to the history of our homeland, even though – or rather: all the more so because – this history includes dark and grievous episodes and events. This work is addressed to the people of our homeland, both old and young, as well as to future generations."

In the preparation of vol. 2, dealing with the advance towards the attainment of equality of legal status, Heyen was assisted by Anton Doll, Hans-Josef Schmidt and Manfred Wilmanns. The narrative is divided into sections corresponding to the sub-regions of the State of Rhineland-Palatinate – the former Prussian Administrative Regions of Koblenz and Trier; parts of Nassau; the Birkenfeld district formerly belonging to Oldenburg; the former Bavarian Rhine-Palatinate; and finally Rhine-Hesse – each section being prefaced by a concise historical survey of the social and political situation of the Jews. It is not surprising that in this patchwork of sub-regions the progress of the Jewish population towards equality of legal status was anything but uniform. It was a laborious and fitful process, characterised by wide local variations, piecemeal advances interrupted by frequent setbacks.

The volume includes 180 documents – notably laws, decrees, administrative orders; official announcements and reports; submissions, rejoinders and judicial rulings; expert opinions and minutes of official proceedings and parliamentary debates – mostly dating from the first half of the nineteenth century. Some of the documents have been abridged without diminishing their value as evidence. One of these is a petition filed by the Trier barrister Heinrich Marx (1777–1838), father of Karl Marx, on 18th June 1815 – well before his conversion – taking exception to the repeal of a Napoleonic Decree of 17th March 1808 that had been beneficial to the Jews.

In mid-1982 the concluding vol. 9 of the series was published. It is an inventory of the sources relating to the history of the Jews in Rhineland-Palatinate and the Saar territory 1800–1945, divided into four sub-volumes with a total of 3,733 items, comprising the relevant material available at the principal State Archives in Koblenz, Speyer and Saarbrücken, at municipal archives and a selected number of others, including notably the Federal Archives at Koblenz, the Archives of the Bonn Foreign Office, the League of Nations Archives at Geneva, and the documentary files of 19 Jewish communities in the region, currently held by the Central Archives for the History of the Jewish People in Jerusalem. The volume concludes with an Index of personal and place names extending to almost 200 pages, two columns to each page, a treasure trove for any reader concerned with the post-mediaeval history of the Jews of the region.

ALTENKIRCHEN and the surrounding Westerwald localities of Wissen, Betzdorf, Kirchen, Herdorf and Hamm a.d. Sieg feature in a series of four essays on 'Jewish-German citizens of our homeland' by the Deacon Günter Heuzeroth (Oldenburg).[49] Before 1933, there were some 90 Jewish inhabitants in Altenkirchen, about 60 at Hamm a.d. Sieg, and over 40 at Betzdorf.

The author carefully states his sources (files in the Koblenz and Wiesbaden State Archives, publications on local and regional history, letters from Jewish emigrés as well as statements by mostly unnamed persons in the localities concerned). The text is accompanied by good-quality photographs not confined to tombstones but representative of Jewish life. The present addresses of some Jewish survivors are given. The methodical care expended on this work deserves appreciation; yet it is not Heuzeroth's ambition to produce a work of historiography. He simply wanted to remind his readers, that is to say, above all the local population, of their former Jewish fellow citizens and their ordeal at the hands of the Nazis. He names many Jews from Westerwald localities and members of their families, discusses their genealogical connections, presents some statistics and describes synagogues and cemeteries. Having covered this ground, he then turns at greater length to the time of outlawry, persecution and annihilation. "Only if we draw the lessons of the past," he writes, "can there be any hope for the future, for a truly human future bringing Jewish people and we Germans together."

ALZEY: This small Rhine-Hesse municipality, together with its Antiquarian Society and the local museum, has repeatedly published information about the history of its Jewish fellow-citizens. The latest contributions are contained in an augmented issue of the local historical journal.[50] Beate Linde Weiland discusses the *Memorbuch* maintained by the Alzey Jewish community at the turn of the eighteenth century, which for a long time was thought to have been lost, but is now held by the Jewish National and University Library, Jerusalem. Ralf Zahn

[49]Günter Heuzeroth, 'Jüdisch-deutsche Bürger unserer Heimat' (four instalments, in:) *Heimatjahrbuch des Kreises Altenkirchen (Westerwald) und der angrenzenden Gemeinden*, 1975–1978; issued as a pamphlet under the same title, *Altenkirchen* n.d. (presumably 1978), 52 pp.

[50]*Alzeyer Geschichtsblätter*, No. 15, 15th December 1979.

contributes a University entrance exam paper on the history of the Jewish communities at Wörrstadt and Nieder-Wiesen, two localities in the vicinity of Alzey. Finally, the Mainz theologian and art historian Otto Böcher, well known for previous studies on the history of the Jews of the region,[51] introduces a reprint of the festive oration delivered by the District Rabbi Samuel Adler (born Worms 1809, died New York 1891) on the occasion of the dedication of Alzey's new synagogue on 20th October 1854.

BENDORF-SAYN: "The freight trucks will be loaded with the Jews from the Israelite Nursing Home Bendorf-Sayn." This laconic sentence, contained in a teleprinted message of the Koblenz Gestapo headquarters, dated 11th June 1942, sealed the fate of about 250 inmates and 100 staff of the Jewish psychiatric nursing home.[52] The message is quoted on the cover of Dietrich Schabow's pamphlet on the history of the Jews of Bendorf.[53] As early as 1947, the Koblenz Jewish community published several extant official lists naming 867 Jews deported from Koblenz town and rural district. Two of these lists, dated respectively 30th April and 15th June 1942, deal exclusively with Bendorf-Sayn, featuring 447 names. An earlier list, dated 22nd March 1942, mentions 100 persons at the address Bendorf-Sayn, Hindenburgstraße 49, which indicates that the total number of Jews deported from Bendorf must have totalled some 550. Schabow's pamphlet is a reprint of a series of articles published in the local press, with a foreword by the Mayor of Bendorf, Dieter Trennheuser. Apart from a detailed report on the terrible end, substantiated by the names and dates, Schabow reprints documents relating to the history of the Jews of Bendorf, Sayn and nearby localities during the time before 1350, and again from 1700. Following a decision by the Town Council, a memorial tablet was unveiled in the summer of 1979 at the site of the former synagogue in Spitalgasse (formerly Judengasse). The Town Council's decision, the Mayor states in his foreword,

> "appeared a suitable occasion for gathering some facts from the history of the Bendorf Jews. For centuries Christians and Jews lived side by side in Bendorf. Several Jewish citizens acquired a high reputation and, especially during the early decades of this century, took an active part in the public life of the town of Bendorf and the commune of Sayn/Mülhofen. Persecution and destruction were meted out to Jewish fellow citizens who, no less than all the others, felt that their roots were in Bendorf or Sayn."

KAISERSLAUTERN (in the former Bavarian Palatinate) did not have a proper Jewish community until 1823, when the synagogue was dedicated followed in 1827 by the appointment of a rabbi and in 1858 by the establishment of a Jewish cemetery. A new synagogue was built between 1883 and 1886. The number of Jews in the town rose steadily from 60 in 1827 in 149 in 1849, 184 in

[51] Cf. *LBI Year Book XI*, pp. 308 f.; *XV*, p. 230; and *XXIII*, p. 293, notes 56 and 57.

[52] Founded in 1869 as the private *Jacobysche Heil- und Pflegeanstalt für jüdische Nerven- und Gemütskranke in Sayn bei Koblenz*. On 3rd February 1939 the proprietors, the physicians Paul Jacoby (Sayn 1899–Montevideo 1969) and Fritz Jacoby (Sayn 1888–New York 1966) were ordered by the Regierungspräsident in Koblenz to reserve the "Jewish mental institution of Bendorf-Sayn" exclusively for Jewish patients. Subsequently, ownership was vested in the *Reichsvereinigung der Juden in Deutschland* (Berlin).

[53] Dietrich Schabow, *Zur Geschichte der Juden in Bendorf*, published by Hedwig-Dransfeld-Haus in conjunction with the Bendorf Ecumenical Working Group, Bendorf 1977, 30 pp.

1852, 616 in 1871, 741 in 1900 and 744 in 1925, then declining to 648 at the beginning of 1933. The decline rapidly accelerated to 395 in 1937 and 85 in 1939. Some 50 of these were deported in the course of the Bürckel Operation to the Gurs camp in Southern France.

Rabbi Sally Baron (born Berlin 1874, died abroad after emigrating), who headed the Kaiserslautern community from 1921 to 1938, published towards the end of his period of office an essay on the history of this community.[54] In 1965/1966 the Head of the Municipal Archives, Heinz Friedel, wrote a series of three articles on the same subject in the local Evangelical weekly.[55] He is also the author of a wide-ranging book on the history of Kaiserslautern from 1914 to 1940,[56] which includes only a few references to Jews and Jewish life in the town: a service of supplication at the synagogue on the outbreak of the First World War; relief contributions by the Julius Plotke (B'nai B'rith) Lodge; hero's death of the engineer Friedrich Mayer on the Western front in September 1914; donation made by the synagogue choir for bereaved relatives of fallen soldiers; the wreckage of the synagogue after it had been blown up (as early as October 1938); tombstones and memorial stones at the Jewish cemetery.

LINZ AM RHEIN celebrated its 1,100th anniversary in 1974. The *Festschrift* published on the occasion[57] had very little to say about the existence of Jews, the Jewish community and its institutions (such as the synagogue and the school attached to it), and nothing at all about the fate that befell the Jewish citizens in the end. It was only in 1978 that some record sheets of the *Einwohnermeldeamt* of the town turned up, which provide some information about the fate of the Linz Jews after 1933.[58] The list contains names, dates of birth and records of their moves relating to 84 persons. It is noted that 24 emigrated between 1933 and 1940, half of them to the USA; 6 died a natural death; one perished at Buchenwald; 10 were deported to Theresienstadt; 12 were recorded on 30th March 1942 as "moved away, destination unknown"; 29 reported their departure to 11 different German towns; lastly, 2 left "for the purpose of travel". It is doubtful whether these figures will ever be published by the Linz Municipality. Jubilees and books commemorating them, after all, do not come every year. These data should have been in the publication of 1974. Their omission can hardly be remedied now, hence the indication of the contents given here.

SAARLAND

Prior to the completion in 1982 of the monumental nine-volume documentation on the history of the Jews in Rhineland-Palatinate and the Saarland,[59] little was written about the Jews of this territory, even though communities with more

[54] *Bayerische Israelitische Gemeindezeitung*, 1936.
[55] *Gemeindergruß. Evangelisches Sonntagsblatt* (Kaiserslautern).
[56] Heinz Friedel, *Gehörtes und Erlebtes*, Otterbach-Kaiserslautern 1980, 128 pp.
[57] Hans Peter Petri (ed.), *Elfhundert Jahr Linz am Rhein 874–1974*, Linz 1974, 384 pp. Cf. *LBI Year Book XXIII*, p. 292.
[58] Not published but made available to the author.
[59] See notes 47 and 48 above. For Hugo Steinthal's pre-war series of articles on the history and sociology of the Saarland Jews cf. *LBI Year Book XXIII*, p. 292, note 49.

than 100 members continued to exist even after 1933, apart from Saarbrücken, also at Dillingen, Illingen, Merzig, Saarlouis, Saarwellingen and St. Wendel.

ILLINGEN: In response to a suggestion by the *Christlich-jüdische Arbeitsgemeinschaft des Saarlandes*, a documentation on the small industrial town of Illingen was published in 1980.[60] The author was evidently unaware of Steinthal's pre-war work. Thus, when Neuhauser notes that in the early 1930s just over 100 Jews lived at Illingen, he could have added (according to Steinthal) that in 1885 there were as many as 225 Jewish inhabitants, and as late as 1927 there were still 162. The new documentation, based in the main on research in the public archives of Illingen, Saarbrücken and Koblenz, covers the period of at least 220 years during which the Illingen Jewish community existed. However, the documents are presented one after the other without any comment or a narrative that could be classified as historiography. Even so, in spite of the random arrangement and the difficulty of deciphering some of the documents reproduced in facsimile, the whole conveys an impression of collective as well as individual development and destiny. Registers of births, marriages and deaths from the period 1800–1936 are given pride of place. Together with lists of names (for 1817, 1824, 1859 and subsequent years) and a list of graves, they comprise nearly half the book. The remaining half contains documents relating to the assignment of surnames in 1808 and the internal organisation of the community, local associations, education, the cemetery and questions of personnel, ranging from the Napoleonic to the Nazi era.

III. HESSE

In June 1979 the Exhibition "Jews in Hesse"[61] was officially opened at Friedberg. Since then it has been shown in 30 localities.[62] The bulk of the material consists of photographic reproductions of documents and other texts as well as illustrations covering the period from the Middle Ages up to our time. Attention is focused chiefly on the persecutions of Jews in Germany, both in the distant and recent past, while the period of 60 to 70 years before 1933 – years of social and political advance and a measure of economic prosperity – are treated rather cavalierly by comparison. This applies in particular to the growth of a Jewish middle class in rural areas. Some of the places in which the exhibition was shown added local

[60] Otto Neuhauser, *Die Jüdische Gemeinde zu Illingen*, published by the Illingen Municipality, 1980, 408 pp.

[61] Exhibition *Juden in Hessen*, organised by the Hesse State Archives at Wiesbaden and Darmstadt in conjunction with the Commission for the History of Jews in Hesse. The 67-page catalogue with the same title, published in 1979, comprises four chapters: Jewish life in Hesse before 1800; Emancipation of the Hesse Jews 1800–1933; Persecution under the Nazi dictatorship; Jewish life in Hesse after 1945.

[62] Offenbach, Wiesbaden, Raunheim, Weilburg, Idstein, Büdingen, Frankfurt, Hofgeismar, Darmstadt, Langen, Babenhausen, Pfungstadt, Hanau, Kassel, Karben, Bad Homburg v.d.H., Wetzlar, Butzbach, Rüsselsheim, Hochheim a. Main, Korbach, Frankfurt-Höchst, Oberursel, Herborn, Schlüchtern, Gießen, Vilbel, Staufenberg, also at the Hessenpark near Neu-Anspach and at the Hesse Agency in Bonn.

material of their own to the basic stock of exhibits. One of these, Rüsselsheim, published in addition a separate 40-page catalogue.[63]

CAMBERG, a small town in the Nassau region, published a *Festschrift* in 1981 to mark the 700th anniversary of its municipal charter.[64] One chapter deals with the Jews in Camberg in the nineteenth and twentieth centuries, with "the last Camberg list of Jewish inhabitants" added as an appendix. The author of this chapter is Caspar Hofmann, a Catholic clergyman born in 1900, a freeman of the town and former teacher at the *Wöhlergymnasium* in Frankfurt a. Main. From the early days of his youth he was closely acquainted with Jews and Jewish customs. In his essay he presents a picture of the occupational structure of the Camberg Jews up to 1933, based largely on documents held by the Camberg Municipal Archives. Dealing at length with the personal and economic persecution of Jews during the early years of the Nazi regime, he instances individual cases in the light of official records.

We learn from this essay *inter alia* that when in 1825 a senior official, the Catholic *Regierungsrat* Lieber, launched a foundation endowed with a capital of 25,000 gulden, the statutes declared expressly that Jews fallen on hard times through no fault of their own should not be excluded from the benefits of the foundation. This episode confirms the general impression that relations between the religious communities in Camberg were on a friendly footing. In 1825 the Jewish population of the town numbered some 80, almost 2 per cent of the total population, and this relatively high proportion was maintained until 1933. Most, perhaps two thirds, of the Camberg Jews are likely to have been deported during Nazi rule.

DIEBURG – situated between Darmstadt and Aschaffenburg – also celebrated the 700th anniversary of its municipal charter and issued a handsome *Festschrift* on the occasion in 1977,[65] in which the part played by the Jewish inhabitants is mentioned in different contexts. Georg Schmidt contributes a chapter on the history of the Jewish community, beginning in 1340. Another chapter, by Adi Simon, entitled 'Dieburg from the Weimar Republic to the fall of the Third *Reich*', provides a terse account of the fate of the Dieburg Jews. Even during the early years of the Nazi regime considerable harm was inflicted on the *Israelitische Religionsgemeinde*, its members and its institutions. The majority of the Jews registered in 1923 and 1933 were able to emigrate, but 17 named persons perished.

The information contained in the two chapters is supplemented by three excellent photographs showing respectively the old synagogue 1869–1929; the new synagogue, modern and monumental, erected in 1929 and left standing in 1938 – as far as the outer structure is concerned – since the building was entered in the Land Register as municipal property; finally the tomb of Jakob Lorch at the

[63]"*Juden in Rüsselsheim*" – *Katalog zur Ausstellung vom 12. Oktober bis 31. Dezember 1981* (Schriften des Museums der Stadt Rüsselsheim, 6) 40 pp.

[64]Caspar Hofmann, 'Die Juden in Camberg im 19. und 20. Jahrhundert', in *Camberg – 700 Jahre Stadtrechte*. Beiträge zur Heimatkunde, published by the Municipality, Camberg 1981, 412 pp.

[65]*Dieburg – Beiträge zur Geschichte der Stadt: Zum Jubiläum 700 Jahre erworbener Stadrechte*, Dieburg 1977, 370 pp.

cemetery in Frankfurter Straße. For all its brevity, the information provided here adds up to a rounded picture. The first mention of a Jewish cemetery dates back to around 1530. Presumably it provided the nucleus for the later cemetery which served at the same time some twenty orthodox Jewish rural communities in the neighbourhood. Roughly 1,000 gravestones have been preserved, some reputed to be very ancient.

EBERSTADT – since 1937 incorporated in the municipality of Darmstadt – has set an example showing that, from the point of view of German-Jewish relations, the part can be more advanced than the whole. For whereas Darmstadt has for a long time harboured an intention to sponsor a publication on the history and fate of its Jewish citizens,[66] but has so far not got beyond a preliminary stage of articles in the daily and periodical press, the lot of the Jews of Eberstadt is the subject of a 63-page pamphlet published privately by its author, Robert Heß.[67] The last few pages, dealing with the 23 Jewish families of Eberstadt and their fate under the Nazi regime, are of particular interest. So are the brief, yet detailed reports on the Heyum and Joseph families, and the reference to the large Jewish cemetery in neighbouring Alsbach an der Bergstraße, which in addition to Eberstadt served at the very least twenty Jewish communities in the area. For the rest, this well meant, if haphazardly arranged publication deals with the history and customs of the Jews in general. The pamphlet describes the way in which the Nazi measures affected Eberstadt. The reader gets the impression that before the onset of the time of terror relations between Christians and Jews were generally friendly.

FRANKFURT A. MAIN: The fortieth anniversary of the November pogrom of 1938 was marked by the publication of a comprehensive bibliography of publications on the history of the Frankfurt Jews 1781–1945.[68] The book is the fruit of years of diligent labour. The compilation involved the perusal of over 200 periodicals and reference to nearly 100 German and foreign bibliographies and libraries.

The book – a treasure trove for those interested in the history of the Frankfurt Jews and their communal institutions – is divided into two parts, the bibliography proper being followed by an alphabetical list of "all personages of the Jewish faith or Jewish descent who played a part in public, cultural or economic life and who were born in Frankfurt or lived and worked there for a number of years". The list of some 900 names includes Börne, Buber, Paul Ehrlich, Anne Frank, the rabbis Abraham Geiger, S. R. Hirsch and Georg Salzberger, and also Moritz Oppenheim, Franz Oppenheimer, Gabriel Riesser, Franz Rosenzweig, the Rothschilds and Speyers, as well as Leopold Sonnemann, the newspaper publisher and politician.

The bibliography proper is characterised by the subtitles of the most important sections: emancipation and the granting of full citizens' rights (1781–1864);

[66]Cf. *LBI Year Book XV*, p. 242.

[67]Robert Heß, *Eberstadts jüdische Mitbürger*, Eberstadt 1982, 64 pp.

[68]*Bibliographie zur Geschichte der Frankfurter Juden 1781–1945*, hrsg. von der Kommission zur Erforschung der Geschichte der Frankfurter Juden, bearbeitet von Hans Schlembs mit Verwendung der Vorarbeiten von Ernst Loewy und Rosel Andernacht, Frankfurt a. Main 1978, 680 pp.

assimilation – antisemitism – Zionism (1866–1933); persecution (1933–1945); social welfare work; the economy; religious trends within Jewry; Jewish community and *Israelitische Religionsgesellschaft*; religious lore and teaching; education; science and learning; the arts.

FULDA had over 1,000 Jewish inhabitants in 1933. By 1942 only some 60 were left. A Jewish community was first documented in the eleventh century, but it was only in the eighteenth century that it rose into prominence. Today its memory is preserved in the first place by the cemetery in Heidelsteinstraße (Edelzellerweg) with almost 400 graves, established in 1906. This cemetery is the subject of a brief pamphlet,[69] which notes that it is "maintained in dignified, indeed exemplary fashion" and has been given the status of an historical memorial site. The accompanying photographs of graves are of exceptional quality. Legible inscriptions recall the memory of well-known Fulda Jews, among them community dignitaries, rabbis (e.g. Michael Cahn who died in 1919) and teachers. A list of funerals gives the names, dates of death and grave numbers of the Jews buried there. The Mayor of Fulda, Wolfgang Hamberger, introduces the documentation with the motto "Remembrance is the secret of redemption", and a reverent foreword is contributed by Naftali Herbert Sonn (Tel-Aviv), known for an earlier work on the history of the Fulda Jews, written with Paul Horn as co-author.[70]

GIESSEN: A documentation on the Jewish population of the town 1933–1945 was published by the Municipal Archivist Erwin Knauß in 1974.[71] The second augmented edition[72] benefited from the co-operation of a former schoolmate of his, Helmut Stern (born 1921, emigrated 1936 to Palestine), who traced new sources in Israel and established communication with former Gießen Jews in the USA.

In 1980 Stern wrote, in the local historical journal edited by Knauß, an article on the Gießen Jews now in Israel.[73] He presents an important list of some 200 immigrants (stating year of immigration, place of residence as well as other personal data) and gives details about their jobs and the way they managed to settle in. The essay is carefully annotated and illustrated and includes some new documents (written and pictorial) casting light on the situation in Gießen. It thus incidentally makes a contribution to the history of the Gießen Jews. Of special interest is the information on the teacher and educationist Hedwig Burgheim (born Alsleben 1887, died Auschwitz 1943), who from 1918 to 1933 was Head of the Gießen Fröbel-Seminar.

HANAU published a *Festschrift* to mark the 675th anniversary of the Altstadt in 1978.[74] Among the excellent photographs supplementing the text there are two

[69] *Der jüdische Friedhof in Fulda, Dokumentationen zur Stadtgeschichte* 2, published by the Municipality, Fulda 1980, 32 pp.

[70] Cf. *LBI Year Book XV*, pp. 223 f.

[71] Cf. *LBI Year Book XXIII*, pp. 294 f.

[72] Erwin Knauß, *Die jüdische Bevölkerung Gießens 1933–1945*, published by the Commission for the History of the Jews in Hesse, 2nd augmented edition, Wiesbaden 1976, 177 pp.

[73] Helmut Stern, 'Gießen Jews in Israel', *Mitteilungen des Oberhessischen Geschichtsvereins Gießen*, N.F. 65, Gießen 1980, pp. 5–86.

[74] *675 Jahre Altstadt Hanau*, Hanau 1978, 286 pp.

with the caption "Deportation of persons of Jewish descent". The pictures are so well focused that it is possible in two cases to decipher the labels on the luggage the victims were allowed to take with them in 1942.

The main part of the book consists of a reprint of the catalogue of an exhibition held at the Historical Museum of the town on the occasion of the jubilee. The Hanau Jewish community and its institutions are remembered. Two photographs show first the burning, then the burnt-out synagogue in November 1938, in both cases displaying a "For Sale" notice undoubtedly painted by the arsonists. The text notes that the synagogue, situated in Nordstraße, the former *Judengasse*, was erected in 1608 as a Jewish school with one room set aside for worship. A photograph shows the Hesse *Landesrabbiner* I. E. Lichtigfeld with the Hanau Mayor Herbert Dröse attending the dedication in 1964 of a memorial stone erected by the municipality on the site of the destroyed synagogue.

BAD HOMBURG VOR DER HÖHE in the Taunus hills marked its 1,200th anniversary in 1982 with the publication of a well-organised, concise and telling *Festschrift*, accompanied by photographs and a list of sources.[75] One of the 17 brief chapters, no more than three pages of print, deals with the Jews of the town, first mentioned in 1335, with later records dating from the 1500s and the period of the *Judengasse*, 1698 to 1791. The chapter refers to the Jewish places of worship (1731–1864; 1866–1938) and to Jewish life in the nineteenth century when the Homburg congregation became an independent community, from 1852 with a rabbi of its own; Leopold Wreschner, the last of these rabbis, held office from 1922 to 1934. Photographs show the synagogue in Wallstraße and the Jewish cemetery in Gluckensteinerweg. Other illustrations show advertisements placed in the local press by Jewish restaurants. Prominent Jews mentioned by the author include Dr. Curt Pariser who ran a world-famous nursing home where the "Homburg diet" was introduced; furthermore Paul Ehrlich, the discoverer of Salvarsan, as well as the writers Chaim N. Bialik and S. J. Agnon and other members of a circle of distinguished intellectuals of the "Russian-Jewish period", who spent some time at Homburg.

Around 1933, the population of close on 17,000 included 400 Jews. By 1939 the figure had declined to 74. In 1942/1943 the remaining Jews – 42 of them – were deported. The terse chronicle of the town records the *Kristallnacht*.

To make up for the absence of relevant documents in the Municipal Archives, a group of *Jungsozialisten* asked older Social Democrats about life in Homburg under Nazi rule and consulted the files of the local *Taunusbote*. The result is a well illustrated book[76] which can be considered as a complement – or possibly a corrective – to the *Festschrift*. It includes a section of 14 pages on the fate of the Homburg Jews.

An article in a local periodical on religious life in Homburg, as represented by the Churches and the Jewish community[77] recalls the history of the synagogue

[75] Angelika Baeumerth, *1200 Jahre Bad Homburg v.d. Höhe – den Bürgern der Stadt Homburg v.d. Höhe zur 1200-Jahrfeier 1982*, published by the Municipality, 80 pp.

[76] *Das Hakenkreuz über Bad Homburg. Eindrücke und Erlebnisse Bad Homburger Sozialdemokraten*, published by the Homburg branch of the Working Group of Young Socialists in the SPD, 1982, 120 pp.

[77] Harro Kieser, 'Aus Homburgs kirchlichem Leben. Kirchen und Israelitische Kultusgemeinde', *Alt-Homburg*, XXV (1982) 6–7, p. 9.

completed in 1866. The former building of the community has since 1956 housed the adult education institute. The Jewish cemetery was the subject of an earlier article in the same journal.[78]

Following a talk delivered in Homburg in 1978 on the fortieth anniversary of the November pogrom, the Homburg Adult Education Circle published a book of reminiscences and reflections by Yitzhak Sophoni Herz (Rechovot) on Homburg and its 600-year old Jewish community.[79] The volume of over 300 pages consists of 44 brief chapters divided into two parts, the first of which, based largely on material in the Municipal Archives, presents documents, statistics and lists, press cuttings and literary references. The second part is mostly autobiographical. Herz includes a survey of Homburg rabbis, beginning in 1825 and ending with his father, Moses Herz who, cantor and teacher since 1898, added rabbinical functions in 1934. The author, born in 1905, tells about his childhood and his experiences as a young man when he worked as a master (*Erzieher*) at the Dinslaken Jewish orphanage.[80] A refugee in Britain, he was in 1940 deported to Australia where he stayed for several years. Herz claims that the *Agudas Jisroel* was founded at Homburg in 1909. In actual fact, only preliminary talks were held at Homburg, and the formal foundation of the organisation took place at Katowice in 1912.[81] Herz also writes about Homburg as a centre of the Russian intelligentsia from 1921 to 1925. He lists twenty names.

Another chapter on the Jewish publishing house of Kauffmann, where the author worked for five years, is disappointing in that it reports comparatively trivial events, but ends with a wholesale condemnation of "Jews belonging to the German-Jewish cultural circle", an opinion also expressed in other parts of the book. One gets the impression that Herz rejects any German-Jewish existence as sinful.

LANGEN: After the war a monument was erected on the site of the synagogue of the former Jewish community which was in Dieburger Straße in Langen, destroyed in 1938. In 1966 a memorial in honour of the fallen Jewish servicemen of the First World War and of the Jewish victims of Nazi persecution was unveiled by the gate of the Jewish cemetery. In November 1978 an exhibition was mounted by the Town Council to mark the anniversary of the pogrom. On that occasion Gerd J. Grein compiled a documentation on the history and the fate of the Jews in Langen.[82] This unassuming duplicated pamphlet achieves its purpose in an exemplary manner. Without scholarly ambitions, the narrative maintains a dispassionate tone. Archival sources, which apparently yielded little material, are tellingly supplemented by the reproduction of advertisements in the local press.

The pamphlet is divided into three parts: a survey of the history of the Jews in the Rhine-Main region is followed by a brief history of the Langen community.

[78]*Ibid.*, XXIV (1981)/11, pp. 181 f.

[79]Yitzhak Sophoni Herz, *Meine Erinnerung an Bad Homburg und seine 600-jährige jüdische Gemeinde (1335–1942)*, Homburg [?1979], 337 pp.

[80]Cf. *LBI Year Book XXIII*, p. 287.

[81]Cf. Jacob Rosenheim, *Erinnerungen 1870–1920*, Frankfurt a. Main 1970, pp. 111 f.

[82]Gerd J. Grein (ed.), *Geschichte der jüdischen Gemeinde zu Langen und ihrer Synagoge*, Langen 1978, 58 pp.

The final chapter, dealing with the bitter end, concludes with a list of 77 Jews who lived in Langen in 1933, indicating their "further fate".

MELSUNGEN on the river Fulda, once attached to the Hesse-Nassau administrative office in Kassel, had a Jewish community at least since the eighteenth century. A comprehensive history of Melsungen published by the Town Council[83] has no separate chapter about the Jews and the synagogue congregation, but there are illuminating scattered references, mostly concerned with the period of persecution. It emerges that the Jewish population increased from 98 in 1835 to 188 in 1880 (almost equalling the number of Roman Catholics), then declined to 112 in 1905, 76 in 1932 and 62 in 1935. The last figure reflects the situation after mass emigration as well as migration within Germany, even within the region, had started. Nearby Kassel was for many the first place of refuge. Eventually 9 Jews were able to emigrate to the USA; 3 each to Palestine, Belgium, Britain, South Africa; and one to South America. Yet, about 40 stayed behind.

NEU-ISENBURG: The young Frankfurt historian Dieter Rebentisch, already well known as the author of a biography of Ludwig Landmann (1868–1945),[84] has added to his reputation by writing with Angelika Raab as co-author a comprehensive history of Neu-Isenburg during the Third *Reich*,[85] in which tribute is paid in particular to Bertha Pappenheim (1859–1936), the Jewish social worker and women's leader who for many years was active in the town.

The book, published under the auspices of the Municipal Administration, is prefaced by a motto taken from Bertha Pappenheim: "To be aware of wrongdoing and yet remain silent means accepting a share in the guilt." One of the eight chapters of the book is devoted to the persecution of the Jews. Out of 60 Jews residing in the town in 1935, 15 were deported and perished. No reliable information is available on the fate of the inmates and staff of the Home for Girls and Children founded in 1907 by the *Jüdischer Frauenbund*. Their combined number had declined from 76 at the end of 1935 to 19 in March 1942. The chapter on the persecution of the Jews is supplemented by 32 well-chosen documents, including records of the Nazi Police and the *Sicherheitsdienst*, extracts from official circulars, reports in the local Nazi press, depositions made from memory by survivors, sentences passed in post-war trials, etc. In July 1978 a memorial tablet was unveiled at the building that had housed the children's home, and a bust of Bertha Pappenheim was placed in the municipal library.

NIEDENSTEIN in the Fritzlar-Homberg district had a substantial Jewish community, the history of which from 1653 to 1866 is the subject of a monograph by Karl E. Demandt,[86] a senior archivist previously known for his authoritative

[83]Jürgen Schmidt, *Melsungen – die Geschichte einer Stadt*, published by the Municipality, 1978, 433 pp.

[84]Dieter Rebentisch, *Ludwig Landmann, Frankfurter Oberbürgermeister der Weimarer Republik* (Frankfurter Historische Abhandlungen, 18) Wiesbaden 1975, 321 pp.

[85]Dieter Rebentisch and Angelika Raab, *Neu-Isenburg zwischen Anpassung und Widerstand, Dokumente über Lebensbedingungen und politisches Verhalten 1933–1945*, published by the Municipality, 1978, 343 pp. For the November pogrom at Neu-Isenburg see also under Offenbach below (note 91).

[86]Karl E. Demandt, *Bevölkerungs- und Sozialgeschichte der jüdischen Gemeinde Niedenstein 1653–1866*. Ein Beitrag zur Geschichte des Judentums in Kurhessen (Darstellung und Dokumente) (Schriften der Kommission für die Geschichte der Juden in Hessen, 5) Wiesbaden 1980, 473 pp.

Hesse bibliography.[87] It is worth noting in this context that in the years 1861 to 1880 Niedenstein had an exceptionally high proportion of Jewish inhabitants, surpassed or equalled by very few German localities. Niedenstein, with 21 per cent, compares with the small Hesse towns of Grebenstein (25 per cent) and Rhina (up to 60 per cent) and South West German localities like Gailingen (60 per cent) and Haigerloch (16 per cent).[88]

Nearly half the substantial volume is taken up by the genealogy of two extended families or clans, the Heinemanns and Naphtalis, including surnames such as Eichengrün, Nagel, Stern, Michaelis, Lotheim, Wertheim, Goldschmidt, Mansbach, Plaut and Kaiser-Wicker, one of the last-named known locally as the "Kaiserkin" ("das Kaiserche von Niedenstein"). The Heinemann family – the older, richer and more rigid of the two – dominated the community until the middle of the nineteenth century. There were scarcely any marriage links with the Naphtalis, and families from outside, too, found it very hard to gain a foothold in the Niedenstein community.

The introductory section surveys the sources and deals with the legal position of the Jewish community from 1650 to 1866, traces its development and structure from 1653, and the administration of the temporal and religious concerns of the community in the nineteenth century. Altogether a noteworthy scholarly contribution.

OFFENBACH – centre of the leather and chemical industries as well as of the arts – celebrated its millennium throughout the year 1977. An "Historical Calendar"[89] published on the occasion by the Municipal Press and Information Office notes under the date of 2nd January 1708 the coming into force of a "Statute of the Jewish Community", and on 3rd September 1956: "The Offenbach Jewish community dedicates its new synagogue in Kaiserstraße". Thus the first and the last of the scattered references to Jewish institutions and the activities of prominent Jewish citizens are among the 300 to 400 events briefly recorded in this attractively produced chronicle. Seligman Reis, believed to be the first Jewish printer in the town, is mentioned in 1715. In 1791 the funeral took place of "Baron Frank", a false Messiah who was born in Podolia in 1726 and came to Offenbach in 1788. In 1882 Salomon Formstecher, the rabbi of the Offenbach community from 1841 to 1889 was made a freeman of the town. According to a census of 27th December 1840, Offenbach then had 9,700 inhabitants, among them 1,700 Catholics and 1,000 Jews. Between 1900 and the beginning of the First World War the membership of the *Israelitische Religionsgemeinde* rose from 1,200 to 2,000. The trend was reversed in 1927. The number declined to 1,400 in 1933 and 950 in 1938.

The fortieth anniversary of November 1938 was marked by the publication of a booklet compiled by the Offenbach district organisation of the "Historical

[87]Karl E. Demandt, *Schrifttum zur Geschichte und geschichtlichen Landeskunde von Hessen* (Veröffentlichungen der Historischen Kommission für Nassau in Wiesbaden, 17), 3 vols., Wiesbaden 1965–1968.

[88]See below, note 96.

[89]*Offenbacher Historischer Kalender*, folder published by the Municipal Press and Information Office, Offenbach 1977.

Commission of the Anti-fascist Association of the Victims of Nazi Persecution".[90] In his introductory remarks the Offenbach Mayor Walter Buckpesch emphasised the documentary character of the work. Nearly half the booklet is taken up by lists – described as incomplete – of "names and fate of Offenbach Jews" and "former Jewish citizens of towns in the Offenbach district".[91] The lists comprise some 600 persons whose fate is specified respectively as "emigrated", "deported" or "unknown", wherever possible stating the sources of the information, mostly records of municipal authorities as well as cemetery records and private depositions. For the rest, the booklet discusses the Nazi brand of antisemitism but touches only to a minor extent on the specific history of the Jews of Offenbach.

WOLFHAGEN: The municipal administration of this North Hesse town issued a weighty and handsomely produced illustrated volume on the history of the town.[92] "To understand the present, we must know the past", says Mayor Otto Eschl in his introductory remarks. Three-quarters of the book are devoted to the post-war period. As far as Jewish life in the town is concerned, we learn that at one time Wolfhagen was the seat of one of the major Jewish communities. In the sixteenth century there were only a few Jewish inhabitants; during the Thirty Years' War three Jewish families lived in the town. In 1728, there were seven "protected Jews", but towards the end of the century the Jewish population had risen to some 60 persons who had their school and synagogue in Schützebergerstraße. By 1827 the figure had risen to 127, and as a result of the Kurhesse Constitution of 1831 which granted the Jews unfettered freedom and equality of legal status, the community continued to grow, with 236 souls in 1850 and some 300 in 1874, about 10 per cent of the population. The majority of economically active Jews engaged in cattle or horse dealing, others had textile or grocery stores, and there were some artisans, notably butchers, locksmiths and shoemakers. From that peak the Jewish population declined to 80 in 1922, a figure which remained roughly constant for the next twenty years. A new synagogue built in Mittelstraße in 1859 was burnt down in 1938.

The period between 1933 and 1945 is dealt with rather perfunctorily, both in general and as regards the fate of the Jews. In the time chart this period does not rate a mention. In the general chapter devoted to the Third *Reich* the author notes: "The slogan 'Germans do not buy in Jewish shops' led in Wolfhagen as elsewhere to the result that a number of families had to give up their shops, and left the town. What became of them appears to be unknown, apart from a few cases." Berthold Kommallein, a former Mayor, contributes 'Notes on the history of the town' in which the fate of some named Jews is hinted at; in conclusion he states with a sigh of relief: it seems "that no Jewish fellow citizen of Wolfhagen was taken from here to an extermination camp". Here he omits the vital word

[90]Karl Schild and Walter Wöll, *Judenpogrom in Offenbach*, zusammengestellt von der Geschichtskommission des VVN-Bundes der Antifaschisten, Kreisverband Offenbach, with a foreword by Max Willner, Chairman of the Offenbach Jewish community established after the war, Frankfurt a. Main 1978, 82 pp.

[91]Including Dietzenbach, Dreieichen, Egelsbach, Heusenstamm, Klein-Krotzenburg, Langen, Neu-Isenburg and Steinheim.

[92]Paul Görlich, *Wolfhagen – Geschichte einer nordhessischen Stadt*, Wolfhagen 1980, 653 pp.

"directly". It appears that Görlich did not himself pursue inquiries into the fate of the Jewish population of this town.

Considering that the Appendix to the book features long lists of the names of Wolfhagen citizens fallen in the First World War (including the Jewish dead) and detailed personal data of those killed or missing in the Second World War, surely it would have been appropriate to add a memorial tablet with the names and personal data of the former Jewish citizens driven into emigration as well as those who perished in the death camps. Conversely, the reproduction of municipal archive records detailing the housing conditions and property holdings of the Jewish inhabitants in 1933 – a section filling several pages – could well have been dispensed with, all the more so as comparative data about the economic standing of other groups of the population are not vouchsafed.

IV. BADEN-WÜRTTEMBERG

BUCHEN, a small town in the Odenwald, celebrated its 700th anniversary in 1980. A memorial volume sponsored by the Municipal Administration[93] contains many references to the Jewish inhabitants. One of them, we learn, was Jacob Mayer, a textile merchant who had made a name for himself as a folk poet and who in 1939, aged 73, opted to end his own life.* Another was Ludwig Schwerin, a well-known painter and graphic artist who was born at Buchen in 1897 and moved to Palestine in 1939. Now both these men have streets named after them. Until then the only street with Jewish associations was the "Judengäßlein", recalling the history of an ancient Jewish community.

Its development is traced in a brief but well-documented chapter by the main author, the archivist Rainer Trunk. In 1925, there were 40 Jewish inhabitants, 3.1 per cent of the total population, as compared with 125 Jews representing 5.4 per cent of the population one hundred years before. As regards the closing years of the nineteenth century, Trunk quotes a remark in Alfred Schwerin's reminiscences:[94]

> "The Jews of my native city constituted a solid small-town middle class that was in every way at one with the rest of the population, and shared in its joys and sorrows."

Of the 34 Jewish inhabitants left in 1933, nearly half managed to emigrate to Western countries, the others perished; most of them were deported in 1940 to Gurs – and died later in Auschwitz. In addition to the community, its synagogue and school and the religious dignitaries, Trunk briefly discusses the occupational and social structure of the Buchen Jews during the period from 1800 to 1933. They were mostly engaged in cattle dealing and the trade in agricultural produce. One Jewish inhabitant, J. Strauss, was the first editor of the *Buchener Anzeiger*, founded in 1865.

EBERBACH AM NECKAR in North Baden celebrated its 750th anniversary in

[93]Rainer Trunk (ed.), *700 Jahre Stadt Buchen. Beiträge zur Stadtgeschichte*, Buchen 1980, 376 pp.

* On suicide under the Nazi regime see the previously cited essay by Konrad Kwiet in this volume of the Year Book – (Ed.).

[94]Alfred Schwerin, *Erinnerungen an Jugend und Elternhaus*, Basel 1968.

1977 and issued a *Festschrift* on the occasion.[95] Yet this publication contains no mention of the fact that a Jewish community (with some 70 members in 1924) existed until 1940, and that its synagogue was duly burnt down in 1938. On inquiry, the Mayor explained the omission, admittedly an oversight; it had been crowded out because of the limited space allotted to the publication. At the end of 1979, a memorial stone was placed at the site of the former synagogue.

GAILINGEN in Baden, near the Swiss frontier, is one of the few German towns – Rhina in Hesse and Haigerloch in Württemberg are others – where the Jews at one time formed the majority of the population. From 1870 to 1884 Gailingen had a Jewish Mayor, the merchant Leopold Guggenheim (1818–1884). By 1932, the number of Jewish inhabitants had declined to some 400. The memory of those comparatively happy days is preserved by a beautifully kept Jewish cemetery on the outskirts of the town and by a memorial tablet in the town centre at the site of the synagogue built in 1836 and destroyed in 1938.

Virtually unrecorded in the past, the history of the Gailingen Jews is now the subject of a monograph[96] compiled with diligence and compassion by two members of the younger generation with a sense of human as well as scholarly responsibility. The result of their labours is a well illustrated and documented volume. As in most publications of this kind, attention is focused first and foremost on the end of the community and the fate of its members. Relevant documents include reports on the political climate in the town between 1928 and 1934; diary entries of a young Gailingen Jew in 1932/1933; reports on the pogrom of November 1938 and the deportations to Gurs in 1940.* Yet over a third of the book deals with life in Gailingen before the First World War. This is documented in particular by extracts from the "records of the tours of inspection of the Grand-Ducal Regional Office in Constance from 1878 to 1909", which, in addition to matters such as Jewish school education and the Jewish hospital, cover even internal Jewish controversies. The book notes that relations between Jews and Christians were generally good, without denying occasional differences, which in some instances the authors take the trouble to specify and explain. They also inform the reader about Jewish social institutions, e.g. the Jewish Regional Hostel "Friedrichsheim" (today an old people's home of the Constance Rural District), and about Jewish representation on the Gailingen Citizens' Committee. Most of the economically active Jews made a secure but modest living as cattle dealers. Dr. Sigmund Heilbronn, who managed to emigrate in 1939, had for years acted as the Paupers' Physician at the princely salary of 300 Marks p.a. In 1900, the Town Councillor Simon Rothschild donated the official municipal coat of arms, which in 1979 was restored to its place of honour in the Town Hall.

Every year the days preceding the high holidays are marked by reverential

[95]*Festschrift zur Feier des 750-jährigen Bestehens der Stadt Eberbach im Jahre 1977*, Stadt Eberbach/Neckar 1977, 124 pp.

[96]Eckhardt Friedrich and Dagmar Schmieder-Friedrich (eds.), *Die Gailinger Juden. Materialien zur Geschichte der jüdischen Gemeinde Gailingen aus ihrer Blütezeit und den Jahren der gewaltsamen Auflösung* (Schriftenreihe des Arbeitskreises für Regionalgeschichte, 3) Konstanz 1981, 126 pp.

*See the photograph reproduced between pp. 184–185 in the essay by Sybil Milton, 'The Expulsion of Polish Jews from Germany: October 1938 to July 1939 – A Documentation', in this volume of the Year Book – (Ed.).

gatherings at the Jewish memorial sites, organised by the Society for the Preservation of the Gailingen Jewish Cemetery with its seat in neighbouring Diessenhofen, just across the frontier in Switzerland. In 1982 these functions were attended by Rabbi Jehuda Bohrer from Israel, one of the sons of the last Gailingen Rabbi, Mordechai Bohrer, who had died at Dachau in 1938.[97]

GÖPPINGEN and JEBENHAUSEN: In 1900 the village of Jebenhausen was incorporated in the municipality of Göppingen. The first monograph on the Jews in both places, a comprehensive volume, was published in 1927 by Aron Tänzer[98] who was rabbi for the Göppingen region from 1907 to 1937, interrupted only by war service as an army chaplain in the East. Tänzer played a prominent part also as a lecturer and author and in public life, especially in adult education.

The centenary of the dedication of the synagogue in Freihofstraße was the occasion for an exhibition 'Jews in Jebenhausen and Göppingen 1777–1945' and for the publication of a pamphlet with the same title.[99] The pamphlet opens with a section on Jebenhausen, followed by twelve sections on Göppingen. Inserted between the two communal histories is a survey of Jewish festivals and customs, which seems out of place in this context. Its inclusion may have been dictated by the arrangement of the exhibition.

One of the sections on Göppingen is devoted to the centenary of the synagogue, the others deal chiefly with Dr. Tänzer and his activities, with the period of persecution and the early dissolution of the community of roughly 400 Jews residing in Göppingen at the beginning of 1933. Over 300 were able to emigrate. The centenary of the birth of Aron Tänzer in the spring of 1971 was marked by the placing of a memorial tablet at the site of the synagogue destroyed in 1938.

The section on Jebenhausen outlines the legal status and occupational structure of the Jewish inhabitants, who at one time represented a substantial proportion of the total population (238 out of 650 in 1805) and describes the Jewish institutions, notably the rabbinate, the school, the synagogue and the cemetery. It is noted that Heinrich Sontheim, a well-known singer and member of the Stuttgart Court Theatre, who died in 1912, was born at Jebenhausen.

HOCKENHEIM, a small town near Mannheim known for its asparagus and tobacco cultivation, was the subject of a book published in 1933 on the 1,200th anniversary of the town, which included a well-documented section on the Jews.[100] The same author, Ernst Brauch, published in 1965 another comprehensive book on the town, presented in a popular style.[101] A brief chapter deals with the history of the Jews, opening with a sketchy review of conditions in the eighteenth and nineteenth centuries. In 1932 the *Israelitische Gemeinde* of the town numbered 50 persons. Turning to the period of the Third *Reich*, the author attempts to give information about the fate of individual Jewish families, above

[97]Cf. E. G. Lowenthal (ed.), *Bewährung im Untergang. Ein Gedenkbuch*, Stuttgart 1965, pp. 29 f.

[98]Aron Tänzer, *Die Geschichte der Juden in Jebenhausen und Göppingen*, Stuttgart 1927, 573 pp.

[99]Dieter Kauß, *Die Juden in Jebenhausen und Göppingen 1777 bis 1945* (Veröffentlichungen des Stadtarchivs Göppingen, 16), Göppingen 1981, 39 pp.

[100]Ernst Brauch, *Das Hockenheimer Heimatbuch. Aus zwölf Jahrhunderten Geschichte Hockenheims*, Hockenheim 1933, 207 pp.

[101]Ernst Brauch, *Hockenheim-Stadt im Auf- und Umbruch*, Hockenheim 1965, 462 pp. The chapter on the fate of the Hockenheim Jews pp. 185–194.

all of those who were able to emigrate and thus escape the mass deportations of Baden Jews in October 1940. Only a few succeeded; the author lists their names.[102]

MANNHEIM: On the occasion of the fortieth anniversary of the deportation of the Jews of Baden to Gurs, a former Mayor of Mannheim, Karl Otto Watzinger, wrote an essay in *Mannheimer Hefte* on the Jewish community during the Weimar period.[103] This journal had repeatedly recalled the memory of prominent Mannheim Jews or citizens of Jewish descent. Watzinger's essay is in two parts. In the first, after briefly outlining the position of the Jewish community within the municipal polity, he proceeds to a more detailed study of the organisational set-up of the commune, based largely on the former *Mannheimer Israelitisches Gemeindeblatt* and supplemented by statistical tables. The second part is devoted to the lives and activities of sixteen Jewish personages who played a prominent part in the public life of the town. The series, mostly illustrated with good photographs, begins with Alice Bensheimer (1864–1935), who was active in the women's movement, and ends with Heinrich Wetzlar (1868–1943), a Regional Court judge who perished at Theresienstadt. The others include the Rabbi Isaak Unna (who died in 1948 in Jerusalem) and Rabbi Max Gruenewald, now the President of the Leo Baeck Institute.

A year later, Watzinger followed up this essay with a study of the Mannheim Jewish community during the period of the Grand Duchy (1803–1918), when both the town and its Jewish community prospered.[104] This study, too, is in two parts, dealing on the one hand with the internal development of the community (reform movement, schism; community statutes; social welfare work; occupational structure of the Jews and their part in the economic life of the town, etc.), and presenting on the other hand pen-portraits of sixteen prominent Jews, eight of them not from Mannheim itself, but from smaller localities, mostly in South West Germany: Ludwig Frank (1874–1914), barrister and Social Democrat politician from Nonnenweier;[105] the social welfare worker Elise Gutmann (-Cahn, 1848–1923) from Jählingen (near Durlach); Felix Hecht (1847–1910) a banker and writer on economic policy, from Friedberg (Hesse); Bernhard Herschel (1837-1920), a tobacco merchant and Municipal Councillor, from Emmerich; Bertha Hirsch (born 1850 at Worms, resident in Mannheim since 1858), who was the centre of a circle of intellectuals; Moritz Lenel (1811–1876), a merchant with interests in politics and economic policy, a member of the Synagogue Council, from Ladenburg; the judge Nathan Stein (1857–1927) from Neckarsulm; and the educationist Simon Wolff (1789–1860) from Hechingen. The remaining eight were natives of Mannheim.

A more recent essay in *Mannheimer Hefte* is devoted to the history of the main synagogue completed in 1855 on the site of its predecessor which had become too

[102] Cf. also Franz Hundsnurscher and Gerhard Taddey, *Die jüdischen Gemeinden in Baden, Denkmale, Geschichte, Schicksale*, Stuttgart 1968, pp. 133 f. See also *LBI Year Book XV*, p. 232.

[103] Karl Otto Watzinger, 'Die jüdische Gemeinde Mannheim in der Weimarer Republik', *Mannheimer Hefte*, 1980, No. 2, pp. 70–92.

[104] Karl Otto Watzinger, 'Die jüdische Gemeinde Mannheims in der großherzoglichen Zeit (1803–1918)', *ibid.* 1981, No. 2, pp. 91–114.

[105] See under Nonnenweier below.

small for the community.[106] Work on the erection of the new synagogue had started in 1851. The author deals at length with the lay-out and equipment of the synagogue, which included an organ; with the solemn dedication of the building, and with its destruction in the course of the pogrom of November 1938. He also touches on aspects relating to the history of architecture, which have been treated in greater detail by the art historian Harold Hammer-Schenk.[107] The essay is accompanied by striking photographs showing the exterior and interior of the two synagogues and the destruction of the second one.

NONNENWEIER, a rural commune near Lahr, had a substantial Jewish community from 1707 on, which in 1925 still numbered 80 souls, or about 5 per cent of the population, as the survey of the Jewish communities in Baden[108] briefly notes. The detailed structure of the Nonnenweier community and the social, economic and religious life of the local Jews are the subject of a scholarly monograph[109] based on material at the Stuttgart Central State Archives and – more importantly – on the questioning of former Jewish inhabitants of Nonnenweier, now scattered over three continents, in Alsace, USA and Israel, and of a few Christian citizens, some of whom, however, were not entirely free of prejudice.

Some people may still remember that Ludwig Frank, the Mannheim barrister and Social Democrat politician (*Reichstag* Deputy since 1907), who was killed during the early stages of the First World War, was born in 1874 at Nonnenweier. In 1974, a *Bundeswehr* barracks in Mannheim was named after him. Very few, especially among the young generation, are likely to remember Alexander Moch (1889–1977), a farmer who took over the direction of Jewish agricultural training establishments (Neuendorf near Berlin, England, Kenya, Israel), who also was a native of Nonnenweier.

SCHWETZINGEN in North Baden witnessed in the years 1976 to 1978 a novel and indeed exemplary enterprise. In the school year 1976/1977, Albrecht Lohrbächer, doubling as parson and teacher, introduced in the Evangelical Religion lessons in the seventh form of the *Hebel-Gymnasium* the project 'Jews and Judaism'. To begin with the pupils ascertained the names of former Jewish inhabitants, gathered recollections of some of the older Schwetzingen citizens and sent out about 130 letters, most of them addressed to former Jewish citizens, requesting them to co-operate with the scheme. In addition the Archives were searched for relevant material, the voluminous regional literature was scanned, and Yad Vashem in Jerusalem was consulted. Many replies were received from many countries, some of them including documents or photographs. These facts are reported in Lohrbächer's concluding remarks, winding up the documentation

[106] Volker Keller in *Mannheimer Hefte*, 1982, No. 1, pp. 2–14.

[107] Harold Hammer-Schenk, *Synagogen in Deutschland. Geschichte einer Baugattung im 19. und 20. Jahrhundert (1780–1933)* (Hamburger Beiträge zur Geschichte der deutschen Juden, VIII), 2 vols., Hamburg 1981, 975 pp.

[108] Hundsnurscher/Taddey, *op. cit.*

[109] Elfriede Labsch-Benz, *Die jüdische Gemeinde Nonnenweier. Jüdisches Leben und Brauchtum in einer badischen Landgemeinde zu Beginn des 20. Jahrhunderts*, master's thesis, Strasbourg 1977, 144 pp.

that was the fruit of this enterprise, published under the title *They belonged among us*.[110]

The duplicated study contains a list of names of the members of 31 families (stating personal data as well as details of housing conditions, occupation and fate), that is to say, the names of all Jews who resided at least temporarily in Schwetzingen between 30th January 1933 and 22nd October 1940 (the day when the Jews of Baden were deported to Gurs). In 1933 Schwetzingen had some 90 Jewish inhabitants, roughly 1 per cent of the population. More than one in four of the Schwetzingen Jews were deported and perished.

Without Lohrbächer's understanding and his personal commitment combined with his strict methodical approach it would not have been possible to compile this documentation, which constitutes a welcome, and in its comprehensiveness so far unprecedented contribution above all to the social and personal history of Schwetzingen's former *Israelitische Gemeinde*, even though a history and family book of the Schwetzingen Jews written by the teachers and cantors Simon Eichstetter (1865–1927) and Heinrich Bloch (1885–1949) are listed among "other than printed sources". The usefulness of the documentation can be gauged from chapter headings such as 'From the protected Jew living on sufferance to the respected citizen (Jews in Schwetzingen 1700–1933)', 'The Jewish community in Schwetzingen, its peculiar traits and its activities', 'The end: suffering, expulsion and extermination of Schwetzingen Jews in the Third *Reich*'.

This documentation can be considered a model and example, presenting a coherent and comprehensive account, not restricted exclusively or predominantly to the period of persecution. Here it has been done, and, granted diligence and some imagination, it can be done again.

V. BAVARIA

Before 1933, there were some 41,000 persons of the Jewish faith in Bavaria, of whom 18,600 lived in the biggest cities, Munich and Nuremberg; 5,900 in Würzburg, Fürth and Augsburg; 3,400 in six other sizeable towns; the remaining 13,000 were scattered over some 200 small or very small rural communes, more than half of them in Lower Franconia (also known as Mainfranken). Until recently, the only source available for the detailed structure of the Jewish communities in Bavaria was the last pre-war guide to the Jewish communities throughout Germany published in 1932 by the *Zentralwohlfahrtsstelle*.[111]

Now a comprehensive survey of the Bavarian Jewish communites, published in 1979, is available.[112] It forms part of the project on *Resistance and Persecution in Bavaria 1933–1945*, launched by the Munich Institute of Contemporary History in

[110] Albrecht Lohrbächer, *Sie gehörten zu uns. Geschichte und Schicksal der Schwetzinger Juden*, published by the Mayor's Office, Schwetzingen 1978, duplicated, 125 pp.

[111] *Führer durch die jüdische Gemeindeverwaltung und Wohlfahrtspflege in Deutschland 1932–33*, hrsg. von der Zentralwohlfahrtsstelle der deutschen Juden, Berlin n.d., 594 pp.

[112] *Die jüdischen Gemeinden in Bayern 1918–1945. Geschichte und Zerstörung*, edited by Baruch Z. Ophir (Jerusalem) and Falk Wiesemann (Munich), Munich-Vienna 1979, 511 pp.

conjunction with the Bavarian State Archives. The book is based on the Hebrew work *Pinkas Hakehilloth, Germany – Bavaria*, published in 1972 by Yad Vashem in Jerusalem. The lexico-chronological reports on the communities are arranged alphabetically for each of the seven Bavarian Administrative Regions. Attention is focused predominantly on the period of persecution, in particular on the pogrom of November 1938, as the beginning of the final catastrophe. The Weimar period is treated much less fully, which creates a certain imbalance, since the economic and social development during the fifteen years of the Weimar Republic cannot be downgraded as a "prelude", but deserves to be studied for its own sake.

As regards the rural localities, the facts and data provided (demographic statistics; institutions and organisations; antisemitic occurrences, including economic boycott; emigration and "final solution") generally meet their purpose. The same cannot be said about the treatment of the towns, where far more extensive material relating to Jewish communal life, organisations, internal Jewish trends as well as to individual personages is available and could have been used. The selection of material is not always balanced and objective. At times the reader is given the impression that in the eleven major communities, in which after all 70 per cent of Bavaria's Jewish population were living, the Orthodox element was both numerically stronger and more influential than the groups of more Bavarian-Jewish or Jewish-liberal tendencies. To mention only two typical instances, pride of place is given to Nuremberg's smaller Orthodox *Adat Jisrael* Community founded in 1875 and to Munich's Orthodox *Ohel Jacob* Association rather than to the larger main congregations such as the *Israelitische Kultusgemeinde* in Nuremberg. Why, one wonders, is the numerically and organisationally important German-Jewish sector, which was so active in the communities and in Jewish politics treated so cavalierly? One must not lose sight of the fact that in Bavaria as in the rest of Germany, already during the Weimar period and even more decisively after 1933, Jewish life was supported, fashioned and financed by the broad and economically strong strata of the Jewish commercial and academic middle class whose orientation was predominantly German-liberal and Jewish-liberal. This is not even marginally noted, whereas on dozens of occasions attention is drawn to local branches of the Jewish National Fund. Nor do we find any recognition of the fact that, right from the beginning of 1933 to the end of 1938 the *Zentralausschuß für Hilfe und Aufbau* in Berlin, which soon afterwards became the Finance Department of the *Reichsvertretung*, had systematically organised the collection of funds in order to maintain Jewish life and Jewish work in Germany – and that includes Bavaria – as effectively as possible in the circumstances.

In other respects, too, those responsible for the compilation have not always lived up to the desirable standards of care, consistency and clarity (as regards names, designation of offices, titles). Furthermore, one has to ask what criteria were adopted in singling out individuals who had made significant contributions to Jewish public life in Bavaria. Looking back on an historical period such as that from 1918 to 1945, it would have been of special interest to "re-live" the events as fully as possible. Instances of misplaced emphasis as well as factual errors suggest that for the sake of greater scholarly objectivity alone, in the event of a new edition a revision would be needed involving corrections and amplifications as well as cuts and the elimination of longueurs. Lastly, in a work as ambitious as this one is, some care ought to be given to proper source references, which are indispensable.

ALTENSTADT: A carefully illustrated, unassuming book on the history of this small Swabian market town, published to mark the completion of the new Catholic parish church in 1965,[113] has a concluding chapter on the Jews of Altenstadt, based largely on a private research paper published in 1931 by the teacher Hermann Rose (1870–1936), a native of the town and its last Jewish religious official.[114]

In 1980 or 1981, the Administrative Officer of the Neu-Ulm Rural District arranged for the publication of a photographic reprint of Rose's paper that had long been out of print. The presence of several Jewish families in Altenstadt, it appears, is documented as early as 1650, but a Jewish community in the proper sense existed only since 1719. Rose quotes the relevant *Schutzbrief*. In a narrative embroidered with many episodes and details of human interest, Rose describes the development in the nineteenth century as well as during the First World War and the post-war period. Much space is given to the history of the two synagogues (1725–1802; 1803–1938), the Jewish primary school and the Jewish cemetery. The Jewish population of Altenstadt reached a peak of over 400 in 1834. By 1850 the number had declined to 250, and by 1931 to a mere 50, owing to large-scale migration to bigger towns.

Rose's study is "dedicated in profound reverence and gratitude to Sir Hugo Hirst, Bt., London, a loyal son and helpful supporter of the local Jewish community, as well as to all other generous helpers who have contributed to this work of reverent remembrance". Hirst (1863–1943), who was later raised to the peerage, was born at Altenstadt, when his name was Hirsch. In his youth he moved from Munich to London where for many years he was at the head of the General Electric Company.

ERLANGEN: Over fifty years ago, Leopold David wrote a history of the Erlangen Jewish community.[115] A recent pamphlet sponsored jointly by the municipality and the regional Society for Christian-Jewish Co-operation and written by Ilse Sponsel, widow of Fritz Sponsel, for many years Social Democrat Mayor of the town, concentrates on the fate of the Jewish community under Nazi rule.[116] The reader gathers from somewhat scattered data that Jews had settled in Erlangen since 1861; in 1878 the town had some 180 Jewish inhabitants, a figure that rose to 224 in 1914, subsequently dropping to 160 in 1926, 117 in 1933 and a

[113]See *LBI Year Book XI*, pp. 332 f.

[114]Hermann Rose, *Geschichtliches der Israelitischen Kultusgemeinde Altenstadt*, Altenstadt 1931, 93 pp.; reprinted 1981.

[115]Leopold David, *Geschichte der Israelitischen Kultusgemeinde Erlangen*, Erlangen 1931.

[116]Ilse Sponsel, *Das Schicksal der Erlanger Judengemeinde in der NS-Zeit* (Erlanger Materialien, No. 4), published jointly by the Erlangen Municipality and the Society for Christian-Jewish Co-operation Nürnberg-Fürth-Erlangen-Bamberg, Erlangen 1982, 43 pp. The pamphlet is the slightly re-edited offprint of a chapter in: Jürgen Sandweg and Helmut Richter (eds.), *Erlangen – Von der Strumpfer- zur Siemensstadt*, Erlangen 1982.

mere 63 in 1935. Between May 1938 and the end of 1939, 30 Jews must have left the town. Only 19 remained by the spring of 1940.

The author notes that the study was undertaken at the suggestion of former Jewish citizens who had emigrated. Some of the footnotes – totalling over 100 – indicate that relations with such ex-citizens abroad have lately been intensified. Otherwise the notes consist of references to the available literature[117] and documentation. Records kept by the Municipal Archives, the University and some schools were instrumental in ascertaining many details, especially those pertaining to individuals.

In the general narrative, too little space is given to events specific to Erlangen as distinct from the wider scene in Bavaria and Germany as a whole. The arrangement of the material follows naturally from the gathering pace of the persecution. The value of the pamphlet is due at least as much to the photographs illustrating local conditions and events as to the text. It might have been better in the circumstances to embark on a comprehensive history of the Erlangen Jews instead of restricting the scope of the study to the destruction of the community.

Some years earlier, on the occasion of the *Woche der Brüderlichkeit* in 1978, Ilse Sponsel contributed two essays to a local journal. One of them dealt with the history of Erlangen's Jewish cemetery,[118] the other was devoted to three University professors: the surgeon Jakob Hertz (Bayreuth 1816-Erlangen 1871), the physiologist Isidor Rosenthal (Labischin, East Prussia 1836–Erlangen 1915), and the great mathematician Emmy Noether, born 1882 at Erlangen, Professor at Göttingen 1922–1934, subsequently at Bryn Mawr College in Pennsylvania, where she died in 1935.[119]

FLOSS in the Upper Palatinate issued a *Festschrift* on its millennium in 1976, which dealt also with the history of Jewish settlement in the town.[120] In 1684 four Jews received permission to settle on the Judenberg, which became an independent political commune, a ghetto with its own house numbers, its own mayor, its own night watchman, etc. It survived until 1850, as the last ghetto in Bavaria, comprising at the time 72 Jewish families totalling 391 souls. Joseph Goldmann, a teacher of religion, wrote in 1845 an "historical-topographic description of the Judenberg near Floß". He noted the "frugal living" of the Jewish population and the great age which many of them attained. They were artisans (weavers, tanners, furriers), traders or shopkeepers. Goldmann pointed out that "in recent times" the population had substantially declined, a remark that refers presumably to the increasing emigration to the USA. In 1920 the *Israelitische Kultusgemeinde* numbered barely 20; even so a religious official (Hirsch Worimklein, Moritz Moses) continued to be engaged.

The first synagogue, built in 1719 by eight families with funds raised partly by levies, partly by voluntary contributions, was burnt down in 1813. A new

[117]Notably to *Die jüdischen Gemeinden in Bayern . . . , op. cit.*

[118]Ilse Sponsel, 'Die Geschichte des jüdischen Friedhofs in Erlangen', *Das Neue Erlangen, Zeitschrift für Wissenschaft, Wirtschaft und kulturelles Leben*, No. 45, March 1978, pp. 3321 ff.

[119]Ilse Sponsel, 'Drei Lebensbilder – Jüdische Schicksale in unserer Stadt', *ibid.*, pp. 3308 ff.

[120]Adolf Wolfgang Schuster, *100 Jahre Floß. Zum Heimatfest 1976 des Marktes Floß im Oberpfälzer Wald*, published by the Floß Municipality, 1976, pp. 334–344.

stone-built synagogue, which took two years to build, was completed in 1817. We know that the small community celebrated its 250th anniversary in 1934.[121] No Jew is living in Floß today, but a monument placed at the Jewish cemetery recalls the memory of the victims of the nearby Flossenbürg concentration camp.

MUNICH: Both before and after his emigration, the economist and social scientist Werner J. Cahnman (Munich 1902-New York 1980)[122] wrote historical-sociological studies on the Jews of his native town.[123] The last paper, written one year before his death, is given a highly personal note by some of the author's reminiscences. Cahnman, who went to school and university in Munich, was from 1930 to 1933 the *Syndikus* of the Bavarian regional organisation of the *Centralverein deutscher Staatsbürger jüdischen Glaubens* (C.V.), with its seat in Munich. Until he emigrated shortly before the outbreak of the war, he was in close touch with Jewish life in Munich and in Bavaria. Of the five chapters of the study (structure of the Jewish community; antisemitism and Jewish reaction; the C.V. in Munich; isolation, atomisation, annihilation; flight and death), the first and the last two appear to be the most interesting. The first chapter, with its survey of the demographic structure, the community and Jewish organisation, provides a point of departure. The last two chapters recall the main events in the life of the Munich Jews between 1933 and 1939. The study derives much of its value from the author's rich fund of memories. Certain episodes, such as the early destruction of the main synagogue in Herzog-Max-Straße – carried out in June 1938 on Hitler's personal orders – are treated at somewhat greater length.

WÜRZBURG, centre of MAINFRANKEN: A doctoral thesis of over 1,000 pages has been devoted to the Jews in Mainfranken, and in particular to the deportations of Würzburg Jews.[124]

The author begins with the statement that

> "during the search for material . . . I encountered in some cases a decisively negative attitude manifested for instance by the fact that written inquiries to official bodies often remained unanswered".

The text of the monograph runs to nearly 650 pages. To this is added an extensive appendix with frequently instructive footnotes and a series of photographs of varying quality, published here probably for the first time. Even so, the author points out, the study cannot claim to have covered the subject completely, since many documents (particularly in regard to Schweinfurt) had been lost in the course of the war; also he had had no access to the records of

[121]See *C.-V.-Zeitung* of 21st September and 5th October 1934.

[122]Cf. *LBI Year Book IV* (1959), IX (1964) and XIX (1974).

[123]See Werner J. Cahnman, 'Die Münchner Judenbeschreibung von 1804', *Zeitschrift für die Geschichte der Juden in Deutschland*, 1937, pp. 180–188; also 'Die soziale Gliederung der Münchner jüdischen Gemeinde und ihre Wandlungen', in Hans Lamm, *Von Juden in München*, Munich 1958, pp. 31–42; 'The decline of the Munich Jewish community 1933–38', *Jewish Social Studies*, III/3 (1941) pp. 285–300; and 'Die Juden in München 1918–1943', *Zeitschrift für Bayerische Landesgeschichte*, 42 (1979), pp. 403–461.

[124]Herbert Schultheis, *Juden in Mainfranken 1933–1945. Unter besonderer Berücksichtigung der Deportationen Würzburger Juden* (Bad Neustädter Beiträge zur Geschichte und Heimatkunde Frankens, 1), doctoral thesis, Neustadt a.d. Saale 1980, 1040 pp.

criminal court and tribunal proceedings; nor had he been able, in the absence of records, to investigate the history of the students' corporation *Salia*. Schultheis's narrative deals not only with November 1938 and what was to come but also with the events of the early years of the Third *Reich*.

The following 21 towns of Mainfranken and Lower Franconia are considered: Alzenau, Aschaffenburg, Brückenau, Ebern, Gemünden, Gerolzhofen, Hammelburg, Haßfurt, Hofheim, Karlstadt, Bad Kissingen, Kitzingen, Königshofen im Grabfeld, Lohr, Marktheidenfeld, Mellrichstadt, Miltenberg, Neustadt a.d. Saale, Oberburg, Ochsenfurt and Würzburg. In 1933 there existed some 125 Jewish communities in this area, each with a synagogue or at least a prayer room of its own. They are listed in this work. In nearly every case the year of construction is placed on record, and the fate of the building is briefly indicated. Some of the listed synagogues date back to the early years of the eighteenth century, notably those at Marktbreit (1714), Höchberg (1721) and Veitshöchheim (prior to 1730).

VI. LOWER SAXONY

After laborious investigations Rabbi Zvi Asaria completed his history of the Jews in the territory of the present Federal State of Lower Saxony in 1979.[125] Undoubtedly a great deal of time and effort went into the collection of the relevant material relating to the last 150 to 200 years. As regards "ancient times", little information of substance is presented. Here, "the sources fall silent", as the author repeatedly notes.

The book is divided into sections covering the six regional rabbinates, which functioned well into the mid-1930s: Hanover, Stade, Eastern Friesland and Hildesheim with a combined total of 15,000 Jews in 1932, furthermore Brunswick with 1,750 and Oldenburg with 1,500 Jews at the time. In 1980 no more than 540 Jews were registered with their communities in the whole of Lower Saxony, nearly 400 of them in Hanover.

Asaria is interested above all in the development of the organisation of Jewish religious life. He deals with the rabbis and their status, teachers and their remuneration, statutes and institutions of the Jewish communities, Jewish schools and education. More or less prominent "secular" Jewish citizens are considered for inclusion only in second place, in so far as the author deems them to be truly representative or typical of Lower Saxony. His preoccupation with the growth of antisemitism in Germany leads to a lack of balance in the presentation of Jewish history. The text is interspersed with theological reflections and lengthy digressions about the Jewish mission.

The content of this handsome volume does not live up to its ambitious title. The author relies in the main on three sources: firstly, on records of the public archives, but only those designated as pertaining to Jewish affairs, while neglecting other files which nevertheless may contain relevant material;

[125] Zvi Asaria, *Die Juden in Niedersachsen von den ältesten Zeiten bis zur Gegenwart*, Leer (Ostfriesland) 1979, 676 pp.

secondly, on recent, and to a less extent on older publications in the field of local, regional and Jewish communal history; thirdly, on personal information supplied by a limited number of individuals, in the main Jewish emigrants, as well as on data obtained from many municipalities and communes. About 20 per cent of the book consists of documents or reports presented in such a way that the reader is often left guessing where a quotation ends and the author's comment begins. Then, again, the local literature is cited at length – some passages running into several pages – verbatim or near verbatim without proper acknowledgement, particularly with regard to Brunswick, Göttingen, Nordhorn, Oldenburg and Schöningen. In addition, some distortions arise as a result of the author's subjective attitude. It would appear that he accepts as Jews only those who were either Orthodox or Zionists or had come from Eastern Europe. Jews who up till 1933 looked upon themselves as German citizens, who indeed were patriots, feeling at home in Germany are the butt of his strictures. He thus betrays the inadequacy of his knowledge and understanding of the conditions of that period as well as of his acquaintance with the relevant literature. Asaria does not shrink from openly displaying his dislike and disrespect. Whereas Orthodox rabbis are invariably described in eulogistic terms as "well known", "famous" or "eminent", those of divergent views are presented in very different terms. Thus, Dr. Leo Baeck, who after all was the last great spiritual leader of the entire body of German Jewry, is introduced as plain "Rabbi Baeck", divested of his academic status, and in one place he is described as the "chief exponent of liberal Judaism so-called"! Brunswick's liberal senior rabbis Paul Rieger, Hugo Schiff and Kurt Wilhelm are given short shrift. The last-named scholar who has done so much to expound and further Jewish studies,[126] is wrongly described as a "publicist". The last rabbi at Hildesheim, Josef Schwarz, is altogether left out. According to Asaria, the Hildesheim community and *B'nai B'rith* lodge were "anti-Zionist". His bias is also manifest in his references to the *Centralverein*, after all the largest organisation of German Jews, with a branch in Hanover as well. He gives it a number of assorted names, culminating in "C.V. jüdischer Frontsoldaten".

Nor is the book free of contradictions. Whereas in his own introduction he praises the Jewish professors in Göttingen as "pillars of science", he mentions only two of them in the section on Göttingen. The rest are left out – the author explains – since they maintained "virtually no relations with the Jewish community". Other shortcomings of this work, in particular with regard to the scholarly apparatus are too numerous to mention here in detail.

BRUNSWICK: A brief sketch of the history of the Jews in Brunswick[127] is contained in a pamphlet published on the occasion of the placing of a memorial tablet at the site of the synagogue built in 1875 by the Brunswick architect Konstantin Uhde and demolished in 1940. In 1975, a local "Brunswick Synagogue Committee" decided to place the tablet. The ceremony took place on

[126]Cf. Robert Weltsch in the Introduction to *LBI Year Book XII* (1967), p. XI.

[127]Ralph Busch, 'Zur Geschichte der Juden in Braunschweig', in *Der ehemaligen Jüdischen Gemeinde Braunschweigs zum Gedenken* (Veröffentlichungen des Braunschweigischen Landesmuseums, 11) Brunswick 1977, pp. 9–13.

23rd September 1976. Busch's essay is largely based on an earlier Book of Remembrance for the Jewish citizens.[128]

GÖTTINGEN: In his introduction to Peter Wilhelm's book on the Göttingen Jewish community, published in 1973,[129] Cuno Ch. Lehrmann (1905–1977), who ended his career as the Chief Rabbi of Lower Saxony, regretted that the book was stopping short at the very point where "the great German-Jewish symbiosis initiated by Moses Mendelssohn came into full bloom". It appears that the author heeded this remark when five years later he published a study on the Synagogengemeinde in Göttingen, Rosdorf and Geismar 1880–1942.[130]

The first part of the book, a history of the community up to 1920, based on the records of the Municipal Archives, concentrates almost exclusively on internal Jewish organisation; the second part, almost as long as the first and no less illuminating, deals with anti-Jewish actions during the Nazi era till 1942. This somewhat lopsided arrangement is probably due to the erratic availability of sources. There are several lists: 440 members of the community during the period 1850–1942 (giving their dates of birth and death, accompanied in most cases by occupational data); shopkeepers; landed proprietors; secondary school pupils; some 80 Göttingen University professors (only a few of whom were members of the community). A list of 'Rabbis and teachers 1850–1938', placed at the beginning of the book, does not in every respect stand up to scrutiny.

HANOVER: An exhibition mounted on the fortieth anniversary of the pogrom of November 1938 by the Hanover Historical Museum, the Municipal Archives, the Historical Institute of the local University and the Municipal Cultural Committee was accompanied by an informative, copiously illustrated booklet.[131] One of the contributions is a report of his personal experiences by the Hanover barrister Horst Berkowitz, a man severely disabled in the First World War. He survived a spell at Buchenwald in 1938, and towards the end of the war the labour camp at Ahlem near Hanover, the site of the former *Israelitische Gartenbauschule*.[132] A biography of Berkowitz was published in 1979.[133] Born at Königsberg in 1898, from 1902 residing in Hanover, Berkowitz had a life dogged by tragedy, in which, however, humanity always triumphed over justice, grief and persecution. The narrative centres on Berkowitz's activity at the bar, which, thanks to his being married to a non-Jewish wife, he was able to continue from 1938 to 1945 as a so-called Jewish consultant. Seen from this angle, the book makes a contribution to the history of the Jewish community in Hanover.

IMBSHAUSEN near Northeim at one time had an independent Jewish community, but since the early 1880s, owing to the very small number of Jewish inhabitants, only a so-called *Anschlußgemeinde*. Nevertheless, Kurt Richter found

[128] *Brunsvicensia Judaica, Gedenkbuch für die jüdischen Mitbürger der Stadt Braunschweig 1933–1945*, Brunswick 1966; cf. *LBI Year Book XV*, p. 236.

[129] See *LBI Year Book XXIII*, p. 301.

[130] Peter Wilhelm, *Die Synagogengemeinde Göttingen, Rosdorf und Geismar 1850–1942* (Studien zur Geschichte der Stadt Göttingen, hrsg. von der Stadt Göttingen, 11), Göttingen 1978, 124 pp.

[131] *"Reichskristallnacht" in Hannover. Eine Ausstellung zur 40. Wiederkehr des 9. November 1938*, Hanover, Historisches Museum 1978, 136 pp.

[132] Cf. *LBI Year Book XIV* (1969), pp. 165–181.

[133] Ulrich Beer, *Versehrt, verfolgt, versöhnt: Horst Berkowitz – ein jüdisches Anwaltsleben*, Essen 1979, 164 pp.

this minute community sufficiently attractive to study its history and publish the results.[134] His sources are the Main Lower Saxony State Archives in Hanover, the Church Records of St. Mark's Church at Imbshausen, and communications from some of the older inhabitants. In the introduction he writes:

> "For more than two centuries, presumably from the end of the seventeenth to the beginning of the twentieth century Jews were living at Imbshausen. In the eighteenth and nineteenth centuries their number was on average about 40, sometimes as high as 60. Indeed, during a long period in the eighteenth century more Jews were living in little Imbshausen than in the town of Göttingen. They formed a genuine Jewish community, with a Head, a synagogue and a cemetery. For twenty years in the middle of the last century they maintained a Jewish primary school with a Jewish teacher."

The last burial at the Jewish cemetery – now the property of the Lower Saxony State Association of Jewish Communities – took place in 1908. The last Jewish inhabitant, a woman, died at Imbshausen in 1939 and was buried at Northeim.

SEESEN, by the Harz mountains, no longer has a Jewish community. One, founded in 1814, was liquidated by the Nazis; another one, established after the war by displaced persons, was short-lived. This emerges from the history of the Seesen Jews[135] by Gerhard Ballin, son of an old Jewish family in Seesen and a highly reputed scholar, who pursued his researches for many years and is known as the author of many publications on urban history and genealogical subjects. Five years earlier he had contributed an essay to a *Festschrift* on the millennium of the town in 1974.[136] His subject then was the progressive and widely known Jacobson School which was founded at Seesen in 1801 by Israel Jacobson (Halberstadt 1768-Berlin 1828) and for over a hundred years remained a centre of Jewish life.

Ballin's monograph, based largely on the records at the Lower Saxony State Archives at Wolfenbüttel, is divided into two parts of equal length, dealing respectively with the history of the community from 1814 to 1941, and with the genealogy of some fifty Jewish families. It is hardly surprising that most of them had some links with the Jacobson School. Today the local *Gymnasium* and a Seesen street are named after Israel Jacobson.

VII. BERLIN

BERLIN had a Jewish population of some 172,000 in 1932. Today's Jewish community with 6,000 members is again the largest in Germany. The absence of a coherent and comprehensive work on the history of the Berlin Jews was deplored in the last instalment of this series.[137] It must be stated with regret that the situation has not improved in the meantime. It is true, a number of essays on aspects of the subject has appeared in periodicals and collective works, and these

[134]Kurt Richter, 'Ein wichtiges Kapitel der Dorfgeschichte' (three instalments in *Northeimer Neueste Nachrichten* supplement, 14th–27th March 1981).

[135]Gerhard Ballin, *Geschichte der Juden in Seesen*, published by the Municipality, Seesen 1979, 286 pp.

[136]Gerhard Ballin, 'Die Jacobson-Schule in Seesen. Ein Beitrag zu ihrer Geschichte', in *Tausend Jahre Seesen 974–1974, Beiträge zur Geschichte der Stadt Seesen am Harz*, Seesen 1974, pp. 349–440.

[137]*LBI Year Book XXIII*, p. 300.

may be building blocks but certainly no substitute for the comprehensive work that is needed. The reasons are varied. The partition of the city places obstacles in the way of research. There are very few competent scholars – Jewish or non-Jewish – currently pursuing this subject – which is not to say that the coming generation may not one day produce historians attracted by this specialised theme. Some signs of such development can be discerned already: Berlin has lately been the exclusive topic of new historical research institutions, of public and semi-public exhibitions, talks and lectures, discussions, colloquia, symposia, often mounted by the media.

Yet, it is remarkable that even the *Preußenjahr* observed in Berlin in 1981 has neither produced nor stimulated a direct contribution to Jewish communal history in Germany, apart from the widely-noted travelling exhibition *Juden in Preußen*. However, a biographical volume of the same title[138] may be regarded as an indirect contribution, since it contains much material on the history of hundreds of Jewish communities in Prussia between 1780 and 1930. Most of the roughly 2,000 men and women briefly listed in this publication are likely to have represented Jewish communities, associations and institutions in Berlin. However, all the Prussian Provinces are represented in this work, including those in the East, notably Poznań which for so long was a "Jewish reservoir" for Berlin. It is hoped that this book as well as a few other publications reviewed below may have a stimulating effect on future work.

A booklet on Jewish cemeteries in Berlin[139] contains 50 excellent photographs of gravestones, including those of the resistance fighter Herbert Baum, murdered by the Nazis in 1942; Rabbi Simon Bernfeld; Micha Bin Gorion, a collector of Jewish folk tales and legends; the parliamentarian Oskar Cassel; the philosopher Hermann Cohen; the writer Karl Emil Franzos; the cantor Leo Gollanin; the social policy experts Max Hirsch and Lina Morgenstern; Salomon Kalischer, a mathematician at the Charlottenburg Technical University; Rudolf Mosse; Martin Riesenburger, rabbi in East Berlin from 1953 to 1965; the bibliographer Moritz Steinschneider; the philologist Heymann Steinthal; Lesser Ury and Theodor Wolff.

These are among the many personages associated with the Berlin community who were buried in the *Ehrenreihen* of the famous Weißensee Cemetery, and whose names and personal data are placed on record in this publication. Photographs show inter alia the Memorial Stone for the Jewish victims of Nazi persecution, the Monuments for the Jewish Soldiers Fallen in the First World War and for the members of the resistance group Baum, executed in 1942/1943, and the memorial site for Kurt Tucholsky's parents.

Other photographs in the booklet show the gravestone of Moses Mendelssohn (1729–1786) at the cemetery in the Große Hamburger Straße, which was closed in 1827 and destroyed by the Nazis, and the memorial stone erected after the end

[138]Ernst G. Lowenthal, *Juden in Preußen. Ein repräsentativer Querschnitt*, Berlin 1981, ²1982, 256 pp.

[139]Alfred Etzold, Peter Kirchner and Heinz Knobloch, *Jüdische Friedhöfe in Berlin* (Schriftenreihe "Historische Friedhöfe in der Deutschen Demokratischen Republik" 1), published on behalf of the GDR Ministry for Culture by the Berlin Institute for the Preservation of Ancient Monuments in conjunction with the (East) Berlin Jewish community, East Berlin n.d. [1980], 64 pp.

of the war next to the location of that grave. The second oldest former Jewish cemetery, in the Schönhauser Allee, is represented by photographs of the gravestone of Giacomo Meyerbeer, and the tomb of the family of Max Liebermann, in addition to a ground plan on which are marked the gravestones of Reichenheim, Ludwig Geiger, Leopold Zunz, Meno Burg, Joseph Mendelssohn, Leopold Ullstein, Gerson von Bleichröder and others.

Note is taken also of the cemetery at Weißensee established in 1878 by the *Austritts-Gemeinde Adass-Jisroel*, as well as of the mediaeval cemetery and of the Spandau cemetery established in 1859.

The *Jahrbuch des Vereins für die Geschichte Berlins* featured an essay listing the Elders, the Chairmen and their Deputies of Berlin's Main Jewish Community, altogether some 40 persons.[140] The material is arranged in four sections corresponding to the historical periods: up to the middle of the nineteenth century; the age of emancipation; the Weimar Republic; the Third *Reich*. The list does not include the chairmen of independent break-away communities such as the Jewish Reform Community and *Adass-Jisroel*. Dates of birth and death are given in all cases, from 1841 on largely with the help of the *Adress-Kalender für Berlin und Potsdam* as well as Jacob Jacobson's *Judenbürgerbücher*.[141]

A *Festschrift* of over 700 pages on the 275th anniversary of CHARLOTTENBURG contains fourteen contributions, two of them dealing with religious aspects. A brief survey of the development of the Evangelical Church is followed by an essay on the Charlottenburg centre of the Jewish community.[142]

The reconstitution of the Berlin Jewish community and the Community House, unquestionably relevant in this context, take up over one third of the essay. It is less clear whether this is the right place for a detailed treatment of internal Jewish differences, not only within the local framework but also at the level of the former German *Reich* as a whole. There is a striking disproportion between the detailed passages on the new community centre at Fasanenstraße 79/80 and the brief mention of the House Kantstraße 158 – only a stone's throw away – which before 1933, and even more so after that watershed, housed the headquarters of many national and regional Jewish organisations: the *Preußischer Landesverband jüdischer Gemeinden*, the *Zentralwohlfahrtsstelle*, the *Zentralausschuß für Hilfe und Aufbau*, the *Reichsvertretung der deutschen Juden* (a title compulsorily changed in 1939 to *Reichsvereinigung der Juden in Deutschland*), the Children's and Youth Aliyah, the *Jüdischer Frauenbund* and others.

This (incomplete) enumeration of the names of organisations omitted from this publication appears to be all the more necessary, since it has become a habit of authors – Jewish or pro-Jewish – to present Jewish history in Germany from a close-range perspective, that is to say in the light of post-1945 moods and events,

[140]Ernst G. Lowenthal, 'Von Moritz Veit bis Heinrich Stahl. Beitrag zur Geschichte der Juden in Berlin', in *Bär von Berlin. Jahrbuch des Vereins für die Geschichte Berlins*, edited by Gerhard Kutzsch and Claus P. Mader, 28, Berlin–Bonn 1979, pp. 79–92.

[141]*Die Judenbürgerbücher der Stadt Berlin*, (Veröffentlichungen der Historischen Kommission zu Berlin, 4), Berlin 1962.

[142]Burkhard Asmuss and Andreas Nachama, 'Zur Geschichte der Juden in Berlin und das Jüdische Gemeindezentrum in Charlottenburg', in Wolfgang Ribbe (ed.), *Von der City zur Residenz – 275 Jahre Charlottenburg*, Berlin 1980, pp. 165–228.

while the developments and achievements of Jewish life up till 1933 or 1943 tend to be treated perfunctorily if not ignored altogether, even in a book like the present one, which after all is dedicated to the history of 275 years, beginning in 1705.

VIII. HAMBURG, ALTONA, WANDSBEK

As in the case of Berlin, a comprehensive scholarly or popular account of the history of Jewish settlement in Hamburg has not yet been written. A monograph on the amalgamated Jewish community of Hamburg, Altona and Wandsbek, published in 1960 to mark the dedication of Hamburg's post-war synagogue,[143] is incomplete and not entirely free either of factual errors or of bias in the presentation of internal Jewish affairs. Unlike the case of Berlin, however, competent studies cover some of the ground. This applies to the periods 1800–1850 and 1848–1918,[144] while the period beginning in 1941 is represented by a Memorial Volume for the Victims of National Socialism in Hamburg, giving the names and personal data of over 6,000 individuals.[145]

It may be opportune in this context to mention a few shorter essays which throw some light on the history of Jews in Hamburg. Peter Freimark, in a brief essay on Jews at the *Johanneum*[146] confines his treatment to a few Jewish pupils of that famous *Gymnasium* who attained prominence in the nineteenth century. Here the question arises as to whether it would not have been preferable to widen the scope of the study to the history of Jews who were educated at the *Johanneum* in more recent times. This, indeed, would have involved the school authorities in a far more difficult enterprise. Yet, to tackle this enterprise – and not only at this particular school – may well be considered a debt of honour in the context of local history, as those alumni who perished under the Nazi regime would have to be included. After all, the sumptuous tablets displayed in countless schools to honour pupils and masters fallen in the wars of 1870–1871 and 1914–1918 are still vividly remembered.

Of Erich Lüth's continuing output of Hamburgensia it is proposed to mention here only his essay on the Heine garden-house in Elbchaussee,[147] at the former summer seat of the Hamburg banker Salomon Heine, the poet's generous uncle. Heinrich Heine stayed there as a visitor in 1843 and 1844. Thanks to an initiative on the part of local citizens, a preservation order was placed on the building over twelve years ago to save it from complete dilapidation.

Günter Marwedel, who in 1976 edited and prefaced a noteworthy work on the privileges of *Hochdeutsche* and Portuguese Jews in Altona (1584–1863),[148] followed

[143]Oskar Wolfsberg-Aviad *et al.*, *Die Drei-Gemeinde. Aus der Geschichte der jüdischen Gemeinden Altona-Hamburg-Wandsbek*, Hamburg 1960, 188 pp.

[144]Cf. *LBI Year Book XV*, p. 239.

[145]*Gedenkbuch für die jüdischen Opfer des Nationalsozialismus in Hamburg*, cf. *LBI Year Book XI*, p. 333.

[146]Peter Freimark, 'Juden auf dem Johanneum', in *450 Jahre Gelehrtenschule des Johanneums zu Hamburg 1979*, Hamburg 1979, pp. 123–129.

[147]Erich Lüth, 'Das Heine-Gartenhaus', *Europäische Hefte*, April 1981, pp. 65–77. (This periodical is published by the Stiftung F.V.S. zu Hamburg and the Johann Wolfgang Goethe-Stiftung, Basel).

[148]Günter Marwedel (ed.), *Die Privilegien der Juden in Altona* (Hamburger Beiträge zur Geschichte der deutschen Juden, 5), Hamburg 1976, 432 pp.

this up in 1982 with the publication of an expanded lecture on the history of the Jews in Hamburg, Altona and Wandsbek.[149] The general introduction as well as the description of the early days in Hamburg and Altona, based chiefly on the well known memoirs of Glückel of Hameln (1645–1724), and the account of the development of the Sephardic and Ashkenasi Jews (well into the nineteenth century) provide an expert and instructive survey.

On the other hand, the more recent history, especially of the Weimar period, receives only marginal treatment. This part of the essay at any rate does not live up to the promise of the title. Moreover, some generalisations and certain, occasionally somewhat dismissive value judgements derived from them, cannot be left unchallenged. This applies in particular to trends evident in Hamburg's Jewry during the past 100 years or so: declining attendances at the synagogue; migration within the urban territory into specific, preferred residential areas; failure to face up to and combat antisemitism; attitude to East German Jews passing through Hamburg in transit; the problematic issue of Jewish integration in Hamburg (in the author's view a lost cause); the formation of the German-Jewish youth movement: all these points – from the angle of local history of minor significance – are raised by the author with a hint of reproach, as if to say the Jews could and should have foreseen the political fate that was in store for them.

In contrast, other facets are missing – such as the civic awareness of the Hamburg Jews, their social commitment manifested in humanitarian foundations for the benefit both of the general public and indigent Jews, who did exist, although that fact is nowhere indicated. Similarly, the bibliography omits to refer to the pamphlet on the Jewish hospital,[150] one of the oldest, and to this day most conspicuous, examples of Jewish charities. The publication of the manuscript of Marwedel's lecture could well have provided a point of departure for a future comprehensive history of Hamburg's Jewry, with special emphasis on the period since 1871.

IX. GERMANY'S FORMER EASTERN TERRITORIES

UPPER SILESIA: In connection with the foundation in the spring of 1979 of an Association for Research on the History of the Jews in Upper Silesia,[151] the present writer provided a brief outline of the demography of the Jews in former Upper Silesia,[152] with the intention of stimulating further research. The essay deals in a summary fashion with the main Jewish communities that existed in the region, with their members and their rabbis.

GRAUDENZ (GRUDZIADZ) figures largely in the memoirs of the eminent surgeon, Professor Paul Rosenstein[153] (Graudenz 1875–Rio de Janeiro 1962).

[149]Günter Marwedel, *Geschichte der Juden in Hamburg, Altona und Wandsbek*, Hamburg 1982, 50 pp.

[150]Mary Lindemann, *140 Jahre Israelitisches Krankenhaus in Hamburg. Vorgeschichte und Entwicklung*, Hamburg 1981, 100 pp.

[151]Verein zur Erforschung der Geschichte der Juden in Oberschlesien, with its seat at Wolfenbüttel.

[152]Ernst G. Lowenthal, 'Zur Demographie der Juden im früheren Oberschlesien', *Zeitschrift für Ostforschung. Länder und Völker im östlichen Mitteleuropa*, 28 (1979), No. 1, pp. 81–84.

[153]Paul Rosenstein, *Narben bleiben zurück*, Munich 1954.

One of eight children of the Graudenz rabbi, he tells about the origin of his family, the parental home and his youth in Graudenz.

This is in marked contrast to a book commemorating "seven centuries of German history" in Graudenz town and Rural District.[154] All we learn from this book about the presence of Jews is the fact that there were 152 of them in the Rural District in 1910, and that 100 out of 2,600 inhabitants of the locality of Lessen, near Graudenz, were Jews. This, surely, is inadequate, especially in view of the title, which would appear to indicate that the book is not concerned exclusively with the expulsion of the population of Graudenz towards the end of the Second World War. That some 800 Jews lived in Graudenz town at the turn of the century is a fact which the editors could readily have found in the 1897 or 1908 editions of *Meyers Lexikon*. Then it might have dawned on them that at that time and at least till 1919 there was a substantial Jewish community in the town, and that it would have been right, and indeed necessary, to explore the fate of those citizens with the same care that has been bestowed on the illustrated history of the Church congregations and schools, and even of the Mennonites.

LANDSBERG/WARTHE (GORZÓW WIELKOPOLSKO), formerly a Brandenburg district town, is the subject of a *Heimatbuch* published in 1976 and going back to 1257.[155] Looking at this book, it seems that the existence of hundreds of Jews was a matter of no account. Even in the Appendix, comprising a 'Thousand Year Chronicle' and bibliography, there is no relevant reference. Yet, in 1925, this town, with a population of 43,000, had 500 to 600 Jewish inhabitants, about 1.3 per cent of the population, next to 3,600 Catholics and 2,300 "others". Well-reputed families, like the Klemperers and Boas, came from Landsberg. Till the end of the 1930s, Landsberg had a normal and well functioning Jewish community, headed for decades by rabbis with academic qualifications, which can be taken as a measure of the size, prosperity and reputation of the community. Yet, even the Chronicle, which gives statistics for the population of the town in 1925 according to religious affiliation, treats the Jews as non-persons whose existence is not to be acknowledged.

The Nazi period is glibly dismissed in the light of insignificant details about building projects, some statistical figures, etc. Can it be that in Landsberg of all places nothing at all worthy of note happened? Can it be that 1st April 1933 and 9th November 1938 by-passed Landsberg? Were no Jews molested, boycotted, arrested, driven away, deported to the death camps? The list of sources is also incomplete. There is no reference to Oswald Lassally's essay on the Jews of Landsberg.[156]

The *Heimatbuch* is the first volume of a series sponsored by a working group on

[154]Nordewin von Diest-Körber, *Die Stadt und der Landkreis Graudenz. Aus sieben Jahrhunderten deutscher Geschichte*, published by the Graudenz branch of the Westpreußen Regional Association (*Landsmannschaft*), Münster 1976.

[155]Hans Beske and Ernst Handke (eds.), *Landsberg an der Warthe 1257, 1945, 1976 – Stadt und Land im Umbruch der Zeiten* (Schriftenreihe der Bundesarbeitsgemeinschaft Landsberg/Warthe, 1), with a foreword by Peter-Paul Nahm, Bielefeld 1976, 350 pp.

[156]Oswald Lassally, 'Die Geschichte der Juden in Landsberg an der Warthe', Monatsschrift für Geschichte und Wissenschaft des Judentums, Breslau 1936, pp. 403–415.

Landsberg. The second volume of the series,[157] under the title *Kultur und Gesellschaft*, contains some 80 contributions of which two have a bearing on Jewish affairs. One is a chapter from an autobiographical novel (*Kindheitsmuster*) by the East Berlin writer Christa Wolf, who was born in Landsberg. The chapter describes the burning of the synagogue, but says nothing about the existence or fate of the Jews in that city. The second contribution with a Jewish context deals with the neighbouring town of Vietz (see below).

STARGARD (Szczecinski) in what used to be Pomerania had in 1932 close to 300 Jewish inhabitants, nearly 1 per cent of the total population (which by 1936 had risen to 40,000). The long-serving rabbi of their Jewish community, in office from 1900 to 1936, was Emil Silberstein, widely known in the town and the neighbouring localities of Pyritz, Labes, Freienwalde and Falkenburg. What happened to the 300 Stargard Jews after 1933 cannot readily be ascertained without thorough and laborious searches and inquiries.

A book on the history of the town was published in 1974,[158] but says very little about the Jews who lived there. What we do learn is that "the synagogue on the inner-urban arm of the Ihna, erected next to the salt store, has attracted general attention by a gable which, seen from Peter-Groening-Straße, has a striking oriental aspect". The author adds that the synagogue "comprised a meeting room and several ancillary rooms. It had an excellent organ. The adjoining house with a frontage to Speicherstraße contained several flats. The rabbi and the cantor lived there." And that is all.

Whereas the churches of the town as well as many secular buildings are shown in drawings, there is no illustration of the synagogue with its "oriental aspect". The clergymen and civic representatives of the town are named, not so the last rabbi and last Jewish teacher (Hermann Schüler).

Again, the reader gathers the impression that during the Nazi era nothing much happened apart from the Second World War (air raids, the entry of the Russian troops), with an honourable mention reserved for the defence of Stargard by the Walloons under the command of the Belgian fascist ("Rexist") leader Léon Degrelle.

VIETZ, a small town West of Landsberg once had a minute Jewish community, which is the subject of an essay in the collective volume on Landsberg just mentioned. The author gives the figure of 31 members in 1856. If he had taken the trouble he could have given the data likewise for 1924 and 1932.[159] Instead, he notes soothingly:

> "After 1933 only a few citizens of Vietz were prepared to treat the Jews with the disrespect ordained by the propaganda machine. Generally they were left alone. Fortunately, most of them managed to emigrate to Palestine, South America or England. As far as is known, there were only two women, a mother and daughter, who would not be persuaded of the seriousness of the situation. They moved to a Berlin ghetto and were later taken to Theresienstadt."

[157]Bielefeld 1978, 317 pp.

[158]Joachim Stampa, *Stargard in Pommern. Schicksale einer Stadt*, Elmshorn 1974, [3]1978, 251 pp.

[159]Cf. *Handbuch der jüdischen Gemeindeverwaltung und Wohlfahrtspflege 1924/25* (place and date of publication not given), p. 13; and *Führer durch die jüdische Gemeindeverwaltung und Wohlfahrtspflege in Deutschland 1932–33*, pp. 66 f.

X. AUSTRIA

Forty years after the *Anschluß* a native of Vienna, the historian Herbert Rosenkranz, since 1955 a research worker with Yad Vashem in Jerusalem, published a book on the persecution and the constructive response of Austrian Jews 1938–1945,[160] apparently the first comprehensive work on this specialised topic. It is in the nature of things that the situation in Vienna dominates the narrative with its 33 chapters. The author provides an exhaustive chronicle of events, documented by hundreds of source references. In a previous, no less thoroughly researched paper[161] Rosenkranz had established that out of the 185,000 Jews living in Austria in 1938, nearly 68,000 perished in East European ghettos, concentration and extermination camps. The meaning of *Selbstbehauptung* (holding one's own) in the title is explained in the author's foreword: it is a question of success or failure in rising to the challenge. Rosenkranz deals at length with organisation and the specific measures of Jewish self-help, such as occupational retraining, schooling, *Kulturbund*, sports movement, illegal emigration.

The book has three valuable indexes, though it is hard to fathom why the subject index features certain irrelevant entries, such as "Bastardehe", "Galgenhumor", "Luach" (and underneath "Luchoth").

HOHENEMS in Vorarlberg is the birthplace of Salomon Sulzer. A memorial tablet unveiled in 1976 at the house in which he was born notes that he was born on 18th March 1804 and died in Vienna on 17th January 1890; that he was cantor at Hohenems 1820–1826, subsequently *Oberkantor* in Vienna, Professor at the Conservatoire, founder of the *Wiener Liedertafel*, initiator of the modern mode of singing in the synagogues, and a friend of Franz Schubert. This event had interesting antecedents, revealed the year before in the first volume of a history of Hohenems.[162] The author, Director of the Municipal Archives, states that a memorial tablet was displayed at the house for a long time, but was "later" removed. However, the tablet was not lost, "so that its restoration to its proper place is urgently called for", since Sulzer had "never forgotten the love and affection extended to him in Hohenems".

Generally, the development of the Jewish community is treated at some length in this book. In 1765, when the town was taken over by Austria, the Jews represented 10 per cent of the population. They formed a separate corporation, at times with their own mayor. Later the town was the seat of the rabbinate for Tirol and Vorarlberg. In his survey of earlier works on the subject, Burmeister refers above all to Aron Tänzer's history of the Jews in Hohenems[163] and Lothar

[160]Herbert Rosenkranz, *Verfolgung und Selbstbehauptung: Die Juden in Österreich 1938–1945*, Vienna 1978, 399 pp.

[161]Herbert Rosenkranz, 'The Anschluss and the Tragedy of Austrian Jewry 1938–1945', in Josef Fraenkel (ed.), *The Jews of Austria. Essays on their Life, History and Destruction*, London 1967, pp. 479–566.

[162]Karl-Heinz Burmeister, *Geschichte von Hohenems*, vol. 1, published by the Hohenems Municipality, 1975, 202 pp.

[163]Aron Tänzer, *Geschichte der Juden in Hohenems*, Meran 1905.

Rothschild's report in a book of remembrance for Austria's Jews.[164] Burmeister deals briefly with the development of the Jewish community until 1769, and after that on the basis of the official records introduced in that year up to 1890, and lastly with the steady decline of the Jewish population as a result of migration to St. Gall and Lengnau in Switzerland, Randegg in South Baden, Vienna, Trieste and other places, leading up to the end of the community in the 1930s.

CONCLUSION

In the first three instalments of the present series some 200 new publications were reviewed. The present fourth instalment has added at least 70 more. Even so, this survey cannot claim to be exhaustive, for we are dealing here with publications which in many cases are not distributed through the book trade, and which therefore may come to public notice only after considerable delay. At a rough estimate, about 300 Jewish communities have so far been covered. This means that out of about 1,500 Jewish communities which existed at least up to the beginning of 1933, and in most cases much longer, within the frontiers of the German *Reich*, one in five is the subject of a publication, a creditable proportion.

It seems likely that the present trend will continue in the coming years, though the rate of progress may be limited by a shortage of funds, manifested in the budgets of public bodies. As far as is known, in mid-1982 (when this fourth instalment was completed), work on the history of local Jewish communities was in progress in the following towns: Aachen, Aschaffenburg, Bamberg, Bielefeld, Düsseldorf, Duisburg, Erlangen, Euskirchen/Voreifel, Gladenbach, Hanover, Heidelberg, Heilbronn, Lüneburg, Michelstadt, Mülheim/Ruhr, Nauheim, Paderborn, Würzburg and Wuppertal. This list, undoubtedly incomplete, together with the repeated public requests and appeals for co-operation in the collection of material for such projects, clearly indicates that interest in this sphere is certainly not flagging.

[164]Lothar Rothschild writes on the Jews of Hohenems in H. Gold, *Geschichte der Juden in Österreich. Ein Gedenkbuch*, Tel-Aviv 1971, pp. 27–32.

Post-War Publications on German Jewry

A Selected Bibliography of Books and Articles 1983

Compiled by
IRMGARD FOERG and ANNETTE PRINGLE

Leo Baeck Institute
4 Devonshire Street
London W.1.

CONTENTS

BIBLIOGRAPHY 1983

I. HISTORY

A. General

19751. Angress, Werner T.: *The impact of the 'Judenwahlen' of 1912 on the Jewish Question.* A synthesis. [In]: LBI Year Book XXVIII, London, 1983. Pp. 367–410, footnotes, ports.

19752. Aschheim, Steven E.: *Eastern Jews, German Jews and Germany's Ostpolitik in the First World War.* [In]: LBI Year Book XXVIII, London, 1983. Pp. 351–365, footnotes. [See also review on Aschheim's 'Brothers and strangers' (see No. 19204/YB XXVIII): Apparitions from the East (Robert S. Wistrich) [in]: TLS, London, 13. Apr. 1984, p. 407.]

19753. Bach, Hans, ed.: *The German Jew: a synthesis of Judaism and Western civilization, 1730–1930.* Rutherford, N.J.: Fairleigh Dickinson Univ. Press, 1983. 650 pp. [Anthology of writings by German Jews, with commentary on the history and biogr. notes on the authors; incl., a.o., Moses Mendelssohn, Heinrich Heine, Hermann Cohen, Martin Buber, Franz Rosenzweig.]

19754. Bautz, Franz J., ed.: *Geschichte der Juden; von der biblischen Zeit bis zur Gegenwart.* (Mit einer Zeittafel und 13 Karten.) München: Beck, 1983. 247 pp., maps. (Beck'sche schwarze Reihe, Bd. 268.) [Incl.: Der preussisch-deutsche Weg der Judenemanzipation (Walter Grab, 140–164). Antisemitismus, Zionismus und Staat Israel (Hermann Greive, 165–183).]

19755. Berding, Helmut: *L'émancipation des juifs dans la Confédération du Rhin.* [In]: Revue de l'Institut Napoléon, 139, Paris, 1982. Pp. 51–62, notes.

19756. Bristow, Edward: *The German-Jewish fight against white slavery.* [In]: LBI Year Book XXVIII, London, 1983. Pp. 301–328.

19757. Degany, Ben-Zion: *Anti-Jewish public opinion as a factor towards the expulsion of the Jews from German towns (1440–1530).* [In Hebrew, with English summary]. Jerusalem, Hebrew Univ., Diss., May 1982. 2 vols. 370, IV, 6 pp.).

19758. Dobkowski, Michael N./Wallimann, Isidor, eds.: *Towards the Holocaust; the social and economic collapse of the Weimar Republic.* Westport, Conn.: Greenwood Press, 1983. 422 pp.

19759. Duchhardt, Heinz: *Karl VI., die Reichsritterschaft und der 'Opferpfennig' der Juden.* [In]: Zeitschrift für Historische Forschung, Bd. 10, H. 2, Berlin, 1983. Pp. 149–167, footnotes.

19760. Elbogen, Ismar/Sterling, Eleonore: *Die Geschichte der Juden in Deutschland.* Wiesbaden: Fourier, 1982. 335 pp., bibl. (321–334). [I. Elbogen's 'Geschichte der Juden in Deutschland' (Berlin, Jüd. Buch-Vereinigung, 1935) was revised and supplemented by E. Sterling in 1966; this is a re-issue of No. 5594/YB XII. See also: Lehre und Geschichte des Judentums: zum 40. Todestag des Historikers Ismar Elbogen (Ernst G. Lowenthal) [in]: 'Allgemeine', Nr. 30, Düsseldorf, 23. Juli 1983, p. 9 [and in]: Isr. Wochenblatt, Nr. 31, Zürich, 5. Aug. 1983, pp. 10–11 [and in]: MB, Nr. 30, Tel-Aviv, 5. Aug. 1983, p. 5. Erinnerungen an I. Elbogen (I. O. Lehman) [in]: Aufbau, Nr. 34, New York, Aug. 26, 1983, p. 21.] [I.E., Sept. 1, 1874 Schildberg – Aug. 1, 1943 New York, historian.]

19761. Ersch, Johann Samuel/Gruber, Johann Gottfried, eds.: *Allgemeine Encyklopädie der Wissenschaften und Künste.* (Unveränd. Nachdr. der 1847–1884 bei F. A. Brockhaus in Leipzig erschienenen Ausg.) Sektion 2, T. 26–28. Graz: Akademische Druck- & Verlagsanstalt, 1983. *T. 26: Italiener – Jüdeln.* 432 pp. *T. 27: Juden – Jüdische Literatur.* 471 pp. *T. 28: Jüdische Münzen – Jungermannia.* 478 pp.

19762. Fahlbusch, Friedrich Bernward: *Städte und Königtum im frühen 15. Jahrhundert; ein Beitrag zur Geschichte Sigmunds von Luxemburg.* Köln: Böhlau, 1983. 52, 263 pp. (Städteforschung, Bd. 17.) [Also on 'Judenschutz'.]

19763. Frey, Sabine: *Rechtsschutz der Juden gegen Ausweisungen im 16. Jahrhundert.* Frankfurt am Main: Lang, 1983. XVII, 158 pp. (Rechtshistorische Reihe, Bd. 30.) Zugl.: Kiel, Univ., Diss., 1983. [Incl. also chap. on Josel von Rosheim.]

19764. *Gegenseitige Einflüsse deutscher und jüdischer Kultur: von der Epoche der Aufklärung bis zur Weimarer Republik.* Internationales Symposium, April 1982. Leitung: Walter Grab. Tel-Aviv: Nateev-Printing, 1982. 341 pp., footnotes. (Jahrbuch des Instituts für Deutsche Geschichte, Beiheft 4.) [Cont.: The genesis of Rosenzweig's Stern der Erlösung' (Amos Funkenstein, 17–29) Jüdischer Pseudomessianismus und deutsche Kultur: der Weg der frankistischen Familie Dobruschka-Schönfeld im Zeitalter der Aufklärung (Josef Karniel, 31–54). Juden,

Wissenschaft und Universitäten: zur Sozialgeschichte der jüdischen Intelligenz und der akademischen Judenfeindschaft 1780–1848 (Monika Richarz, 55–73). Die Sprache als Problem der jüdischen Einordnung im deutschen Kulturraum (Jacob Toury, 75–96). Berliner Salons als Ort deutsch-jüdischer Symbiose (Horst Meixner, 97–109; on Henriette Herz and Rahel Varnhagen). Eine Jugend in Deutschland: Heinrich Heine und die Burschenschaft (Jost Hermand, 111–135). Die revolutionäre Agitation und die Kerkerhaft Leopold Eichelbergs (Walter Grab, 137–173; L. Eichelberg, Marburg 1804–1879, physician, democratic politician). Emanzipierte rheinische Juden im französisch-deutschen Kulturgefälle: das Beispiel Moses Hess (Shlomo Na'aman, 175–201; also on Karl Marx). Jüdisch-deutsche Schriftsteller in Böhmen im 19. Jahrhundert (Margarita Pazi, 203–258; on Moritz Hartmann, Siegfried Kapper, Leopold Kompert). Die Ideologiekritik von Karl Kraus in seiner Tragödie 'Die letzten Tage der Menschheit' (Silvio Vietta, 259–279). Messianisches Denken und pazifistische Utopie im Werk Kurt Eisners (Heinz Sproll, 281–336).]

19765. Höxter, Julius: *Quellenbuch zur jüdischen Geschichte und Literatur*. T. 1–5. Reprint [der Ausg. Frankfurt am Main, Kauffmann 1930]. Bd. 1–2. Zürich: Verlag Morascha, 1983. 2 vols. (in various pagings). [*T. 5: Neueste Zeit, 1789 bis zur Gegenwart* incl.: Deutschland (pp. 17–40). Aus dem inneren Leben der Juden, besonders in Deutschland (pp. 65–169).]

19766. Holeczek, Heinz: *The Jews and the German liberals*. [In]: LBI Year Book XXVIII, London, 1983. Pp. 77–91, footnotes, tabs.

19767. Israel, Jonathan I.: *Central European Jewry during the Thirty Years' War*. [In]: Central European History, Vol. 16, No. 1, Atlanta, Ga., March 1983. Pp. 3–30, notes.

19768. *Jews in Germany: from Roman times to the Weimar Republic = Juden in Deutschland: von den Tagen Roms bis zur Weimarer Epoche*. [Exhibition catalogue. Concept and realization: Nachum T. Gidal. Ed.: Uri Ram.] Winter [1983/] 1984. Tel-Aviv: Beth Hatefutsoth, The Nahum Goldmann Museum of the Jewish Diaspora, Winter [1983/] 1984. 1 vol. (unpaged), illus., ports., facsims. [Incl. essays (in English, German, and Hebrew): On the heritage of German Jewry (Uriel Tal, 3 pp.). The German way of Jewish emancipation (Walter Grab, 5 pp.). Jews in Germany (Nachum T. Gidal, 7 pp.).]

19769. *Juden im Vormärz und in der Revolution von 1848*. Internationales Symposium, Feb. 1982. Leitung: Walter Grab und Julius H. Schoeps. Stuttgart-Bonn: Burg-Verl., 1983. 400 pp., notes, list of names (392–400). (Jahrbuch des Instituts für Deutsche Geschichte, Beiheft 5.) [Also publ. in the series]: (Studien zur Geistesgeschichte, hrsg. von Julius H. Schoeps, Bd. 3.) [Cont.: Heinrich Heine: über die Interdependenz von jüdischer, deutscher und europäischer Identität in seinem Werk (Michael Werner, 9–28). Ludwig Börne als politischer Publizist, 1818–1837 (Wolfgang Labuhn, 29–57). Jüdische Schriftsteller und das Dilemma der Assimilation im böhmischen Vormärz (Michael A. Riff, 58–82). Sigmund Engländer: Kritiker des Vormärz, Satiriker der Wiener Revolution und Freund Friedrich Hebbels (Wolfgang Häusler, 83–137). Moritz Saphir und Karl Beck: zwei vormärzliche Literaten Österreichs (Jacob Toury, 138–156). Die hebräischsprachige Publizistik in Österreich um 1850 (Jacob Allerhand, 157–168). Moses Hess' Einfluss auf die Entfremdungstheorie von Karl Marx (Zwi Rosen, 169–198). Karl Marx zur 'Judenfrage' und zu Juden: eine weiterführende Metakritik? (Helmut Hirsch, 199–213). Die Anfänge des Kults um Rahel Varnhagen und seine Kritiker (Konrad Feilchenfeldt, 214–232). Fanny Lewald: das Echo der Revolution von 1848 in ihren Schriften (Margarita Pazi, 233–271). Politische Zielvorstellungen jüdischer Intellektueller aus dem Rheinland und aus Westfalen im Vormärz und in der Revolution von 1848 (Arno Herzig, 272–311). Revolutionstheorie und revolutionäre Praxis bei Ferdinand Lassalle (Shlomo Na'aman, 312–330). An der Seite der Unterdrückten: Ludwig Kalisch, 1814–1882, im Vormärz, in der Revolution von 1848 und im französischen Exil (Julius H. Schoeps, 331–351). Der deutsch-jüdische Freiheitskämpfer Johann Jacoby (Walter Grab, 352–374). Debatten (375–385).]

19770. *Juden in Deutschland zwischen Assimilation und Verfolgung*. Hrsg. dieses Heftes: Reinhard Rürup. Göttingen: Vandenhoeck & Ruprecht, 1983. Pp. 331–478, footnotes. (Geschichte und Gesellschaft, Jg. 9, H. 3.) [Incl.: Jüdische Assimilation und jüdische Eigenart im Deutschen Kaiserreich: ein Versuch (Shulamit Volkov, pp. 331–348, footnotes). Further contributions are listed according to subject.]

19771. Kaplan, Marion: *Prostitution, morality crusades and feminism: German-Jewish feminists and the campaign against white slavery*. [In]: Women's Studies International Forum, Vol. 5, No. 6, London, 1982. Pp. 619–627.

19772. KNIGHT, GERSHOM A.: *The Rothschild-Bleichröder axis in action: an Anglo-German cooperative 1877–1878.* [In]: LBI Year Book XXVIII, London, 1983. Pp. 43–57, footnotes.

19773. *Kulturpolitisches Wörterbuch: Bundesrepublik Deutschland/Deutsche Demokratische Republik: im Vergleich.* Hrsg. von Wolfgang R. Langenbucher, Ralf Rytlewski und Bernd Weyergraf. Stuttgart: Metzler, 1983. [Incl.: Kultur, jüdische: I. Jüd. Kultur in der Diaspora; II. NS-Vernichtungspolitik und Emigration; III. Juden in beiden deutschen Staaten; IV. Jüd. Kultur heute (Monika Richarz, pp. 347–352, bibl.]

—— LIEBESCHÜTZ, HANS: *Synagoge und Ecclesia.* [See No. 20736.]

19774. LOWENSTEIN, STEVEN M.: *Jewish residential concentration in post-emancipation Germany.* [In]: LBI Year Book XXVIII, London, 1983. Pp. 471–495, footnotes, tabs., maps. [Especially on Berlin, Frankfurt am Main, Hamburg.]

19775. NIEWYK, DONALD L.: *The Impact of inflation and depression on the German Jews.* [And comments]: *Inflation and depression as Hitler's pace makers* (Gerald D. Feldman). [In]: LBI Year Book XXVIII, London, 1983. Pp. 19–36, footnotes, tab.; [& comments]: pp. 37–40, footnotes.

19776. PULZER, PETER: *Religion and judicial appointments in Germany 1869–1918.* [In]: LBI Year Book XXVIII, London, 1983. Pp. 185–204, footnotes, tabs., appendix.

19777. REICHOLD, HARTMUT: *Dr. jur. David Morgenstern: Juden in der Burschenschaft des Vormärz.* [In]: Nachrichten für den jüdischen Bürger Fürths, Hrsg.: Isr. Kultusgemeinde, Fürth (Blumenstr. 31), Sept. 1983. Pp. 15–18, port., bibl. [D.M., March 7, 1814 Büschenbach near Erlangen – Nov. 2, 1882 Fürth, democratic politician, the first Jewish member of the Bavarian Landtag.]

19778. *Revolution and evolution: 1848 in German-Jewish history.* Ed. by Werner E. Mosse, Arnold Paucker, Reinhard Rürup. (Robert Weltsch on his 90th birthday in grateful appreciation.) Tübingen: Mohr, 1981. XII, 431 pp., footnotes, tabs., indexes of names and subjects (411–416, 417–423). (Schriftenreihe wissenschaftlicher Abhandlungen des Leo Baeck Instituts, 39.) [See No. 17885/YB XXVII.] *Selected reviews* [continuation of No. 18823/YB XXVIII]: Review (Jack Wertheimer [in]: German Studies Review, No. 1, Tempe, Ariz., 1984, p. 158. Review [in]: Internat. Review of Social History, No. 3, Amsterdam, 1982, p. 385. Ergänzung zur Geschichte des deutschen Judentums [in]: Isr. Wochenblatt, Nr. 16, Zürich, 20. Apr. 1984, p. 54. Review [in]: Kiryat Sefer, Vol. 57, No. 1, Jerusalem, Jan. 1982, No. 404. Review (Todd M. Endelman) [in]: Religious Studies Review, Vol. 9, No. 2, Waterloo, Ont., Canada, Apr. 1983, p. 187. Besprechung (Harald Müller) [in]: Zeitschrift für Geschichtswissenschaft, Jg. 32, H. 2, Berlin/East, 1984, pp. 167–168.

19779. REINICKE, HELMUT: *Gaunerwirtschaft; die erstaunlichen Abenteuer hebräischer Spitzbuben in Deutschland.* Berlin: Transit, 1983. 224 pp., illus., bibl. (pp. 218–223).

19780. RICHARZ, MONIKA, ed.: *Jüdisches Leben in Deutschland: Selbstzeugnisse zur Sozialgeschichte. Bd. 1: 1780–1871. Bd. 2: Im Kaiserreich. Bd. 3: 1918–1945.* Hrsg. und eingeleitet. Stuttgart: Deutsche Verlags-Anstalt, 1976; 1979; 1982. 3 vols., illus., ports., facsims., biogr. notes, bibl. notes, indexes. (Jüdisches Leben in Deutschland, Bd. 1–3.) (Veröffentlichungen des Leo Baeck Instituts.) [See Nos. 13397/YB XXII, 15838/YB XXV, 18824/YB XXVIII.) *Selected reviews* [continuation]: Germany's Jews between Weimar and the Holocaust (Egon Larsen) [in]: AJR Information, London, Dec. 1983, pp. 1–2. Zur jüd. Sozialgeschichte; Interview mit Monika Richarz (Alfred Joachim Fischer) [in]: 'Allgemeine', Nr. 22, Düsseldorf, 3. Juni 1983, p. 8. Besprechung (Hans-Jürgen Löwenstein) [in]: Archiv für Hessische Geschichte und Altertumskunde, 41, Darmstadt, 1983, pp. 444–445. Besprechung (Jürgen Kocka) [in]: Frankfurter Allgemeine Zeitung, Nr. 202, 1. Sept. 1983, p. 25. Aus der bürgerlichen Mittelschicht (Jane E. Gilbert) [in]: Frankfurter Rundschau, 2. Aug. 1983. Lebensgeschichten jüd. Menschen in Deutschland (Dirk Blasius) [in]: Geschichte und Gesellschaft, Jg. 9, H. 3, Göttingen, 1983, pp. 453–461. Besprechung (Ernst Walter Zeeden) [in]: Historisches Jahrbuch, Bd. 103/II, Freiburg i. Br., 1983, pp. 493–494). Besprechung (Nachum Orland) [in]: Das Historisch-Politische Buch, Jg. 31, H. 4, Göttingen, 1983, pp. 133–134. Interview mit M. Richarz (A. J. Fischer) [in]: MB, Nr. 11/12, Tel-Aviv, 28. März 1983, pp. 9–10. Erinnerungen deutscher Juden (N. Orland) [in]: Das Parlament, Nr. 49, Bonn, 10. Dez. 1983, p. 14. Zeitzeugen gefragt: wie es wirklich war [in]: Die Presse, Wien, 21./22./23. Mai 1983. Jüd. Selbstbehauptung (Hilde Ahemm) [in]: Stuttgarter Zeitung, 13. Juni 1983. Juden in Deutschland (Peter Gralla) [in]: Der Tagesspiegel, Berlin, 8. Dez. 1983. Integriert, isoliert (Alphons Silbermann) [in]: Die Welt, Hamburg, 9. Juli 1983. Besprechung (Peter Freimark) [in]: Zeitschrift des Vereins für Hamburgische Geschichte, Bd. 69, Hamburg, 1983, pp. 225–226. Montagsrezension (Hilde Ahemm) [in]: Sendung Radio Bremen, 28.

Feb. 1983. Besprechung (Helga Prollius) [in]: Sendung 'Himmel und Erde zu Zeugen nehmen . . .', Deutschlandfunk, Köln, 10. Mai 1983. Besprechung (Dieter Döllken) [in]: Sendung 'Politik in Büchern und Zeitschriften', Norddeutscher Rundfunk 1 & Westdeutscher Rundfunk 1, 17. Juli 1983. Besprechung (Franz Richard Reiter) [in]: Sendung 'Magazin der Wissenschaft', Österr. Rundfunk, Wien, 9. Jan. 1983. Besprechung (Julius H. Schoeps) [in]: Sendung 'Das Politische Buch', Südwestfunk, Baden-Baden, 16. Jan. 1983.

19781. RUIZ, ALAIN: *Leben und politische Publizistik Heymann Salomon Pappenheimers in Hamburg zur Zeit der Französischen Revolution.* [In]: Jahrbuch des Instituts für Deutsche Geschichte, Bd. 12, Tel-Aviv, 1983. Pp. 129–187, footnotes. [Biographical essay, also on the history of Jewish emancipation; will be continued. See also the author's essay 'Auf dem Wege zur Emanzipation; der politisch-ideologische Werdegang des . . . H. S. Pappenheimer' in No. 16900/YB XXVI.] [Chaim (Heymann) S. Pappenheimer, Apr. 10, 1769 Lublinitz, Silesia – July 2, 1832 Munich, writer and scholars, 'Heereslieferant' in Bavaria ennobled as Heinrich Sigmund Edler von Kerstorf.]

19782. SHEEHAN, JAMES J.: *Der deutsche Liberalismus von den Anfängen im 18. Jahrhundert bis zum Ersten Weltkrieg, 1770–1914.* (Aus dem Engl. übers. von Karl Heinz Siber.) München: Beck, 1983. 454 pp., bibl. (415–440). [Transl. of No. 17886/YB XXVII. Deals also with Jewish emancipation, Jews and liberalism, antisemitism, Ludwig Bamberger, Eduard Lasker, and others.]

19783. THIEME, HANS: *Friedrich Pilger: ein vergessener Vorkämpfer der Juden-Emanzipation.* [In]: Recht und Staat im sozialen Wandel; Festschrift für Hans Ulrich Scupin, hrsg. von Norbert Achterberg [et al.]. Berlin: Duncker & Humblot, 1983. Pp. 183–194, footnotes. [Pilger's 'Ideen über die Behandlung der Juden in Deutschland freimüthig entworfen' appeared in Wetzlar in 1791.]

19784. VAGO, BELA, ed.: *Jewish assimilation in modern times.* Boulder, Colo.: Westview Press, 1981. X, 220 pp. [Incl.: European Jewry and the politics of assimilation (Michael R. Marrus). Jewish assimilation vis-à-vis German nationalism in the Weimar Republic (L. Yahil). The assimilation of Jews in Austria (W. O. McCagg, Jr.). Cf.: Review (Marsha L. Rozenblit) [in]: Jewish Social Studies, Vol. 44, Nos. 3–4, New York, Summer-Fall 1982, pp. 334–335.]

19785. WANDEL, ECKHARD G.: *Germany's political morale and morals during the Great Depression.* [And comments]: *Inflation and depression as Hitler's pace makers* (Gerald D. Feldman). [In]: LBI Year Book XXVIII, London, 1983. Pp. 11–17 [& comments]: pp. 37–40, footnotes.

19786. WASSERMANN, HENRY: *The Fliegende Blätter as a source for the social history of German Jewry.* [In]: LBI Year Book XXVIII, London, 1983. Pp. 93–138, footnotes, illus.

19787. WERTHEIMER, JACK: *Between Tsar and Kaiser: the radicalisation of Russian-Jewish university students in Germany.* [In]: LBI Year Book XXVIII, London, 1983. Pp. 329–349, footnotes.

Linguistics/Western Yiddish

19788. EICHENBAUM, EDZARD: *Jekuthiel Ben Isaak Blitz: ein Wittmunder legte im Jahre 1676 die erste jüdisch-deutsche Bibelübersetzung vor.* [In]: Anzeiger für Harlingerland, Jg. 119, Nr. 36, 12. Feb. 1983. [J.B.I. Blitz, ca. 1620 Wittmund – ca. 1680 Amsterdam[?]; his transl. of the complete Bible into Yiddish appeared in Amsterdam 1676–1678.]

—— FREIMARK, PETER: *Kuggel und Lockschen in Hamburg; ein Beitrag zur jüdischen Schiller-Rezeption im 19. Jahrhundert.* [See in No. 19824.]

19789. GARRIN, STEPHEN H.: *Johann Christoff Wagenseils 'Belehrung der Teutsch-Hebräischen [sic] Red- und Schreibart': a significant contribution to Yiddish scholarship.* [in]: Michigan Germanic Studies, Vol. 9, No. 1, Ann Arbor, Mich., Spring 1983. Pp. 33–44, notes. [J.Ch. Wagenseil, 1633–1705, Christian Hebraist, publ. his 'Johann Christof Wagenseils Belehrung der Jüdisch-Teutschen Red- und Schreibart' in Königsberg in 1699.]

19790. HEMMERLE, JOACHIM: *Jiddisches Theater im Spiegel deutschsprachiger Kritik von der Jahrhundertwende bis 1928.* Eine Dokumentation. (In): Beter und Rebellen. Hrsg. von Michael Brocke. Frankfurt am Main: Deutscher Koordinierungsrat für Christl.-Jüd. Zusammenarbeit, 1983. Pp. 277–311, bibl. (306–311).

19791. HOPKINS, SIMON: *A Geniza fragment of Pirqe Avot in Old Yiddish.* [In Hebrew, with English summary]. [In]: Tarbiz, Vol. 52, No. 3, Jerusalem, Apr.-June 1983. Pp. 459–467, facsim.

[On the Cambridge Geniza fragment T-S E 3.114, attributed to the 15th century; article is a revised version of No. 18838/YB XXVIII.]

19792. Katz, Dovid: *Explorations in the history of the Semitic component in Yiddish.* London, Univ. of London, Ph.D. Diss., 1982. 607 pp. in 2 vols. [Deals extensively with Western Yiddish.]

19793. Katz, Dovid: *Zur Dialektologie des Jiddischen.* (Autorisierte Übers. von Manfred Görlach.) [In]: Dialektologie; ein Handbuch zur deutschen und allgemeinen Dialektforschung. Hrsg. von Werner Besch [et al.]. Halbbd. 2. Berlin: de Gruyter, 1983. Pp. 1018–1041, bibl. (1035–1041). [Also on Western Yiddish.]

19794. Kern, Brigitte: *'Jüdisch-deutsche' Privatbriefe aus dem 17. Jahrhundert.* [In]: Frankfurter Judaistische Beiträge, H. 10, Frankfurt am Main, Dez. 1982. Pp. 111–153, footnotes. [Transcription of 6 Yiddish letters and reproduction of the orig. Hebrew script.]

19795. Süss, Hermann: *Salman Zvi und sein 'Jüdischer Theriak', Hanau 1615.* [In]: Nachrichten für den jüdischen Bürger Fürths, Hrsg.: Kultusgemeinde, Fürth (Blumenstr. 31), Sept. 1983. Pp. 41–45, facsims. [Polemic, in Yiddish (in Hebrew script), against 'Jüdischer abgestreifter Schlangen-Balg', 1614, a pamphlet by the apostate and anti-Jewish agitator Samuel Friedrich Brenz.]

—— Toury, Jacob: *Die Sprache als Problem der jüdischen Einordnung im deutschen Kulturraum.* [See pp. 75–96 in No. 19764.]

B. Communal and Regional History

1. Germany

19796. BAMBERG. Endres, Rudolf: *Ein antisemitischer Bauernaufstand im Hochstift Bamberg im Jahre 1699.* [In]: Historischer Verein für die Pflege der Geschichte des ehemaligen Fürstbistums Bamberg, Bericht 117, Bamberg, 1981. Pp. 67–81.

19797. BAVARIA. Seidl, Günter H.: *Jüdische Sendboten und bayerische Zedakah im 18. Jahrhundert.* Ein kleiner Beitrag zur Geschichte der Familie Asulai. [In]: Nachrichten für den jüdischen Bürger Fürths, Hrsg.: Isr. Kultusgemeinde, Fürth (Blumenstr. 31), Sept. 1983. Pp. 33–37, map, facsims., tabs., bibl.

19798. BERGHEIM. Friedt, Heinz Gerd/Esser, Norbert: *Die Geschichte der jüdischen Gemeinde in Bergheim 1239–1945.* Bergheim: Verein der Heimatfreunde von Niederaussem und Auenheim, 1983. 300 pp., illus., ports., facsims., maps, bibl. (284–290).

19799. BERLIN. Diamant, Adolf: *150 Jahre jüdische Wohlfahrtspflege in Berlin.* [In]: 'Allgemeine', Nr. 47, Düsseldorf, 25. Nov. 1983. P. 10.

—— — Lowenstein, Steven M.: *Jewish residential concentration.* [See No. 19774.]

—— — Meixner, Horst: *Berliner Salons.* [See in No. 19764.]

19800. — *Nachrichtenblatt* des Verbandes der Jüdischen Gemeinden in der Deutschen Demokratischen Republik. Red.: Helmut Aris [et al.]. Dresden, März, Juni, Sept., Dez. 1983. 4 issues, illus. [*März* incl.: Berliner jüd. Friedhöfe aus kunsthistorischer Sicht (Renate Petras, pp. 6–7). Max Ring: Arzt und Schriftsteller (Detlef Thieke, p. 7; M. Ring, Aug. 4, 1817 Zauditz – March 28, 1901 Berlin). Orthopädische Tradition in Bleicherode (Sabine Pax, pp. 8–9; on Dr. med. Wolf Fränkel, Bleicherode Apr. 9, 1807 - Apr. 3, 1848). *June*: Agudath Achim: Erinnerungen an die Synagoge in Berlin-Pankow (Fritz Selbiger, pp. 3–4). Further contributions are listed according to subject.]

—— — Silberman, Lou H.: *Das Falkenberg'sche Gebetbuch.* [See in No. 20186.]

19801. — Simon, Heinrich: *Organisation des religiösen Lebens der Juden in Berlin um die Jahrhundertwende.* [In]: Kairos, N. F. 25, H. 1–2, Salzburg, 1983. Pp. 86–99, notes.

19802. — Simon, Hermann: *Das Berliner Jüdische Museum in der Oranienburger Strasse.* Geschichte einer zerstörten Kulturstätte. Berlin: Berlin Museum, 1983. 99 pp., illus., ports., facsims., notes (90–99). (Stadtgeschichtliche Publikationen, 2.)

19803. — *Synagogen in Berlin; zur Geschichte einer zerstörten Architektur.* T. 1–2. [Ausstellung im] Berlin Museum 1983. (Ausstellung und Katalog von Veronika Bendt und Rolf Bothe.) Berlin: Arenhövel, 1983. 2 pts. (224; 152 pp.), illus., facsims., plans, notes, bibl. (pt. 2, pp. 137–143). (Stadtgeschichtliche Publikationen, 1.) [Cont. *Pt. 1:* Historische Einführung (Harold Hammer-Schenk, 21–70). Die Gemeindesynagogen: Katalog; Zeichnungen und Pläne, Bilddokumente und Schriftstücke (Rolf Bothe/Hans Hirschberg, 71–182). Die Bedeutung der Orgel in Berliner Synagogen (Hans Hirschberg, 183–195). Die Sabbatfeier und ihre

'Heiligen Geräte'; Kle hakodesch (Veronika Bendt, 197–224). *Pt. 2*: Die Vereinssynagogen (Michael Engel, 9–47), Die Synagogen unter dem Nationalsozialismus (Veronika Bendt, 49–123). Anhang (125–152). Exhibition incl. loans from the LBI New York. Cf.: Review (Helen Rosenau) [in]: AJR Information, London, June 1983, p. 9 [and] Letter to the Editor (Hans Hirschberg) [in]: AJR Information, Nov. 1983, p. 6.]

19804. BIRKENFELD. Kronenberger, Friedrich L.: *Die jüdischen Vieh- und Pferdehändler im Birkenfelder Land und in Gemeinden des Hunsrücks.* Birkenfeld: Kreisvolkshochschule, 1983. 23 pp., illus. (Schriftenreihe der Kreisvolkshochschule Birkenfeld, Bd. 8.)

19805. BOCHOLT. Rohr, Fritz: *Fritz Rohr erzählt von früheren Zeiten, wie sie sein Grossvater, S. B. Löwenstein, erlebte.* [In]: Bocholter Borkener Volksblatt, Nr. 1, Bocholt, 2. Jan. 1982. [On S. B. Löwenstein, born about 1820, and other members of the family L. in Bocholt and Rhede. See also No. 20025.]

19806. — *Wichtige Dokumente [in der Ausstellung] 'Juden in Bocholt – Geschichte als Mahnung'.* [In]: Bocholter-Borkener Volksblatt, Bocholt (Postfach 66), 9. Nov. 1983. [Review of exhibition, incl. survey on the history of Jews in Bocholt, 1396–1942.]

19807. BODENSEE. Sauer, Paul: *Die Judengemeinden im nördlichen Bodenseeraum.* [In]: Zeitschrift für die Geschichte des Oberrheins, Bd. 128, Stuttgart, 1980. Pp. 327–343.

19808. BORKEN. *Studien zur Geschichte der Juden im Kreis Borken.* Eine Aufsatzsammlung. Mit Beiträgen von Diethard Aschoff [et al.]. Vreden: Heimatverein, 1983. 184 pp., illus. (Beiträge des Heimatvereins Vreden zur Landes- und Volkskunde, H. 26.)

19809. BRANDENBURG. Cohen, Daniel J.: *Die Landjudenschaften der brandenburgisch-preussischen Staaten im 17. und 18. Jahrhundert.* Jhre Beziehungen untereinander aufgrund neuerschlossener jüdischer Quellen. [In]: Ständetum und Staatsbildung in Brandenburg-Preussen. Hrsg. von Peter Baumgardt. Berlin: de Gruyter, 1983. (Veröffentlichung der Histor. Kommission zu Berlin, Bd. 55.) Pp. 208–229, notes (225–229).

19810. BREISIG. Radday, Yehuda T./Hommen, Carl Bertram: *Die Grabmale von Burg Rheineck. Zur Geschichte der Juden im ehemaligen Ländchen Breisig und der früheren Herrschaft Rheineck.* Essen: Historischer Verein für Stadt und Stift Essen, 1983. 91 pp., 60 illus., facsims. (Beiträge zur Geschichte von Stadt und Stift Essen, H. 97.)

19811. COLOGNE. *Die verschwundene Synagoge von Köln-Mülheim.* Hrsg. von der Evangelischen Kirchengemeinde Mülheim am Rhein und der Katholischen Pfarrgemeinde Liebfrauen. [Schülerheft.] Köln-Mülheim, 1983. 19 pp., 22 illus. [Obtainable from Josef Metternich, Adamsstr. 15, D-5000 Köln 80.] [Incl. taped reminiscences on Mülheim by Erwin Schild, now rabbi in Toronto.]

19812. DANZIG. Stern, Eliyahu: *The Jews of Danzig, 1840–1943; integration, struggle, rescue.* [In Hebrew]. Kibbutz Lohamei Haghettaot: Ghetto Fighters' House; Tel-Aviv: Hakibbutz Hameuchad, 1983. 339 pp. [Cf.: Die Juden Danzigs [in]: MB, Nr. 22, Tel-Aviv, 10. Juni 1983, pp. 5 & 7.]

19813. FRANCONIA. Schubert, Ernst: *Arme Leute, Bettler und Gauner im Franken des 18. Jahrhunderts.* Neustadt a.d. Aisch: Degener, 1983. 486 pp. (Veröffentlichungen der Gesellschaft für fränkische Geschichte, Reihe 9, Bd. 26.) [Also on rural Jewry in Franconia.]

19814. — Schwierz, Israel: *Zeugnisse jüdischer Vergangenheit in Unterfranken.* Hrsg.: Rudolf Sussmann. Bamberg: Bayerische Verlagsanstalt, 1983. 136 pp., illus.

19815. FRANKFURT am Main. Arnsberg, Paul: *Die Geschichte der Frankfurter Juden seit der Französischen Revolution.* Bd. 1–3. Hrsg. vom Kuratorium für Jüdische Geschichte, Frankfurt am Main. Bearb. und vollendet durch Hans-Otto Schembs. Darmstadt: Roether, 1983. 3 vols., illus., ports., facsims., folding plan, footnotes. *Bd. 1: Der Gang der Ereignisse (1789–1933).* 913 pp. *Bd. 2: Struktur und Aktivitäten der Frankfurter Juden von 1789 bis zu deren Vernichtung in der nationalsozialistischen Ära.* Handbuch. 595 pp. *Bd. 3: Biographisches Lexikon der Juden in den Bereichen: Wissenschaft, Kultur, Bildung, Öffentlichkeitsarbeit in Frankfurt am Main.* 660 pp., bibl. (545–563), index to vols. 1–3 (564–660). [*Vol. 2* covers the activities within the Jewish community including the communities Bockenheim, Heddernheim, Höchst, Niederursel, Rödelheim; also on Jewish participation in the public life of Frankfurt; incl. chaps: Die jüd. Presse; Jüd. Ärzte; Jüd. Advokaten; Im Jahr 1933 entlassene jüd. Dozenten der Frankfurter Universität; Juden in der allgemeinen Wohlfahrtspflege; Juden als Kriegsteilnehmer. *Vol. 3* includes appendix: Frankfurter Juden in der Kommunalpolitik (527–541).] [P. Arnsberg, Frankfurt am Main Dec. 26, 1899 – Dec. 10, 1978, historian, emigrated to Palestine in 1933, returned in 1958.]

—— — Lowenstein, Steven M.: *Jewish residential concentration.* [See No. 19774.]

19816. — SCHIVELBUSCH, WOLFGANG: *Intellektuellendämmerung*. Zur Lage der Frankfurter Intelligenz in den 20er Jahren: die Universität; das Freie Jüdische Lehrhaus; die Frankfurter Zeitung; Radio Frankfurt; der Goethe-Preis und Sigmund Freud; das Institut für Sozialforschung. Frankfurt am Main: Insel, 1982. 141 pp. (Die Hessen-Bibliothek.)

19817. FREUDENTAL. NEBEL, THEOBALD: *Die Geschichte der Freudentaler Juden*. [In]: Ludwigsburger Geschichtsblätter, H. 34, Ludwigsburg, 1982. Pp. 36–74.

19818. FRIEDBERG. HERRMANN, FRITZ H.: *Judentaufen in Burg-Friedberg*. [In]: Wetterauer Geschichtsblätter, Bd. 30, Friedberg, 1981. Pp. 63–68.

19819. — HERRMANN, FRITZ H.: *Vom 'Opferpfennig' befreit – die 'Kronsteuer' erfolgreich verweigert*. [In]: Wetterauer Geschichtsblätter, Bd. 32, Friedberg, 1983. Pp. 119–123.

19820. FÜRTH/BAVARIA. *Nachrichten für den jüdischen Bürger Fürths*. Hrsg.: Isr. Kultusgemeinde Fürth. Red.: Ruben J. Rosenfeld. Fürth (Blumenstr. 31), Sept. 1983. 51 pp., ports., facsims., bibl. [Incl.: Aus dem Tagebuch, 1842–1847, des Abraham Kohn, geb. 1824 in Fürth (10–12; reprinted from 'Jüdisches Leben in Deutschland, 1780–1871', ed. by Monika Richarz, see No. 19780). Dr. Jakob Frank: das Schicksal eines Fürther Juden, der an die Emanzipation glaubte (Werner Heymann, 13–14; J. Frank, May 19, 1871 Baiersdorf –1953 USA). Jüd. Hochzeitsbräuche in Fürth (Jitzchak Rosenfeld, 19–21). Selichot: das Bussgebet; mit einer Bibliographie aller in Fürth gedruckten Selichot (Mosche N. Rosenfeld, 22–32, facsims.). Leben und Wirken des Univ.professors und Arztes Jakob Herz (Ilse Sponsel, 38–40; J. Herz, Feb. 2, 1816 Bayreuth – Sept. 27, 1871 Erlangen). Further contributions are listed according to subject.]

19821. GIESSEN. STUMPF, OTTO: *Bussgeldlisten aus den Rechnungen des Amtes Giessen von 1568–1599*. [In]: Mitteilungen des Oberhessischen Geschichtsvereins Giessen, N.F. Bd. 66, Giessen, 1981. Pp. 203–219. [Refers also to 'Judenschutzgeld'.]

19822. GRÜNSFELD. WEISS, ELMAR: *Die Geschichte der Juden in Grünsfeld*. [In]: Weiss, Elmar: Geschichte der Stadt Grünsfeld. Grünsfeld: Stadtverwaltung, 1981. Pp. 553–581, illus., facsims., footnotes.

19823. HALLE. GERICKE, WERNER/MASCH, FRIEDRICH: *Die israelitische Kultusgemeinde*. [In]: Halles Minderheiten. Bd. 2. [Hrsg. von der] Vereinigung ehemaliger Hallenser. Bornheim-Sechtem (Graue-Burg-Str. 95): A. Deutschbein, 1981. 37 pp.

—— HAMBURG. FREIMARK, PETER: *Juden in Hamburg*. [See in No. 19841].

19824. — FREIMARK, PETER/LORENZ, INA/MARWEDEL, GÜNTER: *Judentore, Kuggel, Steuerkonten; Untersuchungen zur Geschichte der deutschen Juden, vornehmlich im Hamburger Raum*. Hamburg: Christians, 1983. 297 pp., illus., port., facsims., plans, bibl. references. (Hamburger Beiträge zur Geschichte der deutschen Juden, Bd. 9.) [Cont.: Eruw/'Judentore': zur Geschichte einer rituellen Institution im Hamburger Raum und anderswo (Peter Freimark, 10–69). Glückel von Hameln und ihre Familie in den Steuerkontenbüchern der aschkenasischen Gemeinde Altona (Günter Marwedel, 70–97). Das Altonaer Oberrabbinat und die Juden in Fredericia (G. Marwedel, 98–168). Kuggel und Lockschen in Hamburg: ein Beitrag zur jüdischen Schiller-Rezeption im 19. Jahrhundert (P. Freimark, 169–220). Sozialistische Gesellschaft in Palästina; ein Briefwechsel Ernst Tollers mit einer Hamburger Zionistin, 1925 (Ina Lorenz, 221–292).]

19825. — HERZIG, ARNO [et al.], eds.: *Arbeiter in Hamburg*. Unterschichten, Arbeiter und Arbeiterbewegung seit dem ausgehenden 18. Jahrhundert. Hamburg: Verlag Erziehung und Wissenschaft, 1983. (Veröffentlichung des Hamburger Arbeitskreises für Regionalgeschichte.) [Incl.: Antijüdischer Sozialprotest? Proteste von Unter- und Mittelschichten 1819–1835 (Mosche Zimmermann, 89–94). Die politischen und sozialen Impulse bei der Gründung der organisierten Arbeiterbewegung in Hamburg (Shlomo Na'aman, 153–163; refers, a.o., to Ferdinand Lassalle).]

—— — LOWENSTEIN, STEVEN M.: *Jewish residential concentration*. [See No. 19774.]

19826. — POPPEL, STEPHEN M.: *The politics of religious leadership: the rabbinate in nineteenth-century Hamburg*. [In]: LBI Year Book XXVIII, London, 1983. Pp. 439–470, footnotes.

19827. — *Wegweiser zu den ehemaligen Stätten jüdischen Lebens oder Leidens in Hamburg*. Hrsg. von der Deutsch-Jüdischen Gesellschaft Hamburg. *Heft 1: Die Stadtteile Neustadt und St. Pauli*. Bearb. von W. Mosel. Hamburg, 1983. 115 pp., notes, bibl. [First of 10 issues.]

19828. HEILBRONN. HOPPE, GÜNTER: *Juden in der deutschen Provinz; die Geschichte einer Minderheit am Beispiel der Stadt Heilbronn*. [1–2]. [In]: Tribüne, Jg. 22, H. 88 (pp. 134–142) [&] Jg. 23, H. 89 (pp. 140–146, bibl.). Frankfurt am Main, 1983–1984. [Also on the Nazi Period.]

19829. HESSE. BATTENBERG, FRIEDRICH/KROPAT, WOLF-ARNO: *Emanzipation und Verfolgung;*

Geschichte der Juden in Hessen. (Red. und Sachbearb.: Erwin Wiegand.) Frankfurt am Main: Staatliche Landesbildstelle Hessen, 1981. 80 pp., 33 illus., bibl. (Beiheft zur Farblichtbildreihe, 108104.)

19830. — KEIM, ANTON MARIA: *Die Judenfrage im Landtag des Grossherzogtums Hessen 1820–1849.* Ein Beitrag zur Geschichte der Juden im Vormärz. Darmstadt: Hessische Historische Kommission; Marburg: Historische Kommission für Hessen, 1983. 258 pp., bibl. (236–244). (Quellen und Forschungen zur hessischen Geschichte, 46.)

19831. — KÜNZL, HANNELORE: *Synagogenbauten in Rheinhessen.* [In]: Alzeyer Geschichtsblätter, H. 16, Alzey, 1981. Pp. 104–122.

19832. — *Neunhundert Jahre Geschichte der Juden in Hessen.* Beiträge zum politischen, wirtschaftlichen und kulturellen Leben. (Red.: Christiane Heinemann.) Wiesbaden (Mainzer Str. 80): Kommission für die Geschichte der Juden in Hessen, 1983. 512 pp., illus., notes, bibl. (509–512). (Schriften der Kommission für die Geschichte der Juden in Hessen, 6.) [Cont.: Gestaltung und Krisis: Juden und Nichtjuden in Deutschland vom Mittelalter bis zur Neuzeit (Peter Herde, 1–40). Bischof, Stadt und Judengemeinde von Worms im Mittelalter, 1349–1526 (Fritz Reuter, 41–82). Judenordnungen der frühen Neuzeit in Hessen (F. Battenberg, 83–122). Assenheimer Judenpogrome vor dem Reichskammergericht; die Prozesse der Grafschaften Hanau, Isenburg und Solms um die Ausübung des Judenregals 1567–1573 (F. Battenberg, 123–150). Die Landjudenschaften in Hessen-Darmstadt bis zur Emanzipation als Organe der jüd. Selbstverwaltung (Daniel J. Cohen, 151–214). Joseph Süss Oppenheimer – 'Jud Süss' – und die Darmstädter Goldmünze: ein Beitrag zur hessen-darmstädtischen Finanzpolitik unter Landgraf Ernst Ludwig (Jürgen Rainer Wolf, 215–262). Juden an den hessischen Hochschulen im 18. Jh. (Rüdiger Mack, 263–302), Der erste jüd. Goldschmied im Fürstentum Waldeck: Nathan Schwerin, 1792–1859; ein Kapitel aus dem Kampf um die Zulassung der Juden zum zünftigen Handwerk (Bernhard Brilling, 303–324). Die Emanzipation der Juden in Kurhessen und in Nassau im 19. Jh. (Wolf-Arno Kropat, 325–350). Synagogen in Hessen um 1900 (Annie Bardon, 351–376). Otto Böckel und die antisemitische Bauernbewegung in Hessen 1887–1894 (R. Mack, 377–410). Die hessischen Juden im Alltag der NS-Diktatur 1933–1939 (W.-A. Kropat, 411–446). Jüd. Gemeinden, Wiedergutmachung, Rechtsradikalismus und Antisemitismus nach 1945 (W.-A. Kropat, 447 ff.]

—— KASSEL. HALLO, RUDOLF: *Geschichte der jüdischen Gemeinde Kassel. Bd. 1: Kasseler Synagogengeschichte* [et al.]. [See in No. 20236.]

19833. KÖNIGSBERG. JACOBY, YORAM K.: *Jüdisches Leben in Königsberg/Preussen.* Würzburg: Holzner, 1983. 169 pp., footnotes. [Also on Jews in the economic and cultural life; incl. the Nazi period.]

19834. KÖNIGSTEIN. STURM-GODRAMSTEIN, HEINZ: *Juden in Königstein.* Leben – Bedeutung – Schicksale. Hrsg. vom Magistrat der Stadt Königstein/Ts.: Stadtarchiv, 1983. 221 pp., illus., ports., facsims., bibl. (110–111). [Also on the Nazi period.]

19835. LIPPSTADT. MÜHLE, EDUARD: *Zur Geschichte der Juden in Lippstadt bis zum Ende des dreissigjährigen Krieges.* [In]: Der Märker, 31, H. 2, Altena, 1982. Pp. 49–57.

19836. LÜDINGHAUSEN. BRILLING, BERNHARD: *Die jüdische Gemeinde Lüdinghausen.* [In]: 675 Jahre Stadt Lüdinghausen. Hrsg.: Heimatverein Lüdinghausen. 1983. Pp. 125–129.

19837. MAINZ. SCHÜTZ, FRIEDRICH: *'Ihr weint Tränen der treuen Erinnerung . . .': zum 100. Geburtstag von Dr. Sali Levi, dem letzten Mainzer Rabbiner.* [In]: Mainz, Jg. 3, H. 4, Mainz, 1983. Pp. 108–112, ports. [See also: Erinnerung an Mainz: Rabbiner Dr. S. Levi wäre 100 geworden (E. G. Lowenthal) [in]: Aufbau, No. 47, New York, Nov. 25, 1983, p. 2.] [S. Levi, Nov. 2, 1883 Walldorf, Baden – Apr. 25, 1941 Berlin, rabbi, historian.]

19838. NEUWIED. DEETERS, DOROTHEA ELISABETH: *Sie lebten mit uns; zur Geschichte der Wied-Neuwiedischen Landjuden, für die Zeit von 1817–1942 dargestellt an Dorf und Synagogenbezirk Oberbieber.* Hrsg. von der Evang. Kirchengemeinde Oberbieber. Neuwied-Oberbieber: Offsetdruck Veith, 1983. 64 pp.

19839. OLDENBURG. TÖLLNER, JOHANNES-FRITZ, comp.: *Die jüdischen Friedhöfe im Oldenburger Land.* Bestandsaufnahme der erhaltenen Grabsteine. In Zusammenarbeit mit Wouter J. van Bekkum [et al.]. Oldenburg: Holzberg, 1983. 700 pp., illus. (Oldenburger Studien, Bd. 25.)

19840. PLAUEN. SCHMIDT, HANNES: *Zur Geschichte der Israelitischen Religionsgemeinde Plauen im Vogtland.* [In]: Nachrichtenblatt des Verbandes der Jüd. Gemeinden in der DDR, Dresden, Dez. 1983. Pp. 10–12, illus.

19841. PRUSSIA. FREIMARK, PETER, ed.: *Juden in Preussen – Juden in Hamburg.* Hamburg: Christians, 1983. 116 pp., notes, list of names (115–116). (Hamburger Beiträge zur Geschichte der deutschen Juden, Bd. 10.) [Cont.: Die Herausbildung eines 'preussischen' Judentums 1671–1815 (Stefi Jersch-Wenzel, 11–31). Die Juden in Preussen im 19. Jh. (Arno Herzig, 32–58). Juden in Hamburg (Peter Freimark, 59–80). Zur Geschichte der Hamburger Juden 1919–1939 (Baruch Z. Ophir, 81–97). Minoritätenstatus und Toleranz (Hermann Greive, 98–112).]

19842. — PASTOLOVE, YVONNE E.: *'Jewish' porcelain.* [In]: Jewish Spectator, Vol. 48, No. 2, Santa Monica, Calif., Summer 1983. Pp. 38–39.

19843. — SCHOEPS, JULIUS H.: *Christlicher Staat und jüdische Gleichberechtigung: der Antisemitismus der Konservativen und der jüdische Abwehrkampf im Reaktionsjahrzehnt in Preussen 1850–1858.* [In]: Konservatismus – eine Gefahr für die Freiheit? Für Iring Fetscher. München: Piper, 1983. Pp. 38–54.

19844. — WOLFF, RAYMOND: *Das Judenporzellan.* [In]: Der Bär von Berlin, Folge 32, Berlin, 1983. Pp. 67–84, illus., facsims., notes.

19845. — ZIMMERMANN, VOLKER: *Ein besonderer Eid für jüdische Ärzte und Wundärzte in Preussen.* [In]: Medizinhistorisches Journal, Bd. 17, Nr. 1–2, Stuttgart, 1982. Pp. 78–88.

19846. RECKLINGHAUSEN. SCHNEIDER, WERNER: *Jüdische Heimat im Vest; Gedenkbuch der jüdischen Gemeinden im Kreis Recklinghausen.* Recklinghausen: Winkelmann, 1983. 216 pp., illus., port., facsims., list of families (211–214), bibl. (216). [Incl. sections on the Jewish communities of Bottrop, Buer, Castrop-Rauxel, Datteln, Dorsten, Gladbeck, Haltern, Horst, Recklinghausen, Waltrop; also on the Nazi period.]

19847. REGENSBURG. SCHLICHTING, GÜNTER: *Impressionen aus der Regensburger jüdischen Geschichte.* Vortrag vor der Regensburger 'Gesellschaft für christlich-jüdische Zusammenarbeit' am 10. Nov. 1981. No imprint [Tübingen: Institutum Judaicum der Univ., 1983?]. 15 pp., bibl.

19848. RHINELAND. BARKAI, AVRAHAM: *Die sozio-ökonomische Entwicklung der Juden in Rheinland-Westfalen in der Industrialisierung (1850–1910).* [In]: Bulletin des LBI, 66, Königstein/Ts., 1983. Pp. 53–81, diagrs., notes (77–81).

19849. — DUCHHARDT, HEINZ: *Judenpolitik am Mittelrhein nach dem 30jährigen Krieg.* [In]: Jahrbuch für Westdeutsche Landesgeschichte, 8, Koblenz, 1982. Pp. 13–24, footnotes.

—— — HERZIG, ARNO: *Politische Zielsetzung jüdischer Intellektueller.* [See in No. 19769.]

19850. — LINN, HEINRICH: *Juden an Rhein und Sieg.* Unter Mitarb. von Horst Dahlhaus [et al.]. (Ausstellung des Archivs des Rhein-Sieg-Kreises, Mai–Sept. 1983.) [Katalog]. Siegburg: Franz Schmitt, 1983. XI, 672 pp., illus., ports., facsims. (633–672), maps, geneal., bibl. (621–628). [Cont. chaps. (headings condensed): Jüdische Feste und Riten. Juden vor 1800. Die Emanzipation. Die 'assimilierten' Juden in Kaiserreich und Weimarer Republik, 1871–1933 (refers, a.o., to the historian Wilhelm Levison, 1876–1947; Hermann Levy, Hennef 1860–1936; Sanitätsrat Dr. Moritz Herzfeld, Ruppichteroth 1860–1931). Soziale Stellung und wirtschaftliche Bedeutung. Nationalsozialistische Herrschaft, 1933–1945. Die einzelnen Synagogengemeinden (Siegburg; Mondorf; Hennef-Geistingen; Ruppichteroth; Rosbach/Sieg; Königswinter; Honnef; Bornheim/Hersel/Alfter; Heimerzheim; Rheinbach; Meckenheim; Bonn vor 1945; Jüd. Friedhöfe; Statistik). Neubeginn nach 1945. Katalogteil (pp. 409 ff.).]

19851. — RESMINI, BERTRAM: *Juden am Mittelrhein im 16. Jahrhundert.* [In]: Jahrbuch für Westdeutsche Landesgeschichte, Bd. 7, Koblenz, 1981. Pp. 75–104.

19852. SCHERMBECK. KAMMEIER, ANDREA: *Die ehemalige jüdische Gemeinde in Schermbeck.* Schermbeck: Evang. Kirchengemeinde, 1982. 14 pp., illus. [Incl. list of Jews formerly living in Schermbeck (12–13).]

19853. SCHLITZ/Hess. SIPPEL, HEINRICH: *Die Schlitzer Juden.* (Studien zur Schlitzer Geschichte, H. 10, März 1983.) [Obtainable from the author, Ingendorfer Höhe 20, D-5024 Pulheim 3.]

19854. SCHOPFLOCH. PHILIPP, KARL: *Lachoudisch; Geheimsprache Schopflochs.* Dinkelsbuhl: C. W. Wengg, 1983. 52 pp. [Refers also to Jewish life in Schopfloch. Cf.: Lachoudisch: Jiddisch oder Geheimsprache? (W. Wagner/B. Sabrautzki [in]: Neue Jüd. Nachrichten, Nr. 31, München, 23. Dez. 1983, p. 8.]

19855. SEGEBERG. TSCHENTSCHER, HORST: *Als Juden Segeberger Bürger wurden.* Bad Segeberg: Wäser, 1981. 16 pp., 1 illus.

19856. — TSCHENTSCHER, HORST: *Juden im Segeberger Bürgerbuch, 1744–1813.* [In]: Familienkundliches Jahrbuch Schleswig-Holstein, 20, Kiel, 1981. Pp. 78–89.

19857. SILESIA. BARTSCH, HEINRICH: *Die Städte Schlesiens (in den Grenzen des Jahres 1937).* Daten und Fakten zu ihrer landes-, kultur-, wirtschafts- und sozialgeschichtlichen Entwicklung und Bedeutung. 2., verbesserte Aufl. Frankfurt am Main: Weidlich, 1983. 372, XVI pp., illus., maps, bibl. (365–369). (Veröffentlichungen der Forschungsstelle Ostmitteleuropa in Dortmund, Reihe A, Nr. 32.) [Incl. for each town: size of Jewish population up to 1937; also references to synagogues, Jewish schools and cemeteries, especially detailed in the Breslau chapter.]

19858. SPEYER. *Geschichte der Stadt Speyer.* Hrsg. von der Stadt Speyer. Red.: Wolfgang Eger. 2., durchgesehene Aufl. Bd. 1–2. Stuttgart: Kohlhammer, 1983. 2 vols., illus. [Incl. in vol. 2: Die Speyerer Juden 1871–1914 (Hans Fenske, 253–254). Juden (Karl Heinz Debus, 472–477; on the Jewish Community).]

19859. SPRENDLINGEN. *Die Sprendlinger Juden.* Verfasst und bearb. von: Arno Baumbusch [et al.]. Sprendlingen: Freunde Sprendlingens, Heimatkundliche Arbeitsgemeinschaft, 1983. 203 pp., illus. [Also on the Nazi period.]

19860. STOMMELN. *Juden in Stommeln; Geschichte einer jüdischen Gemeinde im Kölner Umland.* Bd. 1. Pulheim (Adamistr. 9): Verein für Geschichte und Heimatkunde, 1983. 1 vol., illus., facsims., plans, bibl. (Pulheimer Beiträge zur Geschichte und Heimatkunde.)

19861. TIENGEN. Petri, Dieter: *Die Tiengener Juden.* Konstanz (Marktstätte 22), 1982. 151, [5] pp., illus., ports., facsims., plans, tabs., bibl. (Schriften des Arbeitskreises für Regionalgeschichte, 4.) [Also on the Nazi period.]

19862. VOREIFEL. Arntz, H.-Dieter: *Judaica: Juden in der Voreifel.* Euskirchen: Kümpel, 1983. 539 pp., illus., ports., facsims., tabs., maps, bibl. (535–539). [Mainly on Euskirchen; incl. the Nazi period.]

19863. WESTPHALIA. Aschoff, Diethard: *Die Feme und die Juden.* [In]: Beiträge zur Geschichte Dortmunds und der Grafschaft Mark, Bd. 72, 1980. Pp. 31–47. [Refers to Westphalia during the Middle Ages.]

19864. — Aschoff, Diethard: *Die Juden in Westfalen zwischen Schwarzem Tod und Reformation.* Studien zur Geschichte der Juden in Westfalen. [In]: Westfälische Forschungen, Bd. 30, Münster, 1980. Pp. 78–106.

19865. — Berding, Helmut: *Die Emanzipation der Juden im Königreich Westfalen (1807–1813).* [In]: Archiv für Sozialgeschichte, Bd. 23, Bonn, 1983. Pp. 25–50, footnotes.

19866. — Brilling, Bernhard: *Die jüdischen Gemeinden [in Westfalen].* [In]: Westfälische Geschichte. Bd. 2. Hrsg. von Wilhelm Kohl. Düsseldorf: Schwann, 1983. Pp. 417–430.

—— WORMS. Reuter, Fritz: *Bischof, Stadt und Judengemeinde von Worms im Mittelalter.* [See in No. 19832.]

19867. WÜRTTEMBERG. Tänzer, Aaron: *Die Geschichte der Juden in Württemberg.* Unveränd. Nachdr. der Ausg. Frankfurt am Main, Kauffmann-Verl., 1937. Frankfurt am Main: Weidlich, 1983. XV, 190 pp., bibl. (174–179). (Weidlich-Reprints.)

1a. **Alsace**

19868. Caron, Vicki: *Patriotism or profit? The emigration of Alsace-Lorraine Jews to France, 1871–1872.* [In]: LBI Year Book XXVIII, London, 1983. Pp. 139–168, tabs., appendix.

19869. Raphael, Freddy: *Les juifs de la campagne alsacienne: les marchands de bestiaux.* [In]: Revue des Sciences Sociales de la France de l'Est, No. 8, Strasbourg, 1979. Pp. 166–184.

19870. Weyl, Robert: *Le cahier de doléance des juifs d'Alsace.* [In]: Revue Alsace, 108 (No. 587), 1983. Pp. 65–80.

2. **Austria**

19871. Bunzl, John/Marin, Bernd: *Antisemitismus in Österreich.* Sozialhistorische und soziologische Studien. Mit einem Vorwort von Anton Pelinka. Innsbruck: Inn-Verl., 1983. 226 pp., 72 pp. of charts, bibl. (Vergleichende Gesellschaftsgeschichte und politische Ideengeschichte der Neuzeit, Bd. 3.) [Cont.: Zur Geschichte des Antisemitismus in Österreich (John Bunzl, 9–88). 'Die Juden' in der Kronen-Zeitung; textanalytisches Fragment zur Mythenproduktion 1974 (Bernd Marin, 89–170; refers to 'Die Juden in Österreich', a series of 42 articles by Viktor Reimann publ. in the Kronen-Zeitung, Vienna, Apr. 7–May 14, 1974). Ein historisch neuartiger 'Antisemitismus ohne Antisemiten'? (Bernd Marin, 171–192). Nachwirkungen des Nazismus (Bernd Marin, 193–224). Umfragebefunde zum Antisemitismus in Österreich 1946–1982 (Bernd Marin, 225 ff.).]

—— GRAB, WALTER/SCHOEPS, JULIUS H., eds.: *Juden im Vormärz und in der Revolution von 1848.* [See No. 19769.]

19872. KARNIEL, JOSEF: *Fürst Kaunitz und die Juden.* [In]: Jahrbuch des Instituts für Deutsche Geschichte, Bd. 12, Tel-Aviv, 1983. Pp. 15–27, footnotes.

—— KARNIEL, JOSEF: *Jüdischer Pseudomessianismus und deutsche Kultur.* [See in No. 19764.]

—— McCAGG JR., WILLIAM O.: *The assimilation of Jews in Austria.* [See in No. 19784.]

19873. POLLEROSS, FRIEDRICH B.: *Hundert Jahre Antisemitismus im Waldviertel.* Krems an der Donau: Waldviertler Heimatbund, Faber-Verl., 1983. 122, XII pp., illus. (Schriftenreihe des Waldviertler Heimatbundes, Bd. 25.)

19874. SOTRIFFER, KRISTIAN, ed.: *Das grössere Österreich: geistiges und soziales Leben von 1880 bis zur Gegenwart.* Wien: Edition Tusch, 1982. 551 pp., 550 illus., ports., facsims. [Incl.: 'Deutsche Worte' oder wer ein Jude ist (Johny Moser). Mit Juden kein Staat zu machen: Theodor Herzl und die Folgen (Jonny Moser). Die Leopoldstadt: Paradoxien des jüd. Schicksals (Jonny Moser). Theater im Vorkriegswien: Jura Soyfer und der Widerstand (Monika Meister). Der grosse Exodus: wo Österreich am Leben blieb (Elisabeth Freundlich). Dachau: eine österreichische Kolonie (Wolfgang Neugebauer). Der letzte Kapitalist: Louis Nathaniel von Rothschild (Fritz Weber). 'Das Malschiff': 'Arier' und 'Entartete' (Bernhard Peithner-Lichtenfels). Also essays on Alfred Adler, Hermann Broch, Sigmund Freud, Hugo von Hofmannsthal, Franz Kafka, Karl Kraus, Max Reinhardt, Joseph Roth, Arnold Schönberg, Otto Weininger, Ludwig Wittgenstein.]

19875. SPITZER, SHLOMO: *Hebrew deeds of sale from the 14th century in Austria.* [In Hebrew, with English summary]. [In]: Bar-Ilan; Annual of Bar-Ilan Univ., Vol. 20/21, Ramat-Gan, 1983. Pp. 192–213, facsim. [Incl. texts of 10 deeds.]

19876. TOURY, JACOB: *Die jüdische Presse im österreichischen Kaiserreich; ein Beitrag zur Problematik der Akkulturation 1802–1918.* Tübingen: Mohr, 1983. VIII, 171 pp., bibl. (159–163). (Schriftenreihe wissenschaftlicher Abhandlungen des Leo Baeck Instituts, 41.) [Cf.: Austro-Hungarian press [in]: AJR Information, London, March 1984, p. 11. Besprechung [in]: Aufbau, No. 47, New York, Nov. 25, 1983, p. 13.]

19877. WACHTER, ANDREA: *Antisemitismus im österreichischen Vereinswesen für Leibesübungen 1918–38 am Beispiel der Geschichte ausgewählter Vereine.* Wien, Univ., Diss., 1983. V, 250 pp., 24 facsims.

19878. WEINZIERL, ERIKA/SKALNIK, KURT, eds.: *Österreich 1918–1938; Geschichte der Ersten Republik.* Graz: Styria, 1983. 2 vols. [Refers to antisemitism in the essays on the Christian-Social Party (Anton Staudinger) and on the Church and politics (Erika Weinzierl).]

19879. GALICIA. MARKOVITZ, ANDREI S./SYSYN, FRANK E., eds.: *Nationbuilding and the politics of nationalism.* Essays on Austrian Galicia. Cambridge, Mass.: Harvard Univ. Press, 1982. VIII, 343 pp., map, footnotes. (Harvard Ukrainian Research Institute, monograph series.) [Incl.: Jewish assimilation in L'vov: the case of Wilhelm Feldman (E. Mendelsohn). The rise of Jewish national politics in Galicia, 1905–1907 (L. P. Everett).]

19880. VIENNA. ANDICS, HELLMUT: *Ringstrassenwelt: Wien 1867–1887; Luegers Aufstieg.* Wien: Jugend & Volk, 1983. 327 pp., illus., ports., bibl. [See also No. 20754.]

19881. — LOHRMANN, KLAUS: *Die Juden in Wien zur Zeit der Türkenkriege.* [In]: Die Türken vor Wien; Europa und die Entscheidung an der Donau 1683. Katalog der 82. Sonderausstellung des Historischen Museums der Stadt Wien. 1983. Pp. 298–301. [Largely on the Court Factor Samuel Oppenheimer.]

19882. — WALKER, COLIN: *Nestroy's 'Judith und Holofernes' and antisemitism in Vienna.* [In]: Oxford German Studies, 12, Oxford, Aug. 1981. Pp. 85–110, footnotes.

19883. ZISLEITHANIEN. GAISBAUER, ADOLF: *Zionismus und jüdischer Nationalismus in Zisleithanien (1882–1918).* Bd. 1–2. Wien, Univ., Diss., 1981. 855 pp.

3. **Czechoslovakia**

19884. *Informationsbulletin.* Hrsg. vom Rat der Jüd. Religionsgemeinden in der Tschechischen Sozialistischen Republik zu Prag und vom Zentralverband der Jüd. Religionsgemeinden in der Slowakischen Sozialistischen Republik zu Bratislava. Nr. 1 & 2–3 (März & Sept.). Red.: Desider Galsky. Prag: Zentralkirchenverlag, 1983. 2 issues, with English summaries. [*Nr. 1* incl.: Michler Mysterien: Geschichte der gewesenen Synagoge in Prag-Michle (24–27). Leben im Dunkeln: Oskar Baum (33–34; O.B., 1883–1941, expressionist writer). *Nr. 2–3:* Schüsse in Marienbad: Ermordung Theodor Lessings, 30. Aug. 1933 (21–24). Geschichte der Juden in Eger und Königsberg an der Eger (25–28). Professor Dr. Emil Utitz (29–33; E.U., 1883–1956, philosopher and psychologist). Zum 80. Jahrestag seit dem Tode von Hieronymus Lorm (34–35; H.L., 1821–1902, orig. Heinrich Landesmann, writer and philosopher). Jüd. Musikkultur in Böhmen (35–39).]

19885. *Judaica Bohemiae*. Vol. 19, Nos. 1–2. Publication du Musée juif d'Etat, Prague. Rédacteur en chef: Otokar Petřík. Praha: Státní židovské muzeum v Praze, 1983. 60; 63–124 pp., illus., footnotes. [2 issues.] [Incl.: Social aspects in the work of Prague Rabbi Löw = Maharal, 1512–1609 (Vladimír Sadek, No. 1, pp. 3–21). Further contributions are listed according to subject.]

19886. *Die Juden in den böhmischen Ländern*. Vorträge der Tagung des Collegium Carolinum in Bad Wiessee vom 27. bis 29. Nov. 1981. Hrsg. von Ferdinand Seibt. München: Oldenbourg, 1983. 368 pp., illus., tabs., 2 folding plans, bibl. references. [Cont.: Die Juden in Böhmen und Mähren im Mittelalter und die ersten Privilegien (Peter Hilsch). Die Luxemburger und die Juden (Wilhelm Hanisch). Böhmische Judengemeinden, 1348–1519 (Maria Tischler). Juden im Ständestaat; zur politischen, wirtschaftlichen und sozialen Geschichte der Juden in Mähren zwischen 1526 und 1620 (Helmut Teufel). Jüd. Gemeinden in Böhmen und Mähren im 17. und 18. Jh. (Vladimir Lipscher). Das Ghetto von Prag (Wilfried Brosche). Die Juden in den böhmischen Ländern zur Zeit des landesfürstlichen Absolutismus (Anna M. Drabek). Toleranzedikt und Emanzipation (Eila Hassenpflug-Elzholz). Identifikation der Prager Juden vor und während der Assimilation (Ruth Gladstein-Kestenberg). Heinrich Friedjung (Harald Bachmann). Der Anteil der Juden am Wirtschaftsleben der böhmischen Länder seit dem Beginn der Industrialisierung (Gustav Otruba). Die soziale und politische Stellung der Juden in der Ersten Republik (Landislav Lipscher). 'Schicksalswende' und 'Der ewige Jude': antisemitische Filmpropaganda am Anfang der NS-Ostexpansion (Stephan Dolezel). Die deutschsprachige jüd. Emigration aus der Tschechoslowakei nach Grossbritannien 1938–1945 (Eva Schmidt-Hartmann). Juden und Nichtjuden in der Geschichte der böhmischen Länder (Hans Lemberg). Übersicht über die nationalsozialistische 'Endlösung der jüd. Frage' in den böhmischen Ländern (Eva Schmidt-Hartmann). Statistische Materialien zur Geschichte der Juden in den böhmischen Ländern seit dem Ausgang des 18. Jh. (G. Otruba).]

—— Pazi, Margarita: *Jüdisch-deutsche Schrifteller in Böhmen im 19. Jahrhundert*. [See in No. 19764.]

—— Riff, Michael A.: *Jüdische Schriftsteller und das Dilemma der Assimilation im Böhmischen Vormärz*. [See in No. 19769.]

4. **Switzerland**

19887. Dreifuss, Emil: *Juden in Bern*. Ein Gang durch die Jahrhunderte. Im Anhang: Judentum – was ist das eigentlich? Bern: Betadruck, 1983. 64 pp., illus., facsims., bibl.

19888. Guggenheim-Grünberg, Florence: *Historisches aus Lengnau: die Vorfahren der Familien Weil*. [In]: Isr. Wochenblatt, Nr. 51, Zürich, 23. Dez. 1983. Pp. 23–24. [And]: *Wie kamen die Oppenheims ins Surbtal*. [In]: Isr. Wochenblatt, Nr. 36, Zürich, 9. Sept. 1983. P. 74.

19889. *Vielen unbekannt: die Jüdische Cultusgemeinde Bremgarten*. [In]: Isr. Wochenblatt, Nr. 49, Zürich, 9. Dez. 1983. Pp. 25–26.

C. **German Jews in Various Countries**

19890. Berroll, Selma C.: *In their image: German Jews and the Americanization of the Ost Juden in New York City*. [In]: New York History, Oct. 1982. Pp. 417–433, illus., ports., footnotes.

19891. Edelman, Joseph: *The centenary of Jewish immigration to the United States, 1881–1981*. [In]: Judaism, Vol. 32, No. 2, New York, Spring 1983. Pp. 215–229. [Incl. German-Jewish immigrants and refugees.]

19892. EXILE. *Biographisches Handbuch der deutschsprachigen Emigration nach 1933 = International biographical dictionary of Central European émigrés 1933–1945*. Hrsg. vom Institut für Zeitgeschichte München und von der Research Foundation for Jewish Immigration, Inc., New York, unter der Gesamtleitung von Werner Röder und Herbert A. Strauss. Bd. 1–3. München; New York; London; Paris: Saur, 1980–1983. 3 vols. in 4.
Bd. 1: Politik, Wirtschaft, Öffentliches Leben. 1980. [See No. 17040/YB XXVI.]

Vol. 2, pts. 1–2 [under the title]: *International biographical dictionary of Central European émigrés 1933–1945: The arts, sciences, and literature.* General eds.: Herbert A. Strauss – Werner Röder, with Hannah Caplan, Egon Radvany – Horst Möller, Dieter Marc Schneider. Research, writing and editing at the Research Foundation for Jewish Immigration: Fred Bilenkis [et al.]; at the Institut für Zeitgeschichte: Brigitte Bruns [et al.]. Eds.: Hannah Caplan (managing), Belinda Rosenblatt. *Pt. 1: A–K. Pt. 2: L–Z.* 1983. 1 vol. in 2 pts. (XCIV, 677; 678–1316 pp.), key for use of dictionary, glossary, list of pseud., bibl. (1308–1311). [Incl.: Prefaces (Curt C. Silberman/Martin Broszat, IX–X). Introductions: Jews in German history: persecution, emigration, acculturation (Herbert A. Strauss, XI–XXVI, tabs.); The political exiles: their politics and their contribution to post-war reconstruction (Werner Röder, XXVII–XL, tabs.); From Weimar to Bonn: the arts and humanities in exile and return, 1933–1980 (Horst Möller, XLI–LXVI); The migration of the academic intellectuals (Herbert A. Strauss, LXVII–LXXVII, tabs.); Some demographic and occupational characteristics of émigrés included in vol. 2 of the 'Dictionary' (Herbert A. Strauss, LXXVIII–LXXXVI, tabs.).]

Bd. 3: Gesamtregister = Index. Unter der Leitung von Werner Röder zusammengestellt von Sybille Claus, Daniel Niederland und Beatrix Schmidt. Leitung der Red.: Sybille Claus. XX. 281 pp. [Cont.: List of persons, pseudonyms, cover names and name changes (1–51). Index of countries of intermediate emigration and final settlement (53–163). Index of occupations (165–205). Index of parties, associations, institutions (207–269). Index of members of parliaments and of governments (271–277). List of Nobel Prize winners (281).]

19893. — Groth, Michael: *The road to New York; the emigration of Berlin journalists, 1933–1945.* Univ. of Iowa, Phil. Diss., 1983. V, 384 pp., bibl. (371–384). [Typescript.]

19894. — Grothusen, Klaus-Detlev: *Zuflucht bei Kemal Atatürk: die deutsche Emigration in der Türkei 1933–1945 und ihre Auswirkungen auf die Reform des Bildungswesens.* [In]: Südosteuropa-Mitteilungen, Jg. 21, H. 4, 1981. Pp. 49–60.

19895. — Heilbut, Anthony: *Exiled in paradise; German refugee artists and intellectuals in America from the 1930's to the present.* New York: Viking Press, 1983. XIV, 506 pp., ports., notes.

19896. — Hirschfeld, Gerhard, ed.: *Exil in Grossbritannien; zur Emigration aus dem nationalsozialistischen Deutschland.* Stuttgart: Klett-Cotta, 1983. 300 pp., footnotes. (Veröffentlichungen des Deutschen Historischen Instituts London, Bd. 14.) [Cont.: Einleitung (Gerhard Hirschfeld, 7 ff.). Das nationalsozialistische Deutschland und die Emigration nach Grossbritannien (John P. Fox, 14 ff.). Britische Regierungen und die deutsche Emigration 1933–1945 (Bernard Wasserstein, 44 ff.). Das deutsche politische Exil in London 1939–1945 (Anthony Glees, 62 ff.). Der Einfluss der deutschen Emigranten auf die britische Kriegszielpolitik (Lothar Kettenacker, 80 ff.). Deutsche Emigranten und britische Propaganda: zur Tätigkeit deutscher Emigranten bei britischen Geheimsendern (Conrad Pütter, 106 ff.). Deutsche Emigranten in Grossbritannien 1933–1945 (Francis L. Carsten, 138 ff.). 'His Majesty's most loyal internees': die Internierung und Deportation deutscher und österreichischer Flüchtlinge als 'enemy aliens' (Michael Seyfert, 155 ff.). Die Künste in der Emigration (John Willett, 183 ff.). Flüchtlingsunternehmen in den wirtschaftlichen Krisengebieten Grossbritanniens (Herbert Loebl, 205 ff.). Emigranten und aufnehmende Gesellschaft im Spannungsfeld: zur Geschichte deutsch-jüdischer Flüchtlinge in Schottland (Rainer Kölmel, 236 ff.). Deutsche Juden in England: zu einigen Aspekten des Assimilations- und Integrationsprozesses (Marion Berghahn, 268 ff.). English edn. forthcoming in 1984.]

19897. — Jackman, Jarrell C./Borden, Carla M., eds.; *The muses flee Hitler; cultural transfer and adaptation, 1930–1945.* Washington, D.C.: Smithsonian Institution Press, 1983. 348 pp., notes, bibl. (321–323). [Cont.: *First pt. 'Background and migration'*: Anti-intellectualism . . . under the Nazis (Alan Beyerchen, 29–44); The movement of people in a time of crisis (Herbert A. Strauss, 45–59). American refugee policy in historical perspective (Roger Daniels, 61–78); 'Wanted by the Gestapo: saved by America': Varian Fry and the Emergency Rescue Committee (Cynthia Jaffee McCabe, 79–94). *Second pt. 'The muses in America'*: German émigrés in Southern California (J. C. Jackman, 95–110); Essays on émigrés in the US: Sociologists (H. Stuart Hughes, 111–122); Writers (Alfred Kazin, 123–150); Architects (Christian F. Otto, 151–168); Physicists (Gerald Holton, 169–188); Chemists (P. Thomas Carroll, 189–204); Mathematicians (Nathan Reingold, 205–234). *Third pt. 'Cultural adaptation in worldwide perspective'*: Essays on refugees in: Switzerland (Helmut F. Pfanner, 235–248); Britain (Bernard Wasserstein, 249–256); Canada (Irving Abella/Harold Troper [&] Paula Jean Draper, 257–270; 271–282); Shanghai (Renata Berg-Pan, 283–289);

Circum-Caribbean (Judith Laikin Elkin, 291–302); Southern South America (Ronald C. Newton, 303–314).]

19898. — KOEBNER, THOMAS: *Vom 'Pazifismus' der dreissiger Jahre: der Aktivismus deutscher Intellektueller im Exil (1933–1945)*. [In]: Aus Politik und Zeitgeschichte, Beilage zur Wochenzeitung Das Parlament, B 40–41, Bonn, 8. Okt. 1983. Pp. 9–16.

19899. — PEN INTERNATIONAL: *PEN symposium report [May 6–7, 1983]; half a century writing in German abroad*. London: International PEN, 1983. 60 pp. [Mimeog.] [Incl.: They burnt their books but not their spirit (Will Schaber, 9–14). Egon Larsen zu seinem Film 'Sie kamen nach London: ein Bericht über Emigrantenschicksale' (18). Deutsche Literaten in England (H. G. Adler, 19–21). Cf.: German writers in exile (Margot Pottlitzer) [in]: AJR Information, London, July 1983, p. 3.]

19900. — — *Unsere Mitglieder in kurzer Selbstdarstellung*. Mit ausgewählter Bibliographie. (Hrsg. von Arno und Karin Reinfrank. Mit einer Einleitung von Gabriele Tergit.) London: PEN Zentrum deutschsprachiger Autoren im Ausland, 1982. 69 pp. [Cf.: Buch der Trauer: eine vernichtende Rezension unseres Landes (Klaus Jeziorkowski) [in]: Die Zeit, Nr. 15, Hamburg, 8. Apr. 1983, p. 48.]

19901. — PFANNER, HELMUT F.: *Exile in New York: German and Austrian writers after 1933*. Detroit: Wayne State Univ. Press, 1983. 252 pp., ports., notes, bibl. of exile authors and their works (199–232), bibl. (241–245).

—— — SCHMIDT-HARTMANN, EVA: *Die deutschsprachige jüdische Emigration aus der Tschechoslowakei nach Grossbritannien 1938–1945*. [See in No. 19886.]

—— STRAUSS, HERBERT A.: *Social and communal acculturation of German-Jewish immigrants of the Nazi period in the U.S.* [See in No. 20365.]

19902. — TAYLOR, JOHN RUSSELL: *Strangers in paradise; the Hollywood émigrés 1933–1950*. London: Faber; New York: Holt, Rinehart and Winston, 1983. 256 pp., bibl. (249–252). [Incl. many German-Jewish writers, composers, actors, film and theatre directors. Cf.: 'New Weimar' in Hollywood (Egon Larsen) [in]: AJR Information, London, June 1983, pp. 1–2. Exiles in never-never-land (Peter Conrad) [in]: The Observer, London, March 20, 1983, p. 33. Colonists in California (S. S. Prawer) [in]: TLS, London, March 11, 1983, p. 233.]

19903. KISSINGER, HENRY. FRESCO-KAUTSKY, EDITH J.: *Henry A. Kissinger; Historiker und Staatsmann*. Köln: Böhlau, 1983. VIII, 322 pp., diagrs. (Dissertationen zur neueren Geschichte, 13.)

19904. — HERSH, SEYMOUR M.: *The price of power: Kissinger in the Nixon White House*. London: Faber; New York: Summit Books, 1983. 699 pp., illus. [Cf.: S. Hershs grosse Attacke gegen Kissinger (Richard Yaffe) [in]: Aufbau, Nr. 32, New York, Aug. 12, 1983, p. 10. 'Getting' Kissinger (Michael Ledeen) [in]: Commentary, Vol. 76, No. 3, New York, Sept. 1983, pp. 76–79).]

19905. MARCUS, JACOB RADER: *The American Jewish woman*. A documentary history. New York: Ktav, 1981. 1047 pp., illus., notes, list of documents. [Cont. extensive material on German-Jewish women who came to America.]

19906. MARX, HENRY: *Deutsche in der Neuen Welt*. Braunschweig: Westermann, 1983. 432 pp., illus., tabs., bibl. (420–423). Also on German-Jewish immigrants and refugees.]

19907. MELTZER, MILTON: *The Jewish Americans*. A history in their own words 1650–1950. New York: Cromwell, 1982. 1974 pp., illus. [Incl. Jews from Germany and material on the Holocaust.]

19908. MESINGER, JONATHAN S.: *Reconstructing the social geography of the nineteenth-century Jewish community from primary statistical sources*. [In]: American Jewish History, Vol. 82, No. 3, Waltham, Mass., 1983. Pp. 354–368, tabs., maps. [Deals also with German Jews living in various American cities during 2nd half of 19th century and their concentration in specific areas.]

19909. MOSER, SIR CLAUS. *Inside outsider*. David Nathan meets Sir Claus Moser, Chairman of the Royal Opera House. [In]: Jewish Chronicle, London, Dec. 16, 1983. P. 18. [Sir C.M., born 1922 in Berlin, economist, banker.]

19910. ROTHSCHILD FAMILY. DAVIS, RICHARD: *The English Rothschilds*. Chapel Hill, NC.: Univ. of North Carolina Press, 1983. 264 pp. [Concentrates on Nathan Mayer (1777–1836), on his son Lionel Nathan (1808–1879) and his grandson Nathaniel Mayer (1840–1915); examines their financial and political careers, their relationships with their families, their part in the campaign for Jewish emancipation, and in shaping English attitudes towards the Jews; based on the Rothschild family archives.] [See also No. 19772.]

19911. — MUHLSTEIN, ANKA: *Baron James; the rise of the French Rothschilds*. New York: Vendome Press, 1983. 223 pp. [Author is a descendant of the Frankfurt Mayer Amschel. Cf.: A family and its fortunes (Gabriele Annan) [in]: The New York Review of Books, Aug. 18, 1983, pp. 22–25.] [James (Jacob) R., 1792–1868.]

II. RESEARCH AND BIBLIOGRAPHY

A. Libraries and Institutes

19912. DEUTSCHES LITERATURARCHIV, MARBACH AM NECKAR. *Jahrbuch der Deutschen Schillergesellschaft.* Jg. 27. Im Auftrag des Vorstands hrsg. von Fritz Martini, Walter Müller-Seidel, Bernhard Zeller. Stuttgart: Kröner, 1983. VII, 599 pp., footnotes. [Incl.: Essay on Karl Kraus (Helmut Pfotenhauer, 326–344); on the literary criticism of Georg Lukács and Herbert Marcuse (Bernhard Schubert, 396–434. See also No. 20692.]

19913. DUISBURG, UNIVERSITÄT – GESAMTHOCHSCHULE, ed.: *Forschungsschwerpunkt 'Geschichte und Religion des Judentums'; Forschungsbericht 1973–1982.* (Red.: Stephan Rotthaus.) Duisburg, 1983. 65 pp.

19914. INSTITUT FÜR DEUTSCHE GESCHICHTE. *Jahrbuch des Instituts für Deutsche Geschichte, Universität Tel-Aviv.* Bd. 12, 1983. Hrsg. und eingeleitet von Walter Grab. (Red.-Sekretär: M. Zuckermann.) Tel-Aviv: Nateev-Printing, 1983. 586, XV (summaries in Hebrew) pp., footnotes. [Contributions relevant to German Jewry are listed according to subject.] [For Jahrbuch . . . , Beiheft 4 & 5, see Nos. 19764, 19769.]

19915. LEO BAECK INSTITUTE. *Bulletin des Leo Baeck Instituts.* Nr. 64–66. Hrsg. von Joseph Walk, Daniel Brecher und Eve Strauss. Königstein/Ts.: Jüdischer Verl., 1983. 95; 86; 81 pp., notes. [3 issues.] [*Nr. 64* incl.: Namensregister 1982 (87–95). Miszelle (Eva Michaelis-Stern, 85–86; some corrections for 'Ahnen und Verwandte Walter Benjamins' by G. Scholem, see No. 19333/YB XXVIII). Individual contributions are listed according to subject.] [Cf.: Besprechungen (E. G. Lowenthal) [in]: 'Allgemeine', Nr. 41, Düsseldorf, 14. Okt. 1983, p. 7; [in]: Aufbau, No. 25, New York, June 25, 1983, p. 17 & No. 46, Nov. 18, 1983, p. 13; [in]: Isr. Wochenblatt, Nr. 25, Zürich, 24. Juni 1983, p. 57; [in]: MB, Nr. 26, Tel-Aviv, 8. Juli 1983, p. 4 & Nr. 9, 2. März 1984, p. 5.]

19916. — *Year Book XXVIII.* Jewry in the German Reich II. Ed.: Arnold Paucker. (Robert Weltsch who founded the Year Book of the Leo Baeck Institute died on the 22nd December 1982; this volume is dedicated to his memory.) London: Secker & Warburg, 1983. XIII, 607 pp., illus., ports., facsims., maps, tabs., footnotes, bibl. (pp. 497–588). [Cont.: Robert Weltsch in memoriam (Max Gruenewald, pp. IX, 2 ports. R. Weltsch, 1891–1982). Preface (Arnold Paucker, pp. XI–XIII; incl. obituary for R. Weltsch, p. XI). Individual contributions are listed according to subject.] [Cf. *selected reviews:* Rivista YB XXIII [in]: Rivista delle Società, Anno 27, fasc. 4–5, Milano, luglio-ott. 1982, p. 1104. Review YB XXVI (F. L. Carsten) [in]: The Slavonic and East European Review, Vol. 61, Pt. 2, London, 1983, pp. 287–288. Besprechung YB XXVI & XXVII (Nachum Orland) [in]: Das Parlament, Nr. 9–10, Bonn, 3./10. März 1984, p. 19. Besprechung YB XXVII [in]: deutschland-berichte, Jg. 19, Nr. 6, Bonn, Juni 1983, p. 22. Constructive tension: the German Jewish past assessed = YB XXVII & Index Vol. (Werner Rosenstock) [in]: AJR Information, London, July 1983, pp. 1–2. Brief note on YB XXVII [in]: TLS, London, Sept. 3, 1983. Das 28. Jb. des LBI erinnert wie es vorher war (Ernst G. Lowenthal) [in]: 'Allgemeine', Nr. 51, Düsseldorf, 23. Dez. 1983, p. 6. Besprechung YB XXVIII [in]: Aufbau, No. 47, New York, Nov. 25, 1983, p. 13. Deutschlands Juden in Kaiserreich und Republik (Hans Steinitz) [in]: Aufbau, No. 14, New York, Apr. 6, 1984, p. 11. LBI Jb. XXVIII zu Ehren von Robert Weltsch (E. G. Lowenthal) [in]: Isr. Wochenblatt, Nr. 49, Zürich, 9. Dez. 1983, pp. 21, 23, 25. Besprechung (E. G. Lowenthal) [in]: MB, Nr. 46, Tel-Aviv, 16. Dez. 1983, p. 4. Brief notes on YB XXVIII [in]: TLS, London, Dec. 2, 1983. [&]: (James Joll) [in]: TLS, London, Feb. 17, 1984, p. 162.]

19917. — LBI New York. *Library and Archives News.* Ed.: Gabrielle Bamberger. Nos. 18–19. New York: Leo Baeck Institute, June & Dec. 1983. 8; 8 pp. [2 issues.]

19918. — — *LBI News.* Ed.: Gabrielle Bamberger. No. 46 (Summer 1983) – No. 47 (Winter 1984). New York: Leo Baeck Institute, 1983–1984. 16; 16 pp., front illus., illus., ports., facsims. [2 issues.] [*No. 46* incl.: Jewish businessmen and industrialists (1–8; on the 'Copper' Hirsches of Halberstadt; Emil Rathenau, Felix Deutsch and the AEG; the Oppenheimers of Michelfeld and Bruchsal; Berthold Nothmann). Reports on LBI events. Tribute: Nahum N. Glatzer on his 80th birthday. Obituary: Robert Weltsch in memoriam, 1891–1982. *No. 47:* 'Exotic' destinations: a tale of difficult adjustments (1–5; on Shanghai and other countries). Three women report on far-away countries (6–7). Reports on LBI events. Tribute: Fred Grubel: a congratulatory message. Obituary: David Nachmansohn 1899–1983, biochemist.] [See also reports on German President Karl Carstens' visit to the LBI New York on Oct. 14, 1983 [in]: AJR Information, London, Dec. 1983, p. 2 [& in]: 'Allgemeine', Nr. 42, Düsseldorf, 21. Okt. 1983, p. 7 [& in]: Aufbau, No. 42, New York, Oct. 21, 1983, p. 2 [& in]: Neue Jüd. Nachrichten, Nr. 29, München, 25. Nov. 1983, p. 3 (= address by K. Carstens).]

19919. — — PROLLIUS, HELGA: *'Himmel und Erde zu Zeugen nehmen . . .'; das Leo-Baeck-Institut in New York.* Manuskript einer Sendung des Deutschlandfunkes, 10. Mai 1983. Köln: Deutschlandfunk, 1983. 9 pp. [Mimeog.] [Interview with Fred Grubel and review of 'Jüdisches Leben in Deutschland', 3 vols., ed. by Monika Richarz.]

19920. — FREEDEN, HERBERT: *Deutsches Judentum und die Juden in der Welt.* [In]: 'Allgemeine', Nr. 14, Düsseldorf, Apr. 8, 1983. Pp. 4–5 [& in]: MB, Nr. 13, Tel-Aviv, 8. Apr. 1983, p. 5 [& in]: Das Neue Israel, Jg. 36, H. 6, Zürich, Dez. 1983, p. 29. [Report on a three-day symposium of the LBI in Haifa on the subject 'Modernes deutsches Judentum im 19. Jh. und sein Einfluss auf die Entwicklung des Weltjudentums'.]

19921. — LAMM, HANS: *Kulturelles Erbe des einstigen deutschen Judentums: Kuratorium der Freunde und Förderer des Leo-Baeck-Instituts traf sich in Bonn.* [In]: 'Allgemeine', Nr. 43, Düsseldorf, 28. Okt. 1983. P. 7. [Reports also [in]: MB, Nr. 37, Tel-Aviv, 14. Okt. 1983, p. 6 [& in]: Neue Jüd. Nachrichten, Nr. 27, München, 28. Okt. 1983, p. 7.]

—— — SEIDENBERG, HANS: *Eine Lücke in der deutschen Geschichtsschreibung: zur Forschungsarbeit des Leo-Baeck-Instituts.* [And]: *Das Leo-Baeck-Institut* (Freunde und Förderer des Leo-Baeck-Instituts e.V.). [See in No. 20135.]

19922. — STRAUSS, HERBERT A.: *Die Leo Baeck Institute und die Erforschung der deutsch-jüdischen Geschichte.* [In]: Geschichte und Gesellschaft, Jg. 9, H. 3, Göttingen, 1983. Pp. 471–478.

19923. — WALK, JOSEPH: *Entwicklung und Verjüngung: von Aufgabe und Wirken des Leo Baeck Instituts.* [In]: MB, Nr. 34/35, Tel-Aviv, 7. Sept. 1983. P. 7.

19924. — *Zur Forschungsarbeit des Leo-Baeck-Institutes.* [In]: Geschichte in Wissenschaft und Unterricht, Jg. 34, H. 8, Stuttgart, Aug. 1983. Pp. IV–V.

19925. WIENER LIBRARY, London. *The Wiener Library Bulletin.* Special issue: *50 years of the Wiener Library.* London: The Institute of Contemporary History and Wiener Library, [1983]. 61 pp. [Issue, specially prepared for the exhibition commemorating 50 years of the Wiener Library. Incl.: Dr. Wiener's Library 1933–1960 (Walter Laqueur, 3–9). Alfred Wiener – the German Jew [1965] (Eva G. Reichmann, 10–13). Leonard Montefiore: 'the father of the Wiener Library' [1962] (Alfred Wiener, 14). Seeds of goodwill: Prof. Heuss in the Wiener Library [1958] (17–19). In memoriam Robert Weltsch, 1891–1982 (Arnold Paucker/Eva G. Reichmann, 51–55).] [A. Wiener, March 16, 1885 Potsdam – Feb. 4, 1964 London, Syndicus of C.V. from 1919, founder-director of the Wiener Library 1933 in Amsterdam and from 1939 in London.]

19926. — *On the track of tyranny 1933–1983.* An exhibition to mark fifty years of the Wiener Library London, 19th Apr.–13th May 1983. London: Wiener Library, 1983. 1 folded leaf, illus., map. [Descriptive guide, introd. by A. J. Wells, exhibition organiser. See also: Bericht anlässlich der Jubiläumsausstellung [in]: NZZ, Nr, 88, Zürich, 16./17. Apr. 1983, p. 4.]

B. **Bibliographies and Catalogues**

—— *Bibliographisches Handbuch der deutschsprachigen Emigration nach 1933.* [See No. 19892.]

19927. CANTOR, AVIVA, comp.: *The Jewish woman, 1900–1980.* Bibliography. Compiled and annotated. 2nd edn. Fresh Meadows, N.Y.: Biblio Press, 1982. 88 pp., 9 pp. supplement. [Also on German-Jewish women.]

19928. EPPLER, ELIZABETH E., ed.: *International bibliography of Jewish affairs, 1976–1977.* A selectively annotated list of books and articles publ. in the Diaspora. Boulder, Col.: Westview Press, 1983. XIII, 402 pp.

19929. KUSSMAUL, INGRID, comp.: *Die Nachlässe und Sammlungen des Deutschen Literaturarchivs Marbach am Neckar.* Ein Verzeichnis. Marbach a.N.: Deutsche Schillergesellschaft, 1983. XXX, 836 cols., facsims., list of names (585–812). (Deutsches Literaturarchiv, Verzeichnisse, 10.) [Cont. résumés of 573 literary estates, incl. German and Austrian Jewish authors.]

19930. MOMMSEN, WOLFGANG A.: *Die Nachlässe in den deutschen Archiven (mit Ergänzungen aus anderen*

Beständen). Teil 2. Boppard: Boldt, 1983. X, pp. 583–1648. (Verzeichnis der schriftlichen Nachlässe in deutschen Archiven und Bibliotheken, Bd. 1,2.) (Schriften des Bundesarchivs, 17,2.) [Incl. literary estates of German Jews, also of German-Jewish émigrés in foreign archives, especially in the GDR, Israel, and the USA. Pt. 1, publ. in 1971, comprises XXXIX, 582 pp. For vol. 2 of 'Verzeichnis der schriftlichen Nachlässe . . .' see No. 18047/ YB XXVII.]

19931. *Post-war publications on German Jewry; a selected bibliography of books and articles 1982*. Compiled by Irmgard Foerg and Annette Pringle. [In]: LBI Year Book XXVIII, London, 1983. Pp. 497–588.

19932. SALAMANDER, RACHEL, ed.: *Literatur zum Judentum*. [Katalog.] München (Fürstenstr. 17): Literatur zum Judentum Handel und Verlag, 1983. 265 pp. [Catalogue of Judaica in print, incl. German Jewry.]

19933. SCHOCHOW, WERNER: *Judaica und Antisemitica in der Staatsbibliothek*. [In]: Mitteilungen der Staatsbibliothek Preussischer Kulturbesitz, Berlin, Nov. 1983. Pp. 150–155.

19934. STUTTGART, HAUPTSTAATSARCHIV. *Quellen zur Geschichte der Juden bis zum Jahr 1600 im Hauptstaatsarchiv Stuttgart und im Staatsarchiv Ludwigsburg*. Bearb. von Wilfried Braunn. Stuttgart, 1982. 339 pp. (Hauptstaatsarchiv Stuttgart: Thematische Repertorien, Bd. 1.)

19935. WIENER LIBRARY at Tel-Aviv University. *Bibliography of new acquisitions*. 1983/1–1983/2–3. (Publ. by the Wiener Library, Sourasky Central Library, Tel-Aviv University. Comp. and ed.: Edith Straschitz.) Tel-Aviv (P.O. Box 39038): Wiener Library, May; Dec. 1983. 2 issues, subject & author indexes.

19936. ZEITLIN, WILLIAMS: *Bibliotheca hebraica post-Mendelssohniana*. Bibliographisches Handbuch der neuhebräischen Literatur seit Beginn der Mendelssohn'schen Epoche bis zum Jahre 1890. Nachdr. der 2., neu bearb. und erweiterten Aufl., Leipzig, Koehler, 1891. Hildesheim: Olms, 1983. IV, 548 pp.

III. THE NAZI PERIOD

19937. AUGSBURG. FILSER, KARL/THIEME, HANS, ed.: *Hakenkreuz und Zirbelnuss; Augsburg im Dritten Reich*. Augsburg: Himmer, 1983. 80 pp., illus., bibl. (Quellen zur Geschichte Bayerisch-Schwabens für den historisch-politischen Unterricht.) [Incl.: Das Schicksal der Augsburger Juden (40–44).]

19938. AUSTRIA. [See also Nos. 19874, 19877.] BUKEY, EVAN B.: *Hitler's hometown under Nazi rule: Linz, Austria, 1939–1945*. [In]: Central European History, Vol. 16, No. 2, Atlanta, Ga., June 1983. Pp. 171–186, notes. [Deals also with persecution of the Linz Jewry.]

19939. — HANISCH, ERNST: *Nationalsozialistische Herrschaft in der Provinz: Salzburg im Dritten Reich*. Salzburg: Landespressebüro, 1983. 364 pp., illus., notes, bibl. [Incl. chap.: Rassische und politische Verfolgungen (105–111); refers also to one Book Burning in 1938 (p. 92).]

19940. — WALZL, AUGUST: *Juden in Kärnten: der Fall Preis als Exempel*. [In]: Zeitgeschichte, Jg. 10, H. 5, Wien, Feb. 1983. Pp. 183–193, notes. [On the persecution of the family Preis, Klagenfurt.]

19941. BAD SODEN. '*. . . als wenn nichts geschehen wäre*'. Fragen an Zeitzeugen zu ihrem Leben im Faschismus. Dokumente aus Bad Soden, Schwalbach und Hofheim. Hrsg.: Bund Deutscher Pfadfinder Main-Taunus. Schwalbach: Eigendruck BDP, 1982. 89 pp., illus. [Also on persecution of Jews in Bad Soden.]

19942. BADEN. GRILL, JOHNPETER HORST: *The Nazi movement in Baden 1920–1945*. Chapel Hill: Univ. of North Carolina Press, 1983. 720 pp. [Incl. persecution of the Jews.]

19943. BAMBERG. ALBART, RUDOLF: *Vom Hakenkreuz zum Sternenbanner*. Ein Bamberg-Report. Bamberg (Luitpoldstr. 10): Selbstverlag, [1983?]. 208 pp., illus. [Incl.: Die Vernichtung der jud. Gemeinde in Bamberg (52–64).]

19944. BAVARIA. BROSZAT, MARTIN/MEHRINGER, HARTMUT, eds.: *Bayern in der NS-Zeit. Bd. 6:* FRÖHLICH, ELKE: *Die Herausforderung des Einzelnen; Geschichten über Widerstand und Verfolgung*. München: Oldenbourg, 1983. 262 pp., footnotes. [Incl. sections on the persecution of Jews in Bavaria. For vols. 1–4 see No. 18070/YB XXVII.]

19945. — KERSHAW, IAN: *Popular opinion and political dissent in the Third Reich: Bavaria 1933–1945*. Oxford: Clarendon Press, 1983. XV, 425 pp., map, tabs., bibl. (398–411). [Incl. chaps.: Reactions to the persecution of the Jews. Popular opinion and the extermination of the Jews. Cf.: The view from below (John P. Fox) [in]: Patterns of Prejudice, Vol. 17, No. 3, London, July 1983, pp. 52–55. Focusing on the Führer (J. D. Noakes) [in]: TLS, London, July 1st,

1983, p. 689.] [See also: The persecution of the Jews and German popular opinion in the Third Reich (Ian Kershaw) [in]: LBI Year Book XXVI, London, 1981, pp. 261–289, footnotes.]

19946. Begov, Lucie: *Mit meinen Augen; Botschaft einer Auschwitz-Überlebenden.* Mit einem Nachwort von Simon Wiesenthal. Gerlingen: Bleicher, 1983. 318 pp.

19947. Belke, Ingrid, ed.: *In den Katakomben: jüdische Verlage in Deutschland 1933–1938.* [Kabinett-Ausstellung im Schiller-Nationalmuseum, 18. Feb.–19. Juni 1983.] Marbach a.N.: Deutsche Schillergesellschaft, 1983. 95, 16 pp., facsims. (Marbacher Magazin, 25.) [Incl.: Jüdische Autoren, Buchhändler und Verleger 1933–1942: eine Chronik mit Dokumenten (65–93). Ich werde seinesgleichen nicht mehr sehen: Erinnerungen an Salman Schocken (Gershom Schocken, 19–53).]

—— BERGHEIM. [See No. 19798.]

19948. BERLIN. Bering, Dietz: *Der Kampf um den Namen Isidor: Polizeipräsident Bernhard Weiss gegen Gauleiter Joseph Goebbels.* [In]: Beiträge zur Namensforschung, N.F. Bd. 18, H. 2, Heidelberg, 1983. Pp. 121–153 [& in]: Wissenschaftskolleg – Institute for Advanced Study – zu Berlin, Jahrbuch 1981/82, Berlin, Quadriga Verl., 1983, pp. 17–34, notes, bibl. [B. Weiss data, see No. 18075/YB XXVII.]

19949. — Bering, Dietz: *Von der Notwendigkeit politischer Beleidigungsprozesse: der Beginn der Auseinandersetzung zwischen Polizeipräsident Bernhard Weiss und der NSDAP.* [In]: Berlin in Geschichte und Gegenwart; Jahrbuch des Landesarchivs Berlin 1983, hrsg. von Hans J. Reichhardt. Berlin: Siedler, 1983. Pp. 87–112.

19950. — Berlinische Galerie: *Aus Berlin emigriert; Werke Berliner Künstler, die nach 1933 Deutschland verlassen mussten.* (Ausstellung und Katalog: Eberhard Roters, Gisela-Ingeborg Bolduan.) Berlin: Berlinische Galerie, 1983. 90 pp., illus., ports. [Incl.: Vor 50 Jahren: Aufzeichnungen aus den Erinnerungen (Albert Klein, 11–26). Catalogue incl. short biographies.]

19951. — Brass, Arthur: *Rettung und Rückkehr der Thora-Rollen.* [In]: Mitteilungen des Vereins für die Geschichte Berlins, Jg. 79, H. 2, Berlin, Apr. 1983. Pp. 54–57, illus. [Refers to more than 400 Thora scrolls stored in the cemetery Berlin-Weissensee during the war and distributed afterwards to Jewish communities in Germany and other countries. See also: The Weissensee cemetery (A. Brass) [in]: AJR Information, London, Sept. 1983, p. 9.]

19952. — Burkert, Hans Norbert/Matussek, Klaus/Wippermann, Wolfgang: *'Machtergreifung' Berlin 1933.* Berlin: Edition Hentrich im Rembrandt Verl., 1982. 263 pp., illus., bibl. (253–256). (Stätten der Geschichte Berlins, Bd. 2.) [Incl. early persecution of the Berlin Jews (113–130).]

19953. — Gross, Leonard: *The last Jews in Berlin.* London: Sidgwick & Jackson, 1983. 349 pp. [Edn. for England of No. 18999/YB XXVIII; also transl. under the title]: *Versteckt: wie Juden in Berlin die Nazi-Zeit überlebten.* Deutsch von Cornelia Holfelder-v.d. Tann. Reinbek: Rowohlt, 1983. 379 pp. [Cf.: Surviving in Berlin: some remarkable escapes (William Guttmann) [in]: AJR Information, London, Nov. 1983, p. 1. The Germans who saved Jews (T. R. Fyvel) [in]: Jewish Chronicle, London, Sept. 1983. Jewish U-boats (Bernard Levin) [in]: The Observer, London, Aug. 7, 1983. Berlin's righteous gentiles (Norman Stone) [in]: The Sunday Times, London, Aug. 14, 1983.]

19954. — Sandvoss, Hans Rainer: *Widerstand in einem Arbeiterbezirk [Wedding].* Berlin: Informationszentrum, Gedenk- und Bildungsstätte Stauffenbergstrasse, 1983. 108 pp., illus. (Widerstand in Berlin, 1.) [Refers also to Jews in Berlin, a.o., to the physician Friedrich Aron (1888 Birkenfeld – 1962 New York).]

19955. BIELEFELD. *Im Zeichen des Hakenkreuzes: Bielefeld 1933–1945.* Eine Ausstellung des Stadtarchivs. Katalog. Text: Reinhard Vogelsang [et al.] Bielefeld: Stadtarchiv und Landesgeschichtliche Bibliothek, 1983. 222 pp., illus., bibl. [Also on persecution of the Jews.]

19956. — Meynert, Joachim/Schäffer, Friedhelm: *Die Juden in der Stadt Bielefeld während der Zeit des Nationalsozialismus.* Bielefeld: Stadtarchiv, 1983. 208 pp., illus. (Bielefeld: Stadtarchiv, 1983. 208 pp., illus. (Bielefelder Beiträge zur Stadt- und Regionalgeschichte, 3.)

—— *Biographisches Handbuch der deutschsprachigen Emigration nach 1933.* [See No. 19892; for German-speaking Jews in exile 1933–1945 see also Nos. 19893–19902.]

—— The BOOK BURNING. [Selection, titles partly shortened; all books refer to Jewish authors and their situation on May 10, 1933.]

19957. — Austria. *Die verbrannten Bücher 10.5.1933.* Red.: Alfred Pfoser, Friedrich Stadler. Wien: Institut für Wissenschaft und Kunst, 1983. 52 pp., illus., bibl. (50–52). [Incl.: Öffentliche

Reaktion in Österreich auf die Bücherverbrennungen 1933 (Alfred Pfoser, 4–9). Zur Bücherverbrennung in Salzburg am 30.Apr. 1938 (Ernst Hanisch, 22). Auszug aus 'Liste des schädlichen und unerwünschten Schrifttums' mit Schwerpunkt Österreich (38–47).]

19958. — BERLIN, AKADEMIE DER KÜNSTE: *'Das war ein Vorspiel nur . . .'. Bücherverbrennung Deutschland 1933: Voraussetzungen und Folgen.* (Ausstellung und Katalog: Hermann Haarmann, Walter Huder, Klaus Siebenhaar.) Berlin: Medusa, 1983. 471 pp., illus., list of names (461–468), bibl. (455–456). (Akademie-Katalog, 137.)

19959. — — JENS, WALTER: *'Die alten Zeiten niemals zu verwinden'.* Rede aus Anlass des 50. Jahrestages der Bücherverbrennung, gehalten am 8. Mai 1983 im Studio der Akademie der Künste Berlin zur Eröffnung der Ausstellung 'Das war ein Vorspiel nur. . .'. Berlin: Akademie der Künste, 1983. 23 pp. (Anmerkungen zur Zeit, 20.) [Refers to persecution of the Jews.]

19960. — DORTMUND, STADT- und LANDESBIBLIOTHEK: *Verboten, verbrannt, vergessen.* Literaturhinweise. Dortmund, 1983. 103 pp.

19961. — DREWS, RICHARD/KANTOROWICZ, ALFRED, eds.: *Verboten und verbrannt: deutsche Literatur 12 Jahre unterdrückt.* Neu hrsg. mit einem Vorwort von Helmut Kindler und einem Nachwort von Walter Jens. Neuaufl. [der Ausg. 1947]. München: Kindler, 1983. 299 pp. [New edn. of the first post-war anthology of authors banned by the Nazis.]

19962. — *europäische ideen.* H. 56: *Bücher-, Menschenverbrennungen.* Berlin: Verlag Europäische Ideen, 1983. 53 pp. (Cont. contributions by Jewish authors.]

19963. — HAMBURG, FREIE AKADEMIE DER KÜNSTE: *Zum 50. Jahrestag der Bücherverbrennung.* Ansprachen anlässlich der Gedenkveranstaltung . . . [von] Klaus von Dohnanyi, Walter Jens, Armin Sandig; und eine Dokumentation der Ausstellung Alfred Kantorowicz. Hamburg, 1983. 67 pp., illus. (Schriften der Freien Akademie der Künste, 8.)

19964. — HEIDELBERG. *Bücherverbrennung; Zensur, Verbot, Vernichtung unter dem Nationalsozialismus in Heidelberg.* Hrsg. von Joachim-Felix Leonhard. Mit Beiträgen von Walter Engel [et al.]. Heidelberg: Heidelberger Verlagsanstalt, 1983. 243 pp., illus. (Heidelberger Bibliotheksschriften, 7.)

19965. — — WOLF-HAUSCHILD, REGINE: *Verzeichnis vergessene Autoren – wieder zu entdecken.* Ausstellung der Univ. bibliothek und der Stadtbücherei. Heidelberg, 1983. 71 pp.

19966. — HEILBRONN, STADTBÜCHEREI: *Verboten und verbrannt; die Bücherverbrennung vom 10. Mai 1933 und ihre Folgen.* Eine Ausstellung. Heilbronn, 1983. 19 pp. [Short description of 454 exhibits; acknowledges assistance of the LBI New York.]

19967. — — *Verboten und verbrannt; die Bücherverbrennung vom 10. Mai 1933 und ihre Folgen.* Ansprachen zur Eröffnung der Ausstellung. Heilbronn: Stadtverwaltung, 1983. 40 pp. [Incl. lecture by Dietrich Aigner (11–36) with references to Jewish authors.]

19968. — KROCKOW, CHRISTIAN Graf von: *Scheiterhaufen; Grösse und Elend des deutschen Geistes.* Berlin: Severin & Siedler, 1983. 213 pp.

19969. — RASSLER, GERDA: *Die Beiträge zum Tag der Bücherverbrennung in der Exilzeitung 'Pariser Tageblatt'.* [In]: Weimarer Beiträge, Jg. 29, H. 5, Berlin/East, 1983. Pp. 893–912, notes.

19970. — SAUDER, GERHARD, ed.: *Die Bücherverbrennung: zum 10. Mai 1933.* München: Hanser, 1983. 339 pp., illus., bibl. [Collection of contemporary documents and texts, also by German Jews.]

19971. — SCHÖFFLING, KLAUS, ed.: *Dort wo man Bücher verbrennt; Stimmen der Betroffenen.* Frankfurt am Main: Suhrkamp, 1983. 483 pp., bibl. (Suhrkamp-Taschenbuch, 905.)

19972. — *Verboten und verbrannt; deutsche Literatur im Exil 1933–1945.* [Ausstellungskatalog für die Internat. Jerusalemer Buchwoche, Frühjahr 1983.] Hamburg: Barsortiment Lingenbrinck 1983. 88 pp., illus. [Incl. bibl. of books in print by émigré authors.]

19973. — WALBERER, ULRICH, ed.: *10. Mai 1933: Bücherverbrennung in Deutschland und die Folgen.* Frankfurt am Main: Fischer, 1983. 317 pp. (Fischer-Taschenbücher, 4245.) [Orig. edn.]

19974. — WIESNER, MARGOT, comp.: *Verbrannte Bücher – verfemte Dichter.* Deutsche Literatur: 1933–1945 unterdrückt und verboten, heute lieferbar. Frankfurt am Main: Buchhändler-Vereinigung, 1983. 82 pp., illus.

19975. — ZWEIG, ARNOLD: *Rückblick auf Barbarei und Bücherverbrennung.* (1934). [In]: Börsenblatt für den Deutschen Buchhandel, Jg. 39, Nr. 11, Frankfurt am Main, 8. Feb. 1983. Pp. 307–310.

19976. CHURCH. *Judaism and Christianity under the impact of National-Socialism, 1919–1945.* Papers presented to the Internat. Symposium in June 1982. Jerusalem: Historical Society of Israel, 1982. 484 pp. [This volume was prepared for publ. by Yitzchak Mais and the manuscripts were duplicated without further editing or proofreading. Incl.: Zum Verhalten des deutschen Katholizismus gegenüber den Juden in der Zeit der Weimarer Republik (Rudolf

Lill, 103–130). Ambivalent dialogue: Jewish-Christian theological encounter in the Weimar period (Paul R. Mendes-Flohr, 131–182). Judentum und Christentum in der Ideologie und Politik des Nationalsozialismus 1919–1945 (Klaus Scholder, 183–200). German Protestantism and the Jews in the Third Reich (Richard Gutteridge, 201–226). Popular Christian attitudes in the Third Reich to National-Socialist policies towards the Jews (Otto D. Kulka, 227–252).]

19977. COLOGNE. Haupts, Leo/Mölich, Georg, eds.: *Aspekte der nationalsozialistischen Herrschaft in Köln und im Rheinland.* Beiträge und Quellen. Köln: dme-Verl., 1983. 114 pp. (Geschichte in Köln, Sonderheft 3.) [Cont.: Verfolgung und Widerstand (G. Brunn). Rassismus (Reiner Pommerin). 'Gleichschaltung' der Univ. Köln (F. Golczewski).]

19978. — Klein, Adolf: *Köln im Dritten Reich.* Köln: Greven, 1983. 303 pp., illus., bibl. (Aus der Kölner Stadtgeschichte.) [Also on persecution of the Jews.]

19979. CZECHOSLOVAKIA. [See also Nos. 19886, 20106.] Campion, Joan: *Gisi Fleischmann and the Jewish fight for survival.* Bethlehem, Pa.: Dvorion Books, 1983. IV, 126 pp., illus. [Incl. letters by G. Fleischmann, née Fischer, Jan. 21, 1894 Bratislava – Oct. 1944 deported to Auschwitz, Zionist, head of local branch of HICEM.]

19980. — Landré, B.: *Jüdische Zwangsarbeit in Prag.* [In]: Zeitgeschichte, Jg. 9, Wien, Aug.–Sept. 1982. Pp. 365–377.

19981. DACHAU, Holzhaider, Hans: *Vor Sonnenaufgang: das Schicksal der jüdischen Bürger Dachaus.* [In]: Dachau Neueste, Nov. 9–Dec. 12, 1983. [Ten-part series of articles, available in the LBI New York.]

—— DANZIG. [See No. 19812.]

19982. Dipper, Christof: *Der deutsche Widerstand und die Juden.* [In]: Geschichte und Gesellschaft, Jg. 9, H. 3, Göttingen, 1983. Pp. 349–380, footnotes.

19983. DORSTEN. Hartwich, Dirk/Stegemann, Wolf, eds.: *Dorsten unterm Hakenkreuz: die jüdische Gemeinde.* Dorsten: Heimeshoff, 1983. 112 pp., illus. (Eine Dokumentation zur Zeitgeschichte, Bd. 1.)

19984. Drewniak, Boguslaw: *Das Theater im NS-Staat.* Szenarium deutscher Zeitgeschichte, 1933–1945. Düsseldorf: Droste, 1983. 456 pp., illus., bibl. [Also on the Nazi policy towards German-Jewish actors and musicians.]

19985. DÜSSELDORF. Voigt, Angelika/Wiesemann, Falk: *Juden in Düsseldorf; die Zerstörung der jüdischen Gemeinde während der nationalsozialistischen Herrschaft.* Dokumente, Erläuterungen, Darstellung. Münster: Aschendorf, 1983. 55 documents, 12 pp. text, in folder.

19986. EICHMANN, ADOLF. Lang, Jochen von, ed.: *Eichmann interrogated.* Transcript from the archives of the Israeli police. Transl. from the German by Ralph Manheim. Introd. by Avner W. Less. New York: Farrar, Straus & Giroux; London: Bodley Head, 1983. XXI, 293 pp., ports. [Transl. of No. 19014/YB XXVIII. Cf.: Organizing the Holocaust (A. J. Sherman) [in]: TLS, London, Apr. 13, 1984, p. 407.]

19987. Feidel-Mertz, Hildegard, ed.: *Schulen im Exil; die verdrängte Pädagogik nach 1933.* Reinbek: Rowohlt, 1983. 252 pp., illus., bibl. (rororo, 7789.) [Also on Jewish schools in Germany until 1938 and in exile.]

19988. Feuchtwanger, Lion: *Der Teufel in Frankreich.* Ein Erlebnisbericht. Mit einem Nachwort von Marta Feuchtwanger. München: Langen Müller, 1983. 266 pp. [Report on F.'s experiences in the internment camps of Milles and San Nicola, first publ. 1942 in Mexico under the title 'Unholdes Frankreich', now augmented by Marta F.]

19989. — Monk, Egon: *Fernsehfilm 'Die Geschwister Oppermann'.* Nach dem Roman von Lion Feuchtwanger. Hrsg. vom Zweiten Deutschen Fernsehen. Frankfurt am Main: Fischer, 1982. 173 pp., illus. (Fischer-Taschenbücher, 3685.) [Two-part TV film 'The Oppermanns', based on Feuchtwanger's 1933 novel, about the effect on a Jewish family of the Nazi rise to power; made by German TV, the film was shown in Germany, Britain, and Israel on Jan. 30 and 31, 1983, and later in the USA. See also: Hints of the Holocaust: interview with F.'s widow Marta in Los Angeles (Colman Andrews) [in]: Radio Times, London, Jan. 29– Feb. 4, 1983, pp. 16–17.]

—— FILM. Dolezel, Stephen: *'Schicksalswende' und 'Der ewige Jude'.* [See in No. 19886.]

19990. — Hollstein, Dorothea: *'Jud Süss' und die Deutschen; antisemitische Vorurteile im nationalsozialistischen Spielfilm.* Frankfurt am Main: Ullstein, 1983. 378 pp., bibl. (357–362). (Ullstein-Buch, Nr. 35169.) [Augmented edn. of No. 9383/YB XVII. Discusses antisemitism in 25 films.]

19991. — Knilli, Friedrich/Maurer, Thomas/Radevagen, Thomas/Zielinski, Siegfried: *'Jud*

Süss': Film-Protokoll, Programmheft und Einzelanalysen. Berlin: Spiess, 1983. 220 pp., illus., bibl.

19992. — WELCH, DAVID: *Propaganda and the German cinema 1933–1945.* Oxford: Clarendon Press, 1983. 352 pp., illus., bibl. [Incl. survey of Nazi antisemitic propaganda films, a.o., 'Jud Süss'. Cf.: Screening the party line (Ian Kershaw) [in]: TLS, London, May 6, 1983, p. 454.]

19993. FRANKFURT am Main. [See also No. 19815.] DIAMANT, ADOLF: *Durch Freitod aus dem Leben geschiedene Frankfurter Juden, 1938–1943.* Frankfurt am Main (Voelckerstr. 9): A. Diamant, 1983. V, 16 pp.

19994. FREEDEN, HERBERT: *Das Ende der jüdischen Presse in Nazideutschland.* [In]: Bulletin des LBI, 65, Königstein/Ts., 1983. Pp. 3–21, notes (19–21).

19995. FREEDEN, HERBERT: *Der 1. April 1933 [Judenboykott]: Anfang vom Ende der deutschen Judenheit.* [In]: MB, Nr. 11/12, Tel-Aviv, 28. März 1983. Pp. 7–8 [& in]: 'Allgemeine', Nr. 9, Düsseldorf, 4. März 1983, p. 18.

19996. FULDA. BERGE, OTTO: *Namensverzeichnis ehemaliger jüdischer Einwohner in Fulda.* Fulda (An St. Johann 21): O. Berge, 1980. [33] pp.

19997. GIESSEN. KRALOVITZ, ROLF & BRIGITTE: *Da war nachher nichts mehr da.* Ein Dokumentarbericht. Giessen: Brühlscher Verl., 1983. 27 pp., illus. [On persecution and deportation of the Jews.]

19998. GÖTTINGEN. *Göttingen unterm Hakenkreuz.* Nationalsozialistischer Alltag in einer deutschen Stadt. Texte und Materialien. Göttingen: Kulturdezernat, 1983. 167 pp., illus. [Also on the persecution of Jews (Hans-Georg Schmeling, 149–154).]

19999. *Die Greuelpropaganda ist eine Lügenpropaganda sagen die deutschen Juden selbst = Atrocity propaganda is based on lies say the Jews of Germany themselves.* Photomechan. Nachdr. der Ausg. Berlin-Charlottenburg, Trachtenberg, 1933. Wobbenbüll/Husum: Verlag für Ganzheitliche Forschung und Kultur, 1982. 142 pp. [Reprint of a publication recommended by neo-Nazi circles. Cont. quotations from papers and Jewish official personages, obviously extorted under pressure; identical text in German, English and French.]

20000. HAMBURG. [See also No. 19827 & Ophir in No. 19841.] BÜTTNER, URSULA/JOCHMANN, WERNER: *Hamburg auf dem Weg ins Dritte Reich.* Entwicklungsjahre 1931–1933. Hamburg, 1983. 220 pp., facsims., bibl. (Veröffentlichung der Landeszentrale für politische Bildung, Hamburg.) [Incl. text and documentation on persecution of the Jews (52–54, 147–159).]

20001. HEIDELBERG. WECKBECKER, ARNO: *Gedenkbuch an die ehemaligen Heidelberger Bürger jüdischer Herkunft.* Dokumentation ihrer Namen und Schicksale 1933–1945. Heidelberg: Stadtverwaltung, 1983. 218 pp.

— HEILBRONN. [See No. 19828.]

20002. HELLFAIER, DETLEV, comp.: *Judenverfolgung im 'Dritten Reich'.* Literatur des letzten Jahrzehnts in der Universitätsbibliothek der Freien Univ. Berlin. Literaturverzeichnis zu einer Ausstellung. Berlin, 1983. 70 pp., illus. (Ausstellungsführer der Univ. bibliothek der Freien Univ. Berlin, 9.)

— HESSE. [See No. 19829 & Kropat in No. 19832.]

20003. HILLESUM, ETTY: *Etty: a diary, 1941–1943.* Introd. by J. G. Gaarlandt. Transl. by Arnold J. Pomerans. London: Cape, 1983. XIV, 226 pp., notes. [Also American edn. under the title]: *An interrupted life; the diaries of Etty Hillesum, 1941–1943.* New York: Pantheon Books, 1983. [And German transl.]: *Das denkende Herz der Baracke; die Tagebücher von Etty Hillesum 1941–1943.* Freiburg i. Br.: Kerle, 1983. 238 pp., illus. [Journal of a young Jewish Dutch woman on persecution and transportation to Westerbork and points east; also covers her relationship with the Frankfurt-born Jewish psychochirologist Julius Spier.]

20004. HITLER. PALDIEL, MORDECAI: *Dualism and genocide; the religious nature of Hitler's antisemitism.* Philadelphia, Temple Univ., Phil. Diss., 1982. 392 pp.

20005. — WEYL, NATHANIEL: *The Marx Hitler Holocaust enigma.* [In]: Midstream, Vol. 29, No. 9, New York, Nov. 1983. Pp. 11–15, notes. [On Marx's antisemitism and how it may have been used by Hitler.]

20006. HOLLANDER, ALFRED: *The tribulations of Jewish dermatologists under the Nazi regime.* [In]: The American Journal of Dermatopathology, Vol. 5, No. 1, New York, Feb. 1983. Pp. 19–26, facsim.

20007. HOLOCAUST. ARAD, YITZHAK/GUTMAN, YISRAEL/MARGALIOT, ABRAHAM, eds.: *Documents on the Holocaust.* Selected sources on the destruction of the Jews of Germany and Austria, Poland and the Soviet Union. New York: Ktav, for Yad Vashem and the Anti-Defamation League, 1982. 504 pp. [For Hebrew edn. see No. 16005/YB XXV.]

20008. — EISENBERG, AZRIEL: *Witness to the Holocaust.* New York: The Pilgrim Press, 1981. 649 pp.

[Collection of memoirs, diaries and documents by survivors, witnesses and historians; incl. extensive material on German Jews as well as chap. 'Postwar Germany and the Jews'.]

20009. HOLOCAUST ART. COSTANZA, MARY S.: *Bilder der Apokalypse; Kunst in Konzentrationslagern und Ghettos.* München: Kindler, 1983. 222 pp., illus. [Transl. of No. 19035/YB XXVIII.]

20010. — ŠKOCHOVÁ, JARMILA: *Das literarische Vermächtnis von Friedl Dicker-Brandejsová.* Zu ihren Gedanken über den Zeichenunterricht der Kinder im Konzentrationslager Terezín. [In]: Judaica Bohemiae, Vol. 19, No. 1, Praha, 1983. Pp. 43–51, notes. [Incl. two texts by F. Dicker-Brandejsová, July 30, 1898 Vienna – Oct. 1944 Auschwitz, artist, deported to Terezín in 1942, became art instructor for children; some 4000 drawings of her pupils are now in the State Jewish Museum in Prague.]

20011. HOLOCAUST KNOWLEDGE. LIPSTADT, DEBORAH E.: *The Christian Science Monitor's reaction to the first phase of Nazi persecution of Jews.* [In]: Jewish Social Studies, Vol. 45, No. 2, New York, Spring 1983. Pp. 95–112. [See also the author's essay 'The American press and the persecution of German Jewry: the early years 1933–1935' [in]: LBI Year Book XXIX, London, 1984, pp. 27–55.]

20012. — LIPSTADT, DEBORAH E.: *Witness to the persecution: the Allies and the Holocaust.* A review essay. [In]: Modern Judaism, Vol. 3, No. 3, Baltimore, Oct. 1983. Pp. 319–335, notes.

20013. — PENKOWER, MONTY NOAM: *The Jews were expendable; free world diplomacy and the Holocaust.* Chicago: Univ. of Illinois Press, 1983. 429 pp., notes, bibl. (382–403).

20014. — PINSKY, EDWARD: *American Jewish unity during the Holocaust: the Joint Emergency Committee, 1943.* [In]: American Jewish History, Vol. 72, No. 4, Waltham, Mass., June 1983. Pp. 477–494.

20015. HORTMEYER, GERD: *Die Rendite des Rassenwahns; als reiche Deutsche noch für Enteignung waren.* [In]: Trans Atlantik, 10, München, Okt. 1983. Pp. 66–73 & 75. [On 'aryanisation' of prominent Jewish industrial and banking firms in Germany and Austria.]

20016. IDAR-OBERSTEIN. REDMER, AXEL: *Die 'Reichskristallnacht' in Idar-Oberstein.* [In]: Heimatkalender für den Landkreis Birkenfeld, 1982. Pp. 54–57, illus., bibl.

20017. KATER, MICHAEL H.: *The Nazi party; a social profile of members and leaders, 1919–1945.* Oxford: Blackwell; Cambridge, Mass.: Harvard Univ. Press, 1983. 415 pp., tabl., notes. [Incl. Nazi policies towards Jews; Jews in Nazi ideology and propaganda.]

20018. KEIM, ANTON MARIA, ed.: *Yad Vashem: die Judenretter aus Deutschland.* (Aus dem Hebr. übers. von Benyamin Z. Barslai.) Mainz: Grünewald; München: Kaiser, 1983. 160 pp. [Documentation on Germans who helped Jews during the Nazi period.]

20019. KERBS, DIETHART [et al.], eds.: *Die Gleichschaltung der Bilder; zur Geschichte der Pressefotografie 1930–1936.* Berlin: Frölich & Kaufmann, 1983. 208 pp., illus. [Incl. persecution of the Jews and its presentation in the news media; also on German-Jewish photo-journalists who had to leave Germany after 1933 and brought modern photo-journalism to Britain and the USA.]

20020. KIEL. HOFFMANN, ERICH/WULF, PETER: *'Wir bauen das Reich'; Aufstieg und erste Herrschaftsjahre des Nationalsozialismus in Schleswig-Holstein.* Neumünster: Wachholtz, 1983. 460 pp. (Quellen und Forschungen zur Geschichte Schleswig-Holsteins, Bd. 81.) [Incl.: Vom Judenboykott zum Judenmord: der 1. Apr. 1933 in Kiel (Dietrich Hauschildt). Aus der Erlebniswelt eines jüd. Jugendlichen in Kiel anfang der dreissiger Jahre (Reuven Golan).]

20021. *Klassiker in finsteren Zeiten 1933–1945.* Eine Ausstellung des Deutschen Literaturarchivs im Schiller-Nationalmuseum Marbach am Neckar. Bd. 1–2. (Ausstellung und Katalog: Bernhard Zeller, in Zusammenarbeit mit Friederike Brüggemann [et al.]). Stuttgart: Klett, 1983. 2 vols. (448; 384 pp.), illus., list of names (vol. 2, 351–379). (Marbacher Kataloge, 38.) [Refers also to discrimination, dismissal and exile of Jews. Incl. chaps. *Vol. 1:* 'Säuberung' und 'Gleichschaltung' der Literatur (Jochen Meyer, 113–129). Vertreibung, Anpassung, Verweigerung (Reinhard Tgahrt, 263–286). *Vol. 2:* Klassiker im Exil (Ludwig Greve, 255–299).]

— KÖNIGSBERG. [See No. 19833.]

— KÖNIGSTEIN. [See No. 19834.]

20022. KULKA, OTTO DOV: *'Public opinion' in Nazi Germany and the 'Jewish Question'.* [And pt. 2]: *'Public opinion' in Nazi Germany: the Final Solution.* [In]: The Jerusalem Quarterly, No. 25, Fall 1982 [&] No. 26, Winter 1983. Pp. 121–144; 34–45.

20023. LANDSTUHL. PAUL, ROLAND: *Die jüdische Gemeinde in Landstuhl.* Anmerkungen zu ihrem Schicksal im Dritten Reich. [In]: Heimatkalender für Stadt- und Landkreis Kaiserslautern, 1982. Pp. 60–64.

20024. LANGEN. FOGEL, HEIDI: *Eine Stadt zwischen Demokratie und Diktatur; Dokumentation zur*

Geschichte Langens von 1918–1945. Langen: Stadt Langen, 1983. 237 pp., illus. [Incl.: Jüdische Gemeinde und nationalsozialistische Judenverfolgung (179–224, illus.).]

20025. Löwenstein, Anna: *Aus dem Tagebuch der Anna Löwenstein*. T. 1–5. [In]: Bocholter-Borkener Volksblatt, Bocholt, 10., 12., 15., 17., 19. Juni 1982. 5 pts. [Excerpts from the diary 1897–1943 of A. Andorn, née Löwenstein, July 14, 1885 Bocholt – May 5, 1945 Theresienstadt.]

20026. LOWER SAXONY. *Vor 50 Jahren: Nationalsozialistische Machtergreifung in Niedersachsen*. Hannover: Hannov. Allg. Zeitung, 1983. 12, XVI pp., illus. [Incl.: Terror und KZ-Lager (Dieter Tasch, 10–12). Also on boycott of Jewish shops (Wolfgang Steinweg, XIII).]

20027. LUX, STEFAN. Pollack, Irwin: *The tragedy of Stefan Lux*. [In]: Jewish Frontier, Vol. 50, No. 4, New York, Apr. 1983. Pp. 21–23. [St. L., 1888 Vienna – July 3, 1936 Geneva, film producer, Weltbühne journalist, shot himself in the press gallery of the League of Nations Assembly Hall in protest against treatment of Jews in Germany.]

20028. MACHTERGREIFUNG. Aronsfeld, C. C.: *How it happened there*. 50 years ago Hitler came to power. [&]: *Government of the big lie*. Seizure of power and the Reichstag fire. [&]: *Boycott day fifty years ago*. Nazis' first shot in the coming war. [Series of three articles in]: AJR Information, London, Jan., Feb., Apr. 1983. Pp. 1–2 [in each issue].

20029. — Becker, Josef & Ruth, eds.: *Hitlers Machtergreifung*. Dokumente vom Machtantritt Hitlers 30. Jan. 1933 bis zur Besiegelung des Einheitsparteienstaates 14. Juli 1933. München: Deutscher Taschenbuch-Verl., 1983. 433 pp., notes, bibl. (409–412). [dtv, 2938.) [Incl. documents on the persecution of Jews, on antisemitism (a.o. by Carl Schmitt), on the critical evaluation of Nazism (a.o. by Joseph Roth).]

20030. — *Deutschlands Weg in die Diktatur*. Internat. Konferenz zur nationalsozialistischen Machtübernahme im Reichstagsgebäude zu Berlin. Referate und Diskussionen; ein Protokoll. Im Auftrage der Histor. Kommission zu Berlin [et al.] hrsg. von Martin Broszat [et al.]. Berlin: Siedler, 1983. 399 pp., bibl. [The conference also dealt with 'Rassenfanatismus und antijüdische Massnahmen'. See also: Bericht über die Konferenz [&] Interview mit Fred Grubel (Rolf Vogel) [in]: deutschland-berichte, Jg. 19, Nr. 2, Bonn, Feb. 1983, pp. 20–26.]

20031. — *The night of the miracle: Adolf Hitler's conquest of power*. A 45-minute radio feature, written and presented by Christopher Andrew, produced by Peter Everett. Reader: Geoffrey Wheeler. Transmitted by BBC, Radio 4, 30th Jan. 1983. Transcript. London: BBC, 1983. 22 pp. [Mimeog.] [Transcript also in: The Listener, London, Feb. 3, 1983, pp. 9–10. Feature with the participation of German–Jewish eye witnesses, a.o., Hans Feld, Arnold Paucker, Eva G. Reichmann, Werner Rosenstock. Cf.: Review [in]: AJR Information, London, March 1983, p. 4.]

20032. — Stachura, Peter D., ed.: *The Nazi Machtergreifung*. London: Allen & Unwin, 1983. 191 pp., notes. [A collection of essays, also on antisemitism and the degree of its appeal to Nazism. Cf.: Review (Richard Grunberger) [in]: AJR Information, London, Jan. 1984, p. 1.]

20033. MAINZ. *Die Machtergreifung der Nationalsozialisten 1933 in Mainz*. Eine Dokumentation. Quellenband zur Ausstellung der Stadt Mainz. (Leitung: Anton Maria Keim. Bearbeitung: Friedrich Schütz.) Mainz, 1983. 395 pp., illus. [Incl. documents on life and persecution of the Jews.]

20034. Mommsen, Hans: *Die Realisierung des Utopischen: die 'Endlösung der Judenfrage' im 'Dritten Reich'*. [In]: Geschichte und Gesellschaft, Jg. 9, H. 3, Göttingen, 1983. Pp. 381–420, footnotes.

20035. Mieder, Wolfgang: *Proverbs in Nazi Germany: the promulgation of anti-Semitism and stereotypes through folklore*. [In]: Journal of American Folklore, 95, Lancaster, Pa., Oct.–Dec. 1982. Pp. 435–464.

20036. Mieder, Wolfgang: *Sprichwörter unterm Hakenkreuz*. [In]: Muttersprache, Jg. 93, H. 1–2, Wiesbaden, 1983. Pp. 1–30. [Deals especially with proverbs used to incite agitation against Jews.]

20037. MOERS. Billstein, Aurel, ed.: *Judendeportationen aus der Stadt und dem Landkreis Moers in die Vernichtungslager*. Namenslisten über Juden, die in die Massenvernichtungslager transportiert wurden; der amtliche Bericht eines Transportführers und Erlebnisberichte von Überlebenden. Krefeld (Flur 115): A. Billstein, [1983?]. 75 pp., illus.

20038. MUCH. Reifenrath, Bruno H.: *Die Internierung der Juden in Much*. Ein Buch des Gedenkens. Siegburg, 1982. 167 pp., illus., map. (Veröffentlichung des Geschichts- und Altertumsvereins für Siegburg und den Rhein-Sieg-Kreis, 15.)

20039. MÜNSTER. *Münster – Spuren aus der Zeit des Faschismus*. Münster: Edition Westfälisches Dampfboot, 1983. (Arbeitshefte zur materialistischen Wissenschaft, 19.) [Incl.: Die Deportation der Juden aus dem Münsterland (Arno Herzig, 157–165). Das Verzeichnis der

Münster'schen Juden aus den Jahren 1933–1945 (Bernhard Brilling/Ulrich Diekmann, 167–186). Ablauf der Vergasungen in Auschwitz-Birkenau (187–193).]

20040. *Nationalsozialistische Massentötungen durch Giftgas.* Eine Dokumentation. Hrsg. von Eugen Kogon, Hermann Langbein, Adalbert Rückerl [et al.]. Frankfurt am Main: S. Fischer, 1983. 350 pp., facsims., diagrs.

—— NEUWIED. [See No. 19838.]

20041. NOVEMBER POGROM. Maas, Angela: *Die 'Reichskristallnacht' im Spiegel der Wiener Presse.* Wien, Univ., Diplomarbeit, 1983. 207 pp.

20042. — Pätzold, Kurt: *Der historische Platz des antijüdischen Pogroms von 1938.* Zu einer Kontroverse. [In]: Jahrbuch für Geschichte, 26, Berlin/East, 1982. Pp. 195–216.

20043. — Petersen, Charlotte: *Novembertage 1938: eine Besuchsreise nach der 'Reichskristallnacht'.* [In]: Tribüne, Jg. 22, H. 87, Frankfurt am Main, 1983. Pp. 157–166. [A German woman visits Jewish friends in Rexingen.]

20044. NUREMBERG. Fritzsch, Robert: *Nürnberg unterm Hakenkreuz im Dritten Reich 1933–1939.* Düsseldorf: Droste, 1983. 109 pp., illus. [Also on persecution of the Jews.]

20045. NUREMBERG LAWS. Gruchmann, Lothar: *'Blutschutzgesetz' und Justiz.* Zu Entstehung und Auswirkung des Nürnberger Gesetzes vom 15. Sept. 1935. [In]: Vierteljahrshefte für Zeitgeschichte, Jg. 31, H. 3, Stuttgart, Juli 1983. Pp. 418–442, footnotes.

20046. NUREMBERG TRIALS. Conot, Robert E.: *Justice at Nuremberg.* London: Weidenfeld and Nicolson; New York: Harper & Row, 1983. XIII, 593 pp., illus., bibl. [Covers persecution of German Jewry prior to 1939 also. Cf.: Winner takes all (John Keegan) [in]: The Sunday Times, London, Feb. 5, 1984. Indicted for agression (Wolfgang Mommsen) [in]: TLS, London, Feb. 3, 1984, p. 120.]

20047. — Tusa, Ann & John: *The Nuremberg Trial.* London: Macmillan, 1983. 519 pp., illus., bibl. [Covers also persecution of German Jewry. Cf.: Both reviews of preceding entry.]

20048. OFFENBACH. *Anschriftenverzeichnis ehemaliger jüdischer Einwohner Offenbachs.* Hrsg.: Magistrat. Offenbach am Main (Stadthof 15): Presse- und Informationsamt, 1983. 21 pp.

20049. Ostler, Fritz: *Rechtsanwälte in der NS-Zeit.* Fakten und Erinnerungen. [In]: Anwaltsblatt, H. 2, Bonn, Feb. 1983. Pp. 50–59, footnotes. [Refers mostly to Jewish lawyers.]

20050. *Over Germany.* A 47-minute film, directed by Ian Sellar, shown in Britain at the 27th London Film Festival in 1983. [Autobiographical recollection of the film-maker's first trip to Germany as a child to visit his Jewish grandmother.]

20051. PASSAU. Rosmus-Wenninger, Anja: *Widerstand und Verfolgung: am Beispiel Passaus 1933–1939.* Mit einem Vorwort von Martin Hirsch. Passau: Andreas-Haller-Verl., 1983. 191 pp., illus. [Incl. chap.: Rassistische Verfolgung (57–79).]

20052. PFORZHEIM. *Gurs – Vorhölle von Auschwitz; Antisemitismus in Pforzheim 1920–1980.* Dokumente, Fotos, Berichte. (Zusammenstellung: Gerhard Brändle.) Pforzheim: Stadt, 1980. 237 pp., illus. notes, bibl. (235–237).

20053. Platner, Geert, ed.: *Schule im Dritten Reich – Erziehung zum Tod?* Eine Dokumentation. Hrsg. in Zusammenarbeit mit Schülern der Gerhart-Hauptmann-Schule in Kassel. München: Deutscher Taschenbuch-Verl., 1983. 281 pp., illus., bibl. (dtv, 10119.) [Especially on racism and antisemitism; incl. reports by Jews who were formerly pupils in Kassel.]

20054. Poliakov, Léon/Wulf, Joseph, eds.: *Das Dritte Reich und die Juden.* Unveränd. Nachdr. der im Arani-Verl., Berlin, erschienenen 2., durchgesehenen Aufl. Frankfurt am Main: Ullstein, 1983. X, 457 pp., illus. (Ullstein-Buch, Nr. 33036.) [See also by same editors the reprints]: *Das Dritte Reich und seine Denker.* 1983. XI, 560 pp. (Ullstein-Buch, Nr. 33038.) [Also on antisemitism.] *Das Dritte Reich und seine Diener.* 1983. XV, 540 pp. (Ullstein-Buch, Nr. 33037.) [Also on persecution of the Jews.]

20055. Pommerin, Reiner: *The fate of mixed blood children in Germany.* [In]: German Studies Review, Vol. 5, Tempe, Ariz., 1982. Pp. 315–323.

20056. Prolingheuer, Hans: *Ausgetan aus dem Land der Lebendigen.* Leidensgeschichten unter Kreuz und Hakenkreuz. Neukirchen-Vluyn: Neukirchener Verl., 1983. 236 pp., illus. [Also on persecution of German Jews.]

—— RECKLINGHAUSEN. [See No. 19846.]

20057. REFUGEE POLICY. Abella, Irving/Troper, Harold: *None is too many; Canada and the Jews of Europe, 1933–1948.* Toronto: Lester and Orpen Dennys, 1982; New York: Random House, 1983. XIII, 336 pp., illus., notes (290–325). [Deals with very restrictive Canadian policy with regard to Jewish immigration 1933–1948. Cf.: Review (Roger Daniels) [in]: American Jewish Archives, No. 1, Cincinnati, Apr. 1983, pp. 72–75, notes. Review (Gershon

D. Hundert) [in]: The Canadian Historical Review, No. 1, Toronto, March 1983, pp. 55–56.]

20058. — ALDERMAN, GEOFFREY: *The Jewish community in British politics*. Oxford: Clarendon Press, 1983. 232 pp., tabs. [Also on the attitude of non-Jews and Jews in Britain towards the Jewish refugees from Nazi Europa.]

20059. — BAUMEL, JUDITH TYDOR: *Twice a refugee: the Jewish refugee children in Great Britain during evacuation, 1939–1943*. [In]: Jewish Social Studies, Vol. 45, No. 2, New York, Spring 1983. Pp. 175–184, notes. [Also on German-Jewish refugee children; see also No. 18132/YB XXVII.]

—— — BRITAIN. [See also in Nos. 19896, 19897.]

20060. — EYCK, U. F. J.: *G. P. Gooch: a study in history and politics*. London: Macmillan, 1982. XV, 498 pp. [Incl. chap XI on the Nazi regime in the Second World War which deals extensively with the immigration of German Jews to Great Britain (406–436).]

20061. — EYCK, U. F. J.: *Psychological warfare and newspaper control in British-occupied Germany*. A personal account. [In]: Men at war: politics, technology and innovation in the 20th century. Ed. by Timothy Travers and Christon Archer. Chicago: Precedent, 1982. 228 pp. [Story of a German-Jewish refugee whom the British army used in propaganda against the German army and later in producing newspapers in German in occupied Germany.]

20062. — HALLIE, PHILIP P.: *. . . dass nicht unschuldig Blut vergossen werde: die Geschichte des Dorfes Le Chambon und wie dort Gutes geschah*. Aus dem Amerikan. übers. von Heidi und Georg Wolfgang Schimpf. Neukirchen-Vluyn: Neukirchener Verl., 1983. 303 pp., illus. [Transl. of No. 16131/YB XXV. A documentary report on the rescue of Jewish and non-Jewish refugees in 1940–1944 in southern France.]

20063. — KANTOROWICZ, ALFRED: *Exil in Frankreich: Merkwürdigkeiten und Denkwürdigkeiten*. (2. Aufl.) Hamburg: Christians, 1983 (c1971). 252 pp.

20064. — KINGSTON, PAUL J.: *Anti-Semitism in France during the 1930s*. Organisations, personalities and propaganda. Hull: Hull Univ. Press, 1983. 165 pp. [Also on the German-Jewish refugees' experience of French antisemitism.]

20065. — KLARSFELD, SERGE: *Memorial to the Jews deported from France 1942–1944*. Documentation of the deportation of the victims of the Final Solution in France. New York: Beate Klarsfeld Foundation, 1983. XXXIX, 663 pp., illus., bibl. [Incl. German- and Austrian-Jewish refugees.]

20066. — KOCHAN, MIRIAM: *Britain's internees in the Second World War*. London: Macmillan, 1983. XIII, 182 pp., illus., maps, bibl. [Study, based on interviews with former internees, on life in the various camps, including camps on the Isle of Man, in Australia and Canada. Cf.: Out of the frying-pan (Rosemary Friedman) [in]: Jewish Chronicle, London, March 9, 1984.]

20067. — LÜHE, BARBARA von der: *'Aus Kindern werden Briefe . . .': zur Auswanderung jüdischer Kinder aus Deutschland (1933 bis 1939)*. [In]: Tribüne, Jg. 22, H. 87, Frankfurt am Main, 1983. Pp. 123–132, footnotes. [On the efforts to bring Jewish children out of Germany, and on the immigration restrictions of the various countries.]

20068. — MAYER, JACOB: *James McDonald and the refugees, 1933–1946*. [In Hebrew, with English summary]. Ramat-Gan, Bar-Ilan Univ., Diss., 1982. V, 413, 3 pp., bibl. (404–413). [Cont.: The office of the High Commissioner for Refugees from Germany, 1933–1935. President Roosevelt's Advisory Committee on Political Refugees, 1938–1945. The Anglo-American Commission of Inquiry on Palestine, 1946.]

20069. — OFER, DALIA: *The rescue of European Jewry and illegal immigration 1940: possibilities and reality*. [In Hebrew, with English summary]. [In]: Yahadut Zemanenu (Contemporary Jewry); a Research Annual, Vol. 1, Jerusalem, 1983. Pp. 179–197. [Discusses rescue operations organised by Berthold Storfer, a Viennese Jew.]

20070. REXIN, MANFRED: *'Regime unter dem Hakenkreuz'*. Eine Sendereihe in 25 Folgen im RIAS-Bildungsprogramm. [In]: RIAS Quartal, IV, Berlin 1983. Pp. 3–7. [Report of the author on his 25 pt. TV documentary series, shown between Jan.–Dec. 1983. Ms. of series (mimeog.) in the LBI New York; incl.: Verfolgung der Juden 1933–1938 (pt. 13); Endlösung; die Verfolgung der europäischen Juden 1939–1945 (pt. 22).]

20071. RHINELAND. [See also No. 19850.] DOLL, ANTON, ed.: *Nationalsozialismus im Alltag*. Quellen zur Geschichte der NS-Herrschaft im Gebiet des Landes Rheinland-Pfalz aus dem Landeshauptarchiv Koblenz und dem Landesarchiv Speyer. Mappe 1–2. Speyer:

landesarchiv, 1983. 2 vols. (XI, 162; 163–318 pp.), bibl. [*Mappe 1* incl.: Judenverfolgung (Dokumente Nr. 73–116 = pp. 128–158).]

20072. SASSIN, HORST R.: *Widerstand, Verfolgung und Emigration Liberaler 1933–1945.* (Hrsg. und verantwortlich: Friedrich-Naumann-Stiftung.) [Ausstellungskatalog.] Bonn: Liberal-Verl., 1983. 120 pp., illus. bibl. [Also on the persecution of Jewish liberals.]

20073. SCHEUER, LISA: *Vom Tode, der nicht stattfand: Theresienstadt, Auschwitz, Freiberg, Mauthausen; eine Frau überlebt.* Reinbek: Rowohlt, 1983. 121 pp., illus. (rororo, 5239.) [L. Sch., deported from Prague, lives in Cologne.]

20074. SCHLICKER, WOLFGANG/GLASER, JOSEF: *Tendenzen und Konsequenzen faschistischer Wissenschaftspolitik nach dem 30. Jan. 1933.* [In]: Zeitschrift für Geschichtswissenschaft, Jg. 31, H. 10, Berlin/East, 1983. Pp. 881–895, footnotes. [On persecution and dismissal of Jewish scientists at Prussian universities and industrial firms; mentions many names.]

20075. SCHMID, HANS-DIETER/SCHNEIDER, GERHARD/SOMMER, WILHELM, eds.: *Juden unterm Hakenkreuz.* Dokumente und Berichte zur Verfolgung und Vernichtung durch die Nationalsozialisten 1933–1945. *Bd. 1: Verdrängung und Verfolgung. Bd. 2: Vertreibung und Vernichtung.* Düsseldorf: Schwann, 1983. 2 vols., illus., maps, bibl. (179; 288 pp.). (Geschichtsdidaktik, Bd. 16–17.)

20076. *Das Schwarzbuch. Tatsachen und Dokumente: die Lage der Juden in Deutschland 1933.* Hrsg. vom Comité des Délégations Juives. [Nachdr. der Ausg.] Paris, 1934. Frankfurt am Main: Ullstein, 1983. 535 pp. [Documents on the persecution of the Jews in Germany and their elimination from public and cultural life. Cf.: Schon 1933 dokumentiert (Julius H. Schoeps) [in]: Die Zeit, Nr. 39, Hamburg, 23. Sept. 1983, p. 13.]

20077. SCHWERIN. HAMBURGER, MARIELUISE: *Das Ende der jüdischen Gemeinde in Schwerin.* [In]: Nachrichtenblatt des Verbandes der Jüd. Gemeinden in der DDR, Dresden, Sept. 1983. Pp. 7–8.

20078. SIEGEN. [See also No. 19850.]. DIETERMANN, KLAUS: *Siegen unterm Hakenkreuz.* Eine alternative Stadtrundfahrt. 2., verbesserte Aufl. Siegen: Verlag der Gesellschaft für christlich-jüdische Zusammenarbeit Siegerland, 1983. 50 pp., illus., bibl. [Incl.: Die Siegener Synagoge. Kaufhaus Tietz. Gedenkstätte Jüd. Friedhof.]

20079. SILESIA. BRUGEL, J. W.: *The Bernheim petition: a challenge to Nazi Germany in 1933.* [In]: Patterns of Prejudice, Vol. 17, No. 3, London, July 1983. Pp. 17–25, notes. [Franz Bernheim, a German-Jewish refugee, sued the Hitler government before the League of Nations and secured exemption for the Jews in German Upper Silesia from Hitler's anti-Jewish measures for 4 more years.]

—— SPRENDLINGEN. [See No. 19859.]

20080. STACHURA, PETER D.: *Gregor Strasser and the rise of Nazism.* London: Allen and Unwin, 1983. 208 pp. [Discusses also Strasser's antisemitism and anti-Jewish propaganda. Cf.: A Nazi on the left (Richard Grunberger) [in]: AJR Information, Jan. 1984, p. 1. Building up the party (F. L. Carsten) [in]: TLS, London, Aug. 12, 1983, p. 851.]

20081. STREICHER, JULIUS. BYTWERK, RANDALL L.: *Julius Streicher: the man who persuaded a nation to hate Jews.* New York: Stein and Day, 1982. 208 pp., illus.

20082. — SHOWALTER, DENNIS E.: *Little man, what now? 'Der Stürmer' in the Weimar Republic.* Hamden, Conn.: Archon, 1982. XVI, 285 pp., illus., bibl. [Cf.: Review (Gary D. Stark) [in]: American Historical Review, Vol. 88, No. 3, Washington, D.C., June 1983, p. 706. Aryanism for the masses (J. D. Noakes) [in]: TLS, London, June 17, 1983, p. 640.] [See also: Letters to 'Der Stürmer': the mobilization of hostility in the Weimar Republic (Dennis E. Showalter) [in]: Modern Judaism, Vol. 3, No. 2, Baltimore, 1983, pp. 173–187, notes.]

20083. SWABIA. RÖMER, GERNOT: *Der Leidensweg der Juden in Schwaben.* Schicksale von 1933–1945 in Berichten, Dokumenten und Zahlen. Unter Mitarbeit von Ellen Römer. Augsburg: Presse-, Druck- und Verlags GmbH, 1983. 188 pp., illus. [On Augsburg and 19 smaller places in Swabia.]

20084. SWITZERLAND. BONJOUR, EDGAR: *Die Schweizer Juden in Frankreich 1942/43.* [In]: Schweizerische Zeitschrift für Geschichte, Jg. 33, No. 2, Basel, 1983. Pp. 217–221.

20085. — GOLDNER, FRANZ: *Flucht in die Schweiz; die neutrale Schweiz und die österreichische Emigration 1938 bis 1945.* Wien: Europaverlag, 1983. 174 pp., bibl.

20086. — HILDEBRANDT, IRMA: *In der Fremde zu Hause.* Freiburg i.Br.: Herder, 1983. 128 pp. (Herder-Bücherei, 967.) [Incl. interviews with German-Jewish emigrants, 1933–1945.]

20087. — KÜHNER, CLAUDIA: *'. . . die Verjudung zu verhindern': die Schweiz in der Nazizeit – und ihre Emigranten.* [In]: Tribüne, Jg. 22, H. 87, Frankfurt am Main, 1983. Pp. 134–139. [Also on Heinrich Rothmund, chief of the Swiss 'Fremdenpolizei' during the Nazi period.]

20088. — LASSERRE, ANDRÉ: *À propos de la lettre du Dr. Rothmund.* [In]: Schweizerische Zeitschrift für Geschichte, Jg. 32, No. 4, Basel, 1982. Pp. 561–562.

20089. — MYSYROWICZ, LADISLAS: *Le Dr. Rothmund et le problème juif (Février 1941).* [In]: Schweizerische Zeitschrift für Geschichte, Jg. 32, Basel, 1982. Pp. 348–355.

20090. SYDOW, ROLF von: *Angst zu atmen.* Frankfurt am Main: Ullstein, 1983. 160 pp. [Recollections by R. v. S., born 1924 in Wiesbaden, how his partly Jewish descent affected his youth in Nazi Germany.]

20091. TAL, URIEL: *Law and theology: on the status of German Jewry at the outset of the Third Reich (1933/4).* Tel-Aviv: Tel-Aviv Univ., [1983]. 54 pp., facsims. (37–54), footnotes. (Third annual lecture of the Jacob M. and Shoshana Schreiber Chair of Contemporary Jewish History, June 30, 1982.)

20092. THERESIENSTADT. ŠKOCHOVÁ, JARMILA: *Theater im Konzentrationslager Theresienstadt.* [In]: Judaica Bohemiae, Vol. 19, No. 2, Praha, 1983. Pp. 63–71, footnotes, illus. [In same issue also]: KÁRNÝ, MIROSLAV: *Vorgeschichte, Sinn und Folge des 23. Juni 1944 in Theresienstadt.* Pp. 72–98, footnotes. [On the inspection of Th. by a delegation of the Internat. Committee of the Red Cross.]

20093. THIMME, ANNELISE: *Friedrich Thimme und der Nationalsozialismus.* [In]: Antidoron; Festschrift für Jürgen Thimme, hrsg. von Dieter Metzler [et al.]. Karlsruhe: C. F. Müller, 1983. Pp. 193–201, facsims., notes. [Incl. letters by Friedrich Thimme, 1868–1938, historian, which express his condemnation of National Socialism and its anti-Jewish measures.]

—— TIENGEN. [See No. 19861.]

20094. TRIER. CHRISTOFFEL, EDGAR: *Der Weg durch die Nacht; Verfolgung und Widerstand im Trierer Land während der Zeit des Nationalsozialismus.* Verfolgte aus Trier und dem Trierer Land durchleben die Konzentrationslager und Zuchthäuser des 'Dritten Reiches'. Trier: NCO Verl. Neu, 1983. 256 pp., illus., bibl. (250–255). [Also on persecution of the Jews.]

—— VOREIFEL. [See No. 19862.]

20095. WARBURG. HERMES, HERMANN: *Deportationsziel Riga; Schicksale Warburger Juden.* Warburg: Hermes, 1982. 148 pp., illus., map.

20096. WEIDEN. BRENNER, MICHAEL: *Am Beispiel Weiden: jüdischer Alltag im Nationalsozialismus.* Würzburg: Arena, 1983. 173 pp., illus., ports., facsims., bibl. (73).

20097. WEINBERG, WERNER: *Why I did not leave Nazi Germany in time.* [In]: The Christian Century, Vol. 99, No. 14, Chicago, Apr. 21, 1982. Pp. 478–481.

20098. WELTSCH, ROBERT: *Jüdische Rundschau.* Jg. 38, Berlin 1933. [Wiederabdruck historisch einmaliger Artikel, 31. Jan.–30. Mai 1933. Mit einer Schlussbemerkung von Arno Lustiger.] Hrsg.: Zionistische Organisation in Deutschland. Red.: Z. Ben-Jischai. Frankfurt am Main (Liebigstr. 24), [Mai] 1983. 8 pp. [Cont. reprints of articles by R. Weltsch [incl. 'Tragt ihn mit Stolz . . .'), Martin Buber, and Kurt Blumenfeld (from 'Das Jüd. Echo'). See also reprints of R. Weltsch's articles orig. publ. 1933 in 'Jüd. Rundschau' [in]: 'Allgemeine', Nr. 14, Düsseldorf, 8. Apr. 1983, pp. 1–2 [& in]: MB, Nr. 47, Tel-Aviv, 23. Dez. 1983, p. 3.]

20099. WESEL. BAUMGART, BERND/HEITKAMP, KLAUS: *Die Geschichte der jüdischen Gemeinde Wesel von 1933 bis 1945.* Duisburg, Univ., Schriftl. Hausarbeit . . . , 14. Sept. 1982. 195 pp., illus., facsims., plans, bibl. (173–177). [Typescript. Available at the library of the LBI New York.]

20100. — PRIEUR, JUTTA: *Wesel 1933–1945.* Unter Mitarbeit weiterer Autoren. (Ausstellung.) Köln: Rheinland-Verl., 1983. 122 pp., illus. (Weseler Museumsschriften, Bd. 7.) [Incl.: Die jüd. Gemeinde in Wesel (Bernd Baumgart/ Klaus Heitkamp, 53–59).]

20101. WISTRICH, ROBERT: *Wer war wer im Dritten Reich.* Anhänger, Mitläufer, Gegner aus Politik, Wirtschaft, Militär, Kunst und Wissenschaft. (Aus dem Engl. übers. von Joachim Rehork.) Überarb., erweiterte und illus. deutsche Ausg. München: Harnack, 1983. 319 pp., 290 ports., bibl. (307–313). [Revised and augmented German edn. of No. 19083/YB XXVIII. Cf. (cont.): Review (Donald M. McKale) [in]: American Historical Review, Vol. 88, No. 3, Washington, D.C., June 1983. Review (Roger Manvell) [in]: British Book News, Dec. 1982. Portraits (Nissim Rejwan) [in]: The Jerusalem Post, 5. Nov. 1982. Hitler and Co. (William Gutmann) [in]: The Observer, London, 25. July 1982. Besprechung [in]: Die Zeit, Nr. 11, Hamburg, 9. März 1984, p. 49.)

20102. WOLFFHEIM, ELSBETH: *Freitod im Exil; Emigrantenschicksale während des Dritten Reiches.* [In]: NZZ, Nr. 106, Zürich, 7./8. Mai 1983. Pp. 69–70.

20103. WÜRZBURG. ROCKENMAIER, DIETER W.: *Das Dritte Reich und Würzburg.* Versuch einer Bestandsaufnahme. Würzburg: Mainpresse Richter, 1983. 262 pp. [Incl. chap.: Buchführung des Todes (117–166), on persecution and deportation of the Jewish population.]

20104. — SCHULTHEIS, HERBERT: *Juden in der Diözese Würzburg 1933–1945.* Bad Neustadt/Saale: Rötter,

1983. 32 pp.

20105. WULF, JOSEPH, ed.: *Theater und Film im Dritten Reich.* Eine Dokumentation. Frankfurt am Main: Ullstein, 1983. 486 pp. (Ullstein-Buch, Nr. 33031.) [Incl. chaps: Artfremdes Theater; Artfremder Film; referring to Jewish actors, also to antisemitic theatre and films. See also the editor's]: *Presse und Funk im Dritten Reich.* 417 pp. *Literatur und Dichtung im Dritten Reich.* 535 pp. *Die bildenden Künste im Dritten Reich.* 456 pp. *Musik im Dritten Reich.* 500 pp. (Ullstein-Buch, Nr. 33028–33030; 33032.) [All vols. are reprints, orig. publ. 1963/64; incl. documentations on persecution and elimination of Jews from the arts.]

20106. *Yad Vashem Studies.* 14. Ed. by Livia Rothkirchen. Jerusalem: Yad Vashem Martyrs' and Heroes' Remembrance Authority, 1981. 370 pp., illus. [Incl.: The defiant few: Jews and Czech 'Inside Front', 1938–1942 (Livia Rothkirchen, 35–88). Palestinian POWs in German captivity (Yoav Gelber, 89–138). The Committee for Jewish Refugees in Holland, 1933–1940 (Dan Michman, 205–232).]

20107. ZISCHKA, JOHANNES: *Aspekte der NS-Rassenideologie.* Eine ideologiekritische Untersuchung. [Nebst] Zusammenfassung. Graz, Univ., Diss., 1982. 217, 6, 6 pp.

20108. ZÜRNDORFER, HANNELE: *The ninth of November.* London: Quartet, 1983. 192 pp., illus. [Autobiography; story of a Jewish family in Germany in the late 1930s, of the author's and her sister's emigration to England and their early years in foster homes. Cf.: A broken childhood (Vivian Hassan) [in]: Jewish Chronicle, London, Dec. 9, 1983.]

IV. **POST WAR**

A. **General**

—— AUSTRIA. [See No. 19871.]

20109. CZECHOSLOVAKIA. WÖRSTER, PETER: *Die Juden in den böhmischen Ländern nach 1945.* Materialien zu ihrer Geschichte. Marburg an der Lahn: Johann-Gottfried-Herder-Institut, Dez. 1982. 110 pp., notes (94–108). (Dokumentation Ostmitteleuropa, Jg. 8 (32), H. 5/6, pp. 235–344.)

20110. FEDERAL GERMAN REPUBLIC. [See also No. 19773.] *Bericht aus Landesverbänden und Gemeinden.* [And]: *Die jüdische Gemeinschaft in Zahlen.* [In]: Jüdischer Pressedienst, Nr. 5/6, Düsseldorf, Okt. 1983. Pp. 3–18; 21–25.

20111. — DÜSSELDORF. *Anschriften ehemaliger Düsseldorfer jüdischer Mitbürger.* 2., ergänzte Aufl. Düsseldorf: Kulturdezernat, 1983. [54] pp.

20112. — JOSEPH, NADINE: *The new Germany: 'We feel like strangers'.* [In]: Present Tense, Vol. 10, No. 4, New York, Summer 1983. Pp. 29–33. [Also excerpts, transl. into German, under the title]: *'Die neuen Juden von Deutschland' oder 'Das neue Deutschland'?* [In]: Jüdischer Pressedienst, Nr. 7/8, Düsseldorf, Dez. 1983, pp. 10–12 [& in]: MB, Nr. 45, Tel-Aviv, 9. Dez. 1983, pp. 3–4. [On Jews living in present day Germany.]

20113. — *Juden in Deutschland 1983 – integriert oder diskriminiert?* Ein Symposium. (Hrsg.: Kurt E. Becker [et al.] im Auftrag der Pegulan-Werke-AG.) Landau/Pfalz: Pfälzische Verlagsanstalt, 1983. 190 pp. (Reihe 'Frankenthaler Gespräche' in der PVA.)

20114. — RUBINSTEIN, W. D.: *The left, the right and the Jews.* London: Croom Helm, 1982; New York: Universe Books, 1983. 256 pp. [Advances a thesis as to why Jews in Western capitalist societies have moved to the right since World War II; incl. post war German Jews. Cf.: Jews and the left (Arthur Liebman) [in]: American Jewish History, Vol. 73, No. 1, Waltham, Mass., Sept. 1983, pp. 99–108. Review (Dan Cohn-Sherbok) [in]: Jewish Spectator, Vol. 48, No. 3, New York, Fall 1983, pp. 50–52; reviews, a.o., also 'Socialism and the Jews' by R. S. Wistrich, see No. 18833/YB XXVIII).]

20115. — STUTTGART. *Ehemalige jüdische Mitbürger in Stuttgart.* Dokumentation des Besuches vom 12.–27. Juni 1983. Stuttgart: Kulturamt, 1983. 72 pp., illus.

20116. — WOLFFSOHN, MICHAEL: *Leben im Land der Mörder; Deutschlands Juden im Spannungsfeld zwischen Israel und Diaspora.* [In]: Die Zeit, Nr. 22, Hamburg, 27. Mai 1983. Pp. 9–10.

20117. GERMAN DEMOCRATIC REPUBLIC. [See also No. 19773.] DIAMANT, ADOLF: *Materialien zur Geschichte der Juden in der Deutschen Demokratischen Republik.* Ein wissenschaftliches Fragment. Frankfurt am Main (Voelckerstr. 9): A. Diamant, 1984 [publ. 1983]. 277 pp., illus., bibl.

20118. — DI NAPOLI, THOMAS: *Reception of the Holocaust in the German Democratic Republic: a philatelic commentary.* [In]: Jewish Social Studies, Vol. 44, Nos. 3–4, New York, Summer-Fall, 1982. Pp. 255–261, notes.

20119. HOLOCAUST TV-FILM. Insdorf, Annette: *Indelible shadows: film and the Holocaust.* New York: Random House, 1983. 234 pp., illus., notes, filmogr. (217–223), bibl. (225–229). [Also Vintage Paperback.] [Discusses 75 films on the Nazi period.]

20120. — Knilli, Friedrich/Zielinski, Siegfried, eds.: *Betrifft 'Holocaust': Zuschauer schreiben an den WDR [Westdeutschen Rundfunk].* Ein Projektbericht. Berlin: Spiess, 1983. 407 pp., bibl. (403–407). (Preprints zur Medienwissenschaft, 4.)

20121. — Lübbe, Hermann: *Der Nationalsozialismus im deutschen Nachkriegsbewusstsein.* [In]: Historische Zeitschrift, Bd. 236, H. 3, München, Juni 1983. Pp. 579–599, notes. [Also on Holocaust film.]

20122. HOLOCAUST TRAUMA. Moskovitz, Sarah: *Love despite hate; child survivors of the Holocaust and their adult lives.* New York: Schocken, 1983. XV, 245 pp., illus., notes. [Deals with the home for refugee children in London run by the German-Jewish refugee Alice Goldberger with the help of Anna Freud; cont. 24 interviews.]

20123. PROSECUTION OF NAZI CRIMES. Vogel, Rolf: *Verfolgung von NS-Verbrechen: 25 Jahre Zentrale Stelle der Landesjustizverwaltungen in Ludwigsburg.* Gespräch mit dem Leiter, Oberstaatsanwalt Dr. Adalbert Rückerl. [In]: Das Parlament, Nr. 51–52, Bonn, 24./31. Dez. 1983. P. 20.

B. Restitution

— Kropat, Wolf-Arno: *Jüdische Gemeinden in Hessen, Wiedergutmachung, Rechtsradikalismus und Antisemitismus nach 1945.* [See pp. 447 ff in No. 19832.]

20124. Schwarz, Walter: *Zum letzten Kapitel der Wiedergutmachung.* [In]: Aufbau, Nr. 2, New York, Jan. 14, 1983. P. 17 [& in]: MB, Nr. 4, Tel-Aviv, 28. Jan. 1983, pp. 3–4.

C. Antisemitism, Judaism, Nazism in Education and Teaching

20125. Gradwohl, Roland: *Was ist der Talmud?* Einführung in die 'Mündliche Tradition' Israels. Stuttgart: Calwer Verl., 1983. 80 pp., illus. (Calwer Paperback.)

20126. Schatzker, Chaim: *Jewish history in contemporary [West] German history textbooks.* [In Hebrew, with English summary]. [In]: Yahadut Zemanenu (Contemporary Jewry); a Research Annual, Vol. 1, Jerusalem, 1983. Pp. 121–135.

20127. *Shoah.* Vol. 3, No. 2–3: *Special double issue on Holocaust education.* New York, Fall–Winter 1982–1983. 45 pp., illus., notes. [Incl.: The Holocaust in West German textbooks (Walter Renn, 26–30). Propaganda in education (Eric Goldhagen, 31–32; on Nazi antisemitism).]

20128. Stöhr, Martin, ed.: *Judentum im christlichen Religionsunterricht.* Frankfurt am Main: Haag und Herchen, 1983. 175 pp., bibl. (170–175). (Arnoldshainer Texte, Bd. 15.)

V. JUDAISM

A. Jewish Learning and Scholars

20129. ALTMANN, ALEXANDER: *Enlightenment and culture; the spiritual image of Moses Mendelssohn.* [In]: Hagut u-ma'ase [Thought and action; essays in memory of Simon Rawidowicz on the 25th anniversary of his death]. Ed. by A. A. Greenbaum, Alfred L. Ivry. Tel-Aviv: Tcherikover, for the Univ. of Haifa, 1983. Pp. 91–99.

20130. — Altmann, Alexander: *Lurianic Kabbala in a platonic key: Abraham Cohen Herrera's Puerta del Cielo.* [In]: Hebrew Union College Annual, Vol. 53 (1982), Cincinnati, 1983. Pp. 317–355, notes.

20131. Amir, Yehoshua: *Deraschot; jüdische Predigten.* Hrsg. von Peter von der Osten-Sacken. Berlin: Selbstverlag Institut Kirche und Judentum, 1983. 82 pp. (Veröffentlichungen aus dem Institut Kirche und Judentum, Bd. 14.) [Sermons 1939–1982 by Y.A., orig. Hermann Neumark.]

20132. ASHER BEN JEHIEL. Ellinson, Elyakim G.: *Toward the study of the Rosh's halakhic decisions (his disregard of ashkenazic regulations).* [In Hebrew, title transl.]. [In]: Sinai, Vol. 93, No. 5/6, Jerusalem, Av/Elul 5743 [July/Aug. 1983]. Pp. 234–244. [A.b.J., also known as Rosh, ca.

1250–1327, became the acknowledged leader of German Jewry after the imprisonment of Meir ben Baruch of Rothenburg, left Germany in 1303, rabbi in Toledo.]

20133. BAECK, LEO. GOLLAN, CLAUDIA: *Jüdische Existenz in der Verfolgung; Grundpositionen der Theologie Leo Baecks.* Würzburg, Univ., Theol. Diplomarbeit, 1982. 85 pp., bibl. (79–84).

20134. — LEITER, ROBERT: *Beyond survival: the life of Leo Baeck.* [In]: Friday; publ. by the Jewish Exponent, Philadelphia, Nov. 26, 1982. Pp. 1–4, ports.

20135. — LICHARZ, WERNER, ed.: *Leo Baeck: Lehrer und Helfer in schwerer Zeit.* Frankfurt am Main: Haag und Herchen, 1983. 197 pp., illus., ports., bibl. (194). (Arnoldshainer Texte, Bd. 20.) [Cont.: Selection of L. Baeck's writings (11–45). Leo Baeck: eine Lebensskizze (Werner Licharz, 4–10). Essays on L.B. (H. G. Adler, Jehoshua Amir, Ernst Ludwig Ehrlich, Albert H. Friedlander, Robert Raphael Geis, Pinchas Lapide, Nathan Peter Levinson, Friedrich-Wilhelm Marquardt, Ernst Simon). Eine Lücke in der deutschen Geschichtsschreibung: zur Forschungsarbeit des Leo-Baeck-Instituts (Hans Seidenberg, 186–188). Das Leo-Baeck-Institut (Freunde und Förderer des LBI, 189–193).]

20136. BRESSELAU, MEYER ISRAEL. FRIEDLANDER, YEHUDA: *On 'Herev Nokemet Nekam-Berit' by Meyer Israel Bresselau.* [In Hebrew, with English summary]. [In]: Tarbiz, Vol. 52, No. 1, Jerusalem, Oct.–Dec. 1982. Pp. 111–127. [M.I.B., Hebrew writer, one of the leaders of the Reform movement, state notary for the Jews of Hamburg, died 1839.]

20137. BREUER, ISAAC. BREUER, MORDECAI: *My father.* [In Hebrew, title transl.]. [In]: Ha-Ma'ayan, Vol. 23, No. 4, Jerusalem, Tammuz 5743 [June 1983]. Pp. 3–8. [I.B. data, see No. 17248/YB XXVI.]

20138. — WOHLGELERNTER, ISRAEL ELIEZER: *Rabbi Isaac Breuer: man of vision and of thought.* [In Hebrew, title transl.]. [In]: Ha-Ma'ayan, Vol. 24, No. 1, Jerusalem, Tishrei 5744 [Aug./Sept. 1983]. Pp. 10–19.

20139. BUBER, MARTIN: *Ich und Du.* 11., durchgesehene Aufl. Heidelberg: Lambert Schneider, 1983. 163 pp. (Sammlung Weltliteratur.)

20140. — BERRY, WANDA WARREN: *Judaism without covenant: Breslauer on Buber.* [In]: Jewish Social Studies, Vol. 45, No. 1, Winter 1983. Pp. 31–42. [Refers to No. 19121/YB XXVIII.]

20141. — BLOCH, JOCHANAN/GORDON, HAIM, eds.: *Martin Buber; Bilanz seines Denkens.* Aus dem Hebr. von Yehoshua Amir. Freiburg i.Br.: Herder, 1983. 528 pp.

20142. — BONI, S.: *The self and the other in the ontologies of Sartre and Buber.* Washington, D.C.: Univ Press of America, 1983. 202 pp.

20143. — BROCKE, MICHAEL: *Martin Bubers misreading des R. Nachman von Bratslaw: die unbekannte 'Geschichte von der fahrenden Prinzessin'.* [In]: Spiel-Räume, hrsg. von Hans-Günter Heimbrock. Neukirchen-Vluyn: Neukirchener Verl., 1983. Pp. 56–85, footnotes. [Incl Buber's hitherto unpubl. transl. of the story 'Von Kaiser und König' by Rabbi Nachman.]

20144. — COHEN, ADIR: *The educational philosophy of Martin Buber.* Rutherford, N.J.: Fairleigh Dickinson Univ. Press; London: Associated Univ. Presses, 1983. 350 pp. [Corrected entry of No. 19122/YB XXVIII.]

20145. — DILGER, IRENE: *Das dialogische Prinzip bei Martin Buber.* Frankfurt am Main: Haag und Herchen, 1983. III, 115 pp.

20146. — FRIEDMAN, MAURICE S.: *Martin Buber's life and work; the middle years 1923–1945.* New York Dutton, 1983. XVIII, 398 pp., ports., notes (327–373). [Cf.: Martin Buber revisited (Dan Cohn-Sherbok) [in]: Jewish Spectator, Vol. 48, No. 4, Santa Monica, Calif., Winter 1983 pp. 49–51 (also on No. 20144). For preceding vol. see No. 18216/YB XXVII.]

20147. — HALLAMISH, MOSHE/KASHER, ASA, eds.: *Israeli philosophy.* A selection of articles on general and Jewish philosophy. [In Hebrew, title transl.]. Tel-Aviv: Papyrus Publ.; Tel-Aviv Univ. 1983. 272 pp. [Incl.: Anarchism and theocracy in the thought of M. Buber (Zev Harvey, 9–19). The social philosophy of Buber as political thought (Avraham Yassour, 20–26). Buber and questions of 'the essence of Judaism' (Rachel Skichor, 27–33). In the footsteps of Buber realistic personalism according to Emanuel Mounier (Theodor Dreyfus, 34–47).]

20148. — HORWITZ, RIVKA: *Buber and Ebner: intellectual cross-fertilization between a Catholic and a Jew* [In]: Judaism, Vol. 32, No. 2, New York, Spring 1983. Pp. 188–195.

20149. — LEVY, ZE'EV: *Sören Kierkegaard and Martin Buber on good and evil, and on original sin.* [In Hebrew, title transl.] [In]: Alei-Siah; Literary Conversations, No. 17/18, Tel-Aviv, 1983 Pp. 196–210.

20150. — MURPHY, JOHN W.: *The social philosophy of Martin Buber; the social world as a human dimension* Washington, D.C.: Univ. Press of America, 1983. 176 pp.

20151. — OBERPARLEITER, HERMANN: *Martin Buber und die Philosophie.* Die Auseinandersetzung

Martin Bubers mit der wissenschaftlichen Philosophie. Frankfurt am Main: Lang, 1983. 117 pp. (Judentum und Umwelt, Bd. 7.) Zugl.: München, Univ., Diss., 1981.

20152. — SCHWEID, ELIEZER: *Martin Buber as a philosophical interpreter of the Bible.* [In Hebrew with English summary]. [In]: Mechkerei Yerushalayim be-Machshevet Yisrael (Jerusalem Studies in Jewish Thought), Vol. 2, No. 4, Jerusalem, Summer 1983. Pp. 570–612.

20153. — WEINRICH, MICHAEL: *Gottesfinsternis; die bleibende Anfrage Martin Bubers an uns.* [In]: Evangelische Theologie, Jg. 43, H. 1, München, Jan./Feb. 1983. Pp. 65–80, footnotes.

20154. CARLEBACH, ALEXANDER: *Men and ideas; a Jewish miscellany.* Selected writings 1935–1980. Jerusalem: Koren, 1982. 458, 31 (Hebrew) pp., illus., bibl. A. Carlebach (417–435). [Incl. chaps.: Of German Jewry (17–86). Family portraits: Salomon Carlebach (381–404); Emanuel Carlebach (405–409); and article on Joseph Zvi Carlebach (in Hebrew section, 29–31).]

20155. COHEN, HERMANN. GOLDSCHMIDT, HERMANN LEVIN: *Hermann Cohens Weg zum Judentum.* [Gedenkrede zum 25. Todestag von H. Cohen am 4. Apr. 1943. Wiederabdruck unter dem Titel]: *Ein seltenes Jubiläum.* [In]: Isr. Wochenblatt, Nr. 47, Zürich, 25. Nov. 1983. Pp. 27, 29, 31. [Republ. from: Isr. Wochenblatt, Apr. 9, 1943.] [See also Steinberg essay in No. 20207.]

20156. — SCHWEID, ELIEZER: *Hermann Cohen as a biblical exegete.* [In Hebrew, with English summary]. [In]: Daat, No. 10, Ramat-Gan, Winter 1983. Pp. 93–122.

20157. ELIEZER BEN JOEL HA-LEVI OF BONN. HANDELSMAN, YITZCHAK: *The views of Rabbi Eliezer ben Joel ha-Levi on communal leadership.* [In Hebrew]. [In]: Zion, Vol. 48, No. 1, Jerusalem, 1983. Pp. 21–54. [E. ben Joel ha-Levi, 1140–1225, scholar, rabbi in Cologne.]

20158. ELLENSON, DAVID: *The role of reform in selected German-Jewish orthodox responsa.* A sociological analysis. [In]: Hebrew Union College Annual, Vol. 53 (1982), Cincinnati, 1983. Pp. 357–380, notes. [Deals especially with Esriel Hildesheimer, David Hoffmann, Marcus Horowitz.]

20159. FACKENHEIM, EMIL: *Quest for past and future.* Essays in Jewish theology. Westport, Conn.: Greenwood, 1983. 336 pp. [Reprint of 1968 edn.]

20160. — FACKENHEIM, EMIL: *To mend the world; foundations of future Jewish thought.* New York: Schocken, 1982. XII, 363 pp. [Cf.: Review (Arthur A. Cohen) [in]: Modern Judaism, Vol. 3, No. 2, Baltimore, May 1983, pp. 225–236.]

20161. FRANK, JACOB. WACHOLDER, BEN ZION: *Jacob Frank and the Frankists' Hebrew Zoharic letters.* [In]: Hebrew Union College Annual, Vol. 53 (1982), Cincinnati, 1983. Pp. 265–293, notes.

20162. GLATZER, NAHUM N. CASH, DEBRA: *Nahum Glatzer at 80.* [In]: Jewish Monthly, Vol. 98, No. 4, Washington, D.C., 1983. Pp. 22–31. [See also tributes (E.G. Lowenthal) [in]: Aufbau, No. 15, New York, Apr. 15, 1983, p. 4. (Max Gruenewald) [in]: MB, Nr. 11/12, Tel-Aviv, 28. März 1983, p. 14.]

20163. GRAETZ, HEINRICH. MARK, B.: *At the grave-site of Zvi Hirsch Graetz.* An essay. [In Hebrew]. [In]: Massuah; a Yearbook, No. 10, Tel-Aviv, Apr. 1982. Pp. 131–147. [Transl. from the Yiddish, written in 1947; incl. description of 19th century Breslau.]

20164. GREIVE, HERMANN. *Obituaries and reports in commemoration of Professor Hermann Greive*, Apr. 7, 1935 Walstedde, Westphalia – Jan. 25, 1984 Cologne, professor of religious history at the Martin-Buber-Institut für Judaistik of the University Cologne. (Selection): Professor murdered in Cologne [in]: AJR Information, London, Apr. 1984, p. 5. Nachruf (Günther Bernd Ginzel) [in]: 'Allgemeine', Nr. 5, Düsseldorf, 3. Feb. 1984, p. 5. Tod in Köln: Opfer eines Wahns? (Peter Freimark) [in]: Deutsches Allg. Sonntagsblatt, Hamburg, 5. Feb. 1984, p. 28. Professor im Hörsaal erschossen: ehemalige Studentin festgenommen [in]: Frankfurter Allg. Zeitung, 26. Jan. 1984. Report [in]: Ha'aretz, Jerusalem, Jan. 26, 1984. Er galt als die Seele des Instituts: Tod des international geschätzten Gelehrten Greive löste Trauer aus [in]: Kölner Stadt-Anzeiger, 26. Jan. 1984. Gedenken an den ermordeten Professor Greive [an der Kölner Univ.] [in]: Kölner Stadt-Anzeiger, 1. Feb. 1984. Kleines Institut, grosser Ruf: ein schreckliches Verbrechen rückte Kölner Judaisten in den Blickpunkt [in]: Kölnische Rundschau, 25. Jan. 1984. Greive international anerkannt: Dienst als Anliegen [in]: Kölnische Rundschau, Jan. 26, 1984. Miteinander ohne Vorbehalt [in]: Kölnische Rundschau, 12. März 1984 (report on a lecture by Hermann Greive delivered posthumously by Werner Jochmann at the occasion of the 'Woche der Brüderlichkeit' 1984). Obituary (Arnold Paucker) [in]: LBI Year Book XXIX, London, 1984, p. viii. H. Greive zum Gedenken (Alex Bein) [in]: MB, Nr. 9, Tel-Aviv, 2. März 1984, p. 4. Mordanschlag auf Professoren für Judaistik: ein Todesopfer (Reuter) [in]: NZZ, Nr. 21, Zürich, 26. Jan. 1983, p. 9. Mord im Hörsaal vermutlich aus religiösem Wahn [in]: SZ, Nr.

21, München, 26. Jan. 1984, p. 44. Mörderin von Kölner Professor in psychiatrischer Anstalt (dpa) [in]: SZ, Nr. 40, München, 17. Feb. 1984, p. 47. Professor während der Vorlesung tödlich verletzt [in]: Die Welt, Essen, 26. Jan. 1984. Cologne professor dies after lecture shooting [in]: Times, London, 26. Jan. 1984.

20165. GROSSMAN, AVRAHAM: *The origins and essence of the custom of 'stopping-the-service'.* [In Hebrew]. [In]: Milet; Everyman's Univ. Studies in Jewish History and Culture, Vol. 1, Tel-Aviv, 1983. Pp. 199–219. [On the custom as practised in German synagogues in the Middle Ages.]

20166. HESCHEL, ABRAHAM JOSHUA: *Maimonides.* A biography. Transl. by Joachim Neugroschel. London: Faber; New York: Farrar, Straus & Giroux, 1983. 284 pp.

20167. — BARNARD, DAVID: *Abraham Heschel's attitude toward religion and psychology.* [In]: The Journal of Religion, Vol. 63, No. 1, Chicago, Jan. 1983. Pp. 26–43, footnotes.

20168. — DRESNER, SAMUEL H.: *The contribution of Abraham Joshua Heschel.* [In]: Judaism, Vol. 32, No. 1, New York, Winter 1983. Pp. 57–69.

20169. HIRSCH, SAMSON RAPHAEL: *Passover Haggadah with the commentary Nachalat ha-Sar, from the writings of Rabbi Samson Raphael Hirsch.* [In Hebrew, title transl.]. Compiled and transl. by Mordechai ben Samson Breuer. Tel-Aviv: Sifriati, 5742 [1982]. 160 pp. [See also No. 20182.]

20170. JOST, ISAAC MARCUS. MICHAEL, REUVEN: *I. M. Jost – founder of the modern Jewish historiography.* [In Hebrew]. Jerusalem: The Magnes Press; The Hebrew Univ., 1983. 8, 218, 6 pp., port. (Texts and studies.)

20171. JUDAH LOEW BEN BEZALEL. AVICHAYIL, DAVID: *Eretz Israel in the thought of the Maharal.* [In Hebrew, title transl.]. [In]: Merchavim, No. 1, Jerusalem, Sivan 5743 [May 1983]. Pp. 96–112.

20172. LUCAS, LEOPOLD. *Toleranz.* [Festvorträge von] Ben-Chorin, Sambursky, Scharf, Bethge, Staniloae, Popper, Rahner zur Verleihung des Dr.-Leopold-Lucas-Preises. Mit Einleitung 'Religion und Kultur in Europa' von Jürgen Moltmann. Hrsg. von Dieter Stuhlmacher und Luise Abramowski. Tübingen: Attempto-Verl., 1982. 213 pp., illus. (Tübinger Universitätsreden, Bd. 31.) [Lectures by the recipients of the prize, a.o.,: Juden – Christen – Deutsche (Kurt Scharf). Dieter Bonhoeffer und die Juden (Eberhard Bethge). Incl. also biogr. essay on L. Lucas (Jürgen Moltmann).] [Leopold Lucas, 1872 Marburg – Sept. 10, 1943 Theresienstadt, rabbi and historian, founder of the 'Gesellschaft zur Förderung der Wissenschaft des Judentums' in 1902; the prize in his memory, founded by his son in 1972, is conferred every year.]

20173. MARGULES, DAVID SAMUEL. LIEBERMAN, J. NINA: *He came to Cambridge: Rabbi David Samuel Margules.* Sketch by daughter J. Nina Lieberman, and commentary by Beaumont. Orwell, Cambs: Ellisons' Editions, [1983] c1982. 35 pp., illus. [D.S.M., Sept. 21, 1884 Lemberg, rabbi of Salzburg 1919–1938, from 1941 in Cambridge where he died.]

20174. MENDELSSOHN, MOSES: *Jerusalem or On religious power and Judaism.* Transl. by Allan Arkush. Introd. and commentary by Alexander Altmann. Hanover, N.H.; London: Univ. Press of New England, 1983. 264 pp.

20175. — MENDELSSOHN, MOSES: *Schriften zum Judentum II.* Bearb. von Alexander Altmann. Stuttgart: Frommann-Holzboog, 1983. XCI, 375 pp. (Mendelssohn, Moses: Gesammelte Schriften; Jubiläumsausgabe, Bd. 8. In Gemeinschaft mit Fritz Bamberger [et al.] begonnen von Ismar Elbogen [et al.], fortgesetzt von Alexander Altmann in Gemeinschaft mit Haim Bar-Dayan [et al.].) [For vol. 1 of 'Schriften zum Judentum', 1974, see No. 12101/YB XX.] [See also No. 20129.]

20176. — ALBRECHT, MICHAEL: *Moses Mendelssohn; ein Forschungsbericht 1965–1980.* [In]: Deutsche Vierteljahrsschrift für Literaturwissenschaft und Geistesgeschichte, Jg. 57, H. 1, Stuttgart, März 1983. Pp. 64–166, footnotes, names and subject index.

20177. — ENGEL, EVA J.: *Habent sua fata libelli: a response to John Brown; Moses Mendelssohn on evolution and change in poetry.* [In]: Hebrew Union College Annual, Vol. 53 (1982), Cincinnati, 1983. Pp. 165–177, notes. [M.M.'s observations on John Brown's 'Dissertation on the rise, union and power, the progression and corruption of poetry and music'.]

20178. — LOWENSTEIN, STEVEN M.: *The readership of Mendelssohn's bible translation.* [In]: Hebrew Union College Annual, Vol. 53 (1982), Cincinnati, 1983. Pp. 179–213, notes, tabs. (194–213).

20179. — WEINBERG, WERNER: *Moses Mendelssohn's 'Biur', two hundred years later.* [In]: Jewish Book Annual, Vol. 40, New York, 1982–1983. Pp. 97–104.

20180. — ZAC, SYLVAIN: *Le spinozisme épuré de Lessing vu par Moses Mendelssohn.* [In]: Revue de Métaphysique et de Morale, Année 87, No. 4, Paris, Oct.–Déc. 1982. Pp. 450–477.

20181. MEYER, MICHAEL A.: *Methodological prolegomena to a history of the Reform movement in modern Jewry.* [In]: Hebrew Union College Annual, Vol. 53 (1982), Cincinnati, 1983. Pp. 309–316, notes. [Essay, dedicated to Fritz Bamberger, deals also with the Reform movement in Germany.]

20182. NEUSNER, JACOB, ed.: *Take Judaism for example.* Studies toward the comparison of religions. Chicago: Univ. of Chicago Press, 1983. 244 pp. [Incl. essays on Jewish pietists in the 12th century in the Rhineland; and on Samson Raphael Hirsch.]

20183. NOBEL, NEHEMIA ANTON. ROSENBLÜTH, PINCHAS: *Rabbi Nehemia Nobel – his personality and his thought.* [In Hebrew, title transl.]. [In]: Bi-Shevilei ha-techiya [In the paths of renewal; studies in religious Zionism], ed. by Avraham Rubinstein. Ramat-Gan: Bar-Ilan Univ., 1983. Pp. 9–31.

20184. PELLI, MOSHE: *The beginning of Hebrew periodical literature: Tishrei 5544-Tishrei 5744, 200 years 'Ha-Me'assef'.* [In Hebrew, title transl.]. [In]: Hadoar, Vol. 62, No. 34, New York, 2. Sept. 1983. Pp. 561–562.

20185. PETUCHOWSKI, ELIZABETH: *Ein Rabbi kommt selten allein.* Rabbinergeschichten aus Frankfurt und anderswo. Mit einem Nachwort von Jakob J. Petuchowski. Freiburg i.Br.: Herder, 1983. 127 pp., bibl.

20186. PLAUT, W. GUNTHER. *Through the sound of many voices.* Writings, contributed on the occasion of the 70th birthday of W. Gunther Plaut. Ed. by Jonathan V. Plaut. Toronto: Lester & Orpen Dennys, 1982. XII, 308 pp., port., notes, bibl. W. G. Plaut (265–302). [Incl.: Franz Werfel's look at genocide (Gregory Baum, 184–195). Ahad Ha-Am and Leopold Zunz: two perspectives on the 'Wissenschaft des Judentums' (Alfred Gottschalk, pp. 196–208; see also No. 18280/YB XXVII). Das Falkenberg'sche Gebetbuch: a bibliographic adventure (Lou H. Silberman, 209–219; on the author's search for the prayer-book, publ. by the liberal Synagogue Berlin Norden during the 1920s and 1930s; sheds light on the activities of this community and the role Rabbi Jonas Plaut, father of W.G.P., played in it).] [W.G.P., born 1912 in Münster, grew up in Berlin, rabbi in Toronto, columnist, artist, sculptor.]

20187. ROSENZWEIG, FRANZ: *Le secret formel du récit biblique.* [And introduction]: *Franz Rosenzweig et la structure dialogale du récit biblique* (Stéphane Mosès). [In]: L'Infini, 1, Paris, 1983. Pp. 31–38; 27–30, footnotes. [See also Funkenstein essay in No. 19764.]

20188. — LEVINAS, EMMANUEL: *Franz Rosenzweig.* [In]: Midstream, Vol. 29, No. 9, New York, Nov. 1983. Pp. 33–40.

20189. — LÖWENSTEIN, JULIUS I.: *Das Judentum im säkularisierten Zeitalter; Betrachtung zur Neuausgabe von Rosenzweigs Briefen.* [In]: Jahrbuch des Instituts für Deutsche Geschichte, Bd. 12, Tel-Aviv, 1983. Pp. 353–376, footnotes. [For R.'s letters see No. 16277/YB XXV.]

20190. — LUZ, EHUD: *Zionism and messianism in the thought of Franz Rosenzweig.* [In Hebrew, with English summary]. [In]: Mechkerei Yerushalayim be-Machshevet Yisrael (Jerusalem Studies in Jewish Thought), Vol. 2, No. 3, Jerusalem, Nissan 5743 [March/Apr. 1983]. Pp. 472–489.

20191. — PERCHENET, A.: *Franz Rosenzweig 'notre grand contemporain' et 'L'étoile de la rédemption'.* [In]: Sens, No. 12, Paris, Déc. 1982.

20192. — PETITDEMANGE, G.: *La provocation de Franz Rosenzweig.* [In]: Recherches de Science Religieuse, No. 4, Paris, 1982. Pp. 499–523.

20193. SCHEIBER, ALEXANDER: *Jewish inscriptions in Hungary from the 3rd century to 1686.* Leiden: Brill, 1983. 434 pp., illus. [Cont. 154 inscriptions; the ones from the Middle Ages show the influence of Rhineland, South-German, Austrian, and Bohemian Moravian Jewish communities; also on the origin and distribution of names used by Jews.]

20194. SCHOLEM, GERSHOM: *Le nom et les symboles de Dieu dans la mystique juive.* Trad. de Maurice R. Hayoun et Georges Vajda. Paris: Editions du Cerf, 1983. 205 pp.

20195. — SCHOLEM, GERSHOM: *Die Stellung der Kabbala in der europäischen Geistesgeschichte.* [In]: Wissenschaftskolleg – Institute for Advanced Study – zu Berlin, Jahrbuch 1981/82, Berlin, Quadriga Verl., 1983. Pp. 281–289. [The first Jahrbuch of the Wissenschaftskolleg zu Berlin is dedicated to the memory of G. Scholem.]

20196. — BEN-SHLOMO, YOSEF: *The spiritual universe of Gershom Scholem.* [In]: The Jerusalem Quarterly, No. 29, Jerusalem, Fall 1983. Pp. 127–144. [Orig. Hebrew text in]: Skira Chodshit, Vol. 30, No. 1, Tel-Aviv, Jan. 1983, pp. 23–32.

20197. — Biale, David: *Gershom Scholem: 1897–1982.* [In]: Jewish Book Annual, Vol. 40, New York, 1982–1983. Pp. 154–161. [See also: Memories of G. Scholem (Howard Schwartz) [in]: Ariel, No. 53, Jerusalem, 1983, pp. 76–79. Zum Tod von G. Sch. (Nathan Rotenstreich] [in]: Frankfurter Hefte, Jg. 38, H. 3, 1983, pp. 11–13. Erinnerungen an G. Sch. (Lotte Cohn) [in]: MB, Nr. 11/12, Tel-Aviv, 28. März 1983, pp. 13–14.]

20198. — Biale, David: *Gershom Scholem and anarchism as a Jewish philosophy.* [In]: Judaism, Vol. 32, No. 1, New York, Winter, 1983. Pp. 70–76.

20199. — *Gershom Scholem: the man and his work.* Addresses delivered on the 30th day after his death. [In Hebrew, title transl.]. Jerusalem: Israel Academy of Sciences [&] Magnes Press, The Hebrew Univ. [&] Mossad Bialik, 5743 [1983]. 88 pp., port. [Cont.: G. Scholem and Jewish studies (E. E. Urbach). G. Sch.'s research on pantheism in Kabbala (Y. Ben-Shlomo). G. Sch.'s contribution to research on the Zohar (Y. Tishby). G. Sch.'s interpretation of Hassidism as an expression of his idealistic beliefs (R. Schatz). G. Sch.'s attitude towards books and libraries (M. Beit-Arie). On G. Sch.'s nationalistic philosophy (N. Rotenstreich). Conclusion (E. E. Urbach). (All articles in Hebrew, titles transl.)]

20200. — Maccoby, Hyam: *The greatness of Gershom Scholem.* [In]: Commentary, Vol. 76, No. 3, New York, Sept. 1983. Pp. 37–46.

20201. — Schweid, Eliezer: *Mysticism and Judaism according to Gershom Scholem; a critical analysis.* [In Hebrew, with English summary]. Jerusalem: Magnes Press, Hebrew Univ., 1983. 88, VII pp. (Jerusalem studies in Jewish thought, Supplement No. 2.) [Cf.: A critique of G. Scholem – after his death [in Hebrew, title transl.] (Yaakov Rabi) [in]: Hadoar, Vol. 63, No. 3, New York, Nov. 18, 1983, pp. 42–43.]

20202. SCHORSCH, EMIL. Schorsch, Ismar: *Rabbi Emil Schorsch.* [In]: The Rabbinical Assembly Proceedings of the 1982 Convention, 1982. Pp. 164–168. [E.Sch., Jan. 12, 1899 Hüngheim, Baden – March 3, 1982 USA, rabbi in Hanover.]

20203. Schorsch, Ismar: *The emergence of historical consciousness in modern Judaism.* [In]: LBI Year Book XXVIII, London, 1983. Pp. 413–437, footnotes.

20204. SEGAL, MORDECHAI MODEL. Hildesheimer, Meir: *A pesak-din of Rabbi Mordechai Model Segal of 1655.* [In Hebrew, with English summary]. [In]: Bar-Ilan; Annual of Bar-Ilan Univ., Vol. 20/21, Ramat-Gan, 1983. Pp. 229–241. [M.M.S. was rabbi in Schnaittach, Bavaria.]

20205. SIMON, AKIVA ERNST. Luz, Ehud: *The 'second innocence'; Jewish humanism in the work of Akiva Ernst Simon.* [In Hebrew, with English summary]. [In]: Mechkerei Yerushalayim be-Machshevet Yisrael (Jerusalem Studies in Jewish Thought), Vol. 2, No. 4, Jerusalem, Summer 1983. Pp. 613–644.

20206. SOFER, MOSES. Birnbaum, Paltiel: *Rabbi Moses Sofer: a sage of many accomplishments.* [In Hebrew, title transl.]. [In]: Bitzaron, Vol. 5, No. 19/20, New York, Summer/Fall 1983. Pp. 101–103. [M.S., 1762 Frankfurt am Main – 1839 Pressburg, rabbi, halakhic authority.]

20207. Steinberg, Aaron: *History as experience; aspects of historical thought – universal and Jewish.* Selected essays and studies. New York: Ktav, 1983. 486 pp. [Incl.: A. Steinberg: a portrait (Gerhart M. Riegner, 1–6). Introduction: on the thought of A. St. (Uriel Tal, 7–34). Hermann Cohen as educator (Aaron Steinberg, 122–139). [A.St., June 12, 1891 Dünaburg – Aug. 17, 1975 London, professor of philosophy, educated in Heidelberg and St. Petersburg, from 1922 in Berlin, emigrated to England in 1934, joined leadership of World Jewish Congress, head of its cultural department until 1971, acted as a representative at UNESCO from 1945.]

20208. STEINSCHNEIDER, MORITZ. Schorsch, Ismar: *Moritz Steinschneider on liturgical reform.* [In]: Hebrew Union College Annual, Vol. 53 (1982), Cincinnati, 1983. Pp. 241–264, notes. [The occasion for this essay is the discovery in the Zunz Archives of substantial material on liturgical reform by Steinschneider, publ. and transl. here for the first time; deals also with the history of the Berlin Jewish community, especially the Synagogue Oranienburger Strasse.]

20209. WELTSCH, ROBERT. Simon, Ernst: *Robert Weltsch als Politiker, Historiker und Erzieher im Vergleich mit Buber und Scholem.* [In]: Bulletin des LBI, 64, Königstein/Ts., 1983. Pp. 15–28.

20210. WESSELY, NAPHTALI HERZ. Pelli, Moshe: *Education and Haskalah in Naphtali Herz Wessely's writings.* [In Hebrew]. [In]: Sheviley ha-Hinnukh, Vol. 42, No. 2, New York, Winter 1982/83. Pp. 121–128. [For preceding parts of this essay see No. 19198/YB XXVIII.]

20211. — Rosenbloom, Noah H.: *The Exodus epic of the enlightenment and exegesis; thought and exegesis in Wessely's 'Songs of splendor'.* [In Hebrew]. Jerusalem: R. Mass, 1983. 447 pp.

20212. ZIMMER, ERIC: *Aspects of the rabbinate in 16th century Germany.* [In Hebrew, with English summary]. [In]: Bar-Ilan; Annual of Bar-Ilan Univ., Vol. 20/21, Ramat-Gan, 1983. Pp. 214–228.

B. The Jewish Problem

20213. *Dialectical Anthropology.* Vol. 8, Nos. 1–2, special issue: *The Jewish Question.* Amsterdam: Elsevier, Oct. 1983. 1 issue, notes. [Incl.: Marx on the Jewish Question (Joel Kovel, 31–46). The Jew as pariah: Hannah Arendt's political philosophy (Leon Botstein, 47–73). The dialectic of desire: the Holocaust, monopoly capitalism and radical anamnesis (Ben Agger, 75–86). Israel and Jewish identity (Richard Falk, 87–111).]

20214. BODEMANN, Y. MICHAL: *Opfer zu Komplizen gemacht? Der jüdisch-deutsche Bruch und die verlorene Identität.* Anmerkungen zu einer Rückkehr in die Bundesrepublik. [In]: Die Zeit, Nr. 1, Hamburg, 30. Dez. 1983. P. 28. [See also: Von Opfern und Komplizen: zu einem Artikel in der 'Zeit' (N. Peter Levinson) [in]: 'Allgemeine', Nr. 3, Düsseldorf, 20. Jan. 1984, p. 3 [&]: Von Opfern, Komplizen und tabusierten Themen: zu dem Artikel von N. P. Levinson (Y. Michal Bodemann) [in]: 'Allgemeine', Nr. 8, Düsseldorf, 24. Feb. 1984, p. 4.]

20215. HESS, MOSHE GERHARD: *Deutsches Judentum; ein Versuch zur Klärung des Selbstverständnisses.* [In]: Tribüne, Jg. 22, H. 88, Frankfurt am Main, 1983. Pp. 126–132.

20216. KLEPFISZ, HESZEL: *Bergson, Freud and Marx: their Jewish problem.* [In]: Midstream, Vol. 29, No. 10, New York, Dec. 1983. Pp. 11–17.

20217. SILBERNER, EDMUND: *Kommunisten zur Judenfrage.* Zur Geschichte von Theorie und Praxis des Kommunismus. Opladen: Westdeutscher Verl., 1983. 402 pp., bibl. (362–388). [Incl., a.o., Rosa Luxemburg, Karl Marx.]

C. Jewish Life and Organisations

20218. BERNFELD, SIEGFRIED. WOLFRUM, VERENA: *Anspruch und Wirklichkeit im Werk von Siegfried Bernfeld anhand von ausgewählten Schriften aus den Jahren 1912–1933.* Würzburg: Königshausen & Neumann, 1983. 278 pp. (Unipress, Pädagogik, Bd. 4.) [Also on B.'s work for the Jewish youth movement and welfare.] [S.B., May 7, 1892 Lemberg – 1953 San Francisco, educationalist, psychoanalyst in Vienna and Berlin.]

20219. CENTRALVEREIN (C.V.). BERING, DIETZ: *Geeinte Zwienatur: zur Struktur politischer Perspektiven im 'Central-Verein deutscher Staatsbürger jüdischen Glaubens'.* [In]: Weimars Ende, hrsg. von Thomas Koebner. Frankfurt am Main, 1982. (Suhrkamp Taschenbuch, 2018). Pp. 182–204, notes (198–202), bibl. (202–204).

20220. HIRSCH, BARON MAURICE DE. SWITZER, KENNEE BETH: *Baron de Hirsch, the Jewish Colonization Association and Canada, 1891–1914.* London, The London School of Economics and Political Science, Ph.D. Thesis, Aug. 1982. 308 pp., bibl. [M.H. data, see No. 19212/YB XXVIII.]

20221. ISRAEL, WILFRID. LOWENTHAL, ERNST G.: *Hoch klingt das Lied . . . : zum 40. Todestag von Wilfrid Israel.* [In]: MB, Nr. 21, Tel-Aviv, 3. Juni 1983. P. 6 [& in]: Isr. Wochenblatt, Nr. 21, Zürich, 27. Mai 1983, pp. 21 & 23. [W.I., July 11, 1899 London – June 1, 1943, died in a plane shot down by the Luftwaffe, merchant, philanthropist.]

20222. JEWISH PRESS. [See also Nos. 19876, 19994, 20230.] *German-Jewish periodicals 1845–1938.* 7 titles on 13 reels. Munchen; New York; London; Paris: Saur, 1983. 13 35-mm-microfilms. [Cont., titles condensed: Der Jude, 1768–1772. Blätter des Jüd. Frauenbundes. Der jüd. Handwerker. Die Menschenrechte. Nathanael. Der Sabbath. Selbstwehr. Continuation of No. 19209/YB XXVIII; 52 periodicals are now available, singly or in a set, all microfilmed from the holdings of the LBI New York.]

20223. JEWISH SPORT. [See also No. 19877.] EISEN, GEORGE: *Zionism, nationalism and the emergence of the Jüdische Turnerschaft.* [In]: LBI Year Book XXVIII, London, 1983. Pp. 247–262, footnotes, illus., ports.

20224. — FRANKL, WALTER: *Erinnerungen an Hakoah Wien 1909–1938.* [In]: Bulletin des LBI, 64, Königstein/Ts., 1983. Pp. 55–84.

20225. JÜDISCHES JUGEND- UND LEHRHEIM. WALK, JOSEPH: *Das Ende des Jüdischen*

Jugend- und Lehrheims Wolzig (1933). [In]: Bulletin des LBI, 66, Königstein/Ts., 1983. Pp. 3–22, notes (19–22).

20226. KAPLAN, MARION A.: *For love or money: the marriage strategies of Jews in Imperial Germany.* [In]: LBI Year Book XXVIII, London, 1983. Pp. 263–300, footnotes, ports., facsim.

20227. KATZ, JAKOB: *Vom Ghetto zum Zionismus: gegenseitige Beeinflussung von Ost und West.* (Aus dem Englischen von Eve Strauss.) [In]: Bulletin des LBI, 64, Königstein/Ts., 1983. Pp. 3–14.

—— KERN, BRIGITTE: *'Jüdisch-deutsche' Privatbriefe aus dem 17. Jahrhundert.* [See No. 19794.]

20228. METZGER, THÉRÈSE & MENDEL: *Jewish life in the Middle Ages.* Illuminated Hebrew manuscripts of the 13th to the 16th centuries. (Transl. from the French.) New York: Alpine Fine Arts Collection, 1982. 316 pp., illus., bibl. [Also German transl.]: *Jüdisches Leben im Mittelalter nach illuminierten hebräischen Handschriften vom 13.–16. Jahrhundert.* Würzburg: Edition Popp, 1983. 324 pp., 396 illus. [Corrected publ. date of No. 17339/YB XXVI.] [Refers also to Jewish life and customs in Germany. Cf.: Besprechung (Julius H. Schoeps) [in]: Das Historisch-Politische Buch, Jg. 32, H. 1, Göttingen, 1984, pp. 5–6.]

20229. MONETA, DALIA: *Von der Zeddakah zur Sozialarbeit: zur Geschichte der jüdischen Wohlfahrtspflege in Deutschland.* Frankfurt am Main, Univ., Diplomarbeit, 1982. VIII, 214 pp., bibl. (209–214). [Typescript.]

20230. SHEDLETZKY, ITTA: *Some observations on the popular Zeitroman in the Jewish weeklies in Germany from 1870 to 1900.* [In]: Canadian Review of Comparative Literature, Vol. 9, No. 3, Edmonton, Sept. 1982. Pp. 349–360.

20231. YUVAL, ISRAEL: *An appeal against the proliferation of divorce in 15th-century Germany.* [In Hebrew, with English summary]. [In]: Zion, Vol. 48, No. 2, Jerusalem, 1983. Pp. 177–216, appendix (209–215: manifesto of Rabbi Seligmann Bing from MS Oxford, Opp. 93).

20232. ZENTRALWOHLFAHRTSSTELLE. DIAMANT, ADOLF: *Vor 75 Jahren Gründung der Zentralwohlfahrtsstelle der deutschen Juden.* [In]: Das Neue Israel, Jg. 36, H. 1 & 2, Zürich, Juli & Aug. 1983. Pp. 24–25; 22–24.

D. **Jewish Art and Music**

—— BERLIN. [See Nos. 19802–19803.]

20233. *Bilder sind nicht verboten; Kunstwerke seit der Mitte des 19. Jahrhunderts mit ausgewählten Kultgeräten aus dem Zeitalter der Aufklärung.* Eine Ausstellung zur Vertiefung des Dialogs zwischen Christen und Juden anlässlich des 87. Deutschen Katholikentages in Düsseldorf 1982. [Red.: Jürgen Harten.] Düsseldorf: Städtische Kunsthalle, 1982. 269 pp., illus., bibl.

20234. CZECHOSLOVAKIA. ALTSHULER, DAVID, ed.: *The precious legacy; Judaic treasures from the Czechoslovak State Collection.* New York: Summit Books; Washington: Smithsonian Institution Travelling Exhibition Service, 1983. 288 pp., illus., bibl. (280–284). [Catalogue of Judaic objects from the State Jewish Museum in Prague.]

20235. — DOLEŽELOVÁ, JANA: *Thoraschilde aus den Werkstätten der Prager Silberschmiede in den Sammlungen des Staatlichen Jüdischen Museums.* [In]: Judaica Bohemiae, Vol. 19, No. 1, Praha, 1983. Pp. 22–34, illus., diagrs., footnotes, bibl.

20236. HALLO, RUDOLF: *Schriften zur Kunstgeschichte in Kassel; Sammlungen, Denkmäler, Judaica.* Im Auftrag der Gesamthochschule Kassel und des Vereins für Hessische Geschichte und Landeskunde hrsg. von Gunter Schweikhart. Mit Beiträgen von Wolfgang Adler [et al.]. Kassel: Gesamthochschule, 1983. 709 pp., illus., ports., facsims., notes (583–606), bibl. R. Hallo (705–709). [Incl. reprints of: Jüd. Kult- und Kunstdenkmäler im Hessischen Landesmuseum; 1928 (259–287). Jüd. Kultaltertümer aus Edelmetall in der Ausstellung Religiöse Kunst in Hessen und Nassau; 1928 (289–317) Jüd. Volkskunst in Hessen; 1928 (319–393). Jüd. Kunst aus Hessen und Nassau; 1933 (395–503). Geschichte der jüd. Gemeinde Kassel, Bd. 1: Kasseler Synagogengeschichte; Synagogen und Friedhöfe, Kunst und Handwerk der Juden in Kassel; 1931 (505–657). Nachlese zum ersten Band der Geschichte der jüd. Gemeinde Kassel; 1932 (659–662). Der Tempel Salomos (663 ff.). Also essay: Rudolf Hallo, Leben und Werk (Horst Keller, 11–29).] [R.H., Sept. 26, 1896 Kassel – Jan. 26, 1933 Hamburg, art historian.]

20237. HEIMANN, FELICITAS: *Die Illustrationen in der 2. Darmstädter Pesach Haggada.* Darmstadt, Hess. Landes- und Hochschulbibliothek, Cod Or 28. [In]: Kairos, N.F. 25, H. 1–2, Salzburg, 1983. Pp. 18–35, notes.

20238. MANDELL, ERIC, Collection. VICTOR, WARNER S.: *Rare books from the Eric Mandell*

Collection [in the] Bertha & Monte H. Tyson Music Department, Gratz College. Pt. 2. Philadelphia: Gratz College, [1983]. 33 pp., facsims., biogr.-bibl. (7–32), bibl. (33). [Mimeog., cover title.] [Part 2 of an annotated catalogue, describes 26 books (nos. 33–58) mostly in the field of Jewish music, 14 of which printed in Germany and Austria between 1810 and 1916; incl. biogr.-bibl. notes concerning the authors. For pt. 1 see No. 18303/YB XXVII.]

20239. OPPENHEIM, MORITZ. DAVIDOWITZ, DAVID: *The artist as witness and recorder; the paintings of Moritz Oppenheim are evidence of forgotten customs.* [In Hebrew, title transl.]. [In]: Eit-mol, Vol. 8, No. 4 (48), Tel-Aviv, March 1983. pp. 3–5. [M.O., Jan. 7, 1799 Hanau – Feb. 26, 1882 Frankfurt am Main.]

20240. — *Moritz Oppenheim, the first Jewish painter.* [In English and Hebrew]. (Exhibition curator: Elisheva Cohen.) Jerusalem: Israel Museum, 1983. 91, 61 pp., illus., bibl. [Incl.: Art as social history: Oppenheim and the German Jewish vision of emancipation (Ismar Schorsch, 31–62).]

20241. SCHALIT, HEINRICH. HIRSCHBERG, JEHOASH: *Heinrich Schalit and Paul Ben-Haim in Munich.* [In]: Yuval, Vol. 4, Jerusalem, 1982. Pp. 131–149. [H. Sch. data, see No. 17347/YB XXVI.]

20242. SCHUBERT, KURT: *Die Illustrationen in der Wiener Genesis im Lichte der rabbinischen Tradition.* [In]: Kairos, N. F. 25, H. 1–2, Salzburg, 1983. Pp. 1–17, notes.

20243. SCHUBERT, URSULA & KURT: *Jüdische Buchkunst.* T. 1. Graz: Akademische Druck- und Verlagsanstalt, 1983. 159 pp., 72 pp. illus. (Buchkunst im Wandel der Zeiten, 3,1.)

20244. *Synagogues in 19th century Germany.* [Catalogue of an exhibition. In English and Hebrew]. Tel-Aviv: Beth Hatefutsoth, The Nahum Goldmann Museum of the Jewish Diaspora, 1982. [48] pp., chiefly illus., plans.

VI. ZIONISM AND ISRAEL

20245. ACHAD HA-AM [orig. Ascher Ginsberg]. KORNBERG, JACQUES, ed.: *At the crossroads: essays on Ahad Ha'Am.* Albany, N.Y.: State Univ. of New York Press, 1983. 242 pp. (Modern Jewish history series.) [Incl.: Ahad Ha-Am, Martin Buber, and German Zionism (Jehuda Reinharz, pp. 142–155, notes (198–202).]

20246. BODENHEIMER, HENRIETTE HANNAH: *Von den Geburtswehen der zionistischen Organisation.* Jerusalem: Kiriat Sefer Ltd., 1983. 32 pp. [Selection from the correspondence 1892–1897 between Max Bodenheimer (1865–1940) and Rahel Apfel.]

20247. BRENNER, LENNI: *Zionism in the age of the dictators.* A reappraisal. London: Croom Helm; Westport, Conn.: Lawrence Hill, 1983. XIV, 277 pp., bibl. references. [Incl. sections 'German Zionism and the collapse of the Weimar Republic' and 'German Zionism offers to collaborate with Nazism' (purports, using largely second-hand sources, to make out a case for so-called Zionist-Nazi 'collaboration'). Cf.: Pathological anti-Zionism and the 'revisionism' of the left (Bryan Cheyette) [in]: Patterns of Prejudice, Vol. 17, No. 3, London, July 1983, pp. 49–51. The evidence of 'Zionist racism'? Letter to the Editor (Lenni Brenner) & reply by the Editor [in]: Patterns of Prejudice, Vol. 18, No. 1, London, Jan. 1984, pp. 53–54. Contradiction, collusion and controversy (Edward Mortimer) [in]: The Times, London, Feb. 11, 1984.]

20248. BRODER, HENRYK M.: *Einordnung und frühes Leid: 'Orient' – eine deutsche Zeitschrift in Palästina 1942/43.* [In]: Die Zeit, Nr. 49, Hamburg, 2. Dez. 1983. P. 50. [Review essay of the 'Orient' reprint, see No. 19292/YB XXVIII.]

20249. BUBER, MARTIN: *A land of two peoples: Martin Buber on Jews and Arabs.* Ed. with commentary by Paul R. Mendes-Flohr. London; New York: Oxford Univ. Press, 1983. XIII, 319 pp. [Also German edn.]: *Ein Land und zwei Völker: zur jüdisch-arabischen Frage.* Hrsg. und eingeleitet von Paul R. Mendes-Flohr. Frankfurt am Main: Insel, 1983. 382 pp. [Cf.: Israel und der Zionismus: Frieden ist möglich (Julius H. Schoeps) [in]: Die Zeit, Nr. 4, Hamburg, 20. Jan. 1984, p. 37.] [See also J. Reinharz: Ahad Ha-Am, Martin Buber, and German Zionism, in No. 20245.]

20250. CARPI, DANIEL: *The Mufti of Jerusalem, Amin el-Husseini, and his diplomatic activity during World War II (Oct. 1941–July 1943).* [In]: Studies in Zionism, No. 7, Tel-Aviv, Spring 1983. Pp. 101–131. [On the Mufti's visits to Berlin and negotiations with Hitler.]

20251. DORON, JOACHIM: *Social concepts prevalent in German Zionism: 1883–1914.* [In]: Studies in Zionism, No. 5, Tel-Aviv, Spring 1982. Pp. 1–31, footnotes.

20252. Erel, Shlomo: *Neue Wurzeln; 50 Jahre Immigration deutschsprachiger Juden in Israel.* Gerlingen: Bleicher, 1983. 312 pp., ports., bibl. (294–300). [Cont. chaps.: Der Beitrag der Juden des deutschen Kulturkreises zum Aufbau Israels. Die Akademiker kommen. Die Ärzte aus Berlin und Wien. Martin Buber und Brit Schalom. Zwei Frauen und ihr Weg (Recha Freier; Senta Josephthal). Zentraleuropäische Juden in der Presse Israels (a.o. Gershom Schocken; Schocken Verlag; Esriel Carlebach 1908–1956). Die Politker. Anhang 1–5 (a.o.: In Deutschland und Österreich geborene Generale; Universitätslehrer vor 1933).]

20253. Greive, Hermann: *Zionism and Jewish Orthodoxy (II).* [In]: LBI Year Book XXVIII, London, 1983. Pp. 241–246, footnotes. [Part I [in]: LBI Year Book XXV, London, 1980, pp. 173–195, footnotes; see No. 17356/YB XXVI.]

20254. Heenen, Susann: *Die unheilvolle Kollaboration; Nationalsozialisten und Zionisten im Dritten Reich.* Funkmanuskript einer Sendung des Norddeutschen Rundfunks, 23. März 1983. Hamburg, 1983. 29 pp. [Mimeog.]

20255. HERZBERG, WILHELM. Michael, Reuven: *Dr. Wilhelm Herzberg (1827–1897): eine lückenhafte Biographie.* [In]: Bulletin des LBI, 65, Königstein/Ts., 1983. Pp. 53–85, notes (83–85). [W.H., author of 'Jüdische Familienpapiere – Briefe eines Missionärs' 1868, educationalist and community worker in Palestine 1877–1891, director, a.o., of the first Jewish orphanage in Jerusalem.]

20256. HERZL, THEODOR. [See also Nos. 20267, 20685.] Bein, Alex: *Theodor Herzl.* Biographie. (Für die Taschenbuch-Edition vom Autor neu eingerichtete Ausg.) Frankfurt am Main: Ullstein, 1983. 366 pp., illus., bibl. Herzl & bibl. (343–352). (Ullstein-Buch, Nr. 35163.)

20257. — Brude-Firnau, Gisela: *Der Toleranzbegriff Theodor Herzls.* [In]: Seminar, 19, No. 1, Toronto, 1983. Pp. 20–32.

20258. — Handler, Andrew Dori: *The life and times of Theodor Herzl in Budapest 1860–1878.* University, Ala.: Univ. of Alabama Press, 1983. 176 pp., illus. (Judaic Studies.)

20259. — Melamed, Yisrael: *Religious Zionism and the philosophy of Herzl.* [In Hebrew, title transl.]. [In]: Hadoar, Vol. 62, No. 30, New York, 8 July 1983. P. 482.

20260. — Toury, Jacob: *Herzl's newspapers: the creation of 'Die Welt'.* [In]: Zionism, Vol. 1, No. 2, Tel-Aviv, Autumn 1980. Pp. 159–172.

20261. Kedourie, Elie/Haim, Sylvia G., eds.: *Palestine & Israel in the nineteenth and twentieth centuries.* Totowa, N.J.: Frank Cass, 1982. VIII, 278 pp. [Incl.: European Jews in Muslim Palestine (Emile Marmorstein). Nazi Germany and the Palestine question (R. Melka). The Third Reich and Palestine (David Yisraeli).]

20262. IRGUN OLEJ MERKAS EUROPA. *MB; Wochenzeitung des Irgun Olej Merkas Europa.* Jg. 51, Nr. 34/35: Sonderausgabe: *50 Jahre 'Fünfte Alijah'.* Tel-Aviv, 7. Sept. 1983. 36 pp. [Incl. (titles condensed): Ein halbes Jahrhundert (Hans Capell). Die deutschen Zionisten in der Landespolitik (Kurt Kanowitz). Deutschsprachige Dichtung in Israel (Schalom Ben-Chorin). Von Aufgabe und Wirken des Leo Baeck Instituts (Joseph Walk). Medizin und Mediziner der 5. Alijah (Julius Kleeberg). Architekten (Gideon Kaminka). 50 Jahre Rechtsschöpfung und Rechtseinfluss (James Yaakov Rosenthal). Alijah der Musik (Peter Gradenwitz). Deutschsprachige Presse (Gabriel Ilan). Das religiöse Judentum der 5. Alijah (Pinchas E. Rosenblüth). Sport (Robert Atlasz). Abschied von Robert Weltsch (Amos Elon; from Haarez Feb. 2, 1983). Further contributions by Herbert Freeden, Zwi Karliner, Georg Landauer, Erich M. Lehmann, Gerda Luft, Shlomo Mautner, Ludwig Pinner, Joseph Porat, Abraham Tobias.]

20263. — Ilan, Gabriel: *Feierstunde der 'Fünften Alijah' beim Staatspräsidenten Navon.* [Bericht]. [In]: MB, Nr. 11/12, Tel-Aviv, 28. März 1983. Pp. 1–2. [Also in same issue: Chefzi-Bah: Pessach-Gedanken über die Alijah aus Deutschland (Eli Rothschild, pp. 15–16). See also: Israel würdigt die Einwanderung aus Deutschland [mit einer Sonderbriefmarke '50th anniversary of Aliya from Germany'] (Ilan Hameiri) [in]: Neue Jüd. Nachrichten, Nr. 1, München, 13. Jan. 1984, p. 1, illus.]

20264. Luft, Gerda: *Chronik eines Lebens für Israel.* Stuttgart: Edition Erdmann in Thienemanns Verl., 1983. 205 pp. [G.L., born Apr. 20, 1898 in Königsberg, journalist, married to Chaim Arlosoroff, settled in Palestine in 1924.]

20265. Michaelis-Stern, Eva: *Die Jugend-Alijah in Europa.* 1–16. [In]: MB, Jg. 51, Nr. 45–48; Jg. 52, Nr. 1–12, Tel-Aviv, 9. Dez. 1983–23. März 1984. [See also: 1933 bis 1983: fünfzig Jahre Jugend-Alijah (Lore Hartmann-von Monakow) [in]: Das Neue Israel, Jg. 36, H. 5, Zürich, Nov. 1983, pp. 23–27, tab.]

20266. Niederland, Doron: *Influence of German-Jewish immigrant doctors on medicine in Eretz-Israel*

(1933–1948). [In Hebrew]. [In]: Cathedra, No. 30, Jerusalem, Dec. 1983. Pp. 111–160, illus. [Summary of an M.A. Thesis, Hebrew Univ. Cf.: Besprechung (H. Steinitz) [in]: MB, Nr. 14, Tel-Aviv, 6. Apr. 1984, p. 5.]

20267. NORDAU, MAX. FRIESEL, EVYATAR: *Max Nordau, 1914; an evaluation of Herzl's political activity*. [In]: Studies in Zionism, No. 7, Tel-Aviv, Spring 1983. Pp. 65–70, notes.

20268. PERL, WILLIAM R.: *Operation Action: rescue from the Holocaust*. New York: Ungar, 1983. 442 pp. [Incl. illegal immigration of German and Austrian Jews to Palestine. Cf.: By hulk to Palestine (A. J. Sherman) [in]: TLS, London, Jan. 27, 1983, p. 92.]

20269. REINHARZ, JEHUDA: *The German Zionist challenge to the faith in emancipation 1897–1914*. Tel-Aviv: Tel-Aviv Univ., 1982. 32 pp., notes (26–32). (Spiegel lectures in European Jewish history, 2.) [Also on the Centralverein (C.V.).]

20270. REINHARZ, JEHUDA, ed.: *Dokumente zur Geschichte des deutschen Zionismus, 1882–1933*. Hrsg. und eingeleitet. Tübingen: Mohr, 1981. IL, 580 pp., footnotes. (Schriftenreihe wissenschaftlicher Abhandlungen des Leo Baeck Instituts, 37.) [See No. 18318/YB XXVII.] *Selected reviews* (continuation): Zionismus in Deutschland (Judith Klein) [in]: 'Allgemeine', Nr. 35, Düsseldorf, 2. Sept. 1983, p. 40. Besprechung [in]: Aufbau, No. 47, New York, Nov. 25, 1983, p. 13. Review [in Hebrew] (Nachum Orland) [in]: Gesher, No. 108, Jerusalem, Winter/Spring 1983, pp. 135–138. Review (Donald L. Niewyk) [in]: Religious Studies Review, Vol. 9, No. 2, Waterloo, Ont., Canada, Apr. 1983, p. 187. Zionismus in Deutschland (Nachum Orland) [in]: Tribüne, Jg. 22, H. 86, Frankfurt am Main, 1983, pp. 184 & 186.

20271. SCHOLEM, GERSHOM: *If only it were possible to relate how we became Zionists*. [In Hebrew, title transl.]. [In]: Moznaim, Vol. 57, No. 5/6, Tel-Aviv, Oct./Nov. 1983. Pp. 10–11. [Two excerpts from Scholem's literary estate, written 1919 & 1921, transl. from the German.]

20272. SCHWARZ-GARDOS, ALICE, ed.: *Heimat ist anderswo; deutsche Schriftsteller in Israel*. Erzählungen und Gedichte. Vorwort von Martin Gregor-Dellin. Freiburg i.Br.: Herder, 1983. 189 pp. (Herder-Bücherei, Bd. 1064.)

20273. SCHWARZ-GARDOS, ALICE: *Paradies mit Schönheitsfehlern; so lebt man in Israel*. Freiburg i.Br.: Herder, 1983. 128 pp. (Herder-Bücherei, Bd. 944.)

20274. WETZEL, DIETRICH, ed.: *Die Verlängerung von Geschichte: Deutsche, Juden und der Palästinakonflikt*. Frankfurt am Main: Verlag Neue Kritik, 1983. 134 pp., [Incl.: Israel und das Trauma der Massenvernichtung: über Elemente jüdischer Deutungsmuster im Palästinakonflikt (Dan Diner, 25–42). Das Dritte Reich, die zionistische Bewegung und der Palästinakonflikt (Alexander Schölch, 65–92, notes; republ. of No. 19256/YB XXVIII). Deutsche Linke, linke Juden und der Zionismus (Susann Heenen, 103–112).]

VII. PARTICIPATION IN CULTURAL AND PUBLIC LIFE

A. General

—— AUSTRIA. [See No. 19874.]

—— BANKING. [See also Nos. 19772, 19910–19911, 20562–20563, 20577.]

20275. — BORN, KARL ERICH: *International banking in the 19th and 20th centuries*. (Transl. from the German by V. R. Berghahn.) Leamington Spa, England: Berg Publ., 1983. 360 pp., bibl. [Refers also to German- and Austrian-Jewish banks.]

20276. — *Deutsche Bankengeschichte*. Hrsg. im Auftrag des Instituts für Bankhistorische Forschung e.V. von seinem wissenschaftlichen Beirat: Günter Ashauer [et al.]. Bd. 1–3. Frankfurt am Main: Knapp, 1982–1983. *Bd. 1–2*. 1982 [See No. 19262/YB XXVIII.] *Bd. 3: Vom Ersten Weltkrieg bis zur Gegenwart*. 1983. 424 pp. [Incl.: Vom Beginn des 1. Weltkrieges bis zum Ende der Weimarer Republik 1914–1933 (Karl Erich Born); also on the participation of Jews in German banking.]

20277. — SHERMAN, A. J.: *German-Jewish bankers in world politics: the financing of the Russo-Japanese War*. [In]: LBI Year Book XXVIII, London, 1983. Pp. 59–73, footnotes. [Especially on Jacob H. Schiff, Sir Ernest Cassel, and Max Warburg.]

20278. BERLIN. ROTERS, EBERHARD, ed.: *Berlin 1910–1933: die visuellen Künste*. Berlin: Rembrandt; Berlin: Kunstbuch-Verl., 1983. 292 pp., 302 illus., bibl. [Refers also to the contributions of German Jews to the visual arts in Berlin; cont. chaps.: On Herwarth Walden and the 'Sturm' circle (Ernst Roters). On the film, a.o., Fritz Lang, Ernst Lubitsch (Ulrich Gregor). On the theatre, a.o., Leopold Jessner, Max Reinhardt (Arno Paul). On architecture (Janos Frescot/Sonja Günther). On sculpture (Joachim Heusinger von Waldeck).] [See also No. 19950.]

20279. BERMAN, RUSSELL A.: *Between Fontane and Tucholsky; literary criticism and the public sphere in Imperial Germany.* New York; Berne: Lang, 1983. 176 pp., bibl. (New York Univ. Ottendorfer series, N.F. Bd. 17.) [Refers, a.o., to Otto Brahm, Paul Lindau, Kerr, Tucholsky.]

—— The BOOK BURNING. [See Nos. 19957–19975.]

20280. BRONNER, STEPHEN ERIC/KELLENER, DOUGLAS, eds.: *Passion and rebellion: the expressionist heritage.* London: Croom Helm, 1983. 468 pp., illus. [Incl. Ernst Bloch, Döblin, Kafka, Lukács.]

20281. COLIN, AMY DIANA: *An den Schnittpunkten der Tradition: Deutsch in der Bukowina.* [In]: Neue Deutsche Hefte, 180, Berlin, 1983. Pp. 739–769, notes. [Refers, a.o., to Aaron Appelfeld, Rose Ausländer, Paul Celan, Karl Emil Franzos, Manès Sperber.]

20282. CZIFFRA, GEZA von: *Der [Anton] Kuh im Kaffeehaus.* Die Goldenen Zwanziger in Anekdoten. München: Droemer Knaur, 1983. 300 pp., list of names. (Knaur-Taschenbücher, 1049.) [Refers to many German and Austrian Jewish writers and actors.]

20283. DAVID, CLAUDE: *Ordnung des Kunstwerks.* Aufsätze zur deutschsprachigen Literatur zwischen Goethe und Kafka. Hrsg. von Theo Buck und Etienne Mazingue. Göttingen: Vandenhoeck & Ruprecht, 1983. 239 pp., bibl. (Sammlung Vandenhoeck.) [Incl.: Gundolf und George (135–155). Kraus und die Literatur seiner Zeit (200–214). Kafkas 'Schloss '- Roman als theologische Fabel (215–232.)

20284. *Drama und Theater im 20. Jahrhundert.* Festschrift für Walter Hinck. Hrsg. von Hans Dietrich Irmscher und Werner Keller. Göttingen: Vandenhoeck & Ruprecht, 1983. 485 pp. [Incl. essays on Hofmannsthal, Stephan Lackner, Schnitzler, Carl Sternheim, Peter Weiss, Werfel.]

—— EXILE LITERATURE. [See also Nos. 19892–19902, 19957–19975.]

20285. — ALBRECHT, RICHARD: *Exil-Forschung.* Eine Zwischenbilanz (I). [In]: Neue Politische Literatur, Jg. 28, H. 2, Wiesbaden, 1983. Pp. 174–201, notes. [Review essay.]

20286. — ALBRECHT, RICHARD: *Exil-Publizistik 1933–1935.* Broschüren aus dem deutschen antifaschistischen Exil. [In]: Publizistik Jg. 28, H. 4, Konstanz, 1983. Pp. 547–573, notes. [Refers, a.o., to Bruno Frei, Theodor Lessing, Rudolf Olden, Franz Carl Weiskopf.]

20287. — *Exil.* Forschung, Erkenntnisse, Ergebnisse. Jg. 1983, Nr. 1. Gegr. von Joachim H. Koch. Hrsg. von Edita Koch. Maintal (Goethestr. 122): E. Koch, 1983. 92 pp., notes. [Incl.: On the publishers Allert de Lange and Querido 1933–1940 (Frithjof Trapp, 12–18). Biography on Hugo Simon and autobiogr. text by him (Edita Koch, 48–51; 52–60; H. Simon, Sept. 1, 1880 Usch, Poznań – July 4, 1950 Sao Paulo, Brazil, banker and politician, emigrated from Berlin to France in 1933 and, under the name Hubert Studenic, to Brazil in 1941). Autobiogr. sketch by Stella Rotenberg (61–66; St.R., born March 27, 1916 in Vienna, poet, emigrated in 1939, lives in England).]

20288. — *Exilforschung.* Ein internationales Jahrbuch. Hrsg. im Auftrag der Gesellschaft für Exilforschung. Bd. 1. Hrsg. von Thomas Koebner, Wulf Köpke und Joachim Radkau. München: Edition Text & Kritik, 1983. 391 pp. [Incl. a sequence of essays on 'Stalin und die Intellektuellen'; essays on the 'Neue Weltbühne' and the 'Aufbau', New York (Lieselotte Maas), and on Ernst Bloch (Heinz-B. Heller); also essay on Ernst Glaeser and his antisemitic writings (Gilbert Badia/René Geoffroy).]

20289. — LANSBURGH, WERNER/MATTHIES, FRANK-WOLF: *Exil – ein Briefwechsel.* Mit Essays, Gedichten und Dokumenten. Köln: Internat. Literaturfabrik im Bund-Verl., 1983. 139 pp., illus. [W. Lansburgh, born 1912 in Berlin, emigrated in 1933. F.-W. Matthies, born in 1951, left the GDR in 1980, lives in West-Berlin.]

20290. — PAZI, MARGARITA: *Deutsche Schriftsteller im Exil; Phasen ihrer Emigration nach 1933.* [1–2]. [In]: Tribüne, Jg. 22, H. 88 (pp. 143–148) [&]: Jg. 23, H. 89 (pp. 148–155, footnotes). Frankfurt am Main, 1983–1984.

20291. — STRELKA, JOSEPH: *Exilliteratur; Grundprobleme der Theorie, Aspekte der Geschichte und Kritik.* Bern: Lang, 1983. 237 pp., bibl. (231–237).

20292. — TRAPP, FRITHJOF: *Deutsche Literatur zwischen den Weltkriegen II: Literatur im Exil.* Bern: Lang, 1983. 250 pp., bio-bibl. of mentioned authors. (Germanistische Lehrbuchsammlung, Bd. 42.)

20293. EXPRESSIONISM. ANZ, THOMAS/STARK, MICHAEL, eds.: *Expressionismus: Manifeste und*

Dokumente zur deutschen Literatur 1910–1920. Mit Einleitungen und Kommentaren. Stuttgart: Metzler, 1982. XXIII, 741 pp., bibl. (711–712). [Incl. texts by many German-Jewish writers, also chap.: Der jüd. Künstler (374–387).]

20294. — Hüppauf, Bernd, ed.: *Expressionismus und Kulturkrise.* Heidelberg: Winter, 1983. 299 pp. (Reihe Siegen, Bd. 42.) [Incl. (titles condensed): Die Maske als Ausdruck der Herrschaftskrise: Carl Sternheim (Maike Leffers, 131–146). Die Situation der deutsch-jüd. Intellektuellen, 1910–1920 (John Milfull, 147–158). W. Rathenau: Intellektueller oder Industrieller? (James Joll, 159–182). 'Das Kabinett des Dr. Caligari' [Regisseur Robert Wiene] (Peter Gerdes, 245–262). Brecht-Lukács-Debatte gegen Expressionismus (Maria Shevtsova, 263–290).]

20295. — Michaels, Jennifer E.: *Anarchy and eros; Otto Gross' impact on German expressionist writers.* Bern; New York: Lang, 1983. 230 pp., bibl. (Utah studies in literature and linguistics, vol. 24.) [Incl.: Max Brod, Walter Hasenclever, Kafka, Werfel.]

20296. — Sheppard, Richard, ed.: *Die Schriften des Neuen Clubs 1908–1914, Band 2.* Hildesheim: Gerstenberg, 1983. 685 pp., ports., notes, bibl. (607–636). [Incl. short biographies of the members of the 'Neue Club', a.o., David Baumgardt, Ernst Blass, Wilhelm Simon Ghuttmann, Oskar Goldberg, Kurt Hiller, Jakob van Hoddis (orig. Hans Davidsohn), Fritz Koffka, Arthur Kronfeld, Erwin Loewenson, Erich Unger (579–604). For vol. 1 see No. 17373/YB XXVI.]

—— FRANKFURT am Main. Arnsberg, Paul: *Biographisches Lexikon der Juden in den Bereichen: Wissenschaft, Kultur [et al.] in Frankfurt.* [See vol. 3 of No. 19815.]

20297. The FRANKFURT SCHOOL. Brumlik, Micha: *Der revolutionäre Messianismus der Frankfurter Schule.* [In]: Merkur, Jg. 37, H. 2 (416), Stuttgart, März 1983. Pp. 228–231.

20298. —Jay, Martin: *A reply to Lewis S. Feuer; misrepresentations of the Frankfurt School.* [And]: Feuer, Lewis S.: *A rejoinder: the social role of the Frankfurt Marxists.* [In]: Survey, Vol. 26, London, Spring 1982. Pp. 131–141; 150–170.

20299. — Rohrmoser, Günter: *Krise der politischen Kultur.* Mainz: von Hase & Koehler, 1983. 412 pp. [Incl. chaps.: Das Elend der kritischen Theorie. Aktionismus und Dezisionismus: G. Lukács 'Geschichte und Klassenbewusstsein'. Benjamins Gewaltkritik.]

20300. — Stern, Laurent: *On the Frankfurt School.* [In]: History of European Ideas, Vol. 4, No. 1, Elmsford, N.Y., 1983. Pp. 83–90, notes.

20301. Graetz, Michael: *Jews as initiators in the 18th century.* [In Hebrew, title transl.]. [In]: Siach, la-Moreh le-Historia, No. 19, Jerusalem, Adar 5743 [Feb./March 1983]. Pp. 16–26. [On economic initiatives of Jews, particularly in Prussia.]

20302. Habermas, Jürgen: *Philosophical-political profiles.* Transl. by Frederick Lawrence. Cambridge, Mass.: MIT Press, 1983. [Transl. of No. 18347/YB XXVII. Refers, a.o., to Adorno, Hannah Arendt, Walter Benjamin, Ernst Bloch, Horkheimer, Leo Löwenthal, Karl Löwith, Herbert Marcuse, Helmuth Plessner, Gershom Scholem.]

20303. Hasenclever, Volker F. W., ed.: *Denken als Widerspruch; Plädoyers gegen die Irrationalität oder Ist Vernunft nicht mehr gefragt?* Frankfurt am Main: Eichborn, 1982. 231 pp. [Eulogies and lectures at the Lessing-Preis awards, conferred by the Town of Hamburg every three years. Incl.: Von der Menschlichkeit in finsteren Zeiten (Hannah Arendt; & eulogy by Hans H. Biermann-Ratjen). Laokoon oder Über die Grenzen der Sprache (Peter Weiss). Der Gang der Wissenschaft und der des Glaubens (Max Horkheimer; & eulogy by Alfred Schmidt). Aufklärung als 'Philosophie perennis' (Jean Améry; & eulogy by Axel Eggebrecht).]

20304. Henrich, Dieter/Iser, Wolfgang, eds.: *Theorien der Kunst.* Frankfurt am Main: Suhrkamp, 1982. 636 pp., bibl. (593–635). [Incl. essays by Adorno, Rudolf Arnheim, Ernst H. Gombrich, Georg Lukács, Georg Simmel.]

20305. Hinck, Walter: *Germanistik als Literaturkritik.* Zur Gegenwartsliteratur. Frankfurt am Main: Suhrkamp, 1983. 316 pp. (Suhrkamp-Taschenbuch, 885.) [Incl. essays on Ilse Aichinger, Hermann Broch, Elias Canetti, Hilde Domin, Erich Fried.]

20306. Hinderer, Walter, ed.: *Geschichte der deutschen Lyrik vom Mittelalter bis zur Gegenwart.* Stuttgart: Reclam, 1983. 659 pp., bibl. (605–636). [Incl. German-Jewish poets through the decades; also chap.: Im Exil (Manfred Durzak, 502–550).]

20307. Horst, Eberhard: *Geh ein Wort weiter.* Aufsätze zur Literatur. Düsseldorf: Claassen, 1983. 224 pp. [Incl. essays on Ilse Aichinger, Canetti, Hilde Domin, Ivan Goll, Hermann Kesten, Gertrud Kolmar, Elisabeth Langgässer, Else Lasker-Schüler.]

20308. Meja, Volker/Stehr, Nico, eds.: *Der Streit um die Wissenssoziologie.* Bd. 1–2. Frankfurt am

Main: Suhrkamp, 1982. 2 vols. (973 pp.), bibl. (Suhrkamp-Taschenbuch Wissenschaft, 361.) [Incl. texts by Max Adler, Hannah Arendt, Norbert Elias, Paul Eppstein, Hans Grüneberg, Horkheimer, Hans Jonas, Emil Lederer, Adolph Löwe, Karl Mannheim, Siegfried Marck, Herbert Marcuse, Helmuth Plessner, Max Scheler, Hans Speier, Kurt Singer.]

20309. MUNICH. SACKETT, ROBERT EBEN: *Popular entertainment, class and politics in Munich, 1900–1923*. London: Harvard Univ. Press, 1983. 208 pp., bibl. [Study in cultural history, incl. participation of Jews; explores the roots of Nazism, also on hostility toward Jews.]

20310. PERIODICALS. *Der Gegen-Angriff*. Antifaschistische Wochenschrift. Chefredakteur: Bruno Frei. Jg. 1–4. Mit satirischer Beilage: Roter Pfeffer. Nr. 1–6 (1933) & 1–7 (1934). [No more published]. Vollst. Nachdr. der Ausg. Prag; Zürich; Basel; Paris, Ende Apr. 1933 – 14. März 1936. Mit einem Geleitwort von Bruno Frei und einem Kommentar von Silvia Schlenstedt. Leipzig: Zentralantiquariat der DDR; Nendeln, Liechtenstein: Kraus, 1982. 3 vols., illus. [Incl. German-Jewish contributors. B. Frei data, see No. 17176/YB XXVI.]

20311. — — KRÄMER, WOLFGANG/MÜLLER, GERHARD: *Der Gegenangriff: Autoren, Personen- und Sachregister*. Worms: Heintz, 1982. VIII, 510 pp. (Deutsches Exil 1933–45, Bd. 15.)

20312. — *Neue Rheinische Zeitung*. Politisch-ökonomische Revue. Redigiert von Karl Marx. H. 1–6. [No more published]. London, 1850. [Reprint mit] Einleitung und Verzeichnis von Druck- und Sachfehlern von Martin Hundt. Leipzig: Zentralantiquariat der DDR, 1982. 500 pp.

20313. — Die Weltbühne. MADRASCH-GROSCHOPP, URSULA: *Die Weltbühne; Porträt einer Zeitschrift*. Berlin/East: Buchverlag Der Morgen; Königstein/Ts.: Athenäum, 1983. 439 pp., illus., list of ca. 600 names, bibl. [For reprints see Nos. 15395/YB XXIV; 17392/YB XXVI.]

20314. PINTHUS, KURT, ed.: *Das Kinobuch*. Kinostücke, hrsg. und eingeleitet. Mit einer Nachbemerkung von Walter Schobert. Frankfurt am Main: Fischer, 1983. 159 pp. (Fischer-Taschenbücher, 3688.) [First edn. 1914. Incl. contributions by Richard A. Bermann (pseud.: Arnold Höllriegel), Max Brod, Albert Ehrenstein, Walter Hasenclever, Julie Jolowicz, Else Lasker-Schüler, Otto Pick, Ludwig Rubiner.]

20315. REICH-RANICKI, MARCEL: *Deutsche Literatur in West und Ost*. Erweiterte Neuausg. Stuttgart: Deutsche Verlags-Anstalt, 1983. 415 pp. [On, a.o., Hermann Kesten, Ludwig Marcuse, Robert Neumann, Anna Seghers, Arnold Zweig.]

20316. *Spiegel und Gleichnis; Festschrift für Jacob Taubes*. Hrsg. von Norbert W. Bolz, Wolfgang Hübener. Würzburg: Königshausen & Neumann, 1983. 426 pp. [Incl.: Wittgenstein's Pilgrim's Progress (Avishai Margalit, 233–238). Walter Benjamins politischer Dezisionismus im theologischen Kontext (Klaus-M. Kodalle, 301–317). Kant, Hegel und Marx in Lukács' Theorie der Verdinglichung; Destruktion eines neomarxistischen 'Klassikers' (Winfried Menninghaus, 318–330). Adorno als Sprachphilosoph (Martin Puder, 331–342). Von Nietzsche zu Freud: sympathy for the devil (Norbert Bolz, 388–403).]

20317. WEIMAR REPUBLIC. BANCE, ALAN, ed.: *Weimar Germany: writers and politics*. Edinburgh: Scottish Academic Press, 1982; New York: Columbia Univ. Press, 1983. VIII, 183 pp. [Incl. essays on Broch's 'Die Schlafwandler', Döblin's 'Berlin Alexanderplatz', Feuchtwanger's 'Erfolg'. Cf.: Review (Richard Sheppard) [in]: Journal of European Studies, Vol. 13, Pt. 3, No. 51, Chalfont St. Giles, Sept. 1983, p. 246.]

20318. — KAES, ANTON, ed.: *Weimarer Republik; Manifeste und Dokumente zur deutschen Literatur 1918–1933*. Mit einer Einleitung und Kommentaren. Stuttgart: Metzler, 1983. LIII, 709 pp., bibl. (690–694). [Incl. texts by many German-Jewish writers.]

20319. — KOEBNER, THOMAS, ed.: *Weimars Ende; Prognosen und Diagnosen in der deutschen Literatur und politischen Publizistik 1930–1933*. Frankfurt am Main: Suhrkamp, 1982. 433 pp., notes. (Suhrkamp-Taschenbuch, 2018.) [Incl. (titles condensed): Die Weltbühne als falscher Prophet? (Joachim Radkau, 57–79). Das Ende Weimars aus der Perspektive Walter Benjamins (Rolf-Peter Janz, 261–270). Alfred Kerrs kritisches Temperament gegenüber der Weimarer Republik (Walter Huder, 303–317). Alfred Döblins Überparteilichkeit (Wulf Köpke, 318–329). Frühe Auseinandersetzungen mit dem Ende Weimars im Exilroman (Siegrid Schneider, 376–396). See also No. 20219.]

20320. — REINHARDT, STEPHAN, ed.: *Weimarer Republik; deutsche Schriftsteller und ihr Staat von 1918 bis 1933*. Berlin: Wagenbach, 1982. 254 pp., bibl. [Anthology with excerpts from the writings of many contemporary German-Jewish authors; incl. also chaps.: Antisemitismus (81–84); Der Fall Gumbel (114–115); Die Ausscheidung der Juden aus dem Leben (215–221).]

20321. WORBS, MICHAEL: *Nervenkunst; Literatur und Psychoanalyse im Wien der Jahrhundertwende*. Frankfurt am Main: Europäische Verlagsanstalt, 1983. 383 pp., illus. [Refers to Freud, Hofmannsthal, Kraus, Schnitzler, based on hitherto unpubl. material.]

B. Individual

20322. ADLER, ALFRED: *Psychotherapie und Erziehung.* Ausgewählte Aufsätze. *Bd. 3: 1933–1937.* Hrsg. von Heinz L. Ansbacher und Robert F. Antoch. Frankfurt am Main: Fischer, 1983. 216 pp., bibl. (Fischer-Taschenbücher, 6748.) [For vols. 1–2 see No. 19305/YB XXVIII.]

20323. — Bruder-Bezzel, Almuth: *Alfred Adler; die Entstehungsgeschichte einer Theorie im historischen Milieu Wiens.* Göttingen: Vandenhoeck & Ruprecht, 1983. 169 pp., bibl. (155–166).

20324. — Sperber, Manès: *Alfred Adler oder Das Elend der Psychologie.* Frankfurt am Main: Ullstein, 1983. 288 pp. (Ullstein-Buch, Nr. 39074.) [Paperback edn. of No. 8781/YB XVI.]

20325. ADORNO, THEODOR W. *Adorno-Konferenz 1983.* Hrsg. von Ludwig von Friedeburg und Jürgen Habermas. Frankfurt am Main: Suhrkamp, 1983. 471 pp., bibl. Adorno & bibl. (404–471). (Suhrkamp-Taschenbuch Wissenschaft, 460.)

20326. — Arnold, Heinz Ludwig, ed.: *Theodor W. Adorno.* 2., erweiterte Aufl. München: Edition Text & Kritik, 1983. 196 pp., bibl. (176–193). (text + kritik, Sonderband.)

—— — Lunn, Eugene: *Marxism and modernism.* [See No. 20533.] [See also Puder in No. 20316.]

20327. ANDRIAN, LEOPOLD von. Rieckmann, Jens: *Narziss und Dionysos: Leopold von Adrians 'Der Garten der Erkenntnis'.* [In]: Modern Austrian Literature, Vol. 16, No. 2, Riverside, Calif., 1983. Pp. 65–81, notes. [L.v.A., May 9, 1875 Vienna – Nov. 19, 1951 Fribourg, writer, grandson of Giacomo Meyerbeer, emigrated to Brazil.]

20328. ARENDT, HANNAH. Barnouw, Dagme: *The secularity of evil: Hannah Arendt and the Eichmann controversy.* [In]: Modern Judaism, Vol. 3, No. 1, Baltimore, Feb. 1983. Pp. 75–94, notes.

20329. — Kateb, George: *Hannah Arendt; politics, conscience, evil.* Totowa, N.J.: Rowman & Allanheld, 1983. Oxford: Martin, Robertson, 1984. 224 pp.

20330. — Luban, David: *Explaining dark times: Hannah Arendt's theory of theory.* [In]: Social Research, Vol. 50, No. 1 New York, Spring 1983. Pp. 215–248, footnotes.

20331. — *Salmagundi.* No. 60 [with the issue title]: *Politics and the social contract: on Hannah Arendt.* Saratoga Springs, N.Y., Spring-Summer 1983. Pp. I-XVI, 1–139, notes. [Incl.: Action, story and history: on re-reading 'The human condition' (Paul Ricoeur, 60–72). Liberating the pariah: politics, the Jews and Hannah Arendt (Leon Botstein, 73–106).]

20332. — Young-Bruehl, Elisabeth: *Hannah Arendt: for love of the world.* New Haven; London: Yale Univ. Press, 1983. 587 pp. [Paperback edn. of No. 19320/YB XXVIII. Cf. (continued): A critic of our time (Ronald Stent) [in]: AJR Information, No. 2, London, Feb. 1984, pp. 1–2. The riddle of H. A. (Herbert S. Frankel) [in]: Journal of Jewish Studies, Vol. 34, No. 1, Oxford, Spring 1983, pp. 93–100. War immer sie selbst (Thomas Nipperdey) [in]: Die Zeit, Nr. 51, Hamburg, 16. Dez. 1983, p. 14.]

20333. AUERBACH, BERTHOLD. Kaiser, Nancy A.: *Berthold Auerbach: the dilemma of the Jewish humanist from 'Vormärz' to empire.* [In]: German Studies Review, Vol. 6, No. 3, Tempe, Ariz., Oct. 1983. Pp. 399–419.

20334. — Katz, Jacob: *Berthold Auerbach's anticipation of the German-Jewish tragedy.* [In]: Hebrew Union College Annual, Vol. 53 (1982), Cincinnati, 1983. Pp. 215–240, notes.

20335. AUERBACH, ERICH. Green, Geoffrey: *Literary criticism and the structures of history: Erich Auerbach and Leo Spitzer.* Lincoln, Neb.; London: Univ. of Nebraska Press, 1983. X, 186 pp. [E. Auerbach, Nov. 9, 1892 Berlin – Oct. 13, 1957 New Haven, professor of Romance literature, emigrated to Turkey, from 1947 in the USA. L. Spitzer, Feb. 7, 1887 Vienna – Sept. 16, 1960 Forte dei Marmi, Italy, professor of Romance philology, emigrated via Turkey to the USA.]

20336. AUSLÄNDER, ROSE: *Doppelspiel.* Frankfurt am Main: S. Fischer, 1983. 72 pp.

20337. BALLIN, ALBERT. Tibbon, Eliezer: *Friend of the Kaiser – Albert Ballin.* [In Hebrew, title transl.]. [In]: Eit-mol, Vol. 9, No. 1 (51), Tel-Aviv, Sept. 1983. Pp. 22–23.

20338. BAUER, LEO. Brandt, Peter/Schumacher, Jörg/Schwarzrock, Götz/Suhl, Klaus: *Karrieren eines Aussenseiters: Leo Bauer zwischen Kommunismus und Sozialdemokratie 1912–1972.* Bonn: Verlag Dietz Nachf., 1983. 360 pp., illus. [L.B., Dec. 18, 1912 Skalat, Galicia – Sept. 18, 1972 Bonn, communist, later socialist politician and journalist, from 1933 in exile, returned to West-Germany in 1945, later to East Berlin, sentenced to death by a Soviet military tribunal, pardoned, from 1955 in the Federal German Republic.]

20339. BAUER, OTTO. Rabinbach, Anson: *The crisis of Austrian socialism; from red Vienna to civil war, 1927–1934.* Chicago: Univ. of Chicago Press, 1983. 296 pp. [Incl. major portrait of Otto Bauer, Sept. 5, 1881 Vienna – July 4, 1938 Paris, socialist politician.]

20340. BEER-HOFMANN, RICHARD. Bein, Alex: *Richard Beer-Hofmann: der Dichter und der Mensch.* [In]: Zeitschrift für Religions- und Geistesgeschichte, Bd. 35, H. 1, Köln, 1983. Pp.

50–66, bibl. [See also: Besuch bei Mirjam B.-H. (Rainer Hank) [in]: 'Allgemeine', Nr. 6, Düsseldorf, 14. Feb. 1983, p. 7.]

20341. — ELSTUN, ESTHER N: *Richard Beer-Hofmann; his life and work.* University Park: Pennsylvania State Univ. Press, 1983. IX, 214 pp., bibl. (205–211).

20342. — HARRIS, KATHLEEN/SHEIRICH, RICHARD: *Richard Beer-Hofmann: a bibliography.* [In]: Modern Austrian Literature, Vol. 15, No. 1, Riverside, Calif., 1982. Pp. 1–60.

20343. BENDER, ARNOLD. MÜLLER, HANS CHRISTIAN, ed.: *Kleines Leben in England: Arnold Bender, 1904–1978; ein Dortmunder Schriftsteller im Exil.* Dortmund, 1982. 90 pp., port. (Stadt- und Landesbibliothek Dortmund, Mitteilungen, N.F. H. 16.) [Incl. excerpts from B.'s diary and selection of his work.] [A.B., June 12, 1904 Bochum-Werne – Apr. 16, 1978 Port Isaac, Cornwall, writer.]

20344. BEN-HAIM, PAUL. HIRSCHBERG, JEHOASH: *Paul Ben-Haim; his life and works.* [In Hebrew]. Tel-Aviv: Am Oved, 1983. 277 pp., illus, bibl. Ben-Haim (251–270). [P.B.-H., orig. Frankenburger, July 5, 1897 Munich – Jan. 15, 1984 Tel-Aviv, composer, emigrated in 1933.]

—— — HIRSCHBERG, JEHOASH: *Heinrich Schalit and P. Ben-Haim in Munich.* [See No. 20241.]

—— BENJAMIN, WALTER. BEICKEN, PETER: *Kafkas 'Prozess' und seine Richter: zur Debatte Brecht-Benjamin und Benjamin-Scholem.* [See in No. 20624.]

20345. — BRANDT, HANS-JÜRGEN: *'Benjamin und kein Ende?' Zur Filmtheorie Walter Benjamins.* [In]: Frankfurter Hefte, Jg. 38, H. 3, Frankfurt am Main, März 1983. Pp. 48–54.

20346. — BUCK-MORSS, SUSAN: *Benjamin's Passagen-Werk: redeeming mass culture for the revolution.* [In]: new german critique, No. 29, Milwaukee, Univ. of Wis., Spring-Summer, 1983. Pp. 211– 240, notes.

—— — FIGAL, GÜNTER: *Selbsterhaltung und Selbstverzicht.* [See No. 20462.]

20347. — HERING, CHRISTOPH: *Die Rekonstruktion der Revolution: Walter Benjamins messianischer Materialismus in den Thesen 'Über den Begriff der Geschichte'.* Frankfurt am Main: Lang, 1983. 218 pp. (Europäische Hochschulschriften: Reihe 20, Bd. 94.)

—— — JANZ, ROLF-PETER: *Das Ende Weimars aus der Perspektive Walter Benjamins.* [See in No. 20319.] [See also Kodalle in No. 20316; & No. 20533.]

20348. — KAMBAS, CHRYSSOULA: *Walter Benjamin im Exil.* Zum Verhältnis von Literaturpolitik und Ästhetik. Tübingen: Niemeyer, 1983. XI, 247 pp. (Studien zur Sozialgeschichte, Bd. 11.)

20349. — *The Philosophical Forum.* Vol. 15, No. 1–2 [with the issue title]: *Walter Benjamin: philosophy, history and aesthetics.* Guest ed.: Gary Smith. New York: Baruch College of CUNY, Fall-Winter 1983–84. 1 issue. [Incl.: Texts by W. Benjamin, a.o. from the Arcades project. Benjamin and Rosenzweig (Stéphane Moses; Engl. version of No. 19332/YB XXVIII). Essays on W.B., a.o., by Adorno, Leo Löwenthal, Rolf Tiedemann.]

20350. — ROBERTS, JULIAN, ed.: *Walter Benjamin.* London: Macmillan, 1983. 264 pp. [Cf.: The wizened dwarf at work (S.S. Prawer) [in]: TLS, London, April 1st, 1983, p. 339.]

20351. — SCHOLEM, GERSHOM: *Walter Benjamin und sein Engel.* Vierzehn Aufsätze und kleine Beiträge. Hrsg. von Rolf Tiedemann. Frankfurt am Main: Suhrkamp, 1983. 223 pp., port. [Incl. four hitherto unpubl. essays.]

20352. — STOESSEL, MARLEEN: *Aura: das vergessene Menschliche; zu Sprache und Erfahrung bei Walter Benjamin.* München: Hanser, 1983. 255 pp., bibl. (250–255).

20353. — TAUBES, JACOB, ed.: *Religionstheorie und politische Theologie. Bd. 1: Der Fürst dieser Welt: Carl Schmitt und die Folgen.* München: Fink, 1983. 321 pp. [Incl.: Charisma und Souveränität: Carl Schmitt und Walter Benjamin im Schatten Max Webers (Norbert W. Bolz). Fritz Lieb – Walter Benjamin – Karl Barth (Chryssoula Kambas).]

20354. — WOHLFARTH, IRVING: *Sur quelques motifs juifs chez Benjamin.* [In]: Revue d'Esthétique, No. 1, Toulouse, 1981. Pp. 141–162.

20355. BERNSTEIN, EDUARD. FLETCHER, ROGER A.: *Cobden as educator: the free-trade internationalism of Eduard Bernstein, 1899–1914.* [In]: American Historical Review, Vol. 88, No. 3, Washington, D.C., June 1983. Pp. 561–578. [Deals also with Hugo Haase, Rudolf Hilferding, Rosa Luxemburg.]

20356. — FLETCHER, ROGER: *Revisionism and militarism: war and peace in the pre-1914 thought of Eduard Bernstein.* [In]: Militärgeschichtl. Mitteilungen, Jg. 31, Nr. 1, Karlsruhe, 1982. Pp. 23–36.

20357. BLOCH, ERNEST. BERGER, SALOMÉ: *Ernest Bloch: a composer between two worlds.* [In]: Midstream, Vol. 29, No. 1, New York, Jan. 1983. Pp. 43–44. [E.B., 1880 Geneva – 1959 Agate Beach, Oregon.]

20358. BLOCH, ERNST. DEUSER, HERMANN/STEINACKER, PETER, eds.: *Ernst Blochs Vermittlungen zur Theologie*. München: Kaiser, 1983. 222 pp., bibl. (211–220).

20359. — SCHMIDT, BURGHART, ed.: *Seminar: zur Philosophie Ernst Blochs*. Frankfurt am Main: Suhrkamp, 1983. 327 pp. (Suhrkamp-Taschenbuch Wissenschaft, 268.) [Incl.: Über den Tod im Denken E.B.'s (E. Lévinas). Zu Blochs Freudkritik (K. Binder).]

20360. BORCHARDT, RUDOLF. GRANGE, JACQUES: *Rudolf Borchardt, 1877–1945*. Contribution à l'étude de la pensée conservatrice et de la poésie en Allemagne dans la moitié du.20. siècle. 1–2. Bern: Lang, 1983. 1396 pp. in 2 vols., bibl. Borchardt (1278–1302). (Publications universitaires européennes: Sér. 1, Vol. 553.)

20361. BORN, MAX. LEMMERICH, JOST, ed.: *Science and conscience: the world of two atomic scientists*. Transl. from the German. London: Science Museum, South Kensington, 1983. 1 vol., illus. [German edn. see No. 19347/YB XXVIII. Refers also to James Franck. See also No. 20399.]

20362. BRAUNTHAL, JULIUS. ROBACH, BRIGITTE: *Julius Braunthal als politischer Publizist*. Ein Leben im Dienste des Sozialismus. Wien, Univ., Diss., 1983. 615 pp., illus.

20363. BROCH, HERMANN. LÜTZELER, PAUL MICHAEL, ed.: *Brochs 'Verzauberung'*. Frankfurt am Main: Suhrkamp, 1983. 295 pp. (Suhrkamp-Taschenbuch, 2039.)

20364. BRUCKNER, FERDINAND: *Elisabeth von England*. Schauspiel. Mit einem Nachwort von Fritz Schwiefert. Stuttgart: Reclam, 1983. 152 pp. (Universal-Bibliothek, Nr. 8433.) [F.B., orig. Theodor Tagger, data see No. 18404/YB XXVII.]

20365. CAHNMAN, WERNER J. *Ethnicity, identity and history: essays in memory of Werner J. Cahnman*. Ed. by Joseph B. Maier and Chaim I. Waxman. New Brunswick: Transaction Books, 1983. 345 pp., bibl. Cahnman (321–331). [Incl.: Werner J. Cahnman: an introduction to his life and work (J. B. Maier/Ch. I. Waxman, 1–12). Social and communal acculturation of German-Jewish immigrants of the Nazi period in the U.S. (Herbert A. Strauss, 227–248).] [W. J. Cahnman, Sept. 30, 1902 Munich – Sept. 29, 1980 New York, formerly syndic of the Bavarian C.V., professor of sociology.]

20366. CANETTI, ELIAS: *Comedy of vanity and Life terms*. Introd. by Klaus Völker. Transl. by Gitta Honegger. New York: Performing Arts Journal Publ., 1983. 158 pp.

20367. — *Modern Austrian Literature*. Vol. 16, No. 3–4: *Special Elias Canetti issue*. Riverside, Calif., 1983. 1 issue. [Incl.: E. C. und Karl Kraus (Gerald Stieg, 197–210).]

20368. CASSIRER, ERNST: *'Mind' and 'life': Heidegger*. An unpublished manuscript. [And]: *Cassirer's unpublished critique of Heidegger*. (John Michael Krois). [In]: Philosophy and Rhetoric, Vol. 16, No. 3, University Park, Pa., 1983. Pp. 160–166 [in English and German]; 147–159.

20369. CELAN, PAUL: *Gesammelte Werke in fünf Bänden*. Hrsg. von Beda Allemann und Stefan Reichert unter Mitwirkung von Rudolf Bücher. Frankfurt am Main: Suhrkamp, 1983. 5 vols., facsims., notes. [Cf.: Die erste Gesamtausgabe: fünf Bände – zu spät und zu früh (Peter Horst Neumann) [&]: Paul Celan – noch immer zu entdecken: Erinnerung an den jungen Dichter, der gerade der Vernichtung entkommen, ein deutsches Lied vom Tode sang (Helmut Niemeyer) [in]: Die Zeit, Nr. 10, Hamburg, 2. März 1984, pp. 48–49, ports., facsims.]

20370. — ALLERHAND, JACOB: *Paul Celan: Aspekte seines Judentums*. Schriftstellerische und jüdische Einsamkeit. [In]: Literatur und Kritik, H. 179/180, Wien, Nov./Dez. 1983. Pp. 511–523, notes.

20371. — BOGUMIL, SIEGHILD: *Celans Wandern im Wort; Entwicklungslinien in der Lyrik Paul Celans, II*. [In]: Neue Rundschau, Jg. 94, H. 1, Frankfurt am Main, 1983. Pp. 88–105, notes. [Continuation of No. 19360/YB XXVIII.]

20372. CHARGAFF, ERWIN: *Kritik der Zukunft*. Stuttgart: Klett-Cotta, 1983. 142 pp. (Cotta's Bibliothek der Moderne, 18.) [E.Ch. data, see No. 18120/YB XXVII.]

20373. COHEN-BLIND, FERDINAND. FRANZ, GÜNTHER: *Ferdinand Cohen-Blind und sein Attentat auf Bismarck 1866*. [In]: Zeitschrift für Württembergische Landesgeschichte, Jg. 40, (1981), Stuttgart, 1982. Pp. 387–397. [F.C.-B., March 25, 1844 Mannheim – May 8, 1866 Berlin, suicide, son of the merchant Jacob Abraham Cohen and Friedericke, née Etlinger from Mannheim who after Cohen's death married Carl Blind.]

20374. COPER, HANS. BIRKS, TONY: *Hans Coper*. London: Collins, 1983. 208 pp., illus. [H.C., born 1920 in Germany, died in England, ceramic artist.]

20375. DEUTSCH, OTTO ERICH: *Admiral Nelson und Joseph Haydn; ein britisch-österreichisches Gipfeltreffen*. Hrsg. von Gitta Deutsch und Rudolf Klein. Wien: Österr. Bundesverlag, 1982. 136 pp., illus. [First German edn.; Engl. transl. was publ. 1941.] [O.E.D., Vienna Sept. 5,

1883–Nov. 25, 1967, musicologist, emigrated to England 1939–1952, especially known for his 1951 catalogue of Schubert's works which are now designated by D numbers.]

20376. DÖBLIN, ALFRED: *A people betrayed. November 1918: a German revolution.* A novel. Transl. from the German by John E. Woods. Foreword: Günter Grass on Alfred Döblin. New York: Fromm Internat., 1983. 642 pp. [First two parts of the author's 'November 1918', orig. publ. 1939–1950; for German edn. and details see No. 15464/YB XXIV .]

20377. — Döblin, Alfred: *Karl and Rosa. November 1918: a German revolution.* A novel. Transl. from the German by John E. Woods. New York: Fromm Internat., 1983. 547 pp. [Third part of the author's 'November 1918'; focuses on Karl Liebknecht and Rosa Luxemburg.]

20378. — Döblin, Alfred: *Drama, Hörspiel, Film.* (Hrsg.: Erich Kleinschmidt.) Olten: Walter, 1983. 669 pp. (Döblin, Alfred: Ausgewählte Werke in Einzelbänden.)

20379. — Anders, Günther: *Erinnerung an Döblin.* [In]: Neue Rundschau, Jg. 94, H. 4, Frankfurt am Main, 1983. Pp. 5–9.

—— — Köpke, Wulf: *Alfred Döblins Überparteilichkeit.* [See in No. 20319.]

20380. — Koopmann, Helmut: *Der klassisch-moderne Roman in Deutschland: Thomas Mann, Alfred Döblin, Hermann Broch.* Stuttgart: Kohlhammer, 1983. 188 pp. (Sprache und Literatur, 113.)

20381. EHRENSTEIN, ALBERT: *Tubutsch.* Eine Erzählung. Zürich: edition moderne, 1983. 74 pp. [A.E., Dec. 23, 1886 Vienna – Apr. 8, 1950 New York, expressionist writer.]

20382. — Laugwitz, Uwe: *Albert Ehrenstein und Karl Kraus; Entwicklung einer literarischen Polemik, 1910–1920.* Hamburg, Univ., Diss., 1982. 108 pp., bibl. (105–108).

—— EICHELBERG, LEOPOLD. Grab, Walter: *Die revolutionäre Agitation und die Kerkerhaft Leopold Eichelbergs.* [See in No. 19764.] [L.E., Marburg 1804–1879, physician, politician.]

20383. EINSTEIN, ALBERT. Dank, Milton: *Albert Einstein.* New York; London: Franklin Watts, 1983. 122 pp., illus., diagr.

20384. — Hermanns, William: *Einstein and the poet: in search of the cosmic man.* Brookline, Mass.: Branden Press, 1983. 152 pp., illus., facsims. [Based on four long interviews with A.E. between 1930–1954 by the German-born anti-Nazi sociologist and poet W. Hermanns.]

20385. — Trbuhovic-Gjuric, Desanka: *Im Schatten Albert Einsteins: das tragische Leben der Mileva Einstein-Maric.* Bern: Haupt, 1983. 189 pp., illus. [M. Maric, 1875–1948, scientist, first wife of Albert Einstein from 1903 to 1919, mother of their two sons.]

20386. EINSTEIN, CARL. Williams, Rhys W.: *Primitivism in the works of Carl Einstein, Carl Sternheim and Gottfried Benn.* [In]: Journal of European Studies, Vol. 13, Pt. 4, Chalfont St. Giles, Dec. 1983. Pp. 247–267, notes.

20387. EINSTEIN, SIEGFRIED. Gerth, Siegfried: *Siegfried Einstein; zum Gedenken an einen Unbehausten.* [In]: Mannheimer Hefte, H. 2, Mannheim, 1983. Pp. 58–59. [S.E., Nov. 30, 1919 Laupheim – Apr. 25, 1983 Mannheim, journalist, emigrated to Switzerland in 1934.]

20388. EISLER, HANNS. Grabs, Manfred, ed.: *Wer war Hanns Eisler.* Auffassungen aus 6 Jahrzehnten, ausgewählt und eingeleitet. Westberlin: Verlag Das Europäische Buch, 1983. 542 pp., illus.

—— EISNER, KURT. Sproll, Heinz: *Messianisches Denken und pazifistische Utopie im Werk Kurt Eisners.* [See in No. 19764.]

20389. EISNER, LOTTE. *Obituaries.* [In]: The Guardian, London, Nov. 29, 1983. [In]: The Times, London, Dec. 3, 1983. Die Arbeiterin des Films (Peter W. Jansen) [in]: Die Zeit, Nr. 49, Hamburg, 2. Dez. 1983, p. 50. [L.E., March 5, 1896 Berlin – Nov. 25, 1983 Garches near Paris, film critic and historian, emigrated to Paris in 1933, one of the founders and conservatrice-en-chef 1945–1974 of the Cinemathèque Française.]

20390. ELIAS, NORBERT: *Engagement und Distanzierung; Arbeiten zur Wissenssoziologie I.* Hrsg. und aus dem Engl. übers. von Michael Schröter. Frankfurt am Main: Suhrkamp, 1983. 272 pp.

20391. — Elias, Norbert: *Über den Rückzug der Soziologen auf die Gegenwart.* [In]: Kölner Zeitschrift für Soziologie und Sozialpsychologie, Jg. 35, H. 1, Opladen, 1983. Pp. 29–40, notes.

20392. ELIASBERG, PAUL. Jensen, Jens Christian: *Paul Eliasberg; das Gesamtwerk der Druckgraphik 1957–1983.* Hamburg: Christians, 1983. 237 pp., illus. [P.E., 1907 Munich – Oct. 1, 1983 Hamburg, painter and graphic artist, son of the literary historian Alexander E., emigrated to France.]

20393. EPPSTEIN, PAUL. Wendling, Willi: *Die Mannheimer Abendakademie und Volkshochschule.* Ihre Geschichte im Rahmen der örtlichen Erwachsenenbildung von den Anfängen im 19. Jahrhundert bis 1953. Heidelberg: Heidelberger Verlagsanstalt, 1983. 248 pp., illus., ports. (Sonderveröffentlichung des Stadtarchivs Mannheim, Nr. 7.) [Incl. chap.: Erwachsenenbildung in der Weimarer Republik: die Volkshochschule unter der Leitung von Dr. Paul

Eppstein (65–94); and three essays by P. Eppstein: Die Mannheimer Volkshochschule: Stellung und Ziel [1929]; Aktualität als Programm? [1929]; Kulturelle Erwerbslosenhilfe [1931/32] (pp. 192–202).] [P.E., March 4, 1901 Mannheim – Sept. 28, 1944 Theresienstadt, sociologist, director of the Mannheimer Volkshochschule, functionary of Reichsvertretung and Reichsvereinigung.]

20394. FECHENBACH, FELIX. STEINBACH, PETER, ed.: *'Das Schicksal hat bestimmt, dass ich hierbleibe'. Zur Erinnerung an Felix Fechenbach (1894–1933).* Mit der Zusammenstellung der Artikel von 'Nazi-Jüsken'. Berlin: Wissenschaftlicher Autoren-Verl., 1983. 157 pp. [Cont. the articles by F.F. which he wrote under his pseud. 'Nazi-Jüsken'; and articles on F.F.]

20395. FEUCHTWANGER, LION: *Die Jüdin von Toledo.* Roman. Frankfurt am Main: Fischer, 1983. 467 pp. (Fischer-Taschenbücher, 5732.)

20396. — KÖPKE, WULF: *Lion Feuchtwanger.* München: Beck; München: Verlag Edition Text & Kritik, 1983. 184 pp., bibl. Feuchtwanger & bibl. (181–184). (Autorenbücher, 35.)

20397. — *Lion Feuchtwanger.* München: Verlag Edition & Kritik, 1983. 148 pp., bibl. Feuchtwanger & bibl. (text + kritik, H. 79/80.) [See also No. 20682.]

20398. — PISCHEL, JOSEPH: *Lion Feuchtwangers 'Jud Süss'.* [In]: Weimarer Beiträge, Jg. 29, H. 12, Berlin/East, 1983. Pp. 2112–2129.

20399. FRANCK, JAMES. *James Franck und Max Born in Göttingen.* Reden zur akademischen Feier aus Anlass der 100. Wiederkehr ihres Geburtsjahres. Göttingen: Vandenhoeck & Ruprecht, 1983. 37 pp. (Göttinger Universitätsreden, 69.) [See also No. 20361.]

20400. FRANZOS, KARL EMIL. GELBER, MARK H.: *Ethnic pluralism and Germanization in the works of Karl Emil Franzos.* [In]: The German Quarterly, Vol. 56, No. 3, Cherry Hill, N.J., May 1983. Pp. 376–385, notes.

20401. FREUD, ANNA. *Eine Kinderanalyse bei Anna Freud (1929–1932).* Retrospektive von Peter Heller. Mit Dokumentation und Notizen von Anna Freud. Kommentar von Günther Bittner. Würzburg: Königshausen & Neumann, 1983. 300 pp., illus.

20402. FREUD, SIGMUND: *Lettre au Dr. Alfons Paquet.* [&]: *Discours dans la maison de Goethe à Francfort (inédit).* [And]: *Énigmatiques: Freud et Goethe* (Philippe Boyer). [In]: L'Infini, 2, Paris, 1983. Pp. 106–110, footnotes; 90–105.

20403. — ANDREAS-SALOMÉ, LOU: *In der Schule bei Freud.* Tagebuch eines Jahres 1912/1913. (Aus dem Nachlass hrsg. von Ernst Pfeiffer.) Frankfurt am Main: Ullstein, 1983. 300 pp., illus., notes. (Ullstein-Buch, Nr. 35174.) [First edn. 1958.]

20404. — BETTELHEIM, BRUNO: *Freud and man's soul.* London: Chatto & Windus; New York: Knopf, 1983. 128 pp. [On the inadequacy of English translations of Freud's works.]

20405. — BROME, VINCENT: *Ernest Jones: Freud's alter ego.* London: Caliban Books, 1983. 250 pp.

20406. — DIAMOND, SIGMUND: *Sigmund Freud, his Jewishness and scientific method; the seen and the unseen as evidence.* [In]: Journal of the History of Ideas, Vol. 43, No. 4, New York, Oct.–Dec. 1982. Pp. 613–634.

20407. — GAY, PETER: *Six names in search of an interpretation: a contribution on the debate over Sigmund Freud's Jewishness.* [In]: Hebrew Union College Annual, Vol. 53 (1982), Cincinnati, 1983. Pp. 295–316, notes.

—— — KLEPFISZ, HESZEL: *Bergson, Freud and Marx – their Jewish problem.* [See No. 20216.]

20408. — STEINER, GEORGE: *The historicity of dreams; (two questions to Freud).* [In]: Salmagundi, No. 61, Saratoga Springs, N.Y., Fall 1983. Pp. 6–21.

20409. FRIED, ERICH: *Angst und Trost; Erzählungen und Gedichte über Juden und Nazis.* Grafiken von David Fried. Erstveröffentlichung. Frankfurt am Main: Alibaba, 1983. 100 pp. [Cf.: E. Fried, der rasende Verworter: drei Bände mit seiner Lyrik und Prosa (Walter Hinck) [in]: Frankfurter Allgemeine Zeitung, Nr. 12, 14. Jan. 1984, Beilage.]

20410. — FRIED, ERICH: *Es ist was es ist: Liebesgedichte, Angstgedichte, Zorngedichte.* Berlin: Wagenbach, 1983. 105 pp. (Quarthefte, 124.)

20411. — FRIED, ERICH: *Höre Israel.* Gedichte und Fussnoten. Neue und erweiterte Aufl. Frankfurt am Main: Syndikat, 1983. 160 pp. (Taschenbücher Syndikat, EVA, Bd. 19.)

20412. FRIEDELL, EGON: *Selbstanzeige.* Essays ab 1918. Hrsg. und mit einem Nachwort 'Der ganze Friedell?' von Heribert Illig. Wien: Löcker, 1983. 256 pp., port. [Sequel to No. 19400/ YB XXVIII.]

20413. FROMM, ERICH: *The working class in Weimar Germany.* A psychological and sociological study. (Transl. from the German by Barbara Weinberger.) With an introd. by Wolfgang Bonss: 'Critical theory and empirical social research'. Leamington Spa, England: Berg Publ., 1983. 320 pp. [Transl. of No. 16530/YB XXV.]

20414. — Fromm, Erich: *Über die Liebe zum Leben.* Rundfunksendungen. Hrsg. von Hans Jürgen Schultz. Stuttgart: Deutsche Verlags-Anstalt, 1983. 183 pp.

20415. — Funk, Rainer: *Erich Fromm.* Mit Selbstzeugnissen und Bilddokumenten dargestellt. Reinbek: Rowohlt, 1983. 153 pp., illus., ports., bibl. E. Fromm & bibl. (146–150). (Rowohlts Monographien, 322.)

20416. FURTMÜLLER, CARL: *Denken und Handeln.* Schriften zur Psychologie 1905–1950. Von den Anfängen der Psychoanalyse zur Anwendung der Individualpsychologie. Hrsg. von Lux Furtmüller. Mit einem Vorwort von Marie Jahoda. München: Ernst Reinhardt, 1983. 318 pp., port. [On Freud and Alfred Adler; incl. biogr. essay on C.F.]

20417. GERNSHEIM, HELMUT: *Geschichte der Photographie; die ersten 100 Jahre.* (Aus dem Engl. übers. von Matthias Fienbork.) Frankfurt am Main: Propyläen, 1983. 792 pp., 560 illus. (Propyläen-Kunstgeschichte, Sonderbd. 3.) [Incl. the German-Jewish photographers.] [H.G., born March 1, 1913 in Munich, historian of photography, emigrated to England in 1937, lives in Switzerland.]

20418. GOMBRICH, ERNST H.: *Die Krise der Kulturgeschichte.* Gedanken zum Wertproblem in der Geisteswissenschaft. (Aus dem Engl. übertr. von Lisbeth Gombrich.) Stuttgart: Klett-Cotta, 1983. 248 pp., illus.

20419. — Gombrich, Ernst H.: *The sense of order.* A study in the psychology of decorative art. Ithaca, N.Y.: Cornell Univ. Press, 1983. 422 pp., illus. [For German transl. see No. 19407/YB XXVIII.]

20420. GRÜNBAUM, FRITZ: *Fritz Grünbaum.* [And]: *Der junge Karl Farkas.* Historische Aufnahmen. Wien: Preiser, [1983?]. 1 disk [Order No. PR 9999]. [F. Grünbaum, Apr. 7, 1880 Brünn, Moravia – Jan. 14, 1941 Dachau, the 'king of Viennese cabaret', theatre and film actor and playwright. K. Farkas, Vienna Oct. 28, 1893 – May 16, 1971, together with F. Grünbaum head of the cabaret 'Simpl' in Vienna, emigrated after 1938, returned to Vienna in 1946, head of the new 'Simpl'.]

20421. — Böhm, Maxi: *Bei uns in Reichenberg.* Unvollendete Memoiren. Fertig erzählt von Georg Markus. Vorwort Alfred Böhm. Wien: Amalthea, 1983. 319 pp., illus. [The Austrian cabaret performer M.B. became Farkas' partner at the new 'Simpl' in Vienna; incl. reminiscences especially on F. Grünbaum.]

20422. HALLBERGER, LOUIS & EDUARD. Berner, Felix: *Louis und Eduard Hallberger: die Gründer der Deutschen Verlags-Anstalt.* Stuttgart: Deutsche Verlags-Anstalt, 1983. 93 pp., illus. (Sonderdruck aus: Lebensbilder aus Schwaben und Franken, Bd. 15.) [Louis H., 1796–1879. Eduard H., 1822–1880.]

20423. Hamburger, Michael: *A proliferation of prophets; essays on German writers from Nietzsche to Brecht.* Manchester: Carcanet New Press, 1983. 328 pp., bibl.(313–319). (Essays in modern German literature, vol. 1.) [Incl. Benjamin, Hofmannsthal, Kafka, Lichtenstein, Scholem, Wolfskehl. Cf.: Triumph of persistence (Idris Parry) [in]: TLS, London, 20. Apr. 1984, p. 434.]

20424. HARDEN, MAXIMILIAN: *Kaiserpanorama; literarische und politische Publizistik.* Hrsg. und mit einem Nachwort von Ruth Greuner. Berlin/East: Buchverlag Der Morgen, 1983. 384 pp., illus. [See also No. 20589.]

20425. HASENCLEVER, WALTER. Hoelzel, Alfred: *Walter Hasenclever's humanitarianism: themes of protest in his works.* Berne, New York: Lang, 1983. VIII, 264 pp., bibl. (255–257). (European university studies: Ser. 1, Vol. 696.)

20426. — Wilder, Ania: *Die Komödien Walter Hasenclevers; ein Beitrag zur Literatur der Zwanziger Jahre.* Frankfurt am Main: Lang, 1983. 181 pp. (Europäische Hochschulschriften: Reihe 1, Bd. 694.)

20427. HAUSER, ARNOLD: *The sociology of art.* Transl. by Kenneth J. Northcott. London: Routledge and Kegan Paul; Chicago: Univ. of Chicago Press, 1982. 776 pp. [Also German paperback edn.]: *Soziologie der Kunst.* München: Deutscher Taschenbuch-Verl., 1983. XVI, 823 pp. (dtv, 4415.) [Augmented and finalized version of the author's 'Social history of art'; German edn. appeared in 1974.] [A.H., May 8, 1892 Temesvar, Hungary – Jan. 28, 1978 England, sociologist, art and literary historian, from 1921 in Berlin, emigrated in 1939.]

20428. HECHT, HERMANN: *Die Entstehung des Rhenania-Konzerns; die ersten dreissig Jahre. (1940).* Heidelberg: Brausdruck, 1983. 72 pp., illus. [H.H., 1878 Gondelsheim – 1969 New York, founded the 'Rhenania Schiffahrts- und Speditionsgesellschaft' on March 8, 1908, emigrated via Switzerland to the USA in 1937.]

20429. HEINE, HEINRICH: *Der Rabbi von Bacharach*. Ein Fragment. Hrsg. von Hartmut Kirchner. Stuttgart: Reclam, 1983. 87 pp. (Universal-Bibliothek, Nr. 2350.)

20430. — Bech, Françoise: *Heines Pariser Exil zwischen Spätromantik und Wirklichkeit, Kunst und Politik*. Frankfurt am Main: Lang, 1983. 330 pp. (Europäische Hochschulschriften: Reihe 1, Bd. 728.)

20431. — Grappin, Pierre: *Heinrich Heine in Paris, 1831–1856*. [In]: Geschichte in Wissenschaft und Unterricht, Jg. 34, H. 8, Stuttgart, Aug. 1983. Pp. 501–511, notes.

20432. — Hamburger, Käte: *Heine und das Judentum*. Vortrag. Stuttgart: Württ. Bibliotheksgesellschaft, 1982. 19 pp.

20433. — *Heine-Jahrbuch 1983*. Jg. 22. Hrsg. von Joseph A. Kruse, Heinrich-Heine-Institut der Landeshauptstadt Düsseldorf. Hamburg: Hoffmann & Campe, 1983. 276 pp., illus., notes, bibl. [Incl.: Das Junge Deutschland als literarische Opposition (Manfred Windfuhr, 47–69; also on Ludwig Börne). Eulogy of a lost cause: Heine's essay 'Ludwig Marcus' (Catherine Creecy, 83–95). Heines 'Prinzessin Sabbat' – hebräisch verkleidet (Dafna Mach, 96–120). Neue Heine-Briefe (Joseph A. Kruse, 121–134). Zu Heines 'Briefen aus Berlin' (Paul Derks, 200–201). Bestandsverzeichnis der Düsseldorfer Heine-Autographen, 1975–1982 (Inge Hermstrüwer, 202–209). Heine-Literatur 1981/82 mit Nachträgen (Heike von Berkholz, 240–252).]

20434. — *Heinrich Heine 1797–1856*. Internationaler Veranstaltungszyklus zum 125. Todesjahr 1981. Trier, 1981. 204 pp. (Schriften aus dem Karl-Marx-Haus, 26.) [Incl.: H. Heine und Moses Hess (Michel Espagne, 80–97). Börne und Heine (Inge Rippmann, 98–119). General Marx –Hund Heine (Klaus Briegleb, 153–181.]

—— — Hermand, Jost: *Eine Jugend in Deutschland*. [See in No. 19764. See also No. 20453.]

20435. — Kraft, Werner: *Heine, der Dichter*. München: Edition Text & Kritik, 1983. 168 pp.

20436. — Kruse, Joseph A.: *Heinrich Heine; Leben und Werk in Daten und Bildern*. Frankfurt am Main: Insel, 1983. 352 pp., illus., bibl. (313–317). (Insel-Taschenbuch, 615.)

20437. — Mende, Fritz: *Heinrich Heine; Studien zu seinem Leben und Werk*. Berlin/East: Akademie-Verl., 1983. 243 pp., bibl. (231–237).

20438. — Nobis, Helmut: *Heines Krankheit; zu Ironie, Parodie, Humor und Spott in den Lamentationen des 'Romanzero'*. [In]: Zeitschrift für Deutsche Philologie, Bd. 102, H. 4, Berlin, 1983. Pp. 521–541, footnotes.

20439. — Oellers, N.: *Friedrich Wilhelm Krummachers Gedicht 'Am Lurleifelsen' – eine Quelle für Heine?* Mit einer methodologischen Vorbemerkung. [In]: Sammeln und sichten; Festschrift für Oscar Fambach, hrsg. von Joachim Krause [et al.]. Bonn: Bouvier, 1982. Pp. 283–293.

20440. — Prawer, S. S.: *Heine's Jewish comedy; a study of his portraits of Jews and Judaism*. Oxford: Clarendon Press; New York: Oxford Univ. Press, 1983. VII, 841 pp., notes, bibl. (805–817). [Cont. pts.: 1. German-Jewish dilemmas. 2. Parisian perspectives. 3. Roads from Damascus. 4. View from a mattress crypt. Cf.: Miniature masterpieces (Chimen Abramsky) [in]: Jewish Chronicle, London, Sept. 30, 1983. The defrocked romantic (Gabriele Annan) [in]: The New York Review of Books, Feb. 16, 1984, pp. 11–13. Heines jüdische Komödie (Hans Reiss) [in]: NZZ, Nr. 8, Zürich, 11. Jan. 1984, p. 37. Imperatives in the blood (John Gross) [in]: The Observer, London, Aug. 14, 1983. The matrix of ambiguity (Sander L. Gilman) [in]: TLS, London, Dec. 2, 1983, p. 1343.] [See also the author's: Heine's portraits of German and French Jews on the eve of the 1848 revolution [in]: Revolution and evolution: 1848 in German-Jewish history, pp. 353–383 (see in No. 17885/YB XXVII).]

20441. — Sammons, Jeffrey L.: *Heinrich Heine; a selected critical bibliography of secondary literature, 1956–1980*. New York; London: Garland, 1982. XVIII, 194 pp.

—— — Werner, Michael: *Heinrich Heine: über die Interdependenz von jüdischer, deutscher und europäischer Identität in seinem Werk*. [See in No. 19769.]

20442. HEINE, THOMAS THEODOR: *Der Teufel im Warenhaus*. Die Märchen des Simplizissimus-Zeichners, vom Autor illustriert. Frankfurt am Main: Robinson, 1983. 64 pp., illus. [Th. Th. H., Feb. 28, 1867 Leipzig – Jan. 26, 1948 Stockholm, emigrated in 1933.]

20443. HELLER, HERMANN: *Staatslehre*. In der Bearb. von Gerhart Niemeyer. 6., revidierte Aufl. Tübingen: Mohr, 1983. VI, 337 pp. [The author's major work, publ. posthumously in 1934.] [H.H., July 17, 1891 Teschen – Nov. 5, 1933 Madrid, political scientist, professor of public law in Berlin and Frankfurt am Main.]

20444. — Albrecht, Stephen: *Hermann Hellers Staats- und Demokratieauffassung*. Frankfurt am Main; New York: Campus, 1983. 262 pp., bibl. (Campus: Forschung, Bd. 326.)

20445. — Schluchter, Wolfgang: *Entscheidung für den sozialen Rechtsstaat; Hermann Heller und die staatstheoretische Diskussion in der Weimarer Republik*. Baden-Baden: Nomos, 1983. 300 pp., bibl. (291–298).

20446. HERMANN, GEORG. KÄHLER, HERMANN: *Erinnerung an Georg Hermann*. [In]: Weimarer Beiträge, Jg. 29, No. 5, Berlin/East, 1983. Pp. 879–883, notes, [G.H., orig. Georg Hermann Borchardt, Oct. 7, 1871 Berlin – Nov. 19, 1943 Auschwitz, writer.]

20447. HERMLIN, STEPHAN: *Äusserungen 1944–1982*. Hrsg. von Ulrich Dietzel. Berlin/East: Aufbau, 1983. 454 pp.

20448. HESS, MOSES. AVINERI, SHLOMO: *Socialism and Judaism in Moses Hess's 'Holy history of mankind'*. [In]: The Review of Politics, Vol. 45, No. 2, Notre Dame, Ind., Apr. 1983. Pp. 234–253, footnotes.

—— — ESPAGNE, MICHEL: *Heine und Moses Hess*. [See in No. 20434.]

20449. — FISHMAN, ARYEI: *Moses Hess on Judaism and its aptness for a socialist civilization*. [In]: Journal of Religion, Vol. 63, No. 2, Chicago, Apr. 1983. Pp. 143–158, footnotes.

—— — NA'AMAN, SHLOMO: *Emanzipierte rheinische Juden im französisch-deutschen Kulturgefälle: das Beispiel Moses Hess*. [See in No. 19764.]

20450. — ROSEN, ZWI: *Moses Hess und Karl Marx*. Ein Beitrag zur Entstehung der Marxschen Theorie. Hamburg: Christians, 1983. 228 pp., notes (189–218), bibl. (219–225). (Hamburger Beiträge zur Sozial- und Zeitgeschichte, Bd. 18.) [See also the author's article in No. 19769.]

20451. — VOLKOV, SHULAMIT: *Religion and faith in the thought of Moses Hess*. [In]: Zionism, Vol. 2, No. 1, Tel-Aviv, Spring 1981. Pp. 1–16.

20452. HESSEL, FRANZ: *Der Kramladen des Glücks*. Roman. Nachwort von Bernd Witte. Frankfurt am Main: Suhrkamp, 1983. 253 pp. (Bibliothek Suhrkamp, 822.) [Autobiographical novel, written in 1913.] [F.H. data, see No. 18485/YB XXVII.]

20453. HEYM, STEFAN: *Atta Troll; Versuch einer Analyse*. München: Bertelsmann, 1983. 109 pp. [St.H.'s essay on Heine is his M.A. thesis submitted 1936 to the Univ. of Chicago, now publ. on the occasion of H.'s 70th birthday on Apr. 10, 1983 in a limited edn.]

20454. HILDESHEIMER, WOLFGANG: *Marbot*. A biography. Transl. by Patricia Crampton. New York: Braziller, 1983. [Cf.: The man who wasn't there (Gert Schiff) [in]: The New York Review of Books, May 12, 1983, pp. 43–45.]

20455. — HILDESHEIMER, WOLFGANG: *Mozart*. Transl. by Marion Faber. New York: Farrar, Straus & Giroux, 1982; London: Dent, 1983. 416 pp., illus. [Also Vintage Paperback.] [Cf.: What we don't know about Mozart (Peter Gay) [in]: London Review of Books, 3–17 March 1983, p. 12. Amadevious (Alan Tyson) [in]: The New York Review of Books, Nov. 18, 1982, pp. 3 & 6–7. What was he like? (Peter Heyworth) [in]: The Observer, London, 1983.]

20456. HIRSCH, HELMUT. *Bibliographie Helmut Hirsch*. [Hrsg. von der] Univ. Duisburg Gesamthochschule. [Red.: Gabriele Kohaupt.] Duisburg, 1983. 30 pp. [H.H., born Sept. 2, 1907 in Wuppertal-Barmen, historian, returned from USA emigration to Germany in 1957.]

20457. HIRSCHFELD, MAGNUS. HAEBERLE, ERWIN J.: *The birth of sexology*. A brief history in documents, selected and annotated with an introduction. Foreword by Wilhelm A. Kewenig. Washington, D.C., 1983. 47 pp., illus. [On Magnus Hirschfeld (data see No. 18492/YB XXVII), and other German-Jewish sexologists.]

20458. — HAEBERLE, ERWIN J.: *The Jewish contribution to the development of sexology*. [In]: The Journal of Sex Research, Vol. 18, No. 4, Philadelphia, Nov. 1982. Pp. 305–323, footnotes.

20459. HOFMANNSTHAL, HUGO von. *Hofmannsthal-Blätter*. H. 27. Hrsg. von Leonhard M. Fiedler. Frankfurt am Main: Hugo von Hofmannsthal-Gesellschaft, Frühjahr 1983. 125 pp., notes, bibl. Hofmannsthal (113–[126]). [Incl.: 'Ein widerwärtiger Anblick': Karl Kraus als Verteidiger Hofmannsthals gegen unberechtigte Sprachkritik (Hans Eberhard Goldschmidt, 59–61). Hofmannsthal und Kafka (L. M. Fiedler) [&]: Kafka und Hofmannsthal (Hans Sahl) [&]: Franz Kafka: Das Schloss; eine Rezension (Hans Sahl, 62–71). Peter Altenbergs Postkarten (L. M. Fiedler) [&]: 'Keine Ansiedlungen': P. Altenbergs Texte der fünf Orchesterlieder Alban Bergs op. 4 (Gert Mattenklott, 72–91, 7 post card reproductions). Über Rudolf Borchardt und seine 'Jamben' (Werner Vordtriede, 92–106).]

20460. HOLITSCHER, ARTHUR. SEIFERT, HERIBERT: *'Bitte streicht mich nicht aus!' Erinnerungen an den Schriftsteller Arthur Holitscher (1869–1941)*. [In]: NZZ, Nr. 66, Zürich, 19./20. März 1983. P. 66, port. [A.H., Aug. 22, 1869 Budapest – Oct. 14, 1941 Geneva, writer.]

20461. HOLZAPFEL, RUDOLF MARIA: *Hauptwerke*. Bd. 1–2. Aarau: Sauerländer, 1983. 2 vols. (632; 606 pp.). [R.M.H., 1874 Krakow – 1930 Switzerland, philosopher, educated in Switzerland, married to Bettina, daughter of the philosopher Theodor Gomperz.]

20462. HORKHEIMER, MAX. FIGAL, GÜNTER: *Selbsterhaltung und Selbstverzicht; zur Kritik der neuzeitlichen Subjektivität bei Max Horkheimer und Walter Benjamin.* [In]: Zeitschrift für Philosophische Forschung, Bd. 32, H. 2, Meisenheim, Apr.-Juni 1983. Pp. 161–179, footnotes.

—— HUSSERL, EDMUND. BARON, LAWRENCE: *Discipleship and dissent: Theodor Lessing and Edmund Husserl.* [See No. 20520.]

20463. — CHEUNG, CHAN-FAI: *Der anfängliche Boden der Phänomenologie; Heideggers Auseinandersetzung mit der Phänomenologie Husserls in seinen Marburger Vorlesungen.* Frankfurt am Main: Lang, 1983. 235 pp. (Europäische Hochschulschriften: Reihe 20, Bd. 110.)

20464. JACOB, HEINRICH EDUARD: *Der Zwanzigjährige.* Ein symphonischer Roman. Mit einem Nachwort von Hannes Schwenger. Berlin: Agora-Verl., 1983. 295 pp. (Schriftenreihe Agora, Bd. 33.) [First edn. 1918.] [H.E.J., Oct. 7, 1889 Berlin – Oct. 25, 1967 Salzburg, writer.]

—— JACOBY, JOHANN. GRAB, WALTER: *Der deutsch-jüdische Freiheitskämpfer Johann Jacoby.* [See in No. 19769.]

20465. JAHODA, MARIE. KREUZER, FRANZ: *Des Menschen hohe Braut; Arbeit, Freizeit, Arbeitslosigkeit.* Franz Kreuzer im Gespräch mit Marie Jahoda fünfzig Jahre nach der Untersuchung 'Die Arbeitslosen von Marienthal'. [Hrsg.: Österr. Radio und Fernsehen] ORF, Nachtstudio. Wien: Deuticke, 1983. 136 pp. [M.J., born Jan. 26, 1907 in Vienna, sociologist, socialist politician, emigrated in 1938, lives in England.]

20466. JUNGK, ROBERT: *Menschenbeben; der Aufstand gegen das Unerträgliche.* Ein Bericht. München: Bertelsmann, 1983. 222 pp.

20467. KAFKA, FRANZ: *The complete novels: The trial. The castle. America.* Transl. by Willa and Edwin Muir. London: Penguin, 1983. 638 pp. [Cf.: Difficulties of the Kafkaesque (S. S. Prawer) [in]: TLS, London, Oct. 14, 1983.

20468. — KAFKA, FRANZ: *The complete short stories.* Transl. by Willa and Edwin Muir. Ed. by Nahum N. Glatzer, London: Penguin; New York: Schocken, 1983. 486 pp. [Cf.: Kafka's short stories (John Updike) [in]: The New Yorker, May 9, 1983, pp. 121–133.]

20469. — KAFKA, FRANZ: *Kritische Ausgabe: Schriften, Tagebücher, Briefe.* Hrsg. von Jürgen Born [et al.] unter Beratung von Nahum Glatzer [et al.]. Frankfurt am Main: S. Fischer, 1982 ff.
— *Der Verschollene.* Hrsg. von Jost Schillemeit. Text- & Apparatband. 1983. 2 vols. (419; 272 pp., 3 facsims.). [For previously publ. vol. of 'Kritische Ausgabe' see No. 19443/YB XXVIII. Cf.: 'Der Verschollene' (Hartmut Binder) [in]: NZZ, Nr. 271, Zürich, 19./20. Nov. 1983, p. 68. Not by Brod alone (Ritchie Robertson) [in]: TLS, London, 1983.]

20470. — KAFKA, FRANZ: *Der Verschollene.* Roman. Hrsg. von Jost Schillemeit. Frankfurt am Main: S. Fischer, 1983. 426 pp. (Kafka, Franz: Gesammelte Werke in Einzelbänden in der Fassung der Handschrift.) [For previously publ. vol. of 'Gesammelte Werke' see No. 19444/YB XXVIII.]

20471. — ABRAHAM, ULF: *Mose 'Vor dem Gesetz': eine unbekannte Vorlage zu Kafkas 'Türhüterlegende'.* [In]: Deutsche Vierteljahrsschrift für Literaturwissenschaft und Geistesgeschichte, Jg. 57, H. 4, Stuttgart, Dez. 1983. Pp. 636–650, footnotes. [In same issue also essay on 'Das Schloss' (Peter Nutting, 651–678).]

—— — BEICKEN, PETER: *Kafkas 'Prozess' und seine Richter: zur Debatte Brecht-Benjamin und Benjamin-Scholem.* [See in No. 20624.]

20472. — BEZZEL, CHRIS: *Kafka-Chronik; Daten zu Leben und Werk.* München: Deutscher Taschenbuch-Verl., 1983. 216 pp., bibl. Kafka & bibl. (200–208). (dtv, 3252.)

20473. — BORN, JÜRGEN, ed.: *Franz Kafka; Kritik und Rezeption: 1924–1938.* Hrsg. unter Mitwirkung von Elke Koch [et al.]. Frankfurt am Main: S. Fischer, 1983. 508 pp., facsims. [For preceding vol. see No. 16584/YB XXV.]

20474. — FIEDLER, LEONHARD M.: *Zwischen 'Wahrheit' und 'Methode'.* Kafka-Rede in Mainz. [In]: Neue Rundschau, Jg. 94, H. 4, Frankfurt am Main, 1983. Pp. 184–204, facsim. [Incl. a hitherto unknown Kafka-letter to Hans Marderstein, and M.'s reply; also publ. [in]: Die Zeit, Nr. 31, Hamburg, 29. Juli 1983, p. 33.] [See also: Hofmannsthal und Kafka (Fiedler/Hans Sahl) in No. 20459.]

20475. — *Franz Kafka 1883–1924.* [In Hebrew, titles transl.]. [In]: Moznaim, Vol. 57, No. 3, Tel-Aviv, Aug. 1983. Pp. 13–31. [Special section dedicated to Kafka, incl. (in Hebrew): Memories of F. Kafka (S. H. Bergmann, 14–16). 'The trial' by Kafka (Gershom Scholem, 17; a paragraph found in Sch.'s literary estate, written 1926). Judaism and Christianity in the works of F.K. (Hillel Barzel, 20–22).]

20476. — GOLDSTÜCKER, EDUARD: *Über Franz Kafkas 'jüdische Dinge'*. [In]: 'Allgemeine', Nr. 24, Düsseldorf, 17. Juni 1983. P. 3.

20477. — HACKERMÜLLER, ROTRAUD: *Die Zeugen von Kierling: Franz Kafkas letzte Tage*. [And]: *Kannten Sie Kafka?* Der Nachforschungen zweiter Teil. [In]: Morgen, Jg. 7, Nr. 28 [&]: 32, St. Pölten, Apr. [&] Dez. 1983. Pp. 69–76; 341–345, illus., ports.

20478. — HAYMAN, RONALD: *Kafka: sein Leben, seine Welt, sein Werk*. Übers. aus dem Engl. des vom Autor für die deutsche Fassung neu überarb. Werks von Karl A. Klewer.) Bern: Scherz, 1983. 399 pp. [Transl. of a revised version of No. 18505/YB XXVII.]

20479. — JESSEN, NORBERT: *'Pua . . . ist ganz verschollen': Begegnung mit Franz Kafkas Hebräisch-Lehrerin*. [In]: 'Allgemeine', Nr. 37, Düsseldorf, 16. Sept. 1983, p. 8 [& in]: Aufbau, No. 30, New York, July 29, 1983, p. 11. [Refers to Pua Menczel-Bentovim who lives in Jerusalem.]

20480. — MAGRIS, CLAUDIO: *Bis an die Schwelle der Wahrheit; Kafkas Lebensangst und Sehnsucht nach der ostjüdischen Welt*. [And]: ENGEL, PETER: *Eine Dichterfreundschaft: Franz Kafka und Ernst Weiss*. [In]: NZZ, Nr. 152, Zürich, 2./3. Juli 1983. Pp. 57–58. [In same issue are 4 more literary essays on F.K. (58–60).]

20481. — NAGEL, BERT: *Kafka und die Weltliteratur; Zusammenhänge und Wechselwirkungen*. München: Winkler, 1983. 447 pp., notes. [Incl. chap.: Jüdisches Erbe.]

20482. — PÜTZ, JÜRGEN: *Kafkas 'Verschollener' – ein Bildungsroman?* Die Sonderstellung von Kafkas Romanfragment 'Der Verschollene' in der Tradition des Bildungsromans. Frankfurt am Main: Lang, 1983. 84 pp., illus., bibl. (75–81). (Europäische Hochschulschriften: Reihe 1, Bd. 690.)

20483. — ROBERTSON, RITCHIE: *Kafka's Zürau aphorisms*. [In]: Oxford German Studies, 14, Oxford, 1983. Pp. 73–91, notes. [Also on K.'s interest in Zionism and Jewish mysticism.]

20484. — STROLZ, WALTER: *Kafkas Vertrauen zum Unzerstörbaren im Menschen*. [In]: Frankfurter Hefte, Jg. 38, H. 11, Frankfurt am Main, 1983. Pp. 53–63, footnotes. [On the biblical Jewish tradition in K.'s writings.]

20485. — TAKAHASH, Y.: *Der Einfluss des jiddischen Theaters auf Kafka; zu 'Eine Geschichte: Das Urteil'*. [In Japanese, with German summary]. [In]: Doitsu Bungaku, No. 70, Tokyo, Frühling 1983. Pp. 118–127, notes.

20486. — *Thema: Franz Kafka, nachgestellt*. [In]: Freibeuter, 16, Berlin, 1983. Pp. 33–90, illus., notes [Incl.: Kafka-Familienlexikon: ein kleiner Überblick über erfolgreiche und weniger erfolgreiche Verwandte (Anthony Northey, 48–59). Drei Sanatorien K.'s: ihre Bauten und Gebräuche (Klaus Wagenbach, 77–90).]

20487. — UEDA, KAZUO: *Franz Kafka und die jiddische Literatur; über M[eyer] Pinès' 'L'histoire de la littérature judéo-allemande'*. [In]: Research Reports of the Kôchi University, Vol. 31–32, Kôchi, 1982–1983. 2 pts. in 1. [Available in the LBI New York.]

20488. — WAGENBACH, KLAUS, ed.: *Franz Kafka: Bilder aus seinem Leben*. Berlin: Wagenbach, 1983. 191 pp., mostly illus., ports., facsims.

20489. — WINEGARTEN, RENEE: *The Kafka legacy*. [In]: The Jewish Quarterly, Vol. 30, No. 4, London, Spring-Summer 1983. Pp. 26–29.

20490. KALÉKO, MASCHA: *Hat alles seine zwei Schattenseiten*. Sinn- und Unsinngedichte. Mit dem 'Kasseler Vortrag' 'Die paar leuchtenden Jahre'. Hrsg. und mit einem Nachwort von Gisela Zoch-Westphal. Berlin: arani, 1983. 89 pp., illus.

—— KALISCH, LUDWIG. SCHOEPS, JULIUS H.: *An der Seite der Unterdrückten: Ludwig Kalisch (1813–1882)*. [See in No. 19769.]

20491. KAMNITZER, HEINZ: *Heimsuchung und Testament*. 2., erweiterte Aufl. Leipzig: Reclam, 1983. 325 pp. (Reclams Universal-Bibliothek, Bd. 875.) [Collection of essays, a.o., on Feuchtwanger, Anna Seghers, Arnold Zweig.] [H.K., born May 10, 1917 in Berlin, historian, returned from exile in England to the GDR.]

20492. KASTEIN, JOSEF. DREYER, ALFRED: *Josef Kastein: Entscheidung für Erez Israel [1935–1946]*. [In]: Bulletin des LBI, 66, Königstein/Ts., 1983. Pp. 23–51, notes (42–51). [For essays by the author on Kastein's earlier years, see No. 18512/YB XXVII.] [J.K., orig. Katzenstein, Oct. 6, 1890 Bremen – June 13, 1946 Haifa, writer and biographer.]

20493. KAUFMANN, GEBRÜDER. ROHLÉN-WOHLGEMUTH, HILDE: *Gebrüder Kaufmann, Elberfeld; die Geschichte eines jüdischen Kaufhauses 1894–1936*. [In]: Zeitschrift des Bergischen Geschichtsvereins, Bd. 90 (1982/1983), Elberfeld, 1983. Pp. 83–142, illus., footnotes.

20494. KELSEN, HANS. *Gesellschaft, Staat und Recht*. Untersuchungen zur reinen Rechtslehre. Festschrift Hans Kelsen zum 50. Geburtstage gewidmet. Unter Mitarbeit von J. Dobretsberger [et al.] hrsg. von Alfred Verdross. Unveränd. Neudr. der Ausg. Wien,

Springer, 1931. Liechtenstein: Topos, 1983. 441 pp., bibl. Kelsen (417–441). [H.K. data, see No. 18514/YB XXVII.]

495. KERR, ALFRED. CARR, G. J.: *'Organic' contradictions in Alfred Kerr's theatre criticism.* [In]: Oxford German Studies, 14, Oxford, 1983. Pp. 111–124, notes.

— — HUDER, WALTER: *Kerrs kritisches Temperament gegenüber der Weimarer Republik.* [See in No. 20319.]

496. — MIDDELL, EIKE: *Der verbrannte Kritiker Alfred Kerr.* [In]: Weimarer Beiträge, Jg. 29, H. 5, Berlin/East, 1983. Pp. 867–878, notes.

497. KESTEN, HERMANN, ed.: *24 neue deutsche Erzähler.* Reprint mit einer Nachbemerkung von Wulf Kirsten. 3. Aufl., unveränd. Nachdr. der 2. Aufl. 1929. Leipzig: Kiepenheuer, 1983. 429 pp.

498. KISCH, EGON ERWIN: *Karl Marx in Karlsbad.* Berlin/East: Aufbau, 1983. 79 pp., illus.

499. — KISCH, EGON ERWIN: *Mein Leben für die Zeitung.* Journalistische Texte. Bd. 1: 1906–1925. Bd. 2: 1926–1947. Berlin/East: Aufbau, 1983. 2 vols. (535; 581 pp.), bibl. (Kisch, E.E.: Gesammelte Werke, Bd. 8–9.)

500. — KISCH, EGON ERWIN: *Der rasende Reporter.* Mit einem Nachwort von Hans-Albert Walter. Köln: Kiepenheuer & Witsch, 1983. 409 pp.

501. — SCHANNE, KARIN: *Anschläge; der rasende Reporter Egon Erwin Kisch.* Stuttgart: Klett, 1983. 205 pp., illus. (Klett-Kaktus.) [Biography.]

0502. — ZAMIS, GUIDO: *Egon Erwin Kisch und die Wiener Rote Garde.* [In]: Beiträge zur Geschichte der Arbeiterbewegung, Jg. 24, Nr. 5, Berlin/East, 1982. Pp. 719–733.

0503. KLEMPERER, OTTO. HEYWORTH, PETER: *Otto Klemperer: his life and times. Vol. 1: 1885–1933.* Cambridge: Cambridge Univ. Press, 1983. 492 pp., illus.

0504. KOENIG, ALMA JOHANNA. RAYNAUD, FRANZISKA: *Alma Johanna Koenig (1887–1942?): Leben und Dichten einer Wienerin.* [In]: Bulletin des LBI, 64, Königstein/Ts., 1983. Pp. 29–54, notes (52–54), bibl. Koenig (50–51). [A.J.K. data, see No. 18794/YB XXVII.]

0505. KOESTLER, ARTHUR. *The life and death of Arthur Koestler; memoirs, tributes, documents.* [In]: Encounter, Vol. 61, No. 1 & 2, London, July-Aug. & Sept.-Oct. 1983. Pp. 9–37; 45–64. [*No. 1* incl.: A writer's greatness (Raymond Aron, 9–12). Biographee (Ian Hamilton, 18–22). Author (Harold Harris, 23–25). *No. 2:* Jew (Hyam Maccoby, 50–53). 'Micromemoirs'; pages from an unpubl. manuscript (A. Koestler, 57–59). Remembering (Melvin J. Lasky, 59–64).] [See also Nos. 20690–20691.]

0506. — *Obituaries and articles in commemoration of Arthur Koestler,* Sept. 5, 1905 Budapest – March 3, 1983 London (selection): A.K. and his wife are found dead [in]: Internat. Herald Tribune, Zürich, March 4, 1983, pp. 1 & 3. A.K.'s Suizid und seine geistig-weltanschaulichen Hintergründe (Günter Gödde) [in]: Neue Deutsche Hefte, 180, Berlin, 1983, pp. 776–787. A.K. and wife suicides in London (Eric Page) [&]: A.K., an intellectual and man of action (Walter Goodman) [in]: The New York Times, March 4, 1983. Koestlers Sprung in die Tiefe (Joachim Kaiser) [in]: SZ, Nr. 52, München, 4. März 1983, p. 47. A.K. and wife found dead in flat (John Witherow) [&]: Obituary [in]: The Times, London, March 4, 1983. So spielt niemand mehr (Karl-Heinz Wocker) [in]: Die Zeit, Nr. 11, Hamburg, 11. März 1983, p. 60.]

0507. KOLMAR, GERTRUD: *Gedichte.* Auswahl und Nachwort von Ulla Hahn. Frankfurt am Main: Suhrkamp, 1983. 186 pp., port. (Bibliothek Suhrkamp, Bd. 815.) [G.K., orig. Chodziesner, Dec. 10, 1894 Berlin – 1943 deported, date and place of death not known, writer.]

0508. KRAMER, THEODOR: *Orgel aus Staub.* Gesammelte Gedichte. Ausgewählt von Erwin Chvojka. Mit einem Nachwort von Hans Jurgen Fröhlich. München: Hanser, 1983. 170 pp. [Th.K., Jan. 1, 1897 Niederhollabrunn, Austria – Apr. 3, 1958 Vienna, poet, emigrated to England in 1939, from 1957 in Austria.]

0509. — KRAMER, THEODOR: *Verbannt aus Österreich.* Neue Gedichte. [Neudr. der Originalausg. des Austrian PEN, London, 1943.] Wien: Böhlau, 1983. 48 pp.

0510. — KAISER, KONSTANTIN, ed.: *Theodor Kramer, 1897–1958, Dichter im Exil.* Aufsätze und Dokumente. Wien (Gumpendorferstr. 15): Dokumentationsstelle für Neuere Österr. Literatur, 1983. 141 pp., bibl. (136–141). (Zirkular, Sondernummer 4.)

0511. KRAUS, KARL. *Kraus-Hefte.* H. 25–28. München: Edition Text & Kritik, Jan., Juli, Okt. 1983. 3 issues. [Issue titles]: H. 25: LIEGLER, LEOPOLD: *Meine Erinnerungen an Karl Kraus.* [L. Liegler, 1882–1949, editorial assistant of K.K. from 1915–1924, wrote these reminiscences in the 1940s, now publ. for the first time]. H. 26/27: HALL, MURRAY G. *Verlage um K.K.* H. 28: *Vermischte Beiträge.*

20512. — MITMASSER, PETER F.: *Der Gesinnungswandel von Karl Kraus zu Monarchie, Kaiserhaus und Ade in der Darstellung der 'Fackel' (1899–1936).* Wien, Univ., Diss., 1983. VI, 285 pp.

—— — VIETTA, SILVIO: *Die Ideologiekritik von Karl Kraus.* [See in No. 19764. See also: A. Ehrenstei und K.K. (No. 20382); K.K. als Verteidiger Hofmannsthals (in No. 20459).]

20513. KUH, ANTON: *Zeitgeist im Literatur-Café.* Feuilletons, Essays und Publizistik. Neu Sammlung. Hrsg. und mit einem Nachwort von Ulrike Lehner. Wien: Löcker, 1983. 287 pp [For preceding vol. see No. 18528/YB XXVII. See also No. 20282.]

20514. KURZ, SELMA. HALBAN, DESI, ed.: *Selma Kurz; die Sängerin und ihre Zeit.* Hrsg. unte Mitarb. von Ursula Ebbers. Stuttgart: Belser, 1983. 224 pp., illus. [Incl. letters by Gusta Mahler.] [S.K., 1874 Bielitz – May 1933 Vienna, singer.]

20515. LASKER-SCHÜLER, ELSE: *Der Malik; eine Kaisergeschichte.* Mit Zeichnungen von Els Lasker-Schüler. Mit einem Nachwort von Erich Fried. Kiel: Neuer Malik-Verl., 1983. 18 pp. [1st edn. 1919.]

20516. — HARTENSTEIN, ELFI: *Wenn auch meine Paläste zerfallen sind: Else Lasker-Schüler 1909/191* Erzählung. Bremen: Schreiben Frauenliteraturverl., 1983. 165 pp.

20517. — HESSING, JAKOB: *Else Lasker-Schüler: Dichterin ohne Geschichte.* Die jüdischen, christliche und deutschen Mythen in ihrer Nachkriegsrezeption. [In]: Bulletin des LBI, 65 Königstein/Ts., 1983. Pp. 23–52, notes (50–52).

20518. — SIMA, MIRON: *Evening and parting: Else Lasker-Schüler in Jerusalem.* Sketches and memories [In Hebrew]. Givatayim: Massada, 1983. [40] pp., ports.

—— LASSALLE, FERDINAND. NA'AMAN, SHLOMO: *Revolutionstheorie und revolutionäre Praxis be Ferdinand Lassalle.* [See in No. 19769. See also the author's essay in No. 19825.]

20519. LESSING, THEODOR: *Geschichte als Sinngebung des Sinnlosen.* Mit einem Nachwort von Rit Bischof. München: Matthes & Seitz, 1983. 291 pp., illus. (Batterien, 17.)

20520. — BARON, LAWRENCE: *Discipleship and dissent: Theodor Lessing and Edmund Husserl.* [In] Proceedings of the American Philosophical Society, 127 (No. 1), Philadelphia, 1983. Pp 32–49.

20521. — MA'OR, YITZCHAK: *For you have struggled with hatred; Theodor Lessing in confrontation with self hatred – 50 years since his murder.* [In Hebrew, title transl.]. [In]: Shdemot, No. 86/87, Tel-Aviv Sept. 1983. Pp. 89–100.

20522. — SCHOEPS, JULIUS H.: *Der ungeliebte Aussenseiter: zum 50. Todestag des Philosophen un Schriftstellers Theodor Lessing.* [In]: Tribüne, Jg. 22, H. 88, Frankfurt am Main, 1983. Pp 150–160.

20523. LEVI, PAUL, QUACK, SIBYLLE: *Geistig frei und niemandes Knecht. Paul Levi – Rosa Luxemburg politische Arbeit und persönliche Beziehung.* Mit 50 unveröffentlichten Briefen. Köln Kiepenheuer & Witsch, 1983. 295 pp., illus., bibl. (285–296). [P.L., March 11, 188 Hechingen – Feb. 9, 1930 Berlin, lawyer, socialist politician, defence lawyer of Ros Luxemburg.] [See also Charlotte Beradt's first biography of P. Levi and her collection of L.' writings and letters, Nos. 8130–8131/YB XV.]

20524. LEWIN, KURT: *Kurt-Lewin-Werkausgabe.* Hrsg. von Carl-Friedrich Graumann. *Bd. 2 Wissenschaftstheorie, 2.* Hrsg. von Alexandre Métraux. Bern: Huber; Stuttgart: Klett-Cotta 1983. 531 pp., illus., bibl. [For previously publ. vols. 1, 4 & 6 see Nos. 18538/YB XXVII & 19481/YB XXVIII.]

20525. LEWIN, LOUIS: *Die Gifte in der Weltgeschichte.* Toxikologische allgemeinverständlich Untersuchungen der historischen Quellen. Hildesheim: Gerstenberg, 1983. 596 pp. [L.L data, see No. 17576/YB XXVI.]

20526. LÖWENTHAL, RICHARD: *Weltpolitische Betrachtungen.* Essays aus zwei Jahrzehnten Hrsg. und eingeleitet von Heinrich August Winkler. Göttingen: Vandenhoeck & Ruprecht 1983. 313 pp.

20527. LÖWITH, KARL: *Sämtliche Schriften 2: Weltgeschichte und Heilsgeschehen; zur Kritik de Geschichtsphilosophie.* Stuttgart: Metzler, 1983. 617 pp. [For vol. 1 see No. 18539/YB XXVII.]

20528. LOWE, ADOLPH: *Was Freiheit bedeuten kann.* [In]: Die Zeit, Nr. 31, Hamburg, 29. Juli 1983 P. 28. [Address on the occasion of the receipt of an honorary doctorate from the Univ. o Bremen.] [A.L., orig. Löwe, born March 4, 1893 in Stuttgart, economist, emigrated t England in 1933, after 1940 professor at the New School for Social Research in New York.]

20529. — *Social Research.* Vol. 50, No. 2 [with the issue title]: *Value, growth and economic policy: essays i tribute to Adolph Lowe.* Guest ed.: Edward Nell. New York, Summer 1983. [Incl.: A. Lowe at 9

(Edward Nell, 251–252). An overlooked chapter of economic thought: the 'New School's' effort to salvage Weimar's economy (Claus-Dieter Krohn, 452–468, footnotes; especially on A. Lowe, also on, a.o. Eduard Heimann, Emil Lederer).]

20530. LUBITSCH, ERNST. PAUL, WILLIAM: *Ernst Lubitsch's American comedy*. Foreword by Andrew Sarris. New York: Columbia Univ. Press, 1983. 359 pp., illus. [Cf.: Touching Lubitsch (Rhoda Koenig) [in]: The New York Review of Books, Feb. 16, 1984, pp. 34–36.] [E.L., Jan. 28, 1892 Berlin – Nov. 28, 1947 Hollywood, film producer and director, from 1922 in Los Angeles.]

20531. LUKÁCS, GEORG. CONGDON, LEE: *The young Lukács*. Chapel Hill, N.C.: Univ. of North Carolina Press, 1983. XIII, 235 pp. [Cf.: The Marxian matrix (Martin Jay) [in]: TLS, London, Oct. 7, 1983, p. 1092.]

20532. — HELLER, AGNES, ed.: *Lukács reappraised*. New York: Columbia Univ. Press, 1983. 204 pp.

20533. — LUNN, EUGENE: *Marxism and modernism; an historical study of Lukács, Brecht, Benjamin and Adorno*. Berkeley: Univ. of California Press, 1982. VI, 330 pp., bibl. (289–322). [Cf.: Review (Terry Eagleton) [in]: Journal of Modern History, Vol. 56, No. 1, Chicago, March 1984.]

20534. — RADDATZ, FRITZ J.: *Tränen hinter der Maske; Georg Lukács: 'Briefwechsel 1902–1917': eine literarische Entdeckung*. [In]: Die Zeit, Nr. 46, Hamburg, 11. Nov. 1983. P. Lit. 4. [Review essay on No. 19630/YB XXVIII.]

—— — SHEVTSOVA, MARIA: *Die Brecht-Lukács-Debatte gegen den Expressionismus*. [See in No. 20294.]

—— LUXEMBURG, ROSA. QUACK, SIBYLLE: *Geistig frei und niemandes Knecht: Paul Levi – Rosa Luxemburg*. [See No. 20523.]

20535. MAHLER, GUSTAV. MONSON, KAREN: *Alma Mahler: muse to genius*. Boston: Houghton Mifflin, 1983. London: Collins, 1984. 348 pp. [Cf.: Having it all (Gabriele Annan) [in]: The New York Review of Books, Sept. 29, 1983, pp. 4–10.]

20536. — WESSLING, BERNDT W.: *Alma: Gefährtin von Gustav Mahler, Oskar Kokoschka, Walter Gropius, Franz Werfel*. Düsseldorf: Claassen, 1983. 302 pp., illus.

20537. MARCUSE, HERBERT. AKARD, PATRICK: *The 'theory-praxis nexus' in Marcuse's theory*. [In]: Dialectical Anthropology, Vol. 8, No. 3, Amsterdam, Dec. 1983. Pp. 207–215, notes.

—— MARX, KARL: *Neue Rheinische Zeitung*. Redigiert von Karl Marx. [See No. 20312.]

20538. — MARX, KARL: *Zur Judenfrage*. Die antisemitischen Schriften, hrsg. von Hartwig Brandt. Berlin: Reichmann, 1982. 55 pp. [See also: Der Judenfeind Karl Marx (Hans Lamm) [in]: 'Allgemeine', Nr. 11, Düsseldorf, 18. März 1983, p. 7.]

20539. — ANDREAS, BERT: *Karl Marx, Friedrich Engels, das Ende der klassischen deutschen Philosophie; Bibliographie*. Deutsch von Elisabeth Krieger. Trier: Karl-Marx-Haus, 1983. 248 pp. (Schriften aus dem Karl-Marx-Haus Trier, Nr. 28.)

20540. — BILLSTEIN, HEINRICH: *Marx in Köln*. Mit einem Beitrag von Karl Obermann. Köln: Pahl-Rugenstein, 1983. 218 pp. (Kleine Bibliothek, 287.) [See also: Karl Marx und Köln 1842–1852; Ausstellung zum 100. Todestag. Bearb.: Everhard Kleinertz. Köln: Histor. Archiv, 1983. 178 pp., illus.]

20541. — FEUER, LEWIS S.: *The case of the revolutionist's daughter; Sherlock Holmes meets Karl Marx*. Buffalo, N.Y.: Prometheus Books, 1983. 159 pp. [Novel about the life and death of Marx's daughter Eleanor. Cf.: Karl Marx and Sherlock Holmes (Nathaniel Weyl) [in]: Midstream, Vol. 30, No. 3, New York, March 1984, pp. 58–59.]

20542. — FLECHTHEIM, OSSIP K., ed.: *Marx heute – pro und contra*. Hamburg: Hoffmann & Campe, 1983. 336 pp. [Cont. 17 essays, a.o., by Helmut Hirsch, Leo Kofler, Richard Löwenthal, Ernest Mandel.]

20543. — FONER, PHILIP S., ed.: *Karl Marx remembered; comments at the time of his death*. San Francisco, Calif.: Synthesis Publ., 1983. 304 pp. [Paperback edn.]

20544. — HERFERTH, WILLI: *Sachregister zu den Werken Karl Marx, Friedrich Engels = Subject index to the works Karl Marx, Friedrich Engels*. Hrsg. und eingeleitet von Hans Jörg Sandkühler. Köln: Pahl-Rugenstein, 1983. LXIV, 918 pp. (Studien zur Dialektik.)

20545. — HIRSCH, HELMUT/PELGER, HANS: *Ein unveröffentlichter Brief von Karl Marx an Sophie von Hatzfeldt; zum Streit mit Karl Blind nach Ferdinand Lassalles Tod*. Erweiterter Separat-Abdr. aus International Review of Social History, Vol. 27 (1982), Pt. 2. Trier: Karl-Marx-Haus, 1983. 65 pp., illus., footnotes. (Schriften aus dem Karl-Marx-Haus Trier, Nr. 27.)

—— — HIRSCH, HELMUT: *Karl Marx zur 'Judenfrage' und zu Juden*. [See in No. 19769.]

20546. — KAPP, YVONNE: *Karl Marx's children*. [In]: New Left Review, No. 138, London, March-Apr. 1983 [Marx centenary issue]. Pp. 69–84, notes. [On M.'s private life.]

—— — KLEPFISZ, HESZEL: *Bergson, Freud and Marx – their Jewish problem*. [See No. 20216.]

20547. — KOVEL, JOEL: *Marx on the Jewish Question.* [In]: Dialectical Anthropology, Vol. 8, Nos. 1–2, Amsterdam, 1983. Pp. 31–46, notes.

20548. — LEVENBERG, S.: *The place of Karl Marx in history.* [In]: The Jewish Quarterly, Vol. 30, No. 4, London, Spring-Summer, 1983. Pp. 9–12.

20549. — MCLELLAN, DAVID, ed.: *Marx: the first hundred years.* London: Pinter, 1983. 288 pp. [Also paperback]: London: Fontana, 1983. 320 pp. [See also: Marx in England (David McLellan) [in]: History Today, Vol. 33, London, March 1983, pp. 5–10, illus.]

20550. — PRAWER, SIEGBERT S.: *Karl Marx und die Weltliteratur.* Aus dem Engl. übers. von Christian Spiel. München: Beck, 1983. 405 pp., bibl. Marx & bibl. (387–394). [Cf.: Ein nicht mehr überbietbares Standard-Werk (Rolf Schneider) [in]: Die Zeit, Nr. 1, 30. Dez. 1983, p. 11. For Engl. orig. and reviews see No. 13939/YB XXII; for review essay see No. 14746/YB XXIII.]

—— — ROSEN, ZWI: *Moses Hess' Einfluss auf die Entfremdungstheorie von Karl Marx.* [See in No. 19769; see also No. 20450.]

20551. — RUBINSTEIN, W. D.: *Marx reconsidered.* [In]: Midstream, Vol. 29, No. 1, New York, Jan. 1983. Pp. 56–58. [Deals with Marx's racialist attitudes and refers to the book 'Karl Marx: racist' by Nathaniel Weyl, New Rochelle, Arlington House, 1979.]

20552. — WALICKI, ANDRZEJ: *Marx and freedom.* [In]: The New York Review of Books, Nov. 24, 1983. Pp. 50–55. [Also on M.'s 'On the Jewish Question'.]

20553. — WILCKE, GERO von: *Karl Marx' Trierer Verwandtschaftskreis.* Zu seinem 100. Geburtstag. [In]: Genealogie, Jg. 32, H. 12, Neustadt/Aisch, Dez. 1983. Pp. 761–782, ports., facsims., geneal. tab., footnotes.

20554. MAUTHNER, FRITZ: *Sprache und Sozialismus.* [In]: Holzfeuer im hölzernen Ofen; Aufsätze zur politischen Sprachkritik. Hrsg.: Hans Jürgen Heringer. Tübingen: Narr, 1982. Pp. 37–47.

20555. MAYER, HANS: *Ein Denkmal für Johannes Brahms; Versuche über Musik und Literatur.* Frankfurt am Main: Suhrkamp, 1983. 209 pp. (Bibliothek Suhrkamp, Bd. 812.) [Incl.: Über den 'Lobgesang' opus 52 von Felix Mendelssohn Bartholdy. Hugo von Hofmannsthal und Richard Strauss. Gustav Mahler und die Literatur. Zeitgenosse Arnold Schönberg.]

20556. MEHRING, WALTER: *Die Nacht des Tyrannen.* Roman. Düsseldorf: Claassen, 1983. 143 pp. (Mehring, Walter: Werke, Bd. 10.) [1st edn. Zürich, Oprecht, 1937.]

20557. — MEHRING, WALTER: *Verrufene Malerei.* Erinnerungen eines Zeitgenossen und 14 Essais zur Kunst. Berlin Dada. Düsseldorf: Claassen, 1983. 332 pp., illus. (Mehring, Walter: Werke.)

20558. — HELLBERG, FRANK: *Walter Mehring – Schriftsteller zwischen Kabarett und Avantgarde.* Bonn: Bouvier, 1983. 305 pp.

20559. — *Walter Mehring.* München: Edition Text & Kritik, 1983. 83 pp., bibl. Mehring & bibl. (72–81). (text + kritik, H. 78.)

20560. MEITNER, LISE. STOLZ, W.: *Otto Hahn – Lise Meitner.* Leipzig: Teubner, 1983. 100 pp., illus. (Biographien hervorragender Naturwissenschaftler, Bd. 64.) [L.M., Nov. 7, 1878 Vienna – Oct. 27, 1968 Cambridge, England, nuclear physicist.]

20561. MENDELSOHN, ERICH. ZEVI, BRUNO: *Erich Mendelsohn.* (Aus dem Ital. übers.) Zürich: Verlag für Architektur Artemis, 1983. 208 pp., illus., bibl. (204–208). (Studio-Paperback.) [E.M. data, see No. 18557/YB XXVII.]

20562. MENDELSSOHN FAMILY. ELVERS, RUDOLF: *Besondere Erwerbungen: Dokumente zur Geschichte des Bankhauses Mendelssohn.* [In]: Mitteilungen der Staatsbibliothek Preussischer Kulturbesitz, Berlin, Nov. 1983. Pp. 192–193.

20563. — *Die Mendelssohns in Berlin: eine Familie und ihre Stadt.* Ausstellung des Mendelssohn-Archivs der Staatsbibliothek Preussischer Kulturbesitz Berlin. Katalog. (Bearb. von Rudolf Elvers und Hans-Günter Klein.) Wiesbaden: Reichert, 1983. 266 pp., illus., ports., facsims., geneal. [Incl. 11 essays.]

20564. — WILCKE, GERO von: *Die Mendelssohns in Leipzig, Vorfahren und Nachkommen.* [In]: Genealogie, Jg. 32, H. 4, Neustadt/Aisch, Apr. 1983. Pp. 497–519, illus., ports., geneal. tabs.

20565. MENDELSSOHN, PETER de: *Die Kathedrale; ein Sommernachtmahr.* Mit einem Nachwort von Hilde Spiel. Hamburg: Knaus, 1983. 263 pp. [Cf.: Ein Vermächtnis (Albert von Schirnding) [in]: SZ, Nr. 124, München, 1./2. Juni 1983, p. 13.]

20566. MENDELSSOHN BARTHOLDY, FELIX. BODLEIAN LIBRARY, Oxford: *Catalogue of the Mendelssohn papers in the Bodleian Library, Oxford. Vol. 2: Music and papers.* Comp. by Margaret Crum. Tutzing: Schneider, 1983. XII, 133 pp. (Musikbibliographische Arbeiten, Bd. 8.) [For vol. 1 see No. 18558/YB XXVII.]

20567. MOSSE, ALBERT. MOSSE, WERNER E.: *Albert Mosse: a Jewish judge in Imperial Germany.* [In]: LBI Year Book XXVIII, London, 1983. Pp. 169–184, footnotes, ports. [A.M., 1846 Grätz, Poznań – 1925 Berlin.]

20568. MÜHSAM, ERICH: *Gesamtausgabe. Bd. 1: Gedichte.* Hrsg. von Günther Emig. Berlin: Verlag Europäische Ideen, 1983. 736 pp. [For previously publ. vols. 2–4 see No. 15632/YB XXIV; the final vol. 5 will follow.]

20569. — MÜHSAM, ERICH: *Ich bin verdammt zu warten in einem Bürgergarten.* Hrsg. von Wolfgang Haug. Bd. 1–2. Orig.-Ausg. Darmstadt: Luchterhand, 1983. 2 vols., bibl. Mühsam & bibl. (Sammlung Luchterhand, 467–468.) *Bd. 1: Gedichte, Stücke, Prosa.* 183 pp. *Bd. 2: Literarische und politische Aufsätze.* 197 pp. [Cf.: Der ewige Bismarxismus: Erinnerung an E. Mühsam (Karl Riha) [in]: Die Zeit, Nr. 46, Hamburg, 11. Nov. 1983, p. Lit. 3.]

20570. — KAUFFELDT, ROLF: *Erich Mühsam; Literatur und Anarchie.* München: Fink, 1983. 398 pp., illus. (Uni-Taschenbücher, 1259.)

20571. — SCHIEWE, JÜRGEN: *Zur anarchistischen Ästhetik Erich Mühsams.* [In]: Wirkendes Wort, Jg. 32, H. 6, Düsseldorf, Nov./Dez. 1982. Pp. 419–431, notes.

20572. MÜNZER, FRIEDRICH. KNEPPE, ALFRED/WIESEHÖFER, JOSEF: *Friedrich Münzer; ein Althistoriker zwischen Kaiserreich und Nationalsozialismus.* Zum 20. Okt. 1982. Mit einem kommentierten Schriftenverzeichnis von Hans-Joachim Drexhage. Bonn: Habelt, 1983. VIII, 310 pp., illus., bibl. Münzer (159–259), bibl. (280–300). [F.M., Apr. 22, 1868 Oppeln – Oct. 20, 1942 Theresienstadt, historian.]

20573. NA'AMAN, SHLOMO. *Arbeiterbewegung und Geschichte; Festschrift für Shlomo Na'aman zum 70. Geburtstag.* Hrsg.: Hans-Peter Harstick, Arno Herzig, Hans Pelger. Trier: Karl-Marx-Haus, 1983. 240 pp., illus., bibl. Na'aman (233–237). (Schriften aus dem Karl-Marx-Haus Trier, 29.) [Incl.: Shlomo Na'aman als Historiker der deutschen Arbeiterbewegung (Gerhard A. Ritter, 9–19). Julius Moses: seine 'jüdische Epoche' (Daniel Nadav, 82–100). Also documents and studies on Karl Marx.] [Sh.N., born 1912 in Essen, emeritus professor of social history at the Univ. Tel-Aviv.]

20574. NAPHTALI, FRITZ. RIEMER, JEHUDA: *Nach dem Zusammenbruch: Fritz Naphtali im Briefwechsel 1933–34.* [In]: Internat. Review of Social History, Vol. 27, Pt. 3, Assen, Netherlands, 1982. Pp. 324–356, footnotes. [F.N. data, see No. 18563/YB XXVII.]

20575. NEUMANN, ROBERT. BROERMAN, BRUCE M.: *Robert Neumann's 'Struensee': potboiler or patent parody?* [In]: Modern Austrian Literature, Vol. 16, No. 2, Riverside, Calif., 1983. Pp. 105–119, notes. [R.N., May 22, 1897 Vienna – Jan. 3, 1975 Munich, writer, emigrated to England in 1934.]

20576. NEUMANN, SALOMON. KARBE, KARL-HEINZ: *Salomon Neumann, 1819–1908; Wegbereiter sozialmedizinischen Denkens und Handelns.* Leipzig: J. A. Barth, 1983. 219 pp., illus., bibl. [Cont. biogr. essay (K.-H. Karbe, 11–86) and selected texts from S.N.'s writings.] [S.N., Oct. 22, 1819 Pyritz – Sept. 20, 1908 Berlin, physician, statistician, democratic politician, co-founder of the Lehranstalt (Hochschule) für die Wissenschaft des Judentums.]

20577. OPPENHEIM, SALOMON jr. TREUE, WILHELM: *Das Schicksal des Bankhauses Sal. Oppenheim jr. & Cie. und seiner Inhaber im Dritten Reich.* Wiesbaden: Steiner, 1983. VII, 117 pp. (Zeitschrift für Unternehmensgeschichte, Beih. 27.)

20578. OPPENHEIMER, JOSEF SÜSSKIND. EMBERGER, GUDRUN: *Verdruss, Sorg und Widerwärtigkeiten: die Inventur und Verwaltung des Jud Süssischen Vermögens 1737–1772.* [In]: Zeitschrift für Württembergische Landesgeschichte, Jg. 40 (1981), Stuttgart, 1982. Pp. 369–375, footnotes. [J.S.O., 'Jud Süss', Feb. 12, 1692 Heidelberg – Feb. 5, 1738 Stuttgart, Court Jew.]

—— — WOLF, JÜRGEN RAINER: *Joseph Süss Oppenheimer ('Jud Süss') und die Darmstädter Goldmünze.* [See in No. 19832.]

20579. ORLIK, EMIL. SCHÜTTE, MARGRET: *Emil Orlik: Graphik im Berliner Kupferstichkabinett.* Berlin: Mann, 1983. 94 pp., mostly illus. (Bilderhefte der Staatlichen Museen Preuss. Kulturbesitz Berlin, H. 43/44.) [E.O. data, see No. 19519/YB XXVIII.]

20580. PEVSNER, NIKOLAUS: *Wegbereiter moderner Formgebung von Morris bis Gropius.* Mit einem Nachwort von Wolfgang Pehnt. Neuausg. des 1957 bei Rowohlt, Reinbek, in der autoris. Übers. aus dem Engl. von Elisabeth Knauth erschienenen Buchs. Köln: DuMont, 1983. 260 pp., 247 illus., bibl. (215–236). (DuMont-Taschenbücher, 137.) [Orig. title: Pioneers of modern design.]

20581. — *Obituaries Sir Nikolaus Pevsner,* Jan. 30, 1902 Leipzig – Aug. 18, 1983 London (selection): Sir N. Pevsner [in]: AJR Information, London, Oct. 1983, p. 7. Magnificent obsession (J. M. Richards) [in]: The Observer, London, Aug. 21, 1983. Enshrined in immortal epithets

(Simon Jenkins) [in]: The Sunday Times, London, Aug. 21, 1983. N. P. gestorben [in]: SZ, Nr. 190, München, 20./21. Aug. 1983, p. 11. Sir N.P., art historian and chronicler of buildings of England [in]: The Times, London, Aug. 19, 1983. The Englishness of Kunstgeschichte [in]: The Times, London, Aug. 20, 1983. See also LBI YB XXIX, p. viii.

20582. PLESSNER, HELMUTH: *Gesammelte Schriften.* Hrsg. von Günter Dux [et al.] unter Mitwirkung von Richard W. Schmidt [et al.]. Frankfurt am Main: Suhrkamp, 1980 ff. *Bd. 8: Conditio humana.* 1983. 413 pp. [For previously publ. vols. 1–7 see No. 19522/YB XXVIII.]

20583. POLGAR, ALFRED: *Kleine Schriften. Bd. 2: Kreislauf.* Hrsg. von Marcel Reich-Ranicki in Zusammenarbeit mit Ulrich Weinzierl. Reinbek: Rowohlt, 1983. XII, 415 pp., illus. [For vol. 1 see No. 19524/YB XXVIII.]

20584. POLITZER, HEINZ. Seidlin, Oskar: *In memoriam Heinz Politzer.* [In]: Modern Austrian Literature, Vol. 16, No. 2, Riverside, Calif., 1983. Pp. 155–163. [H.P., Dec. 31, 1910 Vienna –July 30, 1978 Berkeley, professor of German literature.]

20585. POPPER, KARL R. Gröbl, Evelyn: *Geltung und Gegenstand; zur Metaphysik im Frühwerk Karl R. Poppers.* Frankfurt am Main; New York: Campus, 1983. 131 pp., bibl. (Campus Forschung, 319.)

20586. — Kreuzer, Franz: *Offene Gesellschaft – offenes Universum.* Franz Kreuzer im Gespräch mit Karl R. Popper. Aus Anlass des 80. Geburtstages des grossen österr. Philosophen. 2., von Karl R. Popper verbesserte Aufl. [Hrsg.: Österr. Radio und Fernsehen] ORF, Nachtstudio. Wien: Deuticke, 1983. 119 pp.

20587. RANK, OTTO. Menaker, Esther: *Otto Rank; a rediscovered legacy.* New York: Columbia Univ. Press, 1982. 192 pp. [O.R., orig. Rosenfeld, Apr. 22, 1884 Vienna – Oct. 31, 1939 New York, psychoanalyst.]

20588. RATHENAU, EMIL. Wiedner, Wolfgang/Schallenberger, E. Horst: *Ein Gestalter der Zeit, die noch nachwirkt: Emil Rathenau, Preusse und Jude, Schöpfer der AEG.* [In]: Tribüne, Jg. 22, H. 86, Frankfurt am Main, 1983. Pp. 127–138.

20589. RATHENAU, WALTHER: *Walther Rathenau – Maximilian Harden: Briefwechsel 1897–1920.* Mit einer einleitenden Studie hrsg. von Hans Dieter Hellige. München: Gotthold Müller; Heidelberg: Lambert Schneider, 1983. 1078 pp., illus., facsims., bibl. (947–982). (Walther-Rathenau-Gesamtausgabe, Bd. 6.) [Incl. introd. study: Rathenau und Harden in der Gesellschaft des Deutschen Kaiserreichs; eine sozialgeschichtlich-biographische Studie zur Entstehung neokonservativer Positionen bei Unternehmern und Intellektuellen (15–299, notes 201–299). Cf.: Symptome eines deutschen Schicksals (Nicolaus Sombart) [in]: SZ, Nr. 65, München, 17./18. März 1984, p. II. The conservative reaction (James Joll) [in]: TLS, London, Feb. 17, 1984, p. 162. For previously publ. vol. 2 of 'Gesamtausg.' see No. 14777/ YB XXIII.]

20590. — Hecker, Gerhard: *Walther Rathenau und sein Verhältnis zu Militär und Krieg.* Boppard am Rhein: Boldt, 1983. 542 pp., illus. (Wehrwissenschaftl. Forschungen, Abt. Militärgeschichtl. Studien, 30.)

—— — Joll, James: *Walther Rathenau: Intellektueller oder Industrieller.* [See in No. 20294.]

20591. REICH, WILHELM: *Frühe Schriften. Bd. 1: Aus den Jahren 1920–1925.* Frankfurt am Main: Fischer, 1983. 340 pp. (Fischer-Taschenbücher, 6756.)

20592. — Sharaf, Myron: *Fury on earth: a biography of Wilhelm Reich.* London: Deutsch; New York: St. Martin's Press-Marek, 1983. 550 pp., illus. [Cf.: Review (John Corry) [in]: Internat. Herald Tribune, Zürich, Apr. 14, 1983, p. 18. Science and hocus-pocus (John Gross) [in]: The Observer, London, May 22, 1983, p. 30. Wilhelm Reich: the deviant disciple (Robert Harbison) [in]: Sunday Times, London, May 22, 1983. W.R. data, see No. 18571/YB XXVII.]

20593. REICHENBACH, HANS: *Erfahrung und Prognose.* Eine Analyse der Grundlagen und der Struktur der Erkenntnis. Mit Erläuterungen von Alberto Coffa. (Aus dem Engl. übers. von Maria Reichenbach und Hermann Vetter.) Braunschweig: Vieweg, 1983. XII, 310 pp. (Reichenbach, Hans: Gesammelte Werke in 9 Bänden, Bd. 4.) [1st German edn. of 'Experience and prediction', orig. publ. in 1938. For previously publ. vols. 1–3 see No. 17636/YB XXVI.]

20594. REINHARDT, MAX. Dreifuss, Alfred: *Deutsches Theater Berlin Schumannstr. 13a.* Fünf Kapitel aus der Geschichte einer Schauspielbühne. Berlin/East: Henschel, 1983. 252 pp., 128 illus. [Refers, a.o., to Otto Brahm and Max Reinhardt.]

20595. — Huesmann, Heinrich: *Welttheater Reinhardt; Bauten, Spielstätten, Inszenierungen.* Mit einem

Beitrag 'Max Reinhardts amerikanische Spielpläne' von Leonhard M. Fiedler, München: Prestel, 1983. 616 pp., 157 illus. (Materialien zur Kunst des 19. Jh., Bd. 27.)

20596. — KUSCHNIA, MICHAEL, ed.: *100 Jahre Deutsches Theater Berlin*. Berlin/East: Henschel, 1983. 528 pp., 870 illus., bibl. [Incl. essays by, a.o., Otto Brahm, Siegfried Jacobsohn, Alfred Kerr, Max Reinhardt; refers also to many Jewish actors.]

20597. — STERN, ERNST: *Bühnenbildner bei Max Reinhardt*. Erinnerungen. Mit 27 Zeichnungen des Verfassers. Berlin/East: Henschel, 1983. 155 pp., ports. (dialog.)

20598. — THOMSEN, CHRISTIAN W.: *Leopoldskron; frühe Historie, die Ära Reinhardt, das Salzburg-Seminar*. Siegen: Vorländer; Freilassing: Huemer, 1983. 148 pp., illus. [Text in German and English.]

20599. — WILLIAMS, SIMON: *The director in the German theatre: harmony, spectacle and ensemble*. [In]: new german critique, No. 29, Milwaukee, Univ. of Wis., Spring-Summer 1983. Pp. 107–131. [Incl. long passage on M. Reinhardt.]

20600. RODA RODA, ALEXANDER. STIASSNY-BAUMGARTNER, ILSE: *Roda Rodas Tätigkeit im Kriegspressequartier*. Zur propagandistischen Arbeit österr. Schriftsteller im Ersten Weltkrieg. Wien, Univ., Diss., 1982. 241, 124, 28 pp. [A.R.R., orig. Ladislaus Rosenfeld, Apr. 13, 1872 Puszta Zdenci, Hungary – Aug. 20, 1945 New York, writer, emigrated from Germany.]

20601. ROSENAU, HELEN: *The ideal city; its architectural evolution in Europe*. 3rd, revised and augmented edn. London; New York: Methuen, 1983. XII, 195 pp., illus. [H.R., born March 27, 1900 in Monte Carlo, art historian, emigrated to England in 1933.]

20602. ROSENBERG, ARTHUR: *Entstehung und Geschichte der Weimarer Republik*. (Hrsg. und eingeleitet von Kurt Kersten.) Frankfurt am Main: Europäische Verlagsanstalt, 1983. 1 vol. (265; 226 pp.). (Taschenbücher Syndikat, EVA, Bd. 2.) [Cont.: 'Entstehung der W.R.', 1st edn. 1928; and 'Geschichte der W.R.', 1st edn. 1935.] [A.R., Dec. 19, 1889 Berlin – Feb. 7, 1943 New York, historian, member of the Reichstag.]

20603. ROTH, JOSEPH: *Job; the story of a simple man*. Transl. by Dorothy Thompson. London: Chatto & Windus, Hogarth Press, 1983. 238 pp. [A re-issue of the transl. first publ. in 1933. Cf.: Trials of the simple man (Michael Hofmann) [in]: TLS, London, Apr. 22, 1983, p. 399.]

20604. — ROTH, JOSEPH: *Panoptikum; Gestalten und Kulissen*. Köln: Kiepenheuer & Witsch, 1983. 108 pp. (KiWi, 35.) [Collection of feuilletons, 1st edn. 1930.]

20605. — CZIFFRA, GÉZA von: *Der heilige Trinker*. [Erinnerungen an Joseph Roth.] Bergisch-Gladbach: Lübbe, 1983. 143 pp. (Bastei Lübbe, 10215.)

20606. — FREY, REINER: *Kein Weg ins Freie: Joseph Roths Amerikabild*. Frankfurt am Main: Lang, 1983. VI, 207 pp. (Europäische Hochschulschriften: Reihe 1, Bd. 623.) [Incl.: Ostjüdische Perspektive: Amerika.]

20607. — MENHENNET, ALAN: *Flight of a 'broken eagle': Joseph Roth's 'Radetzkymarsch'*. [In]: New German Studies, Vol. 11, No. 1, Hull, Spring, 1983. Pp. 47–65, notes.

20608. ROTHFELS, HANS. CONZE, WERNER: *Hans Rothfels*. [In]: Historische Zeitschrift, Bd. 237, H. 2, München, Okt. 1983. Pp. 311–360, notes. [H.R., Apr. 12, 1891 Kassel – June 22, 1976 Tübingen, historian, emigrated via England in 1940 to the USA, from 1951 in Germany.]

20609. SACHS, NELLY. KRIEG, MATTHIAS: *Schmetterlingsweisheit; die Todesbilder der Nelly Sachs*. Berlin: Institut Kirche und Judentum, 1983. 136 pp., bibl. (Studien zu jüdischem Volk und christlicher Gemeinde, Bd. 4.)

20610. SALOMON, ALICE. BARON, RÜDEGER, ed.: *Sozialarbeit und soziale Reform; zur Geschichte eines Berufs zwischen Frauenbewegung und öffentlicher Verwaltung*. Festschrift zum 75jährigen Bestehen der Sozialen Frauenschule Berlin-Schöneberg/Fachhochschule für Sozialarbeit und Sozialpädagogik Berlin. Weinheim: Beltz, 1983. XI, 144 pp., illus., bibl. references. [Also on Alice Salomon, founder of the 'Soziale Frauenschule Berlin-Schöneberg' in 1908. See also No. 20705.]

20611. SALOMON, ERICH. *Erich Salomon: aus dem Leben eines Fotografen, 1886 1944*. (Eine Ausstellung der Berlinischen Galerie. Red.: Elisabeth Moortgat. Text: Wolfgang Oehler.) Berlin: Museumpädagogischer Dienst, 1983. 19 pp., mostly illus. (Ausstellungsmagazin, Nr. 14.)

—— SAPHIR, MORITZ. TOURY, JACOB: *Moritz Saphir und Karl Beck*. [See in No. 19769.]

20612. SCHATZKI, WALTER. SCHUMANN, RICHARD: *Walter Schatzki: Frankfurt – New York*. [In]: Aus dem Antiquariat, 2, [Beilage zum] Börsenblatt für den Deutschen Buchhandel, Nr. 16, Frankfurt am Main, 25. Feb. 1983. Pp. A76-A78. [W.Sch., Aug. 26, 1899 Siegen – Jan. 29, 1983 New York, antiquarian bookseller.]

20613. SCHNITZLER, ARTHUR: *Plays and stories*. Ed. by Egon Schwarz, with a foreword by Stanley Elkin. New York: Continuum, 1983. 279 pp. (The German Library, No. 55.) [Cf.:

The return of La ronde (Gabriele Annan) [in]: The New York Review of Books, July 21, 1983, pp. 14–17.]

20614. — BERLIN, JEFFREY B.: *Arthur Schnitzler-Bibliographie for 1977–1981.* [In]: Modern Austrian Literature, Vol. 15, No. 1, Riverside, Calif., 1982. Pp. 61–83.

—— — KUHN, ANNA K.: *Max Ophüls' adaptations of 'Liebelei' and 'Reigen'.* [See in No. 20624.]

20615. — TARNOWSKI-SEIDEL, HEIDE: *Arthur Schnitzler: Flucht in die Finsternis.* Eine produktionsästhetische Untersuchung. München: Fink, 1983. 175 pp., bibl. (168–175).

20616. SCHNITZLER, HEINRICH. BAUMANN, GERHART: *Gedenkblatt für Heinrich Schnitzler.* [In]: Modern Austrian Literature, Vol. 16, No. 1, Riverside, Calif., 1983. Pp. I–III. [H.Sch., Vienna Aug. 9, 1902 – July 14, 1982, son of Arthur Schnitzler, returned from emigration to Vienna, assistant director of the 'Theater in der Josefstadt'.]

20617. SEGHERS ANNA: *Ausgewählte Erzählungen.* Hrsg. und mit einem Nachwort von Christa Wolf. Darmstadt: Luchterhand, 1983. 372 pp. [A.S., orig. Netty Reiling, Nov. 19, 1900 Mainz – June 1, 1983 East Berlin, writer, returned from emigration in Mexico to the GDR in 1947. See selected obituaries: Engagiertes Schreiben (Anton Krättli) [in]: NZZ, Nr. 127, Zürich, 3. Juni 1983, p. 39. In memoriam A.S. [in]: Sinn und Form, Jg. 35, H. 6, Berlin/East, Nov./Dez. 1983, pp. 1154–1170 (personal reminiscences by friends). Stimme der Hoffnung (Klaus Sauer) [in]: SZ, Nr. 125, München, 3. Juni 1983, p. 45. Anna Seghers [in]: The Times, London, June 3rd, 1983.]

20618. — MILFULL, JOHN: *Juden, Frauen, Mulatten, Neger: Probleme der Emanzipation in Anna Seghers 'Karibischen Erzählungen'.* [In]: Frauenliteratur. Hrsg. von Manfred Jurgensen. Bern: Lang, 1983. Pp. 45–55.

20619. — RICHTER, HANS: *Der Kafka der Seghers.* [In]: Sinn und Form, Jg. 35, H. 6, Berlin/East, Nov./Dez. 1983. Pp. 1171–1179.

20620. SERNER, WALTER: *Das gesamte Werk.* Hrsg. von Thomas Milch. *Suppl.-Bd. 2: Das fette Fluchen: ein Walter-Serner-Gaunerwörterbuch.* München: Renner, 1983. 46 pp. [For previously publ. vols. see Nos. 19555–19556/YB XXVIII.]

20621. SIMMEL, GEORG: *Philosophische Kultur.* Über das Abenteuer, die Geschlechter und die Krise der Moderne. Gesammelte Essays. Mit einem Nachwort von Jürgen Habermas. Berlin: Wagenbach, 1983. 251 pp. [Cf.: Der wiederentdeckte G. Simmel (Caroline Neubaur) [in]: Frankfurter Allgemeine Zeitung, Nr. 271, 22. Nov. 1983, p. L 9.]

20622. — SIMMEL, GEORG: *Schriften zur Soziologie.* Eine Auswahl. Hrsg. und eingeleitet von Heinz-Jürgen Dahme und Otthein Rammstedt. Frankfurt am Main: Suhrkamp, 1983. 308 pp. (Suhrkamp-Taschenbuch Wissenschaft, 434.)

20623. SIMON, JAMES. KNOPP, WERNER/GIRARDET, CELLA-MARGARETHA: *Zum 50. Todestag von James Simon.* [Zwei Essays]. [In]: Jahrbuch Preussischer Kulturbesitz, Bd. 19, Berlin, 1983. Pp. 75–76; 77–98, illus. [J.S., Berlin Sept. 17, 1851 – May 23, 1932, industrialist, philanthropist.]

20624. SOKEL, WALTER. *Probleme der Moderne; Studien zur deutschen Literatur von Nietzsche bis Brecht; Festschrift für Walter Sokel.* Hrsg. von Benjamin Bennett [et al.]. Tübingen: Niemeyer, 1983. XI, 498 pp., port. [Incl.: The romantization of Arthur Schnitzler: Max Ophüls' adaptations of 'Liebelei' and 'Reigen' (Anna K. Kuhn, 83–99). Kafkas 'Prozess' und seine Richter: zur Debatte Brecht-Benjamin und Benjamin-Scholem (Peter Beicken, 343–368). Also essays by Käte Hamburger (on Theodor A. Meyer), and Egon Schwarz (on Julio Cambas); literary essays on Hofmannsthal (1), and Kafka (4).] [W.S., born Dec. 17, 1917 in Vienna, professor of German literature, Univ. of Virginia, Fellow of the LBI New York.]

20625. SONNENFELS, JOSEPH von. LINDNER, DOLF: *Der Mann ohne Vorurteil: Joseph von Sonnenfels 1733–1817.* Wien: Österr. Bundesverl., 1983. 212 pp., bibl. (210–212). [J.v.S., 1733 Nikolsburg – Apr. 25, 1817 Vienna, political scientist.]

20626. SONNENSCHEIN, HUGO. GAUSS, KARL MARCUS: *Die Legende vom weltverkommenen Sonka; wer war Hugo Sonnenschein?* [In]: Literatur und Kritik, H. 179/180, Wien, Nov./Dez. 1983. Pp. 524–530. [H.S., May 25, 1889 Gaya, Moravia – 1953 Mirov, Czechoslovakia (in prison), poet, wrote under the pseud. Sonka.]

20627. SPERBER, MANÈS. *Manès Sperber. Ansprachen aus Anlass der Verleihung des Friedenspreises des Deutschen Buchhandels e.V., Frankfurt am Main.* [16. Okt. 1983.] Frankfurt am Main: Buchhändler-Vereinigung, 1983. 56 pp. [Incl. the address by M. Sperber. See also: Die erhabene Heuchelei der Ideologie; Interview mit dem diesjährigen Preisträger Manès Sperber [in]: Börsenblatt für den Deutschen Buchhandel, Nr. 42, Frankfurt am Main, 27.

Mai 1983, pp. 1311–1318, ports.] [M.Sp., Dec. 12, 1905 Zablotow, Galicia – Feb. 5, 1984 Paris.]

0628. — Sperber, Manès: *Die Wirklichkeit in der Literatur des 20. Jahrhunderts. Der Freiheitsgedanke in der europäischen Literatur.* Zwei Vorträge. München: Nymphenburger, 1983. 70 pp. (Positionen, Bd. 1.)

— SPITZER, LEO. Green, Geoffrey: *Literary criticism and the structure of history.* [See No. 20335.]

0629. STAHL, FRIEDRICH JULIUS. Nabrings, Arie: *Friedrich Julius Stahl: Rechtsphilosophie und Kirchenpolitik.* Bielefeld: Luther-Verl., 1983. 258 pp. [F.J.St. data, see No. 17682/YB XXVI.]

0630. STEIN, EDITH. Herbstrith, Waltraud, ed.: *Edith Stein: ein neues Lebensbild in Zeugnissen und Selbstzeugnissen.* Hrsg. und eingeleitet. Freiburg i.B.: Herder, 1983. 188 pp. (Herderbücherei, Bd. 1035.) [E.St. data, see No. 18609/YB XXVII.]

0631. — Leuven, Romaeus: *Heil im Unheil; das Leben Edith Steins: Reife und Vollendung.* [Übers. aus dem Holländ.) Freiburg i.Br.: Herder, 1983. 195 pp. (Stein, Edith: Werke, Bd. 10.)

0632. — Neyer, Maria Amalta: *Nochmals – Edith Stein: 'Märtyrerin'?* [And]: Moosen, Inge: *Antwort auf Sr. Maria Amalta Neyer OCD.* [In]: Frankfurter Hefte, Jg. 38, N. 3 & 4, Frankfurt am Main, März & Apr. 1983. Pp. 13–15; 10–11. [Refers to essay by I. Moosen, see No. 19560/YB XXVIII.]

20633. STERNHEIM, CARL. Budde, Bernhard: *Über die Wahrheit und über die Lüge des radikalen, antibürgerlichen Individualismus; eine Studie zum erzählerischen und essayistischen Werk Carl Sternheims.* Frankfurt am Main: Lang, 1983. 215 pp. (Europäische Hochschulschriften: Reihe 1, Bd. 679.) [See also No. 20386.]

20634. — Reiss, H. S.: *'Sternheim – ein Satiriker!'?* [In]: Deutsche Vierteljahrsschrift für Literaturwissenschaft und Geistesgeschichte, Jg. 57, H. 2, Stuttgart, Juni 1983. Pp. 321–342, footnotes.

20635. STROHEIM, ERICH von. Koszarski, Richard: *The man you loved to hate: Erich von Stroheim and Hollywood.* Oxford: Oxford Univ. Press, 1983. XII, 343 pp., illus., notes, bibl. [Also paperback edn., 386 pp. Cf.: Stroheim (Jonathan Rosenbaum) [in]: Sight and Sound, Internat. Film Quarterly, Vol. 53, No. 1, London, Winter 1983, p. 68. Under the mask of a Hollywood legend [in]: The Times, London, Nov. 12, 1983. Degeneracy incarnate (Geoffrey Nowell-Smith) [in]: TLS, London, Nov. 18, 1983, p. 1277.] [E.v.St., orig. Erich Oswald Stroheim, 1885 Austria – 1957 USA, film actor and director, from 1923 in Hollywood, famous for his Teutonic roles.]

20636. STURMANN, MANFRED: *Heimkehr in die Wirklichkeit.* Novelle. [Neudr. der Ausg. 1928.] Berlin: Verlag Europäische Ideen, 1983. 27 pp. [M.St., born Apr. 6, 1903 in Königsberg, writer, lives in Jerusalem.]

20637. SUESS, EDUARD. Hamann, Günther, ed.: *Eduard Suess zum Gedenken (20.8.1831–26.4.1914).* Wien: Verlag der Österr. Akademie der Wissenschaften, 1983. 100 pp., illus. [E.S., professor of geology in Vienna, liberal politician.]

20638. SUSMAN, MARGARETE. Nigg, Walter: *Ein Zentrum ohne Peripherie: Margarete Susman.* [In]: Nigg, Walter: Heilige and Dichter. Olten: Walter, 1982. Pp. 180–202. [M.S., Oct. 14, 1874 Hamburg – Jan. 16, 1966 Zürich, writer, emigrated in 1933; for her autobiography, see No. 4878/YB X.]

20639. TAUSK, VIKTOR: *Gesammelte psychoanalytische und literarische Schriften.* Hrsg. von Hans-Joachim Metzger. Wien: Medusa, 1983. 563 pp., illus., bibl. [Incl.: Wer war Viktor Tausk? ein biogr. Versuch von seinem Sohn Marius (498–563).] [V.T., March 12, 1877 Zsilina, Slovakia – July 3, 1919 Vienna, psychologist, one of Freud's earliest pupils.]

20640. TOLLER, ERNST. Rothe, Wolfgang: *Ernst Toller in Selbstzeugnissen und Bilddokumenten.* Reinbek: Rowohlt, 1983. 152 pp., illus., ports., facsims., bibl. Toller & bibl. (144–149). (Rowohlts Mongraphien, 312.) [See also Ina Lorenz contribution in No. 19824.]

20641. TUCHOLSKY, KURT: *Gedichte.* Hrsg. von Mary Gerold-Tucholsky. Reinbek: Rowohlt, 1983. 834 pp. [Combines for the first time all poems publ. during T.'s lifetime; incl. also 4 poems from his literary estate.]

20642. — Tucholsky, Kurt: *Das Kurt Tucholsky Chanson Buch.* Texte und Noten (Hrsg. von Mary Gerold-Tucholsky und Hans George Heepe.) Reinbek: Rowohlt, 1983. 367 pp., illus. scores.

20643. — Grenville, Bryan P.: *Kurt Tucholsky.* Unter Mitarbeit von Gerhard Kraus. München: Beck; München: Edition Text & Kritik, 1983. 143 pp., bibl. (138–141). (Autorenbücher, 36.)

20644. — King, William John: *Kurt Tucholsky als politischer Publizist.* Eine politische Biographie Frankfurt am Main: Lang, 1983. 230 pp., bibl. (216–226). (Europäische Hochschulschrif ten: Reihe 1, Bd. 579.)

20645. — Tucholsky, Mary/Lambert, Friedrich, eds.: *Kurt Tucholsky und Deutschlands Marsch in Dritte Reich.* (Katalog zur Ausstellung 'Ein Zeitalter wird berichtigt'.) Berlin: Verla Hentrich, 1983. 123 pp., mostly illus. (Stätten der Geschichte Berlins, Bd. 3.)

20646. VARNHAGEN, RAHEL: *Rahel-Bibliothek: Gesammelte Werke.* Hrsg. von Konrad Feilchen feldt, Uwe Schweikert und Rahel E. Steiner. Bd. 1–10. München: Matthes & Seitz, 1983 10 vols., [in vol. 10]: illus., ports., facsims., chron., list of correspondents, list of names bibl. (451–466). [Vols. 1–8 are facsimile reprints, vols. 9–10 publ. for the first time. Cont. Bd. 1–3: *Rahel; ein Buch des Andenkens für ihre Freunde.* (1834). Bd. 4–6: *Briefwechsel zwische Varnhagen und Rahel.* (1874–1875). Bd. 7: *Briefwechsel zwischen Rahel und David Veit.* (1861) Bd. 8: *Aus Rahel's Herzensleben.* Briefe und Tagebuchblätter, hrsg. von Ludmilla Assing (1877) [&]: *Angelus Silesius und Saint-Martin; Auszüge und Bemerkungen von Rahel,* hrsg. von K A. Varnhagen von Ense (3., vermehrte Aufl., 1849). Bd. 9: *Briefe und Tagebücher au verstreuten Quellen,* hrsg. von Konrad Feilchenfeldt. 959 pp. Bd. 10: *Studien, Materialien Register.* 544 pp. [Cf.: Urworte, nicht orphisch, sondern weiblich (Sybille Wirsing) [in] Frankfurter Allgemeine Zeitung, Nr. 18, 21. Jan. 1984, Beilage. 'Freunde, Gleichgesinnte herein!' (Friedhelm Kemp) [in]: NZZ, Nr. 293, Zürich, 15. Dez. 1983, p. 41. See also No 20710.]

—— — Feilchenfeldt, Konrad: *Die Anfänge des Kults um Rahel Varnhagen und seine Kritiker.* [See in No. 19769. See also Horst Meixner contribution in No. 19764.]

20647. — Goodman, Kay: *Poesis and praxis in Rahel Varnhagen's letters.* [In]: new german critique No. 27, Milwaukee, Univ. of Wis., 1982. Pp. 123–139, notes.

20648. — Pazi, Margarita: *'Eine schöne Seele': Rahel Levin, 1771–1833.* [In]: MB, Nr. 9, Tel-Aviv 4. März 1983. Pp. 5–6. [See also: Rahel Varnhagen in neuer Sicht: Perspektiven anlässlich ihres 150. Todestags, 7. März (Konrad Feilchenfeldt) [in]: NZZ, Nr. 54, Zürich, 5./6 März 1983, p. 39.]

20649. VICKY [orig. Victor Weisz]. Silver, Eric: *From Vicky, to Inge.* [In]: The Observer Colour Supplement, London, 13th Feb. 1983. Pp. 12–15, illus., facsims. [Incl. excerpts and drawings from hitherto unpubl. letters by Vicky to his wife Inge Lew; the c.300 letters are now in the Brynmore Jones Library at Hull University.] [Vicky, 1913 Berlin – Feb. 23 1966 London, political cartoonist.]

20650. WALDEN, HERWARTH. Brühl, Georg: *Herwarth Walden und 'Der Sturm'.* Köln DuMont; Leipzig: Edition Leipzig, 1983. 344 pp., 377 illus., bibl. [See also in No. 20278.] [H.W., orig. Georg Lewin, Sept. 16, 1878 Berlin – Oct. 31, 1941 Saratow, USSR (in prison).]

20651. WARBURG, OTTO. Krebs, Hans with the collaboration of Roswitha Schmidt: *Otto Warburg: cell physiologist, biochemist and eccentric.* Transl. by Hans Krebs and Anne Marten Oxford: Clarendon Press; New York: Oxford Univ. Press, 1981. 154 pp., 23 illus. [For orig. German edn. see No. 16730/YB XXV.] [O.W., Oct. 8, 1883 Freiburg i.Br. – Aug. 1, 1970 Berlin, Nobel Prize 1931.]

20652. WARSCHAUER, FRANK. Lerg, Winfried B: *Frank Warschauer und die Anfänge der Rundfunkkritik.* [In]: Publizistik, Jg. 27, München, Juli-Sept. 1982. Pp. 349–360. [F.W., Apr. 22, 1892 Darmstadt – May 18, 1940 Holland, journalist.]

20653. WEICHMANN, HERBERT. Fahning, Hans, ed.: *Herbert Weichmann zum Gedächtnis.* Hamburg nimmt Abschied von seinem Bürgermeister. Hamburg: Knaus, 1983. 92 pp. [Further obituaries (selection): Publizist, Politiker und Vorbild für viele (Ernst G. Lowenthal) [in]: 'Allgemeine', Nr. 42, Düsseldorf, 21. Okt. 1983, p. 7. Abschied von H. W. (Robert M. W. Kempner) [in]: Aufbau, No. 42, New York, Oct. 21, 1983. Ein preussischer Sozialdemokrat (Karsten Plog) [in]: Frankfurter Rundschau, 11. Okt. 1983. Ein grosser deutsch-jüdischer Politiker (Erich Lüth) [in]: Isr. Wochenblatt, Nr. 41. Okt. 1983, pp. 21 & 23. Obituary [in]: Jewish Chronicle, London, Oct. 14, 1983. Anwalt der Freiheit (Jürgen Wahl) [in]: Rheinischer Merkur, Koblenz, 14. Okt. 1983. Er war einer der Grossen (Rainer Barzel) [in]: Welt am Sonntag, Nr. 42, 16. Okt. 1983, p. 4. Preusse, Hanseat und Staatsmann (Helmut Schmidt) [in]: Die Zeit, Nr. 42, Hamburg, 14. Okt. 1983, p. 7.] [H.W., Feb. 23, 1896 Landsberg O/S. – Oct. 9, 1983 Hamburg, jurist, socialist politician, emigrated 1933 via various countries to the USA, returned to Germany in 1948, Lord Mayor of Hamburg 1965–1971.]

20654. — Loose, Hans-Dieter: *Rückkehr aus der Emigration: Briefe Herbert Weichmanns aus Hamburg im Juni 1948.* [In]: Zeitschrift des Vereins für Hamburgische Geschichte, Bd. 67, Hamburg, 1981. Pp. 177–205. [Documentation.]

20655. — Weichmann, Elsbeth: *Zuflucht: Jahre des Exils.* Mit einem Vorwort von Siegfried Lenz. Hamburg: Knaus, 1983. 208 pp. [Autobiography of the non-Jewish wife of Herbert Weichmann.]

20656. WEIGEL, HANS: *1001 Premiere; Hymnen und Verrisse.* Bd. 1–2. Graz: Styria, 1983. 851 pp. in 2 vols.

20657. WEILL, KURT. Jarman, Douglas: *Kurt Weill.* An illustrated biography. London: Orbis; Bloomington, Ind.: Indiana Univ. Press, 1983. 160 pp., 50 illus. [Cf.: K. Weill and his music (Egon Larsen) [in]: AJR Information, London, Sept. 1983, pp. 1–2.]

20658. — Schebera, Jürgen: *Kurt Weill: Leben und Werk.* Mit Texten und Materialien von und über Kurt Weill. Leipzig: Deutscher Verl. für Musik; Königstein/Ts.: Athenäum, 1983. 352 pp., illus. [Incl. many photos from the literary estate of Lotte Lenya, publ. for the first time.]

20659. WEININGER, OTTO: *Fragments et aphorismes.* Textes inédits. (Choisis et traduits de l'allemand par Michel-François Demet et Jacques Le Rider.) [And]: Le Rider, Jacques: *Modernisme-féminisme/modernité-virilité: Otto Weininger et la modernité viennoise.* [In]: L'Infini, 4, Paris, 1983. Pp. 21–31, footnotes; 5–20, footnotes. [O.W., Vienna Apr. 3, 1880 – Oct. 4, 1903, philosopher.]

20660. — Le Rider, Jacques: *Le cas Otto Weininger.* Paris: Presses Universitaires de France, 1983 [?]. [Cf.: Otto Weininger, le juif dont Hitler avait fait l'elogé (Paul Giniewski) [in]: Das Neue Israel, Jg. 35, H. 10, Zürich, Apr. 1983, pp. 358–359.]

20661. — Sobol, Yehoshua: *The soul of a Jew; the last night of Otto Weininger.* [In Hebrew, title transl.]. Tel-Aviv: Or-Am, 1982. 122 pp. [A play, performed in Israel, also at the Edinburgh Festival and at the Riverside Studios in London during summer 1983. Cf.: Otto Weininger: a portrait of divided solitude [in Hebrew] (Zvi Raphaeli) [in]: Bamah; Drama Quarterly, No. 94, Jerusalem, Winter 1983, pp. 123–125. The origins of self-hatred (Zinovy Zinik) [in]: TLS, London, Sept. 9, 1983, p. 960.]

20662. WEISKOPF, FRANZ CARL. Gallmeister, Petra: *Die historischen Romane von Franz Carl Weiskopf 'Abschied vom Frieden' und 'Inmitten des Stroms'.* Frankfurt am Main: Lang, 1983. 232 pp. (Europäische Hochschulschriften: Reihe 1, Bd. 622.) [F.C.W. data, see No. 17372/YB XXVI.]

20663. WEISS, PETER. Kesting, Hanjo: *The writer's resistance.* [In]: New Left Review, No. 139, London, May-June 1983. Pp. 95–97. [On the author Peter Weiss.]

20664. WEISSKOPF VICTOR F. Kreuzer, Franz: *Sternenfeuer in Menschenhand.* Quarks, Quantenleiter; Zähmung der Wasserstoffbombe. Franz Kreuzer im Gespräch mit Victor F. Weisskopf und Hans Motz. [Hrsg.: Österr. Radio und Fernsehen] ORF, Nachtstudio. Wien: Deuticke, 1983. 94 pp. [V.F.W., born Sept. 19, 1908 in Vienna, physicist, worked on the atomic bomb project in Los Alamos, from 1965 head of the Physics Department of the Mass. Institute of Technology.]

—— WERFEL, FRANZ. Baum, Gregory: *Franz Werfel's look at genocide.* [See in No. 20186. See also (on Alma Mahler-Werfel) Nos. 20535–20536.]

20665. WERTHEIMER, SAMSON. Mevorakh, Barukh: *The 'Hoffaktor' Wertheimer.* [In Hebrew, title transl.]. [In]: Eit-mol, Vol. 9, No. 1 (51), Tel-Aviv, Sept. 1983. P. 21.

20666. WINDER, LUDWIG: *Die jüdische Orgel.* Roman. Nachwort von Ružena Grebeníčková. Olten: Walter, 1983. 170 pp. (Walter-Literarium, Bd. 19.) [L.W., Feb. 7, 1889 Schaffa, Moravia – June 16, 1946 Baldock, Herts., writer, emigrated to England in 1939.]

20667. WITTGENSTEIN, LUDWIG. Bartley, William Warren: *Wittgenstein; eine Leben.* München: Matthes & Seitz, 1983. 222 pp., illus., bibl. (219–222). (Liebhaber-Bibliothek, 3.) [See also A. Margalit contribution in No. 20316.]

20668. — Nedo, Michael/Ranchetti, Michele, eds.: *Ludwig Wittgenstein; sein Leben in Bildern und Texten.* Vorwort von B. F. McGuinness. Frankfurt am Main: Suhrkamp, 1983. XV, 394 pp., mostly illus. [Cf.: Wittgenstein im Bild (Willy Hochkeppel) [in]: Die Zeit, Nr. 49, Hamburg, 2. Dez. 1983, p. Lit. 2.]

20669. WOLF, FRIEDRICH. *Friedrich Wolf: die Jahre in Stuttgart 1927–1933; ein Beispiel.* (Katalogtext und Bildauswahl: Michael Kienzle, Dirk Mende.) Stuttgart: Projekt Zeitgeschichte im Kulturamt, 1983. 382 pp., illus. (Ausstellungsreihe Stuttgart im Dritten Reich.) [See also No. 20712.] [F.W., Dec. 23, 1888 Neuwied – Oct. 5, 1953 East Berlin, physician, dramatist, emigrated in 1934 via various countries to the USSR.]

20670. WOLF, KONRAD. *Konrad Wolf, 1925–1982*. (Zusammenstellung: Rüdiger Koschnitzki.) Frankfurt am Main: Deutsches Institut für Filmkunde, 1983. 51 pp., illus. (Die Information, 1983, H. 1.) [See also No. 20712] [K.W., Oct. 20, 1925 Hechingen – March 7, 1982 GDR, film director, son of Friedrich Wolf.]

20671. WOLFENSTEIN, ALFRED. PANTHEL, HANS WALTER: *Leben im Niedergang; frühe und letzte Autographen Alfred Wolfensteins (1883–1945)*. [In]: Tribüne, Jg. 22, H. 88, Frankfurt am Main, 1983. Pp. 170–176, footnotes. [Incl. letters.]

20672. WOLFSKEHL, KARL. KLUSSMANN, PAUL GERHARD, ed.: *Karl-Wolfskehl-Kolloquium (1978, Bonn)*. Vorträge, Berichte, Dokumente. Hrsg. in Verbindung mit Jörg-Ulrich Fechner und Karlhans Kluncker. Amsterdam: Castrum-Peregrini-Presse, 1983. 329 pp., illus. [Incl.: Karl Wolfskehl: deutscher Dichter und Jude (Frederick P. Bargebuhr). Erinnerungen (Mea Nijland-Verwey [&] Margot Ruben). Drei Briefe aus dem Exil (K. Wolfskehl, Einführung von M. Ruben). W.'s Entwurf eines neuen Dramas: das Beispiel der Saul-Dichtung (P. G. Klussmann). INRI oder die Vier Tafeln (Renate Koch). Wolfskehl in der kosmischen Runde (Hans Eggert Schröder). K.W. und Stefan George (K. Kluncker). Drei frühe Essays über Stefan George (Karl Wolfskehl, erläutert von H.-U. Fechner.).]

20673. ZUCKMAYER, CARL. WAGENER, HANS: *Carl Zuckmayer*. München: Beck; München: Edition Text & Kritik, 1983. 190 pp., bibl. (Autorenbücher, 34.)

20674. ZWEIG, ARNOLD: *Traum ist teuer*. Berlin/East: Aufbau, 1983. 357 pp. [Novel on World War II in Northern Africa; 1st publ. 1962, see No. 3468/YB VIII.]

20675. — KAMNITZER, HEINZ: *Der Tod des Dichters*. 2. Aufl. Berlin/East: Der Morgen, 1981 (c1974). 144 pp. [Also on A.Z.'s attitude towards antisemitism and Zionism.]

20676. — WIZNITZER, MANUEL: *Arnold Zweig; das Leben eines deutsch-jüdischen Schriftstellers*. Königstein/Ts.: Athenäum, 1983. 226 pp., illus., bibl. A. Zweig & bibl. (215–221).

20677. ZWEIG, STEFAN: *Gesammelte Werke in Einzelbänden*. Hrsg. und mit Nachbemerkungen versehen von Knut Beck. [1–5: Erzählungen, Essays, Nachdichtungen.] Frankfurt am Main: S. Fischer, 1983. 5 vols. (cased). [Sequel to the 10 vol. box 1981, see No. 18648/YB XXVII; and the first 5 vol. box 1982, see No. 19600/YB XXVIII.]

20678. — ZWEIG, STEFAN, ed.: *Honoré de Balzac: Über die Liebe. Sein Weltbild aus seinen Werken*. Zusammengestellt und mit einem Essay hrsg. Frankfurt am Main: Insel, 1983. 161 pp. (Insel-Taschenbuch, 715.) [1st edn. 1908, republ. for the first time.]

20679. — KIESSLING, WOLFGANG: *Der Weg nach Petropolis: Stefan Zweig*. [In]: Sinn und Form, Jg. 35, H. 2, Berlin/East, März/Apr. 1983. Pp. 376–392. [On life in exile.]

VIII. AUTOBIOGRAPHY, MEMOIRS, LETTER, GENEALOGY

—— AUERNHEIMER, RAOUL. [See No. 20713.]

—— BEER-HOFMANN, RICHARD. [See No. 20713.]

20680. BERCZELLER, RICHARD: *Verweht*. Aus dem Amerian. von Mathias Gabriel. Eisenstadt: Roetzer, 1983. 319 pp. [On youth in the Burgenland, first years as physician in Mattersburg, flight from the Nazis 1938.] [R.B., born Feb. 4, 1902 in Ödenburg, physician, writer.]

20681. COBLENZ, IDA. GEORGE, STEFAN/COBLENZ, IDA: *Briefwechsel*. Hrsg. von Georg Peter Landmann und Elisabeth Höpker-Herberg. Stuttgart: Klett-Cotta, 1983. 107 pp., port. [On Ida Coblenz see also: Frau Isi: Materialien zur Biographie Ida Dehmels (Elisabeth Höpker-Herberg) [in]: LBI Year Book XII, London, 1967, pp. 103–134, illus., footnotes.] [I.C., Jan. 14, 1870 Bingen – Sept. 29, 1942 Hamburg (suicide), married first Leopold Auerbach, merchant in Berlin, then Richard Dehmel.]

20682. FEUCHTWANGER, MARTA: *Nur eine Frau: Jahre, Tage, Stunden*. München: Langen Müller, 1983. 326 pp., illus. [M.F., née Löffler, born 1891, married to Lion Feuchtwanger in 1912.]

20683. GUMPERT, MARTIN: *Hölle im Paradies*. Selbstdarstellung eines Arztes. Mit einem Vorwort von Frithjof Trapp. Neudr. der Ausg. Stockholm, Berman-Fischer, 1939. Hildesheim: Gerstenberg, 1983. XXIII, 280 pp. (Exilliteratur, Bd. 17.) [M.G., Nov. 13, 1897 Berlin – Apr. 18, 1955 New York, physician, writer, emigrated to New York in 1933.]

20684. HAAS, WILLY: *Die literarische Welt*. Lebenserinnerungen. Frankfurt am Main: Fischer, 1983. 315 pp. (Fischer-Taschenbücher, 5607.) [Paperback edn. of No. 1177/YB III.] [W.H., June 7, 1891 Prague – Sept. 4, 1973 Hamburg, literary critic, writer.]

20685. HERZL, THEODOR: *Briefe und Tagebücher*. Hrsg. von Alex Bein, Hermann Greive, Moshe Schaerf, Julius H. Schoeps. *Bd. 1: Briefe und autobiographische Notizen, 1866–1895*. Bearb. von

Johannes Wachten, in Zusammenarbeit mit Chaya Harel [et al.]. Berlin: Propyläen, 1983. 939 pp., notes (693–840), list and short biogr. of those to whom he wrote (869–872; 873–880), list of names and subjects (895–910; 911–939), bibl. (881–894). [Incl. introduction by Alex Bein (11–54). This edn. will comprise 5 vols. of letters and 2 vols. of diaries. Cf.: Eine hervorragende Arbeit (Barbara Suchy) [in]: 'Allgemeine', Nr. 44, Düsseldorf, 4. Nov. 1983, pp. 6 & 7. Ein Revolutionär wider Willen (Leonid Luks) [in]: Die Zeit, Nr. 26, Hamburg, 24. Juni 1983, p. 35.

20686. HOFMANNSTHAL, HUGO von: *'Was ist das Leben für ein Mysterium'*. Unveröffentlichte Briefe, mitgeteilt und kommentiert von Rudolf Hirsch. [In]: NZZ, Nr, 181, Zürich, 6./7. Aug. 1983. Pp. 41–42. [Incl. letters to Gerty von Hofmannsthal, Yella Oppenheimer, Hans Schlesinger (brother of H.'s wife), Oscar A. H. Schmitz, Franz Werfel, Bertha Zuckerkandl.]

20687. KAFKA, FRANZ: *Letters to Milena*. Ed. by Willy Haas, transl. by Tani and James Stern. London: Penguin, 1983. 188 pp. [Also German edn.]: *Briefe an Milena*. Hrsg. von Jürgen Born und Michael Müller, Erweiterte und neu geordnete Ausg. Frankfurt am Main: S. Fischer, 1983. 423 pp. [Cf.: Happy birthday, Mr. Kafka (Ronald Hayman) [in]: Jewish Chronicle, London, July 1, 1983, p. 11. Kafka renewed (Martin Amis) [in]: The Observer, London, Apr. 24, 1983. Difficulties of the Kafkaesque (S. S. Prawer) [in]: TLS, London, Oct. 14, 1983.]

20688. KEMPENICH, HEINRICH: *[Erinnerungen]*. [In]: Juden in Geldern. 1982. (Veröffentlichung des Historischen Vereins für Geldern und Umgebung, 82.) Pp. 9–58, illus., footnotes. [Cont.: Heinrich Kempenich und seine 'Erinnerungen' (Gregor Hövelmann, 9–22). Aus den 'Erinnerungen' (Heinrich Kempenich, 23–58). Augmented entry of No. 18871/YB XXVIII.] [H.K., Aug. 27, 1866 Geldern – March 5, 1932 Dortmund, lawyer and notary.]

20689. KEMPNER, ROBERT M. W.: *Ankläger einer Epoche*. Lebenserinnerungen. In Zusammenarbeit mit Jörg Friedrich. Frankfurt am Main: Ullstein, 1983. 474 pp., illus., bibl. (463–466). [Cf.: Epochales Geschichtswerk (Hans Lamm) [in]: 'Allgemeine', Nr. 2, Düsseldorf, 19. Jan. 1984, p. 12. Faszinierende Erinnerungen (Rudolf Wassermann) [in]: Das Parlament, Nr. 8, Bonn, 25. Feb. 1984, p. 14.] [R.M.W.K., born Oct. 17, 1899 in Freiburg i.Br., lawyer, emigrated to the USA in 1935, returned to Germany in 1945 to become deputy chief prosecuting counsel at the Nuremberg trials.]

20690. KOESTLER, ARTHUR: *Als Zeuge der Zeit; das Abenteuer meines Lebens*. (Übers. aus dem Engl. von Franziska Becker [et al.]. Vom Verfasser autorisierte Bearbeitung.) Bern: Scherz, 1983. 448 pp. [See also Nos. 20505–20506.]

20691. — KOESTLER, ARTHUR & CYNTHIA: *The stranger on the square*. London: Hutchinson, 1983. 256 pp. [Finished after their deaths, the final vol. of K.'s autobiogr. trilogy which began with 'Arrow in the blue', followed by 'The invisible writing'.]

20692. KORNFELD, PAUL. PAZI, MARGARITA: *Zu Kornfelds Leben und Werk: Tagebücher aus seiner Frankfurter Zeit 1914–1921*. [In]: Jahrbuch der Deutschen Schillergesellschaft, Jg. 27, Stuttgart, 1983. Pp. 59–85, footnotes. [P.K., Dec. 11, 1889 Prague – Jan. 1942 Ghetto Lodz, expressionist writer.]

20693. KUCZYNSKI, JÜRGEN: *Memoiren: die Erziehung des J.K. zum Kommunisten und Wissenschaftler*. Köln: Pahl-Rugenstein, 1983. 458 pp. [J.K., born Sept. 17, 1904 in Elberfeld, professor of statistics and economic history, emigrated to England in 1936, returned to the GDR in 1945.]

—— LAZARUS, MORITZ: *Moritz Lazarus und Heymann Steinthal*. [See No. 20707.]

20694. LIND, JAKOV: *Selbstportrait*. Berlin: Wagenbach, 1983. 157 pp., port. (Wagenbachs Taschenbücherei, 105.) [German edn. of 'Counting my steps'. London, 1970, see No. 9123/YB XVI. Recollections of childhood in Nazi Vienna, antisemitism, life as child refugee.] [J.L., orig. Jakob Landwirt, born Feb. 10, 1927 in Vienna, emigrated to the Netherlands, to Palestine in 1945, now in London.]

20695. LOEWENSTEIN, KARL: *Thomas Mann – Karl Loewenstein Briefwechsel. T. 2: 1938–1955*. Hrsg. von Eva Schiffer. [In]: Blätter der Thomas Mann Gesellschaft, Nr. 19, Zürich, 1982. Pp. 3–40, notes (34–40). [For pt. 1 and K.L. data, see No. 18679/YB XXVII.]

20696. MAERZ FAMILY. *Genealogie einer maehrisch-juedischen Familie (Familie Maerz)*. Verfasst von David Paul Meretz (frueher Paul Maerz). Jerusalem: Priv. print by the author's sons, 1983. 79, [5] pp. [Mimeog.] [Genealogy from the 19th–20th centuries.] [D.P.M., 1894 Ungarisch Hradisch – 1981 Jerusalem, Zionist leader in Czechoslovakia, emigration to Palestine in 1939, served in Israel's Ministry of Interior.]

20697. MAHLER, GUSTAV: *Unbekannte Briefe.* Hrsg. von Herta Blaukopf. Mit Beiträgen von Kurt Blaukopf [et al.]. Wien: Zsolnay, 1983. 256 pp., illus. (Bibliothek der Internat. Gustav-Mahler-Gesellschaft.) [150 hitherto unpubl. letters to 17 people.]

20698. MARX, KARL: *Der Briefwechsel Karl Marx – Friedrich Engels, 1844–1883.* Mit einem Essay von Hermann Oncken. Bd. 1–4. Nachdr. der Ausg. Berlin 1929–1931. München: Deutscher Taschenbuch-Verl., 1983. 4 vols. (cased), bibl. (dtv, 5991.)

20699. MEYERBEER, GIACOMO: *Giacomo Meyerbeer: ein Leben in Briefen.* [Hrsg. von] Heinz und Gudrun Becker. Wilhelmshaven: Heinrichshofen, 1983. 298 pp., illus., bibl. (263–265). (Taschenbücher zur Musikwissenschaft, 85.)

20700. MICHAELIS-JENA, RUTH: *Heritage of the Kaiser's children.* An autobiography. Edinburgh: Canongate, 1983. 156 pp. [Born to a Jewish family in Detmold, the author emigrated to England in 1934 and became a bookseller in Edinburgh.]

20701. PACHTER, HENRY: *Weimar études.* New York: Columbia Univ. Press, 1982. XVII, 397 pp., illus., notes & bibl. (363–379). [Partly autobiographical, deals with the author's experiences in left wing youth movement in Berlin, also refers to, a.o., Benjamin, Einstein, Rathenau. Cf.: The great cabaret (Jim Miller) [in]: Newsweek, New York, Sept. 1982. Henry Pachter and Weimar (George Mosse) [in]: Salmagundi, No. 60, Saratoga Springs, N.Y., Spring-Summer 1983, pp. 170–175.] [H.P., orig. Heinz Pächter, Jan. 22, 1907 Berlin – Dec. 10, 1980 New York, historian, journalist.]

20702. PARKER, ERWIN: *Mein Schauspielhaus; Erinnerungen an die Zürcher Theaterjahre 1933–1947.* Zürich: Pendo-Verl., 1983. 183 pp. [Refers, a.o., to Therese Giehse, Ernst Ginsberg, Kurt Hirschfeld, Kurt Horwitz, Wolfgang Langhoff, Leopold Lindtberg, Leonard Steckel.] [E.P., orig. Pincus, born June 26, 1903 in Berlin, actor, emigrated in 1934 via Holland to Switzerland.]

—— RATHENAU, WALTHER/HARDEN, MAXIMILIAN: *Briefwechsel 1897–1920.* [See No. 20589.]

20703. REIK, THEODOR. BERLIN, JEFFREY B./LINDKEN, HANS ULRICH: *Theodor Reiks unveröffentlichte Briefe an Arthur Schnitzler.* Unter Berücksichtigung einiger Briefe Reiks an Richard Beer-Hofmann. [In]: Literatur und Kritik, H. 173/174, Wien, Apr./Mai 1983. Pp. 182–197, notes. [Th.R., May 12, 1888 Vienna – Oct. 31, 1969 New York, psychoanalyst, emigrated in 1934 via Holland to the USA.]

—— ROTH, JOSEPH. [See No. 20714.]

20704. SAHL, HANS: *Memoiren eines Moralisten.* Erinnerungen 1. Zürich: Ammann, 1983. 231 pp. (Sahl, Hans: Gesammelte Werke, hrsg. von Klaus Schöffling, Bd. 5,1.) [First vol. of the author's 'Collected works' planned to comprise 8 vols.] [H.S., born May 20, 1902 in Dresden, writer, film and theatre critic, emigrated in 1941 via various countries to the USA.]

20705. SALOMON, ALICE: *Charakter ist Schicksal.* Lebenserinnerungen. Aus dem Engl. übers. von Rolf Landwehr. Hrsg. von Rüdeger Baron und Rolf Landwehr. Mit einem Nachwort von Joachim Wieler. Weinheim: Beltz, 1983. 349 pp., illus., footnotes. [Memoirs especially on the author's social work, orig. written in English but never publ. See also No. 20610.] [A.S. data, see No. 18584/YB XXVII.]

20706. SCHNITZLER, ARTHUR: *Tagebuch 1913–1916.* Unter Mitwirkung von Peter Michael Braunwarth [et al.] hrsg. von der Kommission für Literarische Gebrauchsformen der Österr. Akademie der Wissenschaften. Obmann: Werner Welzig. Wien: Verlag der Österr. Akademie der Wissenschaften, 1983. 432 pp. [For preceding vol. see No. 18692/YB XXVII. Cf.: A.Sch.'s occasions: reflections on the 'Tagebuch 1909–1912' (Martin Swales) [in]: German Life and Letters, Vol. 36, New series, No. 4, Oxford, July 1983, pp. 368–373, notes. 'Die verschlossenen schweren Tore in mir' (Hansres Jacobi) [in]: NZZ, Nr. 23, Zürich, 28./29. Jan. 1984, p. 69. Incongruities of war (Edward Timms) [in]: TLS, London, Apr. 20, 1984, p. 434.]

20707. STEINTHAL, HEYMANN: *Moritz Lazarus und Heymann Steinthal; die Begründer der Völkerpsychologie in ihren Briefen.* Bd. 2/1. Mit einer Einleitung hrsg. von Ingrid Belke. Tübingen: Mohr, 1983. LIII, 367 pp., illus., ports., facsims. (Schriftenreihe wissenschaftlicher Abhandlungen des Leo Baeck Instituts, 40.) [Cont. the complete correspondence between H. Steinthal and Gustav Glogau (1844–1899), professor of philosophy in Zürich, Halle and Kiel. For vol. 1, publ. in 1971, see No. 10042/YB XVII.] [H.St., May 16, 1823 Gröbzig – March 14, 1899 Berlin, philologist, one of the founders of ethno-psychology.]

20708. TERGIT, GABRIELE: *Etwas Seltenes überhaupt.* Erinnerungen. Orig .-Ausg. Frankfurt am

Main: Ullstein, 1983. 239 pp. (Ullstein-Buch, Nr. 20324.) [G.T., orig. Elise Reifenberg, née Hirschmann, March 4, 1894 Berlin – July 25, 1982 London, journalist, writer.]

20709. TORBERG, FRIEDRICH: *Pegasus im Joch; Briefwechsel mit Verlegern und Redakteuren.* (Hrsg. von David Axmann und Marietta Torberg.) München: Langen Müller, 1983. 283 pp. (Torberg, Friedrich: Gesammelte Werke in Einzelausgaben, Bd. 14.) [For preceding two vols. of letters see No. 19642/YB XXVIII.] [F.T. data, see No. 18621/YB XXVII.]

20710. VARNHAGEN, RAHEL: *Jeder Wunsch wird Frivolität genannt.* Briefe und Tagebücher. Ausgewählt und hrsg. von Marlis Gerhardt. Orig.-Ausg. Darmstadt: Luchterhand, 1983. 138 pp., bibl. (Sammlung Luchterhand, 426.) [See also No. 20646.]

20711. WEISS, GITTEL: *Ein Lebensbericht.* Berlin/East: Interessengemeinschaft für Denkmalpflege, Kultur und Geschichte der Hauptstadt Berlin, 1982. 95 pp., illus. [G.W., 1903 Galicia – 1983 East Berlin, grew up in the Eastern Jewish 'Scheunenviertel' of Berlin, communist, worked in the law-office of Hilde Benjamin, married to a German worker, survived in Berlin.]

20712. WOLF, FRIEDRICH: *Briefwechsel* [mit Annemarie Langen-Koffler, 1948–1953]. [And]: *Konrad Wolf an Friedrich Wolf [1944].* [In]: Sinn und Form, Jg. 35, H. 6, Berlin/East, Nov./Dez. 1983. Pp. 1133–1148; 1149–1153. [See also Nos. 20669–20670.]

20713. ZWEIG, STEFAN: *The correspondence of Stefan Zweig with Raoul Auernheimer*; ed. with an introd. and notes by Donald G. Daviau and Jorun B. Johns; *and with Richard Beer-Hofmann;* ed. with commentary and notes by Jeffrey B. Berlin. Columbia, S.C.: Camden House, 1983. X, 273 pp., bibl. (Studies in German literature, linguistics, and culture, vol. 20.) [Cont.: The correspondence of St. Zweig and Raoul Auernheimer (1–163). The correspondence of St. Zweig and Richard Beer-Hofmann with unpubl. letters to Sol Liptzin and Ben Huebsch (167–235).] [R. Auernheimer, Apr. 15, 1876 Vienna – Jan. 7, 1948 Oakland, Ca., journalist, cousin of Theodor Herzl and his successor at the Neue Freie Presse, emigrated after 1938 to the USA.]

20714. — SHAKED, GERSHON: *The grace of reason and the grace of misery: Zweig and Roth – a correspondence.* [In]: The Hebrew Univ. Studies in Literature, Vol. 10, No. 2, Jerusalem, Autumn 1982. Pp. 247–270, bibl. reference. [Also in Hebrew under the title]: The grace of reason and the disgrace of misery [in]: Zmanim, No. 13, Tel-Aviv, Fall 1983, pp. 4–13, ports. [Covers the years 1927–1938.]

IX. GERMAN-JEWISH RELATIONS

A. General

20715. BEN-CHORIN, SCHALOM. *Der Mann, der Friede heisst; Begegnungen, Texte, Bilder für Schalom Ben-Chorin.* Aus Anlass seines 70. Geburtstages im Juli 1983, hrsg. und eingeleitet von Heinz M. Bleicher. Gerlingen: Bleicher, 1983. 151, 32 pp., illus., ports.

—— BETHGE, EBERHARD: *Dieter Bonhoeffer und die Juden.* [See in No. 20172.]

20716. *Briefe an junge Deutsche; Juden antworten deutschen Schülern auf einen Leserbrief in der Jerusalem Post.* Hrsg. von F. Angern [et al.]. Düsseldorf (Morsestr. 5): Der Kleine Verlag, 1983. 112 pp. [Refers to the gulf between German Jews who survived Nazi persecution and Germans.]

20717. DAY, INGEBORG: *Geisterwalzer.* (Aus dem Amerikan.) Salzburg: Residenz-Verl., 1983. 195 pp. [Report of a young Austrian woman, born during World War II, on her father's Nazi past and her shocked discovery of her own prejudices; transl. of 'Ghost waltz', publ. 1980 in the USA.]

20718. *Deutsche, Linke, Juden.* Berlin: Ästhetik und Kommunikation Verlag, 1983. 127 pp., illus. (Ästhetik und Kommunikation, Jg. 14, H. 51, Juni 1983.) [Incl.: Fragmente von Unterwegs: über jüd. und politische Identität in Deutschland (Dany Diner, 5–16). Wovon berührt? vom jüd. Trauma? von den Traumata der Eltern? (Olav Münzberg, 24–26). Verlängerung des Schweigens (Eberhard Knödler-Bunte, 33–47). Gespräch mit Eva Reichmann 'Tragt ihn mit Stolz, den gelben Fleck'; [&]: Gespräch mit Maria Jahoda 'Für mich ist mein Judentum erst mit Hitler eine wirkliche Identifikation geworden' (Hajo Funke, 51–70; 71–89). Cf.: Tödliches Gerede: eine Polemik (Henryk M. Broder) [&]: Tödliches Schweigen: eine Antwort (Eberhard Knödler-Bunte) [in]: Die Zeit, Nr. 39, Hamburg, 23. Sept. 1983, pp. 45–46.]

20719. JENS, WALTER: *Nathan der Weise aus der Sicht von Auschwitz; Juden und Christen in Deutschland.* Zur Erinnerung an den 30. Jan. 1933. Vortrag. Hamburg, 1983. 18 pp. (Schriften der Freien Akademie der Künste in Hamburg, 7.)

20720. KEUN, IRMGARD: *Wenn wir alle gut wären.* Hrsg. und mit einem Nachwort von Wilhelm Unger. Köln: Kiepenheuer & Witsch, 1983. 268 pp., illus. [Incl. autobiographical texts referring to the author's emigration and her Jewish friends.] [I.K., Feb. 6, 1910 Berlin – May 5, 1982 Cologne, writer, non-Jewish companion of Joseph Roth, in exile, returned during the war with false papers.]

20721. LIPSTADT, DEBORAH E.: *Present-day Germany.* [In]: Midstream, Vol. 29, No. 9, New York, Nov. 1983. Pp. 25–29, notes. [Deals also with the Germans' attitudes to the past, to Jews, to antisemitism.]

—— SCHARF, KURT: *Juden – Christen – Deutsche.* [See in No. 20172.]

20722. SCHMELZKOPF, CHRISTIANE: *Zur Gestaltung jüdischer Figuren in der deutschsprachigen Literatur nach 1945.* Hildesheim; New York: Olms, 1983. 277 pp. (Germaistische Texte, Bd. 16.)

20723. SOMBART, NICOLAUS: *Jugend in Berlin.* [In]: Merkur, Jg. 37, H. 4 (418), Stuttgart, Juni 1983. Pp. 384–395. [Reminiscences of N.S., born 1923, son of Werner Sombart; incl. chaps. 'Die Juden' and 'Carl Schmitt', refers to antisemitism, and the knowledge of the Final Solution.]

20724. TAL, URIEL: *Young German intellectuals at the beginning of the 19th century – on romanticism and Judaism.* [In Hebrew]. [In]: Zmanim, No. 11, Tel-Aviv, Spring 1983. Pp. 14–19.

20725. *Tribüne.* Zeitschrift zum Verständnis des Judentums. Jg. 22, H. 85–88. Hrsg. von Elisabeth Reisch. Frankfurt am Main: Tribüne-Verl., 1983. 4 issues. [*H. 81* incl.: Eine Generation nach dem Holocaust (Herbert Freeden, 18–24). Das Menschliche und das Unmenschliche: Erörterungen zur Judenhassfrage (Hilde Rubinstein, 136–152). *H. 86*: In einer Vergangenheit leben, die keine Zukunft hatte: Requiem für die Jeckes in Israel (Herbert Freeden, 80–88). Drei Spielarten der Judenfeindschaft: Antijudaismus – Antisemitismus – Antizionismus (Rudolf Pfisterer, 114–126). *H. 87*: Herbstreise in Deutschland: eine Episode am Rande von Bergen-Belsen (Dietrich Gronau, 168–170). Reflexionen über ein beschädigtes Leben: ein Versuch über Hans Mayer (Walter Boehlich, 172–176). *H. 88*: Antisemitismus – Vorstufe zum Judenmord (Robert M. W. Kempner, 20–24). Antisemitismus ohne Antisemiten: über die jüngste Variante eines alten Vorurteils (Henryk M. Broder, 75–87). Further contributions are listed according to subject.]

B. German-Israeli Relations

20726. DEUTSCHKRON, INGE: *Israel und die Deutschen; das besondere Verhältnis.* 2., erweiterte und aktualisierte Aufl. Köln: Verlag Wissenschaft und Politik, 1983. 456 pp. [For first edn. and edn. in English 'Bonn and Jerusalem', 1970, see No. 9148/YB XVI.]

20727. *deutschland-berichte.* Hrsg.: Rolf Vogel. Jg. 19, Nr. 1–12. Bonn, 1983. 11 issues & Themenregister (15 pp). [*Nr. 6* incl.: Alex Bein berichtet über seinen Weg im Zionismus (14– 15). Meir Faerber berichtet über seinen Kampf um die deutsche Sprache in Israel (15– 17). *Nr. 7/8*: Seit 1941: Deutscher literarischer Zirkel in Israel (Nadja Taussig/Rolf Vogel, 16–17). *Nr. 9*: Die wissenschaftlichen Beziehungen zwischen Israel und der Bundesrepublik Deutschland (Günter Lehr, 23–27). Further contributions are listed according to subject.]

20728. HEINEMANN, GÜNTER, ed.: *Die Partnerschaft mit Rehovot wurde vollzogen; nach dem Heidelberg-Treffen in Haifa.* Dokumentation der Informations- und Studienreise einer Gemeindedelegation nach Israel vom 1.–8. Mai 1983. Heidelberg: Stadt, 1983. 37 pp., illus.

20729. TSCHEPE, EBERHARD: *Annahme verweigert; Augenblicke zwischen Sylt und Sinai.* Mit einem Nachwort von Henryk M. Broder. Gerlingen: Bleicher, 1983. 228 pp. [E.T., born 1936 in Guben into a Nazi family, worked in Israel for the 'Aktion Sühnezeichen'.]

C. Church and Synagogue

20730. BEN-CHORIN, SCHALOM: *Vom Kirchenvater Abraham und anderen Ungereimtheiten; Randerlebnisse im christlich-jüdischen Dialog.* Wuppertal: Brockhaus, 1983. 112 pp., illus.

20731. BAUMANN, ARNULF H., ed.: *Was jeder vom Judentum wissen muss.* Im Auftrag des Arbeitskreises

Kirche und Judentum der Vereinigten Evang.-Luther. Kirche Deutschlands und des Deutschen Nationalkomitees des Luther. Weltbundes hrsg. Gütersloh: Mohn, 1983. 208 pp., illus., bibl. (188–196). (Gütersloher Taschenbücher Siebenstern, 1063.)

20732. *Christian Jewish Relations.* A documentary survey. Vol. 16, Nos. 1–4. Ed.: C. C. Aronsfeld. London: Institute of Jewish Affairs in association with the World Jewish Congress, 1983. 4 issues. [*No. 1* incl.: The Jewish Bible and its anti-Jewish interpretation (Rolf Rendtorff, 3–20, bibl.). Antisemitism and the conflict in the Churches since 1945 (John S. Conway, 21–37, notes). The Protestant press of the USA: 1933–1945 (Carl Hermann Voss, 54–61; review article of 'So it was true' by Robert W. Ross, see No. 17153/YB XXVI). *No. 2*: Christians and Judaism: Austrian Catholic Bishops' Declaration, Apr. 1982. (21–31). Judaism in German Catholic education (Waltraud Hermes, 32–36). *No. 3*: Luther, Lutheranism and the Jews; second Jewish/Lutheran Consultation, Stockholm, 11–13 July 1983 (17–22).]

20733. Ericksen, Robert P.: *Zur Auseinandersetzung mit und um Gerhard Kittels Antisemitismus.* [In]: Evangelische Theologie, Jg. 43, H. 3, München, Mai/Juni 1983. Pp. 250–270, footnotes.

20734. Hallo, Rudolf: *Christian Hebraists.* Transl. from German by Gertrude Hallo and postscript by William Hallo. [In]: Modern Judaism, Vol. 3, No. 1, Baltimore, Feb. 1983. Pp. 95–116, notes. [Transl. of 'Die christliche Wissenschaft vom Judentum', a lecture held at the Frankfurt Lehrhaus in 1924 and first publ. [in]: Der Morgen, Jg. 10, 1934, pp. 283–294; 359–365.]

20735. Lapide, Pinchas/Rahner, Karl: *Heil von den Juden?* Ein Gespräch. Mainz: Matthias-Grünewald-Verl., 1983. 123 pp.

20736. Liebeschütz, Hans: *Synagoge und Ecclesia; religionsgeschichtliche Studien über die Auseinandersetzung der Kirche mit dem Judentum im Hochmittelalter.* (Aus dem Nachlass hrsg., mit einem Nachwort und einer 'Bibliographie Hans Liebeschütz' versehen von Alexander Patschovsky. Mit einem Geleitwort von Franz Martini und Peter de Mendelssohn.) Heidelberg: Schneider, 1983. 263 pp., footnotes, bibl. (245–251). (Veröffentlichung der Deutschen Akademie für Sprache und Dichtung, Darmstadt, 55.) [First publ. of a manuscript whose printing was prevented in 1938; cont. chaps.: Die Lehre vom alten und neuen Gottesvolk. Die soziale Stellung der Juden im Karolingerreich. Die karolingische Reichskirche und Erzbischof Agobard von Lyon. Kreuzzugsbewegung und Judentum. Volksfrömmigkeit und religiöse Symbolik. Soziale Wandlungen. Das Judentum im System der Kirchenpolitik und der Scholastik des 13. Jh. Discusses also economic aspects.] [H.L., Dec. 3, 1893 Hamburg – Oct. 28, 1978 Liverpool, historian, medievalist, philosopher, member of London LBI executive board.]

20737. LUTHER, MARTIN. Ben-Chorin, Schalom: *Enttäuschte Hoffnung: Martin Luther und die Juden.* [And]: Kremers, Heinz/Schallenberger, E. Horst: *Keine Tabus um Luther: der Reformator und sein Verhältnis zum Judentum.* [In]: Tribüne, Jg. 22, H. 87, Frankfurt am Main, 1983. Pp. 140–150; 151–156.

20738. — Gritsch, Eric W./Tanenbaum, Marc H.: *Luther and the Jews.* New York: Lutheran Council in the USA, 1983. 17 pp. [See also: World Lutherans adopt historic declaration on 'Luther and the Jews'; religious commentary (Marc H. Tanenbaum) [in]: Canvas, Issue No. 3, Vancouver, Canada, July 27, 1983. 1 p.]

20739. — Gruenewald, Max: *Martin Luther and the Jews.* [In]: The Jewish News, Vauxhall, N.J., Sept. 1, 1983. Pp. C 29 – C 31.

20740. — *Luther und die Juden.* Basel: Stiftung für Kirche und Judentum, Sept. 1983. Pp. 129–208, notes. (Judaica, Jg. 39, H. 3.) [Incl.: Luther und die Juden (Ernst Ludwig Ehrlich, 131–149). Jüd. Reaktionen auf die Reformation (Stefan Schreiner, 150–165). Erbarmen für Luther? (Peter Maser, 166–178; review essay of the books by Walther Bienert, see No. 19684/YB XXVIII; and by Heiko A. Oberman, see No. 18757/YB XXVII). Kein Platz für die Juden? (Reiner Jansen, 179–192).]

20741. — Oberman, Heiko A.: *Luthers Beziehungen zu den Juden: Ahnen und Geahndete.* [In]: Leben und Werk Martin Luthers von 1526 bis 1546, hrsg. von Helmar Junghans. Göttingen: Vandenhoeck & Ruprecht, 1983. Vol. 1, pp. 519–530, notes. [See also: Luther, Israel und die Juden: befangen in mittelalterlicher Tradition (Heiko A. Oberman) [in]: Das Parlament, Nr. 3, Bonn, 22. Jan. 1983, p. 12. Tribut an den Geist der Zeit: M. Luthers Stellung zu den Juden (G. Müller) [&]: Luther und die Juden: Kontroverse mit H. Oberman [in]: Evangelische Kommentare, 6, Stuttgart, 1983, pp. 305–308; 329–330.]

20742. — Schultz, Hans Jürgen, ed.: *Luther kontrovers.* Stuttgart: Kreuz-Verl., 1983. 317 pp. [Incl.: Homo politicus (Helmut Gollwitzer). Rückfragen und Ausblicke aus der Sicht eines Juden (Albert H. Friedlander).]

20743. — ZAHRNT, HEINZ: *Martin Luther in seiner Zeit – für unsere Zeit*. München: Süddeutscher Verl., 1983. 259 pp., 278 illus. [Also on Luther's attitude towards Jews.]

20744. MOLITOR, FRANZ J. SACHS, SHIMON: *A Jewish 'Philanthrop' – Franz Molitor*. [In Hebrew, title transl.]. [In]: Ha-Umma (The Nation), No. 73, Tel-Aviv, Winter 1983/4. Pp. 373–377. [F.J.M., 1779 Oberursel – 1860, Christian philosopher and kabbalist.]

20745. MÜLLER, KARLHEINZ: *Das Judentum in der religionsgeschichtlichen Arbeit am Neuen Testament*. Eine kritische Rückschau auf die Entwicklung einer Methodik bis zu den Qumranfunden. Frankfurt am Main: Lang, 1983. 227 pp. (Judentum und Umwelt, Bd. 6.)

20746. SIEGMUND, GEORG: *Judentum und Christentum; Zeugnisse zu ihrem gegenseitigen Verständnis*. Stein am Rhein: Christiana-Verl., 1983. 80 pp.

20747. STROH, HANS: *Juden und Christen: schwierige Partner*. Begegnungen, Erfahrungen, Erkenntnisse. Stuttgart: Quell-Verl., 1983. 117 pp. [Incl.: Die 'Reichskristallnacht': das tödliche Nebeneinander. Evangelische Christen und die Stuttgarter Juden.]

20748. VOLKEN, LAURENZ: *Jesus der Jude und das Jüdische im Christentum*. Mit einem Geleitwort von Erich Zenger. Düsseldorf: Patmos, 1983. 263 pp., bibl.

D. Antisemitism

—— AUSTRIA. [See Nos. 19871, 19873, 19877–19878, 19882, 20754, 20790.]

—— BRODER, HENRYK M.: *Antisemitismus ohne Antisemiten*. [See in No. 20725.]

20749. ETTINGER, SHMUEL: *The Young Hegelians; a source of modern anti-Semitism?* [In]: The Jerusalem Quarterly, No. 28, Jerusalem, Summer 1983. Pp. 73–82.

20750. GADE, RICHARD E.: *A historical survey of anti-Semitism*. Grand Rapids, Mich.: Baker Book House, 1981. 147 pp., notes, bibl. [Incl.: The enlightenment, Germany in the 19th century, Holocaust.]

20751. GREIVE, HERMANN: *Geschichte des modernen Antisemitismus in Deutschland*. Darmstadt: Wissenschaftliche Buchgesellschaft, 1983. IX, 224 pp., bibl. (187–193). (Grundzüge, Bd. 53.) [From the time of enlightenment to neo-Nazism. Cf.: Besprechung (Günther B. Ginzel) [in]: 'Allgemeine', Nr. 6, Düsseldorf, 10. Feb. 1984, p. 4.] [See also Greive in No. 19754.]

20752. KAMPE, NORBERT: *Bildungsbürgertum und Antisemitismus im deutschen Kaiserreich; der studentische Anteil an der Durchsetzung einer gesellschaftlichen Norm*. Berlin, Techn. Univ., Phil. Diss., 1983. 709 pp., bibl.

20753. KATZ, JACOB: *Misreadings of anti-Semitism*. [In]: Commentary, Vol. 76, No. 1, New York, July 1983. Pp. 39–44, notes. [Also on German and Nazi antisemitism.]

20754. LUEGER, KARL: *'I decide who is a Jew!'* The papers of Karl Lueger, introd., transl. and ed. by Richard S. Geehr. Washington, D.C.: Univ. Press of America, 1982. VII, 360 pp., illus., ports., bibl. (355–360). [See also No. 19880.]

—— MACK, RÜDIGER: *Otto Böckel und die antisemitische Bauernbewegung in Hessen 1887–1894*. [See pp. 377–410 in No. 19832.]

20755. MITSCHERLICH-NIELSEN, MARGARETE: *Antisemitismus – eine Männerkrankheit?* [In]: Psyche, Jg. 37, H. 1, Stuttgart, Jan. 1983. Pp. 41–54, notes, English summary.

20756. NEMITZ, KURT: *Antisemitismus in der Wissenschaftspolitik der Weimarer Republik: der 'Fall Ludwig Schemann'*. [In]: Jahrbuch des Instituts für deutsche Geschichte, Bd. 12, Tel-Aviv, 1983. Pp. 377–407, footnotes, documents.

20757. OBERMAN, HEIKO A.: *The roots of anti-Semitism in the age of Renaissance and Reformation*. Transl. from German by James I. Porter. Philadelphia: Fortress, 1983. 160 pp. [Transl. of No. 18757/YB XXVII. Refers also to Luther. [See also Nos. 20737–20743.]

20758. *Patterns of Prejudice*. Vol. 17, Nos. 1–4. Ed.: C. C. Aronsfeld. London: Institute of Jewish Affairs in association with the World Jewish Congress, 1983. 4 issues. [*No. 1* incl.: The Holocaust and today's generation (John P. Fox, 3–24, notes; review essay on recent books). *No. 2*: 50 years after Hitler: thoughts of a 'German rebellion' (C. C. Aronsfeld, 21–29). *No. 4*: How to combat antisemitism (Milton Ellerin [et al.], 3–18; respond to the symposium on 'Antisemitism today' publ. in No. 4, 1982, of Patterns of Prejudice, see No. 19708/YB XXVIII). Antisemitism in Austria (Marie Jahoda, 46–48). Further contributions are listed according to subject.]

20759. POLIAKOV, LÉON: *Die Aufklärung und ihre judenfeindliche Tendenz*. (Übers.: Rudolf Pfisterer.) Worms: Heintz, 1983. 269 pp. (Poliakov, Léon: Geschichte des Antisemitismus, Bd. 5.)

20760. POLIAKOV, LÉON: *The history of anti-Semitism. Vol. 4: Suicidal Europe, 1817–1933*. New York: Vanguard, 1983. 528 pp.

— RICHARZ, MONIKA: *Juden, Wissenschaft und Universitäten.* [See in No. 19764.]

20761. RINGER, FRITZ K.: *Die Gelehrten; der Niedergang der deutschen Mandarine 1890–1933.* (Aus dem Amerikan. von Klaus Laermann.) Mit einem Nachwort von Dietrich Goldschmidt. Stuttgart: Klett-Cotta, 1983. 452 pp., bibl. (425–444). [Refers to antisemitism at German universities. For American orig., 1969, see No. 8350/YB XV.]

20762. RINGER, FRITZ K.: *Inflation, antisemitism and the German academic community of the Weimar period.* [And comments]: *Inflation and depression as Hitler's pace makers* (Gerald D. Feldman). [In]: LBI Year Book XXVIII, London, 1983. Pp. 3–9, footnotes; [& comments]: 37–40, footnotes.

20763. SCHANNER, BRIGITTE: *Flugschrift und Pasquill als Kampfmittel gegen die Juden.* Ein Beitrag zur frühen Publizistik des 16. und 17. Jahrhunderts. Wien, Univ., Diss., 1983. 371 pp.

20764. SCHOTTLAENDER, RUDOLF: *Vom Judenhass dreier Grosser: Nachbemerkungen zum Luther-Marx-Wagner-Gedenkjahr.* [In]: Frankfurter Hefte, Jg. 38, H. 12, Frankfurt am Main, Dez. 1983. Pp. 37–46.

20765. SINGERMAN, ROBERT: *Antisemitic propaganda.* An annotated bibliography and research guide. Foreword Colin Holmes. New York: Garland, 1982. XXXVII, 448 pp. (Garland reference library . . . vol. 112.) [Incl. German pre-Nazi and Nazi period material publ. in English covering the period 1871–1981; also on the Elders of Zion myth.]

20766. SUCHY, BARBARA: *The Verein zur Abwehr des Antisemitismus (I): from its beginnings to the First World War.* [In]: LBI Year Book XXVIII, London, 1983. Pp. 205–239, footnotes, illus.

20767. TRACHTENBERG, JOSHUA: *The devil and the Jews.* The medieval conception of the Jew and its relation to modern anti-Semitism. Foreword by Marc Saperstein. Philadelphia: Jewish Publ. Society, 1983. 278 pp., illus., bibl. (256–267), notes. [Incl. German medieval antisemitism, ritual murder accusation, blood libel. 2nd paperback edn., first publ. in 1943.]

20768. WISTRICH, ROBERT S.: *Antisemitism as a 'radical ideology' in the 19th century.* [In]: The Jerusalem Quarterly, No. 28, Jerusalem, Summer 1983. Pp. 83–95. [On Germany and Austria.]

20769. WISTRICH, ROBERT S.: *The pitfalls of false prophecy.* [In]: Jewish Chronicle, London, 9. Dec. 1983. [On Luther, Marx, Wagner, Hitler, and the Jews.]

20770. ZENTRUM FÜR ANTISEMITISMUSFORSCHUNG, Berlin. STRAUSS, HERBERT A.: *Alter und neuer Antisemitismus; das Zentrum für Antisemitismusforschung der Technischen Universität Berlin.* [In]: Aktuell, Nr. 37, Berlin, Nov. 1983. Pp. 4–5, illus. [See also: 'Es gibt nichts richtig Vergleichbares'; Interview (Herbert A. Strauss/Jochen Maes) [in]: 'Allgemeine', Nr. 23, Düsseldorf, 10. Juni 1983, pp. 1–2. Fourth lecture: 'Defence against antisemitism, 1893–1933' by Arnold Paucker (Review note) [in]: AJR Information, London, Aug. 1983, p. 4 [& in]: 'Allgemeine', Nr. 25, Düsseldorf, 24. Juni 1983, p. 4.]

20771. — STRAUSS, HERBERT A.: *Antisemitismusforschung als Wissenschaft.* [In]: Aus Politik und Zeitgeschichte, Beilage zur Wochenzeitung Das Parlament, B 30, Bonn, 30. Juli 1983. Pp. 3–10. [Inaugural lecture of the director of the 'Zentrum' on Nov. 9, 1982; see also No. 19713/YB XXVIII.]

20772. — STRAUSS, HERBERT A.: *Zentrum für Antisemitismusforschung.* [In]: Tribüne, Jg. 22, H. 86, Frankfurt am Main, 1983. Pp. 43–50.

E. **Noted Germans and Jews**

20773. BRAHMS, JOHANNES. HAAS, FRITHJOF: *Johannes Brahms und Hermann Levi.* [In]: Johannes Brahms in Baden-Baden und Karlsruhe; eine Ausstellung. [Katalog.] Karlsruhe: Badische Landesbibliothek, 1983. Pp. 58–82, illus., bibl. (81–82). [H. Levi, Nov. 7, 1839 Giessen – May 13, 1900 München, conductor.]

20774. BRECHT, BERTOLD. HAYMAN, RONALD: *Brecht.* A biography. London: Weidenfeld & Nicolson; New York: Oxford Univ. Press, 1983. 423 pp., illus. [Also on B.'s relations with many German Jews.]

20775. FREYTAG, GUSTAV. GELBER, MARK H.: *An alternate reading of the role of the Jewish scholar in Gustav Freytag's 'Soll und Haben'.* [In]: The Germanic Review, Vol. 58, No. 2, Washington, D.C., Spring 1983. Pp. 83–88, notes.

— GEORGE, STEFAN: *Briefwechsel Stefan George – Ida Coblenz.* [See No. 20681.]

20776. — YARROW, ANDREW L.: *Humanism and Deutschtum: the origins, development and consequences of the politics of poetry in the George-Kreis.* [In]: The Germanic Review, Vol. 58, No. 1,

Washington, D.C., Winter 1983. Pp. 1–11, notes. [Refers, a.o., to Gundolf and E. Kantorowicz.]

—— HEBBEL, FRIEDRICH. Häusler, Wolfgang: *Sigmund Engländer . . . Freund F. Hebbels.* [See in No. 19769.]

20777. KLEIST, HEINRICH: *Heinrich von Kleist an Friedrich de la Motte Fouqué, 1810.* [Kommentiert von Hans Joachim Kreutzer.] Veröffentlicht von der Heinrich-von-Kleist-Gesellschaft und der Staatsbibliothek Preuss. Kulturbesitz. Berlin, 1983. [2] pp., & Facsim. [Facsim. and transcription of a hitherto unpubl. letter; refers to K.'s connections with Julius Eduard Hitzig and Ludwig Robert, R. Varnhagen's brother; refutes K.'s alleged anti-Jewish attitude.]

20778. LESSING, GOTTHOLD EPHRAIM. Thiemann, Ronald F.: *Gotthold Ephraim Lessing: an enlightened view of Judaism.* [In]: Journal of Ecumenical Studies, 18, Philadelphia, Summer 1981. Pp. 401–422. [See also No. 20180.]

20779. MANN, THOMAS: *Diaries 1918–1939.* Selection and foreword by Hermann Kesten. Transl. by Richard and Clara Winston. London: Deutsch, 1983. 471 pp., illus. [Incl. M.'s many Jewis associations, views on Judaism, antisemitism. Cf.: Education of a democrat (S. S. Prawer) [in]: TLS, London, Feb. 25, 1983, pp. 171–173. For American edn. see No. 19728/YB XXVIII. See also: Besprechung von Th. Manns Tagebücher 1918–1921 & 1937–1939 (Hermann Meier-Cronemeyer) [in]: Jahrbuch des Instituts für Deutsche Geschichte, 12, Tel-Aviv, 1983, pp. 526–537 (refers also to antisemitic entries in M.'s diaries.]

—— — Mann, Thomas: *Thomas Mann – Karl Loewenstein Briefwechsel.* [See No. 20695.]

20780. — Gelber, Mark H.: *Thomas Mann and antisemitism.* [In]: Patterns of Prejudice, Vol. 17, No. 4, London, Oct. 1983. Pp. 31–40, notes.

20781. NIETZSCHE, FRIEDRICH. Golomb, Jacob: *Nietzsche's image of the Jew, Judaism and Zionism.* [In Hebrew, with English summary]. [In]: Mechkerei Yerushalayim be-Machshevet Yisrael (Jerusalem Studies in Jewish Thought), Vol. 2, No. 3, Jerusalem, Nissan 5743 [March/Apr. 1983]. Pp. 439–471.

20782. — Peters, Heinz Frederick: *Zarathustras Schwester; Fritz und Lieschen Nietzsche – ein deutsches Trauerspiel.* München: Kindler, 1983. 327 pp., illus., notes, bibl. [Elisabeth N. was married to the German antisemite Bernhard Förster. Transl. and augmented edn. of the American orig., New York, Crown, 1977.]

20783. SCHMITT, CARL. Bendersky, Joseph W.: *Carl Schmitt: theorist for the Third Reich.* Princeton: Princeton Univ. Press, 1983. 320 pp. [Cf.: Freund oder Feind: Parlamentarismus oder Diktatur: die unheimliche Aktualität und Kontinuität des Carl Schmitt (Christian Graf von Krockow) [in]: Die Zeit, Nr. 46, Hamburg, 11. Nov. 1983, p. 15.]

20784. — Neumann, Volker: *Carl Schmitt und die Linke.* Zum 95. Geburtstag des Rechtsphilosophen und Staatsrechtlers. [In]: Die Zeit, Nr. 28, Hamburg, 8. Juli 1983. P. 32. [C.Sch., born July 11, 1888, German theorist of public law in the Weimar Republic, became the most prominent supporter of the Nazi regime in legal matters, publ. the antisemitic pamphlet 'Die deutsche Rechtswissenschaft im Kampf gegen den jüdischen Geist'; article discusses Sch.'s influence on leading jurists such as Ernst Fraenkel, Otto Kirchheimer, Franz Neumann.]

20785. STIFTER, ADALBERT. Zettl, Walter: *Hiob im Böhmerwald; Anmerkungen zu Adalbert Stifters Erzählung 'Abdias'.* [In]: Literatur und Kritik, H. 179/180, Wien, Nov./Dez. 1983. Pp. 450–454, notes. [On the Jewish elements in St.'s 'Abdias'; and on his attitude towards Jews.]

20786. WAGNER, RICHARD: *Briefe.* Ausgewählt, eingeleitet und kommentiert von Hanjo Kesting. München: Piper, 1983. 677 pp., bibl. [Also on W.'s antisemitism.]

20787. — Gans, Haim: *Who's afraid of Richard Wagner?* [In Hebrew]. [In]: Iyyun, Vol. 32, No. 1/2, Jerusalem, Jan.–Apr. 1983. Pp. 92–109. [On the discussion in Israel whether to play W.'s music.]

20788. — Gregor-Dellin, Martin: *Richard Wagner: his life, his work, his century.* Transl. by J. Maxwell Brownjohn. London: Collins; New York: Harcourt Brace Jovanovich, 1983. 575 pp. [Also on Wagner and the Jews, covers W.'s antisemitism with leniency; abridged version of the German orig., München, Piper, 1980, 930 pp. For review see No. 20789.]

20789. — Kerman, Joseph: *Wagner and Wagnerism.* [In]: The New York Review of Books, Dec. 22, 1983. Pp. 27–37. [Review article on 15 recent books; refers especially to 'In search of Wagner' by Theodor Adorno (see No. 18375/YB XXVIII); discusses W.'s antisemitism.]

20790. — Wagner, Nike: *Parsifal et l'antisémitisme juif à Vienne, dans les années 1900.* Trad. de l'anglais par J.-L. Houdebine. [In]: L'Infini, 3, Paris, Été 1983. Pp. 22–32, footnotes.

20791. — Watson, D.: *The noble anti-Semitism of Richard Wagner.* [In]: Historical Journal, 25, Cambridge, England, 1982. Pp. 751–763. [Review article.]

20792. — WESSLING, BERDNT W., ed.: *Bayreuth im Dritten Reich; Richard Wagners politische Erben*. Eine Dokumentation. Weinheim: Beltz, 1983. 336 pp., illus. [Incl. antisemitic and racial texts.]

20793. — ZELINSKY, HARTMUT, ed.: *Richard Wagner – ein deutsches Thema*. Eine Dokumentation zur Wirkungsgeschichte Richard Wagners 1876–1976. 3., korrigierte Aufl. Berlin: Medusa, 1983. 292 pp., illus., bibl. [On the effect of W.'s work and Weltanschauung, also on antisemitism; first edn., 1976, see No. 14164/YB XXII.]

20794. — ZUCKERMANN, MOSHE: *Richard Wagner – a reactionary rebel*. [In Hebrew]. [In]: Zmanim, No. 12, Tel-Aviv, Summer 1983. Pp. 61–73. [Discusses W.'s reactionary and racist views as opposed to his revolutionary contribution to music.]

20795. WEBER, MAX. SCHÄFER-LICHTENBERGER, CHRISTA: *Stadt und Eidgenossenschaft im Alten Testament; eine Auseinandersetzung mit Max Webers Studie 'Das antike Judentum'*. Berlin: de Gruyter, 1983. XI, 485 pp. (Zeitschrift für die Alttestamentliche Wissenschaft, Beiheft 156.)

X. FICTION, POETRY AND HUMOUR

20796. AGEL, JEROME/BOE, EUGENE: *Deliverance in Shanghai*. A novel. New York: Dembner Books, 1983. 361 pp. [On Jewish refugees in Shanghai 1939–1945; incl. chap. '1938, Lübeck, Germany'.]

20797. APPELFELD, AHARON: *Tzili; the story of a life*. Transl. from the Hebrew by Dalya Bilu. New York: Dutton, 1983. 185 pp. [Story of a feeble-minded Jewish girl abandoned by her family and how she survives the Holocaust. See also: An interview with A. Appelfeld (Albert H. Friedlander) [in]: European Judaism, Vol. 17, No. 2, London, Winter 1983–84, pp. 2–3. An interview with A. Appelfeld, the recipient of the State of Israel Prize for Literature 1983 (Anita Susan Grossman) [in]: The Jewish Quarterly, Vol. 30, No. 4, London, Spring-Summer, 1983. Pp. 31–36.] [A.A., born 1932 in Czernowitz into an assimilated German-speaking Jewish family, escaped at the age of eight from a concentration camp, lived in the forests for three years, eventually reached Palestine in 1946; teaches Hebrew literature at the Univ. in Beer Sheva.]

20798. BEHRENS, KATJA: *Die dreizehnte Fee*. Düsseldorf: Claassen, 1983. 199 pp. [Chronicle of three women, a Jewish grandmother, her daughter and grand-daughter; refers also to the November pogrom and life in a Jewish middle-class family.]

20799. FAERBER, MEIR M.: *Brennende Eifersucht*. Erzählungen. Gerlingen: Bleicher, 1983. 143 pp. [M.M.F., born Apr. 29, 1908 in Mährisch-Ostrau, writer, lives in Israel.]

20800. HAMPTON, CHRISTOPHER: *Tales from Hollywood*. A play in repertory at the National Theatre, London, 1983 (review) [in]: AJR Information, London, Nov. 1983, p. 12. [On the life of exiles in Hollywood, deals, a.o., with Lion Feuchtwanger. For German version 'Geschichten aus Hollywood', on stage in Düsseldorf, see reviews: Flüchtlingsschicksale, europäische Erstaufführung (Hermann Lewy) [in]: 'Allgemeine', Nr. 14, Düsseldorf, 8. Apr. 1983, p. 7. Die ausgebeuteten Dichter (Heinrich Vormweg) [in]: SZ, Nr. 74, München, 30. März 1983, p. 14.]

20801. HIRSCH, RUDOLF: *Patria Israel*. Roman. Rudolstadt: Greifenverlag, 1983. 326 pp. [Autobiographical novel; the story of Jewish emigrants on board the French ship 'Patria' which was sunk in Haifa harbour in 1940.] [R.H., born Nov. 17, 1907, lives in the GDR.]

20802. KENEALLY, THOMAS: *Schindlers Liste*. Roman. (Aus dem Engl. von Günther Danehl.) München: Bertelsmann, 1983. 381 pp., illus. [Also paperback of English edn.]: *Schindler's list*. London; New York: Penguin, 1983. [Documentary novel on the industrialist Oskar Schindler who from 1939 to 1944 employed Jewish slave labourers and contrived against all the odds to save them from extermination. For Engl. and American edns. see No. 19742/YB XXVIII.]

20803. KIPPHARDT, HEINAR: *Bruder Eichmann*. Schauspiel. Reinbek: Rowohlt, 1983. 160 pp. (Das neue Buch.) [Cf.: Eine letzte, missverständliche Warnung: H. K.'s 'Bruder Eichmann' im Münchner Residenztheater uraufgeführt (C. Bernd Sucher) [in]: SZ, Nr. 18, München, 24. Jan. 1983, p. 24.]

20804. NEMES, LÁSZLÓ: *The age of Herostratus*. [In Hungarian, title transl.]. Budapest: Szépirodalmi Könyvkiadó, 1983. 318 pp. [Novel by a Hungarian-Jewish writer with autobiographical elements; contains a section on a unit of the British Royal Engineers in which many German-Jewish refugees served.]

Index to Bibliography

List of Contributors

Blakeney, Michael Leslie, M.A., b. 1948 in England. Barrister of the Supreme Court of New South Wales and Senior Lecturer, Faculty of Law, University of NSW. Author of *Media Law in Australia* (1983); *Advertising Regulation* (1983); *Price Discrimination and the Regulation of Market Behaviour* (1982).

Boas, Jacob, Ph.D., b. 1943 in Westerbork (Holland). Now lives in San Francisco. Teacher and writer. Author of i.a., 'The Holocaust and Man', in *Alternatives* (1981); 'German Jewry's Search for Renewal in the Hitler Era as Reflected in the Major Jewish Newspapers (1933–1938)', in *Journal of Modern History* (1981); *Boulevard des Misères, The Story of Transit Camp Westerbork* (forthcoming). (Contributor to Year Book XXVII.)

Feinberg, Anat, Ph.D., b. 1951 in Tel-Aviv. Lecturer in the Department of English, Tel-Aviv University and novelist. Author of two novels in Hebrew, *Shadow over All the Days* (1973) and *Still Walking towards Him* (1978); and of i.a., 'Schiller und Brecht und "Grips" auf Hebräisch: Deutsche Theaterstücke auf israelischen Bühnen', in *Die Deutsche Bühne* (July 1982); 'Das jüdische Schicksal in der österreichischen Nachkriegsdramatik', in *Forum* (1982); 'Erwin Sylvanus and the Theatre of the Holocaust', in *Studien zur Dramatik in der Bundesrepublik Deutschland*, Bd. 16, 1983.

Figes, Orlando G., B.A., b. 1959 in London. Research student in Russian History at Trinity College, Cambridge. Author of review articles, 'Autocracy of Public Silence', (1984) and on Dorothy Atkinson's, 'The End of the Russian Land Commune' (1984). Currently working on *The Russian Peasant World, 1917–1921: Peasant Revolts in the Saratov Region* (diss.).

Friedlander, Henry, Ph.D., b. 1930 in Berlin. Professor of Judaic Studies, Brooklyn College of the City University of New York. Author of *The German Revolution, 1918–1919* (Univ. Microfilms 1968). Co-author of *Guides to German Records Microfilmed at Alexandria, Va.*, Nos. 5, 8, 11, 13 and 23 (National Archives 1958–1961); *Art of the Holocaust* (1981); *Jewish Immigrants of the Nazi Period in the USA*, vol. 2 (1981). Co-editor of i.a., *The Holocaust: Ideology, Bureaucracy, and Genocide* (1981); and of the *Simon Wiesenthal Center Annual*, vol. 2 ff. Author of various articles dealing with the Holocaust period and Nazi war crimes.

Helfand, Jonathan Isaac, Ph.D., b. 1945 in New York. Assistant Professor of Jewish History, Department of Jewish History, Brooklyn College. Author of i.a., 'The Election of the Grand Rabbi of France, 1842–1846', in *Proceedings of the Eighth World Congress of Jewish Studies, Division B* (1982); 'Halakhah and the

Holocaust: Historical Perspectives', in *Perspectives on the Holocaust* (1983); and of *French Jewry during the Second Republic and Second Empire* (1979, diss.).

Kwiet, Konrad, Dr.phil., b. 1941 in Swinemünde. Associate Professor, School of German Studies, University of New South Wales. Author of *Reichskommissariat Niederlande* (1968); *Van Jodenhoed tot Gele Ster* (1973); and of various articles in historical journals. Co-author with Helmut Eschwege of *Selbstbehauptung und Widerstand. Deutsche Juden im Kampf um Existenz und Menschenwürde 1933–1945* (1984). (Contributor to Year Books XXI and XXIV.)

Lease, Gary, Dr. theol., b. 1940 in Hollywood. Associate Professor, History of Consciousness, University of California, Santa Cruz. Author of 'Hitler's National Socialism as a Religious Movement', in *Journal of the American Academy of Religion* (1977); 'The Origins of National Socialism: Some Fruits of Religion and Nationalism,' in Peter Merkl and Ninian Smart (eds.), *Religion and Politics in the Modern World* (1983); and of numerous articles on theology and religious history.

Levy, Ze'ev, Ph.D., b. 1921 in Dresden. Professor of Philosophy and Modern Jewish Thought, University of Haifa. Author of i.a., *Precursor of Jewish Existentialism: The Philosophy of Franz Rosenzweig* (1969); *Spinoza and the Concept of Judaism* (1972, enlarged edn. 1983); *Between Yafeth and Sem; on the Relation between Jewish and General Philosophy* (1982); all in Hebrew. Editor and author of numerous other publications.

Lipstadt, Deborah E., Ph.D., b. 1947 in New York. Assistant Professor, Jewish Studies, University of California, Los Angeles. Author of i.a. *Zionist Career of Louis Lipsky*; 'Pious Sympathies and Sincere Regrets: The American News Media and the Holocaust from Krystalnacht to Bermuda, 1938–1943', in *Modern Judaism* (1982). Currently writing a book on the American press and public opinion during the Holocaust.

Lowenthal, Ernst Gottfried, Dr. rer. pol., b. 1904 in Cologne. Now lives in Berlin. Journalist. Formerly Deputy Editor of the *C.V.-Zeitung*; Editor of the *Zeitschrift für die Geschichte der Juden in Deutschland* (1930–1938); *Philo-Atlas* (1938); *Bewährung in Untergang* (1965); co-editor of *Lexikon des Judentums (1967)*, etc. Author of i.a. *Juden in Preussen; biographisches Verzeichnis* (1981). Member of the London and New York Boards of the LBI. (Contributor to Year Books XI, XIV, XV and XXIII.)

Milton, Sybil, Ph.D., b. 1941 in New York. Director of Archives, Leo Baeck Institute, New York. Translator and editor of *The Stroop Report* (1979). Co-author of *Art of the Holocaust* (1981). Co-editor of, and contributor to, *The Holocaust: Ideology, Bureaucracy, and Genocide* (1981); *Genocide: Critical Issues of the Holocaust* (1983); *Simon Wiesenthal Center Annual*, vol. 2 ff (1984); and author of various essays on the Holocaust.

Moore, Bob, Ph.D., b. 1954 in Brighton. Lecturer in Social and Political History

(Dept. of European Studies), University of Manchester Institute of Science and Technology. Author of various articles on the impact of Nazism on German workers in Holland and on Dutch-German relations in the 1930s. Currently preparing a book on the Dutch government and the refugees in the 1930s.

PETUCHOWSKI, Jakob J., Ph.D., Dr.phil. h.c., D.Litt. h.c., Rabbinical Dipl., b. 1925 in Berlin. The Sol and Arlene Bronstein Research Professor of Judaeo-Christian Studies, Hebrew Union College–Jewish Institute of Religion, Cincinnati. Author of numerous books including *Gottesdienst des Herzens* (1981); *Wie unsere Meister die Schrift Erklären* (1982); *Our Masters Taught. Rabbinic Stories and Sayings* (1982); and of innumerable articles published in English, Hebrew and German. (Contributor to Year Book XXII.)

SCHWARZSCHILD, Henry, b. 1925 in Berlin, studied political theory at the City College of New York and Columbia University. Civil-rights and civil-liberties activist (with the late Martin Luther King), now Director of the Capital Punishment Project of the American Civil Liberties Union. Author of several articles on racial justice, problems of peace and justice in the Near East, the death penalty, etc.

SCHWARZSCHILD, Steven S., D.H.L., D.D. h.c., b. 1924 in Frankfurt a. Main. Formerly rabbi, now Professor of Philosophy, Washington University, St. Louis, Missouri. Author of i.a., Introductions to *Hermann Cohen, Werke*, vols. *Ethik des reinen Willens* and *Religion der Vernunft . . .* (1981 and forthcoming); and of numerous articles including 'J.-P. Sartre', in *Modern Judaism* (1983) and 'Karl Marx's Jewish Theory of Usury', in *Gesher* (1978).

WEINBERG, Werner, Ph.D., b. 1915 in Rheda (Germany). Professor of Hebrew Language and Literature, Hebrew Union College-Jewish Institute of Religion, Cincinnati. Author of i.a., *Die Reste des Jüdischdeutschen* (1966, 1973); *The Reform of Hebrew Orthography* (1972, in Hebrew); *A General-Purpose Romanization of Hebrew* (1976); *A Concise History of the Hebrew Language* (1981). Contributor to the *Encyclopaedia Judaica* in the field of Modern Hebrew Literature and author of numerous other articles and reviews in the areas of Hebrew and Yiddish.

Abstracts of articles in this Year Book are included in *Historical Abstracts* and *America: History and Life*.

General Index to Year Book XXIX of the Leo Baeck Institute